ISBN 978-0-483-15197-0
PIBN 10784078

Friends' Intelligencer

ESTABLISHED 1844 PHILADELPHIA, FIRST MONTH 7, 1922 VOLUME 79 NUMBER 1

Vitalizing Our Libraries

By HUBERT W. PEET

The following paper is based on a talk to Preparative Meeting Librarians, given at Ackworth, England, October 25, 1921. Though prepared with English Meetings in mind, it should prove equally helpful to American Friends who are interested in Meeting Libraries. A selected list of books recommended by THE INTELLIGENCER *for American Meeting Libraries will be found elsewhere in this issue.*

MEETING HOUSE libraries are not grandiose substitutes for wall paper nor are they archæological museums. Unfortunately too often they are looked upon as fulfilling these functions rather than of being one of the most important of the agencies at our command today for publishing truth. Through them we can not only help to build up those attending meeting, but also to reach those who perhaps never come within our doors, and one of the proofs of a healthy meeting is to find a library whose books are in constant circulation.

Personally, I feel that one of the greatest enemies to the full usefulness of the library is the possession of a bookcase which has glass doors that are usually kept locked. Disuse is a far greater enemy to books than dust and it is worth while running the risk of occasionally losing a book rather than that they should be kept clean.

Too many meetings also are inclined to think that their library is a good one if it is big, oblivious to the fact that one shelf of books vital to the need of today is worth a dozen full of leather bound volumes of out-of-date works which will interest nobody but the research student. I know of one meeting that has taken its courage in its hands and gone carefully through its old stock. Anything of real historical value it has kept or passed on to the Reference Library at Devonshire House, if they wish to have it while the bulk, having little intrinsic or sentimental value, have been sold. With the small sum received new books have been purchased which are now in regular use. If, however, there is a difficulty about disposing of old volumes, let the books that have a small historical value be placed on one side, and the newer literature concentrated in an easily accessible position..

One Essential

The greatest asset, however, of any library, is a keen librarian. Books do not lend themselves. A Friend is wanted who will keep an eye on what is being published and even if the Preparative Meeting funds will not allow of many books being purchased, he will see that at least there is an occasional new book added. He should make it his business to know about books which it is not possible to buy and be able to talk intelligently about them. It is not possible always to spare time to read either all the books in the library, or others that may be of interest, but usually with the number of reviews that are published a librarian can get an idea of what volumes are worth while. The personal recommendation of the librarian is probably the best way to get books into circulation. I know of one meeting where the librarian makes the library a point of contact with any visitor. Whereas often one can only think of platitudes about the weather as an item of conversation, he always puts the question, "Won't you come and see the library?" and it is seldom that newcomers go away without a book with them, and the necessity of its return means a second visit.

However, there is too much tendency to think that the books on our library shelves are mainly, if not solely, for seekers and attenders, and that members of the meeting know all about everything already. This is a very grave mistake. It is often the members who are in greater need of edification than those who are keenly enquiring.. There should, therefore, be some sort of notice board on which the advent of new volumes to the library can be announced to members of the meeting. If this can take the form of one of the many inexpensive moveable letter boards on the market it will attract more attention than a mere written notice. It can also be utilized not only to draw attention to new ones, but to old ones having a topical interest for the moment. Another good plan is to have a small table book rack at some point, preferably right inside the meeting house, where every Friend passing in and out can see it. Here should be placed a small selection of books Sunday by Sunday, constantly changed.

Talks On Books.

Publishers know that one of the best advertisements they can possibly get for a book is to get it mentioned from a pulpit. The Library, therefore, will form an excellent subject for a Sunday evening address in which the speaker may deal with either its general contents or some specific volume giving an outline of its scope and bearing. Such books as the two volumes of Rufus M. Jones' Later Period of Quakerism, form admirable material for either one or a series of addresses, just because there is so much in them and many people may at first be frightened from attempting to read them. An address will both help to pass on something of their message to those who are really unable to give time to reading, while it will also whet the appetite of those who can.

Small libraries which cannot purchase new books can usually get the loan of them from some members of either the Preparative or Monthly Meeting. The very fact that the book or books are only lent for a certain period provides a reason why the librarian should bring them more definitely before the notice of possible borrowers, pointing out that it is "Now" or perhaps "Never." Friends often will be found willing to give volumes to the library if they are books in which they are particularly interested, either in the way of a special copy or by passing on their own after they have read it, while a good plan when perhaps no grant can be got from a central fund, and a new book is particularly wanted, is to collect for its purchase a sufficient number of sixpences or shillings from members after morning meeting. Usually the required sum will be forthcoming if the book is comparatively inexpensive. A plan that is worth while trying in certain cases where it is particularly desirable to keep the books in constant use, is to consider the selling of books that have had two or three years' run, if they are not of real permanent importance, and devoting the proceeds to the purchase of books of the moment. It is not sufficiently recognized up and down the country also that book boxes are obtainable on loan from the Woodbrooke Extension Committee, and the Peace Committee, while Friends can always borrow single volumes from the Northern Friends' Peace Board, the War and Social Order Committee, the Central Education Committee's "Work Among Children" Section (late F. B. D. S. A.) and also from the Friends' Reference Library at Devonshire House. In certain areas, too, there is a central Monthly Meeting library which circulates round to particular meetings books for a certain period.

A Wider Sphere

We should not only make our libraries as accessible as possible to those coming within the Meeting House walls, but also I think help to spread our message to others who may be interested.. This applies especially to clergymen of other denominations, many of whom will be glad to borrow from the Friends' Library some books which they perhaps cannot purchase for themselves. A knowledge of this can be conveyed by personal call, or as has been done in some cases, by writing a letter to the local paper expressing the Meeting's willingness to loan books to all of any or no church that care to apply for them. The librarian may also fruitfully extend his work by making it his business to see whether there are at least some Standard Friend books in the public libraries. So often any that are on the shelves are woefully out of date but more often than not the sending of some particulars of recent books to the Library Committee will lead to the purchase of the volumes. The Standard Rowntree History, of which a handy prospectus is obtainable, and Edward Grubb's "What is Quakerism?" are particularly suitable for this purpose.

As regards the type of book, librarians can of course be purely Quaker or they can have a wider outlook even, as in some cases, having a big sociological section. In most cases, however, owing to the necessity for husbanding resources it may only be possible to have a definitely Quaker and theological section, and to add a few of the more, important and less expensive books on current matters. The actual books recommended are outlined in The Quaker Bookshelf list, published in 1920, and in the Supplement, recently issued, which can be obtained, together, from the Central Literature Council, Bishopgate, London, E. C. 2 (2½d. by post),

If the librarian is also responsible for the pamphlet case, he should apply exactly the same principles of freshness and variety as he would to his bookshelves.. Dusty out-of-date pamphlets are unlikely to attract the casual visitor and even if a clean stock be unearthed unexpectedly, see that it is vital to the needs of today and not dated 1872 as was the case with a clean but utterly antiquated collection I have met with in at least two Meeting Houses. There will always be a great wastage of pamphlets, as they so soon suff[illegible] from exposure, but it will be worth while to keep them constantly renewed, if they are to be constantly taken away by visitors.

Suggested Books for Meeting Libraries

The following brief list includes the suggestions of several Friends and is made up of books that are readable and not too voluminous for widespread use. The editor will be glad to see that more detailed suggestions are sent to any so desiring. Information concerning prices and publishers may be obtained from Walter H. Jenkins, 140 North Fifteenth Street, Philadelphia, Pa.

Religious Essays, etc.

William Penn; The Fruits of Solitude.
Edward Grubb; Authority and the Light Within.
Henry T. Hodgkins; Lay Religion.
Rufus M. Jones; A Dynamic Faith, and The Inner Light
John Wilhelm Rowntree; Essays and Addresses.
John William Graham; The Faith of a Quaker.
Swarthmore Lectures; especially Silent Worship, The Way of Wonder, by E. Violet Hodgkin. Quakerism, A Religion of Life, and The Nature and Authority of Conscience, by Rufus M. Jones; and Spiritual Guidance in Quaker Experience, by William C. Braithwaite.

THE FRIENDS' INTELLIGENCER is published weekly at 140 N. 15th St., Philadelphia, by FRIENDS' INTELLIGENCER ASSOCIATION, Ltd. Telephone, Spruce 5-75. Entered at Philadelphia Post-Office as second class matter. Subscription in the United States, Mexico, Cuba and Panama, $2.50 a Year. Subscriptions may begin at any time. Subscription in Canada and other foreign countries (on account of extra postage charges), $3.00 a year. Single copies, 6 cents. Make checks payable to FRIENDS' INTELLIGENCER ASSN., LTD.

Historical and Biographical

George Fox, An Autobiography; edited by Rufus M. Jones.

John Woolman's Journal.

John William Graham; The Life of William Penn.

Elizabeth B. Emmott; The Story of Quakerism.

Isaac Sharpless; A Quaker Experiment in Government.

Allen C. Thomas; A History of the Society of Friends in America.

A. Neave Brayshaw; The Quakers: Their Story and Message.

Rufus M. Jones and Wm. C. Braithwaite; History of Friends, in six volumes.

Rufus M. Jones; A Service of Love in Wartime.

D. Owen Stephens; With Quakers in France.

Social and Industrial Problems

Maurice L. Rowntree; Social Freedom.

Herbert Cory; Intellectuals and the Wage Workers.

Pamphlets issued by the Church League For Industrial Democracy, to be obtained from Richard W. Hogue, Secretary, 129 W. Nippon St., Germantown, Pa.

Kirby Page; Industrial Facts.

For Younger Readers

The Children's Story Garden.

Maude Robinson; The Time of Her Life, and Nicholas, The Weaver.

L. Violet Hodgkin; Book of Quaker Saints.

E. F. O'Brien; An Admiral's Son (William Penn).

Pamphlets

Pamphlets are often effective where longer works fail to gain attention. Pamphlets on Friends' principles may be obtained upon request from J. Barnard Walton, Secty., Advancement Committee of Friends' General Conference, 140 N. 15th St., Philadelphia, Pa

Practical Steps Against Future Wars

Cultivate in your own hearts the "will to peace."

Consolidate the sentiment against war so that the strength that comes from union of forces may be exerted. Arouse the community to active service.

See that school children are taught the beauty of peace and the horrors of warfare and war's far-reaching influence. Offer prizes for essays in the schools.

Form groups in churches, Sunday-Schools, clubs, granges, etc., for the study of questions that bear on peace and war, and right international relations.

Get proper printed matter in local papers and distribute literature. Put up posters. Send clippings and editorials to the National Council for Limitation of Armaments, 532 Seventeenth St., N. W., Washington, D. C.

Contribute funds generously, for they are needed in our work.

Urge the abolition of Fear, Suspicion and Greed from the minds of men and between nations.

Express your opinion in the form of statements, or resolutions, or private letters, and send them to those in positions of power.

Urge that all nations become associated for purposes of the maintenance of peace through justice and good-will, all nations co-operating for the benefit of all.

Become well-informed yourself; talk in private, and speak in public for the cause.

Secure a Disarmament Shelf in your local library.

Organize a committee of representative people to work, through successive steps, to make another war impossible.

Urge your senators to favor ratification of the treaties as to relations in the Pacific. Also write to your member in the House of Representatives opposing measures for the military training of young men.

O. Edward Janney.

What Shall We Leave for Our Children?

What shall we leave for our children
When for us the day is done,
When our harvest has all been garnered
And we rest at set of sun?

Shall they gather the treasures of ages,
The gifts of the human soul?
Shall they learn at the lips of the sages,
Or shall we give them—gold?

Shall we search through nature's volumes,
For laws of the universe,
And attune life's music to them?
Or shall we leave—a purse?

Shall we live by the teachings of Jesus,
Making equal the chances of life?
Shall we leave co-operation?
Or hate and industrial strife?

Shall we leave to them faith in Goodness?
That spark Divine, which alas!
Too often we crush in our brother,
Or the gift of the poisoned gas?

Shall we push aside racial barriers,
And level our tariff walls?
Or shall we bequeath them airplanes,
From which destruction falls?

Shall we broaden our love of country,
Till it spreads the wide earth o'er?
Shall we leave the concourse of peoples,
Or the hideous crime of war?

What shall we leave for our children,
When for us life's journey is o'er?
We gather our treasures for them,
E'er we push our barques from shore.

Cornelia J. Shoemaker.

FRIENDS' INTELLIGENCER

The religion of Friends is based on faith in the "INWARD LIGHT," or direct revelation of God's spirit and will in every seeking soul.

The INTELLIGENCER is interested in all who bear the name of Friends in every part of the world, and aims to promote love, unity and intercourse among all branches and with all religious societies.

Editorial and business offices, 140 N. 15th Street, Philadelphia, Pa. For information regarding subscription rates, etc., see foot of second page.

PHILADELPHIA, FIRST MONTH 7, 1922

IN THIS ISSUE

Every new evidence of the unceasing spirit of unity between our branches should be a cause of rejoicing. It is evidence of growth toward the greater Society of Friends to which we are called by our highest ideals. We are glad, therefore, to pass the following quotation on to our readers. It is from a recent letter, written by one of our more elderly Friends, to a member of Cornwall Monthly Meeting, New York.

"I am praying and hoping that the sad mistake among Friends in the long-ago will soon be a thing of the past and that both Meetings will be one, as Jesus meant it should be when He said, "a new commandment I give unto you, that ye love one another." With that principle lived as He intended it to be, we would be a united band of Friends and a power for good to the world by showing that we live the peace principles we profess.

It would perhaps be hard for some to give up our way and conform to the other, but one Meeting *must do so* if we are to be re-united, and I should be glad if ours were the ones to follow Christ's wish when He said, "be ye kindly considerate of each other, in honor preferring one another." And we can live up to the Light Within under *all* conditions."

We want the *Intelligencer* to go officially on record, and we wish that every individual Friend and the Society as a whole might do the same, as uncompromisingly opposed to the continued incarceration of 'political' prisoners—men whose only offense, in the cases with which we are familiar, was that they held beliefs in opposition to hysterical war legislation, and that they did not fear to express those beliefs when such expression was most needed and most difficult to give.

The following letter, from John T. Doran, which came to us a few days ago with a check for ten dollars, throws light on the type of many of the men who are at this moment enduring the rack of penitentiary life because of allegiance to their convictions:

"I am a political prisoner at the U. S. Penitentiary at Leavenworth, Kansas. The inclosed ten dollars was sent to me by a friend with the statement, "It goes to you with faith that Christmas will have its meaning for you as well as for me."

"There is nothing in the world that I need as greatly as do the children of devastated Russia and Europe need food. I ask you to please have this money turned over to the Friends' Service—I do not know the address. They will make this ten dollars go much further than I could myself.

"My friend had the joy of giving the money to me—symbolic of a kindly, sincere interest in me—I had the joy of receiving it, and now, let us hope, some child shall know the joy of food safely stowed away in a little starved stomach."

When one remembers that such an offering means self-denial of even the few good things which can be bought to supplement the usual coarse prison fare, the gift takes on deep spiritual significance. Others of the political prisoners with whom we have personally corresponded are likewise men of earnest ideals. (We add in proofreading that, since writing this editorial, we have received a similar letter from James H. Manning, another political prisoner at Leavenworth, likewise inclosing a check for Russian Relief.)

Whether our particular social theories agree with those of all of these men, we do not know. Probably some of them do not. But as to that we were not set up to judge. The great point is that they are men of earnest ideals, who had the courage to stand for their ideals at a time when every manifestation of the individual 'Light' was certain to be snuffed out by the hurricane of war. They are true conscientious objectors. Their continued imprisonment, especially when the political prisoners of the European nations were long since granted amnesty, is a violation of those principles of freedom and justice for which America ought to stand, and a challenge to a religious society which holds sacred the guidance of the individual conscience.

The *New Republic* for December 28, contains an article exposing conditions in the federal penitentiary at Leavenworth, and challenging the nation which allows the continued imprisonment of political offenders. This article is from the pen of Brent Dow Allison, a former C. O. and present Friends' relief worker in Europe.

Looking upon the situation through the eyes of the disinterested Europeans whom he meets, the author denounces the imprisonment of intelligent men on the sole grounds of belief as a denial of every American ideal. A reader, who believes that Friends should more earnestly face this situation, has volunteered to send a free marked copy of this issue of the *New Republic* to anyone who so requests from the Intelligencer office.

The Washington Conference

VIII

By William I. Hull

The fifth plenary session of the Conference and its settlement of the submarine and naval questions, which has been anxiously awaited during the past ten days, has not yet been held. The British proposition of last week to abolish submarines for both offensive and defensive was promptly followed by a demand from France to be permitted to build 90,000 tons of submarines, and by a proposition from the United States to restrict the submarine tonnage of Great Britain and the United States to 60,000 each, and of France, Japan and Italy to 31,500, 31,500 and 21,150, respectively. Japan and Italy were ready to accept this proposal, approximately; but the French delegation referred it to the French cabinet, which insisted on its original demand of 90,000 tons, or at least on an equality with Great Britain and the United States. Since this would be greatly in excess, for submarines and other auxiliary craft, of the ratio agreed upon for capital ships, Great Britain and the United States would not yield to the French demand, and Italy, too, was wholly adverse to accepting either naval inferiority to France or the necessity of increasing greatly its own submarine and other auxiliary tonnage. Italian spokesmen said that they were willing to cut their submarine preparedness down to a single torpedo, but as a Mediterranean Power their country deemed it necessary to maintain equality with France.

Thus the Conference was face to face with a grave crisis, and was obliged to choose between the alternative of adopting an agreement which would leave France in isolation, or of deferring the whole question of submarine and other auxiliary craft to a future conference. It was the latter alternative which France naturally desired; for, having failed to secure an American guarantee against Germany, by refusing to reduce and limit her armies, she has left no stone unturned to secure a British guarantee against Germany, and has put forward, first her capital ship, and then her submarine demands, hoping to secure by their surrender either a British naval alliance or another Conference in which the supreme French demand for an anti-Germany alliance might have a better chance of being granted than in this Conference at Washington.

During the animated debate in the Conference over the question of submarines, two British spokesmen, Lord Lee, the first lord of the admiralty, and Arthur J. Balfour, the head of the delegation, presented a powerful argument and appeal against all submarine warfare which have made a profound impression upon American public opinion and, through it, upon the American government.. In response to this two-fold pressure, the United States has not yielded entirely to the British proposal, but it has cut down its original limit on submarine tonnage from 90,000 to 60,000, and has proposed drastic rules for the curbing of these "demons of the sea."

The British argument and appeal are to be repeated *in extenso* at the next plenary session of the Conference, the British spokesmen say; and this will greatly strengthen the campaign of publicity and education which is being carried on. The Advisory Committee of the American Delegation reported, prematurely that the American public favored the retention of submarines for defensive war but the National Council on the Limitation of Armaments, under Frederick J. Libby's energetic guidance, is endeavoring to convince the Advisory Committee that it was mistaken in this judgment. Numerous evidences have come through my hands to show that Friends, individually and in their corporate capacity, are taking an active part in the campaign of education against preparations for submarine warfare. This campaign will be necessary for some years to come: for the French are insisting on their right to build a great submarine fleet and America and other powers have not yet been entirely converted to a belief in the futility and wickedness of submarine warfare. The Washington Conference has therefore come most regretfully to the conclusion that a drastic reduction and limitation in submarine building is not possible at this time, and will probably refer the question to a future Conference to be held at the expiration of, say, seven years.

The British are emphasizing the competition which will doubtless set in meanwhile between submarines and an infinite variety and number of anti-submarine devices. The pecuniary cost of this competition, they are glad to admit, will be far less than that between capital ships, and, they are glad to reflect, will be less for them than for any other country. This latter fact is due to the very large number of steel-built, steam-propelled trawlers and other craft which are engaged in the British fisheries, and which can be equipped with anti-submarine devices. Far worse than the expense of this competition, of course, is the atmosphere of suspicion and hostility which it will increase between France and Great Britain and, to a less extent, between other countries as well.

To mitigate in some degree this deplorable condition, the Conference is working today over proposals made by Secretary Hughes for the curbing of submarine activities when engaged in actual warfare, and for the limitation of the size of auxiliary warships to a maximum of 10,000 tons' displacement, of capital ship guns to 16-inch calibre, of auxiliary ship guns to 8-inch calibre, of airplane carrier guns to 8-inch calibre and of total airplane carrier, tonnage to 80,000, 80,000, 48,000, 28,000, and 28,000 for Great Britain, the United States, Japan, France and Italy respectively.

If these proposals are adopted there will be at least *some* reduction and limitation in auxiliary battleships, airplane carriers, and submarine activities. But the outstanding achievement of the Washington Conference, as far as checking preparations for war is concerned, is the great blow struck at dreadnaughts and super-dreadnaughts.. Other instruments of naval warfare, air warfare, chemical warfare, economic warfare and land armaments, still stand like mountains in our path.. Fortunately, we have set our faces resolutely toward them, "the first great step has been taken, and if we proceed steadily on our journey, "sustained by faith and matchless fortitude," we will find these mountains also dwindling into mole-hills and will leave them, too, behind us in the great upward march of civilization and Christianity.

In welcoming the New Year, shall we not turn over another new leaf and write upon it continued devotion and redoubled effort in behalf of the Great Cause of our time?

Washington, D. C., December 29th, 1921.

The Wisdom of the Peoples

COMPILED BY JAMES WALDO FAWCETT

VIII

THE PROVERBS OF OLD CHINA

Better do a good deed near home than go far to burn incense.

If you injure others, you injure yourself.

One generation plants the trees; another sits in the shade.

Better die than turn your back on reason.

When men come face to face their differences vanish.

The cleverest doctor cannot save himself.

God loves all men.

The cure of ignorance is study, as meat is that of hunger.

Among mortals, who is faultless?

If riches can be acquired with propriety, then acquire them; but let not unjust wealth be sought for with violence.

Better be upright with poverty than depraved in abundance.

Do not anxiously hope for what is not yet come; do not vainly regret what is already past.

The man of worth is really great without being proud; the mean man is proud without being really great.

In enacting laws, rigor is desirable; in executing them, mercy.

He who tells me of my faults is my teacher; he who tells me of my virtues does me harm.

Knowing what is right, without practicing it, denotes a want of proper resolution.

A man is ignorant of his own feelings as the ox is unconscious of his great strength.

As it is impossible to please men in all things, our only care should be to satisfy our own consciences.

A single conversation across the table with a wise man is better than ten years' study of books.

Prudence will carry a man all over the world, but the impetuous find every step difficult.

By a single day's practice of virtue, though happiness may not be attained, yet misery may be kept at a distance; by a single day of ill doing, happiness is prevented.

No medicine can procure long life even to the ministers of the emperor; no money can purchase for any man a virtuous posterity..

Knowledge is boundless, and the capacity of man is limited.

It is easy to convince a wise man, but to reason with a fool is a difficult undertaking.

As a light of a single star tinges the mountains of many regions, so a single unguarded expression injures the virtue of a whole life.

The fame of men's good actions seldom goes beyond their own door, but their evil deeds are carried to a thousand miles' distance.

When you put on your clothes, remember the labor of the weaver; when you eat your daily bread, think of the hardships of the husbandman.

Man is born without knowledge, and when he has obtained it, very soon becomes old; when his experience is ripe, death suddenly seizes him.

Let your words be few and your companions select; thus you will avoid remorse and repentance, thus you will avoid sorrow and shame.

As the scream of the eagle is heard when she has passed over, so a man's name remains after his death.

Scholars are their country's treasure and the richest ornaments of the feast.

He who prides himself upon wealth and honor hastens his own downfall.

Mighty is he who conquers himself.

(*End of Series.*)

Winter

As Friends' Service Workers Find It In Poland

The Polish winter has begun at last. Autumn lingered and lingered, covering the wide marshes with golden and brown colours, which grew a deeper and deeper brown day after day. The leaves fell reluctantly in the warmth of the sun until only the coppery leaves of the birch shoots were left, waving briskly in the wind from a thousand silver stems. And then even the birch leaves fell and all the trees and woods waited in winter dress for the winter. But autumn refused to go, and an occasional butterfly was certain that autumn was never going this year. A week ago the wind changed. The butterfly vanished hastily. Great masses of dark clouds hung all day on the horizon and at night the moon and stars were whiter and frostier than before. The wind grew colder and keener. Wild gusts of rain poured down.. The golden brown marshes changed suddenly to grey, and the whole landscape became grey.

Two days ago the snow arrived, and for the last two days it has snowed steadily.. The wind has dropped, and the flakes drift down sleepily and gently..

The villages of little wooden houses and the trees have all turned into Christmas cards.. The long straggling lanes between the houses are inches deep now. The dark tree branches lean over under the weight and brush against the tiny windows, making the rooms of the cottages even darker than before.

The snow is crisp and the air is clear. The wind has dropped completely. In America there would be scores of gay children making snow-men, throwing snowballs, fighting snow-fights, running, laughing and shouting. Small toboggans would be coming out of their dusty lairs, and slides would be made down every available slope. Indoors there would be huge warm fires, and holly, and anticipation of Christmas, and mysterious stirring of plum puddings and saving of pennies for Christmas cards and presents. Everyone would be brisk and good-tempered. There is something about the first fall of snow which makes everyone cheerful, especially if the air is clear and the snow crisp, and if the wind has fallen completely.

In Polish villages there are just as many children as in American villages, and children are the same at heart all the world over. But there are no children playing at snow-man or snow-fights in the lanes. There is no sound of laughter or shouting across the white marshes. There is no holly in the houses.

Winter in an American home can be very pleasant. But the same winter, the same snow, the same cold is death in Poland. There are houses with no glass to the windows, and the snow drifts remorselessly through cracks and crevices. There are houses with no doors, and the snow slips past the tattered canvas which hangs in this doorway. There are houses which are not houses at all, but shelters of tin and stray pieces of log and mud. Some families have fuel for the fires, but others have none and must go out into the woods to collect it with blue, cold fingers, and carry it with thin arms back to their hovels. And others have lost all their strength in the four months' journey from the famine provinces of Russia and cannot even collect wood.

There are orphans living in shelters or cottages who must go out themselves for fuel. There is none to go for them, and the poor half-starved children must do the best they can for themselves. When the snow is coming slowly but steadily through doors and windows and roof, it is better to have a roaring fire in the room.

It is also good to have a pot boiling on that fire, with something good to eat inside it. Not necessarily a turkey and plum pudding. People can live on less than turkey and plum puddings. But it is good to have something nourishing to eat in cold weather.

These people in Poland sometimes have potatoes in their pot on the fire. In America they eat potatoes also, potatoes with their meat for example, or sometimes potato soup, or potato salad. But potatoes without the meat, mashed potatoes wihout the sausages. every day of the week is rather different. The Polish peasant who can cook potatoes for every meal every day is luckier than most of his neighbors. Those who have no potatoes must do the best they can with mushrooms and bark and roots gathered in the fields. But now that the snow has come, how can one find roots in the fields? Some have stores of acorns which will be baked into bread ultimately, mixed with potato peelings or rye husks or straw, to eat after the roots are finished. And when the acorns are finished—

In many of these hovels with the poor fires or with no fires, with the snow coming in, with the small heap of acorns in the corner and the heap of potato-peelings beside them, there are very often four or five families, ten, twelve, twenty souls, in the one single room. And often several of these are ill. Under a heap of clothes or sacks, tiny children lie moaning sometimes, or absolutely silent. Typhus is beginning once again in these ruined districts and there are few medicines and few hospitals and doctors. The sick children in these crowded rooms add the last touch of horror and tragedy. Even the children who are not sick with any disease are pinched and blue and scared. And there is no heart for snowballing here. If there was any holly they would boil the berries for soup. There is no laughter. And still the snow drifts down, and the winter comes on remorselessly.

And between them and the winter the Quakers stand—stand, in the spirit of Christ, and when their arms are filled with gifts from the homes of the happy, fortunate Americans, they stoop down and give.

Fashion: The Modern Idol

A review of "The Glass of Fashion," by "A Gentleman With a Duster." G. P. Putnam, New York, 1921.

This book is a study of "fashion" in morals, delicacy, good taste, common sense and out of these qualities—as flagrantly shown in two recent volumes, Margot Asquith's Autobiography and Colonel Repington's Diaries. The author contends, and I think, proves, that these "best sellers" are debasing morals and taste not alone, but inspiring a contempt for English aristocracy or a lack of confidence in English statesmanship, especially evil at this time. "I do not think I exaggerate in saying that this effect is disastrous. For is it altogether unreasonable to suppose that if there exists at this time a deep affection and a profound confidence between the Republic of the United States and the British Commonwealth such a great step might be taken toward disarmament as might lead in a generation to the peace of the world?"

He gives as comparison to sickening and banal quotations from the books mentioned certain extracts from the biography of Catherine Gladstone, a nobler woman, and wife of a greater Prime Minister. The contrast is reflecting.

The "Gentleman with a Duster" was his homely weapon to high purpose in this book. He is evidently a member of the aristocracy, who was intimately connected with the government during the war. I have not read his "Mirrors of Downing Street, or of Washington. They may be over caustic, but none can doubt the deep sincerity of one who, writing on Morals, says, "Man can no more stop at morality than the elephant can go forward to mathematics or music—The Sermon on the Mount was not a plagiarism of Sinai nor a paraphrase of the Tables of Stone; it was in an altogether different region—it was a discourse on manners—Morals, with Christ, had to do with man as he was; Manners with what he was becoming. His blessings were on the springs of behavior, on meekness and gentleness, on humanity and lowliness, on hunger and thirst after perfection, on mercy, purity of heart, and long suffering."

The author considers Pessimism a greater danger than Bolshevism. "In the sphere of manners I am convinced that the example of Fashion makes powerfully for this danger of Pessimism." The root cause of all bad manners, whatever form they take, he points out to be *selfishness*. "And selfishness, what is it, if we examine it with attention, but a deep and most disfiguring *spiritual* defect?" The most powerful of all our leaders—is Fashion—not Parliament, not Church, not Press—but Fashion. If, then, we would go in a right direction instead of a wrong direction, those who set the nation its most conspicuous example must be, not equivocally, not half-heartedly, not wearily, but enthusiastically on the side of Excellence." "Fashion, because of its conspicuous position in the state, exercises the greatest of all influence on the nation."

"Goodness is not enough. There is something beyond morality. Love is God; how different from obedience to the Mosaic Law!" And in the conclusion he sees hope. "I am going to believe that we may now be moving toward another and a far greater renaissance than that which ended the drowse of the middle ages. I feel that this present darkness has become so stifling, and this present confusion so inextricable, that we may expect humanity to rescue itself from a reversion to barbarism by one of those great forward movements which at long intervals in history have saved evolution from a fatal halt or a disastrous recession.

Advertised by its predecessors, this book should attract many who come to scoff (as they think) with the author, but who haply, under his trenchant words, will remain to pray.

New York. JOHN COX, JR.

What Doth Our Membership Require of Us?

In a work of fiction a devout woman, in answer to a youth who feels he is under no obligation to the call of the church, places the responsibility of the individual differently than we are wont to express it and directs him to "sonship." We usually think of error on the part of the meeting, elders, possibly parents. I wonder, if we should reverse our arguments, or the responsibility, and think of "birthright" in terms of "sonship," would it solve our problem as to what sort of change would adequately satisfy the spiritual development of our youth and vitally attach them to the meeting?

That I can see a helpful note in the admonition of this fictitious character for our drifting members is because of a statement of a minister that, "Our Infant Baptism Is Your Birthright Membership, Only the Form Is Different."

"If God really calls you, you have to say no to *Him*, not to me. You are mistaken that you haven't anything to do with the church. When you were a little baby six months old, your father and mother brought you home to our house; and the first Sunday they were there they took you to the old church, where all the children and grandchildren had been christened for years, and they stood up and assented to the vows that gave you to God. And they promised for themselves that they would bring you up in the nurture and admonition of the Lord until you came to years and could finish the bond by giving yourself to God. I shall never forget the sweet, serious look on the face of your lovely mother when she bowed her head in answer to the minister's question, 'Do you thus promise'?"

"You know that ceremony was not all on your father's and mother's part; it entailed some responsibility upon you. It was part of your heritage, and you have no right to waste it any more than if it were gold or bank stock or houses or lands. It was your title to a heavenly sonship, and it gave God the right to call upon you to do whatever He wants you to do. It's between you and God now, and you'll have to settle it for yourself. It's not anything I can settle for you either way. You must answer God, and you must answer Him from the heart either way; so nobody else has anything to do with it."

Each generation will find weaknesses in the forms of the passing one and may we of this day seek "sonship," since it is only spiritual values that are really lasting. If "sonship" seems to limit the relationship, may we substitute "Christ-likeness?"

ELLA R. BICKNELL.

A Gift of Love and Sympathy

I want to relate a little incident which has touched me very much. A short time ago my telephone rang and I found myself called up by a stranger. The person at the other end—a lady—told me that her sister had just died and that one of her last requests was that I should be asked to attend her funeral. She had said: "He does not know me nor do I know him but I know that he does not believe in war and that he held this faith when many other Christians were preaching in favor of it. I do not want any minister to speak at my funeral who preached in favor of it. I want someone who followed Christ's way of love."

I went to the funeral and spoke the words of comfort which I felt upon my heart to say.. A few days later I received a letter from the sister asking me to let her know what my fee was, that she might send me a check for the amount. I quite naturally replied I desired no fee and could not accept one, as the simple service which I had rendered had been given in love and sympathy and for no other reason.

A few days ago I received in the same handwriting a check for $500, "to be used for the relief of little children who are suffering in Russia." It was likewise a gift of love and sympathy.

RUFUS M. JONES.

Prison Comfort Club Notes

The Philadelphia Branch of the Worker's National Prison Comfort Club sent to political prisoners—to the limit of its treasury—a money order for one dollar each as a Christmas greeting. A cheery card, bearing a happy flash of color and appropriate verse, accompanied the order, as did also the following message:

"'The greatest among you is he who serves,' was said by the fellow-worker whose birthday is remembered on the twenty-fifth of this month. He himself served to the uttermost, and reminded us that for a long time to come all who cared to do the same—loyal to principle, to their ideals, to the truth as they see the truth—would doubtless be misunderstood and mistreated as He was. Shorn of all the theologies and creeds barnacled about it, it is a big story—the things He stood for and the life He lived. For He stood

gard their work as service, have caught the real purpose of life.

(b) *In the community.* What is our attitude toward our community? Do we realize that the way to make the world better is to start in our own community? There are numerous things needing to be done—civic, political, and educational!

(c) *In the meeting.* The fact that we are members of the Society of Friends should be sufficient to show that we believe that Friends have a real service to render. Are we living as though we believe that? Are we alive to the opportunities and responsibilities that are everywhere pressing upon Friends? What are we doing in our meetings for worship, in our business meetings, in all Friendly activities, to help make them such organizations that they will be *alive* with the Friendly message?

Service at home has the right to make a very real demand on each and every one of us. Let us think deeply before we try to live without it!

Service abroad, home service and service at home are the three fields that are not merely open to us, but that are calling to us as young Friends: "A Happy New Year!" Let us put real meaning into the phrase, let us *live* it.

From the Executive Committee of the Young Friends' Movement of Philadelphia Yearly Meeting.

Thomas A. Foulke — Edward N. Wright
Esther F. Holmes — David D. Griscom
Lindsley H. Noble — D. Herbert Way
L. Elizabeth Jones — Eliza M. Ambler.

Friendly News Notes

The two branches of Friends in Lansdowne have temporarily combined the adult classes of their First-day Schools for the purpose of joint discussion of the general topic that is first in all our minds—the Washington Conference. The group alternates between the two meeting houses at 9.45 A. M. The discussion is quite general, under the leadership and direction of Vincent D. Nicholson, and pertains to whatever special topics seem most important of the Conference.

Anyone interested to attend will be, of course, most welcome. The committee in charge is Walter Haviland, John H. Meader, Anna P. Maris, William J. Hicks.

W. D. W.

The News Letter of Baltimore Meeting of Friends, Park Avenue and Laurens Street, has the right idea in stating that "During the coming year our meeting opens wide its doors to all who mourn and need comfort; to all who are tired and need rest; to all who are friendless and want friendship; to all who are lonely and need companionship; to all who are homeless and want sheltering love; to all who pray, and to all who do not but ought; to whoever will."

The closing sentence of the letter, "All things come to him who hustles while he waits," shows that Bliss Forbush, the secretary, realizes that opening the doors is not all that is needed.

Anna J. Haines, who, since her arrival in this country in October, has contributed greatly in many important circles toward the development of public opinion in favor of Russian famine relief, has had so many calls for her story that she has arranged to remain in this country through the month of January. She will be speaking mostly under the auspices of the Russian Famine Fund, and requests for her time should be addressed to that organization at 15 Park Row, New York City. Comments of almost superlative praise have been made upon Anna Haines' addresses, as she has given them from Boston to Minneapolis.

The meetings held under the direction of Dr. O. Edward Janney during the past month have been reported from their respective centers. The following extracts have been made from a report covering the period from Eleventh month 22nd to Twelfth month 22nd.

"Much correspondence has been carried on in regard to various meetings and literature. During the past two weeks there has been a falling off in the number of meetings held, due to the fact that these have now been conducted in nearly every Friendly locality, and the need of others does not seem so imperative. A compact and responsive organization has been completed, co-extensive with our seven Yearly Meetings, and should an emergency arise, calling for action, this organization may be depended on for immediate service.

"The important centers of influence among Friends have been reached, and the floating sentiment in opposition to war consolidated into a firm determination to use every effort to prevent future wars, and to continue such efforts until this object be at length attained."

Japanese business men now in Washington observing the wind-up of the Conference are the heroes of an amusing anecdote that has Philadelphia for its locale. A group of them was recently entertained at dinner at a Broad street club. A member of the party from Nippon asked if there were any Quakers present—explained Pennsylvania meant Quakerism to most Japanese. Two members of the Friends' Society were pointed out. Both happened to be ostentatiously bald. That prompted the Japanese directly to inquire if there is anything in the Quaker creed requiring its devotees to wear their heads clean-shaved.

Later the man of Nippon explained that according to the understanding prevailing in Japan "regular" Friends had to be born in England, serve a novitiate in the United States and then return to the land of their birth. The last shot fired by the Japanese was a request for all available literature about Quakers because, he said, "it's my intention when I get home to start a lodge in Japan."—*Public Ledger* (Phila.)

F. W. W.

YOUNG FRIENDS' CONFERENCE IN NEW YORK

New York Young Friends are planning with great zest for the coming conference with delegates from Baltimore and Philadelphia, on the 21st and 22nd. The occasion is noteworthy, not only because of the guests, but because the younger members of the Orthodox Meetings are assisting in the preparations and the entertainment, are taking their full share in both.

Last summer the "dormitory" of the Seminary building in New York was used for the housing of the Orthodox Friends who were visiting New York for the Christian Endeavor Convention. This winter, Orthodox Friends are likely to help house the delegates to this conference. Thirty or forty visitors are expected, though the number is not at all certain, as yet.

The program is not yet well worked out. It seems certain, though, that there will be a social in the Fifteenth Street Meeting House on Seventh-day night. The visitors will be distributed around New York and Brooklyn for the night, and will attend the four meetings in the two cities the next morning. First-day there will be a general conference of all members of the Young Friends' Movement, followed, if there is time, by a short sight-seeing trip. The afternoon will end by the group attending in a body the Tea Meeting at the Twentieth Street Meeting House. The program for this meeting will be a part of the conference.

ENGLISH NEWS NOTES

All who were in any way connected with the C. O. movement in Great Britain will welcome the news of the wedding on December 17th, of Clifford Allen, Chairman of the No-Conscription Fellowship, and Miss Joan Gill. Clifford Allen, though not yet able to undertake public work, has sufficiently recovered from his serious illnesses in prison, and on his visit to Russia as a member of the Labor Party Delegation there, to be able to live in this country. The C. O. movement and with it, we think we may rightly say the Society of Friends itself, owes Clifford Allen such a debt for his sincere, clear-headed and high moral leadership, both of the N. C. F., and of the Joint Advisory Committee of that body, the Friends' Service Committee and the F. O. R., that there can be none but the best wishes for their united happiness.

J. W. Graham, principal of Dalton Hall, Manchester, on November 29th, gave his contribution on "The Society of Friends" to the series of lectures "Some Leading Phases of Christian Belief," organized by the Court of Governors of Zion College, London. This body is actually one of the ancient city companies dating from the reign of James I, and was originally devoted to the benefit of the clergy "of the City of London and outlying hamlets," though now its membership includes the whole of the metropolitan area.

Principal J. W. Graham had an audience of Church of England clergy and a few ladies, and after speaking for fifty minutes was urged to go on. Forty minutes were afterwards devoted to questions and two speakers described the occasion as an outstanding event in their lives. It appeared to have introduced them to regions of religious thought quite new to them.

H. W. PEET.

Publications of Interest

A list of publications of the General Education Board, 61 Broadway, New York, contains titles which should interest all who are concerned with educational endeavor. Among them are papers on "The Country School of Tomorrow," by Frederick T. Gates; "Changes Needed In American Secondary Education," by Charles W. Eliot, and "A Modern School," by Abraham Flexner. The complete list and any of the publications will be sent free upon request.

GEORGE LLOYD HODGKIN

I have just been reading the beautiful story of a beautiful life—The Life and Letters of George Hodgkin (1880-1918), edited by his gifted sister, L. Violet Hodgkin. His life, his ideals and his Quaker faith were formed and shaped under the immediate influence of two of the most remarkable Friends of the nineteenth century—that of his father, Dr. Thomas Hodgkin, and the famous "nun" of Cambridge, Caroline Stephen. He visited America in 1912 as a representative of the English Young Friends and he attended the Five Years' Meeting of that date, followed by a mem-

followers of Christ to give this question their thought." The platform adopted by the directors declares for a reasonable living wage to the lowest paid workman, constant employment for every member of the organization, and an application of the Golden Rule to all relations between employee and employer.

Quite as interesting as these declarations is Mr. Eagan's comment on the publicity which his announcement received. He remarked that it was an unfortunate commentary on modern business life that when a Christian, among Christians, announced a simple Christian program, the papers should treat it as "news."

Public opinion against the provision by Congress of funds for the execution of the militaristic programs of the War and Navy Departments of the national government, should be expressed to your Washington representatives, and to the army and navy sub-committees. The members of the latter, all to be addressed at the House Office Building, Washington, D. C., are:

Army sub-committee: Daniel R. Anthony, Jr., Chairman, Wm. H. Stafford, C. Bascom Slemp, Thomas U. Sisson, and Thomas W. Harrison.

Navy sub-committee: Patrick H. Kelley, Chairman, Burton L. French, Chas. R. Davis, Jas. F. Brynes and Wm. B. Oliver.

One session of the annual convention of the Federal Council of Churches this year was devoted to a consideration of the topic, "Brotherhood In Industry." The principal speakers were a large employer of labor and a labor union official, both members of the Christian church. At the close of the meeting, Dean Shailer Mathews, who had acted as chairman, remarked: "When I look back twenty years to the beginning of the recognition of the social side of the Gospel and then hear tonight the great report made by the Commission on the Church and Social Service, the progress that has been made seems almost miraculous."

THE OPEN FORUM

This column is intended to afford free expression of opinion by readers on questions of interest. The INTELLIGENCER *is not responsible for any such opinions. Letters must be brief, and the editor reserves the right to omit parts if necessary to save space.*

To the Editor:

From articles in THE INTELLIGENCER I judge that at least some Friends have looked into the case of Sacco and Vanzetti, and have acquitted the two Italians of the crime for which they were sentenced to the electric chair. Believing them innocent, may I ask in all friendliness, why the Society of Friends, as a whole, has not officially taken a stand on the important spiritual issue involved in this case?

The Friends are a powerful group; they possess the respect and affection of all thoughtful people. Through their relief work in Russia and elsewhere, they are becoming known to the keen-witted cynical proletariat. The workers all over the world have been watching them, and are beginning to realize that the Friends' work has no ulterior motive, but is done with the earnest belief in brotherhood, in service; in the practicality of putting Christ's theories into instant practice. But having been fooled many times by other organizations, the workers are still watching! Does your group begin to realize the immense influence you could now wield for peaceful methods as against industrial warfare; for brotherhood instead of enmity, if you took a bold stand in a demand for justice in this new world-famous case of Sacco and Vanzetti?

The proletariat say, with truth, that they cannot get justice in our courts, or by peaceful methods; that under the present system force is the only course open to them. A bomb* thrown at the United States Legation in Paris was in answer to the hypocritical and outrageous sentence accorded their two comrades by the courts of Massachusetts. They believe that an injury to one is an injury to all. Do we? If not, are we Christians? Christ said, "Offenses must come, but woe unto them through whom the offense cometh." Are not all of us who know the injustice done these two Italians, responsible for that bomb—that offense? Surely we are; convicted of guilt by our mental laziness, or cowardice, or lack of initiative in insisting upon justice being given to all by the public servants we put into office.

What is genuine brotherhood but the standing *with* the down and out, *suffering with those in distress*, until we know through our *own discomfort* that we must hold other men's lives as dear as, or dearer than, our own, and, remembering the old saying, that "one with God is a majority," insist upon justice to the workers and their families as we would demand it for our own children.

Before our entrance into the war, the Friends published as an advertisement in many magazines and papers a strong and beautiful protest against war and for brotherhood between nations. Will you not make the same appeal for peace for industrial groups by broadcasting your protest against injustice; setting your candle upon a candlestick that it may give light to all that are in the house? Also sending your protest to the President, the State Department, Judge Thayer and the Governor of Massachusetts? As Moses needed his hand upheld during the passage of the Israelites through the Red Sea, so men in high positions nowadays need *forceful public opinion* to show them that they are set in such positions *merely to be of service to their fellow-men.*

The workers are making an appeal to every high-minded man and woman. They say: "Help us by peaceful methods to get justice, the God-given right of every human being."

Is our answer to be an ignorant silence?

South Danbury, N. H. E. HILLSMITH.

*From a correspondent in Paris at that time comes this word: "In so far as the bombs are concerned—one was thrown at Salle Wagram, another found under a park bench: and their somewhat paradoxical appearance at demonstrations otherwise peaceful gave rise to various conjectures. Some Frenchmen maintain that their origin was similar to that of the Palmer bombs. In all events they furnished a plausible excuse for the mobilizing of thousands of police and soldiers for the two most important demonstrations in Paris."—I. O'Neil in the LIBERATOR of January.—E. H.

BIRTHS.

PETTIT—On Twelfth Month, 26th., to Frank C. and Frances Coles Pettit of Woodstown, New Jersey, a daughter, named Elizabeth A. Pettit.

MARRIAGES.

WEBB-PURDY.—At the Friends' Church, Yorktown Heights, Westchester Co., New York, by Friends' Ceremony Twelfth Month, thirtieth, 1921, Norval E. Webb, of Russiaville, Indiana, to Amie Anna, daughter of Theodore and Sarah H. Purdy, of Yorktown Heights, New York. A reception, at their home immediately followed.

DEATHS.

JANNEY—At Haverford, Pa., on Twelfth Month 31st., Matilda E., wife of Jacob Janney, in her 93d year.

LEEDS—At Moorestown, N. J., First Month 2nd, Susan P. Leeds, aged 71.

LIPPINCOTT—At Marlton, N. J., Twelfth Month 29th. Emma, widow of Samuel Lippincott.

LIPPINCOTT.—At Philadelphia, Pa., on Twelfth Month 27th, Hilles, husband of Elizabeth A. Lippincott.

SHEPPARD.—In Philadelphia, Pa., on Twelfth Month 23d, 1921, William C. Sheppard, in his 95th year.

TEST.—Near Moorestown, N. J., First Month 1st, William P. Test, husband of Virginia B. Test, in his 89th year.

THATCHER.—At West Chester on Twelfth Month. 28th, Enos S. Thatcher, in his 77th year.

COMING EVENTS

FIRST MONTH

6th.—The Brooklyn sewing-group will resume work at 3 P. M., at the Meeting-house, 110 Schermerhorn St. All women are urged to come to sew or knit, and to take sewing home, for the Service Committee.

7th—There will be a recital by the Philadelphia Male Quartette, at George School, Pa., at 8.15 p. m. General admission, 50 cents.

8th—West Philadelphia Bible Class, 35th and Lancaster Avenue, at 10 a. m. Subject—The Christ that was, that is, and that is to come. All welcome.

8th—Conference Class at 15th and Race Streets, Philadelphia, at close of meeting for worship, at 11.40 a. m. Leader, Ida P. Stabler. Topic, Early Friends and Education.

8th—Preparative Meeting will be held in New York and Brooklyn after meeting.

9th—New York Monthly Meeting, at Fifteenth St., and Rutherford Place, New York, at 7.30 P. M. Supper will be served at 6 o'clock.

9th—Friends' Association at Friends' Select School, Chester, Pa., at 8 p. m. Lloyd Balderston will give an illustrated lecture on Japan.

9th—Regular meeting of P. Y. F. A. in Auditorium at 8 P. M.—third lecture on "The Four Gospels," by Dr. Elbert Russell.

9th—New York Monthly Meeting at 221 East 15th St. New York. Meeting for Ministry and Counsel at 5 P. M. Supper at 6 for all present.

14th—Social at the Schermerhorn St., Brooklyn, Meeting-house, at 8 P. M. All cordially invited.

16th—Meeting at 17th Street and Girard Avenue, Philadelphia, at 8 P. M., to be addressed by Elbert Russell. See notice.

18th—Monthly Meeting of Friends of Philadelphia, 15th and Race Streets, 7.30 P. M. See notice.

19th—Green Street Monthly Meeting of Friends of Philadelphia, School House Lane, Germantown, 7.30 P. M.

21st and 22nd—Young Friends' Conference in New York. Social at New York Meeting-house, night of 21st. The delegates from Baltimore and Philadelphia will attend various Meetings First-day morning, a Conference session, First-day afternoon, and The Tea-Meeting at Twentieth Street Meeting-house. All young Friends are urged to extend their circle of acquaintance and inspiration by being present.

22nd—Chester, (Pa.), Monthly Meeting, at Providence, at 2.30 p. m.

24th—Western Quarterly Meeting, at Kennett Square, Pa.

26th—Caen Quarterly Meeting, at Christiana, Pa.

27th—Meeting of Philadelphia Yearly Meeting's Committee on Philanthropic Labor, in Room No. 4 of Race Street Meeting-house, at 2.30 P. M. Talks on the House of Correction and on Motion Pictures. All are cordially invited.

NOTICE—Supper will be served by the Best Interests Committee before Monthly Meeting at Fifteenth and Race Streets, Philadelphia, on First month 18th, in Friends' Central School Lunch Room, at 6 o'clock. Tickets 65 cents. Please purchase tickets before First month 16th, 1922. Anna W. Cloud, 140 North Fifteenth Street.

NOTICE—The Conference Class at Fifteenth and Race Streets, Philadelphia, will be under the care of the Committee on Education of Philadelphia Yearly Meeting during First month. On the 8th, Ida P. Stabler will lead the class, the subject being 'Early Friends and Education." On the 15th, Edward C. Wilson will speak on "Our Friend's School." The subject for the 22nd will be "Vocational Education," but the speaker has not yet been announced. On the 29th, Dr. Paul M. Pearson will address the class on the topic "The Education of Adults."

NOTICE—Elbert Russell will address a meeting to be held First month 16th., at 8 P. M., in the meeting house at 17th Street and Girard Ave., Philadelphia. Subject—The Need of Religious Education. The meeting will be under the joint auspices of Girard Avenue First-day School, Girard Avenue School, and the Best Interest Committee of Race Street Monthly Meeting. A general invitation is extended to all interested.

NOTICE—The Secretary of the Interior, Albert B. Fall, and the Commissioner of Indian Affairs, Charles H. Burke, are expected to be present and speak at the annual meeting of the Indian Rights Association, which this year will be held at 8 P. M., in the Meeting House on Twelfth Street, First month 12th. While the interest of Friends in Indian problems is largely a traditional one, still there are many still active in Indian work who are ready to use their influence and give their support in looking after the best interests of these wards of the nation.

Those who have thought that former Senator Fall was not friendly to work among the Indians, will here have a first-hand chance to learn just what his position is. All interested friends are invited.

GRISCOM HALL

The annual meeting of Stockholders of the Griscom Hall Association will be held in Room No. 1 of the Meeting-house, 15th and Race Streets, Philadelphia, Pa., at 2.30 P. M., Seventh-day, First month (January) 7, 1922. All Stockholders are urged to be present in person if possible.

GRISCOM HALL ASSOCIATION.

American Friends' Service Committee

WILBUR K. THOMAS, Ex. Sec.
20 S. 12th St. Philadelphia

CASH CONTRIBUTIONS

Week Ending December 23

Five Years' Meetings	$497.50
Philadelphia Yearly Meeting	15.00
Other Meetings	
Goose Creek Monthly Meeting, Wrightstown, Pa.	50.00
Solesbury Monthly Meeting	5.00
Lansdowne First-day School	11.27
Alexandria Monthly Meeting	25.00
Lake Stevens Friends' Sunday School	4.80
Goose Creek Monthly Meeting	30.00
Salem Friends	51.00
Flushing Monthly Meeting	9.00
Colerain Friends and Community	110.00
Third Haven Monthly Meeting	43.00
College Park Society of Friends	5.50
Faithful Friends' Class of Woodstown	5.00
Norristown Prep. Mtg.	10.00
Cornwall First-day School	37.50
Contributions for General	2,318.11
For Germany	10,201.66
For Poland	125.00
For Austria	218.79
For Syria	35.00
For Russia	23,630.06
For Russian Overhead	901.35
For Clothing	22.50
Refunds	38.30
	$38,400.34

Shipments received during week ending December 24, 1921—172 boxes and packages received; 4 for German Relief; 8 anonymous.

FUN.

"Carson is the most absent-minded chap I ever saw." "What's he been doing now?" "This morning he thought he had left his watch at home, and then proceeded to take it out of his pocket to see if he had time to go home and get it." "But he doesn't beat the man who went out of his office and put a card on the door saying he would be back at 3 o'clock, and finding that he had forgotten something, went back to the office, read the notice on the door and sat down on the stairs to wait until 3 o'clock."—*Kind Words.*

HOTELS.

SCHOOLS.

To the Lot Holders and others interested in Fairhill Burial Ground:

GREEN STREET Monthly Meeting has funds available for the encouragement of the practice of cremating the dead to be interred in Fairhill Burial Ground. We wish to bring this fact as prominently as possible to those who may be interested. We are prepared to undertake the expense of cremation in case any lot holder desires us to do so.

Those interested should communicate with William H. Gaskill, Treasurer of the Committee of Interments, Green Street Monthly Meeting, or any of the following members of the Committee.

William H. Gaskill, 3201 Arch St.

Samuel N. Longstreth, 1218 Chestnut St.

Charles F. Jenkins, 232 South Seventh St.

Stuart S. Graves, 3033 Germantown Ave.

INTELLIGENCER, for Help Wanted, Positions Wanted, Rooms for Rent, Notices, and other classified advertisements without display, for each insertion, 2 cents per word, including name, initials and address. Answers may be sent to a box at the INTELLIGENCER office, if so directed.

For display advertising the rate is 10 cents per agate line, or $1.40 per column inch, each insertion. On ten or more insertions in a year from date of order, ten per cent. discount. Thus a four-inch single-column or two-inch double-column advertisement costs $5.60 each insertion, less ten per cent., or 5.04 net each time for ten or more insertions. Matter may be changed whenever desired, without extra charge.

Experience has proved the INTELLIGENCER to be a remarkably good advertising medium. All advertisements must "pass the censor!"

Address 140 N. 15th St., Philadelphia

Friends' Intelligencer

ESTABLISHED 1844 PHILADELPHIA, FIRST MONTH 14, 1922 VOLUME 79 NUMBER 2

The Quakerism of George Fox

BY ELBERT RUSSELL

First bi-weekly installment of a series of selected quotations. with comment, from the writings of early Friends. The series, which will bear the general heading "The Quakerism of the Founders," is designed to afford a brief analysis of the convictions of our early leaders regarding questions of current importance.

The Quaker Experience

UT as I had forsaken the priests, so I left the separate preachers also, and those esteemed the most experienced people; for I saw there was none among them all that could speak to my condition. When all my hopes in them and in all men were gone, so that I had nothing outwardly to help me, nor could I tell what to do, then, oh, then, I heard a voice which said, 'There is one, even Christ Jesus, that can speak to thy condition'; and when I heard it, my heart did leap for joy.

"Then the Lord let me see why there was none upon the earth that could speak to my condition, namely, that I might give Him all the glory. For all are concluded under sin, and shut up in unbelief, as I had been; that Jesus Christ might have the preeminence, who enlightens, and gives grace, and faith, and power. Thus when God doth work, who shall hinder it? and *this I knew experimentally*."—*George Fox*: *An Autobiography*, p. 82.

This experience of George Fox was the creative moment in the history of Quakerism. It came to him alone, unmediated by any person or institution. It proved that the mediation of priests, sacraments, and church is unnecessary.

It was not unprepared for, however. He had godly parents. He had sat from childhood under the preaching of a great theologian. He had saturated himself with the thought and language of the Bible until he could repeat most of it from memory. He had consulted many of the priests of neighboring parishes; and associated with many non-conformists sects. This gave him an unusually full religious education. It was, as he found, not a substitute for personal knowledge of God, but it gave him the benefit of other men's knowledge of God, and set him on the way in which he found Him for himself.

The Universal Light

"Now the Lord God opened to me by His invisible power that every man was enlightened by the divine Light of Christ, and I saw it shine through all; and that they that believed in it, came out of condemnation to the Light of life, and became the children of it; but they that hated it, and did not believe in it, were condemned by it, though they made a profession of Christ. This I saw in the pure openings of the Light without the help of any man; neither did I then know where to find it in the Scriptures; though afterwards, searching the Scriptures, I found it. For I saw, in that Light and Spirit which was before the Scriptures were given forth, and which led the holy men of God to give them forth, that all, if they would know God or Christ, or the Scriptures aright, must come to that Spirit by which they that gave them forth were led and taught."—*George Fox*: *An Autobiography*, pp. 101-102.

This is the fundamental principle of Protestantism; involved in Luther's claim that he himself must be convinced by Scripture or plain reason, or he could not change his assertions, because "it is never safe to go against one's conscience."

However, the Protestant leaders had not allowed the same liberty of following the "inward light" to other men, nor did they believe a church or state could be founded on this principle alone.

George Fox trusted it for *all* men as sufficient for all their needs and relations. He believed in the potential divine sonship of all men. It is the true basis of the church universal, the foundation of true democracy, and the hope of universal brotherhood.

The Scriptures

"I was sent to turn people from darkness to the Light, that they might receive Christ Jesus; for to as many as should receive Him in His Light, I saw He would give power to become the sons of God; which power I had obtained by receiving Christ. I was to direct people to the Spirit that gave forth the Scriptures, by which they might be led into all truth, and up to Christ and God, as those had been who gave them forth.

"Yet I had no slight esteem of the holy Scriptures. They were very precious to me; for I was in that Spirit by which they were given forth; and what the Lord opened in me I afterwards found was agreeable to them. I could speak much of these things, and many volumes might be written upon them; but all would prove too short to set forth the infinite love, wisdom, and power of God, in preparing, fitting, and furnishing me for the service to which He had appointed me; letting me see the depths of Satan on the one hand, and opening to me, on the other hand, the divine mysteries of His own everlasting kingdom."—*George Fox: An Autobiography*, pp. 102, 103.

"Concerning the Holy Scriptures: We believe they were given forth by the Holy Spirit of God, through the holy men of God, who (as the Scripture itself declares, 2 Pet. i, 21) spoke as they were moved by the Holy Ghost; we believe they are to be read, believed, and fulfilled (he that fulfills them is Christ) and they are profitable for reproof, for correction, and for instruction in righteousness, that the man of God may be perfect, thoroughly furnished unto all good works, 2 Tim. iii. 19, and are able to make wise unto salvation, through faith in Christ Jesus."—*George Fox: Letter to the Governor and Council of Barbadoes.*

These passages show how George Fox valued and used the Scriptures without being brought into bondage to the letter. They became an aid to the experience of Divine things, a test, and confirmation. He says: "When I had openings, they answered one to another, and answered the Scriptures, for I had great openings of the Scriptures." (*George Fox: An Autobiography*, p. 78.)

Quaker Radicalism

"When the Lord God and His Son Jesus Christ sent me forth into the world to preach His everlasting gospel and kingdom, I was glad that I was commanded to turn people to that inward Light, Spirit and Grace, by which all might know their salvation and their way to God; even that Divine Spirit which would lead them into all truth, and which I infallibly knew would never deceive any.

"But with and by this divine power and Spirit of God, and the Light of Jesus, I was to bring people off from all their own ways, to Christ, the new and living way; and from their churches, which men had made and gathered, to the Church in God, the general assembly written in heaven, of which Christ is the head. And I was to bring them off from the world's teachers, made by men, to learn of Christ, who is the Way, the Truth, and the Life, of whom the Father said, 'This is my beloved Son, hear ye Him'; and off from all the world's worships, to know the Spirit of Truth in the inward parts, and to be led thereby; that in it they might worship the Father of spirits, who seeks such to worship Him. And I saw that they that worshipped not in the Spirit of Truth, knew not what they worshipped."—*George Fox: An Autobiography*, pp. 103-104.

Quakerism involved not only a new basis of faith and duty but a radical change in worship and manner of life. Following the above passage, George Fox goes on to enumerate the customs he was commanded to "bring men off from."

Is our present conformity to the ways of the world about us due to the fact that it has been "brought off from" all that is contrary to the inward Light of Christ or have we declined into conformity with the ways of the world? Is it a healthy sign that we have grown to be conservative as to the business and political ways of the world about us and are very fearful of becoming or being considered radical?

Social Righteousness

"At a certain time, when I was at Mansfield, there was a sitting of the justices about hiring of servants; and it was upon me from the Lord to go and speak to the justices, that they should not oppress the servants in their wages.

"When I was come to the house where they were, and many servants with them, I exhorted the justices not to oppress the servants in their wages, but to do that which was right and just to them; and I exhorted the servants to do their duties, and serve honestly. They all received my exhortation kindly; and I was moved of the Lord therein.

"Moreover, I was moved to go to several courts and steeple-houses at Mansfield, and other places, to warn them to leave off oppression and oaths, and to turn from deceit to the Lord, and to do justly.

"About this time I was sorely exercised in going to their courts to cry for justice, in speaking and writing to judges and justices to do justly; in warning such as kept public houses for entertainment that they should not let people have more drink than would do them good; in testifying against wakes, feasts, May-games, sports, plays, and shows, which trained up people to vanity and looseness, and led them from the fear of God; and the days set forth for holidays were usually the times wherein they most dishonoured God by these things.

"In fairs, also, and in markets, I was made to declare against their deceitful merchandise, cheating, and cozening; warning all to deal justly, to speak the truth, to let their yea be yea, and their nay be nay, and to do unto others as they would have others do unto them; forewarning them of the great and terrible day of the Lord, which would come upon them all."—*George Fox: An Autobiography*, pp. 95, 96, 106. 107.

The effort to follow the Spirit of Christ manifest in their hearts led George Fox, and his co-workers, as later it was to lead John Woolman, to feel the essential wrong of certain social customs, and of phases of the social order, as well as the wickedness of individual men.

The attempt to live out the mind of Christ must lead to social changes as well as to personal reformation before there is room for "the seed to reign."

Education

"Then, returning towards London by Waltham, I advised the setting up of a school there for teaching boys; and also a woman's school to be opened at Shacklewell, for instructing girls and young maidens in whatsoever things were civil and useful in the creation."—*George Fox: An Autobiography*, p. 461.

Fox was keenly conscious of the limitations his own lack of higher education imposed on his service. He supplemented his lack of linguistic and Biblical learning by using liberally the scholarship of the more learned group about him. "The Battle-Door" is perhaps the most noteworthy

THE FRIENDS' INTELLIGENCER is published weekly at 140 N. 15th St., Philadelphia, by FRIENDS' INTELLIGENCER ASSOCIATION, Ltd. Telephone, Spruce 5-75. Entered at Philadelphia Post-Office as second class matter. Subscription in the United States, Mexico, Cuba and Panama, $2.50 a Year. Subscriptions may begin at any time. Subscription in Canada and other foreign countries (on account of extra postage charges), $3.00 a year. Single copies, 6 cents. Make checks payable to FRIENDS' INTELLIGENCER ASSN., LTD.

example of how he drew upon the learning of his associates.

He gave the Society this advice:

"See that schoolmasters and mistresses who are faithful Friends and well qualified be placed and encouraged in all cities and great towns and where they may be needed: the masters to be diligent to forward their scholars in learning and in the frequent reading of the Holy Scriptures and other good books, that being thus *seasoned with the truth*, sanctified to God and taught our holy, self-denying way, they may be instrumental to the glory of God and the generation." (Quoted in *The Later Periods of Quakerism*, by R. M. Jones, Vol. II, p. 666.)

"Fox cherished some large educational views. * * * He proposed that William Tomlinson should set up a school to teach languages, 'together with the nature of herbs, roots, plants and trees.'"

"At his death Fox desired that a part of the Philadelphia property given him by Penn should be enclosed 'for a garden, and to be planted with all sorts of physical plants, for lads and lasses to learn simples there, and the uses to convert them to—distilled waters, oils, ointments, etc.' (*Fells of Swarthmoor Hall*, pp. 366-369; and *Camb. Journ.* ii. 494 note.)"—*Braithwaite, Second Period of Quakerism*, p. 528 and Note 5.

Foreign Missions

"Things beyond seas are pretty well and Truth is spreading: and Truth spread(s) in the Barbados, as we have heard and letters from thence; and spreads in New England; and there is love and unity amongst Friends, though there is one lately put to death and several in prison by the rage of the rulers who drink the blood of the saints. And, in Holland and Germany and other parts that way, Truth spreads and hath a good report. And several more Friends are gone for Barbados and New England; and in Bermudas and Virginia and Maryland and other places Truth spreads; and Friends in the Isle of Man are under sufferings. Charles Bayly, who had been prisoner in Rome and came along with John Perrot is now prisoner in France for crying against their idol priests and their idols; one pretty Friend who is a Frenchman is lately gone over into France. Robert Malins is gone for Jamaica, and many others are preparing to go after him."—Letter of Fox to Friends, Aug. 1661. (Swarthm. Coll. vii. III.)

"This year several Friends were moved to go beyond the seas, to publish Truth in foreign countries. John Stubbs, and Henry Fell, and Richard Costrop were moved to go towards China and Prester John's country; but no masters of ships would carry them."—*George Fox: An Autobiography*, pp. 385, 386.

"They carried with them epistles from Fox, mostly in Latin and English, to the King of Spain, the Pope, the King of France, the magistrates of Malta, the Turk, the Emperor of China, Prester John, and, as a last epistle, one addressed 'To all the nations under the whole heavens.'"—*Braithwaite, Beginnings of Quakerism*, p. 429.

It was a great loss to Friends when they lost this world-wide outlook of Fox and the missionary zeal of the first generation of "Publishers of Truth." Our renewed interest in carrying the Quaker message in word and work to other peoples is both a sign of new spiritual life and an aid to it.

German Thoughts on Silent Worship

"Scheigender Dienst," under which title Violet Hodgkin's Swarthmore Lecture, "Silent Worship," has been published in German with a preface by Dr. Otto, has been reviewed in the "Frankfurter Zeitung," by M. Deutschbein, Professor of English at Marburg University.

He says: "In view of the keen interest in Quakerism in Germany at the present time, this little pamphlet by Violet Hodgkin deserves our attention. It treats of a peculiarity of the divine worship of the Quakers, viz., the so-called silent worship, the only sacrament of the Quakers, if one can use such an expression. Silent Worship, Silent Service, or Spiritual devotion in the silence, or through silence, has for the Quakers the significance of an immediate realization of the divine. The "Silent Service," which, however, implies the highest activity, has, according to Dr. Otto, a threefold aim: the inner union of the many in the oneness and fellowship of the Spirit which arises out of the depth, the waiting for the breaking forth of the Spirit in free discussion or prayer, and finally the quiet resting in the presence of the Highest and its strengthening and illuminating fellowship even without words.

"Violet Hodgkin refers to a number of parallels and prototypes of this kind of worship. They are to be found in not only non-Christian religions, but also in early Christian times, and in the middle ages. The small sects and communities of early modern times have particularly close points of contact. Among the Quakers themselves, the history of "Silent Service," is of course very thoroughly treated. An interesting book from the psychological and historical-religious point of view, very tastefully got up (with a picture of the listening Angel in the Cathedral of Southwell); and in its excellent German translation, should edify and elevate many readers in the quiet hour."

The German translation is obtainable through the Friends' Bookshop, 140 Bishopgate, London, E. C. 2, for 1/6.

Q. Q.

The Creed

Whoever was begotten by pure love,
And came desired and welcomed into life,
Is of immaculate conception. He
Whose heart is full of tenderness and truth,
Who loves mankind more than he loves himself,
And cannot find room in his heart for hate,
May be another Christ. We all may be
The Saviours of the world, if we believe
In the Divinity which dwells in us
And worship it, and nail our grosser selves,
Our tempers, greeds, and our unworthy aims,
Upon the cross. Who giveth love to all,
Pays kindness for unkindness, smiles for frowns,
And lends new courage to each fainting heart,
And strengthens hope and scatters joy abroad,
He, too, is a redeemer, Son of God.

—*Ella Wheeler Wilcox.*

SELECTED BY MARY H. WHITSON.

FRIENDS' INTELLIGENCER

The religion of Friends is based on faith in the "INWARD LIGHT," or direct revelation of God's spirit and will in every seeking soul.

The INTELLIGENCER is interested in all who bear the name of Friends in every part of the world, and aims to promote love, unity and intercourse among all branches and with all religious societies.

Editorial and business offices, 140 N. 15th Street, Philadelphia, Pa. For information regarding subscription rates, etc., see foot of second page.

PHILADELPHIA, FIRST MONTH 14, 1922

IN THIS ISSUE

The Society of Friends is a group of men and women held together by a common spiritual tradition. At its best, that tradition is not inert, but is plastic and developing, responsive to new needs as new generations turn to it for the solution of new problems. But it has behind it centers of insight and inspiration, sources from which it has taken purpose and direction, in the lives and the thoughts of men and women who labored for its development in the past.

While, therefore, we should not lack the initiative nor the courage to square our present activities with present world needs, we may refresh our vision of the central ideals of our religious movement, by turning back occasionally to the records of its past efforts and aspirations.

In the spiritual influence of the personalities, the convictions, and the lives of its founders and former leaders reside the true sources of Quaker tradition. More important than the Meeting-houses which early generations have left to us, more important than the quaint heirlooms and historic scenes, is the spirit with which these generations bore themselves. From what sources did they draw the vision and courage which led them to endure privation and imprisonment for the sake of their ideals? Along what lines did they seek to aid in world progress? What did they consider to be the true relationship between the "spiritual" and the "social service" aspects of religious idealism. What was their attitude toward "radicalism"? The attitude toward life, which we may induce from the answers to such questions as these, constitutes the real Quaker tradition. A clear conception of the exact nature of this tradition is one of the surest guides which our Society can hold before it in working its way forward through the trying present age.

Most of us, however, find no time for a detailed sifting out of the great mass of early Quaker literature. We need some synopsis of the whole field which can give us the upshot of the matter in a brief and useable form.

With such thoughts as these in mind, the *Intelligencer* has arranged with Elbert Russell to select a series of short quotations on important topics, from the works of early Quaker leaders, and to follow each of these quotations with brief comments suggestive of its bearing on the problems of the present. "The Quakerism of George Fox," our leading article this week, introduces the series. Bi-weekly installments will follow under the general heading, "The Quakerism of the Founders."

It is our hope that this review of Quaker tradition, as formulated in the writings of the Society's early leaders, may aid in leading toward the deepened vision, and the more resolutely consecrated way of life, to which the present world challenge calls us.

A recent number of *The American Friend* contains a fine review, by Amy Winslow, of the pamphlet "Industrial Facts," by Kirby Page (George H. Doran Co., New York. Price 10 cents). The paragraphs with which the writer introduces her subject give excellent expression to the point of view which looks upon the relation of Friends to industrial evolution as a matter of religious concern.

This point of view the *Intelligencer* seeks to champion, regarding it as probably the most vital single issue before our Society at the present time. We are glad, therefore, to be able to quote the following from another Friends' paper:

> "This task of living on equality with our brother is so bound up with the complexities and inequalities of modern life and industry that the application of the Christian principles of Love and Justice is not the simple matter of individual adjustment which we find in our personal relationships. We become involved in matters of finance, production, trade, mass hatreds, old and inherited prejudices and instincts and a hundred other complex situations too difficult for overnight solution or mere personal goodwill.
>
> "Understanding of these problems and of proposed solutions we find more and more necessary. They challenge us on every side. The Christian conscience can no longer rest in comfort without some personal effort being put forth to ease the growing tension in industry, the swelling unrest in the ranks of unhappy and dissatisfied labor."

To those desiring a broad introductory view of the whole industrial problem and of the solutions being attempted at present, we agree with Amy Winslow in recommending the pamphlet, "Industrial Facts."

"The Quaker Challenge," by Charles R. Simpson, an article from *The Quaker* just printed in pamphlet form by the Friends' Bookshop (English), is likewise to be recommended. It traces the concern which Friends have had regarding the social problems of the past and relates that concern to the social problem presented today by the industrial order. Another new Quaker review of the problem, somewhat more detailed in scope, but readable in the course of a few evenings, is Maurice L. Rowntree's "Social Freedom." Copies of the latter works may be obtained ordered through all Friends' bookshops.

The Washington Conference

IX.

By William I. Hull

Submarines: Shall they be increased and unlimited in number and size; or reduced and limited; or totally abolished? This is the question that has been the subject of animated debate within the Conference Committee during the past two weeks. France has demanded the right to increase her submarine fleet to 90,000 tons' displacement (the limit proposed by Secretary Hughes for Great Britain and the United States), without any limitation on their size; the United States has proposed a reduction in the present number of submarines of all nations and a limitation upon them in the future; Great Britain has urged their entire abolition. The French have been victorious in the Committee, and the Conference at its next open session will doubtless confirm this result. The American proposal, a compromise between the French and British positions, has not been successful; but, on the other hand, our delegation has succeeded in securing unanimous consent to the adoption of rules designed to curb in as drastic a manner as possible the operation of submarines when engaged in warlike activities. The British have served notice on the whole civilized world that they will carry their attack upon any use of the submarine into the open session of the Conference and on to success in the future.

The debate has been an illuminating one, with the balance of logic and humanity inclining to the side of the British. The arguments of the French are thirteen in number. They claim that public opinion, in the discussion of the Treaty of Versailles, during the League of Nations' discussion of the question, and in the report of the American Advisory Committee, has shown itself in favor of the retention of submarines; that they are preeminently a defensive weapon; that they are the natural defense of nations scantily supplied with capital ships, that is, of the weaker and poorer nations; that the number of submarines possessed by any nation should be proportioned only to its national needs; that large submarines are more in accord than smaller ones with the dictates of humanity, since they can rescue the crews of torpedoed ships; that submarines of large cruising radius are needed to defend distant colonies, and to maintain the lines of communication between these and the mother-country; that submarines can be used under honorable conditions just as *any* weapon can be used either honorably or dishonorably; that they cannot gain control and domination of the seas; that the recent war proved the utility of the submarines as a weapon against warships; since the Germans torpedoed three French battleships and five cruisers; that by necessitating a large defensive system, they can weaken the enemy's offensive; that as wireless stations they are very useful for scouting purposes; that the German submarines proved themselves useful auxiliaries to submarine mines in protecting the German and Gallipoli coasts from bombardment; that it is justifiable to wage war against the enemy's merchant marine, and even more humane than more direct means of using force.

The British met these arguments,—or rather foresaw and answered them in advance,—and stated arguments of their own, as follows: Submarines are not adequate to the defense of coasts against bombardment and the landing of troops, since these operations are conducted by swift-moving and powerfully-armed ships fully equipped to nullify submarine attacks. The ineffectiveness of submarines against warships is proved by the experience of Germany which, with 375 U-Boats during the war, had 203 of them sunk and was unable by means of them to sink a single ship of the British Grand Fleet; to prevent British light cruisers from sweeping through the North Sea unhindered; to prevent the crossing and recrossing of the English Channel by 15,000,000 British troops, without the loss of a single life; or to prevent the transport of 2,000,000 American troops across the Atlantic with equal safety. As for the defense of coast lines, the British argued that theirs are four times the circumference of the globe,—almost as long as those of the other four great powers put together; but that so convinced are they of the ineffectiveness of submarines for defending coast-lines that they are willing to give them up. As for defending maritime and other communication between colonies and mother-country, submarines are much stronger in attacking than defending them, and this is especially true when the defending country does not possess the command of the sea on the surface. From the point of view of defense, also, submarines are useless for defense against other submarines; hence, since Great Britain could also build submarines and possesses a large share of the control of the sea on its surface, she could launch a more effective submarine attack against the communications of other nations than others could launch against her.

Both reason and experience show, the British contend, that it is against merchant ships alone that the submarine achieves real success. During the recent war, German submarines sank 12,000,000 tons of merchant shipping, while achieving practically nothing against warships. Admittedly, Great Britain is most exposed to the menace of submarines against merchant ships, and especially against food supplies; for Britain's soil produces only two-fifths of Britons' food, and not more than a seven-weeks' supply can be maintained. Hence, starvation faces Britain in submarine warfare; and this is as grave a danger as any that can confront France. It is not an insuperable one, as Great Britain proved during the recent war. But it is ingratitude, to say the least, for the nations present at the Washington Conference to hint at "starving Great Britain into submission." Without the British navy, which was almost the keystone of the Allied arch, France and Belgium would have been ruined, and even the United States would have been impotent to intervene, or might have been obliged to abandon its army in France. Can France of all nations, run the risk of a disaster to her near neighbor and only certain ally, should the circumstances of 1914 occur again? But other nations, too, have merchant ships and the need of food imported from abroad, which British submarines could attack. Hence Great Britain's desire to abolish submarines is not a purely selfish and unworthy one; for the British believe that they are fighting against submarines in behalf of the whole civilized world.

All the Allied world once believed, and the British still believe, their spokesmen say, that submarines engage in cowardly and inhuman war. Twenty thousand non-combatants, men, women and children, were drowned in the recent submarine war. This was in violation of laws, both human and divine; but the excuse was then, and will always be, that necessity knows no law. Officers and crews of submarines may be honorable men, but they must obey their governments; and submarines by their very nature cannot rescue the passengers and crews of torpedoed ships. The submarine, then, is a weapon of murder and piracy. The Treaty of Versailles forbade Germany to construct any more submarines, whether for military or mercantile purposes, and it was intended thereby to banish all submarines from the sea. For it is not to be assumed that Germany is always to be bad, and other nations are always to be good; it is not logical to have one rule for Germany, and another for the rest of the world.

It is argued that "submarine warfare is cheap and within the reach of all." Even though this were true, warfare should not be made cheap; for when cheap, it is both easy and continuous. But, on the contrary, submarines may cause a very heavy expense to both the offense and defense. For example, there were only nine or ten German submarines at sea at one time, during the recent war, but Great Britain was required to maintain 3,000 anti-submarine craft to deal with them. Let us not, then, expend upon submarines and anti-submarine craft what we save on capital ships. Great Britain, with its very large number of steam-propelled, steel-built fishing boats, which can readily be equipped with anti-submarine devices, is already best equipped of all nations to cope with submarines. She probably has also the largest and most efficient submarine fleet. But she offers to scrap them all and disband their highly trained personnel, thus offering, she believes, a larger sacrifice than any made by her sister nations, and contributing to the cause of humanity a greater boon than even the reduction and limitation of capital ships.

Finally, the British argue, the menace of the submarine can be gotten rid of only by total abolition. Limitation is not sufficient; for submarines are essentially a weapon of offensive war, and a fleet of them can be rapidly expanded if the submarine industry be kept alive and a nucleus of trained personnel be maintained. Unlike poison gas and aerial bombs, the submarine is not the by-product of any industry; it can and should be unconditionally abolished.

The Italian delegation repeated some of the French arguments in favor of submarines for defense, and added that only five nations were represented in the Armament Conference, while many others could build submarines. To this argument, Chairman Hughes added the statement that the five nations represent the potency of competition in capital ships, but not in submarines, for in the building of these, other nations could compete with the five. To forestall this objection, Lord Lee, speaking for Great Britain, had said that the other powers were not likely to defy the opinion of the civilized world, if the five powers in the Washington Conference would abolish submarines; but should they do so and begin to build, the five great sea-powers would surely find some means of protection against the other, smaller ones.

The result of the long debate has been to place no maximum limit on the submarine or other auxiliary tonnage of any nation; and we may expect to see either a competition in the building of these instruments of war, and of devices designed to cope with them, or the development of "the public opinion of the civilized world" which will put an end in some future conference to the competition, and perhaps to the building itself. Friends, applying to the question their principle that all war, all agencies of war and all preparation for war, are wrong, will have no difficulty in deciding where they stand on the much-debated question. But it is well for us to know and sympathetically consider the arguments on both sides, so that we may do our share in bringing about the right decision.

The American proposition to restrict the size of auxiliary ships to 10,000 tons, the British proposition to restrict the size of their guns to eight inches, and the rules proposed for the curbing of submarine activities, including the outlawry and treating as pirates of any submarine crews who violate these rules) have been adopted in committee; and a new debate has just begun on the American proposition to abolish chemical warfare.

Washington, D. C., January 7, 1922.

Native Quakers in Russia

Discovery Reported by Relief Worker

Since undertaking relief work in Russia during the war, the Society of Friends has continually had news of the existence of groups of so-called Quakers, but has never been able to make any contacts with the sect, although they have been well in touch with not dissimilar bodies such as the Doukhobors and the Molekani.

Better fortune, however, has met two of their most recent workers to go to Russia who are now fighting the famine in the Buzuluk area. One of them, Mr. Tom Copeman, a well-known Norwich journalist, describes how they came upon one of these groups as they were picking up all their worldly possessions preparatory to migrating for a more fertile region in the Caucasus. "In the rain the men folk were busy taking their little wagons to pieces and three dromedaries, 'whether their own or borrowed,' looked very miserable and thin."

A meeting was arranged with them before their departure and Mr. Copeman writes:

"As they sat on boxes and benches on the other side of the table, one could not but help being struck by their faces—especially the face of a matronly woman, who sat silent with folded hands. Whether it was her headgear or what I don't know, but it has struck me since that she was a little like Elizabeth Fry as pictured.

The answers they gave to our questions were extraordinarily interesting, especially the fact that according to tradition they had been started about 300 (three hundred) years ago by someone from England, and had been always called Quakers by other people. They looked, I should add, remarkably clean, considering the conditions under which they had been lately living.

"They told us that although they refused to register for military service, they do register in the Commune for agricultural work. In the Czar's time, 609 of them refused to bear arms and were most of them imprisoned, the leader who told us this being one, but being pardoned owing to ill-health.

"Kerensky, at the beginning of his regime knocked off their chains on 11th., March, 1917, and told them to go and register. They, however, refused, and said they would rather stay in prison. After nine days' further imprisonment they were then released. The Soviet Government had excused them from military service on the grounds of their beliefs, but one had however been sentenced to five years by local authorities, ignorant of the decree of the central government or else actuated by spite. As soon as the Soviet Government discovered the fact, (after a year and a half,) he was released. The Government had also excused them some of the requisitions for corn, knowing that they led a communal life and were true to the government in not hiding any supplies as many other peasants did. Unfortunately they had been thrice raided by brigands and because of this and the famine were forced to move.

"Questioned as to oaths, they said that they did not believe in them but in brotherly words. As far as marriage went they registered their marriages with the Government when requested, but believed that in marriage they were guided by the spirit and that registration or oath is unnecessary. They hold a meeting for the purpose of marriage when "the brother declares to the sister that they will be married." If matrimonial troubles arise, another brother says: "Brother you are doing wrong." They do not believe in funeral rites, but if anyone dies, a meeting is called to settle the practical details of the burial. In all they consider that (apart from other slightly different bodies,) they number one million, but as they do not have any form of organization or any test for membership apparently, they said it was hard to say. As far as the Social Order goes, they seem to be very near to Communism, but they seem to desire to be moved entirely by the Spirit and to have no set forms. When a meeting begins they sing together, or talk, or sit in silence, and believe that 'the same brotherly feeling runs through them all.' God is always with them, they said, but they gather to express themselves and for fellowship."

These primitive Russian Quakers are vegetarians, and their life and religion is of the simplest nature. They say there is no need to pay kopecks to the priest, for everyone has equal access to God. They have no special times for their meetings for worship, and at these meetings one and all have liberty to take part. Some of the hymns they sing are marked by a deep spiritual insight and fervour.

The following are prose translations of two of them.

"Hark! Speech is growing, the hour is coming, the voice of God is calling us to stand up for the truth. Be ready with free words or with deeds, at your post, be ready to confront a menacing death and cross. Since long ago we waited for the dawn, for long we lived in slavery, for long we waited for a beam of light to break the chains of darkness. But it is enough for us to wait for freedom; we shall go to meet it, fearing not the thorny way, nor the menacing of the powers. The earthly power shall not rule over our conscience. Be ready to openly stand up for your convictions.

"Do not give your oath, and do not use force, and yet be not a slave to any one; return good for evil, caring not for military honor, respect only the law of love, and reject killing; do not soil your hands with blood. A cruel fight was fought against slavery to gain freedom.

"Most unmerciful enmity has been born everywhere, but we deny force, we go about a different way, and wrestling we conquer darkness by light and evil by good, not by force, not by blood, and with prison. Only with truth and love we shall overcome the reign of darkness.

"My friend, in a moment of irritation do not bury enmity in your heart; you must forgive and like a fog let it all blow away.

"My friend, to those who do evil to you return only good; remember they themselves regret perhaps and suffer for thoughtless acts; we all are subject to mistakes; we all are men not only 'they.'

"With noble hearts and mind are those who forgive with simplicity of soul; you, also, forgive and learn to show your high gift and be not ashamed to be the first to stretch your hand."

HUBERT W. PEET.

Have You a Rose?

Have you a rose for a friend such as I?
Give it to me; don't wait till I die.
Breathing its sweetness and watching its glow
Will give me a joy that the dead can not know.
Say your kind word to my listening ear—
The word which my sad soul is longing to hear:
Life passes swiftly as spring-melted snows;
Share your sweet tokens of love ere it goes.

E. A. Long, in "The Freedman's Friend."

"With Quakers in France"

A review of "With Quakers In France," by D. Owen Stephens. London: C. W. Daniels, Ltd., pp. 336. $4.50. Obtainable from Walter H. Jenkins, 140 North Fifteenth Street, Philadelphia, Pa.

Anyone who wants an intimate knowledge of the work of the Friends in France, cannot do better than read Owen Stephen's book. It is never possible to get acquainted with a new person by being told about him. A "Life and Letters," depends much more on the letters than on the "life;" for the latter is always what some one thinks about the victim of the biography, while the former is the person himself. Owen Stephens has taken us into even closer intimacy, for he has given us his journal. And as this may be considered as letters written both *from* the mission and *to* the mission, it is doubly saturated with the spirit thereof.

The book takes the reader from September, 1917, with the mission in training at Haverford, to March, 1919, after the armistice and in the midst of the Versailles Conference. It includes incident, dialogue, fun, religion and philosophy. We get views of French peasants and soldiers, of German prisoners, of Americans and other allies, and of their more or less bewildered reaction to the point of view of the Quakers.

Occasionally we get a glimpse of matters usually hidden. Thus a woman of the American Relief Department in France is quoted: "The peasants almost always say they would rather have German troops billeted on them than French troops. The Germans are more strict in discipline. Further on we read that some members of the mission took a short walk into the country. We were astonished to see a large, nearly completed Red Cross;—a circle of white plaster chips with a big red cross of crushed brick inside—stretching twenty-five feet or more. On one side of it stood six field guns—across the road, another thirty yards, is a battery of twelve more guns, and twelve carts of ammunition. It seems there was some excuse for bombing "red cross hospitals."

There is a great deal of very good material in the book and it would do our Friends good to read it. The illustrations—seventeen original drawings by the author—add very much to its value.

It may be of interest to add that since his return to America, Owen Stephens has become a member of Swarthmore Meeting.

JESSE H. HOLMES.

"Democracy and the Church"

The *Journal of Religion* for September contains an article under this title by R. W. Frank, of McCormick Theological Seminary, from which the following is taken:

"Nothing short of the redemption of the social order from all its vices, diseases, malformations and maladjustments, should be the goal of the church, and its primary function should be to incite and then enlist men to the consummation of this task. Education will be the principal method. . . . It will be more effective and conative than in the past, a building up of social attitudes, desires and habits, a moralization of the individual. . . . . Should not the basis of church membership be an intelligent willingness to co-operate in the church's enterprise rather than a submissive acceptance of ecclesiastical dogma? Is not loyalty to the humanitarian purposes of Christianity the more excellent and more just test of fitness for church membership?"

What a Pair of Boy's Pants Can Do

Quite an ordinary man appeared one day in the Clothing Department of the Friends' Mission, in Vienna. His face was thin and anxious, his manner helpless and depressed, and he wore the remains of a military uniform. By one hand he held his five-year-old son, and in the other a bundle of clothes which had just been given to him. The helper in charge of the counter took the bundle and began checking the garments from the list made out by the Austrian helper. Counting, "eight, nine, ten—two garments for every person—have you got what you wanted?" she asked mechanically. It is difficult not to become mechanical, when the same thing has to be said three hundred times a day.

"I had hoped," said the man in tones suggestive of despair, "to get some trousers for my little boy, but the Fraulein says that there are none left."

"Yes, that is right, I am sorry there are no more today," said the woman hastily.

She was well used to the tragedy of being out of stock of some particular garment, and hated to enter into a discussion that could only lead to nothing.

"What we have not got we cannot give," she said, a truism that she had carefully learned in Germany to be used for these occasions.

The man picked up the little shirt and knitted scarf that were the boy's share of the family bundle.

"I would willingly give up all the other things for a pair of trousers," he said; "my wife has made shirts for the children out of an old one of mine, but she has no stuff for their suits. If she were here she would know how to explain; but she is in the hospital and I am afraid I do not know about the making of children's clothes. The gracious lady may see for herself that Franz needs trousers very urgently."

He took his son by the shoulder and turned him around for inspection; and the young woman leaning over the table was at once convinced of the urgency of the need. Patching and darning are arts more practiced in Vienna than in other countries to-day; and the young lady had had ample opportunity to study much mended clothes; but such a marvel of patchwork as she saw upon the trousers of the boy had never come to her notice. It was impossible to see the original fabric of Franz's knickerbockers, for every pattern of cloth and serge seemed to be represented on them. The patches varied in size also from a walnut to a melon, and their shape was fantastic. The sight called up a vision of a careful mother, setting her house in order before going to the hospital, judging and contriving and using every shred of her little store of scraps of cloth.

The helper went to the Austrian fraulein, who unpacked and sorted the second-hand clothes from America, and laid the case before her. "Um Gottes Willen," said that lady when she saw the boy and his patches, and she fell upon her orderly piles, turned them all over, dug into half-unpacked bales, but all in vain. Every sort of other garment was there, but no trousers.

"The rush is over," said the helper; "could you find time to go over to the other depot and see if they have anything there? No new trousers have come in to-day, you know, but perhaps among the second-hand bale—" The fraulein waited for no further encouragement, but went.

The man still stood by the table, as though prepared to remain there for ever, and Franz waited beside him, equally patient and quite unconcerned. It was near the end of the day and the work of tidying up the room went on.

At last Fraulein Schmidt appeared in triumph, bearing in her hand a pair of small blue serge knickerbockers. The people in the other depot had hunted through everything, and nearly in despair had found these at the very bottom of a bale. A look of intense relief came over the father's face as though the burden of life had been suddenly lightened. He began some broken thanks, and gathered up his bundle. He bent over the hand which had given such a treasure to his boy. Franz carefully shook hands with the two women, and they went out into the late afternoon together.

Somebody in America brought that unspeakable happiness to that father's heart. Is there, after all, much that can bring more gladness to a father's heart than to be able to provide for his children's needs? Would you like to feel that glow of happiness which would come to you if you knew you were the cause of helping fathers to help their children like that? The way is very simple. Send to the Friends' Storeroom at Fifteenth and Cherry Streets, Philadelphia, all the clothing you can possible spare. You may not know whom you have made glad. But that makes no difference. You will create the happiness and it will live in the world.

Help Poland

Three cents will feed a child for two days with fresh milk.

Three dollars will feed a child for six months with fresh milk.

Twenty cents will buy a spade.

A dollar and a half will buy a plough.

A dollar will buy enough barley for an acre.

A dollar and a quarter will buy enough oats to sow an acre.

A cent will buy three bricks for a stove.

Five dollars will buy enough bricks for a complete stove,

A cent will buy a tile for a roof.

Fourteen dollars will buy a whole roof.

Forty cents will buy a window.

A cent will provide a starving refugee with bread for a day.

Twenty-five cents will feed a family for a week.

Mark your contributions for the destination you want, and send them to The Service Committee, 20 South 12th Street, Philadelphia.

Service Committee Notes

X-Ray Outfit Sent to Russia

In accordance with instructions from Philadelphia, Francis Bacon, of the German Unit, has purchased an X-ray equipment and sent it to Arthur Watts in Russia.

Murray Kenworthy Ill With Typhus

A cable received at the Service Committee headquarters December 28th, stated that Murray Kenworthy, of Wilmington, Ohio, and who sailed in November to become a member of the Russian Unit, was taken with typhus in Buzuluk. A cable received at headquarters on January 3rd, stated that on the eighth day of his illness his condition was favorable. A nurse was sent down from Moscow, and every possible care is being given him.

When Murray Kenworthy reached Russia the Philadelphia headquarters appointed him the acting chief of the American Friends' Unit; and he immediately began the organization of feeding 50,000 children in Buzuluk. His wife and three children are now at Wilmington, Ohio.

Two others of the Unit in Russia have already had typhus since November, they being Anna Louise Strong and Nancy Babb. Both of these are now entirely recovered.

Clothing Needed At Once For Poland

"The supplies of clothing at Baranowice are completely exhausted, especially clothes for women. The refugees are reaching our outpost stations with very insufficient clothing. The weather is now quite severe, and the lack of adequate clothing is causing many deaths. We can save lives provided clothing comes."

So wrote Oscar Moon from Warsaw last week. The need for clothing constantly increases. Every bit of your old clothing can be used. Send everything you can to our storeroom, care of Elizabeth Marot, at 15th and Cherry Streets, Philadelphia, Pa.

Inter-Racial Committee Meeting

Miss Jessie R. Fauset, literary editor of the Crisis, came to Philadelphia to attend the January meeting of the Philadelphia Inter-racial Committee, and at its meeting at Fifteenth and Race streets, gave an interesting story of the Second Pan-African Congress, held for a week last summer in Europe. Miss Fauset has a charming personality and speaks with simple, fluent ease. She holds an A. B. degree from Cornell, and her master's degree from the University of Pennsylvania.

The first Pan-African Congress was held in Paris in 1919. France was chosen because she is the most liberal of all countries in her treatment of people of darker hue. The Congress of 1921 divided its sessions among London, Brussels and Paris. Its meetings were liberally reported by leading journals. One hundred and ten delegates representing about 26 different groups of African descent attended, and from 1000 to 1200 people, white and colored, were present at the sessions.

Eight resolutions were passed with enthusiasm in London demanding: Recognition of civilized men as civilized, despite their race or color; local self-government for backward groups; education in self-knowledge, science and industrial technique undivorced from the art of beauty; freedom in their own religion and customs; co-operation with the rest of the world in government, industry and art on the basis of justice, freedom and peace; defense against the unrestrained greed of invested capital; the establishment of a bureau under the League of Nations for the study of the Negro problems, and for the protection of native labor.

In Brussels the Congress was attended by more white people than colored and there was a noticeable constraint in free speech, the shadow of the Belgian Congo with its rich treasures exploited by white capital hanging over the sessions. The resolutions which for the sake of racial unity were allowed to pass dealt only with racial susceptibility to culture, etc. In Paris the resolutions were again passed with some modifications in regard to capitalism.

Then the final coup, the presentation of the results of the Congress to the Assembly of the League of Nations then meeting in Geneva. This was managed through the social help of a titled English woman and the prestige of Dr. Dubois' name and personality. Three requests were presented on the floor of the Assembly, for a separate section of the League to deal particularly with the conditions and needs of native Negro labor, especially in Africa and the Islands of the Sea; that a man of Negro descent be added to the Mandates Commission; and that the good offices of the League be exercised in behalf of the Negro race and to check the growing feeling that it is permissible to treat civilized men as uncivilized if they are colored.

The Congress counts among its results also the permanent Pan-African Association, with plans to hold a meeting every other year; the startled attention of the white world which had not known that Negroes could organize, finance and manage such a vast business; and last, but not least, the sense of racial consciousness, friendship and reawakened hope.

ANNE BIDDLE STIRLING,

Chairman, Philadelphia Inter-Racial Committee.

Friendly News Notes

A Reformed Church *Intelligencer* of recent date contains a column article on the visit to America of B. Seebohm Rowntree, English Quaker manufacturer. It outlines his work for a more Christian industrial order, and emphasizes the effect which his visit has had upon American manufacturers.

The Grange, at one time the home of Isaac Pennington and of Mary Pennington's daughter Gulielma Springett, prior to her marriage with William Penn, is reported by the London *Friend* as being on the market. It has been altered and enlarged somewhat since Isaac Pennington's day but some of the original structure still remains. Jordans Friends are hoping that it may once more come into the possession of Friends.—*The American Friend.*

Martha Speakman spent Christmas with her parents, Dr. and Mrs. William W. Speakman, of Philadelphia, formerly of Swarthmore. It was the first Christmas in five years she spent at home. Martha Speakman has been abroad in war relief work for several years. She is receiving letters from friends "over there" that tell of terrible conditions abroad. Children cannot go to school bcause of a lack of clothing and shoes. Such meager salaries are paid, for instance, $1.25 a month in our money—not sufficient to buy bread. A recent letter describes the riots in Vienna and the real causes of the same.—*Swarthmore News.*

GERMANTOWN FRIENDS' ASSOCIATION

The Germantown Friends' Association has had an active and interesting winter. A series of current topic talks has been given once a month by Warwick James Price and there have been several social evenings when home talent was in evidence. On the sixth of last month we united with the Coulter Street Friends in giving a supper to over 300. This supper was given at Coulter Street Meeting, and in the evening Anna J. Haines and Rufus Jones spoke on conditions in Russia. The supper gave an opportunity for social mingling and was a very successful affair.

On the 25th of this month a musical evening is planned for by the committee in charge.

CHICAGO EXECUTIVE MEETING

The Advancement Committee of Illinois Yearly Meeting has held several meetings and is planning special activities to be held in connection with Quarterly Meetings, as well as with the meetings for worship. We are hoping to get freer expression in the meetings for worship.

We are discussing the possibility of having an Executive Secretary for the Chicago Meeting, some one who can take an active part in the First-day meeting, and spend some time in looking up those Friends who no longer attend meeting.

During Twelfth month we had the pleasure of having with us Mary Travilla, who was returning to California, and William T. Cope, of West Chester, Pa., who is on his way to Nebraska for the A. F. S. Committee on the Corn Committee. Both these Friends gave helpful and inspiring messages. William Cope spent the week visiting Friends of both meetings in Chicago.

JEANNETTE FLITCRAFT.

Items From Everywhere

The U. S. House of Representatives recently passed a bill to prohibit the sending through the U. S. mails of any newspaper or other printed or written matter giving or purporting to give the odds, bets or wagers being laid on horse races, prizefights or other contests of speed, strength or skill. *The U. S. Senate should promptly pass this bill,* for it would cut the heart out of the great National gambling business in many ways. Letters urging the support of this bill (H. R. Bill, No. 6508) should be sent to the Senators representing one's state at Washington.

Edward A. Filene, President of Wm. Filene's Sons Co., of Boston, has just returned from a study of conditions in Europe and is circulating a petition urging the government of the United States to defer Austria's American debt for twenty years. Such a measure is necessary to prevent the moral and physical breakdown of the Austrian people. Similar measures have already been agreed upon by the other nations interested. Austria's debt to America was incurred by her purchase of food for her starving population, and she is totally incapacitated for payment at present.

An examination of the Attorney General's report discloses that during the year ending, June 30, 1921, Presidents Wilson and Harding pardoned 485 criminals out of 641 applicants. During the preceding year Wilson pardoned 639 criminals out of 664 applicants. In a statement commenting upon these facts, Albert DeSilver, director of the American Civil Liberties Union, says: "It is difficult to understand, that expressions of opinion should be considered by our government as more heinous than murder, robbery or white slavery. That this seems so, is shown by the refusal of President Harding to pardon any substantial number of political prisoners whose only offense was the expression of opinion in war time. Some of these political prisoners were sentenced to terms as long as 20 years, a longer time than is usually imposed for serious crimes against person and property."

MARRIAGES.

Gillam-Stabler—At Swarthmore, Pa., on Twelfth month 31st, under the care of Swarthmore Monthly Meeting of Friends, Cornelia Miller, daughter of Ida Palmer Stabler of Swarthmore, Pa., and the late Charles M. Stabler, and Clifford Riggs Gillam, son of William and Rachel Gillam, of Langhorne, Pa. The ceremony took place in Swarthmore Meeting House, at 4 o'clock in the afternoon.

Weaver-Bradley—At her home near Peach Bottom, Pa., on Twelfth month 31st, 1921, Edith Mabel Bradley, daughter of Martin H. and Katherine S. Bradley, and Arthur Lee Weaver, of Peach Bottom, Pa.

DEATHS.

Brabson—At her home, near Nottingham, Pa., on Twelfth month 25th, 1921, Nancy Jane Brabson, in her 84th year.

Bumgarner—At his home near McNabb, Ills., on Tenth month 5th, 1921, after an illness of less than twenty-four hours, Oscar Bumgarner. He was born in Washington Co., Pa., in 1842. He left a wife, eight children and seven grandchildren. A son-in-law of the late Joshua L. Mills, well known in the Society of Friends.

He was a devoted father and husband. A member of the Clear Creek Monthly Meeting of Friends. Burial at Clear Creek Cemetery.

Canby—Sallie A. R. Canby on First month 1st, 1922, at their beautiful home in Winfield, Iowa. She was the daughter of Caleb and Elizabeth Mathews Russell, both of Maryland. A birthright member of the Society of Friends, she came to Iowa in 1855, was a member of Prairie Grove Meeting, near Winfield, Iowa, and was married here to William H. Canby by Friends' ceremony in 1867. Funeral services were held in the same house First month 3rd, 1922, and she was laid to rest in the cemetery there, which was preceded by appropriate services. She was in her 78th year.

Davis—At Woodstown, N. J., First month 3d, Elizabeth L. Davis, aged 80.

Engle—On First month 4th, 1922, Elizabth H. Engle, daughter of the late Joseph and Emily M. Engle. Interment at Mount Holly, N. J.

Haight—Suddenly at Aiken, S. C., on First month 5th, S. Louisa Haight, superintendent of Schofield School.

Hulme—At Miami, Fla., First month 3d, in the 72nd year of his age, Robert R. Hulme.

Mills—At his home near McNabb, Ills., on Ninth month 9th, 1921, after a long and lingering illness of many months, in his 69th year, Willis B. Mills.

He was a birthright member of the Society of Friends at Clear Creek, a son of the late Pusey and Lydia Mills. A widow, three sons and six grandchildren, also one sister and three brothers were left to mourn his loss. Burial in Friends' Cemetery.

Palmer—In Washington, D. C., on First month 4th, Roberta Dixon Palmer, wife of A. Mitchell Palmer.

Thomas—At the Northwestern Hospital, Philadelphia, on Twelfth month 25th, 1921, Dr. Harry Leedom Thomas, of Langhorne, Pa., son of the late Edwin and Clara Clayton Thomas, aged 51 years and 9 days. Interment private in Middletown Friends' burying ground.

Wierman—At her home near McNabb, Ills., on Ninth month 6th, 1921, Janet Rebecca, in her fourth year. She was the second child of Harry and Ann Wierman. She was a granddaughter of Isaac P. and the late Belle Wierman. Burial in the Clear Creek Friends' Cemetery.

MATILDA E. JANNEY

In Remembrance of

The passing on of this beloved Friend seemed a translation. She came to her closing years "as a shock of grain cometh in in it's season." The changes of nearly a century had been a part of her life-schooling. It was given her to know life as child, as pupil, as teacher, as wife, as mother, as one widowed, and as public teacher. All these phases of life had so fashioned her own that she had sympathetic access to other lives. Her interests broadened with her years; her mental power strengthened with her experiences. In the gathering of friends in her memory, there were those present who bore testimony to the vigor of her mind as well as the breadth of her view, and the stimulus realized in her companionship, along with the general mirthfulness that brightened her own days and theirs.

Such a passing as hers into the realms invisible to us, leaves a trail of light revealing the pathway into the life eternal. E. P. B.

ROBERTA DIXON PALMER

In Loving Memory

It is difficult for our human minds to realize that Roberta Dixon Palmer has passed into the Great Unknown. Her spirit was so buoyant, her wit so sparkling and ever present, her loyalty so true, her love for family and friends so strong, that to those who knew her she will always seem a part of life itself.

This is the first break in her generation of the family of six children of the late Robert B. and Amanda A. Dixon. Roberta was born in the old family homestead, North Bend, near Easton, Maryland, on July 4, 1871. There on the family estate by the river, she spent a free and happy childhood. She was limited in her physical strength, however, by several severe illnesses. This, although handicapping her in one sense, seemed in another to endow her with unusual poise and dignity of manner which she combined very effectively with her love of fun and mirth. A Friendly atmosphere pervaded her parents' home whose traditions she always revered and strove later to emulate in her own. Their family tie was peculiarly strong. Every young person who entered the home was deeply conscious of this and in after years has recalled with gratitude the impress it left in youth.

Roberta attended the Friends' school at Easton and entered Swarthmore College in the fall of 1888. During her three years at college she made many life-long friends. It is scarcely out of place to state here that this little group in which our friend played so large a part, has enjoyed unusually close association. To this group belonged A. Mitchell Palmer, whom she married on November 23, 1898. They lived for a number of years at Stroudsburg, Pa., where her husband practiced law until he was elected to the House of Representatives at Washington. They spent a part of every year in the National capital and have made their home there permanently since her husband's appointment as Attorney-General in Woodrow Wilson's cabinet. Their marriage was blessed with three children, two of whom, however, did not survive early infancy. A daughter, Mary Dixon Palmer, is now twelve years of age.

From childhood, Bertie, as she was intimately known, has been regarded by her family and circle of friends, as the central figure around whom all gathered for cheer and good fellowship. In her college days and after, no occasion was complete without her presence. She was genuine to the very core. Superficialities never appealed to her, and even when engaged in the most formal social activities into which her husband's high official position took her, she was always her same dear natural self. Their homes, both in Stroudsburg and in Washington, were centres of life and interest. She graced them with an unusual charm of hospitality. It was considered a privilege and an inspiration to come within the influence of the Palmer's happy home life, and their friends will ever count it one of their choicest blessings to have shared in it.

Many memories press for utterance—memories of fun and frolic, of kindnesses done and of efforts made for the happiness of others. One is bewildered to know where to lay the greatest emphasis. Sometimes when a life is so full of radiant sunshine as hers was, one questions whether that life could bear real tests and whether such a character could assume great responsibilities. All who knew our friend saw her meet such tests and such responsibilities with ability and equanimity. Her chief mission seemed to be to bring joy and cheer and comfort into the lives of others and this she fulfilled abundantly.

"God calls our loved ones, but we lose not wholly
What He hath given:
They live on earth in thought and deed as truly
As in His Heaven."

H. C. H.

COMING EVENTS

FIRST MONTH

14th—Social at the Schermerhorn St., Brooklyn, Meeting-house, at 8 P. M. All cordially invited.

15th—West Philadelphia Bible Class, 35th and Lancaster Avenue, at 10 A. M. Subject—The Christ that was, that is, and that is to come. All welcome.

15th—Conference Class at 15th and Race Streets, Philadelphia, at close of meeting for worship, at 11.40 A. M. Speaker—Edward C. Wilson, Principal of Baltimore Friends' School. Subject—Our Friends' School.

15th—Dr. O. Edward Janney expects to attend meeting for worship at Swarthmore, Pa., at 11.30 A. M.

16th—Meeting at 17th Street and Girard Avenue, Philadelphia, at 8 P. M., to be addressed by Elbert Russell. See notice.

18th—Monthly Meeting of Friends of Philadelphia, 15th and Race Streets, 7.30 P. M. See notice.

19th—Green Street Monthly Meeting of Friends of Philadelphia, School House Lane, Germantown, 7.30 P. M.

21st and 22nd—Young Friends' Conference in New York. Social at New York Meeting-house, night of 21st. The delegates from Baltimore and Philadelphia will attend various Meetings First-day morning, a Conference session, First-day afternoon, and The Tea-Meeting at Twentieth Street Meeting-house. All young Friends are urged to extend their circle of acquaintance and inspiration by being present.

22nd—Chester (Pa.) Monthly Meeting, at Providence, at 2.30 P. M.

22nd—Daniel Batchellor plans to attend meeting at Chester, Pa., at 10 A. M., and Chester Monthly Meeting at Media at 2.30 P. M.

23rd—P. Y. F. A. Social in the auditorium, 15th and Cherry Sts., Philadelphia, at 8 P. M. Members and their friends are cordially invited.

24th—Western Quarterly Meeting at Kennett Square, Pa. Daniel Batchellor expects to be present.

26th—William Littleboy, former Warden of Woodbrooke, will speak at 15th and Race Streets Meeting House, Philadelphia, Room No. 1, at 8 P. M., on "What can we do with our city meetings—an English solution"?

26th—Caln Quarterly Meeting at Christiana, Pa. Daniel Batchellor will attend.

27th—Meeting of Philadelphia Yearly Meeting's Committee on Philanthropic Labor, in Room No. 4 of Race Street Meeting-house, at 2.30 P. M. Dr. Louis N. Robinson will speak on "Jails near Home," and Mrs. R. R. P. Bradford will present the subject of "Motion Pictures."

28th—Westbury Quarterly Meeting, at Fifteenth St., New York, 10.30 A. M. At 2.30 the second address on the year's topic of "Problems of Human Relations," will be given by Frank P. Walsh, the special subject being "The Problems of Capital and Labor."

29th—Harrisburg Meeting will be held in the W. C. T. U. Rooms in the Patriot Building, at 11 A. M. Daniel Batchellor will be present. A cordial invitation to all interested.

31st—Concord Quarterly Meeting, at Swarthmore, Pa.

NOTICE—"OVERCOMING BY THE SPIRIT." Illustrated by original readings, by Leslie Pinckney Hill; Negro Spirituals sung by the Cheyney Octette; Public Meeting, 15th and Race Sts. Meeting House, Sixth Day (Friday), Jan. 20th, 8 P. M. Under auspices Yearly Meeting Committee, 'In the Interest of Colored Race." All friends of either white or colored race, cordially invited.

NOTICE—Frank D. Slutz, of the Moraine Park School, Dayton, Ohio, will give an address at Friends' Central School, 15th and Race Streets, Philadelphia, on Seventh Day, First month 21, at 10.30 A. M. Subject: "The

Fundamentals of Progressive Education." The Committee on Education extends an invitation to all teachers, members of educational committees and other friends of education to attend this meeting.

Mr. Slutz will speak at 2 o'clock at Friends' Select School, 16th and Cherry Streets, Philadelphia, Pa., under the auspices of Friends' Educational Association. Subject:—The Creative Impulse in Education. They extend an invitation to all.

IDA P. STABLER,
Executive Secretary of Committee on Education.

NOTICE—A conference under the care of Concord Quarterly Meetings' Committee on Philanthropic Labor, will be held in Friends' Meeting House, 4th and West Streets, Wilmington, Del., on First-day, the 15th, at 2.30 o'clock. W. A. Vrooman, executive secretary of the Prisoners' Aid Society of Delaware, will address the meeting on the subject: "Needed penal legislation for better protection of both the public and the criminal."

NOTICE—Elbert Russell will address a meeting to be held First month 16th., at 8 P. M., in the meeting house at 17th Street and Girard Ave., Philadelphia. Subject—The Need of Religious Education. The meeting will be under the joint auspices of Girard Avenue First-day School, Girard Avenue School, and the Best Interest Committee of Race Street Monthly Meeting. A general invitation is extended to all interested.

NOTICE—Supper will be served by the Best Interests Committee before Monthly Meeting at Fifteenth and Race Streets, Philadelphia, on First month 18th, in Friends' Central School Lunch Room, at 6 o'clock. Tickets 65 cents. Please purchase tickets before First month 16th, 1922. Anna W. Cloud, 140 North Fifteenth Street.

NOTICE—The library in the Young Friends' Association will be open on Thursday evenings from 6.30 to 7:30, instead of Wednesday evenings, for the convenience of members of the Study Group and others.

American Friends' Service Committee

WILBUR K. THOMAS, EX. SEC.
20 S. 12th St. Philadelphia

CASH CONTRIBUTIONS
Week Ending December 31, 1921

Five Years Meetings	$552.00
Other Meetings	
Alexandria Monthly Meeting	10.00
Ithaca Friends' Meeting	44.00
West Monthly Meeting, Alliance, Ohio	10.00
Pleasant Plain Monthly Meeting	50.00
Hopewell Friends' First-day School	29.00
Kennett Monthly Meeting	16.50
Sandy Spring Monthly Meeting	50.00
Plato Mount Joy Meeting, Washington, D. C.	15.00
Purchase Monthly Meeting	225.00
Contributions for General	1,869.08
For Germany	1,290.74
For Austria	3,695.31
For Poland	660.00
For Armenia	76.00
For Russia	54,477.24
For Russian Overhead	1,253.59
For Clothing	361.07
Refunds and Payments	30.93
	$64,715.46

CASH CONTRIBUTIONS RECEIVED FROM MEMBERS OF THE PHILADELPHIA YEARLY MEETING OF FRIENDS, HELD 15TH AND RACE STREETS, DURING DECEMBER, 1921.

Richland Monthly Meeting by E. Irene Meredith	$10.00
Orange Grove Mo. by E. D. Hopkins	60.00
Swarthmore Mo. by E. J. Durnall	30.00
Newtown, Del. Co., Prep. by M. T. Dutton	20.00
Members Phila. Yearly Meeting by Arabella Carter, Russian Relief	50.00
Interest on deposit to 12-15-21	10.11
Lansdowne Mo. by C. C. Lippincott	10.00
Abington by D. L. Lewis	50.00
West Chester Friends (High Street) by S. R. Paiste, General Expenses Russian Relief	125.00
Wilmington, by S. H. Stradley	862.00
ditto (Austrian Relief)	127.00
ditto (Aged Women's Pension Fund, Vienna)	50.00
ditto (Relief Ras El Metn)	25.00
Arabella Carter for Russian Famine Fund	30.00
Wrightstown Mo. Mtg. by Hugo L. Hund	20.00
ditto (Relief Vienna)	10.00
ditto (Relief Russia)	5.00
	$1,494.11

Shipments received during week ending December 31, 1921: 104 boxes and packages—1 for German Relief, 2 from Mennonites.

Chartered 1836

Real Estate
Need Not Be Troublesome

This Company's Real Estate Department can relieve you of the care of real property, including selling and renting, prompt payment of taxes and insurance, collection of rents, economical making of repairs, all dealings with tenants, etc.

This Department has in its charge properties in nearly every state of the Union.

GIRARD TRUST COMPANY

Broad & Chestnut Sts., Philadelphia

ABBOTTS CERTIFIED MILK

Produced at
Edgewood Dairies, Woodside, Pa.

Approved by
Philadelphia Pediatric Society

Contains 4 per cent. Butter Fat

Abbotts Alderney Dairies, Inc.
31st & Chestnut Sts.
Philadelphia, Pa.

SEND for catalogues of andirons, firesets, spark screens, mantels and of the Jackson Ventilating Grate—the open fireplace that heats on two floors.

Edwin A. Jackson & Bro., Inc.
51 Beekman St., New York

HOTELS.

Buck Hill Falls

All apple crops in this section of the country were a total failure this Fall, so that in order to keep the basket in the Exchange filled with this health-producing fruit we received a shipment of four hundred boxes of Western apples. They are unusual in size and quality, without any bruises from their long trip. Come up and sample them!

THE WINTER INN

"WEALTH IN HEALTH"

BUCK HILL FALLS, PA.

HOTEL WARWICK

SOUTH CAROLINA AVENUE
ATLANTIC CITY, N. J.
OPEN ALL THE YEAR

First house from beach and boardwalk. Steam heat, electric lights, elevator. Excellent cuisine, quiet, dignified surroundings and attentive service.

Reasonable rates. Write
SARAH H. FULLOM, Prop.

THE WHEELER

Boardwalk at Massachusetts
ATLANTIC CITY, N. J.
Ocean Rooms—Table Guests
MRS. A. W. WHEELER

Strath Haven Tea Room

Dinner 6 to 7:30.
Sunday Special — Chicken and Waffles, 75 cents.
Swarthmore, Pa. Phone 680

ELLWOOD HEACOCK
FUNERAL DIRECTOR
2027 NORTH COLLEGE AVENUE
PHILADELPHIA
CALLS OUT OF CITY ANSWERED PROMPTLY

FRANK PETTIT
ORNAMENTAL IRON WORKS

Iron Fencing, Fire Escapes, Stairs and Ornamental Iron Work.
809 Master Street Philadelphia, Pa.

SCHOOLS.

Woolman School

SWARTHMORE, PA.

Winter Term—First Month 3d to Third Month 18th

Courses in the Bible, Quakerism, Religious Teaching, Rural Problems. Daily meetings for worship.

Personal contact with instructors experienced in social and religious work.

Helpful group life. Recreation.

ELBERT RUSSELL, DIRECTOR.

GEORGE SCHOOL
Near Newtown, Bucks County, Pa.

Under the care of Philadelphia Yearly Meeting of Friends.

Course of study extended and thorough, preparing students either for business or for college. For catalogue apply to

GEORGE A. WALTON, A. M., Principal
George School, Penna.

FRIENDS' CENTRAL SCHOOL SYSTEM

Write for Year Book and Rates.
CHARLES BURTON WALSH, Principal.
15th and Race Sts., Philadelphia.

FRIENDS' ACADEMY
LONG ISLAND, N. Y.

A Boarding and Day School for Boys and Girls, conducted in accordance with the principles of the Society of Friends. For further particulars address

S. ARCHIBALD SMITH, Principal,
Locust Valley, N. Y.

Cream Buttermilk

HEALTHFUL—REFRESHING

Supplee-Wills-Jones Milk Co.
PHILADELPHIA—ATLANTIC CITY

REGULAR MEETINGS.

OAKLAND, CALIF.—A FRIENDS' MEETING is held every First-day at 11 A. M., in the Extension Room, Y. W. C. A. Building, Webster Street, above 14th. Visiting Friends always welcome.

FRIENDS' MEETING IN PASADENA, California—Orange Grove Monthly Meeting of Friends, 520 East Orange Grove Avenue, Pasadena, California. Meeting for worship, First-day, 11 A. M. Monthly Meeting, the second First-day of each month, at 1.45 P. M.

WANTED.

WANTED—KINDERGARTEN TEACHER as nursery governess. Montessori training preferred. Friend's family in California. Write Mrs. G. B. Elliott, 410 East Lake Ave., Watsonville, Cal.

WANTED—MAN AND WIFE TO LIVE in house. In lieu of rent, wife to care for house and answer phone. Man to care for small lawn and care for heaters and furnish one-half of coal for heaters. Privileges garden and fruit. Write Box 199, Malvern, Pa.

POSITION WANTED—BY ACTIVE, elderly useful man, half time in exchange for good home. Penna., Jersey, Maryland. Bank reference. Address S. 21, Friends' Intelligencer.

POSITION WANTED—AS MATRON or housekeeper in institution, or as directress of Tea Room. Experienced; references. Address E. H., 143 De Lacey Ave., Plainfield, N. J.

WANTED—POSITION BY COLLEGE woman as secretary or nurse-companion. Capable of taking full charge of nervous or chronic invalid. Address, Mrs. J. H. Pease, Schofield School, Aiken, S. C.

HIRED STENOGRAPHER—45 years' macroscopic or/and microscopic experience including (22 years' American-trotting public stenography): English, Latin, German; pedagogy, journalism, commerce, transatlantic-inland transportation, metals, stone-quarrying, wheel-making, textiles, paper-making, law, medicine, theology. GEO. B. COCK. Wants night work "Remington 10" home; also "Zentmayer" magnifying 420. Philadelphia Bell Directory.

STENOGRAPHER DESIRES POSITION. Thoroughly competent. Address F 22, Friends' Intelligencer.

VISITORS TO CALIFORNIA CAN find comfortable accommodations at 400 S. Euclid Avenue, Pasadena. For terms, apply to Mary B. Sutton.

FOR RENT.

FOR RENT—FEBRUARY 1ST, LIVING-ROOM, bedroom, bath, second floor, unfurnished. Two rooms, third floor, furnished. Corner house, east-south-west exposure. Gas and heat supplied. Old neighborhood West Philadelphia. Only women. Reasonable. Owner. Address M. 20, Friends' Intelligencer.

FOR RENT BY YEAR OR TERM OF years, or will consider sale—A very attractive small house in Brielle, New Jersey, near river and sea. Hot-water heater and all possible conveniences, including open fireplace. One minute from "bus" line between Lakewood and Asbury Park. Ten minutes from train. Address Box 28, "Applewood," Brielle, N. J.

WE BUY ANTIQUE FURNITURE AND antiques of every kind, old pictures of Washington or any prominent American, old gold, silver, platinum, diamonds and old false teeth. PHILA. ANTIQUE CO., 623 Chestnut St. Phone Walnut 70-26. Established 1866.

To the Lot Holders and others interested in Fairhill Burial Ground:

GREEN STREET Monthly Meeting has funds available for the encouragement of the practice of cremating the dead to be interred in Fairhill Burial Ground. We wish to bring this fact as prominently as possible to those who may be interested. We are prepared to undertake the expense of cremation in case any lot holder desires us to do so.

Those interested should communicate with William H. Gaskill, Treasurer of the Committee of Interments, Green Street Monthly Meeting, or any of the following members of the Committee.

William H. Gaskill, 3201 Arch St.
Samuel N. Longstreth, 1218 Chestnut St.
Charles F. Jenkins, 232 South Seventh St.
Stuart S. Graves, 3033 Germantown Ave.

INTELLIGENCER, for Help Wanted, Positions Wanted, Rooms for Rent, Notices, and other classified advertisements without display, for each insertion, 2 cents per word, including name, initials and address. Answers may be sent to a box at the INTELLIGENCER office, if so directed.

For display advertising the rate is 10 cents per agate line, or $1.40 per column inch, each insertion. On ten or more insertions in a year from date of order, ten per cent. discount. Thus a four-inch single-column or two-inch double-column advertisement costs $5.60 each insertion, less ten per cent., or 5.04 net each time for ten or more insertions. Matter may be changed whenever desired, without extra charge.

Experience has proved the INTELLIGENCER to be a remarkably good advertising medium. All advertisements must "pass the censor!"

Address 140 N. 15th St., Philadelphia

CLEAN HIGH GRADE
COAL

CLEAN HIGH GRADE
COAL

Friends' Intelligencer

ESTABLISHED 1844 | PHILADELPHIA, FIRST MONTH 21, 1922 | VOLUME 79 NUMBER 3

Mosaics

A STONE means nothing to humanity. God means everything. Why should it be that we can see and grasp a stone, while God is forever eluding even the greatest souls; and to millions of men is altogether unknown?

To those who consider the magnitude of the universe for the first time, the human soul appears infinitesimally small and insignificant. We must traverse immeasurable distances, it seems, before we encounter in the stars the first residence of universal grandeur. And to find a sufficient source for an infinite creation, we must press behind the stars into the realm of God. But those who have followed the path behind the stars, know that by some mysterious turn it leads back into the human soul, and that the true realm of God lies within the infinitesimal world of men.

Motion, activity alone, counts for nothing. Today I came upon an eddy by the side of a stream. The water that turned within it was moving as fast, in its own little circle, as was that of the main current; but it was not advancing. It was not *getting down to the sea.*

The human soul is forever seeking widened opportunity. It gropes upward through the spaces to a vision of heaven, outward beyond seas to the magnified opportunities of unknown lands, forward across the years toward the hopes of the future. But the only path that lies open to it leads inward and downward through the unsounded depths of the soul itself. Spaces, continents and centuries avail us nothing. It was as overwhelming a task to build a cathedral in France in the thirteenth century as it is in America in the twentieth. All distant prospects are alluring, all advance toward them fraught with drudgery and discouragement. No situation can offer greater possibilities, no occasion be more auspicious than the immediate surroundings and the present moment. Opportunity is the upshot of vision, resolution and courage, not a circumstance of environment. Whatever is to be accomplished, must be accomplished here and now by the naked determination of strong souls.

The youth looks up to master artists and great prophets with mingled reverence and awe, feeling that they move in a world to which it is beyond his power to attain. But artists and prophets know that the possibilities of boundless achievement lie, not in themselves, but in the youth who dares not yet expect his visions to be realized. Mastery is limited, potentiality is infinite. The master who is truly great stands in awe of his pupils.

The most limiting and unjustifiable thing in the world is to accept yourself for what you are. No human soul *is.* It *is becoming.* You are changing deeply and mysteriously with every passing moment. You cannot remain what you are, even if you wish to do so. Next year you will be either stronger or weaker, nobler or less noble, more prepared or less prepared for your mission in life, than you are today. Which alternative it is to be depends upon the degree of loyalty which you preserve to your most unattainable aspirations.

The free human spirit is not bound by the assumptions of its past. Promise and disadvantage it can set equally at naught. Genius has lost its vision on the threshold of a master career. Men of seeming mediocrity have suddenly and inexplicably risen to greatness at middle life. Remember that your being is profound, mysterious and sacred. Stand in awe of yourself. Tomorrow your lips may proclaim the law of the universe.

If none but practical men had ever existed on earth, the human race would still be confined to savagery. Civilization was the vision of impractical idealists who dared to dream and to teach that large bodies of men might live together for the good of all. The practical cave man refused to consider such "half-baked," "Utopian" ideas. The association of individuals into a society, he pointed out, would not only limit personal freedom and impose oppressive social responsibilities, but for these very reasons was *impossible* of accomplishment, however pleasant to contemplate in theory. Fortunately for us, not all cave men were practical.

One of America's largest electrical companies is the latest exponent of impracticality. Improved illumination, it declares, will not be achieved by perfecting incandescent lamps, any more than incandescent lamps were achieved by perfecting candles. Monumental progress is never made by those who labor to improve candles or carriages or quill pens. It is the work of visionaries who waste their time studying useless forces such as steam or electricity or the spirit, or who dream of impossibilities like locomotives, typewriters and the "federation of the world."

The false theorist is he who refuses to recognize the practicality of anything which has not been accomplished in the past. He forgets that the impossible *has* been accomplished a thousand times in the past, and that through its accomplishment have come all of humanity's greatest practical gains. The most Utopian ideal which can occur to the human mind may be the means of transforming civilization. At some time in its history, every epoch-making invention has been the laughing stock of the world. The man with a vision is the super-practical man. More precious to a nation than oil wells and coal mines are the dreams in the minds of her young men.

There is no highway to the attainment of the ideal. The course lies over the hills and vales, and through the pathless woodlands. Many have gone astray in the quest. But to those who undertake the journey with high purpose, a sign is given in guidance. So long as they hold resolutely to the true course, they find flowers along the way, earth and sky are touched with grandeur, and the faces of those whom they meet on the road glow with delicacy and charm.

The path of the vision cannot be charted to its end in advance. No man knows as he strikes into it on the first day, whither upon the last it will have led him. He is shown only the next step; the fragment of the way which lies between him and the next bend in the road. What lies beyond, he must accept on faith: trusting to find the best, ready to meet the worst. He who is unwilling to take the next step on faith can never see beyond the next bend.

It is not revealed to those who follow the vision how far along its path they shall advance, nor when their journey shall close. Times and distances are not the measure of a pilgrimage. In art, religion and life there is not ultimate. Each day's journey is its own goal. To travel is the end, not to arrive. The only essential is that the traveler daily find the flowers along the roadside.

WALTER H. ABELL

Design

Weave in glad days and sombre nights,
Designer of the passing year;
That with the shadows and the lights
A perfect pattern may appear.

HARRY BOLAND

The Power of Silence

The message which follows was prepared by Walter C. Woodward at the request of the Associated Press. "The American Friend," from which we reprint it, comments editorially on the significance of the fact that a request for such a message should come from the Associated Press, "the great American news agency which girds the globe with its network of news-sentient nerves. That it should consider the place of silence in our rushing modern life as having news value to the hundreds of thousands of newspapers which it serves is of more than passing significance. The request speaks eloquently for the growing realization of the power of the life of the Spirit and for the increasing appreciation of the necessity for quiet, spiritual communion as the basis for right living and for right attitude toward all the complex relations of life."

From the constant clash and confusion which distract it, the world must retire to the inner chamber of the unseen reality of the spirit, if peace and good will are to become regnant. This is the New Year's Message of the Society of Friends. It is uttered on the background of an experience of more than two centuries and a half, during which this small religious group have relied upon "silent waiting before God" as the source of spiritual discernment and as the motive power which has sent them forth to minister to the world's need.

The world is now stirred as never before with aspirations for world brotherhood through righteousness. To become fruitful, these aspirations must indeed be based upon "the will to peace." The attainment of this will is primarily a spiritual, rather than an intellectual process. It must come, if effectively, through spiritual communion with God the Father and through Him with man, the brother. Herein lies the power of silence, through which we may become "in tune with the Infinite."

This is not the silence of seclusion which would lead one from life's responsibilities to the introspection of the monastic cell. It is what Friends term "a living silence" through which men may become spiritually energized for the great tasks of human betterment. From such a silence, as in Longfellow's "The Legend Beautiful" they go forth to feed the hungry at their doors.

It is cause for hope that the realization is becoming more and more general that the peace of God is requisite to the peace of man. "Spiritual things cannot be discerned without quiet and meditation," the western world is reminded by Sadhu Sundar Singh, the Hindoo seer. That American churches are coming to recognize this fundamental principle is illustrated by the clarion call for "spaces of silence" made by *The Churchman,* organ of the Episcopal Church of America. At a time when the soul of America is being stirred to

THE FRIENDS' INTELLIGENCER is published weekly at 140 N. 15th St., Philadelphia, by FRIENDS' INTELLIGENCER ASSOCIATION, Ltd. Telephone, Spruce 5-75. Entered at Philadelphia Post-Office as second class matter. Subscription in the United States, Mexico, Cuba and Panama, $2.50 a Year. Subscriptions may begin at any time. Subscription in Canada and other foreign countries (on account of extra postage charges), $3.00 a year. Single copies, 6 cents. Make checks payable to FRIENDS' INTELLIGENCER ASSN., LTD.

meet the need of the world, may it be purified and strengthened through the power of a living silence. This is the New Year's aspiration breathed by the Friends for themselves and for all friends of peace and good will.

Penology Up To Date

A review of "Penology in the United States," by Louis N. Robinson, Philadelphia, The John C. Winston Co., 1921, 335 pp., $3.00.

The appearance of this new work on penology by a Friend is another evidence that our Society has not entirely lost interest in the problems of prison reform which our leaders in the days of Elizabeth Fry labored at so earnestly and well. Louis N. Robinson has long been interested in the treatment of offenders, and his experience as a teacher of criminology, as a member of the Penal Commission of the State of Pennsylvania, and as chief probation officer of the Philadelphia municipal court has stood him in good stead in writing this volume.

Most of the existing literature of criminology is devoted primarily to a discussion of the nature and causes of crime, and the theory of its treatment; there has been a decided lack of good material describing and criticizing our penal institutions, and practical ways and means of dealing with criminals. It is to this neglected field that Dr. Robinson has bent his energies. Passing over very lightly the theory of punishment, he launches immediately into a historical and descriptive analysis of our jails, houses of correction or workhouses (for there is no difference between these two, our author tells us), penitentiaries, juvenile institutions, and reformatories. This is followed by a discussion of the problem of giving adequate employment to prisoners, and of compensating them therefor; of prison management, of probation and parole, capital punishment, flogging, fining and other means of dealing with crime.

In the reading of this volume one is impressed with the fact that while we have made tremendous strides forward in the direction of greater humaneness and common sense in our attitude toward those who have trangressed the law, our present methods of punishment are woefully inadequate still. We no longer mutilate the bodies of our criminals or put them to death for the slightest offense, nor permit the atrocious conditions that prevailed in the horrible early English jails, yet there are many abuses remain in our prisons, and the best of them are little better than great filing cabinets where human beings are stowed away for a time,—without proper employment, education or other measures designed to make them better men and women,—to be taken back into society after a few months or years, worse, if anything, than when they were committed.

Dr. Robinson does not believe that we have succeeded in making penology a science. He approves of the reformatory idea, and the increased use of probation and parole, but only under the direction of competent staffs of experts to provide the supervision without which these measures must prove a failure. He would have all prisoners employed, not by private contractors, but by the state, the work being selected primarily with reference to its beneficial effect on the criminal. He would have the men paid for their work. He makes a strong plea for the appointment of better officials to be placed in charge of our prisons, and believes that their management can be improved by adequate state supervision. For the county jail he has nothing but criticism, and would have it abolished altogether, to be replaced with state institutions, specially adapted to the needs of different kinds of offenders.

The author is at his best in the discussion of reformatories and of probation. His concluding chapter, in which he reviews the evolution of our penal methods and points the way for future improvement is also excellent. One might wish that the human interest which enlivens it might have been permitted fuller expression in some of the other chapters of the book, particularly those in the earlier part which are at times a little wearisome in their descriptions of our institutions. The reviewer is of the opinion also that a fuller discussion of the theory of penal treatment would have strengthened the work, for many of its readers, doubtless, will not be sufficiently imbued with the modern point of view toward the criminal to appreciate fully the significance of the very desirable reforms advocated by the author. Nevertheless the book is a very good one, and which will fill a long felt need. It is indeed practically the only satisfactory comprehensive analysis of our penal institutions which has appeared. It is sure to be read widely by students of criminology. It is to be hoped also that it will attract the attention of judges, prison administrators and other officials whose task it is to deal with the criminal, and of the general public, that it may prove an effective agent in bringing about a more scientific treatment of offenders than exists at the present time.

RAYMOND T. BYE.

University of Pennsylvania

Little Night Lamp

Little Night Lamp, I lit you myself,
And then I forgot you up there on the shelf;
You dear little glimmering, tiny light,
What a comfort you were as I watched in the night.

You only lit one little spot,
In the great dark corners your light shone not,
But you lessened the fear as I sat in the room,
And watched and watched through the night's long gloom.

But now, Little Lamp, your work is done,
How small you look by the light of the Sun,
He brings such a calm and wonderful light,
Making the darkest corners bright.

And your work is done, I need you not
To brighten even my tiny spot;
I will blow you out and set you away;
My room is lit by the new-born day!

ELEANOR SCOTT SHARPLES.

FRIENDS' INTELLIGENCER

The religion of Friends is based on faith in the "INWARD LIGHT," or direct revelation of God's spirit and will in every seeking soul.

The INTELLIGENCER is interested in all who bear the name of Friends in every part of the world, and aims to promote love, unity and intercourse among all branches and with all religious societies.

Editorial and business offices, 140 N. 15th Street, Philadelphia, Pa. For information regarding subscription rates, etc., see foot of second page.

PHILADELPHIA, FIRST MONTH 21, 1922

IN THIS ISSUE

"We need to emerge from a lot of old ideas that are not up to these times," writes E. S. Martin in the Christmas number of "Life." "That is the burden of a book, 'The Mind in the Making,' by James Harvey Robinson [Harpers] * * * How is he going to lead men up to reconsider their inherited opinions about their relations to their fellow men? That is where religion comes in. Christmas, just passed, celebrates the birth of one who undertook precisely what Doctor Robinson has in mind—to bring mankind to reconsider its inherited opinions about man and his relations to his fellow men."

Judge B. F. Bledsoe, a California jurist of the United States District Court, recently published in the *Los Angeles Times*, the most clear-cut statement which has yet come to our notice of the moral issue involved in the attitude of the American people toward prohibition. We are indebted to J. Russell Lownes, of Riverside, California, for a copy of this statement as reprinted in the *Riverside Daily News*.

We believe that our readers will be glad to see it in full:

To one who sees and thinks, the greatest menace confronting the American people today is the widespread disregard of the plain and positive provisions of the national prohibition law. People of both high and low degree who will not put a curb on their appetites, reckless and necessitous individuals who seek to enjoy extraordinary gains out of unlawful transactions and persons who are so constituted that they resent any interference with their own ideas of individual liberty—all these are joining in one vast unorganized conspiracy to set at naught the constitutionally declared will of the American people.

By subverting in its entirety one law, they are undermining respect and bringing about disregard for all laws. The natural and inevitable result will be that every individual will soon be led to obey only such laws as conform to his own peculiar ideas of fitness and appropriateness; his conduct will be regulated as his own will or his own weakness determine; he will put himself above the law; and in that wise individual tyranny—the very antithesis of government—will result.

Prior to the adoption of the eighteenth amendment, thirty-seven states of the American union were dry by their own deliberate vote. The eighteenth amendment, ratified by the legislatures of forty-five states and upheld by the supreme court of the United States, against every attack, positively and definitely prohibits the manufacture, sale, transportation within, importation into and exportation from, the United States, of intoxicating liquors for beverage purposes. The national prohibition act is but a due and necessary legislative authorization for the practical enforcement of the constitutional prohibitions. The net result of the situation is, that by the law of the land, constitutionally declared and judicially upheld, this is now a dry nation.

To give conscious, practical, wholehearted, unwavering obedience to this law, is therefore the duty of every good citizen—every man who has more regard for the flag than for his appetite; every man who is willing to hold his own desires in restraint in order that the general good of the country may be advanced; every man who wants to live a life of righteousness; every man who has in truth highly resolved "that this government, of the people, for the people and by the people, shall not perish from the earth." We should obey this law, not because it is the prohibition law—in spite, perhaps, of the fact that it is a prohibition law; but simply because it is the law.

The truth is that the time has come for the real patriots of this land to set an example, no less by the exercise of self-restraint than by the display of good citizenship. If they do this, this law, along with all other laws, will be preserved in the majesty and dignity becoming the announced will of a great people; if they do not, they may not be heard to complain that there has been pulled down upon their own heads, the structural supports of the civilization we have erected at so much cost in our midst.

The problem now immediately presented to the American people is really that of the possible continuance of self-government. The wholesale and widespread flouting and circumvention of this law, if continued and persisted in, is going to make it impossible for us to enforce any law—is going to make it impossible for democracy to function.

With governments once more contesting for the right to retain, rather than to abandon, as many as possible of the engines of scientific destruction, every new sign that there is a "better way," is strengthening to those who dream of the new world.

Such a sign is to be found in a letter of gratitude received a few weeks ago, by the Polish mission of the American Friends' Service Committee, from the director of the State School for Teachers, at Chelm, Poland. This letter, written in appreciation of help which the Mission had rendered to the school, is in part as follows:

"We shall never be able to pay you back, as the mighty English and American nations will never

General Pershing and Admiral Rogers, the technical heads of our army and navy, signed this report, and were perhaps chiefly responsible for it. The General Board of the United Stats Navy also coincided with it; and this is especially gratifying, since it is a reversal of the Amercan opposition at the Hague Conferences to the Russian proposal to abolish the use of projectiles exclusively designed to diffuse asphyxiating or other deleterious gases. The American delegation was, in fact, the only one at the Hague Conferences which refused to accept the prohibition, and it did so on the arguments of Admiral Mahan,—arguments which were used by the Germans fifteen years later, and which "the experts" are still insisting upon. Our American experts, at least, have seen a new light; and this light has evidently come from the terrible experiences of the World War and the reaction to them of an outraged public conscience. American public opinion as thus far registered at Washington is indicated by 366,795 votes against gas warfare, and 19 votes for its retention with restricted use.* The Treaty of Versailles (Article 171) forbade Germany to use, manufacture or import gases for military purposes, and the same prohibition was laid by the Allies upon Austria and Hungary; now that this prescription is being adopted for the Allies themselves, there is hope that some more wholesome medicines prescribed by them for Germany,—especially in the reduction and limitation of land armaments,—will be taken by themselves. With the prohibition of gas warfare, for example, the United States can close its gas plant at Edgewood, Maryland, where facilities exist for producing unlimited quantities of the deadliest gases known to science, and can incidentally save $4,500,000 which are asked for the chemical warfare appropriation for the coming year.

It may be noted in passing that, while submarines were not abolished, the rules adopted for the curbing of their activities provide as a penalty the treatment of crews violating the rules as pirates, but that the prohibition of the use of chemical warfare is accompanied by no penalty on nations or individuals resorting to it. Thus, in another agreement, the Washington Conference is relying upon the conscience and public opinion of the civilized world. There is a tendency to deprecate these agreements as mere scraps of paper, supported *only* (!) by the moral sanction; but here again it is possible that reason, experience and religion will convince men that "cheating does not thrive." At all events, the world is brought face to face with a challenge to its sincerity, civilization, and belief in the righteousness and omnipotence of God.

Submarine warfare having been restricted, and chemical warfare prohibited, the question of aerial warfare was next considered by the Armaments Committee. Its sub-committee on aircraft presented a report which emphasized the great desirability of developing by all legitimate means the science and art of aviation, since this would promote commerce and communications and thereby peace among the nations. The report expressed the opinion that no rules could be devised, or would be

---

*It may be noted. also. that 395,000 votes have been recorded for the abolition of submarines. 6,300 for their limitation in size and numbers. and 3.700 for restricting their activities.

observed, whereby civil and commercial or pleasure aircraft can be differentiated from military aircraft, and that to attempt to limit the number and character of any kind of aircraft would interfere with the desirable development of aeronautics. The sub-committee recommended, therefore, that no such limitation be attempted, but that a future conference should be held for the codification of rules designed to restrict the military operations of aircraft of every kind.

This report was adopted without debate by the Armaments Committee which passed a resolution that "it is not at present practicable to impose any effective limitation upon the numbers or characteristics of aircraft." At the same time, Secretary Hughes admitted that "in aircraft there is probably the most formidable military weapon of the future." and he expressed what he believed was felt by all the delegates, namely, "a deep disappointment in being unable to suggest practical limitations on the use of aircraft in war or on the preparation of aircraft for military purposes." This disappointment is bound to be most keenly felt by the world at large which will look with dismay upon a competition in means of aerial warfare. The conference will probably refer to a future conference the question of what rules can be adopted for the safe-guarding of noncombatants from aerial attacks. One who is opposed to all war, by whatever means, cannot but hope that when the world comes to appreciate the difficulty, perhaps the impossibility, of devising and enforcing adequate rules for this purpose, and when it envisages the frightfulness which aerial warfare in the future would involve, it may be helped rapidly along the pathway of abolishing all means of warfare by the abolition of war itself. Fortunately, the ten years' "naval holiday" and the prohibition of chemical warfare should point the way and give a decided impetus toward the goal.

As to the remaining tasks of the Conference, there are various explanations of the delay in their fulfillment. Premier Briand's resignation will probably cause some additional delay, and further progress on Shantung and other Far Eastern questions is desired before another open session of the Conference is held.

Washington, D. C., January 14, 1922.

The Canadian-American Boundary

AND THE ANGLO-AMERICAN AGREEMENT OF 1909

The following extract from a speech by Sir Robert Borden, former Prime Minister of Canada, and a British delegate to the Washington Conference. was distributed by him among the correspondents in Washington, after I had requested him to address them regarding the two subjects above mentioned, and after he had discoursed very earnestly, though extemporaneously, upon them.—W. I. H.

There are no two nations with thousands of miles of boundary so unguarded; no nations bordering on great inland seas whose waters are so untroubled by armed navies. It is almost commonplace to speak of the disarmament agreement of 1817, but it is always timely to recall the fulfillment of the promise that it bore. It was expressed in the simplest language, not even couched in the terms of a solemn treaty, merely the exchange of notes, scraps of paper if you like; yet the record of that agreement is unstained by the blot of any violation. Its terms covered only disarmament on the Great Lakes, but its spirit has extended to the entire boundary.

A century has almost elapsed when another impressive advance was made. It was inevitable that disputes and even controversies should arise in respect of a border line nearly 4,000 miles, much of it extending through great inland waterways, and everywhere intersected by streams rising in one country or the other, and flowing across the invisible boundary. The treaty that established the International Joint Commission ten years ago was almost as notable in its character and far reaching in its effects as the agreement of 1817. It expressed the cardinal and controlling principle of determining international questions by arbitrament of a permanent tribunal. It signified the crowning of each nation's resolve that by methods of peace and justice, not by resort to brute force should the reciprocal rights and duties of each community in such matters be adjusted and determined.

At the Conference in Washington, we can point to no prouder events than these in our common history. They carry a moral and a lesson that the statesmen there assembled may well bear in mind and take to heart. Upon the boundary from Atlantic to Pacific, the two nations laid down their arms more than a hundred years ago. The weapons then discarded have never been resumed. Can you doubt the infinite advantage? Observe the pride of the two peoples in their preparation for peace and their unpreparedness for war upon each other. Consider the hundreds, yes, thousands of millions that might have been squandered on bristling fortifications, on navies, on armaments, along that vast boundary. Bear in mind the suspicions that might have been engendered, the hostile spirit that might have arisen from the mere existence of such warlike preparations.

Is not the later lesson equally manifest? The American and Canadian nations have created a standing tribunal to which they have entrusted the determination of most important and often very difficult questions in connection with the boundary. This experiment has been a remarkable success and I believe it has developed into a permanent system. With the assent of the two Governments and the approval of your Senate the jurisdiction of the Commission may be extended to any question in dispute between our countries. The very fact that such a tribunal exists in a permanent form increases the probability that such disputed questions will be referred thereto. That which has proved of marked and unmistakable advantage to these sister nations must assuredly be for the benefit of all civilized communities. May we not in this retrospect find good omen of what may be accomplished at the great Conference that your President has summoned, and high hope that glad tidings of disarmament and of peace may be borne to a weary, waiting world?

Bettis Academy

A Story and Some Notes

"Bettis Academy's Contribution to Racial Good-will," is the title of an article, by William Anthony Aery, in the November *Southern Workman*. In addition to describing the invaluable service which this fine colored school is rendering through its work in western South Carolina, the author tells the following remarkable story of Alexander Bettis, its founder:

"Long, long ago, perhaps forty-odd years ago, a group of sullen, scowling, armed white men rode slowly over the heavy, sandy roads of Edgefield County, in South Carolina, and halted under a clump of trees near a small house occupied by Alexander Bettis and his faithful wife—two Negro pioneers in Negro education in western South Carolina.

"The leader strolled leisurely but threateningly to the modest Negro home and rapped on the door with a heavy hand. The colored woman within felt that the end of happy days had come for herself and her husband, who was known far and wide among his people as an earnest preacher and a sacrificing teacher. She remembered the repeated warnings that had come to them to refrain from teaching Negroes.

"Not even in this out-of-the-way place in the sand-hill country, some seven miles from the nearest railroad station, were Negroes then allowed to be taught by Negroes. So strong was public sentiment against Negro education that several times Alexander Bettis had had his schoolhouse burned. Again and again he had taken up the unpopular and dangerous task of trying to train his own people to become more intelligent, thrifty, and prosperous.

"Alexander Bettis was a brave Christian, however. He knew that prayer could do more for him and his righteous cause than bullets could do. He opened the door without hesitation and greeted the unwelcome guest as cheerfully as he could.

"'Your time has come, Alec,' said the white leader, who was not unknown to Bettis. 'You have had your warnings. We have come now to kill you. Be quick. Do not keep us waiting.'

"The Negro teacher and preacher realized that these men were not to be trifled with. 'Wife, give these men something to eat. They have come a long way and must be hungry.'

"Then, turning to the leader, who was ready to take the law into his own hand, Bettis said devoutly: 'Since I must die for doing what I believe God wants me to do, let us just speak to God and ask Him to bless you all.'

"Together white man and black man knelt before God. Alexander prayed a long, long time. Then both rose, transformed men: the one was ready to die without resistance for a cause; the other was ready to lay down his life for his black brother.

"The white leader went back to his companions, who had grown restless, and spoke to them earnestly for a few minutes. Then they rode away in silence, never to return to this Negro schoolhouse on the sand hills or even to disturb Alexander Bettis in his school work."

A personality possessed of the spiritual force to overcome a band of lynchers, is certain to leave behind it accomplishments of lasting value, and such an accomplishment Alexander Bettis left in Bettis Institute. His successor, Alfred W. Nicholson, the present principal of the Academy, has shown himself a worthy successor. Henry W. Wilbur esteemed the latter very highly, feeling that he had confronted more obstacles in his work of building up the Academy than had the principal of any of the other southern Negro schools of which he knew.

At present the Academy is in dire need of funds.

A recent letter from Alfred Nicholson says:

"I have been in this school work for forty years, but I have never faced such gloom and discouragement as we have now. Almost the entire cotton crop of this section was destroyed by the boll weevil this year. Many of the colored people who have heretofore contributed very liberally for the support of Bettis Academy are now in a suffering condition themselves. Schools like mine which have been teaching the colored people to help themselves and have been depending upon the colored people for their support, will be great sufferers unless some charitable persons with influence and money will come to their assistance."

Contributions toward the support of the Academy will be instrumental in aiding a hard-pressed and worthy cause. They should be addressed to Alfred W. Nicholson, Bettis Academy, Trenton, South Carolina.

"Cloister Chords"

The remarkable little article which follows is by Sister M. Fides Shepperson, of the Sisters of Mercy. It appeared originally in "Our Dumb Animals," and was recommended for the Intelligencer by Eliza H. Pownall, of Christiana, Pa.

Make me Thy voice, O gentle Christ, to plead for the voiceless. I hear their muted cries; they rise from the troubled depths of our social system, and their pangs, commingling as a reinforcement with the vocal agonies that rise from human wrongs and sufferings, threaten to undermine and totally to overturn that system.

The Christ ideals are the world's best. In the measure in which society approaches to them is its measure of progress; all divergence from them is retrogression; all tendencies diametrically opposed to them lead to degradation and death. Christ's blessing upon the merciful is a tacit condemnation of the merciless. The cries of defenseless right against man's avaricious might is a power calling down wars and pestilences upon the blind social order which laughs at those cries.

The laws of life are inscrutably complex; they are effective and as a whole inclusive of all known forms of life—highest and lowest. As the atom is now conceived to be a miniature solar system having a central nucleus of positive electricity with revolving ions negatively charged, and as herein lies the undermining of all preceding physical hypotheses, so likewise in the larger light that shall be thrown upon life some happier future day, it may be found that the infusoria abounding in the water drop have an essential place in the scale of continuity ranging from the life that sleeps in the mineral, breathes in the plant, wakens to consciousness in the animal, and becomes intelligence in man and spirituality in forms beyond man; this concept of life implies a total undermining and overturning of present-day practices.

When the wealth of nations is devoted to the righting of old wrongs; when principles of justice and of mercy are instilled into the heart of every child; when reverence for the wonderful mystery of life is made part of the ethical training of all schools; when the Christ ideals shall have been brought back, rehabilitated, made effective in social customs accepted throughout the world—then, and not till then, shall there arise and permanently abide an international Court of Justice, universal brotherhood, World Peace. The spirit of Christ is the *ding-an-sich*, the thing-in-itself, the noumenon which under ten thousand phases of phenomena shall yet save the world.

What We Have Done in Poland

By Arthur Gamble

The following is the story of what our Mission of the American Friends' Service Committee accomplished in the Powiat of Hrubieszow:

1.—Thousands of morgs of land are under cultivation, due to the work of our tractors and horses.

2.—The oats and barley crops of this and last year were increased by the distribution of seed that we made in the spring of both seasons.

3.—Farmers are using tools, such as plows and harrows, from our distribution.

4.—Twenty-five farms have been entirely set up with a full outfit of horses, carts, seeds and tools.

5.—The section has a harvest of flax of excellent quality, due to the seed which we brought from the Wilna area.

6.—The village schools have been developed in a large measure by our efforts, and a gardening school for boys is now running on a firm foundation. Funds are being left in the hands of a local committee to aid in the founding of an industrial school.

7.—During the period of this constructive work, the returning refugees, who have arrived helpless, have been given food and encouragement to make a new start by the loan of tools and material and the gifts of medicine and clothing.

What We Can Do In Poland

The constructive work which has been done in the district of Hrubieszow, can be duplicated in many other districts as needy as was this one when we began it.

But the great field for service today in Poland is among returning refugees. Penniless, half-starved, diseased, these people who have for five years been away from their homes are arriving from the horrors of the famine in Russia, being pushed farther and farther west in the search of food and finally returning to where the ashes and charred bricks of their homes are covered with inches of snow, and where the fields, unplowed for five years, are covered with a mass of tangled barbed wire.

In hordes of 2,000 a day they are passing through the great disinfecting camp at Baranowicze and with wasted bodies and hardly any clothing they drag themselves over the weary miles of desolate snow and ice, either on foot or in broken-down wagons, drawn by dying horses.

Will you aid in bringing to these people the life and hope which came to the people of Hrubieszow because the Quakers had money to help them?

American Friends' Service Committee, 20 S. 12th St., Philadelphia, Pa.

Wearing Out Two Million Children

January 29, 1922, is National Child Labor Day.

Lord Dundreary in the old play used to make his audience laugh when he read two advertisements from the same paper. One offered to lend money. The other asked to borrow money. In his inimitable tones, he used to ask why one advertiser didn't lend money to the other.

Many people are asking seriously now, why the jobs of two million children are not given to two million of the adults who are begging for jobs. Seven million was the estimate of unemployed adults in the fall of 1921. Many of these are parents living on the wages of their own children.

Children work for low wages, and are unorganized. Machines are so perfected that even young children can use them. The federal law affects only a small percentage of child workers. There are 48 kinds of state laws, and more than 48 standards of enforcement. All these reasons together, keep children enslaved.

No one can say truthfully, "I don't use goods made by children." Everybody who eats food, wears clothes, uses material, reads anything, or plays with anything, uses articles produced, in part, by child labor. The children's share may have been done far from the store where the customer pays the final price. But somewhere children have slaved, producing, labeling, handling, or packing the goods.

Wearing out two million children is a mean crime.

The richest country in the world can afford to set free all children to learn, to play and to grow.

Palo Alto, Cal. Alice Park.

A Negro Commission on Housing

A small pamphlet of 56 pages contains the third semi-annual report of "The Mission Negro Industrial Commission."

It is of unusual suggestion and significance. This commission "gives to its colored citizenship their first independent state department and right of investigation with recommendatory privileges." Much as the reader is instructed and interested in the findings of this commission, that the colored people themselves are reporting on conditions affecting their own race is the significant fact.

The report emphasizes the fact that bad housing makes for bad morals and the attitude of the landlords generally, increasing rents and unwilling to repair property, arouses a spirit of antagonism in the tenant. The report uses the expression "homeless houses." There are many such outside of mission contributing to the degradation of life in all classes of society. The aim of the social worker who is also rent collector, is to aid in building up the Negro race from within, out, not from without in.

Do you realize that the Negro of Philadelphia cannot rent a house until it is "run down"?

There are 125,000 Negroes in this city and there were 83 applicants for *two* of our houses recently vacated.

Why cannot Philadelphia have a Negro Commission to investigate and report on housing?

SUSAN P. WHARTON.

Woolman School

The winter term at Woolman School opened on First month 4th, with eleven students staying in the house, and a twelfth one came a few days later. With so large a resident group, and several who come in from outside for special classes, the term promises to be a very good one.

Dr. Elbert Russell is giving three courses on "Hebrew Life and Thought," "History of Friends," and "Life of Christ," all of which are most enlightening. A fourth course on "Great Truths of Christianity," just started, will be full of inspiration if all are like the first lecture given.

Mrs. Collins is giving in her thorough way her course on the "Hebrew Prophets." Two courses, one on First-day School work and one on Rural Problems will begin very soon.

With the outside reading to be done the students are kept very busy, but not so much so but that time has been found to enjoy the recent coasting on Swarthmore College campus, some evenings of recreation at the Woolman House, and a delightful afternoon with Barnard Walton and his family.

Perhaps nothing is of greater usefulness to the group than the devotional period each morning before regular class work of the day begins. In Conference one evening with William Littleboy, he impressed upon the group the helpfulness of the spoken prayer. Another conference is planned with William Littleboy for the near future and is much anticipated. Russell Hayes and his family spent an evening at Woolman House and Barnard Walton and William Littleboy have been most helpfully present at some of the daily devotional periods.

S. W. K.

Quakers in Russia

The *Intelligencer* published a week or so ago an article on Russian Quakers. This stated that there are several groups in Russia, who call themselves Quakers, and declare that they were started by traveling Friends in the early days of the Society, when the "Publishers of Truth" made their way to every part of the world.

One of these Russian Quakers called on me the other day. His story of the origin of Quakerism in Russia is so different from that given in the *Intelligencer*, and yet so interesting, that I would like to know more about it. When Napoleon invaded Russia, said he, there were in his great army, two Scotch Quakers. Whether they went as doctors or as soldiers, willingly or unwillingly, the Russian Friend—I really could not get his name—was uncertain.

Be that as it may, they were there, and when Napoleon's army fell to pieces, these two men, with many others, were captured, and were sent, practically as slaves, to a great estate of six thousand serfs. This was their opportunity. To these six thousand serfs, they preached their faith, and before the owner of the estate realized what was happening, many of the serfs were so filled with the "dangerous doctrines," as he considered them, that they were preaching and teaching in their turn.

To break up this forming church, he sent the Scotchmen to Siberia, and scattered the most enlightened serfs in every direction. The result was that Quakerism was spread broadcast. As in the early days in England, every Quaker was a "Publisher of Truth," and a number of Quaker groups were thus formed. Some of them have been stamped out by conscription; others have endured, against all persecution, even to this day.

My visitor was descended from a group which had been sent to the Caucasus. He himself had been born in that district, but had come to the United States several years ago. At his home in California he had received a week before, the first word from his mother in five years. She was still living, but at the verge of starvation, and the son was making all speed for Russia to find her, save her, and bring her to America with him.

Can anybody give me any further information about Quakerism in Russia?

New York City. ANNA L. CURTIS.

Young Friends' Conference in New York

Philadelphia, Baltimore, New York, and (in spirit, at least) Western Young Friends, will meet in more or less solemn conclave in New York, on the 21st and 22nd of First Month, 1922. The program, as far as completed, is as follows:

Seventh-day the 21st.

4 P. M.—Arrival of Philadelphia and Baltimore visitors. They will be brought direct to Fifteenth Street Meeting-house, where all exercises of the day will be held.

4.45—Conference session. Reports of activities in the various Yearly Meetings.

6—Supper.

7—Social and general mix-up.

8.30—Address—The call to young Friends. Speaker not definitely settled at this writing.

9.45—Social period. All Friends, old and young, are cordially invited to the address and what comes after.

First-day the 22nd.

11 A. M.—Meeting. The visitors will be distributed among the four Meetings, of both branches, in New York and Brooklyn, attending Meeting with the persons with whom they have spent the night.

12.45—Box lunch at Fifteenth St. Meeting-house.

1.45—Conference. The work that lies before us.

3.15—A glimpse of New York.

4.30—Tea-meeting at Twentieth St. Meeting-house. Everybody is invited to attend this. The speaking will be chiefly by the visitors, on the aims and work of the movement. There will also be opportunity, here, as on the preceding evening, for all to meet the visiting Friends.

All the Friends of New York seem to be taking a lively interest in the coming Conference. Their homes are thrown open to the visitors, their Meeting-houses are open for Conference sessions, the young Friends of both branches are working together in the arrangements, and the invitation sent to the New York Staters is signed by representatives of both.

Friendly News Notes

It was reported at the Intelligencer office by Elizabeth Marot that six tons of clothing and foodstuffs were shipped to Russia from the storeroom at 15th and Cherry Sts., Philadelphia, on the 16th.

Frank P. Walsh, who is to speak at Westbury Quarterly Meeting at 221 E. 15th St., New York, on the 28th, at 2.30, is a lawyer. He was Chairman of Federal Commission on Industrial Relations, member of National War Labor Board, and has been active in the Congressional hearings on the West Virginia mine situation, and in railroad cases before the Railroad Labor Board. In accepting the invitation to speak, he said: "The Friends have taken such a big and vital part in so many things close to my heart, and in such a fine way, that I do not feel that I could refuse any request from them, particularly one that will give me such pleasure." His topic, in general, will be, "Current Industrial Problems, with special reference to the Situation in West Virginia."

President Aydelotte left Swarthmore today for a ten-day trip to the Middle West. The President's itinerary includes attendance at the meetings of the Association of American Colleges and a dinner to be given in his honor by the Western Swarthmore Club.

Arthur J. Rawson, a member of the Junior Class, was elected to Sigma Tau, national honorary engineers' fraternity, just prior to the Christmas holidays. Rawson is a major in Mechanical Engineering. After the war he served in a Friends' Reconstruction Unit in Serbia.

John F. Park, instructor in the Engineering Department, was also elected to Sigma Tau. Mr. Park is a graduate of Penn State College.—*Swarthmore Phoenix.*

A recent issue of "The Friend" (London) contained the following letter, which we have been asked to reprint.

To the Editor of The Friend.

Dear Friend,—May I suggest the advisability of starting "Helping Hand Societies" throughout the English-speaking world; Christian homes, with work for the workless, where love rules; preference being given to the production of the necessities of life, each man, woman, or child being employed in the most suitable way, according to the locality and the individual; each encouraged to do his best. After supplying their own needs, let the surplus be sent to a Central Clearing Station, to be drawn upon by fellow societies. In process of time, working on communal lines, these Societies might become self-supporting, and comforts added to necessities.—Yours truly,

Whipps Cross, E. 10, Henry C. Whitcop.

The local Advancement Committee of Chicago Executive Meeting has appointed Clement B. Flitcraft, 633 Maple Avenue, Oak Park, Illinois, phone Oak Park 2669, and Charles C. Smith, 4520 Kimball Avenue, Chicago, office phone Harrison 2222, to receive any communications or calls from Friends visiting in Chicago. We would suggest that Friends who are likely to get to Chicago either temporarily or permanently, make a note of these names and get in touch with the Friends there as soon as possible after their arrival.

BALTIMORE NOTES

The News Letter from Baltimore Meeting of Friends which comes to this office weekly contains so much of inspiration that we wish it could reach every First-day School teacher and every interested worker in the Society of Friends. Of course, much of the news is of local interest but the working suggestions are there, and are shown to be workable and working. The various classes in the First day school are engaged in a friendly contest to increase the membership. The Bible Class at present holds the record for new additions, having increased from 9 to 22. The Conference Class has challenged the rest of the school to a contest to see which class will have the most members attending morning Meeting during the next six weeks. Short Bible stories are dramatized before First-day School by the members.

Then there is always the news of what the clubs organized for the younger folks are doing. This week they report the offer of a silver cup by James and Thomas B. Hull for the winner of the Inter-Castle Series of basket, volley and baseball games.

And aside from this kind of information, the letter which is sent out by Bliss Forbush, Secretary of the Monthly Meeting, always contains a suggestive paragraph or two like the following:

"Did you know that the Bible is full of stories? Look up these:

The story of a man who looked pleasant when every thing went wrong, of a man that looked sad when in trouble, and of a man who forgot his best friend. Genesis 40.

The story of a man taken from prison to live in a palace. Genesis 41.

The story of the meeting of a son with a father who for years had given him up for dead. Genesis 46.

The story of a little girl who watched by her brother's odd cradle, and of a mother who was hired to look after her own baby. Exodus 2.

The story of a bush which blazed with fire and yet was not burned up. Exodus 3.

The story of a hard master who told his servants they must make brick for him, and find their own material. Exodus 5."

Of course not all meetings can have a Bliss Forbush to keep them moving, but there is much latent energy that is being wasted through lack of an outlet. And no doubt some of the energy that is active has found the wrong outlet because there was no avenue provided for it within the care of the Meeting.

Items From Everywhere

The Journal of the AmericanMedical Association has issued another statement concerning its survey of the physicians of the country as to how they regard whisky, beer and wine as medicine. This statement asserts that a large majority of physicians in six states replying to the questionnaire say that they do not regard whisky, beer and wine as necessary therapeutic agents. Nearly two-thirds of the doctors say they believe there should be restrictions in prescribing them. About three-fourths of the replies assert there is no case on record where suffering or death was caused by the enforcement of the Prohibition law. The statement is based on replies coming from Idaho, Kansas, Mississippi, Nebraska, and Rhode Island.—*The American Issue.*

On the 16th of this month a campaign will be launched to raise a million or more dollars for the endowment of periodic rewards for "meritorious service, democracy, public welfare, liberal thought or peace through justice." The enterprise will be called the Woodrow Wilson Foundation and the awards will be called the Woodrow Wilson awards.

Boston, Jan. 2.—A working girl may be able to live on seventy-eight cents a day for food and pay car fare, rent, laundry charges and other bills out of what is left of a $12 a week income, as the Massachusetts Minimum Wage Commission insists she can, but three prominent young Boston women, social workers, who doubted it and put it to a personal test broke down under the strain and declared the feat impossible.—*Public Ledger.*

Sunday, January 29, will be observed as Child Labor Day in churches and Sunday schools. The call issued by the National Child Labor Committee contains a statement from Secretary Hoover:

"Child Labor Day is important bcause it reminds us to consider the question of child labor as a national problem. Every child in the country who labors to the prejudice of health and education is a liability to the nation. It is infinitely better to prevent child labor and to compel and support the education of our children today than to look after untrained, inefficient and unhealthy citizens tomorrow."

W. Lewis Abbott, Professor of Business Administration and Banking at Colorado College, and member of Philadelphia Yearly Meeting of Friends, recently opposed the "open shop campaign" in an address at Colorado Springs. His opinion was based upon an impartial personal investigation. Lewis Abbott charged that the open shop movement denied the right of collective bargaining to the workers, had done incalculable harm to business, especially to the small merchant, and that it is bound to pass away because it is bad. He added that the movement was partly an attempt of certain unfair employers to force conservative elements of American labor into a radical reaction.

The Senior class of Hampton Institute is awake to the needs of the times. At the recent Hampton Emancipation Day exercises, it announced as its motto: "Service the aim of our preparation."

During the exercises Dr. James L. Gregg declared that the word "service" expresses the thought which is in many minds and is receiving general attention. "The world," he said, "cannot go on upon any principle of selfish gain. It blocks the wheels, it clogs the machinery, it tangles up the affairs of nations, when that motive is allowed to become dormant."

"There was no science of hydraulics until men were resolved to make water run uphill."

THE OPEN FORUM

This column is intended to afford free expression of opinion by readers on questions of interest. The INTELLIGENCER *is not responsible for any such opinions. Letters must be brief, and the editor reserves the right to omit parts if necessary to save space.*

To the Editor:

I think there must be some mistake in the statement by John Wanamaker, quoted from the *Public Ledger*, in your issue of Twelfth month tenth, that as a young man he breakfasted with Joseph John Gurney. The latter died on Jan. 4th, 1847, just seventy-five years ago. Possibly the person referred to might be his brother, Samuel Gurney, who died in 1856, or more probably Samuel Gurney the younger, son of the last-named, whom I remember seeing at Devonshire House in 1866, and who died in 1882.

Letchworth, Herts, England. EDWARD GRUBB.

To the Editor:

The Baltimore Sun of today, gives an entire column to a most pitiful appeal from one of the mining sections of West Virginia. There have, from time to time through the past few months, been other such appeals from these mining sections of that state, to which (as stated in this latest one) Governor Morgan issued a sort of blanket denial, as to their need.

One can hardly read this one, and not feel, that the situation (though not on the same scale, of course) is, in *kind*, on a par with some of the stricken sections of Europe.

Would it be possible for Friends to make a thorough investigation and subsequent report, followed by prompt and adequate measures of relief, wherever necessary and possible? If we can do such a large part toward winning public opinion to a merciful, brotherly and truly international course toward Russia, should we quail before West Virginia? The bitter cold of winter is here, and time is all too short for anything in the way of general, adequate relief.

I therefore make an earnest appeal to the American Friends' Service Committee, and to Friends generally, to take the case of these sections of West Virginia under consideration, *as soon as possible*, and I venture to suggest, that some one (or more) of our tactful and efficient returned European workers be sent to this field,—first, to investigate and report, and then, wherever needed, to administer relief, to the "Greeks at our door."

Spencerville, Md. MARY JANET MILLER.

BIRTHS.

MILLER—On First month 3rd, in Webster City, Iowa, to Ray and Annie Miller, a son, named Ray Walter. The mother is a grand-daughter of Elizabeth H. Coale, of Holder, Ills.

PARK—On First month 7th, at Wayne, Pa., to George R. and Athalia Evans Park, a son, named George Rodney Park, 3rd.

DEATHS.

ENGLE—At 1313 Jefferson St., Philadelphia, First month 4th, Elizabeth H. Engle, daughter of Joseph and Emily M. Engle, formerly of Mt. Holly, N. J. She was a member of Race St. Monthly Meeting.

ADAMS—At Albany, N. Y., on Twelfth month 9th, 1921, Elizabeth S. Adams, in her 88th year.

BISHOP—On First month 11th, Susanna Lewis, widow of Henry Clay Bishop. Funeral services Middletown Friends' Meeting House.

HAMBLETON—In Paterson, N. J., on Twelfth month 10th, 1921, Sarah Barlow, wife of the late Joseph W. Hambleton, in her 90th year. Interment in Friends' Cemetery, Prospect Park, Brooklyn, N. Y.

MATHER—At Jenkintown, Pa., on First month 9th, Israel H. Mather, in his 88th year.

WOODMAN—Near Wycombe, Pa., First month 7th, Louisa H., wife of Wilson M. Woodman.

COMING EVENTS

FIRST MONTH

21st and 22nd.—Conference of Young Friends from Philadelphia, Baltimore, and New York, at Fifteenth Street and Twentieth Street Meetings, New York. Details given elsewhere.

22nd—Frederick J. Libby, Secretary of the National Council for Limitation of Armaments, will address a Disarmament Meeting, at the League Building, Flushing, N. Y., on First-day, at 3 P. M., under the auspices of Friends. His subject will be "The Washington Conference, as seen by one in close touch with its work." Admission will be by card only. Cards may be obtained from Paul Williams, or the Secretary of Meeting.

22nd.—Conference Class at 15th and Race Streets, Philadelphia, at close of meeting for worship, at 11.40 A. M.

Speaker—Lillian E. Rogers, principal of Friends' School, West Philadelphia. Subject—Vocational Education."

22nd—West Philadelphia Bible Class, 35th and Lancaster Avenue, at 10 A. M. Subject—The Christ that was, that is, and that is to come. All welcome.

22nd—Chester (Pa.) Monthly Meeting, at Providence, at 2.30 P. M.

22nd—Daniel Batchellor plans to attend meeting at Chester, Pa., at 10 A. M., and Chester Monthly Meeting at Media at 2.30 P. M.

23rd—P. Y. F. A. Social in the auditorium, 15th and Cherry Sts., Philadelphia, at 8 P. M. Members and their friends are cordially invited.

24th—Western Quarterly Meeting at Kennett Square. Daniel Batchellor expects to be present.

26th—Concert by Milan Lusk, Negro pupil of Kubelik, at studio of I. Phillip Schmand, Hotel des Artistes, New York. See notice.

26th—William Littleboy, former Warden of Woodbrooke, will speak at 15th and Race Streets Meeting House, Philadelphia, Room No. 1, at 8 P. M., on "What can we do with our city meetings?"

26th—Caln Quarterly Meeting at Christiana, Pa. Daniel Batchellor will attend.

27th—Meeting of Philadelphia Yearly Meeting's Committee on Philanthropic Labor, in Room No. 4 of Race Street Meeting-house, at 2.30 P. M. Dr. Louis N. Robinson will speak on "Jails near Home," and Mrs. R. R. P. Bradford will present the subject of "Motion Pictures."

28th—Westbury Quarterly Meeting at 221 East 15th St., New York, 10.30 A. M. Lunch at noon. The speaker for the afternoon, at 2.30, will be Frank P. Walsh, former chairman of Federal Commission on Industrial Relations. His subject is, in general, "Current Industrial Problems, with special reference to the situation in West Virginia."

29th—Harrisburg Meeting will be held in the W. C. T. U. Rooms in the Patriot Building, at 11 A. M. Daniel Batchellor will be present. A cordial invitation to all interested.

31st—Concord Quarterly Meeting at Swarthmore, Pa.

American Friends' Service Committee

WILBUR K. THOMAS, EX. SEC.
20 S. 12th St. Philadelphia

CASH CONTRIBUTIONS

Five Years Meetings	$1,973.03
Phila. Yearly Mtg. (4th & Arch Sts.)	19.00
Phila. Yearly Mtg. (15th & Cherry Streets)	2,353.11
Other Meetings:	
Highland Meeting	20.00
Coatesville Meeting	12.00
Detroit Meeting	13.00
Makefield Friends	10.00
Villa St. & Galena Avenue Friends Mtg., Pasadena	100.00
Matimecock Prep. Mtg.	5.00
Rahway & Plainfield Monthly Meeting, New York	20.00
Green Street Monthly Meeting, Phila.	500.00
Bauner Friends Church	32.00
Tillson New York Bible School	14.00
Middletown Meeting, First Day School	7.43
Miami Monthly Meeting	93.86
Lansdowne Monthly Meeting	150.00
Prospect Ave. Friends, West Grove	20.00
New Garden Prep. Mtg.	50.00
Salem Friends' Service Comm., N. J.	115.90
First Friends Church, Portsmouth, Virginia	5.20
Woodland Meeting, North Carolina	7.00
Westfield Monthly Meeting	240.00
Norristown Prep. Meeting	120.00
Contributions for General	5,459.04
For Germany	22,998.04
For German Overhead	39.66
For Austria	1,350.59
For Poland	668.37
For Syria	75.00
For Armenia	15.00
For China	18.40
For Russia	41,364.47
For Russian Overhead	2,663.28
For Clothing	107.31
Refunds	149.67
	$80,789.36

Shipments received during week ending January 7th, 1922: 95 boxes and packages; 5 for German relief; 4 anonymous.

NOTICE—The afternoon session of Western Quarterly Meeting, held on First Month 24th, at Kennett Square, will be devoted to the consideration of the situation in Russia, opened with an address by Rufus M. Jones, of Haverford College. It is desired that Friends of both branches and all other persons interested attend this meeting.

NOTICE—The Pennsylvania School for Social Service, 339 South Broad Street, Philadelphia, has arranged for a series of lectures to be given at the school, on Thursday mornings, at 10.45. The course began on January 12th and will continue until May 11th. The fee for the course will be $5. Miss Anne Flanders, Supervisor Community Organization, will be in charge. Another course of twelve lectures will be given on Monday evenings at 7.45, beginning February 6th. The fee will be $7.50 and Dr. Joseph K. Hart, Director of the School, will be in charge. Both these series of lectures will be of great interest and value to those interested in social service work.

NOTICE—Donation Day, First Month 27th, 1922. The Central Employment Association, organized in 1857, will hold its Donation Day, on First Month 27th, at Friends' Meeting House, 17th St. and Girard Ave., Philadelphia. The object of the Association is to give sewing to women in their homes, and the garments thus made are distributed among the worthy poor. Any donations of money or material will be gratefully received by the members of the Association who will be in attendance from 3 to 5 P. M. Elizabeth Y. Webb, Treasurer, No. 2 East 2nd St., Media, Pa.

NOTICE—Friends will recall the interest taken by Henry W. Wilbur in the Industrial School at Fort Valley, Georgia. In aid of the work of mercy in this Black Belt of Georgia, to buy a car for the District Nurse, there will be a concert given by Milan Lusk, a Negro pupil of Kubelik, at the studio of I. Phillip Schmand, Hotel des Artistes, New York, on Fifth-day evening, First month 26th. Mr. Schmand is a member of the National Arts Club and a painter of portraits in the city, and of landscape at his summer studio in Lynne, Connecticut.

NOTICE—"OVERCOMING BY THE SPIRIT," Illustrated by original readings, by Leslie Pinckney Hill; Negro Spirituals sung by the Cheyney Octette; Public Meeting, 15th and Race Sts. Meeting House, Sixth Day (Friday), Jan. 20th, 8 P. M. Under auspices Yearly Meeting Committee, "In the Interest of Colored Race." All friends of either white or colored race, cordially invited.

NOTICE—Frank D. Slutz, of the Moraine Park School, Dayton, Ohio, will give an address at Friends' Central School, 15th and Race Streets, Philadelphia, on Seventh Day, First month 21, at 10.30 A. M. Subject: "The Fundamentals of Progressive Education." The Committee on Education extends an invitation to all teachers, members of educational committees and other friends of education to attend this meeting.

Mr. Slutz will speak at 2 o'clock at Friends' Select School, 16th and Cherry Streets, Philadelphia, Pa., under the auspices of Friends' Educational Association. Subject:—The Creative Impulse in Education. They extend an invitation to all.

IDA P. STABLER,
Executive Secretary of Committee on Education.

FUN.

An earnest preacher in Georgia, who has a custom of telling the Lord all the news in his prayers, recently began a petition for help against the progress of wickedness in his town with the statement: "O thou great Jehovah, crime is on the increase. It is becoming more prevalent daily. I can prove it to you by statistics."—*Everybody's Magazine.*

As Far As They Could

Two ambitious roosters were at the opposite ends of the same worm. The tug of war was strenuous.

Cried the Worm: "Say, have a heart. Aren't you stretching this joke a little too far?"—Selected.

An example of a fine, but it seems proper, distinction is given in this conversation reported in *Harper's Magazine*:

"Mr. Smith," a man asked his tailor, "how is it you have not called on me for my account?"

"Oh, I never ask a gentleman for money."

"Indeed! How, then, do you get on if he doesn't pay?"

"Why," replied the tailor, hesitating, "after a certain time I conclude he is not a gentleman, and then I ask him."—*Youth's Companion.*

Outdoing Einstein

An Irishman was handling dynamite in a quarry. He let a stick drop, and the whole box went up, taking Mike with it. The quarry boss came around later and said to another Irishman:

"Where is Mike?"

"He's gone," replied Pat.

"When will he be back?" asked the boss.

"Well," replied Pat, "if he comes back as fast as he went, he'll be back yesterday."—O. E. R. Bulletin.

The First to Weaken

Pat—"Tomorrow's Saint Patrick's Day, and I challenge you to be the first one up in the morning. If I succeed, I'll make a chalk mark on the door."

Mike—"Foine. I'll go yer. If I get up first, I'll rub it out."—Selected.

A Difference In Ambition

"Don't you wisht you was a bird, Jimmy, and could fly away up in the sky?" mused little Jean, dreamily.

"Naw!" scorned Jimmy. "I'd ruther be a elephant and squirt water through my nose."—Kind Words.

REGULAR MEETINGS.

OAKLAND, CALIF.—A FRIENDS' MEETing is held every First-day at 11 A. M., in the Extension Room, Y. W. C. A. Building, Webster Street, above 14th. Visiting Friends always welcome.

FRIENDS' MEETING IN PASADENA, California—Orange Grove Monthly Meeting of Friends, 520 East Orange Grove Avenue, Pasadena, California. Meeting for worship, First-day, 11 A. M. Monthly Meeting, the second First-day of each month, at 1.45 P. M.

WANTED

WANTED—POSITION BY COLLEGE woman as secretary or nurse-companion. Capable of taking full charge of nervous or chronic invalid. Address, Mrs. J. H. Pease, Schofield School, Aiken, S. C.

WOMAN OF MIDDLE-AGE, NURSE, wants care of invalid. Address P-30, Friends' Intelligencer.

POSITION WANTED—BY NURSE, undergraduate. Refined; accustomed to traveling. Best references. Address D-32, Friends' Intelligencer.

POSITION WANTED—A REFINED widow desires position as housekeeper for widow or widower's family, excellent cook; economical; reliable; best reference. Address T-31, Friends' Intelligencer.

WANTED — MOTHER'S HELPER, white, to assist with housework and care of two children in refined home. References. H. G. Smith, Lansdowne, Pa.

A WORKING HOUSEKEEPER IS needed by Western Community House. May have use of comfortable quarters. Salary. Permanent. A. C. Leeds, 129 N. 12th Street, Philadelphia.

TRANSIENT ACCOMMODATIONS

VISITORS TO CALIFORNIA CAN find comfortable accommodations at 400 S. Euclid Avenue, Pasadena. For terms, apply to Mary B. Sutton.

WASHINGTON, D. C.—ROOMS FOR visitors. Near Station, Capitol, Library. Continuous hot water. Electricity. Garage. Mrs. L. L. Kendig, 120 C. Street, Northwest.

FOR RENT.

FOR RENT BY YEAR OR TERM OF years, or will consider sale—A very attractive small house in Brielle, New Jersey, near river and sea. Hot-water heater and all possible conveniences, including open fireplace. One minute from "bus" line between Lakewood and Asbury Park. Ten minutes from train. Address Box 28, "Applewood," Brielle, N. J.

FUN

Jud Tunkins says what makes him admire a mother's love and marvel at it is a photograph of himself taken at the age of eleven or twelve.—*Washington Star.*

"Did you give the penny to the monkey, dear?"

"Yes, mamma."

"And what did the monkey do with it?"

"He gave it to his father, who played the organ."—Boston Transcript.

To the Lot Holders and others interested in Fairhill Burial Ground:

GREEN STREET Monthly Meeting has funds available for the encouragement of the practice of cremating the dead to be interred in Fairhill Burial Ground. We wish to bring this fact as prominently as possible to those who may be interested. We are prepared to undertake the expense of cremation in case any lot holder desires us to do so.

Those interested should communicate with William H. Gaskill, Treasurer of the Committee of Interments, Green Street Monthly Meeting, or any of the following members of the Committee.

William H. Gaskill, 3201 Arch St.
Samuel N. Longstreth, 1218 Chestnut St.
Charles F. Jenkins, 232 South Seventh St.
Stuart S. Graves, 3033 Germantown Ave.

ADVERTISING RATE in the FRIENDS' INTELLIGENCER, for Help Wanted, Positions Wanted, Rooms for Rent, Notices, and other classified advertisements without display, for each insertion, 2 cents per word, including name, initials and address. Answers may be sent to a box at the INTELLIGENCER office, if so directed.

For display advertising the rate is 10 cents per agate line, or $1.40 per column inch, each insertion. On ten or more insertions in a year from date of order, ten per cent. discount. Thus a four-inch single-column or two-inch double-column advertisement costs $5.60 each insertion, less ten per cent., or 5.04 net each time for ten or more insertions. Matter may be changed whenever desired, without extra charge.

Experience has proved the INTELLIGENCER to be a remarkably good advertising medium. All advertisements must "pass the censor!"

Address 140 N. 15th St., Philadelphia

CLEAN HIGH GRADE
COAL

S
SUPPLEE

CLEAN HIGH GRADE
COAL

Friends' Intelligencer

ESTABLISHED 1844 PHILADELPHIA, FIRST MONTH 28, 1922 VOLUME 79 NUMBER 4

The Quakerism of Robert Barclay

BY ELBERT RUSSELL

Part One

Second installment of the series "The Quakerism of the Founders." This study of Robert Barclay will be concluded in the third installment, to appear in the issue of Second month eleventh.

AMONG the founders of the Society of Friends, Robert Barclay had the most thorough training in Biblical, theological, and ecclesiastical subjects. Both Presbyterians and Catholics had contributed to his education. In consequence he has given the most complete *theological* interpretation of Quakerism. He followed the methods of scholastic reasoning then still current in the schools, and he used the words and expressions of the non-Quaker world for whom he wrote more than most Friends did. His style is precise, logical and detailed, and on the whole difficult for modern readers.

In reading his writings in comparison with those of the other founders, allowance must be made for these peculiarities of interest and expression.

The Seeking Mind and The True Ground of Knowledge

"He that desireth to acquire any art or science, seeketh first those means by which that art or science is obtained. If we ought to do so in things natural and earthly, how much more then in spiritual?

"Thus when a man first proposeth to himself the knowledge of God, from a sense of his own unworthiness, and from the great weariness of his mind, occasioned by the secret checks of his conscience, and the tender, yet real glances of God's light upon his heart; the earnest desires he has to be redeemed from his present trouble, and the fervent breathings he has to be eased of his disordered passions and lusts, and to find quietness and peace in the certain knowledge of God, and in the assurance of his love and good-will towards him, make his heart tender, and ready to receive any impression; and so—not having then a distinct discerning—through forwardness embraceth any thing that brings present ease. If, either through the reverence he bears to certain persons, or from the secret inclination to what doth comply with his natural disposition, he fall upon any principles or means, by which he apprehends he may come to know God, and so doth centre himself, it will be hard to remove him thence again, how wrong so ever they may be: for the first anguish being over, he becomes more hardy; and the enemy being near, creates a false peace, and a certain confidence, which is strengthened by the mind's unwillingness to enter again into new doubtfulness, or the former anxiety of a search."—*Barclay, Apology, Prop. I.*

To-day as much as ever we need from time to time to re-examine the basis of our religious beliefs and to free ourselves from that fear of honest doubt, which is ever the father of superstition.

Immediate Revelation

"Mat. xi. 27. Seeing 'no man knoweth the Father but the Son, and he to whom the Son revealeth him;' and seeing the 'revelation of the Son is in and by the Spirit;' therefore the testimony of the Spirit is that alone by which the true knowledge of God hath been, is, and can be only revealed; who, as, by the moving of his own Spirit, he disposed the chaos of this world into that wonderful order in which it was in the beginning, and created man a living soul, to rule and govern it, so by the revelation of the same Spirit he hath manifested himself all along unto the sons of men, both patriarchs, prophets, and apostles. * * * Moreover, these divine inward revelations, which we make absolutely necessary for the building up of true faith, neither do nor can ever contradict the outward testimony of the scriptures, or right and sound reason. Yet from hence it will not follow, that these divine revelations are to be subjected to the test, either of the outward testimony of the scriptures, or of the natural reason of man, as to a more noble or certain rule and touchstone; for this divine revelation and inward illumination, is that which is evident and clear of itself, forcing, by its own evidence and clearness, the well-disposed understanding to assent, irresistibly moving the same thereunto, even as the common principles of natural truths do move and incline the mind to a natural assent."—*Apology, Prop. II.*

In the original usage of Friends the term "immediate" means "direct," "personal," "without mediators." By one of those subtle shifts of meaning from which so many words and expressions of early Friends suffered, it came afterwards to mean *"extempore,"* "on the spur of the moment," or unpremeditated.

The Scriptures

"In that which we affirm of them [the Scriptures], it doth appear at what high rate we value them, accounting them, without all deceit or equivocation, the most excellent writings in the world; to which not only no other writings are to be preferred, but even in divers respects not comparable thereto.

"Though then we do acknowledge the Scriptures to be very heavenly and divine writings, the use of them to be very comfortable and necessary to the church of Christ, and that we also admire and give praise to the Lord, for his wonderful providence in preserving these writings so pure and uncorrupted as we have them, through so long a night of apostacy, to be a testimony of his truth against the wickedness and abominations even of those whom he made instrumental in preserving them, so that they have kept them to be a witness against themselves; yet we may not call them the principal fountain of all truth and knowledge, nor yet the first adequate rule of faith and manners; because the principal fountain of truth must be the Truth itself; *i. e.*, that whose certainty and authority depends not upon another."—*Apology, Prop. III.*

The True Justification

"And to conclude this proposition, let none be so bold as to mock God, supposing themselves justified and accepted in the sight of God, by virtue of Christ's death and sufferings, while they remain unsanctified and unjustified in their own hearts, and polluted in their sins, lest their hope prove that of the hypocrite, which perisheth. Neither let any foolishly imagine, that they can by their own works, or by the performance of any ceremonies or traditions, or by the giving of gold or money, or by afflicting their bodies in will-worship and voluntary humility, or foolishly striving to conform their way to the outward letter of the law, flatter themselves that they merit before God, or draw a debt upon him, or that any man or men have power to make such kind of things effectual to their justification, lest they be found foolish boasters and strangers to Christ and his righteousness indeed. But blessed for ever are they, that having truly had a sense of their own unworthiness and sinfulness, and having seen all their own endeavours and performances fruitless and vain, and beheld their own emptiness, and the vanity of their vain hopes, faith, and confidence, while they remained inwardly pricked, pursued, and condemned by God's holy witness in their hearts, and so having applied themselves thereto, and suffered his grace to work in them, are become changed and renewed in the spirit of their minds, passed from death to life, and know Jesus arisen in them, working both the will and the deed; and so having 'put on the Lord Jesus Christ,' in effect are clothed with him, and partake of his righteousness and nature; such can draw near to the Lord with boldness, and know their acceptance in and by him; in whom, and in as many as are found in him, the Father is well pleased."—*Apology, Prop. VII.*

Protestant theology was occupied with schemes by means of which a man was to be accounted or reckoned as righteous: Friends insisted that God does not deal in legal fictions; that the object of the mission of Christ and the inworking of his Spirit is to make men actually and fully righteous.

Public Worship

"All true and acceptable worship of God is offered in the inward and immediate moving and drawing of his own Spirit, which is neither limited to places, times, nor persons. For though we are to worship him always, and continually to fear before him; yet as to the outward signification thereof, in prayers, praises or preachings, we ought not to do it in our own will, where and when we will; but where and when we are moved thereunto by the stirring and secret inspiration of the Spirit of God in our hearts; which God heareth and accepteth of, and is never wanting to move us thereunto, when need is; of which he himself is the alone proper judge.

"Fourthly, To come then to the state of the controversy, as to the public worship, we judge it the duty of all to be diligent in the assembling of themselves together, and what we have been, and are, in this matter, our enemies in Great Britain, who have used all means to hinder our assembling together to worship God, may bear witness; and when assembled, the great work of one and all ought to be to wait upon God; and returning out of their own thoughts and imaginations, to feel the Lord's presence, and know a gathering unto his name indeed, where he is in the midst, according to his promise. And as everyone is thus gathered, and so met together inwardly in their spirits, as well as outwardly in their persons, there the secret power and virtue of life is known to refresh the soul, and the pure motions and breathings of God's Spirit are felt to arise; from which, as words of declaration, prayers or praises arise, the acceptable worship is known, which edifies the church, and is well-pleasing to God. Yea, though there be not a word spoken, yet is the true spiritual worship performed, and the body of Christ edified; yea, it may, and hath often fallen out among us, that divers meetings have past without one word; and yet our souls have been greatly edified and refreshed, and our hearts wonderfully overcome with the secret sense of God's power and Spirit, which without words hath been ministered from one vessel to another."—*Apology, Prop. XI.*

The Convincing Power

"For not a few have come to be convinced of the truth after this manner, of which I myself, in part, am a true witness, who not by strength of arguments, or by a particular disquisition of each doctrine, and convincement of my understanding thereby, came to receive and bear witness of the truth, but by being secretly reached by this life; for when I came into the silent assemblies of God's people, I felt a secret power among them, which touched my heart, and as I gave way unto it, I found the evil weakening in me, and the good raised up, and so I became thus knit and united unto them, hungering more and more after the increase of this power and life, whereby I might feel myself perfectly redeemed. And indeed this is the surest way to become a Christian, to whom afterwards the knowledge and understanding of principles will not be wanting, but will grow up so much as is needful, as the natural fruit of this good root, and such a knowledge will not be barren nor unfruitful. After this manner we desire therefore all that come among us to be proselyted, knowing that though thousands should be convinced in their understandings of all the truths we maintain, yet if they were not sensible of this inward life, and their souls not changed from unrighteousness to righteousness, they could add nothing to us."—*Apology, Prop. XI.*

THE FRIENDS' INTELLIGENCER is published weekly at 140 N. 15th St., Philadelphia, by FRIENDS' INTELLIGENCER ASSOCIATION, Ltd. Telephone, Spruce 5-75. Entered at Philadelphia Post-Office as second class matter. Subscription in the United States, Mexico, Cuba and Panama, $2.60 a Year. Subscriptions may begin at any time. Subscription in Canada and other foreign countries (on account of extra postage charges), $3.00 a year. Single copies, 6 cents. Make checks payable to FRIENDS' INTELLIGENCER ASSN., LTD.

the Life of Today," but he will find as he reads on that here is a man who believes that the "Old Testament" is a vital force in the life of 1921 and states his case in a direct forceful style.

There is a fearless freedom that one might not expect from the author's titles and occupation—"Does not history show that religion to be vital must be conceived in terms of contemporary thought and feeling? Is it not necessary, in other words, that each generation shall re-discover and re-interpret God, just as it does everything else in the light of its new knowledge?"

The book should be helpful to anyone who is teaching the Old Testament. The ordinary reader may be tempted to pass it by, ever mindful of the tendency of the time to read about great books rather than to actually study them, but this book will flood all future readings of the Old Testament with new light. There are detailed compact pictures of the different periods. There are suggestive outlines and references. There is phrasing that compels attention:

"Ruth—The claims of the outsider upon the Church."

"Proverbs—The art of getting on in the world."

"Zechariah—The price of permanent peace."

"Malachi—The religion that counts."

"Substitute the ideal of force for the force of the ideal." (You must get this in its setting in order to appreciate it.)

"We are punished by our sins rather than for them."

"Religion must be institutionalized and the institution Christianized—The universe is fluid rather than fixed; a stream rather than a crystal and not even the holiest of all our institutions must be above revision and reconstruction to meet the changing needs of a changing world."

"The conception of the church as an institution for dispensing salvation must now give way to that of an institution for comforting the disconsolate, for rescuing the lost, for educating the child, for Christianizing community life, for making the social ideal of Jesus prevail, for enthroning God in all human experience, everywhere in the world."

There are many citations of authority throughout the book and we wish the author had cited authors and works. This is particularly true when he refers to economic data.

The description of the Psalms made the reviewer wish that he knew Hebrew. The next best thing was to hear a Rabbi who is said to be an especially fine reader of Hebrew.

Do you have to deal with people who believe the Bible literally?—then the account of Genesis and Exodus may be suggestive.

Do you ever ponder the so-called "punishments of God?"—then see the story of Habakkuk.

Have you ever wondered how to teach the Pentateuch to children?—there is an interesting study of parental and teacher responsibility for the correct interpretation of these stories.

You will be interested in the purpose of the church and why men should belong to church.

If you will take time to skim this book, you will take time to read it carefully.

Ventnor City, N. J. HALLIDAY R. JACKSON.

FRIENDS' INTELLIGENCER

The religion of Friends is based on faith in the "INWARD LIGHT," or direct revelation of God's spirit and will in every seeking soul.

The INTELLIGENCER is interested in all who bear the name of Friends in every part of the world, and aims to promote love, unity and intercourse among all branches and with all religious societies.

Editorial and business offices, 140 N. 15th Street, Philadelphia, Pa. For information regarding subscription rates, etc., see foot of second page.

WALTER H. ABELL, *Editor.*
SUE C. YERKES, *Business Manager.*

Editorial Board:
ELIZABETH POWELL BOND, THOMAS A. JENKINS,
J. RUSSELL SMITH, GEORGE A. WALTON.

PHILADELPHIA, FIRST MONTH 28, 1922

IN THIS ISSUE

Second Annual Meeting of the Intelligencer Associates

A meeting of the Friends' Intelligencer Associates was held on First month 18th, 1922, at 2.30 p. m., in Room No. 1, 15th and Race Streets, Philadelphia, Pa.

The number present, 30, did not constitute a quorum, but the usual business of the meeting was carried on with the understanding that the decisions made should stand unless objection should be raised by absent members.

The Executive Committee stated that its report was virtually embodied in the letter which had been sent out to the Associates along with the official ballot.

In addition to this report, however, it was stated that the question of placing the Intelligencer in libraries, colleges, hospitals, etc., had been considered by the committee, and also referred to the Advancement Committee, and through its secretary to the local Advancement Committees. As yet, no tangible evidence of results have appeared. In the case of Purchase Quarterly Meeting, this action had already been taken, the paper having been placed in neighboring libraries, hospitals, etc.

The Treasurer reported that $2,468.75 had been received from Associates during the year, which with the balance of $377.50 from last year made a total of $2,846.25. Of this amount, $2,600 had been paid into the treasury of the Friends' Intelligencer Association, leaving a balance in his hands of $246.25. Six 1921 payments were made without further pledge, and a few 1921 payments have not yet been made. There are now 304 Associates representing an annual total contribution of $2,502.50.

The Board of Managers and the Editor presented reports which are given below. These reports were commented upon most favorably, and two very en couraging letters were read. Several of the Asso ciates made practical suggestions one of these being that some plan should be made to educate the mem bers of the Society concerning financial conditions of Church papers in general, in order that they might realize that the price of our paper is not high and come to understand the need not only for a wider circulation of the paper but also for a greater number of Associates.

It was further suggested that we should endeavor to find circulation for our paper through news stands and among those who are not Friends. A striking incident was given of how the paper appeals in places where we would not dream of finding it this wider circle of readers being made even more possible because of the world-wide interest in the work of the American Friends' Service Committee

As there was not a quorum present at the meeting the proposed amendments were approved and di rected to be submitted to a mail vote the ensuing year for final action.

The following Executive and Nominating Commit tee was elected. In accordance with the By-Laws six Yearly Meetings had proposed official repre sentatives to this committee as follows:

New York—Frank H. Quimby
Philadelphia—William C. Biddle
Baltimore—Gladys Brooke
Indiana—Reuben Roberts
Illinois—Albert Miller
Genesee—Mabel Brown

Six additional names were selected by the meeting as follows:

Walter C. Longstreth
Charles F. Branson
O. Edward Janney
Ellwood Burdsall, Chairman
Bertha L. Broomell, Secretary
Herbert P. Worth, Treasurer

The following officers were elected for the ensuin year:

Chairman—Ellwood Burdsall, Port Cheste N. Y.

Treasurer—Herbert P. Worth, West Cheste Pa.

Secretary—Bertha L. Broomell, Baltimore, M

Managers for the term from 1922 to 1925 we elected as follows:

Annie Hillborn, Swarthmore, Pa.
William C. Biddle, New York, N. Y.
Elwood Hollingshead, Moorestown, N. J.

The meeting was much indebted to George H. H lett, Jr., through whose kindness at the time of t counting of the votes, a most interesting demonstr tion of the Hare System of Proportional Represe tation was given to the Associates present.

ABBY MARY HALL ROBERTS,
Secretary pro tem.

Associates have joined. Since the organization, the number of Associates deceased is ten, and three, unable to continue their pledges, have been released. The present number of Associates is 304, who have pledged an annual income of $2,502.50.

In 1918, the Friends' Intelligencer Association found it necessary to borrow $1,000. This note was carried until Twelfth month 15th, 1921, when it was paid. No interest had been paid on this note. The Friend who loaned the money, when approached by the business manager as to a basis for cancelling this indebtedness, offered to accept $600 as payment in full, thus making a donation of $400 plus the accrued interest. The balance of $600 was raised by a special fund to which the different Yearly Meetings, through individuals and meetings, contributed varying amounts.

After paying off this note for $1,000, the operations for the year left us with a net gain of $725.47. This gain is very encouraging, but we wish to impress upon the Associates the fact that if it were not for their pledges and the donations, there would be a considerable deficit instead of a gain. At present the lowest possible prices are being paid for paper and printing. We would like to use a better quality of paper and have better work done on the printing. We need more Associates to make these improvements possible, and we trust that the present Associates will do all in their power to enlist the interest of others.

Elwood Hollingshead,
Chairman.

Report of the Editor

A Christmas card from a Waynesville, Ohio, Friend to Thomas A. Jenkins, of Chicago, forwarded by the latter to the Intelligencer office, contains the following lines:

> "I take this opportunity to express my appreciation of the Intelligencer. It is improving all the time. I read it through every week and sometimes go over it again. Others in the house have done the same."

These comments are representatives of many that have to come to us during the past year. We feel that they should be encouraging to the Associates, as they have been to us. They indicate that, despite the indifference in many quarters, which is the worst obstacle to the growth, it is exerting a real influence, and is bringing inspiration to many of its readers.

On the other hand, we have at times been conscious of an attitude of questioning on the part of some readers toward some material which the paper has contained. Such questioning, though directly expressed to us on only three or four occasions, has doubtless been felt by many who have not so expressed it. It relates mainly to articles or editorials which some have felt to be "too radical," though others have criticized the paper for not being radical enough.

The editor recognizes that he has made mistakes in the past, and that he doubtless will do so more than once in the future He welcomes comment and criticism of all kinds, desiring nothing so much as

"Shall We Set New Standards For Prison Reform?"

The article under the above caption in the INTELLIGENCER for Twelfth month 17th, greatly impressed me, particularly its second, fourth, fifth and closing paragraphs. At once I read the book to which it referred (Penology in the U. S., by Louis N. Robinson). And then I re-read those paragraphs —which, indeed, had really been in my thoughts ever since my first reading of them—*"many prisoners, though not all, are more comfortable than in Elizabeth Fry's day. But of what importance is this compared with the fact that nearly all are MADE WORSE by their term of imprisonment? It is only those who disbelieve in the soul who can regard this fact with equanimity. Why have Friends failed here?* * * * *To me the time seems ripe for examination of every prison and every criminal, every problem and every policy, from this point of view."*

There is a dynamic force of conviction back of these words. Here, today, may indeed be set up a new milestone in Quaker history. The time indeed "is ripe." To the present writer, such dynamic impulse toward such a service is in itself of the nature of consecration, inspiration.

I am impressed with the emphasis throughout the book, upon the fact that "prisons should be regarded as great social laboratories," "social factories for turning out a definite product"—*character*. A human being is "not of merely economic value to the State." His "state of mind on release" is of infinitely more social importance. Here is the true Quaker emphasis; here could be the starting-point of one of the greatest reforms—most far-reaching in its education, indeed, of *all departments of society*—that the Society of Friends has ever faced.

This book is of value not only because it "outlines the hopes and disappointments of generation after generation of prison reform for some five hundred years of Anglo-Saxon history," but still more for its forward-looking, constructive attitude. Taken together with the article in the INTELLIGENCER, it gives an unforgettable impetus to thought, to desire for service, definite, constructive action.

The quotation of a sentence here and there may perhaps suggest the trend, though of course in such limited space can do no justice to the work as a whole:

"* * * whether the frightful sanitary condition of many prisons, the mingling of sexes and of young and old offenders, the idleness and neglect of all the decencies of life, are the result of the conscious choice of society, or whether they are due solely to neglect, matters not, since what society allows to be done through indifference is perhaps as good an indication of its real wishes as what it purposely performs * * *."

It is suggested that one read in connection with that word "idleness" the statement of a man at one time confined in the Philadelphia County Prison, where very little work can be done, and remember that in other institutions of this State and elsewhere there is provision for work for only about one hundred out of every sixteen hundred men confined.

"We have been unthinkably foolish in that we have not applied to criminals the things that we know to be good for the rest of us—let alone give them the special attention which the fact of their crime warrants us in believing they are in need of. Certainly the sanitation and diet should be such that good health would be assured; work should be interesting, not drudgery of the lowest and most mechanical sort; it should yield some income to the prisoner; there should be educational opportunities and industrial training; and there should be the chance to grow, and leave behind the 'outgrown shell.' Every one of these things can be achieved if we but put our shoulders to the wheel." It is urged that we "educate our own children for this great work, that they may not grow up totally ignorant of this large part of the machinery of government, which will in the future have no hand to guide it but theirs and those of their fellow ignoramuses * * *."

But the present writer disagrees with this book's tentative suggestion to put the whole prison system into the hands of some existing "learned profession" or department of administration. Just here may be recalled the words of the warden of the State Prison at Stillwater, Minn.: "Good politics may be a necessary function of government, but bad politics has, I think, done more to retard and destroy good prison administration than all other causes combined," and also the fact that today only 2 per cent. of our taxes go for educational purposes (as against 90 per cent. for military ends), and that hundreds of thousands of our children are today denied even a seat in a schoolroom and teachers are ill-paid and ill-equipped for their work. And when one recalls the attitude of many of another "learned profession" (medical) toward, for instance, a fellow scientist such as Dr. Lorenz, would not one hesitate to put so crucial a matter as the management of prisons into the hands of such narrow prejudice? Is there not still "a more excellent" way for those of Friendly persuasion?

We must not forget that three generations of malnutrition (brains half-fed with poor blood) breed the congenital-defectives that supply so large a proportion of our so-called "criminals" today. Since it has been demonstrated that it is actually "cheaper" in dollars and cents, to feed the children of one generation than to imprison successive generations, somewhat more thought is now being given to this phase of the problem. But even so, it is merely in terms of dollars and cents; it wholly lacks the Friendly spirit, the impetus of spiritual conviction. From the Quaker point of view—that the Spirit seeks full expression in every human soul and is thwarted of this in deformed and diseased bodies and minds—is not then the greatest blasphemy, perhaps that unpardonable sin against the Holy Spirit, that it is thus denied right-of-way in human life?

To quote again from this book: "Only here and there the searchlight of science has been turned on the problem of human crime" * * * "there will probably be many interesting experiments in the next few years" * * * But "without the backing of informed men and women" (to inform and educate public opinion, including that of churches, school boards, jurors, judges), in the truth that *men* and not things, mere "property," are the crux of the problem, we will not soon achieve the state of mind "when a jail warden is required to be of the calibre of a college president" because considered to hold an equally responsible and honorable position.

Believing the essential Quaker vision to be the most truly spiritual (and hence the sanest and most practical) outlook on life, the present writer urges, *pleads,* that this great work of world-wide importance, the influence of which would inevitably be felt throughout all the future of humanity, be initiated, and *at once,* by a group of "informed men and women" (of which the writer of this book and the writer of the INTELLIGENCER article would naturally form the nucleus), and that the work of this initial group, and indeed throughout the whole great movement, be on the true Quaker basis of *voluntary service* only. A body of *such* workers would be invincible—men and women with, literally, "authority from God," in love with their work, "filled with the Spirit," "*driven* of the Spirit" to the service of their fellow-men in this hideously neglected field. I am profoundly convinced that even a very small group of devoted men and women, "called of God," with no thought but of *service,* could so stir the conscience and move the hearts of people today that a great and unprecedented wave of popular opinion and interest would be aroused and our present barbarous prison-world be civilized, Christianized, in even less than a generation. The time is ripe.

A READER.

Friendly News Notes

Andrew Erskin is soon to leave on a three months' trip to the Black Sea region with one of the Russian Relief Ships.

President Frank Aydelotte was elected secretary-treasurer of the Association of American Colleges at its annual sessions held in Chicago last week. That this is a high tribute to Swarthmore's new executive is attested by the fact that membership in the Association includes approximately 150 colleges of the country.

Pittsburgh Friends were most glad to welcome Rufus M. Jones at meeting on the morning of January 15th, and listened with deep interest to his sermon. He spoke in the afternoon to an audience of about two thousand, in Syria Temple, the mass meeting being the culmination of the Russian Famine Fund Campaign in Pittsburgh.

The members of our Pittsburgh group feel a deep sense of personal loss in the death (the entrance into "the larger life," as he loved to call it) of Erasmus Wilson, known to many thousands of Pittsburgh, Pennsylvania, readers as "The Quiet Observer."

The Quaker Embassy in Paris has recently issued two new French statements of Friends' principles. One is a four-page leaflet by Henry Van Etten, the other a twenty-page pamphlet entitled "A Quaker Witness," by Miriam Reinhart. A French reader of these statements has judged them well-adapted to appeal to the French mind. At this time when the French people are struggling to regain their mental and spiritual equilibrium after the impact of a war which it felt so disastrously, the message of Quakerism, expressed in such statements as these, may exert a vital influence.

At the invitation of Orthodox young Friends, the executive committees of the Young Friends' Movements of both branches in Philadelphia, and a few other guests, met at 20 South Twelfth Street on the evening of First month 16, for supper and an evening around the open fire with William Littleboy. During the evening William Littleboy talked on the subject of what it seemed to him that American Quakerism is today, and what it might be. In the face of the tremendous opportunities of world recognition, he found American Quakers a respectable and respected group, engaged in philanthropic enterprise, yet stooping down to give to the masses in need, rather than stepping down to literally share and dare with them. He felt that as a group, we still lack "the divine spark," which can enable us to meet the need of the world. To seek means of cultivating this perfecting quality, he felt should be first concern of all Friends.

"Overcoming By The Spirit," was the subject of an address by Leslie Pinckney Hill, principal of the Cheyney Training School for Teachers, delivered in the Meeting House at Fifteenth and Race Streets, Philadelphia, on the evening of First month 20th. The burden of the address was that the colored races of the world, and especially of America, must aid in lifting themselves and the white races to the plane of inter-racial brotherhood, not by resentment or force, but by the power of the spirit—by themselves being nobler, more infused with spiritual vision, than those who so often treat them unjustly. The speaker frequently illustrated his point by reading from his recent book of verse, "The Wings of Oppression." The program was beautifully supplemented by the singing of old Negro spirituals by a group of boys and girls from the Cheyney Training School.

Sherwood Eddy, the well-known Y. M. C. A. speaker, is to be in Philadelphia for three days, the 3rd, 4th and 5th of April. His program arranged by the Y. M. C. A. of the University of Pennsylvania, will include two addresses at the noon-time Lenten services at the Garrick Theatre.

Mary N. Chase, Secretary for the Promotion of International Amity of Proctor Academy, Andover, New Hampshire, has been a devoted worker in helping to build up international correspondence; particularly, since the war, correspondence between America and Germany. She has just sent us the name and address of a German gentleman who is much interested in Friends' principles, and who desires to correspond in English with an American Quaker. We shall be glad to forward his name and address to any one who would enjoy entering upon such a correspondence.

An action which has its particular virtue as a gesture of good will among nations is the conferring by the University of Marburg, Germany, of an honorary degree of Doctor of Theology on William Charles Braithwaite, B. A., LL. B., the well-known Quaker historian and banker of Banbury, England. The Faculty in conferring the degree state that "He has rendered signal service to Church History both as a scholar and in research work by his profound books '*The Beginnings of Quakerism*' and '*The Second Period of Quakerism.*' He has labored indefatigably in education and in popular instruction; also in social problems and for the restoration of justice and fellowship in the intercourse of nations. In him we thankfully honor at the same time the actively applied brotherly love of the Quakers of whom he has shown himself a worthy representative."

The references to Dr. Braithwaite's educational work are in connection with his chairmanship of the National Adult School Union and active participation in the work of the Educational Settlements Association.

The Central Committee met in Philadelphia, Pa., First month 21st. The place for holding the next Conference was considered in the light of the difficulties there seemed to be to house the Conference satisfactorily in Cape May, and in light of the earnest desire of Western Friends that now, after the lapse of fourteen years, the Conference should again come into the middle states.

It was agreed to hold the Conference at Richmond, Ind., Eighth month 26th to Ninth month 2nd, 1922. The sessions will be held in the large auditorium of the Methodist Church, only a block away from the North A. Street Meeting House.

Friends will be housed in hotels, boarding houses, private homes, and in a tent colony on the Meeting House lawn. A very strong and attractive program is being arranged.

At Birkenhead, on the 21st ult., the Mayor (Mr. Luke Lees) formally opened a large room in the Friends' meeting-house as a rest room for the unemployed. Friends had heard of the overcrowded condition of a room opened at St. Paul's; hence their offer. The room set apart has three tables well stocked with magazine literature and is well heated, so making the meeting-house a popular center for the unemployed. The Mayor, in his speech, remarked upon the beauty of the accommodation, and said that although the site was removed considerably from the center of the town, the large number of unemployed men who wandered into the Park for relaxation would find the meeting-house an ideal place for rest and recuperation. Our Birkenhead Correspondent suggests that Friends elsewhere, in towns where there is much unemployment and a lack of rest rooms, may advantageously copy this example. We recently reported a similar effort of Sydenham Friends (one night a week and speakers provided) and of Tottenham Friends (with free canteen).—*The London Friend.*

Correction

In the account in last week's INTELLIGENCER of "A Negro Commission on Housing" through an error, the word Missouri was printed Mission. It is in the State of Missouri that this commission has been appointed, "giving to the colored citizenship their first independent state department and right of investigation with recommendatory privileges."

And look, as the wind in the bellows, which would blow out the candle, blows up the fire; even so it often comes to pass that such temptations do enliven the true Christian, awakening the graces of the spirit in him, and by that means discover both the reality and the strength of grace in him.—*Thomas Boston.*

THE OPEN FORUM

This column is intended to afford free expression of opinion by readers on questions of interest. The INTELLIGENCER is not responsible for any such opinions. Letters must be brief, and the editor reserves the right to omit parts if necessary to save space.

An Open Letter To William I. Hull

Dr. William I. Hull, 1-19-1922.
Swarthmore, Pa.

Dear friend:

In thy Washington report of 1st month 14th thee quotes Secretary Hughes as expressing "a deep disappointment in being unable to suggest practical limitations on the use of air craft in war, or on the preparation of air craft for military purposes."

May I venture to suggest that the difficulties would be removed if the scientific work in the perfection of travel by air were transferred from the War Department to a new Department of Peace, or to one of the existing departments for peaceful enterprise. It would then be a simple matter for nations to agree to cut down even to zero the amount to be spent by the military for air craft.

Sincerely thy friend,
J. BARNARD WALTON.

To the Editor:

It appears improper for Friends to take any steps in the Sacco-Vanzetti affair, as requested by E. Hillsmith. These unfortunate men, like all in trouble, have our earnest sympathy, but we can do nothing collectively for several reasons. Here are the facts with which we have to do in the case:—Payroll messengers were robbed and killed. Two men have been arrested for the crime; tried for the crime; convicted by a jury for the crime; and are now awaiting execution for the crime. A motion for a new trial, after consideration which we may suppose to have been careful, has been denied.

It is not for us to select here and there a dubious case of alleged miscarriage of justice. It is rather for us to work with all our strength for the abolition of the death penalty to the end that errors of justice may not pass beyond remedy, and that conviction of crime may not arouse hysteria and false sentiment.

New York City. JOHN COX, JR.

BIRTHS.

WAY—To Darlington H. and Ina A. Way, at their home near Port Matilda, Pa., a daughter, named Rebecca Jane.

MARRIAGES.

SWISHER-CLEMENT—In the Friends' Meeting House, at Oxford, Pa., on Twelfth month 27th, 1921, under the care of Nottingham Monthly Meeting, Helen E. Clement, daughter of Samuel and Mary K. Clement, and Joel C. Swisher of Peach Bottom, Pa., son of Charles Swisher, Wichita, Kansas.

DEATHS.

COCK—At Locust Valley, L. I., on Eleventh month 27th, Elizabeth T., widow of Augustus G. Cock, in her 83rd year. The funeral was attended by many of her friends and neighbors. Albert Lawton and the Rev. Henry C. Whitney, the latter a cousin of the deceased, spoke of the many sterling qualities that entered into the makeup of her exemplary life and character. A birthright member of Westbury Monthly Meeting, she was ever faithful and diligent in attendance at all meetings, until overtaken by the infirmities of age. She was guided by the Light within along the paths of Love and Charity, and will be greatly missed by the afflicted and less fortunate.

COLES—At Palmyra, N. J., on First month 19th, Ellen M. Coles, aged 74 years.

HARRIS—At Curwensville, Pa., on First month 10th, Charles K. Harris, in his 72nd year. A life-long member of Friends, he impressed all whose lives he touched by his devotion and active influence for the true Christian life.

PETTIT—At Germantown, Pa., on First month 17th, Mary L., widow of George W. Pettit.

RIDGWAY—At Jefferson, N. J., on First month 15th, Jacob H. Ridgway, aged 71 years.

UNDERHILL—At Jericho, Long Island, on First month 13th, Catharine Underhill, wife of the late Daniel Underhill, in the 89th year of her age. She was a valued member of Jericho Monthly Meeting.

WASHBURN—On First month 10th, at her White Plains home, Caroline Underhill, widow of Joshua B. Washburn, in her 91st year.

ERASMUS WILSON

Erasmus Wilson passed into the larger life on the morning of January 14th, after a short illness. His death has occasioned a deep sense of loss among Pittsburgh Friends, as well as to hundreds of others in the community.

He was born in Belmont County, Ohio, in 1842. He was the son of Joseph A. and Isabel (Kerr) Wilson, and a grandson of John Wilson, one of three brothers who came from England and settled in Havre de Grace, Md., afterward moving to Ohio, in 1819. Previous to this last migration John Wilson had married Isabel McGirr, of the Quaker community on Pigeon Creek, Pa.

A stirring chapter in the history of Erasmus Wilson was recorded during the Civil War, when he rendered valiant service in the cause that appealed to him as a just and a great one. Immediately after being mustered out, in 1865, he engaged in newspaper work, and continued in this profession up to the time of his death.

His unostentatious character and the high esteem in which he was held by all is well told in the words of a fellow writer:—"His death deprives the local newspaper colony, the Boy Scouts, and the mass of Pittsburgh humanity in general, of one of its humblest and most loyal friends."

Of late years he became impressed with the beneficial effects of the Boy Scout movement, and of all the staunch friends he possessed, none were more devoted than the Boy Scouts of Allegheny County. Deliberate in manner, dignified in mien, though affable withal, over six feet in height, and with the white hair of his years, he received from these young friends the name of "Chief White Pine," and he thoroughly enjoyed mingling with them, and frankly showed a youthful interest in their activities.

Through his column in a Pittsburgh newspaper he became known to thousands of readers as "The Quiet Observer," and they looked daily for this gentle preachment, with its homely wisdom and quiet humor. Fortified with the knowledge gained by many years of keen observation, he had the wisdom—common sense, he would have called it—to know how to apply what he knew. He would quickly match some story of "original badness" in humanity with one showing "original goodness." His religion was really one of service.

He sometimes attended Friends' meeting, as well as the Quaker Round Table gatherings, and though he was a Friend, he was by no means merely sectarian, but was quite at home at a Monday meeting of clergymen, at a Salvation Army gathering, or attending service at a cathedral. While having his own views on questions of theology, he always spoke respectfully—sympathetically—of any faith that gave comfort or served an uplifting purpose.

His personal friend, James Whitcomb Riley, has characterized him in homely but most truthful words, in "Erasmus Wilson," as follows:

"'Ras Wilson, I respect you, 'cause
You're common, like you allus was, . . .
You're common, yit oncommon *more*.
You allus kindo 'pear, to me,
What all mankind had ort to be."

C. E. W.

In remembrance of

S. LOUISA HAIGHT

There must be a large circle of interested and attached Friends who feel more than a common interest in the work of Louisa Haight, and its startling close. It is for such that this brief reply to their sympathetic inquiries is written. Her early life was passed in her Canadian home among Friends. When she came to the desire for college training, she had first the preparation of the Tomlinson School at Swarthmore; then a partial course in Swarthmore College. This, by the aid of one of our interested Friends, was followed by training in a liberal Theological Seminary, after which she spent a few years in the Ministry.

The climax of her interest in the welfare of the world was reached, we may say, when she was appointed to the Superintendency of the Schofield School for Colored Students in Aiken, South Carolina. The last day of her labors there, January 5th, is characteristic of her daily activities. She had done a full day's work.

She had made a wonderful annual report—financial, etc., and had walked over to the town on some business with the local Board-members. In the afternoon she attended to household affairs, and finally proposed washing the dogs, of whom they were very fond. To this, her secretary objected, since she had already had a full day. Her answer was "Yes, I want to round it up." While this was in cheerful progress, she was seen to swerve, and "the spirit had fled."

One of the Trustees makes this summary: "She had remarkable executive ability and poise. She never seemed hurried, but accomplished a great deal. For the colored people and the School she had vision and ambition. Her example of intelligent application to her task, and tireless industry in order to make it successful; also her power to avail herself of everything in a truly economical way will be a lesson that the pupils cannot forget."

One of her co-workers wishes her friends to know that she had never seemed in better health, nor more buoyantly happy than during the few days preceding her death.

There was a very simple memorial service at the house; the colored people congregating on the piazza and singing some of their songs, which she loved so much. There was not a sound of loud crying; everything was quiet and just as near as possible the way she would have wished it to be.

The burial took place at her Canada home. This is a story rather free from dramatic effects; but it is a life-story full of spirit of the Great Teacher—a life that has left its saving power as seed to germinate in many places.

It is a life-story for Friends, and for Swarthmore College to cherish in their annals.

ELIZABETH POWELL BOND.

COMING EVENTS

FIRST MONTH

27th—Meeting of Philadelphia Yearly Meeting's Committee on Philanthropic Labor, in Room No. 4 of Race Street Meeting-house, at 2.30 P. M. Dr. Louis N. Robinson will speak on "Jails near Home," and Mrs. R. R. P. Bradford will present the subject of "Motion Pictures."

28th—Westbury Quarterly Meeting at 221 East 15th St., New York, 10.30 A. M. Lunch at noon. The speaker for the afternoon, at 2.30, will be Frank P. Walsh, former chairman of Federal Commission on Industrial Relations. His subject is, in general, "Current Industrial Problems, with special reference to the situation in West Virginia."

29th—Conference Class at 15th and Race Streets, Philadelphia, at close of meeting for worship, at 11.40 A. M. Speaker, Dr. Paul M. Pearson, of Swarthmore, Pa. Subject, "The Education of Adults." It is expected that Dr. Pearson will attend meeting for worship at 10.30.

29th—Harrisburg Meeting will be held in the W. C. T. U. Rooms in the Patriot Building, at 11 A. M. Daniel Batchellor will be present. A cordial invitation to all interested.

31st—Concord Quarterly Meeting at Swarthmore, Pa.

SECOND MONTH

4th—Recital at George School, Pa. "The Servant in the House," by Phidelah Rice, Boston, Mass. 8.15 P. M. Admission, 50 cents.

4th—Philadelphia Quarterly Meeting, at 15th and Race Sts., Philadelphia, at 1.30 P. M.

5th—Purchase Quarterly Meeting, at Purchase, N. Y., at 10.30 A. M.

9th—Abington Quarterly Meeting, at Abington, Pa. Meeting of Ministry and Counsel, at 9 A. M.

11th—Salem Quarterly Meeting, at Salem, Ohio.

13th—Miami Quarterly Meeting, at Waynesville, Ohio.

18th—Short Creek Quarterly Meeting, at Emerson, Ohio.

18th—Pelham Half-Yearly Meeting, at Coldstream, Ontario.

20th—Fairfax Quarterly Meeting, at Washington, D. C.

20th—Center Quarterly Meeting, at Unionville, Center Co., Pa.

21st—Burlington Quarterly Meeting, at Mt. Holly, N. J.

23rd—Bucks Quarterly Meeting, at Wrightstown, Pa. Meeting for Ministry and Counsel, preceding day, at 11 A. M.

25th—Blue River Quarterly Meeting, at Chicago, Ill.

27th—Warrington Quarterly Meeting, at Menallen, Pa.

American Friends' Service Committee

WILBUR K. THOMAS, EX. SEC.
20 S. 12th St. Philadelphia

CASH CONTRIBUTIONS
WEEK ENDING JANUARY 16.

Five Years Meetings	$1,216.92
Phila. Yearly Meetings (4th & Arch)	10,958.00
New York Monthly Meeting (Hicksite)	400.00
New Garden First-day School	40.00
Kennett Monthly Meeting	10.50
Pittsfield Friends' Bible School	13.00
Mickleton Young Friends' Association	28.60
Hibbert Friends, Canada	10.00
Cambridge Group of Friends	265.00
Westbury Monthly Meeting	200.00
Westbury Monthly Meeting	300.00
Goldstream Friends	11.50
Westerly Meeting	315.00
Contributions for General	1,320.24
For Germany	6,589.59
For Austria	2,381.91
For Poland	25.00
For Syria	5.00
For Russia	33,430.08
For Russian Overhead	25.00
For German Overhead	10.00
For Clothing	38.04
	$57,593.38

Shipments received during week ending January 14th, 1922: 122 boxes and packages received; 5 for German relief; 2 anonymous.

NOTICE—Donation Day, First Month 27th, 1922. The Central Employment Association, organized in 1857, will hold its Donation Day, on First Month 27th, at Friends' Meeting House, 17th St. and Girard Ave., Philadelphia. The object of the Association is to give sewing to women in their homes, and the garments thus made are distributed among the worthy poor. Any donations of money or material will be gratefully received by the members of the Association who will be in attendance from 3 to 5 P. M. Elizabeth Y. Webb, Treasurer, No. 2 East 2nd St., Media, Pa.

BELL, PRESTON 23-74
KEYSTONE, WEST 2661

S. D. HALL

39th and Parrish Streets

FRANK PETTIT
ORNAMENTAL IRON WORKS

Iron Fencing, Fire Escapes, Stairs and Ornamental Iron Work.
809 Master Street Philadelphia, Pa.

WE BUY ANTIQUE FURNITURE AND antiques of every kind, old pictures of Washington or any prominent American, old gold, silver, platinum, diamonds and old false teeth. PHILA. ANTIQUE CO., 623 Chestnut St. Phone Walnut 70-26. Established 1866.

To the Lot Holders and others interested in Fairhill Burial Ground:

GREEN STREET Monthly Meeting has funds available for the encouragement of the practice of cremating the dead to be interred in Fairhill Burial Ground. We wish to bring this fact as prominently as possible to those who may be interested. We are prepared to undertake the expense of cremation in case any lot holder desires us to do so.

Those interested should communicate with William H. Gaskill, Treasurer of the Committee of Interments, Green Street Monthly Meeting, or any of the following members of the Committee.

William H. Gaskill, 3201 Arch St.
Samuel N. Longstreth, 1218 Chestnut St.
Charles F. Jenkins, 232 South Seventh St.
Stuart S. Graves, 3033 Germantown Ave.

ADVERTISING RATE in the FRIENDS' INTELLIGENCER, for Help Wanted, Positions Wanted, Rooms for Rent, Notices, and other classified advertisements without display, for each insertion, 2 cents per word, including name, initials and address. Answers may be sent to a box at the INTELLIGENCER office, if so directed.

For display advertising the rate is 10 cents per agate line, or $1.40 per column inch, each insertion. On ten or more insertions in a year from date of order, ten per cent. discount. Thus a four-inch single-column or two-inch double-column advertisement costs $5.60 each insertion, less ten per cent., or 5.04 net each time for ten or more insertions. Matter may be changed whenever desired, without extra charge.

Experience has proved the INTELLIGENCER to be a remarkably good advertising medium. All advertisements must "pass the censor!"

Address 140 N. 15th St., Philadelphia

FUN.

Teacher—Why do the Chinese farmers not raise many cows?

Boy—Because the Chinese eat with chop sticks, and cows can't.

HOTELS.

Buck Hill Falls

Has it ever occurred to you that the Poconos have many advantages for convalescents?

You are living very close to sea level and the logical place to get the greatest amount of good from a change of scene is in the mountains, and the Pocono Mountains because of their accessibility, unusually stimulating and pure air, good water, comfortable homelike Inns and boarding houses, and last, but not least, not only a change of scene and air but a change of occupation.

For Rest, Recuperation and Recreation come to

THE WINTER INN
"WEALTH IN HEALTH"
BUCK HILL FALLS, PA.

HOTEL WARWICK

SOUTH CAROLINA AVENUE
ATLANTIC CITY, N. J.
OPEN ALL THE YEAR

First house from beach and boardwalk. Steam heat, electric lights, elevator. Excellent cuisine, quiet, dignified surroundings and attentive service.

Reasonable rates. Write
SARAH H. FULLOM, Prop.

THE WHEELER
Boardwalk at Massachusetts
ATLANTIC CITY, N. J.
Ocean Rooms—Table Guests
MRS. A. W. WHEELER

Strath Haven Tea Room

Dinner 6 to 7:30.
Sunday Special — Chicken and Waffles, 75 cents.
Swarthmore, Pa. Phone 680

PINE RIDGE CAMP
ACTUALLY MID THE PINES

Ideal place for outdoor life in Winter. Main house and cabins with sleeping porches. Modern improvements. Pure water. Excellent Table. Rates moderate. Open all the year. Write

MISS SANBORN or MISS CROCKER
Aiken, South Carolina.

Send two or more names of persons who might be interested in Friends by reading the INTELLIGENCER. A good way to get new members.

SCHOOLS.

Woolman School

SWARTHMORE, PA.

Winter Term—First Month 3d to Third Month 18th

Courses in the Bible, Quakerism, Religious Teaching, Rural Problems. Daily meetings for worship.

Personal contact with instructors experienced in social and religious work.

Helpful group life. Recreation.

ELBERT RUSSELL, DIRECTOR.

GEORGE SCHOOL
Near Newtown, Bucks County, Pa.

Under the care of Philadelphia Yearly Meeting of Friends.

Course of study extended and thorough, preparing students either for business or for college. For catalogue apply to

GEORGE A. WALTON, A. M., Principal
George School, Penna.

FRIENDS' CENTRAL SCHOOL SYSTEM

Write for Year Book and Rates.
CHARLES BURTON WALSH, Principal.
15th and Race Sts., Philadelphia.

FRIENDS' ACADEMY
LONG ISLAND, N. Y.

A Boarding and Day School for Boys and Girls, conducted in accordance with the principles of the Society of Friends. For further particulars address

S. ARCHIBALD SMITH, Principal,
Locust Valley, N. Y.

REGULAR MEETINGS.

OAKLAND, CALIF.—A FRIENDS' MEETing is held every First-day at 11 A. M., in the Extension Room, Y. W. C. A. Building, Webster Street, above 14th. Visiting Friends always welcome.

FRIENDS' MEETING IN PASADENA, California—Orange Grove Monthly Meeting of Friends, 520 East Orange Grove Avenue, Pasadena, California. Meeting for worship, First-day, 11 A. M. Monthly Meeting, the second First-day of each month, at 1.45 P. M.

WANTED

WANTED — MOTHER'S HELPER, white, to assist with housework and care of two children in refined home. References. H. G. Smith, Lansdowne, Pa.

POSITION WANTED—BY NURSE, undergraduate. Refined; accustomed to traveling. Best references. Address D-32, Friends' Intelligencer.

WOMAN DESIRES FINE MENDING, table linen, lingerie, hosiery, etc. Repair work of all kinds carefully done. 5818 McMahon Ave., Germantown, Philadelphia.

WANTED—BY EXPERIENCED WOMan, position as companion, or charge of home. Address C. 40, Friends' Intelligencer.

WANTED—BY REFINED YOUNG lady, in two or three weeks, position as housekeeper in widower's family, or care of semi-invalid. Country preferred. Address B. 41, Friends' Intelligencer.

POSITION WANTED—BY EXPERIenced, capable mother's helper, preferably in Friends' family. Has been two years in present position; excellent reason for leaving. Address S. 43, Friends' Intelligencer.

WANTED—POSITION BY REFINED, educated woman, as traveling companion. Has had experience in traveling and nursing. Prefer going to Florida. Mrs. Sarah W. Taylor, 244 Cleveland Ave., Trenton, N. J.

WANTED—GOOD, REFINED LADY to go into family of widower to care for small daughters and help grandmother manage and run home. Address, M. E. White, P. O. Box 117, Norristown, Pa.

TRANSIENT ACCOMMODATIONS

VISITORS TO CALIFORNIA CAN find comfortable accommodations at 400 S. Euclid Avenue, Pasadena. For terms, apply to Mary B. Sutton.

WASHINGTON, D. C.—ROOMS FOR visitors. Near Station, Capitol, Library. Continuous hot water. Electricity. Garage. Mrs. L. L. Kendig, 120 C. Street, Northwest.

FOR RENT.

FOR RENT BY YEAR OR TERM OF years, or will consider sale—A very attractive small house in Brielle, New Jersey, near river and sea. Hot-water heater and all possible conveniences, including open fireplace. One minute from "bus" line between Lakewood and Asbury Park. Ten minutes from train. Address Box 28, "Applewood," Brielle, N. J.

FUN

"I'm afraid that one tire is going to blow out."

"No, it won't. We are too near a garage."—Life.

Friends' Intelligencer

ESTABLISHED 1844 PHILADELPHIA, SECOND MONTH 4, 1922 VOLUME 79 NUMBER 5

A Plea For Good-Will Toward France

The appeal which follows has been issued by the Friends' Council for International Service, with the approval of the Executive Committee of London Yearly Meeting. It is signed by T. Edmund Harvey and Carl Heath, Chairman and Secretary, respectively, of the Council. Though concerned primarily with Anglo-French relations, it applies equally well to the relations between France and the United States, which at present are likewise a matter of concern to the friends of international good-will.

IT is a difficult time through which our world is passing. We must have an active faith and a creative goodwill if we are to realize the peace which all countries need, and which can only come if it come to all, and not just to a privileged group. At the present moment an increasing distrust and misunderstanding is springing up between our own country and France, which, if it be not conquered, will do immeasurable harm, not only to our two countries, but to many others also. Are we doing our part, our utmost, to stem this tide of evil? We have to combat first of all in ourselves the resentment which so readily rises as we read reports in the public press. We must try more whole-heartedly to understand the French point of view, even when we differ and when we may rightly differ from it. It was easy to feel sympathy for France while she was suffering the grievous ills of invasion, and in the glow of generous emotion which led so many volunteers to lay down their lives on French soil. It is harder now. But we must remember that France has suffered a far heavier loss than Britain, both in precious lives and in the devastation of a vast belt of once prosperous country. Her older men and women have seen not one but two great invasions of her territory. We must try to realize the intense longing for security which this has given rise to. If we feel now that France looks to the wrong means for bringing this security about can we blame her, without blaming ourselves too for putting faith in the way of force and domination which begets resentment and hatred rather than in trust and mutual service which lead up to friendship and fellowship.

France has to bear an immensely heavy burden to restore her ruined departments. Could we not do more as a nation to show our willingness to share this and the whole financial burden caused by the war?

We rejoice that our own country's leaders are turning more and more towards the task of rebuilding the shattered economic and industrial life of Europe. If French opinion as yet does not see the unity of this life, we have no right to be impatient. We are jointly responsible for the hopes which led us to a treaty which though it closed the war did not give real peace. France has built upon those hopes and it is harder for her than for Britain to turn towards a new and wholly different policy.

When once nations begin to drift apart, our press, our politicians, and our own instincts themselves, help to hasten the process. We readily resent words spoken and written by others in the glow of patriotic impulse, and in every country there is a less noble element which at such times becomes easily seen by the outsider. Now is the time to think of the nobler, better side of the country we so easily misunderstand. The true France is there all the while, though beneath the surface sometimes. In each country men of good will must appeal to the best in the other, must have faith in those better elements and give them a chance.

From the experience of many of our own members, whose privilege it was to work in the French war zone both during the war and for many months after peace was concluded, we have learned of the patient endurance and courage of those French peasants who bore the war's worst brunt; we know too how in many cases those who had suffered loss of home and dear ones showed their great-hearted humanity in unrecorded acts of generosity and thoughtfulness to the German prisoners. France is too great to be held back by fear from her true pathway. She has lit and kept alight in the past the torch of freedom. In the realm of thought and of letters the whole world is her debtor, and proud of such a debt.

We must never forget it, or the thousand links by which history has bound our people to each other. Let us have greater faith in these enduring forces of good, the only enduring forces. As we make this effort of will we may begin to take the one way by which we and Europe can reach a real peace, in which the peoples now separated from each other draw nearer together in the common task of mutual service, which is also the service of the whole world.

"Can We Still Believe In God?"

By James W. Macdonald

This and the following article constitute extracts from addresses delivered at the convention of the National Federation of Religious Liberals, held at Sioux City, Iowa, December 10-12, 1921. Some facts about the relation of Friends to the National Federation, are given under Friendly News Notes in this issue.

The speaker who delivered the address bearing the above title was a Unitarian minister from Nebraska. "Can we still believe in God?" he said, is a question which many spiritually-minded persons have asked themselves in view of the staggering blow dealt by the war to the religious faith of mankind.

"God is not found," the address continued, "at the end of a chain of physical causes, or at the conclusion of a syllogism whose premises are doubtful. He is to be found in the souls of men, women and children. He is to be found, as George Eliot said of justice, 'not without us as a fact, but within us as a great yearning.'

"In spite of the weakness of the argument from design, in spite of the evil and pain and sorrow in the world, I still believe in God because I believe that God is not the omnipotent and all-wise Creator of the universe and all that is therein. I do not believe either that God, far away in some extra-cosmical vacuity before the beginning of things, devised in perfect wisdom this world system; or that He is looking down on the evil and sorrow of the world, able to prevent it, yet permitting it. That I do not believe. I cannot think of God as separate from his universe in any such way, the universe here and God there. Rather I believe that the very being and life of God is wrapped up in and involved in the warp and woof of the cosmic process itself. Instead of believing that God permits the evil and sorrow of the world, although able to prevent it, I believe rather that the evil and sorrow is part of the experience of God's cosmic soul.

"For instance, I do not believe that God was able to prevent the war, yet permitted it. What I do believe is that the soul of God suffered and travailled because he was not able to prevent it.

"The real question is, not why did God permit the war? but rather, how can God get rid of such a horrible institution as war from the earth? And the answer to that question is—only when enough of the peoples of the earth so respond to the call of the spirit of God within their souls that they shall rise in their moral determination and co-operative might and establish institutions that will not only curb big armaments but also big business and will nip in the bud the economic causes that lead to war. God is incarnate in the hearts of all men who have striven to conquer what they felt was base in themselves and to advance the cause of righteousness in the earth.

"God has toiled and struggled. Today God is struggling for the supreme values of life in my soul and yours and the souls of men everywhere. Wherever righteousness is advanced a step, whether in the individual life or in the life of society, there does God endure struggle and stress and pain."

"God in his ages-long cosmic life has struggled up out of chaos into some degree of order; out of darkness into light; up out of the blind but not merely mechanical action of physico-chemical atoms, into the instinctive, half-conscious life of the plant; and from there has struggled up to the consciousness of the animal and from there with ever-growing power and purpose and will, with the faint stirrings of a definitely moral life within the universe, into the consciousness of the cave-dweller and primitive savage; and from there with ever-widening vision, with an acquisition of mental power and moral will, with an ever-increasing determination to conquer those physical propensities which have survived from a lower stage of cosmic life but are now hindering his progress up the heights of righteousness and purity and love, has struggled up and up until he has expressed himself in a Buddha, a Socrates, a Jesus, a Lincoln, and is today expressing himself most fully in the great souls of his humanity who are filled with his passion for moral and spiritual progress. And yet not in these alone. He is seeking expression in every human being, in all men, women and children, and is struggling to lead them forward to a life of purity, righteousness and love.

"That is why and how I can still believe in God. And I believe that the Cosmic Spirit of God includes, and will include, all human souls, past, present and to come, in his all-embracing life, and is leading and will lead them up and forward into moral and spiritual life ever fuller and more abundant."

"The More Abundant Life"

By Franklin G. Southworth

Extracts from an address delivered at the Sioux City Convention of the National Federation of Religious Liberals.

Religion exists to make a fuller life. It is not an end in itself, but the means toward a more abundant life. A congress of religious liberals is possible only on the assumption that it is standing for the religion of the deed and of life, rather than a religion of the creed. The object at which the church down through the ages seems frequently, if not regularly, to have been aiming, is almost anything rather than life more abundant here and now. The object of life has been supposed to be religion, whereas the idea of Jesus seemed to be that the object of religion was life.

If the church is to hold its own in its struggle for existence it must hold it, not as a theological debating school, but as a life giver.

We try to find God by philosophizing and fail; we seek him in creeds and books and do not find him;

The Friends' Intelligencer is published weekly at 140 N. 15th St., Philadelphia, by Friends' Intelligencer Association, Ltd. Telephone, Spruce 5-75. Entered at Philadelphia Post-Office as second class matter. Subscription in the United States, Mexico, Cuba and Panama, $2.60 a Year. Subscriptions may begin at any time. Subscription in Canada and other foreign countries (on account of extra postage charges), $3.00 a year. Single copies, 6 cents. Make checks payable to Friends' Intelligencer Assn., Ltd.

and then after much vain striving we behold the Eternal Goodness in the face of some familiar friend.

Religion has been counted on as something to be attained by prayers or sacraments or ceremonies. It is something grander. Religion is a possession which exalts and ennobles life, giving it a finer beauty, a more enduring joy. Religion is destined to endure as helper of our joy, as an unfailing spring whence flow the waters of the river of life freely.

The "Next War" Must Be Prevented

Why so much talk about the 'next war,' as though there were a certainty of it in the near future, or even a probability of it? I freely admit there is a possibility of it, which may easily be developed into a probability, and thence into a certainty, if officials in high places continue to talk as if it were necessary to prepare for it, and so long as unscrupulous persons would welcome it as a means of their aggrandizement.

Long years ago it was said, "What shall it profit a man if he gain the whole world and lose his own soul, or what shall a man give in exchange for his soul?" So we might ask, of what value is a man's accumulated wealth when gained at the expense of human life, and devastated countries, famished children and ravished womanhood?

A man feels jealous of his successful neighbor; this is followed by suspicion of his motives, then distrust of his actions, all culminating finally in hatred of the man, whom he is by this time ready to fight on the least pretext. As with the individual, so with the nation, for the nation is composed of individuals. Now had this man looked with generous eyes instead of envious ones on his neighbor's successes, and been sorry for his failures, there would never be any strife between them for enmity can not exist between friends.

The great Conference at Washington is called primarily to discuss the feasability and practicability of proportional disarmament by the three principal naval powers of the world. If this can be accomplished it will be a long step toward procuring lasting peace in the world. But does it not seem like inconsistency that at the same time, officials are talking of defenses and fortifications?

Only the other day I heard the statement of some man whose name I cannot recall, who has spent the greater part of the last two years in visiting in Central Europe, that Belgium, I think, is a country particularly fitted for agriculture, but that the inhabitants are deterred from entering into its pursuit by the fear of war from their neighbors, and are largely engaged in industries that go to the making of implements of war. What a sad moral condition in which to live.

I read with much satisfaction, the account in the Intelligencer a short time ago of the action of the President and government of Mexico. Although Mexico is a small country compared to the United States or Great Britain, yet her natural riches make her a subject of envy among her sister Republics, and bring her into prominence. It seems she is willing to try the plan of peaceful living. Her example is worthy of emulation, also of imitation by others. I have seen nothing of it in other papers.

Ever since the creation of the world, men have resorted to force to obtain what they could not otherwise get, or to gratify their evil passions. In a fit of angry jealousy, Cain slew his brother. What did he gain by it? We are all familiar with his history. And so it has ever been, and yet with the example of centuries before them, men still object to trying any other method of settling difficulties than by force. Instead of spending so much time and money in preparation for the war that should not occur, why not devote it to cultivating the arts of Peace, of Friendship and Good will, keeping thoughts of War well in the background, thinking the best of our neighbors and helping them when needed.

"As a man thinketh in his heart, so is he."

I close as I began, why so much talk about the "next war"?

Holder, Ill. ELIZABETH H. COALE.

"The Light Within"

E. Maria Bishop has brought us the following notes on some remarks made by Violet Hodgkin, at a Summer School in Blakewell, England, several years ago, regarding the "Light Within." Violet Hodgkin is so deaf that she could not have heard the discussion which had preceded her remarks, and those present were struck by the remarkable unity between the thoughts which she expressed and what had already been said. She spoke as follows:

"We have been asked to put aside our fears and to say in great simplicity something of what the words 'Light Within' mean to us individually. They are not merely a legacy from our ancestors. It is difficult to define them but it is worth while for us to try.

"Most of us used to think that to have the light within meant that it would come in some sudden blaze of illumination, that we should ever after see a road stretching straight before us, and have our difficulties and doubts cleared up, but we find it is not so; that the light within is a much more gradual thing, a more divinely natural thing.

"It is an attitude of soul, a surrender, a passing out of our soul to that of another. We find the difficulties and doubts do not disappear, sometimes they get harder, but we cease to try and find our way out of them. We learn that the only place to bring our doubts and difficulties to is the light at our Master's feet and to watch Him working Light into our sinful poor bruised lives.

"The Inward Light and the Outward Light interpret one another.

"If we are asked what do we understand by the "Light Within," we can only reply: 'The shining of His Face.'"

It is not sufficient to make beautiful theories about love. Love must descend from the mind to the heart. It must have not only flowers, but fruit as well. Love is not simply a thought, a desire, a dream. It is action. To love is to act.—*From the French of H. de Faremont.*

FRIENDS' INTELLIGENCER

The religion of Friends is based on faith in the "INWARD LIGHT," or direct revelation of God's spirit and will in every seeking soul.

The INTELLIGENCER is interested in all who bear the name of Friends in every part of the world, and aims to promote love, unity and intercourse among all branches and with all religious societies.

Editorial and business offices, 140 N. 15th Street, Philadelphia, Pa. For information regarding subscription rates, etc., see foot of second page.

PHILADELPHIA, SECOND MONTH 4, 1922

IN THIS ISSUE

Judged by the eye, the moon looks as large as a hundred stars put together, but the mind knows that in reality one star is millions of times larger than the moon.

A recent editorial in *Team Work,* the "little family paper" of the Near East relief service, opens with the following story:

"A man came to three stonemasons cutting stone in a great inclosure.

"'What are you doing?' he asked the first.

"'Working for five dollars a day,' the stonemason answered.

"'What are you doing?' the man asked the second.

"'Trimming this stone—can't you see?' the stonemason replied.

"The man approached the third stonemason. 'What are you doing?'

"'I am building a cathedral,' said the third stonemason."

The third stonemason had learned one of the deepest secrets of life. He, as well as the first, received the means of physical sustenance in return for his labors. He knew that "the laborer is worthy of his hire," and that the lunch hour would come in due course. But he was not thinking primarily of that. In the meantime, his soul was finding an outlet in the high joy of creative labor.

The third stonemason's task, if judged by the outward results of the moment, was as humble as that of the second. Apparently, he too was only "trimming the stone"; but actually he was creating a majestic column, or carving the tracery for a resplendent rose window. His imagination was awake. Beyond the petty details of the day, he saw the vision of the whole as it would at last be realized; the great cathedral which would eventually stand complete as the result of thousands of days of toil from hundreds of humble workmen like himself. And this vision quickened his life and his work with a zest of inspiration which defied the heat of the day, and the frequent strain of the task.

Today, when a sense of responsibility for the solution of world problems is straining thoughtful minds and sensitive hearts to the breaking point, we need to keep before us the third stonemason's vision of infinite outcomes, of the great plan beyond bewildering details of the moment.

In comparison with humanity's need, nothing which we can do appears adequate. The humble tasks of home or field or office, to which most of us must devote our daily energies, seem often petty and without significance in the vast pattern of humanity's destiny.

Then it is that we need to remember that cathedrals cannot be built except through the faithful performance, for the most part by unknown workmen, of thousands of menial daily tasks. There must be the noble conception of the master builder, but there must likewise be the mixing of mortar and the trimming of stone. And it is so with the attainment of human brotherhood. As essential as the dreams of the prophet, are the care and guidance of the little ones in home and school-room, the cultivation of the fields, the manufacture in our shops of material aids to life,—and a thousand other humble occupations, in some of which at least we all share.

We cannot any of us grip systems and civilizations and literally twist them straight in a moment; but we can go on our daily rounds, however humble they may be, with an earnestness and a devotion fitting to one who is engaged in "building a cathedral." Through the efforts and the influence of the invisible guild which thus carries on its labors in harmony with the great design, the key-stone of the vault will eventually be hung—even though it take four centuries, as it did in the case of Gothic architecture, for the inherent principles of order to work themselves out in the fully-developed masterpiece.

Adagio Lamentoso

Now I have gone the lonely path so long
 I seldom meet a comrade's friendly smile,
 I hear a word of cheer once in a while
 But for the most I voice a solo song.
I am not bitter but I think it wrong
 That as I pass each stone which marks the mile
 I leave behind a host who then revile
 The soul of me because it would be strong.

Lonesome, it is this very soul of mine
 Which hungers for the love that they deny,
 Which clings to earth, the while it heeds the sky.
And yet I feel my solitude divine—
 To raise the ones I love above the clod
 'Tis meet I blaze the way unto my God!

HENRY ROENNE.

The Washington Conference

XII

By William I. Hull

The final work of the Conference is being delayed by the problem of Shantung. This problem is not yet entirely solved; but instructions were received this morning from Pekin and Tokio which it is believed will remove the last point of difference between the Chinese and Japanese delegations and enable them to come to a final settlement of the difficult problem.

It will be recalled that the Japanese, having driven the Germans from Kiao-chow, during the World War, were awarded the German rights or claims in Kiao-chow and the Province of Shantung, by the Treaty of Versailles. This treaty was accepted by President Wilson and by seven of the nine powers represented in the Washington Conference, the United States Senate and China alone having refused to accept it. To overcome this handicap, the American government has found to be a difficult and delicate task; and measured by this difficulty, the results achieved by its efforts have been noteworthy and almost entirely satisfactory.

Japan, too, has conceded much. At first, the Japanese delegation took the position that, the question having been settled at Versailles, it should not be revived at Washington. It consented, however, to negotiate the question with the Chinese delegation, the American and the British first delegates acting as counsellors and friends. Thirty-three meetings have been held under this agreement and a number of questions have been satisfactorily settled, such as the withdrawal of the Japanese troops from the province, the surrender of the German lease of the port to China, the ownership and control of the mines and other natural resources, land titles, telegraphs, post offices, etc.

The one remaining question is the railway which runs through the province from Tsingtao to Tsinanfu, the title to which the Japanese secured from the Germans at Versailles for the sum of fifty-three million gold marks. The first offer of the Japanese at Washington was to give the Chinese a one-half interest in the railway; the Chinese offered to buy it for cash; the Japanese offered to lend the Chinese the money with which to buy, provided they could retain a thirty years' control of the road; this term the Japanese reduced to twenty years, then to fifteen, then to ten, and then to five, and finally agreed to accept Chinese treasury notes with deferred payments extending over twelve or fifteen years, with the option of redemption at the end of three years.

The payment for the railway having been agreed upon, the question of its control during the years of deferred payment was struggled with. The Chinese offered to appoint (or accept) a Japanese associate traffic-manager and an assistant auditor, but the Japanese have insisted on nominating the traffic-manager and auditor, leaving to China the exclusive control of the associate and the assistant. The Japanese argument for this demand is that only thus can the financial and commercial interests of Japanese nationals in the railway be adequately protected against Chinese discrimination. There is a parallel argument in certain American commercial circles that a Japanese traffic-manager would discriminate against American goods.

With political and military control of the province and the railway in the hands of the Chinese, the remaining difference in view-point would seem to an impartial mind to be due to Oriental subtlety or to commercial selfishness, and to be capable of speedy and satisfactory adjustment. The Chinese minister appealed to President Harding, on the 25th instant, to use his good offices, for settling the problem, and the President offered a suggestion which may be reflected in the Pekin and Tokio instructions just received.

With the railway problem solved, the province will return to the control of China, twenty-four years after Germany secured it on a ninety-nine years' "lease." The British are willing to return Wei-hai-wei, also, and perhaps France will return Kwang-chow-wang; while the acceptance of the American policy of the "open-door" will mean the surrender of "spheres of influence" by the British in the Yangtse Valley and Thibet, by the French in Yunnan, Kwangsi and Kwantung, and by the Japanese in Fukien.

On the other hand, there appears to be no likelihood that China's other territorial losses to the European powers and Japan, which date back to 1842, will be restored at the Washington Conference. Great Britain will doubtless retain Hongkong, Burma, Sikkim, and Kowloon; France will keep Annam and Tonking; Japan will cling to the islands off the coast, Korea, South Manchuria and Inner Mongolia. A united, reformed and civilized Chinese Republic may regain these provinces in some unseen future; a reconstructed Russian Republic may aid her in this task, at the same time restoring what Old Russia took from China in Turkestan, Outer Mongolia, North Manchuria and Sakhalin; a democratic government in Japan, and less imperialism and more righteousness in every nation may be confidently expected to facilitate the triumph of justice, before China is overtaken by the fate of either an aggressive, militaristic transformation, or a complete decadence, division and annihilation. Meanwhile, the Washington Conference is doing what it can to redress some of the wrongs done to China in the past, and to set up standards of righteousness and justice for the prevention of further wrongs in the future.

As to Siberia, Japan has formally repudiated the charge that she intends to acquire any territory from her much-harassed neighbor, Russia, and has solemly promised to withdraw her troops from Siberia "as soon as political stability is re-established there." Sad experience makes this promise not only indefinite, but far from reassuring. In the midst of our disappointment, however, we Americans should remember that it was on our own government's initiative that Japanese troops first went into Siberia, for military or anti-Bolshevist purposes; and that we ourselves are maintaining troops "until political stability is re-established" in Haiti, the Dominican Republic, Nicaragua and,—until yesterday,—in Cuba. The United States, while accepting at the Washington Conference Japan's promise in regard to Siberia, reserves of course its right to protest if this promise is not carried out in good faith, and this right is not only unimpaired, but is decidedly strengthened, by the Japanese pledge at the Conference. With the revival of mighty Russia, also, another Russian avalanche may be expected to sweep over the frozen lands of Siberia, and before it the Japanese colonists, who love the lands of the sunny south, would retire. And, best of all, with the dawning of the new era of diplomacy in the Far East, we may confidently expect at the hands of Japan, Russia, China, and especially at the hands of the Christian peoples of the West, who have taught civilization and set the example, the keeping of pledges in entire good faith and mutual participation in that righteousness which not only exalteth the nations, but which secures justice and preserves the peace among them. May the sun of this Righteousness be indeed rising in the Far East to cast its life-giving rays around the World!

Washington, D. C., January 28th, 1922.

An Economic Sandwich

The Pessimist said that whenever a new book came out he read an old one. I don't believe people who talk like this and anyhow the old books were new once. But personally I do try to keep an "old" book somewhere in the background of my attempt to read as many as possible of the new ones. Variety is a good habit in everything, and I must thank Theodora Wilson Wilson for driving me back once again to "Cranford" by her quotation of it in her newest novel, "The Last Dividend," in which she shows how a group of rich folk gave up their unearned wealth for the common good.

I had never thought of "Cranford" (especially that delightful edition with the Hugh Thomson illustrations) as an economic handbook, but Theodora Wilson's speaker, Roger, in his argument on our present social system with Peter, Lord Forelands, does. "Even in 'Cranford'" he says, "Miss Matty's tragic comedy lay in the fact that the 'fortune' which gave her position had gone—that mysterious something which grew of itself, spontaneous and eternal and was therefore more honorable than money earned by the sweat of the brow!" "Even Miss Matty," said Peter gently, "when at last she went into business could not make profits of the sweets she sold to the children. She hadn't the heart!" "Miss Matty was up against the entire 'Beggar-my-neighbor' system! How scared she would be if we had told her so! Her pure spirit recoiled. She is the palpitating expression of that spirit of Common Service which is abroad today." "You would, then, seek to build a world in which Miss Matty could be completely happy?" "Yes, exactly."

"The Last Dividend," is of course emotional, like "The Last Weapon," and the author's other books, and this spirit is doubtless not only enjoyed by many readers, but helps to convince them. The more hard-headed and critical, however, appreciating the author's purpose will particularly regret that there should be flagrant topographical slips such as mistaking the "Royal Exhange" for "The Stock Exchange," and calling St. Margaret's, Westminster, "St. Mary's," for the association of ideas in the minds of her antagonistic readers will be that the author's economic facts are equally shaky. Here, as a matter of fact, she is on very much firmer ground than in her knowledge of London.

So I recommend a sandwich. "Cranford" in the middle; "The Last Dividend" one side, and on the other, a third readable book on Economics of the moment, Maurice Rowntree's "Social Freedom." This is a book which has much in common with so many appearing just now, namely the discovery afresh of what Jesus stood for. "The Jesus of History" and especially Nat. Micklem's "The Galilean," stand out in this category. Maurice Rowntree has confined himself to the economic side. His purpose is best put forward in his own words. "The original portrait of Jesus, virile, undaunted, joyful, amazingly sociable, the friend of all, especially of the outcast and oppressed, is being re-discovered. We see what we have always longed to see—the lineaments of a live man in a troubled world, of a great hero, who is always a sympathetic comrade. Men have disputed long and fiercely about his Godhead, they have painted effeminate caricatures of him, with a halo round his head, but they have continually rejected or politely ignored his fundamental message. It was the same in his own day as in this. 'Why call ye me Lord, Lord,' he protested, 'and do not the things which I say.'"

Well, Maurice Rowntree tells us some of these things again today in 20th century language. "Challenge" is the word that continually rises to one's mind as one reads page after page, whether it be the inquiry into the attitude of the sociable Jesus to the Jewish problems of his day; or in our own industrial conditions so vividly portrayed; or again in the suggested remedies for the straightening out of things. "Most of us, though we don't live it, hold in theory perhaps that whereas death is no dishonor, to do evil is always dishonorable. Therefore we should suffer death ourselves rather than inflict an injury on any living soul. . . Does our buying and selling and general mode of life illustrate this belief?"

The answering of this last question will add seasoning to a sandwich I hope many readers will make it their duty to consume, taking to heart Mr. Gladstone's advice to masticate each mouthful ninety times!

And just as a little mustard and cress with this sandwich, don't neglect the two newest Friend pamphlets. There is Charles Simpson's "The Quaker Challenge," taking us back to the Society's attitude to social problems at the beginning of its history and claiming that Quakerism is fundamentally a challenge to our social life, and B. V. Clough's "Letters of A Rich Young Ruler." If you have read "By An Unknown Disciple," or those Christmas card "Letters from Zaccheus," which were so popular a year or two ago, you will enjoy these "Letters" too. A writer in the ***Methodist Times*** calls them "inspired."

H. W. Peet.

The Minutes

I sit and watch the pigeons
As upward they fly—
Against the cloudless blue
They disappear from sight.

So with the minutes
Which the hours bring me.
They hasten away;
They never return.

I have time only,—
So swift is their flight,—
For thoughts that are brightest
With joy and with love.

BERTHA SELLERS.

On the Field With the Service Committee

Schenectady First Hears of the Service From Moscow

A Russian electrical engineer living in Schenectady received a copy of a Moscow paper from some relatives and there read a glowing report of the work of the Friends in Russia and for the first time heard of the American Friends' Service Committee. It is simply an example of the old truth that it is not the bigness of a deed which alone insures its worth, but the quality of it. Not even a distance of 4,000 miles and a strange country and a foreign language could stop the story of an act of good will. The story in the Moscow paper gave the Philadelphia address of the Service Committee, and Mr. Shinkevich, a native Russian who has been in this country for ten years and is now in charge of the foreign work of the General Electric Company, immediately wrote to the Service Committee asking if it would co-operate with him in raising funds from the people of Schenectady for Russian relief. He did not wait until someone came to him, he did not wait until someone talked with him for two or three hours trying to secure his co-operation, but he began the work himself. He then secured a committee of ten of the leading business men and ministers of Schenectady, headed by Dr. Richmond, President of Union College, and has since worked untiringly, practically giving all his time outside of his business, to the task of raising funds. In this the Schenectady Committee has been eminently successful for a city of its size. We are sometimes led to think that because something we do is hidden and obscure it is of little worth. Perhaps some of the work you have done, or can do, is a little like that paragraph which some unknown reporter on a Moscow paper wrote one afternoon never daring to think that what he had done would mean the children would live for fifty or sixty years more, instead of dying in childhood.

Workers Recover From Typhus

It was glad news that a recent cable brought. It said that Anna Louise Strong was able to walk from one room to another in the house in which she is staying in Moscow; that Nancy Babb had so entirely recovered that she was contemplating returning to work without a period of convalescence; and that Murray Kenworthy, the head of our Unit in Russia, is now able to sit up for two hours each day. Dr. Mary Tatum, of Llanerch, Pa., a member of the Polish mission, is recovering from typhus, in Warsaw. Our rejoicing in their recovery is great, not alone because of the saving of their lives to us and to the work, but because of the great lesson they have taught us. What Christ meant when he said that when a man laid down his life willingly for his friends he had reached the ultimate height of all love—has been cut into the reality of life for us.

Vienna Mission Distributes $578,000 From April to September

A report from the Vienna Mission states that $578,015 was distributed by the Friends for the relief of the stricken people of Vienna from April to September of 1921. This fund was from both the American and English Friends.

Openings For Service In Germany

The interest in the Service of Friends in Germany is taking practical shape in the request which comes to the Friends' office in Berlin for teachers of English who will bring with them the Quaker spirit. For two years, John S. Stephens, of Cambridge University, has been a lecturer on English literature in the University of Frankfort. For some time, he has also been lecturing at the University of Giessen, and at the People's High School, Darmstadt. These positions will be vacant next year, as he will be teaching in England, and we are invited to send another young Friend to fill this need. Several secondary schools are also asking for Quaker teachers of English.

The salary connected with these positions will not entirely support the teacher. It would be necessary for him, therefore, to provide his own traveling expenses and some additional funds.

On the other hand, this work presents a very unusual opportunity to express the Quaker message in the formative period of the new Germany, and in the university life where such a message will count in an incredibly effective way. It also gives a splendid chance to learn German and to come into touch with the swirling currents of European thought in this crucial period.

Persons who are qualified and feel a concern for this service, even though not able themselves to meet all the financial responsibilities involved, are invited to write to the INTELLIGENCER office for more complete details.

CAROLENA M. WOOD.

Teachers for Canton Christian College

The Trustees of the Canton Christian College are seeking properly qualified teachers for the College of Arts and Sciences in Canton, China, to begin their service in the next academic year in Ninth month, 1922, in the following departments: Physics, Economics, Business Administration, English and Mathematics and one teacher who will carry both French and German. If possible all of these teachers are to be unmarried.

They wish to engage men only for the positions in Physics, Economics and Business Administration, but for English, Mathematics and Modern Languages it would be possible to use women who have had experience in these lines and at least one woman instructor is desired. In addition to the above, three instructors for the High School are needed including one in General Science. Appointments are made for three or five years.

The Canton Christian College is a non-sectarian institution incorporated under the Regents of the University of the State of New York. One of the Trustees is a member of Philadelphia Yearly Meeting (Arch Street). Six members of the Staff are Friends, one of them being a member of Philadelphia Yearly Meeting (Race Street).

Any one who may be interested in this call to Christian Service in China, may refer to Dr. William W. Cadbury, 200 East Main Street, Moorestown, N. J.

Friendly News Notes

A meeting on Disarmament was held in Flushing, N. Y., January 22nd, under the auspices of the Society of Friends. Paul J. Furnas, of the Twentieth St. Meeting, N. Y., presided. Various organizations showed a keen interest and co-operated with Friends to make it a great success.

Frederick J. Libby spoke upon the work of the Washington Conference. The results, he said, are hopeful, because they are a beginning, but the work must be followed up by other conferences. To that end we must have education for Peace, so that in ten years steps much in advance of the present conference will be possible.

At Cain Quarterly Meeting held at Christiana, Pa., on First month 26th, Daniel Batchellor gave a very helpful message based on the story of the talents. He said that joy and satisfaction come from service, and use of powers and talents given. Every one has talents given by the Divine and only by using are they retained.

The call for Service today is to help forward the kingdom of God on earth and help make this a better world in which to live. Personal responsibility and the way one uses talents, is one way this call could and should be answered.

Later in the meeting, it was emphasized that young people should be given things to do for in them lie the future of Friends' meetings; also that belief is the foundation of all things and should be felt and shown more deeply by friends.

The General Conference Section of Friends' Disarmament Council held a conference on First month 27th, in Philadelphia.

It was unanimously decided that Friends' work for the abolition of war must be pushed during the present year with the utmost possible energy.

A plan of future work was decided upon, in co-operation with the Friends of Arch Street. Our part of the work as planned will require $5,000 to carry out, and it is our hope that our Friends will meet this need without too much effort on our part.

Also we shall need full co-operation on the part of all our friends in order to carry on the educational campaign as outlined at our conference. **Now is the time to act.**

O. Edward Janney, *Executive Secretary.*

The work of the warehouse for clothing for Russia, just opened by New York Friends, is gathering momentum. The warehouse is at 108 Dobbin St., Brooklyn. Here all clothing sent in which is able to stand three months' wear, at least, is baled into bales weighing 200 pounds each. The Meeting-houses at Schermerhorn St., Brooklyn, and Fifteenth Street, New York, have been advertised as receiving-stations, also, for clothing which may be brought by hand. The Meeting-houses at Lafayette Ave., Brooklyn, and Twentieth Street, New York, will very soon be opened, also. It has been arranged, however, that if a church or other organization collects a quantity of clothing in one place, the warehouse truck will call for it.

All clothing sent by parcels-post or express is to be sent to the Service Committee Warehouse, Station G., 108 Dobbin St., Brooklyn, N. Y. Up to the night of Sixth-day the 27th of First month, practically five tons of clothing had come in. It is likely that this will be shipped for Russia about the first of Second month. If it cannot find transportation in Russia at once, it will at least be available whenever transportation is possible.

The Executive Office for this work is at the Meeting-house, 221 East 15th St., New York. A joint committee of all New York Friends is directing it, with Daisy McCoubrey as Executive Secretary, and Cora Haviland Carver as Treasurer.

The Social held at Schermerhorn Street, Brooklyn, on the evening of the 14th was a decided success, according to all who attended it,—about seventy. The entertainment consisted of charades, and a spelling-race, in which each person was labeled with one of the letters of the alphabet, two alphabets being made. As the words were given out, the persons wearing the required letters hurried out of line to form the words, each alphabet-team trying to spell the word before the other could do so. The old gentleman of seventy and the small child of seven seemed to find equal enjoyment in this truly exciting game. No repetition of a letter in a word being possible, the words are usually quite simple.

A little "community singing," enough lemonade and cookies to satisfy even fourteen-year-old boys, and a game of "Going to Jerusalem" finished out the evening. An original touch was a table-full of games and puzzles, which gave much entertainment "in between times" to a number present.

Western Quarterly Meeting, at Kennett Square, Pa., received helpful messages from Daniel Batchellor, George Nutt, Caroline J. Worth and Rufus Jones. The thought was brought out that evolution is slow, and we must be patient if we do not bring to pass all that we wish.

In a discussion of the Queries and the ministry, it was suggested that we do not only need more ministry in the meetings, but more help and encouragement to those around us, and we are all able to give that.

In the afternoon, Rufus M. Jones gave an address on the conditions and needs of Russia. A collection was taken for the Russians, and more have promised to give through their different meetings.

A minute to Western Quarterly Meeting from New Garden Monthly Meeting of Ministry and Council and one also from the Philanthropic Committee brought to the two meetings the great loss sustained in the "Home-going" of Elma M. Preston, as she was always the leader in all good things, faithful, far-sighted, conscientious and always ready with good advice and sound judgment on questions pertaining to the Meeting or the community. Several expressed and all felt the lack of her presence at the meeting and all realize that her place cannot be filled.

The Society of Friends was one of five denominations which met at the eleventh convention of the National Federation of Religious Liberals, held at Sioux City, Iowa, December 10-12. Universalists, Unitarians, Jews and Congregationalists were also represented.

The membership of the Council of the Federation for the coming year includes the names of three Friends, Jesse H. Holmes, who is President of the Federation, O. Edward Janney and J. Barnard Walton. Two other Friends, Elizabeth Powell Bond, and Joseph Swain, were elected honorary vice-presidents.

Bird T. Baldwin, formerly of Swarthmore College, and now of Iowa State University, was one of the speakers at the Convention, giving an illustrated lecture on "What Iowa is Doing for the Children of the State."

From Menallen Meeting comes the following suggestive note:

We had an interesting conference on First-day afternoon somtime ago on the Washington Conference. It was conducted as a Peace Table, with one representative for each of the five powers, Frederic Griest as Secretary Hughes, presiding.

Each in turn was asked to speak from his nation's standpoint on the general subjects, and to be prepared to explain or defend his nation in informal discussion.

The lesser nations were also represented and asked to state briefly what national interests caused their presence at the Washington Conference.

The Woolman School finds its days full of lectures, prescribed reading, the consideration of problems, National and International, interpersed with recreation and the marshmallow toasts by the open fire.

The course on Great Truths of Christianity continues to open up new fields for thought and helps to clarify impressions, that have been made. The Rural Problems Course has begun and in it are studied not only the history of the rural community, but the outlook that will follow a concerted effort on the part of these sections to organize for their mutual welfare and thereby give a wider local horizon and create a tendency toward a richer life for the family.

Most of the group attended the Swarthmore Meeting on the 22nd, where they heard the inspiring message of Wilbur Thomas. He did not refer to the work he has done in feeding starving Europeans, but challenged every one to see that the Christ spirit works through us to benefit the lives of others. He showed that the world is lifted to higher levels not by laws, but by the personal efforts of the few who, like Christ, are not afraid to lose their lives, that in so doing they may help to a more abounding life for others. M. M. E.

"The Happy Grovian" is the name of a new magazine, the first number of which has just been issued by the Students' Council of the Happy Grove School in Jamaica. Its pages reflect the thriving life of this school, which is under the direction of the Foreign Mission work of the Five Years Meeting of Friends, and of which Montclair E. Hoffman is headmaster. Mental, spiritual, social and athletic activities give color to the articles and illustrations. Among the latter, are pictures of Gladys Smith and Lillian E. Hayes, two American Friends, who are members of the teaching staff. An interesting "Personal" concerns Montclair Hoffman's hobbies. Among these are enumerated: developing an athletic field, collecting portraits of notable people, and collecting furniture of native wood made by native tradesmen.

Frank D. Slutz of Moraine Park School, Dayton, Ohio, visited several centers in Philadelphia and vicinity during the past week, and spoke to large and interested audiences upon Education. He met with Mothers-in-Council of Germantown, Mothers' Club of Abington Friends School, Parent-Teachers Association of West Chester, Classes in Education at Swarthmore College and at University of Pennsylvania, Private School Teachers' Association, of Friends' Schools, Friends' Educational Association, and with the teachers and pupils of Westtown School. He was the guest of the City Club of Philadelphia at luncheon and spoke before the Board of Education and the Superintendent of Schools of Philadelphia.

With each group Mr. Slutz discussed the ideas underlying the educational needs of the present day, outlining the essentials of the kind of education necessary to meet these needs. He showed very clearly that as these demands change and as life becomes more complex, those responsible for the education of the children of the generation must concern themselves with the problems incident thereto. Physical education must occupy a more important place in our program. Citizenship must be taught so as to emphasize the relationships of responsibilities growing out of our closer association with others, and to inculcate respect for the laws made by those whom we ourselves elect. Before members of the City Club and at Swarthmore College, Mr. Slutz appealed for a more scientific study of Education, urging that men and women attack its problems as they do those of engineering. Those who heard him and those who have followed his work in Dayton feel satisfied he is making a very decided contribution to Education. IDA P. STABLER,

Executive Secretary of Committe on Education.

A letter from Daniel Oliver, dated Twelfth month 31st, 1921, describes graphically the terrible conditions under which the Armenian refugees around Beyrouth are living. He with William Bacon Evans visited a number of the camps.

We quote from his letter. "We visited still another camp, further out of the city. The general conditions were the same,—a sea of mud everywhere. In one tent a baby had been born the night before. The parents were refined people. In another tent I entered, there were twenty orphan boys, all standing. They had nothing, not a scrap of bedding, matting or any chair, only the wet earth to sit, lie or sleep on. They had no near relatives in the world,—all had been killed in previous massacres. But these boys were young and I imagine they were having some kind of game which we interrupted. They would all gladly have come with us, but we were only going the rounds to see conditions.

One young lad we met had escaped alone of all his family, in a previous massacre. He had been in prison one and a half years. He had no one in the world. He is coming to us of course. We selected about fifty-five of the most desperate cases. They are to be transported by the "Near East" auto-lorries. We are to put them in empty houses here and shall feed them until we can find, if possible, any work for them. They all want work. Alas! in this land of poverty and want, who can find work for all? We could take hundreds more and house them (for people here in Ras have been kind in loaning empty houses without charge). But can we feed them? *That depends on those who read these lines.* If there is a prompt answer in contributions, lives can be saved and great suffering at least lessened. We are told that over 100,000 have fled from Celicia,—Armenians, Greeks and others. Perhaps 30,000 have landed at Beyrouth. Some have gone to Damascus and other points, hoping to find work. More are coming to Beyrouth. There are many thousands at Mersina and at Alexandretta, waiting to get away. The small Armenian Committee in Beyrouth cannot touch more than the fringe of the need."

A postcript to the letter of Daniel Oliver says:

"Later. The first batch of Armenians has just arrived in pouring rain,—men, women and children and some babies. They look wretched, hungry and cold. They are glad to be *safe*. That was about the first question they asked, and being assured that no one will kill them they are content and relieved. After a good meal we have divided them up into various houses and rooms. More are coming tomorrow."

SCHOFIELD SCHOOL.

At a meeting of the directors of Schofield School held in Philadelphia, January 12th, 1922, the following resolution was passed: Whereas, our valued superintendent and co-worker, S. Louisa Haight, has been called into the Larger Life; we, the directors of the Schofield Normal and Industrial School, wish to express our gratitude for her faithful and intelligent service, and our great loss in her removal from the work, which she entered upon with consecration of heart five years ago.

With her desire for wise and balanced education for the negro she combined scholarly interest, marked executive ability and untiring energy. This enabled her to bring the school through a world crisis not only unimpaired, but better equipped for efficiency in educational work.

The school, its directors, and friends have a sense of inestimable loss, but they have also sincere gratitude for her useful life.

Miss Crocker, of Aiken, has been appointed superintendent of Schofield School. She is a cultivated woman of experience and ability, was a friend of Miss Haight's, was strongly recommended by the Aiken directors and has the support of its residents. She has already taken up her work at the school.

SWARTHMORE CLUB OF SOUTHERN CALIFORNIA

The Swarthmore Club of Southern California held its annual meeting at the Hotel Vista del Arroyo, Pasadena, on January 6th. Dr. and Mrs. Joseph Swain were guests of honor at the dinner at which thirty-two guests were present.

Andrew W. Cadwallader, ex-'87, 2085 Garfield Avenue, Pasadena, California, was elected president at the business meeting, Roberts Leinau, ex-'06, Riverside, California, vice-president, Edith Dixon Hopkins, ex-'04, 343 South Madison Avenue, Pasadena, California, secretary-treasurer. Music and toasts followed.

Louise Wood Ferris, ex-'83, gave a fine tribute to Maria L. Sanford. Dr. Swain inspired enthusiasm with his talk on the growth and development of the college during the nineteen years of his administration. Mrs. Swain, after a few remarks, read a beautiful letter from Elizabeth Powell Bond, conveying good wishes to all the members. Mary Travilla, ex-'81, recalled memories of the founders of the college with later impressions of the buildings, campus and commencement days.

Those present were: Dr. and Mrs. Joseph Swain, Mrs. Caroline S. Wood, Andrew W. Cadwallader, ex-'87, and wife, Mary Stebbins Ellis, '92 and husband, Louise Wood Ferris, ex-'83, and husband, P. Frances Foulke, '82, Eleanor Mulford Hamlin, ex-'78, and husband, Edith Dixon Hopkins, ex-'04, Susan Atkinson Howell, ex-'98, Florence Reid Kellam, '92, Alice Pittman, Alice Keim Leinau, '06, and Roberts Leinau, ex-'06, Amy Carpenter Lewis, ex-'10, Annie Lodge Malven, '99, Elizabeth M. Ogden, '82, Katherine Laing Spackman, ex-'78, and husband, Mary Howell Taylor, '98, Mary Travilla, ex-'81, Charles Henry Walton, ex-'93, and wife, Keturah E. Yeo, '96, and mother, Samuel D. Yeo, ex-'99, and wife. P. FRANCES FOULKE, '82, *Secy-Treas.*

There are twenty members of the Swarthmore Club of Southern California. The club is very glad to have the names and addresses of all persons either residents or tourists who are in California and who have been or are connected in any way whatsoever with the college. It hopes that all such will make themselves known to members of the club.

Much Learning In Little Space

Notes on Recent Pamphlets of Value.

The press of Hampton Institute, Hampton, Va., has just issued an essay by Robert T. Kerlin on "Contemporary Poetry of the Negro." Written with insight, and amplified by many quotations from contemporary Negro poets, this appreciation of the modern literature of a poetic race will be valued by all lovers of the Negro and his art.

The essence of Everett Dean Martin's valuable work, "The Behavior of Crowds," (recently reviewed in the INTELLIGENCER by Bliss Forbush) has been reduced to pamphlet form, and is being issued by the American Civil Liberties Union, 138 W. 13th St., New York City. The pamphlet is entitled "The Mob vs. Civil Liberty," and may be obtained for ten cents. It gives a picture of present-day habits of thinking which should influence minds of all opinions toward greater tolerance.

A pamphlet which will interest all concerned for education toward peace is "Outlawry of War," by Salmon O. Levinson. It is issued by the American Committee for the Outlawry of War, 76 West Monroe St., Chicago, Ill. The propositions set forth are the result of years of effort and collaboration by statesmen, international jurists, business men and others. They are designed to form a simple and practical code by which international relations can be civilized and war between nations abolished. The point of view is one with which Friends are in deep accord, making its first premise that war as a means of settling international disputes must be *abolished*, not simply restricted. A codification of international law is proposed to the end of making war definitely illegal. The Association should wield great educational influence by laboring for the expansion of this attitude.

The George H. Doran Company, of New York, has published the second and third of its "Christianity and Industry" series of pamphlets. These are entitled respectively, "Collective Bargaining: An Ethical Evaluation of Some Phases of Trade Unionism and the Open Shop Movement," and "Fellowship: A Means of Building Up the Christian Social Order." The former is by Kirby Page, the latter by Basil Mathews and Harry Bisseker.

Like "Industrial Facts," the first pamphlet of the series, these statements are brief, but they crystallize the results of careful study. They afford an excellent approach to industrial problems in short form and from the Christian point of view. They may be obtained from the publishers at the price of ten cents each.

A "Five Lesson Study Course," four pages in length, has been prepared by the Federal Council of Churches, 105 E. 22nd St., New York City. It is based upon a twenty-page pamphlet written by Sidney L. Gulick, and entitled "Problems of the Pacific and the Far East," which is also issued by the Federal Council. This pamphlet and study outline afford the best short means known to us of getting in touch with the Eastern problems which Christianity is called upon to solve. Single copies of the pamphlet are twenty-five cents; of the study outline, five cents.

Items From Everywhere

Under the auspices of the Junior Red Cross, pupils of the manual training departments of the Berkeley, California, Public Schools made over 3,000 toys which were distributed as Christmas presents among sick and dependent children in various public institutions. They also made two dozen stationery holders for the patients in the United States Public Health Service Hospital at Palo Alto and constructed twenty Nursing Service boxes which were given to the Public Health Nurses to be distributed in towns having need of them.

One hundred years ago next June was passed the first Act of Parliament recognizing the legal rights of animals. The passing of this Act, which is known as Martin's Act, will be celebrated in England by an important public demonstration on the occasion of its centenary. A large number of humanitarian and animal protection Societies are combining to carry out the work.—*Our Dumb Animals.*

Statistics issued by Robert R. Moton, principal of Tuskegee Institute, set the lynching record of the United States for the year of 1921 at 63 persons. Several of the victims were burned at the stake. Four were white. One colored man was lynched for sending a note to a white girl, while several of the other alleged offenses are equally trivial.

The Anti-Saloon League announces that it has received unqualified endorsement of its local enforcement program, and specifically the organization of local law and order sentiment through the "Allied Citizens of America, Inc.," from Internal Revenue Commissioner David H. Blair, who is the superior officer of the Federal Prohibition Commissioner. The letter of Commissioner Blair was in reply to specific queries pursuant to the published report that the Commissioner had disapproved unofficial enforcement efforts.

In one respect virtually all of the reports received by the New York *Herald* and the Philadelphia *Public Ledger* investigation into the results of two years of prohibition agree. In nearly every part of the country there has been a marked decrease in crime in the last two years. A decrease in the number of insanity cases in some sections and, judging by court records, an improvement in domestic relations, also is noted. Whether there has been an improvement in the general public health which can be traced to prohibition the record is not clear.—*Public Ledger.*

"When Disarmament Worked" is the title of an article by Frederick J. Haskin, which reviews the successful venture of William Penn and the Quaker settlers of Pennsylvania in setting up their unarmed colony. The article appeared recently in *The Oil City Derrick*, and was inspired by Violet Oakley's portfolio, "The Holy Experiment." This portfolio contains color reproductions of Violet Oakley's mural paintings in the State Capital at Harrisburg, together with a hand-printed text based upon the author's note of early Pennsylvania history.

The article reports that "It has been suggested that copies of the portfolio be presented to the delegates at the Washington Conference, and this may be done. It is pointed out by advocates of disarmament that the pictures and story might serve a purpose: they would show that America did at one time offer an honest example, not of limited armaments, but of disarmament.

"Miss Oakley regards the 'holy experiment' as a message to the world from Pennsylvania, and a valuable contribution to the disarmament question. Quaker Pennsylvania, she says, is the keystone to the idea of disarmament."

As a phase of the continuous activity for peace to which Christians are called, the Federal Council of Churches is asking all churches to prepare a petition expressing its judgments on the principal proposals of the Washington Conference, and on "the imperative need of America's associating itself with all nations to secure justice, safety and fair opportunity for all through the establishment of a world peace-system." Friends' meetings may render service by taking the same step, and sending their petitions as soon as possible to the two Senators of their state, and to their local newspapers.

The Nation for February 1st contains a full-page poem by William Ellery Leonard, assistant professor of English in the University of Wisconsin, entitled "The Quaker Meeting-House." It employs as symbols of contrasting ways of life, an army training camp during the war, and an adjacent meeting-house; and traces the subsequent product of one in the death struggle of the trenches, of the other in the ministry of relief and reconstruction. The author writes from the point of view of the camp. After the conclusion of the struggle, he meditates upon the quiet meeting-house, and the poem ends:

You cannot guess how beautiful it seems;
Above the Capitol and marble dome,
Above the spired Cathedral and its dreams,
Unto the way-worn sons of men it gleams
Far down the Landmarks to the Ocean Streams,
With windows burning like the Fires of Home.

THE OPEN FORUM

This column is intended to afford free expression of opinion by readers on questions of interest. The INTELLIGENCER *is not responsible for any such opinions. Letters must be brief, and the editor reserves the right to omit parts if necessary to save space.*

"THE FRIENDLY HAND."

To the Editor:

I am more than interested in the suggestion, made to the Editor of *The Friend* and copied in edition of First month 21st, 1922, of the INTELLIGENCER, referring to "advisability of starting 'Helping Hand' societies." As a matter of fact, the Bible Class of West Philadelphia First-day School has now in operation just such a society, only we call it "The Friendly Hand." In forming this society, interested persons are admitted simply upon their request and left free to pay to the cause of helping those in need, such sums as they are prompted to give, but that all may share, from the least to the greatest, a minimum sum of ten dollars per month is fixed as registering one a member of "The Friendly Hand."

Our object is to keep in touch with the sick and see that they are remembered, by sending flowers. A Flower Committee has charge and has done its work so well that something over 300 bouquets have been sent, and usually to the "shut ins," a plant is sent once a month.

We also have an Auxiliary Fund Committee that meets the other numerous needs, as far as their funds enable them. A great deal of quiet help has been given by this committee. We have no salaried officers, and committees bear their own expense in investigating needy cases. The chairman of the Finance Committee is Joseph Baily, 1122 North Sixty-third street. The secretary-treasurer is Elsie Barton, 311 North Thirty-fourth street. Our motto: "Those that help the needy quickly give twice."

W. J. MacWatters,
West Philadelphia, Pa. *President.*

COMMENTS ON PEACE WORK

To the Editor:

O. Edward Janney, in the INTELLIGENCER, dated First month 7th, gives many valuable suggestions to hasten World Peace. I would like to suggest a few more.

One of the greatest causes that leads to war is through the economic relations and entanglements between nations. High tariff walls between nations do not lead to harmony and peace. What about the famous "Fordney Bill," impending just at the time of the last presidential elections? How many, even among Friends, in the last election cared enough for "World Peace" to change their vote from the high tariff party that makes for war, to the free trade party that makes for peace?

In another paragraph Dr. Janney says, "Urge that all nations become associated for purposes of the maintenance of peace through justice and good-will, all nations co-operating for the benefit of all."

I see no hint in this suggestion, only a studied omission, of the "League of Nations for World Peace" already established and active and making good. If the powerful United States nation had seen fit to supplement the noble work of ex-President Wilson and given the League of Nations its moral support and counsel, I believe that half the misery and starvation that has since overtaken Europe would not have been.

Coldstream, Canada. Edgar M. Zavitz.

BIRTHS.

Bloomsburg—On Twelfth month 24th, 1921, in Salmon, Idaho, to Walter G. and Helen Daniels Bloomsburg, a daughter, named Elizabeth Helen Bloomsburg.

Farquhar—On Twelfth month 17th, 1921, at Indianapolis, Ind., to Roger Brooke, Jr., and Margery Holt Farquhar, a son, named Roderick Haldane Farquhar.

MARRIAGES.

Hannum-Smith—On First month 21, at San Francisco, California, William Townsend Hannum, formerly of Rosedale, Penna., and Helen Smith, of San Francisco.

DEATHS.

Bryan—In Philadelphia, on First month 25th, Louis L. Bryan. Interment Haverford Friends' Burying Ground.

Evens—At Marlton, N. J., First month 25th, Elizabeth L., widow of Jacob L. Evens, in her 84th year.

Farquhar—At her home in Speedway, Indiana, near Indianapolis, on First month 17th, Margery Holt Farquhar, wife of Roger Brooke Farquhar, Jr., in the thirty-fourth year of her age. Interment was made at Crown Hill Cemetery, Indianapolis, on First month twentieth.

Stokes—At Riverside, N. J., on First month 20th, Hillyard B., son of Charles and Helene P. Stokes, aged 26.

Wood—On First month 22nd, at the residence of his son-in-law, William S. Kochersperger, Jr., Germantown, Watson T., husband of the late Josephine Wood. Interment at Horsham.

LOUISA H. WOODMAN
In Memory.

"For all her quiet life flowed on
As meadow streamlets flow,
Where fresher green reveals alone
The noiseless ways they go."

. . . . . .

"She kept her line of rectitude
With love's unconscious ease;
Her kindly instincts understood
All gentle courtesies."

Whittier's lines so aptly portray the beauty of the life and character of Louisa H. Woodman, whose mortal body was laid to rest at Wrightstown on First month 10th, that they seem almost to have been written for her.

Louisa Herre was born in Philadelphia, of German parentage, in 1853. When but a small child she was brought by her widowed mother to the home of Edward and Elizabeth H. Atkinson, Wrightstown, where she grew up as a daughter of the family. She early became associated with all Friendly activities of the neighborhood. She received her education at Wrightstown Friends' School, Elizabeth Lloyd being one of her teachers. She attended First-day School, and Meeting, of which she became a member, and in whose affairs she took an active part until a few months before her death when illness prevented. She at one time served the Meeting as overseer, but was an elder during the last years of her life.

On March 4, 1875, she married Wilson M. Woodman, and removed to the old Woodman homestead, which, with the exception of three years in Newtown, was to be her home the remainder of her life. Here her spirit was released from its earthly bonds and passed to the giver of all life.

For many years she was a member of the committee in charge of Friends' Home of Bucks Quarter, and was ever faithful in attendance and to her duties. She will be greatly missed, not only in the general councils of the committee, but, more particularly, as a cherished personal friend of each member of the large Home family. There is a vacant niche which cannot be filled.

She was a good wife and mother; a devoted grandmother; a kind friend and neighbor; a faithful and consistent member of the Society of Friends. "Her children's children shall rise up and call her blessed."

"The dear Lord's best interpreters
Are humble human souls
The Gospel of a life like hers
Is more than books or scrolls.

"From scheme and creed the light goes out,
The saintly fact survives;
The blessed Master none can doubt
Revealed in holy lives."

E. D. A.

S. LOUISA HAIGHT

S. Louisa Haight, superintendent of Schofield School, Aiken, S. C., whose sudden passing from the earthly life on First month 5th, shocked her many friends, was a woman of unusual personality and ability. She was a Friend by birthright, but feeling she had a message which she could best deliver from an established pulpit, she resigned her membership and studied for the ministry. After about fifteen years in the church, she felt called to supervise Girls' clubs in Chicago, and no one can estimate the value of her work among them.

Then after a year of institutional work in New Jersey, she came to Philadelphia confident, as she often remarked, that somewhere there was a position especially needing her. She refused many that were pressed upon her, but finally consented to superintend a temporary home for unruly girls.

When she heard that a superintendent was needed for Schofield School she felt at once that it was a call for her. What her well-poised, capable, far-seeing mind and her untiring devotion to the school and the cause of the colored people have done for it and them only those closely connected with the school can know. The academic department has been strengthened, the industries developed and extended, the number of boarding pupils greatly increased, buildings repaired and others erected, till today Schofield School stands among the leading institutions for colored people in the south.

The call from earth came with startling suddenness, but it found Louisa Haight with every important detail of her life's work finished to that day. Others will carry on the service, but spirits such as hers are sorely needed at this time. The loss to friendship and service is great.

M. H. W.

COMING EVENTS

SECOND MONTH

3rd.—An Evening of Tableaux by Elizabeth and Esther Fisher will be given in the Meeting-house, 221 East 15th St., New York, at 8.15, for the benefit of the Fort Valley, Ga., High and Industrial School for Colored Children. Colored singers will sing Plantation Melodies at intervals. The admission is only fifty cents. There will be a social gathering afterward, in the gymnasium of the Seminary.

4th—Gwynedd Monthly Meeting at Norristown, Pa., at 3.30 p. m. Box Supper at 6 p. m. will be followed by a conference at 7.30 p. m. on the subject, "A Dynamic Faith."

4th—Recital at George School, Pa. "The Servant in the House," by Phidelah Rice, Boston, Mass. 8.15 P. M. Admission, 50 cents.

4th—Philadelphia Quarterly Meeting, at 15th and Race Sts., Philadelphia, at 1.30 P. M.

5th—Purchase Quarterly Meeting, at Purchase, N. Y., at 10.30 A. M.

5th—Conference Class at 15th and Race Streets, Philadelphia, at close of meeting for worship, at 11.40 a. m. Subject—The Fatherhood of God and the Brotherhood of Man. Leader Samuel J. Bunting, Jr.

9th—Abington Quarterly Meeting, at Abington, Penna., 10.30 p. m., Meeting of Ministry and Counsel, at 9 a. m. All trains leaving Reading Terminal between the hours of 8 and 10 o'clock p. m. will be met at Jenkintown Station; also trains going south between those hours.

11th—Salem Quarterly Meeting, at Salem, Ohio.

12th—Preparative Meetings in New York and Brooklyn, after the Meeting for Worship.

13th—New York Monthly Meeting, at Schermerhorn Street, Brooklyn, at 7.30 p. m. Supper will be served at 6 o'clock. The Meeting for Ministry and Counsel will meet at 5.

13th—At the regular meeting of the Philadelphia Young Friends Association, held at 15th and Cherry Streets, Elbert Russell will give the last of his lectures on the Four Gospels. 8 p. m.

13th—Miami Quarterly Meeting, at Waynesville, Ohio.

18th—Short Creek Quarterly Meeting, at Emerson, Ohio.

18th—Pelham Half-Yearly Meeting, at Coldstream, Ontario.

18th and 19th—Pilgrimage under the care of the Young Friends' Movement at Girard Avenue Meeting, Philadelphia.

20th—Fairfax Quarterly Meeting, at Washington, D. C.

20th—Center Quarterly Meeting, at Unionville, Center Co., Pa.

21st—Burlington Quarterly Meeting, at Mt. Holly, N. J.

23rd—Bucks Quarterly Meeting, at Wrightstown, Pa. Meeting for Ministry and Counsel, preceding day, at 11 A. M.

25th—Blue River Quarterly Meeting, at Chicago, Ill.

27th—Warrington Quarterly Meeting, at Menallen, Pa.

NOTICE—The Library Association of the Monthly Meeting of Friends has, with a few exceptions, the "Suggested Books for Meeting Libraries," which was printed in the *Intelligencer* of First month 7, 1922.

FUN.

Little Frances, age three, was eating breakfast at the home of her grandfather. The oatmeal porridge was a little thinner than usual that morning. The little miss looked intently at her grandfather for some time, as he was eating his porridge, and then broke the somewhat protracted silence with the remark: "Grandfather, you sound like soup."—*Christian Intelligencer.*

Teacher—"Swarms of flies descended upon the Egyptians, but there were no flies on the children of Israel."

Smart Boy—"There ain't now, either." —*Cleveland News.*

Maggie—The garbage man is here, sor.

Professor (from deep thought)—My! my! tell him we don't want any. —*Tiger.*

Thoughtful

A Jewish boy, seriously ill with smallpox, asked to see a Catholic priest before he died. When they asked him if he did not want his rabbi, said he, "Certainly not. You don't think I would expose a rabbi to smallpox, do you?"—*Methodist Protestant.*

REGULAR MEETINGS.

OAKLAND, CALIF.—A FRIENDS' MEETING is held every First-day at 11 A. M., in the Extension Room, Y. W. C. A. Building, Webster Street, above 14th. Visiting Friends always welcome.

FRIENDS' MEETING IN PASADENA, California—Orange Grove Monthly Meeting of Friends, 520 East Orange Grove Avenue, Pasadena, California. Meeting for worship, First-day, 11 A. M. Monthly Meeting, the second First-day of each month, at 1.45 P. M.

WANTED

POSITION WANTED—BY EXPERIENCED, capable mother's helper, preferably in Friends' family. Has been two years in present position; excellent reason for leaving. Address S. 43, Friends' Intelligencer.

WORKING HOUSEKEEPER—EXPERIENCED woman desires position in Christian home. Small household and no children; city preferred. Will cook. Highest recommendation from present employer. Open to engagement after March 10th. Address J-54, Friends' Intelligencer.

GOVERNESS WISHES PERMANENT position in Friends' family. Thoroughly experienced, capable and reliable. Excellent references. Address E-52, Friends' Intelligencer.

WANTED—POSITION BY COLLEGE woman, as secretary or nurse-companion. Capable of taking full charge of nervous or chronic invalid. Address P-55, Friends' Intelligencer.

POSITION WANTED—AS COMPANION-attendant to semi-invalid. Will make herself useful. Philadelphia; suburbs. Address B-56, Friends' Intelligencer.

REFINED, CAPABLE MOTHER OF 3 children, wants any kind of employment where it is possible to keep her little ones together and educate them. Can give best of reference. Address K-59, Friends' Intelligencer.

TRANSIENT ACCOMMODATIONS

VISITORS TO CALIFORNIA CAN find comfortable accommodations at 400 S. Euclid Avenue, Pasadena. For terms, apply to Mary B. Sutton.

WASHINGTON, D. C.—ROOMS FOR visitors. Near Station, Capitol, Library. Continuous hot water. Electricity. Garage. Mrs. L. L. Kendig, 120 C. Street, Northwest.

FOR RENT.

FOR RENT BY YEAR OR TERM OF years, or will consider sale—A very attractive small house in Brielle, New Jersey, near river and sea. Hot-water heater and all possible conveniences, including open fireplace. One minute from "bus" line between Lakewood and Asbury Park. Ten minutes from train. Address Box 28, "Applewood," Brielle, N. J.

FUN

Where He Drew the Line

Sociology Professor (to student)—"Mr. H——, I can't blame you for looking at your watch while I'm lecturing, but I do object to your holding it to your ear to make sure it hasn't stopped."—*Chicago Tribune.*

To the Lot Holders and others interested in Fairhill Burial Ground:

GREEN STREET Monthly Meeting has funds available for the encouragement of the practice of cremating the dead to be interred in Fairhill Burial Ground. We wish to bring this fact as prominently as possible to those who may be interested. We are prepared to undertake the expense of cremation in case any lot holder desires us to do so.

Those interested should communicate with William H. Gaskill, Treasurer of the Committee of Interments, Green Street Monthly Meeting, or any of the following members of the Committee.

William H. Gaskill, 3201 Arch St.
Samuel N. Longstreth, 1218 Chestnut St.
Charles F. Jenkins, 232 South Seventh St.
Stuart S. Graves, 3033 Germantown Ave.

ADVERTISING RATE in the FRIENDS' INTELLIGENCER, for Help Wanted, Positions Wanted, Rooms for Rent, Notices, and other classified advertisements without display, for each insertion, 2 cents per word, including name, initials and address. Answers may be sent to a box at the INTELLIGENCER office, if so directed.

For display advertising the rate is 10 cents per agate line, or $1.40 per column inch, each insertion. On ten or more insertions in a year from date of order, ten per cent. discount. Thus a four-inch single-column or two-inch double-column advertisement costs $5.60 each insertion, less ten per cent., or 5.04 net each time for ten or more insertions. Matter may be changed whenever desired, without extra charge.

Experience has proved the INTELLIGENCER to be a remarkably good advertising medium. All advertisements must "pass the censor!"

Address 140 N. 15th St., Philadelphia

The Friends' Intelligencer

ESTABLISHED 1844 | SECOND MONTH 11, 1922 | VOLUME 79 NUMBER 6

Contents

THE FRIENDS' INTELLIGENCER

Published weekly, 140 N. 15th Street, Philadelphia, Pa., by Friends' Intelligencer Association, Ltd.

WALTER H. ABELL, *Editor*
SUE C. YERKES, *Business Manager*

Editorial Board: Elizabeth Powell Bond, Thomas A. Jenkins, J. Russell Smith, George A. Walton.

Board of Managers: Edward Cornell, Alice Hall Paxson, Paul M. Pearson, Annie Hillborn, Elwood Hollingshead, William C. Biddle, Charles F. Jenkins, Edith M. Winder, Frances M. White.

Officers of Intelligencer Associates: Ellwood Burdsall, Chairman; Bertha L. Broomell, Secretary; Herbert P. Worth, Treasurer.

Subscription rates: United States, Mexico, Cuba and Panama, $2.50 per year. Canada and other foreign countries, $3.00 per year. Checks should be made payable to Friends' Intelligencer Association, Ltd.

Entered as Second Class Matter at Philadelphia Post Office.

The Friends' Intelligencer

The religion of Friends is based on faith in the "INWARD LIGHT," or direct revelation of God's spirit and will in every seeking soul.

The INTELLIGENCER is interested in all who bear the name of Friends in every part of the world, and aims to promote love, unity and intercourse among all branches and with all religious societies.

ESTABLISHED 1844 PHILADELPHIA, SECOND MONTH 11, 1922 VOLUME 79 NUMBER 6

Our New Form

With this issue, the INTELLIGENCER takes on a somewhat altered form which we trust will meet with the approval of our readers. The use of our front page as a cover, we believe improves the appearance of the paper, while a slight enlargement in the size of type used for our leading articles should increase their attractiveness and legibility.

To these changes, we hope within a few months to add an improvement in the quality of the paper upon which the INTELLIGENCER is printed. Should this latter advance prove practicable, it will, like those already achieved, be due to the assistance given to the paper by the Intelligencer Associates. We take this occasion, therefore, to express our appreciation of the splendid support which the latter have rendered, and to hope that more Friends will aid in promoting the growth of the INTELLIGENCER by becoming Associates. Details regarding the organization of the Associates will be gladly furnished in response to all inquiries addressed to the INTELLIGENCER office.

Toward Unity In Friends' Educational Work

At a meeting of the General Educational Committee of Philadelphia Yearly Meeting, on First month 28th, it was agreed to invite the Educational Committee of the Fourth and Arch Streets Yearly Meeting to a conference looking toward a closer co-operation in the supervision of the schools under the care of both meetings.

It is hoped that way may open to combine the educational secretaryships of the two Yearly Meetings, one person being thus given charge of the activities now requiring the efforts of two.

The appointment of such a joint educational superintendent would be a most important forward step. Materially, it would be an economy to have one person fill both positions. Constant demands for increases in the personnel and equipment of our schools, make the labors of our educational committees more and more difficult. Every co-ordination and simplification which is possible within our educational systems should, therefore, be taken advantage of as a means toward greater efficiency in the work.

At the same time, the appointment of a joint superintendent would carry forward our present tendency toward the consolidation of the schools themselves. The two schools at Moorestown successfully combined nearly two years ago, while a joint committee has the care and oversight of the school at London Grove. In both cases, greater educational efficiency has resulted from the co-operation.

And every advance in joint educational activity means a gain not only to our schools, but to the vision and effectiveness of the Society of Friends as a whole. Like our joint activities in the cause of peace, and in the work of the American Friends' Service Committee, such advances tend to stimulate, within our own religious body, that broadened vision, that experience of deepened fellowship, which we acclaim as one of the most insistent needs of the world.

A proposal which has such manifest advantages as does that of joint educational supervision deserves thorough and widespread attention. It is our hope that it will meet with immediate and unanimous approval, and that Friends will express such approval to our educational committees, in order that the latter may be encouraged to press forward in their good work. Proper consideration of the plan, and the expression of widespread sentiment in its favor, should make its execution a definite possibility within the near future.

There is growing up a feeling among men who are conscious of the dignity of life that no job is worth doing unless it accomplishes something good, or helps to steady life or wisely reorganize it.—*Henry Ford.*

The Quakerism of Robert Barclay

By Elbert Russell

Part Two

Third installment of the series "The Quakerism of the Founders."

Vocal Service In Worship

"Many are the blessed experiences which I could relate of this silence and manner of worship; yet I do not so much commend and speak of silence as if we had bound ourselves by any law to exclude praying or preaching, or tied ourselves thereunto; not at all: for as our worship consisteth not in words, so neither in silence, as silence; but in a holy dependence of the mind upon God: from which dependence silence necessarily follows in the first place, until words can be brought forth, which are from God's Spirit. And God is not wanting to move in his children to bring forth words of exhortation or prayer, when it is needful; so that of the many gatherings and meetings of such as are convinced of the truth, there is scarce any in whom God raiseth not up some or other to minister to his brethren; and there are few meetings that are altogether silent. For when many are met together in this one life and name, it doth most naturally and frequently excite them to pray to and praise God, and stir up one another by mutual exhortation and instructions; yet we judge it needful there be in the first place some time of silence, during which every one may be gathered inward to the word and gift of grace, from which he that ministereth may receive strength to bring forth what he ministereth; and that they that hear may have a sense to discern betwixt the precious and the vile, and not to hurry into the exercise of these things so soon as the bell rings, as other Christians do."—*Apology, Prop. XI.*

The Needlessness of Sacraments

Baptism

"As there is one Lord, and one faith, so there is one baptism; which is not the putting away the filth of the flesh, but the answer of a good conscience before God, by the resurrection of Jesus Christ. And this baptism is a pure and spiritual thing, to wit, the baptism of the Spirit and fire, by which we are buried with him, that being washed and purged from our sins, we may walk in newness of life: of which the baptism of John was a figure, which was commanded for a time, and not to continue for ever. As to the baptism of infants, it is a mere human tradition, for which neither precept nor practice is to be found in all the scripture."—*Apology, Prop. XII.*

The Lord's Supper

"The communion of the body and blood of Christ is inward and spiritual, which is the participation of his flesh and blood, by which the inward man is daily nourished in the hearts of those in whom Christ dwells. Of which things the breaking of bread by Christ with his disciples was a figure, which even they who had received the substance used in the church for a time, for the sake of the weak; even as abstaining from things strangled, and from blood, the washing one another's feet, and the anointing of the sick with oil; all which are commanded with no less authority and solemnity than the former; yet seeing they are but shadows of better things, they cease in such as have obtained the substance."—*Apology, Prop. XII.*

The Indifference To Outward Forms

"Lastly, if any now at this day, from a true tenderness of spirit, and with real conscience towards God, did practice this ceremony in the same way, method and manner as did the primitive Christians recorded in scripture, I should not doubt to affirm but they might be indulged in it, and the Lord might regard them, and for a season appear to them in the use of these things, as many of us have known him to do to us in the time of our ignorance; providing always they did not seek to obtrude them upon others, nor judge such as found themselves delivered from them, or that they do not pertinaciously adhere to them. For we certainly know that the day is dawned, in which God hath arisen, and hath dismissed all those ceremonies and rites, and is only to be worshipped in Spirit, and that he appears to them who wait upon him, and that to seek God in these things is, with Mary at the sepulchre, to seek the living among the dead: for we know that he is risen, and revealed in Spirit, leading his children out of these rudiments, that they may walk with him in his light: to whom be glory for ever. Amen."—*Apology, Prop. XIII.*

It is well to be reminded by such passages as these what was the true position of early Friends. They insisted that the outward forms could neither give of themselves the substance of true religion, nor did the absence of the form deprive of the substance. On the other hand, they testified that there was no virtue merely in not being baptized, and that it was not impossible to have the spiritual communion in connection with the outward ceremony. We who discontinue the ordinances that others practice are under extra obligations to show that we have the realities of spiritual life. Otherwise our neglect of the outward rites merely puts us in the same class with the ungodly. Sinners also do not practice baptism nor partake of the outward Communion.

The Ministry: Qualifications and Support

"Though then we make not human learning necessary, yet we are far from excluding true learning; to wit, that learning which proceedeth from the inward teachings and instructions of the Spirit, whereby the soul learneth the secret ways of the Lord, becomes acquainted with many inward travails and exercises of the mind; and learneth by a living experience how to overcome evil, and the temptations of it, by following the Lord, and walking in his light, and waiting daily for wisdom and knowledge immediately from the revelation thereof; and so layeth up these heavenly and divine lessons in the good treasure of the heart, as honest Mary did the sayings which she heard, and things which she observed: and also out of this treasure of the soul, as the good scribe, brings forth things new and old, according as the same Spirit moves, and gives true liberty, and as the glory of God requires, for whose glory the soul, which is the temple of God, learneth to do all things. This is that good learning which we think necessary to a true minister; by and through which learning a man can well instruct, teach, and admonish in due season, and testify for God from a certain experience.

"As by the light or gift of God, all true knowledge in things spiritual is received and revealed, so by the same, as it is manifested and received in the heart, by the strength and power thereof, every true minister of the gospel is ordained, prepared, and supplied in the work of the ministry; and by the leading, moving, and drawing hereof, ought every evangelist and Christian pastor to be led and ordered in his labor and work of the gospel, both as to the place where, as to the persons to whom, and as to the time wherein he is to minister. Moreover, they who have this authority may and ought to preach the gospel, though without human commission or literature; as on the other hand, they who want the authority of this divine gift however learned, or authorized by the commission of men and churches, are to be esteemed but as deceivers, and not true ministers of the gospel. Also they who have received this holy and unspotted gift, as they have freely received it, so are they freely to give it, without hire or bargaining, far less to use it as a trade to get money by: yet if God hath called any one from their employment or trades, by which they acquire their livelihood, it may be lawful for such, according to the liberty which they feel given them in the Lord, to receive such temporals (to wit, what may be needful for them for meat and clothing) as are given them freely and cordially by those, to whom they have communicated spirituals."—*Apology. Prop. X.*

It will be seen that the later objection of Friends to the support of foreign missionaries, secretaries, and ministers whose service requires their whole time, for fear of a "hireling" ministry, was not grounded on the real nature of Early Friends' testimony. They were opposing the professional ministry of the English Church, whose support was com- ... by the State.

Freedom of Conscience

"Since God hath assumed to himself the power and dominion of the conscience, who alone can rightly instruct and govern it, therefore it is not lawful for any, whosoever, by virtue of any authority or principality they bear in the government of this world, to force the consciences of others; and therefore all killing, banishing, fining, imprisoning, and other such things which are inflicted upon men for the alone exercise of their conscience, or difference in worship or opinion, proceedeth from the spirit of Cain the murderer, and is contrary to the truth; providing always, that no man, under the pretence of conscience, prejudice his neighbor in his life or estate, or do anything destructive to, or inconsistent with, human society; in which case the law is for the transgressor, and justice is to be administered upon all, without respect of persons."—*Apology, Prop. XIV.*

War

"Sixthly, The last thing to be considered, is revenge and war, an evil as opposite and contrary to the Spirit and doctrine of Christ as light to darkness. For, as is manifest by what is said, through contempt of Christ's law, the world is filled with violence, oppression, murders, ravishing of the women and virgins, spoilings, depredations, burnings, devastations, and all manner of lasciviousness and cruelty: so that it is strange that men, made after the image of God, should have so much degenerated, that they rather bear the image and nature of roaring lions, tearing tigers, devouring wolves, and raging boars, than of rational creatures endued with reason. And is it not yet much more admirable, that this horrid monster should find place, and be fomented, among those men that profess themselves disciples of our peaceable Lord and master Jesus Christ, who by excellency is called the Prince of Peace, and hath expressly prohibited His children all violence; and on the contrary, commanded them, that, according to His example, they should follow patience, charity, forbearance, and other virtues worthy of a Christian?"—*Apology, Prop. XV.*

The Old Meeting-House
Flushing, N. Y.
1695

Poem read at Disarmament Meeting in Flushing, First month 22, 1921.

Calm and ever faithful stands the quiet old brown house,
Apart from all the tumult of the way,—
Where Friend to Friend through silence speaks
In loving fellowship,—at close of day.

In years gone by, when slave beneath the yoke was bent,
A refuge thou! Four-square to thy true intent
Of human liberty, thy sheltering arms outstretched
O'er low defenseless heads—until the foe was spent.

In our today, a world of war and wild alarms,
To friend and foe alike thy message brings
A sanctuary. When false patriotism wrings the bruised heart
Still steadfast thou and to thy strength the troubled spirit clings.

Unto the calmly gathered thought, the Inner Voice
Of right makes known the way. And reconciliation
Soothes deep hate to yield, and in that yielding
Does disclose a broader faith, a world-wide Nation.

A healing touch on wistful seeking hearts is laid,
Through friendly fellowship at close of day,
Where calm and ever faithful stands the quiet old brown house,—
Apart from all the tumult of the way.

JEWELL MILLER PFALTZ.

The Washington Conference

XIII

By William I. Hull

This week, the twelfth of the Conference, has seen the completion of its tasks. Two plenary sessions, the fifth and the sixth, have been held and have formally adopted the agreements reached after long and weary debate in the various committees. The agreements thus reached and adopted in the six plenary sessions have been embodied in eight treaties, which are to be duly signed the first of next week.

The treaties, signed by our own delegation in the name of the President, will then be referred to the Senate for ratification. There are various prophecies as to the senatorial opposition to be encountered by them. It appears probable at this writing that the senators, both Republican and Democratic, with but few exceptions, will vote for ratification. But should serious opposition develop, we should all stand ready to do our utmost to overcome it. The Church Peace Union has already laid its plans to engage at the first sign of necessity in an immediate and country-wide campaign in support of the treaties. There is no doubt that all Friends will participate in that campaign to the utmost of their ability. For with us, it is not a question of partisanship, or even of statesmanship. It lies at the heart of our religion; it is of the very essence of Christianity as we interpret the religion of the Prince of Peace.

To enumerate all of the achievements of the Conference and to estimate the importance of each of them, in a single letter, would make that letter unduly long. Permit me then, in this, to classify and enumerate its achievements, and to defer until the last letter of this series an attempt to estimate the significance of both that which has been done and that which has been attempted. The Conference was summoned for the purpose of limiting armaments, of halting the approach of war in the Pacific, and of removing some of the causes of war in the Far East. It has made progress along each of those lines.

Its limitation of armaments is preceded by a noteworthy *reduction* of naval armaments. Sixty-eight great battleships, of nearly 1,900,000 tons' displacement are to be "scrapped" by the United States, Great Britain and Japan, while these countries, France and Italy together are to retain about the same number of ships with 100,000 tons less displacement. The limitation itself includes: The abandonment of existing programs for the building of capital ships, no more of these to be built during the next fifteen years, except for replacement. The maintenance of the existing ratio of 5:5:3:1.75:1.75 among the five great naval powers, and the consequent cessation of that competitive increase of navies, which has been so prolific a cause of international distrust and of war. The limitation of capital ships built ten years from now,—if any more should be built,—to 35,000 tons' displacement. The restriction of guns, on capital ships, to a calibre of 16 inches. (Plans were laid before the Washington Conference for the building of battleships with 50,000 tons' displacement and 18 inch guns.) The limitation of auxiliary ships (except aircraft carriers) to 10,000 tons, and of their guns to 8 inches. The limitation of aircraft carriers to a total tonnage of 135,000 for the United States; 135,000 for Great Britain; 81,000 for Japan; 60,000 for France; and 60,000 for Italy; and of each aircraft carrier to a maximum of 27,000 tons (except that each nation may build two such carriers with a maximum tonnage of 33,000). The number and size of guns on aircraft carriers are also limited to eight for those over 6 inches, and to a maximum calibre of 8 inches.

The submarine is so curbed in its activities by the rules agreed upon that it is made practically impossible for it to attack merchant ships, and this is followed up by a formal agreement to prohibit the use of submarines as commerce destroyers.

Chemical warfare, or "the use in war of asphyxiating, poisonous or other gases, and all analogous liquids, materials or devices," is prohibited as being justly condemned by the public opinion of the civilized world.

The attempt of the Conference to prevent war in the Pacific includes the limitation of naval armaments as above stated; the agreement of the four great Pacific powers to confer with one another in regard to the peaceful settlement of any grave difference which may arise among them in the future concerning their respective rights and interests in the Pacific; the agreement adopted by them to communicate with one another as to the best way of dealing with a threat of war in the Pacific due to the aggression of any other power; and the agreement adopted by the United States, Great Britain and Japan not to increase their fortifications or naval bases in most of their island possessions in the Pacific. (Some exceptions are enumerated for each of the three nations.) Another by-product of the Conference, which should aid greatly in maintaining the peace in the Pacific, is the settlement between the United States and Japan in regard to the much-disputed status of the cables on the Island of Yap and the other islands in the Pacific, a mandate over which was given to Japan by the Treaty of Versailles.

The agreements arrived at by the Conference in

regard to the Far East include a considerable number which are all designed to restore and establish the territorial integrity and the sovereignty of China and Russia and the maintenance of the Open Door. Still another "by-product" of the Conference is the agreement on the part of Japan to restore Shantung to China and to evacuate Siberia and Sakhalin. Great Britain has surrendered Wei-hai-wei, and France has promised to negotiate with China as to the surrender of Kwang-chow-wang. Chinese troops, railways, post-offices, customs revenue, extraterritoriality, cables, mines and other natural resources, foreign troops and "spheres of influence" have all been carefully discussed and much unexpected progress has been made in the safeguarding of China along all of these lines, and the participation of all nations in mighty China's development on just and equal terms.

This last open session of the Conference in which I am writing these lines has been devoted largely to the many measures designed to promote just dealings with China; and the large audience has repeatedly expressed by applause the warm interest which the world cherishes towards the great ancient people and much harassed youthful republic of the Far East. A thoroughly frank and explicit exchange of views, expressed in firm and even fervent manner, has occurred between the delegates of China, Japan and the United States; and there is a conviction that the traditional policy of America towards China, which is summed up in the phrase "territorial integrity, independent sovereignty and the open door in China," has been placed upon a more solid foundation than ever before.

The very long and fruitful meetings of the Conference in its fifth and sixth plenary sessions cannot be described here in detail. One single incident may be singled out in conclusion. Arthur J. Balfour, in what may well be the swan-song of his long and illustrious career, stressed the importance of the unprecedented steps taken by the Conference, and attributed its success, first, to an earnest attempt on the part of all the delegates to adhere to the path of "simplicity, honor and honesty" for which President Harding appealed in his opening address, and, secondly, to the fact that Secretary Hughes raised so high a standard in the first proposition which he laid before the conference relating to the reduction and limitation of armaments. The British statesman's words must be read in their entirety, to be fully appreciated; but their essence may be expressed in the words of our American poet:

"Whene'er is spoken a noble thought,
Whene'er a noble deed is wrought,
Our hearts, in glad surprise,
To higher levels rise."

Washington, D. C., February 4, 1922.

Appeal For Flour Being Answered

Thirty-six Carloads, Gift of People from California to Pennsylvania, on Way to Seaboard.

Flour, the gift of the American people, is beginning to roll from all parts of the country toward the Atlantic seaboard where ships will take it to the starving people of Russia. A little over a month ago the Friends' appeal for flour to aid in saving the lives of the 15,000,000 starving people of Russia, was sent out to the centers of all the agricultural communities of the United States, and also to the banks and commercial organizations of the cities. The daily press and the religious press of the country carried the news of this appeal; and representatives from the Service Committee's headquarters at Philadelphia followed the appeal into the localities where flour is most abundant.

Since that time the answer of the country has been given unmistakably clear. It has been that the Christian people of America feel the concern that is laid upon them to aid in relieving the agony and suffering and death which is destroying human life to an extent which the mind cannot grasp. The economic condition in our own country which has thrown so many people out of work and lessened the resources of so many others, has cut deep into the amount of the gift which people would ordinarily have made, but the response has shown that many people are giving to an extent which will cause real suffering and sacrifice here.

The millers of the country have with hardly an exception agreed to sell flour at a cost price; and they themselves have each made a contribution out of their own stores before asking others to buy. Community organizations such as chambers of commerce and rotary clubs have co-operated in enlisting the support of their communities behind this object. A typical case is that of Swope Brothers in Johnstown, Pennsylvania, who took the responsibility for selling a carload of flour in the community and with the active support of the agencies of the town the car which will mean life to Russian people has been received at seabord. This action was duplicated by the Yardley Milling Company, of Yardley, Pennsylvania, and by the citizens of Mound Ridge, Kansas, who contributed two carloads; by the Buhler Mills, of Buhler, Kansas, which contributed two carloads. Flory Brothers, of Pequea, Lancaster County, Pennsylvania, sold a carload of flour in their community and that has also been shipped.

Minneapolis has been foremost among the larger communities, having raised a fund with which they purchased six carloads of flour. Kansas City bought four carloads, and St. Louis is now organizing a committee and has set a quota of eight thousand barrels.

These are only a few examples which have been quoted from the many communities and mills and individuals who have co-operated in this campaign. Has your community done anything to aid in this effort? More than that, have you done anything? No matter how much you might secure, it cannot be enough; for there are 15,000,000 people starving in Russia and even with our government appropriation there are funds enough to feed only 4,000,000. You may think that your own barrel of flour, or a carload of flour from your community, is only comparable to a grain of sand on the great beach; but if you were the one who received even a portion of a barrel of flour in Russia because some one person in America sent it, you would feel that it was worth more than all in the world.

If nothing has been done in your community you are the one to begin this work. See your local miller and your bank and your town officials; organize an effort to secure some quota of flour for your community to send. The Service Committee Headquarters will be glad to furnish you with information and other material which you may need. It is something to have good will towards suffering and broken people. But the greatest love of all is that a man will lay down his life for his friends.

An Internationalist Abroad

Review of "Old Trails and New Borders." by Edward A. Steiner. Fleming H. Revell Co. $1.50.

Dr. Steiner, himself born in Slovakia, but thoroughly Americanized, has written many books on immigration and naturalization, also "Tolstoy, the Man and His Message," and I know of no man that might be better qualified to conduct a tour of Americans over "dull, gray," post-war Europe. The author affectionately dedicates the book to his friends "The Friends, both English and American," and acknowledges his indebtedness to the Friends' Service Committee of Philadelphia for making his journey through Europe possible. But while the relief work of the Friends determined the route of the trip and their work is mentioned and praised by the author on all proper occasions, still the book is intended for and can be warmly recommended to the general reader who feels his duty to study the affairs of our planet. This general reader will find the trip in Dr. Steiner's company very pleasant and convenient as well as highly instructive.

Our guide is a linguist, and there need be no trouble about foreign names or phrases. A few lapses must doubtless be charged to the printer. The Friends may gently remind the author that the French call them "Les Amis," or perhaps "L'Ami" or "L'Amie" if the Friend is alone, but never "L'Amis." May not the "brave Pole" rattle his ever ready sword when he sees the name of his hero spelled "Sobijewsky?" The Russian izvdshchik is so well-known a character that misspelling his name "ischvodjik" will not hurt his business.

Our guide never conceals his convictions or sentiments. For the cautious who desire to know his attitude before starting on the trip, the following, quoted from page 179, will be illuminating:

> "The spectre of Bolshevism has given the reactionaries a chance to arrest social progress; while the liberals, the liberated men, the onward moving men, have been hindered and damned by being opprobriously labelled. The reactionaries label them Bolsheviks, and the Bolsheviks call them reactionaries; so between the reactionary Nationalist and the Bolshevist, the Liberal has no choice. Both are materialistic to the core, though one may swear by the Bible and the other by Karl Marx."

And on the last page but one, page 207, we read the following confession:

> "I have grown suddenly old and not a little disillusioned. I know the odds against those of us who see the Kingdom of God afar, and who want to bring it near. Nations do not care to be saved by teachers and preachers, but by politicians and soldiers; theirs is yet the way of the sword, and not of the cross. I would (sic) be a poor patriot, however, if I would not cast my life into the balance, make war upon war, . . ."

The substitution of "would" for "should" is so thoroughly American that there will be no difficulty in accepting the following assurance on the last page:

> "As an American I was never more in love with my country than now, coming as I do out of the tombs of Empires, and from the grave of a civilization. If I could, I would save my country from the doom of Europe, and to that end she must think with the international mind and feel with the international heart."

Los Angeles, Cal. CORNELIUS M. ENNS.

Westbury Quarterly Meeting

At Westbury Quarterly Meeting held at 15th Street and Rutherford Place, New York, on January 28, Raymond Mendenhall of the 20th Street Meeting spoke earnestly and well on the present need of religion. He emphasized the necessity of bringing the practical application of religious teachings as well as the abstract ideals, to humanity. Way back in the days of Jesus' ministry when the people were heavily taxed and starving, when all conditions of life were bad, then, while the more learned turned to philosophy the people crowded around Jesus. They wished to see and to hear this man from the north, this man of humble birth like themselves. He was a mystery and they came to learn his power. He was the medium thru whom they grew to know God.

The Quaker faith exemplifies this fact, that before

preaching about God it is necessary to know God thru love. George Fox said: "There is one who can speak to thee," and many have renewed the power of knowing God thru him. Knowing God himself, he could make the spirit of God manifest to others. But we have not all followed this religion, a thing of the heart deeper than creed. We must have reality. "Why are we here when so many benches are vacant?" In looking back does not our faith come from some one individual who typified all that was fine and true? Does not our faith come from their true and devoted lives by which we can see an ideal realized?

In these times of unrest the world is looking for something true, and "Thou shalt love thy neighbor as thyself," will solve problems that arguments leave untouched, for love and forgiveness alone heal quarrels.

Believing in the spiritual and in God we must bring the practical application before the world. Children want to see Jesus. They need religious teachers. To see a man of high ideals, clean of life and of deep religious views, brings the message to a child as no amount of abstract teaching could do. It is also true of nations and many see in Quakers a foundation for Faith,—foreign children see Jesus thru the administration of Friends. The teachings of Jesus are vitalized as Friends seek to carry out his work of love. But there are starving souls here, as well as across the ocean, and in avoiding the old rituals, Quakerism is falling into new ruts and there are many who fail to see the beauty on which it was based—the inspiration thru ideals.

William W. Cocks said that the spoken word is frequently a thankless service, but the consecrated lives of those who devote themselves to service are of inestimable value. The influence of quietness and conciliation are necessary to the whole world these turbulent days. He also said that Quakers have had a great work intrusted to them because of their faithfulness, their desire to serve, not their own ends, but those of humanity; and as instruments have received credit for much that has been done by others as well as that justly due their own efforts.

E. A. P.

While Westbury Quarterly Meeting waited at the afternoon session for Frank P. Walsh's substitute to appear, Paul Furnas of Twentieth Street Meeting, chairman for the afternoon session, linked our religion with our daily lives in a way that brought out the significant relationship between Friends' principles and the topics discussed in our Quarterly Meeting afternoon programs of the last year. These have covered the fundamental theory of our present prison system contrasted with Christian teachings, the United States as a neighbor to Haiti, disarmament and the Arms Conference and the Far East,—all subjects to be treated adequately only in the light of religious principles.

The talk on Russia by Lewis Gannett which followed, proved a fitting addition to the above list as well as a natural sequel to the morning session when the Friends' work in Russia was discussed. Mr. Gannett, who spent a month in Russia last summer, tried to visualize and humanize the Russians. The background of Russian Communism is in part like our war conditions raised to the nth degree: while we rationed sugar and a few other foods, conditions in Russia required the rationing of all foods; and while we felt the housing shortage, the war made the situation so acute as to require the rationing of rooms in Russia, as in Berlin. The government has an occupational basis instead of our geographical system; it is not wholly democratic for the elections are somewhat controlled, but the same might be said of New York. If one wished to buy a suit of clothes, he applied to his Soviet and a committee decided whether he needed it enough. This method worked when there was a shortage.

Of the leaders of the Russian government Lenin is the thinker who decides how far they shall go toward capitalism under the new economic policy. Trotsky is an almost unequalled administrator. Witness, the conditions out of which he organized an army; the revolution had been made for peace, bread and land; the people quit fighting Germany and called on the German people, over the heads of their leaders at Brest-Litovsk, to stop likewise; the army, utterly disorganized, returned home, sick and tired of war. Trotsky organized a new army that has met all subsequent invasions of Russia.

Now the famine has come upon Russia; there has been nothing like it since 1891. The drought last year was such that in some places grain was picked stalk by stalk! The twenty million dollars appropriated by Congress will feed two million people, the ten million from Russia will feed another million people, and a little more has come from other sources, but the numbers of dead in the streets, the naked and the sick, mean that, give what we will, we cannot save all.

The discussion that followed centered largely around three questions of Communist methods, which Mr. Gannett urged should be judged in the light of Russian history, not our own. He quoted a Russian wireless operator who hates Communism but who said that the Communists are the ones who must lead Russia out, for they are the only group that is organized and disciplined. To the question, "Isn't the Soviet government a one-class government?" Mr. Gannett replied that their rule is "He who does not work does not eat." At first managing was not called work, but Lenin found that, in the absence of trained proletariat, they must have specialists, and to get specialists they must give extra food, which they have been doing now for two years, against working class opposition. Those living on capital are not helped by the government, and some are now pathetically selling their jewels. To be fair we must remember our own "work or fight" laws and other trespasses on personal liberty which all stand at times of national crisis.

The speaker was asked what he thought of a government that puts to death seventeen men by shooting them down in a row. Mr. Gannett, who was a pacifist member of the Friends' Unit in France during the war, had no justification for such methods, but again insisted on judgment in the light of Russia's own bloody past under Ivan the Terrible and the Czar's chopping block, and in the light of methods used in neighbor countries. For instance, in Jugo-Slavia, a country we recognize and to which we lend money, there is a law by which a son or cousin of a criminal may be punished if the criminal cannot be found.

Finally the question of confiscatory taxation of the peasants was raised as explanation of the present condition of Russia. The speaker cited our own war-time taxes and the British war-time income tax, considered confiscatory by many.

Summing up, Mr. Gannett said the Russian government is not the finest government in the world, but it probably has more fine spots than most as well as more brutal spots. We do not get two sides in our papers. We may admire Lloyd-George in spite of the Blacks and Tans in Ireland and in spite of the fact that the British government shut up a hundred Indians in an unventilated car and most were dead by morning. We do not base our judgment of our own country on the Salsedo incident or the neglect of Negro lynchings. So with Lenin and Trotsky it is only fair to compare their sincerity and sense of right with our own insincere politicians, and to remember Russian history, the background of the revolution. E. C. M.

A First-day School Play

On the 27th of January, Baltimore First-day School gave a play which was easily arranged, yet which gave the audience a great deal of amusement. This play, called "Professor Makeoverski's Magic Box," could be easily given by any First-day School as a part or the whole of an evening's entertainment.

All the equipment needed is a stage, on which is placed a large black box made of screens covered with cloth, a table on which are placed bottles of many colored liquids, a vacuum cleaner or other noise producer and home-made costumes. The Professor announces to the audience that he can change anyone into whatever type of personality they desire—for a slight fee—and various members appear who wish to change their mode of life. A little old lady who has no ear for music appears and wishes to become a fine pianist; she is introduced into the box from whence issue strange noises (the vacuum cleaner and boxes full of stones producing the desired effect), and appears again as another person who steps to the piano and plays a beautiful piece. Then a farmer appears who desires to become an artist, his wish is gratified and an artistic appearing gentleman appears and draws some sketches on the blackboard. So in turn appear the "would-be vamp" and the real thing; the spinster who desires a mate; the darky who would be a white man; and finally the young lady who desires to become a man. Here the Professor balks, but the young lady takes matters into her own hands, mixes up the liquids in utter disregard of the consequence, drinks them down and rushes into the machine before the distracted Professor can prevent her. He tries to stop the catastrophe by turning the machine backwards, but in vain, for with a huge explosion the machine is blown to bits as the curtain falls. Such a play as this gives room for a great variety of talent, takes little rehearsal, and is always well received by the audience.

BLISS FORBUSH.

Friends' Reading Contest

The American Friends' Literature Council, desiring to promote interest in the best Quaker and other religious literature, has prepared two courses of reading and is making them the basis of two reading contests.

The first course is designed for "Young Friends in High School." Books to the value of ten, five and three dollars, respectively, will be given to the three young Friends who have read in the prescribed time, at least one volume under each of the six headings given in the course, and have prepared the best short papers giving an intelligent impression of each book read.

The second course is for "Friends Beyond High School." Books to the value of fifteen, ten and five dollars will be given to the three Friends who have read in the prescribed time, the best selection of books from the list furnished: the total number to be not less than six.

We regret that lack of space prevents us from publishing the two book lists in the INTELLIGENCER. They consist largely of standard Friends' works under the subjects of History, Biography, Stories of Friends, Peace, Poetry, Religion, Principles of Quakerism, Missions, Bible Study and Religious Education. Copies of the book lists may be obtaned upon request from the following committee: William B. Harvey, 304 Arch St., Philadelphia, Pa.; Clarence E. Pickett, 101 S. 8th St., Richmond, Ind.; J. Barnard Walton, 140 N. 15th St., Philadelphia, Pa.

Winners of the contests may select their own books, subject to the approval of the committee. All reports must be sent in to one of the members of the committee by Seventh month (July) 1st, 1922.

Service Committee Notes

One Hundred Bales of Clothing Sent to Europe

The storeroom of the American Friends' Service Committee sent its January shipment of clothing to Europe on the 30th, it being one of the largest shipments of the year. In all, 101 bales of clothing were sent, 48 being sent to Austria, 45 to Germany, and 8 were the gift of the college students of America to the college students of Europe, being sent out under the direction of the Y. M. C. A.

Clothing received within the next few weeks will reach Europe in time for use against the cold of the very severe weather of March. All kinds are needed: underwear, shoes, dresses and suits. All clothing which is not specifically marked for some country will be sent to Austria; as the greatest need at the present time is in the unhappy city of Vienna. Will you not send your clothing immediately? Send it care of the American Friends' Service Committee Storeroom, Fifteenth and Cherry Streets, Philadelphia, Pennsylvania.

Poland Needs Seeds

The Friends' Mission in Poland reports that ten thousand dollars is needed immediately for field seeds for this spring and two thousand dollars would provide vegetable seeds for the Baranowice and Pinsk districts. These are the districts where the Friends will be doing their intensive work this spring.

This condition is caused mostly through the returning refugees, coming into Poland at the rate of 2,000 a day, reaching their homes in a destitute condition. By contributing to this need you are contributing to the permanent stabilizing of a nation, and this means the bringing a wild, hopeless existence into the deep peace of security, and hope.

Latest Cables From Russia

January 26.

Mary Pattison died Moscow of typhus. Frank Watts and Elizabeth Colville ill with typhus. Nurse sent to them.

January 22.

Kenworthy sitting up two hours daily. Opened workshop for the remodelling of children's clothes. The number of starving children is increased by the death or desertion of parents. Grave diggers in Soronchinskeye too weak to dig graves.

January 28.

Kenworthy hopes to begin work again within a month. There is a need of tractors for spring plowing. People in the villages of our district are dying at the rate of one per cent. daily. They are too sick to walk and the dead lie around unburied.

Friendly News Notes

M. M. writes from Woolman School that the interesting routine of classwork was suspended in order that the students might attend Concord Quarterly Meeting, held for the first time at Swarthmore, Pa. E. Maria Bishop and William Littleboy who were attending Quarterly Meeting visited the school.

The younger members of the student body attended a conference at the home of Chester and Abby Hall Roberts. Several students attended the Lincoln Day meeting, at which the Negro Club Women of Philadelphia provided a remarkable program. The speakers stressed the point that the colored people should use wisely all opportunities now offered them, with the hope that conditions which are unfavorable now may by degrees cease to prevent the best possible development of each individual.

Phebe Gardner, whose work as secretary here was ended by her going to Earlham College, is greatly missed.

Frederick J. Libby will spend a week, Second month 9th to 16th, among the Friends' Meetings near Philadelphia. A joint meeting of both branches of Friends will be held each day. The idea is to lay plans for the next step ahead in the light of what has been accomplished at the Washington Conference. The meetings as far as arranged will be as follows:

9th, Moorestown, N. J.; 10th, to be arranged; 11th, Media, Pa., Tea Meeting; 12th, Newtown or Edgewood, Pa.; 13th, Germantown, Y. M. C. A. Building; 14th, Lansdowne, Pa.; 15th, Wilmington, Del., Tenth and Harrison Streets Meeting House; 16th, West Chester, Pa.; North High Street Meeting House.

All the meetings will be held in the evening with the exception of the one on First-day, which is in the afternoon.

William L. Jenkins, Swarthmore '10, returned to his alma mater on February 3rd and made an interesting address to the students in Collection on his experiences as United States Consul, and the appeal to young men to enter this form of service for their country.

In his seven years of service William L. Jenkins has been stationed at several posts, in England, Russia, and the Madeira Islands. He has had the experience of several evacuations. He is soon to start for his new post at Nirobe, Colony of Kenya, formerly British East Africa.

The January number of "Outward Bound," the monthly magazine with a world outlook, contains an illustrated article by Hamilton Fyfe, literary editor of the "Daily Mail," on Friends' work in Europe. Its value lies—as its title, "To Peace Through Goodwill" shows—not merely in the publicity given to the need for relief but in its appreciation that the real cure for the world's needs is the deed done and the life lived, out of love. Mr. Fyfe concludes his article as follows: "One of the truest sayings about the cause of war lies to the credit of the novelist, Compton Mackenzie. 'The war,' he wrote, 'was in all our hearts.' And the day when war is no longer a peril, when disarmament is willing and real, will be the day when in all our hearts there is peace, the peace which is the outcome of goodwill."

A letter from a member of Swarthmore, Pa., Monthly Meeting contains the following interesting note: "At monthly meeting last week a committee was appointed to get information about the West Virginia situation, and the whole coal situation, with a view to seeing whether we Friends can't find a way to bring mutual understanding and avoid the impending coal strike, which will bring misery to so many."

Commenting on an appeal for aid received from A. W. Nicholson, President of Bettis Academy, Joel Borton, President of the Pennsylvania Abolition Society, writes:

"I am sure this is a very worthy object and a school in which our friend Henry W. Wilbur was deeply interested and wished very much to see succeed; he and A. W. Nicholson were good friends.

"I would like very much to make an appeal in behalf of Bettis Academy and its president to all our good Friends who can make even a small contribution and those who can afford to send larger amounts do so at once by sending a check to A. W. Nicholson, Trenton, S. C., care Bettis Academy."

The Executive Secretary of the Philadelphia Young Friends' Movement is sending out a special letter to members, urging them to enter the reading contests which are being instituted by the American Friends' Literature Council. The letter says in part:

"'American young Friends are not well read!' We heard this statement again and again from Friends when they returned from the London Conference. Is it true? Are we allowing ourselves to drift along from day to day, busy with each day's work without taking time to educate ourselves through reading worth while books? In these days when thoughtful and well informed young people are needed, Friends should be above, not below the mark!"

Prof. J. Chauncey Shortlidge, Principal of the Maplewood School for Boys, Darling, Delaware county, Pa., presented a portrait of his father, Prof. Joseph Shortlidge, A.M., Yale, to the Pennsylvania State College on Second month 9th. Prof. Joseph Shortlidge was formerly president of this college and his son will present the portrait by invitation of the President and Faculty of the institution.

He will also deliver on this occasion an address, "Two Presidents of Penn State." The first president of Penn State was Dr. Evan Pugh, a first cousin of Prof. Joseph Shortlidge. Both of these presidents were born and raised on farms in Chester county and later attained eminence as educators. They were both members of the Society of Friends. Dr. Evan Pugh was also a noted chemist and gained a wide reputation because of his researches in agricultural chemistry.

CONCORD QUARTERLY MEETING

The motive power of religion and the expression of our spirit in definite service were interwoven at Concord Quarterly Meeting on the 31st. It was the first session to be held in Swarthmore. William Littleboy and E. Maria Bishop, from England, and Edgar Haight, from Canada, were among the visitors.

William Littleboy's message was a challenge to Friends not to be satisfied with the second best. The condition of the Delaware county jail at Media was called to the attention of the meeting with the fact that it is overcrowded, unsanitary, and some of the prison population are compelled to be kept in idleness. A recent investigation placed this as the next to the worst county jail in the state. The Quarterly Meeting appointed the following committee to investigate the conditions at the jail and report what may be done: Julia Kent, Lydia G. Hawkins, William R. Fogg, Louis N. Robinson and Frances Broomall.

To be free, a ministry—it was said—must be given a natural expression, not cast in antiquated language or tone, but a straightforward message, depending for its authority on its truth.

Realizing that not all who are in prison for opposition to war have yet been released, the following petition was adopted by the Quarterly Meeting and sent to President Harding:

"The traditions of our Society are strongly for free speech. Many Friends have suffered imprisonment for testifying for unpopular causes. We feel deeply that only evil can come from suppressing such freedom in a democracy.

"We therefore earnestly petition President Harding to release all prisoners held for the expression of opinion or for membership in organizations expressing opinions."

Items From Everywhere

Our friend Henry Ferris sends us a copy of the 'Weekly Washington Letter" which is being published in the *Army and Navy Journal*, and which is of special interest as an indication of what the friends of big armaments are saying about the disarmament movement. Plainly the writer is on the defensive, being reduced to the rather pathetic turn of calling names. Commenting on the program of the National Council for the Reduction of Armaments, he says: "There is not a suggestion in it that the welfare and the defenses of the nation should be considered. In conclusion, it is announced that 'the goal which the council sets for itself is the reduction not only of navies but of land armaments to a police force.' "(!)

Asked, a few weeks before his death, for comment on "The Church and a Warless World," a pamphlet recently issued by the Federal Council of Churches, the late Viscount James Bryce said: "I do not know that I can offer any suggestions to you, unless perhaps that further illustrations might be given of the tendency which huge armies and fleets exert towards making the idea of war so familiar that nations yield more readily to the temptation to let themselves be drawn into war. The most effective factor in getting rid of armaments would be to substitute for national hatred and rivalries a sense of the brotherhood of nations such as our Lord inculcated upon individual men. The idea that 'we are all members one of another' needs to be applied to *peoples*."

On the Philadelphia Branch of the National Prison Comfort Club's list of political prisoners whose birthdays fall during the current month are: 4th, Charles Bennett and John Martin; 13th, Vincent Santelli; 14th, G. J. Bourg; 15th, Peter Green; 17th, F. G. Gallagher; 18th, Louis Parenti; 22nd, Charles H. MacKinnon; 27th, John Grave. The address of all these men is: P. O. Box 7, Leavenworth, Kansas.

Speaking in the National House of Representatives on January 18th, Representative Meyer London, of New York, said: "I deny to the State the right to inflict capital punishment. I deny that society as a whole is justified in taking human life. I certainly deny that right to the individual or to the mob. Every manifestation of passion, hatred, or violence which results in the destruction of human life is abhorrent to every civilized man. Since the war particularly, since human life has become cheap, and since young men of refinement have been taught to bayonet and kill their fellow men, mob violence has spread throughout the country and mob action has become a national curse."

THE OPEN FORUM

This column is intended to afford free expression of opinion by readers on questions of interest. The INTELLIGENCER *is not responsible for any such opinions. Letters must be brief, and the editor reserves the right to omit parts if necessary to save space.*

AN OPEN LETTER TO A FRIEND

Dear Friend:

For, though my criticism of thy conduct may appear to bear the harsher meaning of that unfortunate word, we are, and will remain, friends. I appeal to all that is in thee against a part that is in thee; for the whole is greater than any part, and ought not be subjugated to it. So appealed one, long before the age of prohibition, from Philip drunk to Philip sober.

From the time of the Paris Conference to the present day thee has, as occasion offered, or as thee could make occasion, spoken and written against the League of Nations there established. Thee is not ignorant of history; in all records of human endeavor has thee found any which had *ab initio* 100 per cent. efficiency? Can thee not therefore now cease to use the phrases, alike objectionable to the heart and the intelligence, which thee has hitherto so frequently applied to that Conference, its leaders, and its document?

I feel confident that solid reflection will show it unnecessary longer to call it a 'wicked League," or longer to speak of the leaders of the larger nations, who necessarily were the leaders at Paris, as "wicked old men." An elimination of other like phrases—a change of thy entire attitude of mind—may occur if thee restudies, in candid sincerity, the whole matter. It is not in thy real nature to write bitterly or to judge harshly. Thee has in the past shown mental poise and considerate thought.

Therefore I ask thee, with all that is in thee, to sit in judgment on a less amiable part that now shows in thee.

And, whether thee succeeds in this or not, I am

Thy friend,

JOHN COX, JR.

"THE VISION OF JOSEPH HOAGE."

To the Editor:

I wonder if any of the older Friends remember "The Vision of Joseph Hoage." I think Joseph Hoage was a Friend. I was nine years old at the beginning of the civil war. We had then had the little pamphlet in the house for some time. My grandmother kept it in an old Bible, and we children used to read it with awe. As I think of it, it began, "I, Joseph Hoage, was handing in a field (I think he was plowing) when a voice said to me that there was going to be a war between the north and the south and the slaves freed." Then in after years, I think that property was to be taken from Friends, or they were to be imprisoned, and we children wondered if it was to be a religious war that would imprison Friends as of old.

I did not see the paper again; I think, after I was twelve, and do not know what became of it. Since the world war and the Friends were imprisoned, it came back to me, but the latter part imperfectly. If any one has the "Vision," I would be glad if they would send it to the FRIENDS' INTELLIGENCER.

Plainfield, N. J. MARY CLIFTON WHITALL.

BIRTHS.

MOORE—On First month 19th, in Coatesville, Pa., to Dr. Lawrence C. and Helen Paschall Moore, of Avondale, Pa., a son, named Hamilton Dent Moore.

DEATHS.

BROWNING—Suddenly, en route to Poughkeepsie, near his country home, "Browning Lodge," on Twelfth month 29th, 1921, James C. Browning, in his 76th year. He was a life-long member of the Society of Friends, and treasurer of Creek Executive Meeting for nearly twenty years, maintaining interest in Nine Partners Half-Yearly Meeting, and was always present at New York Yearly Meeting and Friends' General Conference when possible. At his funeral Rev. James Edge, of Pleasant Plains Presbyterian church, spoke of his integrity and the high ideals of life to which he strove to live up. Interment was in the family plot in Poughkeepsie Rural cemetery.

He enjoyed the liberality of other denominations and was an enrolled member of The Brotherhood of Presbyterians of Albany, his winter home, and interested in affairs of the Legislature as well as those of his home town of Clinton. He was a member of the Dutchess County Historical Society and spent much time at the State Educational Building, in historical research. He leaves to mourn his loss a wife, Caroline Rider, and three brothers, Charles P., of Salt Point; Theron M. and William J. Browning, of Hyde Park, and two nieces, Eunice M., of Hyde Park, and Mildred Browning of White Plains, N. Y. Many friends will remember the hospitality of his former home at Salt Point where all received a hearty welcome, and he will be greatly missed by a large circle of relatives and friends.

"Alone unto our Father's will
One thought hath reconciled—
That he whose love exceedeth ours
Hath taken home his child."

M. B. B.

ENGLE—At Haddonfield, N. J., on Second month 3d, Margaret T. Taylor Engle, widow of Joseph Engle, in her 79th year.

HAINES—Suddenly, at Medford, N. J., First month 30th, George Stanley Haines, aged 22.

HAINES—At Moorestown, N. J., First month 31st, David S., husband of Hannah H. Haines, in his 61st year.

HARRY—At Norristown, Pa., First month 29th, John Wood Harry.

In Memory—At Gwynedd Monthly Meeting, held on the 4th inst., and at the Meeting for Worship held in Norristown on the 5th, there were many beautiful tributes paid to the worth of this true Friend. He exemplified this thought which Longfellow expressed:

"As one lamp lights another nor grows less,
So nobleness enkindleth nobleness."

HAUXHURST—On First month 16th, Elizabeth Hauxhurst, in her 92nd year. Funeral at Sea Cliff, N. Y. Interment at Manhasset.

NEWLIN—At his home near Elam, Delaware County, Pa., on First month 8th, in the 71st year of his age, Thomas H. Newlin, a birthright member of Concord Monthly Meeting, passed into the higher life. He left a wife, son and widowed daughter to mourn a devoted husband and father. After appropriate services, he was laid to rest close by in Elam cemetery. He was the only son of John and Beulah Newlin, Elders of Concord Monthly Meeting.

RICHARDSON—At Byberry, Pa., on First month 3rd, Hannah Richardson.

ROBERTS—At Alexandria, Va., Second month 1st, Dr. George Roberts, son of the late Spencer and Louisa J. Roberts, aged 75 years.

THOMPSON—At Wilmington, Delaware, on Second month 5th, Dr. Hannah M. Thompson, in her 77th year.

COMING EVENTS

SECOND MONTH

11th—Frederick J. Libby will speak on Disarmament at a Tea meeting, at Media, Pa., in the Orthodox Meeting House, under the auspices of both branches of Friends.

12th—E. Maria Bishop expects to attend meeting at Coatesville, Pa., at 10 a. m.

12th—Conference Class at 15th and Race Streets, Philadelphia, at close of meeting for worship, at 11.40 a. m. Leader—Charles H. Harrison. Subject—The Individual and Social Righteousness.

12th—Joel Borton expects to attend meeting for worship at 35th and Lancaster Avenue, West Philadelphia.

12th—Frederick J. Libby will attend the meeting for worship at Fallsington, Pa., at 10 a. m., in the Orthodox Meeting House.

12th—Disarmament meeting to be addressed by Frederick J. Libby will be held in the afternoon at the Edgewood Community House (or in the Newtown Friends' Meeting House).

12th—Preparative Meetings in New York and Brooklyn, after the Meeting for Worship.

13th—New York Monthly Meeting, at Schermerhorn Street, Brooklyn, at 7.30 p. m. Supper will be served at 6 o'clock. The Meeting for Ministry and Counsel will meet at 5.

13th—At the regular meeting of the Philadelphia Young Friends' Association, held at 15th and Cherry Streets, Elbert Russell will give the last of his lectures on the Four Gospels. 8 p. m.

13th—Miami Quarterly Meeting, at Waynesville, Ohio.

13th—Frederick J. Libby will address a public meeting on the next step in disarmament in the Y. M. C. A., Germantown, Pa., at 8 p. m.

14th—Frederick J. Libby will address a meeting on Disarmament, at Lansdowne, Pa., in the evening.

15th—Frederick J. Libby will attend the joint mid-week meeting for worship, at 10th and Harrison Streets, Wilmington, Del., and afterwards will give an address on future disarmament work.

15th—Monthly Meeting of Friends of Philadelphia, 15th and Race Streets, 7.30 p. m. Supper will be served by the Committee on Best Interests in the Lunch Room of the Friends' Central School Building, 15th and Race Streets, at 6 p. m.

16th—Green Street Monthly Meeting of Friends of Philadelphia, School House Lane, Germantown, 7.30 p. m.

16th—Disarmament meeting at North High Street Friends' Meeting House, West Chester, Pa. Address by Frederick J. Libby in the evening.

18th—Short Creek Quarterly Meeting, at Emerson, Ohio.

18th—Pelham Half-Yearly Meeting, at Coldstream, Ontario.

18th and 19th—Pilgrimage under the care of the Young Friends' Movement at Girard Avenue Meeting, Philadelphia.

NOTICE—Supper will be served by the Committee on Best Interests before Monthly Meeting, at Fifteenth and Race Streets, Philadelphia, on Second month 15th, in Friends' Central School Lunch Room, at 6 o'clock. Tickets 65 cents. Please purchase tickets before Second month 13th, 1922. ANNA W. CLOUD, 140 North 15th Street.

CORRECTION—In William J. MacWatter's article in the Open Forum in regard to "The Friendly Hand Society," he inadvertently wrote "a minimum sum of ten dollars per month is fixed as registering one a member of "The Friendly Hand." He wishes to state that the minimum is *ten cents*, not ten dollars.

American Friends' Service Committee

WILBUR K. THOMAS, EX. SEC.

20 S. 12th St. Philadelphia

CASH CONTRIBUTIONS

Week Ending January 30, 1922

Five Years Meetings	$713.13
Other Meetings	
Green Street Monthly Meeting	5.00
Little Britain Monthly Meeting	56.00
Lafayette Ave. Friends' Meeting, Brooklyn	74.00
Sturgeon Bay Monthly Meeting, Wisconsin	30.80
Jericho Monthly Meeting	177.00
Jericho Friends' First Day School	10.00
Pasadena Monthly Meeting	125.00
Friends of Lincoln Meeting	57.00
Japan Friends' Mission	75.00
New Garden Prep. Mtg.	105.00
Oxford Monthly Meeting	100.00
Deer Creek Monthly Meeting	12.00
Kennett Monthly Meeting	10.00
Mullica Hill Friends' Meeting	22.00
Contributions for General	1,652.47
For Germany	6,741.92
For Austria	3,137.25
For Poland	461.35
For China	1.75
For Syria	2.00
For Russia	19,415.86
For Russian Overhead	1,369.22
For German Overhead	9.41
For Clothing	12.00
Refunds	2.28
	$34,377.41

CONTRIBUTIONS RECEIVED, DURING JANUARY, FROM MEMBERS OF PHILADELPHIA YEARLY MEETING OF FRIENDS, HELD AT FIFTEENTH AND RACE STREETS

Greenwich Mo. by Louisa Powell	$100.00
Swarthmore Mo. by E. J. Durnall	30.00
Makefield Mo. by H. G. Miller, Russian Relief	25.52
Philadelphia by Charles M. Biddle	1,261.00
Chester Prep. by Anna B. Griscom	10.00
Richland Mo. by Eleanor Foulke	2.00
Orange Grove Mo. by E. D. Hopkins, Russian Rel.	52.50
Abington Mo. by Davis L. Lewis	50.00
Middletown Prep. by Frances W. Broomall	40.00
Millville Friends by Bernice Eves	14.00
Swarthmore Mo. by E. J. Durnall	51.00
Wilmington Mo. by S. H. Stradley	910.00
Richland Mo. by E. Irene Meredith	12.00
Greenwich Mo. by Louisa Powell	100.00
Newtown (Del. Co.) Prep. by M. J. Dutton	25.00
Middletown Mo. by Henry C. Pickering	90.50
Darby Mo. by W. R. White	60.00
	$2,833.52

Shipments received during week ending January 28, 1922: 136 boxes and packages received; 4 for German Relief; 5 anonymous.

REGULAR MEETINGS.

OAKLAND, CALIF.—A FRIENDS' MEETING is held every First-day at 11 A. M., in the Extension Room, Y. W. C. A. Building, Webster Street, above 14th. Visiting Friends always welcome.

FRIENDS' MEETING IN PASADENA, California—Orange Grove Monthly Meeting of Friends, 520 East Orange Grove Avenue, Pasadena, California. Meeting for worship, First-day, 11 A. M. Monthly Meeting, the second First-day of each month, at 1.45 P. M.

WANTED

WORKING HOUSEKEEPER—EXPERIENCED woman desires position in Christian home. Small household and no children; city preferred. Will cook. Highest recommendation from present employer. Open to engagement after March 10th. Address J-54, Friends' Intelligencer.

WANTED—CARE OF AN ELDERLY lady or convalescent, by an experienced nurse. City or suburbs. Best of reference. Address E. M., Friends' Intelligencer.

AS CARETAKER OF HOME—REFINED widow of ability desires position as housekeeper for widower, or mother of family. Country preferred. $12 weekly. Address T. 61, Friends' Intelligencer.

POSITION WANTED—BY CAPABLE mother's helper. Thoroughly experienced in the care of children from two to twelve years of age. Excellent references. Address B. 60, Friends' Intelligencer.

WANTED—MOTHER'S HELPER, IN Germantown, to help with care of infant and six-year-old boy. Address A. 62, Friends' Intelligencer.

WANTED—BY A CAPABLE AND DEPENDABLE colored woman, general housework (except washing), in a Friend's family. Has excellent references. Address Cecelia Boush, 74 West Duval street, Germantown, Pa.

POSITION WANTED—BY BOY, 17 (Friend), in wholesale house. Has had some training. Willing to start at bottom with chance for advancement. Address F. 63, Friends' Intelligencer.

FOR SALE OR RENT

FOR RENT—APRIL TO OCTOBER, Nine-room house with sleeping porch and garage, near river, at Riverton. Address Box 107, Riverton, N. J.

FOR SALE—41 ACRES OF LAND, five miles north of Wilmington, Del., on the Westchester pike, 14 acres of forest, one thousand feet of pike front. Price $10,000.00. H. C. Passmore, Wilmington, Del.

TRANSIENT ACCOMMODATIONS

WASHINGTON, D. C.—ROOMS FOR visitors. Near Station, Capitol, Library. Continuous hot water. Electricity. Garage. Mrs. L. L. Kendig, 120 C. Street, Northwest.

To the Lot Holders and others interested in Fairhill Burial Ground:

GREEN STREET Monthly Meeting has funds available for the encouragement of the practice of cremating the dead to be interred in Fairhill Burial Ground. We wish to bring this fact as prominently as possible to those who may be interested. We are prepared to undertake the expense of cremation in case any lot holder desires us to do so.

Those interested should communicate with William H. Gaskill, Treasurer of the Committee of Interments, Green Street Monthly Meeting, or any of the following members of the Committee.

William H. Gaskill, 3201 Arch St.
Samuel N. Longstreth, 1218 Chestnut St.
Charles F. Jenkins, 232 South Seventh St.
Stuart S. Graves, 3033 Germantown Ave.

ADVERTISING RATE in the FRIENDS' INTELLIGENCER, for Help Wanted, Positions Wanted, Rooms for Rent, Notices, and other classified advertisements without display, for each insertion, 2 cents per word, including name, initials and address. Answers may be sent to a box at the INTELLIGENCER office, if so directed.

For display advertising the rate is 10 cents per agate line, or $1.40 per column inch, each insertion. On ten or more insertions in a year from date of order, ten per cent. discount. Thus a four-inch single-column or two-inch double-column advertisement costs $5.60 each insertion, less ten per cent., or 5.04 net each time for ten or more insertions. Matter may be changed whenever desired, without extra charge.

Experience has proved the INTELLIGENCER to be a remarkably good advertising medium. All advertisements must "pass the censor!"

Address 140 N. 15th St., Philadelphia

The Friends'
Intelligencer

ESTABLISHED 1844 | SECOND MONTH 18, 1922 | VOLUME 79 NUMBER 7

Contents

EDITORIAL

GENERAL ARTICLES

AMONG OUR MEETINGS

NOTICE—Concise statements of the principles of the Religious Society of Friends and their application to the problems of every day living, including "The Spirit of Quakerism," by Elbert Russell; "Preparation for Life's Greatest Business," by Rufus M. Jones; and other articles by Henry W. Wilbur, Howard M. Jenkins, Elizabeth Lloyd, Jesse H. Holmes, O. Edward Janney, Edward B. Rawson, etc., to be had free on application to Friends' General Conference Advancement Committee, 140 North Fifteenth Street, Philadelphia, Pa.

ADVERTISING RATE in the FRIENDS' INTELLIGENCER, for Help Wanted, Positions Wanted, Rooms for Rent, Notices, and other classified advertisements without display, for each insertion, 2 cents per word, including name, initials and address. Answers may be sent to a box at the INTELLIGENCER office, if so directed.

For display advertising the rate is 10 cents per agate line, or $1.40 per column inch, each insertion. On ten or more insertions in a year from date of order, ten per cent. discount. Thus a four-inch single-column or two-inch double-column advertisement costs $5.60 each insertion, less ten per cent., or 5.04 net each time for ten or more insertions. Matter may be changed whenever desired, without extra charge.

Experience has proved the INTELLIGENCER to be a remarkably good advertising medium. All advertisements must "pass the censor!"

Address 140 N. 15th St., Philadelphia

THE FRIENDS' INTELLIGENCER

Published weekly, 140 N. 15th Street, Philadelphia, Pa., by Friends' Intelligencer Association, Ltd.

WALTER H. ABELL, *Editor*
SUE C. YERKES, *Business Manager*

Editorial Board: Elizabeth Powell Bond, Thomas A. Jenkins, J. Russell Smith, George A. Walton.

Board of Managers: Edward Cornell, Alice Hall Paxson, Paul M. Pearson, Annie Hillborn, Elwood Hollingshead, William C. Biddle, Charles F. Jenkins, Edith M. Winder, Frances M. White.

Officers of Intelligencer Associates: Ellwood Burdsall, Chairman; Bertha L. Broomell, Secretary; Herbert P. Worth, Treasurer.

Subscription rates: United States, Mexico, Cuba and Panama, $2.50 per year. Canada and other foreign countries, $3.00 per year. Checks should be made payable to Friends' Intelligencer Association, Ltd.

Entered as Second Class Matter at Philadelphia Post Office.

FUN

The Definition

The Teacher—"What is a guitar?"

Little Willie—"A disease of the head."

Johnnie Jones—"No, it ain't either. It's a lump growing on the throat."—Reformed Christian Messenger.

NO OFFENSE MEANT

"Why you call my boy a poor nut?" queried an indignant mother, who confronted the dietitian of a New Jersey charities association the other morning at her office door. And the latter has not yet found a way of convincing Mrs. Caruso that "poor nut" on the face of Angelo's card stands for poor nutrition.—*Survey.*

The Friends' Intelligencer

The religion of Friends is based on faith in the "INWARD LIGHT," or direct revelation of God's spirit and will in every seeking soul.

The INTELLIGENCER is interested in all who bear the name of Friends in every part of the world, and aims to promote love, unity and intercourse among all branches and with all religious societies.

ESTABLISHED 1844 | PHILADELPHIA, SECOND MONTH 18, 1922 | VOLUME 79 NUMBER 7

The End of the Beginning

The conclusion of the Washington Conference marks the end of the beginning. The nations have completed their introduction to humanity's great edict of emancipation from war, and have reached the point at which they—or better, we—must begin the composition of the "subject proper," the long hard labor of attainment which lies between the end of the beginning and the beginning of the end.

Opinions vary widely as to what the Conference has actually accomplished. Extremists hail its outcome, on the one hand, as in itself the inauguration of a warless era; on the other, as a mask to the real deep-seated imperialism of the great powers, our own included. Critics of the latter shade, feel that it has left the real roots of war untouched, that it has done nothing which can prevent either the "bursting" of "the next war," or its annihilating destructiveness if it comes.

The greater portion of those commentators who have carefully studied both the Conference and the international situation which forms its background, feel that there are elements of truth in both these points of view. As an excellent summary of this middle estimate, we need scarcely recommend William I. Hull's reports numbers thirteen and fourteen, the final one of which appears in this issue.

The upshot of the matter seems to us to lie in the oft-repeated statement that the Conference has made a good beginning but *only* a beginning, that equally sweeping advances must continue if the dream of world peace is to become a reality, and that the way lies open for such advances *as fast as we can generate the energy to impel them.* The last point is the most important. The Conference went as far as it did—indeed it was called at all—only because the pressure of popular opinion demanded it. Further advances can only come in the same manner. They can come only in proportion as we are *more* interested in international problems, *more* determined to work against war, *more* earnest in following our religious concern for peace, than we have ever been before.

Disarmament has claimed such an overwhelming share of the world's interest for several months that even its staunchest friends are prone to grow somewhat tired of the subject. But to relax our efforts now is to lose everything. Of peace-workers-for-the-moment, there will be more than enough who will withdraw their energies from the cause now that the great wave of interest stimulated by the Conference begins to subside. To every soul which feels the full meaning of the peace crusade as an issue involving the life or death of the race, as a great social and religious concern, comes the call for renewed allegiance.

The following summary of the "immediate program" of the National Council for the Reduction of Armaments indicates several important steps towards the prosecution of which all friends of peace should bend their efforts at once:

First, the immediate ratification of the Conference treaties; second, a drastic reduction in the army and navy appropriation bills to a peace basis; third, the passage of a measure removing the manufacture of munitions from private control; fourth, development of the international organization of peace groups already begun with England and Japan; fifth, an intensive organization of this country through local and state councils; sixth, an educational campaign in connection with colleges, schools, libraries and through a national speakers' bureau; seventh, a legislation committee in Washington which will study all measures before Congress from the point of view of their influence for or against war.

Advances may be made along these lines first of all by giving vigorous support to the National Council itself, through our constituent body, the Friends' Disarmament Council. The National Council has worked with great effect both before and during the Conference, and can work now with increasing effect as pressure from other sources relaxes. It appeals to all Friends, and to all Friends' meetings for their unqualified co-operation—and deserves it.

Individual relations likewise offer all us of widespread spheres of influence. We should bring the force of our convictions to bear upon the Senate in behalf of a speedy ratification of the Conference treaties, and upon Congress as a whole in the interest of a drastic reduction of military appropriations. All of us, likewise, can do educational work. We all have friends and acquaintances who do not see the light against war. Why not make it one of our concerns to talk with as many of these as possible, expressing our conviction of the seriousness of the issue, and endeavoring to win them to our point of view?

Realizing that, whether we consider the first step taken by the Conference to have been great or small, the path now lies open for further steps, and that such steps depend upon us for their attainment, shall we not make our principle reaction to the Conference a determination to renew our dedication to the cause? In proportion as we do so, will the chances be increased that the "beginning of the end," when it comes, will be the dawn of an era in which peace is finally assured, instead of the downfall of civilization.

The Call of Today

In a recent book called "The Galilean," by Nathaniel Micklem, now lecturing at Woodbrooke, England, we find these illuminating sentences:

"That which we need for salvation, is that we should be open to the personal influence of the living Christ revealing to us livingly the will of God, and coming to us in the personal way of 'friendship.'" "Jesus saves us to God and His will, by awakening the soul to that disposition towards God and one's fellows which he had himself. He gives man not primarily a mystical experience or a new theology or orthodoxy, but his own self in friendship and in love." "Jesus is our Savior because he is our Friend."

Is this not a clear modern statement of the experience of George Fox which he describes in the journal: "When all my hopes in them (the priests and preachers) and in all men were gone, so that I had nothing outwardly to help me, nor could I tell what to do, then, oh, then, I heard a Voice which said: 'There is one, even Christ Jesus, that can speak to thy condition,' and when I heard it, my heart did leap for joy." This is undoubtedly the experience in the soul of the founder that gave rise to the Society of Friends. Has each one of us, who calls himself a Friend, had a similar experience? Or are we claiming membership on the basis of somebody else's experience? Are we Friends because we think it is a beautiful thing to be a Friend or because our inner experience tells us of the friendship of God in Christ?

It seems to the writer that the history of the Society of Friends in America, during the last one hundred years is, bluntly speaking, something like this: Because of the effect of the prejudice lingering after the Separation the so-called Orthodox body has emphasized the Bible to the neglect of the soul experience known as the "Inner Light," and that the so-called Hicksite body, has emphasized the Inner Light to the neglect of the Bible. This is the most deplorable result of the Separation. The neglect of the Inner Light leads to the expression of faith in stereotyped phrases, and reliance upon outward authority, the neglect of the Bible leads to a vague knowledge of the character of God revealed in Christ and to a lack of appreciation of his friendship. Combine the two and the original vitalizing power of the Quaker experience is present. The true Friend spreads his Gospel, as the "First Publishers of Truth" spread it—because it has so set him on fire that he *cannot help* spreading it. It shines out of his countenance. It illumines his walk with men. It makes the uninitiated stand in wonder and longing.

This is the food for which the multitude waits. Shall we send them away because we have only the few loaves and fishes? Nay, rather, with compassion, let us share what we have. It will increase in the sharing, and they shall be fed.

How shall we ourselves come to know this dynamic power of the friendship of Christ? Surely by cultivating it, through much more frequent reading of the story of his life and the working out of his ideals by his first little group of followers; by thinking out the application of these ideals to our own life; and by communing with him in the quiet garden of our souls. There we may bring to him all the hard problems of our lives, the disappointed hopes, the realization of our sins, our discouragements, and our joys. All these belong to him, as our closest friend. Have we a right to keep them from him? Is not his deep love for us grieved by our indifference to him, our misunderstanding of the transforming power of his love? What to us is darkness, to him is day.

Since the world is hungry, hungrier than ever before, for the kind of friendship which is inspired by his personality, will we not come to him in simple trust, leaving all the old intellectual perplexities behind, and ask him to teach us how to reveal his love to those who hunger and thirst for friendship? We can do it if we will, busy as we are. How trivial is some of our "precious" work, compared with the enlarging of the Kingdom of Christ! His power spurs us on! He has won us and we are his. Henceforth the roughness of the way has disappeared. Our eyes are on the goal of the Kingdom of Heaven on earth and he is our guide. Life is at last a unity of purpose and endeavor. No longer will we look back upon our dead past, mourning over our failures and mistakes. He has transformed them into stepping stones to success. The future is ours, "and we are Christ's and Christ is God's." Do we not hear his voice: "Feed my sheep!" "Feed my lambs!"

February 3rd, 1922. E. M. W.

The Washington Conference

XIV

By William I. Hull

The appraisement of the Washington Conference may well begin with the fact that it was held at all. After America's rejection of the League of Nations, there was grave danger lest our country should hold entirely aloof from the efforts of the nations of the Old World to co-operate in the alleviation of the miseries of the last war and the prevention of the next one. The rightly dreaded isolation might well have been accompanied by an excessive nationalism expressed in the building up of armaments which no other nation or combination of nations could have excelled or equalled, but which would have supplied them with an incentive to do their utmost in that direction.

The holding of the Conference, therefore, has enabled America to express her belief in genuine internationalism and to lead her sister-nations upon a path which they appeared to be incapable of pursuing without her. This path has for its goal the prevention of war by the cessation of armament and the exclusive resort to peaceful methods of settling international disputes without the sanction of military force or economic coercion.

The fundamental lesson has been learned that competitive increase of armament is not "insurance against war," but on the contrary a powerful, perhaps an irresistible, incitement to it. Hence the drastic reduction in naval armament and the acceptance of a fixed ratio of naval strength on the part of the five chief naval powers have a pacifist, as well as an economic significance. An immense expenditure of public revenue will be diverted from the production and maintenance of means of destruction to the satisfaction of genuine social needs; or, the burden of oppressive taxation will be lightened, and the people will expend their own money in their own way. But far beyond this economic boon, the scrapping of sixty-eight dreadnoughts, the cessation of competitive building of others and the ten years' naval holiday will remove a powerful incitement to distrust, hostility and war, and will enable men's minds to turn away from the field of Mars to the temple of Justice.

The various other limitations on capital and auxiliary ships and on the size of their guns, on aircraft carriers and on submarine warfare, together with the prohibition of chemical warfare, should aid greatly both to stamp war and preparation for war as wicked, and impel men to beat many more of their swords into plowshares and to learn war no more. At long, long last the great powers of the earth have turned their faces in the right direction,—have entered on the path which leads to disarmament, and have taken a very real and important stride towards that goal. What a cloud of witnesses,—the saints and sages of the past, the sinful, suffering, sorrowing world of today,—are rejoicing over this step and striving onwards toward the next!

Meanwhile, the Conference has also endeavored to remove some of the grave causes of war connected with the Pacific and the Far East, and to provide for a peaceful settlement of such causes as may arise in the future. With China, Russia, and Japan, the United States, Great Britain, France and a score of other Western powers, bordering upon and vitally interested in the vast world of the Pacific, it is easy to see why the questions associated with it are of transcendant importance at the present stage of human development. How relatively insignificant now appear such European questions as the Rhine, the Ruhr, Silesia and the like! The prevention of naval offensives; the halting of fortifications and naval bases; the settlement of cable disputes in Yap and elsewhere; the restoration to China of large portions of Chinese lands and peoples, and the solemn promise in the presence of the world as witness to restore other portions; the progress made in the restoration of China's sovereignty over railways, post-offices, customs revenue, cables, mines, and courts of justice; the abrogation of the Anglo-Japanese Alliance; the surrender of "spheres of influence" and special interests in the world's greatest market and workshop, and the re-establishment of "the open door" on a far more solid basis than ever before; all these achievements of the Conference are fraught both with justice to long suffering China and with amity, equity and good-will among other nations. As with a flash of lightning and a summer shower, the whole international atmosphere overhanging the great ocean and its farther shore has been cleared and purified.

With so much at stake in the world of the Pacific and the Far East, and with human nature such as it is, we cannot expect that no more clouds will rise on the horizon. But to cope with new causes of misunderstanding by peaceful means, the Conference has provided for an international Board of Reference, for an international financial Consortium, and for another conference in case of urgent need.

All the agreements at Washington were arrived at without a show or threat of force, by unanimous consent among governments with equal vote; hence no ill-will has been engendered, no seeds of future war have been sown. The promise and pledges mutually exchanged in the presence of all the world (thanks to the unprecedented publicity given to the proceedings), are not to be enforced by military or economic coercion of any kind; but their fulfillment is consigned to the persuasive influences of enlightened self-interest, public opinion, national honor, and the collective conscience of mankind. Surely, with such sanctions as these, which are the agencies of God himself, the very stars in their courses will withstand any future Sisera who may attempt to ignore or defy them.

The Conference, despite its varied successes, was not without its failures. China was not completely restored; Russia's territorial integrity was pledged, but she was not recognized in the Conference either as a member of it or of the family of nations, or as vastly interested in the welfare of the Pacific and the Far East; land armaments were not reduced or limited; aerial warfare was not prohibited (although an international commission was provided for the curbing of it); submarines were scotched, but not killed; war itself was not outlawed.

The aftermath of the world war, with its clouds of imperialism, militarism and unreasoning fear, and the prevalent distrust of Bolshevism, held the Conference in thrall to that extent. President Harding, in his address at the close of the Conference, said: "It has been the fortune of this Conference to sit in a day far enough removed from war's bitterness, yet near enough to war's horrors, to gain the benefit of both the hatred of war and the yearning for peace." This is true; and it doubtless accounts partly for the successes of the Conference. On the other hand, it is partly responsible for the Conference's failures. It would be more just, perhaps, to speak of these as attempts, rather than as failures. For as men return to the sanity disturbed by the war; as they climb to higher levels of morality and religion; as they seek safety and prosperity by better means than mutual slaughter and preparations for "armageddons," these failures of yesterday and attempts of to-day will be converted into the achievements of to-morrow.

The Washington Conference, with its world-prominence and its unprecedented and unexpected successes, has bequeathed to us a great opportunity and a heavy responsibility. It demands a deep searching of our souls for the strength and wisdom requisite to the task of abolishing all preparations for war and war itself, and of substituting mutual concession and co-operative service among all nations. As I sit here in this last meeting of the Conference, witnessing the formal signing and sealing of the various treaties, resolutions and declarations adopted by it, my thoughts go out to the multitudes of men and women who can, if they will, make these documents no mere scraps of paper, but the living realities of human security, justice, prosperity and mutual service.

President Harding is now reading the last words of his address: "It is all so fine, so gratifying, so reassuring, so full of promise, that above the murmurings of a world sorrow, not yet silenced, above the groans which come of excessive burdens not yet lifted, but now to be lightened, above the discouragement of a world yet struggling to find itself after surpassing upheaval, there is the note of rejoicing, which is not alone ours or yours, or of all of us, but comes from the hearts of men of all the whole world."

Yes, thanks be to God, that is gloriously true. But with the note of rejoicing, we needs must hear the insistent note of duty and of opportunity for further fulfillment of God's will.

Washington, D. C., February 6, 1922.

The Queen of the Pillowed Throne

Dedicated to Sara Linton Ross

There lived a Queen;
Her rank was not proclaimed by pomp or wealth or jewels of intrinsic value rare,

Hers was a quiet life;
She counted not her coins, but happy years four score and five, and snow-white was her hair,

She had a throne;
'Twas not the kind where potentates and kings could boast their pow'r to sway a sceptered hand,

And yet, with regal strength
She lay upon her pillowed throne with dignity of spirit few could understand.

Her subjects came;
They paused for inspiration by her side and passed her message to the outer world:

That courage thus revealed
Gives proof of heroes in Life's daily battle quite as much as under flags unfurled.

Years are but naught
When one can live and reign as does this queen of patience, showing resignation's strength;

She shall not be displaced,
Her kingdom shall extend beyond this earth,—its boundaries are infinite in length.

ANNA ANDREWS THOMAS.

A Letter on the Christmas Spirit

The article which follows constitutes the first chapter of a book now being written by Elsie Hillsmith. It consists, word for word, of the utterances of a Jewish boy, now resident on the author's farm at South Danbury, N. H. Formerly "an idealistic child," this boy is now broken in body, mind and character by the conditions which he had to face, first in his native Russia, later as an immigrant to America.

We are publishing his words in the INTELLIGENCER *because his attitude, which is shared by millions of other workers the world over, is a fundamental fact with which the world has to deal, involving one of the biggest problems which spiritual leadership is at present called upon to solve.*

To what degree are this boy's charges justified? Have we, individually or corporately, shared in the "indifference" of which he speaks? Can we Friends lead the way toward any solution of this problem of the masses, which will avoid the disasters consequent to the armed revolution that they now regard as their only resort?

To my Friend.

Although you do not belong to the working class I am beginning to think you are honest and my friend. It is for this reason that I answer with frankness that question you put to me on December 25th, "Why not try today to have the Christmas Spirit?"

All your life you have been comfortable; you have had happy Christmas after happy Christmas; you have had a clean and beautiful home; you have received love and given it. Always you have been fed, warmed, clothed, and had the certainty that you had a place to sleep. No doubt that you have had grief, but it was a normal sorrow, given by life, not forced upon you by the greed of men. As you look back pleasant memories unroll themselves before you, so that even if you lost all now, the past would be a candle to light the Present and Future. To you, therefore, it should be easy to have the Christmas Spirit, not just upon one day, but the year round.

But have such as you the right to demand from me and my type—the Down and Outs—that we should feel Peace and Goodwill towards men? Are we not uneducated, wretched, without ambition, living in filthy dens in the slums, hungry, cold, because you are thoughtless? Can you, with justice, demand from us the high virtues you love, while you travel through life on our backs? While by your lack of *intelligence* you bear with a system which traffics in the necessaries of life? Your Jesus said "Let him that is without sin cast the first stone." Are any of your class without sin while such as I exist?

And what manner of man am I? A Russian Jew of 22, illiterate, without a trade, unhealthy, the eighth child in a poverty-stricken family. We were not poor through any fault of ours. We all worked, sometimes twelve, sometimes fourteen hours a day, at tailoring. We were illiterate because there was neither time nor opportunity for such children to be educated. Born in Russia, my only knowledge of Christmas was that it was a day of pogroms, which Jews spent in hiding, if possible, because the Christians celebrated it by crucifying the Jewish men or stabbing them, even dragging them behind galloping horses. Our women were raped, our children maimed or killed, our synagogues burned. Nor were the Jews the only ones to suffer. Christian peasants we saw beaten with the lash till they lay in a welter of blood, stripped of the little they possessed for some trivial, or imagined crime, sent to Siberia if they resented brutality towards wife and child. Does this provoke the Christmas Spirit in a child's mind, especially if for the rest of the year his empty belly aches for food, and his frozen hands and feet make day and night hideous to him? Can you who have never known such a life, realize what it means, or how it warps the brain, as well as the body, even breaking down all desire to make good? Those higher virtues you love—are they for us? No, you give us no chance to think of anything beyond our animal wants—you leave us neither outward nor inward peace.

Do not ask me to believe that England and America knew nothing of all our sufferings under the Tzar. *You did know.* But like the Pharisee you passed us by until the suffering masses, in their despair, rose and overthrew the Tzar and his immoral court. The Communists gave land to the peasant, fed and educated children, regardless of class or creed, ended pogroms, relieved the economic pressure which sent girls upon the streets, and taught the willing masses Peace and Goodwill towards men. They gave us life, but the capitalistic countries, fearing us clear-eyed and living, interfered. England blockaded us, America sent arms, ammunition, food to our Tzarist oppressors; France, the home of Democracy, financed the Polish and Finnish Junkers, and now thanks to the Christian countries, Russia, great, big hearted Soviet Russia, lies dying of starvation, and the diseases which follow in its wake.

Do you think that when I get letters from my people imploring me for aid to keep them all from dying, help which I cannot give because for months —through no fault of my own—I have been without work, that I feel the Christmas Spirit?

No, no, no, and again no. I hate—with my whole

being I hate, those whose stupid lack of intelligence has brought about such havoc among us. Why I tell you it will take a hundred years to eradicate the distrust you have engendered in us. Yet you think one kindly action, a moment's friendliness, will do away with such bitterness. Why are you so dull? What right have you to be stupid, to lack even elementary understanding of real life, you who have education, health, happiness and lack that insistent worry of never knowing where your next meal is to be found? You are guilty of gross stupidity, you lack intelligence. Once more I ask, Why are you so dull? Why do you bring upon us all a bloody revolution? For *it is YOU* who bring it. The Workers know that they will bear the brunt of suffering in a revolution. They resort to it only after years of torture, when ill treatment has made them desperate; when they realize that hope in peaceful methods lies dead.

Peace and Good Will! You killed it in Soviet Russia, so do not ask us, the toiling masses, to practice what you only preach. That is childish nonsense.

So although you say you are my friend, I cannot be yours, nor feel the Christmas Spirit even on one day out of the 365. But, O! what happiness *to be able to feel it.* To say, from a singing heart, *Comrade* to *All The World.*

Lord Bryce on Democracy and Religion

Selected by Thomas A. Jenkins from an editorial in "The Christian Century."

The death of Lord Bryce is a bereavement to the whole English-speaking world. Alexis de Tocqueville was the first great observer of our democratic experiment in America, but he came too early to judge results. James Bryce, by virtue of his long life, shared a large part of our stupendous development, witnessed it with keen, intelligent and discerning eye, and wrote the noblest interpretation of it ever written in his "American Commonwealth." Always a convinced believer, without being an inflamed enthusiast, he lived to see the glowing promise become a perplexity. He closed his "American Commonwealth" with a question mark, wondering what would happen when America had ceased to be an economic utopia of free lands and endless room. His monumental study of "Modern Democracies," published last year—a survey of all the free states of the world, except Britain, which he modestly left for a more impartial hand—closed with even deeper questionings; often, indeed, hard to know from misgivings, though he wisely put aside " the pessimism of experience."

If Democracy Fails, What Then?

Democracy, Lord Bryce saw at the end of his life, has not brought us much nearer to the goal of human brotherhood. Freedom has not proved a panacea for our ills, much less a reconciler of our disputes. Self-government has not purified politics or redeemed us from the pernicious power which money exerts, nor has it exorcised the spirit of revolution and unrest. But, he added, "If democracy is flouted, what remains? There was a Greek proverb, If water chokes, what can one drink to stop the choking? If the light of democracy be turned to darkness, how great is that darkness!" He lived to see democracies turned to autocracies for purposes of war— suspending the very liberties which it had cost so much to win—and none knew better than he that it was a step back toward the old night. No sentence in his later writings is more poignant than that in which he says that one of the keenest woes of life is for a man to see his race choose the wrong road, and be unable to prevent it. Lord Bryce was not only a great statesman, ambassador, and publicist; he was a sincere and humble-hearted Christian. He saw that democracy is the inevitable destiny of humanity, but he feared for its future unless it is to be led by moral intelligence and spiritual vision. The stately closing pages of his "American Commonwealth," if put alongside the chapter on "Democracy and Religion" in his last volumes, tell us what was in his heart. "Christianity has never been put into practice," alas, that tells the tragedy of it all. But there lies our hope, if we are to defeat the "new, uprising, emancipated, atheistic democracy" which is at our door. But neither Christianity nor democracy has failed, so long as they can give us men like James Bryce—men of exalted character and clear intellect, touched with human sympathy and Christian vision, dedicated to the disinterested service of the common good.

For forms of government let fools contest;
Whatever is best administered is best:
For modes of faith let graceless zealots fight;
His can't be wrong whose life is in the right:
In faith and hope the world will disagree,
But all mankind's concern is charity:
All must be false that thwart this one great end;
And all of God, that bless mankind or mend.

Man, like the generous vine, supported lives;
The strength he gains, is from the embrace he gives.
On their own axis as the planets run,
Yet make at once their circle round the sun;
So two consistent motions act the soul;
And one regards itself, and one the whole.

Thus God and Nature link'd the general frame,
And bade self-love and social be the same.

—Pope's "Essay on Man."

Selected by Hannah P. Husband, Street, Md.

"Why The Common People Don't Stop War"

The following article was inspired by another of the same title which appeared recently in the Intelligencer. Its author served as an American soldier in France, sustaining serious effects from gas attacks, so that he knows the tragic intensity with which many sections of the world are crying for "Peace!"

"Peace!" is the cry of the hour. "Peace!" is the heartbreaking plea coming from the hearts of a misguided race in agonies. "Peace!" it is the sacred duty of the organized church to propagate, uphold, and hold up as the true and only true banner which can bring mankind to the goal it aims. "Peace!" is the echo of the world's whimsical press which was finally aroused to the dangers that the negation of peace involves. But, if "Peace" is the universal cry, why don't the peoples of the world stop war and have peace?

But as members of the Western Civilization, we ought to be very careful with the term of "peoples." For our belief is that "everybody" in the Nation makes the people. And the everybody includes: The tens and thousands that voluntarily flock to the recruiting offices and fill our armies and navies and do not pray for a lasting eclipse of the military sun; the thousands of military "experts" who include some of our most prominent fellow citizens and who do not, body and soul, yearn for a warless world; the average citizen who, when approached with an innocent exchange of opinions, hesitatingly and too often unhesitatingly desires to have "business protected" from foreign aggression—tho his political economy be of the poorest on market; the officials who *do have* the final "Yes" and "No" on the subject, and who think *more* of the "ratio" that would neutralize the ultimate strength of the lawless piratical schemes of professional buccaneering than of means and ways to pacify and actually to tame the aggressively irrational egotism that infests the race of men with despair and pestilence and strife. And finally, the "people" also includes our Christianity which is found on the crossroad—not knowing which Master to serve,—the State and its inhuman demands based upon irrational policies or the Commandments and the Wisdom of the Gospels.

It is well to wish "good luck" to associations and leagues and conferences of "men in power" who are obliged to gather to "do something" that would make the peoples of the world breathe easier. It is commendable to encourage "limitations" of any brutality, more so, of the greatest insane brutality of an organized society which holds itself ready (and publicly claims its duty to hold itself ready) for the most barbarous annihilation of human beings and their happiness. But *do they really do* something for the approach of the day when "Peace" turns to a reality?

The will for a warless world is not a new desire and not a dream. It is centuries old; and is clearer now than ever. If civilized society shoots, hangs, and electrocutes individuals for *one act* which deprives one human being of its right to live, what should not be the legal punishment for those responsible governments who organize and foster systems that ultimately lead to wholesale murder of innocent men, women and children? And yet it becomes a certainty with every day, that when the present wave of "limitation talk" is passed, the *status quo*, with its grave consequences, remains inviolable. The "rations" for destruction may be slightly limited in quantity, but not in quality!

Though "Peace" is the cry of the hour, the sentiment of the peoples, the spirit of the day, the avowed purpose of the Church, and the topic of the press, behind all that is a "cruel and mocking reality." Behind the popular will that cries for a saner life there is felt a hand, a mighty hand, that makes the *status quo* inviolable. That hand overshadows all the popular sentiments and aspirations from making an end to that savage habit of man slaughter which is made legal by a sophisticated mind and degraded morality. It is the ever-present, ever-victorious consideration of economy and materialism that grips the peoples every-day, and that is able to make them live and act just the contrary to their "popular and aroused will."

Is it not well to remember in face of these facts, that as long as Governments and Assemblies of peoples' representatives *avoid* the discussion of the "economic phase" that is so deeply felt by great and small, as long as that dark veil is not raised by the men who claim to work for peace and raised with the sincere desire to rid the human race of the burden of war, as long as they—the men of power—prefer to gamble with peoples and their problems instead of striving honestly for Peace, as long as the devastating *status quo* remains inviolable, the problem of a warless world shall continue to remain unsolved and its knockings be heard at our doors, and the human race praying and paying with human blood for the delay. Tend the "roots" of the plant, and the plant will grow; care for the boughs, and the fruits are made possible to live and ripen; neglect the "roots," and no labor above and around will correct those defects only the proper cultivation *of the source* can do.

Silver Spring, Md. DAVID GITTLEMAN.

WHAT'S gone, and what's past help, should be past grief.—*Shakespeare*.

Red Cross to Distribute Through Friends

The statement which follows is being sent to all local chapters of the American Red Cross from the National Red Cross headquarters in Washington. In giving Friends complete charge of the distribution of clothing produced or contributed by its members, the Red Cross has paid a splendid tribute to the American Friends' Service Committee.

The statement, as originally sent to the local chapters, included directions for Junior Red Cross co-operation in the production of garments, and a copy of an unsolicited appeal, which appeared in the Ladies' Home Journal. The latter urges all women's organizations, as a special Lenten activity, to co-operate with the Red Cross in producing clothing for European relief.

Owing to the gradual withdrawal of the Red Cross from Europe, the Paris Office has requested that no more shipments of garments be made from this country for distribution by the Red Cross to their Child Health Stations in European countries. A sufficient supply of clothing is on hand now to cover the immediate needs, and since these stations will be handed over to native committees for administration not later than July 1, 1922, other agencies must hereafter be relied on for distribution of the clothing provided for them.

The immediate need in certain European countries for garments of all kinds, adult as well as children's, is so serious, however, that it is earnestly hoped the chapters will continue production with unabated enthusiasm.

Arrangements have been made with the American Friends' Service Committee by which they will transport and deliver Red Cross garments in the European countries where they are already operating: namely, Austria, Russia and Poland, giving full credit to the Red Cross for their contribution, and keeping the chapters supplied with informational matter covering the needs at the points in which their work is being carried on and their method of distributing chapter produced garments.

The situation in Russia is especially appealing, and it is planned to ship children's garments there as rapidly as possible.

The co-operation of the American Friends' Service Committee provides an adequate and well managed outlet for our Chapter production after the discontinuance of our own distributing agencies in Europe.

The immediate effect of this will be that the material received from chapters and other Red Cross sources will be picked up at the Bush Terminal, Brooklyn, New York, by the American Friends' Service Committee and conveyed to their warehouse, 108-126 Dobbin Street, Brooklyn, for shipment overseas.

The Campaign for Flour and Corn

Greater Co-operation Needed From Friends

The campaign of the American Friends' Service Committee for flour and corn is gradually gaining headway.

The appeal to the millers direct to co-operate with the Service Committee in securing gifts of flour was a new idea, and it has required a little time to work out a plan of action. Perhaps the depression in milling conditions may have had something to do with the difficulty of getting the campaign under way. Whatever the cause, apparently it is being overcome, for results are being secured.

At present we have thirty thousand barrels of flour moving toward Russia.

We need volunteers to stir up enthusiasm and interest in every community to get a campaign started for flour.

We have some workers in the middle west. Those able to help should notify our nearest representative. Clarence Griffiths is located at Miami, Okla.; Edmund Stanley at Wichita, Kans., is assisted by Norwood H. Andrews, from the Philadelphia office. Others are: John Newlin, Lawrence, Kans.; George S. Wise, Kansas City, Mo.; S. Edgar Nicholson, Richmond, Ind.; Alvin E. Wildman, Selma, Ohio; and William T. Cope, Y. M. C. A., Lincoln, Neb. So far Missouri has not been organized. The Minnesota Russian Relief Committee is taking charge of Minnesota, North and South Dakota.

Great help is being received from Chambers of Commerce, Granges, Rotary and Kiwanis Clubs and other local organizations. Confidence is expressed that the campaign will succeed, especially if Friends throughout the country will do their part.

Moundridge, Kansas, a town of seven hundred people has shipped two cars of flour for famine relief. What community cannot give a car of flour if the campaign is undertaken with spirit?

Can any Christian "pass by on the other side" while 15,000,000 Russians starve? Have you provided a place with your money or by your effort for the relief of your stricken brothers as did the good Samaritan?

Very few communities in the East have been organized. Friends are numerous there. Cannot they stop in their tasks long enough to help save lives?

The talent of success is nothing more than doing what you can do well, and doing well whatever you do, without thought of fame.—*Longfellow.*

Friendly News Notes

Among those in attendance at Abington Quarterly Meeting were Isaac Wilson, Dr. O. Edward Janney, Jane P. Rushmore and Walter H. Abell. In connection with the answer to the Seventh Query, Dr. Janney gave a good report of the Washington Conference, and urged the Monthly Meetings to keep up the organizations for continuing the work of raising funds to defray the expenses that have already been incurred, and for holding the prestige that we have gained.

The Advisory Committee of Baltimore Monthly Meeting reports that:

Thirty members have joined the Meeting during the past year; the last five recorded years show 20, 19, 18, 14 and 20 for a year's increase.

The First-day School membership is now 131 not counting the cradle roll or the home department. A year ago the membership was 80, an increase of 51.

The membership of the three girls and boys clubs is now 40.

The Secretary has seen 827 individuals in their homes as the result of 455 visits.

Approximately 100 people are doing active Meeting work weekly.

All Friends who are interested in the foreign relief work will be glad to see the following summary of the contributions for the month of January:

Received for Germany approximately	$160,000
Received for all other countries, mainly for Russia	249,000
Garden seeds contributed by seedsmen:—	
Approximately 75,000 pounds, valued at	37,500
Flour, valued at approximately	45,000
Corn, valued at approximately	15,000
	$506,500
In addition to the above: Clothing, 500 bales, at approximately $125 per bale	$62,500

The American public believe in the Society of Friends; and they trust us with money and supplies. Do we believe in ourselves? Do we believe in our message?

The fourteenth annual report of the Woodbrooke Settlement in England contains many indications of the valuable educational work being carried on by this institution along religious, social and international lines. The students in attendance, varying in number from thirty to forty-four during different terms of 1920-21, constituted a thoroughly international group—Scandinavia, Holland, Germany, France and South Africa being represented, in addition to England. The report states that "It has been exceptional and disappointing to have no representative from the U. S. A. this year." The Woodbrooke Extension Committee has been active both in carrying Woodbrooke ideals afield, and in drawing students from the groups in which it has worked.

Professor Charles Foster Kent has accepted the invitation of Friends' General Conference to give a series of four addresses at the Conference at Richmond, Indiana, August 26th to September 2nd, 1922. Professor Kent will come to Richmond direct from his trip to Palestine.

On Second month 3rd, an evening of their "Living Paintings" was given in the New York Meeting-house, by Elizabeth and Esther Fisher, for the benefit of the Fort Valley, Ga., High and Industrial School for Colored Children. Four colored singers sang the old plantation songs and "spirituals." Thirty-six boys and girls, from the New York First-day School took the characters represented in the twenty-seven "Paintings." They were portraits in the manner of 16th, 17th, 18th, and 19th century artists; and pictures from books, as Romola, Olivia and Squire Thornhill, etc. It was a remarkable entertainment, which should have brought in much more than it did. Considering, however, the very short notice on which it was given, with the correspondingly smaller chance for advertising it, and considering, too, the growing influenza epidemic, which kept many away, the net profit of about $75.00 is very satisfactory.

If any one who reads of the Prison Comfort Club in the INTELLIGENCER, has an occasional half hour to spare from his or her own affairs, there are many men in prison today for "conscience sake"—for an ideal, a principle, who would be very glad to get a letter "from the outside." The P. C. C. already has the names of more than two hundred, and others neglected or overlooked continue to come in. For instance, a certain organization sending names of prisoners to the Club, listed "A. Gross and nine others" under a certain war-time indictment. Only with difficulty and after much effort the P. C. C. is getting into personal touch with these "nine others" and the many, many more similarly situated—splendidly loyal to their principles in the face of such terrible odds—and of our own utter indifference! A letter is an event inside prison walls. And correspondence with a man or woman who has the courage to do what these people are doing ought to be a liberal education for many of us.

There are three birthday dates that have just reached the Club and for this reason were not included with others in the last issue—February 21, Eugene Bennett, Box 520, Walla Walla, Wash.; Frank Sherman (No. 35768), San Quentin Penitentiary, San Quentin, California; February 29, L. Allen (No. 35714), San Quentin Penitentiary, San Quentin, California. Will not some one who reads this determine to write not only to these three, but unfailingly month by month to all whose names and birthday dates will be given? Just writing to a prisoner constitutes membership in the P. C. C. There are no "dues" or any material obligations—no one connected with the organization has any salary or commission or remuneration of any sort. Would it not be possible to form similar groups in other places? Any desired information will gladly be supplied if request is made through the INTELLIGENCER office. A group of even three could do valuable service. "Where two or three are gathered in my name, there am I in their midst."

PURCHASE QUARTERLY MEETING

About one hundred people gathered at Purchase for the mid-winter Quarterly Meeting on Second month 5th, and, although a number of familiar faces were absent due to sickness or other causes, a Friendly atmosphere pervaded as always.

The morning meeting was filled with rich thoughts from old and young. Albert Lawton, quoting Whittier, spoke of the instinctive desire of mankind for outward symbols as expressions of high ideals and cited the

American Flag and the Cross as examples. As long as men need these outward reminders they will and should continue to be cherished by all. Raymond Mendenhall recalled to mind pictures of beautiful characters of the past, such as George Fox and William Penn, whose "minds were staid on the Master," and spoke of the need today, not for those who periodically turned their minds in worship to God, but for those whose minds were continually "staid upon Him," who lived so close to Him that their daily lives would be an expression of His will. William Yarnall, formerly of Philadelphia, presented the old true text, "Ye can not serve both God and Mammon," in a new and interesting way, laying particular stress on the necessity of "seeking first the Kingdom of Heaven" in each individual heart. Among a number of other speakers was Harold Laity, a returned "Missionite," now teaching in the Oakwood School at Poughkeepsie, N. Y. He stated that we should get more into the attitude of "not my will but Thine be done" and that this can be attained if we have complete faith in the power of the Divine to carry us over the rough places in life.

After lunch and the usual delightful social mingling, Miss McNeil, of the Near East Relief, gave a graphic description of the wretched conditions under which the women and children of Armenia and the other Asia Minor countries are living at the hands of the Moslems, and of the splendid, though inadequate, work done by her organization. Over $375 was collected in cash and pledges for this work at the meeting. Among other speakers at the afternoon meeting was Mrs. Daisy McCoubrey who told of the opening of the warehouse in New York for the storage of clothing to be shipped to Russia.

An active part in the meeting was taken by members of both branches of Friends, a fact which is significant of the spirit of harmony and unity prevailing in this vicinity.

At the business meeting it was decided, as last year, to subscribe to the INTELLIGENCER to be sent to hospitals and reading rooms in and around Purchase.

ABINGTON QUARTERLY MEETING

At Abington Quarterly Meeting, Jane P. Rushmore spoke of the persistent quest for God, which in itself bears evidence of his being a necessity in the lives of men. That there are two distinct currents manifested in this search to her mind showed no lack of sincerity. That one group essayed to bring him into nearness and the other gloried in the vision which kept him remote, only showed varying human needs. She felt that silent worship might be an obstacle by its very inertia, and wished to lay emphasis on the fact that worship is not forced, and it is easy not to worship. Not inertia but positive search is the proper attitude.

In the discussion of the Queries, Dr. Janney brought out the idea that growth is not the result of *silent* meetings, and growth should be our aim. "Free gospel ministry," he said, "refers not only to payment, but if we suppress the message within ourselves, ours is not a free gospel ministry." Dr. Janney also urged Friends to continue the work begun by the Washington Conference by organizing in every locality for the distribution of literature, the sending of messages to Congress, looking for proper text-books in our schools, etc.

Isaac Michener spoke in tribute to the results of the Arms Conference, and on suggestion of Mary W. Lippincott, it was decided letters should be sent to President Harding and the four United States representatives to the Conference, expressive of the appreciation of this Quarter for what has been accomplished.

In considering the Eleventh Query, it was brought out that little had been done in an organized way to instruct the ninety-four young people within the specified ages, in regard to their responsibilities as Friends. It was felt that First-day School workers and Overseers should look after this, and the responsibility of parents was mentioned as of the utmost importance. A. C.

Items From Everywhere

If the total amount lost in the United States through fires during the last five years, $1,672,722,677, had been used constructively instead if being literally thrown away, the sum would have built 334,540 dwellings, costing on the average $5,000 each, thus supplying homes for 1,672,720 people. This exceeds the total population of Connecticut, Nevada and Wyoming. Or it would have constructed 16,727 schoolhouses, costing $100,000 apiece.—*The National Board of Fire Underwriters.*

Unless Congress enacts immigration legislation, the present emergency restrictive act will expire on June 30 of this year, and we return to the old law allowing practically unrestricted legislation except for those diseased or grossly immoral.

In view of present economic conditions, the Committee on Constructive Immigration Legislation, composed of 1,500 leading American citizens, is asking Congress to enact constructive immigration legislation. This legislation is known as the Sterling and Vaile Bill (Senate Bill No. S. 1253 and House Bill No. H. R. 9880. A descriptive folder concerning this bill may be obtained for twenty-five cents from the National Committee for Constructive Legislation, 105 E. 22nd St., New York City.

"That the Negro in just over half a century should have increased his homes owned from 12,000 to 650,000, of farms operated from 20,000 to 1,000,000, of businesses conducted from 2,100 to 60,000, of literacy from 10 to 80 per cent., of teachers from 600 to 43,000, of voluntary contributions to education from $80,000 to $2,700,000, of churches from 700 to 45,000, of Sunday-school pupils from 50,000 to 2,250,000, of church property from $1,500,000 to $90,000,000—this is an extraordinary record full of reassurance to those who like to believe in human improvability."—*Anson Stokes Phelps, in an address at Hampton Institute.*

At a congress in Copenhagen, July 1 and 2, 1921, the Northern Peace Union, consisting of the peace societies of Sweden, Norway and Denmark, adopted a resolution recommending English as the most suitable language for international use, calling upon the governments of the world and the League of Nations to choose it, or if preferable some other tongue, as an international language, and to introduce the language chosen into the curriculum of the schools and colleges of all nations.

A table of statistics has been issued concerning the constituent bodies of the Federal Council of Churches. The figures for the Five Years Meeting, the only body of Friends belonging to the Council, are as follows: Churches, 820; ministers, 1,296; members, 96,135; gain in membership during last five years, 3,756. The figures for the constituent bodies as a whole, which include the leading protestant denominations of the United States, are: Churches, 142,472; ministers, 113,761; members, 19,933.115; gain during five years, 1,206,881.

THE OPEN FORUM

This column is intended to afford free expression of opinion by readers on questions of interest. The INTELLIGENCER is not responsible for any such opinions. Letters must be brief, and the editor reserves the right to omit parts if necessary to save space.

ARE WE TOO UNAGGRESSIVE?

To the Editor:

As I have been puzzled by the attitude of some Friends since I joined the Society, I should be glad to see in the columns of the INTELLIGENCER some answers to the following questions:

Can Friends consistently join in with the Orthodox churches in their efforts at church union?

Are the fundamental teachings of the Friends and the Orthodox churches the same?

If these questions are answered in the affirmative, why do Friends seek to maintain a separate existence? If such were the case (which I do not for a moment think is the case), I would feel I had made a sad mistake throwing my lot in with the Friends.

If there is a vital difference between the interpretation of the Bible which Friends give and that which others give, should not the differences be arranged and classified a little more clearly, so that every member could if necessary give a reason for the faith that is in him?

Union, Ont., Canada. NANIE WEBSTER.

ADVANTAGES OF NOT BEING AN ANGEL

To the Editor:

I am glad I am not an angel, for if I were I should be bathed in tears. For was not the recent conclave of Statesmen at Washington calculated and staged to make angels weep?

Being a human mortal, I can rejoice and be thankful for the strides toward permanent peace which I am told the Conference has taken—subject to the approval of the Senate. As a man I am not oppressed by the sorrowful humor of the situation. But to an angel what a ludicrous tragedy it must be! Statesmen, men intrusted with the direction of the affairs of millions of their fellows, only a few years after the great war to end war, meeting to agree upon a limitation of the severity with which they may knock each other on the head in the next war!

If they really think they can, by agreement, eliminate poison gas and confine their slaughter to carving and smashing, why do they think they cannot eliminate the butchery and make the next war a peaceable contest between champions in chess or craps?

That the world is not ready for the abolition of war can hardly be maintained in the face of the fact that men gave their lives and children their pennies that the war against war should be won. It was known that the German people didn't want war and the people of all Europe hailed Wilson and America as deliverers from war and wars. But the Statesmen! Well, I am glad I am a gullible mortal who can shout Hurrah! because in the next war my fellow mortals will be only torn and broken and not asphyxiated. Were I an angel, I should weep at the funny antics of the little great ones who take themselves so seriously.

Arlington, Vermont. EDWARD B. RAWSON.

BIRTHS

MARSHALL—On First month 10, 1922, to T. Elwood and Bertha K. C. Marshall, a daughter, named Florence Nightingale Marshall.

DEATHS

BREWER—In Germantown, Pa., suddenly, on Twelfth month 13th, 1921, Bertha C. Brewer.

BROOKES—On Second month 6th, at the home of her niece, Annie B. Grevemeyer, Mary E. Brookes, widow of the late Edward Brookes in the 82nd year of her age. Member of Deer Creek Monthly Meeting.

CLOTHIER—At Buffalo, N. Y., on Second month 6th, William P., son of the late Caleb and Hannah Fletcher Clothier, in his eighty-fourth year.

REEDER—At New Hope, Pa., Second month 6th, Watson K. Reeder, aged 67.

ROBERTS—Dr. George Roberts, now of Alexandria, Va., but for many years past a resident of Lincoln, Va., died in the Alexandria Hospital on February 1, in the seventy-fifth year of his age. His remains were interred in the Lincoln Cemetery.

Dr. Roberts was the son of Spencer and Louisa J. Roberts, of Philadelphia, and was graduated from the University of Pennsylvania in 1868. Two years later he was appointed physician for the Santee Indians on the Santee Agency in Nebraska. For several years Dr. Roberts worked among our red brothers and then he took a homestead near Center, Nebr. In 1880 he moved to Creighton, Nebr., and was one of the first residents in that place. Dr. Roberts lived here many years and reared a family of eight children. During this time he held many positions of trust and honor, among which was the appointment as regent of the University of Nebraska, which position he filled for many years. In 1900, Dr. Roberts moved his family to Lincoln, Va., in search of a quiet, retired life among the Society of Friends.

A useful, well-rounded life has ended, but the loving remembrance will always live in the hearts of those who knew him best. He is survived by a brother, an invalid wife, a son, four daughters, seventeen grandchildren and two great-grandchildren.

COMING EVENTS

SECOND MONTH

18th—Short Creek Quarterly Meeting, at Emerson, Ohio.

18th—Pelham Half-Yearly Meeting, at Coldstream, Ontario.

18th and 19th—Pilgrimage under the care of the Young Friends' Movement at Girard Avenue Meeting, Philadelphia.

19th—10 a. m., Moving Pictures of the Life of Christ, in the Brooklyn First-day School. All are invited. 11 a. m., Carolena Wood will attend Brooklyn Meeting, and will lead a Conference in the afternoon at 2 o'clock, on Relief Work in Central Europe. Friends are asked to bring box lunch, to be served between Meeting and the Conference.

5.30 p. m. James Norton, Assistant Secretary of the Service Committee, will attend the Tea-Meeting at the Meeting-house, 144 East 20th Street, and will speak on "The Meaning of the Friends' Service Committee." All are cordially invited.

19th—Conference Class at 15th and Race Streets, Philadelphia, at close of meeting for worship, at 11.40 a. m. Speaker—William J. MacWatters. Subject—Standards of the Kingdom I. Sacrifice the Measure of Steadfastness.

19th—E. Maria Bishop expects to attend meeting for worship at 15th and Race Streets, Philadelphia, at 10.30 a. m.

19th—William Littleboy will attend the meeting for worship at Cambridge, Mass., in Phillips Brooks House, at 3.30 p. m.

19th—Elbert Russell will attend meeting for worship at Oxford, Pa., at 10.30 a. m. In the afternoon at 2 o'clock, he will give the third lecture on the Life of Jesus.

20th—Center Quarterly Meeting, at Unionville, Center County, Pa. Joel Borton expects to attend.

20th—Fairfax Quarterly Meeting, at Washington, D. C. Dr. O. Edward Janney expects to attend.

21st—Burlington Quarterly Meeting, at Mt. Holly, N. J. Isaac Wilson, Dr. O. Edward Janney and J. Barnard Walton expect to attend.

23rd—Lecture at Pennsylvania School for Social Service, 339 S. Broad Street, Philadelphia. Subject—Adolescent Boys' Organization and Program. Speaker—Mr. Charles W. Bainbridge, Supt. Germantown Boys' Club.

23rd—Bucks Quarterly Meeting, at Wrightstown, Pa. Meeting for Ministry and Counsel, preceding day, at 11 a. m. Dr. O. Edward Janney expects to attend.

25th—Blue River Quarterly Meeting at Chicago, Ill., Fine Arts Building, South Michigan Ave. Friendly Social in the evening, addressed by J. Barnard Walton on "The International Service of the Society of Friends."

26th—At Oxford, Pa., Elbert Russell will give his fourth lecture on the Life of Jesus, at 2 p. m.

26th—William Littleboy will attend the meeting for worship at Cornell in Barnes Hall at 8.15 p. m.

27th—Warrington Quarterly Meeting, at Menallen, Pa.

THIRD MONTH

5th—3 p. m. A meeting for divine worship will be held at Chester Friends' Meeting House under the care of a Committee of Concord Quarterly Meeting. Friends of both branches are asked to attend. The desire is to make it a community meeting to which all persons are welcome; and the co-operation of young persons is solicited. Come and bring another.

NOTICE—Of interest to all friends of Woolman School. Effie Danforth McAfee, who was one of our representatives at the International Congress of Women in Stockholm, and the American Friend who has been asked to deliver the Nobel Salon lecture on Friends' Principles, will be in Swarthmore, Seventh-day, Second month 18th.

In Whittier House, at 3.30 p. m., she will give an illustrated talk, especially for children, on "Our Northern Cousins of Norway." At 8 p. m., the subject of her address will be "A Friend Abroad in Denmark."

Mrs. McAfee is coming to Swarthmore for the benefit of Woolman School, so there will be a charge of ten cents for children and thirty-five cents for adults at each lecture. To further help Woolman School, there will be sale of cake and candy in the afternoon. It is hoped that all who live near enough will take advantage of this privilege to hear Mrs. McAfee and to help Woolman School.

NOTICE—Dr. Lloyd Balderston, who has recently returned after spending four years as a Professor in the Imperial University at Sapporo, Japan, will deliver an illustrated lecture on the subject, "Outstanding Features in Japanese Life and Character," at Friends' Select School, 16th and Cherry Streets, Sixth-day, Second month 24th, at 7.45 p. m. A general invitation is extended to all interested.

American Friends' Service Committee

WILBUR K. THOMAS, Ex. Sec.

20 S. 12th St. Philadelphia

CASH CONTRIBUTIONS

Week Ending February 6.

Five Years Meetings	$1,578.30
Phila. Yearly Meeting (4th and Arch)	5.00
Phila. Yearly Meeting (15th and Race)	2,891.52
Other Meetings—	
Kennett Monthly Meeting	13.00
Germantown Monthly Meeting	20.00
Birmingham Monthly Meeting	5.00
Miami Monthly Meeting	70.78
Villa St. & Galena Avenue Meeting	28.00
Jericho Monthly Meeting	28.00
Chester Monthly Meeting	100.00
West Branch Monthly Meeting, Md.	45.00
Unionville Prep. Meeting	20.00
Little Falls Monthly Meeting	32.91
Contributions for General	776.66
For Germany	371.21
For Austria	4,046.66
For Poland	687.12
For Armenia	10.00
For Syria	10.00
For Russia	7,077.89
For Russian Overhead	211.25
For Clothing	37.50
Refunds and payments	252.85
	$18,308.65

CASH CONTRIBUTIONS

WEEK ENDING JANUARY 23RD.

Five Years Meetings	$736.87
Other Meetings—	
Medford Monthly Meeting	10.00
Westerly Meeting	200.00
Birmingham Monthly Meeting	25.00
London Grove Monthly Meeting	67.00
Cuban Mission	2.00
Moorestown War Victims Relief	150.00
Stavanger Monthly Meeting, Iowa.	25.00
Alexandria Monthly Meeting	219.00
Villa St. & Galena Ave. Friends Mtg.	100.00
West Chester Meeting	100.00
Newton Prep. Meeting	190.00
Crosswicks Prep. Meeting	6.00
Buckingham First-day School	1.50
Concord Monthly Meeting	22.00
Yarmouth Prep. Meeting, Canada	11.00
Contributions for General	1,430.24
For Germany	398.19
For Austria	841.66
For Poland	26.00
For Syria	75.00
For Russia	31,542.75
For Russian Overhead	787.92
For Clothing	41.70
Refunds and Payments	431.71
	$34,440.54

Shipments received during week ending February 4th, 1922. 108 boxes and packages received; 4 anonymous.

REGULAR MEETINGS

OAKLAND, CALIF.—A FRIENDS' MEETING is held every First-day at 11 A. M., in the Extension Room, Y. W. C. A. Building, Webster Street, above 14th. Visiting Friends always welcome.

FRIENDS' MEETING IN PASADENA, California—Orange Grove Monthly Meeting of Friends, 520 East Orange Grove Avenue, Pasadena, California. Meeting for worship, First-day, 11 A. M. Monthly Meeting, the second First-day of each month, at 1.45 P. M.

WANTED

WORKING HOUSEKEEPER—EXPERIENCED woman desires position in Christian home. Small household and no children; city preferred. Will cook. Highest recommendation from present employer. Open to engagement after March 10th. Address J-54, Friends' Intelligencer.

ART TEACHER—EXPERIENCED traveler—is forming party of ten for Europe. Passion Play—art galleries—battlefields. About June 24th to September 5th. Early application necessary. Box 70, Friends' Intelligencer.

WANTED—BY CULTURED MAN, well traveled, and experienced, position of trust and companionship with Christian gentleman, who may also need secretarial work, as well as congenial social relationship; or the charge of a young man needing guidance and fatherly care. Interview necessary. References exchanged. Address D. D., Friends' Intelligencer.

POSITION WANTED—BY GIRL, 16, strong and willing, as mother's helper. Country preferred. References. Address P. 71, Friends' Intelligencer.

REFINED, CAPABLE MOTHER OF 3 children, wants any kind of employment where it is possible to keep her little ones together and educate them. Can give best of reference. Address K-59, Friends' Intelligencer.

WANTED—NURSE, ENGLISH PROTestant preferred; care of three children, 8, 6 and 2. Summer in Rhode Island. Address M. 72, Friends' Intelligencer.

WANTED—AN UNFURNISHED house at Swarthmore, with all conveniences; hot water heat; on high ground, not in village. Please answer, giving all particulars. Mrs. J. R. B. Moore, 44 East 73rd street, New York.

TRANSIENT ACCOMMODATIONS

WASHINGTON, D. C.—ROOMS FOR visitors. Near Station, Capitol, Library. Continuous hot water. Electricity. Garage. Mrs. L. L. Kendig, 120 C. Street, Northwest.

FOR RENT

FOR RENT—APRIL TO OCTOBER. Nine-room house with sleeping porch and garage, near river, at Riverton. Address Helen Lippincott, Riverton, N. J.

FUN

"Father," said little Rollo, "what is meant by 'a Sabbath day's journey'?" "I am afraid, my son, that in too many cases it means twice around the golf links."—*Edinburgh Scotsman.*

Not in the Business.

"I'm not quite sure about your washing machine. Will you demonstrate it again?"

"No, madam. We only do one week's washing."—*Louisville Courier-Journal.*

FUN

Brown—"That new cook of ours makes everything out of the cook book."

Derby—"Then that must have been one of the covers I tasted in the pie last night."—*Kind Words.*

Reassuring.

Nervous Tourist—"What if the bridge should break and the train fall into the river?"

Conductor—"Don't worry, sir. This road won't miss it. It has a lot of trains."—*Erie Railroad Magazine.*

To the Lot Holders and others interested in Fairhill Burial Ground:

GREEN STREET Monthly Meeting has funds available for the encouragement of the practice of cremating the dead to be interred in Fairhill Burial Ground. We wish to bring this fact as prominently as possible to those who may be interested. We are prepared to undertake the expense of cremation in case any lot holder desires us to do so.

Those interested should communicate with William H. Gaskill, Treasurer of the Committee of Interments, Green Street Monthly Meeting, or any of the following members of the Committee.

William H. Gaskill, 3201 Arch St.
Samuel N. Longstreth, 1218 Chestnut St.
Charles F. Jenkins, 232 South Seventh St.
Stuart S. Graves, 3033 Germantown Ave.

The Friends' Intelligencer

ESTABLISHED 1844 | THIRD MONTH 4, 1922 | VOLUME 79 NUMBER 9

Contents

THE FRIENDS' INTELLIGENCER

Published weekly, 140 N. 15th Street, Philadelphia, Pa., by Friends' Intelligencer Association, Ltd.

WALTER H. ABELL, *Editor*
SUE C. YERKES, *Business Manager*

Editorial Board: Elizabeth Powell Bond, Thomas A. Jenkins, J. Russell Smith, George A. Walton.

Board of Managers: Edward Cornell, Alice Hall Paxson, Paul M. Pearson, Annie Hillborn, Elwood Hollingshead, William C. Biddle, Charles F. Jenkins, Edith M. Winder, Frances M. White.

Officers of Intelligencer Associates: Elwood Burdsall, Chairman; Bertha L. Broomell, Secretary; Herbert P. Worth, Treasurer.

Subscription rates: United States, Mexico, Cuba and Panama, $2.50 per year. Canada and other foreign countries, $3.00 per year. Checks should be made payable to Friends' Intelligencer Association, Ltd.

Entered as Second Class Matter at Philadelphia Post Office.

The Friends' Intelligencer

The religion of Friends is based on faith in the "INWARD LIGHT," or direct revelation of God's spirit and will in every seeking soul.

The INTELLIGENCER is interested in all who bear the name of Friends in every part of the world, and aims to promote love, unity and intercourse among all branches and with all religious societies.

ESTABLISHED 1844 | PHILADELPHIA, THIRD MONTH 4, 1922 | VOLUME 79 NUMBER 9

A Spiritual Function for An Age of Chaos

We have seen no other utterance which spoke words of greater hope to the social and spiritual seeker of today than one of the recent articles on "Mr. Ford's Page" of the *Dearborn Independent.* This article is an analysis of the way great forward movements arise, and of the relation of the individual to such movements.

It begins with a reference to the large masses of men and women who today are giving "the very substance of their souls to feel out or think out or work out some better way of life for the multitude." "It would be difficult for persons of limited opportunity to realize how many, many people have two businesses in life; one that earns their bread and butter, the other that looks toward building a better world." They come from all classes, these seekers; many of them simple folk of farm and village, many groping forward through "the greater loneliness of vast cities"; some with definitely conceived plans for advancing the "Great Cause, which is the bringing in of a righteous social order," others condemned to feel the need without being able to crystallize any definite answer to it. And most of the programs to which these earnest souls are giving their best life energies will not be the ones finally adopted, nor will most of those who seek the trail today live to tread the broad highway that must eventually be opened if humanity is to find its God and its goal. Is, then, the effort which we make today bound to be lost in the final outcome?

"That is the question," the article continues. "Is it a failure to espouse a cause and then to die before the cause is established? Is it failure to espouse a cause and see it come to light on a plan different than we hoped it would come?

"It is worth while knowing how all the great progressive changes arrive at the plan of actuality.

"There is first a deep moving of sensitive spirits who feel the wrongness of things and who see in imagination an order of life wherein all wrongs could be corrected. There is where Destiny begins the work of its great overturns. It begins in the obscure and inarticulate world of the common human soul. Men are exercised about the wrongness of things. Often they cannot put their finger on the specific thing that is wrong. Often they are at a total loss to suggest a method of correction. But down in the great mass of sensitive humanity, in that part of humanity capable of weaving from itself a new order of life, there is a moving spirit prophetic of changes.

"The faith of the people—that is to say, the raw material, as it were, of all good things to come—is not as vague or meaningless a thing as it appears. For the faith of the people is the protoplasm out of which the new order evolves.

"Now, it is plain to see that whoever by the stress of his spirit and the action of his mind tends to increase the supply of this raw material of progress, or by his attention and desire tends to increase its vitality, is serving the great movement. Every edifice has its foundations deeply hidden from the eye. The mud mortar of the lowest course of masonry is as necessary to the structure as the pinnacle that crowns it."

Despite the material comfort which special circumstances give to many of us, despite the sense of steadfast support which many have found in the experience of personal religion, despite even the conviction that the tides of destiny have already begun to turn toward a happier era, all of us know that we live in an age of disintegration; an age in which old systems are crumbling and new have not yet been found, an age which cannot be set right except by the gradual revival of those spiritual attributes of personality which have been so largely mistrusted and crushed since the Renaissance. We are at one of the early springtimes of human destiny, in which what Turgeniev calls the "virgin soil" of humanity must bear the deep cut of the plow and be rebroken in preparation for a new sowing. It is a time when no personal security or possesion, whether material or spiritual, can give us permanent peace or satisfaction if our eyes are open to the condition of the world about us. It is a time when, though our personal experience of God were as complete as was that of Jesus, we must nevertheless, like Jesus, yearn to see the "more abundant life" brought to the whole human brotherhood about us. And with millions starving, millions disinherited of the opportunity to gain a livelihood through honest labor, millions torn with unrest and the suppression of personality, we know that the trail must be long before the highway is gained.

The conviction that corporately, as well as individually, "They that seek shall find," must come with refreshing stimulus to those who feel this burden of the world's need. In the midst of a negative era, it opens to every individual, regardless of rank, creed or position, a positive, God-freeing function which is essential to all subsequent constructive movements. Original Quakerism sprang out of a century of unrest and seeking. In a world so vastly more knit and articulate than was that of George Fox, how much greater shall the movement not be which answers to today's unrest.

Let us be vital protoplasm in humanity's evolving organism. Scorning smug comfort and respectability, let us pour our individual drops of the spirit into the arteries of a spiritually awakening race. Let us undertake the sorrows of brotherhood in openly facing the facts of world imperialism, of Russia's attempted answer with its successes and its failures, of starving millions, of strife rampant throughout the body social. From a sharing of the burden, an unrest and a seeking, shall come at last a finding. "Thrice happy are they that hunger and thirst after righteousness—."

West Virginia Calls to the Churches

Two Friendly organs are now concerned with the mine war-fare in West Virginia. Mary Janet Miller's letter in the Open Forum of the INTELLIGENCER, appealing for relief work among the miners, was brought before the American Friends' Service Committee, and the possibilities of entering this field of home service were turned over to the Executive Committee for investigation. Independently of the Service Committee's effort, a committee was appointed by Swarthmore Monthly Meeting to investigate the same problem from the standpoint of possibly clarifying the spiritual atmosphere which prevents its solution.

Of special interest in connection with these actions is an article by Harry F. Ward, which is being released to the religious press of the country and which bears the title: "The Challenge of West Virginia to the Churches." The writer reviews the U. S. Senate investigation of the West Virginia trouble, and supports the conclusion of Senator Kenyon, Chairman of the Senate Committee, that it is "the ruthless denial by the operators of a right (the right to organize) which they continually exercise themselves, that is the primary cause of the violence and bloodshed in West Virginia and its cost and consequences to the United States." The article concludes:

"Herein lies the challenge to the churches. Have not the leading protestant denominations declared, separately and collectively—through the Federal Council of Churches—for the 'equal right of employers and employees alike to organize.' But the root of all the evil in the non-union coal counties of West Virginia is the denial by the organized operators of this 'equal right' to the miners. What then will the churches do about it? Will they officially declare judgment? Will they send their national representatives into West Virginia to address the churches on the single issue of 'equal rights to organize' and so strengthen the hands of those true citizens of that state who have publicly opposed the continued use of its authority to deny 'equal rights' to miners? Is it possible that the voice of religion could create a public conscience and thereby succeed in righting a situation wherein Government has manifestly failed?"

Whatever the eventual decision of the Service Committee regarding the possibilities of administering physical relief, does not the above call imply *spiritual* opportunities directly in line with the concern of Swarthmore Monthly Meeting? We hope that Swarthmore and other meetings will press forward in this matter, and that Quakerism may play its part in answering this call to the churches to bring peace to West Virginia.

It Takes Courage

Not to bend to popular prejudice.

To live according to your conviction.

To refuse to make a living in a questionable vocation.

To say "No," squarely to something wrong when those around you say, "Yes."

To remain in honest poverty while others grow rich by questionable methods.

To live honestly within your means, and not dishonestly upon the means of others.

To speak the truth when, by a little prevarication, you can secure some seeming advantage.

To do your duty in silence, obscurity and poverty, while others about you prosper through neglecting or violating sacred obligations.

To refuse to do a thing which you think is wrong because it is customary and is done in trade.

To face slander and lies, and to carry yourself with cheerfulness, grace and dignity for years before the lie can be corrected.

To throw up a position with a good salary when it is the only business you know, and you have a family dependent upon you because it does not have the unqualified approval of conscience.—*Young People.*

Ambition and Aspiration

All education is a "leading out." It is the putting forth in growth of the inherent power of a unit of life. It is the same with all kinds of education, whether it concerns what is called a self-educated person or a pupil of the schools, or a disciple of the higher learning. There is, however, no definite product in any of these unless two conditions exist: first, a certain vigor in the germ of the life; second, appropriate food and opportunity through which growth is made possible for it. Superimposed upon this growth, in conjunction with it there must be guidance, if an enduring development be attained.

If we trace the life history of a vigorous human germ in its physical unfolding it is seen that it is protected, nurtured and guided in a marvelous manner up to the birth of the individual, its advent in the world; while for many years after it normally receives a very large measure of protection and definite guidance while it is learning to live; during which time the family and the home are or should be its "refuge and strength."

In this body and mind development comes consciousness of the surge of the life forces, of the desire to achieve, the reaching out for new difficulties and new conquests, the love of success for its own sake, the impulse to outdo and surpass, and a passion for power in a boundless hope and purpose. One may properly define this great marshalling of the physical powers under the domination of an alert mind by just one word, in essence including and comprising all of the outward man, the word ambition.

But linked with all this is something else. It is of later growth and of varying degrees of consciousness in different individuals but always there —the germ of a soul, the beginning of the imperishable personality, the awakening of the Spirit life in a man,—the voice of his God calling to him. It is an inseparable part of him; more real than the body, more illuminating than the mind, more enduring than either. What does this soul feed on to develop its powers and what part is it destined to play in the man's life? The food and the occasion of its development are the exercise of love, kindness, service, courage, tenderness, pity, purity, unselfishness, forgiveness,—all the spiritual verities. It is destined to sustain and uplift in the stress of life and is characterized by a hunger of soul that is called prayer,—by breadth and height of aim, by vision and hope, by faith in the good in other men and above all by the possibility of a divine power of leadership in controlling the body and mind. There would seem to be one word that defines this soul life reaching up to God; that word is aspiration.

And we have the contrast, ambition and aspiration. Which of the two should rule the man? The answer is both and together. If the first, alone, it will ruin the life after ruling it. It must have the second for guidance. For this earthly life these two natures are linked, but men have conceived the idea that they must choose between them; either that they must be of the earth, earthy, or else, in their weak aspiration or narrow understanding of God, "not of this world." Both ideals are erroneous. Ye are of differing members but one personality and destiny. The true man on earth must reconcile his members and really live his life. He must honor his body, respect his mind and believe in his soul. Ambition and aspiration must be joined.

Ambition by itself leads to unsatisfied aims and ever increasing desires to greed and lust of power, passion for reputation or applause but all on a dead level of unbridled expansion; not always low in aim but not high, merely material and transitory. The more ambition discovers of nature's secrets, the more of mastery of material things it achieves the more dangerous and destructive in its essential aims it may become. It is a high-powered machine and if without a sane hand at the throttle, the more of power the more danger. The power of mere ambitious desire has always wrecked something,—all along the way from reckless motor-driving to attempted world domination.

By contrast, the function of the soul is to control. Happy is the man who can grow to experience the realization that his developed soul or Spirit has come into its own in his heart, for verily it means for him the being born again and the more blessed if it can come to him in his younger years.

Blessed are ye who mourn for the reconciliation of your members for ye shall be comforted; and the world at large likewise. For when the old and false antagonism of the outward man against his soul and the Spirit of life; or the equally false idea of mortification of the body and mutilation of the mind by a blind and undeveloped soul, shall cease to pervert the Divine plan of life for man, then can the world go forward in a unity and a fullness of life undreamed of, for the accomplishment of all that ambition uplifted in the aspiration for God may crave or the heart of humanity hope for. C. P.

Reality In Religion

Review of "The Spirit," edited by B. H. Streeter. The Macmillan Company, New York, $2.25.

Among the references given by Prof. Charles Foster Kent at the Summer School at George School was the chapter on "The Psychology of Power" in this book. He quoted some of the examples of unusual power displayed under great emotional stress.

One of my patients, suffering from an obstinate neurasthenia, asked for leave one day because his wife, the mother of six little children, had fallen ill with pneumonia consequent on influenza, and, owing to the epidemic, could secure no doctor except for the one visit in which her condition had been diagnosed. He had been a most despondent and depressed individual, scarcely ever speaking to any one else in the ward, and left, still suffering from the tiredness and exhaustion typical of neurasthenia. He returned some days after, looking bright and cheerful, and almost his first words to me were, "I shall never doubt the power of prayer again, sir." In addition to the worry with the children, he had had the great anxiety of nursing his wife through a very serious illness without the aid of a doctor, and had been up day and night in his devoted labours. It is only those who have passed through a strain of that kind who know what it means; but it is equally true that they alone know the mighty resources that come to our aid in the time of extremity. In this case, his keenness to bring about the recovery of his wife, and the conviction of divine assistance, buoyed him up during the time of anxiety; and after the strain was over, the exhilaration of triumph saved him from the relapse that people too often bring on themselves by their lack of confidence.

This story and similar cases are quoted not as oddities, but as phenomena of experience which science is coming to take into account. Both religion and science have suffered by ignoring the field of experience covered by the other. The book we are reviewing is a serious attempt to work out the basis in psychology, philosophy and art of a theory of life that will be scientific and at the same time take into account the spiritual elements that are a part of life. Obviously such an investigation requires the mind of an expert, and as no one person can have accomplished a mastery in all the subjects vitally connected with the quest, the work is the result of the co-operation of several contributors. By a series of conference-retreats it was possible to focus on a single point the results of the first-hand study of each.

In the development of religious thought man has struggled between two conflicting ideas of God. In the one view, God is remote from the world, "of too pure eyes to behold evil." His mighty power and qualities of omniscience are so dwelt upon as to behold evil." His mighty power and qualities of omniscience are so dwelt upon as to make Him seem unapproachable. Finally He becomes the Unknown and Unknowable. This is Deism—a Transcendent God. In contrast other groups of men have emphasized the immanence of God in the world. He is present in every work of creation. God and Nature are identified. Every creation is therefore equally good and there is no room for moral distinctions. All creation is equally perfect. This is pantheism.

To modern philosophy these two views cannot be kept separate. There is unity in the idea of God, at the same time transcendent and immanent. "It is the presence of the Infinite in our finite lives that alone explains the essential nature of man."

The reviewers cannot refrain here from observing that it was the old dualistic philosophy which occasioned the quarrel of a century ago over the nature of the relationship of Christ and God. In the face of the new philosophy this conflict disappears.

The secret of power in the illustration quoted above is that there are untold resources of power not usually tapped. These resources of power refuse to respond to the will, but are at the command of the emotion, especially the deeper instinctive emotions. The problem is to so develop and train these fundamental instincts that their powers may be applied to helpful and social ends instead of running blindly in selfish and hurtful passion.

Other chapters treat of the Psychology of Grace, the Psychology of Inspiration, What Happened at Pentecost, Christ the Constructive Revolutionary, etc. The development of the idea of God as spirit is traced in the Old Testament. The relation of ritual and spiritual worship is discussed. The two kinds of experience are contrasted, the scientific and the aesthetic.

In relation to the latter subject, valuable chapters by A. Clutton-Brock discuss the relation of the "Fairy Angel," Art, to religion. Emphasis is laid on the fact that aesthetic experience brings us in touch with "the personal" of the universe, as contrasted with the impersonality of science. Art offers one of the rare mediums through which spiritual experience may be conveyed directly to others as spiritual experience, and at the same time offers a field of ideal endeavor within which many find their first perception of the laws of the spirit.

The book makes the reader wonder whether Friends have not suffered greatly in maintaining a traditional opposition to the arts.

There can be no complete worship without art. But for all spiritual experience, whether of art or of life, we need a self-surrender, a willing removal of obstructions in our minds, a sacrifice of the obvious, of what is called common sense. We must forget what the ego habitually says to us, so that we may hear something else, speak; we need to deny ourselves and follow. There is a joy in this humility, we are filled with esprit de corps, but the corps is the universe itself; and to be of the universe and proud of it, to surrender your identity to it, and then to have it given back a thousand times enriched, that is happiness compared with which all other is counterfeit.

The action of the Spirit upon man makes for fellowship. The power of its influence at Pentecost is most seen in the way the group of disciples were drawn together into common purpose and brotherly love. In their life all else was subordinate to that which made for the common life of the whole. The most grievous sin was that which marred the common life of the group.

If our prayers are answered and the spirit comes with power today we should expect: (1) that the experience would be stated in different language—rather psychic than physical; (2) that the experience would be given to a group, not an individual; (3) that the first result would be the removal of the barriers that prevent a wider fellowship among us.

"The group, whether small or large, would discover its power to assimilate individuals or other groups which, while spiritually akin to it, were separated from it by differences of taste, social standing, or intellectual outlook."

There would be a great enhancement of powers already operative, but also an uprush of others which had been dormant.

"We should see an overmastering sense of brotherhood, a serenity of mind and temper, and a restoration of religious joy such as Paul noted as the fruit of the Spirit; and accompanying these a marked increase of qualities whose social value we have been inclined to under-estimate—long-temperedness, kindness, goodness, as well as of others the world has always valued—honour, considerateness, self-control."

J. BARNARD WALTON,
RACHEL DAVIS-DUBOIS.

Regarding Children

Review of "Ourselves When Young," by H. T. Sheringham. New York. G. P. Putman's Sons; $1.75.

Books about children range themselves naturally into three general classes: Books to be read to or by children, of which there is happily an increasing number and variety; books to be enjoyed—in different ways—by children and grown-ups, of which "Alice in Wonderland" is a classic example; and books about children to be read by grown-ups, that give them glimpses of what they once did and were, of which perhaps the best is Kenneth Grahame's "The Golden Age." In this latter class, some little way below the top, is this newcomer. It is an English book, about English children, but they get into the same mischiefs and transient tragedies that attend healthy children everywhere. There is a quiet vein of humor and much food for thought in this father's attitude of mind toward the child-mind, and the book may be useful, as well as amusing, to some young parents. Chapter VI, discribing the parent trying to coin a golden story for a questioning pair of hearers will be appreciated by those who have thus failed.

Here is a bit of good philosophy. "Primarily childhood is not interested in toys but in *things,* as an old shoe, a cardboard box, a cigarette case, and so on. These give imagination scope and stimulate ingenuity. Also, it may be, they are a reminder that life is real and earnest, which is no doubt useful when one feels like that. The Powers that Are, on the other hand are for the most part blase about *things,* but fascinated by toys, which to them are a reminder that life need not be wholly real and earnest. That is largely why toy-merchants flourish and why uncles bring such large parcels."

Had the author been intent on imparting advice he doubtless would have (very properly) urged letting the child develop its invention and imagination more with the things about it and less with ready-made toys. But he was only trying to write an interesting little book, and has succeeded.

JOHN COX, JR.

A Prayer

"God, who art Giver of all good gifts and Lover of Concord,—

"Kindle my lips with the live coal from the hands of the Seraph,

"Give me the voice of humility, give me the word of imagination, give me the tongue of love. Give me the gift of understanding all men, that I may be understood of all men. For His sake who came that we might have life, and that we might have it more abundantly."

—From "Soul's Medicine," in "Garments of Praise," by Florence Converse. Selected by E Maria Bishop.

More Patience, God

Give me more patience, God,
  With those who do not see,
The strong and loving kind,
  Like thine with me.

Thou seest me as a child,
  And knowest I may grow,
Help me to look at them,
  And see them so.

Give me more patience, God,
  With those who do not see,
The strong, the tender kind,
  Like thine with me.

ELEANOR SCOTT SHARPLES.

The Nation Back of Flour Campaign

The two outstanding examples of the way America has gotten under the task of sending flour to the starving people of Russia are given by two cities, one in the East and one in the West.

In the city of St. Louis the American Federated Russian Relief Committee combined with the organization established there by our Service Committee and is conducting a campaign under the name of the St. Louis Committee of the American Friends' Service Committee for Russian Relief. Mr. E. C. Dreyer, one of the leading business men of St. Louis, is chairman of the committee which is now securing 200 of the leading business men of St. Louis to become members of the committee. Part of its program includes the organization of the whole State of Missouri with branch committees in every community. Dr. Armstrong, the Secretary of the St. Louis Federation of Churches, has promised that every minister in the city will call the attention of his congregation to the need. The committee has also planned to give the heads of the larger industries of the city a subscription sheet asking them to ask each employee to contribute something. Every Missourian is asked to at once get in touch with this committee, whose office is at 215 Merchants Exchange.

In Trenton, N. J., the Mercer County Russian Famine Fund has been organized, with headquarters in the Chamber of Commerce. Arthur E. Moon is chairman of this committee. They have already placed booths in the various stores of the city, and have collected a considerable amount of money in that way. They have organized a tag day for pedestrians and automobiles, and have made a most attractive tag which can be tied to automobiles, using the cut of the barrel of flour which has become the sign of the flour campaign. If any other community would be interested in using this idea, the Service Committee would be glad to furnish a sample of this kind of publicity.

Have you an organization in your community? If not, you are the one to begin it. Write today to J. Augustus Cadwallader, Secretary for the Flour Campaign, 20 South 12th street, Philadelphia, and he can secure literature containing information and methods of work.

Notes from the Service Field

Accompanying the publicity material received this week from the American Friends' Service Committee, but too long for us to publish in full, is a report of the work of the Friends' Mission in Vienna for the year 1921. To read this report is

kitchen were rapidly erected and the relief efforts undoubtedly prevented what might have been an epidemic, for the refugees made no sanitary arrangements whatever for themselves, and in the hot, damp climate the danger of the spreading of disease was very great."

After describing the work of Friends in other sections of Russia, the writer concludes: "Moreover, although for a time they fell under a shadow of the suspicion with which all philanthropic organizations were regarded, especially those under foreign management, their obviously disinterested and non-partisan character finally convinced everyone that they had no part to play beyond ministering to the sick without regard to creed, race or politics. In both of the Russian capitals they have distributed food, clothing and medicine, and though small in number their labors have always been fruitful. No one who has come into touch with them can fail to be convinced that theirs is a work of grace that will help to revive in body and spirit a now abject people."

Friendly News Notes

In a letter to M. Louise Baker, Constance Allen writes that James G. Douglas, well-known to many Friends here as a prominent member of Dublin Yearly Meeting, is a member of the Committee appointed to draft the Constitution of the Irish Free State.

Word has been received from Joseph and Edith Platt, of their safe arrival on January 27th, in Mukden, China, where they are engaged in Y. M. C. A. work. They sailed from Vancouver, B. C., on January 5th.

David Gittleman informs us that in our introductory note to his recent article, "Why The Common People Don't Stop War," we misstated the manner in which he sustained injury during his war service. He was a member of a detachment which was retained in this country, and after eighteen months of unusually strenuous service, suffered an attack of cerebro-spinal meningitis.

A standing committee for disarmament service composed of both branches of Friends in West Grove and vicinity, arranged for a meeting to be addressed by Frederick J. Libby. In considering the best place to hold the meeting, it was decided it would seriously limit its usefulness to hold it in one of the meeting-houses. It resulted in a well-advertised community meeting in the Borough Hall with no charge for admission. A free-will offering was taken.

Frederick Libby gave a true and interesting account of what had been done at the Washington Conference, and what vital duties yet remain for us to take part in that permanent Peace may be established, based on economic and industrial relations that bespeak a Christian brotherhood. The High School children seemed much impressed with his knowledge and power.

The Committee felt well rewarded in giving this opportunity to the entire community rather than to enlighten ourselves only in one of our own meeting-houses. Should not Friends more frequently follow this course?

Patience W. Kent.

We note in the Swarthmore *Phoenix* that former President and Mrs. Swain have arrived in Honolulu. In accordance with the old Hawaiian custom, when they stepped from the steamer they were "wreathed" by a party of friends, among whom were Anna Satterthwaite, '13, and Edward Caum, '14. Dr. and Mrs. Swain plan to remain in Hawaii until April 1st, when they will embark for Japan.

Also, that Amos J. Peaslee, '07, is to practice before the Permanent Court of International Justice at the Hague. The *Phoenix* writes:

"Mr. Peaslee, while attached to the American Peace Commission, urged recognition of the work of the Hague Conferences, and more prominence to the World Court of the League of Nations. He has made a careful study of the problem of the Permanent Court, and in a special article in the New York *Times* of February 5th, 1922, he has set forth his conclusion that the nations of the world have as much need for 'an adequate system for the realization of justice' as the United States have for the Supreme Court.

"In the same article Mr. Peaslee continues, 'Until some satisfactory mechanism is smoothly functioning to which aggrieved parties can apply when international wrongs are threatened or committed, for a determination and protection of their basis of the facts and the justice of rights by impartial tribunals on the case, the aggrieved parties and their champions will continue to resort to force in an endeavor to realize justice thru the only means that they find available."

In addition to the series of meetings addressed by Frederick J. Libby and the series of addresses given at Quarterly Meetings, Dr. O. Edward Janney, Executive Secretary of the General Conference Section of Friends' Disarmament Council, reports the following activities for the last month:

Letters arranged so that monthly subscriptions, collected quarterly, could be conveniently made, have been sent to all keymen, together with letters of instructions, in sufficient quantities to send out to a selected list of their members. This plan seems to be working well, the amount received in cash and promises to date being $784.50.

About 6000 pages of telling literature has gone out, with orders coming in for much more.

A vicious militia bill, involving conscription, being about to pass the Maryland legislature, the Executive Secretary, with others, visited Annapolis on this matter. The objectionable features were eliminated.

Efforts to have essays prepared by school children on "World Peace and how we may help to secure it," is meeting with success. In Baltimore, for instance, the pupils in eight high schools, are busily at work on them.

Our Section and that of Philadelphia are working together with good results and very pleasantly. The Treasurer of this Section is Anna B. Griscom, Moorestown, N. J.

The week-end of Second month 25th and 26th was a busy one for Friends in Baltimore. The Orthodox group has just completed the construction of a new meeting house in the Homewood district, opposite the campus of Johns Hopkins University. An invitation was extended to our Friends to join in the dedication of this new center. On Seventh-day evening, a reception was given. Rufus M. Jones was asked to speak impromptu on this occasion.

Referring, among other things, to "the terrible tragedy" of the separation of 1827, he expressed his hope that before the first century of separation ends in 1927, Friends will be one. If we are unable to have peace among ourselves, he said, we cannot expect to preach peace effectively to the world.

On First-day morning, Rufus M. Jones preached in the new meeting house, while in the evening Elbert Russell delivered an address on "What Friends Stand For." He defined Quakerism as "social Christian mysticism," and in his exposition of these three terms outlined the essential Friends' principles.

The new Homewood meeting house at Baltimore, Md., is interesting as one of the rare Quaker meeting houses built during the twentieth century. Its exterior is of brick, and the whole, though plain, is planned with elegance. In addition to the large auditorium for meetings, there are rooms for First-day school, study groups and social activities, a tastefully appointed library, and an office for the new Secretary of the Meeting. Several of the rooms contain open fire-places.

Walter and Marcelle Abell visited the Park Avenue Baltimore Friends during the same weekend which marked the above events. Speaking in the morning meeting for worship, the former expressed his conviction that only by deepening our own experience of God, and by working out in every relation of our own personal lives the social urge which such an experience brings, can we help lead the world to peace. We must live our principles, rather than talk them. Friends must beware that class distinctions blind none to the full implications of the doctrine of love. "Bolshevist" and "political prisoner" are our brothers, just as Jesus regarded the outcast of his day as his brothers. By our attitude toward such as these, whom the world despises, do we show whether "love" is a reality in our lives, or simply a word.

Bliss Forbush, O. Edward Janney and others also delivered messages.

On First-day evening, the Young Friends held their monthly Firelight Supper, following which Walter and Marcelle Abell collaborated in an illustrated talk on France and the French.

NEW YORK NOTES

A goodly number of New York and Brooklyn Friends put in "a full day" on the 16th of Second month. The Schermerhorn St. Meeting held a Conference led by Carolena Wood, on the relief work in Central Europe, and the needs of that section, at 2 o'clock. Carolena Wood attended the Meeting for Worship in the morning. Friends were asked to bring a box lunch, which was served in the dining-room at 12.45. Friends from all four Meetings were present at the morning Meeting, and at the "community" lunch, and many more came in for the Conference, which was very large and interesting. Its key-note was struck in the words of Carolena Wood, 'However hungry of body these people may be,—and some of them are very hungry,—they are even more hungry spiritually."

The 19th happened to be the day for the Tea-meeting at the Twentieth St. Meeting-house at 5.30, and by a coincidence, the speaker of the day was James Norton, of the Service Committee, on the topic, "The Meaning of Friends' Service." Twenty or more Friends, therefore, "made a day of it," and went to this gathering also, which was unusually large, and as varied in its makeup as the afternoon Conference. James Norton gave a brief account of the present work of the Service Committee in Europe, and then spoke of the slowly maturing plans for "home Service" work for young Friends.

Clothing comes in so rapidly to the Service Committee's warehouse at 108 Dobbin Street, Brooklyn, from those who would help relieve the suffering in Russia, that the statements of one day are far out-paced on the next. The Secretary for the work prepared an appeal recently, saying that the warehouse was receiving five tons of clothing a week, and asking for co-operation to raise this to a ton a day. Before the circular was printed, clothing was coming at more than the asked-for rate.—It has been sent out, nevertheless.—What is a ton of clothing among millions of people?

The week of the 6th of Second month, ten tons of clothing were shipped to Russia. On the 21st, 22 tons were on hand, baled and expecting to go, by the port of Reval, on the 24th; twenty-two tons of clothing came in between the 6th and the 21st. A little over half of this comes from the various Red Cross Chapters throughout the country, which are sending to Dobbin St. the clothing that they have been for some time gathering. But very nearly half is from other sources,—from Friends, the friends of Friends, and those who have received invitations to co-operate in the work.

A. L. C.

WOOLMAN SCHOOL

The days at Woolman School are full of work and pleasure. At different times during Second month, various members of the school have attended the following: The last of Dr. Russell's lectures on the Four Gospels, given before the Young Friends' Association, Philadelphia; a box supper at Media, by invitation of Media Orthodox Friends, to hear Frederick J. Libby's address on "The Washington Conference. What Next?"; Abington Quarterly Meeting and Quarterly Meeting (Orthodox) at Media, Pa., both being inspiring and helpful occasions; a Young Friends' pilgrimage at 17th and Girard Avenue, Philadelphia; Meeting for worship at Newtown, and Young Friends' Association Meeting at Wrightstown, Pa.

Effie Danforth McAfee's lectures given for the benefit of Woolman School were delightfully interesting. We all enjoyed the visit of William R. Fogg and wife, who showed us a number of pictures and photographs collected by him during his year of service in foreign relief work in Germany and Poland.

Josephine Pennock, of Kennett Square, Pa., Grace Brown and Edith Winder, of George School, Rachel DuBois and others were recent guests. We also entertained a number of Swarthmore College friends on the 23rd.

As we enter on our last three weeks here we look forward to a helpful course on "Success in Teaching Religion," by E. Morris Ferguson.

All good things must come to an end as with regret we realize two of our most interesting and helpful courses have ended,—that by Dr. Russell on "Hebrew Life and Thought" and the course by Mrs. Collins, on the "Hebrew Prophets." Only one who has had the privilege of attending Woolman School can know the wonderful inspiration, lasting help and benefit to each member of the group in the daily morning devotional period led by Dr. Russell, the beautiful and inspiring truths and lessons of the New Testament as interpreted by one divinely gifted, one through whom we glimpse the vision of what it means to be a friend of Christ.

M. R. H.

BURLINGTON QUARTERLY MEETING

Burlington Quarterly Meeting was held at Mt. Holly, N. J., on Second month 21st. There was a large attendance. Dr. O. Edward Janney, Sarah T. Linvill, Keziah R. Wilkins, and Daniel Willets gave helpful messages in the meeting for worship.

At the business meeting, presided over by Franklin S. Zelley, Clerk, the Managers of the Friends' Boarding Home at Trenton, N. J., reported having had a very satisfactory and prosperous year, both financially and for the benefit of those living at the Home.

At the close of the business session, Dr. Janney gave his message in regard to the disarmament work, and resolutions were formulated, adopted and directed to be forwarded to each of our Senators and members of Congress from New Jersey, in regard to the limitation of armaments.

At the close of the meeting a lunch was served to all those who were present at the meeting, which is a step forward in the line of hospitality, good-will and the future welfare of the Society. F. S. Z.

CENTRE QUARTERLY MEETING

Centre Quarterly Meeting was held at Unionville, Pa., Second month 20th. Representatives were in attendance from all the Monthly meetings comprising the Quarterly Meeting. Much splendid real service work has been in progress as reported from all the meetings, in the line of contributions to the European Relief Funds. The meeting was not forgetful to send letters of appreciation to the American Delegates to the Limitation of Armaments. Also a letter of approval of the treaties urging their speedy ratification to our Senators. The memorial of our departed Friend Uriah Blackburn, Fishertown, Pa., was approved by the meeting and directed to be preserved with the minutes. He was Centre Quarterly Meeting Recorder for many years. E. Howard Blackburn was appointed to fill the vacancy.

Joel Borton of Woodstown, N. J., was in attendance at all of the sessions. Some of the boys from State College, Pa., were in attendance at some of the sessions, taking part and contributing much to the splendid spirit of helpfulness.

Foster Heacock, of Bedford, Pa., George T. Underwood, of Clearfield, Pa., and Joel Borton were especially favored in presenting to a good gathering of people on First-day afternoon, "Present-day Peace Prospects and Citizenship Ideals." Sue Fox presided at this meeting, and everything was seemingly a blended inspiration of good thought never to be forgotten by those in attendance.

A parlor meeting was held at the home of our beloved deceased friend Louisa A. W. Russell. Several friends gave testimonials of loving tribute to her memory.

The First-day School Association contributed to the upbuilding of Centre's First-day Schools. Reports indicate a live wide-awake interest.

The meeting of Ministry and Counsel was held as usual and out of its membership there appeared to be coming into sight some new vocal ministry of which our meeting heartily approves. GEO. T. UNDERWOOD.

FAIRFAX QUARTERLY MEETING

Fairfax Quarterly Meeting was held at Washington, D. C., on Second month 20th, Lewis Pidgeon, Clerk, presiding. In the meeting for worship Dr. O. Edward Janney spoke on love and brotherhood, the foundations of Christianity, and the necessity of a sustaining faith. Daniel Batchellor contrasted the two dominating factors in our lives—intelligence and emotion. M. B. Cotsworth, of Vancouver, B. C., urged Friends to use their influence to further the cause of peace, citing an instance of a decision made by Richard Rush which influenced England to abandon the idea of fortifications and the maintenance of a navy on the Canadian border.

Two resolutions were adopted, one to be sent to the House of Representatives urging the reduction of armaments, the other to the Senate asking for prompt ratification of the treaties now under consideration. Letters of commendation were also sent to President Harding and Secretary Hughes.

Following discussion of the Ninth Query, a committee was appointed to visit schools, Normal schools, Parent-Teacher Associations, to urge teachers to foster and encourage the love of nations rather than to emphasize the hatred of nations, and by every means possible to promote the cause of permanent peace through education.

Frederick J. Libby, in a stirring address, pointed out two ways in which work for permanent peace may be carried on,—first through the schools in teaching the new and broader idea of patriotism; secondly, through influencing legislation. Everyone should keep two tests in mind and apply them to every question that comes up. I. Does this legislation lead toward international conferences and better understanding among nations? II. Does it tend toward reduction of armaments? If so, work for it. Friends are in the limelight now, and our influence is greater, perhaps, than we realize.

The First-day School Association met First-day afternoon, class exercises being given by classes from Woodlawn and Washington Schools. In the discussion of the question, "How can the First-day School teach Disarmament?", it was suggested that a broadening influence is gained by the study of the history and good points of other religions, by stories of the children of other lands, and also that we substitute heroes of peace for war heroes. Thomas B. Hull spoke of the change on the part of several prominent men in their attitude toward preparedness, and made many valuable suggestions for First-day school teaching on the subject of disarmament.

Items From Everywhere

The editor of the St. Louis *Christian Advocate* (Methodist) in its issue for January 25, outlines the opportunities and duties of the religious press as he sees them in relation to social and industrial questions. He pleads for attention to these questions because they are "pre-eminently the issues which have to do with human happiness, human relationships, international peace or war," and because they "concern intimately and oftimes wholly condition the physical, mental and spiritual opportunities of men and women and children." Not only the principles but the facts must be presented with reference to social situations that offer a moral challenge to the Christian community. The church press has peculiar responsibility in this connection because "it is the one channel of publicity which can be expected to be impartial and disinterested in the presentation of the facts."

Mary H. Whitson sends us a highly commendable clipping from a Kokomo, Indiana, daily paper, emphasizing the futility of fines as a method of overcoming intoxication, and the hardship which such a method frequently imposes upon innocent members of the family. "Those charged with intoxication," it says, "cannot be reformed, cannot be helped, by transferring money from the pockets of their wives, their children, their dependents to the pockets of the prosecuting attorney and to the city of Kokomo. This money is needed, in almost every instance, by the families of the men from whom it is thoughtlessly taken. How foolish, how heartless, how brutal it is to use the strong forces of the law to take the hard earnings of these men, the victims, in many instances, of looseness in law enforcement against those who sell liquor illegally, either with official approval or through official inefficiency.

"Men who become drunk are sick men, mentally and physically. They should not be sent to jail or fined; they should be cured and brought out of their false sense of pleasure, their bondage to evil influences.

"Public sentiment should demand more mercy, more intelligence, more sympathy for those who are diseased and become the victims of their appetites."

The Federal Council of Churches, 105 E. 22nd St., New York City, is issuing a third call to 150,000 churches to press forward in the "Church campaign for a warless world."

The Council now urges the churches:

1. "To start an immediate drive in each locality, by community mass meetings or otherwise, for prompt and intelligent discussion of the treaties now before the Senate.

2. "To promote the study of the moral significance of the proposed treaties in various groups in all our churches.

3. "To arrange that large numbers of petitions and personal letters shall go at once to Senators, expressing the conclusions reached in regard to the ratification of the treaties."

In case the treaties are ratified by the Senate the churches are further urged to use the Sunday following ratification as an occasion for special thanksgiving for 'the new epoch on which the world is starting, and to use their influence to secure popular meetings of rejoicing and celebration throughout the country."

This urge within the churches themselves should offer an opportunity for Friends to co-operate with other denominations in pressing forward in the crusade for peace.

The Prison Comfort Club's list of those in prison "for conscience's sake" whose birthdays fall during March is as follows:

2nd, Britt Smith; 4th, Ray Becker; 16th, C. Bland; these three to be addressed: Box 520, Walla Walla, Washington.

The remainder are all to be addressed: Box 7, Leavenworth, Kansas, and are: 9th, Stanley J. Clark; 10th, H. F. Kane; 12th, Arthur Boose; 13th, George F. Voetter; 18th, James Slovick; 20th, Ed. Quigly; 22nd, Wm. Hood; 25th, Wm. Moran; 27th, Godfrey Ebel; 28th, Joe Greber. Several of these dates fall early in the month, but a card or letter will be just as welcome even though late. "It is good to be remembered by those on the outside," these men write. "It helps a lot to know we are not forgotten." This is *so little* for *us* to do, in comparison with what *they* are doing. Those in Walla Walla prison are allowed to write only one letter each week, but they may *receive* any number. Those in Leavenworth are allowed 3 letters weekly. If any one reading this would care to have detailed information about any of these men, this will gladly be supplied by the Prison Comfort Club, if inquiry is sent in care of the INTELLIGENCER.

THE OPEN FORUM

This column is intended to afford free expression of opinion by readers on questions of interest. The INTELLIGENCER is not responsible for any such opinions. Letters must be brief, and the editor reserves the right to omit parts if necessary to save space.

FROM A VISITOR TO LAING SCHOOL

To the Editor:

On Second month 3rd, while on our way home from Florida, my husband and I visited the Laing School. What I saw and heard there stirred me deeply and, in the hope that others may be led to feel as I do, I am writing to FRIENDS' INTELLIGENCER.

First, dear friends, please do not send odd shoes to Laing or, indeed, anywhere else. I was shown a barrel of these, except, perhaps for an odd piece of leather, now and then, utterly useless, not worth the freight that was paid on them.

The needs of Laing are urgent. As may be known to many of your readers, the school authorities of Charleston County have heretofore been paying the salaries of four teachers in the School for nine months each year. Now, pleading lack of funds, they have reduced the school term to seven months and refuse to pay these four teachers for a longer time. At $50 per month this deficit, to be made up by us, is $400. Surely, by each contributor's increasing his or her subscription by, say, one half, this and other things can easily be done.

The attendance at Laing, I was told, is not so large as it would otherwise be, because the authorities of Charleston County are trying to force the children to go to the miserable little crowded country schools that they have set up. In a number of cases the children have persevered and still walk from four to six miles each morning to Laing School.

This school ought to be larger and better equipped.

In conclusion I must pay my tribute of admiration to Charlotte B. Ross, principal, and her corps of assistants, whose courtesy, ability, energy and enthusiasm make them an example and an honor to their own people and ought to arouse our deep interest and sympathy.

Bird-in-Hand, Pa. MARIANNA G. BRUBAKER.

FRIENDS AND THE CHURCHES

To the Editor:

The following are my answers to the questions recently asked by Nanie Webster in the Open Forum:

Whether a Friend can consistently join in with the Orthodox churches in their efforts at "church union," depends upon the basis of the proposed union. In a union of "Orthodox" churches Friends can have no place since "orthodox" is a term that cannot properly be applied to Friends. The word implies a standard of belief; Friends have no such standard. Consistency in a Friend is faithfulness to his own conception of truth and not conformity to rules of conduct or of thought formulated by another or by an organization.

If the union of churches is to be based upon a relegation of creeds to the privacy of the individual sanctuary and every member is to be permitted to enjoy his pet heresies or his cherished beliefs, and no questions asked, I see nothing to hinder the co-operation of Friends. If, however, there is to be even a residuum of a minimum of theological qualification for membership, the Friend, tho able to pass, ought not join. For with a Friend the question is not, "Can I subscribe to the required belief," but, "Is any particular belief required?" The protest of Friends has not been against the teachings of orthodoxy, but against the claim that there is such a thing as orthodoxy in teachings.

"The fundamental teachings of Friends and (of) the Orthodox churches" are not the same. The difference I have just pointed out.

But there can be no "vital difference between the interpretation of the Bible which Friends give and that which others give," since Friends do not assume to give any official interpretation at all. Each Friend makes his own and is free to announce it; but he must grant to every other person the same liberty.

It is impossible to "arrange and clarify" what cannot even be stated. The student who performs a mathematical operation because "that is the way we were taught to do it," has not grasped his mathematics. The Friend who, as a reason for the faith that is in him refers to "the way Friends interpret" Bible passages has not grasped Quakerism. EDWARD B. RAWSON.

BIRTHS

BROOMELL—On Second month 21st, at Germantown, Pa., to George Lupton and Anna Pettit Broomell, a daughter, named Hannah Thompson Broomell.

MARRIAGES

COOMBS-HIRES—On Second month 18th, at the home of the bride's parents, "Hiresdale," Salem, N. J., under the care of Salem Monthly Meeting, Marvin H. Coombs to Letitia Fogg Hires, daughter of Charles R. and Anna Fogg Hires.

HAINES-HANCOCK—On Twelfth month 21st, 1921, at Mt. Holly, N. J., R. Shannon Haines and Lydia L. Hancock, both of Mt. Holly, N. J.

DEATHS

JARRETT—At Moorestown, N. J., on Second month 25, Joseph W., husband of M. Ella Jarrett (nee Jones), in his 60th year. Funeral Abington Friends' Meeting House.

KENDERDINE—At Newtown, Pa., on Second month 17th, Thaddeus S. Kenderdine, in the 86th year of his age.

LADD—On First month 28th, at Lodi, California, Emeline C. Ladd, aged 95 years. Emeline Ladd was for many years a subscriber and ardent supporter of the FRIENDS' INTELLIGENCER, and a member of Clear Creek Monthly Meeting of Illinois Yearly Meeting of Friends. She came to Lodi twenty-six years ago, where she has since resided.

A. E. S.

POWELL—Suddenly at Pasadena, California, G. Harold Powell, son of George T. and Marcia C. Powell of Brookfield, Mass.

The death of this man, just past fifty, seems literally a translation. He was in a pleasant dinner-party of friends, when in a moment's pause in conversation, he passed into the life beyond. He was a graduate of Cornell University. He knew the blessedness of marriage and fatherhood. His life-work had been in the field of Horticulture. If he had not "made two blades of grass grow where one grew before," perhaps it might be said of him that he made two oranges grow where one grew before; and that he had conquered the insect enemies of the orange. Perhaps it was not the least of his conquests, that one of his fellow-workers reported of him early in his career: "Oh, yes, I know him well. He is the man who can tell you that you are doing everything wrong, and not make you mad!"

It can truly be said of him that he emanated light!

Not long ago he wrote in an "Appreciation" of Ethan Allen Chase, of California, these words, which are not less true of himself:

"But the greatest triumph of the man was the making of his own individuality. He united a rare beauty and graciousness of spirit with great intellectual attainments; in him farseeing vision, poise and integrity were combined with a sublime faith and a deep religous aspiration. Such fruitage is the test of a man's life."

ELIZABETH POWELL BOND.

ROBERTS—In Baltimore, Md., on Second month 20th, Ellen T., daughter of the late Josiah and Lydia Roberts. Interment was made in Friends' Burying Ground in Baltimore.

WILBUR—At Providence, R. I., on Second month 23rd, Eliza M., wife of the late Henry W. Wilbur, in her 73rd year. Interment at Flushing, N. Y.

WILLIAM BROWN

Loudoun County sustained a loss when William Brown passed on to the higher life, at his home in Lincoln, Va., on Second month 7th. Had he lived until the 22nd, he would have been 83 years of age.

William Brown was born at Circleville, Va. In 1866, he married Lydia N. Janney, daughter of Asa M. Janney. He is survived by his widow, one son, one daughter and several grandchildren.

In the meeting where he was "Cousin Will" to most of us, and which he loved and served next to his family circle, he was the unofficial moderator. Generous of impulse and just in his judgments, his ready wit with his decisive manner solved many a problem in business meetings.

Always interested in young people, one of the joys of these later years in Lincoln was the High School, and the pupils, past and present, feel a personal loss.

Realizing for two years that his health was failing, he approached the end as naturally and as confidently as he had lived, saying to a friend "God has been good to me here. I believe he will be good hereafter and the best is yet to come."

While deeply feeling his going 'There are memories too precious for tears" and a wonderful feeling of thankfulness to our Heavenly Father fills our hearts for a life so full and bright and useful. L. S. H.

HANNAH M. THOMPSON, M. D.

Hannah M. Thompson, physician, preacher, wide awake, worthy citizen of Wilmington, Delaware, died after several weeks' illness, on the 5th of Second month, 1922, aged 76 years and 6 months. This was a woman who *lived* not merely existed; who took her part in the activities of the community, vitalizing to a degree the air of her surroundings; who was not content to be simply carried along on the inevitable current of things, but who stepped in bravely, bearing her flag aloft; willing to *do*, and to *be used*, to the extent of her ability. From a child she thirsted to *know* things. Her lack of robust health induced her to seek the reason why, and if possible to find the remedy, and in that seeking on her own account, she became permanently and absorbingly interested for the benefit of her fellow-beings who suffered, and so was led to devote herself to a thorough study of physiology and therapeutics up to the latest unfoldings of science, graduating after a full and extended course at the Woman's Medical College at Philadelphia, about 1883 or 1884. She began the general practice of medicine in Wilmington, and continued it with success and the great confidence and respect of her patrons till she relinquished it quite recently, still keeping her place on the boards of charitable institutions, and kindly serving many suffering ones who came privately to her for help and advice. Her public ministrations in the meeting, and on other occasions, were thoughtful, encouraging and original; the meaning of her subject often brought out and enforced by illustrations from her daily experiences. She was born on the home farm in Mill Creek Hundred, Delaware, the third daughter of Lewis and Lydia Pusey Thompson, who were among the founders of Mill Creek meeting, a branch of New Garden monthly meeting, Pa. Many tributes of respect and appreciation were paid at her funeral, which took place at Wilmington Meeting-house on the 8th instant. EMMA WORRELL.

COMING EVENTS

THIRD MONTH.

3rd—Pupils of Friends' Seminary will give Conan Doyle's play, "Waterloo," at 8 o'clock, in the Seminary gymnasium. The money received for admissions will be used to send the School basketball team to play the Wilmington Friends School.

4th—Nottingham Quarterly Meeting, at Oxford, Pa., at 10.30 a. m. Conference at 2 o'clock, on Disarmament.

4th—Whitewater Quarterly Meeting, at Richmond, Indiana.

5th—Oxford Preparative meeting, at 7.30 p. m. Bliss Forbush will attend.

4th—Recital by the Hahn String Quartette at George School, Pa., at 8.15. Single admission, fifty cents.

4th—Gwynedd Monthly Meeting at Plymouth Meeting, Pa., at 3.30 p. m. Box supper at 6. William J. Reagan will address a meeting held at 7.30.

5th—3 p. m. A meeting for divine worship will be held at Chester Friends' Meeting House under the care of a Committee of Concord Quarterly Meeting. Friends of both branches are asked to attend. The desire is to make it a community meeting to which all persons are welcome; and the co-operation of young persons is solicited. Come and bring another.

5th—Conference class at 15th and Race Streets, Philadelphia, at close of meeting for worship, at 11.40 a. m. Speaker—Abigail Blackburn. Subject—Standards of the Kingdom III. Service the Final Test of Character.

9th—Salem Quarterly Meeting, at Woodstown, N. J.

11th—Burlington First-day School Union will be held at Mt. Holly Meeting House at 10.30 a. m.

11th and 12th—Pilgrimage under care of the Young Friends' Movement, at Norristown, Pa.

12th.—The Advancement Committee of Westbury Quarterly Meeting will attend Meeting at Fifteenth Street, New York. In the afternoon at 2 o'clock there will be a Conference on some phase of "Civil Liberties." Friends are asked to bring a box lunch, in order that the Conference may begin on time.

12th—Walter Abell, Editor of the FRIENDS' INTELLIGENCER, will attend Meeting at Schermerhorn Street, Brooklyn.

13th—New York Monthly Meeting will be held at the Meeting-house, 221 East 15th Street, New York, at 7.30. Supper will be served at 6 o'clock. The Meeting for Ministry and Counsel will meet at 5.

13th—Baltimore Quarterly Meeting, at Baltimore, Md.

16th—Haddonfield Quarterly Meeting at Moorestown, N. J.

18th—An Evening of Magic, by Paul Fleming, at George School, Pa. Admission, fifty cents.

NOTICE—Whiting Williams will be giving a number of addresses in Philadelphia during the week of Third month 13th. Under the title "Full Up and Fed Up" he describes conditions and attitudes among some of the workers in Europe. His schedule includes the following: Third month 14th, Third-day, 11 a. m. and 5 p. m., Wharton School, University of Pennsylvania; 8 p. m. City Club, 313 South Broad Street. Tickets for last mentioned address obtainable from George B. Comfort, Miller Lock Company, Philadelphia. It is understood that Whiting Williams may also speak at a City Club Long Table Luncheon on Fourth-day, Third month 15th.

American Friends' Service Committee

WILBUR K. THOMAS, EX. SEC.
20 S. 12th St. Philadelphia.

CASH CONTRIBUTIONS
WEEK ENDING FEBRUARY 22.

Five Years Meetings	$719.37
Other Meetings—	
Center Monthly Meeting	15.00
Norristown Prep. Meeting	200.00
Western Quarterly Meeting	327.00
Buckingham Monthly Meeting	5.00
Rahway & Plainfield Monthly Meeting	100.00
Orange Grove Friends of Pasadena	15.00
Germantown Monthly Meeting	50.00
Little Britain Monthly Meeting	11.03
Park Avenue Meeting, Baltimore, Md.	200.00
West Grove First-day School	5.00
Cleveland Friends Service Committee	20.00
West Branch Monthly Meeting, Iowa	20.00
Merion Prep. Meeting	100.00
Gunpowder Monthly Meeting	15.00
Pipe Creek Monthly Meeting	20.00
College Park Association, California	215.00
Villa St. & Galena Avenue Friends	50.00
Lincoln Friends	110.00
Barnesville Unit Friends' Service Committee	67.50
Cornwall Monthly Meeting	15.00
Contributions for General	631.89
For Germany	9,267.21
For Austria	106.08
For Poland	70.02
For Armenia	9.25
For Syria	44.50
For Russia	17,475.59
For Russian Overhead	269.47
For German Overhead	10.00
Refunds	17.82
	$30,182.23

Shipments received during week ending February 18th, 1922: 119 boxes and packages received; 1 for German relief; 4 anonymous.

REGULAR MEETINGS

OAKLAND, CALIF.—A FRIENDS' MEETing is held every First-day at 11 A. M., in the Extension Room, Y. W. C. A. Building, Webster Street, above 14th. Visiting Friends always welcome.

FRIENDS' MEETING IN PASADENA, California—Orange Grove Monthly Meeting of Friends, 520 East Orange Grove Avenue, Pasadena, California. Meeting for worship, First-day, 11 A. M. Monthly Meeting, the second First-day of each month, at 1.45 P. M.

CENTRAL MEETING OF FRIENDS (Chicago), meets every First-day in Room 601, 410 South Michigan Avenue, at 10.45 a. m. Visitors are invited.

WANTED

POSITION WANTED—BY GENTLEwoman of refinement, past middle age, but active and in good health, in a family of means, as companion to elderly or semi-invalid lady. Good reader. Congenial surroundings rather than highest salary. K. B., 24 Lennox Avenue, East Orange, N. J.

POSITION WANTED—NURSE, MIDdle-aged, wants care of invalid. Would manage housekeeping. Address P. 90, Friends' Intelligencer.

BOOK WANTED—FRIENDS' MISCELlany, Vol. 10, containing the Journals of the lives of Joshua Evans and John Hunt. Philadelphia 1837. Anyone having a copy which he would sell, address Benjamin Ashman, 309 S. Henry St., Madison, Wisconsin.

PARTY OF EIGHT NOW ORGANIZing for 58-day trip—Paris, Switzerland, Passion Play, Holland, England. Starting about July 1. Rates reasonable. Apply without delay to Bertha L. Stover, 31 Westview St., Germantown, Philadelphia.

EXPERIENCED, RELIABLE MIDDLE aged woman desires position as housekeeper in small family. Address S. 91, Friends' Intelligencer.

WANTED—CAPABLE AND DEPENDable woman for general housework in family of three adults; suburban town. Must be good cook. Good wages and permanent home for the right person. Reference required. Address T. 92, Friends' Intelligencer.

AT WALLINGFORD—WILL SHARE attractive, furnished, five-room bungalow, with congenial woman. Phone Media 668 J., before 9 a. m.

REFINED, CAPABLE MOTHER OF 3 children, wants any kind of employment where it is possible to keep her little ones together and educate them. Can give best of reference. Address K. 59, Friends' Intelligencer.

FOR RENT

FOR RENT—APRIL TO OCTOBER, Nine-room house with sleeping porch and garage, near river, at Riverton. Address Helen Lippincott, Riverton, N. J.

FOR RENT—AT WALLINGFORD, PA. —$75.—Old colonial house. 5 bedrooms, 2 baths, hot water heat. Convenient to station and trolley. Phone Media 668 J., before 9 a. m.

TRANSIENT ACCOMMODATIONS

WASHINGTON, D. C.—ROOMS FOR visitors. Near Station, Capitol, Library. Continuous hot water. Electricity. Garage. Mrs. L. L. Kendig, 120 C. Street, Northwest.

To the Lot Holders and others interested in Fairhill Burial Ground:

GREEN STREET Monthly Meeting has funds available for the encouragement of the practice of cremating the dead to be interred in Fairhill Burial Ground. We wish to bring this fact as prominently as possible to those who may be interested. We are prepared to undertake the expense of cremation in case any lot holder desires us to do so.

Those interested should communicate with William H. Gaskill, Treasurer of the Committee of Interments, Green Street Monthly Meeting, or any of the following members of the Committee.

William H. Gaskill, 3201 Arch St.
Samuel N. Longstreth, 1218 Chestnut St.
Charles F. Jenkins, 232 South Seventh St.
Stuart S. Graves, 3033 Germantown Ave.

The Friends'
Intelligencer

ESTABLISHED 1844 | THIRD MONTH 11, 1922 | VOLUME 79 NUMBER 10

Contents

EDITORIAL

HOTELS.

GRISCOM HALL

The Hall will open this year for the Memorial Day holiday—on May 27—as last year. Weekly rates are unchanged. Stockholders in the Griscom Hall Association have the first choice of accommodations up to March 15.

Rate cards and room plans may be obtained from the Registrar, 230 South 7th Street, Philadelphia; correspondence in regard to reservations should be addressed to

GRISCOM HALL,
Margaret Eastburn, Manager,
Buck Hill Falls, Pa.

HOTEL WARWICK

SOUTH CAROLINA AVENUE
ATLANTIC CITY, N. J.
OPEN ALL THE YEAR

First house from beach and boardwalk. Steam heat, electric lights, elevator. Excellent cuisine, quiet, dignified surroundings and attentive service.

Reasonable rates. Write
SARAH H. FULLOM, Prop.

THE WHEELER

Boardwalk at Massachusetts
ATLANTIC CITY, N. J.
Ocean Rooms—Table Guests
MRS. A. W. WHEELER

Strath Haven Tea Room

Dinner 6 to 7:30.

Sunday Special — Chicken and Waffles, 85 cents.

Swarthmore, Pa. Phone 680

FRANK PETTIT
ORNAMENTAL IRON WORKS

Iron Fencing, Fire Escapes, Stairs and Ornamental Iron Work.
809 Master Street **Philadelphia, Pa.**

THE FRIENDS' INTELLIGENCER

Published weekly, 140 N. 15th Street, Philadelphia, Pa., by Friends' Intelligencer Association, Ltd.

WALTER H. ABELL, *Editor*
SUE C. YERKES, *Business Manager*

***Editorial Board*: Elizabeth Powell Bond, Thomas A. Jenkins, J. Russell Smith, George A. Walton.**

***Board of Managers*: Edward Cornell, Alice Hall Paxson, Paul M. Pearson, Annie Hillborn, Elwood Hollingshead, William C. Biddle, Charles F. Jenkins, Edith M. Winder, Frances M. White.**

***Officers of Intelligencer Associates*: Ellwood Burdsall, Chairman; Bertha L. Broomell, Secretary; Herbert P. Worth, Treasurer.**

***Subscription rates*: United States, Mexico, Cuba and Panama, $2.50 per year. Canada and other foreign countries, $3.00 per year. Checks should be made payable to Friends' Intelligencer Association, Ltd.**

Entered as Second Class Matter at Philadelphia Post Office.

HOTELS.

Buck Hill Falls

Between March 1st and March 15th of each year our guests of the previous season may indicate the accommodations they desire for the coming summer months. The requests for reservations are taken up in the order received with first consideration given to those of long season. Many have been disappointed by postponing their request.

This is to remind those who are planning a summer at Buck Hill Falls, either in The Inn or in a cottage, to indicate their wishes now.

THE INN

"WEALTH IN HEALTH"

BUCK HILL FALLS, PA.

SHOWS in colors and by many photo-engravings the true form of the Vegetables and Flowers offered and gives expert cultural instructions.

It is the best Garden Book we have ever published and offers the choicest Vegetable and Flower Seeds, Lawn Grass and Agricultural Seeds, Plants of all kinds, including the newest Roses, Dahlias, Hardy Perennials, etc.

You should have this book, a copy of which will be sent free if you mention this publication. Write today.

HENRY A. DREER
714-716 Chestnut St. Philadelphia, Pa.

Send two or more names of persons who might be interested in Friends by reading the INTELLIGENCER. A good way to get new members.

SCHOOLS.

Woolman School

SWARTHMORE, PA.

Winter Term—First Month 3d to Third Month 18th

Courses in the Bible, Quakerism, Religious Teaching, Rural Problems. Daily meetings for worship.

Personal contact with instructors experienced in social and religious work.

Helpful group life. Recreation.

ELBERT RUSSELL, DIRECTOR.

GEORGE SCHOOL

Near Newtown, Bucks County, Pa.

Under the care of Philadelphia Yearly Meeting of Friends.

Course of study extended and thorough, preparing students either for business or for college. For catalogue apply to

GEORGE A. WALTON, A. M., Principal
George School, Penna.

FRIENDS' CENTRAL SCHOOL SYSTEM

Write for Year Book and Rates.
CHARLES BURTON WALSH, Principal.
15th and Race Sts., Philadelphia.

FRIENDS' ACADEMY

LONG ISLAND, N. Y.

A Boarding and Day School for Boys and Girls, conducted in accordance with the principles of the Society of Friends. For further particulars address

S. ARCHIBALD SMITH, Principal,
Locust Valley, N. Y.

Cream Buttermilk

HEALTHFUL—REFRESHING

Supplee-Wills-Jones Milk Co.

PHILADELPHIA—ATLANTIC CITY

The Friends' Intelligencer

The religion of Friends is based on faith in the "INWARD LIGHT," or direct revelation of God's spirit and will in every seeking soul.

The INTELLIGENCER is interested in all who bear the name of Friends in every part of the world, and aims to promote love, unity and intercourse among all branches and with all religious societies.

ESTABLISHED 1844 PHILADELPHIA, THIRD MONTH 11, 1922 VOLUME 79 NUMBER 10

How Can We Answer a Great Appeal?

Under the title "A Word For The Hour," we publish in this issue an appeal to Friends from a Friend who is widely loved for his leadership among us—Rufus M. Jones. It is not an appeal for funds, even in support of the great work of the American Friends' Service Committee, of which its author is the chairman. It is an appeal for a "deeper and more complete devotion to the spiritual mission of the Society of Friends." It has quickened our own thoughts along the same line. We hope that it will strike fire in the hearts of our readers.

And the question comes, "How shall we gird ourselves to meet the opportunity for spiritual leadership which challenges Friends on every side?"

Shall it be through increasing the vitality of our meetings for worship? Partly, without doubt; and yet we cannot attain this end by simply turning our attention to those meetings. A meeting for worship is not a detachable circumstance in itself, subject to alteration or improvement at will. The religious life of an individual or a society is like an iceberg: seven-eighths of it are under water. Meetings for worship are an *outcome;* one phase, when they are vital, of the natural welling forth of religious experience which has its sources in hourly communion with the infinite, and its expression in every act of daily life.

If then, we as Friends must experience a quickening in order to fit ourselves for our mission, and if we cannot turn to even the most fundamental of our group activities as the primary source of new life, to what *shall* we turn? Within what sphere may we, *must* we, take the first definite steps toward the deepened vitality for which we long? Within that sphere which, rather than doctrines or forms, Friends have always insisted must be the basis of all earnest religion—our *way of life.*

In this sphere we have not escaped questioning; either from the world, or from the hearts of many, at least, of our own members. A book note recently received from the English Friends' 'Central Literature Council' gives a significant comment from an outsider upon this subject. It is taken from an appreciative review, by Cannon Quisk, of Rufus Jones' "Later Periods of Quakerism." Referring to Friends' testimony against war, the reviewer says:

> "That it has not done more to convert the world to pacifism is in part due to the fact that Quakers have themselves been involved, and with considerable financial success, in the competitive commerce and industry which go far to cause wars, and in part to the fact that as a body they have been content to be 'prophetic'—to give their testimony against an evil—and have ignored the call to provide a Christian statesmanship which shall devise means to achieve the ideal."

Is not this criticism largely true? Have we not been a people who have inherited a great tradition; who have clung to a great ideal, seeing a distant vision of what the world needs; who have done great things for the world in its hour of need during and since the war; but who, except in scattered instances, have not ourselves attained to an actual way of life which inculcates the great ideals of which we talk and dream?

The following queries suggest themselves as a means by which we may roughly test out our individual and group life, to see what degree of conformity it holds to our fundamental religious principles:

Do I find time *every day* for the cultivation of the spirit? Are there regular periods in my daily life for enjoyment of beauty, communion with truth as expressed in the Bible and other inspired writings, for a full and unrushed experience of that seeking and upbuilding which the ages have called prayer? If our days are over-crowded with activities, if they lack "court-yards" through which the infinite air and sunlight may enter our little personal dwellings, they cannot permanently radiate spiritual vitality.

In how many respects does my way of life stand out in the community in which I live, as more ideal than that of the accepted standard?

Am I really putting spirit above matter; seeking first "things spiritual," and caring for financial and similar considerations only in so far as they are necessary to maintain a simple existence or to serve others? Am I seriously striving to follow an ideal of inspired simplicity; holding and using only as many material possessions as my daily life and those of my dependents require; and offering for free circulation through love to those in greater need, whatever else of material benefits present social relationships, or my own abilities, may bring to me?

Am I living in the real spirit of brotherhood, completely above the barriers of individual or group prejudice? Do I see the earnestness and fineness of countless people who disagree with me in the petty matter of opinion? Can I work toward a common end with men of different convictions than my own? Am I fearless in my championship of right, whether the oppressed be a Belgian child caught in the maelstrom of war; or a sister republic like Haiti, which is this day held subject to imperialistic American interests; or an "I. W. W." who is being confined in a deadening, and in some cases, disease-breeding, prison, for an expression of opinion regarding an issue which is long since past?

Other promptings to self-examination throng into our minds under the stimulus of the great flood of primitive Christian, and primitive Quaker, idealism. Yet why go further? We who write have not succeeded in *living* even this many of our ideals. But they do stand before us as concrete goals to be definitely striven for in *our own* life, not primarily to be urged upon someone else. To attempt to work them out as a genuine way of life is our impelling aspiration. Does not the quest before our religious Society lie somewhat over the same trail? And, if successfully ventured, will not one of the outcomes of this quest be a corporate "holy passion for the spread of light and love?"

The Quakerism of the Founders

By Elbert Russell

III

The Quakerism of Isaac Pennington

(*In Two Parts—Part Two*)

The Authority of Scripture

"The Scriptures give testimony concerning the one thing necessary to salvation; but the thing itself, Christ himself, the seed itself, is not contained in the scriptures, but revealed in the shinings of the true light, and so received or rejected inwardly in the heart.

"That which enlightens and gives life to my soul, is somewhat from Christ, even a measure or appearance of his pure Spirit; it is no less; and the law of life written inwardly is more to the soul than words written outwardly, though all the words that ever come from God's Holy Spirit are very precious, and greatly useful, to those to whom he vouchsafeth to give the understanding of them.

"Time was, when we also did believe that the scriptures were the only rule of faith and practice; and so bent ourselves to search out and observe what we found written therein, hoping thereby to have attained to that which our souls desired after. But we found all the directions thereof weak as to us, through the flesh, and sin had still power over us; and we knew not what it was to be made free by the Son; free by the truth, free indeed from that which stood near to tempt and draw us into sin. But when the light of God's Holy Spirit shined upon us, and our minds were by him turned thereto, and his law written on our hearts, in and by the new covenant, which he revealed in us, and made with us, in and through his Son; then we felt the ministration of the power of the endless life, and were experimentally assured, that in the gospel-administration, which is an administration of the Spirit and power, nothing less than Spirit and power can be the rule.

"Mark; In the old covenant, (the) letter (or outward directions) was a rule; but the living commandment, or Word in the heart, is the rule in the new covenant; living laws; laws livingly written; laws that give life to them in whom they are written; they are the living, powerful, and effectual rule.

"Nor do we undervalue the scriptures in thus giving honour to Christ and his Spirit; for it is their honor to testify of Christ and of his Spirit, who is the pure, certain, infallible rule of the new life, and who gives to fulfill all the holy directions, which are written in the scriptures, concerning the way of life."—*Pp. 42, 43.*

The Mystery of the New Life

"I confess the power doth not so flow forth to man, as man expects it; but the power of life works man out of death in a mystery, and begins in him as weakness. There is all the strength, all the power of the enemy, against the work of God in the heart.

There is but a little thing (like a grain of mustard-seed), a weak thing, a foolish thing, even that which is not, (to man's eye), to overcome all this; and yet in this is the power. And here is the great deceit of man; he looks for a great manifest power in or upon him to begin with, and doth not see how the power is in the little weak stirrings of life in the heart, in the rising up of somewhat against the mighty strength of corruption in him; which he returning towards, cleaving to, and waiting upon the Lord in, the strength of the Lord will be made manifest in its season, and he will be drawn nearer and nearer to the Lord, and his enemies be overcome and fall he knows not how. But he that waits for such a mighty appearance of power at first, looking so to begin, and after that manner to be preserved and carried on, can never in this capacity so much as walk in the path eternal; nor is not in the way of receiving the power, which springs up as weakness, and leads on and overcomes enemies in a mysterious way of working, and not in such a manifest and direct way of conquest, as man's wisdom expects.

"The seed of the kingdom is sown man knows not how, even by a sound of the eternal Spirit, which he is not a fit judge of; and it grows up he knows not how; and the power appears and works in it, in a way that he is not aware of."—*Pp. 63, 64.*

Inner Transformation

"Yet let but any man come rightly to distinguish in himself between that which God begets in the heart, and all other births, and let that speak and judge in them, that will soon confess that our testimony is of God, and given forth in the authority and by the commission of his own Spirit. True wisdom is justified by the children that are born of her; it is the other birth that doth not, nor can own her. The other birth can own former dispensations (according to the letter of them); but not the life and power of the present.

"I have known the breaking down of much in me by the powerful hand of the Lord, and a parting with much (though not too much) for Christ's sake. The Lord hath brought the day of distress and inward judgment over my heart; he hath arisen to shake terribly the earthly part in me (yea, what if I should say that the powers of heaven have been shaken also) that he might make me capable to receive and bring me into that kingdom which cannot be shaken."—*Pp. 36, 37.*

The Cross

"This I dare positively hold forth as a standing truth, which hath been sealed unto me by constant experience. That no man can fall in with and obey the light wherewith he is enlightened, but he must deny himself, and take up a cross to his own wisdom and will; which cross is the cross of Christ, which is the power of God to the salvation of the soul. And he that takes it up daily, and waits upon the Lord therein, shall witness the power of the Lord Jesus Christ to the redemption of his soul; yea, then he shall be able in true understanding to say: This is light indeed, life indeed, power indeed. That powerful arm which hath saved me from sin, and breaks the snares, devices, and strength of the enemy before me (delivering me daily when none else can, and when my own strength and wisdom is as nothing) I cannot but call Christ, the living power and wisdom of God revealed in me, who will not give his glory to another. For he is the Lord God of pure power and life for evermore; and beside him there is no such Saviour."—*Pp. 38, 39.*

Church Government

"The spirit of the prophets is subject to the prophets. Here is the government; here is the law of rule and subjection in the life. Everyone feeling a measure of the Spirit in himself, is thereby taught to and subject to a greater measure of the same Spirit in another. He that hath no measure of the Spirit of God, he is not of God, he is none of Christ's; and he that hath received a measure of the Spirit, in the same Spirit feels another's measure, and owneth it in its place and service, and knoweth its moving, and cannot quench it, but giveth way to it with joy and delight. When the Spirit moves in any one to speak, the same Spirit moves in the other to be subject and give way: and so everyone keeping to his own measure in the Spirit, here can be no disorder, but true subjection of every Spirit; and where this is wanting it cannot be supplied by any outward rule or order set up in the church by common consent; or that is fleshly, and lets in the flesh, and destroys the true order, rule, and subjection."—*Pp. 77, 78*

Silent Worship

"And this is the manner of their worship. They are to wait upon the Lord, to meet in the silence of flesh, and to watch for the stirrings of his life, and the breakings forth of his power amongst them. And in the breakings forth of that power they may pray, speak, exhort, rebuke, sing, or mourn, etc., according as the Spirit teaches, requires, and gives utterance. But if the Spirit do not require to speak, and give to utter, then everyone is to sit still in his place (in his heavenly place I mean) feeling his own measure, feeding thereupon, receiving therefrom (into his spirit) what the Lord giveth. Now in this is edifying, pure edifying, precious edifying; his soul who thus waits, is hereby particularly edified by the Spirit of the Lord at every meeting. And then also there is the life of the whole felt in every vessel that is turned to its measure; insomuch as the warmth of life in each vessel doth not only warm the particular, but they are like an heap of fresh and living coals, warming one another, insomuch as a great strength, freshness, and vigour of life flows into all. And if any be burthened, tempted, buffeted by Satan, bowed down, overborne, languishing, afflicted, distressed, etc., the estate of such is felt in Spirit, and secret cries, or open (as the Lord pleaseth) ascent up to the Lord for them, and they many times find ease and relief, in a few words spoken, or without words, if it be the season of their help and relief with the Lord.

"For absolutely silent meetings (wherein there is a resolution not to speak) we know not; but we wait on the Lord, either to feel him in words, or in silence of Spirit without words, as he pleaseth. And that which we aim at, and are instructed to by the Spirit of the Lord, as to silent meetings, is that the flesh in everyone be kept silent, and that there be no building up but in the Spirit and power of the Lord."—*Pp. 82, 83.*

Life Renewed

The ground is ugly, cold and bare in winter;
We welcome snow upon the dreary earth,
Sharp corners change to loveliness and beauty,
With joy we look upon the world transformed.
The shapes of buildings made by man are changed
When covered by the blanket pure and white,
Harsh sounds are muffled, discords hushed by snow,

And beauty, peace and quiet fill the world.
The snow protects the roots and seeds from cold,
And slumbering in warmth thru' wint'ry months
The trees have dreams of new and fuller life
In spring, refreshed by rest and winter's care.

So is it in the lives of men on earth
When tired of cares, and worn by worldly things
They go away to rest in quiet nooks
Where thoughts of God refresh their souls and minds.

When minds are free and hearts receive His love,
New strength is felt with plans for fuller life,
Then God transforms the selfish, restless lives
To useful ones, of beauty, love and peace.

SARAH P. MENDINHALL.

A Word for the Hour

I have sent out at times of crisis various appeals to Friends to get behind the work of relief in Europe and I have always met a quick and generous response. It has given me deep inward joy to see how ready Friends really are to take their share in tasks and responsibilities when the call comes to them.

But I feel impelled today to send out another kind of call. It is not for money; it is not for clothes; it is not for volunteers to go to distant lands. It is for a deeper and more complete devotion to the spiritual mission of the Society of Friends. It is primarily, of course, an appeal to young Friends, but we must be very careful not to divide our forces into two groups—the young and the elderly. The only way we can get a good crop of noble dedicated young Friends is to have those who are fathers and mothers thoroughly awake to the significance of our spiritual mission in the world. After all it is not a question of age, it is a question of vision, of loyalty, of devotion, of holy passion for the spread of light and love. The earlier the awakening comes the better. The more years that are given to this great business of life and service so much more is the true joy of living realized. But whatever may be one's age, let the business begin now and let no one say: "I am an old derelict and my time to contribute is past. This is the day of the young and the strong." No, not that. This is the day of the devoted and loyal worker, the faithful servant, even though an eleventh-hour-comer. The all important thing is the awakening and the readiness for the business in hand. I have been deeply stirred by the death of my great friend and fellow-laborer, William Charles Braithwaite. He is a magnificent revelation of what can be done with a life devoted to a cause. He has been a great leader, a real prophet of present-day Quaker life and thought. He has interpreted our ideals, he has expressed our historical aims, he has exhibited our social hopes, he has preached our gospel of spiritual religion, and his life has proved to be a powerful force for righteousness. I know many young Friends in America today who have just as great a chance as he had to make their lives count toward these ends as he did. It was not alone his unusual powers of mind that raised him, like the incoming tides, above the common level. It was his spirit, his heart, his attitude, his dedicated will that made him different from the rank and file.

The hour calls for others who will follow in his train. The spirit which we have shown in our foreign work of relief and reconstruction we must now show within the area of our own home field. Every Quaker Meeting in America, in the world, needs a revival of personal devotion to the truth which lies at the heart of our religion—devotion to Christ and to the kingdom of love which He is building in this world where we live. We do not need to blow the trumpet of our particular denomination and set it into rivalry with other forms of faith. We want no campaign of sectarianism. Not that. But here is the point. Religion cannot be disembodied. It must express itself in and through a group. It must find its organs and exponents among people who have inherited ideals and hopes out of the past, and who have the inspiration of leaders and prophets and martyrs behind them.

That great background is ours. Freely we have received a tremendous heritage. What we need to do is to *understand* it, to appreciate it, to prize it, to appropriate it, and then to transmit it. Such chances as have come to us at the present time in history do not often come to a religious body. Earnest, eager people in our towns and cities are begging us to interpret our faith to them. They ask for books, they ask for lectures, they ask for messages, they ask for quiet personal talks. They want to find a real spiritual religion. Shall we disappoint them or shall we let them see the day-dawn and the day-star in our lives?

One thing is certain. This situation cannot be met by formal, easy-going Christians whose religion is superficial and second-hand. Nothing will work here but a religion that goes down to the rock-bottom foundation. It must be a religion that has cost something, and that is why I am putting the emphasis on loyalty and consecration. Our service, if it is to count for great things, must spring out of living experience of God. Our efforts to better the world must have the force and energy which comes from depth of life. Our love and sympathy will have real healing power only when we go out with "the mighty ordination of the pierced hands."

RUFUS M. JONES.

The Present Need in Poland

By HILDA P. HOLME

Former member of the Friends' Polish Unit, just returned to America.

In Poland lies much of the richest agricultural land of Europe. This has long been the natural granary of Europe.

Today hundreds of miles of fertile land along the old eastern battlefront lie unploughed. The peasants, refugees in Russia since 1914, are returning at the rate of 4,000 a day. There are 500,000 who are registered and are still to come back. Two hundred and fifty thousand have already returned. Of these, many returned too late to plough and plant their land. They must live on whatever their neighbors can give, a few potatoes, or a handful of sunflower seeds.

The Poles lack almost everything that is needed for reconstruction, horses, ploughs, seeds, spades and saws.

The government is endeavoring to help, but is not able to meet the tremendous problem. It furnishes lumber for rebuilding the destroyed homes, and has furnished 1,000 horses for woodhauling and ploughing under the supervision of the Friends' Unit.

Forty thousand dollars is urgently needed for agricultural implements and seeds in this work of ploughing and planting in Poland.

$1.50 will buy a plough.

$1.25 will buy enough oats to plant an acre.

2c. will buy a spade.

To meet the need for clothing in a constructive manner, sheep are needed to restock the eastern section. There were thousands of sheep in this district before the war; but the continual passing of the armies destroyed every vestige of the old flocks. The peasants of Poland all spin and weave their own linen and woolen cloth. Since 1914 but little flax has been grown, and the death of the sheep has exhausted the wool. Their stocks of clothing are now gone. Sheep can be bought in Southern Poland and transported to the devastated areas.

The most economical and the most constructive way, because it is a permanent way, of rehabilitating the clothing of Poland, is to supply sheep. The Service Committee is, therefore, asking money to purchase sheep. One sheep costs $1.50. How many sheep will you give? Send your money to the Service Committee, marking it "For sheep for Poland."

News Notes From the Unit in Germany

A recent allocation of $50,000 by the Three-Million-Dollar Drive, for the purpose of buying clothing for the German children, is causing great joy in the hearts of 67,000 children in this country. The clothing is being bought through the agency of the Friends in Berlin, and the Friends are cooperating in distributing the clothing with the German Central Committee for Foreign Relief and with the Welfare Committees in each of the 300 cities and towns where distributions will be made. Each boy or girl will receive two sets of underwear and two pairs of stockings. The balance of the money will be invested in hundreds of yards of material for making clothes for tiny babies. One of the most real joys in connection with this clothing is that it comes in January. With the whole country now shrouded in snow and ice, warm clothing is a prime necessity.

One tremendous need which we have not yet been able to touch is that of linen for confinement cases. Some cities have already obtained lending sets of such linen,—obviously an emergency measure,—but it is very expensive, and many city governments are too poor to appropriate sufficient funds to meet this need.

Letters of appreciation of the work done in Germany through the agency of Friends flow freely into the Berlin office. The other day a beautifully engraved letter came from the city of Frankfurt am Main. The Oberbuergermeister of the city, in expressing his warm thanks and regard, stated that it was the intention of the city to name a street within its environs "Quaker Strasse" as a lasting memorial in the eyes of the children of Frankfurt.

One of the ways to get a matter before the eyes of all the people of a community in Europe nowadays is to have something concerning it printed on the paper money which circulates locally. At the present time such paper money is made in denominations which have less than one cent exchange value. This means wide circulation. Recently the city of Gotha in Thuringia printed on its paper money a picture of a (supposed) Quaker, distributing food to hungry children, with the following verse:

(Translation.)

"In times of need long, long ago
St. Augustin gave us bread, you know.
The Quakers today from a faraway land
Bring bread to put in each little hand."

The city has also coined a piece of money in porcelain which bears on the reverse side the imprint of the Friends Relief Star. Each of these pieces of money has an exchange value of about one cent American.

American Friends will be interested, in view of their co-operation with American Mennonites during the war in France, to know that the Mennonites in Holland are pursuing much the same course as we with regard to Russia. John Fleischer, head of the Mennonite Church at Winterswijk, Holland, writes us under date of January 12th, that his congregation has sent its first shipload of supplies to Russia. As these relief materials are meant mainly for Mennonites in Russia, and as Russian Mennonites exist mainly in the South of that country, their relief supplies are sent in by way of the Black Sea and Odessa. Mr. Fleischer visited the Berlin office some time ago, and told us at that time that Holland Mennonites had plans for bringing back Russian children in their empty ships to keep them in Holland until conditions in Russia justify their return. He told us that Dutch Mennonites would be willing to care for 1,000 Russian children in this way. This little group of people in Holland is more nearly giving to the limit of its ability than most groups of the world.

Working With the Working Woman

Review of "Working With the Working Woman," by Cornelia Stratton Parker, author of "An American Idyll." New York, Harper & Bros. 1922. $2.00.

Those who have read Whiting Williams' book "What's on the Worker's Mind," and his various articles that have been appearing in the recent numbers of Colliers, will be distinctly surprised at the point of view which Cornelia Stratton Parker has taken in her latest book "Working With the Working Woman." Here is no picture of the cruel system crushing out the individuality of the worker, no harsh plant policeman lording it over the waiting lines of men who, with hat in hand, plead for work—for a day's job. Instead, we have a picture of careless, carefree women working doggedly at uncongenial tasks, without complaint, and with little thought to bettering their conditions; and the problem of the unemployed as taken up is rather the point of view of the gum chewing girl who having her feelings hurt by the under boss, or disgruntled at some especially trying bit of work, throws her job up and goes off on the hunt for something better.

Perhaps the view point is not correct, and perhaps Whiting Williams is mistaken also. Let us hope both are, and that somewhere in between is that middle course which is trod by those whom we call the "working class."

If you are looking for the picture of the worker, ground between the millstones of capital, of the boss standing over his flagging help with a whip in hand (figuratively speaking), don't read this book. But if you would like to pass a few hours among the women who wear long earrings, bob their hair and continually chew gum, you will find the Parker adventures most amusing.

One could give an excellent paper before a club from the facts "Connie" gained in her factory days, but the facts would be rather superficial and if a social worker were in the room he might ask some embarassing questions.

With the exception of the carefree attitude which Mrs. Parker has her workers adopt, the most striking thing about them is their language, and Mrs. Parker does not expurgate! In explanation she writes this paragraph. "The proportion who read and write books, especially the female folk, live and die in the belief that it is the worst sort of taste, to say the least, to use the name of the Creator in vain, or mention hell for any purpose whatsoever. Yet suddenly, overnight, you find yourself in a group who would snap their fingers at the notions. Sweet-faced, curly-haired Annie wants another box of caramels. Elizabeth Witherspoon would call, "Fannie, would you be so kind as to bring me another box of caramels?" Annie, without stopping her work, raises her voice and calls down the room—and in her heart she is the same exactly as Elizabeth W.—"Fannie, you bum, bring me a box of car'mels or I'll knock hell clean out o' ya." According to Elizabeth's notions Fannie should answer her, "One moment, Miss Elizabeth; I'm busy just now." What Fannie (with her soul as pure as drifted snow) does call back to Annie is, "My Gawd! Keep your mouth shut. 'Aint't you got sense enough to see I'm busy!"

What Mrs. Parker looses by never working more than three weeks in one place she makes up for by the number of industries she enters. First it is packing chocolates—and after reading her comments one will stick to home-made fudge; then she tries a foundry, tho a week at this is sufficient to show her that it is no place for a woman; next it is a laundry with conditions much better; a dress factory where her impressions are rather confused; a cloth factory of the type Samuel Gompers would go into ecstacy over; and last of all, a Hotel that we all would like to put up at. And the characters in all of these! But what is the use of my describing them—write Harper & Brothers yourself and see how quaint they are.

BLISS FORBUSH.

Friendly News Notes

Thirty-six tons of clothing were shipped to Russia from the Service Committee warehouse at 108 Dobbin Street, Brooklyn, during Second Month. About half of this came from the stores of the Red Cross; the remainder from Friends and others all over the country.

"The Meeting," a little paper published in connection with Haverford Meeting (Orthodox) contains a beautiful tribute to our Friend Matilda F. Janney, who died on Twelfth month 31st, 1921, in her 93d year. It says, in part: "Gifted to a remarkable degree she had all her life been the joy of a large circle of friends, but by none of her friends will she be more missed than by the small group which has known her only since she came to Haverford. She was beloved by all who knew her, and the breadth of her interest, the keenness of her witty comments, and the loving kindness of her spirit made her an extraordinarily delightful companion. Those who had the privilege of being admitted to her intimacy came to her again and again for help, inspiration and enjoyment, sure always of finding her actively interested in the affairs of the world, and eager to discuss them with the wisdom of her long experience and also with a remarkably youthful and modern point of view.

Maynard, Minnesota, with a population of only 550, has given the Friends' Service Committee three cars of corn for Russian relief. Assuming that corn is worth twenty-five cents a bushel in Maynard, the village is giving an average of one dollar for every man, woman and child of its population. Were the entire state of Minnesota to do the same, it would result in saving 477,274 lives. Were the whole United States to give on the same scale, the Russian famine problem would be solved.

At Baltimore Quarterly Meeting to be held Third month 11th to 13th, inclusive, at Baltimore, Md., an address will be given by Elbert Russell at 8 p. m., on Seventh-day. George A. Walton and Elbert Russell expect to attend the meeting for worship on First-day, and at 7 p. m. George A. Walton will speak on "Quaker Worship" at a meeting under care of the Young People's Movement. The notice sent to the office also states that all are welcome to attend the meeting of Ministry and Counsel to be held at 3 p. m. on the 11th.

In connection with the "Vision" of Joseph Hoag, which recently appeared in our columns, William B. Kirkbride, of Trenton, N. J., refers us to a book which may not be known to all our readers. It is entitled "Southern Heroes, or The Friends in War Time," and is by Fernando G. Cartland. It is based chiefly upon the experience of Friends in the South during the Civil War, and contains a discussion of the "Vision" in question.

In an article circulated by the Far and Near Press Bureau, Harry T. Silcock, Secretary of the Friends' Foreign Mission Association (English), writes as follows on "The Coming World Student Conference at Pekin": "What can be done to follow up the work of Washington and help China on to her feet? The World's Student Christian Federation has been alive to this question and has arranged its eleventh international Conference to be held at Peking from April 4 to 9, 1922. The theme of the Conference will be 'Christ in World Reconstruction.' It is significant that the scope of the discussions is to be so broad, and that in spite of the urgent national needs of China, her Christian student leaders have decided to take the whole world as their parish.

"The Conference is to be held at Tsinghua College, a few miles outside Peking. When America returned to China the Boxer Indemnity to be used in sending Chinese students to America, this College was built to give the necessary preliminary training before the students leave China."

Lowndes Taylor, of West Chester, Pa., sends us the following quotation, with interpolated queries of his own, from "The Philosophy of Religion," by J. Caird:

"Neither thought nor the aspirations of the religious nature can be satisfied with the rationalistic notion of a merely subjective religion—(Does this apply to the Society of Friends? Was it intended to so apply?)—of opinions and beliefs wrought out by the purely spontaneous activity of the human mind, and implying nothing more on the divine side than is involved in the original creation of man's rational nature."

Joel Borton, President of the Abolition Society, informs us that William C. Biddle has just returned from a visit to Laing School, giving a splendid report of the working conditions there. Their present needs are: Money to assist in paying the teachers, which amounts to about $600 a month; equipment for gymnasium, in which Miss Ross is taking special interest for the girls, and George Dunlap for the boys; needed equipment for the playground, such as basket-ball and inside games; boxes of clothing, partly worn shoes that need mending to keep our cobbling department busy; remnants and pieces of clothing of any real value can be made into small garments and are very acceptable.

All money contributions should be sent to the Treasurer, Walter Hall, Salem, New Jersey.

All boxes, barrels of clothing, shoes, books, games, magazines or anything for the Laing School should be sent to "Miss Charlotte B. Ross, Laing School, Mount Pleasant, via Charleston, S. C.," plainly marked.

CAROLENA WOOD AT BROOKLYN MEETING

Report of a discussion group under the auspices of Westbury Quarterly Meeting Advancement Committee

A German child rushed home to its mother all upset by the sight of a youngster knocked down and almost run over, "and a Quaker came and picked him up." How did he know it was a Quaker? "Why of course it was a Quaker, because they are the ones who take care of little children!"

A letter from another child to a Quaker in Germany recounted the plight of the American Indians whose lands have been taken away from them. He knew how they felt, for Silesia has been taken from Germany. Would the Quaker please speak to her government about it?

"All our lives we have heard of Christianity, but now we see it." Such is the challenge of Germany to the Quakers—the tremendously humbling challenge—as it came out in Carolena Wood's story of her recent experiences in Central Europe, told at the request of Westbury Quarterly Meeting Advancement Committee, at Brooklyn Meeting House, February 19, before a group that combined Meeting members and returned workers who were invited to share box lunches between Meeting and Carolena Wood's talk, and then continue their reunion in a Tea Meeting at 20th Street, New York.

"How does it happen you come to feed our children?" is being asked on various sides by Catholic, Protestant and Jew. Some have just swallowed food, but most realize there is a deeper content in the Friends' message brought from the heart of America. Can Friends leave Germany without going beyond "saying it with food"?

"The state churches are as empty as our hearts" that are reaching out after the World Father, but everywhere the old-form priest stands in the way of reaching true religion. We cannot do it alone, and do not want to quit the state church with nothing to put in its place. Will the United States, after fighting to make the world safe for democracy, withdraw from European affairs, or try to make the world safe for God?

In response to this longing have come the Friends' Meetings in Berlin and Frankfurt, and the "Friends of Friends," organized to study Friends' principles. There are now about fifteen such groups and new ones are forming at the rate of about three a month. Another big, hopeful movement is the Frei Deutsche Jugend, who, feeling the past has failed and they must build up a fine future, are discussing the most fundamental questions everywhere.

Questions brought out the fact that there are other reactions to Friends' work: some think it is good politics and good business; others, that we are salving our consciences for having starved the Germans out; and there are probably others. But Carolena Wood has dealt with officials high and low, and feels they have been deeply touched. Moreover, conditions are such that the feeding should be carried on another year to save the work already done. Thank God that America *can* give!

FRIENDS IN GERMANTOWN

While in some localities the attendance and membership of our meetings does not seem to be on the increase, it is gratifying to hear from meetings where both have advanced. The Friends' Meeting in Germantown has shown a marked increase in attendance in the last year, 39 persons having joined our meeting. More than half of these are young people, many attend meeting who are not Friends, in the majority of these cases "Grandmother was a Friend."

Visits have been exchanged with the Orthodox Friends, when 18 or 20 visit the meeting of the other branch.

Our First-day School has an enrollment of 100; of these 30 are not members of the Society of Friends.

There is an average attendance of 72. There is also a cradle roll of 16. The difficulty of finding teachers is a problem. Once a month we have a Bible Class, which is led by Elbert Russell. A light supper is served at six o'clock, average attendance of 135.

The Germantown Friends' Association with a membership of over 200, aims to provide a program for an all round development, giving opportunities for social mingling, and for many to take active parts. This winter the Germantown Friends' Association has mapped out the following program:

6 Current Topic Talks, Joint Supper and Meeting with Orthodox, Christmas Party with First-day School, 8 Monthly Meeting Suppers, County Fair, Musicale, Provide entertainment for Quarterly Meeting, Calendar issued once a month, Executive Committee Meeting every month. Once a week a group meets to sew for the Friends' Neighborhood Guild.

It will be a privilege to welcome Friends, or those in any way interested, to our activities. The social room is open daily. E. L. B. P.

BLUE RIVER QUARTERLY MEETING

Blue River Quarterly Meeting held at Chicago, Illinois, on Second month 25th and 26th was well attended. The most important business transacted was the changing of the local meeting from an Executive Meeting to a Monthly Meeting, which will now be known as the Chicago Monthly Meeting of Friends.

A most interesting letter addressed to the Quarterly Meeting from Elizabeth H. Coale, of Holder, Ill., was read and extracts sent to various local papers. In the evening, J. Barnard Walton gave an informal talk on "The International Service of Friends." A number of visitors attended the Meeting for worship on First-day, among them, Dr. Chauncey Shortledge, of Darling, Pa., Ellis W. Bacon of Philadelphia, Mary Anna T. Miller, of Salem, N. J., and J. Barnard Walton, of Swarthmore, Pa.

The local Advancement Committee invited J. Barnard Walton to attend the Quarterly Meeting, and to discuss the need of an executive secretary in Chicago. After spending a week with Friends in Chicago, he left to attend Quarterly Meeting at Richmond, Indiana.

A. Jeannette Flitcraft.

Publications of Interest

Friends of the Negro and lovers of poetry may both resort to Leslie Pinckney Hill's recent book of verse, "The Wings of Oppression" with the certainty of finding food for the spirit. The publishers call this collection "a serious, dignified and artistic expression of the ideals of the Negro race." It is this; and being so is more. It gives expression to a spirit which rises above race and shares all humanity's quest of the ideal. All its several divisions, "Poems of My People," "Poems of The Spirit," and others, radiate the force of a personality which sees the vision of "Overcoming by the Spirit." "The Wings of Oppression" is published by the Stratford Company, Publishers, Boston, Mass., 1921, price, $2.00.

The Friends' Bookstore, 304 Arch St., Philadelphia, has imported 250 copies of a little book, "Selections from the Writings of Clement of Alexandria," edited some years ago by Rufus M. Jones. Copies may be had for the low price of fifty cents each. Rufus M. Jones has a concern that present-day Christians should become acquainted with the writings of this great man. In a note concerning the matter, he writes: "I have long felt that there are very few Christian writers of the early centuries who have such a great, fresh, vital message for the present-day world as has Clement, and this little book gives the cream of his message. I very much want present-day ministers to know him and love him as I do. It is very striking how close his conceptions of Christianity are to those of Phillips Brooks."

"Triumphant Plutocracy," the Story of American Public Life from 1870 to 1920, by R. F. Pettigrew, formerly United States Senator from South Dakota. Direct Sales Book Agency, 31 Union Square, New York City. 1921. Pp. 245. Price: Cloth, $1.00; paper, 50 cents. Former Senator Pettigrew has written this book in the belief that "the American people should know the truth about American public life." His viewpoint, which he marshals the facts of his public life to support, is summed up in the following passage:

"I believe that my country is in danger; I believe that the liberties of the American people are already well-nigh destroyed; I believe that we are moving forward to a crisis of immense significance to the future of the American people, and the ideas and ideals for which the United States has stood before the world. We are far along the road to empire, and we are traveling faster towards that goal than any nation in history ever traveled."

"He Knew Lincoln, and other Billy Brown Stories," by Ida M. Tarbell. New York. The Macmillan Co. 1922. Pp. 179. $1.50. A new edition of the three classic Lincoln stories. Appealing in their charm, and fraught with meaning to all idealists, because they emphasize one of the great traits of a great man—ability to enter into fellowship with all men and all classes. "Lincoln, the Greatest Man of the Nineteenth Century," by Charles R. Brown (pp. 77; $1.00), is another recent Macmillan publication treating of the same subject.

"What is Social Case Work?; An Introductory Description," by Mary E. Richmond. New York. The Russell Sage Foundation. 1922 Price $1.00. This little book gives examples of various social "cases" to show that, "by direct and indirect insights, and direct and indirect action upon the minds of the clients, their social relations can be improved and their personalities developed." Valuable to the social worker and to all interested in improved social relationships. The social case worker who quietly permeates undeveloped strata of humanity with the leaven suggested in these pages is close to him who works for the Kingdom of God.

The Representative Committee of Philadelphia Yearly Meeting is issuing a four-page summary of the treaties, resolutions and declarations adopted by, or in connection with, the Washington Conference. It is written by William I. Hull, and forms an excellent condensed memorandum for reference and distribution. Copies may be obtained from the Central Bureau, 154 N. 15th Street, Philadelphia, Pa.

Items From Everywhere

Raymond T. Bye, a Friend who is a member of the faculty of the University of Pennsylvania, sends us a significant clipping from the *Frankfurter Zeitung* regarding Friends' relief work in Germany. The clipping, which was given him by Dr. Karl Scholz, one of his colleagues at the University, pays a glowing tribute to the Quaker relief mission. After outlining the extent and the importance of the actual physical relief provided, it touches on the spiritual significance of the work in the following words:

"And if among all the hardships which a lost war has imposed upon us, we have as yet discovered very little which might strengthen our faith in the all-conquering power of a superior humanity, the deeds of the Society of Friends, the Quakers, are showering their blessings upon us."

The National Catholic Welfare Council *Bulletin* for January enumerates editorially the "four outstanding and immediate requirements for industrial peace." They are (1) universal recognition of the living wage principle; (2) freedom for labor unions to function effectively; (3) reform in anti-social policies of many labor unions, which "can easily be brought about once the union leaders realize that the war against unionism has definitely ceased"; (4) a comprehensive plan for conciliation and arbitration of disputes, "established by law and involving authoritative decisions, but not compulsory acceptance of the decisions by either party."

Ella Kent Barnard sends us a copy of an interesting letter received from William Ellery Leonard, of the University of Wisconsin, in response to enquiries concerning his recently published poem, "The Quaker Meeting House." He writes in part as follows:

"I was not in the war, my knowledge of barrack's life being from observation and from intimate talks with soldier-boy friends and conscientious objectors. The armistice came just after men of my age had registered and I was schooling myself for the conscientious objector's position. My attitude to the war is recorded in the enclosed off-print ("The Man With The Yellow Streak," from "The Nation.") I have seen nothing in subsequent events to make me question the validity of my vision. It was the greatest swindle, and the greatest moral and spiritual delusion of all time—and the end is not yet—(tho many have awakened).

"As to the origins of the poem, I had known of the Quaker relief work from the beginning and subscribed for it—particularly the work in Central Europe, where two of my friends (not Quakers, one a German woman from the states, one an American) have been active. I have heard also direct from Germans whose children you are feeding. Long since, this work in all the countries had appealed both to my intelligence and imagination as the most tremendous and sublime act of all these terrible years—sublime in its quiet and simplicity, tremendous in its spiritual import. The Quaker Meeting House prevails over Barracks, State and Church—that is the meaning of my poem—and has "kept the home-fires burning" for a distracted mankind."

THE OPEN FORUM

This column is intended to afford free expression of opinion by readers on questions of interest. The INTELLIGENCER *is not responsible for any such opinions. Letters must be brief, and the editor reserves the right to omit parts if necessary to save space.*

ENDORSEMENT OF JOINT PROJECT

To the Editor:

I am much gratified by the proposal to have a joint Secretary of Education for the two Philadelphia Yearly Meetings.

I believe every step toward unity and co-operation to be a step toward bringing the Kingdom of God upon earth.

I hope that the campaign for internationalism will be waged with spirit and energy, and that we shall soon learn a definite program in which most of us can have definite work to do.

Mill Valley, Cal. JESSIE L. HOOPES.

MORE ON RELATIONS WITH THE CHURCHES

To the Editor:

In the issue of the INTELLIGENCER, of the 18th of Second month, a reader asks: "Can Friends consistently join in with the orthodox churches in their efforts at church union?" I would answer that one *may*, if he has the discernment of spiritual values, so as to be sure whether or not they—the orthodox—come out to him in fellowship and friendship as far as they wish him to do to them. That is, if they love and respect our conception of realities as much as they wish us to love and respect theirs.

Second: "Are the fundamental teachings of the Friends and the orthodox churches the same?" Probably, ethically and morally they are, mainly, in the direction of building character. "Then why do Friends seek to maintain a separate existence?" My first answer would be: "Why seek in forms and outward things, the deeper answer inward, and outward, silence brings?" And, as we do not wish to take up the discussion of "doctrine"—probably the following quotations will shed some light on the inquirer's mind. "If it is well that a body of people should continue to show to the world that piety (a fair degree of devotion to sincerity, of honesty of purpose, of right doing along as many lines—byways and highways—as can possibly be); rectitude and spiritual growth can exist without priests or creeds; that luxurious living is not necessary to happiness, nor guile to reasonable prosperity in business; that high intelligence is compatible with simplicity and inexpensiveness; that love and unity are practicable amid the clash and contention of modern life, then such a body as the Society of Friends, or a larger number of individuals possessed of similar far-reaching, quick and deep insight, is still needed, and may be of use in the world."

Keystone, Ind. THOMAS E. SCOTT.

BIRTHS

KIRK—On Eleventh month 18th, 1921, to Dr. Clair B. and Elizabeth Blackburn Kirk, of Mill Hall, Pa., a son, named David Blackburn Kirk.

THOMAS—On Third month 2nd, to Carl Burton and Lilian Ambler Thomas, a son whose name is David Lawrence Thomas.

DEATHS

BORDEN—At Mickleton, N. J., on Second month 14th, Anna Owen, wife of William H. Borden, and daughter of the late Benjamin and Hope Owen, in her 66th year. Although a great sufferer for many years, she never lost her interest in the Meeting, First-day School or the W. C. T. U., a member of the two latter since their organization.

FREDERICK—On First month 30th, at the home of her son-in-law, George Roger North, Lyndell, Pa., Catharine T. Frederick, in her 82nd year. She is survived by two children by her first marriage, William F. Velotte and Sara K. Velotte North.

JACKSON—In West Chester, Pa., Second month 27th. Thomas H. Jackson in his 74th year.

The son of Halliday and Caroline Hoopes Jackson, he was a birthright member of Birmingham Monthly Meeting, in all the concerns of which he was deeply interested.

He was a life-long lover and student of Nature, being widely known as an ornithologist. His knowledge of bird life was thorough and intimate, he contributed frequently to "Bird Lore" and similar publications and possessed one of the largest collections of birds' eggs in the country. His ability as an expert amateur photographer enabled him to make excellent pictures and lantern slides of birds and their nests which were widely used in illustrations of magazine articles and lectures.

Modest and retiring by nature, he nevertheless gave freely the benefit of his knowledge to others, and the sweetness and kindliness of his character had created an unusually tender bond between him and a large circle of friends, which was testified to in many heartfelt expressions at the time of his funeral.

KENDERDINE—In Newtown, Pa., on Second month 17th, Thaddeus S. Kenderdine, in his 86th year.

He was the last survivor of the sons of John E. and Martha Quinby Kenderdine, and was born at Lumberton, Pa., in 1836. One sister, Elizabeth N. Fell, of Germantown, survives. After three winters in boarding schools, he from the age of sixteen until thirty, worked in and about his father's mills on the historic Cuttalossa creek, near his birthplace, except while he was traveling or in the army. In 1858 he joined as a driver on an ox train leaving Leavenworth, Kansas, for Salt Lake City. From the latter place he made his way to San Francisco, and returned home the next year by way of the Isthmus of Panama. At the close of the Civil War, he engaged in business with a brother at Lumberton, removing after a few years to Ambler, Pa., thence to Newtown in 1875, where most of his active life was spent.

He did a great deal of literary work, both prose and poetry, contributing to the newspapers when a youth. His first book, "A California Tramp" appearing in 1888 was followed by a number of others, the last a volume of personal recollections being published in 1921. A genealogical work,

"The Kenderdines of America," represented a great amount of labor and has had a wide circulation.

The deceased was a birthright Friend and was strongly attached to that religious body, and particularly in the latter years of his life, he was a devoted attendant, on week-days as well as First-days, of the meeting at Newtown. Interment was made in New town Cemetery.

WESLEY HALDEMAN.

LEEDS—At West Chester, Pa., on Second month 24th, Deborah Crenshaw, widow Josiah W. Leeds, in her 74th year.

WATSON—At Fallsington, Pa., on Second month 9th, William E. Watson, aged 66 years. Interment in Friends' ground, Fallsington.

AGNES SIMPSON PALMER

Entered into rest on Second month 14th, Agnes Simpson, widow of David Palmer. She was born First month 5th, 1842, in Solebury Township, her parents being John and Letitia Buckman Simpson. She was married in 1867 and went to Lower Makefield Township where they lived until 1897, when they went to Newtown to assume charge of Friends' Boarding Home which opened Fifth month 3rd of that year.

David Palmer died in 1900, but his widow continued as matron of the Home until 1913. Deceased was a birthright member of the Society of Friends and her life was lived in close sympathy with its principles and testimonies, which she exemplified in her life. Careful in speech, solicitious for the welfare of humanity always ready with a word for the right, her quiet, unobtrusive life was a well-spent and useful one.

Her membership since marriage had been with Falls Monthly Meeting in which she took a deep interest and served it in many ways, being an overseer, clerk of Women's Branch of Monthly Meeting for a time and for nearly 30 years as elder. The community has lost a precious friend and helpmate. There was mentioned at her funeral many of her rare attributes and yet all were inadequate when it comes to summing up for the great total.

COMING EVENTS

THIRD MONTH.

11th—Burlington First-day School Union will be held at Mt. Holly Meeting House at 10.30 a. m.

11th and 12th—Pilgrimage under care of the Young Friends' Movement, at Norristown, Pa.

12th—The Advancement Committee of Westbury Quarterly Meeting will attend New York Meeting. It is hoped that President Aydelotte, of Swarthmore, will also be present. In the afternoon there will be a Conference on "Do Trade Unions Find Justice in the Courts?" Albert De Silver, of the Civil Liberties League, will speak. Friends are asked to bring a box lunch. This will be served at 12.45. All are cordially invited.

12th—Conference class at 15th and Race Streets, Philadelphia, at close of meeting for worship, at 11.40 a. m. Speaker—Arabella Carter. Subject—Some Tasks of the Kingdom. I.

12th—Walter Abell, Editor of the FRIENDS' INTELLIGENCER, will attend Meeting at Schermerhorn Street, Brooklyn.

13th—New York Monthly Meeting will be held at the Meeting-house, 221 East 15th Street, New York, at 7.30. Supper will be served at 6 o'clock. The Meeting for Ministry and Counsel will meet at 5.

13th—Friends' Association at Friends' School building, Media, at 8 p. m. A play—"A Rag Carpet Bee," will be given by home talent. Music. Admission, 35 cents.

13th—Baltimore Quarterly Meeting, at Baltimore, Md.

16th—Haddonfield Quarterly Meeting at Moorestown, N. J.

18th—An Evening of Magic, by Paul Fleming, at George School, Pa. Admission, fifty cents.

25th—A Meeting Social in the Gymnasium of Friends Seminary, 226 East 16th Street. All are cordially invited, 8 o'clock.

American Friends' Service Committee

WILBUR K. THOMAS, EX. SEC.
20 S. 12th St. Philadelphia.

CASH CONTRIBUTIONS

WEEK ENDING FEBRUARY 27

Five Years Meetings	$704.56
Upper Springfield Monthly Meeting	5.00
Park Avenue Meeting, Baltimore, Maryland	125.00
Westtown Community First-day School	7.00
Wrightstown Monthly Meeting, Penna.	49.00
Lansdowne First-day School	12.00
Birmingham Prep. Meeting	18.50
Adrian Quarterly Meeting	6.00
Easton Monthly Meeting	22.00
Swarthmore Branch of Friends	20.00
Buckingham Monthly Meeting	10.00
Menallen Monthly Meeting	100.00
Berkeley Friends' Meeting	20.00
Pasadena Monthly Meeting, Villa St. and Galena Ave.	200.00
Contributions for General	472.00
For Germany	2,740.92
For Austria	1,376.75
For Poland	412.00
For Serbia	300.00
For Syria	37.00
For Armenia	50.00
For Russia	49,141.75
For Russian Overhead	1,988.45
For German Overhead	129.91
Refunds	90.85
	$58,038.69

CASH CONTRIBUTIONS RECEIVED FROM MEMBERS OF PHILADELPHIA YEARLY MEETING OF FRIENDS, FIFTEENTH AND RACE STREETS, PHILADELPHIA, PA., DURING FEBRUARY.

15th St. & Race St. Mtg. by Charles M. Biddle	$1,442.40
Swarthmore Mo. by E. J. Durnall	70.00
Wrightstown Mo. by H. L. Hund	42.10
West Chester Mtg. High St. by S. R. Paist, Russian expenses	23.00
Woodbury Prep. by Warner Underwood	39.00
Woodbury Prep. by Warner Underwood for Polish Relief	5.00
Greenwich Mo. by Louisa Powell	100.00
Hancock's Bridge W. C. T. U. by Louisa Powell Russian flour	5.00
Hancock's Bridge Friends by Louisa Powell, Russian flour	15.00

Swarthmore Mo. by E. J. Durnall	35.00
Abington Mo. by D. L. Lewis	50.00
Swarthmore Mo. by E. J. Durnall	150.00
Wilmington Mo. by S. H. Stradley	1,009.00
Middletown Mo. by H. C. Pickering, Russian Rel.	8.00
Newtown, Del. Co., Prep. by M. T. Dutton........	42.00
Swarthmore Mo. by E. J. Durnall (Russian Relief)	25.00
Lansdowne Mo. by C. C. Lippincott	30.00
	$3,090.50

Shipments received during week ending February 25th, 138 boxes and packages received; 8 anonymous; 2 Mennonites.

NOTICE.—The P. Y. F. A. will give "The Passing on the Third Floor Back" on March 24th and 25th in the Auditorium of the P. Y. F. A., 15th and Cherry Streets, Philadelphia. Tickets, $1.00, include dancing. The proceeds will go to the Margaret Hallowell Riggs Fund for support of the work in Canton Christian College, China.

NOTICE—Supper will be served by the Best Interests Committee before Monthly Meeting at 15th and Race Streets, Philadelphia, Third month 22nd, in the Friends' Central School Lunch Room, at 6 o'clock. Tickets, 65 cents. Please purchase tickets before Third month 20th. Anna W. Cloud, 140 N. 15th Street, Philadelphia.

NOTICE—On Third month 24th, a meeting, under the joint auspices of the West Philadelphia First-day School and the Committee on Best Interests of the Monthly Meeting of Friends of Philadelphia, will be held at the Meeting House, 35th Street and Lancaster Avenue, at 8 o'clock P. M. Vincent D. Nicholson will deliver an address on "The Society of Friends of 1922." This address will be followed by a Social.

LUKE 2. 14—AMERICA'S ANGELUS

"Glory to God in the highest, and on earth peace, good will toward men."

Stand back of President Harding in Prayer for Universal Peace by meditating daily, at noon, on the fourteenth verse of the second chapter of Luke.

Ask your friends to help make this a Universal Meditation for Universal Peace

Pass it on ***Friends in Christ***

REGULAR MEETINGS

OAKLAND, CALIF.—A FRIENDS' MEETING is held every First-day at 11 A. M., in the Extension Room, Y. W. C. A. Building, Webster Street, above 14th. Visiting Friends always welcome.

FRIENDS' MEETING IN PASADENA, California—Orange Grove Monthly Meeting of Friends, 520 East Orange Grove Avenue, Pasadena, California. Meeting for worship, First-day, 11 A. M. Monthly Meeting, the second First-day of each month, at 1.45 P. M.

CENTRAL MEETING OF FRIENDS (Chicago), meets every First-day in Room 706, 410 South Michigan Avenue, at 10.45 a. m. Visitors are invited.

WANTED

PARTY OF EIGHT NOW ORGANIZING for 58-day trip—Paris, Switzerland, Passion Play, Holland, England. Starting about July 1. Rates reasonable. Apply without delay to Bertha L. Stover, 31 Westview St., Germantown, Philadelphia.

WANTED—CAPABLE AND DEPENDABLE woman for general housework in family of three adults; suburban town. Must be good cook. Good wages and permanent home for the right person. Reference required. Address T. 92, Friends' Intelligencer.

POSITION WANTED—BY AN HONEST, respectable colored woman, as chambermaid, waitress, or general housework. Celia Boush, 6433 Jefferson Street, Germantown, Pa.

REFINED FRIEND WILL TAKE POsition; assist light house duties. One or two adults only. Or will take room; assist part time. Address F. 102, Friends' Intelligencer.

ROOM WANTED

FRIEND WISHES ROOM IN PHILAdelphia, one week, last of March. Accessible; reasonable. Address F. 101, Friends' Intelligencer.

FOR RENT

FOR RENT—APRIL TO OCTOBER, Nine-room house with sleeping porch and garage, near river, at Riverton. Address. Helen Lippincott, Riverton, N. J.

FOR RENT—TO TWO OR THREE adults, furnished house; seven rooms and bath. June 20th to September 8th. $150 for season. Address, Helen D. Wells, Riverton, New Jersey.

FOR SALE

FOR SALE—BRICK AND FRAME detached residence, well built; 10 rooms, bath, sleeping porch, glassed in; gas and electricity, modern conveniences; near Friends' School and Meeting House, Lansdowne, Pa. Apply J. 100, Friends' Intelligencer.

TRANSIENT ACCOMMODATIONS

WASHINGTON, D. C.—ROOMS FOR visitors. Near Station, Capitol, Library. Continuous hot water. Electricity. Garage. Mrs. L. L. Kendig, 120 C. Street, Northwest.

ELLWOOD HEACOCK
FUNERAL DIRECTOR
2027 NORTH COLLEGE AVENUE
PHILADELPHIA
CALLS OUT OF CITY ANSWERED PROMPTLY

WE BUY ANTIQUE FURNITURE and antiques of every kind, old pictures of Washington or any prominent American, old gold, silver, platinum, diamonds and old false teeth. PHILA. ANTIQUE CO., 700 Chestnut St. Phone Walnut 70-26. Established 1866.

Strawbridge & Clothier

Coat Suits, Cape Suits and "Sportabockers" All Incline to Tweeds

And Tweeds are so varied, in weaves, finish and colorings this season that all types of women can wear them.

Tweed Suits, $25.00 to $32.50

Coat and skirt and long circular cape and skirt. The Coat Suits in belted straight-line styles, unbelted semi-fitting effects and models that can be worn with or without the belt. Our Skibo Tweeds and cassavant twill. Blue, rose, tan, gray and heliotrope.

Tweed Suits, $35.00 to $77.50

High-grade herringbone tweeds, Dent tweeds, hair-line effects, various checks, melrosa mixtures and the imported Canongate tweed. All the shades of Spring.

Strawbridge & Clothier—Second Floor, Centre

Women's New Coats and Capes at Moderate Prices

Coats in the new materials and shades, some plain-tailored to severity, some trimmed with stitching or braid, or gracefully fringed—the plainer types including many of the well-liked tweeds. Prices, $22.50 to $60.00.

Capes of serge in black and navy blue, silk-lined, at $20.00. Others braid-, button- or fringe-trimmed, or trimmed with nail heads combined with chenille embroidery. Also a very fine assortment of Tweed Capes. Prices, $20.00 to $60.00.

Strawbridge & Clothier—Second Floor, Centre

STRAWBRIDGE & CLOTHIER

MARKET STREET EIGHTH STREET FILBERT STREET
PHILADELPHIA, PA.

To the Lot Holders and others interested in Fairhill Burial Ground:

GREEN STREET Monthly Meeting has funds available for the encouragement of the practice of cremating the dead to be interred in Fairhill Burial Ground. We wish to bring this fact as prominently as possible to those who may be interested. We are prepared to undertake the expense of cremation in case any lot holder desires us to do so.

Those interested should communicate with William H. Gaskill, Treasurer of the Committee of Interments, Green Street Monthly Meeting, or any of the following members of the Committee.

William H. Gaskill, 3201 Arch St.
Samuel N. Longstreth, 1218 Chestnut St.
Charles F. Jenkins, 232 South Seventh St.
Stuart S. Graves, 3033 Germantown Ave.

ADVERTISING RATE in the FRIENDS' INTELLIGENCER, for Help Wanted, Positions Wanted, Rooms for Rent, Notices, and other classified advertisements without display, for each insertion, 2 cents per word, including name, initials and address. Answers may be sent to a box at the INTELLIGENCER office, if so directed.

For display advertising the rate is 10 cents per agate line, or $1.40 per column inch, each insertion. On ten or more insertions in a year from date of order, ten per cent. discount. Thus a four-inch single-column or two-inch double-column advertisement costs $5.60 each insertion, less ten per cent., or 5.04 net each time for ten or more insertions. Matter may be changed whenever desired, without extra charge.

Experience has proved the INTELLIGENCER to be a remarkably good advertising medium. All advertisements must "pass the censor!"

Address 140 N. 15th St., Philadelphia

CLEAN HIGH GRADE
COAL

CLEAN HIGH GRADE
COAL

The Friends' Intelligencer

ESTABLISHED 1844 | THIRD MONTH 18, 1922 | VOLUME 79 NUMBER 11

Contents

THE FRIENDS' INTELLIGENCER

Published weekly, 140 N. 15th Street, Philadelphia, Pa., by Friends' Intelligencer Association, Ltd.

WALTER H. ABELL, *Editor*
SUE C. YERKES, *Business Manager*

Editorial Board: Elizabeth Powell Bond, Thomas A. Jenkins, J. Russell Smith, George A. Walton.

Board of Managers: Edward Cornell, Alice Hall Paxson, Paul M. Pearson, Annie Hillborn, Elwood Hollingshead, William C. Biddle, Charles F. Jenkins, Edith M. Winder, Frances M. White.

Officers of Intelligencer Associates: Ellwood Burdsall, Chairman; Bertha L. Broomell, Secretary; Herbert P. Worth, Treasurer.

Subscription rates: United States, Mexico, Cuba and Panama, $2.50 per year. Canada and other foreign countries, $3.00 per year. Checks should be made payable to Friends' Intelligencer Association, Ltd.

Entered as Second Class Matter at Philadelphia Post Office.

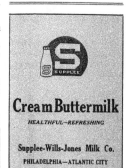

The Friends' Intelligencer

The religion of Friends is based on faith in the "INWARD LIGHT," or direct revelation of God's spirit and will in every seeking soul.

The INTELLIGENCER is interested in all who bear the name of Friends in every part of the world, and aims to promote love, unity and intercourse among all branches and with all religious societies.

ESTABLISHED 1844 — PHILADELPHIA, THIRD MONTH 18, 1922 — VOLUME 79 NUMBER 11

A Cry of Alarm!

This is a *Cry of Alarm* to every city and village and farm!

The Treaties now before the Senate are in danger! Unless ratified the wonderful work of the Conference for the Limitation of Armaments will go for naught. Unless ratified *promptly* the United States will be discredited in the eyes of all nations. The welfare of the world depends upon action by our Senate.

We ask immediate action on the following request: Get scores of private letters written, telegrams sent and resolutions passed by all kinds of gatherings, churches, Friends' Meetings, clubs, women's associations, Y. M. C. A., W. C. T. U., fraternal orders, Granges, Labor Associations and other such bodies.

These should be sent to your Senators at the earliest moment, worded somewhat as follows:

"We urge our Senators that they do their utmost to effect the *prompt* ratification of the treaties growing out of the Washington Conference."

This needs attention and immediate action!

O. EDWARD JANNEY, *Ex. Sec. General Conference Section, Friends' Disarmament Council.*

Our Declining Country Meetings

Not all of our country meetings are declining, but the unfortunate facts remain that many of them are. What can we do to check their decline; to convert them into the active centers of vision and spiritual power which every community needs, and which every Friends' meeting ought to be?

Clues to an answer to this question are given in a recent bulletin issued by the Social Order Committee of the Fourth and Arch Streets Philadelphia Yearly Meeting. The report of the "Farmers' Group" of this committee, of which James F. Walker is chairman, consists of the following paragraphs:

Prof. H. N. Morse, recently of the Inter-Church World Movement, addressed the Farmers' Group December 9th. His talk was based on a survey made by this organization in some 300 rural communities over the U. S. In the course of his work Prof. Morse had come in close contact with Friends and discussed the problems of Friends' Meetings in rural communities. "Friends Rural Meetings are declining faster than the churches of other denominations," Prof. Morse stated. "If nothing is done such meetings will probably disappear completely within fifty years."

He had two suggestions as to a remedy; one to supply thru the meeting a more popular style of service, including present day attractions. The other was for the whole Society to get behind an effort to build up a sound economic and social community in which every family and individual in the community would be reached and held interested, regardless of race or creed.

Both of Prof. Morse's proposed remedies seem to us valuable, though not of equal importance. His first suggestion calls for modification in the type of religious observances held by the meeting. We are sure that he does not desire his "more popular form of service" to supplant silent worship. The latter meets a basic need, and will certainly persist as a primary feature in the life of every Friends' group.

On the other hand, silent worship is the most difficult of all forms of religious excercise. Many individuals and groups are not prepared for it. Nor is it the *only* form. Many who enter into it fully, also find inspiration in other types of service.

There are some who can be helped by the regular invitation of outside speakers, either in conjunction with the meeting for worship or at other times. Forums for the discussion of topics related to community and world ideals have frequently proved valuable. And there may be some in attendance who need music as a part of their religious life. Beauty and truth are inseparable aspects of a single whole, and many spiritual realities which lie too deep for words can be expressed through the symbols of aesthetic expression. Music and other forms of art, if they are inspired by a genuine longing to seek and to express the ideal, may be profoundly religious. The feeling that there is a clash between different forms of worship, that because one seems best suited to certain needs, others are wrong, is a vestige of sectarianism from which Christians of all denominations need to escape.

It should certainly not be the policy of Friends to arbitrarily institute musical or other new types of service. But should it not be the primary concern of those who direct our meetings to have the services under its care *meet the needs* of all its members, and of the community as a whole? If there are those who *desire* inspiration in ways less traditional among Friends, they should be encouraged to develop means of fulfilling this desire under the care of the meeting; and not be confronted by an immovable tradition which lets their need go unanswered, or which drives them elsewhere for their spiritual food.

But though additional forms of service might increase the size of meeting, they alone could not guarantee the social-spiritual power upon which must finally depend the vitality of a religious organization. Prof. Morse's second suggestion, therefore, appeals to us as more fundamental. It offers a new goal toward which to labor—or rather the reassertion of an old one—the building up of a "sound economic and social community." We believe that if a meeting were to set its hand wholeheartedly to the accomplishment of this task, there would be no need to entertain fears of its "disap-

To do so, it would first of all have to rise above all sectarianism. It would have to appeal to the whole community for the good of the whole community, and be willing to learn and to take, as well as to give. The result, if the experiment were whole-hearted and successful, would be a "community church"—but it would be a bigger community church because of the many fine traditions which a Friendly element could contribute to it. It would be a "community meeting."

Perfecting a community, which amounts to achieving the Kingdom of God within one small social group, never was, and never will be, an easy task. It cannot be accomplished without high spiritual qualities of vision and courage. But "to them that ask shall be given"—those that undertake a real task develop real strength.

Faced with the danger of eventual extinction as it is, why do not some of our country meetings consider this suggestion, perhaps asking Prof. Morse for a more detailed statement of the ideas which prompted him to make it. One successful venture in community service impelled by high spiritual ideals, might inspire city and country meetings alike with new life and new power.

"There is no winter in the heart
Of him who does a kindly deed;
Of what he gives he hath a part,
And this supplieth all his need."

Some Thoughts on Friends' Principles

The article which follows was inspired by the questions regarding the relation of Friends to other religious bodies asked by Nannie Webster in the Open Forum of Second month 18th.

What is the relation of Friends' principles to the beliefs of the "orthodox" churches? How far can we unite with the latter in their efforts at church union. I am glad to see these questions asked in the Intelligencer, and I wish to attempt to answer them. It has often struck me that many Friends do not realize just wherein lies their distinctiveness, and do not appreciate enough the discomforts of many members of orthodox families who cannot believe just what their fathers and mothers and brethren have believed, and do not know where to turn to find a body of people who believe in religion, and brotherhood, and the teachings and life of Jesus, and yet will leave each free as to his individual beliefs.

I may say first of all that the difference between Friends and other denominations does not lie in a difference in the interpretation of the Bible. The difference is far more fundamental. It lies for one thing in the difference in the place accorded to the Bible. It lies in a difference as to the source of authority. The "orthodox" churches regard the Bible as the Word of God, and think that their present and future welfare is dependent upon their interpretation of the Bible. This Bible is the ultimate, or chief, source of their authority. Friends derive their only *authority* from what they call the Inner Light, that is the Word of God within them. To the Friend revelation is believed to be continuous; to the average member of orthodox churches revelation is regarded as almost wholly confined within the covers of the Bible.

But bear in mind that orthodox Christians do not deny the existence of the Inner Light—they call it the Holy Ghost. All of them, consciously or unconsciously, live by it—insofar as they live the Christian life, all of them interpret the Bible by it, and some of them acknowledge its authority as supreme; but not many of them are willing to believe that those who differ from them are led by it. The case might be summed up thus: "orthodox" Christians believe that the Bible is the supreme authority, and is infallible, that all regenerate men have the Holy Ghost to interpret the Bible, and to aid them in matters on which the Bible throws no light. Some of them believe that this authority extends to moral and spiritual matters only; some of them believe that its authority extends to history and science also. Friends believe that the Bible is the written record of how the Inner Light dealt with certain historical characters, many of them of exceptional spiritual power, they believe that these scriptural records are preserved to help us and guide us, but they do not believe that it is to the Bible that we must go with our difficulties; rather we must go to the same source from which the scriptural characters got their light and strength: to God, the indwelling spirit.

Now the orthodox Christian, claiming the Bible as the source of authority, lays down obedience to God *in believing the Bible* as the test of true Christianity, and believes that, obedient to God in this respect, he will be given the power to do and think aright. The Friend believes that the true Christian, giving his whole allegiance to the Inner Light, and seeking with his whole heart to obey its dictates, will be given the power to do and think aright.

These two seem very much alike. But herein lie some differences. The Friend is free. He does not have to measure the divine teaching, or secular matters, by the Bible; he does not become confused between two texts that seem to contradict each other, and he is not tempted to quote the Bible as authority to support a matter which is questionable. Then, too, he is not a sectarian. Orthodox Christians lay stress on the interpretation of the Bible, and if their various interpretations differ, they are split up into sects; where their interpretations agree they formulate them into creeds. The Friend lays stress on the Inner Light; if two Friends differ each can only make the difference a reason for seeking the guidance of the Inner Light, lest he himself be wrong; but there is no reason for forming a new sect, unless he is going to deny that his friend has access to the Inner Light, and this no Friend would do.

It is only when one body of Christians sets itself up to be the only possessor of the Inner Light, the only correct interpreter of the scriptures; the only judge of right conduct, that creeds are needed, and sects arise. When the Orthodox Friends decided that Hicks was misrepresenting the meaning and purpose of the life of Jesus there was a division, and the Orthodox Friends made as it were a small creed; that Friends should believe that Jesus was the only begotten Son of God, and that his death was an atonement. Had the Hicksites denied these things they too would have had a creed; but they did not; they are Hicksite not because they demand adherence to the teaching of Hicks; but because they *permit* their members to follow the teaching of Hicks, and to preach those teachings if they feel called to do so.

Friends have a right, therefore, to existence as a separate body because they have no right to existence in any other body. They occupy the ground that is most spacious, I believe, in the whole range of Christian bodies, despite their lack of numbers. It is as if there were a number of people on a group of islands and on the main land; a few on the main land, the islands crowded. You would not expect the few to crowd on the islands and abandon the land where there was room for all simply because their numbers were small.

Now as to Friends joining with other denominations in their efforts at church union. This attempt is a move toward that position of liberality which is a characteristically Friendly position, and which both Orthodox and Liberal (Hicksite) Friends share, so we cannot but foster this movement. And we can truly unite with them, provided they do not demand that we accept their creed; the creed which contains those articles from their various creeds which all of them hold in common. This Friends cannot do, because it would cause them to deny their only distinctive doctrine; the right of every man to be guided by the Inner Light, and to express to others what that Light has taught him.

We do not believe that a man seeking the guidance of the Inner Light is always right; but we believe that the only way for him to be right is to get more and more guidance from the Inner Light, so that his religion will suit *his* needs; so that his expression of it may be sincere and genuine, not formal, not empty, not hypocritical; so that his very perplexities will drive him into closer communion with God who is the source of his life.

It is this belief in the Inner Light that makes us depend not on a paid ministry but on a free gospel ministry, for a man paid by a set of believers in a certain creed can scarcely feel free to let the Divine Light shine freely through him to others and even if his convincement of that creed is such that the Divine Light shining through him is sure to take the color of that creed and please his employers, his very position causes him to interfere with the free expression of others, since he tends to monopolize the time of worship. It is this belief in the Inner Light also which causes Friends to lay no stress on the exact interpretation of the Bible, but rather on communion with God, and obedience to the light which he sends. Free from the necessity of interpreting the scriptures exactly, and of deciding just what we believe as to certain historical events, we have more time to contemplate justly our relations to our fellows, and so greater responsibility in this matter. We likewise feel no need to classify and arrange differences between ourselves and others, and feel sure that the Inner Light will enable each of us individually to give a reason for the faith that is in us. But faith is not a body of belief; faith is trust in that power to which we claim allegiance.

If you talk seriously to most orthodox Christians they will own that what we think most fundamental they also think fundamental, the life lived in communion and obedience to the living God. But they seem to deny that we can live it, and to think that God will not help us to live it unless we believe as they do about what they regard as fundamental. But can you imagine a God like that?

One who does not enjoy the freedom of holding his own belief until it is changed by Divine Light without being considered reprehensible by others, who does not seek a body of people who are content to walk together in the Light without questioning just what color that light may seem to each individual to have; one who does not aspire to work out with God his own salvation, I fear will be disappointed in Friends as a sect.

I believe that the writer of the questions to which I referred above, like myself, would like to be sure that all our members realize on just what grounds Friends' distinctiveness is based, and that they will not let their desire for church unity to lead them to abandon that ground, just when that position is being appreciated outside the Society. To return to the metaphor of the crowded islands and the scarcely populated mainland—we cannot but see that the inhabitants of the islands, in many cases, merely have their residence there, but do business, carry on their Christian life, on the mainland we occupy. We should like to see, I take it, our position defined and advertised, so others like ourselves may know of it, and may know of a body of Christians who adhere to that position; and may, if they like, join us, and so be free from the necessity of making the stormy passage from the island, the creed-bound position, to the open country of liberality every time they do business—that is think.

NORMA G. MILLER.

The Door

The following poem, reprinted from the 'New York Times,' was written by a member of Brooklyn Monthly Meeting when she was fourteen years old. A reader who forwards it to us, writes: "These lines lamenting the death of an Irish terrier puppy, are the more appealing when we recall the very general charge against youth of today in regard to the lack of all religious feeling."

My little dog is dead! And yet I seem to hear
His footfalls on the long-neglected stair;
I hear his baby cry and see his eyes
As, sad, he stood without the hindering door—
So big to him, that door—so small to me!

What echoing stair now bears those footfalls dear?
What eager air his baby cry repeats?
What door stands he before, so still and sad?
So big to me, that door—so small to God!

HELEN CLARKSON MCCLOY.

Lotteries and the Like

The following paper was prepared last year, by Mary E. McDowell, for the Social Reconstruction Committee of New York Yearly Meeting. It was intended to afford a basis for discussion in small meeting groups. We hope to publish in the INTELLIGENCER, from time to time, other analyses of the implications of Friends' "Advices" in modern social life.

One of the striking features of our Discipline is the emphasis on the avoiding of laying wagers, horse racing, any kind of gambling, and lotteries, "even though speciously and enticingly presented in the form of benevolent or philanthropic enterprises." It is worth while to consider wherein lies the harm of lotteries and the like.

Of course these things involve a great waste of money and a great risk of losing it; but this cannot be the fundamental objection, for it would hardly apply in the case of philanthropic enterprises. The inherent evil is a moral evil; it is the result of getting something for nothing at the expense of other people. Even when we receive gifts we usually feel some moral obligation to make a return in gratitude or friendliness, or to pass on to others some of the blessing that has come to us freely. When there is no such feeling it is possible for even gifts to be demoralizing. But in a lottery one takes from others what they all want for themselves, and not even gratitude is given in return. The winner takes something to which he has no moral right; and the effect is that both he and the losers have a thirst to try again. The effect is similar to that of habit-forming drugs; with moderate use the bad effects are hardly noticeable, but there is a tendency to greater and greater indulgence, and the extreme addict in both cases is a moral wreck. Indeed, the wives of confirmed gamblers say that gambling is worse than drink. Remember, for instance, the grandfather of Little Nell in "Old Curiosity Shop." The widespread demoralizing effect of some forms of gambling has been recognized by laws against public lotteries and betting at races.

Probably the worst form of gambling is gambling with stocks. By buying and selling on a margin, a man may become rich overnight without doing a stroke of productive work; he gets his wealth by taking it in some way from other people, often by ruining many others, sometimes it comes out of consumers in high prices for foodstuffs. The moral degradation that is apt to befall stock gamblers is well known by many a tale of fact and fiction. Frank Norris' novel, "The Pit," gives a good illustration.

There is a deadly fascination about the chance to make easy money. Lest you infer that it is the excitement of chance rather than the getting something for nothing which is the attraction, realize that you never heard of the excitement in marbles or cards reaching a dangerous stage unless they were played for "keeps." Excitement in itself is often good if it is unconnected with anything immoral; taking chances, running risks, in a noble cause is often the highest duty of the Christian.

Suppose I own stock paying 5%, bought honestly as a permanent investment; a few years later I get 10% for the stock. What have I done to increase that value? Nothing at all. But somebody, or group of people, created that increased value. If I take it, I take it away from those who deserve it because they made it. It may be due to increased efficiency of managers and workers in a factory, and it may belong to them by moral right; it may have been caused by the growth of the community and belong morally to the community. Is it possible that there may be some demoralizing effect in an arrangement which allows me to get something for nothing, as in lotteries and gambling?

Suppose I have a piece of land bought for $500; the village in the neighborhood grows more prosperous and I sell the land, which I have not touched, for $1,000. The increased value has been produced by the community; but I take it. Of course, it is according to law and custom; but is it not possible that there is something immoral about this taking something for nothing?

You may say that the gains in the two instances mentioned need not involve taking something away from the people who made the increased value. I admit there is another possible explanation of the gains mentioned above. Often such gains do not represent a real increase in value or production; they are often at least partially fictitious gains obtained by withholding from use land or products that are needed till they attain an inflated price. In that case it is the consumer, the general public, who pays our unearned gain by higher prices. With my $500 I am able to purchase the products of other people's labor, having given no labor in return.

Is there any demoralizing effect on society from such opportunities to get something for nothing? There might be without our noticing it because the situation is so common. Nearly all of us are getting something for which we perform no service, or we are trying to. Of course, all cannot succeed. The great mass of the people have to do the work that pays the tribute to the few lucky ones. Wealth never comes from nothing; somebody always produces it, with the help of God and nature. And it is only in the realm of the spirit that one can give and be no poorer.

There are repeated signs of unrest and turmoil in industrial relations today. Is it possible that such situations as described above may have something to do with it?

How We Look to the Dean of St Paul's

A remarkable article on "The Quakers" appears from the pen of Dr. Inge, Dean of St. Paul's (London) in the *Contemporary Review* for February (3/6). It is really an essay on the Society written round Rufus M. Jones' "Later Periods of Quakerism."

Right at the beginning of his article he refers to the attitude of Friends to the late war regarding which he says: "There is a growing conviction that it was a ghastly and unnecessary blunder. It has been said bluntly but not irreverently that the only person who has emerged with intellectual credit from this tragic business is Jesus Christ because if the belligerents had listened to his precepts they would not now be weltering in bankruptcy and misery. The Quakers also in their uncompromising condemnation of war have testified consistently to their belief in the wisdom of the New Testament. . . . It is not surprising then that some notable conversions to Quakerism among persons of high intellectual culture have lately occurred and that even in the Anglican Church attempts have been made to introduce the most characteristic Quaker service, the silent prayer meeting."

The modern science of religious psychology, he points out, has awakened a new interest in the one religious body which has always based faith on the witness of the Inner Light.

"The new Quakerism, apart from its social activities is almost purely mystical, not Puritan. Its mysticism is of a well-known and traditional type and it enlists many more sympathizers than adherents."

He deals appreciatively with the lives of Woolman and Whittier, but he is not afraid to be critical where he thinks he should be. "Worldly prosperity has not promoted faithfulness to the Quaker tradition. Some of the best-known Quaker families have joined the Established Church in a body and are valuable members of it. But the Society has suffered less by these defections than by the infiltration of the prevailing evangelical opinions into the body itself. For a considerable time, especially in America, the majority of Quakers fell under the influence of traditional orthodoxy as held by Protestant Christians in general and thereby lost their main reason for existing as a distinct sect. They lost also the inner freedom of the mystic which gives him so great an advantage, in times of theological unsettlement."

"What is likely to be the future of this brave little body of Christian mystics?" the Dean asks in conclusion. "They are threatened with two dangers —one being assimilated to other Protestant organizations and so losing their distinctive testimony and their peculiar strength, the other that of being entangled in social politics and so carried out of the religious atmosphere altogether. They will probably escape both dangers; for the mystical foundation of Quakerism is now once more increasingly recognized by Friends themselves and they have less than other and larger bodies to gain by unworthy political alliances. H. W. PEET.

Facing the Famine

Why is There Famine in Russia?

Famine is not a new thing in Russia, states Professor James Mavor, in a recent article in the *Wall Street Journal*. The government of Catharine II, encountered the danger when the population of Russia was only a fraction of the present numbers. The czarist government during the nineteenth century repeatedly encountered it, and did its best to deal with the distress it occasioned.

There are four reasons for a famine situation in any country and perhaps, most of all in Russia, apart from the variation of the seasons. These are:

1. The rapid growth of population which renders necessary an increase in food beyond the temporary means of supply.
2. Habitual self-containedness of the population involving the absence of commercial mechanism for the introduction of occasional necessary additions to the local supply of food.
3. Inferior and primitive cultivation of peasant lands, resulting in absence of reserves of grain to insure against want in years of deficient crops.
4. Absence of means of transportation elastic enough to admit a sudden increase of external food supply.

In the fall of 1920 the farmers of the Volga Valley planted their wheat and rye as usual. Then the drought commenced. No rain fell until the end of July and no harvests were gathered. The result has been widespread suffering and starvation among 15,000,000 people, and 15,000,000 more are vitally affected by the shortage of food. Today they are dying by the thousands. Fifteen million are absolutely dependent upon outside help. The terrible incident of famine, in addition to the actual want, is the disease to which the lack of nutrition exposes the people. Typhus, cholera and what is usually called influenza become epidemic, and the influence of the famine is spread far beyond the region afflicted by want of food.

America's Aid

Congress has voted $20,000,000 to help save these desperate people who see death at every hand overwhelming them. The Americans' private subscriptions at the present time total $10,000,000. The Soviet Government is expending $10,000,000 in gold in this country for wheat and seed. But this total of $40,000,000 can only save 5,000,000 of the starving. Who will help save the other 10,000,000?

The Present Need

There are only two American relief agencies working in the Russian famine area today—the American Relief Administration, of which Herbert Hoover is Chairman, and the American Friends' Service Committee. In spite of all that can be humanly done, Dr. Nansen estimates that 5,000,000 of these peasants will die before summer. The problem before the American people is the saving of the 5,000,000 others who have not yet been provided for but who can be saved by a prompt and generous response. The American Friends' Service Committee will accept contributions for these famine victims.

Will You Give Corn?

The large crop of corn last year and its present low price make it possible for rural communities to save life by giving corn. Five bushels of corn will save the life of one of those hungry little waifs along the Volga. The Service Committee will accept carloads of shelled corn at any point, pay all the cost of transportation, convert the corn into hominy and grits and distribute it to the famine victims in Russia without any deduction. Six thousand elevators in the corn belt of our Central West have been appealed to for free service in receiving, shelling, storing and loading corn. They have responded nobly. Any person or organization interested in collecting corn for the famine sufferers is asked to notify the Service Committee at Philadelphia.

Will You Give Flour?

From people who do not have corn to give flour is asked. The American millers have been asked, and have generously agreed, to sell flour for Russian relief at cost. Every community should be able to raise a flour fund for famine relief. A barrel of flour will save a life. The Service Committee will accept flour at any point, pay all transportation cost, and distribute it in the famine area. Every pound of flour given in America will mean a pound of food in Russia where children cry for a crust of bread. The Quakers are feeding in a definitely assigned area in the district of Buzuluk, which has been apportioned to them in conference with the American Relief Administration, and for which they are entirely responsible. These people are entirely dependent upon America's gifts as no congressional aid will go toward these sufferers.

America can save these sufferers. Everyone should help. Somebody must lead in every community. Volunteers are needed to collect food and money to enable the Quaker volunteers in Russia to save some of the starving millions. If no one is collecting in your community, you are the one to do it. Write today to the Service Committee, 20 South 12th Street, Philadelphia, for particulars and instructions.

Schofield School's Call

In the early morning of the 3rd inst., the large Boys' Dormitory, with its recently installed heating plant, harness shop, and printing room, at the Schofield School, Aiken, S. C., was completely destroyed by fire, presumably from a defective wire, and a very heavy loss, in excess of the limited insurance, was sustained. The telegraphic information was a great shock to the writer, whose privilege it was, within the preceding month, to inspect the building in company with J. Lawrence and Caroline Biddle Lippincott, and other friends, and to observe the apparent commendable interest of the management and students reflected in its good order and neatness throughout. It was most fortunate that no injury or fatality occurred, though there were many narrow escapes in the students' endeavor to save the few of their belongings, possible.

The following letter from the Founder to John G. Whittier best reveals the history of this hall, named, as it was, after Deborah Fisher Wharton:

JOHN G. WHITTIER, "8-28-1889.

Dear Friend:

As thee lived in Philadelphia in the early abolition days, thee may be glad to know we are soon to build on these grounds—the Deborah F. Wharton Industrial Hall, where our students will be taught various industries to make them more useful men & women. To have such a building & name it for her had long been in my secret thought, but knowing her modesty did not speak of it. Last summer she was called higher & this spring I went North and gained the consent of her children. Her sons Joseph & Charles giving half the $6,000 needed. Her immortal thought will still be one of helpfulness and she can see now how her name and life will be helpful as an example of simplicity, frugality, industry & adherence to the right. As a representative woman of our Society her religious principles can contribute to the growth and upbuilding of any character, harming none. The greatest blessing of my life has been the inheritance and education of a Christian faith that can cover all creeds as being one—the spirit of Christ. Who would have prophesied that ere the crowning of thy life such a school—with such a name would stand on the soil of South Carolina. The Father's workers should never be discouraged, for we know that underneath all are the Everlasting Arms. The divine love in me goes out with a tenderness that touches thy advancing years with a halo of blessing.

Truly thy friend
Martha Schofield."

The following letter from the poet reflects his sympathetic interest:

"Amesbury, Mass.

My dear Friend:

I am glad to hear once more from thee and of thy noble and christian work of love, and that that work has been blest by our Heavenly Father so unmistakably, and I sympathize fully with thy assurance that the teachings of the Holy Spirit—the Light within, and the worship in spirit and in truth will continue to be taught in thy school. I do not wish to be a sectarian—I love and recognize the good in all—but the older I grow, the more precious to me are the doctrines and testimonies of our Society. That the Divine Help may be given thee abundantly is the prayer of thy aged friend. John G. Whittier."

With the inspiration of the foregoing, will not the many friends of Martha Schofield rise to help meet this first calamity in the history of her beloved school.

G. HERBERT JENKINS.

An Appeal for a Meeting-House

Nearly eight years ago a Friends' Meeting was organized in Berkeley, California, by a small group of Friends of both branches, living in and near San Francisco.

For a few months they met in San Francisco, but for more than seven years the meetings have been held every First-day morning without intermission in various rooms rented for the purpose in Oakland, and changed from time to time, as became necessary.

In the midst of a population of about a million people there is no other place of worship where meetings are held after the manner of early Friends, and if this meeting is to continue and furnish a centre for Friends and Friendly influences in the community, it seems almost imperative that it should have a permanent home. Hence its members are making active efforts to acquire means to build a small Meeting House.

They have already, collected and promised, about $3,500.00.

A visiting Friend who attended the meetings last summer has given $500.00 and offers $1,000.00 more if enough can be raised before the first of Fourth month next, to make the sum $6,000.00.

Being but a small group, and believing there is a real need here for a meeting that may fill a great want, they are asking the help of other Friends, who may feel that there is especial need now to present to the world at large, the ideals and principles of the Society of Friends. Contributions may be sent to Charles E. Cox, Treasurer, 855 Chapman Street, San Jose, and will be very gratefully received.

Signed on behalf of Oakland Meeting,

DONALD ERSKINE, *Clerk.*

Friendly News Notes

In an address at the Poor Richard Club, Philadelphia, recently, Dr. Paul M. Pearson, director of the Swarthmore Chautauqua Association, said that getting one's second wind is not only essential sometimes in winning a race, but there is such a thing as a spiritual second wind. "We are living at a time that requires the expenditure of spiritual energy," he said, "and there can be no satisfactory solution of political and economic problems without such expenditure. The business of the world is no better than the spiritual qualities of the men behind it."

We have received word of the engagement of Lucretia M. Kester, daughter of Reuben P. and Myrtle M. Kester, of Newtown, Pa., to Albert C. Mammel, son of B. Wallace and Ada C. Mammel, of North Wales, Pa. Also the engagement of Phoebe A. Hollingsworth, daughter of Robert and Elizabeth Hollingsworth, to Israel Hough, son of Dr. Mary P. H. Hough, all of Ambler, Pa.

A letter from Butler M. Hoag, Greenwich, N. Y., tells us of an error made in the introduction to the "Vision of Joseph Hoag." It stated that his parents were Presbyterians, but according to Joseph Hoag's Journal, four generations of his ancestors were Friends. Butler Hoag writes, "Joseph's grandfather and my great-great-grandfather were brothers."

Personal letters from Joseph and Edith Stratton Platt tell of their arrival in Moukden, Manchuria. On their way they made a short call in Japan and had a conference with Gilbert Bowles and several of the Friends' mission in Tokio. They were particularly anxious to learn through Gilbert Bowles of the best side of the Japanese, because in Manchuria they see enough of the worst side.

While Henry T. Hodgkin was in Canton, Margaret Hallowell Riggs arranged two meetings for him to speak to the girls at the True Light Middle School of Canton Christian College where she is teaching. How the girls appreciated his message is shown by the following item from their school paper:

> Dr. Henry T. Hodgkin, who is connected with the Fellowship of Reconciliation, gave us two talks during September. On the twenty-sixth he talked about the needs of China, and on the twenty-seventh about the Kingdom of God. Many of our hard problems were solved by his interesting and wonderful thought.

The total destruction by fire of Wharton Hall, at Schofield School, on the third inst., was the first fire which has occurred in the entire history of the school of over fifty years. The usual night inspection had been made, but shortly after midnight flames started in the third story. Notwithstanding the good discipline, and heroic work of the boys and fire department, the building was entirely consumed, with its recently installed heating apparatus. This is a severe blow to the school, coming as it does so soon after the sudden death of its most efficient superintendent, S. Louisa Haight, and at the beginning of the new management under Miss Georgia Crocker, who must look to the many friends of the school to rally around her in this serious emergency.

Martha J. Warner writes that Ohio Friends are much interested in their Parent-Teacher Association, and to remedy undernourishment among school children have been serving them with something warm for the noon-day lunch. Friends have also organized a Missionary Society, which is a community affair. It includes Foreign and Home missions and work in Serbia. One of the members, Edna Wildman, married Harold Peterson last fall, and they went to India to engage in Y. M. C. A. work. Harold had formerly been working in Calcutta.

WOOLMAN SCHOOL

With but one more week of work at Woolman School we are at the point where we realize that all good things come to a close sooner or later.

During the last two weeks we have been enjoying a course on "Success in Teaching Religion" as given by E. Morris Ferguson, A.M., D.D., Secretary of the Associated Sunday School Work in Massachusetts. The course is quite practical and is to cover (a) Good physical conditions for work, (b) Good conditions of organization, (c) Good conditions of Personal Preparation.

Two more of our courses finish this week—that on International Relations by Vincent D. Nicholson, and that on Rural Social Problems by Herman T. Morse. Both of these courses have been very helpful in broadening our viewpoint of social problems at home and abroad.

Not only our studies, but even our social privileges are assuming a rush-hour aspect.

Mr. and Mrs. Louis Robinson entertained the group one evening last week at which time we enjoyed a chapter of Mrs. Robinson's forthcoming text-book on Sociology.

On March 1st we visited Haverford College under the care and guidance of the students of the Thomas Wistar Brown Graduate School. They favored us with a return visit on the following First-day. On Second-day the group hiked over to Rose Valley and visited the Anna H. Shaw House. On Fourth-day we spent a most enjoyable evening at Dr. Russell's home.

We, the "Woolmanites of 1922," wish to extend our appreciation of the efforts put forth by our able instructors—Dr. Elbert Russell, Vincent D. Nicholson, Mrs. Elizabeth W. Collins, Herman T. Morse and E. Morris Ferguson.

May the innumerable succeeding classes appreciate the opportunities for knowledge and joy of lasting friendship as we have done in our brief sojourn here.

March 10, 1922. J. B. H.

SWARTHMORE COLLEGE OPEN SCHOLARSHIPS 1922

Swarthmore College announces the establishment experimentally of five annual open competitive scholarships for men, not confined to any particular school, locality, subject of study, or religious denomination. These scholarships are to be based upon the general plan of the Rhodes Scholarships and are to be given to candidates who show greatest promise in:

(1) Qualities of manhood, force of character and leadership.

(2) Literary and scholastic ability and attainments.

(3) Physical vigor, as shown by interest in outdoor sports or in other ways.

The regulations under which these scholarships will be awarded are as follows:

The stipend of a Swarthmore College Open Scholarship will be five hundred dollars ($500) a year, which will cover the greater part of a man's college expenses.

Each scholarship is tenable for four consecutive years, subject to the maintenance of a high standing in the college.

A candidate to be eligible must:

(*a*) Be between the ages of 16 and 21 on September 1st of the year for which he is elected.

(*b*) Be qualified to enter Swarthmore College on certificate with fifteen units of credit as prescribed in the college catalogue, pages 36-38.

(*c*) Not have attended another college or university.

Each candidate must secure the endorsement of the principal of his preparatory school and not more than two candidates may be selected to represent a particular school in the competition for any one year.

Scholars will be selected without written examination on the basis (1) of their school record, and (2) of a personal interview with some representative of the college. It is expected that these interviews can be arranged in practically any part of the United States so as to make it unnecessary for candidates to travel any considerable distance. Application blanks duly filled out and accompanied by the material specified must reach the Dean of Swarthmore College on or before April 15, 1922. References will be followed up, interviews arranged in various parts of the country, and the awards announced about June 15.

MEETING OF OAKLAND FRIENDS

Friends at Oakland, California, recently held a meeting of unusual interest. All the people in or near San Francisco, Berkeley, and Oakland, who have membership or close association with the Society of Friends, were sent cordial invitations to attend. Between sixty and eighty Friends attended the various meetings. At the morning session William C. Allen, Elizabeth H. Shelley (Isaac Sharp's daughter), Lydia Cox and Donald Erskine spoke with a unity of exercise which was felt to be enforced by the fellowship of silence in the assembly.

At the afternoon session, after a devotional opening, Russian relief, Poland's need of sheep, and the present call to support the national anti-Lynching Bill, were presented. Anna Brinton then conducted the program on Reminiscences of Friends' Secondary Schools, which was participated in by representatives of the various schools. It was regretted that the young Friend who was expected to represent George School could not be present, and that the speaker for Vermillion Academy was obliged to leave early. Other schools that were represented were Ackworth, Westtown, Sidcot, Moses Brown School and the Boarding Schools at Barnesville, Ohio, and Pickering, Canada.

The afternoon was one of those social-religious occasions, so characteristic of and so essential to a Quaker community. One could not help feeling that there is a place and a need among this group of that which a Friends' Meeting alone can fully supply, and though its regular attendance may be small, since distances and pressure of life are felt, it will be a center of spiritual life and a gathering place of hungering hearts.

NOTTINGHAM QUARTERLY MEETING

At Nottingham Quarterly Meeting, held at Oxford, Pa., Robert K. Wood, Clerk, Dr. O. Edward Janney spoke in the meeting for worship on the text, "What Must I Do to Inherit Eternal Life?" He spoke of the many things we all lack, as did the Jew of old, but we develop the finest traits of character in the conflict between right and wrong, and if we but have faith in God, the hardest task will become easy.

At the afternoon conference Dr. Evan Stubbs spoke of the need of disarmament and Isaac Walton told of the economic results of the Washington Conference. Dr. Janney closed the conference with a talk in which he gave the accomplishments of the Washington Conference, and he showed the immense influence of a united people demanding action in their appeals to President Harding and Secretary Hughes. Resolutions were adopted by the meeting, asking our Senators to ratify the treaties as adopted by the Conference and our Representatives to vote to reduce the appropriation for the army and navy.

A letter from Seth L. Kinsey, of York, Pa., to the Quarterly Meeting was read, in which he regretted his inability to attend the meeting. He wrote in part:

"I want you all to know that I will be with you in earnestness of thought and feeling; and a sincere desire to experience with you a portion of the spiritual strengthening and uplift which is characteristic of Friends' meetings; manifest sometimes in the silence of communion; and sometimes in the voicing of counsel or prayer; but always through the touch of the Father's hand upon our hearts."

He then speaks of the need for preparation for the ministry, "*not* the formal preparation of words and sentences, but the *preparation of study*, of the Scriptures; of human life with its joys and sorrows, its successes and failures; of nature in its various moods and activities; of the beauty, yes, even the homeliness; of the harmony and even of the discords, which our eyes see and our ears hear; coming more and more to a realization of the presence, the touch, the influence, the control, of the Divine, in things animate and inanimate. From such a course of study comes a *full heart* as well as a full mind; and as 'Out of the fullness of the heart the mouth speaketh,' hence the heart becomes the overflowing reservoir, using and controlling the brain and speech as instruments of conveyance to those who hear. Such a *study filled* life gradually becomes a *spirit filled* one that influences other lives by the power; not so much of brain or eloquence; but of the Spirit. And there is in the great heart of humanity a responsive chord that vibrates to the touch of love, both human and Divine."

SALEM QUARTERLY MEETING

At Salem Quarterly Meeting, held at Woodstown, N. J., on Third month 9th, Warner Underwood, Clerk, the reverential silence was broken by a prayer of thanksgiving by Rachel M. Lippincott. J. Barnard Walton's message was based on the text, "Ye shall know the truth and the truth shall make you free," and Rachel Davis DuBois spoke on the brotherhood of man. Jane P. Rushmore quoted, "We may hope and resolve and aspire and pray," but if we fail to act with our resolves and aspirations, we have made but little progress toward bettering the world.

Joel Borton, Emily R. Kirby, Louisa Powell and Laura E. Holmes also gave inspiring messages. The Baptist minister of Woodstown was present and supplicated for strength to do our duty as we see it.

At the business meeting all the thirty-three representatives appointed were present, with the exception of one who was prevented by illness. The subject of the "political prisoners" was brought up for discussion, but as there was not unity in the matter, no action was taken.

The meeting was a large one and, after a lunch provided by the Woodstown Friends, J. Barnard Walton gave a most interesting account of his visit to White Water Quarterly Meeting and an outline of the approaching conference at Richmond, Indiana.

RACHEL L. BORDEN.
Assistant Clerk.

PELHAM HALF-YEARLY MEETING

Pelham Half-Yearly Meeting was held at Coldstream, Ontario, on Second month 18th and 19th. Samuel P. Brown and Elston E. Wilson, Clerks, presiding. The meeting for worship was full of messages that were helpful and inspiring. One Friend read a selection containing the thought that "To know God's laws is first to know the life of God in us." Another speaker brought the thought that the still, small voice is the voice of God awakening conscience. It was emphasized that we should accept the Christ Spirit as an ever-present Savior keeping us from sin. Also, a waiting attitude in our members is not enough for the success of our meetings for worship. We must have our inner ear attuned to that still small voice and be willing to do our part.

At the business meeting, the following request, sent by Lobo Monthly Meeting of Friends to the premier and parliament of Canada, was read: "We, the members of the Religious Society of Friends of Western Ontario, do request that the parliament of the Dominion of Canada send a liberal sum of money, or provide its value in available food-stuffs, for the immediate relief of the starving inhabitants of the Volga region of Russia. We know that our taxes are high and Canada's debt is great, but who with a loaf of bread can deny a starving child a crust?"

The Young Friends' Association was held at the home of Florence and Edward Bycraft on First-day evening. A paper was prepared by each of the three Friendly centres represented, Pelham, Yarmouth and Lobo.

Items From Everywhere

One of the men in Leavenworth prison "for conscience's sake" has written to the Philadelphia branch of the Prison Comfort Club, expressing his desire for a Gibson mandolin. Music would be a great gift to him and to many of his companions. Has anyone a good mandolin they could give for this purpose, or something to contribute toward a fund for purchasing one? Contributions may be sent to the INTELLIGENCER office.

The Pennsylvania Department of Forestry will develop thirteen public camp grounds in the State Forests this spring. They will be fully equipped for the convenience of campers and sportsmen and will be ready for use when the trout-fishing season opens, April 15.

To promote wider use of the State Forests and to encourage out-door recreation in Pennsylvania, the Department will provide open-front shelters, or lean-to's, stone fireplaces, walled-up and covered springs, comfort stations, and in some instances, public telephones at the various public camp grounds. Use of the camp grounds will be free, but permits issued by the local forest officers will be required when campers occupy a camp for more than two days.

How far shall Congress reduce the army and navy of the United States? The National Council for Reduction of Armaments, Frederick J. Libby, Executive Secretary, answers this question as follows in its latest bulletin:

"With regard to the Army, the question has narrowed down practically to a difference of opinion as between an Army of 75,000 men and an Army of 100,000, or thereabouts. With regard to the Navy, the figures run between 50,000 and 80,000. A Navy of more than 80,000 men or an Army running much over 100,000 men is not even being considered seriously.

"We support the 50% cut in the appropriations, from $790,000,000 to $400,000,000 for the two arms of defense, and leave it to our Congressmen to allocate this sum according to their own judgment."

After outlining the various reasons why a 50% reduction is not excessive, and the progress which the appropriation bills have made in committee, the article ends:

"If you are in favor of a drastic cut in the army and navy appropriations, *let your Congressman know*. It is not too soon."

An editorial in the *Christian Advocate* discusses prohibition from a significant angle under the title, "Where Law Enforcement Must Begin." It points out that whereas sentiment leading up to the adoption of the prohibition amendment was gradually cultivated in local communities through educational work, enforcement of the amendment is in the opposite direction—from the top down to the community. This method cannot succeed, because it is "too long a reach down from the heights of Federal authority to the local law-breaker.

"The remedy is clear. Local public sentiment in favor of law enforcement must be aroused as local public sentiment was marshalled to vote out the saloon. It must show results in the passage of ordinances in every municipality making possible the suppression of the outlaw traffic by the local police. And it must be so organized and directed as to hold the local officials to their duty in enforcing the law.

"This is a perfectly simple and practical program. One earnest citizen could set it in motion in any locality (as in the old days one earnest woman often set in motion the movement to vote a town dry). A men's Bible Class or a federation of Bible Classes might be the nucleus. The main thing is to make a local beginning of the law enforcement program. It will spread from town to county, from county to state and from state to nation, as did the Prohibition legislation. And Prohibition will not have its perfect work until this solid groundwork is laid, until the nation-wide fabric of law enforcement is built from the grass-roots up!"

THE OPEN FORUM

This column is intended to afford free expression of opinion by readers on questions of interest. The INTELLIGENCER is not responsible for any such opinions. Letters must be brief, and the editor reserves the right to omit parts if necessary to save space.

To the Editor:

In FRIENDS' INTELLIGENCER of First month 28th, is a communication from John Cox, Jr., counselling Friends to take no part in the effort now being made to save the two unfortunate Italians, Sacco and Vanzetti, now under sentence in Massachusetts, from the electric chair. It seems to me that this advice must be the result of ignorance of this case. I have taken pains to go over it with some care and I do not see how any one that reads an abstract of the evidence can believe these men to be guilty.

If we are to allow every man that is unjustly convicted to suffer, why has the National Association for the Advancement of Colored People carried to the Supreme Court of the United States the cases of the unfortunate colored men sentenced to death as the result of a race riot started by *white* men because the colored people of Elaine, Arkansas, organized peaceably in order to employ counsel to represent them in cases against their white landlords in the courts?

I rejoice at the efforts of Friends, hitherto largely unfruitful, to get rid of capital punishment, but if, until the death penalty is abolished, we allow every unjustly convicted man to be put to death, heavy will be our guilt in the sight of a justly offended Deity.

Third month 7th. MARIANNA G. BRUBAKER.

I wish to speak a word to thee, and to the readers of the INTELLIGENCER; particularly to most or all of those who have been appointed as members of the "Advancement Committee" of all of the several "inferior" and "superior" meetings; and even to those who are properly belonging to that class, though their appointment may be that of their having learned to obey the call of an "invisible presence" within their best selves.

Probably our great set-back with our people has been not to really and fully become acquainted with our own individualized selves, or personalities. To find out, *if possible*, why we act as we do in so many instances, in relation to our human affairs that have been forced upon the human family, it may be in the course of evolution, or by divine appointment—under the law of compensation.

It seems quite probable that with all our *intellectual equipment* we are not as well qualified for the tasks of our time as were those who stood out on the front line for the first hundred years after Fox, Penn and others had prepared *some line* on which to advance.

I earnestly wish to recommend that all procure and read, in the January number of *The World Tomorrow*, Richard Robert's article "Disarming Our Minds." Much is told here that many of us thought we knew, but after we have read the article, we feel glad that some one has told it so well.

Keystone, Ind. THOMAS E. SCOTT.

BIRTHS

WAY—On Third month 8th, at Wilmington, Delaware, to D. Herbert and Edith Williams Way, a son, named David Spencer Way.

MARRIAGES

THOMAS-SAURMAN—On Third month 4th, at the home of the bride's parents, Warminster, Pa., under the care of Horsham Monthly Meeting, Charles Edwin Thomas, son of Charles L. and Amy Thomas, of King-of-Prussia, and Anna Elizabeth Saurman, daughter of Atlee B. and Mary Walton Saurman.

DEATHS

CADWALLADER—At Norristown, Pa., on Third month 4th, Elizabeth S., aged 87 years. Interment in Friends' Burial Ground, Quakertown, Pa.

COMLY—At Jacksonville, Fla., on Second month 28th, Newton M., husband of Margaret Richardson Comly, of Bustleton, Pa., aged 57 years.

GRISCOM—In Frankford, Pa., on Third month 7th, Mary Ann Bassett, wife of Leslie Griscom, in her 81st year.

LAMBERT—Suddenly in Philadelphia, Pa., on Second month 21st, Elizabeth J., widow of Samuel C. Lambert.

STRADLING—Third month 5th, at Lansford, Pa., Susanna C., widow of George W. Stradling. Interment Newtown Friends' Burial Ground.

WORRALL—At the residence of his son-in-law, Thomas P. Worth, Marshallton, Pa., on Second month 17th, J. Ellwood Worrall, son of the late Richard T. and Mary Ann Wilson Worrall. He was in his 81st year and was a member of Kenneth Monthly Meeting of Friends.

MARY BURGESS ANDREWS

Mary Burgess Andrews, widow of James B. Andrews, of Baltimore, passed away on Third month 4th. She was born in Bucks County, Pennsylvania, in 1838, and was a daughter of the late Amos and Elizabeth (Smith) Burgess. She is survived by one daughter, Anna Andrews Thomas, wife of Prof. Thaddeus P. Thomas, of Goucher College, and two sisters, Mrs. Sara Linton Ross, of Baltimore, and Mrs. Anna B. Andrews, of Allston, Massachusetts, and one brother, Thomas S. Burgess, of Newark, N. J.

She was a birthright member of the Religious Society of Friends, and for more than fifty years previous to her death a member of the Park Avenue Meeting, Baltimore, Md. At the funeral Dr. O. Edward Janney, Anne W. Janney and Pauline W. Holme bore testimony to her beautiful, loving and Christian life. The funeral was attended by a large number of sorrowing relatives and friends; for she was, indeed, everybody's friend—such as one seldom meets in a lifetime. As some one said of her, "She had all the qualities that are most lovable in human nature—unselfish, always thinking of others, generous and charitable." Sweet and pure herself, she saw only the best in others.

While her life was quiet and unostentatious, she was always deeply interested in progressive and uplifting works. Her keen intellect and clear judgment made her wise counsel ever helpful. This world is better for lives like hers. The influence of a beautiful life does not die, but still abides in the minds and hearts and lives of others.

"Out of its tomb of snow—the flower,
Out of life's bitterest woe—more power,
Out of the dreariest dusk—the morn,
Out of the withering husk—the corn,
Out of this form of clay—the soul,
Out of earth's winding way—the goal."

ELIZABETH B. SATTERTHWAITE.

WILLIAM CHARLES BRAITHWAITE

Many American Friends join with English Friends in mourning the loss of William Charles Braithwaite, Quaker Historian, Banker of Banbury, England, whose sudden death occurred on January 28th.

A memoir by Sir George Newman, who was, with Arnold S. Rowntree, one of his closest fellow-workers, says in part: "In the first place, he had a comprehensive and catholic spirit. His broad-mindedness and innate common-sense served him well all through the forty years of his public service. Unlike many other good and religious men, his faith seemed to be based upon an immovable foundation which had in it the *substance* of things hoped for. For him neither orthodoxy nor heterodoxy seemed to have either terror or interest. He stood all square to the four winds and however much other people might drift or "wobble," he seemed to his friends to remain always fixed, immovable, with a wonderful invisible magnetic needle within him that pointed to the Pole Star. This solidity and stabality was his outstanding characteristic, and it proved invaluable in all the varied activities of his life.

Then, in the next place, William Braithwaite was a learned man. He had been brought up in a home where intellectual control and humanistic and classical learning were held in repute and almost in reverence. He held the Degrees of Bachelor of Arts and Bachelor of Laws in the University of London, and only a few weeks ago received an honorary degree in theology from the University of Marburg. But these academic honors did not represent the wealth of his learning. Classics and history were his strongest points, particularly the history of religious movements and especially Quakerism in the Seventeenth Century. His two volumes on "The Beginnings of Quakerism" and the "Second Period of Quakerism" are masterpieces of profound knowledge and exact workmanship.

A third characteristic was his public spirit. Of him it may be said that his idea of love was service. He was an idealist and a practical mystic combined, and, taking him all round, he was probably the sanest embodiment of the modern Quaker spirit who has worked among us for a generation. There has been no loss to the Society of Friends compared with this since John Wilhelm Rowntree died in New York.

Lastly, there was a personal trait in William Braithwaite which we shall always remember with delight, that was his humor. He possessed in a wonderful degree the true sense of humor.

So when we think of him the memory will always be fresh and green, for his courageous life and his hard work and his sense of seriousness of living were enriched by his humanity and his humor. His has been a very happy life, full to the brim of useful and splendid work—happy in his ideals, happy in seeing their fruition and fulfilment, happy in his wife and family, above all, happy and confident in his Faith.

COMING EVENTS

THIRD MONTH.

18th—An evening of Magic, by Paul Fleming, at George School, Pa. Admission, fifty cents.

19th—Whiting Williams will be present at Swarthmore meeting at 11.30 a. m.

19th—William Littleboy expects to attend the Friends' meeting at Atlantic City at 11 a. m.

19th—E. Maria Bishop is expecting to be in attendance at Solebury meeting at 10 a. m.

19th—Conference class at 15th and Race Streets, Philadelphia, at close of meeting for worship, at 11.40 a. m. Speaker—Edith M. Winder. Subject—Some Tasks of the Kingdom II.

19th—At Oxford, Pa., Elbert Russell will give his fifth lecture on the Life of Jesus, 2 p. m. in Meeting House.

22d—Monthly Meeting of Friends of Philadelphia, 15th and Race Streets, 7.30 p. m. See notice.

23d—Green Street Monthly Meeting of Friends of Philadelphia, School House Lane, Germantown, 7.30 p. m.

24th and 25th—P. Y. F. A. play—"The Passing of the Third Floor Back." See notice.

25th—A Meeting Social in the Gymnasium of Friends' Seminary, 226 East 16th Street. All are cordially invited. 8 o'clock.

26th—Elbert Russell will give the last lecture on the Life of Jesus, in Oxford Meeting House, at 2 p. m.

26th—J. Nevin Sayre, editor of *The World Tomorrow*, will be at Swarthmore—meeting in the morning, college Y. M. and Y. M. C. A. in the evening, and a group meeting of the Fellowship of Reconciliation the evening before.

NOTICE—The P. Y. F. A. will give "The Passing of the Third Floor Back" on March 24th and 25th in the Auditorium of the P. Y. F. A., 15th and Cherry Streets, Philadelphia. Tickets, $1.00, include dancing, now on sale at the P. Y. F. A. desk (reserved seats). The proceeds will go to the Margaret Hallowell Riggs Fund for support of the work in Canton Christian College, China.

NOTICE—Dr. James Moffatt, of Glasgow, Scotland, will give the Boardman Lectures in Christian Ethics under the auspices of the University of Pennsylvania on the evenings of Third month 27th and 28th at 8.15 p. m. at Asbury Church on Chestnut Street between 33d and 34th Streets, Philadelphia. Dr. Moffatt is the well-known Biblical scholar and translator of the New Testament. The Boardman Lectureship in Christian Ethics was founded for the purpose of teaching the "practical application of the precepts and behaviour of Jesus Christ to everyday life."

NOTICE—Supper will be served by the Best Interests Committee before Monthly Meeting at 15th and Race Streets, Philadelphia, Third month 22nd, in the Friends' Central School Lunch Room, at 6 o'clock. Tickets, 65 cents. Please purchase tickets before Third month 20th. Anna W. Cloud, 140 N. 15th Street, Philadelphia.

NOTICE—On Third month 24th, a meeting, under the joint auspices of the West Philadelphia First-day School and the Committee on Best Interests of the Monthly Meeting of Friends of Philadelphia, will be held at the Meeting House, 35th Street and Lancaster Avenue, at 8 o'clock P. M. Vincent D. Nicholson will deliver an address on "The Society of Friends of 1922." This address will be followed by a Social.

NOTICE—The First-day School Union of Western Quarter will be held at the New Garden Meeting House, March 18th. Morning session at 10 o'clock. Subject for discussion, "Beginners' Classes. Address, Mary C. Pyle. The afternoon session will be addressed by Elizabeth W. Collins.

American Friends' Service Committee

WILBUR K. THOMAS, EX. SEC.

20 S. 12th St. Philadelphia.

CASH CONTRIBUTIONS

WEEK ENDING MARCH 6, 1922.

Five Years Meetings	$871.90
Phila. Yearly Meeting (4th & Arch)	5,647.05
Phila. Yearly Meeting (15th & Cherry Street)	3,090.30
New York Monthly Meeting	400.00
Wrightstown Quarterly Meeting	60.00
Oakland Branch of the College Park Asso. of Friends	11.00
Old Merion First-day School	10.00
Oxford Monthly Meeting	100.00
Solesbury Monthly Meeting	15.00
New Garden Prep. Meeting	50.00
First Friends Church, Cleveland	28.00
Buffalo Meeting	24.02
Contributions for General	178.65
For Germany	674.82
For Austria	3,916.13
For Poland	55.50
For Syria	31.00
For Russia	30,529.29
For Russian Overhead	19.00
For Clothing	591.63
Refunds	67.22
	$46,370.51

Shipments received during week ending March 4th, 106 boxes and packages received; 2 for German Relief.

REGULAR MEETINGS

OAKLAND, CALIF.—A FRIENDS' MEETing is held every First-day at 11 A. M., in the Extension Room, Y. W. C. A. Building, Webster Street, above 14th. Visiting Friends always welcome.

FRIENDS' MEETING IN PASADENA, California—Orange Grove Monthly Meeting of Friends, 520 East Orange Grove Avenue, Pasadena, California. Meeting for worship, First-day, 11 A. M. Monthly Meeting, the second First-day of each month, at 1.45 P. M.

CENTRAL MEETING OF FRIENDS (Chicago), meets every First-day in Room 706, 410 South Michigan Avenue, at 10.45 a. m. Visitors are invited.

WANTED

PARTY OF EIGHT NOW ORGANIZing for 58-day trip—Paris, Switzerland, Passion Play, Holland, England. Starting about July 1. Rates reasonable. Apply without delay to Bertha L. Stover, 31 Westview St., Germantown, Philadelphia.

POSITION WANTED IN PHILADELphia or near vicinity. A middle aged man with considerable experience in positions of trust, with tact and sense of responsibility, with thorough knowledge of figures and accounting, desires a position that will occupy his time and give him a small income. J. 110, Friends' Intelligencer.

WANTED — AN ACTIVE, MIDDLEaged person, Friend preferred, to assist with the care of child (four years), with mending and light household duties. Suburbs of Philadelphia. Servants kept. Address W. 111, Friends' Intelligencer.

THOROUGHLY EXPERIENCED farmer, single, Christian, would like work on farm with Friends. Address A. 112, Friends' Intelligencer.

POSITION WANTED — PRACTICAL nurse wishes permanent position; care of lady or gentleman; good references. F. M. W., 5921 N. Broad St., Phila., Telephone Wyoming 4518 W.

POSITION WANTED — AS HOUSEkeeper, mountain or seashore hotel. Address M. W., 5115 Walton Ave., Philadelphia.

WANTED—SUMMER BOARD IN A private family on a farm in New York or Pennsylvania, for two ladies and son 12 years old. Third week in July to third week in September. Mary H. Kirby, 4926 Cedar Ave., West Philadelphia, Pa.

FOR RENT

FOR RENT—APRIL TO OCTOBER, Nine-room house with sleeping porch and garage, near river, at Riverton. Address Helen Lippincott, Riverton, N. J.

FOR RENT — FOUR-ROOM APARTment, on third floor, with bath and kitchenette. Also room and bath. Nothing furnished. Apply 133 E. Main St., Moorestown, N. J.

FOR SALE

FOR SALE—BRICK AND FRAME detached residence, well built; 10 rooms, bath, sleeping porch, glassed in; gas and electricity, modern conveniences; near Friends' School and Meeting House, Lansdowne, Pa. Apply J. 100, Friends' Intelligencer.

TRANSIENT ACCOMMODATIONS

WASHINGTON, D. C.—ROOMS FOR visitors. Near Station, Capitol, Library. Continuous hot water. Electricity. Garage. Mrs. L. L. Kendig, 120 C. Street, Northwest.

WE BUY ANTIQUE FURNITURE and antiques of every kind, old pictures of Washington or any prominent American, old gold, silver, platinum, diamonds and old false teeth. PHILA. ANTIQUE CO., 700 Chestnut St. Phone Walnut 70-26. Established 1866.

To the Lot Holders and others interested in Fairhill Burial Ground:

GREEN STREET Monthly Meeting has funds available for the encouragement of the practice of cremating the dead to be interred in Fairhill Burial Ground. We wish to bring this fact as prominently as possible to those who may be interested. We are prepared to undertake the expense of cremation in case any lot holder desires us to do so.

Those interested should communicate with William H. Gaskill, Treasurer of the Committee of Interments, Green Street Monthly Meeting, or any of the following members of the Committee.

William H. Gaskill, 3201 Arch St.
Samuel N. Longstreth, 1218 Chestnut St.
Charles F. Jenkins, 232 South Seventh St.
Stuart S. Graves, 3033 Germantown Ave.

ADVERTISING RATE in the FRIENDS' INTELLIGENCER, for Help Wanted, Positions Wanted, Rooms for Rent, Notices, and other classified advertisements without display, for each insertion, 2 cents per word, including name, initials and address. Answers may be sent to a box at the INTELLIGENCER office, if so directed.

For display advertising the rate is 10 cents per agate line, or $1.40 per column inch, each insertion. On ten or more insertions in a year from date of order, ten per cent. discount. Thus a four-inch single-column or two-inch double-column advertisement costs $5.60 each insertion, less ten per cent., or 5.04 net each time for ten or more insertions. Matter may be changed whenever desired, without extra charge.

Experience has proved the INTELLIGENCER to be a remarkably good advertising medium. All advertisements must "pass the censor!"

Address 140 N. 15th St., Philadelphia

The Friends' Intelligencer

ESTABLISHED 1844 | THIRD MONTH 25, 1922 | VOLUME 79 NUMBER 12

Contents

THE FRIENDS' INTELLIGENCER

Published weekly, 140 N. 15th Street, Philadelphia, Pa., by Friends' Intelligencer Association, Ltd.

WALTER H. ABELL, *Editor*
SUE C. YERKES, *Business Manager*

Editorial Board: Elizabeth Powell Bond, Thomas A. Jenkins, J. Russell Smith, George A. Walton.

Board of Managers: Edward Cornell, Alice Hall Paxson, Paul M. Pearson, Annie Hillborn, Elwood Hollingshead, William C. Biddle, Charles F. Jenkins, Edith M. Winder, Frances M. White.

Officers of Intelligencer Associates: Ellwood Burdsall, Chairman; Bertha L. Broomell, Secretary; Herbert P. Worth, Treasurer.

Subscription rates: United States, Mexico, Cuba and Panama, $2.50 per year. Canada and other foreign countries, $3.00 per year. Checks should be made payable to Friends' Intelligencer Association, Ltd.

Entered as Second Class Matter at Philadelphia Post Office.

The Friends' Intelligencer

The religion of Friends is based on faith in the "INWARD LIGHT," or direct revelation of God's spirit and will in every seeking soul.

The INTELLIGENCER is interested in all who bear the name of Friends in every part of the world, and aims to promote love, unity and intercourse among all branches and with all religious societies.

ESTABLISHED 1844 | PHILADELPHIA, THIRD MONTH 25, 1922 | VOLUME 79 NUMBER 12

"The Young Quaker"

From the English Young Friends' Movement comes the first number of its new "official organ," *The Young Quaker*. It is a four-page monthly, printed for the most part in small type, so that it includes an astonishing amount of material, and designed to afford a means of communication between the scattered groups of English young Friends. It will "aim in its editorial articles to give an opinion, from a younger point of view, on the current affairs of the Society and on wider matters which may call for attention." The annual foreign subscription rate is only four shillings, and we hope that many American Friends will encourage the new organ by subscribing. Subscriptions should be sent to the Publisher, "The Young Quaker," Friends' Institute, 138, Bishopsgate, London, E. C. 2.

The first number affords an interesting indication of what "the younger point of view" is among English Friends today.

As expressed in *The Young Quaker*, it is a point of view with sound foundations in the will to seek, and to allow others to seek. The editorial, "We Explain Ourselves," champions a free and vigorous conception of truth:

> Having no tradition to maintain, it (*The Young Quaker*) will be free to open its columns to a full expression of ideas from all sources. Knowing that Truth is something ultimate which will prevail through all heresies and wrong doctrines, it will have no fear in placing before its readers any contributions which it feels spring from an honest conviction."

If Friends, young or old, could grasp and live this spirit of unrestricted fellowship with truth-seekers of whatever mind, though they did nothing else, they would be injecting waters of healing into a sick world. In every nation, every class, every sect, there are seekers today. Because few have wholly found as yet, few wholly agree in the details of conclusion. To realize that such disagreement does not necessarily mean that either side is wrong, but that all are converging gradually toward the ultimate point of truth, is to have caught the meaning of fellowship. If the limits of our experience of brotherhood are set by the limits of those whose opinions we share, there is little chance either of our approximating final truth, or of our breaking through convention into the boundlessness of true fellowship. May this free spirit of *The Young Quaker* be the spirit of Friends everywhere!

Two other tendencies come into evidence in this number; one to take from modern science whatever it has to offer for the enrichment of life and religion; the other to reweave the tie between religion and art,—a tie which abnormal circumstances forced the earlier Society of Friends to sever to its own loss. Articles on "The Place of Music in Religion," and "Architecture—An Art of Life," give expression to this urge toward aesthetic expression. Relative to the appreciation of the scientific contribution, are articles on "The Atom" and on "Psychology and Christianity."

Finally, the attitude of the young English group toward the established traditions of Quakerism is indicated in the editorial comment on a proposal, introduced by two English Quarterly Meetings, that the Advices and Queries should be revised:

> The Advices and Queries cannot be remodelled completely. All that is in them is good, but it may rightly be objected that there is much that might be there that is not.
>
> They are too quietist, and inclined to be parochial. Each generation needs to find new implications of old truths to modern conditions.
>
> The path of reform lies along the road of adding to the already existing queries, others which will express new concerns and more vital pronouncements, corresponding with the wider age in which we are living.

As far as the past has gone, well and good; but the present *must go farther*. Not to destroy, but to build higher on old foundations, is the aspiration of English young Friends as expressed in the first number of their new organ. It is an aspiration which all Friends, without limits of age or nationality, should share; an aspiration which will work its leaven with quickening effect throughout our Society. We rejoice that English young Friends, and *The Young Quaker*, are generating this impulse toward an active, untrammeled religion of life.

The Quakerism of the Founders

By Elbert Russell

IV

The Quakerism of William Penn

(In Two Parts—Part One)

The writings of Penn present a greater variety of style and interest than those of the other great founders of the Society of Friends. His special contribution was in working out the political and social implications of Quakerism. His place in history rests largely in his defense of the right of trial by jury in the Old Baily Court, the charter and founding of Pennsylvania Colony, and his proposal for a World Parliament.

But his writings are not confined to political subjects. It was a theological essay, "The Sandy Foundation Shaken," which cost him eight months' imprisonment in the Tower of London at the beginning of his Quaker career. His "Rise and Progress of the People Called Quakers" is a standard statement of Quaker principles and polity. His "No Cross No Crown" is the work of a profound student of human motives and customs; and the maxims of "Some Fruits of Solitude" reveal fruitful meditations on the springs and fruits of conduct.

In making selections I have not thought it necessary to make extensive quotations bearing on the fundamental topics already fully illustrated from Fox, Barclay, and Pennington, on which he agreed with them essentially. The quotations given rather express the special contribution of Penn, either in the practical application or original statement of Quaker principles. While applications of principles to practical problems involve great difficulties of judgment, and must change with changing conditions, Penn's judgment has stood the test of time remarkably well, and his admonitions are still timely. His social ideals anticipate John Woolman in a striking way.

The True Cross

"Sect. 1. The cross of Christ is a figurative speech, borrowed from the outward tree, or wooden cross, on which Christ submitted to the will of God, in permitting him to suffer death at the hands of evil men. So that the cross mystical is that divine grace and power, which crosses the carnal wills of men, and gives a contradiction to their corrupt affections, and that constantly opposeth itself to the inordinate and fleshly appetite of their minds, and so may be justly termed the instrument of man's holy dying to the world, and being made conformable to the will of God. For nothing else can mortify sin, or make it easy for us to submit to the divine will, in things otherwise very contrary to o[ur] own.

"Sect. 3. Well, but then where does this cro[ss] appear, and must it be taken up?

"I answer within: that is, in the heart and sou[l] for where the sin is, the cross must be. Now, a[ll] evil comes from within: this Christ taught. 'Fro[m] within (saith Christ) out of the heart of men pr[o]ceed evil thoughts, adulteries, fornications, murder[s,] thefts, covetousness, wickedness, deceit, lasciviou[s]ness, an evil eye, blasphemy, pride, foolishness: a[ll] these evils come from within, and defile the man.'

"The heart of man is the seat of sin, and whe[re] he is defiled, he must be sanctified; and where si[n] lives, there it must die: it must be crucified."—*N[o] Cross No Crown.*

The Christian Life

"Two things are to be considered; the doctri[ne] they (The First Publishers of Truth) taught, an[d] the example they led among all people. I have a[l]ready touched upon their fundamental principl[e] which is as the corner-stone of their fabric; an[d] indeed, to speak eminently and properly, their cha[r]acteristic, or main distinguishing point or principl[e] viz., The Light of Christ within, as God's gift f[or] man's salvation. This, I say, is as the root of t[he] goodly tree of doctrines that grew and branched o[ut] from it, which I shall now mention in their natu[ral] and experimental order.

"First, repentance from dead works to serve t[he] living God; which comprehends three operatio[ns:] first, a sight of sin; secondly, a sense and godly s[or]row for it; thirdly, an amendment for the time [to] come. This was the repentance they preached a[nd] pressed, and a natural result from the principle th[ey] turned all people unto.

"From hence sprang a second doctrine they w[ere] led to declare, as the mark of the prize of the hi[gh] calling of all true Christians, viz., perfection fr[om] sin, according to the Scriptures of Truth; wh[ich] testify it to be the end of Christ's coming, and [the] nature of His kingdom, and for which His Sp[irit] was given: viz., to be perfect as our Heave[nly] Father is perfect, and holy because God is h[oly.] And this the Apostle labored for, that the Ch[ris]tian should be sanctified through in body, soul, [and] spirit. But they never held a perfection in wisd[om] and glory in this life, or from natural infirmities, death, as some have, with a weak or ill mind imagined and insinuated against them.

"This they called a redeemed state, regeneration, or the new birth: teaching everywhere, according to their foundation, that without this work were known, there was no inheriting the kingdom of God.

"Thirdly, this leads to an acknowledgment of eternal rewards and punishments, as they have good reason; for else, of all people, certainly they must be the most miserable, who, for above forty years have been exceeding great sufferers for their profession, and in some cases treated worse than the worst of men; yea, as the refuse and off-scouring of all things."—*Rise and Progress of the People Called Quakers.*

The Support of the Ministry

"Another part of the character of this people was, and is, they refuse to pay tithes or maintenance to a national ministry; and that for two reasons: the one is, they believe all compelled maintenance, even to gospel ministers, to be unlawful, because expressly contrary to Christ's command, who said, "Freely you have received, freely give"; at least, that the maintenance of gospel ministers should be free, and not forced. The other reason of their refusal is, because those ministers are not gospel ones, in that the Holy Spirit is not their foundation, but human arts and parts. So that it is not matter of humor or sullenness, but pure conscience towards God, that they cannot help to support national ministries where they dwell, which are but too much and too visibly become ways of worldly advantage and preferment." —*Rise and Progress.*

The Head of the Church

"It is further to be noted, that in these solemn assemblies for the churches' service, there is no one presides among them after the manner of the assemblies of other people; Christ only being their President, as He is pleased to appear in life and wisdom in any one or more of them; to whom, whatever be their capacity or degree, the rest adhere with a firm unity, not of authority, but conviction, which is the divine authority and way of Christ's power and Spirit in his people: making good his blessed promise, that he would be in the midst of his, where and whenever they were met together in his name, even to the end of the world. So be it."—*Rise and Progress.*

Church Discipline

"Now it may be expected, I should here set down what sort of authority is exercised by this people, upon such members of their society as correspond not in their lives with their profession, and that are refractory to this good and wholesome order settled among them; and the rather, because they have not wanted their reproach and sufferings from some tongues and pens, upon this occasion, in a plentiful manner.

"The power they exercise is such as Christ has given to his own people, to the end of the world, in the persons of his disciples, viz., to oversee, exhort, reprove, and after long suffering and waiting upon the disobedient and refractory, to disown them, as any more of their communion, or that they will any longer stand charged in the sight and judgment of God or men, with their conversation or behavior, as any of them, until they repent. The subject-matter about which this authority, in any of the foregoing branches of it, is exercised; is first, in relation to common and general practice; and secondly, about those things that more strictly refer to their own character and profession, and which distinguish them from all other professors of Christianity; avoiding two extremes upon which many split, viz., persecution and libertinism: that is, a coercive power, to whip people into the temple; that such as will not conform, though against faith and conscience, shall be punished in their persons or estates: or leaving all loose and at large, as to practice, and so unaccountable to all but God and the magistrate. . . . In short, what is for the promotion of holiness and charity, that men may practise what they profess, live up to their own principles, and not be at liberty to give the lie to their own profession without rebuke, is their use and limit of Church power. They compel none to join them, but oblige those that are of them to walk suitably, or they are denied by them: that is all the mark they set upon them, and the power they exercise, or judge a Christian society can exercise, upon those that are the members of it."—*Rise and Progress.*

A Free Government

"This settles the divine right of government beyond exception, and that for two ends: first, to terrify evil doers; secondly, to cherish those that do well; which gives government a life beyond corruption, and makes it as durable in the world as good men shall be. So that government seems to me a part of religion itself, a thing sacred in its institution and end; for, if it does not directly remove the cause, it crushes the effects of evil, and is, as such, though a lower, yet an emanation of the same divine power that is both author and object of pure religion; the difference lying here, that the one is more free and mental, the other more corporal and compulsive in its operation; but that is only to evil doers, government itself being otherwise as capable of kindness, goodness, and charity, as a more private society. They weakly err who think there is no other use of government than correction, which is the coarsest part of it. Daily experience tells us, that the care and regulation of many other affairs, more soft and daily necessary, make up much the greatest part of government. . . .

"Any government is free to the people under it, whatever be the frame, where the laws rule and the people are a party to those laws; and more than this is tyranny, oligarchy, or confusion.

"But lastly, when all is said, there is hardly one frame of government in the world so ill-designed by its first founders, that in good hands would not do well enough; and story tells us, that the best in ill ones can do nothing that is great and good; witness the Jewish and Roman states. Governments, like clocks, go from the motion men give them; and as governments are made and moved by men, so by them they are ruined, too. Wherefore governments rather depend upon men than men upon governments. Let men be good, and the government cannot be bad. If it be ill, they will cure it. But if men be bad, let the government be ever so good, they will endeavor to warp and spoil it to their turn."—*Preface from Penn's "Frame of Government," quoted from Janney's "Life" of Penn."*

"To be glad of life, because it gives you the chance to love and work and to play and to look up at the stars, to be satisfied with your possessions, but not contented with yourself until you have made the best of them, to despise nothing in the world except falsehood and meanness, and to fear nothing except cowardice; to be governed by your admirations rather than by your disgusts; to covert nothing that is your neighbor's except his kindness of heart and gentleness of manner; to think seldom of your enemies, often of your friends, and every day of Christ; and to spend as much time as you can, with body and with spirit, in God's out-of-doors; these are little guide-posts on the foot-paths to peace.—*Henry Van Dyke; Selected by Bliss Forbush.*

Chanson Pathetique

I sought to live in the land of song,
But joy is brief and sorrow long,
And only those are moved to sing
Who find some joy in everything.

I sought to live in the land of love
With Heaven's cloudless blue above,
But even there my joys took wing
And I found some sorrow in everything

JAMES WALDO FAWCETT.

rice with us, so I got some out and asked them to boil enough for everybody for the next morning.

"Then we settled down to roost for the night. One woman had a sprained ankle and groaned miserably. She lay down on the floor in front of the stove, and the driver slept on top of it. Another man lay on the floor by the side of the stove, and the others huddled around the bed, Nikolai and I each lying on a bench. Snores and groans then prevailed. Although it was as hot as an oven I felt that I must keep my leather coat on. Even at that my face and my hands were well bitten by the lice. About midnight my head was ready to crack, so I went out into the night. The storm was over, and it was a still night, and I saw that one of the sleighs had been left in the middle of the yard. I went in again and, steering my way with one match, got my great shuba and went out again and lay in the sleigh, even though it was all snowy and frosty, for the rest of the night.

"You will not believe it, but I had a lovely night. It seems madness to think of sleeping out in Russia in midwinter, but a shuba is a wonderful thing. It does not let in wet or cold, and, with coverings on my feet and legs, I was altogether protected.

"The next morning we boiled rice and tea, and leaving a few handfuls of rice and a tin of fish, and receiving a warm invitation for another visit, we started off again.

"It was a lovely day and we made forty versts, arriving at Zoevka at five o'clock, it being Christmas Eve. The camels had kept up an absolutely steady walk all day. We jumped off the sleighs two or three times during the day and walked a bit to stretch our limbs and warm up. There was no road at all, just a track over the steppe, and for a few miles there was not even a track. Nikolai had impressed the driver very strongly that we must have the very best house to sleep in that night, and he took us to the priest's. It was a very modest little house, but it had three rooms and was perfectly clean. We had a lovely welcome, and spent a very happy evening talking to the priest and his wife and their one boy. They have three other children, but they are away at school at Samara. They gave us milk from their cow and their best beds and pillows.

"In the morning, which was Christmas Day, we went on to the village of Gerasimovka, where there seems to be absolutely nothing to eat but grass. There is a little meat now and then when an animal is killed, but there are very few animals left. Already a hundred people have died in this small village this month. It was dreadful to see the people with their faces all drawn with misery and pain, hardly able to drag one foot after the other. One woman stopped us and said she had two children left, three had died of hunger. One of the remaining children was being fed in our kitchen and she wanted to know if we could feed the other one. Her husband had already died.

"The kitchens at Gerasimovka were very good. The manager was one of the best men we have met, and he is so anxious for everything to be as good as it possibly can. His whole heart and soul is in it."

Finding The Common Ground

Extracts from an address delivered by Rabbi Frederick Cohn at the Sioux City Convention of the National Federation of Religious Liberals, December 10-12, 1921.

"Let men unite! Let them put aside their dislikes, differences, disagreements; their hatreds, passions, prejudices, suspicions,—whatever it is that separates them from one another, that builds the barriers of race, creed, country or condition, that arrays brethren in hostile camps where unkind words are said and cruel words are done. Let men remember that their beliefs, opinions, feelings, instincts,—whatever they may be pleased to call them,—are not necessarily right and just because they are *theirs,* because for long time they have entertained them, carefully nursed and nurtured them.

"Let men bear in mind that no one is always right and never wrong, that all human things are fallible, that neither Church nor State nor Science nor Philosophy nor any system or institution yet conceived by man from Moses to Bergson, or from Jesus to Karl Marx, possesses all wisdom or has a monopoly on eternal truth. Truth is indeed one, but it has many aspects like the infinite flashes of iridescent rainbow light from out the shimmering heart of a gem. Let science be less arrogant, philosophy more reverent, economics more humble, governments less brutal, religion more tolerant and humane. Let men seek and they will surely find the common ground upon which all can stand, even as the earth bears us all, 'while heaven is blue above.'"

Strength

In the silence of the night
While I sleep.
Oh, the strength that's being born
To carry on the fight in the morn.

In the silence of the heart
While I pray.
Oh, the Power that's being given
That I may act the part for which I've striven.

RACHEL DAVIS-DUBOIS.

The Mark

Religion consists in treating our fellow men as well as we want them to treat us; in living in fellowship with them.

All earthly endeavor must be one of fellowship; we must not try to get more food and drink and clothing and shelter and social pleasures for ourselves, leaving the d—l to catch the hindmost for all we care. We must seek first to bring about the practice of fellowship and brotherhood, never trying to raise ourselves above our fellowmen, or climb upon their backs and make them support us, but always raise them up with us.

Christianity above all things is not selfish, but is concern for others, to raise others with ourselves. It is co-operative, and active, a builder up, but always in fellowship. With Jesus riches cannot exist, but only common wealth; and to that there is no limit, for that has God's special blessing. Riches are the accumulation of goods for private benefit, which is always a curse, while wealth shared in fellowship is a blessing. No one can refuse to fellowship his fellowman and not draw down upon his own head a curse. The curse is the natural, unavoidable result of his unbrotherly action, akin to handling a hot iron or touching a charged wire.

The whole aim of the scriptures and of the eternal urge of God is to get men to practice brotherhood and fellowship. This is the *Mark* of life. Jesus came expressly that he might enable men to do that by His risen, living spirit, and thus bring to pass upon earth His will as it is done in heaven. Sin is "amartia," missing the mark—transgressing the law, or "anomia." All law is summed up in the *Golden Rule, the eternal urge of God—the Mark.*

There is no other way under heaven to persist through into life but by being willing to do that. Whoso is willing to do that Jesus will enable, empower, vitalize, enliven, help to do just that. This is the gospel or good news, "euaggelia" or good angel.

This is His commandment: That we must believe in the name ("onomati", character, bounden law or rule of life) of His son Jesus Christ, and must love all others ("allelous") as He gave commandment to us.

J. A. WEBSTER.

Union, Ont., Canada.

"In the world of politics, government and society nothing is fixed and final. Mankind has to make its way in this world; by trial and error it must discover the best road; and must then adopt such measures as promise best to provide for the common security and quicken the pace of progress." —*S. Z. B.*

And Then I Sympathized

It happened in my barn. I had raised both of them. It had taken years of selecting and care in breeding, it had taken nursing over some severe sicknesses. I had been up late into some nights. I had studied and worked to give them the best food. There was plenty of food, more than enough. They were not fastened. They could have gone away But they fought. And I had worked for them both. And one of them died. And there was plenty of food. I provided that myself, there was always more than enough. And I had worked so hard for both. And then—then—as I stood looking at it all, then—I sympathized with God.

ELEANOR S. SHARPLES.

Service Committee Notes

Volunteers Needed

The American Friends' Service Committee is organizing a Mending Department to mend clothes which need repair before being sent to Europe. An all-day meeting will be held every Tuesday, beginning at 9.30 a. m., in Room No. 3, 15th and Race Streets, Philadelphia. Every woman who can give this day regularly or occasionally is asked to enroll in this department. The need is urgent. Miss Anna B. Dudley, Secretary of Women's work of the Service Committee, 20 S. 12th Street, Philadelphia, will gladly furnish information concerning this work. Volunteers should get in touch with her regarding what accessories to bring with them.

Cables from the Field

The following cable has been received from Russia: "Men's and children's shoes greatly needed. Women's shoes useless. Unlimited need for bedding and all kinds of clothing."

A cable from Austria says: "Distress in Vienna increasing because of unemployment. Need for large consignment of clothing to be here by May, also for consignment to be ready for October." A consignment of clothes for Austria is now waiting to be completed. Clothing marked "For Austria," or "For Use Where Most Needed," will help to complete this consignment and enable its prompt shipment.

An Appreciation

Friends who attended Darby Meeting during the 30 or 40 years previous to 1912 will remember that kind, gentle, loving Friend, Israel H. Lloyd, and his appealing little messages frequently given to the Meeting and his lessons to the First-day School. Though not possessed of an abundance of this world's goods, a large part of his slender income he used to support a crippled brother and a sister with several small children. He could find more faith and cheerfulness in adversity than most of those on whom fortune seems continually to smile. Since about 1912 he has been in the Friends' Home in West Chester, sincerely thankful for his comforts and still writing those quaint, original and often beautiful little sentiments as of old. Here is a recent one:

TWILIGHT

There is an hour or two every evening between suppertime and dark when it is neither night nor day. It is twilight—"Sunset and Evening Star." We seek the front porch and the easy chair; take a short walk or receive a call. The day's work is done. Still, there is a long hour before night for quiet thought, and rest, and "folding of the hands"—twilight.

And, so there is in many of our lives a time between ordinary health and the last sickness—we are not strong and well, nor are we sick. The eye is a little dim, but not much. The ear is dull but only a little. There is a little ache, or the hand trembles, or we use a cane, the spectacles and a little shawl. Still, there is no pain, no need of a doctor or a nurse. We are in a decline—a kind of twilight—neither sick nor well. O! how generous Nature is—like a mother putting her children to bed. The day's play is over, and we have nothing to boast of but our infirmities. "So fades a summer cloud away"—the change is so gradual—like a long twilight. It may be Moses had this in mind when he wrote: "Honor thy father and thy mother."

W. C. B.

Onward to Peace!

The current bulletin of the National Council for Reduction of Armaments contains a strong appeal that America take the Washington Conference seriously, realize that the danger of war has been averted "beyond our generation," and make 50 per cent. reductions in her Army and Navy appropriations for the coming year. The issue is clearly set forth in the following paragraph:

"Why continue the war hysteria? Why start now a 'race of efficiency' as our naval experts exuberantly advise. Either war has been averted or it hasn't. In the one case we can cut our armaments to a peace footing. In the other, it would be reasonable that they should ask us for an increase. *The middle ground of half-armed suspicion is exceedingly dangerous.* It provokes distrust and it gives the *security neither of preparedness nor of trust and goodwill.* It takes away security and at the same time brings *no compensating relief from the burden of arms.*"

After a discussion of the reasons why a 50 per cent. reduction is justified by the facts of present world conditions, the article concludes:

"*The Army and Navy* are not sacred institutions. They exist *only as we want them*, as Secretary Weeks said recently. We express our wishes through Congress. *Weigh these considerations and write your Congressman your* conclusion, that he may know if he has your support in this vast economy.

"The cry of the people led to the calling of the Conference. The will of the people made it a success. Now let the people see to it that they reap its fruits. *Don't delay! Write now!*"

The National Council is issuing Easter post cards bearing a colored reproduction of a painting especially designed for the purpose. Above widespread fields in which plowmen and sowers are at work, rises a symbolic figure of Peace, bearing in her hands an illumined cross. In the cloud-masses are seen the vague forms of disappearing armies. Below is the motto: "Labor that Life triumphant may banish the blasphemy of war."

These cards may be obtained from the National Council for Reduction of Armaments, 532 17th Street, N. W., Washington, D. C. Expressive as they are of the world's hope for peace, they deserve wide circulation. The rate is two cards for five cents, in any quantity.

We hope that all Friends are giving to the National Council as liberal financial support as their means permit. No Friend is doing more today for the advancement of our ideals than is Frederick J. Libby. He has created an organization of national importance which has for its one goal the abolition of war. He has enlisted the co-operation of groups which approach the crusade from every possible angle. He and the National Council ought to have the support of all Friends in measure running over.

Friends should contribute to the work through their own constituent organization, the Friends' Disarmament Council, of which Anna M. Griscom, Moorestown, N. J., is Treasurer.

Friendly News Notes

Two items gleaned from Bliss Forbush's News Letter are first that "the grandson of Elias Hicks, for whom our branch of the Society of Friends was named, is in a Federal Prison as a political prisoner."

Second, that he quotes George A. Walton as saying that "There are only two things which are holding back the Society of Friends today; one, that it is a divided society; and the second, that it is afraid to try anything new."

Friends at Girard Avenue and Seventeenth Streets, Philadelphia, are arranging for a celebration, on Fifth month 7th, of the fiftieth anniversary of the opening of the meeting house. They hope that all Friends who have ever attended at Girard Avenue will help to make the occasion a success by being present, and especially any who were at the opening meeting.

In connection with the recent destruction by fire of Wharton Hall, at Schofield School, friends are requested to send any contributions they care to make to Mary S. A. Jenkins, Secretary of Board, 920 Commercial Trust Building, Philadelphia, making checks payable to Schofield Normal and Industrial School. The need is very urgent and it is hoped that friends of the school will keep the matter in mind.

All Alumni and ex-students who knew and loved Dr. and Mrs. Charles De Garmo while he was President of Swarthmore will be saddened by the news of the sudden death by accident of Robert Max, the younger son, and the sympathy of all will go out to Dr. and Mrs. De Garmo and Walter in their sorrow.

A most interesting meeting of the members of the Young Friends' Movement of Burlington Quarter was held at Crosswicks, N. J., on Third month 12th. The visiting Friends attended Crosswicks' Meeting for Worship and First-day School. Box-Lunch and coffee were served at noon-time.

In the afternoon a short business meeting was held, at which candidates were nominated for Representatives to Central Committee, a Crosswicks Study Group was organized to be led by Mary Anderson, and plans discussed for sending two or more delegates to Richmond Conference this coming summer. The following committee was appointed: Elizabeth Stiles and Mrs. Mary Anderson, of Crosswicks, and Agnes Woodman and John S. Ruhlman, Jr., of Trenton, N. J.

Any young Friends of Burlington Quarter, wishing to attend the Earlham Conference, should get in touch with one of the above persons at an early date.

There are some extraordinary statements made concerning Friends in the section devoted to them in a little book, "English Sects," by Arthur Reynolds. The chief and most surprising is that "in the opinion of some, the sect owes its origin to the preaching of a fanatical person, James Nayler. . . . With more reason the claim of George Fox to be the founder can be vindicated"; but we also learn that John Howard was a Quaker, and that "sometimes at a funeral a minister bears testimony at the graveside to the dead person's character."

Such errors or half truths make it all the more surprising to find the degree of sympathetic understanding of Mr. Reynolds of the Quaker ideals. Writing evidently from the point of view of an Anglo-Catholic and for that public, he says in reference to silent worship—"It is surprising that, Quakerism, being what it is, there should be a movement among its members in favor of altering the character of the Meetings for Worship with the idea of making them more attractive and entertaining. To an outsider, at any rate, it is that impressive silence that seems to be the most attractive feature." He also quoted appreciatively from Vipont Brown's recent book, "Quaker Aspects of Truth," to the effect that the ideal of a Friends' Meeting is human fellowship in divine communion.

H. W. PEET.

A recent letter from George P. Hayes, one of our young Friends who is teaching at Robert College, Constantinople, contains interesting notes on a talk on John Woolman, which the writer gave at "prayer meeting." Woolman was little known, even to the leaders of thought in the community, and the talk aroused great interest. Commenting on the subject, George writes:

"I suppose few religious societies have had the good fortune to have their ideal realized in human form as the Quaker ideal has been realized in John Woolman.—He is such a satisfying person to talk about because when people have once heard of him, they somehow can't forget him.—It is hard to make Christ's example seem real to us because he lived so long ago and under such different surroundings, but John Woolman is a modern of the moderns with his interest in social questions and his religion of love. To see a saint at such close range is a bit disconcerting. People called him a fool because of his "eccentricities" of dress and his delicate scruples—yet history justifies these saints and forgets the rest of us who called them fools."

It is good to know that we have our Quaker ambassador to carry Woolman's influence to the Near East.

An unfortunately small group gathered in the New York Meeting-house on the afternoon of Third month 12th, to hear Albert de Silver, of the Civil Liberties Union, give an interesting talk on "Do Trade Unions Find Justice in the Courts." The speaker analyzed various test cases upon which American courts have established precedents in this field. He felt that the judges are usually highly trained men, whose training lies in other lines than those of industry, and who are at a disadvantage in attempting to deal with industrial problems. They are apt to deal in legalistic concepts, while neglecting the facts of current economic life.

Albert de Silver felt that, rightly or wrongly, American labor law is developing in such a way that within a few decades it will render the trade union ineffective as a means of increasing the economic advantage of labor; and that should this come to pass, labor would probably organize itself along lines of its own which would refuse to recognize the law. He advocated public education on industrial problems, with resulting wise legislation that would be based upon a knowledge of the needs of both sides. If both labor and capital were highly and effectively organized, he felt that the resulting balance of power would force each side to respect the other and result in the working out of some plan of peaceful relations.

Among other opinions expressed in the discussion which followed was one, with which the speaker agreed, that there could be no final solution of industrial problems without a new spirit on both sides. As long as individual gain is the goal, there must be strife. When service becomes the aim, there will be co-operation.

"The Young Friends' Number" of *The Friend* (Philadelphia), dated Third month 16, wins our hearty admiration for its alertness to many big spiritual issues which Friends of today need to face. An editorial entitled, "The Challenge of our Galleries" puts forward the view that our facing galleries tend to produce a gap between certain regular speakers and the main body of the meeting, thus working against the democratic spirit which should be the foundation of Friends' worship. Under the title "The Greatest Man on Earth Today," Anne G. W. Pennell gives one of the best statements which we have seen of the life of Gandhi and the non-co-operation movement in India. Two other articles protest against the injustice which has been wrought against our "political prisoners." Then there is an article by Alice Edgerton on "Unseen Forces," and a symposium by younger Friends on "What Meeting Means to Me." Finally, S. W. Elkinton and Howard E. Yarnall, Jr., contribute frankly opposite answers to the question, "Shall We Send Delegates to the Five Years' Meeting?" The whole number shows wide-awake thinking and editing, and a willingness to temporarily disagree in seeking the truth, which is very wholesome. We congratulate the young Friends for their fine work!

Unity for March 9th, contains an article by our friend Jesse H. Holmes in which the latter answers the assertion of an "evangelist" that preachers should stop "arguing and explaining," and should "proclaim God and his laws." Dr. Holmes considers the various sources of authority which might justify such an unquestioned and unexplained "proclamation," and rejects the theories of both papal and biblical infallibility. The only thing remaining which the church might "proclaim" would be a code of morals, and the writer states that it has no such code which it is willing to stand by—witness its participation in class and international war. He concludes:

"We recognize that this is a serious charge and it is so intended. It may be summed up in the statement that the Christian church of today is essentially a state church and a class church; that it has no world message; that it stands only for vague and narrow personal respectability and takes no responsibility for the bringing in of the "kingdom on earth." There are many notable and noble exceptions in the individual lives of representatives of Christian churches, and there are a few fine and forward-looking pronouncements from church assemblies; but there is no "church of God" that moves "like a mighty army" in the interest of a genuinely Christian world, and there is no general demand that the lives of members of Christian churches shall be in accord with the things they accept "in principle."

"What shall the church proclaim?"

FRIENDS' CONFERENCE

The sessions of the Friends' Conference are to be held at Richmond, Ind., August 26th to September 2nd, 1922. An interesting program has been planned which includes addresses from prominent men other than Friends, upon the vital topics of the day.

Richmond is well suited for the Conference, both for accommodations and pleasure. Accommodations can be furnished to suit the tastes of everyone, whether they desire the conveniences of a good hotel, or a boarding house; and tents will be erected for those who enjoy camping. Different forms of recreation will be easily accessible, such as tennis, swimming, baseball, golf, and motoring.

WOOLMAN SCHOOL

At the meeting of the Board of Managers of Woolman School on Third month 15th, various propositions were considered for the future of the school, arising out of various degrees of hopefulness or discouragement.

The most encouraging note came from the former students, seventy of whom expressed themselves as unqualifiedly in favor of continuing the school, and only two "left the matter to the judgment of the Managers." These boosting letters were most of them backed up with the pledge of five years contributions.

The Board united to go ahead with the school; and indeed was enthusiastic over the results that have been accomplished, and faced the future in a spirit that promises success.

Elbert Russell is to continue as Director of the school, and a summer term is to be announced immediately.

J. Barnard Walton, *Secretary.*

WESTERN QUARTER FIRST-DAY SCHOOL UNION

The First-day School Union of Western Quarter was held at New Garden on Third month 18th The reports had all been summarized by the Chairman, and a new feature, the supplementary reports, was introduced. Alice Pusey, New Garden; Elma Walker, Kennett, and Cora Hall, West Grove, gave helpful suggestions for the conduct of Primary classes. Mary Pyle, from Wilmington, presented valuable material for help with Primary pupils, emphasizing the importance of the "story" for little people.

Officers for the ensuing year are Ethel Jefferis, Chairman, and Cora F. G. Hall, Secretary and Treasurer.

Caroline H. Engle, hostess of Woolman School, and Mary Magruder, one of the students, were present, each leaving with the Union the "spirit of Woolman School."

At the afternoon session, Elizabeth W. Collins spoke on "The Old Testament Text." She recommended the prophetic stories and the stories of the patriarchs to be the very best stories ever written to be told to children.

The next meeting will be held at Hockessin, Delaware, in Third month, 1923. Cora F. G. Hall, Secretary.

FRIENDS IN CHINA

Most readers of Friends' Intelligencer knew that last year a fund was raised sufficient for the support of Margaret Hallowell Riggs as a teacher at the Christian College, Canton, China. The Philadelphia Y. F. A. and West Philadelphia First-day School were the prime movers and raised a considerable part of the money. The interest spread through a number of meetings, and a volunteer committee was organized including Friends from different parts of the country. This committee is now making its appeal for the renewal of the fund. A letter is going to each meeting asking that some one in the meeting make the collection there. Alfred W. Wright is Chairman, and Linda E. Bicknell, 252 W. Wyoming Ave., Germantown, is Treasurer.

This year the committee is including in its interest not only Margaret Hallowell Riggs, but also Joseph and Edith Stratton Platt, who have just arrived in Moukden, Manchuria. These Friends are working under a call quite similar to that which has prompted the Quaker Embassies in Europe, which are carrying on after the physical relief, the spiritual concern of the American Friends' Service Committee. The points of contact open both in Canton and in Manchuria are strategic. It means much to these Friends to feel that they are representing the spirit of the Society of Friends. It should mean as much to those at home. The appeal urges Friends to make a concrete expression of this feeling that it is good to have our vital message represented in spirit.

BALTIMORE QUARTERLY MEETING

On Seventh day evening preceding Baltimore Quarterly Meeting Elbert Russell gave an eloquent and convincing address on The Spiritual Significance of Disarmament. Some of the main points are as follows: Because of enormous expenditures for military and naval purposes, the education of our children is being neglected. People are paying in war taxes the contributions that should go to charitable and social service work. In consequence, many important organizations have had to curtail their work or assume heavy debts. The church too, is suffering for funds, and has been forced either to go into debt or to call home some of its mission workers from abroad. As an example, the Mission Board of the Five Years Meeting is $60,000 in debt.

The speakers on First-day morning were Isaac Wilson and Daniel Batchellor.

On First-day evening, under the auspices of the Young Friends' Movement, George A. Walton gave a most inspiring and helpful talk on Quaker Worship, speaking of worship as an effort to find strength to overcome our limitations.

Among the interesting and helpful messages given on Second-day morning, George A. Walton reviewed the opportunities that have from its founding come to the Society of Friends, and raised the very pertinent question as to how far we have been true to the responsibility which these opportunities entail.

In the business session, resolutions were adopted urging all State Senators to vote for the Enforcement bill without the Referendum; urging U. S. Senators from Maryland to promptly ratify the Peace Treaties; urging our Representatives at Washington to limit the appropriation for military and naval purposes to the lowest possible point; urging our State Senators to pass the bill against race-track gambling; and urging that steps be taken to have a copy of the law regarding the selling of tobacco to minors placed in the schools of the State and in every place where tobacco is sold.

HADDONFIELD QUARTERLY MEETING

Haddonfield Quarterly Meeting on the 16th at Moorestown, N. J., seemed to take its keynote from Daniel Willett's message beginning "Be ye doers of the Word and not hearers only" for throughout the sessions practical religion claimed first place in all deliberations.

During the consideration of the queries, Henry Coles gave expression to the thought that "service" had come to mean all lines of work and no one but could give service to his fellowman in some way, in business, politics, or internationally—all fields were covered.

Jane Rushmore referred to the time of strain and stress

through which Friends had passed the last few years when the pacifist, militarist and shades of opinion between, had gripped the Society, yet the inherent strength had endured.

A gratifying report of the first year's work of Moorestown School under joint management was given. One of the results had been an increase of love and fellowship between the two branches, which it would seem was a thing worth striving for, apart from scholastic advantages.

In the afternoon a session was held in the schoolhouse to consider ways and means of encouraging attendance at meetings.

Elsie Thomas presided and there were many who contributed of their thought in consideration of this vital matter. Jane P. Rushmore urged that people get their thinking straight in this regard, by getting out of our minds that there is any special sanctity, wisdom, or experience attaches to the ministry, the last remaining remnant of class distinction being taken away a few years back when we ceased to record ministers. She deplored the taking from one meeting those who occasionally speak in order to help another meeting. "Let us get out of our minds that there is a source of supply for ministers for the only way to have vocal expression is for the common lay member to do it, and it is for us to make ourselves equal to the task."

George H. Nutt felt this lack of attendance at places of worship was in no way peculiar to Friends nor, indeed, to religious bodies of any kind. He urged Friends to get away from the endeavor to reproduce Friends' Meetings of a generation or more ago. It cannot be done, nor in the main is it desirable. "In this matter" he said, "let us do as does the engineer, who finds out just what is needed to have accomplished, then work toward its accomplishment by every means possible." He also dropped the thought that young people would follow their elders if the latter were filled themselves with enthusiasm for their meeting, but usually they were lukewarm, yet expected their children to feel the interest which had not been imparted.

Caroline Worth, and others, urged a development of the social side, the personal touch meaning much. The suggestion of a "home-coming day" at local meetings was made also among others to arouse enthusiastic interest.

A. C.

NEW YORK NOTES

There are now 604 children attending the two schools under the care of the New York Monthly Meeting. 247 of these are in the Friends' Seminary in New York, and 357 in the Brooklyn Friends' School. The great problem now before the Trustees is to secure additional space so that the New York School may be increased to the size of the Brooklyn School. The number in attendance in New York is nearly 80% greater than it was twenty years ago; but, especially in the High School, there would be better grading and more economical teaching if there were place for larger classes; while, at the same time, not affecting the essential spirit of the Seminary.

A most encouraging feature in New York Monthly Meeting is the steadily increasing number of members who contribute to the support of the Meeting. The reported membership is about 870. The report just given on the collections of last year shows 315 persons contributing. As the membership includes a number of families, of course, and many children, the ratio of contributors is really surprising. The number of contributors has steadily increased every year for a dozen or more years.

The High School pupils of Friends' Seminary, New York, are publishing a bi-monthly paper, "The Friendly Times." This paper carries, regularly, the advertisement of the Meeting, and, also, on the first page, a column article telling of the various activities of Friends, especially in the relief work abroad.

The Service Committee workers in charge of the warehouse at 108 Dobbin St., Brooklyn, have sent, as they had opportunity, appeals to manufacturers of knitted goods, to shoe manufacturers, and to soap makers, asking for contributions of articles which might, by technical imperfections, be unsalable, yet be quite as useful for relief work. A number of contributions have resulted from these appeals, especially from the soap manufacturers. From one of these last alone, came a donation of 1600 pounds of soap. Others are giving in smaller quantity. The way appears to be opening to secure a large number of gingham dresses and other garments, perfectly new, but of the fashion of a year or two ago. Thirty-six tons of clothing were sent from the warehouse to Russia during Second month. The shipments during Third month will, unless there is a very sudden falling off, greatly exceed this amount.

The Committee is starting a Speakers' Bureau, with Elizabeth Walton as Chairman. A notice of this Bureau, offering to furnish speakers on the Friends' relief work, "without charge and without taking up a collection," is being sent with every letter to persons in or near New York. The Bureau feels that the most important thing to "put over" is the spirit in which Friends have undertaken the work. Returned Service workers will, therefore, take an important part in filling any dates that may be offered. A number of members of the Young Friends' Movement have offered their services, also, and are in training for this important task.

Items From Everywhere

The American Bible Society is producing a small handy volume of Scripture selections for the Blind. The purpose is to have a light book for easy handling by the aged and invalids, and for easy carrying by those who travel. The blind are not only handicapped seriously by blindness, but by the necessary bulk and cost of books in embossed systems. While an ink print Bible can be supplied for 50 cents, an average embossed Bible costs over $50, and weighs over 150 pounds. It takes from eleven to fifty-eight volumes, the pages of which are 13 x 14 inches, on an average.

The small volume will consist of approximately 40 sheets 7 x 14 inches and will weigh about one pound. Inquiries in regard to this volume and gifts to promote its circulation should be addressed to Mr. L. B. Chamberlain, Bible House, Astor Place, New York City.

The United States Navy has another Haiti in the Pacific, according to charges about the treatment of the Samoan Islands published in *The Nation* for March 15. Without any proprietary rights in the Samoan Islands, which have been used for many years as a naval coaling station, our navy is said to have destroyed the independence of the natives, by the same autocratic methods which have been described in the case of Haiti and other Caribbean republics. Complete details are given in the number of *The Nation* mentioned above.

On February 3 of the present year, Senator Rankin introduced into the United States Senate a joint resolution that the United States grant complete independence to the Philippine Islands (H. J. Res. 266). The resolution reviews the various reasons and past utterances which call for such action. The "Press Bulletin" issued by the Philippine Commission of Independence, comes regularly to the INTELLIGENCER with its appeal from the Philippinos themselves for independence. They are obviously capable of enlightened self-government and ought to have it.

A Philadelphia Unitarian Church announces a series of sermons on the general subject, "Religion for an Age of Confusion." The aim of the series is given in the following words:

"To increase faith, to strengthen hope, to broaden charity, to make old thoughts larger, to show that there is a way out of the conflict between modern thought and traditional theology, a conflict which has brought confusion and skepticism to our age, and to set forth the beneficent and eternal elements in Christianity."

A church which makes these its aims, and which starts out recognizing that the age is one of "confusion," to reach those who "find their belief in the old traditions shaken," is on the right track.

The third annual session of the Pilgrimage Play Life of Christ commences Monday, July 10, 1922, at the Pilgrimage Theatre, Cahuenga and Highland avenues, Los Angeles, California. The Pilgrimage Theatre is an open canyon, and the reproduction of the life of Jesus must be particularly striking in the midst of scenery so like that of Judea as is that of Southern California. It is hoped that the Pilgrimage play may develop into "the most accurate historical and beautiful interpretation ever given to the world of the most spiritual life that was ever lived on earth."

On March 11, the Commission of the Church and Social Service of the Federal Council of Churches issued a special bulletin on "Amnesty for Political Prisoners." Correspondence between Secretaries of the Federal Council and Attorney General of the United States is published, together with details of an investigation which showed that many of the statements contained in the Attorney General's letter were not justified by the facts. The Department of Justice was asked for digests of the cases and information on specific charges against the individual prisoners, but these were refused. On March 16, 1922, a public hearing was scheduled, before the House Committee on the Judiciary, on the resolution urging amnesty to political prisoners which was introduced by Representative London (H. R. Res. 60). The Federal Council of Churches says, "There could scarcely be a better way to clear the atmosphere on this matter than to have all the facts brought out before a Congressional Committee and made accessible to the public."

DEATHS

GREEN—At Marion, Illinois, on Third month 9th, Esther J. Green, widow of Thomas J. Green, aged 82 years. She was the daughter of Richard and Anna Janney Lupton, and was born at Wilmington, Ohio. The greater part of her life was spent at Richmond, Indiana, where she was a member of the North "A" Street Friends' Meeting. Since 1908 she has lived with her daughter, Pearl Green Wilson, at Marion. Of cheerful and kindly disposition and helpful nature, her life was a busy one, and until the infirmities of age compelled her to become inactive, her hands were ever ready to perform some kind act for any one in need. Interment was made at Marion.

HALLOWELL—At Bethayres, Pa., on Third month 17th, Thomson Dyer, infant son of Israel R. and Marian Dyer Hallowell, aged 10 months.

HOLLINGSWORTH—In her home in West Liberty, Iowa, Third month 6th, Josephine T. Hollingsworth, widow of the late Mahlon Hollingsworth.

She was the eldest daughter of Carver and Mary Ann Tomlinson, was born in Washington Co., Penna., in 1848. They moved to Illinois in 1852. She was married in 1886 and removed to Iowa.

She passed away after an illness of several months, her husband having preceded her by twenty-one years. She was a member of Clear Creek Monthly Meeting.

HUGHES—At West Grove, Pa., Third month 14th, Lydia V., daughter of Priscilla H. and late Mark Hughes, in her 43d year.

HUSSEY—In Philadelphia, on Third month 11th, Samuel B. Hussey, in his 79th year. Funeral services at Friends' Meeting House, Fallsington, Pa.

MASON—On Second month 23rd, Benjamin Mason, son of Samuel C. and Alice Mason, aged 45 years. Interment in Friends' burial ground at Maple Grove.

PINE—At Riverside, N. J., on Third month 16th, Hannah E. Pine, widow of Elwood Pine, aged 82.

SHERER—At Worcester, Mass., on Third month 17th, Gertrude Roberts Sherer.

STABLER—Suddenly, on Second month 18th, Albina Osburn Stabler, wife of Asa Moore Stabler, of Spencerville, Maryland, in her 79th year.

The many friends who gathered at Sandy Spring Meeting house on the afternoon of February 20th bore testimony to the high esteem in which she was held.

Her sweet, brave spirit in a frail body had struggled nobly for years against discomfort and pain, and she had kept her place as the centre of the hospitable home at Sunnyside long after many would have succumbed to a life of invalidism.

WOOD—At his home in La Jolla, California, on Second month 27th, 1922, William Stroud Wood, son of Christopher C. Wood and Hannah Stockton Wood, and husband of Edith Longstreth Wood.

CAROLINE SHOTWELL WOOD

On Second month, 27th, at her residence in Sierra Madre, California, in her 83rd year, Caroline Shotwell Wood, daughter of the late Henry R. and Margaret G. Shotwell, of Rahway, N. J., and mother of Louise Wood Ferris, passed away. Funeral services were held in the Friends' Meeting House, Orange Grove Avenue, Pasadena, attended by a large gathering of friends—friends who are Friends and many others. John E. Carpenter and Dr. Emily Hunt, of Orange Grove Meeting, and Reynold E. Blight, of Los Angeles, bore witness to the character of Caroline S. Wood as one of rare charm and strength.

At the Monthly Meeting held Third month 12th, a period was given to thoughts and expressions of appreciation of what this dear Friend has been to the meeting, wherein her loss is so deeply and seriously felt. She has lived in California more than thirty years, having been an active member since the inception of Orange Grove Meeting. As a beloved Overseer she was equitable in her judgments and in business meetings always helpful in brief, decisive response upon problems requiring quick and just action.

Caroline S. Wood will be remembered as Dean of Swarthmore College from 1878 to 1882. She never grew old, but was vigorous and full of interest in worthy activities until the very end.

A friend writes: "I think Caroline Wood was an inspiration for good to many more than we realized. All who lived near her felt this and talked about it often. It was always 'Is she not lovely?' I never heard anything less beautiful said of her but many things more beautiful."

The composite thought of last Monthly meeting centered upon her even-mindedness, her sweet spirit, her helpful, quiet manner, her ready wit, refined humor and enjoyment of fun. That strong, calm countenance of love will be greatly missed from the facing seat—a countenance which to look upon was a benediction. MARIANNA BURGESS.

COMING EVENTS

THIRD MONTH.

24th and 25th—P. Y. F. A. play—"The Passing of the Third Floor Back." See notice.

25th—A Meeting Social in the Gymnasium of Friends' Seminary, 226 East 16th Street. All are cordially invited. 8 o'clock.

26th—Elbert Russell will give the last lecture on the Life of Jesus, in Oxford Meeting House, at 2 p. m.

26th—J. Nevin Sayre, editor of *The World Tomorrow*, will be at Swarthmore—meeting in the morning, college Y. W. and Y. M. C. A. in the evening, and a group meeting of the Fellowship of Reconciliation the evening before.

26th—Conference class at 15th and Race Streets, Philadelphia, at close of meeting for worship, at 11.40 a. m. Speaker—Dr. Fletcher Clark. Subject—Some Tasks of the Kingdom. III.

30th—Members of the Young Friends' Movement of New York, and others of appropriate age and condition are invited to the gymnasium of Friends' Seminary for an "unpremeditated evening." Nothing is arranged for but the place. Wear old clothes and tennis shoes. Be ready for anything. Be sure to enter by entrance of Rutherford Place, between 15th and 16th Streets.

FOURTH MONTH.

1st and 2nd—Pilgrimage under care of Young Friends' Movement, at Mickleton, N. J.

2nd—Miss Dwight, head of the Personal Service Bureau of the Near East Relief, will speak after Meeting in New York. Her work is that of uniting separated families, and her talk should be intensely interesting.

2nd—Carolena M. Wood expects to attend Matinecock Meeting in company with the Advancement Committee of Westbury Quarterly Meeting. An afternoon conference will be held on the Future of Friends' Service.

2nd—First-day, 3 p. m. A meeting for divine worship will be held at Providence Friends' Meeting House, near Media, Pa., under care of a Committee of Concord Quarterly Meeting. A community meeting and all denominations welcome. Young people are invited to be present and take part in the services.

NOTICE—G. Sherwood Eddy, the well-known speaker in student Y. M. C. A. groups, is to be in Philadelphia April 3, 4, 5. He will be speaking at the University of Pennsylvania at 7.30 p. m. on each evening of April 3, 4, 5; and at the noon-day Lenten services at Keith's Theatre at 12.15 on the 4th and 5th.

NOTICE—The P. Y. F. A. will give "The Passing of the Third Floor Back" on March 24th and 25th in the Auditorium of the P. Y. F. A., 15th and Cherry Streets, Philadelphia. Tickets, $1.00, include dancing, now on sale at the P. Y. F. A. desk (reserved seats). The proceeds will go to the Margaret Hallowell Riggs Fund for support of the work in Canton Christian College, China.

NOTICE—A special invitation is extended to Friends of all branches to attend the Foreign Missionary Meeting to be held at Twelfth Street Meeting House, Philadelphia, on Fourth-day evening, Third month 29th, at 7.30 o'clock. The chief speaker will be Dr. Frank W. Padelford, of New York City. Dr. Padelford is Executive Secretary of the Educational Board of the Northern Baptist Convention, and also Executive Secretary of the Department of Publicity of the Promotional Board. He has recently spent six or seven months in China as a member of a commission to study the situation and conditions there. His subject at the meeting will be "Christian Obligations to China and Japan." He is regarded as one of the best speakers in the Baptist denomination.

American Friends' Service Committee

WILBUR K. THOMAS, EX. SEC.

20 S. 12th St. Philadelphia.

CASH CONTRIBUTIONS

RECEIVED WEEK ENDING MARCH 13.

Five Years Meetings	$290.77
New York Service Committee	5,500.00
Alum Creek Friends	143.50
Bristol Meeting	75.00
Rahway & Plainfield Monthly Meeting	20.00
Chester Monthly Meeting	1,032.15
Third St. Friends' School, Media	10.00
Harrisburg Friends	7.00
Kennett Monthly Meeting	20.50
Birmingham Prep. Meeting	2.00
Norristown Prep. Meeting	100.00
Alexanria Monthly Meeting	75.00
Contributions for General	1,657.10
For Germany	218.50
For Poland	6,888.01
For Austria	7,147.73
For Syria	35.00
For Russia	21,275.03
For German Overhead	68.42
For Clothing	2.00
Refunds	1,075.97
	$45,668.73

Shipments received during week ending March 11th: 84 boxes and packages received; 1 German Relief; 1 anonymous.

REGULAR MEETINGS

OAKLAND, CALIF.—A FRIENDS' MEETing is held every First-day at 11 A. M., in the Extension Room, Y. W. C. A. Building, Webster Street, above 14th. Visiting Friends always welcome.

FRIENDS' MEETING IN PASADENA, California—Orange Grove Monthly Meeting of Friends, 520 East Orange Grove Avenue, Pasadena, California. Meeting for worship, First-day, 11 A. M. Monthly Meeting, the second First-day of each month, at 1.45 P. M.

CENTRAL MEETING OF FRIENDS (Chicago), meets every First-day in Room 706, 410 South Michigan Avenue, at 10.45 a. m. Visitors are invited.

WANTED

POSITION WANTED IN PHILADELphia or near vicinity. A middle aged man with considerable experience in positions of trust, with tact and sense of responsibility, with thorough knowledge of figures and accounting, desires a position that will occupy his time and give him a small income. J. 110, Friends' Intelligencer.

THOROUGHLY EXPERIENCED farmer, single, Christian, would like work on farm with Friends. Address A. 112, Friends' Intelligencer.

WANTED—POSITION AS MOTHER'S helper for summer. Experienced; can give references. Address W. 120, Friends' Intelligencer.

WANTED — SMALL, FURNISHED house in Germantown, Philadelphia, near Reading Railroad. Address S. C. Willis, 1422 Girard Avenue, Philadelphia.

WANTED — FOR RENT, PREFERably furnished house, suitable for family with children, during summer; neighborhood of Swarthmore, Rose Valley, or Haverford. Address P. O. Box 284, Langhorne, Pa.

WANTED—SUMMER BOARD IN A private family on a farm in New York or Pennsylvania, for two ladies and son 12 years old. Third week in July to third week in September. Mary H. Kirby, 1926 Cedar Ave., West Philadelphia, Pa.

FOR RENT

FOR RENT—APRIL TO OCTOBER. Nine-room house with sleeping porch and garage, near river, at Riverton. Address Helen Lippincott, Riverton, N. J.

FOR RENT — FOUR-ROOM APARTment, on third floor, with bath and kitchenette. Also room and bath. Nothing furnished. Apply 133 E. Main St., Moorestown, N. J.

FOR RENT — AT ATLANTIC CITY, small, fully furnished apartment from now to the first of May. Accommodate three persons. Light housekeeping. Maid service supplied. Mrs. John Kenrick Bangs, 20 S. Pennsylvania Ave.

FOR SALE

FOR SALE—BRICK AND FRAME detached residence, well built; 10 rooms, bath, sleeping porch, glassed in; gas and electricity, modern conveniences; near Friends' School and Meeting House, Lansdowne, Pa. Apply J. 100, Friends' Intelligencer.

TRANSIENT ACCOMMODATIONS

WASHINGTON, D. C.—ROOMS FOR visitors. Near Station, Capitol, Library. Continuous hot water. Electric. Garage. Mrs. L. L. Kendig, 120 C. Street, Northwest.

FUN

"A pipe with a pedigree" is advertised. This reminds us of the pipe a plumber repaired for us the other day; he took all day to find its connections.—*London Opinion.*

To the Lot Holders and others interested in Fairhill Burial Ground:

GREEN STREET Monthly Meeting has funds available for the encouragement of the practice of cremating the dead to be interred in Fairhill Burial Ground. We wish to bring this fact as prominently as possible to those who may be interested. We are prepared to undertake the expense of cremation in case any lot holder desires us to do so.

Those interested should communicate with William H. Gaskill, Treasurer of the Committee of Interments, Green Street Monthly Meeting, or any of the following members of the Committee.

William H. Gaskill, 3201 Arch St.
Samuel N. Longstreth, 1218 Chestnut St.
Charles F. Jenkins, 232 South Seventh St.
Stuart S. Graves, 3033 Germantown Ave.

The Friends' Intelligencer

ESTABLISHED 1844 | FOURTH MONTH 1, 1922 | VOLUME 79 NUMBER 13

Contents

THE FRIENDS' INTELLIGENCER

Published weekly, 140 N. 15th Street, Philadelphia, Pa., by Friends' Intelligencer Association, Ltd.

WALTER H. ABELL, *Editor*
SUE C. YERKES, *Business Manager*

Editorial Board: Elizabeth Powell Bond, Thomas A. Jenkins, J. Russell Smith, George A. Walton.

Board of Managers: Edward Cornell, Alice Hall Paxson, Paul M. Pearson, Annie Hillborn, Elwood Hollingshead, William C. Biddle, Charles F. Jenkins, Edith M. Winder, Frances M. White.

Officers of Intelligencer Associates: Ellwood Burdsall, Chairman; Bertha L. Broomell, Secretary; Herbert P. Worth, Treasurer.

Subscription rates: United States, Mexico, Cuba and Panama, $2.50 per year. Canada and other foreign countries, $3.00 per year. Checks should be made payable to Friends' Intelligencer Association, Ltd.

Entered as Second Class Matter at Philadelphia Post Office.

The Friends' Intelligencer

The religion of Friends is based on faith in the "INWARD LIGHT," or direct revelation of God's spirit and will in every seeking soul.

The INTELLIGENCER is interested in all who bear the name of Friends in every part of the world, and aims to promote love, unity and intercourse among all branches and with all religious societies.

ESTABLISHED 1844 | PHILADELPHIA, FOURTH MONTH 1, 1922 | VOLUME 79 NUMBER 13

Should Industrial Issues Be the Churches' Concern?

Both the Society of Friends and the Christian Church as a whole are divided in their answer to the above question.

One of our readers, in commenting upon a previous editorial reference to this difference of opinion, advised that since it existed, we refrain altogether from the discussion of economic and industrial issues. This Friend was probably one of the group which prefers that religion express itself only on the "spiritual" plane, the group which looks askance at the revolution which would follow from a social application of religious principles. Members of this group appeal frequently for "more old fashioned Christianity and less 'socialism.'"

On the other hand there are many Friends, and many Christians of other denominations, who feel that Christianity as a simple code of beliefs, or as an entirely individualistic experience of mysticism, is only half Christianity. It is not enough to talk and read of the spirit; not enough even to feel its presence as an emotional reality in our own individual lives. The spirit must work itself out in every relationship of social life; it must be regarded as a leaven which shall eventually transform the present ill-adjusted social system into the Kingdom of God.

A Friend of another "branch," serving recently as chairman of a Friends' conference on industrial problems, said: "The devil—if there is such a thing as a personal devil—must have laughed to himself on the day on which he got men to separate their religion from their economic system. He must have known that as long as that separation continued, *he* could rule."

Our economic system holds the reins of present-day life, both individual and social. It determines where and how long the great masses of "the children of God" shall work, and at what tasks; it determines how much they eat, even how much some of them sleep; how much time and energy they have for the cultivation of the higher elements of personality. If it is a bad system, forcing them to work too long and under unfavorable conditions, giving them insufficient food and comfort and rest, insufficient social respect and recreation, then the churches may labor in vain to render more abundant the lives of those whom it thus holds in bondage.

Such a bad system, we believe it to be. That it is so is not the fault of any one group, nor does only one group suffer the consequences. It is a system which has grown up out of the dominant motive of the last century; the motive of acquiring possession of things, of "making a fortune." This ideal governed, and to a large extent still governs, all classes. The poor laborer usually differs from the millionaire capitalist only in respect to circumstance. If he could, he would become a millionaire himself; and he often does so, or at least used to.

The evils of this system based upon self-seeking have piled up to such an extent our eyes are beginning to be opened to them. On a national scale, they brought imperialism, and imperialism brought the world war and countless minor wars. Within the nations, they have disrupted the social fabric; concentrated the control of wealth in the hands of a comparatively small group, created the very rich and the very poor, set class against class in a growing struggle for existence. The declaration of the impending coal strike is a declaration of economic civil war.

If religion is a call to us to help develop the soul, and render more abundant the life, of humanity, it must be a call to remedy such conditions as these. The world's present economic problems can never be solved by economic means. Economic factors alone are tending more and more toward a blind use of force; toward the method of destruction. Such forces, if they continue their blind opposition, will bring upon all the world the death struggle between classes which they brought upon Russia. Only in the light of the spirit can these problems be solved. The ideal of service must be substituted for that of gain; the welfare of all, instead of the advancement of self, must be the goal of each. When this is so, when "love" dominates instead of self-seeking, economic strife will cease automatically.

To preach the vision of this changed motive is the mission of religion in economics. Christianity can never be satisfied until it has attained a Christian social system. Only those engaged in industrial pursuits can directly determine the course of industrial evolution; but every Christian can take his part in standing for the *principle* of Christianity's industrial applications; making sure that he himself is clear of the motive of selfish gain, and helping others to find the motive of service.

As a contribution to the developing body of religious thought on economic problems, we are glad to present on another page the first of a series of articles on "Christianity and Economic Problems," issued by the Federal Council of the Churches of Christ in America. This series is being released to about a dozen of the leading religious journals of the country before being published in booklet form. Lack of space will prevent us from publishing it in full, but we shall at least give a resume of each installment, in order that our readers may be in touch with this important expression of Christian thought on economic problems. We trust that it may help us as a religious society to grow toward unity on the relation of our religion to economic problems.

Christianity and Economic Problems

The study which follows, of which additional installments will be given in subsequent issues, was prepared by direction of the Educational Committee of the Federal Council of the Churches of Christ in America. This committee consists of Kirby Page, Sherwood Eddy, Harrison S. Elliott, Florence Simms, Leslie Blanchard, David Porter, and F. Ernest Johnson.

I
A Divided World

The revolt against the suffering and misery of the present day is world-wide. A never-ending stream of protest is pouring from our printing presses. Many of the titles are significant: "The Salvaging of Civilization," "Social Decay and Regeneration," "Chaos and Order in Industry," "Principles of Social Reconstruction," "Proposed Roads to Freedom," "The New Social Order," "Labor in the Changing World," "What the Workers Want," "The Cry for Justice." Books which defend the present order are also appearing. Such titles as these are significant: "The Case for Capitalism," "A Defense of Wealth."

The unrest and dissatisfaction with things-as-they-are is finding expression in the utterances and actions of the Churches. The Federal Council of the Churches of Christ in America has adopted the "Social Ideals of the Churches." The National Catholic War Council has issued a program of "Social Reconstruction." The Central Conference of American Rabbis has issued a "Social Justice Program." Practically all of the great religious bodies in the United States have made pronouncements dealing with the present social order. "The Church and Industrial Reconstruction," a notable volume published by a group of prominent churchmen, devotes 46 pages to a consideration of the "Un-Christian Aspects of the Present Industrial Order."

In every quarter, the present state of affairs is being challenged. Especially do we find the youth of all lands giving voice to their dissatisfaction with the old order of things. Among old and young it is being recognized increasingly that at present life is almost intolerable for great masses of people. Others are saying that the present social order is doomed. In this connection, Mr. Lloyd George has said: "The old world must and will come to an end. No effort can shore it up much longer. If there be any who feel inclined to maintain it, let them beware lest it fall upon them and overwhelm them and their households in the ruins." Mr. H. G. Wells has recently said: "There are some things that it is almost impossible to tell without seeming to scream and exaggerate, and yet these things may be in reality the soberest matter of fact. I want to say that this civilization in which we are living is tumbling down, and I think tumbling down very fast; that I think rapid, enormous efforts will be needed to save it."

Present Situation Can be Changed

Throughout the literature of protest against present-day misery runs a note of optimism. Conditions can be changed. These are days of transition. If only we have the intelligence and the will, a new and better world may be built.

Perhaps no writer has sounded this note of hope and triumph more vigorously than has Benjamin Kidd, in these words: "We are undoubtedly living in the West in the opening stages of a revolution the like of which has never been experienced in history. We are witnessing the emergence of causes and the marshalling and leaguing of forces utterly unknown to textbooks. They will make history for a thousand years to come. . . . Through all the stress of conflict in the West there swells the deep diapason of the social passion calling for service, for subordination, for sacrifice, for renunciation on a scale unprecedented. . . . We are watching the assembling in the world of the governing forces of new eras of history. . . . The ascending history of the human race is indeed nothing else than the progressive history of the sacrifice of the individual efficient for himself to the meaning of that collective efficiency which is being organized in civilization gradually merging in the universal. The progress of humanity has, therefore, over and above every other feature this meaning. It is the epic of the vast, tragic, ennobling, immortalizing, all-conquering ethic of Renunciation. Within the life of a single generation it can be made to undergo changes so profound, so revolutionary, so permanent, that it would almost appear as if human nature itself had been completely altered in the interval."

. . .

Mr. H. G. Wells closed his series of articles on the Washington Conference with these words: "But I know that I believe so firmly in this great World at Peace that lies so close to our own, ready to come into being as our wills turn towards it, that I must needs go about this present world of disorder and darkness like an exile doing such feeble things as I can towards the world of my desire, now hopefully, now bitterly, as the moods may happen, until I die."

This same note of hopefulness has been expressed by Dr. John A. Hutton. "I sometimes think that in a great, wholesale way we are all of us about to make a wonderful discovery. At times it seems to me as though we were on the edge and moment of a world-shaking Revolution in thought and mood. For a long time now we have been feeling our way in a vast, unlit corridor, contending with others in the dark, striking out at shapes which seemed to be wishing to do us harm, when all the time they, like ourselves, may only have been out upon their business, and, like us, in the dark. I sometimes think that in answer to the cry of our present distress a light is once more about to shine, and by this light we shall see again an open door, and beyond the fair earth and sky."

A Divided World

When we begin to analyze the present situation in the effort to discover the chief causes of misery, we are at once impressed by the obvious fact that we are living in a divided world. All about us are vast chasms. The supreme task of this generation is to bridge the deep gulfs which separate group from group. Modern social cleavages are varied and complex. They are not easy to define, much less easy to surmount.

One of the most comprehensive of these antagonisms is that between races. We are deeply affected by the color of a man's skin, the slant of his eyes, the shape of his nose, or the curl in his hair. One of the most serious questions with which we in the United States are confronted is the so-called "Negro Problem." A vast immigration from every corner of the globe has thrust upon us a complex and dangerous race problem. We hear of a "Yellow Peril" and of "The Rising Tide of Color." We are constantly being warned that the next world war will be a struggle between races.

Then there is the constant clash between nations. Eight years of war and the aftermath have made us all too familiar with the tragic seriousness of the struggles between nations. There is another major cleavage in the modern world, that between religions. Do we not hear of "the menace of Islam"? Are we not told of the bitter resentment and even overt hostility with which Christian missionaries are greeted in various parts of the earth?

The antagonism, however, which comes closest home to most of us, and which most seriously affects our daily lives, is the conflict between classes. Everywhere a terrific struggle is being waged between employer and workers. In most countries this conflict is growing more intense. In our own land we are becoming increasingly aware of it. Strikes and lockouts on a national scale are constantly being threatened. Not only in the basic industries, such as coal, steel, railways, packing houses and building trades, but throughout the whole of industry the conflict is on. Industry is sharply divided into two camps, employers and workers. Organized business is arrayed against organized labor.

The situation is even more complex than this. Each side, in turn, is divided into many conflicting factions. Within the ranks of the employers a bitter struggle is being waged. Is it not considered axiomatic that "competition is the life of trade" and the corner-stone upon which modern business rests? Does not success in business depend upon the degree of victory achieved in vanquishing one's competitors? Is not bitterness and unrestricted warfare inherent and inevitable in a system based upon competition?

The ranks of labor are even more seriously divided. Competing employers have found it to their advantage to unite against labor, and are usually able to present a united front against the common enemy. Labor, on the other hand, in spite of the plea for solidarity which is often made, has not learned to act unitedly. Only a fraction of labor's strength is ever marshalled against the solid ranks of the employers. A bitter and unrelenting warfare is constantly being waged among the various factions within the labor movement.

Consequences of Division

As a result of these manifold antagonisms, humanity is losing much vital blood. It is weak when it might be strong. It is poor when it might be rich. Sufficient strides have been made in mechanical invention and the conquest of nature to make it possible for every person to receive an adequate supply of the material necessities and comforts of life. And yet, because we continue to attack one another, most of the human race is still in physical need.

Not only in China, India, Russia and parts of Europe and the Near East are large masses of the people living in destitution, but even in the United States, the most favored nation of the earth, an appalling proportion of the population is in dire physical need. It was more than thirty years ago that Jacob Riis wrote his notable volume, "How the Other Half Lives," but the situation among our poorer people is still tragic in the extreme. Thousands of families never have enough to eat. Children are deprived of milk and other nourishing food. . . . The supply of clothing is altogether inadequate. Whole families are crowded together in two or three dingy rooms. Health is menaced and morals are endangered. Mental and spiritual growth are stunted. The miracle is that some families find a measure of joy in life even in the midst of sordidness and wretchedness. But these are exceptions. As a rule, the "fruits of the spirit" do not spring from such soil. Instead of love, joy, beauty, peace and hope, we more often find bitterness, misery, squalor, dread, fear and despair.

One of the tragic consequences of the divided state of mankind is to be found in its effect upon brotherhood. It is obvious that the spirit of brotherhood is endangered by the great gulf which exists between the rich and the poor, by racial, national and class struggles, and by the exploitation of the weak. The results of division upon brotherhood are especially visible in the Church. It is, of course, impossible for the Church to proclaim with maximum power the message of Jesus so long as its ranks are divided by race, nationality and class. These divisions constitute an effective barrier to the progress of the Kingdom of God on earth and are an absolute denial of the prayer of our Lord, "That they all may be one."

What Can We Do?

No follower of Jesus can be satisfied with the present state of affairs. Our divisions are a source of regret and unhappiness. We long for a united world. What can we do to hasten its coming?

The first step is an open-minded examination of the facts. It is absolutely essential that we know the real nature of our problems. Only as we know the facts can we hope to find a way out of our present situation. To discover all the facts with regard to our complex problems is difficult indeed. The difficulties are made all the greater because of the social cleavages which separate us from other groups. No single group has access to all the facts. Each group reaches its decisions after an examination of only a portion of the facts. Our problem is intensified by the hostility which exists between different groups or, at best, the prejudice, suspicion and fear with which various groups regard each other.

Still another factor increases our difficulty, namely, the conscious or unconscious tendency to defend the *status quo*. The mere existence throughout several decades or centuries of a given practice or attitude is often the only defense it needs. Prejudice, passion and the tendency to defend things-as-they-are without examining the ethical foundations upon which they rest, block the way to the discovery of the facts. Those persons who are desirous of rendering their maximum contribution to the building of a better world, simply must free themselves from preconceived notions and enter into a sympathetic and open-minded examination of the facts. This is not easy to do. It requires constant watchfulness and effort. And yet this must be accomplished by leaders in various groups if further chaos is to be avoided.

It has been said that "there is no refuge but in truth." In this connection a recent writer has said: "The watchword of conduct that will clear up all our difficulties is the plain truth. Rely upon that watchword, use that key with courage and we can go out of the prison in which we live; we can go right out of the conditions of war, shortage, angry scrambling, mutual thwarting and malice and disease in which we live; we and our kind can go out into sunlight, into a sweet air of understanding, into confident freedoms and a full creative life—forever."

We must also make a careful selection of principles by which we are to judge progress. A mere knowledge of the facts will not solve our problems. We must have a correct scale of values by which the facts are to be tested. In succeeding chapters we shall attempt to discover the principles of Jesus that have a bearing upon the problems under consideration. In the light of these principles we shall examine specific problems and attempt to evaluate various programs of action which are being set forth as ways of building a better world. In other words, we shall endeavor to locate the sources of division and to discover paths to a united world through following in the footsteps of Jesus.

Seeing With the Outward Eye

If one stands on a high hill overlooking a wide expanse of valley the mind takes cognizance of the landscape as a whole rather than of detached parts. The beauty and completeness of the scene stimulate the mind and appeal to the imagination. One may note if one chooses to do so the varying parts and aspects of it and may study in some measure the details of woods and meadow and tilled fields and orchards; but as one gazes a sense of the unity of it all constantly reasserts itself, and if one closes his eyes he may see all the more perfectly the image of the whole with the inner eye of the mind. If a fair stream of water winds through it; flowing on and on unceasingly, the years, the decades, the centuries through,—long before and long after we have come and gazed and passed on;—the eye brightens at the sight of it and the heart thanks the stream that makes perfect the landscape.

Long years ago the Son of Man painted on the minds and hearts of his fellowmen a fair imagery of the home of the Spirit of the human soul for all mankind to gaze upon. For those who have seen it there is on earth no pictured expanse of mere landscape equal to it in beauty. It should be called the panorama of the soul-world. It is the gospel and teaching and the life of Jesus of Nazareth.

As in our valley, so in this scene pictured by the Son of Man, there is a wonderful on-flowing stream. It should be named the river of the Compensations of Life; for it receives and it gives, it washes out and builds up; and it is fed by the springs of God; to purge and wash clean, to serve and to bless the souls of men.

Jesus taught primarily the compensations of life. The very heart of His ministry was the proclaiming of these eternal, unswerving, inescapable compensations,—the recompense of the Spirit.

There is one great phase of this which, although not usually conspicuous, men would do well to dwell more upon,—the reward of trying to see by the inner eye of the soul rather than by the eye of the body alone; and the judging of their fellowmen by the real, if partly hidden, personalities instead of by their outward appearances.

In physical blindness there is the beautiful compensation, at least in part, of added acuteness of the other senses, particularly those of touch and hearing. So, likewise, when we shall voluntarily close our eyes to many of the minor distracting things of life and shall voluntarily be blind to the many frailties and shortcomings of people, the Inward Light may then shine more brightly and the inner eye of the soul see more clearly the true personality each of the other; and seeing, shall understand; and understanding, shall find the way to come near to; and coming near, shall learn to love. Thus shall we the better perceive the real difficulties of daily living and the sooner learn the true solution of the problems of our modern complex social life; by seeing the whole *as a whole*: seeing the whole of the relations and the dependence of men one on another; seeing *all* of the needs, the rivalries, the contentions of nations; and the whole broad survey of the causes of warfare between classes and groups,—if one can only stand on the hill and see and feel the whole as one.

Jesus constantly taught this unity of spirit and the reconciliation of the earthly and the heavenly by the elimination of the trivial and the unworthy things. "Cease to do evil; learn to do well" and receive the compensation provided for the soul in the better living. He was ever teaching the giving up of the lesser thing for the greater; the good thing for the better; the imperfect for the perfect, the transitory for the eternal;—a veritable stream of living compensations flowing on for everybody.

And as for really seeing, how can any man hope to see clearly except by means of the eye of the soul and the Divine illumination? The outward eye contemplates primarily the surface of things only. Unguided what can it perceive or discover of the hidden hopes and fears, the impulses and motives, the ambitions or aspirations of men? "There is nothing hidden that shall not be revealed," but it is not to the worldly wise.

May we then, become as little children of the unspoiled mind that can believe, in perfect trust, and live without fear!

And as we gaze fondly upon the valley of our soul dream may we remember that the beauty of the scene is of the whole of humanity not of any detached part thereof. C. P.

Prepare for Life!

So live that when to thee, each morn, doth come
The call to join the motley crowd
That throngs the streets and thoroughfares,
Each to take part in life's activities—
Thou go, not like the unwilling worker,
Urged to his daily task unready; but sustained
And helped by an unfailing trust
That Truth and Right will yet prevail;
Like him who draws his girdle tight
About him, and with faith invincible
And firm resolve, goes out to join
With others in the race to reach the goal,
And gain the prize that waits
Each victor in the strife.

Holder, Ill. ELIZABETH H. COALE.

Notes From the Service Field

Need for Clothes Continues

Yes, the American Friends' Service Committee still needs clothes to send abroad.

It is not as you may have begun to think, that surely by this time Europe has ceased to need clothes. Instead of that, the real condition is that those brothers and sisters of ours across the seas will need more clothes this winter than they have for any winter in the past five years.

In Austria, Poland and Russia the middle and lower classes are really destitute of clothing. Stocks and reserves were exhausted long ago, and there has been no money to buy clothing even if there had been raw material in Europe out of which clothes might be made.

In Vienna the value of the crown has dwindled so that it practically has no power at all for purchasing. It is now quoted at the rate of 6,182 to the dollar. The people whom this most greatly affects are the middle-class people. They are the office workers, the students, the teachers, the professors in the universities, the doctors and all of those who once held civil positions under the old government. These people are helpless. They cannot leave Vienna, for they are not trained for any other kind of work than their own and there is no place to go which would benefit them. To continue living in Vienna means an existence on a salary which, in the majority of cases, does not exceed the value of twenty-five dollars in purchasing power a year. These are people who are men like ourselves, doing the same kind of work and understanding the same spirit of life and hemmed in by that terrible wall of no resource and the futility of leaving the city. It is just what our condition would be if our money lost its power. These people cannot buy clothes. When they cannot buy food, the purchasing of clothing becomes totally remote. Whatever they wear of clothing must be given to them. Have you something?

In Poland 30,000 refugees a week, most of whom have been exiled from their native land for five years, are returning to Poland. They are coming without money, without household goods, and return to their old homes which they find devastated. Can you understand that their only clothing will be that which is given to them?

In Russia typhus and cholera can only be stopped by cleanliness. They are dirt diseases. Without soap, without fuel or hot water, and starved into such weakness that exertion is impossible, the Russian people cannot hope to prevent their little stock of clothing becoming too dirty for human beings to wear. They need clean clothing but can neither make nor buy.

The people of Europe need clothes. If you have any that is strong and wearable, will you not send it at once to the Friends' Storeroom at Fifteenth and Cherry Streets, Philadelphia?

Don't Forget the Tuesday Sewing Meeting

The Women's Work Committee of the Service Committee asks that every woman who possibly can, will volunteer for work in the Tuesday sewing group which meets all day Tuesdays in Room No. 3 of the 15th and Race Streets (Philadelphia) Meeting House. The garments which will be sent to Europe will be repaired and put into shape for wearing. Every one who can, is asked to bring old lining material which is fit to be used to reline the garments.

An Appeal from the Mothers of Russia

A group of the mothers of Russia recently issued an appeal to the civilized world. It appeared in "Ogin," a Russian newspaper published in Prague. It reads:

"We Russian mothers who are destined to die from starvation and disease implore the people of the whole world to take our children from us that those who are innocent may not share our horrible fate. We implore the world to do this because, even at the cost of a voluntary and eternal separation, we long to repair the wrong we have committed in giving them a life which is worse than death. All of you who have children, or who have lost children, all of you who have children and fear to lose them, in remembrance of the children who are dead and in the name of those who are still living, we beseech you. Have pity upon our children. Do not think of us, we cannot be helped. We have lost all hope, but we shall yet be happy with the only happiness a mother knows—that of the knowledge that her child is safe."

Typhus Grips East Poland

Day after day increases the list of typhus sufferers throughout Poland, but especially along the railroads by which the Polish refugees of the great war are now crowding back from the Volga famine area in Russia. This is the substance of a report which Anna Louise Strong, one of the Friends' workers in Poland, sent to the Service Committee this week. East Poland, that wide section of territory inhabited by White Russians and Ukrainians and only last year annexed to Poland as a result of this war with Russia, is especially afflicted with the scourge, since here live the greatest number of the destitute peasants now returning.

One hundred of the personnel manning the Polish quarantine station at Baranowieze have been reported down with typhus; while six of the American and English relief workers have had typhus during the past few weeks, most of them as a result of a trip to Baranowicze. Three members of the Friends' Mission in Poland have been ill but are recovering, although reports from the Friends' Mission across the border in Russia indicate that 10 of the 30 members, both English and American, have been ill with typhus and two have died.

There seems no possibility of permanently stemming this disease for two or three years, without a greater expenditure than either Russia or Poland will be able to undertake. Summer will, of course, greatly decrease its prevalence, but next winter it will begin again and continue as long as the movement of refugees from Russia back to Poland continues. For these refugees are destitute peasants, who lost their homes in the great war, and who have suffered seven years of exile. They have no change of clothing or underwear. They return in the same sheepskins in which they set out years ago. Under these conditions the stamping out of a louse-carried disease is impossible without spending more money. There are still more than 600,000 refugees to return from Russia; and as long as they are moving along the railroads they will cause serious trouble both in Poland and Russia.

Efficient quarantine would in part stop the spread of the disease. The Friends' Mission is presenting 50 typhus-proof suits for the use of the personnel in the new repatriation camp just opened at Dorchusk. It is hoped that by this means the new camp will be saved the experience of Baranowicze.

A Word Concerning Swarthmore

At a recent meeting of the Swarthmore Alumnæ Club held in Philadelphia, there were interesting and valuable addresses by Dean Raymond Walters, and President Aydelotte. We were given a detailed account of the method of selection of incoming students, from the applicants in excess of the vacancies at the beginning of the new college year. Fitness of preparation, and scholarly aims are taken into account along with the date of application. Another factor in the choice of new students, is the preference to be given, other things being equal, to members of the Society of Friends.

There is a very definite plan to secure justice to the different grades of scholarship in a given class, whereby there shall be justice secured to the quicker minds, and courage and confidence established for those of slower habits of mind. In listening to the plans and methods of this latter day, one feels a kind of intellectual baptism into a new order of things, taking the work of teacher and pupil quite away from lifeless formalism into the stimulating delight of knowledge steadily acquired, and the mental power steadily increased.

One of our poets has written that "Time makes ancient good uncouth." Those of us who may feel that "Time" is putting this stamp upon us, may find satisfaction in remembering that we too have had our opportunity to work for the securing of "better ways" to the young; and while we rest from these labors, we may enter into the joys of the fresh laborers. ELIZABETH POWELL BOND.

Germantown, Pa.

Friendly News Notes

Charles F. Jenkins, Treasurer of the American Friends' Service Committee, expects to sail for Europe on Fourth month 7th. He will give the annual address before the Friends' Historical Society in London, and will spend about two months travelling through England and France.

Edith Stratton Platt writes from Shanghai, China, en route to Moukden with her husband, Joseph Platt, who is the American Secretary of the Y. M. C. A. in the latter city, of meeting Henry T. Hodgkin and his wife. She tells how much he is appreciated among the Y. M. C. A. group, and how great is the work he is doing in China. He is interpreting to the Chinese his belief in the possibility of a thorough-going application of the Christian message of love and good-will, and doing it with enthusiasm.

The Advisory and Executive Committees of the Young Friends' Movement of Philadelphia Yearly Meeting announce that Elizabeth A. Walters has been appointed Executive Secretary of the Movement for the year 1922-23, to succeed Eliza M. Ambler, whose resignation goes into effect on the first of June. Elizabeth A. Walters, better known as "Betty" Walters, is a resident of Swarthmore and a member of the graduating class of Vassar College.

Those who have enjoyed the charming Quaker stories by Violet Hodgkin will be interested to know that on February 14 she was married in the Friends' Meeting House at Truro, England, to John Holdsworth, of New Zealand before a very representative company from almost every Quarterly Meeting in the London Yearly Meeting. Both these Friends were in attendance upon the London Conference in 1920.—*The American Friend.*

Margaret Hallowell Riggs, Friends' representative on the staff of the Canton Christian College, who has been loaned this year by the College to the nearby True Light Middle School for girls, is Faculty Adviser on the staff of the "True Light Y. W. C. A. News Letter." Two copies of the "News Letter" which have recently come to us are well printed and well written. That they are well written shows the progress which the True Light School makes in teaching English, for most of the articles are by the students. One feels in these columns the ideals of China's awakening youth; hopeful, vigorous, and seeing clearly the vision of Christian service.

A feature of the meeting of ministers and elders, preceding the Yearly Meeting of Orthodox Friends, being held this week at Fourth and Arch Streets, Philadelphia, was the presentation of a letter from William C. Allen and his wife, Mary C. B. Allen, of San Jose, Cal. Both are members of Philadelphia Yearly Meeting, and are about to start on a tour for religious work through the Far East. They expect to visit Australia, New Zealand, South Africa, Java, Ceylon and other places en route.

Friends expecting to attend the fiftieth anniversary celebration at 17th Street and Girard Avenue, Philadelphia, on Fifth month 7th, are invited to bring a box lunch and spend the day. The closing session of the First-day School will be held at 9.45, and the meeting for worship at 11 o'clock. The speaker for the afternoon session has not yet been chosen.

Samuel P. Zavitz, of Coldstream, Ontario, sends us the account of a lecture on "The Outlook of Europe," by Professor James T. Shotwell, M. A., Ph. D., of Columbia University, given at Strathroy recently. Professor Shotwell's father was a birthright member of the Society of Friends.

Last summer he visited the countries of Central Europe, to make a survey of the archives, relating to the late war, which have been preserved in many countries. He found them outwardly prosperous, economically unsound. In Germany everybody is busy, plenty of work, amusement and banqueting. He declared the world problem today is not Germany, but Russia, whom the Germans have always feared. He defined why Germany considers herself guiltless of a world war. He lucidly explained the situation in France. His sympathy is with France, but his understanding is with Britain.

Charles F. Jenkins, of Germantown, Pennsylvania, publisher of *The Farm Journal*, while searching in the Congressional Library for Quaker history in the West Indies, discovered that a William Thornton, a young Quaker architect, once lived in Tortola, one of the British Virgin Islands, and later lived in Philadelphia where he married a Philadelphia girl, and returned to Tortola. In a Philadelphia paper sent to him there, he found a prize offer of $500 in cash for the best design for the United States capitol. He competed and his drawing, although arriving after the contest was closed, was so well liked by George Washington that Thornton was declared the winner, and the capitol was built according to his plans. He was born in the West Indies May 27, 1761. He went to Washington in 1793, where he assisted the Commissioners in the early history of the city, and died in 1828. He was also architect of the Octagon House, used by Dolly Madison, the only Quaker wife of a president of the United States, and her husband, President James Madison.—*The American Friend.*

HAVERFORD COLLEGE SCHOLARSHIPS

The Board of Managers of Haverford College, Haverford, Pa., announce three Jacob P. Jones Foundation Scholarships open to young men graduating from accredited Secondary Schools and passing the College Entrance Board Examinations. These scholarships of $300.00 each are awarded on the following basis:

(1) Qualities of manhood, force of character and leadership;
(2) Literary and scholastic attainments;
(3) Physical vigor.

Awards will be made early in June and the scholarships are offered for National Competition.

The Board announces also four Corporation Scholarships with an annual value of $300.00 each, to be awarded without application to the four Freshmen receiving the highest averages in the College Entrance Board examinations in June.

FROM ASSOCIATION FIELD

"Young Friends Active in Charity" was the headline in a daily paper reporting the Spring Executive meeting of Young Friends' Associations, held in Philadelphia on Third month 18th, and was doubtless caused by the reports from so many Associations showing activity in aid of the work of the American Friends' Service Committee, Friends' Neighborhood Guild, as well as definite friendly local work. Yet these reports can give but a faint idea of the amount of work done in these organizations.

During the war some of the erstwhile active Associations ceased work as such, giving themselves to work felt to be more needed then and unable to keep up both. Some of these are now resuming regular meetings, others still branching out into fields shown to be very much worth while. So, while the total number of Associations today is less than the pre-war count, yet it is doubtful if there is not better work being done now than then, the deepening and broadening of intervening experiences being productive of greater things.

Where one Association falls out another one comes into being and the work goes on. The Philadelphia Association, the first one in the field, has undertaken more kinds of work than any other—or one might say than *all* others!

The officers for the coming year are: Thomas P. Bartram, of Media, President, and Julius Hund, Wrightstown, Treasurer; Sarah W. Knight, of Byberry, Secretary.

A committee to look after the holding of the Fall Conference at Makefield, Pa., as guests of that Association, was also named.

Earnest consideration was given various problems which arose from both city and country Associations, and it it was felt to be one of the most worth-while sessions held in years.

A. C.

NEWS FROM ORANGE GROVE MEETING

Orange Grove Monthly Meeting of Friends, Pasadena, California, held Third month 12th, united in sending a letter to President Harding, containing an urgent appeal for him to issue an amnesty proclamation at once to release all federal prisoners convicted under the Espionage Act.

At the morning session for worship George F. Powell spoke at considerable length, the chief concern of his message being the conspicuous lack of spiritual training to students in the average college curriculum and in the general educational system of our country. There must be more of the spirit of Love and less of the spirit of hatred. Mary Travilla was specially favored. William Frame, of Waynesville, Ohio; Cornelius Enns, of Los Angeles, and others gave brief but helpful words of encouragement.

Tourists from various Friendly centers throughout the United States and Canada have been in attendance upon our meetings this winter, and are warmly received. Among others were Oliver and Martha Wilson, Mary L. and Ruth S. Bumgarner, and Anna Mary Mills, of Illinois Yearly Meeting; William and Jessie Greist, of Portland, Indiana, Samuel and Hannah Bartram, Lansdowne, Pa., and the Pratt sisters from Media. Frances M. Robinson with her rich offerings of love and truth, and her two sisters, are almost like "homefolks" with us.

Two socials in the Meeting House Annex, in honor of the tourist Friends have been given under the auspices of the Membership Committee. The first, almost a banquet, was favored with Andrew Cadwallader as toast-master.

MARIANNA BURGESS.

THE 250TH ANNIVERSARY OF BALTIMORE YEARLY MEETING

Fifth Month (May) 4th, 5th, 6th and 7th.

Two hundred and fifty years ago this spring the first General or Yearly Meeting of Friends in Maryland was held on the shore of West River, a dozen miles south of Annapolis.

George Fox, the founder of the Society of Friends, on his journey from England to the American Colonies in 1672, arrived just in time to take part on this occasion.

Such an important and unusual event as this anniversary should have a worthy celebration, and therefore the bodies forming the two Yearly Meetings of Baltimore, equally interested in this event, have appointed committees to jointly celebrate the event.

All Yearly Meetings, as far as possible, have been invited to send official delegates, and several of them have complied with this invitation. Other visitors will be very welcome. All who desire to attend should send their names and wishes as to location to Mary F. Blackburn, Govans, Md., by Fourth month (April) 20th. Those who do not apply by that date will be expected to locate themselves.

The time will be Fifth month 4th, to 7th, inclusive, beginning on the evening of the 4th.

The exercises, according to the preliminary announcements, will consist of addresses by Elizabeth B. Emmott, of England, Frederick J. Libby, Governor William Sproul, of Pennsylvania, Jesse H. Holmes, L. Meachem Thruston, Elbert Russell and Rufus M. Jones. There will also be brief messages from representatives of churches and from the delegates from other Yearly Meetings. On one evening scenes from Quaker history will be shown; and on Seventh-day the 6th of Fifth month, all will sail down Chesapeake Bay to West River and visit the spot where the first Yearly Meeting was held.

Both the New Homewood Meeting-house, 3107 N. Charles Street and that at Park Avenue will be used for the meetings. Visitors on arrival will register at one or the other.

Arrangements are being made whereby board and lodging will be made convenient to all. Accommodations for a limited number of guests will be provided at cost in the two Meeting-houses. Reservations will be made in the order of their reception.

We are looking forward to this event with unusual interest.

THE JOINT COMMITTEE.

Items From Everywhere

According to figures issued by the Federal Council of Churches, 96,338,096 persons in the United States are connected with some religious organization. Roman Catholics number 17,885,646 members. On the same basis the total membership of all Protestant bodies is 74,795,226. The membership of Friends is given for "four bodies" as 117,239. The gain of total church membership over that recorded by the 1916 census is 4,070,345, and the gain in Sunday school membership is 4,008,548. What could not 96,338,096 persons do for the enrichment of human life if each one saw the whole vision which Jesus taught, and acted in the spirit in which Jesus lived!

Two other important documents have been issued during recent weeks by the Federal Council of Churches. One is an appeal, regarding the impending coal strike, issued jointly with the National Catholic Welfare Council, to both mine owners and miners. It calls for a settlement of the controversy upon the grounds of justice and the right human relations rather than upon economic advantage. Secondly, a message has been sent by the Federal Council inviting the churches of Germany to enter into hearty co-operation with the Churches of America. Later, it is planned to send representatives of the American churches to visit the church leaders of Germany. This means the resumption of Friendly relations between the churches of Germany and those of America. While we regard it as essentially un-Christian that those relations were ever broken, we rejoice to see the bonds of international amity thus being rewoven.

A great bronze figure of Booker T. Washington will be unveiled at Tuskegee Institute on April 5th. It is the work of Charles Keck. William Anthony Aery writes of the statue: "To see Mr. Keck's figure of Dr. Washington is to carry away the picture of a man who stood up straight and firm under the heavy burden of millions of Negroes, who carried in the deep lines of his forehead and face the signs of victorious struggle, and who cared less for clothes than for service of his fellow-men."

The New York *American* on March 8, contained the statement that democracy, progressing in many other countries, is in retreat in the United States. Why, it asks, is our politics untrustworthy and inefficient, our captains of industry autocratic and our methods confused and uninspired? The answer is: "Because the soul of America lacks a lode star. We need, to guide us, a spiritual concept of what democracy is. Nothing less can enkindle our emotions, cohere our thinking and direct effectively our restimulated energies." Discussion is invited upon a definition of democracy which shall meet America's need, and the following definition, "thought out by Dr. Charles Fleischer twenty years ago and since subjected successfully to many tests," is forthwith offered: "Democracy is the organization of society on the basis of respect for the individual."

Figures compiled by the Chicago crime commission, a voluntary body prompted by the Association of Commerce, show that major crimes in Chicago, though still disquietingly numerous, have been decreasing during the past three years. In 1919, 1920 and 1921 respectively the number of cases were: Murder, 330, 194 and 190; burglary, 6108, 5495 and 4774; robbery, 2912, 2782 and 2558. It looks a little as if the crime wave were a receding one. It also looks as if prohibition were doing some good.—*Springfield Republican.*

The Prison Comfort Club's list of birthdays of political prisoners for April is as follows, to be addressed Box 7, Leavenworth, Kansas: 4th, John L. Turner; 5th, Frank Westerlund; 10th, James Quinlan; 13th, Ben Fletcher, a Negro; 14th, Charles L. Lambert; 15th, James Phillips; 20th, John Avila. To be addressed Box 520, Walla Walla, Washington: 4th, A. Shoemaker; 5th, George Raney; 21st, Jack Battle; 27th, B. Bland.

Publications of Interest

The Friends' Bookshop, London, has just issued a new edition of William C. Braithwaite's little volume of poems entitled "Red Letter Days." Since the death of its author this year, says a letter from Ernest E. Taylor, "a demand has grown up for this selection of poems which he issued in 1906. From the nature of this demand it is clear that many of these pieces have proven extraordinarily helpful to individuals all over the world." Many of the poems are as fine in art as they are high in spirit, and they form a lasting message from our departed friend. We have received no details for purchasers, but are sure that the volume is very low-priced and that it will be available from American Friends' bookshops.

Recent Macmillan publications include many volumes of moment in the field of religious thought. "A Student's Philosophy of Religion," by William Kelly Wright (472 pp., $3.75), is a general survey of the whole field of religion from the historical, the philosophical and the psychological viewpoints. Its purpose is to furnish college undergraduates and general readers with the facts and theories from which they can work out their own philosophy of religion. Judging by a hasty review of its contents this volume must render in the field of religion much the same sweeping synthetic service which Well's "Outline" contributes to history. "Creative Christianity," by George Cross (164 pp., $1.75), is designed to be "a contribution toward reshaping the inherited forms in which our Protestantism has expressed its inner life for us so that the coming generation nurtured under the changed spiritual tendencies current today may have a form of Christianity better fitted to its needs."

"A Faith That Enquires," by Sir Henry Jones (278 pp., $2.00), is a series of lectures on topics related to the "value and need of a free religion." It appeals for an inquiring spirit as the basis of religious outlook, as opposed to the dogmatic spirit. The author says:

"I believe that our spiritual knowledge and practice, both individual and social, is so crude and rudimentary that we cannot even imagine the splendor of the results which an enquiring religious faith can bring to man." "Property, Its Rights and Uses" (243 pp., $2.00), constitutes a series of essays by seven different writers, considering the subject of property from the historical, philosophical and religious standpoints.

N. H. Motsinger, of Fredonia, Pa., sends us a valuable book on "The Social Center," edited by Edward J. Ward, Adviser in Civic and Social Center Development, of the University of Wisconsin (D. Appleton and Company, 1913). The book is based upon the conviction that before men can make fundamental social progress, they have got to find a way to get together; that before they can act intelligently upon matters of social importance, such as the making of our laws, they must meet as a community and seriously discuss those issues from all points of view. The book proposes the use of the local school house as community center, and outlines a program of activities, including meetings for the consideration of all problems related to community and national life. This volume would afford much help should any of our meetings follow the suggestion of Prof. Morse, quoted in a recent INTELLIGENCER editorial, to "get behind an effort to build up a sound economic and social community."

Achievements of the Conference is the title of a new pamphlet prepared by the Commission on International Justice and Goodwill of the Federal Council of Churches, 105 E. 22d Street, New York City. It puts into figures the decisions of the Conference with reference to armament summarizes its most important achievements and urges prompt enactment of the treaties, without amendment or reservation, as a moral issue. Copies of the pamphlet may be obtained from the Commission at 15 cents a copy; $5.00 a hundred.

"The Carpenter and his Kingdom," by Alexander Irvine, New York. Charles Scribner's Sons, 1922, pp. 247. Price $1.50. A life of Jesus which aims to so present his teachings as to make them the controlling principle in the everyday life of the individual. The author's original material is interspersed with excerpts from the New Testament, which the book follows closely.

"In the Prison Camps of Germany," A Narrative of "Y" Service among Prisoners of War, by Conrad Hoffman. Association Press, 347 Madison Avenue, New York. 1920. Pp. 279.

The life of the prisoners of war, brought together in such numbers as no previous conflict has ever known, is a unique aspect of the World War that is of absorbing human interest. The story is told here by the American who, from August, 1915, to June, 1919, devoted his whole time to the welfare of the British, French, Russian, and Americans in German prison camps.

THE OPEN FORUM

This column is intended to afford free expression of opinion by readers on questions of interest. The INTELLIGENCER is not responsible for any such opinions. Letters must be brief, and the editor reserves the right to omit parts if necessary to save space.

FRIENDS' OPPORTUNITY IN THE ORIENT

To the Editor:

One of the Preparative Meetings which received the letter of appeal for the support of Friends' Work in the Orient, replied that so many calls came to them at this time that they could not render assistance. The multiplicity of calls for aid is well-known to our Committee. We were encouraged to send out ours because we know that these three young Friends in China are a great spiritual asset to the Society. The sum to be raised is not large for the number to whom the appeal has been made, if each will do a small share.

I can hardly imagine the situation where a meeting can do nothing. If each will do his part, these three young Friends will go forward assured that what they are doing for the spread of the Kingdom of God is not alone for the Chinese, but for the awakened missionary spirit of the Friends at home. Thus will they render double service. Just a dollar would have meant "We are helping"; "We can do nothing at this time"—what does this mean?

I trust that the action quoted here is exceptional and that other meetings are appointing Friends to solicit and forward their contributions to Linda E. Bicknell, 252 W. Wyoming Avenue, Germantown, Philadelphia.

ALFRED W. WRIGHT, *Chairman*
Friends' Opportunity in the Orient.

"IT IS EASIER TO FIGHT THAN TO THINK."

To the Editor:

As Friends, we profess to believe in individual interpretation, responsibility. As a Society, Friends would resent, refuse, dictation from any human being, any group, regarding interpretation of scripture, details of daily life, or indeed, anything else. But what better are we doing when we *blindly* follow dictation, "leadership," in international matters? Is the future of humanity of less concern to us than our business or housekeeping? Are we not untrue in essence, disloyal in spirit, to the very foundation of Quaker faith, when we follow *any* majority or propaganda, *indiscriminately?* Then why do we merely clamor for "ratification" of the treaties? And repeat: "Either these pacts must be ratified or efforts to prevent war become a mockery." Which one of us has sincerely studied any of these things? Honest, intelligent study would reveal many things besides "peace," in all those treaties. They have no necessary connection with "disarmament."

What boots it, except in mere dollars and cents, to sell a few obsolete ships and reduce the *paid* army and navy, while hundreds of thousands of young men are given military training in "summer camps," schools and colleges, for the "civilian army," the ship-subsidy bill entails enforced naval training for every employe under it, with the right of conscription for active war still vested in the Government? The daily papers laud the outlawing of "poison gas" on one page, and on the next, report "recruiting for the chemical warfare service." What better than sheer hypocrisy is it to "thank God for disarmament" while we do not even take the trouble to *know* these things? A cynic has recently said of us: "It is easier to fight than to think." It is not enough that Friends attend the wounded and feed the starving *after* a war. Upon the consciences of Friends above all others lies the responsibility to *prevent* war, the individual responsibility to "*know* whereof we speak." Are Friends by their inertia, their refusal to use their *own* minds, lending themselves to indirectness, inequity? Pacific Pacts are indeed internationally desirable, but whether they shall be pacts of peace and justice or of aggression and deceit is directly chargeable to the vision or sloth of individual souls. Of yours and of mine. ESTHER HARLAN.

BIRTHS

GREEN—On Third month 19th, at Swarthmore, Penna., to Sheldon R. and Charlotte Bunting Green, of Brooklyn, N. Y., a daughter, named Patricia Helen Green.

SCHOCH—At Trenton, N. J., on First month 29th, to E. Roland and Florence Pearson Schoch, a son, named Edward Roland Schoch, Jr. A great-grandson to Robert and the late Amanda J. Pearson.

MARRIAGES

PANCOAST-MAYNARD—On Third month 15th, at Buffalo, N. Y., Joseph Davis Pancoast, son of Charles F. and Annie E. Pancoast, of Woodstown, N. J., and Gertrude J. Maynard, of Buffalo, N. Y.

DEATHS

BROOMALL—At Cheyney, Pa., on Third month 22d, Anna B., widow of James Broomall, in her 82d year.

CORSE—At her home in Baltimore, Md., on Third month 22nd, Sarah Sutton Corse, wife of the late Dr. George F. Corse, in her 80th year.

HENDRICKSON—At Crosswicks, N. J., Third month 21, Abbie, widow of Joseph Hendrickson, in her 75th year.

PYLE—At Gradyville, Pa., on Third month 22d, Dr. Jerome Levis Pyle, in his 65th year.

RICE—At Lahaska, Pa., Third month 25th, Euthenia A. Rice.

SULLIVAN—At Moorestown, N. J., Third month 21st, Joseph T. Sullivan, in his 67th year.

G. HAROLD POWELL.

In sending in a biographical sketch of the life of G. Harold Powell, whose death occurred recently at Pasadena, California, Sarah E. Gardner-Magill writes, "Such characters as that of G. Harold Powell are rare, and no better example can be put before our young people than the record of his life." We regret that we cannot reprint in full the sketch as it appeared in a California paper.

"G. Harold Powell's life is marked by accomplishments, too many to mention, but even more important than the things which he guided to success is the spirit of the man which holds its inspiration for those who follow after.

His high purpose was service. He gave of his vision, his mind, his strength and his purse to those movements that he thought worthy of support.

First he gave to all agriculture through the government of the United States.

When the country went to war, he was chosen by Herbert Hoover to head the division of perishable foods of the United States Food Administration.

During the past ten years he has guided the California Fruit Growers' Exchange, the pioneer in co-operative agricultural organizations. Among the many things he accomplished was the solving of the problem of the prevention of fruit decay in storage, especially of apples, peaches and oranges.

With all these large tasks which he accomplished there has been a constant flow of others to which he gave his clear mind and his stabilizing judgment.

He had the right to wear the Cross of the Chevalier of the Order of the Crown, given him by King Albert of Belgium for work in the relief of that country.

G. Harold Powell was a speaker and writer of note, of ability and of charm. One of his statements may best illustrate his faith in men. 'The basis of the co-operative organization is men. Capital cannot co-operate; products cannot co-operate; only men can co-operate.'

His life, his achievements, his spirit, his service combine to form an imperishable monument to G. Harold Powell, the man."

COMING EVENTS

THIRD MONTH.

30th—Members of the Young Friends' Movement of New York, and others of appropriate age and condition are invited to the gymnasium of Friends' Seminary for an "unpremeditated evening." Nothing is arranged for but the place. Wear old clothes and tennis shoes. Be ready for anything. Be sure to enter by entrance of Rutherford Place, between 15th and 16th Streets.

FOURTH MONTH.

1st and 2nd—Pilgrimage under care of Young Friends' Movement, at Mickleton, N. J.

2nd—Miss Dwight, head of the Personal Service Bureau of the Near East Relief, will speak after Meeting in New York. Her work is that of uniting separated families, and her talk should be intensely interesting.

2nd—Carolena M. Wood expects to attend Matinecock Meeting in company with the Advancement Committee of Westbury Quarterly Meeting. An afternoon conference will be held on the Future of Friends' Service.

2nd—First-day. 3 p. m. A meeting for divine worship will be held at Providence Friends' Meeting House, near Media, Pa., under care of a Committee of Concord Quarterly Meeting. A community meeting and all denominations welcome. Young people are invited to be present and take part in the services.

2nd—Public service at Friends' Home for Children, 4011 Aspen St., West Philadelphia. 3 p. m. Those interested in children invited.

2nd—Conference class at 15th and Race Streets, Philadelphia, at close of meeting for worship, at 11.40 a. m.

Speaker—Nicholas Hennessy. Subject—Methods of Church Extension in the Apostolic Age.

5th—William Littleboy expects to attend Baltimore Monthly Meeting at Park Avenue Meeting House.

8th—Lecture at George School, by Tom Daly, on "The Laughing Muse." Admission, fifty cents.

8th—Salem First-day School Union will meet at Mickleton, N. J. Sessions at 10.30 a. m. and 2 p. m. Jane P. Rushmore and Grace Adams (Gloucester Co. S. S. Secretary) will speak during afternoon session on "First-day School Teaching." All cordially invited.

9th—William Littleboy, expects to attend meeting for worship at 1811 I. Street, Washington, D. C., at 11 a. m.

10th—New York Monthly Meeting will be held at 7.30 at 110 Schermerhorn St., Brooklyn. Supper will be served at 6.

15th—Abington First-day School Union at Abington Friends' Meeting House, Jenkintown, Pa.

23rd—Southern Half-Yearly Meeting, at Easton, Md.

25th—Western Quarterly Meeting, at London Grove, Pa.

27th—Cain Quarterly Meeting, at Christiana, Pa.

29th—Westbury Quarterly Meeting, at Brooklyn, N. Y.

NOTICE—Concord First-day School Union, to be held at Swarthmore, has been postponed until Fourth month 22, owing to conflict with Somerville Day at Swarthmore College.

NOTICE—From Fourth month 2nd to 23rd, inclusive, the subject for discussion in the Bible Class at 35th and Lancaster Avenue, Philadelphia, will be "The Christ that is to Come." W. J. MacWatters, leader. 10 a. m. The First-day School has ten classes. Bring the children 9.45.

NOTICE—Witherspoon Hall, Saturday, April 1, at 8.15 p. m. Judge Florence E. Allen of Cleveland, Ohio, will speak on "Justice and Citizenship" under the Auspices of The Philadelphia League of Women Voters. Admission free.

NOTICE—On April 17th, the George School Club of New York have an informal dinner-dance (private room) at the White Rose Restaurant, 981 8th Avenue and 60th Street, at 6.30 p. m. for $3.00 per cover. All former George School pupils and those who are interested are invited. Remit to Edwin Freidel, Treasurer, 2812 Church Avenue, Brooklyn, N. Y.

LUKE 2. 14—AMERICA'S ANGELUS

"Glory to God in the highest, and on earth peace, good will toward men."

Stand back of President Harding in Prayer for Universal Peace by meditating daily, at noon, on the fourteenth verse of the second chapter of Luke.

Ask your friends to help make this a Universal Meditation for Universal Peace

Pass it on *Friends in Christ*

American Friends' Service Committee

WILBUR K. THOMAS, EX. SEC.

20 S. 12th St. Philadelphia.

CASH CONTRIBUTIONS

WEEK ENDING MARCH 20.

Five Years Meeting	$364.60
New York Yearly Meeting	264.03
Other Meetings.	
Makefield Prep. Meeting	3.00
Monkton Ridge Meeting	1.50
Tecumseh Friends	16.00
Center Meeting	20.00
Buckingham Meeting	5.00
Friends at Coldstream	44.00
Cornwall Monthly Meeting	30.00
Contributions for General	395.33
For Germany	38,410.59
For Austria	2,140.10
For Poland	354.15
For Serbia	20.00
For Russia	14,582.38
For Russian Overhead	367.10
For German Overhead	31.83
For Clothing	311.13
Refunds and payments	13.60
	$57,374.34

Shipments received during week ending March 18th, 1922: 121 boxes and packages received; 3 anonymous.

To Our Friends

We want to put the FRIENDS' INTELLIGENCER on the reading table of every Friendly home. Will thee help us? Certainly no family that is not now receiving the paper can refuse to receive it for the next three months, if we will send it to them for that length of time for thirty-five cents. Will thee not ask every Friend with whom thee comes in contact whether they take the INTELLIGENCER, and if not whether thee may not send in their name for a trial subscription?

Don't be put off with the excuse that they see it through some other subscriber, or that they haven't time. Just for the next three months let's have a copy of our own, and if there isn't time for every member of the family to read every page of it, let's have it on the reading table where it is accessible in case anyone does have time.

All we ask thee to do, is to send the name and address to us. We will send bill and coin card to make payment easy.

REGULAR MEETINGS

OAKLAND, CALIF.—A FRIENDS' MEETing is held every First-day at 11 A. M., in the Extension Room, Y. W. C. A. Building, Webster Street, above 14th. Visiting Friends always welcome.

FRIENDS' MEETING IN PASADENA, California—Orange Grove Monthly Meeting of Friends, 520 East Orange Grove Avenue, Pasadena, California. Meeting for worship, First-day, 11 A. M. Monthly Meeting, the second First-day of each month, at 1.45 P. M.

CENTRAL MEETING OF FRIENDS (Chicago), meets every First-day in Room 706, 410 South Michigan Avenue, at 10.45 a. m. Visitors are invited.

WANTED

POSITION WANTED IN PHILADELphia or near vicinity. A middle aged man with considerable experience in positions of trust, with tact and sense of responsibility, with thorough knowledge of figures and accounting, desires a position that will occupy his time and give him a small income. J. 110, Friends' Intelligencer.

WANTED—POSITION AS MOTHER'S helper for summer. Experienced; can give references. Address W. 120, Friends' Intelligencer.

WOMAN OF EXPERIENCE IN PUBlic work desires a position of trust in hotel or institution. Address E. 131, Friends' Intelligencer.

POSITION WANTED—BY EXPERIenced, practical nurse and companion to invalid or elderly person. Assist with household duties. Philadelphia suburbs. Address B. 130, Friends' Intelligencer.

WANTED—WORKING HOUSEKEEPer for father and adult son; no laundry. Within half a square to station. Address D. 132, Friends' Intelligencer.

FOR RENT

FOR RENT—APRIL TO OCTOBER. Nine-room house with sleeping porch and garage, near river, at Riverton. Address Helen Lippincott, Riverton, N. J.

FOR RENT—IN LOWER CHELSEA, new bungalow, six rooms and bath, three bedrooms. Three months, $800. 56 N. DeLancey Place.

HOUSE FOR RENT—UP TO THE minute, two story bungalow, 5 bedrooms, 3 baths, shower. 9 S. Baton Rouge Ave., Ventnor, Atlantic City, N. J.

AT SEASHORE — DESIRABLE rooms; Friends' family. 9 S. Baton Rouge Ave., Ventnor, Atlantic City.

FOR SALE

FOR SALE—BRICK AND FRAME detached residence, well built; 10 rooms, bath, sleeping porch, glassed in; gas and electricity, modern conveniences; near Friends' School and Meeting House, Lansdowne, Pa. Apply J. 100, Friends' Intelligencer.

FUN

HOPEFUL

His relatives telegraphed the undertaker to make a wreath with the inscription "Rest in Peace" on both sides and (if there is room) "We Shall Meet in Heaven." The undertaker was out of town, and his new assistant handled the job. It was a startling floral piece which turned up at the funeral. The ribbon was extra wide and bore the inscription, "Rest in Peace on Both Sides, and if There Is Room We Shall Meet in Heaven."—*Christian Life.*

To the Lot Holders and others interested in Fairhill Burial Ground:

GREEN STREET Monthly Meeting has funds available for the encouragement of the practice of cremating the dead to be interred in Fairhill Burial Ground. We wish to bring this fact as prominently as possible to those who may be interested. We are prepared to undertake the expense of cremation in case any lot holder desires us to do so.

Those interested should communicate with William H. Gaskill, Treasurer of the Committee of Interments, Green Street Monthly Meeting, or any of the following members of the Committee:

William H. Gaskill, 3201 Arch St.
Samuel N. Longstreth, 1218 Chestnut St.
Charles F. Jenkins, 232 South Seventh St.
Stuart S. Graves, 3033 Germantown Ave.

ADVERTISING RATE in the FRIENDS' INTELLIGENCER, for Help Wanted, Positions Wanted, Rooms for Rent, Notices, and other classified advertisements without display, for each insertion, 2 cents per word, including name, initials and address. Answers may be sent to a box at the INTELLIGENCER office, if so directed.

For display advertising the rate is 10 cents per agate line, or $1.40 per column inch, each insertion. On ten or more insertions in a year from date of order, ten per cent. discount. Thus a four-inch single-column or two-inch double-column advertisement costs $5.60 each insertion, less ten per cent., or 5.04 net each time for ten or more insertions. Matter may be changed whenever desired, without extra charge.

Experience has proved the INTELLIGENCER to be a remarkably good advertising medium. All advertisements must "pass the censor!"

Address 140 N. 15th St., Philadelphia

The Friends' Intelligencer

ESTABLISHED 1844 | FOURTH MONTH 8, 1922 | VOLUME 79 NUMBER 14

Contents

REGULAR MEETINGS

OAKLAND, CALIF.—A FRIENDS' MEETing is held every First-day at 11 A. M., in the Extension Room, Y. W. C. A. Building, Webster Street, above 14th. Visiting Friends always welcome.

FRIENDS' MEETING IN PASADENA, California—Orange Grove Monthly Meeting of Friends, 520 East Orange Grove Avenue, Pasadena, California. Meeting for worship, First-day, 11 A. M. Monthly Meeting, the second First-day of each month, at 1.45 P. M.

CENTRAL MEETING OF FRIENDS (Chicago), meets every First-day in Room 706, 410 South Michigan Avenue, at 10.45 a. m. Visitors are invited.

FUN

A Massachusetts boy told the teacher that his sister had the measles. The teacher sent him home and told him to stay there till his sister got well. After he skipped joyfully away another boy held up his hand and said, "Teacher, Jimmy Dolan's sister, what's got the measles, lives in California."—*Kind Words.*

THE FRIENDS' INTELLIGENCER

Published weekly, 140 N. 15th Street, Philadelphia, Pa., by Friends' Intelligencer Association, Ltd.

WALTER H. ABELL, *Editor*
SUE C. YERKES, *Business Manager*

Subscription rates: United States, Mexico, Cuba and Panama, $2.50 per year. Canada and other foreign countries, $3.00 per year. Checks should be made payable to Friends' Intelligencer Association, Ltd.

Entered as Second Class Matter at Philadelphia Post Office.

The Friends' Intelligencer

The religion of Friends is based on faith in the "INWARD LIGHT," or direct revelation of God's spirit and will in every seeking soul.

The INTELLIGENCER is interested in all who bear the name of Friends in every part of the world, and aims to promote love, unity and intercourse among all branches and with all religious societies.

ESTABLISHED 1844 | PHILADELPHIA, FOURTH MONTH 8, 1922 | VOLUME 79 NUMBER 14

End the Lynching Evil

Of the iniquity of lynching in America no civilized person, to say nothing of one whose conscience has been trained in the school of Christ, needs longer to be convinced. Some, however, do not know of its extent, are ignorant of the fact that nearly 3,500 known mob-murders have taken place in our country in the last thirty-two years and, worst of all, that not more than a dozen of these excesses have been prosecuted and punished.

The danger which this form of violence constitutes for orderly government is appallingly obvious. Continued and unpunished disregard of law and legal processes, on the part of lynching mobs, can only weaken the cement that holds the State together.

Beyond its deplorable effect upon citizenship within our country, lynching has a further detrimental influence upon the nation. It shames and humiliates us before the world. Many Americans would doubtless be astonished to learn that our national shame is as well known abroad as at home. America as a Christian nation suffers from the gibes of Turks and Indians, of Japanese and Germans and French and the whole of Latin-America. We cannot expect our moral leadership to be rated very high so long as human beings can be publicly burned at stake, as were four in the United States within the year 1921.

One of the most serious difficulties confronting those who have sought to end lynching is the oft-refuted but still persistent statement that mob-murders occur only in punishment of "the usual crime." In point of fact, the best available statistics go to show that only 570 out of 3,436 lynchings in thirty years, or less than seventeen per cent., have ever been attributed to the crime of rape. In this connection it should also be borne in mind that accusation of this crime is not proof of guilt, for lynching itself renders it impossible to establish guilt by the means provided by law.

Even the Church has not yet awakened to a realization of the extent to which, in the lynching evil, fundamental Christian principles are at stake. The conscience of America must be aroused upon the iniquity of mob law. The nation must be called to repentance and to a better way of life. Friends' traditions in inter-racial work give them a special opportunity to lead in this cause.

Steps have recently been taken to secure suppression of lynching within the borders of the United States by Federal action. The Anti-Lynching Bill introduced into Congress by Representative Dyer of Missouri provides that culpable State officers and participants in mob violence shall be tried for felony; and that the sum of $10,000 may be recovered in a Federal court by the family of the victim from a county in which a lynching takes place.

The Dyer Bill has now passed the House and has been sent to the Senate. In the Senate it has been referred to the Committee on the Judiciary and, in turn, to a sub-committee whose chairman is Senator William E. Borah of Idaho.

Probably the contest over the Bill in the Senate will center on the constitutionality of the measure. Its sponsors maintain, as did Judge Guy D. Goff in his testimony before the House Committee on the Judiciary, that under the 14th Amendment, a failure on the part of the state to protect the lives of its citizens makes it just as incumbent upon the Federal government to supply that protection as though the state had intentionally denied it.

It is furthermore held that lynching is not merely murder, but consists of a conspiracy on the part of the mob to supersede the State, temporarily dethroning it and taking into their hands the power to punish individuals for actual or supposed guilt. In every civilized and Christian country, a person accused of crime is entitled to a trial by due process of law. No person in the United States, guilty or innocent, white or black, should be deprived of that right. This is what the Dyer Bill aims to secure.

Friends have done much good work against the lynching evil, and in supporting the Dyer bill. Now is the time when we should make our convictions of racial brotherhood more than ever known, and our influence in behalf of the Dyer bill doubly felt.

The Quakerism of the Founders

By Elbert Russell

IV

The Quakerism of William Penn

(In Two Parts—Part Two)

Tolerance

"Let the tares grow with the wheat, errors of judgment remain till removed by the power of light and conviction. A religion without it is inhuman, since reason only makes humanity. For my part, I frankly declare that I cannot think that God will damn any man for the errors of his judgment, and God forbid that all or most of the world err willingly in understanding."—*William Penn to the Duke of Ormond. Quoted from Sharpless' "A Quaker Experiment," p. 118, footnote.*

The Folly of Luxury

Such is now become our Delicacy, that we will not eat ordinary Meat, nor drink small pall'd Liquor; we must have the best, and the best cook'd for our Bodies, while our Souls feed on empty or corrupted Things.

In short, Man is spending all upon a bare House, and hath little or no Furniture within to recommend it; which is preferring the Cabinet before the Jewel, a Lease of seven Years before an Inheritance. So absurd a thing is Man, after all his proud Pretences to Wit and Understanding.—*Some Fruits of Solitude.*

Social Evils of Luxury

It is the vanity of the few great ones that make so much toil for the many small; and the great excess of the one occasions the great labour of the other. Would men learn to be contented with few things, such as are necessary and convenient, the ancient Christian life, all things might be at a cheaper rate, and men might live for little. . . . If men never think themselves rich enough, they may never miss of trouble and employment; but those who can take the primitive state and God's creation for their model, may learn with a little to be contented; as knowing that desires after wealth do not only prevent or destroy true faith, but when got, increase snares and trouble.—*No Cross, No Crown.*

Evil of a Privileged Class

Let it be sufficient for us to say, that when people have first learned to fear, worship, and obey their Creator, to pay their numerous vicious debts, to alleviate and abate their oppressed tenants; but above all outward regards, when the pale faces are more commiserated, the pinched bellies relieved, and naked backs clothed; when the famished poor, the distressed widow, and helpless orphan, God's works, and your fellow creatures, are provided for! then I say, if then, it will be time enough for you to plead the indifferency of your pleasures. But that the sweat and tedious labour of the husbandmen, early and late, cold and hot, wet and dry, should be converted into the pleasure, ease, and pastime of a small number of men; that the cart, the plough, the thresh, should be in that continual severity laid upon nineteen parts of the land to feed the inordinate lusts and delicious appetites of the twentieth, is so far from the appointment of the great Governor of the world, and God of the spirits of all flesh, that to imagine such horrible injustice as the effects of his determinations, and not the intemperance of men, were wretched and blasphemous. As on the other side, it would be to deserve no pity, no help, no relief from God Almighty, for people to continue that expense in vanity and pleasure, whilst the great necessities of such objects go unanswered: especially since God hath made the sons of men but stewards to each other's exigencies and relief.—*No Cross, No Crown.*

Vanity of Personal Pride

But personal pride ends not in nobility of blood; it leads folks to a fond value of their persons, be they noble or ignoble; especially if they have any pretence to shape or beauty. It is admirable to see, how much it is possible for some to be taken with themselves, as if nothing else deserved their regard, or the good opinion of others. It would abate their folly, if they could find in their hearts to spare but half the time to think of God, and their latter end, which they most prodigally spend in washing, perfuming, painting, patching, attiring, and dressing. In these things they are precise, and very artificial; and for cost they spare not. But that which aggravates the evil is, the pride of one might comfortably supply the need of ten. "Gross impiety that it is, that a nation's pride should not be spared to a nation's poor!" But what is this for at last? only to be admired, to have reverence, draw love, and command the eyes and affections of beholders. And so fantastic are they in it, as hardly to be pleased, too. Nothing is good, or fine, or fashionable enough for them; the sun itself, the blessing of heaven and comfort of the earth, must not shine upon them, lest it tan them; nor the wind blow, for

when married, according to the way of God's people used amongst Friends, out of whom only choose, strictly keep covenant; avoid occasion of misunderstanding, allow for weaknesses, and variety of constitution and disposition, and take care of showing the least disgust or misunderstanding to others, especially your children. Never lie down with any displeasure in your minds, but avoid occasion of dispute and offence; overlook and cover failings. Seek the Lord for one another; wait upon him together, morning and evening, in his holy fear, which will renew and confirm your love and covenant; give way to nothing that would in the least violate it; use all means of true endearment, that you may recommend and please one another; remembering your relation and union is the figure of Christ to his church; therefore, let the authority of love only bear sway your whole life.—*Penn's Advice to His Children.*

A Day in Thy Courts

I will begin here also with the beginning of time —the morning. So soon as you wake, retire your mind into a pure silence from all thoughts and ideas of worldly things, and in that frame wait upon God, to feel his good presence, to lift up your hearts to him, and commit your whole self into his blessed care and protection. Then rise, if well, immediately; being dressed, read a chapter or more in the Scriptures, and afterwards dispose yourselves for the business of the day, ever remembering that God is present—the overseer of all your thoughts, words, and actions, and demean yourselves, my dear children, accordingly, and do not you dare to do that in his holy, all-seeing presence, which you would be ashamed a man, yea, a child, should see you do. And as you have intervals from your lawful occasions, delight to step home (within yourselves, I mean), commune with your own hearts and be still; and, as Nebuchadnezzar said on another occasion, One like the Son of God you shall find and enjoy with you and in you; a treasure the world knows not of, but is the aim, end, and diadem of the children of God. This will bear you up against all temptations, and carry you sweetly and evenly through your day's business, supporting you under disappointment, and moderating your satisfaction in success and prosperity. The evening come, read again the Holy Scripture, and have your times of retirement, before you close your eyes, as in the morning; that so the Lord may be the Alpha and Omega of every day of your lives.—*Penn's Advice to His Children.*

Public Worship

Keep close to the meetings of God's people; wait diligently at them, to feel the heavenly life in your hearts. Look for that more than words in ministry and you will profit most. Above all, look to the Lord, but despise not instruments, man or woman, young or old, rich or poor, learned or unlearned.—*Penn's Advice to His Children.*

The Value of Silence

We are indebted to Montclair E. Hoffman for the extracts which follow. They are both taken from addresses recently delivered before the Anglican, or Episcopal, Synod of Jamaica. The first extract is by "Miss Turner, the headmistress of the largest Church of England high school in Jamaica; the second, by the "Lord Bishop of Jamaica." "These addresses," writes Montclair Hoffman, "are making us think very much of the message of Friends to Jamaica on the spiritual significance of silence."

"The second great necessity in the training of the Christian servant is the necessity of silence. We are only just beginning to realize that it is a necessity. It is being realized more and more that there is too much noise in the world. And our spiritual leaders are realizing it, too, and are preaching everywhere that Christians cannot be their best selves while they live perpetually in the "Dusty City of external relationships." The surface affairs of life—passing things—have become the only realities. We gauge our life by the amount of activity and excitement which we put into it. And is it not so in religion also? We measure our religious enthusiasm by the amount of bustle we put into our church work. We have no room for quiet. We do not feel the need of it. How many tell us so cheerfully that they hate to be alone, they can't bear their own company. Oh, the pity of such confessions!

"Quite apart from religion it is well known that silence possesses wonderful recreative and healing power. And in this age of over-work and nervous breakdown doctors cry aloud for quiet, for rest of body and mind. Why should we wait until we are ill, before we can be quiet? I want to touch very briefly upon the necessity for quiet as part of our equipment for service. It was Archbishop Faber who said, "How rare it is to find a soul quiet enough to hear God speak." The Bible is full of passages which tell of the value of silence. "Be still and know that I am God"; "My soul waiteth still upon God! We can hear God's voice in the silence. How can we serve if we do not wait and listen for our orders? Why should our prayers be a monologue? What help can we get from a friend if we do all the talking ourselves?

"The idea of silence seems as simple as daylight, but it is astonishing to find how difficult it is when we try to practice it. That is because we allow our words and thoughts to be so undisciplined in our daily life. We allow our thoughts and words to run on and on, and when we want to check them we find it is hard to do so. Yet it is immensely worth while to cultivate the habit of interior silence. As Christian women, it would add so much to our strength of purpose and character if we would check some of the chatter of our daily lives and also try to give silence a place in our prayers. There is tremendous power in silence. The great men of the world have been men of long silences and ponderings. It is the small people of the world who make the most noise—like the small insects?

"Away in the Eastern Hemisphere the peoples have learnt long ago the necessity of silence and contemplation for the building up of character. The young of India are trained in the school of meditation. That great-souled poet and philosopher, Rabinadrath Tagore, has much to teach us and many passages to give us—out of the silence. But it is a hopeful sign that in our day in the West a pioneer of education has included silence in the daily programme. If you go into a Montesorri school and spend a day with the babies you will find that in the midst of the abundant and wholesome activity which that system provides there is the silent period. The room is darkened and the little ones are left alone in silence. After a while, the teacher's voice calls them one by one by name into the next room and out they come with fresh faces and shining eyes manifestly strengthened and refreshed by the silence.

"It is a pity that we have not all had the benefit of such a training from our youth up. But it is never too late to begin, and I do want to plead the importance of silence as giving added power to our lives and enabling us to render better service. There are many attractive and interesting books on the subject. There is 'The Fellowship of Silence,' by Cyril Hepher, and another most inspiring and suggestive book is, 'Creative Prayer,' by W. Hermon. Away in Brown's Town some of us have gathered together weekly in silent fellowship, and we find it exceedingly helpful."

The quotation from the address by the Lord Bishop is as follows:

"I further urge that the clergy should at once invite their faithful laity to the Rectory or, if more convenient, to the Vestry to join with them week by week in united and informal prayer. The spiritual power of such meetings has been constantly experienced in the past. In this connection let me remind you of the value often experienced of corporate silence. The Society of Friends has long known and used that method of approach to God, and have much to teach us. Such silence helps to create that atmosphere of awe and worship which lifts our common prayer to higher levels of power and intensity."

Christianity and Economic Problems
II AND III

Lack of space compels us to greatly abridge Chapters II and III of this series, and to combine the two in one installment. The complete series will be later available in booklet form.

Chapter II deals with the general problem as to what view of poverty we should accept; whether it may be considered an advantage, or whether it be considered a curse. Both these points of view are given in detail. The attitude of Jesus toward poverty is then considered, and the following conclusion is reached regarding it:

"The ultimate test of every institution and every manner of life is to be found in its effects upon human beings. Poverty is neither good or bad in itself. It is good when human beings are uplifted, it is bad when they are degraded. Does Jesus commend or condemn poverty as a way of life? The only answer that can be given is that this depends upon what poverty does to human beings. Does modern poverty uplift or degrade those who live in this condition?"

The chapter as a whole is then summarized as follows:

"Having examined some of the favorable and some of the unfavorable aspects of poverty, are we now prepared to decide whether it is a misfortune or a blessing? Let us summarize the discussion. The more favorable aspects of poverty are: It compels work, prevents idleness and riotous living and consequently tends to develop character. It provides an incentive to achievement. It brings happiness through character and the satisfaction of creation and achievement.

"On the other hand, poverty causes sickness and ill health, leads to unwholesome family life, drives mothers and children into factories and other industrial establishments, produces ignorance, low mentality, criminality and undesirable citizenship, and is a source of bitterness, hatred, inefficiency, misery and despair.

"Is it possible to strike a balance between these two sides? The present writers are not disposed to be dogmatic at this point. There is not the slightest doubt that there are many striking illustrations of sterling character, brilliant achievement and genuine happiness in the midst of poverty. We are strongly convinced, however, that for every such case, there are hundreds of instances where modern enforced poverty is accompanied by ignorance, inefficiency, squalor, wretchedness and despair. The evidence at this point seems to us to be overwhelming. There is surely something in what Henry Ward Beecher used to say: 'Poverty is very good in poems, but very bad in the house. It is very good in maxims and sermons, but very bad in practical life.' "

Chapter III constitutes a study of how widespread this evil of poverty is at present in the United States. The general attitude is to feel that it is not a serious problem in the United States:

"It is recognized, of course, that there are still many cases of poverty and that it will probably be necessary to appropriate public funds and solicit private philanthropy for the support of charitable institutions for a long time to come. But, after all, the opinion prevails that the number of persons who are in need of charitable aid are relatively few; that the great mass of people in the United States are living in comfortable circumstances and are quite able to look after themselves. It is generally recognized that in the Orient and in parts of Europe, poverty is a very serious problem. But in the United States the situation is assumed to be quite different; the volume of poverty is not sufficient to cause alarm."

A detailed attempt is then made to obtain actual statistics, and the conclusion is reached that appallingly large groups are still suffering from poverty in the United States:

"In the light of the wage schedules, income tax returns, and analysis of the national income and minimum budgets, it seems difficult to question the essential accuracy of the conclusion reached by the Federal Commission on Industrial Relations that 'a large part of our industrial population are, as a result of the combination of low wages and unemployment, living in a condition of actual poverty. How large this proportion is cannot be exactly determined, but it is certain that at least one-third and possibly one-half of the families of wage-earners employed in manufacturing and mining earn in the course of the year less than enough to support them in anything like a comfortable and decent condition.' "

If there be some weaker one,
Give me strength to help him on;
If a blinder soul there be,
Let me guide him nearer thee.
Make my mortal dreams come true,
With the work I fain would do;
Clothe with life my weak intent,
Let me be the thing I meant,
Let me find, in thy employ,
Peace, that dearer is than joy;
Out of self to love be led,
And to Heaven acclimated,
Until all things sweet and good
Seem my natural habitude.

—*Whittier; Selected by Keziah R. Wilkins.*

"At Evening Time"

Days of my age,
Ye will shortly be past;
Pains of my age,
Yet awhile ye can last;
Joys of my age,
In true wisdom delight;
Eyes of my age,
Be religion your light;
Thoughts of my age,
Dread ye not the cold sod;
Hopes of my age,
Be ye fixed on your God.
—*St. George Tucker.*

I came across the following a few years ago: "When John Quincy Adams was eighty years of age, he met in the streets of Boston an old friend, who shook his trembling hand and said: 'Good morning, and how is John Quincy Adams today?' 'Thank you,' was the ex-president's answer, 'John Quincy Adams himself is well, quite well, I thank you. But the house in which he lives at present is becoming dilapidated. It is tottering upon its foundation. Time and seasons have nearly destroyed it. Its roof is pretty well worn out. Its walls are much shattered, and it trembles with every wind. The old tenement is becoming almost uninhabitable, and I think John Quincy Adams will have to move out of it soon. But he himself is quite well, quite well!'"

It is good to see old people with an unconquerable spirit. When their earthly course is almost run how often they fearlessly look into the future. It is well when they have such vital faith in God that they think of the worn body, shaken by every wind, as only becoming "uninhabitable," that soon they must "move out of it" as expressed by the venerable ex-president of the United States.

Generally speaking, there are two kinds of old age. One represents an attitude of mind that has become mistrustful or cynical after participating in the great adventure of life. This sort has not laid hold on that restful confidence in "the eternal Goodness" that Whittier sang of. It relinquishes its uncertain hold on this life with doubtfulness or dismay. God pity such—but let these remember that He ever loves them! The other kind of old age reviews its career as a wonderful school in which sweet and bitter lessons have been learned but during which preparation has been made for the mellow years and for the triumphant life beyond. These experiences have developed a firm reliance on the gracious intent of the Great Caretaker of men. The valley of the shadow of death may, in some of the waiting hours, look dark but beyond is the victory and the glory, the beauty and the joy that awaits the faithful child of God!

And now the searching question comes home to each one of us:—are we regulating our lives so that our swiftly passing days shall become fragrant and beautiful if ripe years shall overtake us? Are not youth and middle age the periods in which to form the habit of voluntary obedience to God and to acquire the happiness of unmixed trust in Him? Shall not his fortitude and grace finally sustain us when physical and mental powers shall diminish and our earthly ties are soon to be sundered? I ask my readers to think of the abundant possibilities associated with age and of how it can become a flower-strewn pathway to the gates of heaven! Zachariah, the far-seeing prophet, wrote:

"At evening time there shall be light!"

William C. Allen.

Last Thoughts From the Attic

By M. H. C. H.

If I have failed to be amused by the kind of joy some people seem to get out of life,

I have not been unhappy.

If to me the spectacle of the toiling masses is an enigma which I think absurd,

It is not because I am without sympathy.

If I feel that a crowded tram or a laden omnibus suggests suicide,

It is not because I do not love this life.

If a daily newspaper, a popular orator, or a famous boxer gives me a sickness at heart,

It is not because I consider myself superior in motive.

It is not because thousands succeed where I fail, and thousands fail where I fail too that

I hesitate to line up with the masses in their attempt to achieve.

If for me there is no home where others make theirs,

It is not because the roof of my own head is sufficient shelter.

Who knows that I have not discovered more joy in my attic than explorers ice in the Arctic?

Who knows that I have not known more sunshine than those living near the Equator?

Who knows that I may not have learned more of the stars than the watchers in their high towers of observation?

The philosophy of Life is not written in books, but on the faces of men.

Joy and sympathy are attitudes of mind more than they are pennies thrown to a beggar.

Life is the love of it and room wherein to live it.

Superiority exists only between Man and his

Maker and even there the basis is one of friendship.

Failure never came to anyone who stood alone—if he stood with his face to the Light.

It was in a moment of forgetfulness that we shut out the sky and made the stars to shine on slates.

But there are days ahead of which we only faintly have dreams, and hours that come to us as odors from far lands beyond our ken; and sometimes we feel a meaning in things which we do not understand, and see a light which is as warmth coming down to us; and sometimes we even catch whispers in a language only the heart can interpret from shores no ship ever sailed to!

I count the flights; I reach the door; I am out in the street; and I leave behind me memories unforgetable but travel with a religion yet more real!

Why Save Ignorant Peasants?

Someone has said that if you search far enough back in the history of a prince you will find a peasant, and if you search far enough back in the history of a peasant you will find a prince.

This is one of the deep reasons for saving starving, ignorant peasant children from starvation. Woodrow Wilson, in his book, "The New Freedom," says that life is always being renewed from the soil. And in our search we find that it is true that the great men of the world, those who have been most effective in making their talents play a useful part in the world, have been men who have come out of the loins of peasants, who have taken their strength from the soil.

Have we found ourselves thinking that the Russian people are so ignorant and so cattle-like that to save them is only, after all, to keep cattle alive? Have we thought that they are such clods that it might be better to give of our money and resources to people who offer far more possibility in their lives?

Have not some of us paraphrased that sentence which Nathaniel spoke 1900 years ago when he said: "Can any good thing come out of Nazareth?" And we have said that no good thing can come out of Russia. But Jesus came out of that degraded and miserable and ill-famed village of Nazareth which was despised throughout all his people; and cannot some great, true, useful life come out of even Russia?

Great and healing life has come out of Russia. That gracious apostle of the spirit of Christ, Tolstoy, came out of this Russia. And among this mass of people of the soil there were many who could respond to the appeal of this life which was lived in the spirit of love and mercy and kindly forgiveness.

And is it not strange that we have forgotten the story that for years was one of the forces which kept the soul of the world alive? There was no story that so thrilled our hearts, nor so deeply stirred every passion for liberty and truth and freedom within us, as the story of those brave, undaunted, fearless Russian patriots, who, under the cruelest autocracy the world has ever known, struggled that Russia might be free, and faced the horrible living death of the Siberian prisons for an ideal. These men and women, seeing in their minds the life of the future, free Russia, fought the forces of darkness and evil of a Czar's tyranny, and, torn from family and home and hope, went out unafraid to the frozen deserts of the North.

These men and women were the people of the soil, born of the peasants, reared in the hovels of a people kept ignorant and poverty-stricken by force for generations. These pure, unselfish idealists came out of even the peasants of Russia.

What has come, may come again. Because the lives who fought for freedom under a tyranny and who are still the ones who will lead Russia eventually to the light, came from the soil and the peasants, it is well to save Russian children. Yes, and because He who was born in a stable among the cattle and the lowly of the earth, and worked as a peasant and carpenter, became the One who made the way to God a pathway of light, it is well to save Russian children!

Russia Ever Calls

The latest cable from Murray Kenworthy in Russia states that children are dying in the children's homes and the hospitals because of the total lack of bedding material. It is hardly possible to conceive of places designed to take care of abandoned and orphaned children, and especially hospitals, being without adequate bedding supplies, but there are very few of these places which have any supplies, at all, of this character. The pictures which are being sent in tell the story even more graphically than words can. The children lie mostly upon tables and the floor, and on whatever parts of the iron and wood portions of the bed will hold their bodies. In several of the homes our workers saw rooms which were so filled with children that there was no space for them to all lie down upon the floor at once.

This situation affords the possibility of giving relief in a most effective way. Old bedding which is still of use is valuable; but new bedding material is, of course, most wanted in order to stand the severe wear to which it will be subjected. There is practically no limit to the amount of this which is needed. Stocks are now being made up at the Friends' Storeroom to provide for this need. Whatever you can give will be a most decided help.

The Confusion of Tongues and Sophistry of Speech

In the relation of man to man and of nation to nation the need is conspicuous for sincerity of speech and for abhorrence of hitherto accepted methods in politics and of indirection in world diplomacy. The perversion, conscious or unconscious, of the true meaning of words and the blight of insincerity in purposely attaching widely differing meanings to the same word, befog and cripple the mind itself. It results in a confusion of statement and purpose, fosters misunderstandings, shatters faith in one another and tends to undermine the very foundations of society.

When the descendents of Noah conceived the idea of a tower to reach unto Heaven, and when out of their own self-sufficiency they undertook thus to attain the heavenly things without the guidance of the Infinite God, it is written that the Lord came down to confuse their tongues and to "scatter them abroad upon the face of all the earth" because of their self-sufficiency.

The confusion of tongues is not really differences between languages, for a language as such may be accurately learned. It is rather the sophistry in the use of words of any language when men use them to deceive instead of to enlighten; which even throws around the mind of the man himself a confusion and a self-deception which precludes any exact or clear thinking.

Man can not live without God. If our finite mind arrogates to itself the ability to learn of the infinite things of life by means of its limited and unguided grasp then God has ordained that of necessity it must suffer until it is willing to listen to His voice in the soul.

If black is called white and white, black, the sophistry of life persists, and nothing but God speaking in the heart can illumine the mental path, clear the vision and lead to right thinking.

Many Friends and others in the past have very often had the experience of finding that the most "conclusive" and forceful arguments of the mind repudiated and reversed by the deep "feeling" and pleading of the heart in moments of silent waiting for the Soul to speak and the Lord of Life to lead on. This was what the sons of Noah were required to learn in the dim past and the same that is required of us today.

The Soul is superior to the mind. The Infinite is more than the finite. The Creator is above his creature. The Lord is over all. C. P.

A contented spirit is the sweetness of existence. —*Dickens.*

All We Need

The following anonymous poem was selected by Thomas E. Scott as suggesting the basis upon which must be judged the relation of Friends' principles to those of other church groups.

He who holds a sincere trust
In the wise, the true, the just—
In the worth of noble deeds—
His belief is all he needs.

He who holds to truthfulness—
Dares be true until success—
Fears no scoff, if duty leads—
His belief is all he needs.

Know, O men, that light divine,
Not on one but all doth shine,
Who in love life's lesson reads,
His belief is all he needs.

The Prison Comfort Club

With its March meeting, the Prison Comfort Club of Philadelphia completed its first half year. Nearly $1,200 has been collected and distributed to political prisoners and their families, except a reserve fund of $400, which is to be divided among those ordered deported, when they actually leave this country.

Several hundred letters have been written to and received from prisoners and their families. It may be of interest to quote from a recent letter (from Richard Brazier, serving a twenty-year sentence, slated for deportation to England): ". . . My mother, when a young girl, was a pupil in Miss Helen Cadbury's Sunday School class. Miss Cadbury, as you doubtless know, was a member of the famous Cadbury family of Bournville, amongst the leading Quakers of Great Britain. It was largely through Miss Cadbury's efforts that I came to America—as assistant in charge of a group of orphan boys and girls—emigrants." He incloses the latest of his prison poems, with many protestations, and only because it was especially desired of him. But to the writer, it seems of more than casual interest—

"The Hidden Heavens

"From my high prison window I see fall
The far, soft shadows of the summer eve.
I watch the warm glow climb the towered wall,
Then creep away in slow and lingering leave.
Soft falls the dusk upon the prison yard,
The twittering birds seek rest beneath the eaves,
The evening wind takes up its watch and ward
O'er prisoned flowers and buds and captive leaves,
And Night her sable curtain draws without.
But I can see no moon with silver sheen
The shades of deepest darkness put to rout,
And reign in radiant loveliness as queen
Of distant stars and of earth's lesser lights.
For here, where walls are high and windows barred,
Are hidden from my eyes the heaven of nights—
The heavens full of glory, silver-starred.
Only in dreams my hungry heart can keep
Dear memories of things I loved outside;
And when the bugle sounds the hour of sleep
I see once more what bars and walls would hide."

Have we no responsibility that men so-minded are left to spend twenty years behind iron bars, and only by accident do any of us learn of it? These men in prison, "substituting" for every one of us in the fight for freedom of speech, of thought, of faith, the fight "against the inhumanity of all war," have written again and again that above all else they desire the convictions for which they are paying this price, may be understood by those "on the outside." And nothing could show our friendship for them, could so companion them in their exile, as action born of sincere understanding of the principles for which they are working—and suffering.

Service Committee Notes

The Service Committee, through its Women's Work Department, is arranging for a sale of embroideries this spring. There will be handwork from Russia, Austria and Germany, including laces and linen embroidery. The first consignments of these goods are already on the way to this country in charge of returning workers. The date and place of sale will be announced later.

Beulah Hurley, who has carried the burden of the direction of the Unit in Russia during Murray Kenworthy's sickness, was taken ill with typhus a week ago, according to a cable received March 28th. The cable stated simply that it was a slight case.

Murray Kenworthy is convalescing slowly in Moscow. Nancy Babb is back at work. Cornell Hewson is also recovering from typhus in Minsk. Dr. Mary Tatum, a member of the Polish Unit, is also on the way to complete recovery in Warsaw.

Dr. Lucy Elliott, a physician from Flint, Michigan, who was accepted for service in Russia a month ago, has now arrived in the famine area, and has begun her work in taking care of the health of the Unit.

Friendly News Notes

In the *Swarthmore Phoenix*, we note that Dr. William I. Hull has been appointed one of the American delegates to the conference to be held in Copenhagen next August. This has been called by the World Alliance for International Fellowship through the Churches.

The meeting will consist of 121 delegates from twenty-nine countries, who will consider the possibility of inducing the European governments to undertake the reduction and limitation of land armaments which the recent Conference in Washington failed to accomplish.

Also, that Doctor Isabelle Bronk, head of the French Department, will act as delegate to two conventions of university graduates. During spring vacation she will represent both Swarthmore and the Middle Atlantic States district at a convention of the Association of University Women to be held in Kansas City; during the summer vacation she will attend the international convention of the above organization in the role of an American delegate.

Elizabeth B. Emmott, author of "The Story of Quakerism," and her sister, Anna B. Thomas, arrived recently from England, in time to attend Baltimore Quarterly Meeting, March 24th-25th, and Yearly Meeting at Fourth and Arch Streets, Philadelphia. They are visiting their sister, Mary Caroline Whitney.

The Young Friends' Movement of Philadelphia Yearly Meeting has published the outline "Through the Year with the Bible," copies of which may be obtained by application to the headquarters, 154 N. 15th Street, Philadelphia.

A recent book, "Painted Windows," is a series of "Studies in Religious Personality," and contains an interesting pen picture of Maude Royden. The author writes that the secret of her great appeal is that she preaches Christ as a Power and this discovery, the second great event in her life, she calls it, came about as follows:

"Miss Royden met a lady who had left the Church of England and joined the Quakers, seeking by this change to intensify her spiritual experience, seeking to make faith a deep personal reality in her life. This lady told Miss Royden the following experience:

"One day, at a Quakers' meeting, she had earnestly 'besieged the Throne of Grace' during the silence of prayer, imploring God to manifest Himself to her spirit. So earnestly did she 'besiege the Throne of Grace' in this silent intercession of soul that at last she was physically exhausted and could frame no further words of entreaty. At that moment she heard a voice in her soul, and this voice said to her, 'Yes, I have something to say to you *when you stop your shouting*.'

"From this experience Miss Royden learned to see the tremendous difference between physical and spiritual silence. She cultivated with the peace of soul which is the atmosphere of surrender and dependence, silence of spirit; and out of this silence came a faith against which the gates of hell could not prevail; and out of that faith, winged by her earliest sympathy with all suffering and all sorrow, came a desire to give herself up to the service of God. She had found the secret, she could use the power.

H. W. Peet.

Augustus Brosius, of Avondale, Pa., who has been sojourning at St. Petersburg, Florida, writes to us most enthusiastically of delightful climate and surroundings. The country is beautiful, the nights fine for sleeping, and in summer the mercury seldom rises above ninety degrees, with a good breeze usually prevailing.

He writes: "Among the enjoyments of the many visitors who are members of the Society of Friends, or in sympathy therewith, has been the opportunity of weekly meeting for worship at the beautiful hospitable home of Mrs. Sarah E. Gardner Magill, where the seasons of social and spiritual communion have been appreciated occasions. These gatherings, as well as at the First-day schools that preceded the meetings, have been openings for profitable expression. The bright, genial hostess, with her deep interest in what pertains to the welfare of the Society of Friends, as well as for humanity at large, has for years kindly opened her doors for this assembly of Friendly visitors, and at the closing service on last First-day there seemed to prevail a feeling of regret that the early departure of Mrs. Magill and many other Friends to their northern homes rendered the close necessary, and thus end the pleasant associations of the winter."

FRIENDS' YEARLY MEETING HELD AT FOURTH AND ARCH STREETS, PHILADELPHIA

At the meeting of Orthodox Friends, held during last week, the Representative Committee reported that fifty per cent. more business in the way of publishing Friends' books and pamphlets had been done by the Extension Committee during the last year. The membership of the

Yearly Meeting was shown to be 4,493; of these 170 are new members.

The report of the Committee on Christian Education in Foreign Lands recommended that all foreign missionary work done by Friends in the Philadelphia region be centralized and placed in charge of an especially appointed Yearly Meeting Committee.

After a protracted discussion, it was finally agreed that delegates are to be sent to the Conference at Richmond, to be held next September. Five years ago it was decided not to send delegates, as the Yearly Meeting felt that the beliefs of the Philadelphia body, especially as regards its steadfast objection to "paid ministry," would be compromised thereby. This year the decision was reversed, Friends feeling that the sending of delegates would be distinctly in keeping with Friends' doctrine of co-operation and sympathetic work and would not compromise any views which were held by some of the more conservative of the Philadelphia body.

Items From Everywhere

According to an article in the *Southern Workman*, "two of the twenty policewomen in Washington are colored women, and into their hands for investigation come all cases of first offense among colored women seventeen years or over, and those of all colored girls under seventeen, whether these girls are lawbreakers or merely destitute and dependent. Both of these policewomen bring to their work a wide social experience, one having served overseas as Y. M. C. A. worker during the World War, and the other, a graduate of a Western university, having been identified with representative social agencies in New York."

A saving of five billion dollars to the United States treasury in the next fifteen years as a result of the Washington conference is estimated by naval experts. It gives a little glimpse of what real world peace would mean in money only—which is only a small part of the story.—*Springfield Republican.*

A few months ago a group of men and women, most of them engaged in religious work, met in New York City, for the purpose of associating themselves in a fellowship for the building of a more Christian social order and for the more earnest practice of Christianity as a way of life.

The committee appointed at that meeting has now announced another conference to be held at Lake Mohonk, May 10-11. It is expected that during this conference, although its organization may be of the most informal kind, the Fellowship will come to definite self-consciousness and fit itself to become an educational force in churches and colleges throughout the country. Mr. Sherwood Eddy has been the moving spirit in the effort to form the fellowship. Requests for information may be addressed to the Secretary of the committee, Mr. Kirby Page, 311 Division Avenue, Hasbrouck Heights, New Jersey.

Recent investigations at St. Stephen's College, a college of liberal arts and sciences for men conducted under the oversight of the Episcopal Church which has sent many of its graduates to theological seminaries, show that if the Church is to recruit its ministry from the young men of the country, it must reach them while they are in their teens.

Of thirty-three men now at the college who intend to enter the ministry, only three made the decision after coming to college. Each of the other thirty conceived the idea long before entering St. Stephen's. Evidently if the Church is to reach the men who are suitable material for the ministry it must begin in the Sunday School, rather than after they have made up their minds as to a career and have entered higher educational institutions.

Does this not prove the value and need of First-day School work?

A group of sixty-eight prosecuting attorneys met recently in Albany, N. Y., to make an intensive study of the so-called "crime wave." In summing up the situation, they felt that the open violation of the Prohibition law had much to do with the disregard of all laws. In their appeal to the public they say, "Our so-called reputable and responsible citizens must not wink at the violation of some laws and thus lead to disrespect for all laws."

In order to assist in bringing about a more law-abiding spirit, the General Federation of Women's Clubs is seeking to make widely known the new scientific motion picture entitled "Safeguarding the Nation." The purpose of this film is to make the citizen realize that alcohol is his personal enemy; that its use, even in very small quantities, interferes with his efficiency and so lessens his income, his health, his happiness. Such knowledge, effectively given, will do more to bring about a willingness and a desire to have the Prohibition law enforced than any other one step that can be taken.

The leading temperance organizations are beginning to use it in their work. It should have the widest possible circulation, and for that purpose churches are being urged to show it in their evening services, to secure opportunities for its exhibition in industrial plants and other places where large numbers of men are gathered together. It is a five-reel picture, full of human interest, holding the attention from the first moment to the last. Further information will gladly be given by the Chairman of Motion Pictures for the General Federation of Women's Clubs, 220 W. 42d Street, New York, N. Y.

BIRTHS

KIRK—On Third month 9th, to Lewis Hughes and Laura Garrett Kirk, of Drexel Hill, Pa., a son, named Edwin Laurance Kirk.

WALKER—On Third month 8th, to Harry Thomas and Anna Frederick Walker, of Norristown, Pa., a son, who is named Harry Thomas Walker, Jr.

ZAVITZ—At Coldstream, Ontario, Canada, to Russell W. and Marguerite Haight Zavitz, on First month 13th, a daughter, who is named Elizabeth Evangeline.

MARRIAGES

TIMBRES-JANNEY—On Third month 29th, in Warsaw, Poland, Harry G. Timbres, son of Mr. and Mrs. Harry G. Timbres, of Edmondton, Alberta, Canada, and Rebecca Sinclair Janney, daughter of O. Edward and Anne Webb Janney, of Baltimore, Md.

DEATHS

HARPER—At Fox Chase, Pa., on Third month 27th, Smith Harper, 95 years. Int. Abington Meeting Grounds.

HEALD—In Kennett Square, Pa., Third month 28th, Joshua Heald, in his 83d year.

SHOEMAKER—In Philadelphia, Pa., on Third month 28th, Joanna Lukens, widow of Allen Shoemaker, aged 76 years. Interment Fairhill Friends' Burial Grounds.

COMING EVENTS

FOURTH MONTH

8th—Lecture at George School, by Tom Daly, on "The Laughing Muse." Admission, fifty cents.

8th—Salem First-day School Union will meet at Mickleton, N. J. Sessions at 10.30 a. m. and 2 p. m. Jane P. Rushmore and Grace Adams (Gloucester Co. S. S. Secretary) will speak during afternoon session on "First-day School Teaching." All cordially invited.

9th—Conference class at 15th and Race Streets, Philadelphia, at close of meeting for worship, at 11.40 a. m.

Speaker—J. Barnard Walton. Subject—The Work of Our Advancement Committee.

10th—Regular P. Y. F. A. Meeting. Illustrated lecture by John Henry Frome. Mary M. Baily, violinist.

10th—New York Monthly Meeting will be held at 7.30 at 110 Schermerhorn Street, Brooklyn. Supper will be served at 6.

14th—Joint meeting of Study Groups, and others interested, 15th and Race Street Meeting House, at 7.30 p. m. Led by Elizabeth B. Emmott. Subject—"A Fortnight in Early Quaker History."

15th—Abington First-day School Union at Abington Friends' Meeting House, Jenkintown, Pa.

16th—Elizabeth B. Emmott, author of The Spirit of Quakerism, expects to attend Fairhill Meeting for worship, Germantown Avenue and Cambria Street, Philadelphia, at 3.30 p. m.

23rd—Southern Half-Yearly Meeting, at Easton, Md.

25th—Western Quarterly Meeting, at London Grove, Pa.

27th—Caln Quarterly Meeting, at Christiana, Pa.

29th—Westbury Quarterly Meeting, at Brooklyn, N. Y.

NOTICE—Rummage Sale! Last week in April. Benefit of Friends' Home for Children. Will you help the children by saving rummage? Send direct to Home by April 24, or arrangements for collecting can be made by calling: Lula B. Dixon, 918 S. 49th Street, Woodland 2361-J; Anna Kirby Swope, 4926 Cedar Avenue, Woodland 2858-J; Anna Hall, 5301 Woodbine Avenue, Overbrook 0411.

NOTICE—"A Fortnight in Early Quaker History" will be the subject presented by Elizabeth B. Emmott at a meeting on Sixth-day evening April 14th, at 7.30 p. m., in Room No. 4, 15th and Race Streets Meeting House, Philadelphia. All interested are invited.

NOTICE—Concord First-day School Union, to be held at Swarthmore, has been postponed until Fourth month 22, owing to conflict with Somerville Day at Swarthmore College.

NOTICE—The Fellowship of Reconciliation will be addressed by Bishop Paul Jones, on "Realism in Religion," on Fifth-day, Fourth month 6th, at 8.15 p. m., in the Y. W. C. A. Building, N. E. Cor. Park Avenue and Franklin Street, Baltimore, Md. A general invitation is extended.

CORRECTION—The dinner-dance of the George School Club of New York is to be held Fourth month 7th, not 17th as published last week. The notice submitted contained the date published, but we have been informed that it is incorrect, and are glad to make the correction. The dinner is to be held at the White Rose Restaurant, 981 8th Avenue and 60th Street, at 6.30 p. m. for $3.00 per cover. All former George School pupils and those who are interested are invited. Remit to Edwin Freidel, Treasurer, 2812 Church Avenue, Brooklyn, N. Y.

Unity means oneness. The family that has one pocket-book, one desire, and equal love for all, expressed unity.

The struggle to get for oneself, to win money from others, defeats unity, for it is opposed to the Law of Love.

A body of men and women united for a good purpose are a wonderful power for good. The degree of their harmony, the oneness of their efforts, the completeness of their union, determines their power.

If one thousand brave and true men and women could be brought to work together with entire unity for a good cause, and could totally sink all personal desires, they could move the whole world within a decade.

Therefore—if you believe in your church, work with it. If you believe in your government, work with it. If you believe in your lodge, your club or your chums, work with them.—*Unity.*

LUKE 2. 14—AMERICA'S ANGELUS

"Glory to God in the highest, and on earth peace, good will toward men."

Stand back of President Harding in Prayer for Universal Peace by meditating daily, at noon, on the fourteenth verse of the second chapter of Luke.

Ask your friends to help make this a Universal Meditation for Universal Peace

Pass it on ***Friends in Christ***

FUN

A reader, remarking the cost of $18 per capita of a certain church, sends this:—A Negro preacher after a sermon on "Salvation Free" proceeded to announce a collection. A colored brother took him to task after the service for not practicing as he preached. "Patience, brudder, patience," said the parson. "S'pose yo' was thirsty an' come to a ribber. Yo' could kneel right down and drink yo' fill, couldn't you'? An' it wouldn't cost yo' nothin', would it?" "Ob co'se not. Dat's jes' de bery t'ing— "Well, s'posin' yo' was to hab dat water piped to yo' house, yo'd hab to pay, wouldn't yo'?" "Yassuh, but"—. "Wall, brudder, so it is in dis case. Salvation am free. It's de habin' it piped to yo' dat yo' got to pay for'."—*Christian Register.*

THE UPPER IS LOWER

The man had just informed the Pullman agent that he wanted a Pullman berth.

"Upper or lower?" asked the agent.

"What's the difference?" asked the man.

"A difference of fifty cents," replied the agent. "The lower is higher than the upper. The higher price is for lower. If you want it lower, you'll have to go higher. We sell the upper lower than the lower. In other words, the higher, the lower. Most people don't like the upper, although it is lower on account of it being upper. When you occupy an upper, you have to get up to go to bed, and get down when you get up. You can have the lower, if you pay higher. If you are willing to go lower, it will be higher."

But the poor man had fainted.—*Self-Starter.*

Who Needs the "Friends' Intelligencer?"

1. Every member of the Society of Friends who has joined through convincement. They need to know for what the Society stands.
2. Every newly-formed family of Friends. There is nothing like making a good beginning.
3. Every well-established family of Friends, in order that they may keep in touch with the work of the Society, and the latest presentation of our ideals and principles.
4. Everyone, either Friend or non-Friend, who wants to keep in touch with the relief work abroad.

To thy friends who have only a limited time to spend on reading, recommend the FRIENDS' INTELLIGENCER. It tells much in little space.

A three months' trial subscription, received during the next two months, will cost only thirty-five cents.

FUN

"What, giving up already?" said a gentleman to a youthful angler. "You must bring a little more patience with you next time, my boy." "'Taint patience I'm out of, mister; it's worms," was the reply.—*Boston Transcript.*

American Friends' Service Committee

WILBUR K. THOMAS, EX. SEC.
20 S. 12th St. Philadelphia.

CASH CONTRIBUTIONS
WEEK ENDING MARCH 27.

Five Years Meetings	$254.35
Other Meetings	
Darby Friends' First Day School	5.50
Baltimore Monthly Meeting	130.00
Menallen Monthly Meeting	10.00
Solesbury Monthly Meeting	11.00
Villa St. & Galena Ave. Meeting	18.00
Westbury Monthly Meeting	200.00
First Friends' Church, Cleveland	7.00
Cornwall Monthly Meeting	10.00
Miami Monthly Meeting	22.50
Westerly Meeting, Rhode Island	43.00
Cambridge Group of Friends	490.00
Contributions for Germany	59.50
For Austria	115.15
For Poland	339.50
For Syria	150.00
For Russia	13,480.76
For Russian Overhead	41.85
For General	650.00
For German Overhead	100.83
For Armenia	3.00
Refunds	7,884.56
	$24,026.50

WANTED

POSITION WANTED IN PHILADELPHIA or near vicinity. A middle aged man with considerable experience in positions of trust, with tact and sense of responsibility, with thorough knowledge of figures and accounting, desires a position that will occupy his time and give him a small income. J. 110, Friends' Intelligencer.

WANTED—POSITION AS MOTHER'S helper for summer. Experienced; can give references. Address W. 120, Friends' Intelligencer.

WOMAN OF EXPERIENCE IN PUBLIC work desires a position of trust in hotel or institution. Address E. 131, Friends' Intelligencer.

COMPANION DESIRES POSITION; experienced in care of elderly and semi-invalids. Reference. Address D. 140, Friends' Intelligencer.

WANTED—MOTHER'S HELPER, capable, with refined family. Address, Herschel G. Smith, 28 W. Greenwood Ave., Lansdowne, Pa.

WANTED—ATTENDANT FOR ELDERLY woman. Moderate salary. Address A. 141, Friends' Intelligencer.

WANTED—BY WIDOW AND DAUGHTER, a companionable and competent helper in the home. Phone Gtn. 2808-J before 9 a. m., or write, Mrs. William B. Kinsey, 1015 S. St. Bernard St., West Philadelphia.

PRACTICAL NURSE WISHES PERMANENT position, care of lady or gentleman. Good references. F. M. W., 5921 N. Broad St., Philadelphia, or Phone, Wyoming 4518-W.

POSITION WANTED—BY YOUNG woman, experienced in general office work; school or institution preferred where home is included in compensation. Address B. 142, Friends' Intelligencer.

POSITION WANTED—AS GOVERNESS or mother's helper. Address B. 143, Friends' Intelligencer.

WANTED—MAY 1ST, FRIEND trained in office work. Must be good typist. Apply in writing to X. 146, Friends' Intelligencer.

WOMAN OF REFINEMENT, PAST middle age, but active and in good health, desires position as companion to elderly lady, or one with impaired vision. Good reader. Congenial home rather than highest salary. K. B., 744 Carlton Ave., Plainfield, New Jersey.

WANTED—WORKING HOUSEKEEPER for father and adult son; no laundry. Within half a square to station. Address D. 132, Friends' Intelligencer.

FOR RENT

FOR RENT—APRIL TO OCTOBER. Nine-room house with sleeping porch and garage, near river, at Riverton. Address Helen Lippincott, Riverton, N. J.

FOR RENT—IN LOWER CHELSEA, new bungalow, six rooms and bath, three bedrooms. Three months. 56 N. DeLancey Place.

HOUSE FOR RENT—UP TO THE minute, two story bungalow, 5 bedrooms, 3 baths, shower. 9 S. Baton Rouge Ave., Ventnor, Atlantic City, N. J.

AT SEASHORE — DESIRABLE rooms; Friends' family. 9 S. Baton Rouge Ave., Ventnor, Atlantic City.

FOR RENT—AT BUCK HILL FALLS, cottage, from May 1st to June 5th. Apply, Mary S. A. Jenkins, Gwynedd, Pa.

FOR RENT—FOR THE SUMMER, AT Swarthmore, new house, furnished, two doors from Woolman School, near College Woods. Large living room, sleeping porch, two baths, five bedrooms. Every convenience for the housekeeper. Price $90 to right party. Phone 249-R. Address Juliet C. Kent.

FOR SALE

FOR SALE—BRICK AND FRAME detached residence, well built; 10 rooms, bath, sleeping porch, glassed in; gas and electricity, modern conveniences; near Friends' School and Meeting House, Lansdowne, Pa. Apply J. 100, Friends' Intelligencer.

THE UNFOUND NUMBER

Johnny—"Say, paw, I can't get these 'rithmetic examples. Teacher said somethin' 'bout findin' the great common divisor."

Paw, (in disgust)—"Great Scott! Haven't they found that thing yet? Why they were huntin' for it when I was a boy."

To the Lot Holders and others interested in Fairhill Burial Ground:

GREEN STREET Monthly Meeting has funds available for the encouragement of the practice of cremating the dead to be interred in Fairhill Burial Ground. We wish to bring this fact as prominently as possible to those who may be interested. We are prepared to undertake the expense of cremation in case any lot holder desires us to do so.

Those interested should communicate with William H. Gaskill, Treasurer of the Committee of Interments, Green Street Monthly Meeting, or any of the following members of the Committee.

William H. Gaskill, 3201 Arch St.
Samuel N. Longstreth, 1218 Chestnut St.
Charles F. Jenkins, 232 South Seventh St.
Stuart S. Graves, 3033 Germantown Ave.

The Friends' Intelligencer

ESTABLISHED 1844 | FOURTH MONTH 15, 1922 | VOLUME 79 NUMBER 15

Contents

EDITORIAL

GENERAL ARTICLES

AMONG OUR MEETINGS

FOR SALE

REGULAR MEETINGS

OAKLAND, CALIF. — A FRIENDS' Meeting is held every First-day at 11 A. M., in the Extension Room, Y. W. C. A. Building, Webster Street, above 14th. Visiting Friends always welcome.

FRIENDS' MEETING IN PASADENA, California — Orange Grove Monthly Meeting of Friends, 520 East Orange Grove Avenue, Pasadena, California. Meeting for worship, First-day, 11 A. M. Monthly Meeting, the second First-day of each month, at 1.45 P. M.

CENTRAL MEETING OF FRIENDS (Chicago), meets every First-day in Room 706, 410 South Michigan Avenue, at 10.45 A. M. Visitors are invited.

FUN

A shortsighted old lady went into a large curio shop. After pottering about for some time she asked the assistant, "How much is that Japanese idol worth—the one near the door?" "It is worth a great deal," replied the assistant. "It's the proprietor."—*Christian Register.*

NEEDFUL

On one of the tombstones in an old New England cemetery appears the following inscription:

Here Lies Jonathan Steele—
Good and Upright Citizen
Weighed 250 Pounds
Open Wide Ye Golden Gates
—Ladies Home Journal.

THE FRIENDS' INTELLIGENCER

Published weekly, 140 N. 15th Street, Philadelphia, Pa., by Friends' Intelligencer Association, Ltd.

WALTER H. ABELL, *Editor*

SUE C. YERKES, *Business Manager*

Subscription rates: United States, Mexico, Cuba and Panama, $2.50 per year. Canada and other foreign countries, $3.00 per year. Checks should be made payable to Friends' Intelligencer Association, Ltd.

Entered as Second Class Matter at Philadelphia Post Office.

To the Lot Holders and others interested in Fairhill Burial Ground:

GREEN STREET Monthly Meeting has funds available for the encouragement of the practice of cremating the dead to be interred in Fairhill Burial Ground. We wish to bring this fact as prominently as possible to those who may be interested. We are prepared to undertake the expense of cremation in case any lot holder desires us to do so.

Those interested should communicate with William H. Gaskill, Treasurer of the Committee of Interments, Green Street Monthly Meeting, or any of the following members of the Committee.

William H. Gaskill, 3201 Arch St.
Samuel N. Longstreth, 1218 Chestnut St.
Charles F. Jenkins, 232 South Seventh St.
Stuart S. Graves, 3033 Germantown Ave.

SCHOOLS.

NOTICE—Concise statements of the principles of the Religious Society of Friends and their application to the problems of every day living, including "The Spirit of Quakerism," by Elbert Russell; "Preparation for Life's Greatest Business," by Rufus M. Jones; and other articles by Henry W. Wilbur, Howard M. Jenkins, Elizabeth Lloyd, Jesse H. Holmes, O. Edward Janney, Edward B. Rawson, etc., to be had free on application to Friends' General Conference Advancement Committee, 140 North Fifteenth Street, Philadelphia, Pa.

The Friends' Intelligencer

The religion of Friends is based on faith in the "INWARD LIGHT," or direct revelation of God's spirit and will in every seeking soul.

The INTELLIGENCER is interested in all who bear the name of Friends in every part of the world, and aims to promote love, unity and intercourse among all branches and with all religious societies.

ESTABLISHED 1844 | PHILADELPHIA, FOURTH MONTH 15, 1922 | VOLUME 79 NUMBER 15

On To Richmond!

Though five Yearly Meetings are still to come during the intervening period, it is not too early for Friends to begin planning for the gathering of all our Yearly Meetings in this summer's General Conference.

The Conference is to convene this year, August 26th to September 2d, at Richmond, Indiana. It has not met in Richmond since 1898, the only meeting in Indiana since that time having been at Winona Lake, in 1908.

We rejoice that the Conference meets this year in the middle west. This fact should enable a full attendance of Western Friends, and the energy and enthusiasm generated by the Conference will undoubtedly react as a powerful stimulus upon the surrounding communities of Western Quakerism. Equally important will be the gain to Eastern Friends through fellowship with a large group of Friends from the West.

Two things come to mind as the fundamental bases, whenever one thinks of such a gathering as the General Conference: the program and the fellowship of social contact. The latter calls for little comment. It is the overtone that is struck whenever men gather in a spirit of concerned truth-seeking; an overtone which is as inevitable as it is intangible. Equally with the words we hear and the thoughts we gain, it sends us back to our tasks determined to strive more earnestly that human fellowship in a universal sense may prevail.

The program for the Conference is being built up around the idea of relating our essential religious foundations to the needs of the present world. Charles Foster Kent, of Yale, is to deliver the central lecture course; a course based upon Biblical interpretation. Prof. Kent's writings are too well known, and his course at the Summer School last year is too well remembered, to need comment. He will come to Richmond directly from his trip to Palestine and the Near East. The subjects of his four lectures are to be: "The Basis of Christian Unity," "The Solution of Industry's Problems," "Recreation and Religion," and "The Way to Find Happiness."

Around this central course, will be woven a program of lectures, round tables and discussion groups based upon the relation of our religion to the needs of our world. Prohibition, the industrial problem, Friends' service, education, peace work in general and disarmament in particular, are among the subjects thus far listed to receive attention.

Details concerning the program, transportation and accommodation will be forthcoming as the various committees complete their work, and will be published in future issues of the INTELLIGENCER. But none of us needs to wait for details before deciding to go to Richmond. We all need the stimulus which the Conference will afford, and the Conference needs all of us. Whether it proves a dead and formal gathering, or a dynamo of spiritual vitality depends upon the amount of enthusiasm and life which we take to it. Our committees are providing for all arrangements, and offer the promise of live sessions. Shall not Friends as a whole add the final and most essential contribution to the success of the Conference, by attending in unprecedented numbers? *On to Richmond!*

Jesus taught the doctrine of personal responsibility. Casting aside all traditions of creed, ceremonies and emotionalism, he taught us to worship God through faith in man. It is said that he was the first true Democrat who ever lived. He was a respecter of personality, not of persons. He taught us to deal with our neighbor as man to man and to pray as man to God. He taught that all men are our neighbors, and that whatever injustice we do to the least of these falls likewise on us. He taught the sanctity of human values, that loving man is our only way to the love of God. To the young and strong in this our century comes the call for human service as never before in the lifetime of the world. —*David Starr Jordan, in Unity.*

New Churches for Old

A Book Review

By Jesse H. Holmes

The sub-title of this new volume by John Haynes Holmes,* "minister of the Community Church of New York," is "a plea for Community Religion." It is written, says the preface, "in the deliberate conviction that the churches as they exist today are an intolerable interference with the program of modern life, and are therefore to be transformed or replaced as speedily as possible; that Protestantism in all its forms, both orthodox and liberal, is dead as a religion today." To meet this situation the author undertakes to present "(1) an analysis of the situation today, both inside the churches and out; and (2) a constructive program for the organization of new churches to supplant the old."

The analysis of the situation outlines familiar facts concerning the general collapse of the churches: —empty pulpits, dwindling congregations, lack of influence, lack of leadership. In a time crying aloud for a principle of unity among men, a time when millions are hopelessly entangled in group-hatreds and group-conflicts, the churches concern themselves with ancient formulas and divide endlessly into competing denominations. "Denominationalism may be briefly described as a division of religious forces on trivial issues to the service of private ends." The attempts of the liberal element to "subordinate non-essentials to essentials" have not been successful, producing only more denominations, and not very efficient ones at that. The attempts to federalize the sects have had only slight success.

Meanwhile the religion of Jesus, which "had no theology,—no creed—no church," forsaken by institutions, has appeared again and again in human hearts and lives. The God that "is love" reappears in every generation and among every people. It came to noble expression in the Reformation, and then was institutionalized. It has come again in the struggle for Democracy, and again has been made into a machine. The task is still before us to make a society which shall be ruled by "the King who is present when just men foregather."

To this end we must do some clear thinking and revise our standards of value. We must get rid of the "two compartment mind," and throw down the wall of separation between the so-called "sacred" and "secular." The distinction is a wholly unreal one, and has been used to keep the influence of religion in the regions of abstraction and away from the actual affairs of men. It may be remarked in passing that the appeal often heard among us for keeping our religious "spiritual" is the same effort to prevent the demands of our faith from interfering with our comforts, or unsettling our habits. In fact we know of no values but human values. All institutions justify themselves only by serving men. And as we know only this life, and nothing of the life after death, our institutions must justify themselves by making this world a place of increasing happiness, and of increasing opportunity for the development of human capacities and powers.

Thus the Church must be "the institutional embodiment of a new religion of democracy." It must set aside theology, replacing it by sociology. It must give up creeds, replacing them by fellowship. It must become inclusive instead of exclusive, opening its doors to all members of the community whatever their beliefs or non-beliefs. It may not be narrowly and technically Christian, for Jew, Buddhist or Confucian should be welcomed. Its aim must be that presented by Josiah Royce, as quoted in the author's foreword,—"the creation on earth of the Beloved Community"; all else is "the accident of your special race or nation, or form of worship or training, or accidental personal opinion or devout mystical experience."

Its organization must be purely democratic and its support the same. Its message and work will vary according to the community, but its purpose everywhere and always will be that of arousing, stimulating and developing the higher nature of man. It will be free to seek for God in any way, its theology being not prescribed, but experimental It will be free to consider any plans for the improvement of social conditions, since its purpose is to bring in "the kingdom on earth." It will be the center of intellectual ferment and of social mingling. It will unite classes, races and sects in one inclusive friendliness.

All this should be of special interest to Friends. For the ideal of our Society from the start has been that it should be, as its name implies, a "Society of Friends." It has never accepted a creed as a proper basis for membership, and has made no authoritative demand for any particular set of beliefs. It has no formulated theology, but depends on individual experience with God expressed in varying terms—ac-

*"New Churches for Old," Dodd, Meade and Company. New York. 1922.

cording to peculiarities of person, time and place. It has taken continuous responsibility for social regeneration. Our meeting-houses have been centers for discussion of slavery, temperance, prohibition, woman's suffrage, peace and war, and many other social problems. Our principles, therefore, accord exactly with the ideals proposed for the Community Church; but we have not succeeded in the matter of organization and management. The special form of these, however, is non-essential. Many of our meetings are appointing "executive secretaries" to manage the service of our meeting to the community. Our forms of worship are flexible. We want our silent hour punctuated by spontaneous prayer and testimony; but that does not involve any condemnation of those who desire music and ritual at other times. It should be no small encouragement to us to realize that the trend of religion is toward the personal search for God, a general friendliness to man, and a struggle for a better world. Shall we not recognize our essential unity with this program, and give it our hearty support whenever possible.

Friends will do well to read and consider this new book,—"New Churches for Old," by one who has always been a friend of the Friends.

Religion in the Home

A concern arose in the New York Meeting for Ministry and Counsel that more attention be paid to worship and religious training in the home. In the first place, we felt the need for it in order to prepare children to understand and make use of the meeting for worship. Then we realized that all of us need to devote more attention to cultivating our religious natures at home; parents must feel that periods for religious training are worth while for themselves if they wish to impress their value upon the children. No doubt, all family groups need some form of common religious expression. A small committee collected valuable suggestions from various Friends upon this subject and has summarized them in the following report:

Purpose: We believe that some form of daily group devotion tends to give to our lives greater repose and power by turning our thoughts from the details of our material experiences in search of spiritual strength. Our efforts toward the development of deeper spirituality in our lives undoubtedly will strengthen our influence with all with whom we come in contact.

Avoidance of Formality: We advise Friends to form the habit of having some daily religious exercise; but there is little value in the mere form of devotion. It should be the sincere expression of a desire for higher guidance. Experiments in regard to the character and content of the exercise are useful, and some variety is almost essential. It should be remembered that we should allow ourselves no omissions when trying to form any new habit.

Children: It is easier to begin such a custom with children when they are quite young. Little children are sensitive to spiritual atmosphere and can share in it even if they do not understand the exercise intellectually. But we believe that with care some form of devotion can be started when children are older, though there may be several failures before the right method is discovered. It should be borne in mind that children often have a tendency to conceal, by bluster and opposition and scoffing, the religious impulses that they really have.

Prayer: Prayer is perhaps the most important form of worship. Men used to pray to God in order to change his mind; now we pray to change our own minds so that we may think and live in conformity with his will and receive of his power. Harry Emerson Fosdick's book, "The Meaning of Prayer," is helpful in understanding this subject.

The "silence" that many Friends observe at the beginning of meals should be a brief period of thankfulness and prayer. If it is, the children will feel it; but it may also be worth while to explain to them how to use the silence. Though many of our meals are hurried and irregular, it seems desirable that we take care to have all join in the silence at least once a day. Even upon a child of three the practice of silence before meals has become such a habit that a meal though eaten alone must be preceded by the customary bowing of the head. This one case illustrates the value of well-formed habits which lead later to understanding. The repetition of a simple prayer at bed time is just the foundation of a habit which leads later to priceless periods of communion with the Divine Source. One Friend writes, "If your children feel no conscious need of prayer take their little hands in yours at nightfall and pray in silence. Thus quietly, gently, in time they will be led to feel the Presence of God."

Readings: Daily readings from the Bible, religious poems or hymns, or some other selections that may be helpful are recommended. The close of the evening meal is suggested as a good time for this.

The following books are suggested: Various versions of the Bible; Moffatt, Weymouth, Prof. Kent's "Shorter Bible"; "The Soul of the Bible," etc.; "Daily Strength for Daily Needs"; "The Meaning of Prayer" and "The Meaning of Service," by Fosdick; "Power Through Repose" and "Every Day Living," by Anna Payson Call; Unity Hymns, Whittier's Poems, "Toward Democracy," Edward Carpenter; "The Arm of God," Dunkerly (this is a collection of short accounts of incidents when people were saved by the action of spiritual forces); Rauschenbusch's "Prayers"; Passages from THE INTELLIGENCER.

When there are children in the family, poems and other pieces of good literature that are not distinctly religious may serve the purpose; or a long story read serially may provoke valuable discussions of ethics and moral values. The following books for children are both interesting and religious: "Quaker Saints," Violet Hodgkin; "A Child's Story Garden"; "The Garden of Eden," "The Castle of Zion" and other collections of Bible stories by Hodges; "The King of the Golden River," Ruskin; "The Great Stone Face," "The Golden Touch."

Quakerism: The following suggestions are designed to create an understanding of Quakerism and interest in our meetings:

Home discussion of some good thought as preparation for attendance at meeting. (Many Friends urge the importance of the *entire family* attending meeting.)

Family discussion of the origin and meaning of Quakerism.

Study and discussion of the Book of Discipline by every member of the family old enough to understand, with emphasis upon practice of its precepts.

Discussion of the origin and purpose of our Preparative, Monthly, Quarterly and Yearly Meetings, with advance information as to subjects to be brought up at these meetings.

Other Suggestions in regard to *Children:*

Children can be led to God through nature; through nature study, and through being shown the mysteries of life and growth by the care of plants and animals.

In place of prayer with the children at night an evening talk with them separately or together may be useful sometimes. "What has thee done today to make somebody happy?" is a question that should go deeply into the soul of every child.

Family contest games for children; naming the books of the Bible, the Prophets, the Disciples; naming famous Friends and telling something of their lives.

Learning texts or sentiments and reciting them to the family group.

Family study of beautiful pictures.

Family walks, dwelling on the beauty of the world.

Less family vanity in keeping up with the world; more family effort to serve one's fellows.

In selecting reading and Quakerism material for the children, be careful not to repeat what they have had in school or First-Day School. But what they have in school may often be an excellent basis for further discussion.

Beware of adverse criticism of minor details in connection with anything that you wish your children to respect in its main issues. They will remember the criticism of the detail, and often magnify it out of all proportion, and sometimes completely lose sight of the good in the thing as a whole.

All of these suggestions have been tried and were considered helpful. We hope that they may be suggestive to others in the effort to make our religion a vital power in our lives, so that we may make a contribution toward bringing in the Kingdom of God.

CORA H. CARVER,
Chairman of Sub-committee.

The Sweep of the Ages

A Book Review

I have just finished reading two important books; the "Story of Mankind,"* and the "Outline of History."† I wish that every Friend would read both of them, for no matter how narrow or how broad the reader's mind, it cannot fail to be broadened by the reading. The two books are in no way competitive; they were written from different viewpoints and each has required, and received, serious and long sustained effort.

If only one may be read, the "Outline" is the more important. It gives in orderly sequence, a reasoned view of the elemental causes and effects which have made the history of the various groups of races, of historic, prehistoric, paleolithic, and earlier mankind. I wish especially that all who dislike the thought of being "descended from monkeys" (and who does not?) would read this book and learn how crude and unintelligent a caricature of the process of evolution is that timeworn slogan. A current backsurge of timid thought, most ably expressed by a prominent Chautauqua lecturer (and which may thereby cause the happy effect of a profitable lecture season) shows a belated fear of the doctrine of evolution. To the earnest Friend it ought not matter whether or not the theory of evolution is true, for theology only may be confused by scientific truth; religion being itself true, cannot be confused or injured by any other truth. But the reflective mind cannot well doubt the broad general principle of evolution unless one shuts out all of the archeological and geological knowledge added in the last sixty years, including the proofs found in the cave-floors of France by those abbes, who are none

* The Story of Mankind. Hendrik Van Loon, 1921. $5.00. Boni & Liveright, N. Y.

† The Outline of History. H. G. Wells. Third edition, revised, one volume, 1921. $5.00. McMillan & Co., N. Y.

the less earnest sons of the Church, for all their enthusiastic digging up of bones of men buried 25,000 years.

Wells shows evidence of a deeply religious nature and outlook. His treatment of the principal great religions, and consideration of their effect in humanizing and enriching human life, are well and fairly done. All Friends can agree with most of what he says about religion, past, present and to come, and all might profitably read the remainder with that charity in which it was so evidently written. His consideration of the present condition of human life and society in the world, and his hopes and fears for the future, may not fully meet the approval of all minds, but will quite certainly leave the careful reader in a thoughtful and more earnest state of mind.

His fairness of judgment is illustrated in his conclusive reflection on the character of Nero. "Before a man condemns Nero as a different species of being from himself, he should examine his own thoughts very carefully.".

The "Story of Mankind" was written to give young people a panoramic glimpse of Life, from the scum of the worn sea-floor, up through the lowest forms of life, through amphibian, reptile and furred mammal, up to Man, and something of human life to the present time. The author makes of human life—of all life—a Great Romance. Indeed, it is The Great Romance, though I had not realized the idea until I read his story. The grandsire may read this book with as great profit as the grandchild, for though he may feel that he has heretofore read something of all these matters, he will find in the logical arrangement of facts unknown to his earlier reading, an interest that will seldom let him drop the book through drowsiness.

Therefore I hope all Friends will read both these books.

John Cox, Jr.

William Penn As a Courtier

Lord Macaulay has not been the only person to be critical of the connection of William Penn, founder of Pennsylvania, with the Courts of Charles II and James II, so that the appearance in print for the first time of a reminiscence concerning the "Quaker Courtier" is noteworthy.

This has been handed down in a letter which has just come into the possession of the Society of Friends' Reference Library, Devonshire House, Bishopsgate, London, E. S. 2, from the collection of the late J. J. Green, of Hastings.

"On one occasion," the letter runs, "coming to Reading and being about to proceed thence to London in order to attend at the Court of James II, as was his frequent practice, several Friends manifested their uneasiness at his being so much at the Court, expressing their fears that in such a place, and in such company, he would be in danger of departing from that simplicity of demeanour which Friends believed it their duty to maintain.

"W. Penn, after listening to their observations, expressed his wish to take one of their number with him to the Court of James, and one of them accordingly accompanied him thither. Being duly introduced, he remained with him during the whole time, thus having a full opportunity of observing the tenour of W. P.'s carriage, as well towards the king as towards others with whom he came in contact. Finding that his conduct, mode of address and general conduct were quite in harmony with his profession and practice as a Friend, he was entirely satisfied and was thus put in a position to allay the uneasiness of such of his friends as had entertained doubts on this head."

On another occasion during the visit to Reading several Friends spoke to him after meeting saying they should be glad of his company to dine, but feared they had not suitable accommodation or provision, etc., for him. At last, a plain, honest woman asked him to her house, saying she could furnish all he could require. W. P. accepted her invitation and accompanied her to her very humble dwelling, in which was a small shop where she sold provisions, etc. She took thence some "bread, butter and cheese, and W. Penn made a very sufficient dinner, much enjoyed his visit, and, at parting, heartily thanked her for her hospitality and especially for her cordial kindness and hearty welcome."

These anecdotes are recorded in a letter of Thomas Mounsey, of Sunderland, to Thomas Robson, of Liverpool, according to the current *Journal of the Friends' Historical Society*, dated 10/3/1850. He quotes as his authority Joseph Naish, of Congresbury, who died in 1822, aged 72, who was acquainted with a man whose father knew William Penn when he resided near Reading.

Hubert W. Peet.

Guest Or Refugee?

God is omniscient?
  Yes—lent your mind to know;
And omnipresent—
  Where your feet will go.
All powerful?
  With your hands, power to guide;
But lacking you,
  God is a hope denied.

Walter H. Abell.

Christianity and Economic Problems

IV

Do Great Fortunes Help or Hinder Social Progress?

(Abridged to Summary Form)

"For the purpose of this discussion let us arbitrarily define a great fortune as one valued at a million dollars or with an income of $50,000 per year. It is estimated that in 1918 there were 21,453 millionaires in the United States. We are also told that: 'More than 40 families in the United States have in excess of 100 millions each. More than 100 other families have in excess of 50 millions each. More than 300 other families have in excess of 20 millions each.' The question with which we are concerned in the following paragraphs is this: Is it a good thing or a bad thing for the country as a whole to have this degree of concentration of wealth?

Do the Rich Deserve to be Rich?

"Before we examine both sides of the argument, a prior question must be dealt with. It is often contended that regardless of whether great fortunes are a blessing or a menace to the country, society has no right to interfere because to do so would be an unwarranted invasion of private ownership.

"The basis of this attitude is that wealth is achieved by superior ability, self-control, and a high degree of self-sacrifice. . . .

"There is surely much to be said for this point of view. It is unfortunately true that many people have low intelligence and poor judgment, and that many others are self-indulgent, lacking in thrift and never able to save anything. From the viewpoint of social welfare it is highly questionable whether this latter group should receive the same rewards as are given to the intelligent, industrious and thrifty.

"And yet there are several fallacies in the argument suggested above. As a matter of actual fact, were the fortunes of the 21,000 millionaires in the United States achieved by unusual brain power, hard work, and self-denial? There is considerable doubt as to whether very many, if any, of these great fortunes were achieved solely in this manner. Let us examine the sources of a few of them."

The sources from which several large American fortunes were derived are then considered, among them those of the Astor family, of the Standard Oil Company, and of Andrew Carnegie. It is found that practically all of our fortunes amounting to more than a million dollars have been acquired, not primarily through personal ability, but through the control of natural resources, or through speculation and manipulation of stocks. A study of the income tax returns for 1918 is used to indicate that in fortunes of from $100,000 to $150,000, not more than 41 per cent. of the total income is derived from personal services and business, 59 per cent. being derived from the control of property. The amount derived from the latter source increases as the fortune increases, until in those of $2,000,000 and over, only 4 per cent. of the income is obtained through personal services, while 96 per cent. comes from property.

It is admitted that many men possess business genius which deserves great reward, but it is contended that men in many other walks of life—teachers, physicians, and religious leaders, for example—have equal genius and render equally important service to humanity. Why should the business genius receive more material recompense than they, if service to society is the basis upon which the recompense is made?

Are Great Fortunes a Social Asset?

They give opportunity for leisure, and the cultivation of personality, but they lead to dangers of idleness and intemperance. Jesus warned repeatedly of the dangers of great riches.

Great fortunes are sources of charity, but there are tremendous social dangers in the concentration of wealth. It leads to the control of public institutions, and is responsible for legislation which is more concerned with the protection of property than with the welfare of human life.

Great fortunes make possible large scale production, and many contend that autocracy is essential to modern life. "Government and industry are safer in the hands of the self-controlled few than they would be under the mediocre and undisciplined masses." Even from the basis of material efficiency, this contention is open to question; but regardless of its economic bearing, there is a higher reason why this doctrine is to be questioned:

"Over against this doctrine of paternalism, there is a widespread belief in real democracy. Those who believe in democracy say that the real issue is not the material prosperity of the country so much as it is one of the status and relationship of peoples. A strong case can be made out that many negroes were better fed, clothed and housed while they were slaves than after they were freed. This fact does not necessarily mean that Slavery was better than freedom. The principles involved in this question as to whether paternalism is better than democracy are in a very real sense parallel with those in the issue of slavery. The fundamental issue is that of personal status.

"The ideal of a superior people controlling wealth and privilege and handing down favors to other people is a fundamental contradiction of the worth and dignity of human beings. It is an absolute denial of brotherhood. The continuation of paternalism can have no other result than the creation of a servile people. This is too great a price to pay even if it could be demonstrated beyond doubt that paternalism results in higher production and greater industrial efficiency. After all, a nation's life consists not in the abundance of *things* possessed, but rather in the quality of its men and women. . . ."

"In the present chapter we have not attempted to say whether or not modern business methods are contrary to the principles of Jesus. The ethics of speculation, private exploitation of natural resources, unearned increment and such questions will be discussed in a later chapter, as will also such proposed solutions of the problem of concentrated wealth as the steeply graduated income tax, the inheritance tax and the legal limitation of great fortunes.

"We have sought to raise only one issue in the chapter: Do great fortunes help or hinder social progress? This question will be answered as we answer such questions as these:

"Is the chief end of society the production of goods or the creation of men and women with character and intelligence?

"Is paternalism better adapted than democracy to develop initiative and self-reliance on the part of the workers?

"In the long run, does progress come from above or from below?

"Is vast inequality of wealth and privilege consistent with brotherhood?"

Vision

Sing on, gay bird, with spirit brave,
Sing on of summer flowers,
Though winter's here with wind and sleet,
Thou sing'st of sun and showers.

For thou hast faith that spring will come,
And thou hast vision clear
Of nests in trees 'neath skies of blue,
When summer-time is here.

The lone reformer sings like thee,
And dreams of brighter years,
He strives to right an erring world
In which are doubts and fears.

But faithfully he labors on
While praying for an age
When love will conquer every wrong
And wars no longer rage.

SARAH P. MENDINHALL.

Six Weeks in Russia

"It's a glorious country. I'm frightfully in love with it."

I turned in my chair expecting to see some tourist who had come recently from Switzerland or California. Instead, I confronted Gertrude Ostler, of Manchester, England, who had just stepped off the Courier train from the Russian border. She had been in Russia six weeks, and I gather she would like to spend the rest of her life there.

Miss Ostler has been in charge of the campaign for contributions to the famine fund made through the Manchester Guardian. She was so successful in her efforts that the Society of Friends sent her to Russia to see the famine regions with her own eyes. And she returns to tell us that Russia is a wonderful country.

She is not speaking of scenery or mechanical achievement, or even of forms of government. She is thinking of people when she speaks of Russia. She has been among these people for a few weeks, too short perhaps to make profound analysis of anything in such a vast section of the world, but not too short to catch something of the quality of its people. For she has been among these people in the hour of their greatest misery. She has seen them resisting a mighty natural force—the famine.

Miss Ostler has seen every stage of the Friends' work of relief, from the arrival of the food trains in Moscow to the serving of the cooked food to the children in the kitchens at Buzuluk, and the most distant outpost of the area—as large as Belgium—where the Society of Friends is at work.

One of the villages visited was Novo Alexandrovka, once a community of prosperous small farmers. At the Central Kitchen there she saw rations given out to 50 children. Then she visited one of the families to which the rations went. She gives this picture of it:

"We had noticed a little fellow 9 or 10 years of age who had come to the kitchen for two rations, neither of them for himself. He stumbled away across the snow hugging the can of soup and cup of cocoa with the two bread rations buttoned under his coat. I thought the child would collapse any moment. His face was colorless. His lips drawn back. He was shivering and crying tearlessly as so many do. We went with him to his home and found the mother trying to cook some grass flour mixed with twigs and wood. The soup and bread were handed over to the two younger children and the boy stood watching them, following every movement of the wooden spoons, but not attempting to take anything for himself. Later, we saw him struggling once more across the heavy snow; slipping and stumbling and still crying quietly. We asked that if possible a ration should be given him. *But he is only one of the tens of thousands yet unfed.*"

In one of the villages a peasant pressed to the front of the crowd and handed this note to Miss Ostler: "I beg you to include my children in the feeding center of my village. I have 6 children, 12 to 2 years. These are not included. They are threatened by death from hunger." When she went to see this family she found them rationing out the thatch from the roof to these six children who were living on a stew made from this and animal hair.

In almost any town of any size in Russia there are Children's Homes. These are a part of the tremendous work accomplished in the last four years by the People's Commissariat of Health. These have been established in great numbers. But the famine has more than taxed their capacity to care for the children abandoned by loving but desperate parents who feel that the chances of life are greater in these institutions than in the foodless peasant houses.

The institutions are grim enough; but worse still are the private houses where people die without any attempt at care or medical treatment: . . . "In all the houses we visited, sick and dying people—men, women and children—were lying on the floor or on the big stone stoves. It was difficult to know what to say or what to do. We gave what food we had in our pockets, ashamed to look at their suffering and do nothing, but knowing that they would soon be dead. We found no bread in any of the houses save the bread made of leaves and sticks that tortures the children who eat it."

In all the hospitals that she visited in Buzuluk district she did not see a pillow or a sheet, save in the newly equipped hospital at Andriefka, where they had some mattress covers and pillow-cases made of coarse but clean sacking.

Her footnote to her remarks about all these institutions was: "In the hospitals that I visited the staffs seemed to be doing their best under the appalling conditions, but efficiency is obviously impaired by underfeeding."

Yet in spite of all she has seen Miss Ostler can say that she loves Russia. Perhaps such incidents as these explain it. In a few notes on her travels through the small villages she says: "If you have time to put up the sleigh and see the head-man of the village, you may be absolutely sure of a welcome; and if there is a samovar in the place, it will soon be ready for you. The gracious hospitality of these suffering peasants is a beautiful thing to remember. I think of one village where our meal was spread in the living room. The starving family withdrew lest their presence should embarrass us. Only after much insistence could they be induced to share our tea and bread, and then only after they had been assured that we had enough to see us through our journey."

This is one of the reasons why the Friends' workers love the people to whom they are taking a little food and a little clothing. This is why so many of them say with Gertrude Ostler, "It's a glorious country."

ROBERT DUNN,
Publicity Representative, American Quaker Unit.

Service Committee Notes

Murray Kenworthy has been able to travel to Moscow since his illness and is remaining there for a short period directing the work.

L. Oscar Moon, who has been Assistant Head of the Polish Mission, is seriously ill with typhus. He had been to one of the outposts to attend the funeral of Florence Witherington and contracted the disease there. He is now in Warsaw; and the cables state that the crisis has not yet been reached but he has excellent medical care.

Sydnor Walker and Dorothy North, both members of the Vienna Unit, have been accepted for service in Russia and will proceed there as soon as their passports have been amended.

Robert Dunn, formerly Director of Publicity in the Philadelphia Office, has at last gotten into Russia as a member of the Unit and has gone down into the famine area at Sorochinskaya. He will travel about among the Field Kitchens directing the work, and so learn at first hand the conditions that he may adequately write of them.

Caroline G. Norment, who has been a member of the German Unit for two years, has volunteered for work in Russia and been accepted. She will leave in a month or so for Moscow, taking up her work there at headquarters.

The Poland Committee had a meeting in Philadelphia on Fourth month 3d and decided to continue the Polish Mission until November. The Committee appeals for $20,000 to carry on this work. The presence of a million returned refugees—men, women and children who have returned to their devastated homes without food, clothing or any material with which to begin life anew—has made it impossible to withdraw the Mission. Money given for this work will be doing one of the most effective pieces of reconstruction work possible in the world today; as it means not only giving temporarily, but the reconstruction of whole communities for the future.

Hilda Holme, who for over a year was a member of the Polish Mission, and is now at her home in Baltimore, will gladly speak to any group of people who would be interested in hearing of the needs in Poland and the work which the Polish Unit is doing. Any meeting or group wishing to arrange to have Hilda Holme speak, may do so by addressing her care of the Service Committee.

James MacAffee, a member of New York Yearly Meeting, who went abroad last fall spending most of his time aiding the Vienna Unit, has returned home, and attended a meeting of the Committee on Work in Poland and Russia recently. While in Vienna, he disposed of the entire transport material of the Vienna Mission to a firm in Jugoslavia. He also visited the Mission in Poland and reported on the work being done in both fields.

Parry Paul, of Moorestown, New Jersey, who volunteered for work in the mechanical section of the Russian Unit, reached Moscow a little over a week ago and immediately went into the famine area, where he is engaged in the distribution of supplies.

The largest gift which the Service Committee has received for the relief of the Russian famine sufferers came to the office a few days ago. It was for $65,000, and from a man who only last year made a personal gift of $50,000 for Poland. This gift alone will feed for one month two-thirds of the number of people in Russia whom the Service Committee is now feeding.

Alma Mater

Elizabeth Powell Bond's "word" concerning Swarthmore in last week's INTELLIGENCER has opened a rush of memories of the "words by the way" which during her connection with Swarthmore she planted as seeds in the lives of Swarthmore students.

In the fuller intellectual life which Mrs. Bond's words of appreciation ascribe to the college of today, I would plead for a re-consecration to the "ancient goods" which she ever taught us and which can never grow uncouth; for they were the verities of our Friendly faith, the life germs of growth, the unfailing index which pointed to those things worth while.

Swarthmore, to fulfill her high mission, must preserve a balance between her scholarly aims and a wise preparation for life. She must maintain in the future, as she did in the past, the finest characteristics of the Friends' homes; moderation, appreciation of spiritual values, courage to keep the faith, to lead and not imitate. We need a reconsecration in our homes as in our college.

For the example which our college mother has ever been to us, her sons and daughters rise up and call her blessed.

EMMA HUTCHINSON CONROW.

Friendly News Notes

Friends at Center Preparative Meeting were very glad to have a visit from Isaac Wilson on Third month 26th, on his way to a meeting at Friends' Union, State College, Pa.

An important conference of young Friends will be held this summer in England, July 29th to August 8th. American young Friends who are going abroad this summer should make note of these dates and be in England for this conference. We expect to receive further details later.

The public meeting to be held in Broad Street Theatre, Philadelphia, on Fourth month 30th, at 3 p. m., under the auspices of the Society of Friends is another noteworthy occasion and should have the active support of all Friends. Rufus M. Jones will be the speaker, his subject being "Quakerism—A Way of Life." The meeting is held for the purpose of extending "the faith of the founders of their city, The City of Brotherly Love."

Chicago Friends are actively at work to enlarge the attendance at Monthly Meeting. They have adopted the plan of serving dinner before the meeting in order to have a social get-together time at least once a month. The time of meeting has also been changed from First-day to a day during the week, since a number of Friends did not care to make the trip into the city on First-day. Other meetings might adopt these suggestions with equally good results.

Friends in Toledo are interested to get together and to ascertain the strength of the group of Friends in that city. It is requested that the names and addresses of any Friend, or people interested in Friends, in Toledo be sent to William C. Lawrence, 4203 Fairview Drive, Toledo, Ohio.

Fourth month 2nd was a notable day for the Baltimore First-day School as it set a new high water mark for attendance. 116 teachers and scholars and seventeen visitors, which is the highest mark anyone can remember our school ever reaching.

The number of official delegates to the Baltimore 250th Anniversary is augmenting rapidly, and all indications insure a good attendance. The program for the occasion, beginning on the 4th of Fifth month, in the evening and lasting through the 7th, is attractive. The names of delegates have been received from the following Yearly Meetings: Genesee, Philadelphia (Race street), Indiana (both Meetings), New England, Nebraska and North Carolina, and Elizabeth B. Emmott and her daughter, Margaret, will represent London Yearly Meeting.

At the afternoon session of the Fiftieth Anniversary of the opening of Girard Avenue Meeting House, Jane P. Rushmore will give an address on the subject: Constants and Variables in Fifty Years of Quakerism. It is hoped that there will be a large attendance.

The Quaker Round Table of Pittsburgh, Pa., met at the home of Mr. and Mrs. R. A. Smith, North Side, on the evening of April 8th. The subject for the evening was Barclay's Apology, and Penn's Sandy Foundation Shaken. After a short period of silence J. Howard Hopkins read an interesting review of the two great works, and the reading was followed by appreciative discussion. A special meeting of the Round Table was announced, to be held on the evening of the 22nd instant, when Friends will have an opportunity of meeting Bishop Paul Jones, who will be addressing meetings in Pittsburgh at that time.

After the regular program and the transaction of some special business, the members enjoyed an informal social hour.

W.

Sherwood Eddy, speaking at the Lenten services under the auspices of the Philadelphia Federation of Churches referred to Seebohm Rowntree, the English Quaker employer, as an authority on industrial problems, and as one who is seeking to apply Christian principles in his business.

He quoted from Seebohm Rowntree the five following standards for our dealings with employees:

(1) A living wage,
(2) Regulation of hours,
(3) Insurance against unemployment,
(4) That labor should share in the democratic control of industry,
(5) That labor should receive a fairer share of the production.

In the two addresses which Sherwood Eddy made at these Lenten services, he called, in a most unflinching way, for a thorough application of Christian ideals to politics, the abolition of war, a human attitude toward other races, industry, the church, and the individual life.

NEW YORK NOTES

James McAfee spoke to the children of the Friends' Seminary on the morning of the 5th, telling about his work with the Friends' Service Committee this winter in Vienna and Poland. He had returned only a few days before, and his subject was still a living, vital thing to him, which he presented to the children in vivid fashion. As he told of the miles and miles of devastation in Poland, the little girls gasped in horror, and as he spoke of the falling value of the kronen, the arithmetical boys hastily computed its exact value in terms of fractions of a cent. If ten thousand kronen make a dollar, how much is one kronen worth? His first business in Vienna was with orphan asylums. When he said to the children there that he brought greetings from the children of America they always answered, "Please take them back our sincere thanks."

On the night of Fourth month 6th, Mrs. Alice Geddes-Lloyd and three mountain boys from Pippapass, Kentucky, spoke in the Fifteenth Street Meeting-house, New York, about the work of the Caney Creek Community Center. This Center is in the Kentucky Mountains where live between four and five million of the most pure-blooded Americans in the country. Pure-blooded because cut off by the mountains from the rest of the country, and by these same mountains cut off from the world. Several community centers have now been established in these districts, and are trying to bridge the gap between the seventeenth and the nineteenth centuries for these people.

They are bringing in modern ideas of medicine, modern ways of living, modern ideas of schools, they are helping the people to celebrate Christmas. The first newspaper in the Caney Creek district is published by the boys who have been drawn into the Center. The Centers are stimulating the people to change the roads from mudholes to real highways. The children are drawn in to clubs and groups, which work for libraries in the log-school-houses, for more schooling, which learn something of the outside world, and are prepared to go into other sections of the mountains and carry the modern message to others. At the Caney Creek Community Center alone there are eighty boys and young men who are pledged to remain in the mountains and help their own people.

Most of the message of the evening was given by the three boys accompanying Mrs. Lloyd. They were perhaps twelve or thirteen years of age, but spoke with an astonishing fluency and a self-possession which was remarkable.

When the American Friends' Service Committee summed up on Fourth month 5th the work of the warehouse at 108 Dobbin St., Brooklyn, it found that 653 bales of clothing, weighing 200 pounds each had been sent to Russia, that 50 more bales were all ready to go, and that clothing for 20 bales was on hand ready to be baled. In addition, sixty bales had been sent to Austria, and there have been numerous boxes of soap, food, and even a few toys.

Items From Everywhere

The National Child Welfare Association, 70 Fifth avenue, New York City, announces three illustrated lectures under the titles, "Child Welfare—Everybody's Business," "Makers of American Ideals," and "Warfare or Welfare," for churches, schools and general community gatherings. Each lecture has fifty colored slides and is arranged for use as a special feature of a regular program or as a complete program for a special meeting.

"Child Welfare—Everybody's Business" points out that the most effective child welfare endeavors can be promoted in any community by the simple device of cultivating the normal child's natural inclinations and interests. "Makers of American Ideals" helps young and old to realize their debt to those who have striven for the establishment of America's great ideals and to inspire them with a resolve to pay that debt. "Warfare or Welfare" tells of the nation's endeavors for public betterment through many agencies and suggests what might be accomplished if a part of the money and energy now spent for war purposes were to be devoted to constructive welfare activities. The lectures are available by purchase or rental.

The American Humane Association, Albany, N. Y., is arousing interest in "Be Kind to Animals Week," April 24-29, which ends in "Humane Sunday," April 30. Special services will be held throughout the country in clubs, churches and elsewhere, in the interests of kindness to our dumb friends, the animals. Young artists will be interested in a poster contest which the Humane Association directs, and which ends on May 20th. Cash prizes are offered for winning posters which illustrate the theme of kindness to animals. Details may be obtained by writing to the Association at Albany, N. Y.

A sign of the times is the forthcoming publication of a new international news weekly, *The Interpreter*. It claims as its aim: "To put internationalism above nationalism, humanity above parochialism, mankind and its aspirations above Main Street and its private aims!" *The Interpreter* is to be edited by Frederick Dixon. It will cost six dollars a year in advance, and fifty cents extra for postage in Canada. Details may be obtained from the Interpreter Publishing Corporation, Interpreter Building, 268 West 40th street, New York City.

"No idealism whatever characterizes the Army and Navy bills now before Congress. Both are based frankly on the policy of armed preparedness. *Don't be deceived* by press headlines charging pacifist activities with responsibility for these bills. Hardheaded business sense dictating *necessary economies* is the utmost limit thus far reached by our legislators." So says the current issue of the *Bulletin* of the National Council for Reduction of Armaments. The steps still to be taken, before we have overcome our national reliance on armed preparedness, are many and large. At the same time, the disarmament movement has already influenced the government to such an extent that the proposed Army Bill calls for a saving of $50,000,000, while the proposed Navy Bill will save the country at least $150,000,000.

The Committee of Forty-eight, 15 East 40th street, New York City, which has been laboring for a new liberal political party, is establishing a National Bureau of Information and Education. The object of this bureau will be to present in simple form, through bulletins distributed to the press, the best current information and opinion on the problems confronting the American voter. Editors, professors, scientists, and others are co-operating in this venture, which represents the first attempt of any political organization to do constructive educational work. The

Committee of Forty-eight says that before the country's governmental machinery can be used to the advantage of humanity, the citizens must take an interest in using it. In the last presidential election, only 55 per cent. of the voters went to the polls, while in other recent elections the percentage has been much less.

THE OPEN FORUM

This column is intended to afford free expression of opinion by readers on questions of interest. The INTELLIGENCER is not responsible for any such opinions. Letters must be brief, and the editor reserves the right to omit parts if necessary to save space.

A BASIS FOR THE VALUATION OF LABOR

To the Editor:

Since the INTELLIGENCER is open to the consideration of economic questions, I would call attention to the difference between the demands of Union labor and the returns of labor in farming. After a farmer has paid two or more per cent. taxes for general welfare, paid for fertilizer, machinery, and working stock, and wear and tear of same, he cannot get more for the returns of his labor for a day's work than Union labor demands for an hour's work. It appears to me that what a farmer can make out of the ground should be a basis for the valuation of labor, adding additional for increased skill. H. P. H.

DEATHS

ALLEN—In Media, Pa., on Fourth month 4th, Deborah S., wife of George B. Allen, in her 81st year.

ALLINSON—At Yardville, Pa., on Fourth month 5th, Bernice, daughter of the late Samuel and Ann Allinson, aged 66 years.

CLOTHIER—At residence of David D. Engle, Newark, N. J., Fourth month 5th, Priscilla H. Clothier, in her 92nd year.

FLITCRAFT—At Woodstown, N. J., Fourth month 5th, William Z. Flitcraft, aged 74.

ROBERTS—At Moorestown, N. J., Fourth month 6th, Eliza Lillian, wife of Samuel M. Roberts.

SHARPLESS—Near Landenberg, Pa., Fourth month, 5th, Alfred Sharpless, in his 74th year.

TILLUM—At the residence of her nephew Thomas J. Lea, near Sandy Spring, Maryland, Third month 27th, Ann Pierce Tillum, widow of Dr. B. F. Tillum of Chester County, Pennsylvania, in her 98th year. Her parents moved from Pennsylvania in 1820 and lived here the balance of their lives. She was at the time of her death the oldest birthright member of Sandy Spring Meeting. She is survived by a most untiring and faithful daughter who had been her sole caretaker for many years.

UNDERHILL—In Germantown, Pa., on Fourth month 3rd, Harriet Lukens, wife of the late Reuben Howes Underhill.

JOANNA LUKENS SHOEMAKER

Joanna Lukens Shoemaker, widow of the late Allen Shoemaker, departed this life on Third month 28th.

She was a prominent member of the Religious Society of Friends and came of old Quaker stock, and has lived in the old Shoemaker home, 914 North 8th Street, Philadelphia, for over 51 years, having come there as a bride.

With her beloved husband and family, she has been a regular attendant of Girard Avenue Meeting since it was built and her presence will be greatly missed. She is survived by two sons, Comly Shoemaker and William Kirk Shoemaker, and one grandchild, Eunice Moore Roberts, all members of Green Street Monthly Meeting.

COMING EVENTS

FOURTH MONTH

14th—Joint meeting of Study Groups, and others interested, 15th and Race Street Meeting House, at 7.30 p. m. Led by Elizabeth B. Emmott. Subject—"A Fortnight in Early Quaker History."

15th—Abington First-day School Union at Abington Friends' Meeting House, Jenkintown, Pa.

16th—Conference class at 15th and Race Streets, Philadelphia, at close of meeting for worship, at 11.40 a. m.

Speaker—Clyde Milner. Subject—Methods of English and Western Friends to Extend their work.

16th—Philadelphia Quarterly Meeting's Visiting Committee expects to hold a meeting for worship at Germantown Friends' Home, at 7.30 p. m.

16th—Elizabeth B. Emmott will be at Moorestown, N. J., attending the Orthodox meeting in the morning, and a joint group of Friends in the afternoon.

16th—William Littleboy expects to attend the Friends' meeting at Salem, N. J., at 10 a. m.

16th—E. Maria Bishop expects to attend Friends' meeting at Drumore, Pa., at 11 a. m.

19th—Monthly Meeting of Friends of Philadelphia, 15th and Race Streets, 7.30 p. m. Supper will be served by the Committee on Best Interests in the Lunch Room of the Friends' Central School Building, 15th and Race Streets, at 6.00 p. m.

20th—Green Street Monthly Meeting of Friends of Philadelphia, School House Lane, Germantown, 7.30 p. m.

22nd—Concord First-day School Union. See Notice.

22nd and 23rd—Pilgrimage under care of the Young Friends' Movement at Fair Hill Meeting.

23rd—Philadelphia Quarterly Meeting's Visiting Committee expects to attend meeting at Valley Meeting, at 10.30 a. m. First-day School at 11.30 a. m.

23rd—E. Maria Bishop is expecting to be present at the meeting for worship at Lincoln, Va.

23rd—Southern Half-Yearly Meeting, at Easton, Md.

23rd—Daniel Batchellor is planning to be at the meeting at Hockessin, Del., at 10 a. m., and First-day School following.

25th—Western Quarterly Meeting at London Grove, Pa. Daniel Batchellor expects to attend.

27th—Members of the Young Friends' Movement, and others of appropriate age and condition are invited to the gymnasium of Friends' Seminary, New York, from 8 to 10. Wear old clothes and tennis shoes, and be ready for anything. Use Rutherford Place entrance.

27th—Caln Quarterly Meeting, at Christiana, Pa., Daniel Batchellor expects to attend.

29th—Westbury Quarterly Meeting will be held at 110 Schermerhorn Street, Brooklyn, at 10.30 a. m. Lunch will be served at noon. The subject of the afternoon session at 2.30 will be "Gandhi and Race Problems." Norman Thomas will be the speaker. Daniel Batchellor expects to be present.

29th—First-day School Conference at Oxford, Pa., at 10 a. m. Subject—Duties and Responsibilities of Superintendents. At 2 p. m., adult Bible Work and Dramatization of Bible Stories. Bliss and La Verne Forbush will attend. Box lunch.

29th and 30th—Pilgrimage under care of the Young Friends' Movement at Langhorne and Newtown Meetings.

NOTICE—Concord First-day School Union at Swarthmore, Pa., on Fourth month 22nd, at 10 a. m. Open discussion on question of a field-worker in the schools of our Union. Afternoon session at 2 o'clock. Bliss Forbush will speak on Organization of the First-day School work. La Verne Forbush will tell how to dramatize Bible stories in our schools. Bus meets Media short line at Chester Road on the hour.

NOTICE—Supper will be served by the Committee on Best Interests before Monthly Meeting, at 15th and Race Streets, Fourth month 19th, 1922, in the Friends' Central School Lunch Room, at 6 o'clock. Tickets 65 cents. Please purchase tickets before Fourth month 17th, 1922. Anna W. Cloud, 140 N. 15th Street, Philadelphia.

NOTICE—Address—Quakerism: A Way of Life, by Dr. Rufus M. Jones at the South Broad Street Theatre (Broad Street below Locust Street), Sunday afternoon, April 30th, at three o'clock. An invitation is extended to all to learn the faith of the founders of their city, The City of Brotherly Love.

NOTICE—Friends' Neighborhood Guild invites thee to tea on First-day, April 23rd, 1922, from 3.30 to 5.30; Elbert Russell will speak at four. Exhibition of work done by children in art, millinery, carpentry, and handcraft. R. S. V. P. Friends' Neighborhood Guild, Fourth and Green Streets.

NOTICE—Rummage Sale! Last week in April. Benefit of Friends' Home for Children. Will you help the children by saving rummage? Send direct to Home by April 24, or arrangements for collecting can be made by calling: Lula B. Dixon, 918 S. 49th Street, Woodland 2361-J; Anna Kirby Swope, 4926 Cedar Avenue, Woodland 2858-J; Anna Hall, 5301 Woodbine Avenue, Overbrook 0411.

NOTICE—"A Fortnight in Early Quaker History" will be the subject presented by Elizabeth B. Emmott at a meeting on Sixth-day evening April 14th, at 7.30 p. m., in Room No. 4, 15th and Race Streets Meeting House, Philadelphia. All interested are invited.

Interesting Comments from Some of Our Subscribers

H. R. J., Ventnor, N. J., writes: "A new lease on life. Renew my subscription to INTELLIGENCER when it expires."

D. Z., of Buffalo, N. Y., writes: "I have been inclined to drop the subscription but believe that if I were to do so, it would be so greatly missed that I would be forced to renew it."

J. F. G., of Hollins, Va., writes: "In renewing my subscription to the INTELLIGENCER, I feel that I must express to you and your staff my appreciation of your excellent paper. I recently told one of my friends, to whom I was quoting the INTELLIGENCER: 'If I could have but one magazine of any kind, I should choose the INTELLIGENCER without a moment's hesitation.'"

Perhaps thee too, kind reader, feels this way toward the INTELLIGENCER. Is it not then thy duty to help spread the message the INTELLIGENCER carries, especially to those Friends who are not now subscribing. Thirty-five cents will secure a three months' subscription.

American Friends' Service Committee

WILBUR K. THOMAS, EX. SEC.
20 S. 12th St. Philadelphia.

CASH CONTRIBUTIONS

WEEK ENDING APRIL 3.

Five Years Meetings	$390.23
Phila. Yearly Mtg.	4,504.00
Other Meetings:	
Rahway & Plainfield Mo. Mtg.	10.00
Highland Friends' Mtg., Oregon	10.71
Haverford Mtg. & Friends' School	214.39
Smithville Mo. Mtg., Missouri	9.80
Oakland Branch of the College Park Ass'n	20.00
Chester Mo. Mtg. (Hicksite)	37.00
Purchase Mtg., N. Y.	10.00
Everett Friends' Church, Seattle	14.02
Germany	539.87
Austria	195.31
Poland	789.50
Russia	90,498.45
Russian overhead	67.58
Armenia	7.50
Syria	5.00
General	924.30
German overhead	6.00
Clothing	15.80
Total	$98,269.46

CONTRIBUTIONS RECEIVED FROM MEMBERS OF THE PHILADELPHIA YEARLY MEETING OF FRIENDS HELD AT FIFTEENTH AND RACE STREETS

FOR THE MONTH OF MARCH

Swarthmore Mo. Meeting by Jesse H. Holmes	$30.00
Abington Monthly by D. L. Lewis	50.00
Middletown Prep. by Frances W. Broomall	40.00
Hancocks Bridge W. C. T. U. by Louisa Powell, Russian Flour	5.00
Buckingham Mo. Mtg. by Mary A. Watson, Sheep for Poland	5.00
Through Arabella Carter—overhead expenses	150.00
Wilmington Mo. by L. H. Stradley	956.00
Makefield Mo. by H. G. Miller, Sheep for Poland	1.50
Lansdowne Mo. by C. C. Lippincott	40.00
Darby Mo. by W. R. White, Russian Relief	5.00
	$1,282.50

Shipments received during week ending April 1st: Thirty-eight boxes and packages received.

LUKE 2. 14—AMERICA'S ANGELUS

"Glory to God in the highest, and on earth peace, good will toward men."

Stand back of President Harding in Prayer for Universal Peace by meditating daily, at noon, on the fourteenth verse of the second chapter of Luke.

Ask your friends to help make this a Universal Meditation for Universal Peace

Pass it on *Friends in Christ*

THE BEST FIRM

A pretty good firm is "Watch & Waite,"
And another is "Attit, Early & Layte";
And still another is "Doo & Dairet";
But the best is probably "Grinn & Barrett."

—*Walter G. Doty, in Christian-Evangelist.*

WANTED

WANTED—POSITION AS MOTHER'S helper for summer. Experienced; can give references. Address W. 130, Friends' Intelligencer.

WOMAN OF EXPERIENCE IN PUBlic work desires a position of trust in hotel or institution. Address E. 131, Friends' Intelligencer.

COMPANION DESIRES POSITION; experienced in care of elderly and semi-invalids. Reference. Address D. 140, Friends' Intelligencer.

WANTED — MOTHER'S HELPER, capable, with refined family. Address, Herschel G. Smith, 28 W. Greenwood Ave., Lansdowne, Pa.

WOMAN OF REFINEMENT, PAST middle age, but active and in good health, desires position as companion to elderly lady, or one with impaired vision. Good reader. Congenial home rather than highest salary. K. B., 744 Carlton Ave., Plainfield, New Jersey.

YOUNG MAN, 30, RECENTLY REturned from German Child-feeding Mission of American Friends' Service Committee, seeks responsible position with reliable concern. Headed Transportation work in Germany, formerly purchasing agent large Quaker concern; also has had long experience with large bank with special training in credit department. Robert Gray Taylor, 20 Rigby avenue, Lansdowne, Pa.

SWARTHMORE COLLEGE STUDENT desires position as mother's helper for the summer. Address G. P. K., Box 441, Swarthmore College, Swarthmore, Pa.

WANTED—POSITION AS COMPANion, care of invalid, or housekeeper. Address I. 151, Friends' Intelligencer.

WANTED—POSITION AS A MOTHer's helper, light housework, or place as a companion by a young woman, Friend. Country preferred. Address, Box 66, R. 5, Coatesville, Pa.

WANTED—HOME ON A FARM FOR boy of 12, who has had some training in such work. Useful in the house. Must go to school. Address 2201 Belmont avenue, Philadelphia.

WANTED — HOUSEKEEPER (MANager), capable woman of refinement who desires good permanent home in Philadelphia suburbs with family of three children and male adult. Box S. 150, Friends' Intelligencer.

WOMAN OF MIDDLE AGE, NURSE, wants care of invalid. Address P. 152, Friends' Intelligencer.

WANTED—AN EXPERIENCED teacher for 5th and 6th Grades. Friend preferred. Address Haddonfield Friends' School, Haddonfield, N. J.

WANTED—MAY 1ST, FOR HALFtime work, Friend trained in office work. Must be good typist. Apply in writing to A. 159, Friends' Intelligencer.

WANTED — SUMMER BOARD FOR three adults, with private family on farm. Commuting distance from Philadelphia. Address D. 154, Friends' Intelligencer.

WANTED — ACTIVE MIDDLE-AGED woman with nursing experience to look after nervous cases and have general supervision in absence of owner, in small private sanitarium in Philadelphia suburbs. Give references. Good salary to right person. Address M. 155, Friends' Intelligencer.

WANTED — PRINCIPAL WITH EXperience for Friends' school in country town, 20 miles from Philadelphia. Good salary to teachers employed. Address S. 153, Friends' Intelligencer.

FOR RENT

FOR RENT—THE PACKER COTTAGE at Buck Hill. Accommodations for five or six. Located within fifteen minutes' walk of Inn. For particulars inquire Franklin Packer, Newtown, Pa.

FOR RENT

FOR RENT—APRIL TO OCTOBER, nine-room house (furnished) with sleeping porch and garage, near river, at Riverton. Address Helen Lippincott, Riverton, N. J.

FOR RENT—IN LOWER CHELSEA, new bungalow, six rooms and bath, three bedrooms. Three months. 56 N. DeLancey Place.

FOR RENT—AT BUCK HILL FALLS, cottage, from May 1st to June 5th. Apply, Mary S. A. Jenkins, Gwynedd, Pa.

FOR RENT—FOR THE SUMMER, AT Swarthmore, new house, furnished, two doors from Woolman School, near College Woods. Large living room, sleeping porch, two baths, five bedrooms. Every convenience for the housekeeper. Price $90 to right party. Phone 249-R. Address Juliet C. Kent.

ADVERTISING RATE in the FRIENDS' INTELLIGENCER, for Help Wanted, Positions Wanted, Rooms for Rent, Notices, and other classified advertisements without display, for each insertion, 2 cents per word, including name, initials and address. Answers may be sent to a box at the INTELLIGENCER office, if so directed.

For display advertising the rate is 10 cents per agate line, or $1.40 per column inch, each insertion. On ten or more insertions in a year from date of order, ten per cent. discount. Thus a four-inch single-column or two-inch double-column advertisement costs $5.60 each insertion, less ten per cent., or 5.04 net each time for ten or more insertions. Matter may be changed whenever desired, without extra charge.

Experience has proved the INTELLIGENCER to be a remarkably good advertising medium. All advertisements must "pass the censor!"

Address 140 N. 15th St., Philadelphia

The Friends' Intelligencer

Established 1844 | FOURTH MONTH 22, 1922 | Volume 79 Number 16

Contents

EDITORIAL

THE FRIENDS' INTELLIGENCER

Published weekly, 140 N. 15th Street, Philadelphia, Pa., by Friends' Intelligencer Association, Ltd.

WALTER H. ABELL, *Editor*

SUE C. YERKES, *Business Manager*

Editorial Board: Elizabeth Powell Bond, Thomas A. Jenkins, J. Russell Smith, George A. Walton.

Board of Managers: Edward Cornell, Alice Hall Paxson, Paul M. Pearson, Annie Hillborn, Elwood Hollingshead, William C. Biddle, Charles F. Jenkins, Edith M. Winder, Frances M. White.

Officers of Intelligencer Associates: Elhwood Burdsall, Chairman; Bertha L. Broomell, Secretary; Herbert P. Worth, Treasurer.

Subscription rates: United States, Mexico, Cuba and Panama, $2.50 per year. Canada and other foreign countries, $3.00 per year. Checks should be made payable to Friends' Intelligencer Association, Ltd.

Entered as Second Class Matter at Philadelphia Post Office.

The Friends' Intelligencer

The religion of Friends is based on faith in the "INWARD LIGHT," or direct revelation of God's spirit and will in every seeking soul.

The INTELLIGENCER is interested in all who bear the name of Friends in every part of the world, and aims to promote love, unity and intercourse among all branches and with all religious societies.

ESTABLISHED 1844 PHILADELPHIA, FOURTH MONTH 22, 1922 VOLUME 79 NUMBER 16

Personality and Coal

From the point of its junction with the Kanawha River, Cabin Creek plunges southward into the mountains of West Virginia—rugged in its setting, rugged in the great black coal tipples which line it at intervals of every mile or so to mark a mine and a mining camp, rugged in the human drama of which it forms the scene. It was too early for the single daily train when we reached the mouth of the valley, and the creek was too high to permit the "Jitneys" to cross the fords—there are no bridges on the road up Cabin Creek—so we followed the winding railroad on foot.

Two miles above, at Dry Branch, the first of the valley's mining camps, we asked for the chairman of the local union relief committee; for we had gone to West Virginia to investigate the reported need for relief in the mining regions. One of the men lounging outside the "company store" went in search of the miner for whom we had enquired, and returned after ten minutes to report that he would "be along after a while." We waited for half an hour, but our man did not come. Finally, we had to leave for the next camp without seeing him. The next day, when we returned, we learned that this native-born American had not responded to our request for an interview because he was *afraid to do so.* He had feared that we were state constabulary in plain clothes, and that we had come to arrest him. So far as we could learn from all concerned, he had done nothing wrong. But he was a miner in West Virginia, and he wanted to know who it was that asked for him before he answered. He apologized with considerable embarrassment when he learned that we were Quakers from Philadelphia, and that we came on a mission of good-will, not of malice.

Such incidents as the above left upon us an indellible impression of the *human side* of industrial relations in general, and of coal mining in particular. For an issue of such great national importance, the present coal strike is receiving little enough publicity of any kind in our daily press. But even in such reports as we do receive, the human side is almost entirely lacking. We read of tonnage and wage scales, injunctions and contracts; the whole matter is conceived in terms of coal and dollars. But in West Virginia, the great impression which one receives is that the whole issue is one of humanity; human needs and hopes and fears not only form its basis, but will be the real factors influenced affected by its outcome.

In the same camp at Dry Branch, we came upon a family of mother and six children, of which the father had fled six months ago after the state constabulary had twice entered his house at midnight and sought to arrest him. He was accused of having taken part in the march on Logan and Mingo Counties; he was new at the mines, and afraid of midnight invaders—and so he fled. No one knew whether he had taken part in the march or not. Months passed, and he remained far from his family, "somewhere in the mountains of Virginia."

And there was Mrs. Crawford. Yes, *she* needed medical attention, she replied in answer to our question as to whether she knew of any sickness in the camp, and went on to tell us that she was consumptive. She had spent a month at the state hospital once, and had been much helped, but since the unemployment, she was no longer able to pay the fee of a dollar a day.

"I wish something *could* be done to get me back there," she called after us as we turned to go. "I set my heart on living to see this little girl grow up—and I just feel now that if I don't get taken care of, I can't make it."

. . . .

The streets and yards at Dry Branch were muddy, and littered with tin cans and refuse. Of course, the men had been out of work for nearly a year, and could have cleaned them up if they had wished. A few had done so, but most of them said it was the company's business to do such things, not theirs, and so they continued to live in filth. And what foundation had they for any higher attitude? They could never hope to acquire their homes themselves. The pride of possession and development was completely denied them. The company owned everything—houses, mines, store; the whole camp, and in a very real sense the people in it. They might be evicted from their homes and turned out into the street at any moment—except as unionism might give them sufficient collective strength to demand reasons and call for justice.

Most of the miners above thirty years of age could not read or write—though practically all of them, in the fields which we visited, were native Americans. Their wages, even during periods of normalcy, are seldom more, and are often less than a thousand dollars a year; out of which is automatically deducted payment for all the services which the company controls—rent, heat and light, medical attention, in many cases food and merchandise. The annual income of the West Virginia miner is thus about six hundred dollars less than the "minimum of subsistence" estimated by Prof. W. F. Ogburn of Columbia University, as necessary to the support of a family of five. But even realizing this sub-minimum annual wage, money is not the real issue. Even were the miner twice as well off financially, he could not use his money for his best good. It would still be impossible for him to buy his own home, or to build better schools for the education of his children. In many instances, these limitations and his own lack of education lead him to spend unwisely a part of even what money he does have.

It is not our present aim to discuss the industrial issues which lie at the root of such conditions as these. We simply wish to make clear as possible the human side of the coal mining and the coal controversy. It is an undeniable fact, ascertainable at first hand by whoever cares to visit the fields and investigate for himself, that large sections of our American population, large divisions of our human brotherhood, are at this moment subject to a type of life which is un-American and sub-human. It is a life which is daily crushing and dwarfing unlimited resources of human personality. Its existence ought to be a matter of immediate and unceasing concern to all who are interested in either the maintenance of a true democracy or the attainment of a Christian civilization.

Whatever way the industrial issues of the coal strike are decided, its human issues will continue. They will continue until leadership consecrates itself to service, instead of to personal gain; until human beings and provision for human needs are given first and highest consideration by operators, miners and public alike. Their existence is a challenge to us to study the facts until we have each come as close as possible to the truth of the matter, a challenge to examine our own relations to the cause of such conditions, and to give earnest, mental and spiritual energy to seeking a way forward toward a more enlightened and Christian day.

Such conditions cannot continue permanently. In one way or another they must, and will, change. Upon the attitude of today's rulers, thinkers and idealists will defend the method by which that change is to come. Will it be by the earnest persuasive concern of modern John Woolmans, or shall present indifference allow it to fall to the mailed fist of modern civil war?

Wanted—A Poet

Where are our major poets, men of dreams
Who gain great insights on momentous themes,
And, by their inspiration's steady glow,
Mark out the path and lead men as they go?
The yellow fever has been blotted out.
The white plague has been turned to utter rout.
The words of men are carried everywhere
On slender wires, or through the vibrant air.
Through Arctic wastes men pressed toward their goal
To plant a flag above each frozen pole.
And, soon or late, some daring foot shall rest
Upon the gleaming top of Everest.
At Panama and at Suez we see
Titanic passes cut from sea to sea.
While, after age-long efforts, men have found
A way to soar, on wings, above the ground.
These wonders will add little to our state
If they but serve as ministers of hate.
This added mastery of the air and earth
Has been, and will be, of but doubtful worth,
If it brings men together, more and more,
To wallow in the ghastly hell of war.
Attend, you men of first rate intellect!
The world needs an inspired architect,
Not to plan structures of concrete and steel,
Not to lay down a greater warship's keel,
But to work out the details for a plan
Of life, that shall relate us man to man,
In daily intercourse, and state to state,
So that the outcome shall be love, not hate.
Material structures crumble to decay.
A world so framed shall never pass away.

RAYMON F. FRITZ.

Despised Gifts

It was not bright enough for me,
Who prize the things that shine.
How could I know that it should be
A nugget from God's mine?

HARRY BOLAND.

The Quakerism of the Founders

By Elbert Russell

V

(Concluding Installment)

The Breadth of Quakerism

One who comes to the writings of the founders of the Society of Friends from the standpoint of its later spirit and practices is impressed that the "First Publishers of Truth" breathed a freer air and enjoyed a larger outlook. The later sectarian exclusiveness and bondage to the letter are to a large extent happily lacking. They saw more clearly the distinction between the root and the leaf, between the vital and the non-essential in their own experience. There is a catholicity of sympathy about them. They were able to recognize kindred spirits when they came in contact with them in other nations and religious professions, or wearing other garb than their own. They were willing that religion should have various theological expressions. They dared trust truth to maintain itself by its own inherent strength against error. They believed "God was atop of the devil"; that his love could swallow up the ocean of darkness; that spiritual forces could make righteousness prevail without resort to misrepresentation, contention, hate or force. They had a working faith in "that of God" in other men, and gave it liberty. The following extracts illustrate their breadth of vision and spirit in addition to some already given in previous articles.

The True Believers

"About the beginning of the year 1646, as I was going to Coventry, and approaching towards the gate, a consideration arose in me, how it was said that 'All Christians are believers, both Protestants and Papists,' and the Lord opened to me that if all were believers, then they were all born of God, and passed from death to life; and that none were true believers but such; and, though others said they were believers, yet they were not."—*George Fox, 'Journal.'*

The One Religion

"The *Humble, Meek, Merciful, Just, Pious* and *Devout* Souls are everywhere of one Religion; and when Death has taken off the *Mask,* they will know one another, tho' the divers Liveries they wear here makes them *Strangers.*"—*Penn, 'Some Fruits of Solitude.'*

God's Love

God is sweetness, meekness, gentleness, tenderness; abounding in mercy and loving-kindness, pitying the miserable, and naturally holding forth an helping hand towards them: yea, he is universally thus. There is not one miserable soul, not one perishing creature upon the face of the earth, but as he hath wisdom and power to help it, so he hath tender bowels, and an heart thereunto. And it is not for want of somewhat to be done on his part, that souls perish, but the failing always was, and still is, on the creature's part.

God loveth all his creatures, and cannot but be good to them. He is outwardly good, he is inwardly good to them all. He can do nothing against any one of them, but what stands with his love and mercy.—*Pennington, 'Works.'*

"The Spirit Quickeneth"

Lastly, if any now at this day, from a true tenderness of spirit, and with real conscience towards God, did practice this ceremony [The Lord's Supper] in the same way, method, and manner as did the primitive Christians recorded in Scripture, I should not doubt to affirm but they might be indulged in it, and the Lord might regard them, and for a season appear to them in the use of these things, as many of us have known him to do to us in the time of our ignorance; providing always they did not seek to obtrude them upon others, nor judge such as found themselves delivered from them, or that they do not pertinaciously adhere to them.—*Barclay, 'Apology.'*

Heresies

There is great advantage of errors and heresies to the true church; for the life grows and gets ground by a fair trial and overcoming of them, and the approved are thereby made manifest.—*Pennington, 'Works.'*

Unity and Uniformity

The great error of the ages of the apostasy hath been, to set up an outward order and uniformity, and to make men's consciences bend thereto, either by arguments of wisdom or by force; but the property of the true church-government is, to leave the conscience to its full liberty in the Lord, to preserve it single and entire for the Lord to exercise, and to seek unity in the light and in the Spirit, walking sweetly and harmoniously together in the midst of different practices.—*Pennington, 'Works.'*

Liberty

The perfection of the true liberty lies in the perfection of bonds, in the perfect binding down of that which is out of the life; for the true liberty is the liberty of the life, and of nothing else; and when all that is contrary to the life is perfectly bound down, then the life hath its full scope, without the least control of the fleshly part; and when the life lives, then that which is joined to the life lives also.—*Pennington, 'Works.'*

Fellowship in Spite of Differences

After the meeting I went to John Audland's. There came Joseph Story to me. He lighted his pipe and said, "Will you take a pipe of tobacco? Come, all is ours." I considered him a forward, bold youth. Tobacco I did not take; but it came into my mind that he might think I had not unity with the creation, for I saw he had a flashy empty notion of religion. So I took his pipe and put it to my mouth and gave it to him again, to prevent his saying I had not unity with the creation.—*Fox, Journal (Modernized from the Camb. Ed.).*

One whose name was Cock met me in the street and would have given me a roll of tobacco, for people were then much given to smoking. I accepted his love, but did not receive his tobacco.—*George Fox, 'An Autobiography.'*

Christian Liberty

For it is now gone forty-seven years since we owned the Truth, and all things have gone well and peaceable, till now of late that this narrowness and strictness is entering in; that many meetings were set up for reproving and looking into suspicious and disorderly walking . . . and not (for) private persons to take upon them to make orders and say: This must be done and the other must be done. And can Friends think that those who are taught and guided of God can be subject and follow such low mean orders? . . . We are now coming into Jewism, into that which Christ cried Woe against, minding altogether outward things, neglecting the inward work of Almighty God in our hearts . . . insomuch that poor Friends are mangled in their minds, that they know not what to do. For one Friend says one way and another, another.—*Margaret Fell's 'Address to Friends' (April, 1700).*

Life Not Drab Nor Uniform

But Christ Jesus saith, That we must take no thought what we shall eat or what we shall drink or what we shall put on; but bids us consider the lilies, how they grow in more royalty than Solomon. But, contrary to this, we must not look at no colours, nor make anything that is changeable colours, as the hills are, nor sell them, nor wear them. But we must be all in one dress and one colour.

This is a silly, poor gospel. It is more fit for us to be covered with God's eternal Spirit and clothed with His eternal Light, which leads us and guides us into righteousness; and to live righteously and justly and holily in this present evil world. This is the clothing that God puts on us, and likes, and will bless. This will make our light to shine forth before men . . . for we have God for our Teacher; and we have His promise and His doctrine; and we have the apostles' practice in their day and generation; and we have God's Holy Spirit to lead us and guide us; and we have the blessed Truth that we are made partakers of to be our practice. . . .

Friends, we have one God, and one mediator betwixt God and man—the man Christ Jesus. Let us keep to Him or we are undone.—*Margaret Fell, 'Address to Friends' (April, 1700).*

Turning the World Upside-down

For turning the world upside-down, it is acknowledged: the power of the Lord is come forth to do it. Who would strive to keep the old heavens and the old earth standing, which must be dissolved before the new heavens and the new earth (wherein dwells righteousness) can be formed and brought forth?—*Pennington, 'Works.'*

The New Faith

1. Faith in Nature, and in man as a part of Nature.

2. Faith that Nature's contradictions are due to friction in the process of becoming.

3. Faith that man's highest aspirations reveal the direction of future growth.

4. Faith that a Life which is Spirit is moving to ever new creations, that "blind force" is not fundamental.

5. Faith that there is a solution for every apparently insoluble problem.

6. Faith that a true metaphysics must tally with facts of experience.

7. Faith that the physical is not unreal nor evil, but is as the roots out of which the spiritual shall grow.

8. Faith that justice and compassion will prepare a soul to develop the spiritual.

9. Faith that God, or the Ultimate Reality, is not outside of time, but working in and through it, the deepest fact of our being, here and now.

10. Faith in a power to know such a God, by direct perception, or intuition.

11. Faith that reason deserves as strict allegiance in outward relations as intuition in inward relations.

Since reason has evolved by solving problems of a practical nature and is a necessary means for bringing ideals to outward realization.

Harriet B. Bradbury.

"Thou Shalt Have No Other Gods Before Me"

The paper which follows, was read at a meeting of the Coldstream Young Friends' Association, held at the time of Pelham Half-Yearly Meeting.

The Hebrew people for years had been dwellers in Egypt, and like the Egyptians and the people of other countries of that day, they had many gods. They worshipped Nature-forces; bloody sacrifices formed a chief part in their rites, and even human sacrifices were not unknown.

In the course of time, the Hebrews discarded their various gods and came to look upon Jehovah as their national deity. They considered him "God of Israel," but of Israel alone. Heretofore their gods had been gods belonging immovably to certain places; but Jehovah, they considered, was a god not of a place but of a people—the Hebrew people. They, however, were not yet monotheists. They regarded the gods of other nations as real beings and joined in their worship.

Then on Mt. Sinai "and God spake all these words saying 'I am the Lord thy God which have brought thee out of the land of Egypt, out of the house of bondage. Thou shalt have no other gods before me' ";—This, given by God to Moses, and by Moses to the people, as the first of the ten commandments on which the Hebrew law was built.

This revelation to Moses was not readily or easily taken up by the people. Its adoption takes place gradually through the whole recorded history of the Hebrew people. With every foreign invasion of Israel and Jacob crept in the worship of the agricultural or household gods of the invader. Hundreds of years after Moses had given this commandment, prophets were still begging, pleading and threatening for Israel to give up the worship of idols and return to Jehovah. Hosea protests against idolatry and pictures Jehovah, heart-broken because of the utter faithlessness of Israel, crying out "Woe unto them (the Israelites) for they have fled from me; destruction unto them because they have transgressed against me: though I have redeemed them, yet they have spoken lies about me." Elijah's spectacular abolition of the Baal gods once convinced the people and brought the nation back to Jehovah.

Always the fidelity of some prophet kept alive the ideal of Jehovah and saved the nation from total forgetfulness and extinction.

The present-day stumbling block is not idolatry or the worship of images, but there is perhaps a hint of something very much akin to it keeping back our civilization from its destined prayers, perhaps even as great an evil because less recognized. We have no hesitancy in asserting that we are followers of this first commandment; we consider that we worship but one God—the Giver of Life—the Universal Power; and yet there are other things that creep into our lives and gradually absorb our attention and interest until they become the center of our thoughts—our god. For anything which claims our attention, our interest, our esteem, our love or our service more than God, anything on which we depend more than we depend on God, of that thing are we making a god. Many things, good and estimable in their true perspective come to occupy us too much and crowd out God, assume first place and so become, for the time, a god to us.

Success is greatly to be sought, but there may be legitimate barriers, and Success gained at the expense of kindness along the way is likely to prove a bitter fruit of possession. The search for Fame may usurp the central thought and become a god. Business, if it occupies the mind to the exclusion of God, is our deity. Material progress and accumulation of wealth may so exhaust the energies that God comes in second place. The attainment of social position is paramount with some. Great leaders of men, who have rendered public service to their countries and have tasted popularity become seized with an ambition for power and more power, until they are blinded by self to the "divine in all men" and the less strong and less fortunate are trampled in the rush for the top. Ease and luxury, personal comfort lure some from God's way. Many covet happiness when its price is too high. Education, a good reputation, possessions, all are necessary in the attainment of an object, but when they become the object itself—the perspective of life is lost—God is forgotten and all-unconsciously a false god is set us.

Each of these false gods when realized proves unsatisfying, empty of the thing we sought and thought we were attaining. We must use each of these as God meant them—for our service in helping others—making of them servants and not masters and gods. The value of education lies in helping us to understand people; the value of power and position in widening the circle to whom we may give help; ease and comfort only in releasing our minds from the combat against discomfort and so allowing its powers to go in the direction of others; possessions and wealth only as they are shared with the needy. We must see each not as a primal, only as a secondary, as a step in the fulfilment of God's purpose, always being able to live it up and see past it to God. "Life is but a means unto Beginning, mean and end of all things—an end—the end—God."

And so I say we still need the commandment as a reminder—"Thou shalt have no other gods before me."

LORENA ZAVITZ.

Christianity and Economic Problems

V

What Shall We Do About Luxuries?

(*Abridged to Summary Form*)

"Is luxury a social problem? If so, what shall we do about it? Before we can answer these questions intelligently, we must take into consideration various standards of living and determine whether or not our national income is sufficient to enable the entire population to enjoy the higher standards. We should then analyze the consequences of luxury."

How Much Does a Family Need?

Various estimates are quoted in answer to this question. That of $1,267.76, made in 1919 by a group of manufacturers' associations of Fall River, Mass., is questioned as a sufficient basis for normal family life. An estimate of 2,262.47, for a family of five, was made by the United States Bureau of Labor Statistics in August, 1919. Edward W. Evans, secretary of the Social Order Committee of the Fourth and Arch Streets Yearly Meeting, makes an estimate of $5,625 as adequate means of full family development, beyond which limit Christian families should spend only after a serious examination of each contemplated additional expenditure.

The editors of the present course conclude that a clear case could be made out that any family could find legitimate use for an income of at least $5,000 a year. Statistics are then examined to determine whether our national income is large enough to provide such an income to every family in the country. It is found that if the 49 billion dollars of our national income available for personal use were divided equally among the 21 million families in the United States, each family would receive about $2,330. "These figures show the utter inadequacy of our present national income to provide $5,000 per year for every family."

"As a matter of fact, the number of persons receiving an income as high as $5,000 during 1918 was only 842,458, or less than 3 per cent. of the total number of income receivers. The number of persons who received as much as $2,000 for 1918 was only 5,290,649, or 14 per cent. of the total number. The startling fact is that the total number of persons receiving less than $1,500 during that year was 27,056,344, or 72 per cent. of the total number; while the number receiving less than $1,000 for the year was 14,558,224, or 38 per cent. of the total number."

What Are the Effects of Luxury?

"In view of the present inadequacy of the national income to make it possible for every family to maintain a comfortable standard of living, it naturally follows that excessive luxuries can be enjoyed by the few only as others are deprived of necessities. The consumption of expensive luxuries has three notable effects: (1) it diverts human labor from tasks which are socially more productive; (2) it diverts capital from more beneficial uses; (3) it wastes raw materials which might be used to better advantage."

The Extent of Luxury

The Secretary of the Treasury is quoted as having estimated that the total amount spent in luxuries by the people of the United States during 1919 was $12,260,000,000. The items on which this amount was spent are: Joy riding, pleasure resorts and races; luxurious services, excessively high-priced wearing apparel, carpets and rugs; tobacco and snuff; perfumery and cosmetics; soft drinks, candy and chewing gum, and jewelry.

How Determine an Equitable Distribution of Luxuries?

"In view of the definite limits to production at the present time, four possibilities are open to society: (1) to increase production to the point where there will be enough luxuries for everybody; (2) to cease entirely all luxury production; (3) to provide luxuries for a small class of rich people; (4) to bring about a more equitable distribution by limiting the luxury expenditures of the rich."

The first three proposals are rejected as inadequate to bring a present solution.

"The final possibility is limiting the luxury expenditures of the rich. Does the existing inequality of distribution represent the actual difference in ability, perseverance and thrift? Is the interest of the whole people best served by concentrating great wealth in the hands of a few?

The follower of Jesus will turn again to the record for light. What does Jesus say about luxuries? One of the effective ways of teaching is by action. In this connection the example of Jesus is significant. He did not live a life of ease and luxury. Quite the reverse. His chief concern was not for his own comfort, but rather for the welfare of others. On one occasion he reminded his hearers that he "came not to be ministered unto, but to minister, and to give his life a ransom for many." He also said: "For their sake I consecrate myself."

Jesus issued a stirring challenge to his hearers to live this same kind of life: "If any man would come after me, let him *deny himself*, take up his cross, and follow me." Love is to be dominant in human relations. The second great commandment is: "Thou shalt love thy neighbor as thyself." In the parable of the Good Samaritan one's neighbor is defined as any person who is in need. On another occasion Jesus said: "A new commandment I give unto you, that ye love one another; even as I have loved you, that ye love one another. By this shall all men know that ye are my disciples, if ye have love one to another."

In the parable of the Last Judgment we see pictured the doom of those who neglect the needy: "For I was hungry, and ye did not give me to eat; I was thirsty, and ye gave me no drink; I was a stranger and ye took me not in; naked, and ye clothed me not; sick, and in prison, and ye visited me not."

In the light of the very clear teaching of Jesus and his disciples, should a Christian live in ease and luxury? Can there be real brotherhood between those who dwell in mansions and those who are housed in slums? Does a Christian love his brother as himself when he lives in luxury from rents and dividends, while others through toil are unable to rise above need and squalor?

With the world in physical hunger and spiritual destitution, with the tragic need for men and money everywhere, is it not supreme disloyalty to Jesus and an absolute denial of His Way of Life for a Christion to live in luxury and expend his substance and energies upon his own pleasure and comfort?

Some Queries On the Ministry

The following queries are read occasionally at the New York meeting for Ministry and Council. The Friend who was directed by that meeting to send them to the INTELLIGENCER, *writes concerning them: "Of course they do not apply only to members of ministry and counsel."*

1. Do I frequently read the Bible or other religious books, or such as tend to encourage the spiritual life?
2. Do I "continue steadfastly in prayer"?
3. Am I willing to speak in meeting?
4. Am I willing to devote time to prepare for service in meeting?
5. If I do not speak in meeting, am I sure that it is not from laziness or timidity?
6. If I speak in meeting, am I willing and glad to receive suggestions for the improvement of the service?
7. Do I endeavor to practice personally and to advocate consistently the principles of religion that I profess?

Death

Death brings, I think, such comfort to the soul
(Beyond our knowledge of the ultimate)
As when a runner crossing a great goal,
Heedless to voices inarticulate,
Feels a glad strength for contests yet to be
While sounds the thunder of his victory.

—*Harold Speakman.*

As An Unbiased American Saw Russia

An address given by Mrs. Marguerite E. Harrison at the Philadelphia City Club last week should be reported at length but lack of space forbids. She spent several months in Russia, the last ten in prison; she speaks the language fluently, hence came to know all classes of people intimately. Being a talented woman of wide experience her observations and conclusions are of value. One of her auditors has summarized the strongest points of her address as follows:

The Russian people are kind-hearted, lovers of the fine arts; they are intelligent, but ninety per cent. are uneducated; thousands of schools have been opened by the Bolshevists, and college students are aided by appropriations of money and food. Women have social and political equality. The standard of morality is such that Mrs. Harrison felt safer on the streets of Moscow alone, late at night, than she does on the streets of an American city.

The terms Soviet and Bolshevism must not be confused. The latter refers to a political party, the former to a system of government.

The Russians have always been accustomed to a despotism. Education, and the broader outlook that is coming with the interchange of ideas as men from various sections come together in the Red army, will evolve a different form of government. The Red army is not generally communistic; the common soldiers are non-political, drafted peasants with no idea why they are under arms; the officers are largely from the old imperialistic army.

There is little probability that the Bolshevist party can firmly establish its idea of communism. That would mean nationalization of the land, and the peasants are strongly convinced that the land belongs to them.

Intervention by the allies and encouragement given to the attacks of Poland have greatly strengthened the present dictatorship by uniting all factions in Russia to repel the invaders, even former adherents of the Kerensky party joining forces with the Bolshevists. Lenin is a sincere, hard-working man, possibly big enough to lead the present Russia as it develops into the great Russia of the future.

The Russian church under the monarchy was despotic and the people held it in contempt, but since church and state have been separated and the people are permitted to support the clergy of their choice, the churches are crowded. The present removal of church valuables, and the application of funds thus derived to the relief of the needy, meets with the approval of the people.

MARY H. WHITSON.

Russia's Need Cannot Be Met By Harvest

This Summer's Crop will Alleviate Hunger, But Cholera and Diseases of Malnutrition will Continue To Take Life.

It is being told in many quarters that this summer's crop in Russia will entirely save the Russian people and that, therefore, there will be no further need of foreign relief. If this were true, it would be one of the greatest blessings that could be conferred upon Russia at the present time. This year's crop undoubtedly will contribute to the relief of many millions. That is, of course, taking for granted that there will be no crop failure. But because of lack of seed and lack of man-power to plough and plant, even with favorable weather conditions, it cannot be hoped that the crop which Russia expects will meet the need which has been caused by the present calamity. Fifteen million people have been starving. Five million will have died. Five million others will have been saved by foreign relief; while five million more, if they are able to exist, will be mere wrecks of humanity because of tuberculosis, dysentery, typhus and cholera due to starvation and filth.

The crop which Russia will harvest this summer will bring relief; but it is impossible to hope that the gigantic misery and disease which this year has caused can be met in any adequate way by this means. Without the crop there would possibly be no hope; but the presence of the crop does not mean Russia's salvation. It can only mean that a foundation for rehabilitation has been laid and that upon this foundation of a renewal of the agriculture the new life of Russia may be built. But if you had gone through nine months of living upon grass and roots and then had even been saved by a relief portion of one meal a day, it is very easy to suppose that your body would not be in adequate physical condition to go forward with life. The effects of the Russian famine will not end this summer, no matter how great the crop may be; for the famine will continue to take its toll of life for a generation in disease-ridden bodies of men and women and in undersized bodies and brains of children. The fight against tuberculosis has only begun. The fight against the children's diseases of rickets, and undersized bodies and brains, has not yet begun and must be started.

The hospitals of Russia are destitute even of the supplies which we would ordinarily have in our own homes in case of an emergency. So that at the present time the hospitals may be said to be useless. Bedding has disappeared from the children's homes and, in fact, from most of the private homes of the peasants. Medicines are not known throughout the famine area; and most of the doctors and nurses have died through starvation or disease.

It is a very depressing picture which must be drawn of Russia today; but the true situation must be realized, if any adequate program which will stabilize Russia is to be carried on. Money for food, medicines, hospital supplies, bedding and clothing will be needed for five years, to bring Russia once more back into a normal, healthy and clean life.

The Woman Who Cheated

In one of the villages in Poland where I went once a fortnight, to distribute and collect the work for the cottage industries by which the poorest peasants are kept alive, there was a woman who cheated. She was not the only one. I used to find them occasionally, sometimes very bold, and sometimes trying pitifully to cheat and failing because of want of practice. It is not surprising, for their need is so great.

This woman was returning balls of yarn made from the raw flax we had given her. As soon as I took them in my hand I felt that they were overweight.

"What have you put inside these balls?" I asked. "They do not feel as they should."

"By God, I swear that there is nothing in it," the woman declared loudly.

"No, I am not satisfied," I answered her. "I am putting your balls to one side on this chair; and when I get them home, I will unwind them and see whether or not you speak truly." The woman looked startled and seemed taken aback, but then she went out through the crowd with her new allotment of work. Even though I felt sure she was cheating, I still gave her the largest return of work, for I knew she was poor and might suffer if I reduced her portion.

At the end of the distribution I said to the village President who had been with me, "You see these three balls that were brought in by that woman. I am wrapping them up separately to examine them."

"You are doing well," he said, "for they are too heavy."

When I came home I found that one of the balls contained good thread and one had a large stone inside of it to add weight, while the third had good thread on the outside but such coarse stuff inside that it could not be used even for sacking. It was quite clear that she had cheated and had kept some of the flax.

A fortnight later, when I returned to that village, I brought out the three balls of yarn and laid them on the table. The crowd looked on. A horror-struck silence held them. It was so tense that I wondered at the reason.

"This woman did not do well," I said, and waited for an answer.

The village President gave it. "The woman is dead," he replied.

The peasants are hardened to death. Most of them have lost half their families on the long journey from Russia, and deaths from typhus and relapsing fever occur continually in the village. But I could feel in the air that this death was different. I doubt if they went far enough in their reasoning to suppose that God had punished her because of her false oath. Perhaps they felt merely worried that she died with an unconfessed fault which was discovered afterwards. But there was something not comfortable about it in their minds. Since that time there has been a higher standard of work from that village, and a higher standard of truth-telling.

ANNA LOUISE STRONG.

Friendly News Notes

The Art Classes of the different Friends' Schools are preparing posters for the Friends' General Conference, which will meet in Richmond, Ind., Eighth month 26th to Ninth month 2nd.

L. Oscar Moon, who was taken ill with typhus a short time ago, has now passed the crisis and is on the way to recovery, according to the cable received at the Service Committee headquarters. At the present writing, no further cases of typhus, either in the Polish or Russian Unit, have been reported, and those who still have the disease are reported convalescing as rapidly as can be expected.

In a private letter from England we are informed that John H. Barlow, who was clerk of the London Conference in 1920, is planning to attend, with his wife, the coming session of the Five Years Meeting.—*The American Friend.*

Henry T. Hodgkin and his wife, who have been in religious work in China for an extended time, expect to return to England during the coming summer by way of America.—*The Canadian Friend.*

Rebecca B. Nicholson brought us a copy of the *State Gazette*, of Trenton, N. J., for March 25th, which contains a long and interesting account of the old Stony Brook Meeting House, near Princeton, N. J. Annual sessions are held there by the Society of Friends. The history of the meeting house dates back to 1709, and the article printed in the *Gazette* traces it from that time to the present. Doubtless many Friends would enjoy reading the account, which is too long to be reprinted in the INTELLIGENCER, and we would suggest that copies can probably be obtained by writing to the office of the *State Gazette*, Trenton, N. J.

FRIENDS' MEETING AT ST. PETERSBURG, FLORDIA

The fourth season of Friends' Meeting held at St. Petersburg, Florida, at the home of Sarah E. Gardner-Magill, was opened on Twelfth month 18, 1921, and closed for this season Fourth month 19, 1922. This meeting has been attended by 140 different people from 12 states of the Union.

The weekly attendance has been from 45 to 70 persons, both branches of the Society of Friends having attended these meetings.

A record is being kept of each one attending with their address, both home and city, so they can be easily located, and for future reference.

Friends have manifested much interest in each meeting. No one entirely silent meeting has been held. While a period of living silence pervaded the meeting, the spoken message came frequently, during the season from William Cocks, N. Y., John and Elizabeth Percy, N. Y., Augustus Brosius and Frank M. Bartrum, Chester Co., James Forest, George Row, Bucks Co., Sara E. G. Magill, and several others gave brief messages. At the closing meeting a deep feeling of gratitude prevailed, and expressions of thanks were extended to our Friend for her kindness in making it possible for this large community of Friends to find a meeting place and a warm welcome in her hospitable home.

Phoenixville, Pa. HETTIE Y. HALLOWELL.

221 EAST 15TH ST., NEW YORK CITY

One of the most important events in New York Quaker society for the Fourth month was the Tea-Meeting held at the Orthodox Meeting-house, 144 East Twentieth St. on the 16th. The Tea-Meeting is a monthly event, and is well patronized by every kind of Friend. It is regularly held at 5.30 in the afternoon. Tea, sandwiches, and cake are served. These are followed by a little music, and that again by a talk by somebody worth hearing. The meeting ends at eight, unless somebody forgets about the time, which occasionally happens.

But on the 16th, the Tea-Meeting promoters decided to extend its spirit of hospitality throughout the entire day. Notices were sent to all the out-of-town Friends of both branches, on Long Island, in northern New Jersey, and as far up the Hudson as Poughkeepsie, inviting them to attend Meeting, eat dinner at Twentieth St., amuse themselves as they pleased in the afternoon (with guides, if desired), and attend the Tea-Meeting at 5.30. "Everybody is invited to everything" was the spirit of the day, and a goodly number availed themselves of the opportunity.

Augustus T. Murray spoke to an unusually large Meeting in the morning, on the meaning of Easter, and the inspiration of the resurrection. People then adjourned to the plain but hearty meal which had been provided. Many persons found friends present whom they had not seen for months, and the occasion was one of reunion. This was even more so at the evening meeting, which was attended by about a hundred people. A number, both in New York and nearby towns, who had attended their own meetings in the morning came in for the Tea-Meeting. Augustus T. Murray spoke on "Our Part in Friendly Service," with especial reference to the Home Service work now being planned by the Service Committee.

A number of Friends of the Twentieth Street Meeting are working very hard to make these monthly gatherings representative of and attended by all nearby Friends. Their efforts are meeting with a most hearty response in every direction, and are of a value which cannot yet be estimated.

"The Young Friends' Movement of New York" is to be taken in a geographical sense, almost entirely. It includes in its potential membership all young Friends between the ages of fifteen and thirty-five, living in New York State and northern New Jersey whether they belong to a New York Yearly Meeting or to some other; and other young people who are closely enough connected to wish to ally themselves with the group. Actually, the Movement does not yet include even half of those whom it hopes for, but all these groups are represented in its membership, and its card index of members is steadily lengthening. Those living in and near New York City have arranged for the use of the gymnasium of the Friends' Seminary every other Fifth-day evening, to play basket-ball, and other games, for exercise, fun, and fellowship. As soon as the Seminary closes for the summer, it is planned to convert the largest playground into a tennis-court which will be available throughout the summer for the Young Friends' Movement, and others interested.

MICKLETON FRIENDS

Mickleton has been having an unusual amount of the good things lately! On the 1st and 2nd of this month we had Abigail Blackburn, Eleanor Darnell, David Paul, Eugene Dungan and John Ruhlman with us as Pilgrims. They were a group of earnest, thoughtful young people bringing us their views on "The Present-day Opportunities."

They urged that we guard against the ruts of self-satisfaction and the comfortable feeling of laurels won. On First-day all had some message of love or encouragement for us at meeting or First-day School. One told of the group work and group thinking that is being carried on at their meeting. They find the group thinking much broader than individual thought.

On Seventh-day, the 8th, the F. D. S. Conference met here. Several of the schools have gained in numbers and none report any lack of interest. One school has lengthened its study period fifteen minutes, and two or more report organized classes. Discussion on teacher training took up the rest of the morning session.

Lucy A. H. Tyler having served the meeting as clerk for the past eight years and desiring to be released, the committee offered the name of Ella H. Brown for clerk and Hannah Gaunt for assistant clerk. Both names were heartily united with. A feeling of grateful appreciation for the retiring clerk was expressed.

Jane Rushmore was the first speaker for the afternoon. Her subject was: "F. D. S. Teaching" and she gave us a half hour of stirring thoughts in her usual "hit-the-nail-on-the-head" manner which was full of help. This thought was predominant, "*Believe* your work is worth while, then *make* it so."

Grace Adams, Gloucester County Sunday-school Superintendent, gave the closing address, urging all to greater faithfulness in the work. Her close touch with the county work gives her the ability to bring many interesting illustrations into her talk.

We closed feeling we had had a real feast of good thoughts and ideas left with us to make practical.

R. L. B.

BALTIMORE'S CCL

The symbol "CCL" has been adopted to denote the 250th Anniversary celebration of the founding of Baltimore Yearly Meeting. These Latin numerals signify 250, and the appropriate Latin word is too long and intricate for any but a Russian to use.

The plans for this event are going forward very well indeed, and the program is now passing through the press. Those in the two Baltimore Meetings, young and older, are co-operating with enthusiasm in all of the many details.

The pageant is already arousing much interest even outside of Friendly circles. A beautiful hall—not a theatre—seating 1200 people, has been secured for the occasion. There will be presented fourteen scenes from Quaker history, illustrating in a graphic way, not only striking events of the past, but also the great principles for which our Society has formerly stood, and advocates also at the present time. This will be a real message.

But the pageant is only one of the interesting events. There will be present speakers of international reputation who, in the course of the five sessions will treat of such topics as "The Founding of Quakerism," "Our Duty to Other Peoples," "The Influence of Friends on Colonial Life," "The Founding and Development of Quakerism in Maryland," "The Landing of William Penn," "The New Social Order," and "The Message of Christ to the World of To-day."

Then there is the all-day excursion on the lovely Chesapeake Bay, which will be a revelation of charming scenery and points of historic interest. The steamer will pass the spot where "The Star Spangled Banner" was written.

Publications of Interest

"Peace and Bread in Time of War," by Jane Addams. The Macmillan Co., New York. 1922. Pp. 257. $1.75. Miss Addams states in her "Foreword" that this book is a "brief history of the efforts for peace made by a small group of American women in the United States during the European war, and of their connection with the women of other countries, as together they became organized into the Women's International League for Peace and Freedom." It is a work bound up in a score of ways with the ideals and experience of Friends during the war. Many of our women shared with Miss Addams the brave efforts which she describes to withstand the tide of war psychology. Many of our reconstruction workers will remember the night on which she and Jeanette Rankin visited Grange le Comte in France. All of us will read these pages with sympathy and draw from them much inspiration for the still-unfinished crusade for peace.

"Preaching In London," by Joseph Fort Newton. George H. Doran Co., New York. 1922. Pp. 140. $1.50. This record of an American a "Preacher Ambassador" in England, forms an interesting comparison with Miss Addams' book noted above. It is the account of one who stayed inside humanity's war movement, instead of resisting it, but who saw much of the real meaning of the war during the war, and still more of its meaning when "Peace" came to bring "Chaos." The record of contacts with outstanding figures in English public and cultural life, the comment on men, movements and events, is keen and stimulating; the frank reactions of mind which is quick to perceive that "A conservative in England would be a radical in America, so far are they in advance of us."

"The Book of Job," by Moses Buttenweiser. The Macmillan Co., New York. 1922. Pp. 370. $4.00. A rearranged text with extended comments, both the rearrangement and the notes of which "bring out and sustain a deeper and more satisfactory meaning of the poem, both as to the reason and the literary sense."

Three comparatively brief publications are of outstanding value to the busy Friend who feels a concern to understand the "coal situation." One is the "Coal Number" of the Survey Graphic, issued March 25th, and obtainable from the Survey Associates, 112 E. 19th St., New York City, price 30 cents a copy. This contains articles, on all phases of America's coal problem, by representatives of operators, miners, and the public; and is illustrated with photographs and drawings.

Largely a digest of the above, but containing some new material, is "The Coal Crisis," a special number of the "Information Service" issued by the Commission on the Church and Social Service of the Federal Council of Churches. It is dated April 11. Such surplus copies as are available, may be obtained by writing to the Council offices, 105 E. 22nd St., New York City. Finally, an important pamphlet is just being issued by the Department of Industrial Studies, of the Russell Sage Foundation, New York City. It is by Louis Bloch, and is entitled: "The Coal Miners' Insecurity; Facts about Irregularity of Employment in the Bituminous Coal Industry in the United States." It contains the results of a careful unbiased study, and is made graphic by numerous diagrams and tables.

BIRTHS

CALVERT—Near Selma, Ohio, on Third month 25th, to J. Donald and Mildred Henley Calvert, a daughter, whose name is Martha Jane Calvert.

MARRIAGES

HALL-WASHBURN—On Fourth month 12th, Winfield Scott Hall and Antoinette Kirk Washburn, both of Chappaqua, N. Y.

DEATHS

COX—On Fourth month 10th, at San Jose, California, Lydia Shipley Bean Cox, daughter of Joel Bean, and wife of Charles Cox.

MORRIS—At Philadelphia, on Fourth month 12th, George Spencer Morris, son of late Samuel and Lydia Spencer Morris.

COMING EVENTS

FOURTH MONTH

22nd—Haddonfield First-day School Union will be held at Moorestown, N. J., at 10.30 a. m. Afternoon session at 2.30.

22nd—Concord First-day School Union. See Notice.

22nd and 23rd—Pilgrimage under care of the Young Friends' Movement at Fair Hill Meeting.

23rd—Philadelphia Quarterly Meeting's Visiting Committee expects to attend meeting at Valley Meeting, at 10.30 a. m. First-day School at 11.30 a. m.

23rd—E. Maria Bishop is expecting to be present at the meeting for worship at Lincoln, Va.

23rd—Southern Half-Yearly Meeting, at Easton, Md.

23rd—Daniel Batchellor is planning to be at the meeting at Hockessin, Del., at 10 a. m., and First-day School following.

23rd—William J. MacWatters expects to visit Crosswicks Meeting and First-day School, Crosswicks, N. J.

23rd—Conference class at 15th and Race Streets, Philadelphia, at close of meeting for worship, at 11.40 a. m. Speaker—Edith M. Winder. Subject—Methods of Church Extension in the Day of George Fox and his Followers.

25th—Western Quarterly Meeting at London Grove, Pa. Daniel Batchellor expects to attend.

27th—Members of the Young Friends' Movement, and others of appropriate age and condition are invited to the gymnasium of Friends' Seminary, New York, from 8 to 10. Wear old clothes and tennis shoes, and be ready for any. thing. Use Rutherford Place entrance.

27th—Caln Quarterly Meeting, at Christiana, Pa., Daniel Batchellor expects to attend.

29th—Westbury Quarterly Meeting will be held at 110 Schermerhorn Street, Brooklyn, at 10.30 a. m. Lunch will be served at noon. The subject of the afternoon session at 2.30 will be "Gandhi and Race Problems." Norman Thomas will be the speaker. Daniel Batchellor expects to be present.

29th—First-day School Conference at Oxford, Pa., at 10 a. m. Subject—Duties and Responsibilities of Superintendents. At 2 p. m., adult Bible Work and Dramatization of Bible Stories. Bliss and La Verne Forbush will attend. Box lunch.

29th and 30th—Pilgrimage under care of the Young Friends' Movement at Langhorne and Newtown Meetings.

29th-30th—Farmington Half-Yearly Meeting at Orchard Park. Business session on Seventh-day the 29th, at 3 p. m. Meeting for worship on First-day, the 30th, at 11 a. m., and an afternoon session. Frederick J. Libby and Isaac Wilson are expecting to be present.

30th—E. Maria Bishop will be at Hopewell, Va., attending meeting in the morning at 11 a. m., and a conference in the afternoon.

FIFTH MONTH

2nd—Concord Quarterly Meeting, at Providence Meeting House, Chester, Pa., 10 a. m., Daylight saving time.

4th—Abington Quarterly Meeting at Horsham, Pa., at 10.30 a. m., Standard time.

5th-6th—Pilgrimage under care of the young Friends' Movement, at West Chester, Pa.

6th—Philadelphia Quarterly Meeting will be held in Germantown Meeting House, 45 W. School House Lane, Germantown, on Fifth month 6th, Seventh-day afternoon.

Religious Meeting, 1.30 p. m.; Business Meeting, 2.30 p. m. Box Supper (coffee, ice cream and cake will be served). Entertainment by Germantown Friends' Association 7.30 p. m.

7th—First-day at 3 p. m. The usual semi-annual Community Meeting for worship will be held at Chichester Friends' Meeting House under care of a Committee of Concord Quarterly Meeting. All persons are welcome and young people particularly invited. Joseph H. Willits, of Swarthmore, expects to attend. Train leaves 24th and Chestnut Sts., for Boothwyn at 1.30 p. m.; Darby, 1.43; Chester, 2.00; returning about 4.45 p. m. Trains will stop at cross-road near the Meeting house.

7th—Purchase Quarterly Meeting, at Amawalk, N. Y. See notice.

8th—Nine Partners Half-Yearly Meeting, at Poughkeepsie, N. Y.

8th—Easton and Granville Half-Yearly Meeting, at Granville, N. Y., at 11 a. m. Meeting of Ministry and Counsel, same day, at 10 a. m.

NOTICE—Friends' Neighborhood Guild invites thee to tea on First-day, April 23rd, 1922, from 3.30 to 5.30; Elbert Russell will speak at four. Exhibition of work done by children in art, millinery, carpentry, and handcraft. R. S. V. P. Friends' Neighborhood Guild, Fourth and Green Streets.

NOTICE—Rummage Sale! Last week in April. Benefit of Friends' Home for Children. Will you help the children by saving rummage? Send direct to Home by April 24, or arrangements for collecting can be made by calling: Lula B. Dixon, 918 S. 49th Street, Woodland 2361-J; Anna Kirby Swope, 4926 Cedar Avenue, Woodland 2858-J; Anna Hall, 5301 Woodbine Avenue, Overbrook 0411.

NOTICE—West Philadelphia First-day School, 35th and Lancaster Avenue, has planned a gathering for "Friendly Merriment" on Fourth month 22nd, Seventh-day, at 7.30 p. m. Fun for all ages at no cost to anyone, including ice cream. Children, parents and interested friends are invited. Don't miss it.

NOTICE—Concord First-day School Union at Swarthmore, Pa., on Fourth month 22nd, at 10 a. m. Open discussion on question of a field-worker in the schools of our Union. Afternoon session at 2 o'clock. Bliss Forbush will speak on Organization of the First-day School work. La Verne Forbush will tell how to dramatize Bible stories in our schools. Bus meets Media short line at Chester Road on the hour.

NOTICE—Purchase Quarterly Meeting will be held at Amawalk, at 10.30 a. m., Standard time. Joel Borton will be in attendance. Young Friends' Meeting at 2. p. m. Subject for discussion—"Good Will to Men." Meeting of Ministry and Counsel at 9.30 a. m., same day. Train leaves Sedgwick Avenue, 6.40 a. m., Elmsford, 7.39; Millwood, 8.10. Arrives at Amawalk, 8.34 a. m. Returning leaves Amawalk 4.45.

What a Non-Friend Thinks of the "Intelligencer"

March 17th, 1922.

THE FRIENDS' INTELLIGENCER,
Philadelphia.

My Dear Friends:

Enclosed find my check for another year of the INTELLIGENCER. Your paper is rightly named. I like its spirit. It breathes a great benediction every time it comes to my home.

Sincerely,
ELMER WARD COLE.

Elmer Ward Cole, D.D., is minister of a church in Indiana. If one who is not a Friend feels this way about the INTELLIGENCER, is it not thy duty to help arouse those Friends who do not now read it, to a sense of its value.

Will thee not urge Friends who are not now subscribers to take it for three months at the low price of thirty-five cents? Send us the names and addresses and we will send bill and coin card to make payment easy.

To make experiments is the most practical thing one can do. —*Major Leonard Darwin.*

LUKE 2. 14—AMERICA'S ANGELUS

"Glory to God in the highest, and on earth peace, good will toward men."

Stand back of President Harding in Prayer for Universal Peace by meditating daily, at noon, on the fourteenth verse of the second chapter of Luke.

Ask your friends to help make this a Universal Meditation for Universal Peace

Pass it on *Friends in Christ*

REGULAR MEETINGS

OAKLAND, CALIF. — A FRIENDS' Meeting is held every First-day at 11 A. M., in the Extension Room, Y. W. C. A. Building, Webster Street, above 14th. Visiting Friends always welcome.

FRIENDS' MEETING IN PASADENA, California — Orange Grove Monthly Meeting of Friends, 520 East Orange Grove Avenue, Pasadena, California. Meeting for worship, First-day, 11 A. M. Monthly Meeting, the second First-day of each month, at 1.45 P. M.

CENTRAL MEETING OF FRIENDS (Chicago), meets every First-day in Room 706, 410 South Michigan Avenue, at 10.45 A. M. Visitors are invited.

WANTED

SWARTHMORE COLLEGE STUDENT desires position as mother's helper for the summer. Address G. P. K., Box 441, Swarthmore College, Swarthmore, Pa.

WANTED—POSITION AS COMPANION, care of invalid, or housekeeper. Address I. 151, Friends' Intelligencer.

WANTED — HOUSEKEEPER (MANAGER), capable woman of refinement who desires good permanent home in Philadelphia suburbs with family of three children and male adult. Box S. 150, Friends' Intelligencer.

WANTED—MAY 1ST, FOR HALF-time work, Friend trained in office work. Must be good typist. Apply in writing to A. 159, Friends' Intelligencer.

WANTED — SUMMER BOARD FOR three adults, with private family on farm. Commuting distance from Philadelphia. Address D. 154, Friends' Intelligencer.

WANTED — PRINCIPAL WITH EXPERIENCE for Friends' school in country town, 20 miles from Philadelphia. Good salary to teachers employed. Address S. 153, Friends' Intelligencer.

WANTED — POSITION AS CHAUFFEUR, four years' experience; references. Charles A. Neiman, 915 W. Lehigh Ave., Philadelphia.

WANTED — POSITION AS CHAUFFEUR, 12 years' experience; married; references; country preferred. John C. Elser, 3749 Germantown Ave., Philadelphia.

WANTED — PRINCIPAL WITH EXPERIENCE for Friends' school in country town, 20 miles from Philadelphia. Good salary; two teachers employed. Address S. 153, Friends' Intelligencer.

FOR RENT

FOR RENT—THE PACKER COTTAGE at Buck Hill. Accommodations for five or six. Located within fifteen minutes' walk of Inn. For particulars inquire Franklin Packer, Newtown, Pa.

FOR RENT—AT BUCK HILL FALLS, cottage, from May 1st to June 5th. Apply, Mary S. A. Jenkins, Gwynedd, Pa.

FOR RENT—COOL, TWO-STORY house; furnished; bath. May 15th to October 1st. Address G. 160, Friends' Intelligencer, or phone Media 304-J.

FOR RENT—FOR ALL OR PART OF season, delightful furnished cottage among New Hampshire pines in Quaker neighborhood. Address W. 161, Friends' Intelligencer.

FOR RENT—APARTMENT FOR light housekeeping, in suburban home. Two large rooms, semi-private bath, heat, hot water, electric lights, gas, front and back porches, large yard, old shade. Convenient to train, trolley and bus line. Good roads and convenient garages. Price reasonable. C. B. Llewellynm, Cheltenham, Pa. Bell Phone—Cheltenham 1241-W.

IN FIFTH MONTH, 1922, THE PHILAdelphia Young Friends' Association, Inc., expect to have a few rooms available for permanent guests. Address 140 North 15th Street, Philadelphia.

FOR SALE

FOR SALE—BRICK AND FRAME detached residence, well built; 10 rooms, bath, sleeping porch, glassed in; gas and electricity, modern conveniences; near Friends' School and Meeting House, Lansdowne, Pa. Apply J. 100, Friends' Intelligencer.

Send two or more names of persons who might be interested in Friends by reading the INTELLIGENCER. A good way to get new members.

Strawbridge & Clothier

A Little Clearance of Boys' Clothing!

No boy and no mother in Philadelphia would want to miss this opportunity if they could see the values, now. The best thing to do is to come in and see the values as soon as possible. Just a hurried clear-away of several odd and incomplete lines at prices that will insure quick action.

Wool Suits With Extra Trousers—$8.75

Wonderful value. Mohair-lined coat, full-lined knickerbockers. Sizes 7 to 16 years—$8.75.

Suits With Extra Trousers—$10.75

These all-wool Cheviot Suits, with two pairs of trousers, have just arrived. They should have been here last week, and their late arrival necessitates as unusually low price to insure quick clearance. Sizes 8 to 18 years. Special at $10.75.

Wool Serge Top Coats—$5.75

Of fine twill serge, with chevron on sleeve. Most attractive. Sizes 3 to 8 years—$5.75.

Small Boys' Wash Suits—$1.95

Made of strong, unbleached drill, with self collar, and colored collar in Middy or Oliver Twist styles. Sizes 3 to 8 years. Special—$1.95.

Strawbridge & Clothier—Second Floor, Filbert Street, East

Over-Blouses

A NOTABLE VALUE

$10.00

Of crepe de chine. Elaborate designs in steel beads are lovely against canna, bisque and navy blue crepe de chine. In kimono style, slim in effect, and with short sleeves and collarless neck-line as Fashion decrees. Such Over-Blouses are rare at this price—$10.00.

Second Floor, Centre

White Voile

BLOUSES

MUCH UNDER PRICE

$3.85

Daintily tucked models that you will know at a glance are out of their class as far as price is concerned. Trimmed with imported embroidered organdie panels and Valenciennes lace.

Second Floor, Centre

STRAWBRIDGE & CLOTHIER

MARKET STREET EIGHTH STREET FILBERT STREET

PHILADELPHIA, PA.

To the Lot Holders and others interested in Fairhill Burial Ground:

GREEN STREET Monthly Meeting has funds available for the encouragement of the practice of cremating the dead to be interred in Fairhill Burial Ground. We wish to bring this fact as prominently as possible to those who may be interested. We are prepared to undertake the expense of cremation in case any lot holder desires us to do so.

Those interested should communicate with William H. Gaskill, Treasurer of the Committee of Interments, Green Street Monthly Meeting, or any of the following members of the Committee.

William H. Gaskill, 3201 Arch St.
Samuel N. Longstreth, 1218 Chestnut St.
Charles F. Jenkins, 232 South Seventh St.
Stuart S. Graves, 3033 Germantown Ave.

ADVERTISING RATE in the FRIENDS' INTELLIGENCER, for Help Wanted, Positions Wanted, Rooms for Rent, Notices, and other classified advertisements without display, for each insertion, 2 cents per word, including name, initials and address. Answers may be sent to a box at the INTELLIGENCER office, if so directed.

For display advertising the rate is 10 cents per agate line, or $1.40 per column inch, each insertion. On ten or more insertions in a year from date of order, ten per cent. discount. Thus a four-inch single-column or two-inch double-column advertisement costs $5.60 each insertion, less ten per cent., or 5.04 net each time for ten or more insertions. Matter may be changed whenever desired, without extra charge.

Experience has proved the INTELLIGENCER to be a remarkably good advertising medium. All advertisements must "pass the censor!"

Address 140 N. 15th St., Philadelphia

The Friends' Intelligencer

Established 1844

FOURTH MONTH 29, 1922

Volume 79
Number 17

Contents

EDITORIALS

THE FRIENDS' INTELLIGENCER

Published weekly, 140 N. 15th Street, Philadelphia, Pa., by Friends' Intelligencer Association, Ltd.

WALTER H. ABELL, Editor

SUE C. YERKES, *Business Manager*

Editorial Board: Elizabeth Powell Bond, Thomas A. Jenkins, J. Russell Smith, George A. Walton.

Board of Managers: Edward Cornell, Alice Hall Paxson, Paul M. Pearson, Annie Hillborn, Elwood Hollingshead, William C. Biddle, Charles F. Jenkins, Edith M. Winder, Frances M. White.

Officers of Intelligencer Associates: Ellwood Burdsall, Chairman; Bertha L. Broomell, Secretary; Herbert P. Worth, Treasurer.

Subscription rates: United States, Mexico, Cuba and Panama, $2.50 per year. Canada and other foreign countries, $3.00 per year. Checks should be made payable to Friends' Intelligencer Association, Ltd.

Entered as Second Class Matter at Philadelphia Post Office.

Homes During Yearly Meeting Week.

Friends expecting to attend Philadelphia Yearly Meeting and wishing the assistance of the committee appointed by the two Monthly Meetings of Philadelphia to help Friends in securing suitable homes, are asked to communicate with *Almira P. Harlan*, Fifteenth and Race Streets, Philadelphia, and they will be furnished with a list from which they can select and engage rooms for themselves.

Persons willing to assist in the dining-room during Yearly Meeting week will please communicate with Esther W. Fell, 433 School Lane, Germantown, Philadelphia.

To the Lot Holders and others interested in Fairhill Burial Ground:

GREEN STREET Monthly Meeting has funds available for the encouragement of the practice of cremating the dead to be interred in Fairhill Burial Ground. We wish to bring this fact as prominently as possible to those who may be interested. We are prepared to undertake the expense of cremation in case any lot holder desires us to do so.

Those interested should communicate with William H. Gaskill, Treasurer of the Committee of Interments, Green Street Monthly Meeting, or any of the following members of the Committee.

William H. Gaskill, 3201 Arch St.
Samuel N. Longstreth, 1218 Chestnut St.
Charles F. Jenkins, 232 South Seventh St.
Stuart S. Graves, 3033 Germantown Ave.

The Friends' Intelligencer

The religion of Friends is based on faith in the "INWARD LIGHT," or direct revelation of God's spirit and will in every seeking soul.

The INTELLIGENCER is interested in all who bear the name of Friends in every part of the world, and aims to promote love, unity and intercourse among all branches and with all religious societies.

ESTABLISHED 1844 | PHILADELPHIA, FOURTH MONTH 29, 1922 | VOLUME 79 NUMBER 17

Practical Idealism In Swarthmore Monthly Meeting

Following these editorial notes will be found the first half of a report on the present "coal situation." This report was prepared by Drew Pearson, in conjunction with other members of a committee especially appointed for the purpose by Swarthmore Monthly Meeting.

The action of the Meeting in appointing such a committee seems to us peculiarly significant. All Friends' Meetings stand for the ideal of brotherhood and peace. Their queries call for unstinted effort on the part of their members to promote the extension and practical application of that ideal. "Wars and rumors of wars" in the coal industry come as a challenge to the cause. Shall the Meeting "pass by on the other side"; shall it be content with a traditional and formal answer to its queries—which is really an evasion, not an answer at all—or shall it accept the challenge and do its best to put its ideals to work where they are needed?

Swarthmore Monthly Meeting decided on the latter course. It appointed a committee to study the situation and inform its members as to the facts. Its action seems to us significant for at least three distinct reasons. It has obtained, and extended a knowledge of, the facts themselves; thereby hastening an intelligent settlement of an important industrial strife. In the second place, it has united in a mutual attempt to reach the truth, Friends who differ in their tendencies of economic outlook. By working together and seeking together, we come to understand each other and to build up a basis of fellowship which is broad enough to include, and to profit by, differences of individual opinion. It is such a spirit of fellowship, rather than any of the oft-mooted "isms" in particular, which marks a living expression of our ideals, and which offers the surest hope of a fraternal social order.

Finally, this action on the part of Swarthmore Monthly Meeting is important because it represents another concrete step in relating Friends' traditional ideals to the present needs of the world. Too easily our principles may be accepted on the basis of their relation to the past—to slavery rather than economic status, to wars in general rather than to *this* war, to alcoholic drinks and tobacco rather than to luxury and our general standard of living. Such an attitude means formalism and eventually the death of the spirit. Nothing will do more to alienate from the Meeting the spirit of sincere youth, a spirit sensing something of the world's need, than a feeling on the part our younger members that Meeting activities are formal and routine, that they do not face the present social challenge and attempt to make a contribution toward solving it.

Swarthmore's study of the coal situation stimulates the imagination and the enthusiasm by marking a step toward the union of tradition with present reality. The spirit in which it is being made is worthy of emulation by all our Meetings.

Does This Apply to Thee?

Scores of Friends are living near meetings other than that wherein their membership is recorded. Naturally their interest in the neighboring meeting is less than if by membership they could participate in its business activities. For the strengthening of themselves and the Society, should not these Friends seriously consider the advisability of moving their membership to the nearest Meeting?

Each Meeting would be strengthened by seeking to know Friends of other Meetings living within its limits, by attracting their attendance, and by inviting a transfer of membership.

Every Meeting, at least once a year, should correspond with its non-resident members, to show the continued interest of the home meeting. Only absent members can tell how welcome these letters are.

When these non-resident members are carefully reported to the Central Bureau and the Advancement Committees, those in charge of the wider activities are able to make Friends from distant points known to each other, and thus Friendly groups have been formed in several communities, to the mutual benefit and pleasure of many. The Friendly groups in

Cambridge, Mass., Newark, N. J., Lancaster, Harrisburg, Pittsburgh, Buffalo, Detroit, Des Moines, Denver, Portland, Ore., and Oakland, Cal., have been formed and strengthened by a centralized knowledge of the whereabouts of non-resident members.

We suggest as an aid to greater effectiveness in the Society that Friends make it a general principle to record their membership in the meeting nearest to their place of residence; and that isolated members report their location, not only to their home Meeting, but to the Advancement Committee of the General Conference, 140 N. 15th St., Philadelphia, Pa.

Coal Facts

By Drew Pearson

The Substance of a Report Prepared at the Direction of Swarthmore Monthly Meeting

"Do we maintain a faithful testimony in favor of the peaceful settlement of differences, whether industrial or political, and against all war and preparation for and incitement to it?"

This query, discussed by the Swarthmore Monthly Meeting last winter, led to the conclusion that our Society has much to learn about the industrial problems of our time. Swarthmore Friends felt an especial need for more information concerning the present coal strike. They felt that a satisfactory settlement of the coal problem could be attained only when the public was thoroughly informed of the true facts. As a step in this direction, therefore, a committee was appointed under the chairmanship of J. Russell Smith, to acquaint the Meeting with the issues involved in the coal crisis and to indicate alternate solutions.

The committee decided that it could best lay the problem of coal before the Meeting, by holding a series of forum discussions. At the first of these, held on April 9th, the general survey of the situation, given below, was presented. Conclusions and solutions were left to be discussed at another meeting, when Friends would be more familiar with the problem.

The facts and figures herein presented are based upon such recognized authorities as the Federal Trade Commission and the United States Geological Survey; and also upon personal observation during a visit to the West Virginia coal fields as one of the representatives of the American Friends' Service Committee.

The first thing that strikes a visitor to the West Virginia coal fields is the excess of mines and miners. The coal operator bewails the fact that there are too many mines for all to do business, and the miner bewails the fact that there are too many miners for all to get jobs. Not only is this true of West Virginia but the coal industry thruout the whole of the United States has mines and miners capable of producing 40% more coal than our industries can consume or we can export to foreign markets. Because of this condition, it is recognized that the present strike was precipitated by the operators essentially for the purpose of forcing the surplus mines with their surplus miners out of the coal industry. I stress this at the very start because it is the most essential point necessary to an understanding of the coal strike, and a point which must be kept constantly in mind in considering the position of the operators and miners.

The Bituminous Coal Fields

The position of the operators and miners outlined below, deals only with the bituminous or soft coal fields. The demands of the anthracite or hard coal miners who work only in eastern Pennsylvania, differ in that they seek a 20% wage increase which will put their income on a level with that of the bituminous miner. Because the demands of the two fields are essentially similar, and because the bituminous field is so predominately important, producing 85% of the country's coal, we shall consider only the latter in this report.

However, within the bituminous coal industry itself, there are two kinds of fields—the central competitive field which includes western Pennsylvania, northern West Virginia, Ohio, Indiana and Illinois; and the non-competitive fields which include chiefly southern West Virginia, Tennessee, Kentucky, Alabama, Kansas, and Colorado. The former are called competitive because the operators here compete for the immense iron and steel market in Ohio and Pennsylvania, for the railroad market created by the network of trunk lines between Chicago and New York, and for the Great Lake barge traffic. The other fields, being distant from these industrial centers and trade routes, must pay a higher freight tariff in order to send their coal north. Therefore, in order to offset this higher rate and allow their coal to compete with the coal of Pennsylvania, Ohio, Indiana, and Illinois, the miners in the non-competitive fields to the south, accept a lower wage.

The central competitive field is almost completely unionized. However, in the non-competitive fields of West Virginia, Kentucky, Alabama, and Colorado, about half the miners belong to the union. It is significant that in the solidly unionized fields, the great majority of miners are native Americans, originally of English, Scotch, Welsh, and Irish stock, but having lived in this country more than one generation. On the other hand, foreign born workers predominate in the non-union fields. While the miner in the central competitive field is a progressive member of his community, the miner of West Virginia, Kentucky, Tennessee, and Alabama, even tho he date his ancestry back to Revolutionary days as many of them do, is ignorant and backward. He lives in a cabin in an isolated mountain gulch, has seldom travelled far from home, and can only handle a pick, wheelbarrow, or rifle. He does not realize that his unsteady income is due to a surplus of mines and a surplus of miners; and if he did he lacks the initiative to find a new job and the ability to make a living at another trade.

The Miners' Demands

The miners of all these fields—competitive and non-competitive—unite in demanding:

1. *A continuation of the present wage scale.* The present wage scale was awarded them on March 31, 1920, and was to continue in effect until March 31, 1922.

2. *A five day week.* In making this demand, the miners point out that during the last 30 years they have averaged but 215 days of work per year, or four days per week. And these days have been so scattered—a month on full time or even overtime, then two or three months of idleness—that the miner is never sure of his income, and falls into the demoralizing habit of spasmodic work. Instead the miner now asks to be allowed to work five days per week and by slowing up weekly production, hopes to spread his work out over the entire year, thereby insuring himself of a steady, regular income.

The miner also argues that since there are 40% more miners than are required in the coal industry, that by giving each man a limited number of working days, there may be work for all.

3. *A six hour day.* In asking this, the miners point out that in most mines a miner spends one hour in walking thru the mine to his place of work, and one hour back again, making a total of eight hours underground. Besides, the noon lunch-hour is practically eliminated in the mine, because the miner in his sweating condition, cannot risk injury to his health by remaining inactive in the cool mine.

Furthermore, much time is lost at the start of the day, under the present eight hour system. The miners frequently must wait at the mouth of the mine for new tracks to be laid, for cave-ins to be cleared away, for repairs and for railroad cars. The six-hour day gives the management time to prepare for the day's operations and allows the miner to spend his time 100% in actual work.

Moreover, since a contract miner is paid only according to the number of tons he produces, a six-hour day means no wage increase for him. It means that he works harder during the six hours in order to produce a tonnage equivalent to that which he once produced in eight hours. However, a six-hour day does mean a wage increase for company miners and day laborers who are paid by the hour instead of by the day.

4. *Weekly* instead of bi-weekly *pay*, a *two-year agreement* with the operators, and the *elimination of differentials*—which we shall not discuss, because they are not important enough to block an agreement once the aforementioned major issues are decided.

The Operators' Case

On the other hand, the coal operators oppose the union demands and put forth the following counter arguments:

1. *The margin of profits is so small that a continued operation of many mines is not profitable.* (They point out that Income Tax Reports for 1918, from 1,551 bituminous operators show an average return on investment of 9.72%. 1918 was probably the best year ever enjoyed by the bituminous coal industry. The Bureau of Internal Revenue estimates that the investment return during 1919 was between 8% and 9%. Similar data for the years following is not available; but it is unquestionably true that since the war, the operators' margin of profit has materially decreased.)

2. The operators in the central competitive field claim that the operators in the south—chiefly in Mingo, Logan, Mercer, and McDowell counties, West Virginia—who have succeeded in barring the union, can undersell them in the open market because of reduced labor cost.

3. Pleading as an excuse, the fact that many of the operators and miners are already under an indictment by the Federal Government for a previous attempt to agree on yearly wage rates, the *operators have flatly refused to meet the miners in conference.* (This is an open break of the previous wage agreement drawn up by President Wilson's Bituminous Coal Commission on which sat representatives of the operators, the miners, and the public, and which provided for "an Interstate Joint Conference to be held prior to April 1, 1922." The miners requested the operators to meet with them March 2nd, but the latter refused.)

These are the most essential claims and arguments of the coal operators and miners. The Federal Government has been inclined to let the two factions fight out the issue without intervention. Secretary of Labor Davis has criticised the operators for refusing to confer with the miners, and Attorney General Daugherty has pointed out that the Bituminous Coal Commission agreement was one to which the Government was a party, and therefore the operators have violated a legal contract with the Federal Government.

(A second report on "Coal Facts," to be published in the following issue, will take up in detail miners' wages, operators' profits and methods of private management.)

Quaker Meeting

*Introductory Note**

The following poem written, many years ago, was inspired by the little brick Friends' Meeting House in Homeville, Chester Co., Pa. Although this Meeting House is no longer opened as a place of worship except for special meetings or in time of funerals, the grave yard is kept under careful supervision and the beautiful trees still remain, and beautiful memories which can never fade. Thinking they may awaken a responsive echo in the hearts of the descendants of some who worshipped there, I send these verses to the INTELLIGENCER for publication, at the oft repeated request of my eldest grandson.

High in the maples, overhead,
The robin trills her song
Unmindful of the ancient creed,
Pronouncing music wrong.

And by my side a young girl sits;
Her eyes of beauty speak;
A summer rose is in her hair
A fairer on her cheek.

Some old beliefs will pass away,
The voice of song be heard,
And broad brimmed hats a lesson learn
From flower and from bird.

And may we strive in earnest faith
A broader view to gain,
And casting off those fetters, which
Our onward march detain.

Attain at last a noble height,
From early errors free;
Still showing in our dress and life
A sweet simplicity.

*This introductory note was written by the author in the summer of 1921, during her last illness.

How brightly shines the sun today!
A soft air stirs the trees;
The white fleeced clouds sail through the skies
As vessels sail the seas.

A holy Sabbath stillness reigns;
The working world is still;
Hushed is the plough-boy's whistle
And whirr of busy mill.

And in this quaint brick meeting-house,
Endeared by memories old,
My heart recalls, with sigh or smile,
The changes time has told.

O brightly shone the sun as now,
And balmy was the air,
And gayly beat our youthful hearts
Untouched by toil or care.

When, closely packed by mother's hand
'Neath shady oak and elm,
Our family coach rolled slowly out
With father at the helm.

Though sober horse and driver were,
And placid mother's brow,
The echo of our laughing tones
Steals o'er my memory now.

From bonnets void of flower or bow
Came many a burst of song,
And many a softly whispered prayer
That "meeting won't be long."

Beyond the window where I sit
The little graveyard lies,
And scarcely higher than the grass
The modest tombstones rise.

No "city of the dead" is it,—
A quiet country town;
A hamlet where the weak may rest,
The weary ones lie down.

Green is the grass on father's grave;
His heart was green always,
And though his lips ne'er tuned a hymn
His life was full of praise.

ELIZA R. WHITSON.

"DE reason some of us doesn't git along," said Uncle Eben, "is dat we sits down dreamin' of automobiles when we orter be pushin' a wheelbarrar."

Solving the Study-Group Problem

Every so often there springs into existence some new movement. Possibly it aims to further a reform; to gain adherents for a new sect; to introduce new business or social studies; or for any one of a thousand other purposes. Infrequently there exists actual need for the new group, whereupon it becomes firmly entrenched in our social structure. But most often its life span is measured in months.

A movement will continue to function with increasing interest just so long as there is a place for it. When usefulness is ended, or energies become misdirected it will automatically become a thing of the past.

I have been interested in the groups of young Quakers who have started and are carrying on the Young Friends' Movement. Ofttimes the local members meet during First-day School as a Study Group; in other meetings some week-day evening is given over to this activity. The groups start off with a vim: fellowship, study, service as aims make enthusiasm quite natural. But gradually there is a slackening. Finally it takes a superhuman effort to hold together, especially if the group meet other than in conjunction with First-day School.

What is the trouble? I have visited a number of the Study Groups and to me the reason for waning of interest is apparent. There never has been a successful boy's club whose meetings were given to abstract talks. On the contrary, one finds its business running toward challenges to other teams, methods for raising funds for new athletic equipment, plans for hikes and camp—all definitely active longings sponsoring health, sportsmanship and comradeship. The idea of service is brought home by "kind deeds each day." With such varied work, the interlocking of fellowship, study and service is easily seen.

A Father and Son movement with attendant golf and tennis matches, fishin' trips, etc., bases every reason for success on active participation together—here again is the making of a close spiritual relationship by "doing things," rather than merely talking about them. In political circles interest lags till shortly before election, when necessity for actively corralling votes for one's party and candidate brings enthusiasm to high pitch. It lags between times, because there's nothing concrete to do.

Most of the Young Friends' Groups to which I refer devote the period to Bible study. One never could reach a point where all its contained beauty had been found; or all lessons disclosed; or all thoughts crystallized for making lives finer and nearer to an ideal. The study of the Bible is endless. However, does not the following hold truth? Bring a lad through First-day School from kindergarten to Bible Class, and his fundamentals of right and wrong, his spiritual ideals will be well grounded; far more thoroughly, too, than most of us realize. A few more years in theoretical study would help, surely. But is this desirable? Are these years being put to greatest service to himself and to his community? Could some other method intensify the benefit he would ordinarily have received?

Young men and women in ages from fifteen to thirty-five need action. Put their energies to work. At this period when interest in abstract study cannot possibly be held at a maximum (the words "active" and "abstract" are used throughout in the sense of personal application), groups will rarely hold together.

Assume a group in some meeting plans to meet Sixth-day evening at eight. The novelty brings full attendance for a while. Say the group decides on Bible Study. As certain as fate, unless the personality of the leader is intense, the numbers will dwindle as time passes. Possibly group suppers earlier in the evening might help, but that will be found only a temporary measure. Many a First-day School class may be failing in like measure—simply because the single factor of human nature is being overlooked.

The solution: The Trenton Study Group had it well in hand. I have rarely found a class with greater potential ability, earnestness and stick-to-it-ive-ness; so it is a pleasure to outline what I know of their activity. Last Fall, a public speaking class gave every member of this group opportunity to train in vocal expression. It was felt the younger members too seldom gave expression to thoughts in Meeting, and the training might help overcome conscious resistance.

Some of this group spoke at small public gatherings on disarmament. Every member influenced the sending of letters to President Harding, Senators and others, all of which certainly helped swell the avalanche that awoke our government to the national desire on this great question. A large public meeting on "The conference and after" is tentatively planned. The drive for Russian relief found this group actively engaged in helping send flour to the Russians.

These are but a few of the movements in which *active participation* has served to keep up enthusiasm, knit closely the work of its members, increase good-fellowship; and what is probably most important: it has shown the *practical application of Christianity by putting to use the fundamentals absorbed during past years of Bible and other study.*

I do not advocate our study groups or First-day classes running riot in political questions or adopting any anarchistic social tendencies—trust Friends to keep close watch on themselves in this connection! But I do maintain the time has come when sitting in class with a minority talking of things in the abstract must be succeeded or to a large extent supplemented by an intelligent study of world conditions; and discussions held which will be specific in their decisions as how best to serve humanity. The groups should choose an able leader to direct the application of conclusions. Perhaps the leader may be of their number, perhaps an older Friend—it matters not.

Therein lies the way of bringing the Message of Quakerism forcibly to the front; therein lies the hope of the younger groups and the method of increasing numbers and power. Training in thought and word of the Message we hold for the world is at least temporarily sufficient; now, by deed, let these younger members carry on.

Thought . . . word . . . *action.*

ERWIN LIONEL MALONE.

Friends In Austria

By SYBIL JANE MOORE

*(One of the most devoted workers with the American Friends' Service Committee in Austria was Sybil Jane Moore, who is still actively connected with the work of relief, being now engaged in voluntary service as an Associate Secretary at the Philadelphia headquarters.—*ED.)

The American Friends' Service Committee, in co-operation with the English Friends, has had a Mission in Austria since 1919. Its work has been mainly along four lines:

1st—Feeding of children under six years of age, and nursing and expectant mothers.

2nd—Distribution of clothing.

3rd—Increase in the milk supplies for babies and for children's hospitals.

4th—Relief for the salaried professional and pensioned classes.

The supplying of a balanced ration to undernourished children under six years of age has been the largest piece of work. Under this plan, mothers whose children were too young to go to the American Relief Administration feeding stations, drew a fortnightly ration from a central depot, which was prepared in the home. Bimonthly medical examinations, and visits to the homes by the workers controlled the use of this food. During 1921 and 1922. only children under four years of age, and nursing and expectant mothers, about 25,000 in all, were supplied with rations.

Clothing has been furnished at a very low price to families whose children were entitled to draw rations at the depots. All money received from the sale of clothing, or from any other of the Mission's activities, is turned back into the work. Many other groups have also been supplied by this department, after investigation. The need for clothing increases constantly. On March 9th, we received the following cable:

> "Distress in Vienna Increasing Because of Unemployment. Need for Large Consignment of Clothing to be Here By May. Also for Consignment to be Ready for October."

A department organized in 1920, for purchasing cows in the Tyrol, Switzerland and in Holland, and for placing them with dairymen in the vicinity of Vienna, has been enlarged. The milk was distributed to the welfare centres and hospitals in payment for the cows. In this way, nearly 10,000 children are now being helped.

It was found that the salaried and professional classes were in as great distress as the working people. Their salaries have not been increased. The break-up of the Austrian Empire had in many cases destroyed their fields of occupation. The Mission extended its clothing distribution to individual cases in these classes. It developed an Old Age Relief Department to provide for the aged pensioners, whose pensions in depreciated kronen are wholly inadequate. It arranged an adoption plan by which especially delicate children in these families received extra rations.

Aid is given to students in the trade schools and also to university students and professors, in co-operation with other organizations. A somewhat ambitious house-building program has been undertaken for the skilled workers and salaried classes, who are working along the lines of the garden suburb, with land for adequate gardens attached to their houses.

In 1920 and 1921, the work was financed largely by the English Committee, with grants from the Government and "Save-the-Children's Fund." The American Relief Administration and the American Red Cross also made generous grants. The budget—June 1, 1921, to June 1, 1922—for the combined American and English work, was for $250,000; somewhat over $20,000 a month. We have been able to provide only $69,000, instead of the expected $125,000. In consequence, the work was sharply reduced this winter; for we could not ask the English Friends to carry more than their just proportion.

The Service is now being brought to a close through lack of funds. Certain departments are being turned over to the Austrian organizations, under the supervision of two or three Mission members. The Mission, however, thinks as does the American Relief Administration, that the time has not yet come to withdraw. It considers that its help is still needed for the following purposes:

1st—Feeding of several thousand young children.

2nd—Clothing distribution.

3rd—Old age relief.

4th—Land settlement work.

In view of the terrible need in Poland and Russia, the Mission has been reluctant to ask for a definite sum for the continuation of this work. It thinks, however, that not less an amount than that asked for in 1921-22 ($250,000) will be needed. Relief has been carried on through the winter of 1922, from funds supplied by a group of English and Americans who have the welfare of Austria greatly at heart. With this nucleus of trained relief workers, the service can be extended as rapidly as funds are provided.

Under Quiet Stars

By Anna Louise Strong

Into the night I went,
Under the quiet stars of Moscow,
And said: "I have seen
The strongest thing in the world;
Unconquerable,
Outlasting Governments.
A band of common men
So held by a common aim
That they know how
To be hungry,
And they know how
To be cold,
And they know how to go on
After the day's work,
Working now in the night,
Facing the hostile skies
And the hostile earth
With a laugh
For the whole world's lies."

Laying Up Treasures

The following letter, recently received by the A. F. S. C., is from one who, in the spirit of Christ's teachings, is "laying up treasures in heaven."

"Dear Friends:—

"Enclosed you will find a money order for $1,541.90 for the starving of Russia. It is practically all I have, but I think that perhaps it will never go so far again toward alleviating human suffering, so I am giving it and trusting God for the future.

"There is another matter about which I wished to write. I wish during the rest of my life to feel that I am helping to make the world a better place for humanity and it has occurred to me that one of the ways in which to do this, for a few years at least, would be to help in the Friends' Relief Work in one of the countries of Europe."

Woolman Summer School

An Important Opportunity for Eastern Young Friends

Arrangements are under way to enlarge the scope of the summer term at Woolman School. It seems an opportune time, since there is no important gathering for young Friends east of the Alleghenys this summer, except possibly a conference of New England young Friends. Neither the Haverford nor George School summer school comes this summer. The Earlham Young Friends' Conference, the Friends' General Conference and the Five Years Meeting are all to be held in the Middle West.

The regular six weeks' term is to be held June 27 to Aug 5. There will be five regular courses, three hours a week: The Life of Christ and Quakerism by Elbert Russell: The Poetry of the Old Testament, by Elizabeth W. Collins: An Outline of Social Work, by Elizabeth Wood; and Success in Religious Education by Morris E. Fergusson.

The school wishes to provide for those who might attend a conference or summer school for a few days, but who are only free week-ends or for a few days' vacation. The success of the week-end class the fall term suggested the way. There will be five special week-end programs, Fri. to Sun. evenings, each week-end program complete in itself, and yet arranged so that those who attend all five will get some consecutive work. Among the features planned are lectures by prominent speakers on timely topics such as the labor and industrial questions, international and race relations, foreign missions and political prisoners.

A class for First-day School teachers and a Story telling hour on Seventh-days, and a Bible Class by Dr. Russell and a young Friends' Vesper Conference on First-days are other features.

The managers of Swarthmore College have kindly put the college buildings at our disposal, as far as we need them. For the social advantage of having all together it is proposed to feed all the visitors at Woolman House, if possible, and to house those who can not be accommodated in Woolman House in some of the Swarthmore college cottages. Means of Recreation, such as tennis, croquet, boating, and bathing will be available. Fuller announcements will be made shortly.

Christianity and Economic Problems

VI

Does Modern Industry Help or Hinder The Full Development of Human Beings?

(Abridged to Summary Form)

Is the modern economic system more favorable to the full development of human beings than any preceding system? What are the benefits of modern industry? What are its human costs? In what respects is it in accord with the ethical principles of Jesus? Wherein does it violate his teaching?

The Benefits of Modern Industry

(1) *Increased Production.* The development of modern machinery and industrial organization have enormously increased the productive power of human labor. The United States Department of Agriculture has estimated that the amount of human labor required to produce a bushel of wheat was on the average only 10 minutes in 1896, as compared with three hours and 30 minutes in 1830.

(2) *Saving of Human Energy.* The amount of human energy saved by modern machinery is astounding. A single turbine in New York produces energy equal to that of 400,000 strong workmen.

(3) *Saving of Time.* Leisure was formerly secured only at the expense of slave labor. With the aid of modern machines, men now accomplish in a few hours what formerly required days and consequently have greater opportunities for leisure.

Modern machines and industrial organization, by enormously increasing production, lifting heavy burdens from human shoulders and the saving of time, have made possible a richer and fuller life for the whole people than was ever true before. A broader base has been laid upon which the "good life" may be built.

Human Costs of Modern Industry

(1) *Health and Safety.* Dust, heat, humidity, and poisons produce disease among the workers in 500 hazardous occupations listed by the Bureau of Labor Statistics. The American Red Cross has estimated that industrial accidents cause the deaths of more than 22,000 persons annually in the United States. The number of disabilities resulting from industrial accidents was estimated at 3,400,000. A total of 680,000 workers were incapacitated for at least four weeks.

Repetition and monotony, due to extreme specialization, also have disastrous nervous and mental consequences. A few years at such a task unfits a person for constructive workmanship.

(2) *Decreasing Independence of the Individual.* as witnessed by enforced unemployment, concentration of ownership and control of property, inability of the worker to control his own work.

(3) *Antagonism in Human Relations.* Intense competition and commercial struggle against one's neighbor have resulted in a policy of warfare; every man for himself and the hand of every man raised against his fellows. This struggle not only disrupts national life, but results in international complications and war.

(4) *Moral and Spiritual Losses.* The strife which is inherent in a system based upon self-seeking has played havoc with human brotherhood. A dual code of ethics has grown up. Jesus' principle of brotherhood is still widely accepted as a theory, as an ideal to be realized in the Utopian future. But to base business policies upon the gospel of brotherhood is usually considered utterly impracticable. "Business is business," we are told and it cannot be conducted along sentimental lines.

Is not modern business in so far as it employs this slogan based upon motives which are in fundamental contradiction to the spirit and teaching of Jesus? For the true follower of Jesus the serving of others is far more important than the securing of material luxuries and personal power.

It would never occur to anyone to suggest that a reputable surgeon would vary his skill in an operation in accordance with the size of his fee. And yet over and over again we hear it said that business men cannot be expected to do their best work without the possibility of unlimited material rewards. In other words, a dual standard has been erected, one for business men and another for Christian preachers, teachers, doctors, and other servants of society. Is not this lack of faith in business men and the failure to expect them to respond to the higher motive of service for the common good just as readily as other Christian men, one of the serious losses of the present day?

One of the very serious costs of modern industry is found in its effects upon family life. Behold what modern industry is doing to the family; taking the father away for long hours and returning him exhausted, driving mothers away from home and leaving children unguarded, sending children into distant workshops at the earliest legal age, furnishing dreary and unattractive places of abode, attempting to satisfy the craving for excitement by outside commercial amusements—all these combined present a grave menace to the family.

Let us now summarize the facts set forth in this chapter. Modern industry has enormously increased production and has made possible a higher standard of living. Modern machines have lifted heavy burdens from human shoulders. Modern inventions and transportation facilities have made possible greater leisure. Over against these extraordinary benefits are many heavy human costs; occupational diseases, industrial accidents, monotony and fatigue; the increasing helplessness of the individual by reason of unavoidable unemployment, the concentration of control of industry and the existence of class codes; antagonistic human relations, caused by competition and self-seeking; the causing of wars; the endangering of human brotherhood; the creation of a dual standard of morals; the failure to expect business men to be dominated by the motive of service; the menace to the family.

Are we now in a position to strike a balance? Does modern industry help or hinder the full development of human beings? Do its benefits outweigh its human costs? Upon what groups rest chief responsibility for reducing the human costs of modern industry?

Serving With Joy

"The spirit of love conscious of its divinity" was the definition of the Holy Spirit given by Amrose W. Vernon, in an address on "The Place of the Holy Spirit in the Religion of Liberals," at the Sioux City Convention of the National Federation of Religious Liberals. "Service," he said, "is a great and holy word, and through it we have made a genuine and necessary contribution to the life of our time. It is a word of the will, and the will is not the primary thing about us. Service, to be contagious and redemptive, must be the mark of another's will not only to the man who receives it, but to the man who renders it. In other words, service must spring from a profound emotion, from an inner experience with God that we call love.

"Holy love, divine love, the love of God, the Holy Spirit, possesses a man when he meets a being for whose sake all service becomes his deepest joy. That is why Christ has been taken for God through so many ages.

"The tragedy of the church is that through contact with us the service of all men becomes a joy to so few. We love liberty, but liberty without love is hollow. If the love is deep enough it will make its own liberty. It will free us from all other authority. It is the goal for which creed and ritual and church alike have striven. Are we ready to see that for us the sole object in life will be to make love lord of every business plan, every social activity, every legislative program, every family relationship? Will we do all for the glory and in the power of love?"

Philadelphia's Third Annual Theatre Meeting.

Two years ago, under the pressure of a concern to carry the Quaker message to the general public, the Young Friends' Association of Philadelphia found recourse in one of the earliest Friendly practices—that of meeting the people in a public place. Adapting that old custom to modern conditions, the South Broad Street Theatre was selected as the strategic place to gather an audience of those not familiar with Friends.

The first meeting was a pronounced success, and brought many inquiries regarding our beliefs. Last spring a second meeting was held, drawing even a larger audience; while New York Friends attempting a similar meeting, were thoroughly successful and genuinely enthusiastic.

Theatre meetings have established their merit and have become an institution. We are committed to give our Quaker ideals, spiritual and ethical, to an increasingly receptive public.

Our third theatre meeting will be held First-day afternoon, Fourth month 30th, at 3 o'clock, in the Broad Street Theatre, when an invitation is extended to all, to learn the faith of the founders of our city, the City of Brotherly Love. Dr. Rufus M. Jones will make the address, "Quakerism, a Way of Life."

These meetings are expensive, and we will appreciate any financial aid thee may render; but above all, we desire spiritual support, and the attendance of enough Friends that the speaker and committee will be aided in creating the necessary spiritual atmosphere for the best exposition of our Quaker ideals.

Contributions should be sent to Arabella Carter, Treasurer, 1305 Arch St., Philadelphia, Pa.

J. Harold Watson,
Chairman, Committee of Arrangements.

Friendly News Notes

Friends at Drumore Meeting greatly enjoyed the visit of E. Maria Bishop on Fourth month 16th. She left a beautiful Easter message that will be long remembered.

Friends at Cornwall, N. Y., are looking forward to a visit from William J. Reagan, principal of Oakwood School, Poughkeepsie, N. Y. He expects to attend Cornwall Monthy Meeting on First-day, Fifth month 21st, and will speak at the Association Meeting in the afternoon.

The well known Irish Friend, James Douglas, of Dublin, contributed an article of several columns on "The Irish Free State" to the London *Daily News* of April 4th.

Our Friend Henry J. Cadbury's name is included prominently among the contributors of the second volume of Part I of the important work, "The Beginnings of Christianity" (MacMillan 24/—) of which Dr. F. J. Foakes Jackson and Dr. Kirsopp Lake are the editors.

The history of the C. O. Movement, by John William Graham, Principal of Dalton Hall, Manchester University, England, which is being published under the title of "Conscription and Conscience," is now practically through the printer's hands, and should be ready for publication on May 9th. There was so much matter of permanent historic value that claimed record in the book that it is nearly double the size originally contemplated. There was a danger that the price would be doubled, too, but happily it has been decided to fix this at 12/6d., so that the book might have as wide a circulation as possible. There is a long preface by Clifford Allen, Chairman of the No-Conscription Fellowship. The book is of such historic importance that it should be in every Quaker College and Meeting Library.

Friends who remember Rennie Smith as a student at Woodbrooke will be interested to learn that the *Sheffield Daily Telegraph* announces his recent marriage to Miss Lotte Peemuller. The home of the bride is near Dresden, Germany, and the romance began just before the war in social study group in Berlin.

Margaret Knollenberg, of Richmond, Indiana, returned this week from Europe, after being for eighteen months a member of the German Unit. Her work has been mostly in Saxony and Upper Silesia. She was directing the feeding of the children in Upper Silesia when the Polish Army went through last summer. Miss Knollenberg is en route to her home in Richmond.

The Women's International League for Peace and Freedom announces a speaking tour by Mrs. Annot Robinson, of England, Fraulein Gertrude Baer, of Germany, and Mlle. Therese Pottecher-Arnould, of France. These three distinguished women will speak from the same platforms on world peace, mutual understanding between nations, and the development of the peace spirit in Europe. Each of the speakers has contributed important work and thought to the development of international ideals, both within her own country and between nations.

The visitors are to be in Philadelphia from May 10th to 18th. Among the places at which they will speak during this time are: May 12, 9 a. m., Swarthmore College collection; May 17th, "early supper" at Westtown School; evening of May 18th, Philadelphia Yearly Meeting, 15th and Race Streets.

Engagements for other cities may be obtained from the Women's International League for Peace and Freedom.

The program for the Fiftieth Anniversary of the opening of Girard Avenue Meeting House, 17th Street and Girard Avenue, Philadelphia, Fifth month 7th, will be as follows: 9.45 a. m. First-day School—closing exercises; 11.00 a. m. Meeting for worship; 2.30 p. m. Address—"Constants and Variables in Fifty Years of Quakerism." Speaker, Jane P. Rushmore. All former attenders and interested Friends are cordially invited to attend all sessions of the anniversary.

Pittsburgh Friends met Bishop Paul Jones at a special meeting of the Quaker Round Table, at the home of Mary and Harriet Eck, on April 22nd. An unusually large number were present, and listened with much interest to Bishop Jones' talk on the Fellowship of Reconciliation, and the great need for serious study of present-day problems, especially in the industrial world. Animated general discussion followed the talk, and was prolonged through the enjoyable social hour which ended the meeting.

The Baltimore News Letter contains the following:

"We were pleased to hear in a recent letter from Alexander McDowell, Summerville, N. C., that they are conducting their own First-day School at home. They are using three different F. D. S. quarterlies for the different members of the family. They are all enrolled in our Home Department.

The Advisory Committee has just sent a letter to all non-resident members containing the news of the last three months. This is the sixth letter that has been sent to this group during the past fourteen months."

Isolated or non-resident members of other Monthly Meetings would do well to follow the example of the McDowells, and Advisory or Best Interest Committees, or by whatever name they may be called, should note that instead of once or twice a year, "home news" goes to Baltimore non-resident members practically every other month.

The Philanthropic Committee has secured Sally Lucas Jean, Director of the Child Health Organization of America, to talk on "The Health of Our School Children," Fifth-day evening of Yearly Meeting week, Fifth month 16th, at 7.30 p. m. The Child Health Organization is conducting a nation wide campaign to raise the health standard of the American School Child. It strives to discover the best modern thought on the growth and training of children, and also, to interpret this thought to the understanding of the man in the street and to the imagination of the child in the school room. Their dramatic characters, such as Cho-Cho—the Health Clown, aim to make the teaching of health interesting and its practice attractive. Miss Jean has a message for all interested in any phase of the health movement.

ACCOMMODATIONS FOR THE RICHMOND CONFERENCE

Advance information concerning accommodations for the General Conference, to be held at Richmond, Ind., August 26th to September 2d, has been received from Dorothy E. Dilks, chairman of the Richmond committee on local arrangements.

The Westcott Hotel, which is Richmond's leading hotel, will probably serve as headquarters for conference visitors. It is centrally located, two blocks from the meeting-house and one block from the church in which the Conference sessions are to be held. Rates vary from $1.50 to $2.50 per day per person, European plan.

Rooms will be available in boarding houses and private houses at from $3.50 to $8 per week. Room and board in these houses will be from $10 to $14 per week, while board alone will be about $7 per week. Individual meals are forty cents, with a seventy-five cent Sunday dinner.

Plans are under way for a tent colony on the Meeting House grounds which will take care of about 100. This will be primarily a Young Friends' Movement feature. The definite charge for each person in the tents has not been decided upon, but it will probably be about $5 for the whole week.

There is an apartment house in the same block as the meeting-house which has a dormitory on the third floor. The rooms are small and will be $4 for one person or $8 if there are two in the room. These prices are for the entire week. There are, of course, restaurants, etc., where people can get meals, and the local committee is also planning to have a cafeteria in the basement of the meeting-house. The meals can be gotten there for 30 cents to 40 cents per meal.

It is certain that there will be ample accommodations for all and of a variety to meet all needs.

ELIZABETH EMMOTT AT PHILADELPHIA

Elizabeth Braithwaite Emmott spoke to a small gathering in Room 4 of Race Street, Philadelphia, Meeting-house, on the evening of the 14th. Members of the study groups and others interested composed the audience. Elizabeth

Emmott's authorship of "The Story of Quakerism," a valuable textbook for study circles, makes her personality especially interesting to those who have been studying Quaker history.

Her talk on the 14th was on the Fortnight in the Life of George Fox, in the earlier days of his travelling ministry, when he saw from the top of Pendle Hill the vision of a "great people to be gathered." The fulfillment of this vision among the seekers of the northern counties of England marked the phenomenal growth in the following of Fox, providing, as it did, many of the active leaders of the movement, known as "The First Publishers of Truth."

In the discussion which followed this vivid narrative, one of the questions that was asked was: "Why do we not have this dynamic power in our day?" This is a question to which we need to find an answer. Our own generation seems to be full of seekers. If we lent our time and thought to the study of the needs of our generation, as Fox did to the problems of his day, on the hillside with the sheep; in his business dealings with professing Christians, and in the solitude of his wanderings, this dynamic power latent in us all would not be lacking. It is the earnestness which longs to satisfy the need, whether it be one of moral standards in business or social life, or the spiritual hunger of a meeting for worship, which, with the grace of God, yields dynamic power. George Fox did not wait to have the whole truth made plain to his soul. As soon as he saw one thing clearly, he began to share it with others, who helped to open the way for the revelation of more truth.

Anna Braithwaite Thomas, a sister of Elizabeth Emmott's, took a helpful part in the discussion and in the devotional part of the meeting. Informal gatherings like this certainly meet one of the needs of leadership of Friends today. E. M. W.

BIRTHS

KAIGHN—At Atlantic City, N. J., on Fourth month 3rd, to Dr. Charles B. and Eleanor Chandlee Kaighn, twin daughters, who have been named Joan Jackson and Phyllis Chandlee Kaighn.

SANGER—On Fourth month 21st to Ernest and Etta Borton Sanger, of New York City, a son named Richard Brown Sanger.

STAPLER—At Dallas, Texas, on Fourth month 11th, to R. Russell and Louise Stapler, a son, whose name is R. Russell Stapler, Jr.

DEATHS

BUZBY—At Atlantic City, N. J., Fourth month 14th, George H., son of Walter J. and Emily W. Buzby, in his 26th year. Funeral from Friends' Meeting House, at Moorestown, N. J.

EASTBURN—In Pasadena, California, on Third month [illegible] Margaret Eastburn.

HICKS—At the Hahnemann Hospital, Philadelphia, Pa., on Fourth month 18th, Margaret A., widow of the late Francis W. Hicks, in the 78th year of her age. This Friend has been for a long time a devoted member of London Grove Meeting and profoundly interested in what tended to promote social welfare. Temperance, suffrage, education and other worthy problems elicited her earnest thought. A faithful wife and devoted mother, accompanied by perennial cheerfulness, were characteristics of her career.

COMING EVENTS

FOURTH MONTH

29th—Westbury Quarterly Meeting will be held at 110 Schermerhorn Street, Brooklyn, at 10.30 a. m. Lunch will be served at noon. The subject of the afternoon session at 2.30 will be "Gandhi and Race Problems." Norman Thomas will be the speaker. Daniel Batchellor expects to be present.

29th—First-day School Conference at Oxford, Pa., at 10 a. m. Subject—Duties and Responsibilities of Superintendents. At 2 p. m., adult Bible Work and Dramatization of Bible Stories. Bliss and La Verne Forbush will attend. Box lunch.

29th and 30th—Pilgrimage under care of the Young Friends' Movement at Langhorne and Newtown Meetings, is postponed until Sixth month 4th and 5th.

29th-30th—Farmington Half-Yearly Meeting at Orchard Park. Business session on Seventh-day the 29th, at 3 p. m. Meeting for worship on First-day, the 30th, at 11 a. m., and an afternoon session. Frederick J. Libby and Isaac Wilson are expecting to be present.

30th—E. Maria Bishop will be at Hopewell, Va., attending meeting in the morning at 11 a. m., and a conference in the afternoon.

30th—Members of the Young Men's Christian Association of Gloucester County, N. J., with their group leaders will attend Friends' Meeting at Woodbury, N. J., at 10.30 a. m., in the east end of the Meeting House. Orthodox Friends meet in the west end of the house at the same hour. Joel Borton, of Woodstown, expects to attend the meeting.

30th—Conference class at 15th and Race Streets, Philadelphia, at close of meeting for worship, at 11.40 a. m. Summary of "Methods of Church Extension."

30th—Concord Quarterly Meeting of Ministry and Counsel, at Providence, Delaware County, Pa., at 2 p. m., Standard time.

FIFTH MONTH

2nd—Concord Quarterly Meeting, at Providence Meeting House, Media, Pa., 10 a. m., Daylight saving time.

4th—Abington Quarterly Meeting at Horsham, Pa., at 10.30 a. m., Standard time.

5th-6th—Pilgrimage under care of the young Friends' Movement, at West Chester, Pa.

6th—Philadelphia Quarterly Meeting will be held in Germantown Meeting House, 45 W. School House Lane, Germantown, on Fifth month 6th, Seventh-day afternoon. Religious Meeting, 1.30 p. m.; Business Meeting, 2.30 p. m. Box Supper (coffee, ice cream and cake will be served). Entertainment by Germantown Friends' Association 7.30 p. m.

7th—First-day at 3 p. m., "Daylight saving time." The usual semi-annual Community Meeting for worship will be held at Chichester Friends' Meeting House under care of a Committee of Concord Quarterly Meeting. All persons are welcome and young people particularly invited. Joseph H. Willits, of Swarthmore, expects to attend. Train leaves 24th and Chestnut Sts., for Boothwyn at 1.30 p. m.; Darby, 1.43; Chester, 2.00; returning 5 p. m. All "Daylight saving." Trains will stop at cross-road near the meeting house.

7th—Purchase Quarterly Meeting, at Amawalk, N. Y. See notice.

7th—Nine Partners Half-Yearly Meeting will be held at Clinton Corners, New York.

8th—Easton and Granville Half-Yearly Meeting, at Granville, N. Y., at 11 a. m. Meeting of Ministry and Counsel, same day, at 10 a. m.

NOTICE—The committee in charge of the Friends' Boarding Home of Bucks Quarterly Meeting, situated in Newtown, Pa., invites interested friends to attend the 25th Anniversary of its opening, from 2 to 5 p. m., on Fifth month 3rd.

Train leaves Reading Terminal at 1.23 p. m.

NOTICE—Purchase Quarterly Meeting will be held at Amawalk, at 10.30 a. m., Standard time. Joel Borton will be in attendance. Young Friends' Meeting at 2. p. m. Subject for discussion—"Good Will to Men." Meeting of Ministry and Counsel at 9.30 a. m., same day. Train leaves Sedgwick Avenue, 6.40 a. m., Elmsford, 7.39; Millwood, 8.10. Arrives at Amawalk, 8.34 a. m. Returning leaves Amawalk 4.45.

NOTICE—Rummage Sale! Last week in April. Benefit of Friends' Home for Children. Will you help the children by saving rummage? Send direct to Home by April 24, or arrangements for collecting can be made by calling: Lula B. Dixon, 918 S. 49th Street, Woodland 2361-J; Anna Kirby Swope, 4926 Cedar Avenue, Woodland 2858-J; Anna Hall, 5301 Woodbine Avenue, Overbrook 0411.

From the Baltimore News Letter

"Every family in Baltimore Monthly Meeting should subscribe to the FRIENDS' INTELLIGENCER. Any members who have joined the Society thru convincement should take it in order that they might know just what this paper which represents our Society is saying; and all well-established families of Friends need the paper to keep in touch with what the Society is doing in its many Monthly, Quarterly and Yearly Meetings.

Of our 140 resident families only 51 subscribe at present to the INTELLIGENCER. You will find articles of moment and of interest, you will find articles in it with which you will be in sympathy, and some with which you will not agree. But it would be a commonplace world if we agreed with everything the other fellow said.

The INTELLIGENCER is offering at this time a special three months' get-acquainted rate of thirty-five cents, just half the regular rate. Will you not today send thirty-five cents in stamps to THE FRIENDS' INTELLIGENCER, 140 North 15th Street, Philadelphia? Or, if you would rather, send $2.50 for a full year's subscription."

BLISS FORBUSH, *Secretary.*

The Secretary of Baltimore Monthly Meeting is doing his part in helping to increase the circulation of the INTELLIGENCER. Won't thee help, too?

American Friends' Service Committee

WILBUR K. THOMAS, EX. SEC.
20 S. 12th St. Philadelphia.

CASH CONTRIBUTIONS
WEEK ENDING APRIL 17.

Five Years Meetings	$427.65
Other Meetings:	
Sandy Spring, Monthly Meeting	8.00
Oakland Branch of the College Park Association	22.00
Valley Meeting	49.50
Alexandria Monthly Meeting	30.00
Ladies' Aid of the First Friends' Church, Dayton, Ohio	5.00
Orange Grove Friends of Pasadena	60.00
Friends Group at State College	46.00
First Friends Church, Portsmouth, Va.	3.90
Jamaica Friends Mission	31.11
Contributions for Germany	206.63
For Austria	4,668.67
For Poland	5,512.55
For Serbia	25.00
For Russia	16,302.27
For Russian Overhead	111.63
For General	484.50
Refunds	63.47
	$28,087.88

SHIPMENTS RECEIVED
WEEK ENDING APRIL 15.

97 boxes and packages received; two anonymous.

LUKE 2. 14—AMERICA'S ANGELUS

"Glory to God in the highest, and on earth peace, good will toward men."

Stand back of President Harding in Prayer for Universal Peace by meditating daily, at noon, on the fourteenth verse of the second chapter of Luke.

Ask your friends to help make this a Universal Meditation for Universal Peace

Pass it on *Friends in Christ*

FUN

Wasn't Sure

"I want to get a good novel to read on the train—something pathetic," said a woman to a book salesman.

"Let me see. How would 'The Last Days of Pompeii' do?" asked the salesman.

"Pompeii? I never heard of him. What did he die of?"

"I'm not quite sure, ma'am," replied the salesman; "some kind of eruption I've heard."—*The Paper Book.*

WANTED

WANTED—POSITION AS COMPANION, care of invalid, or housekeeper. Address I. 151, Friends' Intelligencer.

WANTED — HOUSEKEEPER (MANAGER), capable woman of refinement who desires good permanent home in Philadelphia suburbs with family of three children and male adult. Box S. 150, Friends' Intelligencer.

WANTED — SUMMER BOARD FOR three adults, with private family on farm. Commuting distance from Philadelphia. Address D. 154, Friends' Intelligencer.

WANTED — POSITION AS CHAUFFEUR, 12 years' experience; married; references; country preferred. John C. Elser, 3749 Germantown Ave., Philadelphia.

FRIEND OWNING HER HOME NEAR Camden would take an elderly lady to board. Best care and attention given. Address C. 171, Friends' Intelligencer.

THE GRANDOM INSTITUTION HAS furnished coal to the deserving poor of Philadelphia at reduced prices since 1841. To increase this work, gifts or legacies will be welcomed. For further information apply to William Biddle, Secretary, No. 119 S. 4th Street, Philadelphia, Pa.

POSITION WANTED—BY CAPABLE housekeeper or caretaker (Friend) after June 1st. Good cook; economical; kind disposition. Best reference. Give particulars and salary. Address L. 174, Friends' Intelligencer.

POSITION WANTED BY TEACHER, Friend, for summer; also for September term. Address H. 175, Friends' Intelligencer.

WOMAN, EXPERIENCED IN SECRETARIAL work, and who has done much manuscript revision and proofreading, desires work along these lines. Will consider part time or full time employment. Address "Proofreader," care New Century Guild, 1307 Locust Street, Philadelphia.

WANTED—SIMPLE FURNISHED house, minimum five bedrooms, commuting distance from Philadelphia. June 1st to September 15. Reasonable rental. References exchanged. Reply to F. 172, Friends' Intelligencer.

WANTED — MIDDLE-AGED WHITE woman of refinement for cook in private family. Also, woman for chambermaid and waitress; both to go to mountains for three months this summer. Answer by letter only. Address M. 173, Friends' Intelligencer.

WANTED—MOTHER'S HELPER, suburban home, 2 small children, help in housework. Address C. 176, Friends' Intelligencer.

WANTED—A NURSE AT FRIENDS' Home, Swede and Powell streets, Norristown, Pa. Apply, Mary R. Livezey, 908 W. Marshall street, Norristown, Pa.

POSITION WANTED—AS COMPANION-attendant for semi-invalid or elderly person; good sewer and reader; moderate salary; good references. Address K. 177, Friends' Intelligencer.

FOR SALE

FOR SALE—BRICK AND FRAME detached residence, well built; 10 rooms, bath, sleeping porch, glassed in; gas and electricity, modern conveniences; near Friends' School and Meeting House, Lansdowne, Pa. Apply J. 100, Friends' Intelligencer.

FOR RENT

FOR RENT — FOR THE SUMMER, furnished 9-room stone house in Germantown, Pa. Can be seen by appointment. Phone Germantown 4029-W.

FOR RENT—FURNISHED, AN ATTRACTIVE home in Haddonfield, N. J., the three summer months, 6th, 7th and 8th. Address P. 170, Friends' Intelligencer.

FOR RENT

FOR RENT—THE PACKER COTTAGE at Buck Hill. Accommodations for five or six. Located within fifteen minutes' walk of Inn. For particulars inquire Franklin Packer, Newtown, Pa.

FOR RENT—TO REFINED COUPLE, a pleasant second floor corner room, next to bath; with excellent board, good cooking, fresh vegetables, chickens and eggs. Near trolley, and within ten minutes of two lakes for bathing and canoeing. Highest reference required. Bell phone 69-J, or write to 15 Grove Street, Haddonfield, N. J.

FOR RENT — COOL, TWO-STORY house; furnished; bath. May 15th to October 1st. Address G. 160, Friends' Intelligencer, or phone Media 304-J.

FOR RENT—FOR ALL OR PART OF season, delightful furnished cottage among New Hampshire pines in Quaker neighborhood. Address W. 161, Friends' Intelligencer.

FOR RENT—APARTMENT FOR light housekeeping, in suburban home. Two large rooms, semi-private bath, heat, hot water, electric lights, gas, front and back porches, large yard, old shade. Convenient to train, trolley and bus line. Good roads and convenient garages. Price reasonable. C. B. Llewellynm, Cheltenham, Pa. Bell Phone—Cheltenham 1241-W.

IN FIFTH MONTH, 1922, THE PHILADELPHIA Young Friends' Association, Inc., expect to have a few rooms available for permanent guests. Address 140 North 15th Street, Philadelphia.

Woolman Summer School

SWARTHMORE, PA.

JUNE 27 TO AUGUST 5

Regular Courses

Hebrew Poetry—Elizabeth W. Collins
The Life of Christ—Elbert Russell
Quaker History—Elbert Russell
Success in Teaching Religion—E. Morris Fergusson
Outline of Social Work—Elizabeth Wood

Five Special Week-end Programs

for those not able to attend the regular courses: Consecutive lessons on Religious Education, Telling Bible Stories, and Paul's Epistles.

Lectures by leaders on the Race Problem, Labor Movement, Foreign Missions, Boys' Clubs, Internationalism, and Fellowship of Reconciliation.

Write for announcement and full program.

WOOLMAN SCHOOL,
Swarthmore, Pa.

The only Friends' Summer School in the East this summer.

Please help us by patronizing our advertisers. Mention the "Friends' Intelligencer."

The Friends'
Intelligencer

ESTABLISHED 1844 | FIFTH MONTH 6, 1922 | VOLUME 79 NUMBER 18

Contents

EDITORIALS

GENERAL ARTICLES

AMONG OUR MEETINGS

REGULAR MEETINGS

OAKLAND, CALIF. — A FRIENDS' Meeting is held every First-day at 11 A. M., in the Extension Room, Y. W. C. A. Building, Webster Street, above 14th. Visiting Friends always welcome.

FRIENDS' MEETING IN PASADENA, California — Orange Grove Monthly Meeting of Friends, 520 East Orange Grove Avenue, Pasadena, California. Meeting for worship, First-day, 11 A. M. Monthly Meeting, the second First-day of each month, at 1.45 P. M.

CENTRAL MEETING OF FRIENDS (Chicago), meets every First-day in Room 706, 410 South Michigan Avenue, at 10.45 A. M. Visitors are invited.

THE FRIENDS' INTELLIGENCER

Published weekly, 140 N. 15th Street, Philadelphia, Pa., by Friends' Intelligencer Association, Ltd.

WALTER H. ABELL, *Editor*

SUE C. YERKES, *Business Manager*

Editorial Board: Elizabeth Powell Bond, Thomas A. Jenkins, J. Russell Smith, George A. Walton.

Board of Managers: Edward Cornell, Alice Hall Paxson, Paul M. Pearson, Annie Hillborn, Elwood Hollingshead, William C. Biddle, Charles F. Jenkins, Edith M. Winder, Frances M. White.

Officers of Intelligencer Associates: Ellwood Burdsall, Chairman; Bertha L. Broomell, Secretary; Herbert P. Worth, Treasurer.

Subscription rates: United States, Mexico, Cuba and Panama, $2.50 per year. Canada and other foreign countries, $3.00 per year. Checks should be made payable to Friends' Intelligencer Association, Ltd.

Entered as Second Class Matter at Philadelphia Post Office.

The Friends' Intelligencer

The religion of Friends is based on faith in the "INWARD LIGHT," or direct revelation of God's spirit and will in every seeking soul.

The INTELLIGENCER is interested in all who bear the name of Friends in every part of the world, and aims to promote love, unity and intercourse among all branches and with all religious societies.

ESTABLISHED 1844 | PHILADELPHIA, FIFTH MONTH 6, 1922 | VOLUME 79 NUMBER 18

Helping Us Grow More Effective

We trust that our readers are keeping in touch with our energetic campaign to increase our subscription list. Weekly reports of its progress are given in the back of the paper—this time under the heading "What Has Thee Done To Help?"

The effectiveness of the INTELLIGENCER as a medium for the expression of Friends' principles depends upon the number of Friends and others who read it. Every additional subscription likewise means additional material support, with corresponding opportunity for the improvement of the paper. Seventy-nine trial subscriptions have thus far been obtained. We appreciate the help of those who have made this gain possible, and we invite others to join in making the campaign a success.

Philadelphia Yearly Meeting in Prospect

The program for the coming sessions of Philadelphia Yearly Meeting, printed elsewhere in this issue, promises several interesting developments in Yearly Meeting activities.

A number of changes are planned for the business sessions. In response to the press of a constantly increasing agenda, these sessions will begin half an hour earlier both in the morning and afternoon. Formerly scheduled for 10 a. m. and 2.30 p. m., they are now to be opened at 9.30 and 2.

A further time-saving step is to be proposed in connection with the reports of the various committees. Instead of having these read in full to the meeting, it is proposed to present a summary of each, not to exceed ten minutes in length. The full reports will, as usual, be available in printed form. A similar procedure was long ago adopted by London Yearly Meeting. By saving time from routine, it gives greater opportunity for discussion. It marks a step which is inevitable as the business of the Yearly Meeting grows from year to year in answer to the multiple demands now being made for Friendly attention.

In connection with this new procedure, it has been possible to schedule the business throughout, designating in advance the respective sessions at which the various reports are to be considered—a decided advantage in the case of those who are unable to attend all the sessions.

No mention is made on the program as to whether or not joint sessions are to be enjoyed by the meeting. The new order of business, however, will be greatly facilitated by such sessions, and it is not unlikely that a proposal in their favor will be early introduced. If separate sessions of the men's and women's meetings are held, it will be necessary for two Friends to present the summary of each report, or else for the same Friend to go from one meeting to the other. In either of these cases, the meeting is bound to spend more time and energy in arriving at its conclusion than would be required if the business were conducted in joint session. With last year's joint session a decided success, the experimental stage has passed, and there seems every reason for responding to the demands of efficiency in this respect.

A very interesting innovation will be the nursery which is to be conducted in the Elementary School Building, under the direction of the Child Welfare Section of the Committee on Philanthropic Labor. It will be in charge of Lusanna Beaman, one of the teachers in the Elementary School. An official letter regarding the plan says: "Mothers who wish to attend the sessions may leave their children here with the assurance that they will have competent supervision. There will be games and story-telling and suitable accommodations for the comfort and entertainment of little people." The idea is excellent.

The four evening programs are all attractive, a new departure being one in charge of the Representative Committee. The Young Friends' Movement has likewise planned a strong program, with its general meeting, supper and evening of entertainment on Seventh-day, its William Penn Lecture by Sherwood Eddy on "Incentives in Modern Life," and its supper conferences during Yearly Meeting week.

All of these advance plans promise well for the successful issue of the Yearly Meeting. Successful in the real sense, however, it cannot be rendered by any forms or procedures or programs. Only as we are conscious of the tremendous needs of the world and of the hope which is set on Friends to help in answering that need, only as we lay aside our personal standards of position and class to unite in the unfettered search for "pure truth," can we make any Friends' meeting of genuine service to ourselves and to humanity. May Philadelphia Yearly Meeting undertake its labors this year forgetful of the fact that it is Philadelphia Yearly Meeting—a formal organization—and remembering only that it constitutes a group of Christians united in the attempt to follow a leader whose goal was the here-and-now attainment of "the kingdom of God," and who followed that ideal to death in the face of every organized religious convention. "Those who seek shall find." How much nearer will the world be to the kingdom of God when Philadelphia Yearly Meeting adjourns this year than it is at present?

We deeply regret a serious error which occurred in our last issue, that of Fourth month 29th. In the process of printing, the stanzas of the poem "Quaker Meeting," by Eliza R. Whitson, were placed in incorrect order. The five stanzas appearing in the first column should come at the end, instead of at the beginning of the poem. The poem is intended to begin, "How brightly shone the sun that day!"

Coal Facts

By Drew Pearson

The Substance of a Report Prepared at the Direction of Swarthmore Monthly Meeting

(Part II—Conclusion)

Each of the two contending parties in the coal strike have one major argument. The miners claim that their wages must not be reduced, because they do not receive a living wage even at present. The operators claim that they cannot possibly continue to pay present wages and operate the mines at a profit.

A careful analysis of these two arguments is illuminating.

1. Wages.—It is quite true that the present wage scale was fixed in 1920 when the cost of living was at its peak. However, Professor William F. Ogburn, of Columbia, makes an estimate based on prices of December, 1921—just four months ago—that $1,870 is necessary in order to support a man, wife and three dependent children with a minimum amount of comfort. But for the same year—1921—the average annual earning per miner was as follows:

West Virginia	$500
Pittsburgh District	736
Ohio	550
Illinois	1,000
West Kentucky	960

(In the figures given for Illinois and Kentucky the cost of powder, supplies, blacksmithing and tools had not been deducted.)

It is also true that when a mine day-laborer does get a chance to work that he makes $7.50 per day, while a miner makes more than a mine foreman. However, a mine foreman draws his pay every day, while the miner's chances to work were only 170 days during 1921.

Moreover, coal mining is one of our most dangerous industries; 2,500 miners are killed and 30,000 injured every year. Every 260,000 tons of coal costs a human life. Also, the mine has no social compensation. The miner works in monotonous solitude.

Yet, in spite of the dangers which attend his work, and in spite of the fact that he is unable to make a living wage, the miner at present asks only for a continuation of the present scale.

2. Profits.—It is true that during the last year many operators have been making a very small margin of profit. However, in October, 1921, testimony by the National Coal Association before the Interstate Commerce Commission disclosed the fact that labor cost in the production of one ton of coal was $1.972, and the total cost, including labor, was $2.91. But the same coal retailed at $10.41. The question is: what became of the remaining $8.44? The government has attempted to answer this question by the Federal Trade Commission investigation; but the operators blocked the move by an injunction.

Undoubtedly a part of the questionable $8.44 can be accounted for to tribute paid to absentee landlordism. The royalties of the Girard estate on 3,000,000 tons of anthracite rose with the price of coal from $1 to $1.25 to $1.33. How general this is, of course, nobody knows.

It is known, however, that the United States Steel

Corporation owns 85,000 acres of coal land in Mingo and Logan counties, West Virginia; the Norfolk and Western Railroad owns 63,000 acres, or most of the Pocahontas field just adjacent; while the Chesapeake and Ohio Railroad is the chief owner in the New River and Raleigh fields of West Virginia. These lands are leased to independent operators. Just what the nature of the lease, or what the division of profits, the parties concerned have to date successfully held back from the public.

Federal Trade Commission investigation, however, has unearthed the fact that no less than, and probably more than, "45 per cent. of the operators sold through jobbers and sales agencies" and "had no direct connection with the consumer."

The municipality of Lincoln, Nebraska, proved how great the gap between operator and consumer by investing $30,000 in coal, paying transportation and bankers' interest, and distributing it at $5 a ton less than the price of the ordinary local coal.

It would seem, therefore, that while profits to operators certainly are not what they were during the war, and that while many mines are now operated on a very narrow margin of profit or even a loss, yet this is the fault of the operators, because (1) of their loose sales policy, (2) their involved system of ownership and leasing, (3) because they have opened more mines than the country requires.

An Inevitable Strike

Furthermore, it appears that the operators have welcomed the strike, not only as an excuse for boosting prices of the coal stock on hand at present, not only as a means of forcing a wage reduction, but more especially of clubbing out of the industry the 40 per cent. surplus mines and miners.

Under the present system some such "show-down," some strike, was inevitable. According to the United States Geological Survey, the country has active mines capable of supplying 700,000,000 tons; whereas we need only 500,000,000 tons; 150,000 surplus miners staff these mines and thereby cut down the working hours and eat into the net wages of their 500,000 brothers. The condition could not go on. But who was to decide which mine was to close? Who was to decide which miner should pack off his family to another town and hunt another job?

The miners offered their remedy—a six-hour day and a five-day week—by which work might be passed around to all. This, of course, was only a temporary remedy, a making the best of a bad situation. As long as 40 per cent. too many mines gave promise of part-time work, it is only human nature that 40 per cent. too many miners will continue to snatch at that opportunity to work. So under the present system—without governmental authority, without even an active public opinion—the strike was inevitable.

The History of Private Management

The question now arises, is the coal industry to continue in its present chaotic state, with recurrent cycles of depression and disagreements? The answer requires a further review of the coal industry under private management.

We have already discussed private management (*sales methods*, its *complicated system of absentee ownership*, and its policy of *concealing "coal" facts from the public*. There remains an examination of the *overhead cost of maintaining idle mines, methods of work* in the mine, and the *waste of coal* at the mine.

The *overhead cost of maintaining an idle mine* all goes back to the fundamental trouble—40 per cent. too many mines. The average mine remains idle about 40 per cent. of the time, during which fans and pumps must be kept working, roofs must be repaired, and cave-ins cleaned out. Eighteen tons of water must be brought out of an anthracite mine for every ton of coal. The air pumped into and out of a mine on a working day weighs more than the coal that comes out. The total cost of these overhead expenses has been variously estimated at from $500,000,000 to $760,000,000 annually. In other words, if we did away with our 40 per cent. extra mines, the consumer would be saved about half a billion dollars.

Methods of work and training employees in the coal industry has lagged far behind the advanced practices in other industries. "The functions of management are largely left to the judgment of workmen—fixing their own tools, keeping their own records. Machine operation is poorly developed. There is no tool-room; no planning departments. Men are not trained in the best way of performing their work. One foreman frequently has charge of one hundred men scattered over a square mile in isolated passageways.

During the year 1917, the miners were idle 33 1/3 per cent. of their time. Of this idleness 30 per cent. was spent at the mines for the following reasons: 20 per cent. due to lack of cars, 6 per cent. of the time was lost for other managerial causes, and 4 per cent. due to "lack of help." The latter may seem a strange item, when one remembers that labor is idle at least one-quarter of the year. "Yet it is just this unsystematic, sporadic management of mines that breeds unsteady industrial habits among employees."

Waste of coal at the mines is enormous. The United States Geological Survey estimates that 50 per cent. of the coal is wasted under the present form of management. In other words, a mine must produce two tons before one ton is made available to the consumer. The chief causes for this wanton destruction are:

1. A system of mining which leaves a large quantity of coal inside the mines.

2. Wastage of a considerable amount of coal dust or inferior fuel.

3. Abandoning of partially exploited mines.

4. Neglecting to use by-products and multiple products of the mines.

It is estimated that since we began mining in 1844, seven and one-half billion tons have been wasted. If our wastage continues at this rate, it is estimated that our coal supply will last only 100 years. "This means that it will not outlast even our own grandchildren. The toleration of this appalling rate of destruction cannot be justified on technical grounds, for the difficulties of recovery are negligible. Indeed the means are well known and quite simple: mines can be completely scraped of coal and projects have been brought forward to burn out the last remains of fuel and transform it locally into electricity without bringing it to the surface. Coal dust, anthracite culm, could be flushed by water through pipes into nearby power plants, or briqueted.

"The reason why these things are not being done—why mines are abandoned if ash content is found to be high, why various by-products are not derived—is that under the existing mode of financing the mines it is more profitable to the private owners to throw the life and prosperity of our grandchildren away than to incur the expense for the reclamation of waste. Indeed, no coal operator can be blamed for not mining coal at a cost of $4 per ton to sell it at a price of $2, or for refusing to clean excessive amount of ash, slate and bone at a cost exceeding his possible margin.

"Neither can it be expected under the existing economic relations that mine operators will supply the territory, say 300 miles in radius, with electric power made at the mouth of their mines, in addition to such by-products of coal as ammonium sulphate, tar, benzol and other derivatives; although such a scheme at present market prices would realize from eight to ten times more revenue than the sale of raw coal."

Swarthmore's Recommendation to President Harding

Following the presentation of the above facts concerning the coal industry, Swarthmore Monthly Meeting, on Fourth month 25, adopted the official report of its findings which is given below. This report will be sent to President Harding, carried to Concord Quarterly Meeting, and if there approved, will be brought before Philadelphia Yearly Meeting. It is as follows:

"There are obviously many factors involved in the present coal strike, so many that it is beyond the province of your committee to attempt to review them. One fact, however, stands out as fundamental in the controversy—that as claimed by competent authority, there is an excess of producing facilities and of miners of about 40 per cent. over what is necessary to supply our normal annual needs. Unless this condition is changed, irregularity of production and employment, with its corollaries of unemployment, lowered annual wages and strikes, on the one hand, and excessively high costs of production on the other—are inevitable.

"In general, your committee is opposed to the habit of turning to the Government to find the cure for our ills. However, it sees no prospect of an improvement if present conditions are allowed to be left to continue. The continuance of such conditions as have occurred for years in the coal mines endangers the foundations of our own society. Such continuance creates a sense of grievance and hopelessness which makes for revolution. Some improvement must be attempted.

"The committee, therefore, recommends that the President be requested to appoint a commission of competent persons, first, to arbitrate the present dispute (the resulting decision to be enforced by the public opinion of the country), and, secondly, to inquire into the causes of the conditions leading up to this and previous strikes in the industry, to suggest adequate remedies to prevent their recurrence, and protect the public interest, after the fashion already adopted in connection with our forest resources and the public utilities."

We Never Know

I spoke a word
And no one heard;
I wrote a word,
And no one cared
Or seemed to heed;
But after half a score of years
It blossomed in a fragrant deed.
Preachers and teachers all are we—
Sowers of seeds unconsciously;
Our hearers are beyond our ken,
Yet all we give may come again
With usury of joy or pain,
We never know
To what one little word may grow;
See to it then that all your seeds
Be such as bring forth noble deeds.

—*John Oxenham; selected by M. Jane Pancoast.*

Polish School Girls Care for Russian Orphans

"They are poor little orphans who cannot speak Polish, so we must see that they have an especially good Christmas."

This was the view taken of an orphan asylum of white Russian children by Polish school girls in Warsaw. This is one of the by-products of the Friends' Relief Mission work during the past two years, and in a country where national feeling is so strong as in Poland, it is doubly significant.

The peasants from the district which is now Poland are pouring back from Russia at the rate of from fifty to sixty thousand a month. During the great war some seven years ago, their villages were devastated, and they were carried far into the interior of Russia. They are now returning. Large numbers of them die on the way from cold, hunger and disease, and thousands of children are thus left orphans. Although they live in a territory which is now under the Polish Government, most of these peasants are white Russians, and speak only Russian.

Some of the girls in a Secondary School in Warsaw learning of the work which the Society of Friends was doing for these unfortunate refugees, asked if there was any way in which they could help. An assembly was called, and was addressed by two members of the Friends' organization. It was decided that the girls would make long shirts and underwear as part of their domestic science work. The smaller girls made overalls for the children. The Friends supplied the material and distributed the goods later. About 280 new garments were made by the girls in this first school.

Another school heard of it, and asked also for a little lecture about the refugees. After this lecture they decided to make 200 flannelette dresses for the children.

A third school received some grey flannel from the Friends and made 250 women's nightgowns of a kind which are being used by the refugee women alternately as nightgowns and house dresses, since they are in many cases the only whole garment of any warmth.

A mathematics school came forward to make 150 warm clothes for children, and now there are seven schools making 1,500 pillow-cases and sheets for hospitals and outposts.

Not only did the movement grow, but it began to deepen in interest. The first school formed a permanent committee, and asked to be put in touch with orphans which they might help. They were allotted an orphanage at Kobryn. A sister of one of the girls had been a nurse there, and had just died of typhus, and this naturally added to the sympathy which the school felt for the orphans. Four big boxes of food, and three sacks of clothes have been sent there for distribution up to the present.

Other schools also began to form permanent committees to care for orphanages. When the orphanages are located in Warsaw the girls take them toys and colored picture books, as well as the more necessary food and clothing. It was in this connection that the spirit arose regarding the "Poor little children who could not talk Polish" and who therefore must have an especially good Christmas because they were strangers in a strange city.

Volunteers Wanted for Mending

The Mending Room, which is being conducted by the Woman's Work Committee of the Service Committee in the Meeting House at Fifteenth and Cherry Streets, has proven to be a decided success. Many women are volunteering for part, at least, of each Third-day, and many garments contributed for the relief work and which are in need of repair, have been put into wearable condition, and thus made more valuable. The Committee is most grateful to those who have helped in this work.

The sewing room is open on Third-days beginning at 9 o'clock; and all who have an hour or two, or longer, are asked to come and aid in this very important work of mending the old garments. If those who come will bring aprons, they will probably be more comfortable in working.

Sale of Foreign Embroideries

A sale of foreign handwork and embroideries will be held under the auspices of the Woman's Work Committee of the American Friends' Service Committee in the Young Friends' Auditorium at Fifteenth and Cherry Streets, on Friday, May 24th, from 2 until 7 p. m.

This most excellent handicraft and embroidery work has been secured through the Units in Austria, Poland, Russia, Germany and France; and practically all are of the finest possible work and texture. The proceeds from this sale will be sent back to aid the impoverished people who did the work. Because of the low rate of foreign exchange the people who are doing this work are living on practically the value of Three and Four Dollars a month, and so the proceeds from the sale of their work will be of immense value to them.

The work includes many useful as well as handsome articles; and all Friends are asked to bear it in mind, realizing the tremendous aid they will be giving to helpless middle-class people in Europe, and at the same time obtaining purchases of great value, especially for gifts.

Christianity and Economic Problems
VII
Why Is Present Production Inadequate?
(*Reduced to Summary Form*)

It is freely admitted that modern industry is highly injurious to the health, mentality and morals of many workers. But it is often contended that this human cost is one of the prices we have to pay for increased production and a higher standard of life.

Back of such statements is the assumption that at the present time a sufficient quantity of goods is being produced to provide plenty for all. This view is widely prevalent. The truth is the reverse of this. The heads of half the families in the United States have an annual income of less than $1,500. There is simply no escaping the fact that at the present time we are not producing enough goods to go around.

Surely we are confronted with an amazing situation. With fertile soil, favorable climate, vast natural resources, enormous mechanical power, countless inventions and labor saving devices, keen business men, highly trained administrators, skilled engineers and mechanics, and an abundant supply of manual workers—with all these combined we are not producing enough to go around and at least one-third of our people are lacking in the necessities and minimum comforts of life. How are we to account for such an extraordinary state of affairs? Why is present production inadequate? There are four reasons:

1. *Sabotage and Waste.* Only a small fraction of the workers put their whole energy into their tasks. A few deliberately waste materials. Employers likewise practice sabotage. They often deliberately restrict output, in order to keep prices up. Another form of social waste lies in the annual expenditure of ten billion dollars for luxuries. This helps to cause shortage and high prices of necessities.

2. *Ignorance and Bad Management.* Many workers are poorly trained. There is an alarming degree of ignorance and illiteracy, even in the United States. The employer is also frequently subject to criticism for waste. Hoover's committee of engineers found that "over fifty per cent. of the responsibility for these wastes can be placed at the door of management and less than twenty-five per cent. at the door of labor."

3. *Lack of Impelling Motive to Maximum Production.* No appeal is made to the worker except that of financial return for his work. This return he feels is unjustly inadequate. Helplessness and hopelessness is a barrier to efficiency of the workers. Their creative impulses are repressed by modern machine monotony. Business men likewise lack an adequate motive for production. They produce only for profit. When production ceases to pay profits, they cease production, though there may be a crying need for their goods.

We are not attempting to say that at the present time a manufacturer can do anything else other than restrict production when he can no longer produce at a profit. We are merely pointing out the fact that our modern productive processes are not built around the needs of the community but around the profits of the managers or owners.

4. *Lack of Security.* The fear of unemployment frequently leads workers to restrict their output in order to keep their work. They have reason to fear unemployment; there are rarely less than a million unemployed in the United States. The employer likewise restricts production because of his fear that his goods cannot be disposed of. He, too, fears insecurity.

The insecurity of modern business is further increased by the general attitude of the consuming public. Consumers insist on purchasing goods at the very lowest possible price, without regard to whether or not the workers and employers are assured an adequate income for their services. Thus we have a situation where employers and workers are arrayed against each other and where the consumers are arrayed against both employers and workers. By our emphasis upon self-interest we have created a vicious circle of antagonism; we are defeating our own purposes and are standing in the way of our own progress.

The only possible way to get adequate production of needed goods is on a basis of co-operation between employers, workers and consumers. It is futile to expect cordial co-operation between these groups so long as industry is based frankly on private gain—of employer, worker or consumer. We shall not solve the human problems of modern industry until industry is regarded as a public service and goods are produced because they are needed, not merely because they can be sold at a profit. Production for use is the way out of our industrial tangle and our consequent inadequate supply of goods.

There is, however, a very serious question in the minds of many people as to whether the quantity of goods produced would be greater under a system of production for use. Pertinent questions are being asked: What basis is there for believing that production for use would increase the quantity of needed goods? Is not this a theory that is without basis in actual experience? Will it not be necessary to "change human nature" before industry can be placed on a basis of production for use? Even if we were assured of more goods, how shall we bring about the change from production for private profit to production for use?

These are fair questions and they should not be dodged. We propose, therefore, to devote our next chapter to a consideration of the issues involved in production for use.

Prayer

We all pray according to our relationship with God. Saying prayers in a mechanical way will not bring about a vital relationship with God. Real prayer is consciousness of relationship with God. We pray because we know we are his children and can call him "Our Father."

Possibly our first real prayer was our first consciousness of relationship. If we are talking with God in the same vocabulary which we used in childhood, we may be spiritual dwarfs.

Luke 11.1. "Lord, teach us to pray!" A petition which should precede every prayer.

Romans 8.26, 27. The great saints are those who have learned to pray "according to the will of God." If there is anything in prayer, there is everything. Either we are taking it too seriously and wasting too much energy, or we are not intelligent and learning to pray according to God's laws.

Habit is a channel through which good or bad may flow. It may be cultivated in the spiritual realm as in the physical and mental. In this respect you are different from five or ten years ago; i. e., it is harder to change a habit. Be master of physical, mental, and spiritual habits.

Prayer is a spiritual habit which may be cultivated. It makes a channel in character through which good will flow.

Prayer is like a power plant. Our part is to make the connection and realize the power.

Prayer is an investment of time. There is a fire brick in England which is advertized: "For every moment of saturation there is a corresponding moment of illumination."

Prayer is like the wireless. If my will and God's cross, there is discord. If my will and his are parallel, there is harmony and communion.—*Mrs. W. R. Moody, in the "Record of Christian Work."*

Philadelphia Theatre Meeting

With Music Week being inaugurated by musical programs in twelve other theatres of the city, the attendance was nevertheless excellent at this year's theatre meeting under the care of a committee of the Philadelphia Young Friends' Association. The meeting was held as usual in the South Broad Street Theatre, of which the lower floor and a considerable portion of the balcony were filled.

Before presenting the chairman of the afternoon, J. Harold Watson, chairman of the committee in charge, called for a period of silent worship. In this way, he said, those who had come to find out what Quakerism was would experience at once 'the best that Quakerism has to offer." Dr. William I. Hull, of Swarthmore College, served as chairman of the meeting. In introducing the speaker, he mentioned two factors as the basis of Quakerism: mysticism and a practical application of religion to every-day life.

The address was given by Rufus M. Jones, of Haverford College. It is significant of the growing unity within the Society of Friends that the speakers at two of the three theatre meetings thus far held in Philadelphia have been members of a "branch" other than our own. And despite this difference, Rufus Jones gave this year, as did Elbert Russell on a previous occasion, an exposition of Quakerism which set forth all the essential Friends' principles and which Friends of all "branches" could heartily support.

Rufus Jones outlined the essentials of Quakerism simply, illuminating each topic with a wealth of illustrative incident. He chose as the principal points under which to develop his theme: direct connection with, and experience of, God—which meant the overthrowing of formalism and dogma; the importance of meetings for worship in the Quaker way of life; conscience, the voice of God in the soul, as the supreme authority for human conduct; the infinite worth of human personality and the high destiny which every human life should know and which it should set as its goal.

Under the latter heading, the speaker outlined the work of generations of Friends in social reform, and the present labors of the American Friends' Service Committee in Europe. It was at this point, perhaps, that he gripped his hearers most intensely. The ministrations of Friends abroad stood forth as a living demonstration that Quakerism was being tried, and was succeeding, as a "way of life," a practical application of Christian principles.

Transportation Costs to the Richmond Conference

Robert Seaman, Chairman of the Transportation Committee of the Friends' General Conference, writes as follows concerning rates of travel to Richmond:

"To all interested in the Friends' General Conference to be held at Richmond, Ind., August 26 to September 2, 1922, I quote the following rates of fare one way to Richmond, Ind., from various cities:

From	Fare	Lower berth	Upper berth
N. Y. City	$26.74	$8.25	$6.60
Philadelphia	23.50	7.50	6.00
Baltimore	21.82	7.50	6.00
Washington	21.82	7.50	6.00
Harrisburg	19.75	6.38	5.10
Chicago	8.12	3.73	3.00

"A reduction of one and one-half fare on the 'Conference Plan' will apply for the round trip for those attending the Friends' General Conference providing there are 250 traveling *with certification* by the various railroads. If there are any Friends thinking of attending the Conference and do not live near any of the above mentioned cities to take these rates and would like to know their own rate or any further information regarding the transportation, please write me."

Robert Seaman's address is Jericho, N. Y.

These transportation costs, together with the rates of accommodation given in the last issue of the INTELLIGENCER, may be taken as a basis for calculating the total expense of attendance at the Conference. For one going from Philadelphia, or some equally distant point, the minimum cost will be about $60, while $75 will comfortably cover all moderate contingencies. This includes expenses of travel both ways, and accommodations while in Richmond.

Concord First-day School Union

Concord First-day School Union, held at Swarthmore, Pa., on Fourth month 22nd, was fairly well attended. The morning session was largely devoted to the discussion of the question "Shall we have a Field Worker among the First-day Schools of our Union?" Annie Hillborn, in opening the subject, disclosed startling facts in statistics. During the past ten years, out of the thirteen Schools, nine have decreased in the number of teachers, two increased, eight decreased in attendance, four increased, one school closed, and one new school started. If we believe that we have a message to the world, why have we not started more schools?

However, reports show that the teaching has improved, the schools are better organized, graded as to proper material, and are producing better work. But we do need a supervisor to whip us along, bring new ideas and new methods, and show us how to apply them. There is no more important work than teaching our children religious truths.

D. Herbert Way, in continuing the discussion, presented a number of objections, which have been offered from time to time, to the paid Field Worker, and showed how these objections might in many cases prove to be advantages. It was feared also that the Field Worker would suggest expensive equipment which the school could not afford. Can we afford *not* to meet this legitimate expense for equipment which will be of value for the betterment of the child?

The expense of this Field Worker would probably be $250 for the three summer months, the amount to be raised by the Monthly Meetings of the Quarter on a pro rata basis. Besides consecutive intelligent visiting, and the studying and working out of individual problems, the worker would hold training classes for the instruction of teachers.

After careful consideration, the meeting united in trying the experiment for the three summer months. All the Schools, both winter and summer, will share the expense, the former tho not in session during the experiment, will have an opportunity to join the training classes. The following committee was appointed to engage a Field Worker, keep in touch with her work during the summer, and report results in the fall: Ethel Gates Coates, D. Herbert Way, Annie Hilborn, William T. Cope, Anna S. Bartram, Herbert P. Worth, Frances Darlington, William R. Fogg.

La Verne Forbush gave a most interesting and enlightening talk on "Dramatization of Bible stories," by recounting her experiences in Baltimore. It is time, she said, that we adapted day-school methods to our First-day Schools. One-half to two-thirds of our education comes thru the eyes. She has had two aims in her work: (1) The educational value of dramatization. It is not done for entertainment or with the idea of a finished product, but to put the spirit of the story across, to live over the events of that time. (2) To give the young people something to do. Children are fundamentally religious, but their religion is unexpressed.

Bliss Forbush, of Baltimore, gave a most inspiring and instructive talk on "Organization of our First-day School Work." He dwelt upon improved methods, suggesting a program for the day.

The Superintendent should be spiritual not pious. He must be up to date, should read, study, and visit; and if possible attend some school of religious instruction. The teachers should realize their responsibility, be prepared and equipped, and have something to give. The most modern class in the First-day School is the organized class. Each class above the primary department should have a secretary with definite duties.

Bliss Forbush then summed up a number of outside interests which the ideal school should strive to have:

1. Service—Must be definite work and personal, for example, raising money to buy sheep for Poland (in order to visualize, have the school pin a white paper sheep on a black background as sufficient money for each one is collected, aiming for a definite number of sheep), or collect magazines to be sent to lonely lighthouse keepers.

2. Biblical Museums—Make outline maps, clay models, etc.

3. Organize Clubs—Have boys' clubs and girls' clubs as a means of promoting sociability and loyalty to the school. If possible have the clubs meet in the First-day School building.

4. Invite and visit the absentees.

5. Enroll the shut-ins in a home department.

6. Interest non-Friends—those not having a church home.

7. Competition in membership, or in attending the meeting for worship—never in financial matters.

The meeting felt deeply grateful for the inspiration and wealth of suggestions which Bliss Forbush and his wife left with us. ESTHER SMEDLEY CHAMBERS.

Friendly News Notes

A cable from Murray Kenworthy in Moscow, received Fourth month 24th, at the Service Committee, stated that Arthur Watts, the head of the English Unit in the Russian famine area, is ill with typhus. Arthur Watts was one of the first of the Quaker group to enter Russia, going there in the group representing the Friends' International Service in the summer of 1917. After leaving on account of the movement of the armies, he returned in the summer of 1920 and with Anna Haines carried on the entire distribution of the Quaker Relief in Moscow during the winter of 1920-21. When Anna Haines left the famine area last September to return to America, Arthur Watts took her place and began the first of the famine relief feeding. He has been in the famine area ever since.

One of the race of great headmasters has "passed on," in the passing of Frederick Andrews, for forty-two years head master of Ackworth, the famous Quaker School founded by Dr John Fothergill, F. R. S., in Yorkshire in 1779.

The faith of those who made him head of a great school at the age of 27 was abundantly justified. A great educator in the more restricted sense he may not have been, but his claim to be a great headmaster none will challenge.

Q. Q.

NEW YORK YEARLY MEETING

The program for New York Yearly Meeting begins to emerge from the mists of the future.

On the evening of Seventh-day the 27th, Bliss Forbush, of Baltimore Monthly Meeting, will speak; under care of the First-day School Committee.

On Second-day night, the 29th, a series of Biblical

tableaux will be given by First-day School children under the direction of Cora H. Carver, with appropriate music by Josephine Tilton.

Third-day evening James McAfee will give an illustrated talk on his experiences with the Service Committee work in Vienna and Poland.

The Young Friends' Movement, which will have charge of the meeting on First-day night, is planning a big celebration on Seventh-day in honor of its second birthday, and may burst out in unexpected directions during the week.

SOUTHERN HALF-YEARLY MEETING

Southern Half-Yearly Meeting, held at Easton, Maryland, the 23rd of Fourth month, was well attended. Visiting Friends most prominent were Caroline S. Jackson, of Philadelphia, and Elizabeth G. Stapler, of Bucks Quarter. Both spoke acceptably in the religious meeting, emphasizing the duties and responsibilities laid upon individuals of the Society. Wilson M. Tylor arose with the thought, "and they met with one accord in one place." In his address he went to the fundamental principles of mass psychology either in attending to religious or social service; that there could be but one religious "meeting," and that was for the individual to meet with the Spirit of Truth; if we assembled without that desire it was not an ideal Friends' Meeting. He further spoke of the beauty and simplicity of the teaching of Jesus and contrasted in detail the two texts given of the Lord's Prayer, in Matthew and Luke, bringing out much that is overlooked in that familiar petition. John Poole was favored to speak upon practical Christian ethics, in a discourse most acceptable to the meeting. In the business meeting new names for the Representative Committee from Southern were approved.

E. S. H.

FAIRHILL PILGRIMAGE

Fairhill Friends' Meeting House, Germantown Avenue and Cambria Streets, was the Mecca of a Young Friends' Pilgrimage on Fourth month 22nd and 23rd. Members were present from Ambler, Frankford, Haverford, New York, Baltimore and Five Years Meetings.

The program opened on Seventh-day evening with an informal social gathering. On First-day morning a very interesting discussion was led by William Price, on the subject of "Present Day Opportunities."

Friend Price used as the theme of his talk the possibilities of general and specialized service along the lines loved by Friends and known and appreciated the world over. The speaker retold Oscar Wilde's tale of the "Young King" in such a manner as to bring home very strikingly the need for real leadership among Friends. Opportunities for real service, in meeting and out, it was demonstrated are forever surrounding us and although we may often be faced with that old bugaboo "what's the use" in our attempts, like the young king, we must ever keep before us our objective.

"Perhaps we could be of more service if our occupation were different. Is it advisable to change?" "Unquestionably," replies William Price. The returns to self and to society will be more than sufficient to compensate any temporary inconvenience. In reply to a query, it was pointed out that it is not necessary to change one's vocation. There are myriads of possibilities, countless opportunities to all persons, regardless of how they may be situated in the factory of the world's work.

Following the talk, the Pilgrims were the guests of Fairhill Friends at dinner. All remained for First-day School, where William Price once more obliged by relating a story with a moral lesson.

The pilgrimage was brought to a close with an hour of silent meeting for worship.

HENRY BECK.

FRIENDS' OPPORTUNITY IN THE ORIENT

It is now more than a month since a letter was sent out to all Monthly Meetings in the seven Yearly Meetings associated in the General Conference asking for contributions of money for the support of missionary work in China. Fifteen hundred dollars has already been sent to the Trustees of Canton Christian College for the full support for another year of Margaret H. Riggs, who, through last year's efforts, now represents us as a teacher supplied by Friends to further the work of this great undenominational College for the uplift of China's millions. This puts us where we were a year ago. But our present appeal has gone wider and is in behalf of three Friends instead of one. Analysis of returns shows Friends are contributing generously where the three young Missionary Friends are known, a tribute to their sincerity and zeal. They are for the time representatives of a great cause. It is the thought of our committee that the cause is greater than the personality of its self-sacrificing servants. China is now disturbed in the conflict of great social forces. Never was the opportunity greater to carry the Christian Message to a receptive people than right now. We need fully two thousand dollars more to carry through the program outlined in our letters to Friends. Some funds we know are in the hands of collectors who are not yet ready to report. Let everyone do only a small share and the thing will be done. Why delay?

ALFRED W. WRIGHT, *Chairman,*
Friends' Opportunity in the Orient.

WESTERN QUARTERLY MEETING

At the meeting for worship preceding the business meeting of Western Quarterly Meeting held Fourth month 25th, at London Grove, Pa., Sarah T. Linvill brought a message urging Friends to not fill their lives so full of the many interests that claim their attention that they cannot find time for waiting on the Lord and communing with Him for their own growth and help. Daniel Batchellor presented the differences in the accounts of the Resurrection in the various Gospels. He brought to us some pictures of the fine characters throughout history in different sects and nationalities who have been mystics. He pointed out that Friends have a mystical religion, and that we must be mystics to believe in the things of the spirit which cannot be seen to be proven.

In the business meeting the committee in charge of the Friends' Boarding Home reported that there are 37 in family. Much appreciation was felt for the gift of $1,000 to the Home from Augustus and Mary Brosius, which is to be kept in a fund to be known as the "Augustus and Mary Brosius Fund."

In a report from the Philanthropic Committee, Friends were urged to realize their responsibility of attending the primaries on May 16th and voting for the candidates who stand for our principles. Others spoke of the necessity of work being done toward the nomination of good men for governor.

A memorial for Elma M. Preston presented from New Garden Monthly Meeting, brought forth expressions from several of her sterling worth to our meeting and other interests in the community. Her life was a benediction to all who knew her and one which left a lasting impression for good.

ELLA BROOMELL.

Philadelphia Yearly Meeting

FIFTH MONTH 13-19, 1922

Program

Seventh-day, Fifth month 13th

10.00 a. m. and 2.00 p. m.—Meeting of Ministry and Counsel.

4.30 p. m.—Eighth General Conference of Young Friends' Movement. (For details of this and other Young Friends' activities, to many of which *all* are invited, see complete program below.)

First-day, Fifth month 14th

10.00 a. m.—Meetings for Worship in Race Street and Cherry Street Meeting Houses, also in the other city Meeting Houses except Fair Hill.

10.30 a. m.—Meeting in the Central School Building for Children, between the ages of 9 and 14 years, under care of the Yearly Meeting's Committee on First-day Schools.

7.30 p. m.—Meetings for Worship—Race Street and Girard Avenue.

9.00 a. m.—Meeting for Worship each day.

From 9 a. m. to 12 m. and from 1.30 to 4.00 p. m. daily, a nursery will be conducted in the *Elementary School Building*, where children will be cared for during the sessions of the Yearly Meeting

Fourth-day at 1.15 p. m.—Meeting under care of Friends' Neighborhood Guild. *Friends' Central School Lecture Room.*

Business Sessions

Morning Session—9.30 a. m.	Afternoon Session—2.00 p. m.
Second-day, Fifth month 15th	
Organization.	Report of Representative Committee.
Epistles.	First-day School Report.
	Epistles.
Third-day, Fifth month 16th	
Central Bureau Report.	George School Report.
Friends' General Conference Report.	Committee on Interests of Colored Race Report.
General Nominating Committee Report.	Joseph Jeanes Committee Report.
Baltimore Anniversary Report.	
Fourth-day, Fifth month 17th	
Queries.	Peace and Service Report.
	Young Friends' Movement Report.
Fifth-day, Fifth month 18th	
Meeting for Worship—10.30 a. m.	Philanthropic Labor Report.
	Committee on Education Report.
	Auditing Committee Report.
Sixth-day, Fifth month 19th	
Trustees' Report.	Time for completion of business previously introduced.
American Friends' Service Committee Report.	Memorial.
Approval of Epistles to be sent.	

Evening Meetings

Second-day, Fifth month 15th

7.30 p. m.—Under care of the Representative Committee. "STRENGTHENING OUR SOCIETY."

1. Religious Education.—W. Russell Green.
2. Making Our Organization Effective—Jane P. Rushmore.
3. The Relation of Service to Spiritual Life—Hannah Clothier Hull.
4. The Meeting for Worship—Elbert Russell.

Third-day, Fifth month 16th

7.30 p. m.—Under care of the Philanthropic Committee. "THE HEALTH OF OUR SCHOOL CHILDREN"—Miss Sally Lucas Jean, Director, Child Health Organization of America.

Fourth-day, Fifth month 17th

7.30 p. m.—Under care of Committee on Education. "THE CONTRIBUTION OF THE SOCIETY OF FRIENDS TO AMERICAN EDUCATION"—Pres. Frank Aydelotte, of Swarthmore College.

Fifth-day, Fifth month 18th

7.30 p. m.—Under care of Peace and Service Committee. "MUTUAL UNDERSTANDING BETWEEN NATIONS"—Mlle. Therese Pottecher, of France; Fraulein Gertrud Baer, of Germany; Mrs. Annot Robinson, of England.

Young Friends' Yearly Meeting Activities

Eighth General Conference, Young Friends' Movement of Philadelphia Yearly Meeting

FIFTH MONTH 13-18, 1922

Seventh-day, Fifth month 13th

4.30 p. m.—General Meeting of Young People (Cherry Street Meeting House). Opening Remarks by Chairman; Reports of Executive Secretary and Treasurer; Announcement of plans for Camp and other Summer Activities.

Eight-minute talks on the subject:

"THE YOUNG FRIENDS' MOVEMENT—WHAT IS IT?" Helen Hawkins (Five Years' Meeting), speaker to be announced (Arch Street), Lindsley H. Noble (Race Street), Wm. Eves, 3rd.

General discussion.

Concluding remarks by William Littleboy, of England.

6.30 p. m.—Young People's Supper (65 cents).

8.00 p. m.—Readings and Music. (Lecture Room of Friends' Central School.) All Friends are cordially invited.

First-day, Fifth month 14th

2.15 p. m.—Meeting of new Central Committee.

3.00 p. m.—Eighth Wm. Penn Lecture. "INCENTIVES IN MODERN LIFE," by Kirby Page (Race Street Meeting House). All Friends are cordially invited.

4.15 p. m.—YOUNG PEOPLE'S MEETING FOR WORSHIP. (Cherry Street Meeting House.)

Supper Conferences

Young People's Supper Conferences will be held between the afternoon and evening sessions of the Yearly Meeting on Second, Third, Fourth and Fifth-day evenings, from 5.30 p. m. to 7.15 p. m. Acceptances for these should be at Headquarters by 9 a. m. each day.

Second-day, Fifth month 15th

"LEADERSHIP"—Albert E. Rogers, Drew Pearson.

Third-day, Fifth month 16th

"YOUNG FRIENDS IN THEIR HOME COMMUNITIES"—D. Herbert Way, John S. Ruhlman, Jr., Thomas L. Knight.

Fourth-day, Fifth month 17th

"IDEALISM APPLIED"—David G. Paul, Wm. W. Price.

Fifth-day, Fifth month 18th

"THE FOUNDATIONS OF SERVICE"—E. Maria Bishop.

THE OPEN FORUM

This column is intended to afford free expression of opinion by readers on questions of interest. The INTELLIGENCER *is not responsible for any such opinions. Letters must be brief, and the editor reserves the right to omit parts if necessary to save space.*

To the Editor:

May I add to the suggestions, made in the editorial "Personality and Coal" in a recent INTELLIGENCER, as to why the West Virginia miner does not always clean up the premises around his house, two further reasons which are difficult for those living under other conditions to understand:

1. Miners who have worked to improve their living conditions have frequently been evicted from their houses immediately afterward without reason, and the place "rented" to some one else who will pay a trifle more.

2. For half-fed men, physical effort of any kind costs actual flesh and blood with no hope of replenishment.

3. Under-nourishment means anemic blood, which means warped brains. Three generations of mal-nutrition bring on mental deficiency. Men cannot act as we act, or even see as we see, until we share our food with them.

Are not these miners, even in the face of such terrible odds, far more loyal to their ideal than we to the faith we profess?

Philadelphia, Pa. ESTHER HARLAN.

To the Editor:

I wish to express my appreciation of your editorial, "Should Industrial Issues Be the Churches' Concern?" This question is the greatest issue of this or any other age, and it is because we have not answered it in the past that human society now finds itself at such a crisis.

As a result of the church's wilful neglect to answer this question honestly, our material accomplishment has so outrun our spiritual development that society now has the power to destroy itself and will do so unless it achieves a new object, that of service in its social, economic and industrial relations.

Christianity, whatever it may have done for the individual, has failed in leadership for society as a whole. It has failed through ignorance, cowardice and selfishness to answer the question you have asked.

If the church continues to fail to answer this question, it will, nevertheless, be answered as a purely civic problem; and that answer will be harsh indeed.

Our religion must find its chief expression in this life which God has plainly given us for our present field of action rather than seek to express itself on a spiritual plane about which he has vouchsafed to us very little information indeed. There is, then, no better religion, no better expression of the brotherhood of man, than good government as comprehended in all its social, economic and industrial relations. I. DANIEL WEBSTER.

San Diego, Cal.

To the Editor:

Many articles have appeared in the INTELLIGENCER which are interesting and helpful in many ways, and more than any other of recent date I should like to say "thanks" for the one, "Religion in the Home." Just the name brings forward the greatest need of the whole world, and the work and report of this committee deserves the thanks and consideration of all Friends, and especially of those who are parents. Surely our most important "advancement work" should be done by the parents in the homes, as the future of our Society rests largely upon the children.

I hope the INTELLIGENCER will have further articles along the same line of thought from time to time.

Port Washington, Pa. ANNA W. LAPHAM.

MARRIAGES

LIPPINCOTT-WARNER—In Horsham Friends' meeting house, Fourth month 15th, Albert H. Lippincott, of Marlton, N. J., and Marion S. Warner, daughter of Isaac and Mary S. Warner, of Horsham.

DEATHS

BROWN—At Purcellville, Va., Third month 8th, Edwin M., in the 59th year of his age. He is survived by his wife, Lillian Birdsall, and two sons and a daughter.

CORNELL—At the home of her son-in-law, Ellis Tomlinson, Fourth month 26th, Anna B., widow of Theodore Cornell, aged 77.

CUMMONS—On Fourth month 28th, Emma, wife of I. Randall Cummons, aged 73 years. Interment in Middletown Friends' burying ground.

SHARPLESS—Liddia Coale Sharpless, wife of John Clemson Sharpless, of Secane, Pa., died at Spartanburg, S. C., in 81st year. Interment at Downingtown, Pa.

COMING EVENTS

FIFTH MONTH

5th-6th—Pilgrimage under care of the young Friends' Movement, at West Chester, Pa.

6th—Philadelphia Quarterly Meeting will be held in Germantown Meeting House, 45 W. School House Lane, Germantown, on Fifth month 6th, Seventh-day afternoon. Religious Meeting, 1.30 p. m.; Business Meeting, 2.30 p. m. Box Supper (coffee, ice cream and cake will be served). Entertainment by Germantown Friends' Association 7.30 p. m.

7th—First-day at 3 p. m., "Daylight saving time." The usual semi-annual Community Meeting for worship will be held at Chichester Friends' Meeting House under care of a Committee of Concord Quarterly Meeting. All persons are welcome and young people particularly invited. Joseph H. Willits, of Swarthmore, expects to attend. Train leaves 24th and Chestnut Sts., for Boothwyn at 1.30 p. m.; Darby, 1.43; Chester, 2.00; returning 5 p. m. All "Daylight saving." Trains will stop at cross-road near the meeting-house.

7th—Purchase Quarterly Meeting, at Amawalk, N. Y.

7th—Nine Partners Half-Yearly Meeting will be held at Clinton Corners, New York. Business session at 11 a. m. and meeting for worship at 2 p. m. Albert Lawton is expected to be present.

7th—Preparative Meeting in New York and Brooklyn after the Meeting for Worship.

7th—Members of Philadelphia Quarterly Meeting's Visiting Committee will attend meeting at Frankford, Philadelphia. First-day School at 11 a. m. They will also attend a meeting at Germantown Friends' Home, at 7.30 p. m.

8th—At the final Spring meeting of the P. Y. F. A., Ruth Verlenden will give a reading of O'Henry stories. Music. Come and bring thy friends.

8th—New York Monthly Meeting, at 7.30, at 221 East 15th St., New York. Supper will be served at 6. The Meeting for Ministry and Counsel will be at 5.

8th—Easton and Granville Half-Yearly Meeting, at Granville, N. Y., at 11 a. m. Meeting of Ministry and Counsel, same day, at 10 a. m.

11th—Members of the Young Friends' Movement of New York, and others of appropriate age and condition are invited to the gymnasium of Friends' Seminary for another unconventional evening, from 8 to 10. Wear old clothes and tennis shoes. Use entrance on Rutherford Place, between 15th and 16th Sts.

13th—Miami Quarterly Meeting convenes at 10 a. m., at Waynesville, Ohio. Meeting for Ministers and Elders the day before, at 2 p. m.

NOTICE—"Camp Onas"—the fourth annual camp under the direction of the Young Friends' Movement of Philadelphia Yearly Meeting will be held from Sixth month 24th to Seventh month 10th. The site will be selected within the next few weeks and folders giving full particulars will then be ready. As accommodations will be very much limited this year, applications should be sent early to Ruth H. Conrow, Camp Leader, 154 N. 15th Street, Philadelphia.

What Has Thee Done to Help?

The special offer of a three-months' trial subscription for .35 will be withdrawn on Seventh month 1st. To date, 79 people have taken advantage of the offer. In beginning this campaign we wrote to 115 active Friends throughout all our Yearly Meetings asking their co-operation.

Samuel P. Zavitz, of Coldstream, Ontario, went to work in real earnest and sent in 19 names, writing "That will put the INTELLIGENCER in every home for three months." Wasn't that fine work?

A. W. Phillips, Waterford, Va., wrote: "Replying to thine of Third month 25th, I think a copy of the INTELLIGENCER goes into the home of each member of our very small meeting."

Here are two meetings that now have a perfect record. We hear a great deal these days about being "100% American." Is thee helping to make the Society of Friends "100% INTELLIGENCER?"

Won't thee make a special effort to ask every member of thy meeting, whether he gets the INTELLIGENCER, and if not, get his permission to send in his name for three months for .35. We will send bill and coin card if thee does not care to bother with the collection of the money.

American Friends' Service Committee

WILBUR K. THOMAS, EX. SEC.
20 S. 12th St. Philadelphia.

CASH CONTRIBUTIONS
WEEK ENDING APRIL 24TH

Five Years Meetings	$326.60
Other Meetings	
Caln Quarterly Meeting	10.00
Chester Monthly Meeting	12.00
Concord Quarterly Meeting	25.00
Coulter Street Meeting, S. S.	5.00
Woodbury Prep. Meeting	25.00
Valley Meeting	25.00
Cornwall Monthly Meeting	5.00
Manasquan First-day School	11.65
Woodstown First-day School, N. J.	16.25
New York Monthly Meeting (Hicksite)	400.00
Flushing Friends' First-day School	10.00
Park Avenue Meeting	150.00
Contributions for Germany	191.44
" " Austria	1,688.50
" " Poland	2,532.79
" " Russia	25,041.82
" " Russian overhead	136.07
" " Armenia	20.00
" " General	432.50
" " Clothing	12.00
" " Home service	25.00
" " Religious work in Europe	100.00
Refunds	526.09
	$31,727.71

Shipments received during week ending April 22nd: 101 boxes and packages received; 2 from Mennonites.

Homes During Yearly Meeting Week.

Friends expecting to attend Philadelphia Yearly Meeting and wishing the assistance of the committee appointed by the two Monthly Meetings of Philadelphia to help Friends in securing suitable homes, are asked to communicate with *Almira P. Harlan*, Fifteenth and Race Streets, Philadelphia, and they will be furnished with a list from which they can select and engage rooms for themselves.

Persons willing to assist in the dining-room during Yearly Meeting week will please communicate with Esther W. Fell, 433 School Lane, Germantown, Philadelphia.

To the Lot Holders and others interested in Fairhill Burial Ground:

GREEN STREET Monthly Meeting has funds available for the encouragement of the practice of cremating the dead to be interred in Fairhill Burial Ground. We wish to bring this fact as prominently as possible to those who may be interested. We are prepared to undertake the expense of cremation in case any lot holder desires us to do so.

Those interested should communicate with William H. Gaskill, Treasurer of the Committee of Interments, Green Street Monthly Meeting, or any of the following members of the Committee.

William H. Gaskill, 3201 Arch St.
Samuel N. Longstreth, 1218 Chestnut St.
Charles F. Jenkins, 232 South Seventh St.
Stuart S. Graves, 3033 Germantown Ave.

WANTED

WANTED — HOUSEKEEPER (MANager), capable woman of refinement who desires good permanent home in Philadelphia suburbs with family of three children and male adult. Box S. 150, Friends' Intelligencer.

WANTED — SUMMER BOARD FOR three adults, with private family on farm. Commuting distance from Philadelphia. Address D. 154, Friends' Intelligencer.

WANTED — MIDDLE-AGED WHITE woman of refinement for cook in private family. Also, woman for chambermaid and waitress; both to go to mountains for three months this summer. Answer by letter only. Address M. 173, Friends' Intelligencer.

WANTED — POSITION AS CHAUFfeur, four years' experience; references. Charles A. Neiman, 915 West Lehigh avenue, Philadelphia.

POSITION WANTED—BY CAPABLE woman, as companion to semi-invalid, or elderly woman; able to manage house. Philadelphia suburbs. References. Address B. 180, Friends' Intelligencer.

HIRED STENOGRAPHER — HEIR (*crescendo molto!*) Erin-go-bragh's culture through that immigrant progenitor of Pennsylvania judges, Thomas Ross (died Quaker preacher 1786 guest of Lindley Murray, grammarian)—wants, under dock-for-time-off arrangement, occasional swift work at 25c. per 100 words plus expenses. Night telephonic dictations solicited. Served Biennial General Conference Religious Society Friends 9 times, American Electro-Chemical Society 5, annual meeting American Association University Presidents 1, American Medical Association 10 (coast to coast), Homeopathic Medical Society State Pennsylvania 3, Association Colleges Preparatory Schools Middle States Maryland 15, New Jersey State Teachers' Association 7, American Society Chemical Engineers (addressing them once on theory capacity Chinese stomach shrunken through ages underfeeding) 2; law courts Bucks, Chester, Philadelphia, Atlantic and Camden Counties. Geo. B. Cock, Philadelphia Bell Directory.

FOR SALE

FOR SALE—BRICK AND FRAME detached residence, well built; 10 rooms, bath, sleeping porch, glassed in; gas and electricity, modern conveniences; near Friends' School and Meeting House, Lansdowne, Pa. Apply J. 100, Friends' Intelligencer.

FOR RENT

FOR RENT—THE PACKER COTTAGE at Buck Hill. Accommodations for five or six. Located within fifteen minutes' walk of Inn. For particulars inquire Franklin Packer, Newtown, Pa.

FOR RENT—FURNISHED, AN ATtractive home in Haddonfield, N. J., the three summer months, 6th, 7th and 8th. Address P. 170, Friends' Intelligencer.

FOR RENT—FOR ALL OR PART OF season, delightful furnished cottage among New Hampshire pines in Quaker neighborhood. Address W. 161, Friends' Intelligencer.

FOR RENT—APARTMENT FOR light housekeeping, in suburban home. Two large rooms, semi-private bath, heat, hot water, electric lights, gas, front and back porches, large yard, old shade. Convenient to train, trolley and bus line. Good roads and convenient garages. Price reasonable. C. B. Llewellynn, Cheltenham, Pa. Bell Phone—Cheltenham 1241-W.

FOR RENT — FOR THE SUMMER, furnished house in Germantown. Four bedrooms, all conveniences. Near Reading railroad and woods. Address B. 181, Friends' Intelligencer.

FOR RENT

TO RENT—BEAUTIFULLY FURNISHed half of fine summer home at Washington's Crossing for season. Electric lights, six rooms, modern bath. Hot water furnished. Screened sun-parlor. Huge living-room with fire-place. Spacious porches with hammock. Room for motor car. On main concrete highroad to Water Gap. Five minutes' walk to Delaware River with swimming and boating. Hourly motor bus to Trenton. Wonderful lawn with magnificent shade trees, and summer house. Direct train service to Philadelphia. Milk, eggs, fruits and vegetables in season at wholesale prices. An exceptional place for a discriminating family. Address Harry G. Forster, Titusville, N. J., R. F. D. 1.

FOR RENT — FOR SUMMER, TENroom house, furnished; two baths. Carpenter station, Germantown. Nice yard and shade. Apply A. 182, Friends' Intelligencer. Phone Gtn. 2735-J.

FUN

In a general intelligence test in a school one of the questions was, "What is the longest day in the year?" One child answered, "Sunday."—*Christian Register.*

The Friends' Intelligencer

ESTABLISHED 1844 | FIFTH MONTH 27, 1922 | VOLUME 79 NUMBER 21

Contents

EDITORIAL

GENERAL ARTICLES

AMONG OUR MEETINGS

SCHOOLS.

Woolman School

SWARTHMORE, PA.

Summer Term

6th Month 27 to 8th Month 5

Five special week-end programs for those unable to take regular courses. Write for information.

ELBERT RUSSELL, *Director.*

GEORGE SCHOOL
Near Newtown, Bucks County, Pa.

Under the care of Philadelphia Yearly Meeting of Friends.

Course of study extended and thorough, preparing students either for business or for college. For catalogue apply to

GEORGE A. WALTON, A. M., Principal
George School, Penna.

FRIENDS' CENTRAL SCHOOL SYSTEM

Write for Year Book and Rates.

CHARLES BURTON WALSH, Principal.

15th and Race Sts., Philadelphia.

FRIENDS' ACADEMY
LONG ISLAND, N. Y.

A Boarding and Day School for Boys and Girls, conducted in accordance with the principles of the Society of Friends. For further particulars address

S. ARCHIBALD SMITH, Principal,
Locust Valley, N. Y.

THE FRIENDS' INTELLIGENCER

Published weekly, 140 N. 15th Street, Philadelphia, Pa., by Friends' Intelligencer Association, Ltd.

WALTER H. ABELL, *Editor*

SUE C. YERKES, *Business Manager*

Editorial Board: Elizabeth Powell Bond, Thomas A. Jenkins, J. Russell Smith, George A. Walton.

Board of Managers: Edward Cornell, Alice Hall Paxson, Paul M. Pearson, Annie Hillborn, Elwood Hollingshead, William C. Biddle, Charles F. Jenkins, Edith M. Winder, Frances M. White.

Officers of Intelligencer Associates: Ellwood Burdsall, Chairman; Bertha L. Broomell, Secretary; Herbert P. Worth, Treasurer.

Subscription rates: United States, Mexico, Cuba and Panama, $2.50 per year. Canada and other foreign countries, $3.00 per year. Checks should be made payable to Friends' Intelligencer Association, Ltd.

Entered as Second Class Matter at Philadelphia Post Office.

HOTELS.

Ye Longfellow Inn,

130 Eastern Promenade,
PORTLAND, MAINE.
H. H. PEASE, Proprietor.

Overlooking Casco Bay—Ideal Summer Resort.

Opened from June 20th to September 20th.

Philadelphia references given on request.

Can you afford to be without a partial supply of COAL under present conditions in the mining district?

H. F. BRUNER & CO.

16 North 21st Street

Bell, Locust 0243 *Keystone, Race 5661*

BELL, PRESTON 23-74
KEYSTONE, WEST 2661

S. D. HALL

39th and Parrish Streets

Asthma

Hay Fever and Rose Colds are caused by nervous irritations of the delicate membranes in your throat. Chiropractors have proved over and over again that this irritation comes from a misplaced vertebra of the spine which presses upon the throat nerve with a vise-like grip. Adjust this into proper alignment and your distressing illness entirely disappears. Simple, isn't it?

RUDULPH J. SUPLEE, D. C.

3304 HAMILTON STREET,
Philadelphia, Pa.

8 to 10 a.m.—4 to 7 p.m. and by appointment. Baring 0352-J.

HOTELS.

Buck Hill Falls

JUNE—the month of laurel, rhododendron, golf, tennis, riding—all to be found amidst the homey atmosphere of

THE INN

BUCK HILL FALLS, PA.

HOTEL WARWICK

SOUTH CAROLINA AVENUE
ATLANTIC CITY, N. J.
OPEN ALL THE YEAR

First house from beach and boardwalk. Steam heat, electric lights, elevator. Excellent cuisine, quiet, dignified surroundings and attentive service.

Reasonable rates. Write
SARAH H. FULLOM, Prop.

OCEAN CITY, N. J.

Hotel Swarthmore

Capacity 135.

Near beach and attractions; running water thruout; neat white help; cuisine first class.

W. P. & F. R. LIPPINCOTT.

THE WHEELER
Boardwalk at Massachusetts
ATLANTIC CITY, N. J.
Ocean Rooms—Table Guests
MRS. A. W. WHEELER

Strath Haven Tea Room
Dinner 6 to 7:30.
Sunday Special — Chicken and Waffles, 85 cents.
Swarthmore, Pa. Phone 680

TRANSIENT ACCOMMODATIONS

WASHINGTON, D. C.—ROOMS FOR visitors. Near Station, Capitol, Library. Continuous hot water. Electricity. Garage. Mrs. L. L. Kendig, 120 C. Street, Northwest.

When patronizing our advertisers, please mention the "Friends' Intelligencer."

The Friends' Intelligencer

The religion of Friends is based on faith in the "INWARD LIGHT," or direct revelation of God's spirit and will in every seeking soul.

The INTELLIGENCER is interested in all who bear the name of Friends in every part of the world, and aims to promote love, unity and intercourse among all branches and with all religious societies.

ESTABLISHED 1844 | PHILADELPHIA, FIFTH MONTH 27, 1922 | VOLUME 79 NUMBER 21

Impressions of Philadelphia Yearly Meeting

Our main impression of Philadelphia Yearly Meeting this year was one of hope. Not that the Meeting met the need of a "world in ruins," in the sense in which a movement founded by Jesus, and revitalized by such men as Fox and Penn, might be expected to meet that need. But there were manifest in its sessions two tendencies which can grow, and which if they do grow, can render Quakerism increasingly capable of fulfilling its mission.

These tendencies revealed themselves partly in new activities proposed by the Meeting for Ministry and Counsel and by the Representative Committee. They were further expressed by many speakers at the different sessions. Our own impression of them might be summarized as follows:

First, there was the recognition that the function of the Society of Friends is precisely that of meeting the need of the world—a need which we recognize as essentially "spiritual." Said one speaker: "Some of us still incline to think of the Society of Friends as an end in itself; an organization to which we owe our loyalty for its own sake. Such is not the case. It is simply a piece of machinery created for us to use in advancing causes of human uplift. When it can be shown that it is no longer serviceable in advancing such causes, it ought to be abandoned." To bring the "Kingdom," or "leadership" of God in every relationship of personal and social life is, then, our reason for existence and our task. "Quietism" is a "menace." Jane P. Rushmore's stimulating address on "Making Our Organization Effective" was along lines closely related to these thoughts.

In the second place, there was an humble recognition on the part of many that, despite encouraging successes, we have too often failed to fulfil this function of world service. J. Barnard Walton expressed a "real dissatisfaction" that we had failed to reach the world with our message, when we believe that that message is what the world needs. In one of Isaac Wilson's sermons came the challenge: "Let us cease so frequently to ease our consciences. We may sin in the things which we fail to do, even though we are guilty of no positively wrong actions." The loving service of William Littleboy brought to us a sense of the great progress to be made if our meetings for worship are to afford a vital ministry. Jesse H. Holmes, said: "Our ministry is failing. It is not successfully reaching even our own meetings, and we are overlooking the fact that we are a society of ministers, the function of which is to preach, not to ourselves, but to the world." The General Epistle is an appeal for "ever-deepening sincerity and courage in every phase of our individual and corporate lives."

Such a consciousness of our need for increasing power is a wholesome sign. "Those that seek shall find"; or, as Jane P. Rushmore put it: "The first step toward progress is to realize that we lack something." If our vision of the world's need, and our sincere and humble seeking for the power to meet that need are to continue, the Society of Friends may be regarded as a growing, not a dying, force.

The joint sessions were eminently successful. At no one of them were Friends crowded, large spaces in the galleries always remaining vacant, while the consideration of business was greatly facilitated. When the meeting met in separate sessions, those who summarized the reports had to go from one side to the other, and some inefficiency resulted. It is earnestly to be hoped that separate sessions will be entirely abandoned next year, and that joint sessions will henceforward be the accepted rule.

The omission of report reading was another innovation which worked for the good of the meeting. It reduced the time required for routine, and increased that given to consideration and discussion. It further enabled the meeting to receive, not only the actual reports of the various committees, but the stimulus of the more personal appeal given by those who presented the reports. We believe that the practice should be continued, and that the principle of thus reducing formal routine should be extended as widely as possible throughout all business activities, whether of the Yearly or other meetings.

Owing to the space required by our reports of the Baltimore CCL, and of Philadelphia and New York Yearly Meeting, it has been necessary to postpone the remaining three chapters of the series on "Christianity and Economic Problems." These will be published as soon as space permits, probably within the next two or three issues.

To The Churches of Christ in All Countries

An Appeal from the Religious Society of Friends

The following appeal originated in a joint peace committee of Philadelphia Friends, and has been approved by both Philadelphia Yearly Meetings. It is being forwarded to London and other Yearly Meetings for approval, and will be sent to all the Christian churches of the world.

Fellow Christians and Sister Churches in All Lands:

The small fraction of the Christian Church which ventures to address this appeal to you, does so in a spirit of fervent hope that we may give our united strength whole-heartedly to uphold and advance the standards of peace which some followers of Christ have long cherished as a fundamental Christian principle.

Christianity seems to us to face a grave crisis and a divine duty. In this aftermath of history's most terrible war, we see two paths before us. One leads inevitably to another war by renewed preparedness of the most efficient military, economic, educational and religious means of waging it. The other begins with a complete rejection of war, and of all preparations for it, for any purpose and against any people; it demands definite organization for peace.

These two paths lie in opposite directions; we cannot possibly follow them both. There is no shadow of doubt on which of them are found the footprints and the sign-posts of Jesus Christ our Lord. Christ would not send His disciples where He Himself does not lead. "Follow me" has been forever His watchword. Shall not then, the Christian Church follow its Leader with perfect loyalty along this path?

Such loyalty to Christ is consistent with loyalty to one's native land. The higher loyalty includes the lower, and gives to it all its best and brightest substance. The Christian's love of country finds its source, its inspiration and its direction in his love of God and his fellow-men. Christ taught the fatherhood of God and the brotherhood of man; His church transcends all divisions of nationality, all prejudices and hatreds of nation for nation and of class for class. It must rise to the height of its divinely given mission. It must not depend on the leadership of generals or admirals, or financiers; nor await the changing policies of statecraft. In time of war, as in time of peace, it must keep its eye single to God's commands, and must draw constantly its Founder's immortal and stupendous contrast between that which is Caesar's and that which is God's.

As Christians, we are striving for "a warless world." We are firmly convinced that this can be achieved only by refusal to participate in war, simply and sufficiently because war is by its very nature at variance with the message, the spirit, and the life and death of Jesus Christ. We unite in supporting treaties of arbitration and conciliation, limitation and reduction of armaments, international courts of justice, a league or association of nations for the preservation of peace. This is well; it is a great achievement for statesmen to accomplish these things; but it is not sufficient for the Christian Church.

A principle is greater than any or all of its applications. The fundamental peace principle of Christianity demands the utter rejection of war, unequivocally and without compromise. With this principle in its charter the Christian Church can always utter a clear and unmistakable verdict on any specific measure of statesmanship that is proposed; it will not be misled or coerced, by argument or by force, into participating in any kind or degree of preparation for war, or into lending the sanction of Christianity to the waging of any war whatsoever.

The achievement of all the great moral reforms in history has awaited the development of a deep *religious* conviction in the hearts of the people. Vital, uncompromising Christianity when applied to great moral issues, has never failed to bring the Kingdom of Heaven on Earth another step nearer to realization.

The most pressing reform of our time is to abolish war, and to establish exclusively peaceful means of settling disputes and promoting co-operation among the nations. These peaceful means cannot prevail until the nations beat their swords into plowshares and learn war no more. To accomplish these results the Christian Church in practice and profession must condemn the whole system of war unequivocally and finally, relying not upon armed preparedness, but upon the awakened conscience of mankind.

Fellow Christians, we can scarcely exaggerate the loss and suffering of the Great War. There is a bitter Macedonian cry in our afflicted time for physical help and healing, but far more for the things of the Spirit—for faith, and hope and love. What greater message of cheer and reconstruction could be brought to mankind today than the assurance that all who bear the name of Christ in every land have solemnly resolved to have no part in war or in preparation for war, but henceforth to work unitedly for peace by peaceful means alone? Shall we not make this venture of faith together in the love that beareth all things, believeth all things, hopeth all things, endureth all things and that never fails? Shall the torch of spiritual heroism be borne by the Church of the living Christ, or shall leadership in the utter rejection of war pass from our hands to men of braver and truer spirit? Which Master shall we who call ourselves Christians be known by all the world to serve, the God of Battles or the Prince of Peace?

With love and greetings to you all, we are your sincere friends and brothers.

Philadelphia Yearly Meeting

A Summary of the Proceedings

(Continued from last week)

Business Sessions

SECOND-DAY, FIFTH MONTH 15, 1922

Separate sessions of the men's and women's meetings convened at 9 a. m., the hour provisionally set by the Representative Committee. The meetings decided to return to the original hour of 9.30 for opening the morning sessions, but to continue opening the afternoon sessions at 2, half an hour earlier than formerly.

In response to the requests of committees to present reports, joint sessions were approved for Second-day afternoon and all day Fourth-day.

In the men's meeting, Morgan Bunting was reappointed clerk for the ensuing year, and Isaac Michener and Thomas A. Foulke were appointed assistant clerks.

In connection with the reading of the epistles, the concern was expressed that Friends should feel a "real dissatisfaction" with many aspects of their condition, despite progress in other directions. We believe that the Society of Friends has a great message, yet we have not succeeded in convincing the world of that message. If we see the truth, we cannot be satisfied until we have brought the world to share it with us. A spirit of humbleness and a realization of the need for increased power will result in growing efficiency in our work.

The report of the Representative Committee was presented in summary form at the joint afternoon session. The Committee expressed a concern for increasing spiritual life in our Society, and reported meetings with the overseers of our monthly meetings which had led to finding some new light. It is planned to have joint meetings of the Representative Committee, the Overseers, and the members of Ministry and Counsel, from which it is hoped that new impulses of spiritual vitality will spring. The danger of over-organization was emphasized.

Two important actions resulted from matters brought forward by the Representative Committee:

1. It was decided to establish a "more direct and carefully worked out financial system" for the Yearly Meeting. The principle of a budget system was agreed upon. It was decided to appoint a committee of 25, including one member of each active committee, to work out the plan for a budget system, and to present it, together with the estimated amount of the budget for the following year, to next year's Yearly Meeting.

2. A recommendation for a general revision of the Book of Discipline was favorably acted upon. The recommendation originated in Swarthmore Monthly Meeting, and came through Concord Quarterly Meeting. The present Discipline is the result of a general revision made in 1894. Changing conditions due to the world war, to the suffrage and prohibition amendments, and to other causes have rendered portions out of date, while frequent minor changes have destroyed the original unity of the whole, and led to contradictions between some of the parts. Some changes are proposed practically every year; several meetings proposed changes this year. The time seems ripe, therefore, for a general revision.

The appointment of a committee of 60 was approved. This committee, which is to include two men and two women from each Quarterly Meeting, is to consider the need for general revision, and if it deems wise, is empowered to begin the work.

It is hoped that the new discipline, if such is decided upon, may be rendered, not only a statement of principles for our own members, but an inspiring exposition of the Quaker point of view which can be given to all who wish to know the things for which our Society stands. In this latter respect, the newly-revised London Discipline will offer many suggestions.

The report of the Committee on First-day Schools was heartily approved by the meeting. Samuel J.

Bunting, Jr., Chairman of the Committee, urged Friends to increase their efforts in First-day school work. Those denominations are making the most progress, he said, which are giving the greatest attention to the training of their young. In the discussion which followed, it was urged that older Friends attend First-day school as well as our children. We cannot expect the children to take the work seriously if we do not take it so ourselves. If adult classes do not care to undertake courses of study, they may meet to consider the needs of the community. Mary H. Whitson urged that every First-day School send at least one student each year to Woolman School. Such an action would mean one additional leader for the community.

Third-day, Fifth Month 16th

The meeting convened in separate sessions. Sarah Griscom, who has served as clerk of the women's meeting since 1893, asked to be released from further service, receiving widespread tribute from the meeting for her long and faithful services. Jane P. Rushmore was appointed clerk, and Mary S. Bartram and Abby Hall Roberts assistant clerks.

Consideration of reports and the reading of epistles continued. Full committee reports are available in printed form, and lack of space prevents us from giving more than occasional brief references thereto. In connection with its report, the Central Bureau received commendation for its excellent and efficient work. A feature of the report of the General Conference Advancement Committee was its statement that it is being able to shift its attention more and more from work within the Society to that of reaching those on the outside. It is receiving more expressions of interest from non-members than at any previous time in its 17 years of existence, and is hopeful of increasing opportunities for bringing our message to seeking spirits. At present it is receiving requests for literature from one group as far away as the Virgin Islands.

Delegates to the Baltimore CCL celebration reported that the celebration was one full of inspiration, and that the fellowship to which it gave rise should exert a great influence in the direction of understanding and unity between the various groups which attended.

The importance of George School to the Society was expressed in appreciative comments on the report of the George School Committee. The Committee on the Interests of the Colored Race gave evidence of its success in several lines of activity calculated to reduce prejudice against the Negro. One of its activities, the Inter-racial committee, consisting of ten white and ten Negro members, has functioned so successfully that the Philadelphia Federation of Churches has suggested that it be expanded to a municipal scale.

Fourth-day, Fifth Month 17th

The meetings met in joint session. The morning was given to the consideration of the Queries. In recent years it has been felt that the consideration of the Queries had not received sufficient attention, and it was therefore given this entire morning session. The discussion was so extensive as to require a part of the afternoon session as well.

In connection with the Queries on meetings for worship, William Littleboy felt moved to address the meeting with a loving appeal that the spiritual vitality of our meetings for worship be increased. The meeting for worship, he said, is the supreme test of our spiritual vigor as a religious society, and he had frequently found it lacking in the power which it should possess. He had found a certain shrinking from the deepest phases of spiritual life, a frequent introduction into the meeting of irrelevant thought, an absence of the spirit of prayer, and a tendency on the part of members to shirk personal responsibility for the welfare of the meeting. He appealed to Friends to strengthen themselves with regard to all these matters. His words and the spirit which moved them produced a profound impression on the Yearly Meeting. The loving kindness in which he spoke made Friends eager to respond by giving their best service to their meetings.

In connection with the Query on gambling and lottery, Friends were urged to teach their children never to accept anything for which they gave no form of compensation, even in the case of certain kinds of prizes. The Query regarding alcoholic liquors brought out astonishment and shame that we are not altogether clear in this respect. It also gave rise to a plea that those interested in prohibition should actively support the 18th amendment, instead of allowing the "comic supplement to laugh it out of force," due to the indifference of those who should see that it is upheld.

The Query on prompt attendance at meetings called forth a feeling that Friends are not as careful in this respect as answers to the Query frequently imply. If we are to undertake to build up our meetings for worship, it is essential that they be relieved of the disturbing element caused by late arrivals. In connection with the Query on our youth, it was said that it is not enough simply to teach our principles to our younger members. We should give them means of working out those principles in actual meeting activities, so that they will come to feel that the meeting is a live, worth-while organization. By participation with other Friends in concrete service, our younger members may be most deeply imbued with an understanding of Friends' principles.

Relative to Friends' schools disappointment was expressed that so many of the teachers are not members of the Society. Elizabeth Powell Bond, however, said that many not members were earnest in seeking to further Friends' principles. Paul M. Pearson brought forward statistics to show that in most Friends' schools, the compensation offered to teachers is so low that a graduate of Swarthmore College cannot afford to accept such a position. Elbert Russell said that the young person who desires to dedicate himself to education should not alone be forced to make all the financial sacrifice involved. That sacrifice should be made by the Society as a whole in providing him with adequate financial support. The 1400 non-Friends' children in our schools offer a special opportunity for advancement work.

In reporting for the Peace and Service Committee, Jesse H. Holmes urged Friends to carry on the campaign for a warless world, especially since popular interest in this cause is largely receding. Scarcely a beginning has yet been made in bringing about an end to war. Most people and all nations still accept force as the necessary means of settling serious international differences, and as long as that attitude continues, war will continue. Every Friend should be aiding in creating a new public opinion in favor of a world based upon good-will, which practically none of the disarmament programs have yet contemplated. The best individual contribution to the cause of peace is simply to begin to live it.

Frederick J. Libby outlined a three-point program for a warless world. First, there must be some association of nations in which America and all other nations will join. Second, armaments must be progressively reduced to police strength. Third, we must educate for peace in our schools and elsewhere. The only chance of preventing war depends upon how vigorously we are able to "wage peace."

William I. Hull presented a letter to the Christian churches of the world, which was prepared by the joint peace committees of the two Philadelphia Yearly Meetings, and which is printed elsewhere in this issue. The letter had already been adopted by the Yearly Meeting at Fourth and Arch Sts., Philadelphia, and is being sent to London and other Yearly Meetings. It was adopted by our Yearly Meeting with unanimous approval, and with a prayer that we might find strength to live up to its spirit.

The report of the Young Friends' Movement was accepted with much appreciation for the progress which the movement is making in interesting our younger members in our meetings.

Anne Biddle Stirling expressed a concern for greater individual responsibility in committee work. Attendance at committee meetings, she said, is frequently regarded as the most to be expected of committee members. The real purpose of the committee is to accomplish outside work, and meetings are only for reports and suggestions. In themselves they have little value.

Fifth-day, Fifth Month 18th

In connection with the report of the Philanthropic Committee, Friends were urged to keep in touch with the motion pictures shown in their communities, with a view of seeing that a morally high standard is maintained. The committee is reporting to the Pennsylvania Board of Censors any objectionable features found in the films which it passes. In the discussion following the Philanthropic report, it was said that every Friend ought to make a special study of, and become an expert in, at least one of our testimonies. To carry on effective work in the field of any one of our testimonies, we must have minds trained in that field.

The report of the Committee on Education drew forth a discussion of Friends' schools. It was felt that the latter should be the best in their communities, or else that they should be discontinued. Two principles were pointed out as especially applicable in our schools: 1, the value of moral and religious training should be emphasized; 2nd, special attention should be given to the development of the individual student. These principles are the ones which the public school of today is least successful in applying, and by emphasizing them, Friends can help lead the public schools toward them. Jesse H. Holmes felt that our schools should lead in producing "the kind of moral courage that is involved in taking individual stands on new causes and new principles."

As the proposed general revision of the Discipline will take considerable time, an immediate change in the wording of the Sixth Query was approved. The new form of the Query is:

> "Are you clear of the manufacture and use of alcoholic liquors as a drink and for culinary purposes? Are you careful to discourage by precept and example their use as medicine?
>
> "Do you show an active concern for education regarding the injurious effects of alcohol, tobacco and all narcotics? Do you use your influence toward the proper enforcement of laws designed to prohibit the manufacture, sale and use of intoxicants?"

A considerable discussion regarding the ability of the Yearly Meeting to raise funds followed the report of the Auditors. Many Friends felt that increased appropriations were a sign of, and a necessity for, increased activity and usefulness in the

Yearly Meeting's business. Others felt that the resources of the meeting are already strained. A proposed reduction to $2500 of the appropriation for the Educational Committee met with particular regret on the part of many Friends. This appropriation was finally raised to $3500, and the final budget set for the Yearly Meeting for the coming year was $21,750. According to the statistics of total membership, this means a tax of about $2 per member.

Membership statistics were given as 10,594; Concord being the largest of the Quarters. There was a net loss of 42 for the year in the total membership of the Yearly Meeting. J. Harold Watson expressed a sense of shame that our numbers should be decreasing at a time when our principles were so universally respected. Friends were urged to be more active in interesting others to join meeting. We should seek to win those who have not yet come into contact with us, and the overseers should invite into membership those who have shown a sympathy by attending meetings. Many who attend our meetings have never joined because never invited to do so; sometimes we do not even realize that they are not members.

Sixth-day, Fifth Month 19th

In presenting the report of the American Friends' Service Committee, Wilbur K. Thomas told of the esteem with which our relief work has caused Friends to be held abroad. Can we measure up to this standard? Plans have been made for a program of relief and rehabilitation in Russia which will probably take twenty years. The great opportunity which this and similar work affords, lays a tremendous task upon our shoulders. To accomplish it, we must increase in zeal and unity. We must be conscious of the weakness which division within our Society causes us, and must develop spiritual leadership capable of meeting our opportunities. The work that opens before us will be a test, showing whether we have a vital message which is to increase, or whether we are only a dying body with a noble record in the past.

The meeting approved of sending five delegates to a conference to be held at Bluffton College, Bluffton, O., Aug. 4th to 7th. At this conference will gather representatives of all religious bodies having a testimony against war, with a view of giving national expression to the religious objection to war.

The recommendation to President Harding to appoint a coal commission for arbitration and investigation, which arose in Swarthmore Monthly Meeting and was approved by Concord Quarterly Meeting, was also approved by the Yearly Meeting. J. Russell Smith said that good-will and common sense could only function if applied with a knowledge of the facts. The resolution in question calls for a scientific investigation of the facts, so that a permanent national solution of the coal problem may be achieved. The recommendation to the President appeared in the Intelligencer for Fifth month 6th.

The meeting approved of the following request to President Harding, regarding the release of political prisoners:

> "In the feeling that the spirit of war should be eliminated as rapidly as possible from our people, and in sympathy with the desire that is being expressed for the release of those still in prison under war-time legislation, Philadelphia Yearly Meeting of the Religious Society of Friends, now in session, asks the Government to look into the cases of those men and if not found detrimental to the public interest that they be released."

In connection with the approval of the revised budget, William I. Hull commented on the fact, raised by another Friend, that of the $20,000 appropriated by the Yearly Meeting, $12,000 is used in salaries. This fact when it was first stated to him, he said, had surprised him. Upon reflection, he had come to the conclusion that the statement was so misleading as to be unkind and even untrue. His reasons for this conclusion were as follows:

1. The Yearly Meeting committees use many times the $20,000 actually collected from the members. The Peace Committee alone used a total of nearly $9,000 last year. The percentage of overhead, therefore, is not at all what it would seem when we say that twelve of the twenty thousand is used in salaries.

2. The salaried secretaries, carrying on the necessary routine and other central work, make possible the volunteer services of scores of busy Friends who would otherwise be unable to serve the meeting in this way. Hence the salaries in question make possible the work of a great many more Friends than the secretaries themselves.

3. Those receiving these salaries are not simply clerks, but consecrated workers who are giving the best they have to this service. It would not be just to allow their work to lay a financial burden upon them. The service upon which they are engaged is the concern of the Yearly Meeting as a whole, and the meeting as a whole should see that it is adequately supported.

Epistles, exercises and other written material which came before the meeting will be available in the Extracts. As the hour for adjournment drew near, several Friends expressed their gratitude for the labors accomplished by the meeting, and the spirit which it had manifested. Dr. Pusey Heald expressed his feeling that in the many years of his experience with the Yearly Meeting, he could not remember any other year when the exercises seemed to him to have reviewed so many fine concerns expressed and so much accomplished.

(An account of the evening meetings during Yearly Meeting week, and of some of the messages brought to the Meetings for Worship, will be given in our next issue.)

From Famine Fields

(Professor Jerome Davis, of Dartmouth College, recently spoke in one of the churches in the interest of Russian Relief. A woman who was present went home and wrote the following poem, which was published in *The Outlook*, March 22, 1922.—Ed.)

I am a little better than a movie show
Because I speak reality. You know
That I was there, have worked and shared and seen.
And yet, like shadow pictures on the screen,
The scenes I paint bring but a passing thrill
Of pleasant horror. Self-complacent still,
You murmur, "Sad! So sad!" and go your way,
While cards, and tea-rooms, and the latest play
Will reap their easy millions through the week.
You cannot sense the things of which I speak.
You are not heartless. Could I only lay
One baby's body at your feet today,
Or here and now bring swift before your eyes
One mother watching by her child that dies,
You would be pitiful, would strain to give,—
And thousands doomed by apathy would live.
Great God of Nations, give me words to stir
These sleek-fed aisles of broadcloth and of fur!

Martha Haskell Clark.

West Virginia: A Field for Friends

By Drew Pearson

There was once a missionary who went into a certain coal camp in West Virginia. He was a simple, devout man, devoted to his work. His church in this particular mining camp was a long railroad car, one end of which with its benches, held his congregation, the other end was fitted up as kitchen and bed-room for his family. He had performed missionary work all over the United States with tremendous success.

But when he first arrived in this particular camp, he made one mistake. He asked the coal mine owners to install gas and electricity and water in his car. Immediately the entire camp of coal miners became suspicious. The company had befriended him; therefore he was a friend, a tool, of the company's; and therefore he was no friend of theirs. And they never got over this; and his work was greatly hampered because they looked upon him with suspicion.

However, in spite of this, he did a great work. For the children were not suspicious, and his wife taught the girls to sew, and he taught the boys to use tools. Neither the girls nor their mothers knew how to sew. But the girls were anxious to learn, and begged to work almost every minute.

This missionary found that the miners' wives not only did not know how to sew, but did not know how to cook. They lived literally with a can-opener. They spent their husbands' wages the very day they earned them. When their husbands had plenty of work they lived high, when there was no work at the mines, they starved. With these women and with their husbands, the missionary accomplished almost nothing. The men would stand out on their front porches and shoot off their revolvers one after another, on down the line, just for amusement. And when I visited the camp, a bunch of youngsters amused themselves by throwing rocks at the company windows. They were really no worse than any other boys; but instead of taking out their surplus energy on football, the only thing they could think of was to break company windows.

Eleven other missionaries were sent to neighboring camps. They were secretly financed by the mine operators. The miners suspected this and would have nothing to do with them.

That is the really fundamental problem in West Virginia—the problem which is behind the starvation conditions and the martial law and the semi-civil war. The greatest need in West Virginia is education. But the miners are suspicious of education, of anything which comes from the outside world, unless they are sure that it comes from a friendly source. And they will continue to be suspicious. They are native born and have lived in these mountains for a hundred years.

And right here is where we Friends have a great field—a field which we alone can fill. We are about to undertake relief work in West Virginia. We are undertaking this work in the face of severe opposition, in the face of the fact that we know we shall be criticized. But we are undertaking it because we believe that women and children should not suffer whether their husbands and parents happen to be coal miners or Germans or Bolsheviki. In undertaking this work, we shall drive an entering wedge—we shall gain the confidence of these mountaineers. And once having gained their confidence, how great the opportunities for service!

Clothing the Naked

The American Red Cross is now actively engaged in collecting clothing and shoes for the destitute men, women and children of Russia. All of these supplies are being distributed by the relief workers of the American Friends' Service Committee, who state that there is also need for bedding; that children are dying in the homes and hospitals for lack of covering, even during this month of April.

They crouch against the walls or on their beds, hour after hour and day after day. Clothes and bedclothes are almost as necessary as food.

Another case cited of these homes was that of a building in which 400 children were housed, with accommodations of all sorts for forty. Clothes were as non-existent as food, so that in most cases the children are left in their verminous rags, spreading the infection of typhus and cholera.

"In one home," says A. Ruth Fry, secretary of the English Friends' organization in Russia, "by some great effort rather more was done for them. They were washed and dressed in thin cotton shirts, and yet all the staff were down with typhus except one woman doctor. It is difficult to exaggerate the need for clothes; every scrap sent here already has been distributed."

The Liberal Faith

The real traitor against God is the one who refuses to trust the faculties which He has given. The Liberal churches have always stood for the rights of reason. They have nothing to fear from its exercise. They are never convulsed over a new idea. They are hospitable to truth from whatever quarter.

The Liberal faith tries to make one stand upon his feet. No one can grow morally strong, any more than he can grow strong intellectually or physically, until he has been thrown upon his own resources and made to feel his own responsibility. The sin of Adam cannot work our ruin; the holiness of Christ cannot take the place of our obedience. For weal or for woe, the responsibility is with us.

At the very basis of moral manhood and womanhood lies sincerity. The Liberal faith does not seek by any ecclesiastical machinery or threats of divine interference to coerce men into any belief or course of action. The threat of endless torture against those who do not comply with certain conditions of salvation has done more than any other one thing to produce cowardice and falsehood in the things of religion. But the Liberal faith does not leave man without motive. For the lower and withering motive of fear, it substitutes the grander and nobler motive of love—love of God and love for all mankind. Of the work we do in our own characters and in the world, that is the best and strongest and grandest which is wrought under the inspiration of love—love for God, love for those who bear his image!—*Marion D. Shutter, in an address delivered at the Sioux City Convention of the National Federation of Religious Liberals.*

Was Thomas Paine a Quaker?

The Thomas Paine National Museum at New Rochelle, N. Y., has a very interesting engraving depicting Louis XVI on trial for his life. Paine is shown among the members of the Convention before whom Louis XVI was brought for trial, and he is curiously represented in the large wide-brimmed Quaker hat. He is the only member of the tribunal who is wearing a hat. Thomas Paine, of course, did not wear a hat at the trial, and never in his life did he wear a Quaker hat. The artist wished in this way to indicate that Thomas Paine was a Quaker. It is true, of course, that Thomas Paine was of Quaker parentage and that he owed much to his Quaker origin. But he never attended Quaker meetings, and, as a matter of fact, was not affiliated with any religious body. He was, however, neither an atheist nor an agnostic. Theodore Roosevelt did his memory a great wrong in referring to him in his book *Gouverneur Morris* as "a filthy little atheist." Mr. W. M. Van Der Weyde, president of the Thomas Paine National Historical Association, submitted to the late ex-president sufficient proofs of Thomas Paine's theism, but no correction was ever made in the subsequent editions of the book.

MAXIMILIAN RUDWIN.

Deeds, Not Words

Not forever on thy knees
  Would Jehovah have thee found;
There are burdens thou canst ease,
There are griefs Jehovah sees:
  Look around.

Not long prayers, but earnest zeal;
  This is what is wanted more.
Put thy shoulder to the wheel;
Bread unto the famished deal
  From thy store.

Worship God by doing good:
  Help the suffering in their needs.
He who loves God as he should
Makes his heart's love understood
  By kind deeds.

Deeds are powerful, words are weak,
  Battering at high heaven's door.
Let thy love by actions speak;
Wipe the tear from sorrow's cheek;
  Clothe the poor.

—*Anonymous; selected by Keziah R. Wilkins.*

The Library Association of Friends

The library at Fifteenth and Cherry Streets, Philadelphia, has had a very successful year. The efforts of the new librarian have been highly endorsed by the committee in charge, and a number of new volumes have been added to the list available for the use of its patrons. Among the books added recently are;

NON-FICTION

Later Periods of Quakerism ....Rufus M. Jones
Peace and Bread ....Jane Addams
Old Trails and New Borders ....Edward Steiner
Party of the Third Part ....Henry J. Allen
Penology in the U. S. ....Louis Robinson
Outline of History ....H. G. Wells
Vanished Pomps of Yesterday ....Frederic Hamilton
Here, There and Everywhere ....Frederic Hamilton
Working North from Patagonia ....Harry Franck
More That Must Be Told ....Philip Gibbs
Europe—Whither Bound ....Stephen Graham
Mirrors of Washington ....Anon.
Queen Victoria ....Lytton Strachey

FICTION

Mr. Prohack ....Arnold Bennett
Head of the House of Coombe....Francis Hodgson Burnett
To Him That Hath ....Ralph Connor
Mother ....Maxim Gorky
Saint Teresa ....Henry Sydnor Harrison
Maria Chapdelaine ....Louis Hemon
Children of the Market Place ....Edgar Lee Masters
Nicholas The Weaver and Other Quaker Stories
Maud Robinson

JUVENILE

Anderson's Fairy Tales
Robin Hood ....Louis Rhead
Prince and the Pauper ....Mark Twain
Tales from Shakespeare ....Charles and Mary Lamb
Why Lincoln Laughed ....Russell H. Conwell
Mollie and the Unwiseman ....John Kendrick Bangs
Mollie and the Unwiseman Abroad..John Kendrick Bangs
Master Skylark ....John Bennett
Understood Betsy ....Dorothy Canfield
Hans Brinker ....Mary Mapes Dodge
Uncle Remus ....Joel Chandler Harris
Anne of Green Gables ....L. M. Montgomery
Mazli ....Johanna Spyri
Just Patty ....Jean Webster
When Patty Went to College ....Jean Webster

Friendly News Notes

The Fair Hill Friends' Association, Philadelphia, has a regular baseball team. They also have tennis courts on the meeting grounds, and are planning a number of pilgrimages and hikes for the summer.

The senior play at Swarthmore College will be given Friday, June 9; Alumni Day, Saturday, June 10; Baccalaureate address, by Dr. Frank Aydelotte on Sunday, June 11, and the Commencement on Monday, June 12.

Baltimore Young Friends are planning a camp on the South River this summer. A delightful spot has been found and if enough will go, a camp will be held the last two weeks in June. The cost will be between ten and twelve dollars a week. This is opened to Young Friends, the members of Castle Stirling and the Queens of Avalon, and, if possible, a few of the junior Castle boys. The camp will be directed by Mary Blackburn, with the Secretary, Bliss Forbush, on hand to assist.

The Summer School at Woodbrooke is being arranged jointly by the Woodbrooke Extension Committee and the Adult School Union and will be held from August 5th to 14th. The printed program is not yet ready, but it is expected that there will be one period each morning devoted to definite teaching and discussion of Religious, Quaker and Biblical subjects, and a morning and afternoon period each day will be devoted to talks and demonstrations on subjects such as the use of books, preparation of material for addresses, the art of memory, etc.

LONGWOOD YEARLY MEETING

The Seventieth Yearly Meeting of Progressive Friends at Longwood, three miles east of Kennett Square, Pa., on Route 131, will be held June 2nd, 3rd and 4th, and the meetings will open at 9.30 a. m. and 1.30 p. m. Standard time.

Friday, June 2nd, the speakers will be John A. McSparran, Master of State Grange; William Pickens (a Yale graduate), Field Secretary of the National Organization for Advancement of Colored, and Gifford Pinchot, Commissioner of Forestry.

On Saturday, Horace Knowles, one of the Advisory Council of Santo Domingo affairs, will speak on our relations with Haiti. Roger N. Baldwin, attorney of Civil Liberties Bureau, makes a plea for "Political Prisoners," and Syud Hossian, a friend of Gandhi's, will speak on the movement for independence in India. Roger N. Baldwin is also expected to speak on the coal situation.

Rev. Paul Jones, former Bishop of Utah, will conduct the service on Sunday morning.

PURCHASE QUARTERLY MEETING

Purchase Quarterly Meeting, held at Amawalk, N. Y., was one of the largest ever held there. The wonderful beauty of the country at this time of year, through which all those attending had driven, put everyone into a spirit of thankfulness for the promises of nature, and the blessings of life and friends, and this spirit pervaded throughout the whole day.

Short messages were given by Burling Hallock, Gertrude Hallock, Phoebe C. Cornell and others. In the afternoon meeting Joel Borton gave an address on "Good Will Toward Men." Too much stress has been laid in the past on the "Peace" part of the text from which this is quoted. If good will were created and spread, peace would come of itself.

Annual reports from constituent meetings indicated continued work for the Service Committee, not only in money contributed, but in garments made and sent in. Sympathetic attention was given to the work of Friends in China.

E. Morris Burdsall.

Items From Everywhere

The University of Geneva (Switzerland), founded by John Calvin in 1559, has held since 1892 a Summer School with the main object of providing students of non-French speaking countries with the opportunity of improving their practical knowledge of the French language.

This year it is planned to develop the Summer School further by adding to its curriculum the "Study of Contemporaneous International Affairs." It has been considered that such a Summer School, situated at the seat of so many important international institutions, might appeal particularly to undergraduates and graduate students of American Universities. Further information can be secured from "The Institute of International Education," Dr. Stephen P. Duggan, Director, 419 West 117th Street, New York City.

Two forward looking bills have recently been signed by Governor Miller for the state of New York. One is an anti-gambling bill, which seeks to strike at the gambling evil by prohibiting the sale of gambling implements or devices. The other calls for a strict regulation of billiard rooms and pool parlors, which in many communities are now exerting the vicious influence that formerly centered around the saloon. The New York Civic League has been instrumental in bringing about the passage of these bills. Let us hope that thought is also being given toward educating to a higher outlook those who patronized these evils. The problem will not be finally solved until they have been led *not to want* them.

THE OPEN FORUM

This column is intended to afford free expression of opinion by readers on questions of interest. The INTELLIGENCER *is not responsible for any such opinions. Letters must be brief, and the editor reserves the right to omit parts if necessary to save space.*

A COMMENT ON "COAL FACTS"

To the Editor:

I desire to express my appreciation of the splendid review of the mining situation which appeared in your paper under the title: "Coal Facts." I have read page after page of propaganda from both sides of the dispute between miner and operator, but realized that beneath that fight was a cause the public did not understand. There is more in this summing up than I have read in weeks. It would be worth while to print it in pamphlet form for general distribution.

While writing, I may also add my appreciation of the Quaker press for true piety, clearness of vision and fearlessness in presenting the truth.

Dearborn, Mich. M. T. WOODRUFF.

A BRIEF FOR OUR INDUSTRIAL SYSTEM

To the Editor:

There is nothing fundamentally wrong with our system of wage payment and profit taking. Too often letters that "note signs of unrest in industrial relations today," whether knowingly or otherwise, infer that a turn to communism or something similar would raise our business life to an Utopian plane. As a matter of fact, most of these "isms" have been tested without showing the gleam of hope to warrant belief in their ever being of practical service.

Costs of products depend to a large extent on costs of labor; there is at present necessity to bear down on the latter, or have it produce a greater return for a given wage, due to strenuous competition. It is well to state here that in the present business lull capital investors receive dividends only in rare instances; many firms operate at a clear loss, not beginning to cover overhead expenses.

We might just as well realize now that there always will be a group which labors, one which manages, another with investment capital. No isolated community alloting each of its members a definite and equal portion of money, land, tools, etcetera, will long preserve this individual balance. Leaders, industrial and financial, will evolve quite as naturally as the sun rises; and the majority will soon be working for the few. It is doubtful if any material change in their outlooks on life would result—though these same writers lead us to believe an equal distribution of wealth would usher in the millennium of happiness; too often responsibility brings decided misery and discord to those unfitted to accept. On the other hand, wealth concentrated in a few hands may be the life-giving force to that community.

Why must leaders develop? Because no two men are created equal save in the eye of the law; heredity plays too important a part. So do environment, associates, friends, opportunities. The great majority of us are plodders with little energy, initiative, enthusiasm, vision or genius. La Place found less than one-half of one per cent. of all humans actually think. Considering the labor involved in original thought, that is a high figure.

Unrest in laboring ranks may be traced to a myriad of causes: Paid union leaders or trouble-breeders, poor working conditions, unsanitary living quarters, low wages, high wages in one department of a plant, long hours, short hours—Germans struck for a ten-hour day last year when they were working eight; trouble with foremen or managers, open shop, closed shop, or one of a hundred other causes. Nevertheless, strikes as a means of adjustment are as futile as wars between nations; mutual understandings arrived at across a conference table between representatives of workers (*not* radicals, stand-patters or agitators, please note), and all others concerned, will foreshadow the end of this destructive agent.

One hears so much of the "capital and labor problem." Yet there are not two, but three, parties essential for business success: capital, management and labor. And most certainly *all must lend maximum co-operation, all must share profits and losses in just ratio.*

A growing faith in the ability of each party to broadmindedly see the viewpoints of the others, the financial success attending those plants adopting it, lead one to believe this principle of partnership a long step forward toward clarifying our present situation.

Our business life is essentially sound, and the "humanizing" of our industrial relations is the big problem confronting us. And that, like all others, is slowly but surely being solved. ERWIN LIONEL MALONE.

Trenton, N. J.

Pictures of the CCL Pageant and West River Trip

Held at Baltimore, Fifth Month, 1922

1. George Fox in the stocks.
2. First Yearly Meeting wedding.
3. John Woolman, slaveholder and slaves.
4. Lucretia Mott and the mob.
5. Benj. Hallowell at Westtown School.
6. Elizabeth Fry in Newgate prison.
7. Court of the Grand Turk.
8. Mission work—The witch doctor.
9. " " The modern doctor.
10. Park Avenue Meeting-house.
11. Homewood Meeting-house.
12. Galesville steamboat pier.
13. Friends landing at pier.
14. The start of the pilgrimage.
15. West River Burial-ground.
16. Planting the white oak—Dr. Janney, Rufus M. Jones, Benj. H. Miller.
17. " " " " Donald Van Hollen (Geo. Fox).
18. " " " " Children.
19. " " " " Edward P. Thomas.
20. " " " " Mrs. Morris Carey.
21. " " " " John C. Thomas.
22. Elizabeth B. Emmott—Sketching the oak.
23. " " " with daughter—On steamer.
24. Governor Sproul and Edward C. Wilson.
25. Park Avenue Meeting-house with attending Friends.

Full set of postals, $2.00. Single cards, 10 cents. Any view, 5x7, 25 cents. Henry R. Sharpless, 305 Munsey Building, Baltimore, Md.

BIRTHS

SEAMAN—On Fifth month 6th, at Roslyn, Long Island, to Frederick W. and Eda Hicks Seaman, a son whose name is Albertson Hicks Seaman.

WILLARD—On Fourth month 23rd, to Hannah and Earl Willard, of Trevose, Pa., a daughter named Emily Pearl.

DEATHS

GRIEST—At Pasadena, Calif., on Fifth month 16th, John Griest, aged 77 years. He was a native of Pennsylvania, but had lived in California for thirty-six years.

JANNEY—At Meadow Lawn, Lincoln, Virginia, on Third month 19th, Cornelia Janney, daughter of Samuel M. and Elizabeth Janney, in her 90th year.

Her heart was full of love for everybody, and her greatest joy was in giving of her service and of her slender means.

During the later years of his ministry she was her father's constant traveling companion. When, as Superintendent of Indian Affairs, he had to make long and difficult journeys in an unsettled country she was at his side, carrying sewed in her skirts the thousands of dollars which our government dispensed to its wards. Her care of and devotion to her parents in their declining years was very beautiful.

She was deeply interested in the colored people, and as long as her strength would permit she visited the colored school each week, supplying the children with papers suited to their age, and reading to them stories of great men and women, particularly of those of their own race who had lived nobly.

A charter member of the Lincoln W. C. T. U., she was a devoted worker in the temperance movement.

She was for many years a much loved elder of Goose Creek Monthly Meeting and a teacher in our First-day school. At her funeral loving testimony was born to her helpful services.

REED—At Chicago, Ill., Fifth month 16th, Beatrice Magill Reed, only daughter of Thomas A. and Marian M. Jenkins, wife of Collins B. Reed, in her 27th year.

SHOEMAKER—At Meadow Lawn, Lincoln, Virginia, on Third month 27th, William T. Shoemaker, son of Naylor and Sarah Shoemaker, aged 84 years.

Confined to his bed for more than four years, he bore his long illness with wonderful patience. Not once during these years of invalidism was he heard to complain about his physical infirmities. His deep concern for himself and for us all was that we might ever feel our dependence upon the Source of All Good, and might be given strength to follow the Light.

WORTH—At his home, Coatesville, Chester County, Pennsylvania, on Fifth month 4th, John Sharpless Worth, in the 72nd year of his age.

Young Friends' Movement of New York Yearly Meeting

Program of Events

Seventh-day, the 27th

5.00 p. m.—Third annual meeting at 20th Street Meeting-house.

6.00 p. m.—Annual Supper at 20th Street Meeting-house. The charge will be 75 cents.

7.45 p. m.—Return to 15th Street Meeting-house for regular evening session of the Yearly Meeting at 8 o'clock.

First-day, the 28th

3.30 p. m.—Annual bus ride at close of First-day School exercises. The route will be different from any taken before. Tickets will be sold in advance.

7.15 p. m.—Hymn singing.

8.00 p. m.—Evening meeting in charge of Y. F. M. Scott Nearing will give a talk on "Can Economic Relations be Ethical?"

Second-day, the 29th

7.00 p. m.—Illustrated talk by Mrs. Helena H. Weed, of the Haiti-Santo Domingo Independent Society.

Third-day, the 30th

11.00 a. m.—Hike on Long Island. Meet in Long Island waiting-room of the Pennsylvania Station at 11 to take train arriving at Jamaica as near 12 o'clock as possible. Bring lunch.

7.00 p. m.—Y. F. M. Musical at 15th Street Meeting-house.

Fourth-day, the 31st

7.00 p. m.—Frederick Pohl's play, "Gas," will be presented by his students at the 15th Street Meeting-house.

COMING EVENTS

FIFTH MONTH

27th to Sixth month 1st, New York Yearly Meeting.

27th—Stillwater Half-Yearly Meeting, at Richland, Ohio.

27th—Blue River Quarterly Meeting, Highlands Creek Meeting-house, near Salem, Ind.

27th—Nottingham Quarterly Meeting at Deer Creek, Darlington, Md. Daniel Batchellor expects to attend.

28th—Wilbur K. Thomas and family will attend meeting at Oxford, Pa., at 10.30 a. m. At 2.30 p. m. Wilbur Thomas will talk on Friends' Service Work. Standard time.

28th—Philadelphia Quarterly Meeting's Visiting Committee has appointed certain members to attend meeting for worship at Fair Hill Meeting, Philadelphia.

29th—Canada Half-Yearly Meeting, at Bloomfield, Ontario.

SIXTH MONTH

3rd—Prairie Grove Quarterly Meeting, at Winfield, Iowa.

3rd—Whitewater Quarterly Meeting, at Richmond, Ind.

4th—First-day, at 3 p. m., daylight saving time: The regular meeting for worship under care of a Committee of Concord Quarterly Meeting will be held at Middletown Friends' Meeting-house (Delaware County). This is a community meeting in which all interested persons and Friends are invited to participate. Trolleys for Lima connect at Media.

4th—Certain members of Philadelphia Quarterly Meeting's Visiting Committee have been appointed to attend Reading meeting, at 11 a. m.

5th—Chicago Monthly Meeting, at Y. M. C. A. Dinner at 6.30.

5th—Center Quarterly Meeting, at Dunning's Creek, Fishertown, Pa. Dr. O. Edward Janney and Joel Borton expect to be present.

5th—Millville Half-Yearly Meeting, at Millville, Pa. Daniel Batchellor expects to attend.

8th—Salem Quarterly Meeting, at Salem, N. J. Isaac Wilson expects to attend.

11th—Certain members of Philadelphia Quarterly Meeting's Visiting Committee have been appointed to attend Schuylkill Meeting, at 10.30 a. m.

12th—Baltimore Quarterly Meeting, at Sandy Spring, Md.

15th—Haddonfield Quarterly Meeting, at Medford, N. J.

NOTICE—Several changes in the New York Yearly Meeting program have come to the office since our last issue in which the full program was printed. The morning devotional meetings on Second, Third and Fifth-days will be held at 9.15 instead of 9.30. The subject of Scott Nearing's address will be "Can Economic Relations be

Ethical?" On Second-day, the 29th, at 7 p. m., instead of the "Entertainment by Young Friends' Movement," as announced, there will be an illustrated talk by Mrs. Helena H. Weed, of the Haiti-Santo Domingo Independent Society.

NOTICE.—There will be a Summer School at Jordans, arranged jointly by the Hostel Committee and the Woodbrooke Extension Committee, Friday afternoon, July 7th, to Monday afternoon, July 10th. Lectures will be given on "Man's Developing Conceptions of God" (Primitive-Oriental-Christian) by W. Fearon Halliday, M. A., Lecturer, Selly Oak Colleges, and Robert J. Davidson, of West China. Accommodations limited to sixty persons. Early application should be made to Robert Davis, 23, Fox Hill, Selly Oak, Birmingham.

Progress of the Campaign

In the issue of Fifth month 6th, we reported 79 new subscribers taking advantage of our special get-acquainted rate of .35. Since then the number has gone to 123, and we know of a number of others on the way.

This is fine and represents a great deal of work and interest on the part of some of our friends. But we believe a great deal more can be done. We have about 3,000 subscribers. Think what it would mean if each one sent in *only one* new subscription. Thee knows we are glad to carry our message to those outside the Society, so won't thee try to find one person to whom it might be of interest?

If thee does not care to collect the money, just send the name and we will send a bill and coin card. Don't forget, it is only .35 for three months.

American Friends' Service Committee

WILBUR K. THOMAS, EX. SEC.
20 S. 12th St. Philadelphia.

CASH CONTRIBUTIONS
WEEK ENDING MAY 15TH.

Five Years Meetings	$426.76
Other Meetings:	
New Garden Prep. Mtg.	50.00
Orange Grove Friends' First-day School, Clif.	6.50
Rahway and Plainfield Monthly Meeting	10.00
Contributions for Germany	353.75
For Austria	272.54
For Poland	185.81
For Russia	18,731.60
For Russian Overhead	59.27
For General	366.14
For Home Service	15.00
For Armenia	20.00
For German Overhead	171.60
Refunds	13.25
	$20,682.22

Shipments received during week ending May 13th: 38 boxes and packages received.

REGULAR MEETINGS

OAKLAND, CALIF. — A FRIENDS' Meeting is held every First-day at 11 A. M., in the Extension Room, Y. W. C. A. Building, Webster Street, above 14th. Visiting Friends always welcome.

FRIENDS' MEETING IN PASADENA, California — Orange Grove Monthly Meeting of Friends, 520 East Orange Grove Avenue, Pasadena, California. Meeting for worship, First-day, 11 A. M. Monthly Meeting, the second First-day of each month, at 1.45 P. M.

CENTRAL MEETING OF FRIENDS (Chicago), meets every First-day in Room 706, 410 South Michigan Avenue, at 10.45 A. M. Visitors are invited.

WANTED

WANTED — SUMMER BOARD FOR three adults, with private family on farm. Commuting distance from Philadelphia. Address D. 154, Friends' Intelligencer.

WANTED—TWO GIRLS, ONE FOR plain cooking and housework; other for child's nurse. Good wages for competent help. G. L. Corson, Edgewater Park, N. J.

IS THERE AN ELDERLY WIDOWER or widow alone, who would appreciate as housekeeper and companion, a woman of culture and refinement, and possessing all the attributes of a gentlewoman. Sunny disposition, thoroughly domesticated, excellent manager. References. Address G. 210, Friends' Intelligencer.

WANTED — SOMEONE TO ASSIST with housework and care of aged woman, in family of three. Address 307 West Ave., Jenkintown, Pa., stating wages desired.

WANTED — GIRL FOR GENERAL housework with cooking, for three adults. Seashore in summer. Apply Mrs. J. Z. Collings, 638 Cooper St., Camden, N. J.

IN RECENT YEARS THE HIGH COST of coal has checked the ability of The Grandom Institution to supply coal to the worthy poor of Philadelphia, at reduced prices. To aid in this work gifts or legacies will be much appreciated. For further information apply to William Biddle, Secretary, No. 119 South 4th St., Philadelphia, Pa.

WANTED—TWO GIRLS, ONE FOR plain cooking and housework; other for child's nurse. Good wages for competent help. G. L. Cowan, Edgewater Park, N. J.

COMPANIONABLE HOUSEHOLD helper in mountain cottage. Small adult family, pleasant surroundings, light work. Address M. 214, Friends' Intelligencer.

FOR RENT

FOR RENT—THE PACKER COTTAGE at Buck Hill. Accommodations for five or six. Located within fifteen minutes' walk of Inn. For particulars inquire Franklin Packer, Newtown, Pa.

TO RENT FURNISHED—FOR FEW months or for a longer period, attractive 14-room house near college, Swarthmore, Pa. All conveniences, porches and shaded lawn. Large and small fruits and vegetables. No garage. References exchanged. For terms and particulars write or phone, Swarthmore 572, M. S. B., 503 W. Chester Road.

FOR RENT — SUMMER COTTAGE. Half of big sixteen-room, furnished residence on Ocean Drive, Elberon, N. J., between Long Branch and Asbury Park. Cool ocean breezes. Porch and front windows direct view of ocean. Private bathing beach. Large grounds with trees; garage. Rent $125, June 1st to July 15th, and $100 August 15th to October 1st. Will Walter Jackson, 50 Beekman St., New York.

FOR RENT — APARTMENT FOR light housekeeping, in home near West Chester, Pa. Four large rooms, use of bath, large porch, lawn, old shade, electric light, convenient to trolley. Garage for automobile. Good roads. Mrs. E. W. Baker, West Chester, Pa. Bell phone—West Chester, 508-J-4.

FOR RENT — JUNE 1ST-OCTOBER 1st. Small furnished house, old-fashioned garden, on big estate. Five minutes from Fisher's Lane Station on Reading; $75.00 monthly. Wyoming 7503-J. Address G. 211, Friends' Intelligencer.

FOR RENT — PERMANENT ROOM with running water available for Friend at P. Y. F. A., 140 N. 15th St., Philadelphia.

FOR RENT

FOR RENT—TO SMALL FAMILY OF adults, part of my farm house near Mickleton. Convenient to trains. Bus service at the door. Excellent water and shade. Apply R. 212, Friends' Intelligencer.

To the Lot-Holders and others interested in Fairhill Burial Ground:

GREEN STREET Monthly Meeting has funds available for the encouragement of the practice of cremating the dead to be interred in Fairhill Burial Ground. We wish to bring this fact as prominently as possible to those who may be interested. We are prepared to undertake the expense of cremation in case any lot holder desires us to do so.

Those interested should communicate with William H. Gaskill, Treasurer of the Committee of Interments, Green Street Monthly Meeting, or any of the following members of the Committee.

William H. Gaskill, 3201 Arch St.
Samuel N. Longstreth, 1218 Chestnut St.
Charles F. Jenkins, 232 South Seventh St.
Stuart S. Graves, 3633 Germantown Ave.

Send two or more names of persons who might be interested in Friends by reading the INTELLIGENCER. A good way to get new members.

The Friends' Intelligencer

ESTABLISHED 1844 SIXTH MONTH 17, 1922 VOLUME 79 NUMBER 24

Contents

EDITORIAL

THE FRIENDS' INTELLIGENCER

Published weekly, 140 N. 15th Street, Philadelphia, Pa., by Friends' Intelligencer Association, Ltd.

SUE C. YERKES, *Business Manager*

Editorial Board: Elizabeth Powell Bond, Thomas A. Jenkins, J. Russell Smith, George A. Walton.

Board of Managers: Edward Cornell, Alice Hall Paxson, Paul M. Pearson, Annie Hillborn, Elwood Hollingshead, William C. Biddle, Charles F. Jenkins, Edith M. Winder, Frances M. White.

Officers of Intelligencer Associates: Ellwood Burdsall, Chairman; Bertha L. Broomell, Secretary; Herbert P. Worth, Treasurer.

Subscription rates: United States, Mexico, Cuba and Panama, $2.50 per year. Canada and other foreign countries, $3.00 per year. Checks should be made payable to Friends' Intelligencer Association, Ltd.

Entered as Second Class Matter at Philadelphia Post Office.

The Friends' Intelligencer

The religion of Friends is based on faith in the "INWARD LIGHT," or direct revelation of God's spirit and will in every
eking soul.

The INTELLIGENCER is interested in all who bear the name of Friends in every part of the world, and aims to promote love,
ity and intercourse among all branches and with all religious societies.

STABLISHED 1844 | PHILADELPHIA, SIXTH MONTH 17, 1922 | VOLUME 79 NUMBER 24

Penn, the Great Founder

Everybody knows that William Penn was the ounder of Philadelphia, and of the State of Penn- lvania, but not all are aware to what extent he has ecome a national figure—one of the founders of merica. More than this, Penn has also become a orld figure—one of those outstanding great men out whom there is a universal and perennial riosity.

In these days when social friction is the rule and pression of weaker groups is widespread, a multi- de of people the world over are pondering Penn's en and generous dealings with the ignorant In- ans. He offered these primitive people justice d friendship, he told them he expected the same om them in return; neither party to the pact was sappointed. With the experience of Virginia and ew England in his mind, Penn's sheer moral urage is astounding. He made a venture of faith, ith in our common humanity and the result justi- d his courage and insight. Taken all in all, it as one of the great moments in the history of the man race, and such is the tenacity with which men easure up the record of generous acts that the story Penn and the Indians will be told and will in- ence those who hear it, down to the end of time. ike Washington's truthfulness, like Franklin's rift, like Lincoln's integrity, the story of Penn's nture of faith in Indian human nature has taken a kind of immortality; it cannot be forgotten.

And yet it is true also that the facts about Penn's alings with Tammany and the other Indian chiefs e as yet imperfectly known to the public; the "true illiam Penn" himself has not yet been fully re- aled, even to the professional historians.

At the sumptuous rooms of the Historical Society Pennsylvania, the writer spent several hours look- g over the materials collected for the projected new d complete edition of the books and letters of illiam Penn. Here have been assembled, with reless patience and most commendable industry, t merely the writings themselves, but a great mass of illustrative information—genealogies, maps and plans, biographies, anecdotes, photographic views—which, when published, will make the Founder, as never before, a living, active man in a real world of men and affairs.

It was heartening to hear from the Editor, our friend Albert Cook Myers, who undoubtedly knows more about Penn and his times than any other person now living, that his judgment of Penn as an honest, upright man has become even more favorable as the work has progressed and new facts have come to light. Penn's was a soul, a character, which will bear scrutiny: the "fierce light which beats upon the thrones" of world-figures reveals, in his case, no stains, no disheartening weaknesses, nothing to apologize for or to cover up.

To enter into sympathetic understanding of Penn is therefore, to grow in moral stature; his example inoculates against intolerance, fortifies against indolence and despair, inspires to unselfish public spirit. His was one of the greatest and most successful efforts ever made to carry religion into public and private affairs.

In view of the immense importance of Penn's personality to the world, in view of the place which he holds in the American consciousness and in the hearts of the thinking people of Pennsylvania, it is unbelievable that this project to write of William Penn "more fully than has been done of any other Englishman" (as Sir Sidney Lee has said of Albert Cook Myers' work) should now suffer detriment or delay because of lack of financial or other support. The Sesqui-centennial of 1926 would be the right and fitting moment for the work to appear from the press. May all those to whom Penn is more than a mere name, to whom it seems important to keep alive the words and deeds of a moral hero, to whom the present miseries of the world are a burden, may all such rally now to the support and encouragement of this great and unique undertaking. Penn's was an upright, valiant and helpful spirit, and such are cruelly needed today.

Chicago. THOMAS A. JENKINS.

The Moral Basis for a Treaty of Peace

(*Memorandum, issued by the Peace Committee of the Society of Friends.*)

Most of the suggestions for the revision of the Treaty of Versailles are avowedly based on its economic folly (from the point of view of the prosperity of Great Britain and her late allies in the war) or its impossibility (from the point of view of Germany's capacity to pay). It is true that both Keynes and Nitti also insist that the Treaty of Versailles is immoral, largely because it is a violation of the armistice terms. So far, very few active politicians have followed up this line of thought. We believe that if a condition of peace and harmony is to be achieved in Europe this line of thought must be followed much further. Moreover, we believe that public opinion, having been so long fed on expediency, is sick of the diet, and would turn with relief to a policy based on some moral principle.

The vindictive principles on which the 1918 General Election was won are, we believe, being repudiated by an ever-growing number of people in this country, partly from force of circumstances, and partly because mental stability and charity are replacing the madness and hatred of war-time. What is wanted to express this new sentiment is not so much a *revision* of the Treaty of Versailles, clause by clause, as a *new agreement* amongst all the nations, based on wise principles and superseding the treaties dictated by the victorious allies.

Principles That Should Be Absolutely Rejected

1. *The sole responsibility of Germany for the War.*—Quite apart from the diplomatic revelations of the last three years, it is notorious that every nation before 1914 had been making preparations for war, and that the system of alliances and of trust in armaments, acquiesced in by every nation, was largely responsible for the outbreak. Every citizen of Europe must accept some responsibility, and should see to it that he is himself bearing "fruits worthy of repentance" before he insists on visible "repentance" of another.

2. *The right of the victors to dictate terms.* This principle tends to perpetuate the belief in superior military force, the very belief we were told we went to war to exorcise. Yet the Peace Treaties were not even negotiated round a table, as almost every other post-war treaty of modern times has been negotiated, but were forced upon protesting parties.

3. The belief that any nation or group of nations can register the degrees of guilt resting upon others, and assign the reparation due as atonement for such guilt.

What is the True Basis for a New Agreement?

1. *President Wilson's Fourteen Points.*—These were accepted by the Central Powers as the condition of the Armistice and the basis of peace. To deny them in the Treaties is a vast breach of faith.

2. *The Restoration of Prosperity.*—Important as the restoration of prosperity is, we should regard it as a desirable by-product of applying true principles, not as the ultimate test of the truth of these principles.

3. *Forgiveness and Co-operation.*—Let us not deny that every nation has much to forgive. Nor, on the other hand, let us regard full forgiveness as a sign of weakness or a dangerous acquiescence in injustice and crime. Within a State, where defined rules of justice are accepted by all, it may be right that crimes should be punished by approximately impartial judges or tribunals. Similarly, the time may be not far distant when all international disputes can be adjudicated by the Court of International Justice or by an all-inclusive League of Nations.

Meanwhile the application of the higher Christian virtue of forgiveness will do the world no harm, but a great deal of good, and involves that "change of heart" which is so widely advocated. If they have once forgiven the past, the nations will naturally proceed to co-operate on a basis of equality in building a better future; the great desire of each will be to contribute what it can to the general good. The policy for which we should work may be thus summarized: for the past, forgive and forget; for the future, show our goodwill and confidence by disarming, and our desire for the general welfare by contributing what we can to the rebuilding of what has been destroyed and the loyal support of all international humanitarian activities.

Such Conferences as that of Genoa may be the beginning of better things; but we must make sure that British policy does not mean the cajolery of other states into a policy of reconstruction because such a policy is in our interest; we must make it clear that we are prepared to lead the way, to take risks, even to undertake fresh economic burdens, on behalf of human welfare.

John W. Graham, *Chairman;*
Bertram Pickard, *Secretary.*

Devonshire House, 136, Bishopsgate, E.C.2
May, 1922.

service that is directed by thought and knowledge, will make them able warriors in the struggle with evil. Others are too old; physical strength and nerve-force are failing; and for them the days of active warfare are over. Others, again, are for the time compelled by bodily infirmities to stand aside, and leave the conflict to be waged by those more fit. For all these the only answer they can give to the summons is to wait and pray.

So long as we are "in our right place," and are not making our weakness of body or mind or spirit an excuse for indolence, the task of quiet waiting, and of supporting by sympathy and prayer the soldiers of the Lord, is as true a service as any we could render with strength of arm or quickness of brain. God needs His unknown servants, whose place is in the obscurity of home, and not only the active fighters for truth and goodness who gain the public eye. We can help Him more by quiet waiting, by sympathy with their endeavors, and prayer that He will endue them with courage and wisdom and whole-hearted devotion, than we could by restlessly trying to share a task that is not for us.

"Who best
Bear His mild yoke, they serve Him best. His state
Is kingly; thousands at His bidding speed,
And post o'er land and ocean without rest;
They also serve who only stand and wait."

EDWARD GRUBB.

Exhortation of the Dawn

Listen to the exhortation of the dawn,
Look to this day!
For it is life, the very life of life.
In its brief course lie all the
Phases and realities of your existence:

The bliss of growth,
The glory of action,
The splendor of beauty.

For yesterday is but a dream,
And tomorrow is only a vision;
But today, well lived, makes
Every yesterday a dream of happiness
And every tomorrow a vision of hope,
Look well therefore to this day;
Such is the salutation of the dawn.

—*Versed motto from the Sanskrit; selected by M. Jane Pancoast.*

Hunting Lafayette's Home

The Marquis de Lafayette, the early friend of American Independence, apparently does not bulk so large in France as he does in America. There is the handsome equestrian statue of him standing in front of the Louvre, erected by the school children of America, and there may be other monuments to his memory in Paris. When, however, we asked the alert and ever obliging clerk at the hotel, how to find La Grange, Lafayette's old home, he smiled and said he would find it for us and began to look frantically through the telephone book. But neither the concierge, who usually knows everything, nor any one of the six other clerks, or even the proprietor of this very orderly Paris hotel, could throw any light on where Lafayette had lived, and when it was at last conveyed to them that the place was at least thirty kilometers outside of Paris, they gave up entirely.

In the comfortable American library, a half hour's search of the various lives of Lafayette, still left a vague idea as to the exact location. The best we could find was that La Grange was half way between Melun and Meaux, which are thirty miles apart, so we drew a straight line on the map and steered the automobile for the centre. Out through the old walls of Paris, past immense dumps of artillery and army supplies, we soon entered the Forest of Vincennes, a picture of vernal beauty. The ground is carpeted with ivies and other greens, the tree trunks are a soft yellow, covered with moss, and the new soft green leaves were just putting out. Through it all, the sun chased the shadows of a perfect afternoon. Yes, we all agreed Corot was born in the Forest of Vincennes and in the spring time.

We crossed the Marne, for we were bearing south-eastwardly, at a happy suburban town and then on and on across the plains of Brie, through great estates and private forests, where the hares were running and the pheasants mating, by level farm lands with oxen ploughing, in one case, three yokes to a plow, through little villages with their narrow, crooked streets, until finally we reached Fontenoy, which was the spot indicated on the straight line from Melun to Meaux. Here we inquired and found the town we wanted was Rozoy-en-Brie, two miles away, and inquiry in this village located Grange about two kilometers to the south.

But let me quote a writer who in 1817 made the same journey,—"The chateau is so remote from any highway, so wood-embossed, that we had great difficulty in finding it. We passed from one deep entangled glen to another, forded stony brooks, crossed the remains of a Roman road and finally saw the towers of the chateau." This was in the days of poorer roads (Oh, the joy of the roads in France!), and we had no great trouble for a half mile away we saw the conical towers about the trees, but steering straight for them, we wound up in the farm yard instead of entering by the more dignified main entrance.

La Grange was formerly a fortified baronial castle with portcullis and a moat fed by a little stream which winds through the place. The ground is level, so there is no great view except the distant vistas cut through the forest trees on the east and south. Here, Lafayette retired on his return to France, and after he was released from his long imprisonment at Olmutz, and here with his family around him, he spent the remaining days of his life, usually passing part of the year in Paris and occasionally taking part in the affairs of state.

An ancient gate lead from the farm yard to the grounds of the chateau. The moat has been partly filled in, but one-half the mansion is still encircled by it and here a solitary swan, resenting our intrusion, climbed out on the bank and would have driven us off if he could.

The building is in the shape of a square "C," with five round gothic towers at the corners, each surmounted by very tall and steep roofs, like giant candle extinguishers. The building apparently in the dangerous, early days, had a fourth side to complete its defense, leaving a good sized courtyard in the middle. The drawbridge has been replaced by a permanent stone bridge over the moat and we enter the courtyard between two of the conical towers. The buildings are three stories high, of stone, aged and moss-covered and ivy-covered. The interior was not open to the public as the owner, the Marquis de Lasteyric, a collateral descendant of Lafayette, was not in residence and the building is not shown.

One striking feature of the grounds is the way ivy has been used to make what we would call the fences along the drive way and around the courtyard. It is festooned in great ropes from post to post apparently supporting itself. On the wall is a green ivy planted by Charles James Fox, on a visit to La Grange, and in the park are specimen trees that look from their size and location, as if they too, might be mementoes of some cherished friend.

It may have been that Lafayette was influenced by the great devotion of Washington to a real interest in farming, for he gave attention to the intimate details of the place. He was so proud of his set of farm account books that he brought them with him on his memorable visit to America in 1824-25, and unfortunately, they were lost when the steamboat on which he was riding, struck a snag in the Mississippi and sank.

His merino sheep were the best in France and he imported his dairy stock from England and Switzerland. Noted stock breeders sent him pedigreed animals and he followed with deep interest the experiences in farming of those in England and America with whom he corresponded.

He kept as many as 800 sheep and one of the first things that greeted us as we landed in the barnyard, was the bleating of ewes and lambs in the barns. The ewes had been shorn and the wind that cold spring day, was not tempered to the shorn lamb. The farmer said there were 650 of them and it certainly sounded so.

With the exception of the driveway in, and the old gate leading to the chateau grounds, the barnyard was solidly built around. On one side were the sheep barns, on another the sheds for the wagons and tools, on another the home of the farmer and his helper, while chicken houses, hay lofts, rabbit hutches, feed houses, filled the remaining space. In the middle was the immense pile of manure not yet hauled out to the fields. The chateau without its owner, was lonely and deserted, the barnyard was full of the life which Lafayette loved.

We returned to Paris by the direct road, finding the distance to be about thirty miles and we imagined Lafayette toiling over it on horseback or in his carriage, on his frequent visits to Paris. Then we pictured the pleasure he must have found in throwing off the cares of state and once again seeking the quiet and peaceful spot, hidden away near Rozoy-en-Brie. C. F. J.

Paris, Fifth month 5, 1922.

American-English Friends' Conference at Buzuluk, Russia

A conference of relief workers in Russia, held at Buzuluk, April 29th and 30th, brought together a number of workers whose reports were far from encouraging.

Marjorie Rackstraw, who came by camel cart from Alexievka, an English outpost 55 versts from Buzuluk, reported that four-fifths of her territory had Friends' food up to May 2nd, but there would be several days when no supplies would be in the warehouse for distribution. Unless more seeds came quickly, the prospects for a harvest would completely disappear. Miss Rackstraw gave the official, and doubtless conservative, death figures for some of her volosts. Between February and April, between 15 and 30 per cent. of all the people had died.

Muriel Payne, who has been at Boscoye for a month, reported that actually only 49 per cent. were being fed in her district and that the children were not receiving a ration sufficient to keep them alive. She told of 21 children who had been picked up on the steps of the Quaker Dom (House) in Boscoye and taken to the Ispolcom Patronat. Although they had been receiving some of our food, 12 of them died within two weeks. She was somewhat assured to hear that, due to the more generous contributions of the Friends in England, the children's rations for May could be increased.

Dorice White, who has been chief of the Andrievka outpost since last fall, reported the present situation was in many respects as terrible as the one in January and February. Five volosts out of her eight had been unable to receive their supplies at Andrievka, as what few horses and camels they possessed had been sent to Buzuluk for seed grain. Many of them had fallen on the return trip. Several of these volosts had absolutely no food on hand. The results of this would soon be apparent in the death statistics, as it had been in the middle of March when the death rate had doubled, due to a three days' delay in the arrival of the Quaker food.

From Pavlofka, Frank Watts brought news of conditions at present even worse than they were last December, due largely to the irregularities of transport. Two of the volosts of this district were completely cut off from any communication with the warehouse, as the Spring floods had carried away several bridges in strategic positions along the main arteries of transport.

In the absence of Nancy Babb and Anne Herkner, representing the two American outposts, Homer Morris gave a comprehensive report of the feeding operations in the whole of the American section. His picture of the likely effects of the present collapse of a large percentage of the animal transport was as grim as that of the English representatives. If full amount of transport could be secured from the volosts and the products moved to their "ultimate consumers" effectively and speedily, the American section would be feeding approximately 65 per cent. of the child population and 62 per cent. of the adult. The total population of the American area at the moment is officially 186,000. The American Friends' food and the ARA corn should, under the May allotment list, be feeding over 122,000 of this number. How many will actually receive the food in their bodies remains to be decided by the strength of the animals that can be mobilized to drag the food from the full-packed warehouses at Sorochinskaya and Totskoye. The children who are surest of receiving their full ration (and it is one and a half the size of the regular children's dry ration) are the parentless children in the various Children's Homes, Patronats and Collectors. Over 4,000 of these children live in the Homes in the American section.

Edward Balls, the acting chief of the English Mission during the sickness of Arthur Watts, outlined the program of feeding for the English section beginning with May 16th. Of the 200,000 adult population in the west Buzuluk territory the English will feed 180,000 (a much more balanced ration than the ARA corn including flour and beans and herring and soup); and of the 160,000 child population, the English will be feeding, if their May plans are carried out, some 112,000.

While the conference was in progress on Sunday, Parry Paul arrived from Samara, where he had been buying oil and gasoline for the three Fordson tractors that will soon be turning up the black soil near Sorochinskaya. He came in the "teplushka," and brought Rebecca and Harry Timbres with him. They were on their way from Moscow, and stepped into the Quaker coach at Kenel.

A Recent Contribution

The following letter speaks for itself:

"I am enclosing herewith check for fifty-nine dollars forwarded through our office for United Mine Workers' Union, Local No. 2583 of Roslyn, Washington.

"These workers are on strike at the present time but are able, even in their own adversity, to remember those who are suffering so severely in far-away lands."

Those who have suffered are willing to share the little they have with others in need.

The Future of the American Friends' Service Committee

The American Friends' Service Committee has given special consideration to the question of its future activities. The question was discussed at the meeting in Third month and again in Fifth month. As a result the following minute was made a part of the records of the Service Committee meeting that was held on Sixth month 1st. It outlines the present feeling of the Committee in regard to future activities.

"The members of the Committee are all united in believing that the American Friends' Service Committee should seek to maintain the interest in improving international relationships so greatly enlarged by recent joint work of Friends, and either under its present name, or another, continue the organization as a channel for the expression, at home and abroad, of the Christian ideal of service. While it is not expected that such great emergencies as have existed in the past few years will confront us in the next few years, it is felt that there will be many calls for united action on the part of the Society of Friends, outside of any of the existing organizations.

"No matter how large or small the organization may be at any time, it would then constitute a nucleus which could be expanded as occasion demanded and thus enable the whole group of Friends to give united service on any particular occasion."

New York Yearly Meeting

Meetings for Worship

First-day, Fifth month 28th

At the Meeting for Worship on First-day afternoon, Caroline J. Worth reminded us of how all are singing together in God's great harmony, and compared the chorus to that of a congregation in which one strong voice sang at first in discord, but gradually came into tone with the others, until all were singing in perfect harmony.

Daniel Willets said: "We must hear, we must listen to that which is fundamental. Within us is that power upon which we must lean."

Dr. Edward Janney said: "There is a modesty which amounts to a crime—the modesty which prevents people from doing what they can. The little girl who whistled a hymn today did what she could. There was a woman who wondered once what she could do. And while thinking and puzzling, she sang a hymn,—which reached and helped a soul to better things. There often seems so little that we can do. But a loving spirit, the spirit of service, will make us do the best we can."

William Yarnall said: "We are like children in a mighty power-house. One switch gives light for a city, another power, etc. But we do not know which switch to use. It is for us to learn what switch to use. God is always present; His power is available, and we must learn what a wonderful power we always have with us."

Elbert Russell said: "Jonah took ship to Tarshish. Jonah was trying to flee from the presence of God—not from His power, but His love. The writer of this book shows how the mercy of God filled the world. The sailors, heathen, risked their lives to save Jonah, before they finally consented to throw him overboard. The mercy of God was demonstrated in the heathen. The mercy of God was demonstrated in the abyss beneath. Finally Jonah preached in Nineveh, and the city repented, and was saved. So God's mercy to sinners was shown.

"In the last chapter of Jonah, with its story of the gourd, we see the strength of the love of living things, in solitude. It seemed to Jonah that the death of the gourd was the last straw in a world that was not run right. Then said God to Jonah, 'Thou hast had pity on the gourd, and shall I not have mercy on Nineveh?' If we can love those under our care, can we not feel the fatherly love of God for all under His care. We must not shy at the love of God, or let ourselves doubt the mercy, the healing power that sends the rain alike on the just and the unjust.

"The test of Jonah in the modern world would be to see if he were willing to preach to Germany in the hope that the Germans might be saved."

Isaac Wilson said: "In the high experience of God, our eyes will be opened, and our ears unstopped. Let us join in the determination to join in all things with the Master who spoke the words which we long to follow. In the spiritual field of service, we can follow if we but will."

Fourth-day, Fifth month 31st

The Meeting for Worship opened with a prayer from J. Barnard Walton.

Dr. O. Edward Janney said: "And this is the life eternal, to know Thee, the only true God and Jesus Christ, whom thou hast sent." It is surprising to see that there is so much infidelity to law in these days. We see young people growing up indifferent to religious life. We do not wonder when we think of the world experiences of the past few years, that people say "Is there a God, and is He good?" If He is good, why has He allowed the war to occur? The war was not brought on by God: it was brought on by human selfishness and greed—representative qualities that we ascribe to the Evil one. It was because men did not obey the laws that God has laid down for their well-being. War has never been inevitable. So we can ascribe war, not to God, but to men's disobeying the laws of God. So we can relieve our minds of the thought that God brought on war.

Is it possible to relieve our young people of the skepticism and doubt that makes them unhappy?

When we look about the world with all its beauty, when we look at the seasons, and the fertility of the earth's soil, can we doubt that there is a Power that made all things; an Intelligence that thought out all parts of that great machine.

God manifests himself not only in Nature, but in humanity itself. Think of the deeds that have been done in and for the human race. Can we doubt that He works through the human race. The development of the Roman race made it safe for the disciples of Christ to carry the Message along their wonderful roads. The development of the Greek people gave the language in which to carry the message. The development of the Jewish people gave the religious impulse to carry the message. "Through the ages one increasing purpose runs. And the mind of man is broadened with the process of the suns." We see God in the Bible, and how His spirit worked in men who wrote it. It is wonderful how that book has lived into the present day, giving us the living teachings of Jesus Christ, who taught how it is possible for a human being to manifest in his life the spirit of God.

I wish we could think of God as a personal friend. He is not far away, but close at hand,—"closer than breathing, and nearer than hands and feet." Jesus turned to God at every step. Shall we not, too, meet God as a friend. "But," we may say, "I can't visualize God." Can't you visualize your friend who is on a voyage to Europe? Then do the same with God. You can't give Him a form, perhaps, but you know that He is your friend. If we know we are sons and daughters of God, what else matters? Let us ask today for the certainty that we are the sons of God,—"as many as are led by the Spirit of God they are the sons of God." Nothing can take the place of this great possession—the knowledge that God is ours, and we are His.

Isaac Wilson said: "A recognition is possible of the religious element in human nature. We need courage to claim our individual convictions. Jesus had this courage. It is natural for us to love our friends and hate our enemies, but, said Jesus, 'I say unto you, Love your enemies.' I believe the Society of Friends has not been preserved for 250 years to sit in quietude, but for great service. I believe that God takes small groups to do the great work of the world. Our world lies in ruins; can we not help it? The spirit of Jesus Christ is unknown in many places; strife and selfishness are in our own land. We must have the vision of courage and faith, and added to that the light of the Spirit. We look for faith in the world. Is it not our duty to teach the simple faith? Our organization does not look to flight into another world. We should teach our faith in this world."

John Gordon said: "I never thought of Jonah as a man who refused to accept the mercy of God. But can we get away from Love? Can we be Christians, and hate anyone? I have been a professed Christian for years, yet I know that in years past I have led men astray. Something has led me to be active, and I have been active when I should have been patient. They have changed the name of Blackwell's Island to Welfare Island. If I understand what he meant who said, 'I have come that ye might have life,'—then nothing remains for us but to do what we can do. What can we do to make it a *Welfare Island*, a place of blessing to its unfortunate inhabitants?"

William Yarnall said: "When Jesus healed the blind man, the Pharisees were angry because it was done on the Sabbath day. They tried to tangle the man in their questionings, but he answered, 'This one thing I know, that whereas I was blind, now I see.' That was the outstanding fact. We often ask what so-and-so thinks about a thing, without counting the presence of Fact. We need to seek out the underlying truth under all words and ideas. The spiritual man is descended from God."

Carolena Wood said: "The question is asked, 'What manner of men and women are Friends?' We heard of the carrying of the first message, and how it was helped by the universal language. To-day is there any language spoken by so many people as English? The language is there, waiting for the message. We rejoice that the Roman roads were ready for the disciples,—but what of the roads of today, ready for the men and women who have the message? A Hebrew disciple wrote to a group of men and women, saying that they had the will to be saved. Oh, let us feel that call. Let us be saved."

ANNA L. CURTIS.

(Evening meetings in next issue)

A Swarthmorean in China

Nora Waln, a member of the Society of Friends and a former student at Swarthmore College, has been working with the Y. W. C. A. in China. In writing to a friend she speaks of a visit to Kamakura, where they passed under an archway which bore the inscription "Whosoever thou art and whatsoever thy creed, remember as thou entereth here that this place is hallowed and made sacred by the worship of ages." She adds, "There was a calm and quiet peace there that is akin to the peace of a meeting-house at home."

In commenting on Pekin, a visit to the Forbidden City took her through the city which she says is not all beauty for there are dirty parts with ragged professional beggars, but there is space and little rush and hurry and new picturesque wonders at every turning. And there are warm hearts that smile out from strange Chinese faces and a charm about it all which is not all due to the spell of the golden roofs of a departed glory, nor the legends and lore of other days, but it is more than half the life of today, the patience, the good humor of the people, the philosophy of the folks one talks with and, too, it is the potential possibilities of this old new land.

Part of Nora Waln's work, after studying the language, was to write a book of stories for girls' clubs. In substituting for another teacher in one of the Congregational schools, she was much amused at the little girls who rose all together every time she entered the room saying in chorus "Good afternoon." But she says they are much like the children at home and break into peals of laughter at her mistakes in pronouncing their names.

Commenting on the custom of binding the feet of women, she says that it is gradually dying out, but it is slow, for public opinion about beauty is not changed by an edict from the government. However, there are among men's schools, clubs of men who have issued statements that they will not marry girls with small feet.

One letter speaks of attending a meeting of the Fellowship of Reconciliation, which has grown from a small beginning last year into a group that is predominated by Chinese and is truly Chinese in its leadership. Several publications of the more radical type, when translated, proved to be largely a discussion of marriage and marriage customs. Whole columns were filled with debates concerning the method of parents arranging the marriages of their children versus the western way.

One of the last of her letters states that she is returning to Shanghai to begin work at the publication office of the Y. W. C. A., and that she hopes to complete the book of stories for girls in a short time.

Friendly Fundamentals

A copy of the little pamphlet "Friendly Fundamentals" was recently sent to one of the political prisoners in Leavenworth (one of the scores of men still imprisoned for expression of opinion only, and under war-time legislation long since repealed). In response he writes: "I had never thought about Quakers in that way before. Do they really live this way every day? I have believed these things for a long time and tried to live them as best I could. And that is what has brought me where I now am. But I've never counted myself religious at all. That sentence 'It seems to be the will of him who is infinite in wisdom that light upon great subjects should first arise and be gradually spread through the faithfulness of individuals in acting up to their own convictions,' and 'Nowhere else is the same emphasis given to the value of individual initiative as in the Society of Friends'—seems to me truly a big thing. I've tried to act up to my convictions. If I were willing to forget and to recant them, I could be free. But that would be a poor kind of freedom for me. . . . I wish I could talk with some Quaker sometime about all these things. Do you think they would really understand what we are in prison for?"

My thoughts went back to those words of the Discipline: "To bear testimony against all forms of human bondage." Are we all doing this today?

Just now, throughout the country there is a concerted, earnest effort to effect the freedom of these men in prison "for conscience sake." Of all people, can we of Quaker faith escape a deep responsibility for this fundamental concern of human justice and liberty? When men are giving their lives, literally all that they have, all their *future* (some of these men now in prison have sentences of twenty years) for the cause of all humanity, for the right as they see the right,—when such men reach out in questioning toward the ideal that Friends profess, can we fail them through indifference, through inertia, and preoccupation in our personal affairs? One of these men whose five-year sentence is completed and who may soon be going to Italy, has asked if any of us knows a Friendly centre, or even family—or a single Friend—in that country, with whom he may talk when he reaches there? If any Friend has information to give about this, it will be greatly appreciated if sent to the Secretary of the Prison Comfort Club in care of the INTELLIGENCER office. And if anyone cares to have further information about any matter concerning these prisoners, though not caring to join or support any organization, the Secretary will be glad to know of this, and will try to share the results of personal correspondence with all these men as well as study of the subject in general, with anyone who is at all interested.

Friendly News Notes

Daniel Batchellor attended all the sessions of Millville Half-Yearly Meeting held recently. On First-day afternoon, an outdoor service was held at the old log meeting-house at Cattawissa, and as the sun shone through the stately oaks, he, in vivid language, compared this to the way the spirit shines through our lives if we give it a chance.

The engagement of Alice Blackburn, daughter of Allen C. Blackburn, Bedford, Pa., and Harold W. Flitcraft, of Oak Park, Ill., has been announced.

Dr. and Mrs. William I. Hull and daughters will sail for Europe on June 17th. Dr. Hull will attend the International Conference of the Federation of Churches at Copenhagen early in August, and their daughter, Miss Mary Hull, will spend next winter studying at Oxford. Friends from Philadelphia will occupy the Hull residence during their absence.—*Swarthmore News.*

Gertrude Roberts Sherer and her successor, Olive Robins Haviland, superintendents of schools for the Yearly Meeting of Friends held at Fourth and Arch Streets, Philadelphia, have recommended J. Russell Smith's Grammar School Geographies for use in their schools and several of the schools have already adopted them.

These books called "Human Geography," published by the Winston Co., Philadelphia, are a Friend's attempt to promote better international understanding, and therefore international co-operation, by writing a text-book that should be both good geography and good ethics. The second of these books has recently appeared, and is producing favorable comment.

It is not often that a Friend, opposed to war, gets a chance to address the army on the causes of war, but such was the case recently when J. Russell Smith, a member of Swarthmore Monthly Meeting, and Professor of Economic Geography in Columbia University, New York, addressed the War College at Washington.

The War College provides instruction for a body of mature army officers from 35 to 60 years of age, who are being trained to be the brains of the army. Dr. Smith's lecture was on the resources of France and Germany with especial reference to prospective wars.

Thomas Mott Osborne, the former unconventional warden of the Sing Sing Prison, is opening a preparatory school for boys in the old Osborne home at Auburn, New York, his present residence. The policies of the school will be formulated by the boys themselves, who will be allowed the fullest possible amount of control. He holds that scholastic institutions in America do not train for the responsibility of citizenship. "Osborne School" is so named in honor of his father and mother, whose home was a noted place of gathering for the early reformers in the suffrage movement. His grandmother, Martha Wright, was the sister of Lucretia Mott.—*The Friend* (Philadelphia).

Charles Foster Kent, Professor of Biblical Literature at Yale University, will be one of the speakers at Friends' General Conference at Richmond, Ind., August 26th to September 2nd. Prof. Kent has for the last year or two given half of his time to the holding of conferences and series of lectures in different cities. The purpose of this work is to interpret the social principles of the prophets and Jesus in clear modern terms, and to develop practical methods by which these principles may be applied to the present social and industrial situation. Prof. Kent has met an excellent response in this work.

Again we would congratulate the editors of the Young Friends' number of *The Friend* (Philadelphia). Their live number for Fifth month deals with "Youth and Youth Movements." It contains articles on the work of young Friends in all branches of our Society and in England, and also on the youth movements in Germany and Czechoslovakia.

The last of these movements in particular has received little notice in America. An article by a Czechoslovakian student now in America tells how it first rose in response to an appeal from President Masaryk, of the Czechoslovakian Republic, and how it was nurtured by the visits of J. R. Mott, Sherwood Eddy and other American leaders.

At its conference last summer, the movement assumed a definitely religious basis, with the following statement of its aims:

"We associate ourselves in a common work on a religious basis for the regeneration of man, which shall manifest itself through love, through the longing after the knowledge of truth, and through the endeavor to do good. Those of us who strive after regeneration in the spirit of Christ may become regular members of the movement."

The subject of the amount of money paid out in salaries by Philadelphia Yearly Meeting was under discussion at its recent sessions. Later an article in FRIENDS' INTELLIGENCER referred to the salary expenditures as $12,000, which is not quite correct. When considering the wisdom of spending money in this way, we at least ought to have exact knowledge as to the amount we are spending. The total salary list at the Central Bureau, including the Secretary of the Young Friends' Movement, and the Secretary of the Committee on Education, amounts to $6,920.00. The only other salary charge against the Yearly Meeting funds is 60 per cent. of the salaries paid in the Advancement office. This totals for salaries in 1921 and 1922, $9,200.00. Beginning with Seventh month 1st, the $2,000 salary of the Secretary for the Committee on Education will be dispensed with. A salary item, appearing in the report of the Committee on Peace and Service, is not properly chargeable against Yearly Meeting funds, since this Committee raised by subscription last year a sum of money about equal to the salary expended.

So far as we have knowledge, no Yearly Meeting money except as above noted has been expended in salaries. It is of course always possible to consider whether we need salaried officers. The meeting has apparently decided that we do. An expenditure of $9,200 per year as compensation for the services of eight Friends is certainly not extravagant and the Friends included on the payroll may be fairly entitled to consider that they give at least as much volunteer service to the Society as other members who work under our system without remuneration.

JANE P. RUSHMORE.

CENTRE QUARTERLY MEETING

From a spiritual and social standpoint, the Quarterly Meeting held at Dunning's Creek as a rule seems to be most favored. It is the most delightful season of the year and Dunning Creek Friends are live wires in every element required to make a *Friends'* Quarterly Meeting.

Among the visitors were Joel Borton, Dr. O. Edward Janney, Charles P. Blackburn and family, Isaac Walker and wife, and La Verne Forbush. These Friends all contributed to making the three sessions each day a success. On Seventh-day, the 3rd, the First-day School Association met and after routine business was transacted discussed various questions relating to First-day School work.

The meeting of Ministry and Counsel which followed developed that notwithstanding Centre Quarterly Meeting has no recorded minister, there is considerable vocal ministry in some of our meetings, and the question whether acknowledgment and recording by the meeting was an encouragement or the reverse, was discussed.

Four meetings were held on First-day,—First-day School, meeting for worship both morning and evening and a special meeting at 3 p. m. addressed by Dr. Janney and Joel Borton, on the subject 'A Warless World." On Second-day, after the short meeting for worship, the business of the Quarterly Meeting was transacted.

It would be invidious for me to attempt to give a summary of the thoughts presented and report the inspiration of these meetings, but I do want to emphasize the concern of Joel Borton and Dr. Janney for universal and permanent peace. It is not only the moral and religious obligation, but a patriotic duty for Friends to press this matter upon educational lines by all practical means and upon all available occasions.

ISAAC UNDERWOOD.

WHITE WATER QUARTERLY MEETING

At the meeting for worship at White Water Quarterly Meeting held at Richmond, Indiana, recently, much spiritual power developed because several members spoke briefly from hearts that are habitually communicative with the Divine Spirit.

The matter that brought out the most discussion was the deplorable practice prevailing in the various meetings of members attending First-day School and then absenting themselves from the regular meetings for worship. The meeting decided to request subordinate meetings to introduce some means, or make a special effort to improve conditions along this line.

The regular time for holding White Water Quarterly Meeting in Ninth month falls on the last day of the General Conference at Richmond, Indiana. In order to relieve this conflict of dates, it was decided to hold the next session of the Quarterly Meeting on Ninth month 5th, at Lincolnville, Indiana.

A very earnest appeal was made during the discussion of business for a vigorous support of the Prohibition laws of the nation.

FINLEY TOMLINSON, *Clerk.*

JOINT PRESS COMMITTEE OF FAIRFAX QUARTERLY MEETING

At the last meeting of Fairfax Quarter, the Joint Press Committee appointed in Second month to co-operate with the other branch of Friends, in Virginia, to see what could be done toward teaching the constructive side of our national and international life in the normal schools of Virginia and the District of Columbia, reported that they had secured the additional co-operation of the Friends of Homewood, and also through the superintendent of the Yearly Meeting's Committee, included Maryland and the portion of Pennsylvania that is in Baltimore Yearly Meeting.

The Committee recommended that each Monthly Meeting be asked to stress this work *right now*. That we publish peace items in the local papers, and have essays written in all schools. Baltimore Yearly Meeting has offered prizes for essays. That an especially fine peace anthem "O Hear Ye All Nations" be sung when practical at Sunday School conventions and other gatherings; also that speakers be placed on the programs of as many summer gatherings as possible, especially the summer normals, and that an effort be made to reach the student body of the present term.

That we use our influence toward having the best books of history obtainable placed in our public schools, and appoint someone to see what books are used in our Friends' schools in order to have constructive teaching of history in both grade and high schools.

Charles M. Pidgeon was appointed to see what could be done through the University Extension course, Lucretia S. Franklin to draft a circular letter setting forth the aims of this committee to be sent to distant members; Lina S. Stanton to write to the International Lesson Leaf Committee asking for a Peace lesson once a quarter as we have the Temperance lesson. Space is to be asked in the *Union Signal* and our Friends' papers when our course is thoroughly determined and we have books to recommend. "The Sword or the Cross," price ten cents, and the "Folly of Nations" are recommended for circulation.

At a later meeting of the committee, text books were discussed, and it was decided to recommend Beard and Bagley's Histories. It was determined to ask Dr. David Starr Jordan, Dr. William I. Hull, Professor Lunt, of Haverford, Robert Kelley and Dr. Latane, of Hopkins, to review the History situation, and recommend something suitable to the advanced thought of the time.

ELIZABETH H. WILSON, *Chairman;*
LAURA S. HOGE, *Secretary.*

THE OPEN FORUM

This column is intended to afford free expression of opinion by readers on questions of interest. The INTELLIGENCER is not responsible for any such opinions. Letters must be brief, and the editor reserves the right to omit parts if necessary to save space.

To the Editor:

Many expressions of appreciation have come to me concerning M. T. Woodruff's clear and courageous statement of facts (and of the *truth*, which includes all facts and is yet still wider and deeper) in his Forum letter in the INTELLIGENCER for Sixth month 10th. May I add some details that have already helped to make for clarity in the minds of many who are now for the first time trying to understand the problems that today vitally concern the great majority of our fellow human beings: there are really, essentially, only two factors involved—the earth (God-given freely to all humanity) and human labor. Everything that is in the world today came in some way from the earth by means of human work. ("Capital," which is really only distilled, stored-up human labor, past or present, is at bottom only a fictitious factor, a secondary item; it only *seems* an essential today because our thinking is confused, not basic, about this whole matter.) But for those of us who truly believe in the spirit of democracy, for those of us who believe in the word, the life, of Jesus, there are some facts that cannot be ignored:—the workers of the world constitute the overwhelming human majority, yet a very small minority of human beings own and control all the industrial mechanism (all the "jobs" in the world) and can, and do, when they please, decree that great numbers of workers may not continue to work, or must be paid so small an amount that their children slowly starve, growing up with stunted bodies and brains, living distorted lives, and later are called "criminals." Those who have power over the "jobs" of the world, thus really have power over the *whole lives*, the bodies and brains, of all those who work for wages, and these wage-earners are as truly slaves as in the time of chattel-slavery. Once when this was said to an elderly Friend, she protested that at least wage-workers have public schools, as chattel-slaves did not. But this is only nominally true. Hundreds of thousands of children today have only half-time schooling and thousands upon thousands more, no schooling at all, because there are not enough school houses—only about two cents out of every dollar of tax-money we pay, go to education; about ninety cents of every dollar go to war, past or present. But even were there enough school houses and teachers, the increase in "mental defectives" among children (due chiefly to malnutrition) is appalling—they are incapacitated for education. Such statements may seem hardly credible. But they are true.

If anyone who reads this may care to go a little further into the consideration of these things (believing that Jesus' teaching and actions were very explicitly concerned with all such things as he found them in the world at that time also, and that if we are to help in answering his prayer that God's will—(peace and good will)—may be done *on earth*, we must follow Jesus' example)—if anyone feels he has but little time to give and yet would like to put that little to service in the cause of truth, there is a small group of Friends who for some time have tried to study these things conscientiously and in the spirit of Jesus, and who would be glad to share the results of this study with anyone who may care to share it—(quite freely, of course, without entailing the slightest obligation, material or immaterial)—if a letter be sent in care of the INTELLIGENCER office. E. H.

COAL AND HENRY FORD

To the Editor:

It is a most hopeful sign of the times that Friends have taken a real step toward uncovering the coal situation, which is threatening most serious consequences to us all. Drew Pearson's personally conducted investigation discloses facts not presented to readers of the daily press,—but which may be easily inferred by persons whose industrial experiences during the war have brought actual contact with labor conditions which many of us only read about, and never *feel*.

Now that the miners' side of this unequal situation is clearly, honestly and boldly shown, may Friends and other denominations continue to press for the fair play which the miners demand, in their exceptionally hazardous and disagreeable business, from which they only make an uncertain and second-rate livelihood, while the operators live in luxury and security.

Mr. Malone believes that "there is nothing fundamentally wrong with our system of wage payment and profit taking." Really! If there isn't something fundamentally wrong with it, will he kindly explain why we are having such terrible troubles industrially, financially and economically everywhere, under the old system, right now?

One Captain of Industry, Henry Ford, stands alone almost in his successes at this time of trouble, even in the matter of railroading. He did not go to the group of "investment capital" to be placed where he is. He reversed the formula, "Capital, management and labor.". Ford's formula reads,—labor, management, *and* capital.

Ford's formula works. It has been abundantly proven. His autobiography is a classic for its straight, common sense logic and its bold tearing down of ancient stupid methods by which kings, courtiers and politicians become hugely rich at the expense of those on whose labors the whole fabric of civilization rests. Wherever there is trouble, there is something wrong, and "no question is ever settled *until* it is settled right."

Those who differ as to the need for the change in the formula usually accepted as correct, viz., "Capital, management and labor," would do well to read the life of Henry Ford, now running in *McClure's Magazine*, and re-read it if necessary, until the newer and more successfully working ideas have been somewhat assimilated, then look to the concrete evidences of the truths of Ford's ideas, in his works and his increasing wealth, without the aid of "Wall Street" at any time, and in spite of many efforts lately to discredit him. Labor leaders and agitators do not belong to Ford's system. They are unnecessary to it.

Philadelphia, Pa. S. P. BYRNES.

COMING EVENTS

SIXTH MONTH

18th—Certain members of Philadelphia Quarterly Meeting's Visiting Committee expect to attend meeting for worship at Germantown Friends' Home, at 7.30 p. m.

18th—Chester Monthly Meeting, at Chester, Pa., at 2.30 p. m.

18th—W. J. MacWatters expects to visit Haverford Meeting, 10.30 a. m.

21st—Monthly Meeting of Friends of Philadelphia, 15th and Race Streets, 7.30 p. m.

22nd—Green Street Monthly Meeting of Friends of Philadelphia, School House Lane, Germantown, 7.30 p m.

25th—W. J. MacWatters expects to visit Newtown, Bucks County, Pa., meeting, at 11 a. m.

25th—Certain members of Philadelphia Quarterly Meeting's Visiting Committee expect to attend Merion Meeting at 11 a. m. Other members will attend meeting for worship at 15th and Race Streets, Philadelphia, at 10.30 a. m.

SEVENTH MONTH

2nd—First-day, at 2.30 p. m. Daylight Saving Time; a meeting for Divine Worship will be held at Stanton (Delaware) Friends' Meeting-house under care of a committee of Concord Quarterly Meeting. Wilmington Friends' School motor bus will leave 4th and Market Sts. for Stanton about 1.55 o'clock; also trolley cars leave at same place and hour. Friends of both branches as well as all interested persons are invited.

BIRTHS

VAN WAGNER—On Sixth month 10th, at Plainfield, N. J., to Claude and Winifred Stringham Van Wagner, a son, named Willis Conklin Van Wagner.

DEATHS

COALE—On First month 14th, at the age of 57 years, in Los Angeles, Calif., where she and her husband were spending the winter, Clara B., wife of William N. Coale, and daughter of the late Benjamin and Mary Ann Bedell, all of Bennett, Nebraska, and all members of the Society of Friends. Her parents were among the pioneer settlers of Benjaminville, Ill., and were originally from Athens, New York.

HOOPES—In West Collingswood, N. J., on Fifth month 19th, Charles H., husband of the late Annie M. Hoopes, formerly of Chester, Pa., a member of Chester (Pa.) Monthly Meeting.

WALTON—On Sixth month 3rd, at Christiana, Pa., after a lingering illness of ten months, Alban Walton, aged 78 years.

NOTICE—Camp Onas, the camp of the Young Friends' Movement, is to be along the Schuylkill, near Port Indian, Pa., for the two weeks June 24th to July 10th. Plans are progressing nicely and all persons wishing to go should send in their applications at once.

This is our fourth annual camp and we are expecting it to be as successful as the other years. The canoeing and swimming will be especially good and "Mose" is to cook for us again. After this camp we hope that we too will be able to write as did a former camper, "Apart from the duties and formalities of daily routine, we led the simple life in its true sense, and it was little wonder that we all soon became warm friends and were in accord with each other and with God.

For further information address Ruth H. Conrow, 154 N. 15th St., Philadelphia, Pa.

NOTICE—Henry T. Hodgkin is expected to reach Philadelphia June 24th, and to be present at the following meetings: Haverford Meeting (Orthodox) on the 25th at 11 a. m.; Fellowship of Reconciliation at Haverford College on the 26th; a joint meeting of the different interests of the two Philadelphia Yearly Meetings at 4th and Arch Streets, on June 28th or July 5th; and the Woolman School week-end conference June 30th to July 2nd.

Is it Needed?

A piece of machinery if neglected will rust and decay, a beautiful garden will go to ruin unless cared for and cultivated. In fact everything in the material or natural world requires a certain amount of attention to preserve it and bring it to its highest use. So it is in the mental and spiritual world.

Has thee ever considered how much time is spent in reading the daily papers, the magazines and books that are of only passing interest, and how little time in comparison is given to those books and magazines that have messages of uplift?

Thee may be sure that the Friend who says he *hasn't time* to read the INTELLIGENCER, is not reading any other literature that will keep him in touch with Friendly ideals and principles. He may attend meeting regularly, he may see that the property is kept in good condition, but is he keeping his *spiritual* machinery in shape for its highest use?

Will thee not find out whether the Friends with whom thee comes in contact are taking the paper, and if not, tell them of this last chance to get the INTELLIGENCER for three months for thirty-five cents? The offer expires on Seventh month 1st.

American Friends' Service Committee

WILBUR K. THOMAS, EX. SEC.
20 S. 12th St. Philadelphia.

CASH CONTRIBUTIONS
WEEK ENDING JUNE 5TH

Five Years Meetings	$177.05
Other Meetings:	
Wrightstown Monthly Meeting, Pa.	26.00
Contributions for Germany	417.45
For Austria	1,156.00
For Poland	822.37
For Armenia	10.00
For Syria	30.00
For Russia	6,701.69
For Russian Overhead	5.00
For German Overhead	306.26
For Home Service, West Virginia	25.00
For General	592.54
For Clothing	137.61
Refunds	71.97
	$10,478.94

STATEMENT OF CASH CONTRIBUTIONS RECEIVED FOR THE MONTH OF MAY FROM THE PHILADELPHIA YEARLY MEETING OF FRIENDS, HELD AT 15TH AND RACE STREETS

Newtown (Delaware Co.) Prep. by M. T. Dutton	$20.00
Abington Mo. by D. L. Lewis	50.00
Wilmington Mo. by S. H. Stradley	934.00
Darby Mo. by W. R. White	50.00
	$1,054.00

Shipments received during week ending June 3, 1922: 11 packages.

ON TO RICHMOND!

REGULAR MEETINGS

OAKLAND, CALIF. — A FRIENDS' Meeting is held every First-day at 11 A. M., in the Extension Room, Y. W. C. A. Building, Webster Street, above 14th. Visiting Friends always welcome.

FRIENDS' MEETING IN PASADENA, California — Orange Grove Monthly Meeting of Friends, 520 East Orange Grove Avenue, Pasadena, California. Meeting for worship, First-day, 11 A. M. Monthly Meeting, the second First-day of each month, at 1.45 P. M.

CENTRAL MEETING OF FRIENDS (Chicago), meets every First-day in Room 706, 410 South Michigan Avenue, at 10.45 A. M. Visitors are invited.

FUN

Mr. Augustus Linkins, of Sunvillo, Ala., was reading an old newspaper in which he chanced upon an item he thought might interest his friend. "I observes by dis papah," said Mr. Linkins, "dat de smallest cows in de world is to be found in de South Seas. Dis papah says dat de average weight of sich a cow does not exceed one hundred an' fifty pounds." "Does yo' suppose," asked his listener, "dat dat's where dey gits de condensed milk from?"—*Harper's Magazine.*

The Friends' Intelligencer

ESTABLISHED 1844 | SIXTH MONTH 24, 1922 | VOLUME 79 NUMBER 25

Contents

EDITORIALS

REGULAR MEETINGS

OAKLAND, CALIF. — A FRIENDS' Meeting is held every First-day at 11 A. M., in the Extension Room, Y. W. C. A. Building, Webster Street, above 14th. Visiting Friends always welcome.

FRIENDS' MEETING IN PASADENA, California — Orange Grove Monthly Meeting of Friends, 520 East Orange Grove Avenue, Pasadena, California. Meeting for worship, First-day, 11 A. M. Monthly Meeting, the second First-day of each month, at 1.45 P. M.

CENTRAL MEETING OF FRIENDS (Chicago), meets every First-day in Room 706, 410 South Michigan Avenue, at 10.45 A. M. Visitors are invited.

THE FRIENDS' INTELLIGENCER

Published weekly, 140 N. 15th Street, Philadelphia, Pa., by Friends' Intelligencer Association, Ltd.

PAUL W. WAGER, *Editor.*
SUE C. YERKES, *Business Manager*

Subscription rates: United States, Mexico, Cuba and Panama, $2.50 per year. Canada and other foreign countries, $3.00 per year. Checks should be made payable to Friends' Intelligencer Association, Ltd.

Entered as Second Class Matter at Philadelphia Post Office

TRANSIENT ACCOMMODATIONS

SCHOOLS.

To the Lot Holders and others interested in Fairhill Burial Ground:

GREEN STREET Monthly Meeting has funds available for the encouragement of the practice of cremating the dead to be interred in Fairhill Burial Ground. We wish to bring this fact as prominently as possible to those who may be interested. We are prepared to undertake the expense of cremation in case any lot holder desires us to do so.

Those interested should communicate with William H. Gaskill, Treasurer of the Committee of Interments, Green Street Monthly Meeting, or any of the following members of the Committee.

William H. Gaskill, 3201 Arch St.
Samuel N. Longstreth, 1218 Chestnut St.
Charles F. Jenkins, 232 South Seventh St.
Stuart S. Graves, 3033 Germantown Ave.

HOTELS.

The Friends' Intelligencer

The religion of Friends is based on faith in the "INWARD LIGHT," or direct revelation of God's spirit and will in every seeking soul.

The INTELLIGENCER is interested in all who bear the name of Friends in every part of the world, and aims to promote love, unity and intercourse among all branches and with all religious societies.

ESTABLISHED 1844 | PHILADELPHIA, SIXTH MONTH 24, 1922 | VOLUME 79 NUMBER 25

The Lincoln Memorial

Once a year the busy life of a nation pauses to give reverent praise to its honored dead. This year Memorial Day was particularly significant for it witnessed the dedication of the Lincoln Memorial. The fifty-seven years which have elapsed since Lincoln's martyrdom have but served to engrave his name more deeply in the hearts of his countrymen. As President Harding so well says: "The true measure of Lincoln is his place today in the heart of American citizenship."

Like all courageous men Lincoln made many enemies. Unalterable in his defense of right, steadfast in pursuing a single course, he was the victim of violent criticism and abuse. Naturally kindly and sensitive, these attacks must have bruised his tender heart. But time is a great solvent. Hatreds, jealousies, fears have all melted away. Only the things of the spirit,—truth, beauty, and goodness,—are eternal. Today Lincoln is immortally enshrined in the affections of a grateful people and unanimously accorded a place above any of his contemporaries.

At the dedication ceremonies white-haired veterans in Union blue and Confederate gray mingled tears as they saw their common friend honored by a united nation. President Harding in his moving address visioned the joy that would have been Lincoln's could he have been present to see these one-time foes "each with a common pride and all with a common confidence in the future of this reunited country." And finally what finer tribute could have been paid to Lincoln than to choose as the first speaker on this impressive occasion, Dr. Robert R. Moton, President of Tuskegee Institute, and a representative of that race which Lincoln freed from the shackles of slavery.

No Reduction in the Army

Friends of disarmament will find little encouragement in the Senate's action in increasing the army beyond the figure fixed by the House. An army of 115,000 and an appropriation of $288,000,000 was voted by the House. The Senate increases the personnel of the army to 133,000 and the appropriation to $334,000,000. The compromise measure will probably approach the Senate figures, for 130,000 is the minimum army strength demanded by General Pershing and the Administration. This means that next year the army will remain practically as it is now. Though the Treasury is facing a deficit, the government will spend next year more than three times as much for the army as it did in 1914.

Relief in taxation is not, however, the biggest argument for reduction of our military establishment. We have missed a great opportunity to prove to the world our faith in the platform announced at the Washington Conference. We cannot convince the world of our entire sincerity in urging disarmament unless we ourselves are willing to make a venture of faith. We took a bold step in naval reduction and the response of the world was overwhelming. There was a universal sigh of relief for a great load had been lifted. A similar bold step in military reduction would have increased the faith of the world tremendously.

There is something else which will injure the world's faith in us more than our failure to reduce our army. That is to increase the expenditure for experimentation in chemical warfare. This particular appropriation was increased 50 per cent. or from $500,000 to $750,000. The clause in the Naval Treaty which forbids the use of poison gas in warfare was hailed as one of the most humane and important achievements of the conference. If gas warfare has been outlawed what excuse or right have we to experiment further with its possibilities? Some will say how do we know that other nations are not experimenting in secret. The answer is, take them at their word and fulfil our part of the contract. One of the foundation principles of business is the inviolability of contract. Why can there not be in international relations the same degree of good faith and responsibility? By continuing and increasing research in the field of chemical warfare we are certainly violating the spirit of the treaty. Gas warfare is an outlawed institution and the American people ought to see to it that no further appropriations are made for its support. Let us, as Friends, voice our protest without delay.

For Sincerity and Courage

The 1922 General Epistle from Philadelphia Yearly Meeting

DEAR FRIENDS:

Prompted by a concern which has several times found expression in our meetings this year, we feel constrained to center this message to our sister Yearly Meetings around a single point—the need for ever-deepening sincerity and courage in every phase of our individual and corporate lives.

As followers of Jesus of Nazareth, we must be content to measure ourselves by no other standard than that of unflinching sincerity and courage which he established; a standard which condemns self-righteous religious leaders, and which extends fellowship to "publicans and sinners." Measured in the light of that standard, all of us realize the necessity for growth toward a fuller spiritual stature. We realize that we have only haltingly and partially answered the call of humanity for spiritual leadership.

Our service abroad has rendered one splendid contribution by relieving suffering and stimulating faith in Christian idealism, and has won world-wide recognition for our religious Society. Our activities along educational, philanthropic and social lines have in many cases worked toward the development of a more enlightened way of life. The vision, courage and sincerity of the founders of our Society, and of those who have since labored for its ideals, have left us standards which we believe have preserved Friends from many of the common prejudices of our day.

But opposed to these assets, and in the face of the opportunity for leadership which they afford, we recognize many points in which we must strive for higher development. In many of our corporate activities, such as the labors of our committees and the answering of our queries, we must work against a tendency toward formalism; avoiding subservience to the letter, and judging every word and every act in the light of its relation to simple truth and to present-day needs. We must fear the danger of self-complacency, the danger of accepting as though they were universally applied, principles which we have only perceived, or which we have only applied under abnormal conditions abroad.

We must likewise strengthen ourselves in regard to the principle of love, which, rather than that of force, we accept as the basis of our relations with others. We must not only perceive the truth of this principle in theory, but must apply it to all phases of the activity in which we share; to international and social, to racial and industrial, relations. In several of these fields, centuries of tradition have accustomed us, at least in theory, to the application of this principle. In others, do we not find it necessary to overcome in our own minds, the barriers of nationality, social position or economic advantage, before love can find free expression through us?

Whoever attempts uncompromisingly to apply the principle of love to the conditions of his own modern life will find the way tremendously difficult. He will frequently find the path blocked, the trail still to be blazed. But only as we start out in practice to seek the way, however fruitless our first efforts may seem, can the way ever be found. Christianity, Quakerism, is not a challenge which we can throw before the world in words, feeling that we already see the light. It is a challenge to us ourselves to find the way of applying uncompromising love in our own lives, which few of us since the great example of John Woolman have succeeded in doing.

Like all other organized religious bodies, Quakerism stands today at the "cross-roads." If formalism persists, if there is not deepened sincerity, higher courage, new vision along both new lines and old, we cannot permanently hope to offer the forward-looking leadership which the world, for the moment, has come to expect of us.

Sensing humanity's need, kindled to enthusiasm by their first contact with our ideals, members of the coming generation, both within our religious Society and frequently from without, turn to us for far-seeing leadership, for real crusades in which to dare for the coming of the "Kingdom" on earth. If they find that at the heart of our activities is formalism, lack of new vision, inability to adapt ourselves to changing demands of present conditions, they turn away in disillusionment. And in that disillusionment, they may turn not only from faith in organized religious activities, but from all trust in spiritual things.

Conscious of the challenge with which principle, tradition, and present world needs all confront us, shall we not find the vision to choose the true path? We have behind us the inspiring personalities of early Christianity and early Quakerism. Today in India, Mahatma Gandhi is giving a modern example of the power of self-sacrificing love. Shall not we, as Friends of today, likewise follow the adventurous path of spiritual conquest? Shall we not cultivate the humbleness of the little child, seeking to learn rather than feeling that we already know, endeavoring to throw off the fetters which have bound us in the past, striving primarily to apply in our own lives all the high principles which we profess?

Signed on behalf of Philadelphia Yearly Meeting of Friends held at Fifteenth and Race Streets, Fifth month 15th to 19th inclusive.

JANE P. RUSHMORE,
MORGAN BUNTING,
Clerks.

The Meeting for Worship

By ELBERT RUSSELL

First of a series of articles on "Worship"

In the Quaker scheme of life the meeting for worship occupies a central place. What the power plant is to a factory or a detector in the radiophone, the meeting for worship is to the organization and activities of our Society. From our worship we should draw the inspiration for our best service. God is always with us; "in Him we live and move and have our being"; but we are not always conscious of His presence and we need to turn our attention to His presence at times, and listen to His voice. We need to increase our spiritual sensitiveness by the presence, the reverent fellowship, and the spoken experience of other worshippers in order, to be best attuned to the mind of God and most sensitive to his messages. Life cannot be maintained without nitrogen. It constitutes the greater part of the air in which we move and which we breathe, but unless we can assimilate it in some form, it does not add to our life. Certain plants have the power to draw nitrogen from the air and work it up into forms that we can use as food. Means have recently been devised by means of which nitrogen can be taken directly from the air and converted into fertilizers. Worship is a function in which we should be able in like manner to draw directly from God's immanent presence the sustenance of our spiritual life.

The value of the meeting for worship can only be increased by increasing its ministry to men's spiritual needs. We can increase the interest and attendance at meetings permanently only by increasing the reality of the worship. That alone will make it worth while to attend regularly. Various efforts are made by churches to add to the attractiveness of public worship; but these will be only temporary in their results, if they attempt anything else than better ministration to men's spiritual needs. The meeting cannot successfully maintain itself as an amusement or educational centre; it cannot compete with literary clubs, lecture courses, the Chautauqua platform, or "the movies" on their own ground. We need not hope materially to strengthen the Society of Friends unless we can increase the vitality of the meeting for worship. It will be useless to persuade our neighbors to come if they are not fed. It will not be worth while to change or add to the machinery of the organization, unless there is a corresponding increase in spiritual power. As a Society we are face to face with a wonderful opportunity and a serious demand for service. Only by a very great increase in spiritual power and earnestness can we meet this opportunity successfully. Our efforts to gird ourselves for the task should begin with and in the meeting for worship. If we come so vitally into contact with God there that our devotion is intensified, our vision cleared, and our powers enhanced, men will feel the stimulus of our consecration and the attraction of the spirit of Christ through us. Men will begin to say, as the Hebrew prophet predicted of his people, "We will go with you, for we have heard that God is with you."

Christianity and Economic Problems

IX

What Changes In Control Would Most Benefit Industry?

(Reduced to Summary Form)

The first step in determining what sort of control would most benefit industry is the selection of principles as the basis of judgment. It would seem that the value of any system of control depends upon two factors, its effects upon production and its effects upon human relations.

Let us examine various types of control and seek to determine, in the light of the effects upon production and upon human relations, what changes in control would most benefit industry.

(1) *Exclusive control by owners and stockholders.* The only possible answer to this question that occurs to many persons is exclusive control by owners and stockholders. The opinion of Judge E. H. Gary, Chairman of the United States Steel Corporation, concerning the control of industry by security holders, is widely accepted. Judge Gary says: "These must be recognized as rightfully in control. Their capital permits the existence . . . of the corporation. They properly may and ultimately will dictate the personnel, . . rates of compensation to employees, . . . terms and conditions of employment, and all other matters pertaining to the properties and business and management of the corporation. After the honest fulfillment of all obligations to others, they are entitled, not only to a fair and reasonable return on their investments, but to all the net proceeds of the business; otherwise, they could not be expected to leave their capital in the enterprise in question."

Does exclusive control by owners increase efficiency? Does it leave the workers at the mercy of the employers? What are its effects upon the equitable distribution of the proceeds of industry?

(2) *Control Through Employees' Representation.* Many experiments are now being made with various types of shop committees and other forms of employees' representation. The degree of power exercised by the workers varies greatly in the different schemes.

One example is that of William Filene's Sons Company, of Boston, which has an organization of employees known as the Filene Co-operative Association. This is a self-governing body consisting of every employee of the company from the highest paid official to the lowest paid salesgirl. The F. C. A. may initiate new store rules, working conditions or relations, wages or any other matters, except policies of business. Any measure vetoed by the management may be passed over the veto by a ballot vote of two-thirds of the membership of the F. C. A. The Arbitration Board is composed of twelve members, elected by the employees in various sections of the store. The management as such has no representation on the Arbitration Board. Of the eleven members of the Board of Directors of the Company, four are employees nominated by the F. C. A. and elected by the stockholders. The retail clerks are not organized but the company maintains working agreements with various unions of teamsters, printers, engineers, etc. The plan, with modifications, has been in operation for more than twenty years and has met with great success.

In what ways does employees' representation increase or decrease production? In what way does it improve or impair human relations?

(3) *Workers' Control.* This term has been given several different meanings. In certain sections it means exclusive control by hand-workers, "the dictatorship of the proletarist." The number of persons in the United States who believe in this sort of workers' control is exceedingly small.

Another meaning is that the workers shall have representation on the national administrative body of the industry and on the grievance committees in the shop. Many experiments are now being made with this type of workers' control. The degree of power exercised by the workers varies greatly in the different schemes. One of the most notable agreements is that between Hart, Schaffner & Marx, one of the large clothing manufacturers of Chicago, and the Amalgamated Clothing Workers, an unusually strong national union. This agreement has a very wide range and includes wages, hours, preference of union members in hiring, working conditions, discipline, etc. Throughout the ten years of its operation this labor agreement has met with notable success in promoting "such co-operation and good will between employers, foremen, union and workers as will prevent misunderstanding and friction and make for good team work, good business, mutual advantage and mutual respect."

Still another meaning is that the means of production should be entirely in the hands of workers by hand and brain. Under this form of control every person doing useful work in an industry—whether it be as a laborer, mechanic, foreman, clerk or administrative officer—would be regarded as a worker and as such would be entitled to a share in the control of the industry. This would mean the elimination of owners from any share in the control of industry. Owners would be paid a regular rate of interest upon invested capital or there would be co-operative or public ownership of the industry. The National Building Guild of England is making a significant and very successful experiment with this latter method of control.

What effects would an adequate representation of workers by hand and brain on the national administrative body of the industry and on local grievance committees have upon production? Upon human relations? Is it practicable to place entire control of an industry in the hands of the persons employed in that industry—hand-workers, clerical workers and administrative officers? Would it be unfair to investors simply to pay them regular interest on invested capital and relieve them of all responsibility for the control of industry?

(4) *Consumers' Control.* Another type of control of industry is found in the co-operative movement. The primary purpose of the co-operative movement is the elimination of middle men, getting products into the hands of the consumer direct from the producer.

The most successful kind of consumers' co-operation is that known as the Rochdale Plan, so-called because it was first adopted by a group of poor weavers in Rochdale, England. The minimum rate of interest is paid on invested capital. At the end of the year the surplus-savings, or profits, are used for the common social good of the members or distributed as savings-returns in proportion to purchases.

It is estimated that about 30 million families are now represented in the international co-operative movement. In the British Isles, especially, the movement has assumed huge proportions. There are more than 1,400 societies, with more than four million members, and 187,000 employees, with an annual sale for factories, wholesale and retail stores of approximately a billion and a half dollars, and an annual net surplus of 100 million dollars to be divided among the members. A number of "fake" co-operative schemes have failed in America and this has tended to discredit the whole idea of consumers' co-operation in our country. Long experience in many countries, however, has demonstrated that the co-operative movement can be carried on successfully if the Rochdale principles are followed.

Does the co-operative movement provide a way for greater efficiency in the distribution of the products of industry? Is co-operation in distribution more likely or less likely to improve human relations? Are there any types of industry in which co-operation is not practicable?

(6) *State Control.* The question of state control in industry is so complex and important that we propose devoting our next chapter to a consideration of the various aspects of the subject. Our final evaluation of the merits of different types of control in industry must, therefore, await discussion in the succeeding chapter.

The House of Terror

Our daily round, even in the heart of the Russian famine area, is often a normal one of office work, warehousing and household business, or it may be a round of visits to children's homes, hospitals and kitchens—all of them distressing enough, but at least doing the best any one could with his slender resources, and keeping most of the kiddies alive until better times come.

But always in the background runs the plaintive minor note of wailing at our doors, or windows, always a mournful voice begging a bit of bread, a pinched face peering in and pleading for life for another day. They pace the streets by day and always a few filter into the office and sometimes even to our living quarters. Always we must turn them away empty and ignore the pleading. We must feed those we can reach every day; not yet have we enough to touch them all, and our lists are full. So we tell ourselves, but I can never convince myself that is the answer Christ would make. As yet we find no other course. We try not to see them and to forget by plunging hard into the mountain of work always at hand.

But what becomes of these poor bits of human driftwood? Some few find their way into the children's homes, but they have supplies for never more than five new ones each day, and the others must pass on and sleep in sheds or empty houses, or drop down and die in the snow. At last by the earnest efforts of the big-hearted and untiring head of the local Soviet a small house was repaired and some fuel secured. Here each day the current washes up a few more derelicts, and they sit in the sun at the door or herd together inside for greater warmth.

For days and weeks I have passed this house but never entered. I had no business there of any sort, and there is always enough that is harrowing without touching any that is avoidable. That visit could wait until some one wanted to know the worst, and then I could check up on the tales that are told of this House of Terror.

Visits there will be by request only. Our Field Director, who arrived the other day, is very much on the job and wants to see everything. I've not wanted to take the interpreters because they already receive the full brunt of horrors and begging more than we do. However, a new worker came along and wished to see everything before going on to open up her new outpost, so the time had come to see the worst.

It is an attractive enough little one-story house, and the day was a beautiful, still, sunny one, so three mites were basking in the sun on the steps. One could hear the wailing, and, as we pushed open the door of a tiny corridor, it came like the sound of a mournful sea and with it came a horrible smell. The next door, and we faced the two rooms with only a wide built-in bench as furniture. On this bench and the floor and piled against the walls and stove are bundles of ragged moaning wretches, about a hundred of them, some dying, others already dead. Every day the one attendant of the place cleans it and pulls out from 20 to 30 dead bodies to cart off to the burial trench.

March 20, 1922. BEULAH A. HURLEY.

Dear Heart!

Faint not! though hard seems the pressure, dear heart;
Pure gold is had through refining.
'Though fierce and long seems the battle, dear heart;
'Twill aid, doubt not, your refining.

All sunshine kills even a plant, dear heart;
Storms, too, they need to perfect them.
The darkness of night is as needful, dear heart,
As noon-day sun to perfect them.

Then whether in "sunshine" or "tempest," dear heart,
Still trust in God's wisdom and power.
He will pilot you safely through all, dear heart,
And supply your *real* needs every hour.

Just continue to "do your best," dear heart;
'Though discouragements do creep in.
Our Father is still "at the helm," dear heart;
To help you to conquer—to win!

GERTRUD HALLOCK.

New York Yearly Meeting

Evening Meetings

FIRST-DAY, FIFTH MONTH 28TH

"Can Economic Relations be Ethical?" an address by Scott Nearing, under the Young Friends' Movement.

During the last few years, the problems connected with economics have been very important. They will be much more important in the next few years. They are so important because they are vital. We do not notice the processes of digestion unless something goes wrong. We do not notice the social processes until they go wrong.

Now what are economic relations? They are the relations which are connected with the living we get. For purposes of this discussion, let me now define "ethical" as "for the betterment of ourselves or our fellows." Society has, at one stage or another, called many things ethical which do not now seem so to us,—as slavery.

Economic relations refer to the means of making a living. The question is can these economic relations be ethical,—can they be to the advantage of every group of people? I shall not discuss the question of whether they are ethical or not; if they were, we should not hear so much about them.

The United States is one of the richest countries in the world. It could supply its people with all the necessaries of life. Yet industrial depressions come again and again. The present one has lasted since 1920. It is the seventeenth since 1820. Seventeen times the economic machinery has broken down, making the only thought of the people food, when they should have a chance for higher things.

Some of our economic relations can be made ethical by individuals, others only by the community. If I owe you a dollar, and pay it, I am being honest and ethical. There are children in New York City who are hungry because their father's wages are too low. That is a problem which must be met by the community. Now take one or two problems, and let us see how unethical relations can be made ethical.

All that we have is the product of somebody's labors. Therefore, if I wear a suit of clothes, I wear labor; if I drink milk, I drink labor. The normal processes of society stop when labor stops. Who shall do this labor,—make clothes, clean the streets? Somebody must.

Interest is described in economic books as "the result of abstinence." Now, it is the means by which, through my ownership of bonds, securities, etc., I can let somebody else do the work. The income statistics of 1913 show that only a few thousand people had incomes of $200 a week and, generally speaking, these people do not work. Those who really work get $25 a week, $50 a week, $100. The rule should be that each person in the community should produce as much as he takes. Until we do produce as much as we take, we are living an unethical life.

If you steal my three-dollar watch today, you get twenty years. But if you own millions of dollars, you are a great man, and can pass it on to your son, who never lifted a finger to earn it. The economic system will not be ethical until each of us produces as much as he takes, making shoes, or newspapers, or teaching, or singing,—all services that the community wants. Unless you are very young or very old, or crippled, each should do this. We can see how ethical this is, and we can find the command in the Old Testament, "He that will not work, neither shall he eat."

In the second place, it is necessary for each to give as much as he receives. It is also necessary for me to see that my neighbor receives as much as he gives. The report of the New York State Industrial Commission for February, 1922, shows that the average weekly wage at that time was $24.22. The Labor Bureau estimates that for a family of five, the need for decent living is about $45 a week. Yet the average wage is under $25.

In 1918, the payment of dividends was about 285 millions of dollars; in 1921 it was 290 millions. Yet in this year 1921, three and one-half million people were out of work. If we wish ethical advantages to one another, we must see that our neighbors get the value of what they produce. If I get enough money, I can get $100 a week without working at all. The man who makes $100 a week may get only $25 for his work.

In New York City there are hundreds of men and women with hundreds of dollars a week income who give little for it. In New York City, there are thousands of children who suffer because wages are so low. A state where children go hungry is not ethical.

You and I are more or less free economically. If we are not free economically, we go to some man, and say, "May I go to work for the New York Central, or the Steel Corporation?" and are told, "You may go to work," or if there is no work, we are told to move on. If we get the job, we hold it at the will of the employer. We may be turned off any day. Such a man has no status in his job. If I own a job, I am a free man. If I work on another man's job, I am a slave. I am not bound to one particular job, but I am bound to a job. And if I don't get the job, I go hungry. If I own the machine, the rake, the tools, the man who works for me is economically "my man." Such a relation is unethical. The job-taker should be the job-owner. When our right to be economically free as a State is denied, it is an unethical thing, and a community cannot exist on unethical foundations.

The old relation between the job-owner and job-taker breaks down in ethics. For thousands of years, men worked in agricultural communities. On that foundation, we have built an industrial organization, and that is breaking down. That is the price we are paying for progress. But economic relations must be made ethical. In the last analysis, ethical relations are advantageous.

The organization of society must be so constituted that nobody can go without work. Our industrial experiment of one hundred and fifty years' standing was nearly wrecked in Europe. Until these simple problems of food, clothing, shelter, are settled, we cannot feel that we are on an ethical basis.

Sooner or later, society will do its work with the least possible labor, and in the most ethical way, using machinery, etc. We want food, clothing, shelter, education, with time for more important things. It is questionable whether a part of the established order like the church would do anything because it has property. It has pipe-organs, vested choirs, paid ministers, and it has expenses which must be met by propertied people. It should be, however, the spiritual guide of the people. It should seek out the facts, and state the ethics of the facts, without fear.

Second-day, Fifth Month 29th

On Second-day night, the 29th, Helena Hill Weed, Secretary of the Haiti-Santos Domingo Independence League spoke at 7 o'clock, under arrangements made by the Young Friends' Movement, upon the general topic of "Haiti and the American Occupation." Fragmentary notes upon her talk are as follows:

It is a question of financial slavery in Haiti. Haiti does not want a loan, or need a loan. She has a loan now placed in Europe. But that is not due for thirty years, and the interest is paid. Please remember that, for your papers will tell you that Haiti is in debt and in arrears with the interest. Moreover, France does not want this loan paid off. Haiti's financial matters have nothing to do with the occupation.

Yet it is financial interests which have brought it about,—the financial interests of cotton, sugar, etc., which are urging the United States on. The cotton and sugar interests recently got 200,000 acres of the richest land in the country. They are exploiting the land and the people, forcing workers to work here at a fixed wage of twenty cents a day, while in Cuba and Porto Rico, wages are $1.75 a day. This is done in our name; what are we going to do about it?

About 75 per cent. of the people of the cities in Haiti are educated; in the country about 25 per cent. They are a gentle, friendly people. When they broke away from the French in 1804, the population was mainly African slaves. There was a very small leaven of education. They had nothing; no culture, no anything. Their progress has been amazing. Haiti started the movement that abolished slavery in South America.

Here is what we are doing. The European loan is to be paid, in spite of the protests of the European nations who do not want it paid, and of Haiti, who does not want to pay it. The bonds of the National City Bank are to be paid in full. Land is to be developed in the interest of cotton and sugar interests. The whole story is sordid, gross and evil. The interests doing this are to be investigated by the Attorney-General.

The Secretary of the Navy said that we took Haiti because if we had not, Germany would have done so. He forgot to mention that in 1915, France landed sailors there, and Haiti protested. That is never mentioned. But France had actually taken possession. There had been some small outbreaks, but nothing serious.

The civilization of Haiti is like that of southern France. Culture is shown by the care of the dead. Haitian cemeteries, even the small ones, are neat and beautiful. There is more soap per capita imported to Haiti than to any other country in the world. Even in the slum districts, the streets are wide and pretty,—and they were paved before the occupation. They have neatly dressed school children, handsome tropical public buildings, good hospitals, with trim nurses and doctors, all the signs of a developing nation. The Americans went to Haiti and "Jim Crowed" the negroes. For instance, there is a certain hotel in the mountains, a delightful and much frequented resort. The American officers took a fancy to it, and gave orders that no negroes should be served there in future.

Mrs. Weed's pictures illustrated all these points, and showed much of the beautiful scenery and of civilization of Haiti. Her closing pictures showed several men who had been tortured by American Marines to make them confess things about which they knew nothing. One man who had been accused of theft was seared with red-hot irons on one day; on another had alternate cold and boiling water poured over him. On the third day they were about to apply even worse tortures when his innocence was shown. It was two years before he recovered. The speaker was careful to say that not all the commands of Marines were guilty of such things; but that some were, and that the deeds of these have been shielded and covered up. In 1918, an official was asked why the President had not been informed. "Well, you see he is in Paris talking about what the Germans did, and it would embarrass him to know that our men did just as bad things."

ANNA L. CURTIS.

(To be concluded next week)

An Impressive Letter

The following letter was written recently by Miss Alice Butler, a Presbyterian Missionary-teacher in Ginling College, Nanking, China, to her parents at Rockville, Indiana. A friend of the family sent a copy of the letter to Harlow Lindley of Earlham College, thinking that as a Friend and possible acquaintance of Henry T. Hodgkin, he would be interested. The letter is doubly significant, having been written not for publication and with no thought of it even being read by Friends.

Some privileges come to us in far away lands that are rare in the home country and one of these has been ours in Ginling recently. I thought that I had been greatly favored when I had the chance of hearing Fosdick twice daily for eight days, but while I still think he was a very great blessing I think we have had a greater one. I wonder if you have ever heard of Henry T. Hodgkin. He is an English Friend, or Quaker, and one of the original group that started the Fellowship of Reconciliation. As a Friend he was opposed to war, but he makes you feel that war is certainly un-Christ-like. When I first heard of him I would not go to hear him, for I had no use for Pacifists. This fall we heard that he was to be in Nanking for two weeks at Christmas time, and it was suggested that we invite him and his wife to be with us at that time. Well, I was not at all enthusiastic, but I agreed when the others wanted it and so he was asked.

They were ideal guests, they were here for two weeks and though we are a very busy family and have not much leisure for company, we were very loath to have them go and they seemed to hate to leave, too.

The Fellowship of Reconciliation has many other positive convictions in addition to the position of not fighting. Please notice that I do not say non-resistance, for they stand for the strongest kind of resistance, that is spiritual resistance. Peace as a method has not been given a full chance to prove itself and now that war has not brought peace, might we not try peace? For seventy years the Quakers in Pennsylvania with no military force whatever had no trouble with the Indians while all the other colonies were fighting.

I have not yet come to the point of joining the F. O. R. for its standard is so high that it makes you think. And one thing that it makes me think is—why do not the churches have in practice as high a standard or one that challenges as much thought. And I find that I am not the only one of our group, that is doing some strenuous thinking. Two of the strongest of them are having the same questions confronting them, and I do not know how many more.

I hope that I have not given you the impression that Dr. Hodgkin was out here in the interests of this movement only. He was giving lectures before the students of the universities and colleges of Nanking on different topics connected with world politics.

And I hope, too, that I have not made you think that he is down on every one who does not see his way. That is far from true. He realizes the difficulty of taking the step that he has taken and the fact that many honest thinking Christians do not agree that it is right belief. He has all respect for the man who disagrees with his views, and will spend hours answering the questions of a doubter, and as he answers you realize that he has thought out all sides of the question and that it was not a snap judgment.

Of course one of the first questions asked is, "What should one do if his nation goes to war," and he replies to that by saying that he knows the difficulty of that position for his nation did. But it was chance guided by an overruling Providence that made him a citizen of England. He by his own choice later became a citizen of a greater Kingdom, the Kingdom of God, and to this he owes his first allegiance. The early church for three hundred years, or until the church and state became united, thought that Christians should not fight and they refused to take part in wars of those days.

Whether you agree with the conclusions that Dr. Hodgkin and his friends reached or not, you at least have put in some hours of hard thinking that surely are beneficial and constructive.

Please put this name down in your memory so that if you ever have the opportunity to hear him you will not miss it. All of us who have had the chance to get to know them crave for our friends at home the same privilege. Don't let it slip if it ever comes your way.

Extracts from a letter which appeared in full in a recent issue of the American Friend.—ED.

Swarthmore's Fiftieth Commencement

Swarthmore's Fiftieth Commencement was truly a memorable occasion; the spirit of the exercises was expressive of the same spirit of optimism which has guided the College so successfully in the past and promises so much for the future.

One of the features of the morning was the awarding of honorary degrees to M. Carey Thomas, retiring president of Bryn Mawr; Rufus M. Jones, Professor of Philosophy at Haverford, and Thomas A. Jenkins, Professor of French at the University of Chicago. The degree was awarded to President Thomas for her work at Bryn Mawr, to Rufus M. Jones for his contribution to Quaker history and literature, and to Thomas A. Jenkins for his work on old French literature.

Dr. Samuel McChord Crothers, Preacher to Harvard University, delivered the Commencement address. His subject was "The Challenge of George Fox to the Twentieth Century," and he stressed the great need for reconciling wisdom in this world of human relations, pointing out that the George Fox of the Twentieth Century is the one who challenges every institution to show why it should be supported.

President Aydelotte then announced the awarding of the Ivy Medal to Richard W. Slocum, and the newly established Oak Leaf Medal to Barbara Manley. Scholarship and fellowship awards were then made public, and the Commencement exercises of the Class of 1922 were brought to a close when President Aydelotte conferred A. B. degrees upon the ninety-five members of the graduating class.

At the Alumni dinner on Seventh-day, the 10th, both dining-rooms were crowded to capacity and the spirit of all was that there must be still stronger support in the future and greater co-operation between the Alumni and the College for the building of a greater Swarthmore.

(For a very full and interesting account of all the exercises in connection with the Commencement, we suggest sending for a copy of "The Phoenix," for June 12th, from which the above notes were taken.)

Friends' General Conference

Richmond, Ind., August 26th-September 2, 1922

ADVANCE PROGRAM

August 26th

8.00 p. m.—Opening address by the Chairman, Arthur C. Jackson. "Fundamentals," Wilson S. Doan.

August 27th

Meeting for Worship—Morning and Evening

3.00 p. m.—Young Friends' Session, addresses, "The High Road," by William J. Reagan and others.

August 28th

10.00 a. m.—"Enforcement," Commissioner Roy A. Haynes.
11.00 a. m.—Round Table on Enforcement.
2.30 p. m.—Industrial Relations, Alva W. Taylor.
8.00 p. m.—Address on an Educational Subject, Frank Aydelotte.

August 29th

10.00 a. m.—Round Table on Education.
8.00 p. m.—"The Quaker Faith," George A. Walton.

August 30th

10.00 a. m.—"Future Peace Work of the Society of Friends," Jesse H. Holmes.
11.00 a. m.—Round Table on Future Peace Work in the Society of Friends.
8.00 p. m.—"How Can We Abolish War in Our Time?" Frederick J. Libby.

August 31st

10.00 a. m.—"Future Service of the Society of Friends," Lucy Biddle Lewis.
11.00 a. m.—Round Table on Future Service of the Society of Friends.
2.30 p. m.—Conference activities.
8.00 p. m.—"The Basis of Christian Unity," Charles Foster Kent.

September 1st

10.00 a. m.—"The Solution of Industry's Problems," Charles Foster Kent.
11.00 a. m.—Round Table on Prof. Kent's addresses.
2.30 p. m.—"The Causes of War and the Next Steps Toward Peace," J. Russell Smith. "A Next Step—The Teaching of History," Harlow Lindley.
8.00 p. m.—"Recreation and Religion," Charles Foster Kent.

September 2nd

10.00 a. m.—"The Way to Find Happiness," Charles Foster Kent.

Friendly News Notes

Dr. O. Edward Janney, Executive Secretary of the General Conference Section of Friends' Disarmament Council, in summing up the work being done by Friends in this country in the interest of peace states: "We have held a large number of meetings, distributed a vast amount of literature, joined and given much financial support to the National Council for the Reduction of Armaments, and assisted in creating a public sentiment that made the work of the Washington Conference possible. We did our part, too, in urging our Senate to ratify the four treaties placed before it by the Conference."

"Our energies are now directed towards the education of the children of our country. Our first step is to eliminate from all text-books as much reference to the conduct of the wars of the past as possible, but emphasize the causes leading to them. The next step is to reach those who are in training to become teachers, so that, through them the right ideas may be taught to the children in the schools. There are scores of such training schools throughout the country, and as many of these as possible will be reached this summer. At these I shall make an address on 'The Educational Approach to a War-less World.'"

COMMENCEMENT AT GEORGE SCHOOL

On June 15th George School held its twenty-eighth annual commencement. The day was perfect and a large number of alumnæ and friends gathered to enjoy the exercises. There were thirty-five in the graduating class, a number which has never been exceeded, and equalled only twice.

After Bible reading by the Principal, George A. Walton, two of the graduates had place on the program. Mildred A. Michener gave an oration entitled "Unsung Heroes," and Arthur G. Jackson an essay entitled "Retrospect." Both were exceptionally well rendered. The principal address was delivered by Dr. Clifford B. Connelley, Commissioner of Labor and Industry of Pennsylvania. The central theme of his talk was a challenge to the young men and women of today to carry on the unfinished work which the great leaders of yesterday had so nobly begun. Mr. Walton, in a farewell message to the graduates thanked them for their spirit of co-operation and the initiative which they had displayed in assuming responsibility for school discipline. The presentation of diplomas completed the exercises.

SALEM QUARTERLY MEETING

At Salem Quarterly Meeting, held Sixth month 8th, at Salem, N. J., a very good report of the work of the recent Yearly Meeting was given by the representatives and others, and much appreciation of the faithful service of Sarah Griscom was expressed. Rachel M. Lippincott, Isaac Wilson, Emily R. Kirby, Joel Borton and others spoke very acceptably.

Louisa Powell, chairman of the Philanthropic Committee, presented two communications, one protesting against appropriations for the making of gas or any other poisonous liquid; the other, a declaration against any modification of the Volstead Act which would admit wine or beer or otherwise weaken enforcement. The Quarterly Meeting minuted the latter concern, and gave publicity to it in the local papers, stating that the members would do all in their power to insure the election in Eleventh month of members of the United States Congress and State Legislature who will work for the retention and enforcement of the Eighteenth Amendment and the Volstead Code. The resolution was signed by the clerk, Warner Underwood, and forwarded to Washington. RACHEL L. BORDEN.

BALTIMORE QUARTERLY MEETING

Among those present at Baltimore Quarterly Meeting were Frederick J. Libby, who spoke on the importance of the united efforts of Friends; Isaac Wilson, George Warner, Daniel Batchellor, who said "Let us bear Fruit, not leaves only"; and O. Edward Janney, who urged that we hold fast to what has been gained by us in regard to a reasonable faith, which is based on the life and teachings of Jesus.

A strong appeal was adopted asking President Harding to investigate the situation as to the political prisoners still held in Leavenworth prison and to pardon them if conditions justify such action.

Friends in each Monthly Meeting represented were urged to send students to the summer term at Woolman School. Also that each meeting see that one or two young people be encouraged in a practical way to attend the Richmond Conference.

Lunch was served both Sunday and Monday under the shade of the beautiful trees in the grove wherein the vine-covered meeting-house nestles. There was the usual large attendance, many coming long distances.

In the afternoon conference, Hilda P. Holme gave an interesting address on conditions in Poland. This was followed by addresses on "Approaches to a Warless World," by O. Edward Janney, Frederick J. Libby and Rachel D. DuBois. THOMAS B. HULL, *Clerk.*

WOOLMAN SCHOOL WEEK-END CONFERENCES

The Woolman School week-end conferences this summer are appealing to wide groups of Friends and others both in the Philadelphia vicinity and at a greater distance. They offer an opportunity for a refreshing week-end in the country combined with the inspiration of discussing vital problems of today with some of the most able leaders in their respective fields.

Week-enders come Sixth-day evening and stay until First-day evening. The overflow from Woolman School will be housed in the cottages of Swarthmore College, or in Parrish Hall. Accommodations can be arranged for a single night, or those coming for a day can get meals at Woolman School. On Seventh-day, July 1st, when Henry T. Hodgkin is there, it is anticipated that the crowd will surpass the capacity of the Woolman School kitchen, and it is suggested that those coming for the afternoon and evening bring box supper and picnic on the Woolman School lawn. Registrations should be sent as early as possible to Woolman School, Swarthmore, Pa.

The week-end speakers are as follows:

July 1st—Henry T. Hodgkin and Paul Jones.
July 8th—Frederick J. Libby.
July 15th—Dr. William W. Cadbury.
July 22nd—Kirby Page.
July 29th—Dr. Wm. Byron Forbush.

THE OPEN FORUM

This column is intended to afford free expression of opinion by readers on questions of interest. The INTELLIGENCER *is not responsible for any such opinions. Letters must be brief, and the editor reserves the right to omit parts if necessary to save space.*

"PRISON REFORM AND MENTAL HYGIENE"

To the Editor:

When the Philanthropic Committee of the Philadelphia Yearly Meeting recommended to local Philanthropic Committees that the subject of "Prison Reform and Mental Hygiene" be taken up, the Philanthropic Committee of Orange Grove Meeting, Pasadena, Calif., sent an inquiry to the General Committee in Philadelphia in order to get full information as to the nature of the work and best methods, and at the same time invited Miss Miriam Van Waters, the woman referee of our Juvenile Court, to give a lecture on the subject "Prison Reform and Mental Hygiene."

Nothing has been learned from the Philadelphia Committee, as far as the writer can learn. Denominational success in the matter would probably be best insured if the General Committee would plan and outline the work, recommend best methods, even exercise inspection and supervision of work done, but leave execution, administration and financial risks to the local committees. Public Poor Relief in Massachusetts tends to prove that centralization of the development of the right method, the social program, and decentralization of administration, have produced the best results. For us of Orange Grove Meeting who are largely aged retired Easterners, and who no longer care to undertake new experiments of their own, a ready program supplied by the General Committee in Philadelphia would be all the more desirable and beneficial. And this Philadelphia Committee might be able to agree on a common program with other branches of Friends and recommend work and methods at home to the American Friends' Committee.

More encouragement came from the Referee of our Juvenile Court. On First-day afternoon, May 21st, she gave us a lecture in our meeting-house, opened a new world to us, won our hearts, and gladly promised to address the Monthly Meeting whenever convenient.

Our Juvenile Court Law is a wonderful improvement on the old system that cast the juvenile offenders into common jails and into the company of older criminals, but Miss Van Waters showed how very desirable and important it is to inform and interest the public, to shape and promote a wholesome public opinion and to counteract and banish the influence of picture shows and newspaper funny pictures that inculcate an anti-social code.

When governments persecuted Friends and acquainted them with jails, whipping posts, pillory and stake, the Friends could not help exerting a good influence on the persecutors by their passive resistance and did very much to teach them religious tolerance and more humane methods. This young referee of our Juvenile Court, Miss Van Waters, before whom female offenders under 21 and male offenders under 13 are tried, the daughter of an Episcopalian minister, who knows what Elizabeth Fry and the Quakers have done, now invites us to continue our interest in the courts and prisons, altho we as Friends are no longer persecuted, indeed she seems to expect us to turn the tables and to become persecutors, moral persecutors, using spiritual weapons, and to be ever at the heels of public officials who too often get intoxicated with power and sink back into brutality and savagery.

Very sincerely yours,

Los Angeles, Calif., June 2, 1922. C. M. ENNS.

BIRTHS

PAUL—On Fifth month 29th, in Philadelphia, to David G. and Mary Kirk Griest Paul, a daughter, named Mary Catharine.

DEATHS

BARTLETT—On Sixth month 9th, at her home, Juliet Reese, wife of William K. Bartlett, and daughter of the late Edward and Mary A. Reese.

She was a birthright member of Baltimore Monthly Meeting of Friends and had been a resident of Baltimore all her life and of her home on Mt. Royal Terrace for thirty-four years.

She is survived by her husband, two daughters, two grandchildren and two sisters. Her funeral was from her late home and interment at Friends' Burial Ground, Harford Road.

Of but few people can it be said "I never entered her presence without coming away lighter-hearted and more at peace with the world." She was full of a great joy of living, shedding the ray of her enthusiasm on those around her. All who knew her will remember her cordial manner, her wonderful love for her home, and her great gratitude for the smallest favor, which magnified it many times.

Her life is an example to those who would get the greatest joy out of life by giving always of their best to those around them. E. W.

CHASE—At his home in Baltimore, Md., on Fifth month 11th, Emmett C., husband of M. Roberta Chase.

COALE—On Fifth month 30th, Skipwith Peyton Coale was run down and killed by an automobile near his home in Takoma Park, Md. He was the son of Lewis and Mary Catherine Matthews Coale, and was descended from Friendly ancestry extending to the early days of the colony of Maryland. He was in the 45th year of his age and is survived by his wife, Louise Bartlett Coale, and two daughters.

He has been intimately identified with Takoma Park for 20 years, and was Dean of the Faculty of the Bliss Electrical School at the time of his death. The qualities of mind which made him a very successful teacher endeared him to an unusually wide and varied circle of friends. His influence through his pupils is widespread, and has been exerted as much by his personal qualities of geniality, optimism and perseverance as by his technical instruction. His appreciation of human personality was founded on a broad love for all animate nature, and his insight into the life of fields and woods was instinctive and thorough. D. N. SHOEMAKER.

HARDY—In Pendleton, Indiana, on Sixth month 13th, Rebecca P., widow of Solomon F. Hardy, aged 76 years. She was a birthright member of the Society of Friends and an elder of long standing of Fall Creek Monthly Meeting.

PAUL—In Philadelphia, on Sixth month 1st, Mary Catherine, infant daughter of David G. and Mary Griest Paul. Interment in Solesbury Friends' Burying Ground.

WHEATLEY—Elizabeth Starr, wife of Edmund A. Wheatley, and daughter of the late Joseph West, and Eliza Burr Starr, of Diller, Nebraska. The deceased was the granddaughter of Charles W. and Elizabeth Starr, of Richmond, Indiana, and was born at the old Starr homestead at Richmond on January 8, 1866. In 1880 she moved with her parents to Steele City, Nebraska. In 1892 was united in marriage at Chicago, Ill., to Edmund A. Wheatley, of London, England, with whom she lived happily for nearly thirty years. She died February 15th, at her home on Missionary Ridge, Chattanooga. Burial at Forest Hills Cemetery, Chattanooga, Tenn. Besides her beloved husband and a host of friends she leaves to mourn her three brothers and one sister, John Vernon Starr, William B. Starr, Robert Frederick Starr, and Mrs. J. C. Stucker.

JOHN GRIEST

John Griest was born in York County, Pennsylvania, Ninth month 5th, 1844, son of John and Hannah Edmundson Griest, a lineal descendant of the Quaker apostle, William Edmundson. All of his ancestors were members of the Society of Friends from the time of George Fox and William Penn. In 1880, he married Sarah E. Worley, native of Louden County, Va., who survives him. Of the thirty-seven years of California experience, eighteen were lived in Pasadena.

John Griest took conspicuous part in gathering scattered Friends of this section together, and was one of the original twenty-one members which formed Orange Grove Meeting, in 1904—the first and only Hicksite Friends' Meeting west of the Rocky Mountains. This meeting was the outgrowth of the Young Friends' Association in which he took active part in forming, contributing of his means and service as far as he was able. He was chairman of the building committee when the meeting-house was erected, and for years was one of the trustees.

The funeral services of this Friend were largely attended. Isaiah Lightner, Mary Travilla and others were wonderfully favored with loving messages of sympathy and spiritual helpfulness. At Monthly Meeting, Sixth month 11th, there was a general expression of loving tribute to the memory of the good works of our friend, especially in the days of his vigorous health. Dr. Emily Hunt spoke particularly of his loving and careful watching and cultivation of the trees of various rare kinds now luxuriant and beautiful for us all to enjoy. Keturah E. Yeo, Anna Walter Speakman and others voiced remembrance of kindly service. One spoke of his independence of thought, his manifest courage of convictions on topics of the day, and his unscrupulous honesty of purpose. MARIANNA BURGESS.

ALBAN WALTON

"To live in love is to live in everlasting youth. Whoever enters old age by this royal road will find the last of life to be the very best of life."

It was always difficult to associate old age with Alban Walton, so fresh and vivid was his spirit. His life was a beautiful expression of love and truth.

A lifelong, active member of the Society of Friends he was loyal and conscientious, practicing the principles of the Society in every daily act.

His mind was alert and keen, quick to grasp the vital heart of a situation and consequently in the front ranks of progress and reform. Simplicity and truth marked his character. Humorous, loving and tender he was greatly beloved. To the end he kept his sweetness of spirit and a little child's faith in his Heavenly Father.

COMING EVENTS

SIXTH MONTH

25th—Annual Meeting in the old meeting-house at Shrewsbury, N. J., at 2.30 p. m. (Daylight Saving Time) under the care of Squan Meeting and the Yearly Meeting Advancement Committee.

The Meeting-house is located at the corner of Sycamore Avenue and Broad Street in the village of Shrewsbury and can be reached by auto bus from either Red Bank or Long Branch.

Visitors are welcome and we are especially anxious that a goodly number of the members of our beloved Society will be present.

25th—W. J. MacWatters expects to visit Newtown, Bucks County, Pa., meeting, at 11 a. m.

25th—Certain members of Philadelphia Quarterly Meeting's Visiting Committee expect to attend Merion Meeting at 11 a. m. Other members will attend meeting for worship at 15th and Race Streets, Philadelphia, at 10.30 a. m.

25th—Henry T. Hodgkin will be present at Haverford meeting (Orthodox), at 11 a. m.

26th—Henry T. Hodgkin will address a meeting held by the Fellowship of Reconciliation at Haverford College, at 8 p. m. James Manning will speak on Amnesty at 5.45 p. m.

27th—Address on "The Truth About Russia," by Senator Borah. See notice.

28th—A meeting is being planned to be addressed by Henry T. Hodgkin on behalf of all of the interests of the two Philadelphia Yearly Meetings. It is proposed that this meeting be held at 4th and Arch streets on the 28th, or Seventh month 5th.

30th—First Woolman School week-end conference to First-day, Seventh month 2nd, inclusive. Henry T. Hodgkin will speak Seventh-day evening at 7.30.

SEVENTH MONTH

2nd—First-day, at 2.30 p. m. Daylight Saving Time; a meeting for Divine Worship will be held at Stanton (Delaware) Friends' Meeting-house under care of a committee of Concord Quarterly Meeting. Wilmington Friends' School motor bus will leave 4th and Market Sts. for Stanton about 1.55 o'clock; also trolley cars leave at same place and hour. Friends of both branches as well as all interested persons are invited.

2nd—Religious meeting under care of a Committee of Burlington Quarterly Meeting will be held at Arney's Mount Meeting-house, near Mt. Holly, N. J., at 3 p. m. (daylight saving). Isaac Wilson is expected to be in attendance.

NOTICE—Mass Meeting under the auspices of Philadelphia Citizens Committee, Academy of Music, Tuesday, June 27, 1922, 8.15 p. m. Speaker, Senator Borah. Subject, "The Truth About Russia."

Free tickets may be obtained at Heppe's, 1117 Chestnut Street and at the Academy of Music box office.

Seats for those holding tickets reserved until 8 p. m. after which entire house will be thrown open to the public.

NOTICE—At the recent Yearly Meeting of Ministry and Counsel, held at 15th and Race Streets, Philadelphia, it was evident from some of the answers to the Queries that certain of our meetings could be strengthened and helped if some of our ministering and interested Friends might from time to time visit and confer with members of such meetings.

Accordingly a small committee was named to have charge of this special service during the present year. This notice therefore is to suggest that such neighborhoods as may desire help write to the Central Bureau, 15th and Race Streets, or any members of the committee whose names and addresses appear below.

It is the desire of this committee that the subject be given attention in the various Preparative, Monthly and Quarterly Meetings of the Society.

The loyal service of our visiting English Friends in behalf of our smaller meetings and of our younger people should be followed up with full vigor. Our Quaker message is one which can and must be spread in as many localities as possible and an aid to the machinery of such service is now available. Please discuss this problem in your meeting and let us co-operate toward a renewed, energetic Quakerism by putting into operation the following minute adopted at the Meeting of Ministry and Counsel held Fifth month 13, 1922. "It seems both proper and imperative at this time that the Meeting of Ministry and Counsel lends its positive encouragement to the weaker meetings of our membership by the appointment of a committee of conference and counsel to whom such appeals may be made, and to that end we name Ellis W. Bacon, 227 S. 6th Street, Phila.; Frank M. Bartram, Kennett Square, Pa.; Reuben Kester, Newtown, Pa.; Sarah Linvill, 1931 N. Gratz Street, Phila.; Elizabeth F. Newlin, 1210 Shalcross Avenue, Wilmington, Del.; Caroline J. Worth, West Chester, Pa.

The Last Lap

Let us make one last strenuous effort to gather in those Friends who are still outside the INTELLIGENCER circle. They don't realize how much they need it, so they are not as much to blame as those who read the paper, recognize its value, and yet do not pass the word along.

The sin of omission sometimes brings about as dire calamities as that of commission, and not to tell all thy friends about the good things in the INTELLIGENCER is in the same class as not taking thy share of responsibility in the meeting, if thee has a message and fails to give it voice.

So far we have placed 218 new names on the mailing list as the result of the work of those who have realized their responsibility for the success of the INTELLIGENCER. If thee, who reads these lines, has not sent in at least one name, won't thee do it now? *Just one name before Seventh month 1st.* The offer is .35 for three months' trial, three names for $1.

American Friends' Service Committee

WILBUR K. THOMAS, EX. SEC.
20 S. 12th St. Philadelphia.

CASH CONTRIBUTIONS
WEEK ENDING JUNE 12TH

Five Years Meetings		$375.42
Philadelphia Yearly Meeting (Orthodox)		3,375.34
Philadelphia Yearly Meeting (Hicksite)		1,064.00
Other Meetings		
Buckingham Quarterly Meeting		5.00
Baltimore Yearly Meeting:		
Ashton Meeting, Md.	$20.00	
Baltimore Monthly Meeting	45.00	
Bethel Meeting, Va.	5.00	
Fishertown, Penna.	12.55	
Richmond Meeting, Va.	15.00	
Washington Meeting, D. C.	15.00	
		112.55
Goose Creek Mo. Meeting, Wrightstown, Pa.		10.00
Toronto Friends		16.97
Cornwall Monthly Meeting, New York		5.00
Contributions for Germany		103.60
For Austria		387.20
For Poland		72.34
For Russia		8,314.52
For Russian Overhead		3,510.00
Home Service		190.00
German Overhead		33.00
For General		675.45
For Clothing		5.00
Refunds		2.12
		$18,257.51

FUN

Degrees

Said a friend to the proud father of a college graduate who had just been awarded an A. M. degree:

"I suppose Robert will be looking for a Ph.D. next?"

"No. He will be looking for a J. O. B."—*Life.*

FUN

The Irish lad and the Yiddish boy were engaged in verbal combat. First one would insist that his father or mother was better than the other's. Then it was their pet bulldogs and their teachers. Finally the subject came down to respective churches.

"I guess I know that Father Harriety knows more than your Rabbi," the little Irish boy insisted.

"Sure, he does; vy not?" replied the Jew boy. "You tell him everything." —*Treat 'Em Square.*

ADVERTISING RATE in the FRIENDS' INTELLIGENCER, for Help Wanted, Positions Wanted, Rooms for Rent, Notices, and other classified advertisements without display, for each insertion, 2 cents per word, including name, initials and address. Answers may be sent to a box at the INTELLIGENCER office, if so directed.

For display advertising the rate is 10 cents per agate line, or $1.40 per column inch, each insertion. On ten or more insertions in a year from date of order, ten per cent. discount. Thus a four-inch single-column or two-inch double-column advertisement costs $5.60 each insertion, less ten per cent., or 5.04 net each time for ten or more insertions. Matter may be changed whenever desired, without extra charge.

Experience has proved the INTELLIGENCER to be a remarkably good advertising medium. All advertisements must "pass the censor!"

Address 140 N. 15th St., Philadelphia

S
SUPPLEE

The Friends' Intelligencer

ESTABLISHED 1844 | SEVENTH MONTH 1, 1922 | VOLUME 79 NUMBER 26

Contents

REGULAR MEETINGS

OAKLAND, CALIF. — A FRIENDS' Meeting is held every First-day at 11 A. M., in the Extension Room, Y. W. C. A. Building, Webster Street, above 14th. Visiting Friends always welcome.

FRIENDS' MEETING IN PASADENA, California — Orange Grove Monthly Meeting of Friends, 520 East Orange Grove Avenue, Pasadena, California. Meeting for worship, First-day, 11 A. M. Monthly Meeting, the second First-day of each month, at 1.45 P. M.

CENTRAL MEETING OF FRIENDS (Chicago), meets every First-day in Room 706, 410 South Michigan Avenue, at 10.45 A. M. Visitors are invited.

NOTICE—Concise statements of the principles of the Religious Society of Friends and their application to the problems of every day living, including "The Spirit of Quakerism," by Elbert Russell; "Preparation for Life's Greatest Business," by Rufus M. Jones; and other articles by Henry W. Wilbur, Howard M. Jenkins, Elizabeth Lloyd, Jesse H. Holmes, O. Edward Janney, Edward B. Rawson, etc., to be had free on application to Friends' General Conference Advancement Committee, 140 North Fifteenth Street, Philadelphia, Pa.

THE FRIENDS' INTELLIGENCER

Published weekly, 140 N. 15th Street, Philadelphia, Pa., by Friends' Intelligencer Association, Ltd.

PAUL W. WAGER, *Editor*.
SUE C. YERKES, *Business Manager*

Editorial Board: Elizabeth Powell Bond, Thomas A. Jenkins; J. Russell Smith, George A. Walton.

Board of Managers: Edward Cornell, Alice Hall Paxson, Paul M. Pearson, Annie Hillborn, Elwood Hollingshead, William C. Biddle, Charles F. Jenkins, Edith M. Winder, Frances M. White.

Officers of Intelligencer Associates: Ellwood Burdsall, Chairman; Bertha L. Broomell, Secretary; Herbert P. Worth, Treasurer.

Subscription rates: United States, Mexico, Cuba and Panama, $2.50 per year. Canada and other foreign countries, $3.00 per year. Checks should be made payable to Friends' Intelligencer Association, Ltd.

Entered as Second Class Matter at Philadelphia Post Office.

To the Lot Holders and others interested in Fairhill Burial Ground:

GREEN STREET Monthly Meeting has funds available for the encouragement of the practice of cremating the dead to be interred in Fairhill Burial Ground. We wish to bring this fact as prominently as possible to those who may be interested. We are prepared to undertake the expense of cremation in case any lot holder desires us to do so.

Those interested should communicate with William H. Gaskill, Treasurer of the Committee of Interments, Green Street Monthly Meeting, or any of the following members of the Committee.

William H. Gaskill, 3201 Arch St.
Samuel N. Longstreth, 1218 Chestnut St.
Charles F. Jenkins, 232 South Seventh St.
Stuart S. Graves, 3033 Germantown Ave.

The Friends' Intelligencer

The religion of Friends is based on faith in the "INWARD LIGHT," or direct revelation of God's spirit and will in every seeking soul.

The INTELLIGENCER is interested in all who bear the name of Friends in every part of the world, and aims to promote love, unity and intercourse among all branches and with all religious societies.

ESTABLISHED 1844 | PHILADELPHIA, SEVENTH MONTH 1, 1922 | VOLUME 79 NUMBER 26

Patriotism Expressed in Good Citizenship

The nation celebrates again the anniversary of its birth. It is one hundred and forty-six years now since the old bell in Independence Hall rang out the old order of despotism and rang in the new order of freedom.

That first Fourth of July celebration was no solemn occasion. When, after years of irritation and anxiety and doubtful loyalty the tense cords of allegiance finally snapped, the colonists let their pent-up feelings run riot for a day. It was a time of wild enthusiasm. So, with us, it is not improper to celebrate the day with bands, and parades, and patriotic demonstrations. It is a time to be joyful. That does not mean that it need be a day of din, confusion and danger. Noise is not patriotism. The campaign that has been waged in recent years for a "safe and sane" Fourth has resulted in fewer fires, fewer accidents, and a more fitting celebration of the day.

While the colonists hailed the Declaration of Independence with joyous enthusiasm they felt the significance of it in the days which followed. It was one thing to announce their independence and another thing to acquire it. It took fifteen years of arduous labor and untold sacrifice before their independence was secure and their cherished ideals of liberty established in the fundamental law of a new nation.

It is, therefore, right and proper for us on the Fourth of July to proclaim our liberties and indulge in patriotic demonstrations, but it is a hollow and senseless performance unless on the morrow we assume the responsibilities of freedom and self-government. Patriotism is more than sentiment. It is love for one's country expressed in honest, intelligent, aggressive citizenship. Let us see what that involves.

An honest citizen is one who gives value received in all his dealings. He lives by the sweat of his own brow. He has but one standard of honesty. He is as square with the government, or with an invisible corporation as he is with his own brother. He not only pays his material debts but he fulfils his moral obligations. A man, ever so punctilious in paying his bills, who never makes a voluntary contribution for civic or religious purposes, is not a patriotic citizen.

An intelligent citizen is one who possesses both knowledge and judgment. It is the patriotic duty of a citizen to keep himself informed about public affairs. Not all have equal educational advantages but none need be ignorant if he has the ambition to learn. It is not alone the uneducated who are uninformed politically. Well educated people with plenty of leisure often are shamefully ignorant of governmental affairs. Democracy can not endure unless supported by an intelligent electorate. Intelligence implies discrimination, as well as knowledge. A patriotic citizen is tolerant of another's opinion, impartial in his judgment, open-minded. He learns to sift truth from error, the eternal from the transitory. He rises above provincialism. Local patriotism ruined Greece. The growth of nationalism stopped feudal warfare, the growth of internationalism will stop all warfare.

An aggressive citizen is one who does not shirk his responsibilities. He recognizes that the machinery of government is not self-operative. He recognizes, too, that like other machinery it sometimes gets out of adjustment. The price of liberty is eternal vigilance. Even a slight deflection, unless corrected, will steadily grow worse, causing more and more friction. The agencies of society like the tools of industry must be constantly altered to meet new conditions. Civilization must always be making progress. Stagnation means decay. Change is the order of the universe and only the persons and institutions which are constantly adjusting to meet new conditions are really masters of their environment. The aggressive citizen is not the malcontent who sees nothing good as it is. Neither is he the complacent individual who is always satisfied with things as they are. He is the man who adjusts to fit a changing environment. He is the man who succeeds because he has the vision to see and the faith to follow truth.

Love of country must precede any real desire to make it better. One can have little faith in the criticism of an anarchist, even though the particular criticism is sound. Love of country on the other hand should not blind us to its mistakes. A parent corrects the child because he loves it. Constructive criticism of one's country indicates no lack of

A Christian Program

The Washington Conference on Limitation of Armament established a naval holiday, thus saving the country some $4,958,000,000 during the next fifteen years. It also took steps toward assuring peace in the Pacific for ten years. These two achievements give the Churches and Christians of America a "Day of Grace" in which, under relatively favorable conditions, they can push their program of education for a Warless World.

The basis for such an educational program may well be found in the following declarations of the Federal Council of the Churches of Christ in America in regard to the "International Ideals of the Churches" and "America's International Obligations."

International Ideals of the Churches of Christ

1. We believe that nations no less than individuals are subject to God's immutable moral laws.
2. We believe that nations achieve true welfare, greatness and honor only through just dealing and unselfish service.
3. We believe that nations that regard themselves as Christian have special international obligations.
4. We believe that the spirit of Christian brotherliness can remove every unjust barrier of trade, color, creed and race.
5. We believe that Christian patriotism demands the practice of good-will between nations.
6. We believe that international policies should secure equal justice for all races.
7. We believe that all nations should associate themselves permanently for world peace and good-will.
8. We believe in international law, and in the universal use of international courts of justice and boards of arbitration.
9. We believe in a sweeping reduction of armaments by all nations.
10. We believe in a warless world, and dedicate ourselves to its achievement.

understand these causes of war and organize to remove them. They must lead their own nations to abandon aggressive international policies and also to perform positive deeds of good-will in their relations with other nations. They must also help create the necessary agencies for the peaceful settlement of all differences that may arise between nations.

When millions of Christians in Christian lands are as earnest for a Warless World as they were to win the great war, and when they will devote as much energy and thought and time to an organized program for establishing the international institutions of justice, security, honor and liberty under law, which are the essential prerequisites of a Warless World, as they did to establish national security and maintain national honor in a Warring World, the way will be found and the institutions will be created by which the causes of war will be removed, war will be banished forever, and nations will learn war no more.

Every denomination and every church should have a conscious part in this crusade to end war. Every professed Christian should be a loyal and ardent volunteer in this Crusade of the Prince of Peace.

The New Crusade

A mighty crusade against the whole war system is now imperative. The Churches must wage this crusade with the same holy enthusiasm and unflinching devotion that characterized the ancient crusades. We must enroll intelligent crusaders by the million. None others can be efficient. No conscripts can be forced into this war to end war. We have, moreover, priceless values at stake in our crusade, more fundamental and essential to religion and to civilization than the crusaders of the Middle Ages had in theirs.

Americanism

Rev. Ralph E. Hartman

Abolition of all things that tend toward aristocracy in industry, politics, business, society, legislation, government, wealth, labor and all other relations among men. Americanism!

Moving out of America if the things that are written in our American Constitution do not mean anything to the individual, his home, his life, and his moral standards. Americanism!

Entering whole-heartedly into the spirit of wisdom, goodness and truth, so that law and order, justice and peace may everywhere prevail. Encouraging the fear of God and the love of righteousness so that America may become a real blessing to all nations. Americanism!

Reviving the faith of our fathers, in the Lord's Day, the Church, the Bible, the marriage vows, the suppression of evil, the enforcement of laws, the establishment of justice, the assurance of domestic tranquillity, the promotion of good will toward men and reverence toward God. Americanism!

Interest—undivided interest in America's ideals of good schools, good roads, good literature, good music. Healthful recreation, harmless amusement, helpful worship, honest workmanship, and honorable living. Americanism!

Christ's spirit for the brotherhood of man, put into practice. The fulfillment of the words, "whatsoever ye would that men should do to you, do ye even so to them." "Doing justly, loving mercy, and walking humbly with God." "Being kindly affectioned one to another (whosoever) with brotherly love." Americanism!

Abraham Lincoln's spirit of "malice toward none and charity for all." "I am not bound to win, but I am bound to be true." "I have one vote, and shall always cast that against wrong as long as I live." Americanism!

Negotiating with the other nations of the world—strong and weak—in the spirit of righteousness and justice to all, that the horrors of war shall never be again, and the blessings of peace be always to all men in all places. Never forgetting the Prince of Peace, nor ignoring Him. Americanism!

Investing all that we are and all that we have in the institutions that make for righteous citizenship, Christian homes, conscientious balloting, statesmanship above reproach, and world brotherhood. Americanism?

Stretching out the helping hand to the oppressed in the world, the needy and the distressed. Feed the starving, clothe the naked, and teach the ignorant. Americanism!

Men and women who believe in God, in the ideals that are noblest and best, in peace on earth and goodwill toward all men everywhere. Americanism!

Quakertown, Pa.

From *Reformed Church Messenger*.

Forward!

Seek first the highway, seek first the path,
  The foot speeds best on the beaten track;
But if the path and the highway fail,
Challenge the wilderness! Blaze a trail!
  Turn not the vision back.

Walter H. Abell.

Christianity and Economic Problems

X

What Degree of Public Control of Industry Will Best Promote the General Welfare?

Reduced to Summary Form.

The majority of the people in the United States have looked with disfavor upon most phases of state regulation and control of industry. And yet during the past few decades a considerable degree of control has been assumed by the state. Under what circumstances is the public justified in interfering with private control of industry?

1. *Safety and Health Measures.* It is now generally recognized that the protection of the life, health, and energies of the workers is not an individual question. It cannot safely be left to the discretion of the owner or employer. Practically all states now have laws which require the guarding of machinery, the protection of elevators and hoistways, adequate ventilation, lighting, and heating; sanitary provisions, protection from infectious disease, and other safety measures. Various laws have been passed looking to the protection of women and children in industry. During the years from 1911 to 1919 industrial accident compensation laws were passed in forty-two states. Under these laws employers are required to insure their employes against industrial accidents. Adequate compensation for fatal and permanent injuries will do more than all other legislation to promote industrial safety and to encourage genuine rehabilitation.

Most states and municipalities have laws relating to tenement-house construction and to the location of obnoxious establishments. Severe penalties are attached to the provisions for proper disposal of garbage and other sanitary measures. Many municipalities require adequate heat and light in apartment houses.

During the past decade the effort to protect the lowest paid women workers from exploitation has taken the form of a legal minimum wage. Twelve states now have minimum wage laws. These laws were enacted because of the facts brought out in numerous investigations that a large proportion of unskilled women workers received wages which were far too low for decent self-support.

2. *Control of Public Utilities and Semi-Monopolistic Industries.* As a result of the changing conditions, there has been an increasing demand during the past thirty years for legislative action against monopolies and trusts, and in favor of more and more governmental control in industry. Owners of certain kinds of industry now possess only a limited degree of control. This is true of industries, classified as public utilities, and includes steam and electric railways, water transportation lines, express service, telegraph and telephone, light, heat, power, and public water supply. Various types of public-utility commissions fix the rates of payment for such services, determine the grade of service given, and provide for safety measures and working conditions.

The extent of public ownership of property in the United States is not generally recognized. In his annual report for 1921 the Secretary of the Interior stated that 400 million acres of land remain in the Public Domain of the United States and that this contains potential wealth estimated at 150 billion dollars. Considered in the aggregate the amount of property which is publicly owned in the United States is enormous. And yet there is relatively less public ownership in the United States than in almost any other civilized country.

3. *What Further Extensions of Public Control or Ownership Are Desirable?* A number of measures are now being advocated.

Health Insurance. In nine states official commissions have made reports concerning the need for this type of social insurance. Many of the arguments used in advocacy of industrial accident insurance are now being used in favor of compulsory health insurance. Thus far there has been considerable popular opposition to compulsory health insurance and a majority of medical men also seem to be opposed to the idea. Compulsory health legislation has been enacted in a score of foreign countries.

Unemployment Insurance. Within recent years a number of experiments have been made by different municipalities and states in Europe with various types of compulsory unemployment insurance. In England and in Italy national schemes of unemployment insurance are in operation. Under the British scheme each adult male worker pays a premium of about eight cents per week and the employer pays an equal amount. The government adds an amount sufficient to provide an unemployment benefit of fifteen shillings per week (about $3.50) for each adult male worker who is unable to secure employment, and twelve shillings for unemployed women. These sums are, of course, wholly inadequate, and yet even such a small weekly benefit has relieved an immense amount of distress.

Public Ownership of Coal Mines and Railways. There is an increasing demand for public ownership of coal mines and railways. A plan for the public ownership of coal mines has received high official endorsement in England. The United Mine Workers of America are now advocating the nationalization of the coal mines. The American Federation of Labor has officially endorsed the Plumb Plan, calling for public ownership of the railways, and joint operation by representatives of managers, workers, and the public.

Taxation as a Means of Preventing Excessive Concentration of Wealth. That huge fortunes are a possible menace to public welfare is now generally recognized. Taxation is often suggested as one of the most effective ways of limiting the excessive concentration of wealth. In the final report of the Federal Commission on Industrial Relations a recommendation was made that personal fortunes in the United States be limited to one million dollars. If such a limitation seemed desirable to a majority of the people of the country, the means are at hand.

The income tax is now firmly established in this country. In addition to the federal government, many of the states levy an income tax.

The federal income tax has proved to be a huge success as a revenue measure. The amount received from this source has jumped from less than sixty-one million dollars in 1914 to more than 3,956 millions in 1920. Up to the present time, however, it has not succeeded to any considerable extent in limiting the growth of great fortunes. The wealth of many rich men has more than doubled since 1914, when the federal income-tax law became effective, and in many cases the increase has been upwards of 500 per cent. The reasons for this failure are obvious. Even after the 1921 tax is deducted from a million-dollar income, there remains a sum of $336,810, and at the 1922 rate the amount remaining is $449,360. Then, too, there are many ways of evading the tax on large portions of income. Interest from many government bonds and certain other forms of income are non-taxable.

The Inheritance Tax. The inheritance tax is now firmly installed as a permanent part of our federal financial system. Under the Revenue Act of February, 1919, the inheritance tax on estates varied from one per cent. on estates not in excess of $50,000 to twenty-five per cent. on estates above ten millions. Estates under $50,000 are exempt from the inheritance tax. Forty-five of the States also levy inheritance taxes, the rates varying from one per cent. to thirty per cent., according to the amount of the estate and the kinship of the heir.

Inheritance taxes have not thus far been successful in checking the growth of great fortunes, due to three reasons: First, they have not been used on an effective scale for a sufficient length of time; second, the rates have not been sufficiently high, even under the federal tax and the highest state taxes direct heirs may inherit $750,000 out of a million-dollar estate, while indirect heirs may inherit $600,000 out of one million dollars; third, large fortunes are usually distributed prior to the death of the owner.

Are we now ready to reach any conclusions as to what degree of public control of industry will best promote the general welfare? Each proposal should be tested by such questions as these: Is it necessary for the protection of the public health and welfare? Is it the most efficient way of achieving the desired end? Does it tend to place industry on a basis of production for use? Does it promote co-operation in industry? Will it aid in securing an equitable division of the national wealth and income? Will it promote genuine democracy?

The Royal Counties Fair

Like every other country heard from the spring has been backward in England, but a week of unusually hot weather, late in May, with temperature the highest in the history of the weather bureau, has brought out the flowering trees and shrubs in one simultaneous display. They usually follow each other in some sort of an orderly succession, but this year nature has poured out her cornucopia of blooms in glorious profusion.

The English fairs follow each other, as do ours, and began in Oxfordshire some days ago. The second was held at Guildford, the county seat of Surrey, some thirty miles southwest from London. It is called the Royal Counties' Show because it covers the counties of Surrey, Kent, Sussex, Berks and Hampshire and these counties, because they were once separate, ancient kingdoms, are called the Royal Counties.

Our journey out of London, by Wimbledon Common and through the back of Richmond forest where the giant oaks were not yet in full leaf, and the deer were grazing unconcernedly, soon brought us to the open country. The roads were lined with hawthorne hedges in full bloom, mile after mile of it. The horse chestnuts were covered with their upstanding bouquets, the golden yellow laburnums nodded over the gateways and in the gardens; the lilacs, just a little past their time, but still beautiful, were everywhere; with patches of flaming rhododendrons, the gardens full of spring flowers, the fields covered with daisies and buttercups and the woodlands carpeted with blue bells,—you cannot picture it or imagine it no matter how hard you try unless you, too, have been in England in some other wonderful spring and have traveled the back roads. Most of us taking our summer vacations in July and August never see the country at its very best.

The fair at Guildford had been on for three days and we arrived the closing day. It was of special interest to note the English way of running things and comparing them with our own. One outstanding difference was the entire absence of side shows and catch-penny devices. The fair is apparently made a great social affair, the King himself being the patron and dukes and earls and lords and ladies are on the various committees and vie with each other in the show-ring with their horses, cattle, pigs and sheep. As this fair rotates through the various royal counties the local show grounds at Guildford were not fully equipped with permanent buildings, so that a big tent sheltered the very unusual poultry show. The famous Orpington breeds of chickens were originated in Sussex and they with other heavy breeds were shown in unusual size and perfection. The whole display while not as large as some of our big poultry shows was equal to our best in quality.

All over the grounds officers and exhibitors had gone to far more trouble in planning and arranging their displays than is customary with us. The leading seedmen had planted out in the grounds in front of their tasteful booths beds of blooming plants. The grounds were clean and orderly, no peanut shells or empty pop bottles or blowing paper, in fact it was more like a glorified lawn party, where people came who took a keen and intelligent interest in the exhibits or if not this they dressed in their good clothes and strolled around as at a social function.

The President had a big tent, the floor covered with red carpet, with linen covered tables for a hundred people whom he entertained at lunch. You entered it through a temporary flower garden. In front of the Secretary's charming office was a little fence, and in the garden enclosure were chairs for visitors and committees.

There were two contests which aroused the keenest interest. One of farriers or blacksmiths, as we would call them, making special shoes and shoeing horses of different breeds and in different ways and the other a butter making contest in which several score of young women and a few young men took part.

The exhibit of sheep was particularly fine as the southern downs are noted for their mutton and wool. The King breeds Southdowns and had sent a representative exhibit from Sandingham, but a second prize was the best we could find that he had received. Class 113—three ram lambs, had for contestants the King, Lady Fitzgerald, Lady Ludlow, Sir Thomas Colman, Sir Richard Gaston and the Duke of Richmond. The Hampshire downs were in great force, and all of them had been dipped, which had dyed them a mustard brown, this, with their black noses and ears made them very conspicuous. A local breed, Romney Marsh, showed the giants of the sheep world, with backs so flat and broad they could have served for dining tables. Other breeds unknown with us were the Dorsetdowns and the Ryelands.

The cattle display was unusually strong with England's favorite breed, the milking Shorthorns in the lead. In the regular short-horn class it was interesting to note the King and the Prince of Wales competing in two of the classes. Here, as among the sheep, were breeds unknown or little known on our side of the water. Sussex, a handsome, heavy, red cattle and a large display of Dexters—little, black cattle, in size half way between a goat and any ordinary cow, and Kerrys, sleek black little cows from Ireland. Jerseys and Guernseys far outnumbered the Holsteins or British Freisians as our English cousins call them.

Among the hogs, too, were strange and unknown names. Gloucestershire Old Spots, Large Black, a very popular breed, Middle White, Wessex Saddlebacks, Wessex Derby, in addition to Berkshire and Tamworths which we also breed under these names.

It was too early in the year for any display of farm products, but honey and butter were shown. Then there was the usual agricultural implement display, out in the open, and the commercial features were all grouped in one long street in uniform booths.

There was no horse racing—a feature of our county fairs, but jumping, riding, four-in-hand contests, as we have them at our horse shows. All together the Royal Fair was an orderly, well managed, worthwhile event. C. F. J.

Poland Still Needs Our Help

One million refugees who were ordered into Russia by the retreating Russian army in 1915-16 now remain to be repatriated in Poland. They return to land that is often covered with entanglements and gutted with trenches and concrete dug-outs. In any case no ploughing has been done since they left home.

The Friends in Poland have bought 1,000 horses from the Polish Government and are ploughing the land owned by returning peasants. If no ploughing is done this year before November 1, 1922, it will be necessary to wait until 1924 before their crops can be harvested. (1,000) one thousand horses will plough enough land to start 2,000 families every month with at least four acres of broken ground.

More fortunate Polish towns in Western Poland are adopting devastated areas. They raise funds for seeds, ploughs, spades, hoes, scythes, and sickles. They also provide food and medical supplies.

There is the closest co-operation between Polish organizations, both national and private, and the Society of Friends. The Society is proving that the land may be ploughed by columns of horses fully equipped and supervised at the rate of at least half an acre per horse per ploughing day. The Government is following our example with ploughing columns of its own.

The peasants need food and medicine and soap in order to get strong and healthy and clean. We supply these requirements.

Clothing is another dire need. Nearly every peasant woman can spin flax. We pay them at the rate of 30 cents to spin 3¼ pounds of our raw flax. With this money many a family has been able to live during the winter just past. We have also supplied fine linen and paid to have it worked into beautifully embroidered blouses, table covers, towels and mats.

Friends in Poland calculate that we can supervise the ploughing of twenty thousand acres of land by 500 of the 1,000 horses formerly owned by the Polish army. The other 500 horses will be sold at once to poor peasants, preferably widows with children, on long-time credits. The cost for ploughing will be approximately $5.00 per acre. This sum will plough and seed the land, will provide the spade to work it, will give the scythe to harvest the crop. It will also make a well peasant out of an under-nourished one.

It is hoped that the American Friends' Service Committee can contribute $45,000 between now and September 1, 1922.

New York Yearly Meeting

Evening Meetings

(Concluded in this issue)

The Biblical Tableaux

Let us call them Tableaux, for lack of a better word,—though Tableaux they were not. At all events, these Biblical presentations arranged by Cora H. Carver, and participated in by about fifty Friends of all ages, were a new note in our outside-business activities, and gave both interest and inspiration to all who saw them on the evening of the 29th. Only three scenes were presented,—"The Child Samuel in the Temple," "The Charge to the Disciples," and "Suffer Little Children to Come Unto Me"; but these were enough: more would have destroyed the freshness of interest. Josephine Tilton at the piano, and Mary Waterman with violin, gave appropriate music before every scene. The entire stories were read as told in the Bible, by Charles F. Underhill, while the actors gave appropriate action, quietly, but impressively.

Thursday, Fifth Month 30th

The address of the evening was given by James McAfee, who gave an illustrated talk on his experiences and the relief work of Friends in Vienna and Poland. His pictures showed vividly the miles and miles of barbed-wire in Poland,—not one or two lines extending for miles,—but one wire behind another, as far as the eye could see. They showed the holes in the ground, the brush "shacks," the impossible conditions under which people do find it possible to live. His stories of the life and the suffering in both countries, were sometimes funny, sometimes horrible, but always true an interesting. He concluded by showing several pictures of the Russian famine,—some, pictures of the skeletons still living, whom aid now might save, and one a picture of some for whom help is too late,—a heap of hundreds of naked skeleton bodies thrown together in a hideous pile, because the living lacked the strength to bury them.

Fourth-day, Fifth Month 31st

On Fourth-day afternoon, under the care of the Philanthropic Committee, two talks were given, the first by Waldemar Groszman, on "The Preparation for Life of the Exceptional Child," and the second by Ella H. Boole, of the W. C. T. U., on "Problems of Law Enforcement."

Mr. Groszman spoke of the duties of parents and teachers, and tried to show, by concrete instances, how, under the proper training, teaching and environment, what seemed to be extreme disadvantages, could be overcome, and the 'exceptional child' made a desirable part of society, instead of a burden and a menace,—the very qualities which were threatening might be made an asset. He spoke of the old doctrine of "original sin," by which a child's pranks, no matter how innocent, were counted to "original sin," and deprecated as such.

Mrs. Boole said: "We live in a new age, as regards liquor. The Eighteenth Amendment was passed according to law. The Suffrage Amendment had one vote more than enough in the House to pass it; the prohibition Amendment had 9 more than enough. Suffrage has been ratified by 36 states; Prohibition by 46 states. On the face of it, there was much more sentiment for Prohibition than for Suffrage; yet we hear nothing of repealing the Suffrage Amendment.

"There are now thirty-four organizations for the repeal of the Volstead Act, or its loosening. To counteract this, you and I must be boosters for Prohibition. Point out what the former saloons are, now. Find out the attitude of candidates for office. Remember that if beer and wine are brought back, they must be sold somewhere, and there will be a good place to violate the law on other drinks. Beer and wine were 90 per cent. of the liquor trade, anyhow.

"The prohibition law enforcement is now 64 per

cent. efficient. Liquor that once came in by the cart-load, now comes by the suitcase. The liquor traffic is an outlaw. To abolish the last 36 per cent. of the trade, give officials what information you have, and *attend trials*. Commend officials who do their duty, and insist that all shall do it. But each one of us must do his or her part, as well."

The Young Friends' Movement

The Movement deserves a separate word, both for its part in the Yearly Meeting and for the number of young people who attended the sessions. In addition to holding their annual meeting, they conducted the hymn singing, arranged for Scott Nearing's lecture on First-day night, Mrs. Weed's address on Second-day evening, arranged a little musicale on Third-day evening, and on Fourth-day evening, one of their members, Frederick Pohl, read a little original one-act play, "Gas, or Ninety Feet Above Ground," which gave in dramatic form, a vivid idea of the meaning of gas in "the next war." On Memorial Day, about twenty members took a hike on Long Island, on which, aside from the good time, some very serious talking and planning was done.

THE CHILDREN AT YEARLY MEETING

Never before were there so many out. They were everywhere. On Seventh-day, Phebe Wilbur Griffen held a Prohibition Poster Parade in which every available child took part, and many children assisted in the Biblical tableaux. We are beginning to realize that the way to have the children at Yearly Meeting is to have a definite program for them, so there was the bus ride and various other trips. We want to make the Yearly Meeting a time of joy for the children. Our reward is in seeing, as we did this year, a number of those in their middle teens attending the sessions with every appearance of real interest.

ANNA L. CURTIS.

Hope

(*Romans V: 3, 4.*)

Hope is a treasure that's for age to claim,—
The garnered grain of ripe experience;
For courage that o'ercomes, a recompense;
Or, change the metaphor, the sunset's flame.
In youth, strong bars a cramped enclosure frame;
Age, having hewn a gap in the high fence,
Goes out to blaze a trail through brushwood dense,
And so to fields beyond the forest came.

Young eyes, I ween, see only valley lands
And the sky resting on the nearest hill;
Young ploughmen work with blistered, bleeding hands,
And miss the glories that the distance fill.
Who wins the guerdon is the one who stands
On vantage ground attained by patient will.

ANNIE MARGARET PIKE.

An Old Meeting-house

During my attendance at Millville Half-Yearly Meeting, a charming interlude was the visit on First-day afternoon to the old log meeting-house at Catawissa, fifteen miles distant from Millville and five miles from Bloomsburg. Catawissa has about 1,200 inhabitants.

As we turned off from the village street and entered the meeting-house grove, it seemed as if we had been suddenly transported into the life and worship of an earlier age. There, under the shade of fine old trees, stood the little log building, as staunch as when it was built in 1775. The only sign of decay was that the floor had given way under the gallery seats.

Most of our country meeting-houses stand on elevated sites, commanding an extensive view; but this one nestles in a hollow, with a background of wooded hills. Behind a border of trees lies the graveyard, beautiful with a profusion of roses in full bloom. But there is none of the trimness which is generally seen in a Friends' burial ground. There is also an absence of even the plainly carved memorial stones on the graves. The only marks of identification are little slabs of slate, or flat pieces of uncarved rock.

Notwithstanding the late notice of the meeting for worship, there were about 100 people present. To accommodate them the seats were brought out under the trees. Some were crudely made and apparently as old as the building itself. Quite a number of low benches also gave mute evidence of "the little ones" of bygone generations.

The meeting was held in a spirit of deep reverence. The Methodist minister, who was present, offered a beautiful prayer and the meeting closed with singing "Nearer my God, to Thee." The interest expressed by many showed the value of such meetings for spreading the Friendly message.

No description of Catawissa meeting would be complete without some mention of its guardian spirit. Mary Emma Walters, a maiden lady of eighty years, has made it the mission of her life to care for the meeting-house and grounds. There she worships alone and there she spends her days keeping the place in good order. In her loving devotion to that shrine she reminds one of Sir Walter Scott's "Old Mortality."

And yet, she is by no means a recluse. It was pleasant to see her moving around among the interested groups, after the meeting. She likes to entertain the tourists who turn aside to visit the place, and she is always ready to answer questions concerning the faith of Friends.

Whether for scenes of natural beauty, or for historical and human interest, a visit to Catawissa, Columbia Co., Pa., is well worth while.

DANIEL BATCHELLOR.

Service Notes

The following workers have arrived on this side within the last few weeks. Practically every foreign field is represented:

From Germany—Julia Branson, of Lansdowne, Pa., who has been in the work for more than two years; and Frieda Burkle, of Waterbury, Conn., who has had charge of planning the menus in the German mass child-feeding. Julia has been accepted for the Russian field, and after a short holiday in America will depart for her new post.

From Poland—Mary C. Maris, of Lansdowne, Pa.; Dr. Mary Tatum, of Llanerch, Pa.; and Richard Cadbury, of Haverford, Pa.

From France—Melvin A. Cawl, of Brooklyn, N. Y., who designed the Maternity Hospital in Chalons presented by the English and American Friends, as a memorial of our work in France, to the people of the Marne Department. Not only was he the architect, but for three years and more he has been the moving spirit in this work.

From France and Poland—Julianna Tatum, of Llanerch, Pa., who spent a year in Chalons Hospital as nurses' aide and, later, joined her mother in Poland.

From Austria—Dorothy Detzer, of Fort Wayne, Illinois; Caroline Newton, of Philadelphia, Pa.; and Emily C. Poley, of Germantown, Philadelphia, Pa. Dorothy has worked for over a year in connection with the food depots both in Vienna and the provinces. She has taken special interest in the co-operation of the Friends' Mission with the A. R. A. and the A. R. C. She will return in the fall, to join the Russian Unit. Caroline Newton's work was with the Weighing Room children. She is planning to spend next winter in Vienna pursuing her studies in psychoanalysis. Emily Poley's work was with the Mittelstand Department.

From Serbia—Dr. and Mrs. Charles Outland, of Tarboro, N. C. Dr. Outland has been in charge of the Hospital at Pec, which has recently been turned over to the Serbian Government.

The Minnesota Russian Relief Committee has contributed approximately $95,000 in cash and kind to the work of the American Friends' Service Committee.

Friends in America will be glad to learn that Arthur Watts, who has served as Chief of the Russian Unit for the past two years, is convalescing from typhus. Following a very severe case one lung filled up. This has now cleared, and he is so far recovered that he has taken a trip to Norway for a period of rest and recuperation.

Two Points of Danger

The Government, in urging military training in camps and in colleges and similar institutions, would do well to recall the fable of the eagle that perceived that the arrow which struck at its life was furnished with one of the eagle's own feathers.

At the present time there would seem to be little danger to this country from militarism, and yet history proves that the destruction of the great nations of the past was caused chiefly by militarism. In fact a republic cannot carry on war and remain a republic. In the World War we saw extraordinary powers granted to our President, powers, indeed, that would have been extremely dangerous in the hands of an ambitious man. We saw free speech abolished and all industry and transportation mobilized for the purposes of war. To an alarming extent civil authority was superceded by the military. During the period of the war the United States was no longer a republic.

Therefore, in this time of peace, let us not make the mistake of turning the minds of our young men towards war and preparations therefor, but let those ideals which make for the wise development and perpetuity of our country be instilled into the minds of our youth.

Another objection to the proposed military training of young men is that it tends to substitute obedience for personal judgment. There is no value in a course of training which takes away a man's initiative and judgment, and which requires immediate obedience simply upon the order of a "superior." One of the most vital arraignments against war is that it makes a man's conscience practically inoperative. "Their's not to reason why." Can we afford to train men to eliminate conscience and substitute obedience for their sense of right? It is probable that not one of the soldiers who were ordered to shoot Edith Cavell wanted to do it; they "obeyed orders."

Our national and state governments would do well to direct the thoughts of our young people towards the arts of peace rather than towards those of war if we would preserve and strengthen our national ideals.

O. Edward Jannney.

Friendly News Notes

Dr. William I. Hull's summary of the results of the Washington Conference have been sent to over 20,000 clergymen in the United States.

Amelia Mott Gummere's new edition of John Woolman's Journal, which is ready for publication, will contain much new material and include the full journal of Woolman, with numerous illustrations. According to *The Friend* (Phila.), the popular edition edited by John G. Whittier, was not based on the original journal, but on a copy.

Henry T. Hodgkin reached Haverford, Pa., on the 25th, where he was the guest of Rufus M. Jones. He is to be at the Woolman School week-end conference over Seventh month 1st; speaks at 12th Street Meeting-house, Philadelphia, on the 5th; in New York on the evening of the 6th; and sails for England at the end of the week. For times of holding meetings, see "Coming Events."

"Quakerism and Democracy," will be the subject of the address by Frank Aydelotte, President of Swarthmore College, at Friends' General Conference at Richmond, Ind., Eighth month 26th to Ninth month 2nd.

President Aydelotte, coming as he does from a wide educational experience outside the Society of Friends, is in an excellent position to observe the contribution of the Society of Friends to education in a democracy.

The summer term at Woolman School opened on the 27th with an enthusiastic group of students. This group is anticipating the coming each week of the special speakers and the gathering of Friends and friendly people who will come. Henry T. Hodgkin, Paul Jones, and Dr. William Byron Forbush are among the speakers at the first week-end—Sixth month 30th-Seventh month 2nd.

J. Henry Scattergood has recently been elected trustee of Hampton Institute. He gave the principal address when Armstrong Athletic Field, a gift of alumni and former students, was formally presented on May 4th.

A delegation of twelve, mostly young people, from Fair Hill Meeting, Philadelphia, made a pilgrimage to the Schuylkill Meeting, at Phoenixville, Pa., on Sixth month 18th. There was vocal ministry by H. Clara Foulke, Harry Brussel and Stuart S. Graves. Basket lunch was served on the old historic ground.

At Haddonfield Quarterly Meeting held at Medford, N. J., on Sixth month 15th, Caroline J. Worth, Franklin Zelley, Keziah Wilkins, and J. Barnard Walton were present. Messages were given bearing on the great value of getting together for the mutual understanding in the settlement of differences, and also the value of preparation, "the example of the wise virgins."

Laura Collings, as a representative to the Yearly Meeting, gave a very interesting and comprehensive report of the exercises and work of the Yearly Meeting.

Sufficient funds were raised to send a member of the Quarterly Meeting to the Young Friends' Conference at Earlham.

The birthday list for July of political prisoners still confined in American prisons is as follows:

4th—Warren Billings, San Quentin Prison, San Quentin, California.

10th—Harry Brewer, P. O. Box 7, Leavenworth, Kansas.

15th—John Potthast, P. O. Box 7, Leavenworth, Kansas.

25th—Edw. Flogaus, Walla Walla, Washington, Box 520.

26th—James Price, Repressa, California (Folsom Prison).

28th—Charles M. Cline, Huntsville, Texas, Box 32.

On commencement Day, June 16th, Haverford College conferred the degree of Doctor of Laws upon Rufus Matthew Jones, a graduate of Haverford College in the class of 1885 and for 25 years Professor of Philosophy at Haverford. In conferring the degree, President Comfort said: "Rufus Jones is an impenitent optimist, who has discovered the secret of perpetual youth, and who has helped numberless young men find themselves in finding a faith. He is a believer," the president continued, "in the forces of the unseen, who has interpreted these forces to his students by his spoken word and by his living illustration of the power of love."

A feature of London Yearly Meeting this year was an address by Lord Robert Cecil. Such a fine impression did he make on his hearers that the chairman remarked "Though we may not believe *with* our speaker we believe *in* him."

Lord Robert said: "I was brought up to believe war the most terrible of all things and that peace was an international affair and the greatest blessing. I look to complete disarmament as the ideal we should like to see carried out, and I think that the Covenant of the League of Nations with its severe practicality of outlook is a definite step towards this end and far from being the visionary measure that some seem to think it. We must make the League all embracing and then we shall be able more easily to carry out a scheme for real disarmament."

In Lord Robert's opinion the League of Nations relied less on force than anything else with which he was acquainted. It relies, he said, on public opinion and its appeal was to international co-operation.

The Summer Schools of New York Monthly Meeting will open for the summer on Second-day, Seventh month 10th, and will continue until Ninth month 2nd. In New York, under four teachers, there will be a kindergarten class, two classes in sewing, and making hats and dresses, etc., and a manual training class for boys. There will be, too, of course, supervised play, folk-dancing, singing, etc. This school is open only in the morning.

In Brooklyn, the work is carried on more as a playground, under two teachers, the place being open from 10 to 12 in the morning, and 2 to 5 in the afternoon. Here there will be supervised play, with kindergarten handwork, and sewing, weaving, etc.

Last year, nearly 100 children in each school enjoyed the chance to play or work in safety, and comparative coolness. This year, it is hoped to increase the budget, and the attendance, and begin the establishment of permanent equipment in both places. The sum set as the goal for this year is $1,300 which is nearly $200 more than the total receipts of last year.

Items Fom Everywhere

Felony indictments against forty-three high officials and members of the Ku Klux Klan were returned by the Los Angeles County Grand Jury.

Notification that 1,000, or not more than 1,200, officers and men of the American forces in Germany will remain indefinitely at Coblenz was made, according to an official report.

In the name of the American Congress and people, Myron T. Herrick, the American Ambassador, June 4, presented to the city of Verdun the only medal ever given by the United States Government to any community in the world.

The recent acquisition by British oil interests of $28,000,000 worth of stock in the Shell Oil Company, a Dutch concern, is ominous. It looks like the preliminary to a merger of British and Dutch interests to fight American companies. Oil may sometimes quiet troubled waters, but in international relations it is apt to have the opposite effect.

Ignoring local prohibition officials, the Hotel Association of New York has made a direct appeal to President Harding, Secretary of the Treasury Mellon, and Prohibition Commissioner Haynes, to stop the brazen sale of liquors in restaurants and other places in that city.

The result of the new 3 per cent. restrictive immigration law is startling. In the last fiscal year, without this law in force, the net increase of immigration was more than one-half million. For the first nine months of the present fiscal year, operating under this 3 per cent. law, the net increase is but 80,000. Strange to say, this increase consists entirely of women and girls. The male immigrant aliens admitted do not equal those who have departed. The female immigrant aliens admitted exceed in number those who have departed by 80,000.

On June 4 Movie Director Hays sent an ultimatum to the picture industry to clean up the films and keep them clean. This order affects the Motion Picture Producers and Distributors of America, which represents 70 or 80 per cent. of the business in this country. This ultimatum, so press dispatches said, was to be pasted upon the bulletin boards of all Los Angeles studios, calling upon actors, directors, etc., to assist in eliminating objectionable features. The head of each particular company sent a letter with Mr. Hays' order. Every picture of the allied companies is to be filtered through the internal censorship of Mr. Hays' office. The public is asked to report objectionable films.

According to reports Pancho Villa, the former Mexican bandit, is a peace-loving, hard-working, contented rancher, without political ambitions and imbued with a sincere desire to help his people. He has established schools on his ranch and he and his three children are studying English. He is also studying Spanish for he has all his life been illiterate. Agriculture is his hobby and he is attempting to make his ranch a model in modern farming. He declares that he wants Mexico to live in harmonious accord with the United States.

The Loved and Lost

In memory of Marcia S. Doan

Spring comes with its birds and flowers,
Its breezes warm from the south—
New life bursting in bloom,
But they come never again,
Our friends, the loved and lost,
Cut down in their vernal years,
Comrades who walked with us once
Under these campus trees,
Who loved these fields and woods
And all that old Swarthmore gives
Of beauty and wisdom and truth.

In the drip of the silver rains,
In the sigh of the soft June winds,
I hear a lament for them,
An elegy tender and low,
For vanished beauty and charm,
For loyal and kindly hearts

And she was one of the band
Of that sisterhood loved and lost,
She whom we mourn today,
And whose memory now we mark
With these evergreens* vivid and fresh.

But let now this grieving mood
Give way to our certain faith
That her beautiful spirit lives
In some higher sphere, and works
For noble things, for joy,
For sunny and radiant ends!

* * *

Flowers in a peaceful garth,
  Stars on a lonely sea,
Loveliness immortal,
  Blend with our thought of thee,
Blend with our dreaming tears,
Friend of our Swarthmore years.

—John Russell Hayes (in *The Swarthmore Phoenix*).

*A pair of box trees, planted at the north entrance of Science Hall, Swarthmore College.

THE OPEN FORUM

This column is intended to afford free expression of opinion by readers on questions of interest. The Intelligencer is not responsible for any such opinions. Letters must be brief, and the editor reserves the right to omit parts if necessary to save space.

To the Editor:

Today's Intelligencer contains an article in the Open Forum on Labor Cost vs. Finished Product. The assertion is made that "Capital itself never produced anything." Was ever a serious statement more absurdly untrue? Every meadow, forest and mine is a refutation of it. Every electric plant driven by water power is substantially a refutation of the statement.

Practically all of the Baltimore industries—its trolley cars, all of its electric lights, etc., get the power produced by the capital invested in the large electric plant on the Susquehanna, and in the feed wires coming therefrom. The labor (if you can call it labor to oil the machinery) is an almost negligible factor. Of course labor produced the dam and the machinery and the feed wires, but now they are "Capital." Again,—labor produces money—money is invested in a Government bond and this produces interest. The Government gets this "interest" by levying taxes, substantially all of which comes from other interest or dividends from invested Capital. It will be observed that this matter is a very complicated one and impossible to handle in a brief letter in the Open Forum. There seem to be several people who have the idea that "the present industrial system while it could and should be of benefit to all, is not, because it takes from labor the tools that formerly made him independent, and makes him dependent upon so-called Capital for permission to 'earn," and these people write letters to your forum from time to time. Their letters occasionally take the form of protesting against what they call the "profit" system.

Why do they "never produce anything" in the nature of a plan which they think may change things for the better? Are these people laborers? If not, what right have they to speak for labor? If they are, and do not like it, why do they not earn and save some capital? I think it would be very easy for a man to earn and save capital if he has brains enough to change our industrial system.

Have you ever met a man who will not admit, or whose family will not admit for him, that he gets just about what he deserves?

Baltimore, Md., June 10th. Enoch Harlan.

LET'S DO IT!

To the Editor:

I have just returned from witnessing the Dubuque General Sunday School Parade. It is an annual affair and nearly all the Protestant Sunday Schools in the city participate. Following the parade is a picnic. As I watched the various schools I thought, "Where are the Methodists, where are the Baptists, and all the other 'ists' and 'isms'?" The banners mentioned these, but not the faces. There it is; it is the Words that are between us. How significant in John: "The Word was made flesh and dwelt amongst us." Words you may divide, there are many; but not Word, it is one; not even composed of syllables. Why have we squabbled over words? Paul warns us about it. Let us do away, religiously, with Words and just use Word, one Word—Love. G. R. Rogers,

Dubuque, Iowa.

BIRTHS

Deckman—On Fifth month 13th, to William J. and Margaret G. Deckman, of Greene, Pa., a son, named William J. Deckman, Jr.

Grubb—On second month 19th, to Clyde and Alice G. Smith Grubb, Peach Bottom, Pa., a son, named Walter Charles Grubb.

Kirk—On Sixth month 5th, to William J. and Eva M. Kirk, of Peach Bottom, Pa., a daughter, named Marian Estelle Kirk.

MARRIAGES

Wright-Cox—At Media, Pa., on Sixth month 21st, Elizabeth Horsey, daughter of Mr. and Mrs. Robert Feekes Cox, and Edward Needles, son of William and Cornelia N. Wright, of Moylan, Pa.

DEATHS

Beans—Near Moorestown, N. J., on Sixth month 18th, Mary E. Beans, widow of Thomas J. Beans, in her 93rd year. Interment at Neshaminy Cemetery, near Hartsville, Pa.

Bradley—At his home near Peach Bottom, Pa., on Fifth month 25th, Joseph H. Bradley, in his 47th year.

BROWN—On Sixth month 7th, at Moorestown, N. J., Charles L. Brown, in his 84th year. Funeral was held at Friends' Meeting House, Moorestown, and interment made at Westfield, N. J.

KIRKBRIDE—In Trenton, N. J., on Sixth month 3rd, Elizabeth Henderson Kirkbride, wife of William B. Kirkbride.

SHAW—At Friends' Home, Newtown, Pa., on Sixth month 15th, Clementine G. Shaw, at an advanced age. Interment at Carversville.

STEELE—At his home in Birmingham Township, Chester County, Pa., on Fifth month 26th, George Steele, in his 95th year. A member and for many years an Elder of Birmingham Monthly Meeting.

WHITALL—On Sixth month 22nd, at Friends' Boarding Home, Woodstown, N. J., Mary E. Whitall, aged 86 years. Funeral and interment at Woodbury, N. J. A valued member of Woodbury Monthly Meeting.

YERKES—At the residence of her son-in-law, Howard R. Yearsley, Philadelphia, on Sixth month 20th, Elizabeth Walter Yerkes, wife of the late John D. Yerkes, aged 84 years.

COMING EVENTS

SIXTH MONTH

29th—Open-air meeting under auspices of Young Democracy in interest of political prisoners. See notice.

30th—First Woolman School week-end conference to First-day, Seventh month 2nd, inclusive. Henry T. Hodgkin will speak Seventh-day evening at 7.30.

SEVENTH MONTH

1st—Woolman School week-end conference, 4.30 p. m., Paul Jones "Enjoying a Good Scrap." 7.30 p. m. Henry T. Hodgkin, "The Situation in the Far East." (For those coming for this afternoon and evening only, it is suggested that they bring box supper. Accommodations at Woolman School for meals and lodging during the week-end as far as capacity permits.)

2nd—First-day, at 2.30 p. m. Daylight Saving Time; a meeting for Divine Worship will be held at Stanton (Delaware) Friends' Meeting-house under care of a committee of Concord Quarterly Meeting. Wilmington Friends' School motor bus will leave 4th and Market Sts. for Stanton about 1.55 o'clock; also trolley cars leave at same place and hour. Friends of both branches as well as all interested persons are invited.

2nd—Religious meeting under care of a Committee of Burlington Quarterly Meeting will be held at Arney's Mount Meeting-house, near Mt. Holly, N. J., at 3 p. m. (daylight saving). Isaac Wilson is expected to be in attendance.

5th—Henry T. Hodgkin will address a meeting at Friends' Meeting-house, 12th Street below Market, Philadelphia, at 7.30 p. m. Subject, "The Society of Friends and the Far East." A cordial invitation to all.

6th—Henry T. Hodgkin will address a meeting in Friends' Meeting-house, 20th Street and Gramercy Park, New York, at 8 p. m.

8th—Frederick J. Libby will speak at the Woolman School week-end conference at 8 p. m., on "Recent Phases in the World Drama."

9th—Woolman School week-end conference at 4 p. m. "How to Create the International Mind," Dorothy Brooke, Irvin C. Poley and others.

9th—Certain members of Philadelphia Quarterly Meeting's Visiting Committee will attend Valley Meeting, at 10.30 a. m. First-day School at 11.30 a. m.

9th—Preparative Meeting in New York and Brooklyn, after the Meetings for Worship.

10th—New York Monthly Meeting, in New York, at 7.30. Supper will be served at 6 o'clock, as usual.

16th—Certain members of Philadelphia Quarterly Meeting's Visiting Committee will attend a meeting for worship at Germantown Friends' Home, at 7.30 p. m.

29th—Westbury Quarterly Meeting, at Westbury, L. I., at 10.30 a. m. Lunch will be served soon after noon. The afternoon session at 2.30 will be under the care of the Meeting's Advancement Committee.

NOTICE—An open air meeting in the garden of the Art Alliance, 1823 Walnut Street, Philadelphia, on June 29th, at 8 p. m. Rev. John A. Ryan, D. D., Director of the National Catholic Welfare Council, and Mr. James Manning, released lately from Leavenworth Penitentiary, where he served a five-year term as a political prisoner, will address the meeting. Admission free. Collection taken. The meeting is under the auspices of the Young Democracy.

American Friends' Service Committee

WILBUR K. THOMAS, EX. SEC.
20 S. 12th St. Philadelphia.

CASH CONTRIBUTIONS
WEEK ENDING JUNE 19TH

Five Years Meetings	$66.50
Other Meetings—	
Orange Grove Avenue Meeting, of Pasadena	60.00
Alexandria Monthly Meeting and First-day School	35.00
Little Britain Monthly Meeting	20.00
Frends' Meetings (both branches)	250.00
Eastland First-day School	.91
Men's Friendly Bible Class, Baltimore, Md.	40.00
Western Quarter, Kennett Square	30.00
First Friends' Church, Cleveland, Ohio	7.00
Little Britain Monthly Meeting	5.00
Contributions for Germany	194.00
For Austria	82.50
For Poland	27.00
For Russia	2,851.78
For Russian Overhead	193.25
For Home Service	368.00
For Clothing	2.00
For Syria	3.15
For General	668.00
For German Overhead	10.00
Refunds	8.00
	$4,922.09

Shipments received during week ending June 17, 1922: 90 boxes and packages received; 1 from Mennonites.

WANTED

WOMAN OF MIDDLE AGE, NURSE, wants care of invalid. Address P. 250, Friends' Intelligencer.

POSITION WANTED—BY NURSE companion, free July 4th, semi-invalid, or elderly woman; light household duties; sewing; useful. Country; references. Address B. 251, Friends' Intelligencer.

WANTED—CHILDREN TO BOARD in country. Mother's care, best references. Apply to Mrs. F. J. Reeser, Honey Brook, Chester Co., Pa.

COLLEGE GIRL WANTS SUMMER work as mother's helper, camp worker, office assistant, etc. Phone Swarthmore 15-M, or address S. 260, Friends' Intelligencer.

WANTED—A FEW BOARDERS FOR Seventh and Eighth months, in private home. Modern conveniences. Apply to Caroline L. Warrick, Rancocas, N. J.

BLIND TAUGHT TO WRITE, IN four to six months. Lessons by mail. Prices reasonable. Samuel Koons, 633 Eye St., N. W., Washington, D. C.

WANTED—WORKING HOUSE-keeper; no laundry. Good home and pay for capable and satisfactory woman. Mrs. W. Morris Palmer, Exton, Chester Co., Pa.

POSITION WANTED BY PRACTICAL nurse and companion for semi-invalid, or elderly lady. Address 38 Bispham St., Mt. Holly, N. J.

POSITION WANTED—BY NURSE companion, free July 4th, semi-invalid, or elderly woman; light household duties; sewing. Country. Address B. 251, Friends' Intelligencer.

FOR RENT

TO RENT FURNISHED—FOR FEW months or for a longer period, attractive 14-room house near college, Swarthmore, Pa. All conveniences, porches and shaded lawn. Large and small fruits and vegetables. No garage. References exchanged. For terms and particulars write or phone, Swarthmore 572, M. S. B., 503 W. Chester Road.

FOR RENT—DURING AUGUST, AT reasonable rate, new cottage, near Buck Hill; 7 large open-air rooms and bath; fireplace and large porch. Well equipped. Broad mountain view. Address, Edith M. Winder, Cresco, Pa.

TO RENT FURNISHED—FOR FEW months or for a longer period, attractive 14-room house near college, Swarthmore, Pa. All conveniences, porches and shaded lawn. Large and small fruits and vegetables. No garage. References exchanged. For terms and particulars write or phone, Swarthmore 572, M. S. B., 503 N. Chester Road.

FOR RENT—AT POCONO MANOR, Pa., beautiful summer home, 12 rooms, sleeping porch, billiard room; electricity; magnificent view of Delaware Water Gap and mountains; 2 minutes from Inn. Address, Mrs. Alice H. Phillips, 2029 Spruce St., Philadelphia.

FOR RENT—ROOM. CALL EVENings, or phone Swarthmore 606. James Cranston, 17 S. Chester Road, Swarthmore, Pa.

AIRY, DOUBLE ROOM, SECOND floor, private home. Short distance through beautiful shade to boarding house. Mrs. L. H. Marshall, Westtown School, Pa.

FOR SALE

FOR SALE—FIRST MORTGAGE OF three thousand dollars, bearing interest at 6%, on farm of 80 acres desirably located about 25 miles from Philadelphia. Address Floyd S. Platt, Morrisville, Pa.

GENEALOGIST

ELIZABETH B. SATTERTHWAITE,

52 N. Stockton St., Trenton, N. J.

WALTER RHOADS WHITE,

Attorney and Counsellor-at-Law

Lansdowne Trust Co., Lansdowne, Pa.

Also Member of the Delaware County Bar

WE BUY ANTIQUE FURNITURE and antiques of all kinds; old gold, silver, platinum, diamonds and old false teeth. Phila. Antique Co., 633 Chestnut, cor. 7th. Phone Lombard 6398. Est. 1866.

ADVERTISING RATE in the FRIENDS' INTELLIGENCER, for Help Wanted, Positions Wanted, Rooms for Rent, Notices, and other classified advertisements without display, for each insertion, 2 cents per word, including name, initials and address. Answers may be sent to a box at the INTELLIGENCER office, if so directed.

For display advertising the rate is 10 cents per agate line, or $1.40 per column inch, each insertion. On ten or more insertions in a year from date of order, ten per cent. discount. Thus a four-inch single-column or two-inch double-column advertisement costs $5.60 each insertion, less ten per cent., or 5.04 net each time for ten or more insertions. Matter may be changed whenever desired, without extra charge.

Experience has proved the INTELLIGENCER to be a remarkably good advertising medium. All advertisements must "pass the censor!"

Address 140 N. 15th St., Philadelphia

The Friends' Intelligencer

Established 1844 | SEVENTH MONTH 8, 1922 | Volume 79 Number 27

Contents

REGULAR MEETINGS

OAKLAND, CALIF. — A FRIENDS' Meeting is held every First-day at 11 A. M., in the Extension Room, Y. W. C. A. Building, Webster Street, above 14th. Visiting Friends always welcome.

FRIENDS' MEETING IN PASADENA, California — Orange Grove Monthly Meeting of Friends, 520 East Orange Grove Avenue, Pasadena, California. Meeting for worship, First-day, 11 A. M. Monthly Meeting, the second First-day of each month, at 1.45 P. M.

CENTRAL MEETING OF FRIENDS (Chicago), meets every First-day in Room 706, 410 South Michigan Avenue, at 10.45 A. M. Visitors are invited.

NOTICE—Concise statements of the principles of the Religious Society of Friends and their application to the problems of every day living, including "The Spirit of Quakerism," by Elbert Russell; "Preparation for Life's Greatest Business," by Rufus M. Jones; and other articles by Henry W. Wilbur, Howard M. Jenkins, Elizabeth Lloyd, Jesse H. Holmes, O. Edward Janney, Edward B. Rawson, etc., to be had free on application to Friends' General Conference Advancement Committee, 140 North Fifteenth Street, Philadelphia, Pa.

Can you afford to be without a partial supply of COAL under present conditions in the mining district?

H. F. BRUNER & CO.

16 North 21st Street

Bell, Locust 0243 *Keystone, Race 5661*

THE FRIENDS' INTELLIGENCER

Published weekly, 140 N. 15th Street, Philadelphia, Pa., by Friends' Intelligencer Association, Ltd.

PAUL W. WAGER, *Editor.*
SUE C. YERKES, *Business Manager*

Editorial Board: Elizabeth Powell Bond, Thomas A. Jenkins, J. Russell Smith, George A. Walton.

Board of Managers: Edward Cornell, Alice Hall Paxson, Paul M. Pearson, Annie Hillborn, Elwood Hollingshead, William C. Biddle, Charles F. Jenkins, Edith M. Winder, Frances M. White.

Officers of Intelligencer Associates: Ellwood Burdsall, Chairman; Bertha L. Broomell, Secretary; Herbert P. Worth, Treasurer.

Subscription rates: United States, Mexico, Cuba and Panama, $2.50 per year. Canada and other foreign countries, $3.00 per year. Checks should be made payable to Friends' Intelligencer Association, Ltd.

Entered as Second Class Matter at Philadelphia Post Office.

TRANSIENT ACCOMMODATIONS

WASHINGTON, D. C.—ROOMS FOR visitors. Near Station, Capitol, Library. Continuous hot water. Electricity. Garage. Mrs. L. L. Kendig, 120 C. Street, Northwest.

SCHOOLS.

Woolman School

SWARTHMORE, PA.

Summer Term

6th Month 27 to 8th Month 5

Five special week-end programs for those unable to take regular courses. Write for information.

ELBERT RUSSELL, *Director.*

GEORGE SCHOOL
Near Newtown, Bucks County, Pa.

Under the care of Philadelphia Yearly Meeting of Friends.

Course of study extended and thorough, preparing students either for business or for college. For catalogue apply to

GEORGE A. WALTON, A. M., Principal
George School, Penna.

FRIENDS' CENTRAL SCHOOL SYSTEM

Write for Year Book and Rates.

RALSTON THOMAS,
Principal.

15th and Race Sts., Philadelphia.

FRIENDS' ACADEMY
LONG ISLAND, N. Y.

A Boarding and Day School for Boys and Girls, conducted in accordance with the principles of the Society of Friends. For further particulars address

S. ARCHIBALD SMITH, Principal,
Locust Valley, N. Y.

To the Lot Holders and others interested in Fairhill Burial Ground:

GREEN STREET Monthly Meeting has funds available for the encouragement of the practice of cremating the dead to be interred in Fairhill Burial Ground. We wish to bring this fact as prominently as possible to those who may be interested. We are prepared to undertake the expense of cremation in case any lot holder desires us to do so.

Those interested should communicate with William H. Gaskill, Treasurer of the Committee of Interments, Green Street Monthly Meeting, or any of the following members of the Committee.

William H. Gaskill, 3201 Arch St.
Samuel N. Longstreth, 1218 Chestnut St.
Charles F. Jenkins, 232 South Seventh St.
Stuart S. Graves, 3033 Germantown Ave.

ELLWOOD HEACOCK
FUNERAL DIRECTOR
2027 NORTH COLLEGE AVENUE
PHILADELPHIA
CALLS OUT OF CITY ANSWERED PROMPTLY

HOTELS.

Buck Hill Falls

Buck Hill Golf Course—1922.

Schedule of Competitions.

July 25th, 26th, 27th, 28th—Women's Tournament.

August 4th—2-Ball Mixed Foursome.

August 9th, 10th, 11th, 12th—Regular Tournament.

August 23rd—Obstacle Putting Contest.

September 4th — Pocono - Buck Hill Match at Pocono Manor.

THE INN

BUCK HILL FALLS, PA.

HOTEL WARWICK

SOUTH CAROLINA AVENUE
ATLANTIC CITY, N. J.
OPEN ALL THE YEAR

First house from beach and boardwalk. Steam heat, electric lights, elevator. Excellent cuisine, quiet, dignified surroundings and attentive service.

Reasonable rates. Write
SARAH H. FULLOM, Prop.

OCEAN CITY, N. J.

Hotel Swarthmore

Capacity 135.

Near beach and attractions; running water thruout; neat white help; cuisine first class.

W. P. & F. R. LIPPINCOTT.

Congress Hall
Cape May, N. J.

Unsurpassed as to comfort, convenience, service and atmosphere. American Plan. JOHN V. SCOTT, Manager.

THE WHEELER
Boardwalk at Massachusetts
ATLANTIC CITY, N. J.
Ocean Rooms—Table Guests
MRS. A. W. WHEELER

Strath Haven Tea Room
Dinner 6 to 7:30.
Sunday Special — Chicken and Waffles, 85 cents.
Swarthmore, Pa. Phone 680

The Friends' Intelligencer

The religion of Friends is based on faith in the "INWARD LIGHT," or direct revelation of God's spirit and will in every seeking soul.

The INTELLIGENCER is interested in all who bear the name of Friends in every part of the world, and aims to promote love, unity and intercourse among all branches and with all religious societies.

ESTABLISHED 1844 | PHILADELPHIA, SEVENTH MONTH 8, 1922 | VOLUME 79 NUMBER 27

Cross Crossings Cautiously

The malcontents of Europe have yet to learn that assassination is not the road to peace.

Why is the United States the last of the allied nations to set its war-opinion prisoners free?

It is better that a hundred guilty men should go free than that one innocent man should die. Sacco and Vanzetti can never be proved guilty and their death sentence should be commuted.

An automobile without brakes is a very unsafe proposition. It would be equally dangerous to deprive the Supreme Court of its power to annul legislation which it believes to be unconstitutional.

It looks as though the United States government is violating its own prohibition law in permitting the sale of intoxicating liquors on board vessels operated by the United States Shipping Board when these vessels are outside the three-mile limit.

Mr. Lasker, Chairman of the Shipping Board, maintains that the prohibition law is not violated because the Eighteenth Amendment and the Volstead Act do not apply to vessels on the high seas. If this is so, how can vessels flying the American flag expect or demand the protection guaranteed under other articles of the Constitution? Representative Bankhead of Alabama proposes that an amendment be added to the merchant marine bill which would deny government aid to any government ship on which liquor is stored, sold, or otherwise disposed of. The suggestion is good but it does not strike the root of the matter. To quote from "The American Issue," a prohibition paper, "American vessels outside the three-mile limit are either American territory or they are not. If not, what territory are they? If they are American territory, the Eighteenth Amendment applies to them the same as to any other American territory, and if the Volstead Act does not apply, Congress should pass an act making it apply."

This episode only illustrates again that prohibition is not a dead issue in this country and its friends must be ever on the alert. The enemies of prohibition are missing no opportunity to belittle its benefits and to magnify its shortcomings. Every ill with which society is now afflicted is charged to prohibition. The drug habit, the crime wave, strikes, unemployment, high taxes, and the spirit of unrest and lawlessness which is abroad, are all claimed to be the direct result of prohibition. Unfortunately, a lot of honest people are beginning to believe it. They fail to see that they are the victims of a very deliberate propaganda. They should not have forgotten so soon that the liquor interests never make direct frontal attacks.

Every argument that was advanced in favor of prohibition ten years ago is valid today. If prohibition has failed to bring all the benefits that were expected of it there is no reason to be discouraged. Murder was never more rampant than now but no one proposes that the law against murder be repealed. These people who pretend to be so concerned lest prohibition undermine the force of the constitution are usually concealing their real motive. The enemies of prohibition can nearly all be grouped in three classes,—those with parched throats, those whose pocket-book is affected, or those who have a mistaken notion of personal liberty. The members of the last group are either too stupid to be dangerous or intelligent enough to be converted.

Prohibition has come to stay. It would be impossible to secure thirty-six states that would vote for the repeal of the Eighteenth Amendment. But there is grave danger that the Volstead Enforcement Act will be tampered with. The same Congressmen who voted for prohibition because they feared public opinion, will vote for wine and beer if they feel it will win them votes. The friends of prohibition still outnumber its enemies, but the latter are making the most noise. If prohibition can be defended until the present generation of "old topers" has died off, and until money formerly invested in brewery interests has been permanently transferred to other channels of investment, then it will stand alone. Until then we must be on guard.

The Desert Shall Blossom as the Rose

Baccalaureate sermon delivered at Earlham College by Elbert Russell

The desert is a closer neighbor to Palestine than the sea. It spreads its desolation along the whole face of Syria. It enfolds Palestine on the south. The wilderness of Judea rears its desolation from the Jordan to the crest of the highland and peers into the very gates of Jerusalem. The conservative says: "Nature doesn't change. The desert has always been there, and as long as the mountains remain to strip the Mediterranean winds of their moisture, the desert will always be desert."

Yet the prophet-poet is right rather than the practical conservative. It is possible to change nature. Man taps the artesian waters beneath or lifts the waters of low-lying streams into irrigation sluices; he transplants alfalfa, strips the cactus of its spines, learns dry farming, and lo, the desert is carpeted with green, garlanded with flowers, enriched with fruit. By such co-operative industry the Nile Valley is snatched from the desert; and for lack of it the Babylonian plain, once like the garden of the Lord, has become a desolation.

It was, however, human nature which the prophet expected to be reclaimed from its desolation. It is precisely this which we are assured today is hopelessly unchangeable: "You can't change human nature: men have always been clannish, selfish, drunken, lustful, warring, competitive, and they always will be!" So the refrain of resignation runs. There is, of course, a sense in which it is true. Our fundamental instincts, powers, passions, and capacities are pretty much the same as those revealed in the earliest records of human life. Adam puts the blame on Eve, Samuel's sons take bribes, Homer's warriors boast and tremble, pray and fight, lust and loot. Their leaders practice deceit on their own men with propaganda and on the enemy with camouflage in quite modern fashion. Hector comes in from the bloody battlefield to play the role of gentle father and tender husband. He takes off his helmet because it frightens his baby, fondles the child, reassures Andromache, his wife, and kisses both a tender farewell! In its fundamental elements human nature has not changed.

But when it is asserted that human nature as a determining force in conduct and as the basis of our social institutions cannot be changed, the assertion is contradicted by both history and Christian faith. Men may be changed from savage to civilized, from professional fighters to peaceful citizens, from Arab idolaters to Moslem fanatics, from shiftless bachelors to hard-working heads of families, from soldiers of fortune to Knights of the Cross, from sinners to saints. All the old elements may be there, but the dominant motives, the working forces are changed.

The changelessness of human nature is usually put forward as an obstacle to attempted reform. We are told that idealism is impracticable, spiritual and moral reforms impossible because human nature is unchangeable. It is asserted that our animal nature is so primitive and fundamental in us that like beasts, we must always "bark and bite 'cause 'tis our nature to."

This hopelessness overlooks two great truths. One is that you can change animal nature, even as the desert can be made to bloom. The leopard can change his spots and the Ethiopian his skin through breeding and change of environment. The dog was a wolf once. Now he will die to protect a baby. The horse was once a five-toed animal no larger than a fox. Man breeds him into a pony, or a racer, or a draught horse. The animal in us is no less susceptible of domestication and transformation.

Education, training, custom, public opinion, and religious influence can mold and remake character and through it determine conduct. In a thousand ways we inculcate a militant patriotism and then call it natural. History and tradition keep alive the memory of wars. Monuments and patriotic orations exalt the warrior, kindle ambition for military conquest, develop a sense of national honor and independence incompatible with arbitral justice or international courts, as in the United States Senate; keep alive national pride as in France or hope of revenge as in Germany. We have been able to develop a peaceful national spirit in our 48 states between people of many races. It is just as possible to train the citizens of different nations to submit to organized justice and respect one another's rights if we bring the same forces to the task.

Race prejudice is no more an essential part of human nature than the fighting spirit. Children either do not have it or lose it quickly. In the cosmopolitan quarters of our great cities black, white, and yellow play together without discrimination, until the caste prejudices of their elders teach them to ostracize their different colored playmates. Where white and colored meet without artificial restrictions on the borders of our social organizations, wonderful loyalties and friendships often arise. Barriers to brotherhood that are artificially created can be removed by conscious and consecrated effort.

The second great fact is that altruism is as funda-

fair, however eager to win by any means; to observe the laws, abide by the court's decrees, respect our neighbors' rights, whatever our personal opinions or inclinations.

Love may become such a principle of conduct. We can act as though our enemies were our friends, and make lovely our conduct toward the unlovely. And such is human nature, that we come naturally to feel kind toward those whom we treat kindly and to feel love for those with whom we deal lovingly. Love wins love in response. We usually get a response in kind to our dealings with others. The merciful obtain mercy. The friendly make friends. Every wooer knows that to win a maiden's love he must show himself loving. What the world needs amid its strife and desolation, is for us to take Jesus at his word and act like brothers. This will make the world bloom like the desert under the latter rains. Justice can bring ordered security; the fruit of righteousness is peace, but only love can bring the bloom of loveliness.

To this task both the prophet and the need of the age invite us. We are heirs not only of a redemptive faith but of a needy, desolate, disordered world. It is not a task for the fainthearted, the lazy, or selfish. It is for those whose hope is on distant horizons; who can sow, and water, and bear the heat and burden of the day sustained by the glory of the lily on dimly seen horizons and inspired by the perfume of roses on winds from afar.

The reward must be the Creator's joy in his work, the artist's satisfaction with beauty. It is the work of parent, teacher, cleaner, restorer of things unformed, ignorant, soiled, broken. From the selfish point of view the mistakes of a pupil, the waywardness of a child, the discords of a musical beginner, are jarring, unpleasant. Washing soiled clothes, grubbing briar patches, repairing old houses, dealing with graceless people, eating with publicans and sinners is not entertainment. But the joy of seeing grace come to a child's limbs and order to his thinking: the joy of putting beauty for ashes, and garlands for mourning: the joy of seeing clothes and souls alike come from our labors spotless and white, this is a joy no selfish seeking for beauty and happiness can give. It brings us fellowship with the Infinite Father whose Love is both Creator and Redeemer of men. To a divine partnership the prophet invites us; to help God make the human wilderness glad and bring again in the waste places the Garden of the Lord.

Men become great by working nobly at some great task. The elements of greatness may be in them, or in all men, but it needs the great task to make them shine out.—*Louis Tucker.*

Forty-five Years With Friends in Denmark

The Society of Friends is small in Denmark. There are between 60 and 70 Friends in Denmark when the children are included. The group of Friends dates back to 1877-78, when English Friends visited Denmark and established meetings at different places. There are still a few old Friends living of those, who were convinced of the truth through the message of the English visitors. In the past forty-five years' activity of Danish Friends, the Society has not been taking an outwardly conspicuous part in the affairs of Denmark. Yet the influence of the Society has left its mark and the work which has been done has not been in vain. Several of the young men of the Society have been conscientious objectors to military service (conscription) and some have been imprisoned for this reason. Others have emigrated in order to avoid conscription, and a number of these have settled in the United States.

Some of the members have taken a firm stand in the struggle for the abolition of the oath. In many cases the oath has been compulsory; for instance in the court, or when entering into an official position in the service of the state. As a tangible result of a Friend standing for this principle, the oath has in one particular been done away with.

In the earliest years of the life of the Society in Denmark, Friends established a boarding school at Vejle. This was kept going for some few years with the financial support of English Friends. But after a brief but fruitful existence the school was closed—never to open again. Of other kinds of educational work mention should be made of the attempt of Friends to co-operate with non-conformists bodies at one or two places in educating their children in elementary schools independent of the curriculum imposed on the public schools by the state.

It was from the ranks of Friends the Danish temperance movement gained some of its leaders in the early eighties when the movement was still new and unpopular. Friends took an active and sometimes a prominent part in the work, and some of the older and younger Friends are still actively engaged in temperance work.

When the number of Friends was more numerous than now, monthly and quarterly meetings were held regularly in the different towns, where regular meetings for worship were established. In the years 1899-1900 Friends also issued a small monthly page, "The Friendly Message."

Since the foundation of the Society, English Friends have frequently visited Denmark and attended our annual meeting, which is now the only

established in Copenhagen a Quaker centre to link up with the Quaker centres already existing in Paris and Berlin.

At present we are looking forward to a two-days' conference to be held in Copenhagen on the 17th and 18th of Seventh month, immediately after our Yearly Meeting. We hope that one or two members of the American Friends' Service Committee in Berlin will be present. Probably Francis R. Bacon and his wife will be coming. We are also expecting one or two German Friends to this Conference, and one or two Friends from England. We hope these Friends will give us a stimulating and interesting account of the wide work of Friends. We feel that now the international work of Friends requires the sincere co-operation of *all* Friends and of each individual member irrespective of nationality. Remember, *we are all Friends*. Our nationality and our colors and our language is secondary. In the spirit we are all one body.

Vejle, Denmark. PETER GULDBRANDSEN.

Christianity and Economic Problems XI

How Rapidly Can a Christian Economic Order Be Achieved?

Reduced to Summary Form.

1. *Is a Christian Economic Order Practicable?* Many persons say that it is utterly impossible to conduct modern industry on a basis of the spirit of Jesus. Such persons say that it is futile to expect business men to regard their competitors as brothers and to manifest only good will and love toward them, or to transform the antagonisms between employers and workers into mutual service for the common good. The Christian forces have been seeking for nineteen centuries to establish the Kingdom of God on earth. Thus far they have not wholly succeeded.

Lethargy and indifference are responsible for much of our lack of progress. Then too often men do not know "how the other half lives" and are not sufficiently concerned to find out the extent of injustice and suffering. The situation is further complicated by reason of the strong tendency to defend the *status quo*. Tradition, custom, and social habit exert a tremendous influence over a community and can be displaced only with great difficulty.

There is no room for doubt as to the seriousness of the difficulties which confront the follower of Jesus in this day. And yet one of the notable characteristics of true Christians through the ages has been an indomitable optimism, a refusal to be discouraged at the magnitude of the task to be accomplished.

One of the encouraging signs of the times is the new sensitiveness to suffering and injustice. The very fact that a volume of protest is arising and that everywhere men are seeking a way out of the present distress, gives hope for the future. In past ages when men became sensitive to any great evil, made up their minds that it must be abolished, and set about the task with determination, they have succeeded to a marked degree. And so will it be with present evils. They can be overcome. They *must* be overcome. We must refuse to regard as inevitable any evil in modern life. We must refuse to tolerate any immoral practice, no matter how deep rooted in the past it may be or how difficult seems the task of uprooting it.

This attitude is now becoming increasingly characteristic of the churches in the United States. In many quarters there is a new conscience concerning exploitation and injustice in economic life. A multitude of Christian laymen and ministers are insisting that these wrongs must be righted and are exerting themselves strenuously to this end.

One evidence of this fact is found in "The Social Ideals of the Churches" adopted by the Federal Council of the Churches of Christ in America. The Federal Council is composed of official representatives of some thirty-one Protestant religious bodies, the total membership of which is over twenty million persons.

Social Ideals of the Church

I. Equal rights and justice for all men in all stations of life.

II. Protection of the family by the single standard of purity, uniform divorce laws, proper regulation of marriage, proper housing.

III. The fullest possible development of every child, especially by the provision of education and recreation.

IV. Abolition of child labor.

V. Such regulation of the conditions of toil for women as shall safeguard the physical and moral health of the community.

VI. Abatement and prevention of poverty.

VII. Protection of the individual and society from the social, economic, and moral waste of the liquor traffic.

VIII. Conservation of health.

IX. Protection of the worker from dangerous machinery, occupational diseases, and mortality.

X. The right of all men to the opportunity for self-maintenance, for safeguarding this right against encroachments of every kind, for the protection of workers from the hardships of enforced unemployment.

XI. Suitable provision for the old age of the workers, and for those incapacitated by injury.

XII. The right of employes and employers alike to organize; and for the adequate means of conciliation and arbitration in industrial disputes.

XIII. Release from employment one day in seven.

XIV. Gradual and reasonable reduction of hours of labor to the lowest practicable point, and for that degree of leisure for all which is a condition of the highest human life.

XV. A living wage as a minimum in every industry, and for the highest wage that each industry can afford.

XVI. A new emphasis upon the application of Christian principles to the acquisition and use of property, and for the most equitable division of the product of industry that can ultimately be devised.

Facing the social issues involved in reconstruction.

Resolved, That we affirm as Christian Churches:

1. That the teachings of Jesus are those of essential democracy and express themselves through brotherhood and the co-operation of all groups. We deplore class struggle and declare against all class domination, whether of capital or labor. Sympathizing with labor's desire for a better day and an equitable share in the profits and management of industry, we stand for orderly and progressive social reconstruction instead of revolution by violence.

2. That an ordered and constructive democracy in industry is as necessary as political democracy, and that collective bargaining and the sharing of shop control and management are inevitable steps in its attainment.

3. That the first charge upon industry should be that of a wage sufficient to support an American standard of living. To that end we advocate the guarantee of a minimum wage, the control of unemployment through government labor exchanges, public works, land settlement, social insurance, and experimentation in profit sharing and co-operative ownership.

4. We recognize that women played no small part in the winning of the war. We believe that they should have full political and economic equality with equal pay for equal work, and a maximum eight-hour day. We declare for the abolition of night work by women, and the abolition of child labor; and for the provision of adequate safeguards to insure the moral as well as the physical health of the mothers and children of the race.

A pronouncement concerning social reconstruction has been issued by the Administrative Committee of the National Catholic War Council, an official organization of the Roman Catholic Church in the United States. The Central Conference of American Rabbis has also issued a "Social Justice Program."

These official pronouncements by representatives of the three great religious forces in the United States reveal the extent of the interest of the churches in social problems. In addition to these official statements, there are several significant religious movements of an unofficial nature which are exerting themselves on behalf of a new social order.

One of these is the Fellowship of Reconciliation, which has now been operating for about seven years. Another is the Fellowship for a Christian Social Order. In addition to these movements, most of the larger religious bodies have national departments of social service, with bureaus of information and traveling secretaries. In addition, the Church League for Industrial Democracy is doing effective work among members of the Episcopal Church. There are also several other movements within the churches working for social righteousness, such as the Brotherhood of the Kingdom, etc.

Plans are now under way for conducting in 1924 a National Conference on the Meaning of Christianity in Industrial, Racial, and International Relations. A similar conference is to be held in England. A world conference on "Life and Work" is planned for 1924 or 1925.

It is sometimes said that the pronouncements of various religious bodies are only paper programs, mere words, and do not possess any real significance. In reply, it should be pointed out that the statements and activities of these bodies indicate a new sensitiveness to the evils in the present social order and a new determination to overcome them. In past centuries an awakened conscience to great evils and a resolute determination to overcome them has been the basis of moral progress. And so it is in our day. The awakening within the churches during the past few decades with regard to social problems is of tremendous significance for the moral progress of mankind.

2. *How Rapidly Can a Christian Economic Order Be Achieved?* There are two common attitudes toward this question. First, there is the attempt to revolutionize the economic order immediately and the tendency to be impatient with delay. Second, there is the widespread feeling that no considerable progress in the solution of economic problems can be made in a short time, with the consequent tendency to regard proposed solutions as "Utopian."

An examination of the records of history reveals the fact that many far-reaching changes in human affairs have taken place with relatively great speed. It has been said that "for the material advancement of mankind the nineteenth century has done more than all preceding ages combined." Not only with regard to inventions but also in the realm of moral problems great strides have been made within comparatively short periods.

The outstanding problems of the day, however, require an educational basis for their solution. One of the great needs of the present moment is for a thorough application of the spirit of scientific analysis in all realms of modern industry, in the sphere of human relations as well as in mechanics. Another great need of the present moment is fellowship—intimate acquaintance, a sharing of thought and experience, mutual outpouring and ingathering, a common search for truth, a mutual desire to serve, and co-operation in the common task of achieving a Christian economic order. Fellowship in industry can best be promoted by seeking to place industry on a basis of production for use and by intensive experiments with various types of co-operation in industry.

During the nineteenth century we achieved the physical basis of the good life for all the people, and it now seems possible to raise the general standard of living in the United States very considerably during the next few decades. Is it too much to believe that during the twentieth century we shall be able to establish a Christian economic order, in which abundant life will be within the reach of all, and every human being will have opportunity for complete self-development and self-expression?

A Texas Horror

We are reprinting from The Crisis this account of a recent lynching in Texas because it is a typical case. This description is probably reasonably accurate.—Ed.

The National Association for the Advancement of Colored People as soon as it heard of the burnings and lynchings at Kirwin, Texas, sent a special representative there. He has returned with his report and these appear to be the facts:

A white land-holder named King owns many farms in the vicinity. The town is in a backwoods district and everybody, black and white, with only a few exceptions, is backward and illiterate. A road runs past King's house. Next to King lives an old colored man and next to him, a white family,—the Prowls (at least that is the way we spell it—they themselves did not know how it was spelled). King, a man of 65 years had an orphan grand-daughter who was the apple of his eye. She rode to school daily past the Prowls and down the pike about a mile where there was a consolidated white brick school.

Between the Prowls and the Kings there was a long standing feud beginning with an accusation by King of cattle stealing by the Prowls and culminating two years ago in a murderous attack upon one of King's sons by a Prowl who promptly disappeared from the community. Consent for his return had been asked by the family but King offered him "six foot of ground." The Prowls swore vengeance and women folk of the families quarreled.

South of Prowl's home and skirted by the highway to the schools is a dense, impenetrable thicket. Beyond the thicket and to one side is the square of the town with two churches, stores and, further on, the railway. Still further to the south is the Negro part of the town where colored folk work on detached farms owned by King and others. Here lived Snap Curley and several other colored families. Here too was an old shack called the Negro school but it was not in session.

One day King's granddaughter failed to return from school. He telephoned anxiously and traced her as far as the thicket. He said that he had a presentiment that she had suffered harm at the hands of the Prowls. He sent his colored neighbor down to look for her and the neighbor found the horse tied by the road but no trace of the girl. The black man brought the horse back and declares that no sooner had he done this than one of the Prowl women upbraided him and asked what business he had bringing the horse up.

Then the search began. They found the girl in the thicket murdered by knife wounds in the abdomen, but the physician found no evidence of rape. Immediately the neighborhood gathered. There were footsteps leading from the thicket to the Prowl's home. One of the three remaining Prowl men disappeared but another was arrested. He explained the footsteps as leading from his whiskey still. The sheriff did not search for the still. Several parties scoured the neighborhood looking for the missing Prowl and for any other suspicious characters. In the searching party was Snap Curley and other colored men. Finally they came to Negro town. By the time they got there Snap Curley had disappeared. They claimed that his wife said that he had brought home a bloody shirt. Immediately he and two other Negroes were captured. The Kings were urged to kill them immediately, but they did not believe them guilty. They were taken to the jail. That night the mob came. They beat the sheriff black and blue and secured the prisoners. They took the prisoners to the square where there was an old steel plow. One by one the Negroes were seated on the plow, wood piled about them and gasoline poured over them. They were allowed to burn a while and then pulled out by a great wet rope. At last the rope burned and the last man, hugging the red hot plow, refused to come out. The Prowl arrested was released and the whole family, without waiting to sell their property, has gone to Oklahoma.

Afterward another Negro was hanged and a fifth "disappeared." No one in town believes all the Negroes guilty. Curley never confessed. He simply, under torture, named his companions. Some think one or two may have been hired to do the deed. Others think all were innocent.

Found: Eight Dollars

Polya Xitrova, our cook and domestic adviser found them in a sticky grey rain coat we had dug out of one of the Philadelphia clothing bales. We had brought the coat to the house to be worn by the personnel during the April showers. Polya tried it on to have us take her picture in it. As she was taking it off she put her hand in a pocket and drew out a handful of greenish paper. She smoothed it out into seven pieces and laid it on the window sill, and almost forgot about it. In the evening she picked it up and asked us what it was. It was new to her. Was it money? We looked at it. There were six clean one-dollar notes, and a two-dollar one issued by the Federal Reserve Bank of Boston. "We don't have pictures like that on our roubles," she informed us. "Ours say: 'Proletarians of all countries, unite.'"

Thereupon began a lesson in United States currency. Polya showed interest but no astonishment or awe when we explained that one of these little pieces of paper with the "1" on it would bring her a pocketful of high-denomination roubles. For Polya is only slightly interested in money, even legal tender American. She is interested in baking rye bread on the floor of the huge stone oven, in carrying water from the river, in singing, in teaching you Russian if you care to learn by her method. She does not go to the "bazaar" (market) to speculate. She detests "speculants." She is a Communist without a compromise.

If those eight American dollars had been hiding in a coat issued to a peasant he would have been able to buy a plow, a cow or a yellow goat and he would not have been forced to kill his horse for the dinner-pot or live on "lebeda"—bread and ground weeds. He could do this if he could get roubles for his dollars. But American money is not the treasure in demand even in this country of inverted exchange values where a dollar will bring you nearly two million roubles. What goes farther than any amount of paper, Russian or American, with pictures or without, with appeals to foreign proletariat or not, is FOOD.

To peasants who fill a pit in our woodhouse with ice for the summer we pay one pood (36 lbs.) of BEANS.

To a locksmith who tinkers a day with the doors and windows we give ten funts (one funt equals 14½ oz.) of FLOUR.

To the carpenter who makes artistic furniture out of provision boxes and crooked nails, pulled from them, we present a sack of RICE.

The premier currency of the Hunger land is flour. For five poods of it you can buy that pretty little frame cottage on Riverside Street. An old couple who live there will surrender the result of long lives of peasant toil for a sack just large enough to carry them through till the harvest.

But the only sack that large in this volost is across the street in the warehouse of the Ispomgolod (Mutual Aid Committee for the Famine). It came from American Quakers. It will go to Russian children. Eight dollars cannot buy it.

April, 1922. ROBERT W. DUNN.

Friends' Tractor Plowing In Russia

In Buzuluk Uyezd, Samara Gubernia, land is being plowed by tractors. The tractors belong to the Society of Friends' Relief Organizations. The drivers are members of these organizations. The plowed land is being sown with seed furnished by the Soviet Government. The products to be harvested will be used to feed the Children's Homes in the area.

The English section of the Uyezd already has four tractors at work; two are turning up the black steppe within a stone's throw of the Buzuluk railway station, two are at Maximovka, a Quaker outpost, working on land owned by the October School of the Revolution. In seven days the latter two have plowed about 68 acres. They have no definite schedule to accomplish. They are merely plowing at top speed from sunrise to sunset, and they will keep on plowing as long as there is a day left for sowing. Both wheat and garden seeds will be put in the ground near Buzuluk. A large quantity of seed potatoes have been furnished by the Government. The English tractors were brought out originally to serve as transport. They will be utilized for this purpose after the plowing season is passed.

The American section, likewise, has two tracts of land both near Sorochinskaya the home station and warehouse center of the American Friends' work. The first is low land that can be irrigated in case of drought. It comprises some 27 acres along the muddy banks of the Samara river. For this tract the Quakers are to supply the tractors and the tractor drivers. The Government gives a trained agricultural supervisor, an adequate amount of garden seed, workers for sowing and cultivating, and some tools.

A plan to have all the children in the Children's Homes of Sorochinskaya work on their individual plots as well as on the common plot is agreed upon by the Quakers and the Government. In addition to the seeds provided by the latter the Quakers are now advised that 1,450 sacks of garden seeds are on their way from Philadelphia. (By the time this appears these seeds will be in the ground.)

Some of these seeds will, of course, be used on the larger plot of land southwest of the village in the rich black soil where wheat was sown and burnt by the drought last year. "You can have all the land from here to the hills," says the Soviet representative to Homer Morris, the American Field Director, as he points toward some rising ground three or four versts away. The sweep of his arm takes in at least 2,500 acres! The arable land in this section is literally unlimited this year. So many of the peasants have died, so many have left, so many are too weak or too poor in livestock to plow their allotments, that the land to be cut by the plowshares, pulled by the three Fordson tractors, is much more than could be covered by even a thousand tractors in the month remaining before the last Spring grains can be sown. On the larger allotment the Quakers will supervise the planting of buckwheat, millet, Russian maize, potatoes and sunflower seeds, the latter being one of the staple Russian products that will grow in some of the driest lands.

Just as in France and Poland the American tractors pulled the plows for the peasants after the ravages of war, so in Russia after the great sweep of the Hunger has done its worst the tractors will lay open the soil for the harvest that the Spring rains tell us is coming this year. Next winter, perhaps, the Children's Home will have food from the Quaker gardens. And in the Autumn the machines will open the soil again for the Spring rye. This is more than charity. It is reconstruction.

ROBERT W. DUNN.

The Young Friends' General Conference

The Thirteenth Annual Young Friends' General Conference will be held on the Earlham College Campus, Richmond, Indiana, July 21st to 31st.

In the thirteen years of its history this conference has grown until today its place and influence is firmly established. It is recognized as one of the biggest things of the year among Friends. Last year the enrollment was three hundred and fifty.

As in other conferences the mornings are largely devoted to class work. This year's schedule offers this promising choice: Bible Study, Edward E. Nourse; Friends' History, Clarence E. Pickett; Missions, Amelia R. Lindley; Older Girls' Class, Edith E. Wildman; Older Boys' Class, William J. Reagan; Young People and the Church, Ward Applegate; The Teacher, Isadore H. Wilson; The Modern Sunday School, E. T. Albertson; Personal Evangelism, Milo S. Hinckle; Training Class for the World Peace Movement, Frederick J. Libby.

Aside from regular class work each morning, there will be Devotional Bible groups, open forums, vespers and discussion circles. The afternoons are given over to supervised recreation including instruction in methods of conducting community sports. Evenings there will be addresses by prominent speakers including Alexander C. Purdy and Murray S. Kenworthy.

Other attractions are home-grown products to eat, library facilities, cool and comfortable rooms, hot and cold shower baths, and athletic field and equipment.

The expense is nominal, registration fee $2.50, board and room for 10 days $10.00. All young Friends who want to equip themselves for active service should plan to attend this conference and partake of its inspiration and fellowship.

Friendly News Notes

At a luncheon given Third-day, Sixth month 27th, at the home of Mrs. H. P. Wilhelmie, of Overbrook, Mary Craig Bates, formerly of Philadelphia, announced the engagement of her daughter, Mary A. Craig, to John S. Wright, of Newtown, Pa.

The Bulletin of the Friends' Historical Society, in the ten volumes thus far published, has gathered together a large amount of material bearing upon the history of the Society of Friends. Much of it comes from rare sources. Some of it has never been printed before. In order to make this material accessible to Friends and to all students of history, a general index has been compiled and published. It contains more than five thousand entries and is itself a book of about one hundred pages.

Much of the work was done by Amy L. Post, of the Haverford College Library. Amelia Mott Gummere and Elizabeth B. Jones assisted in proof-reading.

At Prairie Grove Quarterly Meeting held on Sixth month 4th, there was only a small attendance, with no visiting Friends, which was very unusual and they were greatly missed. A selection from the FRIENDS' INTELLIGENCER, "The Liberal Faith," was read and called forth remarks from L. W. Canby. He urged that Friends be workers, not drones, for Christian workers are needed to further the kingdom of God on earth. Our principles are as sound today as ever and the walls of sectarianism are being swept away.

Ragnar Johanson, one of the political prisoners still confined in Leavenworth Penitentiary for expression of opinion only, and under war-time legislation long since repealed, asks that his gratitude and appreciation be conveyed through these columns to the many kind friends, known and unknown, who wrote to him on his birthday last month. Since prisoners there are not allowed to write more than three letters a week, and those are due to his most intimate friends and relatives, he finds it quite impossible to reply to each of the birthday letters separately, much as he would like to do so.

Accommodations at the Richmond Conference

The Housing Committee has arranged for accommodations at Richmond, Indiana, during the Conference as follows:

Westcott Hotel.—Can accommodate about 200; two blocks from Meeting-house and one block from the church in which the meetings are to be held. Rooms, without bath, $1.50 to $2.00 per day; with bath, $2.50 for one person, $4.00 and up for two persons in room. Garage will be available within two blocks of hotel. Storage prices, 75 cents for night, $3.00 per week.

Arlington Hotel.—Six blocks from Meeting-house, five from church. Rooms, without bath, $1.50 for one person, $2.50 for two persons in room; with bath, $2.50 to $3.00 for one person, $3.50 to $4.50 for two persons.

Both hotels European plan. There are restaurants and dining-rooms in connection with both hotels.

Boarding Houses.—Not far from Meeting-house, $10 to $14 per week for room and board. Rooms without board, $3 to $8 per week; meals there are $7 per week. There is an apartment house in same block as Meeting-house. The entire third floor will be available at that time; about 20 rooms. Rate, $5 per week for one in a room, or $8 per week, two in a room. These rooms are small.

Meals.—There will be cafeteria meals served in basement of Meeting-house all the time. The price will be from 30 cents to 40 cents with cafeteria service.

Tents.—Accommodations for about 100 young people in tents on Meeting-house grounds. We do not know definitely about the charge, but it will probably be from $4 to $5 per person for the week.

Rooms.—In private houses available, at less than regular boarding houses.

Applications may be addressed to

Dorothy E. Dilks, 46 Thirteenth street, Richmond, Ind.

J. Barnard Walton, 140 N. Fifteenth St., Philadelphia, Pa.

Or to members of the Housing Committee:

James H. Atkinson, 421 Chestnut street, Philadelphia.

Harry A. Hawkins, 57 Pierrepont avenue, W., Rutherford, N. J.

William C. Coles, Moorestown, N. J.

J. Bernard Hilliard, Salem, N. J.

Esther Holmes, Riverton, N. J.

Eliza M. Ambler, Plymouth Meeting, Pa.

Items From Everywhere

The conference to consider Russian affairs opened at The Hague on June 15th. Sixty delegates, representing about thirty countries, were present.

Members of the League of Nations have been requested by the League Council to furnish information to the Committee on Disarmament for use in drawing up disarmament plans.

Protestant churches in America are planning to give to the Protestant churches in France and Belgium $175,000 during the coming year, chiefly for reconstruction work and for the extension of missionary endeavor in the former German colonies.

The Japanese Cabinet has announced its decision to withdraw Japanese forces from Siberia. This is in keeping with the policy announced at the Washington Conference. One of the first moves of Baron Kato, the new Premier, was to reduce the army by 56,000 men.

Dr. Walter Rathenau, the Foreign Minister of Germany, was assassinated on June 24th by Monarchist sympathizers. Dr. Rathenau was recognized as one of the strong men of the new Germany and a man in whose honesty other nations had great faith. His assassination indicates that there is still a group of Junkers who would like to overthrow the Republic.

The American Federation of Labor, at its national convention in Cincinnati, adopted a resolution setting forth the flimsiness of the evidence on which a death verdict was returned against Nicola Sacco and Bartolomeo Vanzetti, and calling for a new trial in their case. The resolution was introduced by the delegates from Boston Central Labor Union. The vote was unanimous.

The American Federation of Labor at its recent convention in Cincinnati committed itself to the following program: A Congressional veto of Supreme Court decisions; the guarantee to workers of the right to organize, to bargain collectively, and to strike; the prohibition of child labor and the adoption of an easier method than the present for changing the Federal Constitution.

Believing that only action by the United States Government can save the remnant of Armenians from further persecution and extermination on account of their faith, the Federal Council of Churches is making a nation-wide appeal to 150,000 congregations in America to urge Congress to take necessary steps to ensure the permanent protection of Christians under Turkish rule. This appeal is being sent in conjunction with the Near East Relief to all pastors.

THE OPEN FORUM

This column is intended to afford free expression of opinion by readers on questions of interest. The INTELLIGENCER *is not responsible for any such opinions. Letters must be brief, and the editor reserves the right to omit parts if necessary to save space.*

AN APPEAL TO THE FRIENDS

To the Editor:

From modest beginnings have sprung up some of the most vital and enduring movements of the world. However small the beginning, it justifies its existence in the long run, if it be made in the right direction. I was very much moved and inspired by what Henry Hodgkin had to say at the conference in regard to his visit to China. The splendid work he did among the Chinese will, I am sure, bear its fruit in the near future. It is this sort of sympathetic approach to their vexed problems that is needed by countries that are in the throes of a new birth like China, Russia and India.

The distinctive contribution of modern times to the thought forces of the world is the dawning of the idea of World-Citizenship. We feel that we are not isolated groups of peoples, whatever part of the world we happen to have been born in—we are instinctively drawn together, one to another. To this New Spirit is to be traced the "concern" we now feel for Russia and for China and in a limited sphere for India. We have reached a stage when I feel that our sphere of concern must be expanded. We who have found the truth must not shirk our responsibilities. For any opportunity that may present itself to us for bettering the lot of our fellow-brothers and for sowing the seeds of mutual understanding and friendship, we must thank God. And we must promptly embrace the opportunity.

India is in the throes of a new birth. She is carrying on a new experiment designed to revolutionize revolution. The Non-Violent Non-Co-operation Program originated by Mahatma Gandhi is based on non-violence and on love—coming as it does after the terrible havoc of the last war, this peaceful program gives us a new hope for man and his destiny. It is especially the concern of Friends who are trying to apply the principles of Jesus Christ to social problems to see to it that this experiment striving for the spiritual regeneration of man, eschewing violence and disregarding armaments, gets the moral support of the world. My suggestion is that the Friends here and in England organize two or more units of relief workers to go to India, study the conditions at first hand and help relieve the famine-stricken areas of misery and starvation. It is a curious coincidence that the introduction of "modern civilization" in India has reduced the land of plenty to chronic famines. Here is enough work for the Friends to do. In 1917-18, in the course of a year, 33 million people died in India during the famine. I strongly feel that Gandhi's work in India follows the same lines as the Friends here and in Europe: if it be so, it is our paramount duty to co-operate in the task; if it is not, all the more reason that the Friends should go and preach the message of Reconciliation and of Non-Resistance. The Friends may not take part in the political movement of India, but they may do relief work in the famine-stricken areas. Let them study the conditions of the people and then come here to tell us the story of India's "religious struggle."

I hope and trust that this suggestion may bring about a beginning in the direction stated above.

Fraternally yours,

Haridas Muzumdar.

Philadelphia, Pa., June 29, 1922.

AN ANSWER TO MR. E. L. MALONE'S LETTER "A BRIEF FOR OUR INDUSTRIAL SYSTEM" (May 27, 1922, number)

To the Editor:

I take issue with Mr. Malone's attitude toward our present Industrial System. As he puts it, "there is nothing fundamentally wrong with our system of wage payment and profit taking." Furthermore, I believe many of his statements are unsupportable and lack that vision necessary for our civilization to progress. From his statements, I quote the following:

(1)—"Most of these 'isms' have been tested without showing the gleam of hope to warrant belief in their being of practical service." (2)—"wealth concentrated in a few hands may be the life giving force to that community." (3)—"La Place found less than one-half of one per cent. of all humans actually think. Considering the labor involved in original thought, that is a high figure."

(4)—"The great majority of us are plodders with little energy, initiative, enthusiasm, vision or genius."

Such a brief is devoid of all human sympathy; it kills faith, hope and idealism and without these life is not worth living. To lose faith in the common people, to assume that they are, and always shall be mere pawns in the hands of the few, is, indeed depressing.

One look at the present chaotic condition of our social structure points to one conclusion—there *is* something fundamentally wrong. When a system functions so inefficiently that part of the world is caught in the grip of pestilence and starvation while another portion is depressed because of an over-supply of food and clothing (with little transfer of goods because there is not enough "profit" in it), it is time the "one-half of one per cent, who actually think" began to wonder whether "our business life *is* essentially sound." When a system breeds wars, crime waves, industrial unrest, unemployment, and business crises perhaps we should not be so keen for its complete "reconstruction." It would seem permissible to regard such a system with the gravest suspicions.

Mr. Malone attributes "unrest in the labor ranks to a myriad of causes," among them such superficial reasons as "paid union leaders or trouble-breeders." However, the principal cause is discontent due to an unfair distribution of wealth. Reliable economists give us the following information:

(1) 2% of the people own 65% of the wealth
33% of the people own 30% of the wealth
65% of the people own 5% of the wealth

(2) The spread between rich and poor is gradually growing greater.

Little wonder we have our social unrest. The poor 65% are at least thinking enough to know that something is wrong. Democracy teaches, "to every one in proportion to what he gives to society." Our present system fails in this. It should go still further by laying the foundation for the time when those who are fortunate, from the standpoint of heredity and environment, willingly share their advantages with the less fortunate.

Our present industrial system is but the offspring of the "Industrial Revolution." From the historical viewpoint this period is only a flash in the space of time; social orders have come and gone. It is presumptuous to assume that we have an infallible system which is the direct road to a distant Utopia. And we cannot afford not to hope and build for a better world; it is a moral obligation. After all, faith and hope, rather than concentration of wealth, should be the life-giving force to a community.

I am not suggesting any "isms" or "cure-alls." I am not advocating any rapid reorganization. But I do maintain that we must have as our ideal a system with a more worthy object for a goal than profits alone.

Our present industrial system is characterized by a "laissez-faire" attitude on the part of society. Ambitions for power and wealth are now looked upon as fitting aims in life. Yet this is but a polite way of spelling selfishness.

When personal success is measured in terms of "service," rather than wealth, then we can truthfully say, "there is nothing fundamentally wrong with our system."

San Diego, Calif. Philip J. Webster.

BIRTHS

Preston—On Sixth month 29th, to Edmond C. and Catherine M. Preston, of Philadelphia, a daughter, named Catherine Eleanor Preston.

MARRIAGES

Keever-Washburn—At Quaker St. Meeting-house, N. Y., Sixth month 28th, by Friends' ceremony, Miriam Margaret, daughter of Charles E. and Elizabeth C. Washburn, of Delanson, N. Y., and Stanley Wynne, son of Dudley and Ida W. Keever, of Centerville, Ohio.

DEATHS

Atkinson—On First-day, Seventh month 2nd, at her summer home, Sunset Cottage, Buck Hill Falls, Pa., Anna

Allen, widow of Wilmer Atkinson and daughter of the late Samuel and Elizabeth Justice Allen. She was a birthright member of Green Street Monthly Meeting, Philadelphia. She is survived by three daughters.

BROWN—At his home in Lincoln, Va., on Fourth month 5th, Nathan T. Brown, son of the late William H. and Martha Jane Brown, in his 79th year. An earnest Friend, a generous and devoted husband and father, a good neighbor; his life has left a lasting impress upon the lives of many who have been privileged to know him and to enjoy the hospitality of his home.

COOPER—At Camden, N. J., on Sixth month 29th, Howard M. Cooper, aged 78.

EYRE—At Norristown, Pa., Seventh month 1st, Caroline Eyre, aged 76.

FUSSELL—On Sixth month 26th, in the hospital at Anderson, Ind., Charles K. Fussell, of Pendleton, Ind., aged 59 years. An active member of Fall Creek Monthly Meeting.

HAINES—At Burlington, N. J., Sixth month 25th, Henry Snowden Haines, in his 88th year.

HANCE—At the home of his daughter, Fairport, N. Y., Sixth month 22nd, Dr. Samuel Hance, in his 97th year. He was born at Marion, Ohio, the son of Thomas and Sarah Hance. He practiced his profession for 47 years. All his life an active Friend he never failed to attend the Half Yearly Meeting at Farmington, N. Y.

HENRIE—On Sixth month 19th, Mary B., wife of C. Herbert Henrie, of Millville, Pa., aged 39 years.

HOOPES—At her home in West Chester, Pa., after a long and suffering illness, Emma Rowland Haines, wife of Edmund D. Hoopes and great granddaughter of the late John Comly, in the 57th year of her age.

LUPTON—On Seventh month 2nd, at the home of his parents near Clearbrook, Va., Hugh S. Lupton 3rd, aged three years and six months. Grandson of the late Hugh S. Lupton and Mary S. Lupton.

MILLER—On Sixth month 24th, Arabella M., widow of the late James Miller and daughter of Mahlon and Susanna Mancil, aged 78 years. A member and regular attendant of Chester Meeting. Funeral at her home in Chester, Pa. Among those who paid loving tribute to her memory were Ella Elliott, Elizabeth Newlin, Edwin J. Durnall and Rev. Edwin D. Riley. Interment at Media.

RUSSELL—On Sixth month 1st at his home in Unionville, Centre County, Pa., Dr. Edward A. Russell, aged 85 years. A member of Centre Monthly Meeting. Had practiced medicine in Unionville for almost fifty years.

SCATTERGOOD—In Philadelphia, Pa., on Sixth month 30th, Mary Davis, wife of Charles C. Scattergood.

SUPLEE—At Malvern, Sixth month 16th, Lydia A., widow of Nathan Suplee, in her 70th year. She was a daughter of the late Joseph and Sarah Thatcher Sutton. A member of High St. Friends' Meeting, West Chester, Pa.

TOMLINSON—In Germantown, Philadelphia, on Sixth month 29th, Achsah A., widow of Aaron Tomlinson.

TOMLINSON—On Sixth month 10th, at Grace Hospital, Kansas City, Mo., J. B. Tomlinson, of Independence, Kansas. He is survived by his wife, Mary A., two children, Lydia and Victor Rees, and two brothers, Samuel and Curtis. He was a son of Paul and Lydia Daniel Tomlinson. He had distinguished himself not only as a lawyer of ability but as a man of integrity.

ZELLEY—At Moorestown, N. J., Seventh month 1st, Mary, wife of Chalkley B. Zelley, in her 79th year. Funeral from Friends' Meeting-house.

COMING EVENTS

SEVENTH MONTH

8th—Frederick J. Libby will speak at the Woolman School week-end conference at 8 p. m., on "Recent Phases in the World Drama."

9th—Woolman School week-end conference at 4 p. m. "How to Create the International Mind," Dorothy Brooke, Irvin C. Poley and James A. Norton.

9th—Preparative Meeting in New York and Brooklyn, after the Meetings for Worship.

10th—New York Monthly Meeting, in New York, at 7.30. Supper will be served at 6 o'clock, as usual.

16th—Certain members of Philadelphia Quarterly Meeting's Visiting Committee will attend a meeting for worship at Germantown Friends' Home, at 7.30 p. m.

23rd—Certain members of Philadelphia Quarterly Meeting's Visiting Committee will attend meeting at Frankford, Philadelphia, at 11 a. m.

29th—Westbury Quarterly Meeting, at Westbury, L. I., at 10.30 a. m. Lunch will be served soon after noon. The afternoon session at 2.30 will be under the care of the Meeting's Advancement Committee.

American Friends' Service Committee

WILBUR K. THOMAS, EX. SEC.
20 S. 12th St. Philadelphia.

CASH CONTRIBUTIONS
WEEK ENDING JUNE 26TH

Five Years Meetings	$2.60
Extension Committee of Phila. Yearly Meeting	250.00
Other Meetings:	
Middletown Meeting and First-day School	3.48
New York Monthly Meeting	400.00
Oakland Branch of the College Park Association of Friends	5.00
Easton Monthly Meeting	22.00
New Garden Prep. Meeting	50.00
Providence Meeting	2.00
Salem Monthly Meeting	68.56
Contributions for Germany	56.25
For Austria	3,764.00
For Poland	2,503.79
For Serbia	455.20
For Russia	6,222.98
For Russian Overhead	250.00
For Home Service	921.25
For Clothing	176.03
For German Overhead	70.10
For General	471.50
Refunds	67.32
	$15,762.06

Shipments received during week ending June 24, 1922: 58 boxes and packages; 7 anonymous.

FUN

It Feels That Way.—The finding of a headless body has caused the arrest of an American dentist. Our experience with dentists is that the head doesn't really come off; it just feels that way.—*Manila Bulletin.*

ADVERTISING RATE in the FRIENDS' INTELLIGENCER, for Help Wanted, Positions Wanted, Rooms for Rent, Notices, and other classified advertisements without display, for each insertion, 2 cents per word, including name, initials and address. Answers may be sent to a box at the INTELLIGENCER office, if so directed.

For display advertising the rate is 10 cents per agate line, or $1.40 per column inch, each insertion. On ten or more insertions in a year from date of order, ten per cent. discount. Thus a four-inch single-column or two-inch double-column advertisement costs $5.60 each insertion, less ten per cent., or 5.04 net each time for ten or more insertions. Matter may be changed whenever desired, without extra charge.

Experience has proved the INTELLIGENCER to be a remarkably good advertising medium. All advertisements must "pass the censor!"

Address 140 N. 15th St., Philadelphia

The Friends' Intelligencer

ESTABLISHED 1844 — SEVENTH MONTH 15, 1922 — VOLUME 79 NUMBER 28

Contents

REGULAR MEETINGS

OAKLAND, CALIF. — A FRIENDS' Meeting is held every First-day at 11 A. M., in the Extension Room, Y. W. C. A. Building, Webster Street, above 14th. Visiting Friends always welcome.

FRIENDS' MEETING IN PASADENA, California — Orange Grove Monthly Meeting of Friends, 520 East Orange Grove Avenue, Pasadena, California. Meeting for worship, First-day, 11 A. M. Monthly Meeting, the second First-day of each month, at 1.45 P. M.

NOTICE—Concise statements of the principles of the Religious Society of Friends and their application to the problems of every day living, including "The Spirit of Quakerism," by Elbert Russell; "Preparation for Life's Greatest Business," by Rufus M. Jones; and other articles by Henry W. Wilbur, Howard M. Jenkins, Elizabeth Lloyd, Jesse H. Holmes, O. Edward Janney, Edward B. Rawson, etc., to be had free on application to Friends' General Conference Advancement Committee, 140 North Fifteenth Street, Philadelphia, Pa.

FUN

Famous Last Words.

"I wonder if it's loaded. I'll look down the barrel and see."

"Oh, listen! That's the train whistle! Step on the accelerator and we'll try to get across before it comes."

"They say these things can't possibly explode, no matter how much you throw them around."

"I wonder whether this rope will hold my weight."

"It's no fun swimming in the surf. I'm going out beyond the life-lines."

"Which one of these is the third rail, anyway?"

"There's only one way to manage a horse. Walk right up behind him and chastise him."

"That firecracker must have gone out. I'll light it again.—*Selected.*

THE FRIENDS' INTELLIGENCER

Published weekly, 140 N. 15th Street, Philadelphia, Pa., by Friends' Intelligencer Association, Ltd.

PAUL W. WAGER, *Editor.*
SUE C. YERKES, *Business Manager*

Editorial Board: Elizabeth Powell Bond, Thomas A. Jenkins, J. Russell Smith, George A. Walton.

Board of Managers: Edward Cornell, Alice Hall Paxson, Paul M. Pearson, Annie Hillborn, Elwood Hollingshead, William C. Biddle, Charles F. Jenkins, Edith M. Winder, Frances M. White.

Officers of Intelligencer Associates: Ellwood Burdsall, Chairman; Bertha L. Broomell, Secretary; Herbert P. Worth, Treasurer.

Subscription rates: United States, Mexico, Cuba and Panama, $2.50 per year. Canada and other foreign countries, $3.00 per year. Checks should be made payable to Friends' Intelligencer Association, Ltd.

Entered as Second Class Matter at Philadelphia Post Office.

To the Lot Holders and others interested in Fairhill Burial Ground:

GREEN STREET Monthly Meeting has funds available for the encouragement of the practice of cremating the dead to be interred in Fairhill Burial Ground. We wish to bring this fact as prominently as possible to those who may be interested. We are prepared to undertake the expense of cremation in case any lot holder desires us to do so.

Those interested should communicate with William H. Gaskill, Treasurer of the Committee of Interments, Green Street Monthly Meeting, or any of the following members of the Committee.

William H. Gaskill, 3201 Arch St.
Samuel N. Longstreth, 1218 Chestnut St.
Charles F. Jenkins, 232 South Seventh St.
Stuart S. Graves, 3033 Germantown Ave.

The Friends' Intelligencer

The religion of Friends is based on faith in the "INWARD LIGHT," or direct revelation of God's spirit and will in every seeking soul.

The INTELLIGENCER is interested in all who bear the name of Friends in every part of the world, and aims to promote love, unity and intercourse among all branches and with all religious societies.

ESTABLISHED 1844 | PHILADELPHIA, SEVENTH MONTH 15, 1922 | VOLUME 79 NUMBER 28

Everyone has a right to be happy.

✖

Cheer up! There may be some women in the next Senate.

✖

It will never be possible to broadcast a Friends' meeting by radio.

✖

If the tariff were taken out of politics there would not be any fun in being a Congressman.

✖

One man's vote is supposed to be worth as much as another's but this year the soldier's vote is at a premium.

✖

It is not unusual for a debtor to fail to recognize his creditor but in the case of Russia it is different, the creditors refuse to recognize the debtor.

✖

Nothing would be more helpful in promoting peace and good-will among nations than an international language. Fewer misunderstandings would arise if all the people of the world could read and speak a common tongue. The League of Nations and other international bodies could function better if their sessions could be conducted in a language understood by all.

This new international language must be an artificial creation, first, because no natural language could be adopted without arousing jealousies, and secondly, no natural language is simple enough to commend it as a universal medium. It must, also, be purely an auxiliary language and in no instance replace the native tongue.

For several years educators and linguists have been experimenting and two or three artificial languages have been devised. Probably the best one is Esperanto. While not perfect, it is remarkably free from irregularities of spelling or grammar. Its vocabulary is essentially a selection and combination of exact, idea word-elements chosen from the common modern Aryan word-stock. The result is that the language is marvelously precise and so simple that it can be learned in a few months.

We hold no brief for Esperanto in particular, but we feel that some international language ought to be agreed upon and then taught, in addition to the native speech, in the high schools and colleges of all civilized countries. One could then travel around the world and converse with people everywhere. We believe the result would be the removal of one of the greatest barriers to international co-operation and peace.

While we await the development of Esperanto or some other auxiliary language there is one international medium of expression which we can use, and which will not be misunderstood. That is the international language of love. It is understood by educated or illiterate, royalty or peasant, black or white, Aryan or Semite, Teuton or Anglo-Saxon. Not only is its message always intelligible, but it is more convincing than any written document or any spoken word. It is a language of the soul and arouses a soul response. Though quiet and invisible it is the most dynamic force in the world. It has overthrown kings, captured armies, opened prisons, conquered passion, and disarmed the forces of iniquity. It is not only a language of power; it is a language of beauty. It inspires poets, enraptures youth, comforts old age, cheers the disconsolate, and transforms lives of sin and despair to lives of honor and achievement. It is a magic language for it kindles ambition, removes fear, awakens hope, and instills strength. It is a God-given language, not vocal but spiritual. It is a gift which man possesses because he is made in the image of God. It becomes articulate and useful only through cultivation. It should be developed as the language of the home, of society, of business, of international relations. When all people have learned the language of love then will the earth no longer be a Babel but East and West, white and yellow, Jew and Gentile, will join their voices in one universal anthem of peace.

If our readers were inclined to marvel at the ingenious (if incongruous) arrangement of la week's editorial column, we must disclaim any the credit. It was entirely the enterprise of t printer. The words "Cross Crossings Cautiousl were intended as an editorial brief and not as caption.—Ed.

The Epistle From London Yearly Meeting

1922

TO FRIENDS EVERYWHERE

Dear Friends:

Man's boasted civilization will destroy him, unless he takes the way of life in time. If, while mastering the forces of Nature, he makes personal advantage the end, and his brother men the means to it, he oppresses them, frustrating God's will for peace. If, fearing to lose his goods, he turns his inventive skill to perfecting guns and poison gases, he will assuredly perish.

Two ways lie before us: that which looks first to self, and that which seeks to become one with all men. The selfish life may seem the way of development and safety, but its fruits are fear and war. It contains within itself the seed of its own destruction. The life that seeks the good of all often seems rash and unwise, but it is the one hope for the world.

This we see in the life and death of Jesus Christ. The carpenter of Nazareth so threw himself into the life of his fellows, that what hurt them hurt him more, what raised them up rejoiced him beyond measure. The powers of bigotry and selfishness nailed him to the cross, but they could not destroy his love.

The life and death of Jesus Christ throb with the message that, as he felt and loved, so God feels and loves. He showed us a Father, who shares to the full the suffering of his children, so that with them he may achieve victory and joy. Each pang in the agony of the starving Russian child the Father feels as his own. Christ our Lord is nailed to the cross afresh whenever a man or a woman is crushed or marred by war, by unemployment, by vice, by despair; he is pierced with grief as we hug our comforts, fearing to follow him in loving unto death.

Grievously as we have failed, we believe that God, as Christ reveals him, enters so completely into the daily life of all of us, that all can become one family in him. We find him indeed in our own hearts, but we find him there far more as we unite in quietness with one another, seeking to forget ourselves and to discover his will.

This realized oneness with God and man is the greatest of all forces: it is the Kingdom of God in germ, the beginning of a world of untold beau and joy, where sin, oppression and squalor shall no more.

God has no human body now upon the earth b ours, yet he calls the bodies of men his own.

"Christ's spirit taketh breath again
Within the lives of holy men.
Each changing age beholds afresh
Its word of God in human flesh."

Do we indeed come to his aid as we see him star ing or unemployed? Are we not driven with sha to confess that again and again we pass him b Should we not strive to find God as Jesus four him in every man, whether we call him British, Ru sian, Chinese, German, Frenchman, Orangeman Sinn Feiner, Communist or Capitalist: above all t find God in those with whom we live and work, eve if they annoy or slight us?

If men fail to do God's will, how can his will o earth be done? "I would fain," said one of old, "t to the Eternal Goodness what his own hand is to man." Are we prepared to be the hands and fe of God? If so, we must hold nothing back, bu whether in our homes, in industry or in internation relations, we must follow in whatever paths he ma lead us. Are we willing, should need arise, for th sake of this great quest, to face suffering and eve death; or, what may be still harder, to accept wha ever new ideals God may show to us?

We dare set no limit to what God can do throug us if we are faithful. Let us, however unworth our past, go forth together to the work, joyfull believing that God can, in very deed, create throug men the new world in which all are made one i him.

There are two ways only before mankind—th way of death and the way of life. Are we to shir the issue, to let fear rule and humanity perish, o dare we, individually and together, surrender our selves utterly to the God who wills this suprem glory for men?

Signed in and on behalf of London Yearly Meeting,

Roger Clark, *Clerk.*

views and no-views are pressed upon men and women by earnest propagandists; from the hardest and crudest rationalism of the blatant 'common-sense' order up to faiths and philosophies, in closer touch with the biology and psychology of scientific researchers. In the most surprising places one comes upon people who have been laid hold of by splendid half-views, who hail them as new revelations, the consummation of Christian thinking. . . . If ever the special conditions of an age called for clear, thoughtful and brave preaching of the Person of Christ, and for the kind and wise guidance of the young to the center of things, it is our own day." Out of the desire to meet this great need, the need of "guidance of the young to the center of things," have grown many organized agencies; among them, one of the newest (in America), and one of the most interesting is the Residential House.

The Residential Hall, or House, is denominational, yet situated at a center of studies founded by some other denomination. After all, is there anything denominational about learning the Hebrew language, or New Testament Greek? There need be no sectarian bias in the teaching of Church History; the lives of Luther, Calvin and Fox have passed the controversial period. "Religious education" is become almost a separate profession in itself. Granted the will to be helpful, the desire to be in fruitful touch with life, the learner wants to know where to go for late and reliable information, where to find recorded the useful experience of others, where to meet those who can point out the path of real progress. All this is the field of the Residential Hall.

Typical of this development in recent years, is the remarkable growth of the Divinity School (Baptist) of the University of Chicago, founded in 1866: this, with an attendance of some 400 students of both sexes, is now planning an extended group of new buildings. Adjoining the University campus are now in operation a Disciples (of Christ) Divinity House, and a Norwegian Baptist House. Besides these, the Congregationalists are planning a seminary, the site having been chosen; the Universalists are organizing a students' home near their Church of St. Paul, on the Midway; the Unitarian Faculty of Meadville, Penna., for the past seven years, have held a summer session next the University, and have now drawn plans for a House which will shelter about twenty postgraduate students. It seems, indeed, as if, in the years to come, Chicago were destined to be one of the world's greatest centers for religious education.

Has this wide-spread movement no echo in the minds and hearts of forward-looking Friends? It is known that our Society has its center of gravity, if membership be considered, west of the Alleghany mountains. Are the young Friends who attend the college and the graduate schools of the University to be always without a denominational Home, where they may be really "at home"? Where the atmosphere is that created by Friendly ideals and Friendly persons? Where counsel and assistance may be had without fee and without price? Where the enthusiasm and loyalty natural to youth may be valued and cherished?

A group of Friends, many of them members of the teaching staff of the University, are now organizing to promote the idea and the fact of a Friends' Hostel, a permanent Friends' Center, primarily for young Friends in attendance at the University of Chicago. They bespeak, from now on, the counsels and the assistance of Friends everywhere. They hope to convert their dream into a project, and their project into the reality; if they succeed, Chicago will yet be an important center of Friends' Service, in the best sense.

THOMAS A. JENKINS.

Friends interested should communicate with the undersigned, or, preferably, with Garfield V. Cox, 1347 E. 62d St., Chicago, Ill.

Relief in the Coal Fields

The proposed relief work of the American Friends' Service Committee to be carried on in West Virginia and Pennsylvania among the families of the miners is under way. Investigations by their representatives and by many other agencies indicate that a very serious condition exists among the children and families dependent upon the mining industry. Already a number are developing tuberculosis, on account of malnutrition. There are hundreds of children who are without necessary food.

Christian people cannot sit by and see people starve. Without discussing any of the issues involved in the present controversy in the coal industry, the Committee believes that it should engage in relief for the most needy cases. Economic strife does not justify the starving of innocent people. No civil or industrial warfare should ever be allowed to progress to the point where the lives of children are at stake or where there is a possibility that they may be dwarfed in body for the years to come. While the officials on both sides of the controversy are coming to an agreement we propose to see that the little ones are helped to such an extent that they may develop into normal men and women and thus become a real asset to society. The work is being undertaken, therefore, with the desire to bring a message of good will to these people in their time of need. Beginning on a small scale in the district around Charleston it will be extended to other sections just as rapidly as funds will permit.

The press is giving the matter favorable publicity, and from all sides sympathy with the work is being evidenced through letters of appreciation and money contributions. Philip Furnas, an instructor at Earlham College; Cyril Harvey, a student, and Lucile Ralston, an experienced dietitian and social worker—one of this year's graduates from the same college—have been chosen for the West Virginia field. Edward Evans, of Philadelphia; Herbert Bowles and Lawrence Dale, students at Earlham College; Luella Jones, of Iowa, and Frieda Burkle, dietitian in the German child-feeding, will constitute the Pennsylvania Unit.

The immediate work will be the feeding of the most under-nourished children and of expectant and nursing mothers. One meal a day will be served for six days in the week. This will consist of the very simplest but most nourishing kinds of food, such as milk, cocoa, rice and fats. The menu will be worked out by expert dietitians and the meal will be made supplementary to that which they receive at home. The closest kind of co-operation will be sought with the community and the owners and operators of mines. Nothing is to be done which will create partisan feeling. The whole work is to be kept on a humanitarian basis. Advice and counsel will be sought from the relief committees among the miners, the men in charge for the operators, local physicians, and others. The character of the work, the manner of conducting it, etc., will be entirely in the hands of the American Friends' Service Committee.

Chalons Hospitals—Old and New

Esther Whitson, now serving as a nurses' aide at the Chalons Maternity Hospital, sends the following letter to Mission members.

DEAR MISSION MEMBERS:

Have you forgotten the days you spent in sunny, muddy France? Have you forgotten Chalons-sur-Marne, with its quaint canals and bridges, its crooked streets and old cathedrals? Can you recall the red-brown wall of the Aziel (poorhouse) just opposite?

You were told that within that walled enclosure Miss Pye of England had started her "French Hospital." When you went inside you saw six huge, bare buildings and a well-kept kitchen-garden. Yo wondered to yourself where were the little childre you had heard Miss Pye talking about. But yo followed the pathway, because the arrow on th weather-beaten sign pointed "MATERNITE."

Your walk soon ended and you came into a littl world of babies. There they were, a dozen of them corralled in a crooked pen in the sunshine—fat happy babies! As you looked you saw others smaller ones, kicking and cooing in their baskets nearby. It was a gala day for these tiny, nameless people, for the blessed sun was shining and they could be out of doors. Each tiny urchin crept or crawled his happy radius as though no fairer expanse there were on earth than the space of his big, grey blanket.

Inside the "Maternite" you ascended a flight of well-worn stairs and came to a ward of "new" babies and their hardy, peasant mothers. They looked contented, but you noticed the rude equipment for their comfort. You wondered how those grey girls, who moved about beneath white veils, could be resigned to work in such crude ways.

Then you met the Directress of this little "Maternite." She was a sturdy Huguenot, embodying the loyalty and tireless enthusiasm necessary to carry on the work. You felt the warmth and earnestness of her spirit and you knew that her workers had caught it, too. You cried within yourself: "Oh! for some one with money, some group of people to build a new and fairer Maison, a cleaner, sweeter shelter, for these brave workers to protect poor, ignorant mothers!"

Your cry has been answered! Come with me and peep inside the wall of our *new* Maison Maternelle! We have watched and waited and worked; we have swept and scrubbed and painted; and now we have our dear, new house. Not a public poorhouse, but a clean, white dwelling. Not an old garden-plot and stumble-stones, but greensward, blossoms and shade trees. Not six, bare buildings, but two fair homes together. Do you recognize it—our "novelle Maison"?

The same white veils are worn, but not now so much for protection. The walls are decorated with stencil-work and pictures—in the Children's Ward a complete border of them around the room. The woodwork is painted, and there are neat, white draperies. Instead of the old stoves we have gas and steam heat. Instead of the bare stone floor of the children's Pouponier, there is a separate play-room for the "kiddies." Instead of the rough, cold barracks that housed the nurses in former days, we have a "Staff House" with a dining-room, a place we call "home." Every day we are trying to make you feel repaid, dear co-workers, in giving this gift to France.

Much is due to our Directress. For five tedious years she has been a loyal friend and helper to us all. Throughout all the changes and vicissitudes, this staunch, steady, undaunted leader has never swerved from her steady purpose to serve and to keep her workers united in serving.

We know we are but a part of the great work for the relief of suffering in Europe. Russia needs our hearts and hands. Everywhere there is need for money. But remember that in the county town of Chalons, one hundred and ten miles east of Paris in the valley of the Marne, there are inscribed over the doorway of a certain house of blessing these significant lines:

MEMORIAL HOSPITAL OF THE MISSION DES AMIS
Opened June 17, 1922
DEDICATED TO INTERNATIONAL FRIENDSHIP

Presented to the people of France by English and American FRIENDS and their Co-workers, who during the agony of the World War and the years that followed, founded and maintained at Chalons LA MAISON MATERNELLE DE LA MARNE.

China Needs Our Help

Henry Hodgkin in an address at 12th St. Meeting-house on Fourth-day evening, Seventh month 5th, held his audience in rapt attention, as he presented the challenge to Friends in the Far East. He said he was pleased to note the start which the Yearly Meeting at Fourth and Arch Sts. had made in foreign missionary enterprise in the closer connection of the Yearly Meeting with the work. He also mentioned his pleasure that Friends of both Yearly Meetings are associated in work in China through Joseph and Edith Stratton Platt in Moukden, and through Margaret Hallowell Riggs and several other Friends in Canton Christian College. Fruitful as the work in Europe has been, he said he felt China and the Far East was an even more promising field.

"The world," he said, "is judging organized Christianity by the standard of Christ and finding it wanting." The Chinese, Japanese, and Indians who come to America see our slums with their poverty and misery; they witness our labor struggles; they see crime and discontent on every hand, and they are convinced that Western civilization is not Christian, or else Christianity is a doubtful good.

Still Christianity is not yet entirely discredited in China because its transforming influence in the lives of Chinese converts is so marked. Christians are being chosen for the most responsible governmental posts because they are not subject to bribery. The young Christian church in China is on trial, or it may be more correct to say, the Chinese are trying out Christianity. They are seeing what Christianity means, and how it can be applied. The Chinese church is passing through a period of crystallization. Friends can render a tremendous service in helping it take shape.

1. They can help China in its effort to discover the authority of truth. Confucius and the sages of

the past have long been held as authority. Modern scholars are now testing these authorities. This means an openness for Christian truth and especially the Quaker idea of an inner light.

2. The testimony of Friends will be valuable in furthering the emancipation of Chinese women. The women of the Far East are awaking to the larger life before them. Here again the Quaker experience can be an example.

3. The young Chinese church needs encouragement as it seeks divine guidance in its corporate life. Many are trying the Quaker way of worship and are finding that it answers their needs. Many feel that a professional ministry cramps the spiritual life of the worshipers, but they do not want to sever the bonds which attach them to denominational missions which have done so much for them.

4. There is a need in China for some body of people who will take Christ seriously. The church has too often adjusted its ideals to its own mediocrity. The East cannot understand how the church can preach peace and practice war. It was Christian missionaries who introduced military training into the schools and colleges of China. The Chinese have the right background to respond to a peace message. Western denominationalism doesn't interest them, but Christianity can be so presented as to reach the best thought of China. It must be presented, however, in its purity. It looks as though the church has inoculated the world with a mild form of Christianity and so made it proof against the real thing.

There is a call comes to the Friends to step up into a larger service. A whole continent is hungry for the Quaker fellowship. It may be that the Christians of the East will yet lead the Christians of the West to a new and fuller appreciation of Jesus.

Quakerism in Tortola

Charles F. Jenkins, of Germantown, Philadelphia, was this year President of the Friends' Historical Society. He delivered the annual address in London, the following report of which appeared in the London *Friend*.

A remote ancestor of Charles Jenkins was one of the many Friends who visited the Quaker community in Tortola in the eighteenth century, and who died there or on the voyage. This led our Friend to take an interest in the obscure history of the happenings on this little island, about twelve miles long and three miles broad—one of the group of the Virgin Isles, not far from Porto Rico in the West Indies. He visited the island with his son in 1913; found, with great difficulty, the foundation masonry of the meeting-house, overgrown with forest trees and prickly pear, and found a few loose bricks as remains of the burying places of Friends no less mighty in their day than Thomas Chalkley, John Cadwalader, and John Estaugh, who died on ministerial service there.

In summary form, the facts of the history are—that an English Friend named Joshua Fielding spent three years, from 1726-29, in traveling in America and the West Indies. He spent three weeks in Tortola, holding many meetings. After returning home, he sent to the father of John Pickering, Lieutenant-Governor of Tortola, three Quaker books. John Pickering's father took up "the way of Quakerism" by himself. His son says that "he lived here as Lot did at Sodom." John Pickering, who is the central figure in Tortolan Quakerism during the whole course of its history, writes to David Barclay, junr., in 1741, of his own condition at that time. "For my part, I owned the Way, but never lived any way answerable to it, but had always a great Love and tenderness for them People above all others, and believe then could have lost my life for them, and has had many quarrels in vindication of them, as my Father's being one, was often hove in my teeth." One more "tender-hearted young man" had been convinced by the elder Pickering.

In 1738 James Birkett traded to Tortola, finding that about half a dozen or more had become Quakerly and "allowed that to be the true way of worship." He persuaded the little group to begin a meeting, which was held in John Pickering's house, his father having died. There seems to have been some outpouring of life in the early days. Of about 900 white people on the island, as many as 100 at one time belonged to Friends. There was no church on the island, and this group of planters lived amongst—and owned—several thousand slaves, who were constantly being imported from Africa. To lead a life of righteousness and self-control, seems to have been the particular qualification for Quakerism in this slave-holding, hard drinking community, where we read that at one time there were only thirteen white women. Friends in Philadelphia were deeply moved when they heard of this marvelous awakening of Quakerism in the tropics of the New World, and many were the visits paid by them to the little community, which stood in great need of stimulus and guidance.

As time went on, it would appear that there was a diminishing faithful nucleus among many backsliders, with numerous disownments, and frequent expressions of feebleness, growing year by year, in the letters sent from the island to London Yearly Meeting. These finally ceased in 1763, after twenty-five years of corporate connection, but a faithful few kept up their meetings, with no hope of finding younger people to follow in their steps, at least till 1770.

The island suffered from wild and dangerous outbreaks of storm. It appears to have been unhealthy physically as well as morally, and it was very difficult for light to shine in a slave-holding community. There were at least two cases of Friends manumitting their slaves on a large scale.

Two personalities of note emerge from the little community. One was Dr. John C. Lettsom, the famous London physician, and successor to Dr. Fothergill, whose life may be found interestingly described in Dr. Hingston Fox's book on Dr. John Fothergill and his friends. Dr. Lettsom was born in the Tortolan group. After being educated at Lancaster in England, he returned to the West Indies, freed his slaves, practiced medicine for a few months with great success, and returned to make a distinguished career in London. The other distinguished Tortolan was also a medical—Dr. Thornton, who, however, became famous as an architect, and was the designer of the Capitol at Washington.

The lecture was beautifully illustrated by a collection of lantern slides. It will be published as a whole—including much for the delivery of which there was no time. The would-be audience was far in excess of the accommodation of the library.

J. W. G.

English Friends' Book of Discipline

(*Revised*)

American Friends will read with interest the little volume just issued by the English Friends entitled "Christian Life, Faith and Thought: *Being the First Part of the Book of Christian Discipline of the Religious Society of Friends in Great Britain.*"

Though pronouncements, dealing with particular doctrinal problems, were issued from time to time, it was not until 1783 that there was issued the volume, which in its later editions, became known as the "Book of Discipline" of the Society. In 1834 a number of important doctrinal passages were incorporated in the book, and these were revised and enlarged in 1861 and 1883.

The present work is much more than a mere revision of the earlier material, it sets forth a collective view of Christian life and thought by means of selections both from individual Quaker writers and from pronouncements made by representative bodies of the Society of Friends from the seventeenth century up to 1920, the date of the "All Friends' Conference."

An entirely new and characteristic feature of the book is the section, forming more than a third of the whole work, entitled: "Illustrative Spiritual Experiences of Friends." Here we have a record of the deepest life experiences of more than thirty men and women, ranging from George Fox and the great pioneers of the seventeenth century, through typical leaders of the intervening years, like John Woolman and Elizabeth Fry, to modern times, with John Wilhelm Roundtree, Caroline E. Stephen, and Thomas Hodgkin. In each case the central fact of their life is a profoundly religious experience and the cumulative effect of this series of biographical narratives conveys to the readers perhaps better than would be possible in any other way the essential spirit of Quakerism.

The book is on sale at The Friends' Bookshop, 140, Bishopsgate, London, E. C. 2, or may be ordered through the office of Walter H. Jenkins, 140 N. 15th street, Philadelphia, Pa.

Henry Hodgkin Addresses F. O. R.

On Seventh month 6th, Henry T. Hodgkin gave a talk in the Twentieth St. Meeting-house, New York, under the Fellowship of Reconciliation, for whom he has just completed a year's work in China. A faint idea of his remarks may be gathered from the following notes:

If I can bring to you something of the inspiration, something of the challenge and call of the Far East, I shall be glad. All during the war, my wife and I thought much of the industrial and international conditions in the East, and felt more and more how important Eastern work must be. There were three chief problems on our minds.

First of all, international relations. When I was first in China, in 1905, at the time of the Russo-Japanese War, China was welcoming Japan as a friend, who was fighting her battles for her. Later, China became suspicious, believing that Japan wished to gain a hold in her territory, and was interested in keeping her weak. I am not stating whether these beliefs were right or wrong. This is the Chinese idea, so that Chinese boycotted Japanese goods, and held no intercourse whatever with the Japanese. Two years ago, even the Chinese Christians were unwilling to send delegates to the World's Sunday-school Convention, held in Japan at that time. In going to the Far East a year ago, my thought was, Here is the Christian Church, which should destroy these differences, but instead seems even to increase them. In Europe, the leaders of the churches watched Europe drift into war, and when the war came, they were too weak to do anything. We thought that if the Christians in the Far East could really be brought together, Christianity might become a real factor in the situation.

The second problem before us was industrial conditions. Even in 1905 the factory system was beginning to enter China. Children six and seven years old were pouring into the factories, working twelve-hour shifts, under deplorable conditions. Now, there are many more factories. The standard of living has perhaps been slightly raised as a result of this new industry, but in spite of this, it is very evident that the physique of the population in the factory districts is already deteriorating. The factories are started by English, American, Japanese, and Chinese capital, and nearly all reproduce the worst features of the Lancashire factories of the last century. This factory development is already sowing the seeds of class separation and class war, such as has never existed in China. China's resources should be developed, but it needs Christian thought, and we went there a year ago, in the hope of getting Christian men to think of it.

The third problem was that of the Christian church. It has a tremendous opportunity in China. A great many young Chinese men and women are intensely interested in psychology, new thought, etc. They paid the expenses of Professor Dewey from the United States, and Bertrand Russell from England, to go to China and lecture for a number of months. Some of these young people are Christians, but very many are indifferent, and many more are even opposed to Christianity, because they think it is joined to capitalism and militarism, as exemplified in the factories, and the European war. I think the real essence of the Christian faith is right in line with the aspirations of these young people. They are internationally-minded, they are social-minded, and they are seeking Truth in a fresh, new way. The Christian Church has here a great opportunity.

And at the very time, when this great chance offered, there was a movement which filled me with dismay,—a movement to lay greater stress on the separate creeds, of the various denominations. The Chinese see no sense in variation of creeds. They want all who believe in Christ to stand together, to put His goodness into others. And for *creeds* now to be a source of division among Christian churches in China is a work of Satan. The time has come when differences in creed must be forgotten. We want to make Christ a living issue in the life of the East today.

The spirit of conciliation is needed. What is the part of the Christian Church in social relations? It must work, not through commercial means, not through political means, but through individuals who have caught the idea, and are infecting others. Our talks last year on these matters were listened to by business men, scholars, Christians, and non-Christians. In Hong-kong, I gave five lectures to very mixed nationalities, and to speak to such a group of Chinese labor, the social revolution, etc., was a most delicate task. I was warned again and again of possible trouble. But I carried through, and as a result of these talks, a fellowship was formed there in Hong-kong, of several hundred members, from all nations, for definite and serious social service. In Shanghai, with a similar constituency, a like fellowship was formed, with a definite purpose to fight the child labor.

In the work for internationalism: I told a group of Chinese Christians, of an English woman Friend who, in the early days of the war, went to the rescue of a German woman in London, who was surrounded by a mob, beating and stoning her. The Friend faced them, unafraid, and, receiving many blows herself, led the German away to safety. Then I asked them, "Would you do that for a Japanese?" The answer was a resounding cheer. The international ideal is deep-grained in the Chinese.

During this past year, I brought together a group of Japanese and Chinese Christians, all of them leaders among their respective groups, and all carefully selected. We met to seek friendly interchange of opinions, and to seek the Divine guidance. These should be the functions of the Christian Church, to talk in friendly manner, of the most dangerous problems, of race, nation, class, etc., meeting on the common basis of our spiritual sonship.

In this group we began our days with an hour of worship. Then came a period of frank discussion. The Chinese gave their case against Japan, fully, frankly, with nothing left out, but without heat. Later, one of the Japanese replied, "We are ashamed that we have not khown of the things that our country has done. We should have known, and we are ashamed, but will try to make them better."

In spite of the Washington Conference, there is still friction between China and Japan. But I think the Conference has helped matters, and there is a better chance for understanding, as China moves to a strong government; I think Japan sees that a strong, independent China will be better for both countries.

Many of the Chinese converts to Christianity were greatly disturbed by the attitude taken by some missionaries during the war. I heard of one case in which an entire congregation rose and left the church when its pastor preached a "war" sermon. A young Chinese who had come to London to study, early in the war, heard one pastor preach after another. All gave "war sermons," until in despair he said, "I have made a mistake. I thought I was following a religion of peace, but it is not." He gave up his Bible and his Christianity, but finally came upon something written by Henry Hodgkin himself, which restored his faith,—"There is someone else in the world, who believes in the same Christ that I believed in."

What does young China want? They watch the west for the Christianity in which they instinctively believe. They thank God when they see one who believes "in the same Christ that we do."

Camp Keewadin—the Baltimore Camp

An automobile filled with young people, and piled high with suit cases and rolls of blankets, with a box of live crabs tied on here and there, made its way out the winding road from the Cove last Seventh-day morning and the first half of the season for Camp Keewadin was over. For two weeks the young people of Baltimore Monthly Meeting, and some Young Friends from other Monthly Meetings nearby, had rowed and swam, fished and crabbed in the Cove, played games and hiked over the surrounding country, and now they gave way to the families who were to spend the next month at the camp.

Camp Keewadin has indeed been a success as the nineteen young people who spent the first week there and the twenty-three occupants of the second week, will testify.

The place itself was a delightful one for a camp. A sandy peninsula, well shaded, jutted out into a cove that in turn lead into the South River and so to the Chesapeake Bay. The equipment consisted of eight tents, some large enough to hold eight people comfortably, the others for groups of two or three, with a covered mess shack and cook shack, and a well of remarkably cold water.

Our personnel was a changing one, though more than half of the number came for both weeks, and varied greatly in age from our mascot of nine to our dignified chaperon. The Camp fell naturally into two groups, however, of those under fifteen and those of the Young Friends age. These latter entered heartily into the spirit of the occasion, helped with the younger ones, taking them out in the boats and on hikes, to say nothing of cutting the necessary wood for the cook stove; and the former were of course right in their element.

Though the daily program varied a good deal the routine was as follows: At seven a whistle woke everyone up, those having the courage going into the water for a morning dip, all others having to wash at the pump. At 7.45, a whistle announced breakfast was nearly ready and called those who were waiting on the tables for that day to their tasks. A second whistle blown a few moments later found all in their places. Silent grace and then all sounds were swallowed up in the onslaught on the cereals, cocoa and flapjacks. After breakfast there was a brief reading from Dr. Fosdick's book "The Meaning of Prayer" and then a scattering to tents to clean up the camp. At nine the tents were all inspected and graded on their appearance, the tent having the highest score winning and holding for the day a banner which they proudly exhibited. After tent inspection came scheduled contests, quoits, baseball and other games being very popular, with a half hour swim at eleven and a hearty meal at noon.

After dinner the camp settled down to a quiet hour when all rested or slept in their tents, following which groups scattered in the different boats or the canoes, or on hikes to nearby places of interest, to return for a second swim at four o'clock. Supper was at six with a camp fire at eight about which we all gathered to sing or tell stories, those of the ghostly variety being especially in demand. At nine came the go-to-bed whistle and at 9.30 a second whistle called for all lights out and quiet.

Thus the days passed all too quickly. There is not space here to tell of all the horse play that our friend from Washington pulled off, of the two trips we took down the Chesapeake Bay with the Captain, of the long hike to Annapolis, and the day spent there, of the visits to the nearby places of interest, or of that exciting moment in the deciding baseball game when, with one run needed and two out X— was a moment too late reaching first base and his disconsolate coach was heard to holla "Hang it, thee's out!" Enough is it to say that we all grew fat, and our "school girl" complexion grew very brown, and we're all coming back next year.

Seventh month 3rd. BLISS FORBUSH.

Swarthmore First-day School

When the First-day School report was read in the Monthly Meeting much appreciative comment was made. The Friends were particularly interested in a plan that has been developed by Ethel G. Coates, superintendent, the object of which was to have unity of thought in the opening and closing exercises. For each First-day a theme was chosen around which all the exercises of the day were grouped—the scripture reading, the hymn, the story, class exercise, or a talk by an invited guest. All were planned to develop and intensify the thought for the day.

This year the philanthropic work seems to have been more successful than usual. An attempt has been made to appeal to the natural interests of different groups of children. Little children like to help other little children, therefore primary classes have sent donations to the Schofield School and to help a French mother and child. The older pupils like better to participate in aiding some great cause. This year the boys in the senior class took up Near East Relief as a project and through their own efforts they collected the $60.00 necessary to support one child in an orphanage for one year. Thus the main philanthropic activity of the school was planned and executed by the children themselves.

The school observed the first First-day in May as children's day. Everybody went to meeting and George A. Walton, of George School, spoke in a manner thoroughly understood and appreciated by his youthful audience. There were no First-day school classes that day but instead a group of boys (age 11 to 13 years) presented two scenes from the life and work of Dr. Wilfred Grenfell. The dramatization was a culmination of several weeks of class study and was especially notable because no dialogue was formally prepared. Instead it came as a result of the knowledge of the subject and the boy's interest in the great work of this modern missionary.

The social activities of the year include a Christmas party when the barrels were packed as Christmas gifts to the needy; several class parties; a mother's and daughter's luncheon at which a surprise program was given by the daughters. One of our Friends who is not able to assume the responsibility of teaching in the First-day School has had a boy's swimming club which meets in the college pool.

Before the school closed for the summer the officers, teachers and committee met for general sociability and a conference supper together. At that time plans were made for opening the school on October 1st. The committee felt that a very healthy enthusiasm was apparent.

From Generation to Generation

Among the Hamptonburgh hills in the country which lies back of Storm King, stands the Bull homestead. It is the oldest house in Orange County, New York (built in 1717) and is affectionately known to the county as the Old Stone House. The builders were evidently not Friends, as the seventeen-inch walls of solid masonry, the small windows and heavy, rough-hewn timbers testify clearly to a fear of the Indians. But now its gray walls are covered by a luxurious growth of Virginia creeper, and its whole aspect is softened by age, and perhaps—shall we say?—by its long identity with the Society of Friends. The interior is a veritable museum of Colonial heirlooms belonging to the Bull family. Friends have known it as a favorite resort for the old-time *parlor meeting.* Many times, we were told, in the past, a group of worshipers have sat breathless in the gathering twilight of its ample rooms with the first moonlight stealing through the tiny panes of the casement, while the Spirit spoke to their condition, through the lips of some consecrated minister.

Ebenezer and Anna Bull, the present owners and occupants, carried out in an inspired way the family traditions when they invited Cornwall Monthly Meeting and its friends to hold a meeting for worship there on First-day, Sixth month 25th.

The company which responded was large. It included members of Cornwall and Smith's Clove preparative meetings, many of the descendants and relatives of the Bull family and neighbors and visiting Friends from across the river and even farther distances. Because of the threatening showers the morning meeting was held indoors. Messages were given by Dr. O. Edward Janney, Samuel Willets, William Bull Cocks, Edward Cornell, John Roberts, and Grace Tower Warren. As the sun came out, one hundred and ten then enjoyed a box luncheon under the trees. A still larger company settled themselves out-of-doors—mostly on the ground—for the advertised afternoon meeting, at which Dr. Janney was the principal speaker, with shorter messages from William H. Stone and two other speakers of the morning. Every one lingered after its close for some time, renewing old friendships and forming new ties; and left with regret, and a backward glance at the Old Stone House which seemed to be bearing almost audible witness that "from generation to generation, Thou art God." G. T. W.

Week-end Conference at Woolman School

Those who were privileged to attend the week-end sessions at Woolman School are unanimous in pronouncing it a most enlightening and inspiring occasion.

On Sixth-day evening Murray S. Kenworthy, recently returned from Russia, gave a full and vivid description of his experiences in that unfortunate country.

On Seventh-day morning Haridas Muzumdar from India, in a brilliant address, told the story of Gandhi and explained the significance of the non-violent revolution which Gandhi has launched.

He was followed by E. Vesta Haines, who is doing field work this summer among the First-day Schools of Concord Quarter. In a most interesting way she set forth the possibilities in the way of dramatization of Bible stories.

At five o'clock there was a story hour conducted by Mrs. Elbert Russell.

In the evening Frederick J. Libby, in his usual vigorous and stimulating manner, presented the latest developments in the world drama which is being enacted. He said that a multiplicity of circumstances were operating so favorably that it was not too much to hope that war would be outlawed in our generation.

First-day morning Elbert Russell gave the second of the series of lectures on Paul's Epistles.

The last session of the week-end was a conference First-day afternoon on the subject: "How to Create the International Mind." Dorothy Brooke, James Norton and Irving Poley presented the subject from the points-of-view of education, travel and literature respectively.

To mention the schedule of the conference is to give but the skeleton of the event. It is the spirit, the fellowship, the music and sociability that gives form and beauty to a gathering of this kind. There are three more of these conferences to come, and each of these promises to be as interesting and helpful as those which have already been held.

Transportation to the Conference

The Friends' General Conference will be held at Richmond, Indiana, August 26th to September 2nd, and in order to make the best transportation arrangements, the Transportation Committee desires to know how many are intending to go. The Committee desires to know who will go by RAILROAD or AUTOMOBILE.

The following rates of fare by railroad, one way to Richmond, Ind., from the various cities, are:

From	Fare	Lower berth	Upper berth
New York City, N. Y.	$26.74	$8.25	$6.60
Philadelphia, Pa.	23.50	7.50	6.00
Baltimore, Md.	21.82	7.50	6.00
Washington, D. C.	21.82	7.50	6.00
Harrisburg, Pa.	19.75	6.38	5.10
Rochester, N. Y.	17.27	6.00	4.80
Chicago, Ill.	8.12	3.75	3.00

A reduction of one and one-half fare on the "CERTIFICATE PLAN" will apply for the round trip, providing there are 250 traveling with certificates by the various railroads. "CERTIFICATES ARE OBTAINED FROM THE AGENT WHEN TICKET IS PURCHASED."

If there are Friends expecting to attend the Conference who do not live near any of the above-mentioned cities to take these rates and who would like to know their own rate or any further information regarding the transportation, please write Robert Seaman, Chairman Transportation Committee, Jericho, N. Y.

Friendly News Notes

Drew Pearson left for Japan, China and India on June 29th. His trip is a journalistic one, and his articles on the Orient will appear in various newspapers throughout the country, including the *Evening Bulletin* and the *Chester Times*. Drew Pearson's traveling partner is W. Lawrence Seaman, of New York, who graduated from Swarthmore in 1915.

Dr. William W. Speakman expects to go abroad the last of July. He will travel through Switzerland, Belgium, England and France, and will see the Passion Play at Oberammergau. His daughter, Janet, who is still serving at the hospital at Chalons, France, will accompany him in his travels.

Former President Joseph Swain, of Swarthmore College, writes that he and Mrs. Swain have spent two months in Japan, having visited Tokyo, Nikko, and many other places. They next go to Kamizama, over 3,000 feet above sea level, for a couple of months, and will then visit China for two months.

Friends are having the opportunity of seeing Gandhi through the eyes of a native of India and a friend and follower of this great religious leader. Haridas Muzumdar is in America as a student. He feels particularly drawn to Friends and finds a kinship between the religious ideals of Friends and his own. He is to speak on Gandhi and India at a meeting under the auspices of the Peace and Service Committee in the auditorium of the P. Y. F. A., 15th and Cherry Streets, Philadelphia, on Sixth-day, July 14th, at 8.15 p. m., to which all are invited.

MEETING AT ARNEY'S MOUNT, N. J.

On First-day, Sixth month 25th, a meeting was held at "The Mount," Arney's Mount, N. J., by Orthodox Friends, with a large attendance. An inspiring prayer and several sermons showed the spirit of Friends was still there,—that spirit that did so much toward making this section of Burlington County in the past, when most of the farms were owned and lived on by Friends.

On Seventh month 2nd, the Liberal Friends held a meeting with a good attendance. Isaac Wilson, the only speaker, gave a message of love.

It is well that interest can still be felt for these old meeting-houses which in former times were filled to overflowing. Through the active interest of some Friends whose ancestors lie in the adjoining burying ground, a fund has been raised, the interest to be used for the perpetual up-keep of the burying ground, lawn and house. Could this be done for all old grounds, wherein lie the pioneer Friends and others, so they could be made pleasant, attractive spots for surrounding neighborhoods, how much better it would be than the lonely, neglected appearance so many now present. Thus could be shown love and respect to those who made it possible to have the present comfortable farms and homes. "The Mount" meeting-house was built in 1775. REBECCA N. HOUGH.

POLISH EMBROIDERIES FOR SALE

The American Friends' Service Committee has received a large consignment of Polish embroideries and some German laces, which will be on sale throughout the summer at the office, 20 South Twelfth Street, Philadelphia, Penna.

The Polish consignment includes tea-cloths, runners, children's dresses, blouses and bags. These articles, which are typical of Polish handcraft, were produced under the direction of our Unit in Poland by women who have no other means of livelihood; and money resulting from the sale of these articles is returned to further the industry.

Those purchasing these articles will not only secure useful as well as beautiful embroideries, but will render a valuable service to the deserving people across the sea.

Items From Everywhere

At the next Pan-American Conference the Chilean President is going to propose disarmament throughout South America.

Forty-six Germans were killed and 109 wounded during every hour the World War was raging, according to German statistics.

Railroad crossings have killed an average of 18,000 persons annually for the past three years, according to the general safety agent of the New York Central Lines.

The brewery that made Milwaukee famous is now turning out chocolates by the ton and helping the candy industry to maintain its position of fifth place in the industries benefited by prohibition.

Final legislative action has been taken on the annual Naval Appropriation Bill and it has now gone to the President for his signature. The bill carries appropriations of $289,000,000 and provision for 86,000 enlisted men.

Next week a delegation of several hundred prominent American citizens will carry to President Harding a million-signature petition urging the release of the 88 remaining war-opinion prisoners. The mammoth roll will be encased in a mahogany cabinet, made by an expert woodworker, one of the I. W. W. members, who lately completed a full five-year term at Leavenworth.

"Christendom for a Warless World," the appeal to the churches throughout the world adopted by the two Yearly Meetings in Philadelphia, is being sent out through the Church Peace Union to a selected list of 20,000 ministers in the United States. The letter is also being sent to the religious press. It has been endorsed by London Yearly Meeting. (For the text of the letter see FRIENDS' INTELLIGENCER of Fifth month 27th.)

Dr. C. W. Saleeby, probably the best-known eugenist in the world, states in a letter to the *Westminster Gazette* that prohibition has increased the consumption of milk in the United States by fifty per cent. He says:

"Before prohibition Americans drank about one-half pint of milk per head per day. The latest American figures are over three-quarters of a pint, and students of modern dietetics, and of that food of foods in particular will realize what these figures mean for public health and especially for childhood.

In the first six months of 1922 there were 30 lynchings. This is 6 less than the number, 36, for the first six months of 1921, and 18 more than the number, 12, for the first six months of 1920. Of the 30 persons put to death, 19 or 63% were in two states, Mississippi (7) and Texas (12). Of those lynched, 2 were whites and 28 were Negroes. Eleven of those put to death were charged with the crime of rape and nineteen were charged with other offenses. Five of those put to death were burned at the stake and 3 were first put to death and then their bodies were burned.

THE OPEN FORUM

This column is intended to afford free expression of opinion by readers on questions of interest. The INTELLIGENCER is not responsible for any such opinions. Letters must be brief, and the editor reserves the right to omit parts if necessary to save space.

To the Editor:

In regard to the miners' trouble, if a miner wishes to work for two dollars a day, which is more than a farmer is able to average, he should be protected in doing so by all the forces of the United States if necessary.

H. P. HUSBAND.

To the Editor:

In a brief but interesting letter by M. T. Woodruff published in the INTELLIGENCER of June 10, 1922, one phrase particularly struck my notice: "The injustice that capitalism has inflicted upon humanity." I do not feel sure what he means.

I think there is much confusion of idea as to what capital and the theory of capital, or capitalism, mean. It appears that there are at least two quite distinct meanings. In one, capital means the mines, or the fertile fields, or the merchant's stock in trade, or the farmer's seed, or the factory and raw material, or whatever else it is to which labor is applied, or it is the money to purchase these things, the money or property convertible into money with which the trader or farmer or manufacturer carries on his business, or it is money or something reserved from immediate consumption and made to serve in future production, as seed reserved by a farmer, or money to buy seed, or money reserved by a trader to buy stock in trade, or as M. T. Woodruff says, it is the accretion of past undivided profits; it is not necessary to enumerate further, but it will probably be agreed that capital is at least all of these. Capitalism may be defined as the theory that such capital is necessary for production, that labor must have such capital to which to apply itself in order to produce wealth. M. T. Woodruff says, probably truly, that "capital itself never produced anything," labor produces. But is it not labor applied to capital, intelligently, of course, the two in combination, that produces? Take either away, and no material wealth will be produced. The necessity of the combination of the two, labor and capital, is, I believe, the capitalistic theory, or capitalism. There is also involved the management of capital to bring best returns. Opposed to this capitalistic theory is the one that labor alone produces.

This brings us to the second meaning. To many persons capitalism denotes the centering of large amounts of capital in a few hands, and the management of such capital to bring largest returns to them; it means the undue power or oppression that some large possessors of capital can exercise and have exercised; it means the human temptation to use great power for selfish ends. To many capitalism is just an epithet connoting evil. Opposers of private ownership of the means and instruments of production, and also those who oppose all private property attack capital and capitalism by name, when in reality it is private ownership or private property they mean to attack, in order to lead the way to the abolition of private ownership and private property and the establishment of public or communal ownership.

There being these two meanings, and I suspect in some minds they are quite confused, it seems to me well for those who attack or speak of capital and capitalism, to consider and indicate in which sense they would be understood, and whether they mean to attack oppression, or whether they are consciously or unconsciously working for public or communal ownership.

"Capital never produced anything,"—that may be true enough, but if so, may it not be equally correct to say that capital never did any wrong, that capitalism never inflicted any injustice on humanity, that it was only greedy, covetous, selfish men who have inflicted injustice when they have had power in government or by reason of wealth, so that it is not government nor capital we should wish to abolish, but greed, covetousness and selfishness wherever found. Perhaps it is not money, but the love of money that is a root of evil. H. M. H.

BIRTHS

WEBSTER—On Sixth month 16th, at Ercildoun, Pa., to Warren L. and Alice Beitler Webster, a son, whose name is Robert Beitler Webster.

MARRIAGES

SIMKINS-KIRK—At Friends' Association Building, 15th and Cherry Streets, Philadelphia, on Sixth month 20th, by Friends' ceremony, Daniel W. Simkins, of Philadelphia, and Martha B. Kirk, of Newtown, Pa.

TOMLINSON-STAPLER—In Friends' meeting-house, Newtown, Pa., on Sixth month 24th, under care of Makefield Monthly Meeting of Friends, Homer A. Tomlinson, of Wrightstown, and Marian E. Stapler, of Edgewood.

DEATHS

BULLOCK—At her home, Salem, N. J., on Seventh month 2nd, Annie Bullock, daughter of the late David B. and Susan E. Bullock.

COMING EVENTS

SEVENTH MONTH

14th—"Gandhi and India," by Haridas Muzumdar, friend of Gandhi. An address under the auspices of the Peace and Service Committee. Auditorium of the P. Y. F. A., 140 North 15th Street, Philadelphia, Pa., at 8.15 p. m. All invited.

14th-16th—Woolman School week-end conference. Address by William W. Cadbury, of Canton Christian College on "The Life of a Modern Missionary," Seventh-day evening, at 8.00 p. m.

16th—W. J. and H. J. MacWatters expect to visit Manasquan Meeting and First-day School, at Manasquan, N. J., 10.30 Daylight Saving time.

16th—Certain members of Philadelphia Quarterly Meeting's Visiting Committee will attend a meeting for worship at Germantown Friends' Home, at 7.30 p. m.

19th—Monthly Meeting of Friends of Philadelphia, 15th and Race Streets, 7.30 p. m. Supper will be served.

20th—Green Street Monthly Meeting of Friends of Philadelphia, School House Lane, Germantown, 7.30 p. m.

22nd—Kirby Page, William Penn Lecturer of 1922, will speak at Woolman School on "Machiavelli or Jesus?" at 8 p. m.

23rd—Certain members of Philadelphia Quarterly Meeting's Visiting Committee will attend meeting at Frankford, Philadelphia, at 11 a. m.

25th—Western Quarterly Meeting, at London Grove, Pa., 10 a. m., Standard time.

29th—Westbury Quarterly Meeting, at Westbury, L. I., at 10.30 a. m. Lunch will be served soon after noon. The afternoon session at 2.30 will be under the care of the Meeting's Advancement Committee.

NOTICE—The Indiana Yearly Meeting convenes on Eighth month 14th, at Waynesville, Ohio. Anyone wishing accommodations, please write to Ethel Mendenhall, Waynesville, Ohio, R. R. 3.

American Friends' Service Committee

WILBUR K. THOMAS, EX. SEC.
20 S. 12th St. Philadelphia.

CASH CONTRIBUTIONS
WEEK ENDING JULY 3RD

Five Years Meetings	$185.49
Phila. Yearly Meeting (4th and Arch Sts.)	3,831.35
15th and Race Streets Meeting, Phila., Penna.	40.00
Other Meetings:	
Oakland Branch of College Park Ass'n	15.00
Westfield Monthly Meeting	236.50
Friends' Church, Portsmouth, Va.	2.75
Contributions for Germany	38.00
For Austria	38.94
For Poland	542.65
For Russia	2,521.13
For Russian Overhead	16.00
For General	84.78
For German Overhead	31.62
For Home Service—West Virginia	178.50
For Home Service—Central Penna.	775.00
For Syria	5.50
Refunds	11.38
	$8,654.59

STATEMENT OF CONTRIBUTIONS RECEIVED FROM MEMBERS OF THE PHILADELPHIA YEARLY MEETING OF FRIENDS HELD AT FIFTEENTH AND RACE STS., PHILADELPHIA, PENNA.

For the month of June

Swarthmore Meeting, G. E. J. Durnall	$35.00
E. Irene Meredith for Russia	12.00
Wilmington Mo., by S. H. Stradley	956.00
A friend—Russian Relief	10.76
Phila. Mo., by Wm. C. Biddle	792.91
Abington Mo., by D. S. Lewis	50.00
Gwynedd Prep., by Walter H. Jenkins	56.36
Woodbury Prep.	11.00
Interest on deposit to 6-15, 1922	11.71
	$1,935.74

Shipments received during week ending July 1: 63 boxes and packages; 4 anonymous.

FUN

The London *Times* reports having seen two youths, made destitute by the World War, sitting on a roadside with two British naval hats they had picked up somewhere. On one hat was "H. M. S. Devastation"; on the other "H. M. S. Broke."

WANTED

WANTED—A FEW BOARDERS FOR Seventh and Eighth months, in private home. Modern conveniences. Apply to Caroline L. Warrick, Rancocas, N. J.

WANTED—POSITION IN HIGH School or private school, as teacher of Expression and Dramatics. Normal School and Emerson College graduate. Address R. Ikeler, 212 W. 5th Street, Bloomsburg, Pa.

WANTED—POSITION AS NURSE-companion to semi-invalid or elderly woman. Light duties. Suburbs. Reference. Address B. 280, Friends' Intelligencer.

WANTED—SUMMER BOARDERS, IN a small country town; rates reasonable. Address P. 281, Friends' Intelligencer.

WOMAN OF MIDDLE AGE, NURSE, wants care of invalid. Address P. 282, Friends' Intelligencer.

POSITION WANTED—BY REFINED woman, with nervous or elderly person; capable of taking full charge; light duties. Address B. 270, Friends' Intelligencer.

ROOM AND BOARD CAN BE HAD IN private family by business man or woman, during 7th and 8th months. No smoking. Box 306, Haverford, Pa.

FOR RENT

FOR RENT—DURING AUGUST, AT reasonable rate, new cottage, near Buck Hill; 7 large open-air rooms and bath; fireplace and large porch. Well equipped. Broad mountain view. Address, Edith M. Winder, Cresco, Pa.

FOR RENT—FURNISHED OR UNfurnished, 84th St., near Central Park, 7-room apartment. Real kitchen, steam, continuous hot water. Clarence Kimball, 115 Broadway, New York. Schuyler 2661.

FOR RENT—THREE ROOMS IN private family, until Labor Day. Rates reasonable. 1402 Asbury Avenue, Ocean City, N. J.

FUN

"Charlie is wonderful," exclaimed young Mrs. Torkins. "I never dreamed that anyone could run a motor car the way he can!"

"What has happened?"

"We took a ride yesterday and went along beautifully in spite of the fact that he had forgotten some of the machinery."

"You were running without machinery?"

"Yes. We had gone at least eleven miles before Charlie discovered that his engine was missing."—*Exchange.*

Sam was reading the paper when suddenly he snorted and addressed Mrs. Sam: "What tomfoolery, Maria! It says here that some idiot has actually paid a thousand dollars for a dog!" "Well, my dear, those well-bred dogs are worth a lot of money, you know," answered his wife. "Yes, of course, I know that. But a thousand dollars! Why, it's a good deal more than I am worth myself!" "Ah, yes, Sam. But those dogs are well bred."—*Glens Falls Post-Star.*

The Friends' Intelligencer

ESTABLISHED 1844 | SEVENTH MONTH 22, 1922 | VOLUME 79 NUMBER 29

Contents

REGULAR MEETINGS

OAKLAND, CALIF. — A FRIENDS' Meeting is held every First-day at 11 A. M., in the Extension Room, Y. W. C. A. Building, Webster Street, above 14th. Visiting Friends always welcome.

PASADENA, CALIFORNIA — Orange Grove Monthly Meeting of Friends, 520 East Orange Grove Avenue. Meeting for worship, First-day, 11 A. M. Monthly Meeting, the second First-day of each month, at 1.45 P. M. First-day School (except Monthly Meeting days) 9.45 A. M.

NOTICE—Concise statements of the principles of the Religious Society of Friends and their application to the problems of every day living, including "The Spirit of Quakerism," by Elbert Russell; "Preparation for Life's Greatest Business," by Rufus M. Jones; and other articles by Henry W. Wilbur, Howard M. Jenkins, Elizabeth Lloyd, Jesse H. Holmes, O. Edward Janney, Edward B. Rawson, etc., to be had free on application to Friends' General Conference Advancement Committee, 140 North Fifteenth Street, Philadelphia, Pa.

FUN

By reason of his absent-mindedness a certain Brooklyn divine is forever perpetrating the most curious "bulls."

"And how is your wife" he recently inquired of a parishioner.

"I regret to say," was the response, "that I am not yet married."

"Ah, how pleasant that is! I take it, then, your wife is single, too."—*Harper's Magazine.*

The professor was ready to perform a chemical experiment before his class. "Should I do anything incorrect in this test," he advised, "we might be blown through the roof. Kindly step a little nearer so that you can follow me better."—*Life.*

THE FRIENDS' INTELLIGENCER

Published weekly, 140 N. 15th Street, Philadelphia, Pa., by Friends' Intelligencer Association, Ltd.

PAUL W. WAGER, *Editor.*
SUE C. YERKES, *Business Manager*

Editorial Board: Elizabeth Powell Bond, Thomas A. Jenkins, J. Russell Smith, George A. Walton.

Board of Managers: Edward Cornell, Alice Hall Paxson, Paul M. Pearson, Annie Hillborn, Elwood Hollingshead, William C. Biddle, Charles F. Jenkins, Edith M. Winder, Frances M. White.

Officers of Intelligencer Associates: Ellwood Burdsall, Chairman; Bertha L. Broomell, Secretary; Herbert P. Worth, Treasurer.

Subscription rates: United States, Mexico, Cuba and Panama, $2.50 per year. Canada and other foreign countries, $3.00 per year. Checks should be made payable to Friends' Intelligencer Association, Ltd.

Entered as Second Class Matter at Philadelphia Post Office

To the Lot Holders and others interested in Fairhill Burial Ground:

GREEN STREET Monthly Meeting has funds available for the encouragement of the practice of cremating the dead to be interred in Fairhill Burial Ground. We wish to bring this fact as prominently as possible to those who may be interested. We are prepared to undertake the expense of cremation in case any lot holder desires us to do so.

Those interested should communicate with William H. Gaskill, Treasurer of the Committee of Interments, Green Street Monthly Meeting, or any of the following members of the Committee.

William H. Gaskill, 3201 Arch St.
Samuel N. Longstreth, 1218 Chestnut St.
Charles F. Jenkins, 232 South Seventh St.
Stuart S. Graves, 3033 Germantown Ave.

The Friends' Intelligencer

The religion of Friends is based on faith in the "INWARD LIGHT," or direct revelation of God's spirit and will in every seeking soul.

The INTELLIGENCER is interested in all who bear the name of Friends in every part of the world, and aims to promote love, unity and intercourse among all branches and with all religious societies.

ESTABLISHED 1844 | PHILADELPHIA, SEVENTH MONTH 22, 1922 | VOLUME 79 NUMBER 29

Both truth and error are winged words; error flies more swiftly, but truth endures the longer.

⌘

Just as Mt. Everest defies man's efforts to scale its highest peak, so in life each new peak ascended reveals others still unscaled.

⌘

Friends must recognize in Mahatma Gandhi a leader after their own hearts. He is the George Fox of India. The non-violent revolution which is sweeping that great country is one of the most stupendous moral undertakings ever attempted anywhere. Yet most of Christendom seems to be hardly conscious of the movement at all. Those who do know of it are holding their breaths for fear it will collapse, yet doing nothing to help it succeed. The least we can do is to inform ourselves about it and then tell others. A favorable public opinion is one of the strongest forces in the world and the one thing which India needs if she is to be successful in this national venture of faith. If we cynically say "it can't be done" we are obstructing the progress of the greatest religious crusade since the days of Martin Luther.

⌘

A few weeks ago Y. M. C. A. workers from all parts of the United States and Canada gathered at Lakehurst, N. J., for the avowed purpose of making the *Christian* more emphatic in the name Young Men's Christian Association. This move indicates the sincere desire on the part of Y. M. C. A. leaders to fortify the good name of its organization. As to all other religious organizations the war brought temptations to compromise its ideals. The Y. M. C. A., in its effort to serve,—and it did serve heroically,—may have yielded somewhat to this temptation. But it is not more or less guilty in this regard than the rest of us, and all of us alike will find it difficult to recover lost ground and regain an untroubled self-respect. "Why does man persist," asks Henry Hodgkin, "in adjusting his ideals to his own mediocrity?"

⌘

We often see religious activity fall short of its aim because one feature is emphasized at the expense of other equally important matters. Religion has three aspects: worship, fellowship and service. They are like the three sides of a triangle, if one is removed the figure collapses.

Worship is essential because it is the only means whereby one may replenish his spiritual reserve from the eternal reservoirs of divine truth. One cannot receive this spiritual nourishment except through prayer and meditation.

Fellowship is a sense of Christian unity. The Fatherhood of God implies the brotherhood of men. Only as Christians work together and worship together as one great family can the Kingdom of Heaven be realized. Individual worship is necessary but it is not sufficient. We need to join with others in public worship. There are times, too, when it is well to work alone, but the world will not be won to Christ unless his followers learn to cooperate.

Service is the practical expression of Christian faith. "If ye love me," said Jesus, "feed my sheep." No one truly loves the Master unless he is willing to minister unto those who are physically or spiritually in need. No one is thoroughly a Christian unless he has dedicated his life to the ideal of service.

Some are kindly, generous, serviceable but fail because they do not renew their strength through worship. Some are pious, earnest workers but fail because they cannot work with others, or understand another's viewpoint. Some are prayerful, sociable, broad-minded but fail because they shrink from hard work. Only as Christians are careful to develop all three sides of their religious life can they hope to approach the stature of Christ, or effectively carry on his work.

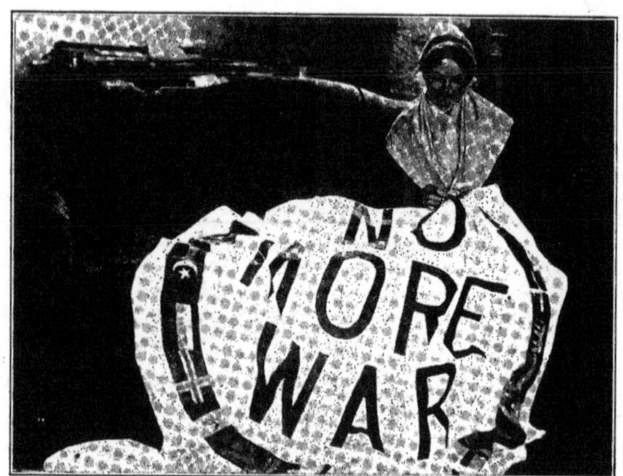

Mrs. Anna C. Easterling, member of the Friends' Disarmament Council, acting as the Betsy Ross of the "No More War" movement, completing the unbroken circle of the flags of all nations carried on the "No More War" banner, which will be raised over the headquarters of the National Council for the Reduction of Armaments, as a part of the international "No More War" demonstrations, July 29th and 30th.

Friends Must Help

An international "No More War" Day will be observed in ten countries on July 29th running over to July 30th and it has become of very great importance that the American people shall renew at this time the demonstration for peace which was so impressive and influential during the period of the Washington Conference. A militaristic revival is on foot and it is under the leadership of members of our War and Navy Departments. Only an overwhelming expression of world opinion in favor of unceasing progress towards the substitution for war of world organization in some form will be adequate to overcome the forces that oppose it. The National Council for Reduction of Armaments, of which Frederick J. Libby is Executive Secretary, appeals to Friends everywhere to rise as one man to meet the situation that confronts us.

The National Council informs us that parades are being arranged in New York City, Milwaukee and elsewhere, similar to those that will be conducted abroad but the day will be observed chiefly in three or four ways in which Friends can well participate.

1. Order posters immediately which bear the slogan, "No More War" from the National Council for Reduction of Armaments, 532 Seventeenth Street, Northwest, Washington, D. C., paying the cost price of 25 cents per hundred, which includes postage. These posters are to appear simultaneously on the morning of July 29th in windows and on automobiles, fences and trees, wherever the law allows, in cities and towns and on country roads, all the way from Eastport, Maine, to Puget Sound. The W. C. T. U., the National Y. W. C. A., the Women's International League, the Foreign Policy Association, the Fellowship of Reconciliation and the National League of Women Voters, have endorsed the idea and their State and City groups in all parts of the country are ordering posters. When other organizations are taking so strong a stand in a "No More War" demonstration, the Friends must join in.

2. Give your local editor the story of "No More War" Day with the request that he participate in the nation-wide expression of the universal longing.

3. Ask the ministers of your town to make clear in the services on First-day, July 30th, that they stand firmly for further progress on practical lines in the direction of world peace. Remember that on this issue Catholics, Protestants and Hebrews are united.

4. On July 29th—and this is particularly important in view of world conditions—write or telegraph President Harding that he will have your support in further steps towards permanent peace. Address

Preparation for Worship

Second of a Series of Articles on Worship by Elbert Russell

Most Friends spend one hour a week only in public worship. Without preparation that hour is all too short for the needs it ought to serve. Too often we come with our minds preoccupied with other interests which intrude themselves even into the meeting hour itself. It is a common experience to have the meeting close just as it is becoming alive. The meeting for worship is often compared to a meal. It is the place where we receive our spiritual food and where our spiritual strength is renewed for the duties of the rest of the week. A good meal must be prepared before we sit down to partake of it; and the meeting for worship requires preparation likewise if it is to serve its ends the best way.

In the first place physical conditions must be right for a live and helpful meeting. Many a meeting is spoiled because the stale and exhausted air of a previous gathering is still in the house and asphyxiates the willing spirit. Often the glare of windows or lights in front of the audience distracts the attention of the worshippers. Many an over-heated house has stifled a good sermon with drowsiness.

The worshippers themselves need to come physically fit. If we come to meeting over-weary, we are unable to listen or worship effectively. In the meeting where I worshipped as a boy, there was one Friend who almost invariably went to sleep in the mid-week meeting. He was distressed at his weakness and consulted some of the elders. They advised him to come in from his work an hour before time to start to meeting, to refresh himself and rest awhile. He followed the advice and found that this was what he needed in order to keep awake.

The preparation often needs to begin with changes in our habits. The real obstacle to effective worship may lie in the fact that some work too long and hard on Seventh-day, or keep late hours Seventh-day night, which leaves them exhausted and dull First-day morning. Others lie in bed too late on First-day morning or spend the time right up to the meeting-hour reading the Sunday paper. I do not regard the Sunday newspaper as essentially wrong, but if it absorbs time and energies that should be spent in preparation for worship and send us to meeting with our minds preoccupied with other interests, it is a decided hindrance to effective worship.

In direct preparation for the hour of worship we need to think of the very great importance of the opportunity and the means by which we can make the most of it. We need to become conscious of our own spiritual needs and earnestly desirous that we find help to overcome our weaknesses and to improve our opportunities. We should come with our hearts open to the divine leading and the divine blessings, conscious of the need of larger light, and praying for strength to be obedient to the heavenly vision, when it comes. We should regard the meeting not only as a means of help to ourselves but to our fellow-worshippers. We should come prayerful that they may be helped and with our minds open as to possible service that may be required of us.

I know that the "ages of quietism" produced a reluctance on the part of Friends either to seek for vocal service or to prepare for it in a meeting for worship. That is not involved, however, in the fundamental principle of Quakerism. When early Friends spoke of "immediate guidance" the word "immediate" meant "without mediation." They were emphasizing the important truth that each individual may be divinely led in worship and in service directly, without the agency of priests or other "mediators." Of course, God, who is immanent in all life, is not shut up to any times or places in his indication of our duty, and there is no obstacle to his making known our duty in advance as well as the time and place of worship. But in the course of time the word "immediate" shifted its meaning; and under the influence of quietism and in the effort to avoid rigid and meaningless forms of worship the word "immediate" came to mean "on the spur of the moment," "extempore."

If our meetings are to become the vital and dynamic occasions they ought to be we must get away from any such limitation of our purposes and of God's leading in regard to worship to the sixty minutes a week in which we are actually assembled. We need to come together with our minds already set on spiritual things and filled with thoughts concerning our own needs and the needs of our neighbors. We should come expectant of help and eager to be helpful to others. I do not think that anyone should come to meeting either determined to abstain from vocal exercise on the one hand or on the other with something prepared to say regardless of the mood and needs of the meeting or of what else may be said on the occasion. Messages that are important may often need to be postponed to a more suitable occasion, but we can come with our minds full of spiritual truth and fully conscious of the adaptation of some particular truths to the spiritual welfare of the worshippers. A meeting may fail quite as much through a predetermination *not* to say anything as through a preparation to say something which may prove unsuitable; neither is likely to happen if we are "in the Spirit" before meeting as well as at meeting.

We should go ready and eager to be of help if the way opens for it; and our ability to be helpful will be in proportion to the richness of our own experience of divine things, the exactness of our thought about them, and our eagerness to share our treasures of knowledge with the others who come, drawn by a like sense of need, to the hour of worship. And when we feel it right to be silent in the worship, the earnestness of our supplication, the fullness of our love, the eagerness of our attention, and the keenness of our sense of God will prove vitally stimulating and helpful even when the meeting is only an occasion of

"silence multiplied
By these still forms on either side."

Gandhi: Fighting Man of Peace

An Introduction for Children

By Blanche Watson

*(The author of the following article believes that religious principles may be instilled most effectively if they are carried to the little children. It is primarily for them that she has written this story of India's modern prophet of love.—*Ed.)

About two thousand years ago there lived a man who said, "He that taketh the sword shall perish by the sword,"—that is, He tried to make people see that war was wrong—that all killing was wrong—because *all* human life was sacred. The world, since that time, has listened to that message, but it has not understood it, or even tried to understand it—all of which means that this man came before the world was ready for Him, and (not being ready) it crucified Him!

When I say the world, I do not mean everybody in it. There were some few people who did understand what Jesus, the Christ, taught, and who tried to live by those teachings.

Now, today, on the other side of the world, in far away India, a man is preaching as did Jesus of Nazareth, "Love your enemies"; "Do good to them that hate you"; Do unto others as you would that they should do unto you." Like Jesus, he goes out under the blue sky and gathers the people around him. Like Jesus, he says "Follow me!" And the people follow him—not by the hundreds—but by the millions—for India is a nation numbering more than 300 million souls!

The people of India want the right to govern themselves as we govern ourselves in this country—as they governed themselves a great many years ago! Usually when a people decide that they want to be independent (as we call it) they "go to war"—that is, they gather together armies and go out and kill one another—forgetting what Jesus said—forgetting that we are all brothers and that God is our Father.

Now this man, who is leading the Indian people—"Saint" Gandhi as he is called—is giving to his people, after all these years, the message of the Man that we Christians call our leader. He, too, says: "He that taketh the sword shall perish by the sword," and—if you will believe it—the British Government, that has held India against its will for a hundred and sixty years, has been more afraid of this man than any "general," that is, any fighting man—that has ever arisen during that time.

Recently they took him and thrust him into prison.

You ask me, "Why"?

Let me tell you. Gandhi, this saint, says, "Don't have anything to do with this government and the people it sends here to rule us; but do not hurt them —do not lift a hand against them: just love them!" But when he said "Do not have anything to do with the Government," Gandhi was guilty of sedition. Like Jesus, he was guilty of "stirring up the people," —and like Jesus he was not afraid to be punished.

Gandhi says to his people, "If you follow my way, you will be a free people; and when he speaks thus— this frail little man who has to sit in a chair on a table when he speaks—no one can disagree with him. No one can look in his wonderful eyes and even *think* that he is wrong. Do you know why this is? Because of the strength of his spirit. It is the spirit—the spirit of God Himself that blazes there, and his word is the word of God.

That is why the British government is so afraid of this great leader. When a man persists in loving you—in spite of all you do to him—you can't keep on hating and mis-using that man forever!

"Mahatma" Gandhi knows that a group of people held together by good-will, by love, is mighty—for love is constructive—that is, it builds.

The English government (and I do not mean the English *people*—that is a different thing) the English government may not know it, but they are afraid of Saint Gandhi simply because he is speaking with the voice of God, even as did Jesus, the Christ— by the Sea of Galilee—hundreds of years ago.

Will the people of India hold out? Is the world to learn the lesson that war is murder—that Christ's way is the better way—that love is the "greatest thing in the world"?

Let us all watch India, and Gandhi!

Consulting a Book in the British Museum

Let me start by saying that what follows is not in anyway to be taken as a criticism of English methods or of the courteous attendants in the British Museum. No one could have been more kind or anxious to help than they. What follows is only intended to show the difference there is in their ways and ours.

In working on a certain line of research it was desirable to consult the "History of the Church of England in the Colonies." It is possibly to be found in some of our libraries, but it seemed easier to get it in London, its native habitat.

This was the operation. In order for an American to become a "reader" in the museum it is necessary to have an introduction from American Embassy in London. To secure this we should in turn secure an introduction to the Ambassador, so that the trail begins in America in first obtaining such a letter from our Secretary of State.

Armed with this, and after waiting a half hour, caused by the fact that our Embassy is lunching up to three o'clock, the proper Secretary telephoned to the museum that an American reader was coming— please give him a reader's ticket.

An important looking official at the gate with a silk hat and red collar and cuffs keeps smokers out of even the grounds, but he and a regulation "bobby" inside the library cheerfully directed the searcher to the dispenser of permits. This was in a somewhat distant room along a passage way, and here another polite official stated he had heard from the American Embassy and issued the ticket. It is only fair to say that I have since heard that tickets have been issued to strangers on the simple recommendation of the Librarian of Friends' Historical Library and possibly that might have been all that was necessary in this case. The ticket is in three parts—one retained in the official's office, the second delivered to another red-cuffed and collared official, who guards the sacred portals of the Library itself, the third part the reader retains to be shown when required.

The reading-room is an immense circular hall with a great dome. The librarians' desks are in the center surrounded by other desks under which are the shelves containing the voluminous index of 1006 volumes.

From there the readers' desks radiate like the spokes of a wheel, fourteen desks in each row. These desks are large and comfortable, supplied with blotter, ink, and pens and pegs on which to hang your hats. You secure your desk, which is numbered, and secure it by placing some personal article on it—your hat, gloves, or stick. Signs warn you not to leave your overcoat or other articles of value, as they are sometimes stolen.

The next step is to consult the catalog. The thousand and more volumes of this are large substantial books, each with a leather loop at the back to pull it out easily. Unfortunately, the index is arranged by authors, and in addition is not strictly alphabetical, though nearly so. If you do not know your author you are deeply at sea. A subject index is under way, but not nearly complete.

Well, who did write the History of the Church of England in the Colonies? No one knew and a half hour's search availed nothing. "England" fills eighteen volumes of the index. Walking up and down through the desks is a courteous helper who came to the rescue. Fortunately it was known that the book was published in 1856 and reference to a printed book of the output for that year gave the author's name as Anderson. Again to the index containing the Andersons who have written books, but alas, they are prolific writers and there are ninety-six pages in double columns to a page. A fairly careful search taking half an hour failed to discover the man we were looking for. Another application to the peripatetic friend, another printed book consulted and the name is disclosed—J. S. M. Anderson.

It is now necessary to fill up an application slip giving your name,. the number of your desk, the number, title, and date of the wanted book. This was just about completed when a young man stood up in the librarian desk and rang a little dinner bell, which meant it was 5.40 p. m., the library would close in a few moments, and no more books would be given out that day.

The Library opens at ten in the morning. At ten minutes past ten the next day the application slip was placed in the proper box along with several others secured previously, and the reader hastened to his desk for the slip distinctly says no book will be delivered unless the reader is seated in his proper place. Later it was found this rule is not rigidly enforced. At 10.50 the book was delivered—just forty minutes' waiting. This, too, was much longer than subsequent orders for books sent through.

Ten minutes disclosed the fact there was nothing in the History of the English Church in the Colonies along the searcher's line, so a full half day was charged up to experience. "Why don't you have a modern card index?" I asked the head of the manuscript division. He looked at me in rather pained surprise. "Do you know what it would cost, and furthermore, where would we put it?" I tried to explain that the great card index in our Congressional Library at Washington takes up less room than their thousand heavy vellum-paper volumes, but I am sure he remained convinced that this was the better plan. Then I asked why they thought it necessary to have so much red tape. He replied by telling a story of two men sitting in a tavern whom he once had overheard talking. One said to the other: "Do you think I am a thief?" to which the other replied, "Perhaps you are—I don't know 'till I try you."

There are no more courteous, obliging and interested officials anywhere than the English if you are properly introduced, and go about the matter strictly according to their good order and rules. They go to any amount of trouble and seem to take pleasure in helping, but they want notice in advance, and do not like the casual and abrupt way we have of doing many things.

But I do think a little more speed at the Museum Library in getting books after you have done your part would not come amiss, and with this conclusion many English friends agree. C. F. J.

London, 5th mo. 17, 1922.

Conditions In the Russian Famine Area

By Murray S. Kenworthy

(Murray S. Kenworthy, chief of the Russian Unit from November 1, 1921, to June 1, 1922, returned home on July 1st. He is the first worker to return since Anna Haines came back last October. His account of conditions during the winter shows that all reports about the severity of the famine are without exaggeration. The following extracts from his comprehensive report to the Service Committee covering every phase of the situation gives an indication of the problems that the Unit has had to meet and of those which still confront it.)

"When I went south of Buzuluk to Andrievka in November, many peasants had already died. Thousands were leaving, seeking more promising areas where food was to be had. Bones of animals which had died were bleaching by the wayside. Peasants were stripping the thatch from their house-roofs to feed their stock. Bread made from grass flour stuck together with glue from horses' hoofs was common. Harness leather broth was not unknown! Cannibalism was more than occasional. The situation was desperate.

When I left Russia the combined efforts of all relief organizations were probably giving relief to well up to 10,000,000 people. But there were large untouched territories begging assistance.

What the total population loss will be is beyond estimation at present. We have statistics for a part of our territory. Present figures indicate that the average loss is 23% for six months. Some volosts have lost 41% in that time. What would have happened if we had not come? Whole villages would have died to the last man. In others, a few would have survived, and, along the railroad, many would have pulled through. The remote peasant villages would have suffered terribly.

Living Conditions for the Personnel

We live in Russian houses which, although the best available, are not equal to those we are accustomed to. Our food is canned or dried goods to a great extent; for we dare not eat raw or uncooked foods, for fear of cholera. Our workers must in consequence go through the summer without green vegetables. There are no places of amusement or recreation. In winter, skating on the Samara river, just back of our home, might be available but for the snow. Skiing and coasting are possible for months on the bluffs beyond the river. A good Edison or Victrola with suitable records would be very acceptable. If a vacation is desired, Moscow is the nearest point, and it offers little real rest; while the trip back and forth spoils all one gets by going.

The danger from disease is very great. We know of no way to avoid the possibility of becoming infected. None of us know where we got the bites giving us typhus. We have tried to use all practical means of protection.

Distribution of Food

One of our most difficult problems lay in selecting those whom we should feed. At first we did not provide food to the people living in the best provided sections.

By June 1st, however, practically every one in our area was getting food, either from us, the A. R. A., or the Central Russian Government. The government was feeding a certain number of children in kitchens under its own management; we were feeding the rest of the children, and distributing American corn to the adults for the A. R. A.

The problem of feeding the inmates of the children's homes was particularly puzzling. If a farmer had 100 piges and only enough food to get 50 of them through the winter, would he select the weakest to be fed? Should we apply these calculating tactics? We did not: our code of ethics somehow got in the way. We did our best to relieve the situation in all its phases.

Transportation

Russia at her best never had an adequate system of railroads. Her lines for the most part are single track, her fuel wood, and in the winter deep snowdrifts block her tracks. At one time it was said that as many as 60% of the trainmen on the Buzuluk section were down with typhus.

When the thaw came and the ports were free, there was congestion, of course. During this period, the railroads were tested to the utmost. Passenger trains were for a time discontinued, and the engines used for freight service. For a brief period, passenger and food trains were sidetracked to allow trains loaded with seed wheat for the spring sowing to pass to the interior. Everything considered I am inclined to praise the Russian railroad officials rather than to find fault.

When one considers the starving populations and the condition of the hungry, underpaid railroad men, it is a marvel that whole carloads of food were not missing.

Relations with the Russian Government

We have experienced no trouble with the central Russian government. There have been times when we felt it necssary to ask for changes in local appointments in the famine area, which have been effected without difficulty.

The government has furnished us with dwelling-houses, often going to trouble and expense to repair them. Furniture has also been supplied. Only in Moscow have we had to buy our own fuel. Gasoline, oil and kerosene for motor transport, as well as garages, have been supplied. Russian helpers have been provided free of cost. Free transportation of personnel and baggage in addition to food supplies has been provided. Of warehouses we had the best available. In other words the government has given us ready assistance all along the line.

Agriculture

The need for an agricultural program was seen early in the work, but the first proposition was to buy hay and feed the horses. This venture did not work out to our satisfaction. At last we ordered tractor outfits from Poland; these on arrival were quickly assembled, and put to work about the middle of May. When I visited the field the end of May these were running day and night. The land plowed was to be planted in potatoes or sown to millet. It was too late for spring wheat. The government was furnishing the fuel and oil, also the seed. The people were planting the potatoes. The people are to harvest the crop and the food is to be distributed among the Children's Homes of our areas.

This kind of work, so far as this year's crop is concerned, must close by the middle of June. Fall plowing may begin by the first week in July. It is quite probable that the fall plowing will include sections in at least two of the outposts. Russian boys were taught to run the tractors, thus training them for usefulness in this line of work.

Russia needs, above everything else material, a modern farming system. The soil is unusually rich. Probably one of the best things we could do would be to inaugurate a good agricultural program.

Crop Prospects

It was too early when I left to get a very accurate estimate, but all reports concur in the opinion that the winter wheat and rye will yield only a moderate amount. The prospect for all Russia is only fair, for the acreage is low. For the spring crops conditions were good, though the weather was cool. There was plenty of moisture—too much, almost.

People were still sowing the first of June, consequently it will be some time before estimates can be made. Undoubtedly Russia will require the assistance of her friends for another year.

Future Work

The Russians are now in rags. Clothing and clothing materials of all kinds are needed in great quantities. The time is probably near at hand when the people should be guided into definite efforts for themselves. They can spin, weave and sew and should be encouraged to do it for themselves.

Some steps might well be taken to give these peasants work during the long winter months. Artificial light would be necessary, for the hours of daylight are few. For months on end, the peasants are housed in, with no well organized industry, no uplifting social, educational or religious activities. Here is a vast field for valuable effort for someone.

As Friends, we would find it easy to take over large tracts of land and farm them with modern methods, or take over land and Children's Homes and establish industrial centers. If we desired, we would certainly be permitted a free hand educationally and religiously with these children, of course within certain limits. Russia has orphans—thousands of them; and her task in caring for them alone is staggering.

A vast amount of medical and sanitary work could be done in the peasant villages. Russia will continue to be a source of danger to the rest of Europe and to America until radical sanitary changes are made.

How much feeding will be required next winter, it is too early to say. Present crop estimates indicate that 50% of the people will not have sufficient food to carry them through next winter. The children in the Homes, of whom there are 4,078 in our district, will in any case need nourishing food.

This new program of effort must be worked out by those now on the field in the light of existing conditions.

Wanted, a Doctor for Russia

The Friends' Unit in Russia needs immediately a good American Doctor, to look after the health of the Unit and organize community welfare work. A wonderful opportunity to help bring the message of good will to the Russian people, minister to thousands of children, render service in the name of the Christ.

Applicant must be in good health, and in full sympathy with Friends. Salary if needed.

AMERICAN FRIENDS' SERVICE COMMITTEE
20 South 12th Street *Philadelphia, Pa.*

A Message from China

Extracts from a letter from Edith Stratton Platt to her friends at home

We are really now living in the country, east of the city, though only about ten minutes from it. Out to the farther south and east there are miles of open gardens to be wandered over and explored. You can walk any place. No fences, only walls around the little home compounds, and paths across any field you take a fancy to. I choose the paths that look alone and rejoice that the birds and sunshine don't think me strange, nor the little wandering pathways which are almost white with blossoms now.

To see these farmer folk working, working along their immaculate rows is to understand the Chinese temperament better. They impress one as such good, genuine men. They live close to Nature and have that patience and industry and wholesomeness that seems to bless people that live close to the soil. They are optimistic, full of laughter and smiles and weird discordant song. They are peace-loving and reasonable and get along extraordinarily well together. As I told one of the boys the other day, "You Chinese must have wonderful dispositions to live in these big patriarchial families and get along so smoothly." Little Chu puckered up his brow and said: "There is a great deal of unhappiness behind those compound walls." I guess he is right. They sit on top of their sorrow and work on with invincible optimism. The outstanding blackness in the picture is the home—the appalling lovelessness of marriage divorced from Christianity, the presence possibly of several wives to one husband and several families under one roof and the hodge-podge resulting. These boys share their distresses with Joe and it makes our hearts ache to think how their lives have been robbed through circumstances beyond their control.

This reminds me of a Better Homes Conference that the Y. M. and Y. W. have had this week. I want to tell you about three sessions of it that I attended. The first was a lecture by Mrs. C. F. Wang who is a Chinese Wellesley girl living here in Moukden and one of the joys of my life! She spoke on the spiritual side of the marriage relation. She could. Her own marriage is one of the beautiful things in Moukden. She and her husband are both returned students from America and their home atmosphere is one of deep devotion and joy. She made two points. One was that the privilege of choosing one's own life partner as in the west did not guarantee a happy union, and the second was that a happy relationship could be worked out even on the old Chinese plan.

After the lecture we divided into four discussion groups on Hygiene, Religious Education in the Home, Training of Children, and Marriage. I went to the Marriage group. Probably about twenty-five men and women were there. They discussed the suitable age for marrying and some such details and then sailed into one of the most fundamental problems of a Chinese home: whether young couples should break away from the parent home and set up one of their own. There seemed to be no dissenting voice to the desire for the reorganization of the home on the basis of each family to itself except one earnest lad who thoughtfully brought up the duty toward caring for their old people that children should feel. It was an eye-opener to me to see those men and women simply leaping into the problem—two or three trying to speak at once in their eagerness for solution, and doing it furthermore together, when not two years ago men and women were so screened off from one another here in the conservative North that the East Moukden Church had a curtain hung between the men's and women's sides! The lad who led this discussion has already made an attempt to bring his own little family apart into a home of their own but has been largely frustrated because relatives of his from the country moved in on top of them and his home is such a bedlam that he retreats to the Y. M. C. A. to get the quiet and settlement that he had attempted to achieve in his home.

One other session of the Conference I must describe—the picnic in the Grove. It was such fun! We had planned various games for grown-ups and children and there were speeches and songs and wonderful eats. What a pity we never thought of our kodak to catch some of the family scenes—a very young father jauntily tossing his fretful scantily-clad progeny on two strong white gloved hands. No other sign of elegance about either. I whispered to Bess, "But why does he wear gloves?" "Because he has them I suppose," was her luminous reply. Or the presiding host of the occasion with a broad-brimmed feminine piece of millinery on his jovial head that made him look sweet sixteen.

I might as well confess to you that I am worth very little to China as yet and that I get very impatient at times about the long, long trail of preparation before me. Perhaps every one of you who reads this letter is accomplishing more than I am and adding more to the sum of human welfare. There is nothing very big or wonderful about it but I am happy. Happy most of all because of the future which beckons and calls with strange and beautiful insistence day and night, night and day, and pauses not but to call more loudly. EDITH STRATTON PLATT.

Friends' Opportunity In the Orient

The committee working under this title met on First-day afternoon at 3 o'clock preceding the afternoon session of Woolman School Week-end Conference on the 16th.

The treasurer's report showed:

Balance from last year	$354.73
Contributions in 1922	2,039.42
Total	$2,393.15

Of this amount $1,500 has been sent to Canton Christian College for the full support of Margaret H. Riggs, and $800 was directed to be sent to the Y. M. C. A. towards the support of Joseph and Edith Stratton Platt, this being $1,700 short of the amount required for their full support.

The committee further decided to bring the subject before the Richmond Conference to secure such indorsement as will insure the permanence of the work begun here.

The visit and addresses of Henry T. Hodgkin have aided materially in awakening Friends to the great service our three young missionaries are rendering and also in impressing upon us the obligation of upholding and supporting them in their chosen fields of service.

The conference which followed and which was addressed by Dr. William W. Cadbury further confirmed this feeling.

ALFRED W. WRIGHT.

Friendly News Notes

Those who are going to attend Friends' General Conference at Richmond will be glad to know that Elbert Russell and William J. Reagan will be present at the conference for the week.

Alva W. Taylor, who is announced to speak at the Richmond Conference on "Christian Ideals for Industry," is Social Welfare Secretary of the Church of Christ (Disciples), with headquarters in Indianapolis. He is an editorial writer for the *Christian Century*, and is also active in the Social Service Department of the Federal Council of the Churches of Christ in America.

Rowntree and Henry Gillett, well known English Friends, are expecting to be in attendance at Friends' General Conference at Richmond, Ind., August 26th to September 2nd. These Friends have been active in connection with the relief work on the continent, and are especially interested in experiments English Friends are making in the application of Christian ideals to industrial problems.

The Detroit Meeting of Friends, composed of Friends of all branches, have formally organized as a Monthly Meeting, and are preparing to build a suitable meeting-house. Certain Friends have signified their willingness to help finance a building project in part, and the 104 members feel confident that with some outside help they can obtain a suitable lot and build a small meeting-house that will take care of the growing meeting in Detroit. They will greatly appreciate any co-operation on the part of our Friends.

Among the speakers at the third week-end conference at Woolman School were Leslie P. Hill, who presented in poetic form the longings and aspirations of the colored race; Dr. Morris Ferguson, who gave the first two of a series of five lectures on "Community Religion"; Dr. William W. Cadbury, from China, who described the life and opportunities of a modern missionary; and Dr. Elbert Russell, who gave the third of his illuminating lectures on Paul's Epistles. Among those who participated in the First-day afternoon conference on "Our Attitude Toward Missionary Work" were Dr. Cadbury, Herbert Way, Sidney Nicholson and Alfred Wright.

"Any nation that forcibly suppresses the expression of honest thought is doomed as a democracy," President Harding is told in a letter addressed to him by the Baltimore Quarterly Meeting of Friends (Quakers), lately held at Sandy Spring, Md. The message was a plea for the release of all persons in prison for violation of the Espionage Act.

"If it is successful," the Friends continue, "it imprisons not only men's bodies but their minds. If it is unsuccessful, it courts revolution. . . . We believe it would be an act of wise statesmanship to release all those now in prison for speeches or action during the war, which would not have been illegal in time of peace."

According to *The Young Quaker*, the official organ of the English Young Friends' Movement, Dublin Yearly Meeting, which met from May 3-9, reflected the tragedy of the internal strife that still hangs over Ireland, and despite an earnest seeking after unity, considerable difference of thought was reflected. But "Irish Friends have a true sense of humor, and this helped to pilot the Yearly Meeting through several difficult waters. Especially was this evident during the discussion which preceded the decision to continue correspondence with Hicksite Yearly Meetings in America."

"Irish Young Friends, like their English cousins at Manchester, are feeling the importance of personal responsibility, a note which was indeed the dominating one throughout the whole Yearly Meeting."

The Friends in the village of Jordans in Buckinghamshire, which is growing up around old Jordans' meeting, where William Penn is buried, have started the publication of a little paper, the *Penn Pioneer*, now in its fourth number. The contents are made up of contributions mainly from among the 150 villagers of Jordans. The editor, F. J. Edminson, is anxious to enlarge the collection of William Penn books and pictures and to start a library that might eventually include an International School of History as representing Penn's broad interest in international relations. They would also like eventually to have a museum and school of art. They have made a start in these matters with the Alfred Thorne bookcase and a collection of neolithic implements presented by the Bucks Archaeological Society. They would welcome any assistance from American Friends.

MID-WEEK MEETINGS AT COLUMBIA

Last year's series of meetings at Columbia University proved so satisfactory in every way that the New York Friends of both branches, with Quaker students at the Columbia University Summer School have again made arrangements for four meetings on the campus, during the four middle weeks of the school. As last year, each meeting will begin with an address and conference on a set topic, the last half of the period being given to a Meeting for Worship on the basis of silence.

The meetings are to be held on the campus facing the east end of the grandstand, on Fifth-day evenings at 7.30. All students who may be interested are invited to come, to participate in the consideration of the following topics, and to join in the Meetings for Worship:

Seventh month 20th—Quakerism and Education.
Seventh month 27th—Quakerism and Industry.
Eighth month 3rd—Quakerism and Peace.
Eighth month 10th—Quakerism and Adventure.

Plans are also under way for a picnic on the Palisades to be given to the Quaker students at Columbia Summer School, by New York Friends, on the afternoon and evening of Eighth month 5th. All Friends in and near New York are invited to attend this picnic and help welcome the visitors.

Books Recently Received at The Friends' Intelligencer Office

What is Social Case Work? *Mary E. Richmond.* Russell Sage Foundation, New York. $1.00.

What's Best Worth Saying. *Rev. Richard Roberts.* George H. Doran Company, New York. $1.25.

Jesus Christ and the World Today. *Grace Hutchins and Anna Rochester.* George H. Doran Company, New York. $1.25.

The Book of Job. *Moses Buttenwieser.* The Macmillan Company, New York. $4.00.

Parenthood and Child Nurture. *Edna Dean Baker, M. A.* The Macmillan Company, New York. $1.50.

Conscription and Conscience. *John W. Graham, M. A.* George Allen and Unwin, Ltd., London. 12/6.

Christian Life, Faith and Thought (*The First Part of the English Friends' Book of Discipline*). The Friends' Bookshop, 140 Bishopsgate, London, E. C. 2. 2/—.

America Faces the Future. *Durant Drake.* The Macmillan Company, New York. $2.00.

The Little Corner Never Conquered—The Story of the American Red Cross Work in Belgium. *John Van Schaick, Jr.* The Macmillan Company, New York. $2.00.

Items From Everywhere

Lloyd George announced in the House of Commons last week that England would be willing to support a proposal for Germany's admission to the League of Nations.

During the first six months of 1922 in the city of Philadelphia 19 persons were killed by trolley cars, 22 by railroad trains, and 105 by automobiles. Beside those killed 3,446 were injured.

Fifty per cent. more money was spent by the people of the United States for perfumes, face powder and cosmetics in 1920 than the total endowment of all the private colleges and universities in the country, according to Treasury Department statistics.

After defeating an amendment to shorten the time of military service in France, the Chamber of Deputies adopted an article providing for active army service of eighteen months, in reserve for eighteen years and six months, and territorial service for ten years. Total, thirty years.

On July 4th more than 100,000 German workmen marched through the streets of Berlin with banners inscribed "For the Republic," "Down with Ludendorf," "Down with Reaction." This is the answer of the masses to the monarchist revival.

Eugene V. Debs has entered a Chicago sanitarium for treatment. The strain of his incarceration at the Atlanta penitentiary affected his heart, and since his release he has been unable to recover his former vitality.

Baptist women in the farm districts of Iowa have agreed to contribute all the eggs laid by their hens on Sundays until the end of April to help finance foreign and home missions. It is believed that the contributions from this source will total more than $75,000.

On May 30th the Chinese Government was notified by the Japanese ambassador, Yukichi Obata, that his government had decided to move its troops from Hankow. The Japanese garrison at Hankow has been maintained for years, the excuse being that it was needed to protect Japanese interests along the Yangtze Valley. Minister Obata stated that the action was in accord with the spirit of the resolutions adopted at the Washington Conference.

The House of Representatives has passed a bill which, if passed by the Senate, gives alien married women substantially the same naturalization and citizenship rights as are now enjoyed by alien men. At present a married woman has the same status as her husband. Under the provisions of this bill an alien married woman, who desires to do so and is qualified, may become naturalized independent of her husband. The bill would also permit American women who marry foreigners to retain their citizenship if they wish, unless they marry aliens ineligible to United States citizenship.

On Flag Day, June 14th, President Harding was the speaker at the dedication of a national memorial on the site of Fort McHenry, near Baltimore, to Francis Scott Key, author of "The Star-Spangled Banner." It was in Fort McHenry in 1814, during an attack by a British fleet, that the flag hung to which the anthem was written. The memorial is a colossal statue in bronze.

German universities now enroll about one hundred and twenty thousand students, of whom more than two-thirds are reported to be suffering from extreme poverty. These are the sons of doctors, lawyers, government officials, and men of small fixed incomes, who feel most keenly the effects of a depreciated currency and the accompanying increase in the cost of living.

President Harding recently interceded for the life of a dog owned by a poor Russian immigrant at Lansdale, Pa. The State of Pennsylvania prohibits any alien from owning a dog, and a justice of the peace at Lansdale fined the poor Russian $25 and ordered the dog to be shot. Mrs. Harding read in a newspaper about it, and she induced the President to write Governor Sproul, who telegraphed the magistrate to spare the life of the dog.

THE OPEN FORUM

This column is intended to afford free expression of opinion by readers on questions of interest. The INTELLIGENCER *is not responsible for any such opinions. Letters must be brief, and the editor reserves the right to omit parts if necessary to save space.*

To the Editor:

To the writer of the Forum letter of Sixth month 17th, which had the signature "E. H.," and which mentioned that money is not an essential, I would like to suggest that she hand over whatever she has of it to some one who has come to consider money an essential by having been deprived of it.

To those who state that labor is *all*, I feel that for them it would be elevating if they could raise their thoughts to the Almighty beneficent Source that gives the milk, the wool, the grains, the grasses which humans have the privilege of gathering in and manipulating. The condition of the dear children comes from its not being arranged that they get abundant sleep; that their food is not well selected and guarded; that their mothers do not make for them home-made bread. Where these attentions to their welfare are neglected, there are the same conditions as where there is plenty of money.

TACIE P. WILLETS.

To the Editor:

May I suggest to the correspondent who contradicts the statement that "Capital produces nothing" that his view of the subject is not broad enough? His conception of Capital is that it is Money entirely. So, too, must such statement be founded on the same conception.

True Capital is Labor. Capital began to produce before Money was invented. Nature has provided the resources through which Capital has been able to make the progress it has. The benefit Money has conferred on humanity has been by facilitating the exchange of products of true Capital. These benefits have been inequitably distributed and Money made the god, the master, instead of the servant.

The great inventions which have made possible the harnessing of electricity and water and oil are the product of Labor, not Money. Possession of Money has enabled others than the inventors to appropriate to themselves the profits, while the real Capitalist too often has not been rewarded for his expenditure of time and study.

Society itself is robbed by this Money, falsely called Capital, for there is not a commodity on earth, not a convenience in home or field, that does not cost more than it should. Investment is swelled by trick, and there is not a public utility which does not exact toll from "watered" stock.

Take the transcontinental railways, endowed with princely generosity by the people. From the start there has been wholesale theft. Construction costs were a matter of getting all possible, absorbing the domain granted by Government without return, and later manipulating stocks and bonds until the interest on obligations is a heavier tax on the public than any cost of operation.

The automobile is another example by which the truth of this argument is established. Money scoffed at the motor-driven vehicle. After failure of Money, or its possessor in control of his first venture, to appreciate his idea, Henry Ford reorganized a new company and began on his own Capital, faith in himself, inexhaustible energy and genius, but without Money. And today, when nearly every other corporation in the same business has failed—for absorption in mergers is neither more nor less than failure—and Capital is seeking a monopoly of the great invention, Henry Ford is the one successful Capitalist who is enjoying an earned reward for time and toil which might well have discouraged him a score of years ago. Money (falsely termed Capital) has control of many plants it did not create.

Realization of the depth of thought in this matter is the best solvent for these academic disputes. They are unimportant in view of the more terrible truth that we are worshiping the Golden Calf. The pulpit itself is too often sacrificing to Baal. I do not charge insincerity, but I do insist that righteous judgment is not always delivered by the professed follower of the Lamb.

A word more and I am done. Your correspondent speaks of the Capitalist "putting *his* Money in a venture" and deserving a proper return. *His* Money? Not always. Statistics show that savings deposits, almost exclusively made by wage earners, aggregate more than the existing amount of Money. Our friend's investment, then, is on borrowed capital. If labor should demand, as it has a moral right, a share in the profits of that borrowed capital, where would he be?

M. T. WOODRUFF.

Dearborn, Mich.

BIRTHS

FURNAS—On Fifth month 29th, to Seth E. and Sarah C. Furnas, of Waynesville, Ohio, a son, named Seth E. Furnas, Jr.

SINCLAIRE—On Seventh month 9th, to J. Kennedy and Louise Andrews Sinclaire, of Rutherford, N. J., a son, named Harry Addison Sinclaire.

MARRIAGES

ADAMS—PIDGEON—At Washington, D. C., on Sixth month 28th, Jane Jackson, daughter of Charles M. and Katie D. Pidgeon, to Elliot Quincy Adams, of Cleveland, Ohio.

DEATHS

HICKS—In Lansdowne, Pa., Seventh month 11th, Mary S. M., wife of Harry K. Hicks, in her 71st year. Interment private at London Grove.

JACOBS—In Philadelphia, Pa., on Seventh month 10th, A. Laura Cleaver Jacobs, wife of Edward E. Jacobs, aged 59 years. Interment Plymouth Meeting.

JONES—At Moorestown, N. J., on Seventh month 16th, Norman S. Jones, son of B. Henry and late Elizabeth S. Jones, aged 16.

COMING EVENTS

SEVENTH MONTH

20th—7.30 p. m., Conference and Meeting for Worship on the campus, under care of Friends attending Summer School of Columbia University. Topic of Conference, "Quakerism and Education." Leader, Clarence W. Maxfield.

22nd—Kirby Page, William Penn Lecturer of 1922, will speak at Woolman School on "Machiavelli or Jesus?" at 8 p. m.

23rd—Meeting for worship at Friends' Meeting-house, North avenue and Third street, Media, Pa., at 3.30 p. m. (daylight saving). All are welcome.

23rd—Certain members of Philadelphia Quarterly Meeting's Visiting Committee will attend meeting at Frankford, Philadelphia, at 11 a. m.

25th—Western Quarterly Meeting, at London Grove, Pa., 10 a. m., standard time. Afternoon meeting will be of especial interest to young people, as George A. Walton, of George School, will speak on "Quakerism, the Religion of Youth."

If names are forwarded to Edw. B. Walton, London Grove, Pa., transportation from the trolleys at Willowdale and the trains at Avondale will be provided.

27th—Cain Quarterly Meeting at Cain, at 11 a. m. Isaac Wilson expects to attend.

27th—7.30 p. m., Conference and Meeting for Worship on the campus, under care of Friends attending Summer School of Columbia University. Topic of Conference, "Quakerism and Industry."

28th-30th—Closing week-end conference at Woolman School. Subject, "Boys' Work." Lectures by William Byron Forbush on First-day School Teaching, Sixth-day evening and Seventh-day evening. Seventh-day morning classes by Dr. Fergusson and Bliss Forbush.

29th—Westbury Quarterly Meeting will be held at Westbury, L. I., at 10.30 a. m. The train from New York City leaves the Long Island terminal of the Penn station at 9.09 a. m. (daylight saving time). Lunch will be served at noon. The afternoon session at 2.30 will be addressed by Robert W. Bruere, of the Bureau of Industrial Research, on the topic, "Personality and Coal." He is in close contact with the situation in the mining regions, is acting as a representative of the Service Committee, and comes through the co-operation of this committee. Isaac Wilson expects to attend.

30th—Certain members of Philadelphia Quarterly Meeting's Visiting Committee expect to attend Haverford meeting at 10.30 a. m., First-day School at 11 a. m.

EIGHTH MONTH

1st—Concord Quarterly Meeting at Concord Meeting-House (Pa.), at 10 a. m., daylight saving time.

3rd—Conference and Meeting for Worship on the campus, under care of Friends attending Summer School of Columbia University. Topic of conference, "Quakerism and Peace."

5th—Picnic on the Palisades, given by New York Friends to Friends at Columbia Summer School. Save the afternoon and evening for this. Notice later.

5th—Philadelphia Quarterly Meeting, at Merion, Pa.

6th—Purchase Quarterly Meeting, at Purchase, N. Y., at 10.30 a. m.

7th—Genesee Yearly Meeting, at Coldstream, Ont.

7th—Miami Quarterly Meeting, at Green Plain, Ohio.

NOTICE—Registrations for the Richmond Conference are now being received in good numbers. There are plenty of comfortable accommodations at Richmond for all, but requests for rooms should be sent as early as possible to Dorothy E. Dilks, 46 South 13th street, Richmond, Ind.

NOTICE—The Indiana Yearly Meeting convenes on Eighth month 14th, at Waynesville, Ohio. Anyone wishing accommodations, please write to Ethel Mendenhall, Waynesville, Ohio, R. R. 3.

A Note of Thanks

We want to thank all those who have in any way helped us in our recent campaign to get new subscribers for the INTELLIGENCER. There were 269 people who in one way or another took advantage of our special offer.

This number may seem small, but if every one who is receiving the paper for this trial period will continue it for the coming year, there will be real benefit to the people themselves and to the Society of Friends; and those Friends who are managing the INTELLIGENCER will be encouraged to go on with the work with renewed zest, feeling that some real progress has been made in thus getting our message to a larger group.

American Friends' Service Committee

WILBUR K. THOMAS, EX. SEC.
20 S. 12th St. Philadelphia.

CASH CONTRIBUTIONS

WEEK ENDING JULY 10, 1922.

Five Years Meetings	$5.00
Phila. Yearly Meeting (15th and Cherry Sts.)	1,934.74
Other Meetings:	
Friends' Meeting Committee	10.00
Minneapolis Monthly Meeting	18.60
Westerly Friends	35.00
Contributions for Germany	122.75
For Austria	449.43
For Poland	428.93
For Russia	625.51
For Russian overhead	25.05
For Home Service—West Virginia	552.00
Central Pennsylvania	1,020.00
For General	212.15
For Armenia	3.00
Refunds	144.73
	$5,586.89

Shipments received during week ending July 8th—39 boxes and packages received; 2 anonymous.

WANTED

WANTED—A FEW BOARDERS FOR Seventh and Eighth months, in private home. Modern conveniences. Apply to Caroline L. Warrick, Rancocas, N. J.

WANTED—POSITION IN HIGH School or private school, as teacher of Expression and Dramatics. Normal School and Emerson College graduate. Address R. Ikeler, 212 W. 5th Street, Bloomsburg, Pa.

WANTED—POSITION AS NURSE-companion to semi-invalid or elderly woman. Light duties. Suburbs. Reference. Address B. 280, Friends' Intelligencer.

WANTED—SUMMER BOARDERS, IN a small country town; rates reasonable. Address P. 281, Friends' Intelligencer.

WOMAN OF MIDDLE AGE, NURSE, wants care of invalid. Address P. 282, Friends' Intelligencer.

RIVER CROFT, CLAYMONT, DEL. Special home care for invalids, or rest and physical upbuilding. Booklet on application. E. H. Speakman.

WANTED—A FRIEND TO TEACH Buckingham Friends' School at Lahaska, Pa. 15 pupils—grades 1-8. Apply to Mary A. Watson, 277 Maple Ave., Doylestown, Pa.

POSITION WANTED—BY REFINED woman, with nervous or elderly person; capable of taking full charge; light duties. Address B. 290, Friends' Intelligencer.

WANTED—AN UNFURNISHED house at Swarthmore, Pa., on high ground. All modern conveniences. Mrs. J. R. B. Moore, Reservoir House, Bridgeton, N. J.

WANTED—BY YOUNG COUPLE BY October 1st, light housekeeping apartments, 2 rooms, bath and kitchenette; within walking distance of University of Pennsylvania. Address B. 291, Friends' Intelligencer.

FOR RENT

FOR RENT—THREE ROOMS IN private family, until Labor Day. Rates reasonable. 1402 Asbury Avenue, Ocean City, N. J.

FOR RENT—FURNISHED OR UNfurnished, 84th St., near Central Park, 7-room apartment. Real kitchen, steam, continuous hot water. Clarence Kimball, 115 Broadway, New York. Schuyler 2661.

ORDER SUPPLIES NOW FOR DELIVERY IN THE FALL.

WALTER H. JENKINS

Successor to Friends' Book Association

140 N. 15th Street, Philadelphia

Bell Telephone—Spruce 2425

NARCISSUS, TULIPS, DAFFODILS

Bulbs Direct from

OLD ENGLISH GARDENS

Moderate Prices

Imported by

JAMES C. BUTT, Dimock, Pa.

Price Lists on Application.

FUN

Harold: "Oh, mother, I got one hundred in school today in two subjects!" Fond Parent (kissing him): "Well, well; in what subjects?" Harold: "Fifty in reading and fifty in arithmetic."—*Christian Register.*

Strawbridge & Clothier

Clearing Out Hundreds of Frocks Women Need Now—at End-of-the-Season Prices

Don't fail to profit by this—it is an economy event without precedent and without counterpart; it is a time for stocking up with all the lovely Frocks you may need for summer, autumn and winter, for many of the loveliest models, are of fine silk crepes, which are always so desirable.

Canton Crepe, Crepe-Knit and Drop-stitch Tricolette Dresses ***$15.00***

Average half price. Not all sizes in each style. A variety of shades, including navy blue; some in black.

Dotted Swiss, Ratine and Gingham Dresses ***$15.00***

Dark Voile and fine Gingham Dresses at ***$7.50***

Sports Dresses of Velette, Crepe de Chine, Serpentine Crepe ***$27.50***

Chiefly small sizes in these. Other models of Canton crepe, crepe de chine and Chammy-knit, in sizes 36 to 46.

Canton Crepe and Crepe Meteor Dresses ***$32.50***

Tub Frocks of Dimity and Tissue Ginghams ***$10.00***

Strawbridge & Clothier—Second Floor, Market Street

STRAWBRIDGE & CLOTHIER

MARKET STREET EIGHTH STREET FILBERT STREET

PHILADELPHIA, PA.

ELLWOOD HEACOCK

FUNERAL DIRECTOR

2027 NORTH COLLEGE AVENUE

PHILADELPHIA

CALLS OUT OF CITY ANSWERED PROMPTLY

WE BUY ANTIQUE FURNITURE and antiques of all kinds; old gold, silver, platinum, diamonds and old false teeth. Phila. Antique Co., 633 Chestnut, cor. 7th. Phone Lombard 6398. Est. 1866.

ADVERTISING RATE in the FRIENDS' INTELLIGENCER, for Help Wanted, Positions Wanted, Rooms for Rent, Notices, and other classified advertisements without display, for each insertion, 2 cents per word, including name, initials and address. Answers may be sent to a box at the INTELLIGENCER office, if so directed.

For display advertising the rate is 10 cents per agate line, or $1.40 per column inch, each insertion. On ten or more insertions in a year from date of order, ten per cent. discount. Thus a four-inch single-column or two-inch double-column advertisement costs $5.60 each insertion, less ten per cent., or 5.04 net each time for ten or more insertions. Matter may be changed whenever desired, without extra charge.

Experience has proved the INTELLIGENCER to be a remarkably good advertising medium. All advertisements must "pass the censor!"

Address 140 N. 15th St., Philadelphia

The Friends' Intelligencer

ESTABLISHED 1844 | SEVENTH MONTH 29, 1922 | VOLUME 79 NUMBER 30

Contents

SCHOOLS.

THE FRIENDS' INTELLIGENCER

Published weekly, 140 N. 15th Street, Philadelphia, Pa., by Friends' Intelligencer Association, Ltd.

PAUL W. WAGER, *Editor*.
SUE C. YERKES, *Business Manager*

Editorial Board: Elizabeth Powell Bond, Thomas A. Jenkins, J. Russell Smith, George A. Walton.

Board of Managers: Edward Cornell, Alice Hall Paxson, Paul M. Pearson, Annie Hillborn, Elwood Hollingshead, William C. Biddle, Charles F. Jenkins, Edith M. Winder, Frances M. White.

Officers of Intelligencer Associates: Ellwood Burdsall, Chairman; Bertha L. Broomell, Secretary; Herbert P. Worth, Treasurer.

Subscription rates: United States, Mexico, Cuba and Panama, $2.50 per year. Canada and other foreign countries, $3.00 per year. Checks should be made payable to Friends' Intelligencer Association, Ltd.

Entered as Second Class Matter at Philadelphia Post Office.

REGULAR MEETINGS

OAKLAND, CALIF. — A FRIENDS' Meeting is held every First-day at 11 A. M., in the Extension Room, Y. W. C. A. Building, Webster Street, above 14th. Visiting Friends always welcome.

PASADENA, CALIFORNIA — Orange Grove Monthly Meeting of Friends, 520 East Orange Grove Avenue. Meeting for worship, First-day, 11 A. M. Monthly Meeting, the second First-day of each month, at 1.45 P. M. First-day School (except Monthly Meeting days) 9.45 A. M.

NOTICE—Concise statements of the principles of the Religious Society of Friends and their application to the problems of every day living, including "The Spirit of Quakerism," by Elbert Russell; "Preparation for Life's Greatest Business," by Rufus M. Jones; and other articles by Henry W. Wilbur, Howard M. Jenkins, Elizabeth Lloyd, Jesse H. Holmes, O. Edward Janney, Edward B. Rawson, etc., to be had free on application to Friends' General Conference Advancement Committee, 140 North Fifteenth Street, Philadelphia, Pa.

To the Lot Holders and others interested in Fairhill Burial Ground:

GREEN STREET Monthly Meeting has funds available for the encouragement of the practice of cremating the dead to be interred in Fairhill Burial Ground. We wish to bring this fact as prominently as possible to those who may be interested. We are prepared to undertake the expense of cremation in case any lot holder desires us to do so.

Those interested should communicate with William H. Gaskill, Treasurer of the Committee of Interments, Green Street Monthly Meeting, or any of the following members of the Committee.

William H. Gaskill, 3201 Arch St.
Samuel N. Longstreth, 1218 Chestnut St.
Charles F. Jenkins, 232 South Seventh St.
Stuart S. Graves, 3033 Germantown Ave.

FUN

With so many radio outfits springing up in Baltimore, funny things are happening. Some sensitive persons are having an awful time getting to sleep because of the bedtime stories catching on the springs of their beds. A row of iron dish rags at a 5 and 10 cent store frightened the lady clerk out of a week's appetite by giving a lecture on careless husbands. Another lady, whose boy is installing a radio outfit, was talking to a neighbor with a potato masher in her hand, when all of a sudden the masher joined in the conversation. Both ladies fainted and the potato masher quit after giving the weather report, the baseball scores and singing a song.—*Middletown (Md.) Register*.

"I taught school among my own people in the Tennessee mountains for several years after I graduated from college," said a southern lecturer. "Funny things happened. Hearing a boy say, 'I ain't gwine thar,' I said to him, 'That's no way to talk. Listen: "I am not going there; thou art not going there; he is not going there; we are not going there; you are not going there; they are not going there." Do you get the idea?'

"'Yessur, I gits it all right. *They ain't nobody gwine.*'"—*The Outlook*.

"Have you heard of the Irish father of an interesting family of three children dwelling in New York?" inquired a reader of *The Register*. We answered in the negative. "Well," said our friend, "one of his acquaintances asked him about the number of his offspring, and he replied that he hoped there would be no more, for according to the papers every fourth child born in New York was a Jew."—*The Christian Register*.

Helen was attending her first party. When refreshments were served she refused a second helping of ice cream with a polite "No, thank you," although her look was wistful. "Oh, do have some more ice cream, dear," her hostess urged. "Mother told me I must say, 'No, thank you,'" explained the little girl, "but I don't believe she knew the dishes were going to be so small."—*New York Evening Post*.

Traffic rule number seven: "When you meet temptation always turn to the right."—*Boston Evening Transcript*.

The Friends' Intelligencer

The religion of Friends is based on faith in the "INWARD LIGHT," or direct revelation of God's spirit and will in every seeking soul.

The INTELLIGENCER is interested in all who bear the name of Friends in every part of the world, and aims to promote love, unity and intercourse among all branches and with all religious societies.

ESTABLISHED 1844 | PHILADELPHIA, SEVENTH MONTH 29, 1922 | VOLUME 79 NUMBER 30

We urge our readers to do their full part in making the "No More War" demonstration impressive and unmistakable. Silence or inaction on your part will mean that you will be registered on the wrong side. We have finally started this old world moving in the right direction. Now let every friend of peace get his shoulder against it and keep it rolling. Individually our influence is imperceptible but all together it is a mighty force. Remember July 29th, and all together, push.

⌘

We are printing as our leading article "What the Society of Friends Stands For." We urge everyone to read the review, or better still, get and read the whole pamphlet. It is fine to have such a clear spokesman as Edward Grubb to present the views of the Society of Friends to the world. But every member of the Society should be able, in some measure at least, to answer without hesitation when asked by an outsider "What does the Society of Friends stand for?" or "Why are you a Quaker?" There are many who are making these inquiries today and we should have a ready answer. Let Edward Grubb, Rufus Jones, or some other leader formulate our answer if we prefer, but then make it our own for constant and ready use.

Quakerism, however, is more than a formula so that words alone will never satisfactorily answer the query. Those who have been the beneficiaries of Friends' service in France, Germany or Russia have a far better appreciation of Quakerism than those even who read Edward Grubb's splendid exposition.

Friends will be known and judged by the way they conduct themselves in business, in politics, in home and community life. Our very smallness in numbers makes us the more conspicuous. Our wartime activities have brought us into public notice. Many are expressing an interest in our position.

Friends have, therefore, a great opportunity but at the same time a great responsibility. We must demonstrate "what we stand for" in every activity in which we are engaged. We must be practical but not compromising. We must be courageous but not fanatical. We must express our religion in the world as it is, and not feel that we must draw apart from it in order to be holy. We must be tolerant of another's point of view, and yet not surrender our own. We must, above all, avoid an air of self-righteousness. Individually, we must so live that when a stranger judges the Society by our conduct, we do not bring dishonor to the Society. Collectively, we must strive not for self-glory or increased membership but happier lives and a better world.

⌘

"At least 1,000,000 people are living in the Near East today who would have perished had it not been for American relief." These significant words appear in the report of the Near East Relief Commission to Congress. Could the $50,000,000 which the American people have contributed for this work have been better spent! Fifty dollars to save a life is certainly a good investment. All whose contributions have saved or helped to save a human life are as truly heroes as if they rescued a child from drowning or from fire. No Carnegie medals will be awarded but the inward joy which they feel must be greater than any award could bring them. Thousands of American people are foster parents of little sweet-faced children in Syria and Armenia whom they will never see. Though the worst is over these little orphans, more than 100,000 of them, are still dependent upon Near East Relief for the necessities of life. Kind-hearted Americans must "carry on" a little longer until native agencies are able to give these children proper care.

Not only has the money given for Near East Relief been a good investment on the part of the individual contributor but for the nation as a whole. "America is a name to conjure with in the Near East," says the report, "because American relief workers have gone there with no commercial or political motives, not for what they could get, but what they could give, and in so doing they have strengthened international good-will for decades to come."

The Society of Friends

And What It Stands for

By Edward Grubb, M. A.

Edward Grubb's paper on the Society of Friends appears as one of the contributions to the interesting volume entitled "What The Churches Stand For," which the Oxford University Press is just publishing. The other papers included in the book deal with the Church of England, Congregationalism, Baptists, and Presbyterianism. Edward Grubb's address has been reprinted in pamphlet form, of which the following is a brief review.

After expressing the honor and the responsibility attached to the task assigned to him, Edward Grubb says:

"The fact that you wish to hear something about the Quakers marks the progress we have made since the seventeenth century, when the saintly Richard Baxter, in his *Quaker's Catechism* (published in 1659), wrote, 'Was there ever a generation of men on whom the image of the Devil was more visible than on these [Quakers]?' "

There is undoubtedly, beneath all our differences, an underlying unity—a fellowship of those who seek the same truth, worship the same Lord, know some measure of the same Christian experience, and desire to follow in the same way of life. To bring to the surface of consciousness this underlying unity is surely the true path towards the Reunion of Christendom; and such opportunities as are afforded by this course of lectures, for gaining mutual knowledge and understanding, appear to me to be of priceless worth.

We think that "what we stand for" is in part the conviction that the essence of Christianity is to be found, not in formulated beliefs or methods of worship or of Church organization, but in a common experience and a common service of men.

"What else the Society of Friends stands for," he says, "may be best seen by looking at its origin." He then relates the experiences of George Fox and of the Society in its formative years. He says the mysticism of George Fox and his followers was a very *practical* mysticism, yet in the real sense of the word, *evangelical.*

Their central affirmation of the Light within their souls, the Light that is, potentially at least, in the souls of all men, he explains as follows:

"It meant, in the first place, if we may express it in modern terms, *an intuitive perception of spiritual truth:* truth, that is, concerning the reality of God, the character of Jesus, and the way of life He requires from us as disciples. This was to them as direct and immediate as is our perception of the beauty of a picture or the excellence of a character; we must discern the value for ourselves if we are to see it at all. But this involved the consequence that the basis and seat of authority in religion was transferred from without to within; truth was to be believed, not because Church or Bible pronounced it true, but because it was inwardly 'seen' to be true.

In the second place, it meant an experience of *Guidance* by the Spirit of God in all the affairs of life—a Guidance which was to be known on condition of obedience. By this was meant something more than the 'natural conscience,' though the Quakers often appealed to conscience as *evidence* of a Light in all men.

There was, it is certain, no thought of denying the reality of Sin, or the need of Atonement and Redemption. But the Quakers always maintained that this must be an *inward* work, changing the man himself into what God required; they could not regard it as an outward or 'forensic' transaction, still less as a piece of make-believe. It was Sin that blinded the eyes of men to the Light within them, and Sin must be effectively removed if the Light were to shine undimmed.

Nor was there any thought of denying the reality and importance of the person and work of Jesus Christ. The affirmation of the 'Christ within' did not mean denial of the 'Christ without'—though some expressions used by the Quakers show that their thoughts were not always clear. Essentially their position was in line with the mysticism of Paul and of the author of the Fourth Gospel: the Light in their souls was, they believed, Christ re-living His own life in the souls of His true followers.

"As to the Bible, they accepted it as inspired, but they would not call it 'the Word of God,' because for them it was not the *final* 'rule' of faith and duty. The Spirit that inspired was above the Scripture, and inspired men still if they would seek it and obey."

He then shows how the principle of the Light within has affected their mode of worship and their ideas of ministry, and how their assumption that the Light was available for *all men* has affected their outlook on human life and the duties of men and nations to one another. It gave to personality a new dignity.

The Quakers very early felt that everything which oppressed and degraded humanity was wrong and must be removed. In the earliest days of his public ministry George Fox pleaded with the magistrates at Mansfield to fix at least a 'living wage' for the laborers in the district. In Cornwall he issued a public protest against the wicked practice of 'wrecking' ships and plundering their cargoes. He appealed to the authorities concerning the cruelties of the penal code and the prison system of that day; and warned the public against the misuse of intoxicating drink.

In the matter of *Slavery*, when Fox was in the West Indies, he wrote to slave-owners to train their "blacks" in Christianity, and to free them as soon as possible. He does not appear to have seen that Slavery in itself is wrong; but some of his followers very soon did so, and the Society of Friends has the honor of having been the first Christian body in America to make membership incompatible with the holding of slaves.

The *Testimony against War* grew out of the belief in the Inner Light. In the first place, belief in Universal Light meant that all men were *brothers* and no man who held it could consent to kill his brethren. Secondly, the Light was felt to be the Light of *Christ*, who was reproducing in his followers His own character and way of life. As He conquered evil, not by force but by the way of the Cross, which was love to the uttermost, so must they. And thirdly, it was held that implicit obedience was due *to Christ alone*, and to His Light in the soul, and that therefore such absolute obedience could not be promised to any human authority: military discipline would not square with allegiance to Christ.

In the matter of *Politics* the Quakers have been more active than most other mystical sects.

Edward Grubb says, "the outlook of the Society of Friends at the present time, in spite of its small numbers, is one of hope. The great war brought its principles to the test as nothing else in its history had ever done, at least since the days of persecution passed away." The various relief enterprises which the Society carried on shows that it desires to maintain its "testimony for Peace" in a more than negative way; to uphold it by deeds of service, to "foes" as well as friends, that may help to break down antagonisms, foster friendship, and destroy the spirit that leads to war.

"Since the war relief work has continued in Austria, Germany and Poland. This has opened to us in a remarkable way a field for spiritual service as well. It has been found that there is a deep hunger for spiritual religion, not only in the countries suffering from war, but also in far-off China and Japan; and the call is urgent to offer such help as we can to the many who mistrust official Christianity, and feel that it has largely failed, yet need a religion to live by. There are 'Seekers' in many lands today, as there were in the days of Fox, and it is for these that we seem to have a special message. But unfortunately we are far too few, and much too weak, to respond to the call as we would. Our call and service for humanity would seem to be to reach and quicken to life the 'Seed of God' in men everywhere, and the little we have been able to do shows that this is not a vain endeavor."

He concludes his address with these words: "We Friends believe that we are rendering a real service to Reunion by standing firm to our convictions, and not giving way for the sake of a superficial uniformity. We are not erecting barriers ourselves; we are trying to prevent barriers from being erected where we are sure there should be none. But we recognize with humility and contrition that we shall only succeed in this if we can convince our fellow-Christians by the evidence of facts that, though we deny the forms which they think needful, we are not strangers to the substance that lies beneath them; that to us, as well as to others, in spite of weakness and unworthiness, the grace of the Spirit has been given—just as in the days of the early Church it was given to Gentiles like Cornelius, whom some Christians, laying stress on outward forms, would have excluded from the Body of Christ."

Quaker Meeting

A sweet thought given to others,
  A beautiful prayer;
A conversation with the Father
  And devotion so rare.
Old and young alike share
  This wonderful meeting;
They all have sweet thoughts
  As the moments go fleeting.

The impression of a mid-week meeting as gathered and expressed by a nine-year-old girl.

Not until right is founded upon reverence will it be secure; not until duty is based upon love will it be complete; not until liberty is based upon eternal principles will it be full, equal, lofty and universal.—*Henry Giles.*

An Invocation

To the Spirit of Wisdom, Beauty and Love

Spirit of Truth, groping ever out of the past into the future, seeking to master the mystery of life, we who seek with thee for truth open our hearts to thee in this hour of prayer, that our searching may be guided by the eternal light. Use us as instruments of thine in this immortal and unending quest. Quench not the hunger for knowledge that drives us onward, but grant to us the undying joy of continual discovery.

Guide thou the seekers who wander today in darkness for whom the landmarks of old faith have vanished. Lead them through the night into the glory of a new day of hope and vision.

Give to us all, we pray, plastic minds to learn unceasingly, leaving without regret the outworn creeds of yesterday that we may live the larger faith that dawns tomorrow.

Spirit of Beauty—thou who hast created dawn and sunset, songs of birds at morning, and splash of waves against the shore—thou who stirreth the heart of sculptor and of poet—stir thou our hearts today, and give to us a new participation in the radiance of life and joy. Teach us to live each day abundantly, with growing understanding of the joy that fills the world.

Spirit of Brotherhood—thou who hast made of one flesh all the peoples of the earth, knit our lives increasingly into the great fabric of humanity, that we may help each other onward in the great adventure of existence in this universe of thine.

So shall we grow in wisdom and in love and in harmony with thy vast purposes forever. Amen.

DR. HORNELL HART.

Selected by R. Luella Jones.

What Is Meant by "Wage Slavery"?

Attending a meeting held on July 8th in one of the largest theaters in Scranton, Pa., by the striking shopmen of the railroads, I was most impressed by the three following statements made by various speakers: (1) That the American worker refused to be a slave of the bosses and managers of the privately-owned railroads and to meekly submit to the insults and abuses to which he has been subjected ever since the roads were released from government control; (2) That the labor unions are the real safeguard in this country against chaos, anarchy and revolution, and if the movement to crush organized labor and substitute the "American Plan" (which the strikers said meant the employment of Hindus, Chinese, negroes and similar classes to take the places of American citizens as at Hoboken, N. J., and other places) should succeed, anarchy would be here; (3) That the fight on the part of organized labor is not only for a wage which will insure a decent American standard of living at present prices, but for a saving wage and for the lasting benefit and fuller life of their children and future workers.

The use of the words "wage slavery" is becoming more and more common. Just what is meant? Is it possible that those workers, who compare the present wage system with the system of black slavery before the Civil War, and that the students of social conditions who describe the "white-collar slave" have definite content to their thought? May it be possible that the Society of Friends has immediately before it a great task in helping to abolish this modern form of slavery? The advices of the New York Yearly Meeting contain the following significant words:

"Friends should be careful to extend aid and sympathy to those in affliction, and they are feelingly advised to yield to every requirement of duty toward removing the causes which produce misery and suffering in the world."

"While we thankfully rejoice that property in man is no longer recognized by the laws of our country, we tenderly solicit Friends, on all proper occasions, to bear our testimony against all forms of human bondage."

Only those who have experienced it know the "misery and suffering" caused when a man with a family to support is "fired" from his "job" and forced to join the great army of unemployed; and all the military and naval forces are always at the command of the owners if necessary to protect "property" in case exasperated workers can control themselves no longer and protest by striking against the "human bondage" of low wages and low standards of living. Surely all must see that the vast majority of people in this country today are salaried or wage workers dependent for a living on a "position" or a "job"—not, of course, any one job, but some job offered or withheld by another's will. If they lose one job they are forced by necessity to take the wage or salary which may be offered by another if they are to earn a living—unless the industry is thoroughly unionized. This simple fact is the basic reason for the announced policy of employers to break the unions, and of their desire to keep a large margin of unemployed always waiting to pull down the wage offer necessary to obtain workers. Perhaps a few examples of the effect of this system may suggest a basis for the feeling of thousands, that they are really no more than slaves. Before considering these, however, let us define the term slavery in its modern sense.

I understand wage slavery to mean the dependence of the worker on the will of another both for the right to work and for the nature and conditions of his labor while working. "According to the theory of modern industry, not only does the factory belong to the employer to do with it what he will; the workman also belongs to the employer during the hours for which his labor has been bought." This new form of bondage is the result of industrial development on the theory just quoted. The owner of the tools of industry has complete control over the labor power of those who use the tools, and can at any time take away their means of livelihood.

That such a form of slavery, a new "master and servant" relation, really exists needs no demonstration. It is just now particularly evident in the fact that millions of workers in this country are unemployed or on strike against a deliberate plan on the part of owners and managers to break the labor unions and regain the control which organized labor has been gradually gaining from them. Their real object is to force the workers back to individual barter in the selling of their labor as a commodity to a buyer highly organized and determined to pay as little as necessary to buy labor power. Lockouts and strikes are the inevitable consequence.

Autocratic control over the lives of thousands of workers is not confined to wage workers only. The civil engineers employed by a large railroad were urged to join a harmless, anti-union national association; many were afraid to do so, fearing to lose their positions, and others did not wish their superiors to know that they had joined. Another railroad received orders to cut down expenses; did the big executives reduce their own salaries or order a general percentage reduction in salaries and wages so that all could retain their means of livelihood? Not at all; instead, certain men through no fault of their own (generally those who last joined the company and probably needed work most) were discharged. A certain professor in a big university had been teaching erroneous principles for years; when pointed out by a new assistant professor who taught the facts, he ordered the assistant to be removed and was upheld by the university authorities.

These typical examples are cited to show that it is owners and their managers who control the very source of livelihood of those who work. If anyone claims that these workers are free to become owners and managers themselves, he should be reminded that about one in ten thousand may possibly do so through money resources, special energy, special opportunity, or special ability and social graces. This is a small chance; it does not change the fact but demonstrates it.

Perhaps some believe that the right to "life, liberty, and the pursuit of happiness" so seriously infringed by the modern salary and wage system is no God-given right, and that there is no way to prevent these injustices or to remedy conditions which are part of our machine age. This right *is* God-given, however, and there are remedies which, if applied in time, may save present civilization from the inevitable crash into chaos which is coming unless something is done. Space limitations prevent discussion of these remedies here; the writer has done so in a previous article.* Those who wish new light should read "Chaos and Order in Industry," by G. D. H. Cole. The articles in the INTELLIGENCER entitled "Christianity and Economic Problems," published during the past several months should also be given serious study. My own present conclusions can be suggested in very condensed form; I believe that modern civilization will not survive unless some or all of the following changes are made:

Transformation by peaceful methods from production for selfish advantage and profits for the few to production for the benefit and service of all at prices fixed according to labor cost and maintenance charges; from ownership by outsiders and stockholders to ownership by all the workers of small production units and by the government of all natural resources and national as well as local public utilities such as railroads, coal mining, lighting and heating plants, ship-building plants, etc.; from management by salaried executives selected by owners or their agents to management by technically trained workers acceptable by election or referendum to the body of workers under them; from a spirit of "getting ahead" regardless of others to a spirit of good will and mutual helpfulness which seeks for each worker full measure of opportunity for creative and soul-satisfying labor; from payment of the lowest wage or salary necessary to buy labor as a commodity on the market to payment in terms of human living primarily according to need and secondarily according to the value produced by the worker.

Members of the Society of Friends in this country, which is now passing through a crisis, have a new call to service in this field which has too long been divorced from religion. Let us dedicate ourselves to the new task and add to the splendid services of relief the constructive and preventive measures which will help to transform society so that such a type of relief work will never be necessary. Thus can we carry out the injunctions contained in our Advices. J. PAUL J. WILLIAMS.

*FRIENDS' INTELLIGENCER, Eighth month 13, 1921.

Modern thought is placing less emphasis on material considerations. It is recognizing that the basis of national progress, whether industrial or social, is the health, efficiency and spiritual development of the people.—*John D. Rockefeller, Jr.*

Superman

A Sage, beneath the dome celestial blue,
Pored o'er a volume bound in radiant light:
The record of creation aeons through,
Earth's history unrolled to human sight
From chaos to the Age of Superman.
Unseen vibrations of eternal might, from star to star,
Flashed love and wisdom's echoes through the span
Twixt Earth and worlds in space—uncounted—far.
And as the scroll unrolled its page on page,
Sweet voices marvelled that the mind of man
Devised such wonders: yet from age to age,
Wars—wretched misery—defiled the plan.
"My Children," spoke the Sage, "the truth is told."
'Twas not the Golden Age—but 'Age of Gold.' "

Sarah Palmer Byrnes.

She Hath Done What She Could

A Little Girl's Contribution for Russian Relief.

DEAR MISS HAINES:

I have tried to earn a little money for the Russians by selling some of the plants that I raised in my garden. I just earned this four dollars and twenty-five cents and I hope it will do some Russian good. I am eleven years old and I hope to be able to give you a large sum of money soon.

I don't think you know me but I hope we'll soon meet.

Your devoted worker,
(Signed) ———

What Did You Do?

During the war many a man was spurred on to enlist by the statement that in the future his own children might ask him: "Father, what did you do during the war?" In some way this same question ought to be brought home to every adult Friend in the United States. At a time when thousands of people are turning to the Society of Friends with questions concerning the way of life, the Service Committee finds itself with a great many applications from people who are not Friends and comparatively few applications from Friends themselves for service abroad. The Committee has been looking for a physician for its work in Russia for a year. Jewish, Russian, Catholic, and doctors without church affiliations have volunteered. There are Friends who would have volunteered if it were not for age limitations and health requirements; but up to the present time no suitable physician has offered his services from the Society of Friends, even though we have offered a small salary in addition to maintenance. A great many people are eager to join in our work in Poland and Austria; but comparatively few Friends are volunteering for this service now that the war is over and it is not the popular thing to do.

It is impossible to carry on our work unless we have a sufficient number of Friends, or those who are grounded in the principles of Friends, to give the right kind of direction to the work. We are glad to have the co-operation and fellowship of so many other people; but we do need more of those who have been born with a sense of responsibility for their fellowman and who are actuated by the desire to serve Jesus Christ by doing such work. This is not a time to make a plea for personnel, but a time for individual heart-searching as to how the question can be answered when put to us—What did you do to make the message of Jesus a living reality to the hungry and the helpless in their time of need?

Thanks from Semenovka

Last week two little villages belonging to the same soviet held a meeting on the public square at Semenovka. All the people came; all the children. It was a holiday and every one had on the best clothes left from the long miserable months of the famine when almost everything was sold to buy food. They all came to give thanks to the Quakers for the food they had given them and still continue to give them.

They brought us this resolution from the meeting. "Resolution: passed by the citizens of Semenovka and Vassilkovka. The Soviet, the village Mutual Aid Committee and all the citizens, men, women and children numbering 273 express their deep-felt thanks to the Quakers for the very great help they have rendered us through the children and adult rations. Once more we thank the Quakers of America.

"We also want to thank the Quaker Mission at Grachovka, Kusminovskaya volost, that is working with the Mutual Aid Committee in extending help to a starving people.

Signed by Simeon Selyantev, President of the Village Mutual Aid.
Feodor Chemykov, Secretary of the Village Soviet.
And 40 citizens, all in the village who are capable of signing their names."

A Parable

"No More War" is the spontaneous cry of millions of people in many lands on this anniversary of the outbreak of the war. We work out the arguments for peace and strive by disarmament to prevent the next war. Why argue in the abstract about war abroad when we have an actual state of war with us in West Virginia?

President Harding has followed the psychology of the country when in dealing with the coal strike he first appealed to arbitration and, that failing, resorts to military force.

Is not President Harding going backwards—from the greater to the lesser force?

What man seeking to cross the ocean in a launch and having failed will try in a row boat? Will he not rather try a steamship?

What man having a load of hay to pull into his barn and having first tried with his team of horses and having failed will resort to wolves and wild cats? Will be not rather invent a tractor?

J. Barnard Walton.

Christian Economics

By Stephen Bell, Foreign Editor *Commerce and Finance.*

This contribution is the result of a letter, written by one of our readers, commending the author for an editorial which appeared in Commerce and Finance.

"Be still, and know that I am God!"

Never, probably, did this poor old world need more than at present this advice to turn from its turmoil of self-made troubles to contemplate the futility of mere human wisdom, which is foolishness unto God.

The Son of Man, sanest of all who have ever trod the earth, in the world but not of it, surveying the tangled web of human relationships from His height of detachment, and speaking specifically of our physical needs, showed us the one sure and certain way of satisfying them abundantly in these few words: "Seek ye first the Kingdom of God and His righteousness, and all these things shall be added unto you."

And in these words is condensed all that is essential to the popular understanding of the science called Political Economy, the abuse of which has caused untold misery to countless millions and again and again has led the nations to mutually destructive warfare.

There is no economic question before the nations today —there never has been—which is not at bottom a moral question, and as they are answered in conformity or non-conformity with sound moral principles humanity is blessed or cursed in the answer, for all things bring forth fruits after their kind and it is vain to expect good results to flow from unrighteous laws and ordinances.

The world on which God has placed us is great and rich and beautiful beyond our utmost needs. To man alone of all animate creation has God given the power to augment indefinitely the natural riches of the earth, for man alone possesses the power of intelligent labor to adapt means to desired ends. Yet on this planet, ample to support manyfold the present population that now inhabits it, we find all nations pinched with poverty and famine stalking in more than one land.

That this is because in their race for domination the nations have made the earth a shambles, instead of seeking the kingdom of righteousness and working together to make it a garden, who can doubt?

It is in vain that we lift our voices in prayer to God to save us from the consequences of our insane acts—indeed it is blasphemy, for it bears the implication that it is God who has brought our miseries upon us. The national laws by which God governs the universe, social as well as physical, are wise and beneficent beyond our ability to appreciate, and He has shown us how we may utilize them to our good as well as ignore or defy them to our hurt.

To nations as well as individuals is the counsel given: "As ye would that others should do unto you, do ye even so unto them."

I would in this short article point to only one particular in which all nations are violating this Golden Rule.

Trade is the lifeblood of civilization. Were we compelled to make each for himself the things he needs we would at once revert to primitive savagery, for none of us can make more than enough to suffice for such an existence. Trade, then, is the national co-operation by which civilization is sustained.

Yet we see all nations engaged in trying to handicap the trade of their neighbors by hostile tariffs, ignorant of the fact that they thus strangle their own trade, until industry and commerce in all lands are sick, unable to sustain the peoples properly.

The Lake Geneva Student Conference

It was my privilege to attend this year, as one of the discussion group leaders from the University of Wisconsin delegation, the annual Y. M. C. A. Student Conference at College Camp, Lake Geneva, Wisconsin. Believing that the readers of The Intelligencer will be interested in a passing account of this noteworthy gathering I am led to attempt a brief survey of its outstanding contributions.

The Lake Geneva Conference holds a unique place in the rapidly developing intercollegiate life of the Middle West. It is a part of the larger Student Christian Association which unites the students of some 700 colleges and universities in the United States, and brings together students in state and regional gatherings such as this one and those meeting simultaneously at Silver Bay, N. Y., Estes Park, Col., and Blue Ridge, N. C. This American Association is joined with other similar national organizations in what is known as the World's Student Christian Federation, comprising the Student Christian organizations of 32 nations. The Peking Conference just closed was a meeting of this World Federation. Mr. David R. Porter, Senior Secretary of the Student Department of the International Committee of the Y. M. C. A., claims that this Federation was the one international society which did not break down from the strain of the war.

This year approximately 700 men, about 125 of whom were foreign students, representing the voluntary religious forces of some 200 colleges and universities from nine states of the Middle West, gathered at Geneva to study the application of Christianity to human relationships. Although the actual numbers present, due largely to the industrial depression, were somewhat less than last year's gathering, the present Conference recognizedly surpassed all others in the freedom and scope of its subject matter, in its team work, and in its purposiveness in actually seeking the application of Christian principles in personal, collegiate, social, economic, racial, national and international relationships.

The subject of both the morning and evening platform meetings bore on the larger aspects of the day's topic as announced for the group discussion meetings. The Conference opened with a consideration of "The Need and Possibility of a New World," the subject which remained throughout the heart of the Conference. This need was presented in the first day's platform addresses by Mr. D. R. Porter, by Mr. C. D. Hurrey, traveling secretary for the World's Student Christian Federation, just returned from Peking and a trip around the world and sailing abroad again this summer, and by Raymond Robins. All three speakers made a most impassioned plea against war and the forces working for a future war. Raymond

Robins saw in the Washington Conference the first break in our mad rush for armaments and what he dares to hope marks the turn in the tide. These appeals were supplemented later by four masterful addresses by Sherwood Eddy, who challenged his "fellow" students to the call first for personal morality, and then to the industrial and social needs of America and of the rest of the world. So powerful were Mr. Eddy's appeals that he was given an extra hour to speak on the importance of the Bible in personal life. He made use of this opportunity by revealing how "the letter killeth but the spirit giveth life."

Perhaps the most outstanding addresses of the entire ten days, if indeed any can be so characterized, were those delivered on the two closing days by Mr. Glenn Frank, editor of the *Century Magazine*. Mr. Frank spoke first on "The New Order and the New Disorder," in which he showed the relative groundlessness of any immediate menace from extreme radicalism, basing his belief on the inherent soundness of the average man's judgment. The best defence, however, against the present disorder and the chief bulwarks of the new order he ascribed to three things or positions, the importance of which needed to be more generally recognized; first, tolerance of opinion, or the position taken that liberty of speech, press and assemblage while evolving a grave responsibility for a democracy is nevertheless far less dangerous than repression; second, democracy of wealth, or the imperative need of our striving toward an economic policy which will insure a juster distribution of wealth; third, the aristocracy of work, emphasizing the Greek derivation of aristocracy implying the rule by the best, *i. e.*, by those best fitted to lead both in industry and in government.

Again, speaking on "The Nature and Possibilities of a New Spiritual Renaissance," he said he did not look to the institutional churches to bring this about. The radiant centers of the new spirituality would be the scientist's laboratory, the humanized industry and factory, the regenerated home, the socialized professions, and the prophetic teachers, editors and ministers. In short, it would be a laity movement.

Thus the Colleges of the Middle West and the Geneva Conference in particular are endeavoring to inspire men for leadership in a day when simple formulæ are put forward for the saving of a world, and when there are comparatively few thoughtfully preparing themselves that they may scientifically, prayerfully, and powerfully build a new world. Inspired by the vision of a science consecrated to human welfare and advancement rather than to human destruction, and by a socialized religion, freed from the dogmas, traditions and limitations of a by-gone age and still conserving the essential contributions of the past there arises the cry not only from the colleges, but from other places as well—business journals, newspapers, statistical bureaus, political assemblies, professional associations, secular and religious periodicals—the cry that but one thing is needed now: the *application* of Christianity to human relationships.

W. RUSSELL TYLOR,
Instructor in Economics and Sociology,
University of Wisconsin.

Friends Meet

By WM. C. ALLEN.

After a few days (in 1922) passed in humid, sweltering, seething Hongkong we left that city for Singapore on the Dutch S. S. *Van Overstraten*. Climbing down from the wharf onto the unsteady launch, for the ship, we settled by the other white cabin passengers and opened conversation with them. There were only six, beside ourselves, and all were bound for Singapore. About two minutes disclosed the fact that of the three women, out of the eight passengers, the parents of one resided in Nottingham, Pa., another came from Trenton, N. J., and the third from Philadelphia. So it came about that of the three women who met in this small Dutch vessel, for a 1,470 miles run across a distant sea little traveled by Americans, 66 2/3 per cent. had been born within a few miles of each other on the other side of the globe. But the truth of the hackneyed phrase that "the world is very small after all" did not stop here. Soon we announced ourselves as Friends. Then the Trenton girl spoke up: "I am a Friend, too." Then my wife discovered that the name of our new acquaintance was Addie Pitman Goodeno, whose husband is connected with the Standard Oil Company in China and who was proceeding to Singapore on business for his company.

We had a very pleasant voyage. The frequently cantankerous China sea was in a quiet mood, although the sailing of our ship had been deferred because of a typhoon. She did not have all the comforts of modern travel, but was adapted to life in the tropics. If I lay in my berth, and desired a "boy" to bring something to me because I did not want to get up, I had to go down the corridor and across the open deck to the pantry to find him, as there were no electric calls on board. But we constituted a happy party and our eight white folks, plus the few cultured Chinese in the cabin, got along very well together.

There were several hundred Chinese coolies on board going down to the equator to work. It was very interesting to watch them on the deck below us. Most of the men were delightfully clad in very little but the brown-yellow skins that kind Nature had endowed them with. Three times a day little groups of them squatted on the deck in circles whilst devouring the strange foods so dear to the coolie—those unholy, highly-seasoned mixtures that accompanied the inevitable rice. But the poorest of these black-haired, swarthy people rejoiced in tiny plates and saucers with pretty decorations on them that would bring pleasure to any housewife in America. At night they had the best of the cabin passengers, who decorously rested in their stuffy little rooms, whilst these coolies reposed on the open deck under the friendly stars in the sweet sea air.

Then we reached picturesque and polyglot Singapore, close to the equator. Here work awaited me after six days of rest among a few people who really understood the meaning of the word "thee." This was the queerest thing of all!

Week-end Conference at Woolman School

The fourth week-end conference at Woolman School varied its program on Sixth-day night by giving a dramatization of Bible stories. Seven scenes from the life of Samuel were presented. Dr. Russell played the part of Samuel and the regular and week-end students took the minor parts. The stage settings were improvised as was the costuming, yet the scenes selected were pretty faithfully reproduced. The play was enacted mainly to illustrate how splendidly Bible stories lend themselves to dramatization and how easy it is for even inexperienced players to stage these scenes effectively. It illustrates the possibilities of this phase of religious education. A considerable number of Swarthmore residents gathered on the Woolman House lawn to enjoy this amateur production.

Seventh-day morning, Dr. Morris Ferguson continued the treatment of the subject, "A Community Religion." Dr. Ferguson's thesis is that religious freedom was purchased at the price of religious unity. Without forfeiting this freedom, he raises the question whether it is not now possible to recover the purchase price. "In the name of religious toleration," he says, "any one may lift the knife of religious propaganda and cut from the once rotund community what sector he will." This "new intolerance" which prevents any one from raising a voice of protest against religious division, is nearly as destructive to religious power in a community as enforced conformity. There is, on the other hand, however, an increasing sentiment against denominationalism. The Sunday School, the Y. M. C. A., the Christian Endeavor and the rural community church all indicate a revival of the spirit of religious unity.

Seventh-day evening, the lecturer was Kirby Page and his theme, "Christ or Machiavelli." In a forceful address, he presented the contrast between the Christian ideal and the selfish attitude typified by Machiavelli. "Modern business is based on the motive of self-interest," he said, "and just as long as it is conducted on that basis there will be strife and warfare. We cannot continue indefinitely to fight each other and survive. The rumblings of discontent which we hear are warnings of serious dangers ahead. There are fourteen million workers in this country who are receiving less than a decent living wage. What can we do to remedy these conditions? The least we can do is to inform ourselves. Then we must take Christ seriously. We must live simply. It is mockery to Jesus Christ to live easily and luxuriously when so many in the world are starving. We must dedicate our whole lives,—time, energy and thought to the cause of the Master."

The First-day afternoon conference continued the discussion of industrial relations, and the application of Christian principles to their solution.

Those who have been privileged to attend all or any of these conferences will testify both to their educational and spiritual value, and to the general spirit of sociability which has pervaded them. Much credit belongs to William and Julia Eves who as host and hostess of Woolman School have been most solicitous for the comfort and happiness of their guests.

Friendly News Notes

"The Mysticism of George Fox," a book which is announced for publication by George Allen and Unwin, is the work of Rachel Knight, whose death occurred last year. Rachel Knight's many friends will look forward to seeing this book which is the result of much study, part of it done at Devonshire House, where she had access to George Fox's Journal in its original form.

In considering the education of the children of London Yearly Meeting, the statement was made that the cost per pupil in the Friends' Schools is just double what it was in 1914. Statistics showed that a little more than 50 per cent. of Friends' children were at Friends' schools. There are approximately 1,500 children in the Yearly Meeting.

A letter from Charlotte L. Postlethwaite, of New Rochelle, N. Y., tells of how one of the requests sent out by New York Monthly Meeting for clothes for Russian relief was forwarded from one to the other until three sets of people were touched, resulting in a large number of garments being sent to the 15th Street Meeting-house to be forwarded. In writing about the appeal one lady said, "So it was the case of casting a pebble into a pool. You never can tell how large a circle it will create, and your one act brought rich results."

In the early part of the 19th century there were only two churches in Richmond, Va., St. John's, on Church Hill, where Patrick Henry spoke, and a Quaker Meeting-house.

In 1665 a fine of 5,000 pounds of tobacco was incurred by any ship-master who should bring in a Quaker, and by any person who should entertain a Quaker in or near his house to preach.

The first mid-week meeting of Friends at Columbia University Summer School was held on the evening of the 20th. The Conference part of the session was addressed by Francis Maxfield on "Quakerism and Education." This was followed by a meeting for worship. It was a successful opening of the series to be held on Fifth-day evenings. Students will lead the next two conference sessions.

For those who are interested in bringing a bit of sunshine and encouragement to those political prisoners who are still in prison, by sending a birthday greeting, we print the following list for August:

1st, John M. Foss; 7th, Wencil Francik; 7th, Carl Ahlteen; 13th, Henry Hammer; 15th, James Rowan; 16th, William Weyh; 17th, J. A. MacDonald; 17th, Librado Rivera; 20th, Dan Buckley; 24th, H. H. Munson; 27th, Mortimer Downing; 27th, Forrest Edwards; 30th, Ralph Chaplin. The address for all the above is P. O. Box 7, Leavenworth, Kansas. Two others, whose address is Box 520, Walla Walla, Washington, are: 15th, James McInery, and 25th, John Lamb.

This startling statement was made in London Yearly Meeting by a Friend but recently returned from Russia. He said that until he reached Russia he had not realized what an immense number of Quakers there were in that country. He was visited by representatives of those calling themselves Quakers, and in mingling with them made the discovery to his surprise that their beliefs were very like those held by Friends. They were absolutely convinced of the unlawfulness of all war to the Christian, and believed in the positive side of communion with the Lord. Those who held the views of the Society of Friends in Russia were reckoned to be quite one million; that is to say, there were more Friends in Russia than in the whole of the rest of the world. It is hoped that there will be some method of getting into touch with these people.—*The Friend* (Philadelphia).

Genesee Yearly Meeting will be held at Coldstream, Ontario, from Eighth month 5th to 10th, inclusive. Friends desiring accommodation should write to C. Harold Zavitz, R. R. 2, Idlerton, Ontario, at once.

The Young Friends' Association will hold a meeting at 8 p. m. on Seventh-day, the 5th. Meetings for worship will be held on First-day at 11 a. m. and 3 p. m., and a meeting in the Park will be held at 8 p. m., to be addressed by Prof. Dorland on the subject, "The World Alliance for International Friendship."

Sessions during the day will be given over largely to the business of the Yearly Meeting. On Second-day evening at 8 o'clock there will be a meeting at which there will be short addresses on "Opening Opportunities of Friends," and on Fourth-day evening at 8 o'clock the "Sunderland P. Gardner Lecture" will be delivered.

A. W. Moore, of Moore's Mills, N. Y., sends the following interesting item, clipped from the *Poughkeepsie Eagle*:

"Millbrook residents are mourning the loss of four giant oak trees, so old that their exact age cannot be estimated, which were blown down during the severe storm on Thursday.

"The four trees stood near the old Brick Meeting-house, which is the old Quaker Church at Mechanic, northeast of Millbrook, often called the meeting-house of the Nine Partners. The trees had been there for many years before the present church, which was erected in 1780, was built. They were big enough, in fact, to provide shelter for the old log meeting-house that stood at Mechanic more than 200 years ago, and their decayed trunks still bear the hitching rings for the horses of those who 'rode to meetin'' at that time. Because of their decayed condition, their age cannot be computed by rings of growth.

"The old landmarks have weathered many storms, and have been fortunate enough to escape the lightning, but Thursday's storm was a terrific one, when the wind blew a gale. At 12.30 o'clock in the afternoon it was at its worst and it was then that the four old trees gave up the fight and crashed to the ground."

E. Vesta Haines, who has been appointed to visit and arrange conferences for the First-day Schools of Concord Quarter, is actively at work. The work has been planned out so that each First-day School in the Quarter will have two visits and four conference groups during the summer. It has been decided to give a co-operative Quaker Pageant illustrating scenes and characters in Quaker history at one of the meetings in Ninth month, and if a success, to reproduce it for the next meeting of the Union at Concordville.

The conference for Seventh month 22nd will be held at Birmingham, and on the 29th at Willistown. The places arranged for Eighth month are as follows: 5th, Concordville; 12th, Birmingham; 19th, Newtown Square; 26th, place not decided. Tentative arrangements have been made for Malvern for Ninth month 9th.

LAING SCHOOL, MT. PLEASANT, S. C.

"By Their Fruits Ye Shall Know Them."

The graduates of 1920 and 1921 have been such successes in entrance examinations and general work and demeanor in schools to which they have gone that Charleston County, South Carolina, is waking up to the fact that Laing School is in her midst.

Never before have there been such large crowds to all of the closing exercises as attended this June. Long before the doors were opened the little platform and steps leading to the main building were crowded with anxious parents. At each of the exercises, which were held Sunday, Monday and Wednesday the week of June 4th, it was necessary for Mr. Purvis and Mr. Dunlap to bring even the stools from the cooking department as seats for our visitors. Many were turned away because there was not standing room.

The exercises were all creditable. Rev. Horry preached a brilliant sermon on Sunday, and the music by the Auroean Orchestra gave that necessary inspiration to the program to make it a delightful one. "A Day in Flowerdom," operetta, was presented by members of the second and third grades on Monday evening, and on Wednesday evening Mr. Jones' address was a most fitting farewell to the graduates.

There are now two more added to the small army of graduates. They will carry Laing's spirit into the world, and by the fruits of these who go through our doors, Laing shall be immortalized.

CHARLOTTE B. ROSS, Principal.

(The above account was written at the request of Joel Borton, who is deeply interested in Laing School, and who desires to enlist the support of Friends in this good work.)

Items from Everywhere

The last of the religious conscientious objectors confined during the war have just been released, according to the American Civil Liberties Union.

Official notification has been received at the State Department that the Japanese Privy Council has approved the nine-power treaty concerning China and the Chinese customs tariff treaty. Both these treaties were negotiated at the Washington Conference on the Limitation of Armament.

The delegation of prominent men and women who interviewed President Harding on July 19th in the interest of general amnesty for all remaining political prisoners returned to their homes much encouraged. The President received them most cordially and promised them that the cases of the 86 prisoners for whom they spoke would receive attention at the earliest possible date.

France is seriously considering Germany's proposal to undertake public works in France as a substitute for reparation payments in cash. The program includes not only the restoration of the devastated areas, but river and harbor improvements, digging canals, and tunneling the Vosges Mountains. German material and German workmen would be used. If the new project is adopted it will be because all other schemes have failed. It is a sensible proposal, however, and would benefit both countries.

There has recently been organized in New York City a People's Tribunal for the speedy, inexpensive and lawful determination of all kinds of controversies and differences (except divorce) by arbitration. Such an open tribunal for the settlement by prominent laymen, acting as arbitrators, of business and other disputes is hailed by judges, lawyers and business men alike as the greatest step in twenty-five years to simplify legal procedure and relieve court congestion.

Two months ago Near East Relief was obliged to make a 25% reduction in all appropriations for orphanage support in Armenia, Anatolia, Syria and Palestine. Receipts had decreased 40%. There was no alternative. The 25% reduction in appropriations meant the inevitable death of thousands of little children whom America had already taken into the orphanages of the Near East—certain Death unless the American public, by increased contributions, "commuted the sentence."

The facts were quickly placed before the public and the public responded. The contributions during April and May increased with the result that the lives of these orphan children were spared.

One check came unsolicited for $100,000 from an anonymous donor, who read in the *Literary Digest* of the threatened slaughter of innocents and responded promptly, generously. This man, by signing that check, literally saved the lives of 2,000 orphaned children as truly as if he had rescued them from a sinking ship or burning building.

There are more than 100,000 of these children wholly dependent upon American philanthropy. Their needs will be as great during the summer months and the coming winter as they were last spring, and it is only by a steady continuance of contributions that a recurrence of the crisis can be avoided. Every possible opportunity is being used to develop all practical self-support and government aid, but until the allied powers have in some way secured stable and friendly government for this area, these children—orphans of our allies—must continue to look to America for the necessities of life and preparation for large future usefulness.

THE OPEN FORUM

This column is intended to afford free expression of opinion by readers on questions of interest. The INTELLIGENCER *is not responsible for any such opinions. Letters must be brief, and the editor reserves the right to omit parts if necessary to save space.*

To the Editor:

Passing along a clear winding stream amid the growing blooming beauty of the woods, I hear the ethereal flute note of the wood thrush. No human throat ever uttered such divine tones. Whence didst thou, O sweet singer of the cool deep woods, learn that song? 'Tis a pæon of love and beauty imbibed from their environment by thy ancestors and by thee too sweet for sordid man to comprehend.

'Tis fit only for joyous, innocent childhood's ears; those of whom the Master said: "Of such is the kingdom of heaven."

If all children were given this natural communion and teaching, which is their right, amid the sweet wild life of the woods and the meadows, they, too, would learn a divine song of love and praise comparable to that of the wood thrush. The understanding of Nature's teachings would always be an ennobling, saving influence in their lives. Millions now never hear the song of a bird or comprehend the meaning of a flower. No decent normal society ever existed where the lives of the masses were cursed by an aristocracy of greed and privilege where even from the cradle lives are blighted and under-nourished due to a "profits system" that exalts its accumulation of dollars above the primal necessities of a decent start in life for the children of its wealth producers.

Society has only commenced to realize its duty to the child. City playgrounds are a splendid thing. Every large city should own and conserve nearby groves and meadows and sparkling streams and have nature teachers in summer to instruct and teach its children the wonders and beauty of Nature.

As I listened to the song of the wood thrush an intense longing possessed my soul that "the new heavens" and "the new earth," socially and spiritually conceived by Jesus should be striven for more radically and earnestly, especially by those who profess to be His followers. I. K. W.

Oxford, Pa.

To the Editor:

To the present writer, the article by Philip J. Webster in the INTELLIGENCER of Seventh month 8th, appears to be very inadequate as an "answer to Mr. Malone's letter" in an earlier issue of the paper. Mr. Webster simply proceeds in the usual Socialistic manner to denounce "our present economic system" as fundamentally wrong because human greed unrestrained by adequate laws has led to an unfair distribution of the proceeds of industry and to the individual exploitation of national resources. But he does not suggest any other system that might be more beneficient in its results.

Our present industrial and economic system rests upon the following fundamental principles which may be regarded as inalienable rights: The right of every one to sell his services and to hire the services of others; the right of those who possess capital honorably acquired to loan it at interest or to employ it in business and to receive for such use of it a portion of the profits of the business; and the right of those who own capital to make such testamentary disposal of such capital as they may see fit. These rights have all been regulated by law and may be further so regulated, but for any "system" to be essentially different from our own, it must absolutely deny them. Such a system, the only alternative to the one we are suffering under, is in operation today in Russia; and if Mr. Webster could be transported to that most wretched of all lands, he would find labor troubles and social unrest; and intensified a thousand fold, the pestilence and starvation which he so naively attributes to our industrial system.

There are large industrial establishments in America and also in Europe from which the simple application of the Golden Rule to business has eliminated all industrial troubles, and the results thus obtained and the methods employed might well be studied by our Socialist Friends as a basis for proposed industrial legislation. Their present line of attack will certainly never get them anywhere.

Bartow, Fla. S. S. GREEN.

MARRIAGES

MORRIS-COMPTON—At the home of the bride's parents, at Plainfield, N. J., on Sixth month 6th, Thomas Maurey Morris, M. D., and Ruth Marion Compton.

DEATHS

JONES—At Moorestown, N. J., on Seventh month 16th, Norman S. Jones, son of B. Henry and the late Elizabeth S. Jones, aged 16 years.

We know the old must die and bow to the inevitable, but when the young, who seem to have but started on life's journey, with all the possibilities of a bright and useful future, have life suddenly ended, we feel bereft indeed.

Norman Jones had just reached his 16th year, but his bright and sunny disposition, his cheerful, willing helpfulness, had endeared him to a host of friends, both young and old.

Though entering vigorously into all boyish sports, he could be just as companionable to older people, and many of his older friends will sadly miss his bright and cordial greetings.

He had lived since infancy with his aunt, M. Ella Jarrett, who has the deepest sympathy of all her friends in her great loss.

"Day after day we think what he is doing
In those bright realms of air,
Year after year, his heavenly course pursuing,
Behold him grown more fair."

KIRBY—At Thorofare, N. J., Seventh month 22d, Chalkley Kirby, husband of Jennie R. Blair, aged 67. Interment Friends' Burying Grounds, Woodstown, N. J.

SMITH—At Lambertville, N. J., on Seventh month 11th, Albert T. Smith, son of Emma E. and the late Jacob Heston Smith. Interment at Buckingham.

SMITH—At Woodbury, N. J., on Seventh month 20th, Elizabeth W., widow of Thomas P. Smith, aged 75. Interment at Horsham, Pa.

WOOD—At Johnsville, Pa., on Seventh month 19th, Mary R., wife of Benjamin G. Wood (nee Kirk), in her 63d year.

COMING EVENTS

SEVENTH MONTH

28th-30th—Closing week-end conference at Woolman School. Subject, "Boys' Work." Lectures by William Byron Forbush on First-day School Teaching, Sixth-day evening and Seventh-day evening. Seventh-day morning classes by Dr. Fergusson and Bliss Forbush.

29th—Westbury Quarterly Meeting, at Westbury, L. I., at 10.30 a. m. Train leaves Pennsylvania Station, New York, at 9.09, and Flatbush Avenue, Brooklyn Station, at 9.12, arriving at Westbury at 10. Isaac Wilson expects to attend the meeting. Lunch will be served soon after noon. The afternoon session at 2.30 will be addressed by Robert Bruyere, of the Bureau of Industrial Research, on "Personality and Coal." The address will treat of the work of Friends in the coal regions of West Virginia and Pennsylvania, where he is acting as a representative or Field Secretary of the American Friends' Service Committee.

30th—Certain members of Philadelphia Quarterly Meeting's Visiting Committee expect to attend Haverford meeting at 10.30 a. m., First-day School at 11. a. m.

30th—2.30 p. m. (daylight saving time), at Byberry Friends' Meeting-house, a lecture by Dr. O. Edward Janney on "The Educational Approach to a Warless World." See Notice.

30th—Concord Quarterly Meeting of Ministry and Counsel, at Concord, 2 p. m. (daylight saving time).

EIGHTH MONTH

1st—Concord Quarterly Meeting at Concord Meeting-House (Pa.), at 10 a. m., daylight saving time.

3rd—Conference and Meeting for Worship on the campus, under care of Friends attending Summer School of Columbia University. Topic of conference, "Quakerism and Peace."

5th—Philadelphia Quarterly Meeting, at Merion, Pa.

6th—Purchase Quarterly Meeting, at Purchase, N. Y., at 10.30 a. m.

6th—First-day, 2.30 p. m., Eastern Standard time. An appointed meeting for divine worship will be held at the Friends' Meeting-house, Newtown Square, Delaware County, Pa., under care of a Committee of Concord Quarter. For young and old, for conservative and liberal; non-sectarians especially invited. Easily reached by trolley from 69th Street station or by pilgrimage.

6th—Conference under care of Yearly Meeting's First-day School Committee at Wrightstown, Pa., 2.30 p. m., Standard time (3.30 daylight saving). Subject, "The Meeting and the First-day School in Co-operation." Box lunch at 1 o'clock.

6th—William J. and Hannah L. MacWatters expect to visit Mt. Holly, N. J., meeting, at 11 a. m. (daylight saving time), and Springfield in the afternoon.

7th—Genesee Yearly Meeting, at Coldstream, Ont.

7th—Miami Quarterly Meeting, at Green Plain, Ohio.

10th—Abington Quarterly Meeting, at Gwynedd, Pa., at 10.30 (daylight saving time). Meeting of Ministry and Counsel, same day, at 9 a. m.

12th—Blue River Quarterly Meeting, at Benjaminville, Ill.

12th—Picnic on the Palisades, given by New York Friends to Quaker students at Columbia University Summer School. All Friends are invited. Fuller notice later.

13th—Certain members of Philadelphia Quarterly Meeting's Visiting Committee will visit Germantown Friends' Home, at 7.30 p. m.

14th—Indiana Yearly Meeting, at Waynesville, Ohio.

NOTICE—Byberry Friends' Meeting is planning an all-day affair for the 30th. Members are desired to attend meeting for worship at 10 o'clock, and Monthly Meeting following, bringing box lunch and enjoying a social time before the lecture by Dr. O. Edward Janney, at 2.30. All nearby churches are announcing this lecture at their services and will co-operate in this "No-More-War Demonstration."

"No More War" Resolution

On July 30th, churches and meetings everywhere should circulate petitions or adopt peace resolutions for immediate transmission to President Harding. Such a petition might read in whole or in part substantially as follows:

To the President,
The White House,
Washington, D. C.

We assure you of our support in further steps along the path on which the world entered at the Washington Conference until war has been outlawed and permanent peace has been achieved. We favor American recognition of the World Court at The Hague, American participation in the reconstruction of Europe, and the outlawry of war by international agreement.

American Friends' Service Committee

WILBUR K. THOMAS, EX. SEC.
20 S. 12th St. Philadelphia.

CASH CONTRIBUTIONS
WEEK ENDING JULY 17TH.

Five Years Meetings	$453.50
Other Meetings:	
Westtown Monthly Meeting	33.00
Cornwall Monthly Meeting	5.50
Oxford Monthly Meeting	100.00
Westbury Monthly Meeting	230.00
Orange Grove Friends of Pasadena	30.00
Contributions for Germany	156.25
For Austria	117.25
For Poland	106.54
For Russia	1,717.23
For Russian overhead	254.17
For Armenia	60.00
West Virginia	206.50
Central Pennsylvania	340.00
For General	218.00
Miscellaneous Sources for General	200.00
For German Overhead	505.77
Continuation Committee	2.00
For Clothing Department	300.39
Refunds and payments	7.08
	$5,043.18

Shipments received during week ending July 15: 41 boxes and packages; 1 for Mennonite relief.

WANTED

WANTED—SUMMER BOARDERS, IN a small country town; rates reasonable. Address P. 281, Friends' Intelligencer.

WOMAN OF MIDDLE AGE, NURSE, wants care of invalid. Address P. 282, Friends' Intelligencer.

RIVER CROFT, CLAYMONT, DEL. Special home care for invalids, or rest and physical upbuilding. Booklet on application. E. H. Speakman.

WANTED — A FRIEND TO TEACH Buckingham Friends' School at Lahaska, Pa. 15 pupils—grades 1-8. Apply to Mary A. Watson, 277 Maple Ave., Doylestown, Pa.

POSITION WANTED—BY REFINED woman, with nervous or elderly person; capable of taking full charge; light duties. Address B. 290, Friends' Intelligencer.

WANTED—BY YOUNG COUPLE BY October 1st, light housekeeping apartments, 2 rooms, bath and kitchenette; within walking distance of University of Pennsylvania. Address B. 291, Friends' Intelligencer.

WANTED—AN EXPERIENCED DIETITIAN for an institution of three hundred persons. Friend preferred. Address F. 301, Friends' Intelligencer.

SEPTEMBER 1ST, BUSINESS WOMAN, Friend, wants unfurnished room and board, in walking distance of Wayne Junction; state terms. Box P. 302, Friends' Intelligencer.

FOR RENT

FOR RENT—THREE ROOMS IN private family, until Labor Day. Rates reasonable. 1402 Asbury Avenue, Ocean City, N. J.

FOR RENT—FURNISHED OR UNFURNISHED, 84th St., near Central Park, 7-room apartment. Real kitchen, steam, continuous hot water. Clarence Kimball, 115 Broadway, New York. Schuyler 2661.

FOR RENT—A RETIRED CITY worker will rent a small, furnished, furnace heated cottage on outskirts of Maine village, to an appreciative tenant at moderate expense. Suitable for a Sabbatical year or for intellectual or artistic workers. Correspondence invited. Address M. 300, Friends' Intelligencer.

FOR RENT—AT OCEAN CITY, N. J.—Attractive furnished rooms; ocean view; fine location near Boardwalk. Address Laura H. Brosius, 820 Sixth St.

FUN

"It is the duty of every one to make at least one person happy during the week," said a Sunday school teacher. "Have you done so, Freddy?" "Yes." "What did you do?" "I went to see my aunt, and she was happy when I went home."—*Exchange.*

A village newspaper contains this reference to the local hospital achievements: "Our esteemed fellow-citizen Abner Brown will go to the hospital tomorrow to be operated on for appendicitis. He will leave a wife and two children."—*The Christian Register.*

"Where's the capital of the United States?" "In Europe."—*Lehigh Burr.*

ADVERTISING RATE in the FRIENDS' INTELLIGENCER, for Help Wanted, Positions Wanted, Rooms for Rent, Notices, and other classified advertisements without display, for each insertion, 2 cents per word, including name, initials and address. Answers may be sent to a box at the INTELLIGENCER office, if so directed.

For display advertising the rate is 10 cents per agate line, or $1.40 per column inch, each insertion. On ten or more insertions in a year from date of order, ten per cent. discount. Thus a four-inch single-column or two-inch double-column advertisement costs $5.60 each insertion, less ten per cent., or 5.04 net each time for ten or more insertions. Matter may be changed whenever desired, without extra charge.

Experience has proved the INTELLIGENCER to be a remarkably good advertising medium. All advertisements must "pass the censor!"

Address 140 N. 15th St., Philadelphia

The Friends' Intelligencer

ESTABLISHED 1844 | EIGHTH MONTH 5, 1922 | VOLUME 79 NUMBER 31

Contents

THE FRIENDS' INTELLIGENCER

Published weekly, 140 N. 15th Street, Philadelphia, Pa., by Friends' Intelligencer Association, Ltd.

PAUL W. WAGER, *Editor.*
SUE C. YERKES, *Business Manager*

Editorial Board: Elizabeth Powell Bond, Thomas A. Jenkins, J. Russell Smith, George A. Walton.

Board of Managers: Edward Cornell, Alice Hall Paxson, Paul M. Pearson, Annie Hillborn, Elwood Hollingshead, William C. Biddle, Charles F. Jenkins, Edith M. Winder, Frances M. White.

Officers of Intelligencer Associates: Ellwood Burdsall, Chairman; Bertha L. Broomell, Secretary; Herbert P. Worth, Treasurer.

Subscription rates: United States, Mexico, Cuba and Panama, $2.50 per year. Canada and other foreign countries, $3.00 per year. Checks should be made payable to Friends' Intelligencer Association, Ltd.

Entered as Second Class Matter at Philadelphia Post Office.

REGULAR MEETINGS

OAKLAND, CALIF. — A FRIENDS' Meeting is held every First-day at 11 A. M., in the Extension Room, Y. W. C. A. Building, Webster Street, above 14th. Visiting Friends always welcome.

PASADENA, CALIFORNIA — Orange Grove Monthly Meeting of Friends, 520 East Orange Grove Avenue. Meeting for worship, First-day, 11 A. M. Monthly Meeting, the second First-day of each month, at 1.45 P. M. First-day School (except Monthly Meeting days) 9.45 A. M.

NOTICE—Concise statements of the principles of the Religious Society of Friends and their application to the problems of every day living, including "The Spirit of Quakerism," by Elbert Russell; "Preparation for Life's Greatest Business," by Rufus M. Jones; and other articles by Henry W. Wilbur, Howard M. Jenkins, Elizabeth Lloyd, Jesse H. Holmes, O. Edward Janney, Edward B. Rawson, etc., to be had free on application to Friends' General Conference Advancement Committee, 140 North Fifteenth Street, Philadelphia, Pa.

FUN

Mrs. Cobb decided to visit London and spend the day with a friend.

Her grocer had not called by the time she was ready to leave, so she wrote on a card: "All out. Don't leave anything," and tacked it on the door.

Upon her return at night she discovered that the house had been ransacked. On the card which she had left on the door these words had been added:

"Thanks, but we couldn't take the heavy furniture."—*Epworth Herald.*

The Friends' Intelligencer

The religion of Friends is based on faith in the "INWARD LIGHT," or direct revelation of God's spirit and will in every seeking soul.

The INTELLIGENCER is interested in all who bear the name of Friends in every part of the world, and aims to promote love, unity and intercourse among all branches and with all religious societies.

ESTABLISHED 1844 | PHILADELPHIA, EIGHTH MONTH 5, 1922 | VOLUME 79 NUMBER 31

A larger measure of the spirit of Christian brotherhood is the only cure for all these industrial ills.

✖

It may be hard to love the unlovely and to be tolerant of the intolerant but it is the acid test of Christianity.

✖

The way of love works ninety-nine times out of a hundred and the one failure may be used to measure the successes by.

✖

We asked a very-much-concerned Friend what, in his opinion, was the solution of the open-shop question. "There is none," he replied, "until the matter is approached, from both sides, in a different spirit."

✖

Richmond, Indiana, where the Conference is to be held, is not so far "West" as some people seem to think. In fact, it is only fifty miles from Cincinnati, and Cincinnati is a railroad center. "On to Richmond!"

✖

We learn with sincerest regret that there is serious question whether *Friends' Fellowship Papers,* now in their thirteenth volume, will be continued beyond next November. This little journal, ably edited by Elizabeth Fox Howard, has been a welcome monthly visitor in many American homes. It has brought with it a breath from foreign lands, from a wider Quakerism than most of us had been accustomed to, and its glimpses of Friends' mission posts have been not only interesting but thought-provoking. We hope this financial crisis can be safely passed. The American agent is Grace W. Blair, Media, Penna., and the annual subscription is one dollar.

✖

This nation was founded on a religious basis. It was settled by men and women who sought freedom to worship God. The constitution was drafted in an atmosphere of prayer. Religious toleration and the separation of church and state were accepted as fundamental principles of our republic. To further protect and promote religion the government has always recognized the Sabbath as a day for rest and worship. Our chief executives from Washington to Harding have reverenced the day and set it apart as a Holy Day. It has been one of the bulwarks of our national character but there is now grave danger lest the beauty and sanctity of the day shall be destroyed.

There are those who want to repeal all the old colonial statutes which were designed to protect and foster religious worship. It is true that they have long ceased to serve any useful purpose and until recently were slumbering in repose. There is probably no logical reason why they should be preserved, nor perhaps why they should be repealed. They are about as useless and as harmless as grandmother's spinning wheel in the attic. It has a certain sentimental value but since closet room is so scarce in our modern houses it can be sacrificed. So with these innocent "blue laws," if it is going to make anyone feel any better we can relegate them to the scrap heap. But be not deceived. Those who are most insistent in urging their repeal have other motives than to preserve the respect for law.

There are interests which want to commercialize the Sabbath. They want a chance to consume the contents of Saturday's pay envelopes on Sunday. They want a chance to exploit the wage-earners every hour that they are "off duty." It is certainly true that what people spend on First-day (except what little the churches get) is practically wasted. We compel the grocer, the clothier and the furniture dealer to close their stores, but let the movies (in some places), the ice cream parlors, the railroads and the Coney Islands to extract all that they can from the people.

But that is not the worst aspect of Sabbath desecration. The day is ceasing to be observed for rest and worship and the Christian people themselves are largely responsible for the laxity which prevails. They practice in a small way what they condemn others for doing in a larger way. They go to church in the morning (none too regularly) and then spend the rest of the day like any other holiday. We cannot secure reverence for the day through legislation; we cannot compel church attendance; but much can be accomplished through example. If the Christian people of America want to see the Sabbath kept sacred they must set an example in consecration and reverence. They must create the atmosphere in which religion flourishes. We cannot classify our activities into things which it is *right* to do on the Sabbath and others which it is *wrong* to do. It is not so simple a problem. Our only criterion must be—does it edify? At the close of the day can we feel that sense of benediction that comes only when our souls have been earnestly seeking for God?

We are sometimes inclined to scoff at the Puritanism of our fathers. It is true we may be more tolerant, more liberal in our religious views. We ought to be. But is our gain as great as our loss if we lose their devotion and reverence? They erred in dividing life into sacred and secular; we err in making nothing sacred. If First-day, like any holiday, is given over to travel, entertainment and frivolity, people fail to secure that soul refreshment which alone lifts them to God. Unless God has a place in the lives of its people, any nation will perish no matter how rich or powerful it may be. America is in danger of losing its soul unless the Sabbath is preserved as a day conducive to worship.

To Those "Contemplating the Engagement of Marriage"

By

Gwen & Corder Catchpool

In these times of social unrest at home, social chaos in many countries abroad, and social revolution in at least one of them, the problems involved must press for the attention of every earnest, thoughtful mind, and therefore *a priori*, we are inclined to say, for the attention of Young Friends.

These problems are of two kinds, viz.: those concerned with analysis of existing evils and their causes, to which a good deal of thought has been given by Friends in the past, and those which contemplate wide reconstructive change in the future. Consideration of both is essential if we are to pass quietly from the old order to the new.

Methods of violent transformation scarcely harmonize with Quaker mentality, and they have completely broken down in the recent practice of Bolshevism; but even if the change come gradually, the time is at hand for us to set our minds resolutely towards the new order. Come it must, and lacking the active co-operation of people of goodwill—especially of young people—it may well come with all the futility and instability of conquest by force.

The Danger Zone

There can be no doubt that the "snare of accumulating wealth," although probably remote from most of us by reason of our present circumstances, is a real one to many people, and we need to put the old query seriously, asking if we are ***in the spirit*** that would save us from becoming potential victims.

Recent experience in collecting funds for Russia has revealed a terrible contrast between the readiness of the poor of this world to give, even at the cost of personal privation, and the reverse on the part of the well-to-do. The spirit of money-making for its own sake is a deadly, cumulative narcotic to the spirit of freely giving.

But the trouble goes far deeper than that. We may have realized that to the Christian there can be no race or color bar. We have not altogether realized that class barriers sometimes isolate more effectually than national or ethnological frontiers, hindering that perfect "unity with all creation" which Quakers should be the first amongst Christians to emphasize and practice.

Even in the advertisement columns of *The Friend* one sees enquiries for "Lady" help where "woman" is kept "to do the rough work." The barrier of large houses and establishments, segregated in class-areas in the pleasanter parts of our cities, must be obvious to all. The multiplying of possessions absorbs time and energy—Life—in caring for them, and we cling to them with a pathetic hold that shackles freedom of response to the call for service. "There are two classes of people: those who think the world owes them a living, and those who think they owe the world a life."

There is a freedom and elasticity about youth—an enthusiasm and love of adventure, that usually keeps these perils at a distance. It is when we marry, "settle down," start an establishment of our own, that we enter the danger zone. In realizing one ideal, we sometimes lose another. We become bourgeois. We take class-sides, and before we realize it, we are handicapped in advance should there stir within us the longing to live and work for a better social order.

If we are right in thinking that this danger exists we want to save young Friends "contemplating the engagement of marriage" from going blindly towards it.

The Experiment

To-day the class-war is being preached by extreme Socialists. It may or may not be possible now to avoid it, but there is one simple way in which it might be sidetracked, if sufficient recruits could be enlisted for a great experiment, and that is by building up as quickly as possible in the midst of the old contending classes a new class that is no class. It is not an easy matter to be obviously no class, and requires a lot of thought, but Young Friends will come to it from first Quaker principles, and not wait till some crisis makes it inevitable.

Needless to say, to work out an ideal in married life demands absolute co-operation in spirit and in deed between husband and wife. The first step is to fix the style of living. Many are prepared to start in a small way, and this is good; but maybe they are only content to do so because of the implicit understanding that they will enlarge as soon as opportunity offers. We would suggest that there is a right standard which can and should be more or less determined in advance. The guide in this matter is the no-class principle, which will require the home to be neither too pretentious nor too mean; neither too luxurious nor bare to the point of discomfort. Beauty will be found compatible with simplicity—perhaps even incompatible with anything else.

Books, pictures (these should grow with our homes and never be a mere branch of furnishing), music, all the means to a liberal education, are part of personality, and should be within reach of ourselves *and of all around us*. Obvious class-areas will be avoided and fortunately the garden suburb movement should be making this easier than it was a generation ago. We want to be valued for what we are, not for the goods we possess, and unless we are really living a simple life we cannot always be sure that this is the case. We may even have to consider how rightly to dispose of surplus wealth if circumstances should have endowed us with it.

The ideal home is a means to life, our own and others' and not an end in itself. No woman's life should be devoted, as so many are, *solely* to providing meals and keeping everything clean and in order, good and useful as that may be. (The care of a family lies in a different category.)

Home Making

Home-making is an art. Perhaps the Divine in human life—its sacramental aspect—may come nearer to realization in the home than anywhere else, not excluding places of worship. The ideal home is a centre of fellowship—not for the family only, but for the neighborhood, and occasionally perhaps—guests from abroad for example—for a much wider circle. Spiritually conceived the limits of its influence are of course, infinite.

Much has been heard of the "atmosphere" of the old Quaker home. The early Friends were for the most part simple folk—hand or land workers, and their home life, from such glimpses as we have of it, was very sweet. But the old Quaker home with its "atmosphere" more often conjures up before our minds the abode of the wealthy in generations which had lost the early simplicity; where the beautiful Quaker spirit broods, to be sure, amidst all the accompaniments of affluence.

One cannot escape the thought that the very calm with which life flows in these retreats is due in part to the staff of superior and well-treated domestics who minister to the needs of their masters. A story is told of Elizabeth Fry, who had a praiseworthy habit of early rising. When staying on one occasion with Friends, she asked for coffee at 6 a. m., and on coming down next morning expressed surprise at finding one of the servants already astir. "Thee about so early?" she queried, naively unconscious that the girl had had to rise half an hour earlier to get her the coffee she had ordered overnight.

The problem of domestic servants is at the centre of the whole complex. We must face it resolutely and without compromise. We can never hope to defy the barriers of class distinction if we install the class system on our very hearths. Broadly speaking, a healthy and active young married couple should be able to do all their own work, and might at least begin by trying to do it. There will, of course, be exceptional cases, and later on help in some form or other will, in all probability, be generally desirable.

The husband must in any case be prepared to take some share in the housework. His sphere in the home, and his wife's cannot be divided into water-tight compartments.

If and when outside help becomes necessary (note that the poor women with large families around us *have* to do without it), we must absolutely bar out any shadow of class difference; we must do a fair share of the dirty work; and we must remember that if such help is right for us, it is right for all, and must see to it that others obtain their rights.

The Abundant Life

It is our task to recapture the old peaceful Quaker atmosphere for our work-a-day twentieth century homes. We can get it, and with much beside in the wonderful joy of an universal unclouded fellowship.

We have said that home-making is an art. It is also in some aspects a science. The home portrayed above is impossible of realization in many of the houses—even the small ones—that we know to-day, and without relinquishing some of the middle class traditions in which we have been brought up.

Young people who are in earnest about living out the vision will find that much can be done in the way of simplification. Slight and uncostly changes of arrangement and method may cut out whole needless processes, but to touch on some of these would require a further article.

In conclusion we would say that intense joy may be experienced in thinking out together a really labor-saving menage, because behind it all is the great purpose of releasing souls from bondage to the material, and launching out into the more abundant life.

Reprinted from "The Young Quaker," London.

Life's Varied Round

With just enough of cloud and shade
To make the sun more bright,
And just enough of honest toil
To fit one for the fight;
With just enough of strain and stress
To keep the courage strong,
And just enough of minor chords
To strengthen life's glad song;
With just enough of weariness
To make rest seem more sweet,
And just enough of varying scenes
To make the days complete;
With life expanding to the needs
Of tasks abounding here,
That heart and mind and soul be trained
For heaven's enlarging sphere.

Fred Scott Shepard, in "The Christian Advocate."

Attitudes in Worship

Third article on worship by Elbert Russell

By attitudes I do not mean physical postures. Such questions as whether the worshippers should kneel or stand in prayer are relatively unimportant. The attitude of spirit is the important thing in worship. In such intangible matters one cannot draw hard and fast lines or make rigid classifications, but we may be helped by noting four attitudes that in their times and places are essential to the fullest and most effective worship.

Fundamental is the *attitude of devotion.* It involves something more than the feeling of devoutness. It requires a self-discipline so as to *devote* oneself during the hour of worship wholly to the task. To bring all the powers of mind and spirit and use them in the worship with consecration and singleness of purpose. This hour is to be devoted wholly, fully, and to the utmost to worshipping God together and to finding the supply of our deepest individual and common needs. We should come to meeting and "settle down" attentive to the task in hand, determined that nothing shall divert us from it. It is especially the attitude for coming into the meeting for worship.

The second attitude is the *passive or receptive* attitude. No doubt Quietism overstressed this attitude. But the Quietist ideal contains an important element of truth. In its proper place it is necessary to the fullest fruition of worship. At certain times we derive our greatest physical benefits from complete relaxation. We can only recover from certain kinds of illness by giving up all mental and physical exertion and simply lying in bed. Convalescence comes sometimes by idling at the seashore or basking in mountain sunlight and letting the great curative forces of Nature have full play upon us and within us. A certain woman relates that she frequently found herself at the limit of her strength and patience seemingly unable to bear her burdens longer, but feeling that everything depended on her "carrying on." At such times she would lie down and relax completely, saying over and over again, "I did not make the world and I do not have to keep it going." Her attitude was really one of trust, and from it she received needed strength to go on, so we find healing and renewed strength when we simply wait on God and trust in Him. The passive attitude also gives God opportunity to speak to us of things we do not readily hear, when other matters occupy our minds and attention and which may be drowned out by the din of the physical machinery, when it is running. I remember the first time, as a boy, I slept outdoors at night I was surprised at hearing in the "small hours" many sounds that I had never heard before. They were noises always to be heard but the ordinary routine of work and sleep had kept them from my notice. It is often only "in the quiet" that we grow conscious of weaknesses, passions, desires, or motives growing up unnoticed within us amid the stress and preoccupation of our ordinary life. Likewise we may discover duties neglected, opportunities missed, powers atrophying from disuse, or needs overlooked, as we give God opportunity to point out to us the things overlooked, or to reveal us fully to ourselves, as He makes Himself felt and heard afresh. We need the passive attitude as an antidote to the "world that is too much with us."

The third is the *seeking* attitude. Jesus assures us that he that seeketh shall find. Too much of the passive attitude may lead to emptiness of mind or spiritual laziness. There is a suspension of mental activity closely akin to the unconsciousness of sleep. There are times when we need to give our lives a definite and vigorous overhauling. Too much introspection, to be sure, is not healthful. It is not good for us to go about with a spiritual fever-thermometer in our consciences and our fingers on our emotional pulse all the time. But on the other hand, it *is* good to look for weaknesses before they become serious enough to cause a break down. There are times when duty requires us to drive a motor car regardless of squeaks and knocks. But it is wise to overhaul it between times, pay careful heed to lost motion, friction, and unusual noises, and remedy the trouble in time. So our souls need frequent overhauling. We may regard J. J. Gurney's daily examination by means of a private set of queries or his quarterly examination of his spiritual state and progress as overdone. It is more important frequently to inspect our spiritual affairs than it is to take frequent inventories of our temporal business; and for this the meeting for worship provides opportunity.

Besides this there should be a definite seeking after enlargement of our knowledge of God, of our usefulness, and powers. Jesus came that we might have life abundantly. This greater abundance we should seek after: the larger love, the deeper knowledge, the fuller consecration, the more fruitful worship, the freer communion with God.

Among the many secrets of power in the first generation of Friends was the fact that so many of them had been Seekers, before they became Friends, and carried into the gatherings of Friends the seeker attitude. Some precious things come to those who wait on God; there are others which only he that asketh receiveth, or he that seeketh findeth.

"Forty Acres and a Mule'

To the Polish peasant no less than to the American freed slave, land and stock represent all this world's blessings to which one can aspire. More fortunate than the Negro, the peasant already owns the acres and the Friends' Mission is trying to supply the mule.

Throughout the years when the peasants of Eastern Poland were pushed back by the armies and swept into Russia, they were sustained by the memory of the home-land and the hope of return to their own fields and the simple laborious life that meant happiness to them. After the war they began to return. They had but fled from one tragedy to encounter another. There was no place to live, there were neither horses nor cows, there were no implements nor seeds. They returned enfeebled, with empty hands, to begin life anew.

It is no easy matter to cultivate the wilderness and to obliterate the traces of seven years of war. Acres of fertile fields are now overgrown with weeds and grass. The woods have encroached upon the meadows, covering them with a growth of young birch trees sometimes fifteen feet high. Barbed wire entanglements still cover miles of territory, and everywhere the earth is broken by trenches. It was a feat for the refugees to discover in this scene of desolation the plots of ground to which they could claim ownership. Sometimes they were recognizable by the fruit trees standing by the scattered heap of bricks, once the oven, which was all that remained of the house. Sometimes there was nothing—not even a square yard of cultivable ground—to show where house and garden had been. Disappointing as they found their homecoming, at least they were refugees no longer, and they set to work to put their land in condition.

It was a heartbreaking task, lightened only by the help received from the Mission. It was necessary to supply food, implements, material for house building, seeds and aid in tilling the soil. Assistance in getting the land under cultivation was the most important form of relief. In the spring of 1921 tractor plowing was undertaken. Small tracts were plowed for the neediest peasants, and afterwards larger tracts for those who agreed to plant them to grain in order to increase the bread supply. Because of the costs and delays in tractor plowing, this method was superseded by horse plowing. An observer describes the difficulty of this work. The peasant leads a two-horse plow, his wife following behind, turning over with her hands the sods too heavy for the plow to turn. Every five or six yards the man has to stop and help her. A second plowing is necessary before the seed can be sown. Only the strongest peasants can get much land in condition unaided. This spring the Mission bought the horses from the Government for about $7.00 a piece. It was money well spent. The use of a seven-dollar horse, a German trench spade, and a few seeds puts a family on its feet by the end of the first harvest.

Most of the horses were organized in plowing columns which are plowing a piece of land for as many returning peasants as possible. At the present rate, these columns can plow enough land to start 2,000 families each month with at least 4 acres of broken ground. All the spring the columns worked at terrific pressure to prepare the ground for planting, which went on as late as there was any hope that the seed would grow. Crop reports are favorable and everything indicates that the peasants with their Mission sickles and scythes will reap a good harvest. As soon as the crops are gathered, fall plowing will be begun. Then the horses will be sold to the neediest peasants and the proceeds from the sale will be used for permanent local improvements.

So rapid has been the improvement in the districts where the Friends are working that the Ministry of

Repatriation has been studying their system and recommending its adoption in other districts. Oscar Moon, assistant head of the Mission, who was present at a conference of all the County Starostas, reports that they showed great interest in the work of the Friends. Whether they can secure the maximum results depends on the help received from America. The plan of plowing 4 acres for 2,000 families every month from August to November, with all the incidental relief calls for $40,000. The shortage of money is so great that the Mission has had to discontinue giving a week's ration of food to each newly-arrived refugee family. Without our help the return to normal life is indefinitely delayed. The acres are there but what avails ownership without food and seed and plows and horses?

Only those who have lived among the peasants know what our aid means to them. Oscar Moon thus describes their attitude. "Their appreciation is pathetic. Most of them attempt to kiss the hand in token of gratitude, but why not? Have not the Quakers given them an acre of plowing, and does not that one acre spell the difference between life and death to them? Why should they not look upon these people as saviors? So they kiss the hands that have helped them."

Quakerism, the Religion of Youth

(Address by George A. Walton at Western Quarterly Meeting)

"The Society of Friends was established as a growing organization by men and women between the ages of twenty and thirty. It was conceived, fought for, bled for, by young people. But the times changed and there came into our Society a different spirit, and the duties gradually came to rest on the shoulders of the older people. If there had been young blood among the leaders of Quakerism in 1822 we would not have divided our forces and partially paralyzed our growth by splitting up into small groups in 1827, each group consisting of those who used the same forms of expression, not realizing that man is not able to set up a dogma to which we can all conform: that the words that we use are but pointers to a view, not the thing itself.

'In England they did not separate, although they had the same differences, the same extremes of doctrinal opinion. They were not afraid to disagree and yet they always remembered that they were a Society of Friends and not a Society of Enemies. Very soon after the division of the American Friends the leaders all began to realize that something was wrong and, in the 50 years following there was founding of educational centers: the First-day School Movement was instigated, and the General Conference was set up as a scheme for interesting the young Friends, but these all left ground still to be gained.

"The Society did not grow as it should. At the present time the prospects are brighter as the young people are coming to the front. Our most famous Friends, such as Elizabeth Fry, George Fox and John Woolman never gave way to the popular fallacy that religion belongs to women and old men. There are today many who live a pretty thin, outward, formal religious life who, after they retire from business turn to religion at the age of 60 or 70. But they are not the glowing lights of our Society. Those who have done big things for Quakerism have had a concern from youth.

"Religious awakening usually comes in the adolescent period between the ages of 14 and 22. If one is led aright during this vital period his growth will keep on. Man is incurably religious. In the heart of man, even the savage, there is the yearning after an affiliation with a Deity. This religious surging in the hearts of our youth is often carefully concealed and denied by them. We must not expect them to express themselves as we would. Men of one generation have never been able to formulate a set of words which will express the ideas of the next generation. The best that comes into our hearts is when we are alone with God.

"Religion is like a wind that bloweth where it listeth. The older generation have always denounced and belabored the younger people for their shortcomings, but the world is young yet, and although we are unable to develop the faultless person, we might at least help to inject an unadulterated dose of primitive Quakerism into the hearts of Young America. Religion should be a force which multiplies the innate powers of men and women. The first fruits of religion that God commands of us is a more useful personality. The intellectual poverty of the members of our Society has been deeply felt. Many of the early leaders were not educated men and women. Today we would not stand by a haystack three hours to hear George Fox, or anyone else, speak for that length of time, but it took him that long to express, and his hearers to understand, what an educated man of today could put in a 30 or 40 minute sermon.

"We have the power today to comprehend the thoughts of others as well as to express ourselves and would that we could combine the education of today with the religious fervor, strength and enthusiasm of the first half century of the Society's history. Many feel that lack of educated leaders was responsible for the dying out of the heat in the movement during those early days. Many of our members were convinced that intellectuality and spirituality could not be combined in the same person, but the impossible has been accomplished. St. Paul, William Penn, Martin Luther combined the two.

"Our religion is satisfactory to young people if they can take it in their own hands and make it what they will. They may lean far toward Orthodoxy or far toward Unitarianism, but their oneness of spirit with God, to get as near as possible to the God-foundation, will lead to the great spiritual, Christian unity.

"We welcome the Young Friends' Movement, the study of the Discipline and of the history of our Society, and we should storm the doors of our institutions of learning for the knowledge which they can give us. Knowledge is not fire, but there has never been a big fire unless much combustible material has been collected. Let our young people collect this material. Some of it is dry, but it will burn much better. Then set this knowledge on fire by the Divine Spark.'

Ethel W. Martin, *Secretary.*

A Plea for a Larger Conception of God

By S. E. Gibbs, M. D.

Many years ago the Westminster Assembly defined God as "a Spirit, infinite, eternal and unchangeable, in His being, wisdom, power, holiness, justice, goodness and truth." To all of which we agree, but would add, a Power, inscrutable, omnipotent, omnipresent and omniscient, which presides over and governs the entire universe. It

nearer to the Divine Spirit, and know more in the hereafter. We must humbly try to follow that "Inner Light" which, unless it be heedlessly quenched, will guide us safely through life and sustain us in death. We do not know where the universe begins, nor where it ends; neither do we know where God begins and ends. Is it not more honest to admit that we do not know what God is or what His Divine purposes are than to pretend, as some do, that we perfectly understand all? The so-called Agnosticism is simply a humble confession that we do not know all.

In conclusion, what I would emphasize is, that our conception of God has been too limited, too small, more like the fairy tales of our childhood. As grown men and women we should enlarge our conception of the Supreme Being, at the same time keeping in mind that in one sense we are still children, in that we have much to learn, humble, teachable, reverent, endeavoring to learn the truth and ready at all times to use our God-given reason, even in religious matters, ever obeying the voice of conscience and following that "Inner Light" which, while in some it shines but dimly, yet is capable of development in every one of us.

The Last Hill

(Being the last chapter of "The History of the Last War of Men," published in 1982, by the Secretary of Education for free distribution.)

Colonel Young received the secret order to proceed at once with his men—picked from the armies of the twenty-four nations in arms to vindicate the rights of those victors and vanquished who, after sixty years of despair, finally revolted against the inhuman and unworkable arrangements that followed the World War of 1914-18. The order was brief, "March at once forward and *do not return* without the report that the last hill of the enemy's position is taken." It was something unusual to have an attack launched in daylight, on Sunday, and especially in an hour when friend and foe worshipped the Prince of Peace. But orders were orders. The chaplains were astonished to have their eloquence interrupted, but had to console themselves with another prayer. As to the rank and file,—they had been trained so well to believe and obey that nothing on earth could force their minds to shake off the moral lethargy, mental inertia, and general indifference to life, mind and matter that would impel them to reason. Even the lack of the intoxicating drum sounds did not disturb them.

Quietly, sneakingly, like huge, plotting snakes, they made their way through the barbed wire entanglements and finally entered the narrow passage leading through the woods to the last enemy position. But as they ascended the hill a restlessness was betrayed upon the petrified faces of the once smiling and loving fathers and sons and bridegrooms. They passed the first enemy cannons and not a sign of the enemy, though the huge monsters were in perfect order and ready for action. The second and third platforms revealed the same surprise. Was it a trap? And the men felt for the first time the need of a last prayer, expecting every second the deadly bullets from the snipers. Finally they began to near their destination; and there was no doubt that the enemy forces were massed on the plateau. With balanced bayonets the men followed their indomitable leader who, with drawn rapier, signalled forward. They reached the edge of the thickness and halted, not trusting their own eyes.

A great, brave army was kneeling before an open-air altar. Surrounding the rude platform stood the army chaplains in their denominational garb with hands in supplication. Immediately above, in the dazzling colors of the rainbow, stood the majestic figure of Christ with a white banner in his right hand upon which golden letters read, "NO MORE WAR!" Celestial music incensed the air, while every word He uttered was clearly heard by the remotest soldier in hiding. And He spoke as of yore,—"If any man have an ear let him hear. He that leadeth into captivity shall go into captivity; he that killeth with the sword must be killed with the sword. I am not the Christ of war, but of peace. I am not the prophet of human beasts, but of loving men. Hearken and learn—There can be no lasting peace, no lasting friendship, no lasting happiness begotten by the sword; and there can be no Christian nation where swords Christians kill. Lay down, then, your murderous weapons and return to your homes. Care for your neglected mothers and children, for your distant and near. Think of your neighbors as ye think of yourself, for all are the children of one fatherly love. Look ye yonder, behind those woods; there, look, are children as you in deed—ready to murder, to sacrifice all. Why? What for? Remember, he that gaineth with the sword must lose by the sword!" With His last words, He offered the banner to the multitude.

A sudden commotion went through the worshipping and amazed army. They became aware of the presence of the enemy who took advantage of the Sabbath hour to surprise them with an attack. But an invisible force prevented them from taking arms. In the meantime, led by the colonel, legions began to pour from the treacherous woods; but instead of uttering the war cry and thrusting forward with the glittering bayonets, they followed their leader who rushed to the altar and the first grasped the banner offered by Christ, flinging the sword aside. The face of the Lord shone as it never did before, and He gave the warrior His blessing. With the banner over his head, the officer faced the two armies and ordered, "Let's vow, NO MORE WAR AMONG CHRISTIAN NATIONS!" In reply, all weapons of both armies went to the ground, and one mighty army took up the vow which was heard over the entire surface of the globe, "NO MORE WAR! NO MORE WAR!" And there was not a home, Heathen or Christian, upon this earth that failed to re-echo the new order.

Thus came to an end the last war of men which brought to a final extinction that most hideous practice of men-slaughter which sacked mankind for years thousands.

DAVID GITTLEMAN.

Friendly News Notes

During the last week our Friend and friend, Daniel Batchellor, has been visiting and carrying messages of cheer to a number of "shut-ins" between Washington, D. C., and Kennett Square, Pa. His presence was also most helpful at London Grove Quarterly Meeting on Seventh month 25th.

Friends and sympathizers are urged to write to Mr. Votaw, Superintendent of Prisons, Washington, D. C., in behalf of Roy P. Conner, a political prisoner at Leavenworth, Kansas. He has been isolated for three years, as a result of a general complaint about the food in prison. This information has been supplied by the Philadelphia Branch of the Prison Comfort Club, and no doubt those Friends who were interested in that work, as well as many others, will want to file a protest against such inhuman treatment.

According to a recent issue of the *American Friend*, the following English Friends expect to attend the coming Five Years Meeting as fraternal delegates from London Yearly Meeting:

John H. Barlow, Ex-Clerk of London Yearly Meeting, and Clerk of the London Conference, and his wife, Mabel C. Barlow; Barrow and Geraldine S. Cadbury and their daughters, Dorothy and Geraldine Mary; M. Catharine Albright, Henry T. Gillett and J. Rowntree Gillett, Herbert Corder and Corder and Gwen Catchpool. There is also a possibility that T. Edmund Harvey may also be present.

The following delegates have been appointed by Dublin Yearly Meeting: Samuel A. Bell, Henrietta Bulla, Charles B. and Charlotte C. Lamb and Joseph T. Wigham.

William I. Hull, of Swarthmore, Pa., attended the Meeting for Sufferings, London, on Seventh month 7th. During the discussion regarding the Appeal to the Churches he referred to the motive and hopes behind the Appeal. There was an underlying consciousness that the Peace Movement would never be entirely successful until it was based altogether on Christian principles. He believed that the psychological moment had come for the religious appeal. As a representative of one of the Philadelphia Yearly Meetings, he rejoiced that London Yearly Meeting had endorsed the Appeal.—*The Friend* (London).

The closing week-end at Woolman School saw the usual number present to enjoy the benefit of programs mainly devoted to First-day School work. On Seventh-day evening, William Byron Forbush gave an instructive talk on paintings of Bible scenes and characters and how to best interpret them to the First-day School class.

On First-day, Dr. Russell gave the last of his very illuminating series of Bible lessons on Paul's Epistles, and in the afternoon Bliss Forbush conducted an interesting conference on methods of work for First-day School classes and clubs for boys.

All have felt that the weeks at Woolman School have been most instructive and enjoyable and with regret enter upon the final week of the Summer School. M. R. H.

INDIANA YEARLY MEETING NEWS NOTES

Isaac Wilson, Charles H. Harrison, Grace E. Clevenger, Edith Winder and George H. Nutt have announced their intention of attending Indiana Yearly Meeting. Phebe Seaman, of New York, may also attend.

Humphreys Baynes, of Salem, Ind., and Ruby Davis, of Pendleton, will join Frederick Swain and John Allen as students at George School. Douglass Hoskins, of Indianapolis, is a possible candidate.

The President, Executive Secretary and at least two other members of our Young Friends' Movement are attending the Earlham Conference. One of these, Lillian Wood, is secretary of Fall Creek First-day School.

Among the young Friends from Philadelphia Yearly Meeting now attending the Earlham Conference are Mary Sands and Margaret Henrie, of Millville, Pa. On their return they are to attend the Conference of Religious Bodies Opposed to War to be held at Bluffton College, Bluffton, Ohio, August 4-7. The hope is expressed that Ralph Howell, of Yellow Springs, Ohio, will represent our Yearly Meeting at Bluffton.

CALN QUARTERLY MEETING

At Caln Quarterly Meeting held at Caln, Pa., on Seventh month 27th, Isaac Wilson was present. His message was based on "What I say unto one, I say unto all—Watch."

There are greater doors of opportunity today than ever before and through evidence of faith, truth and righteousness they can be opened. Grow in harmony one with another and the saving and sustaining power acquired, demonstrated through human lives, should help save the world. As a man doeth he is known, and as he thinketh, so is he. Do your own thinking and know yourself.

At the business session the subject of disarmament was discussed and posters distributed. A letter was sent to President Harding asking him to use his efforts that this country continue its work for world peace.

HETTIE E. THOMAS.

WESTERN QUARTERLY MEETING

At the meeting for worship, Daniel Batchellor compared the present form of Christianity to the Christianity in Christ's day, and felt that altho our progress has been slow, we have advanced. Alfred W. Wright urged us to "look up—look out—look forward, and to lend a hand." George A. Walton felt that the kingdom of God is on earth, but will not come into its full power until everyone—man, woman and child—of every denomination and every race does his or her best by exercising all their faculties for the good of humanity. Mary Heald Way offered a beautiful prayer.

At the business session an interesting report from the Young Friends' Movement of Western Quarter was read, and an appropriation of $25 was granted for necessary expenses. In the Philanthropic Committee's report, it was stated that a meeting concerning "Gambling and Lotteries" will be held in September, the time and place to be announced later.

In the afternoon, a lecture on "Quakerism, the Religion of Youth," was given by George A. Walton. A full report of this lecture is given elsewhere in this issue.

EMELIE L. MITCHELL.

THE QUAKER HILL MEETING

The presence of more than two hundred people at the meeting held at Quaker Hill last First-day, the twenty-third, made it one of deep inspiration. All those who found words to express themselves seemed to feel the spell of the glorious view from the hill-top where it is located, and the time-honored history of the plain, shingled building. Joel Borton spoke on the text, "That ye might have life and have it more abundantly." He spoke from a full heart about the joys, the comforts, the pleasures that are at our disposal in the world today; how the auto makes possible such gatherings as that; and how great is our responsibility that our spiritual response be in proportion to these blessings. Alfred Moore was moved to recall the names of several of the Friends who in his memory had occupied those facing seats and broken that same silence with words of power. Both branches were represented. There was no lack of speaking; the messages following in close succession, and a spirit of unity prevailing. Toward the end, a resident expressed his appreciation for the community. He said that the people of the neighborhood looked forward to these meetings and felt that they were a great benefit.

Even the shower of rain which greeted the dispersing company could not spoil the charm of the spot; and every one shook hands with Elizabeth Hallock Post with a feeling of gratitude for her efforts and generous hospitality which had made the occasion possible. G. T. W.

FRIENDS' NEIGHBORHOOD GUILD WORK

The playground at the Friends' Neighborhood Guild, Fourth and Green streets, Philadelphia, opened for the season all day Seventh month 5th. In Sixth month it was was open from 3.30 to 8.30.

The playground has the usual equipment,—swings, sliding boards, etc. The Book Corner in a shady spot is quite an attraction where all sorts of picture books and magazines can be found to amuse the children tired of playing.

Last, but the most important equipment on the playground, is the bathing pool called by the children the "swimmin' hole." It is only a tiny affair twenty feet long by eight feet wide, at its deepest spot two feet, and holding about thirty children.

It is open mornings and afternoons with fresh water in it each time. Thirty at a time they dip,—girls first hour, boys second. There is always a long line waiting for the first thirty to finish and as one comes out another is admitted. When the whistle signals time up for the girls the joyful cheers of the impatient boys can be heard for blocks.

Average attendance: 45 girls and 50 boys in the morning and 60 girls and 50 boys in the afternoon. On one of the hot afternoons 95 girls and 80 boys dipped and splashed.

The playground is open from 9 to 12, 2 to 5 and 7 to 8.30, making long and strenuous hours with our small staff in charge.

The Guild Savings Fund continues to function one evening a week during the summer with approximately 450 depositors and about $900 in bank. Men, women and children of the neighborhood make use of it and the deposits vary from five cents to five dollars.

Come pay us a visit and see how we take care of the children during the summer. H. F. P.

CAMP ONAS

Camp Onas, the camp of the Young Friends' Movement of Philadelphia Yearly Meeting, was held this year from Sixth month 24 to Seventh month 10, on the Schuylkill River between Betzwood and Port Indian. Valley Forge was a little further up the river on the other bank, and we took trips there on foot and in canoes. We also made one trip up the Perkiomen in canoe, and another time we walked over to Seven County View. It was a wonderful view, but unfortunately we had no one with us who could point out all seven counties.

Each day, directly after breakfast, one of the campers would read from Rufus Jones' "The Inner Life," while the rest listened; we each took a turn at this and at leading Discussion Group. Discussion Group came later in the day and everyone took part, two campers being chosen each day to lead the discussion, which was based on Richard La Rue Swain's book, "What and Where is God?"

Every day we did something interesting. Sometimes an all-day canoe trip, sometimes a hike or a short canoe trip in the morning and a swim in the afternoon. In the evening we sat around the campfire, or went up the river in the canoes and then, joining all the canoes together, we drifted down to camp, singing in the moonlight.

Among the visitors to camp were Dr. and Mrs. Henry T. Hodgkin, Mr. and Mrs. Henry Scattergood and Haridas Mazumdar, a friend of Ghandi.

Probably camp's greatest claim to being worth while is the fact that it gives to the campers friends well worth knowing, as well as a pleasant, healthful vacation.

A CAMPER.

Items From Everywhere

There are four mutual savings and loan associations engaged in co-operative banking in Spokane, with 12,000 depositors, and $6,000,000 in savings accounts. The dividend disbursements of July 1 were $135,000 or five per cent. annually.

County agents of California have the rank of assistant professors in the university and are entitled to all the rights and privileges of the resident teaching force. One county agent who has served eight years has been granted sabbatical leave. He will travel in Europe studying rural co-operation.

Many thousands of women and girls in the Near East, held captive during the war, have obtained their liberty and found refuge in Near East Relief homes. Seven of these homes are being operated with 749 inmates, who at the first opportunity are re-established in some form of self-supporting employment. Industrial work of various types suitable for women is conducted in all of these homes.

The International Sunday School Convention held at Kansas City June 21-27 registered the largest attendance ever attained by the organization, there being almost seven thousand registered delegates. The most important action taken by the body was the adoption of a plan for the complete merging of the International Sunday School Association and the Sunday School Council of Evangelical Denominations. The new organization is to be known as the International Sunday School Council of Religious Education. Dr. Hugh S. Magill, who has been Field Secretary of the National Education Association since 1919, was chosen General Secretary. Dr. Magill is a member of the National Disarmament Council.

Taking issue with Samuel Gompers on labor's attitude towards prohibition, John B. Cooper, U. S. Representative, Ohio, for 19 years employed by the Pennsylvania Railroad, and today a member of the Brotherhood of Locomotive Engineers, says: "It is not the working people of our country who are clamoring for the return of the liquor traffic. It is far from the facts when anyone makes the statement that organized labor as a whole favors the return of wine and beer.—I do not challenge the right of Mr. Gompers, or any other leader, to express his own views and sentiments in favor of the repeal of the prohibition laws, but I do challenge the right of anyone to speak for the thousands of law abiding working men and women of our country who joined hands with others and banished this un-American institution from the land." "Ninety-five per cent. of the railroad men would vote dry if prohibition were put up to them," is the declaration of a prominent union official.—*The Evangelical.*

THE OPEN FORUM

This column is intended to afford free expression of opinion by readers on questions of interest. The* Intelligencer *is not responsible for any such opinions. Letters must be brief, and the editor reserves the right to omit parts if necessary to save space.

To the Editor:

When H. P. Husband says: "If a miner wishes to work for $2 a day, which is more than a farmer is able to average, he should be protected in doing so by all the forces of the United States if necessary," she ignores the essential fact in the situation, which is that the miners would then be compelled to take whatever the mine-owners are willing to pay them, even as we at present are also compelled to pay whatever the mine-owners demand for coal.

By this system, which exists with the consent of a majority of the people, because they are misled by the beneficiaries of the system who control press and pulpit and school, the mine-owners accumulate billions of profits and become the imperial government of that phase of industry and finance.

Again, if the farmers average only $2 a day it is because they, with the rest of the dupes (there is no other word) maintain the system by which the controlling business interests set their own prices for everything the farmer buys from them and everything the farmer sells to them; and thus they accumulate billions of profits and inevitably become part of the invisible financial government, back of the visible government at Washington and in the states.

Now, the Intelligencer has long and frequent exhortations for the lion and the lamb to lie down *side by side*, but the testimony of all history shows that the lamb is always *inside* the lion; and human nature does not change.

The incentive of big, possible and legal profits overcome the restraints of religion and altruism in most good people, even as healthy people yield to epidemics and become sick. Remove the cause, in one case as in the other, and most of those who are now so often unjustly reproached will naturally become good citizens.

The private ownership by a decreasing few of the means by which an increasing many make their living is obviously the imperialism which causes all our problems.

The collective ownership and management of these means of making a living, which have become too expensive and too extensive for the individual to own and to operate by himself, is the only means to restore democracy and self-government and to give every individual that mutual interest in, and responsibility for, the affairs of his own maintenance, which are necessary for the development of good citizenship and the higher life.

I have presented all this many times, but the critics neither discuss this nor present any other remedy.

There is a great deal of pious cant in the frequent appeals to think carefully and prayerfully, and then to courageously present our opinions; but that is what the wise and the prudent and the popular do not want and will not discuss.

But there is no hope, except as we break down the conservatism of the *status quo* and get new ideas discussed.

White Plains, N. Y. Jonathan C. Pierce.

To the Editor:

Your correspondent, H. M. H., and I do not disagree at all, except that I used the word "capital" to designate a system. Had "capitalism" been used it would have been better, perhaps, but in our language the popular word really conveys a better idea of the thought. "Capitalism" has come, from common application, to mean something more than the accumulation of wealth, just as "bolsheviki" and "soviet," two innocent words meaning "majority" and "association," have acquired a not very desirable significance. It is human selfishness, human cupidity and human lust of power, to which all injustice is blamable, and it is the misuse of the blessings equally deserved by all that causes the misery and sorrow in the world. And it is our duty to combat this wherever it is found. It is to that end I wrote as I did and I am gratified to find such reaction to my thought as is evidenced by the correspondence that has resulted. M. T. Woodruff.

Dearborn, Mich.

Indiana Yearly Meeting of Friends

Eighth month 12 to 17, 1922

PROGRAM

SEVENTH-DAY, THE 12TH

2.00 p. m.—Meeting of Ministers and Elders. All interested Friends invited to attend.
7.00 p. m.—Executive Committee Meeting.
7.45 p. m.—Advancement Committee Meeting.
8.15 p. m.—Social Gathering—Welcome to Strangers.

FIRST-DAY, THE 13TH

10.00 a. m.—Meeting for Worship.
10.00 a. m.—Story Hour for Children Under Ten.
2.30 p. m.—Address, "God and Immortality," Wilson S. Doan.

SECOND-DAY, THE 14TH

First General Session of the Yearly Meeting

8.30 a. m.—Executive Committee Meeting.
9.30 a. m.—Half Hour Devotional Meeting.
10.00 a. m.—Business Session—Opening Minute, Roll Call of Representatives, Minutes of Visiting Friends, Report of Nominating Committee, Quarterly Meeting Reports, Revising Committee's Report, Miscellaneous Reports, New Business.
2.00 p. m.—Report of Representatives on the Nominations for Clerks, Advancement Committee Report, Report of Committee of Friends' General Conference, Reading of Epistles from Other Yearly Meetings, New Business.
7.30 p. m.—Biblical Play Presented by Young Friends of Waynesville, Ohio.

THIRD-DAY, THE 15TH

9.30 a. m.—Half Hour Devotional Meeting.
10.00 a. m.—Business Session. New Business, Reading of Epistles from Other Yearly Meetings, Philanthropic Committee's Report, Friends' Home Report.
2.00 p. m.—Public Meeting of the Young Friends' Movement. Address by Charles H. Harrison.
7.30 p. m.—Open Meeting Young Friends' Movement. (Program not announced.)

FOURTH-DAY, THE 16TH

10.00 a. m.—Fourth-day Devotional Meeting.
2.00 p. m.—Business Session. First-day School Report, Friends' Service Committee's Report, Queries and General Statement, Report of Committee on the Revision of the Discipline, New Business.
7.30 p. m.—Russian Relief Work—Illustrated. Address by Murray Kenworthy.

FIFTH-DAY, THE 17TH

9.30 a. m.—Half Hour Devotional Meeting.
10.00 a. m.—Business Session. Report of Legislative and George School Committees, Treasurer's Report, Report of Delegates to the 250th Anniversary of Baltimore Yearly Meeting, Minutes of Executive Committee.
2.00 p. m.—Report of Epistolary Committee, Report of Exercise Committee. Adjournment.

J. LINDLEY MENDENHALL, *Clerk*,
Waynesville, Ohio.

Accommodations at the Richmond Conference

The Housing Committee has arranged for accommodations at Richmond, Indiana, during the Conference as follows:

Westcott Hotel.—Can accommodate about 200; two blocks from Meeting-house and one block from the church in which the meetings are to be held. Rooms, without bath, $1.50 to $2.00 per day; with bath, $2.50 for one person, $4.00 and up for two persons in room. Garage will be available within two blocks of hotel. Storage prices, 75 cents for night, $3.00 per week.

Arlington Hotel.—Six blocks from Meeting-house, five from church. Rooms, without bath, $1.50 for one person, $2.50 for two persons in room; with bath, $2.50 to $3.00 for one person, $3.50 to $4.50 for two persons.

Both hotels European plan. There are restaurants and dining-rooms in connection with both hotels.

Boarding Houses.—Not far from Meeting-house, $10 to $14 per week for room and board. Rooms without board, $3 to $8 per week; meals there are $7 per week. There is an apartment house in same block as Meeting-house. The entire third floor will be available at that time; about 20 rooms. Rate, $5 per week for one in a room, or $8 per week, two in a room. These rooms are small.

Meals.—There will be cafeteria meals served in basement of Meeting-house all the time. The price will be from 30 cents to 40 cents with cafeteria service.

Tents.—Accommodations for about 100 young people in tents on Meeting-house grounds. We do not know definitely about the charge, but it will probably be from $4 to $5 per person for the week.

Rooms.—In private houses available, at less than regular boarding houses.

Applications may be addressed to

Dorothy E. Dilks, 46 Thirteenth street, Richmond, Ind.
J. Barnard Walton, 140 N. Fifteenth St., Philadelphia, Pa.
Or to members of the Housing Committee:
James H. Atkinson, 421 Chestnut street, Philadelphia.
Harry A. Hawkins, 57 Pierrepont avenue, W., Rutherford, N. J.
William C. Coles, Moorestown, N. J.
J. Bernard Hilliard, Salem, N. J.
Esther Holmes, Riverton, N. J.
Eliza M. Ambler, Plymouth Meeting, Pa.

BIRTHS

FLITCRAFT—On Seventh month 13th, at Woodstown, N. J., to H. Milton and Edna Crispen Flitcraft, a son, who is named Howard Crispen Flitcraft.

MARRIAGES

RAMEY—MOORE—At the home of the bride's parents, Plainfield, Sandy Spring, Maryland, on Seventh month 20th, Howard Knox Ramey and Martha Ellicott Moore.

DEATHS

BOSTON—At her home in Pendleton, Indiana, on Seventh month 26th, Eliza A. Boston, aged 78 years. She was an active member of Fall Creek Monthly Meeting of Friends.

LUKENS—In Germantown, Pa., on Seventh month 30th, George W. Lukens.

WORTHINGTON—At Hulmeville, Pa., on Seventh

month 30th, Amy, widow of Benjamin M. Worthington. Interment at Somerton, Pa.

HANNAH MARY GOOD.

Suddenly, on Seventh month 8th, the spirit of Hannah Mary Good passed into the higher life, in the 70th year of her age, after an illness of several months. She was the daughter of the late Samuel and Rachel B. Gatchell and was a birthright member of Little Britain Monthly Meeting. In 1877 she married Lewis Good, son of Jesse and Amanda Good, of West Grove, Pa. This very happy union was blest with one son, Raymond S., who survives with his wife and four grandchildren. Her husband's early death was a sad bereavement to her, but she took up the burden of life and gave the best of herself for others. Her nearly 45 years of widowhood were years of service. She taught many years in the public schools of Lancaster County and as her mother grew feeble with age, she cared for her devotedly.

Not only her own family mourn her loss, but also those who have known her and lived closely to her through life are better, see life through nature in a different way. She was interested in the birds, the plants, flowers and even in the weeds she saw much to enjoy.

Everything to her had beauty,
Flowers that fade and leaves that fall;
She would spare the meanest insect,
Saying, "One Creator made us all."

After beautiful and impressive words by Howard Coates, Alice M. Coates and Caroline J. Worth, she was laid to rest in Penn Hill graveyard, where lay in peaceful sleep those of her family gone before. H. W.

COMING EVENTS

EIGHTH MONTH

3rd—7.30 p. m., Conference, and Meeting for Worship, on the campus of Columbia University, under care of Friends attending Summer School. Topic of Conference, "Quakerism and Peace," led by Mark Balderston.

5th—Philadelphia Quarterly Meeting, at Merion, Pa.

6th—Purchase Quarterly Meeting, at Purchase, N. Y. Train leaves the Grand Central Station, New York City, at 9.08 a. m., Daylight Saving Time (8.08 E. S.).

6th—First-day, 2.30 p. m., Eastern Standard time. An appointed meeting for divine worship will be held at the Friends' Meeting-house, Newtown Square, Delaware County, Pa., under care of a Committee of Concord Quarter. For young and old, for conservative and liberal; non-sectarians especially invited. Easily reached by trolley from 69th Street station or by pilgrimage.

6th—Conference under care of Yearly Meeting's First-day School Committee at Wrightstown, Pa., 2.30 p. m., Standard time (3.30 daylight saving). Subject, "The Meeting and the First-day School in Co-operation." Box lunch at 1 o'clock.

6th—William J. and Hannah L. MacWatters expect to visit Mt. Holly, N. J., meeting, at 11 a. m. (daylight saving time), and Springfield in the afternoon.

7th—Genesee Yearly Meeting, at Coldstream, Ont.

7th—Miami Quarterly Meeting, at Green Plain, Ohio.

10th—Abington Quarterly Meeting, at Gwynedd, Pa., at 10.30 (daylight saving time). Meeting of Ministry and Counsel, same day, at 9 a. m.

10th—7.30 p. m., Conference, and Meeting for Worship, on the campus of Columbia University, under care of Friends attending Summer School. Topic of Conference, "Quakerism and Adventure," led by Carolena Wood.

12th—Blue River Quarterly Meeting, at Benjaminville, Ill.

12th—Picnic on the Palisades, given by New York Friends to Quaker students at Columbia University Summer School. All Friends are invited. Fuller notice later.

13th—Certain members of Philadelphia Quarterly Meeting's Visiting Committee will visit Germantown Friends' Home, at 7.30 p. m.

14th—Indiana Yearly Meeting, at Waynesville, Ohio. Program on another page.

14th—New York Monthly Meeting, at 7.30 p. m., at 110 Schermerhorn street, Brooklyn. Supper will be served at 6 o'clock.

19th—Short Creek Quarterly Meeting, at Emerson, Ohio.

19th—Pelham Half-Yearly Meeting, at Sparta, Ontario.

NOTICE—A religious meeting under care of Committee of Burlington Quarterly Meeting, will be held at "Old Springfield" Meeting-house, near Jacksonville, N. J., on First-day, Eighth month 6th, at 3 o'clock, Daylight Saving Time. All are cordially invited.

NOTICE—Students who are Friends, attending the University of Chicago, may find rooms in Friends' families by addressing the Housing Bureau, stating their desire.

NOTICE—There is available ten shares of stock in Friends' Student Hostel, $10 each. It is the desire to keep a wide-spread interest in this undertaking of conducting a house in a Friendly spirit at Pennsylvania State College. Purchasers of the stock will therefore be welcome in quantities of one or more shares. Address J. Barnard Walton, Secretary-Treasurer, 140 N. Fifteenth street, Philadelphia, Pa.

American Friends' Service Committee

WILBUR K. THOMAS, EX. SEC.
20 S. 12th St. Philadelphia.

CASH CONTRIBUTIONS
WEEK ENDING JULY 24TH

Five Years Meeting	$112.60
Other Meetings:	
Fifteenth and Race Streets Meeting	200.00
Contributions for Germany	208.47
For Poland	109.55
For Austria	250.25
For Russia	9,990.60
For West Virginia	250.27
For Central Pennsylvania	647.78
For General	53.54
Miscellaneous Sources for General	9.18
For Syria	10.00
Refunds and payments	5.38
	$11,847.62

Contributions received during week ending July 22nd: 27 boxes and packages received.

WANTED

RIVER CROFT, CLAYMONT, DEL. Special home care for invalids, or rest and physical upbuilding. Booklet on application. E. H. Speakman.

WANTED—A FRIEND TO TEACH Buckingham Friends' School at Lahaska, Pa. 15 pupils—grades 1-8. Apply to Mary A. Watson, 277 Maple Ave., Doylestown, Pa.

SEPTEMBER 1ST, BUSINESS WOMan, Friend, wants unfurnished room and board, in walking distance of Wayne Junction; state terms. Box P. 302, Friends' Intelligencer.

WANTED—POSITION TO TAKE charge of a home for family away for the summer or any position of trust. Best reference. Moderate salary. Address G. 303, Friends' Intelligencer.

REFINED, EDUCATED, TRUSTworthy German girl (speaks English), wishes situation. Experienced with children, sewing, chamber work. Reference. $10.00 per week. Address Mrs. Joseph Steinmetz, 736 Westview St., Germantown, Pa. Germantown 2035.

WANTED—COMPANION OR PRACtical nurse for elderly lady. Address L. 304, Friends' Intelligencer.

FOR RENT

FOR RENT—AT OCEAN CITY, N. J.—Attractive furnished rooms; ocean view; fine location near Boardwalk. Address Laura H. Brosius, 820 Sixth St.

FUN

The golfing novice, after disturbing much turf, turned for reassurance to his caddie and said, "I have a brother in Australia who plays this game awfully well." "Well, carry on, sir," was the dry reply, "you'll soon dig him up."—*London Post.*

A little girl in Southern California was having her first glimpse of snow in the recent phenomenal blizzard near Los Angeles. "Oh, mother, what is it—what is it?" she shouted excitedly. "Why, that is *snow*, Peggy. Whatever did you think it was?" "Snow? Why, it looks like *popped rain!*"—*Life.*

Thomas A. Edison is not much given to humor—he is far too busy for that—but he has one pet yarn that he is never tired of repeating.

A man from the country one day came to town and put up at a first-class hotel. He went to the office and asked the clerk what were the times of the meals.

"Breakfast, seven to eleven," answered the clerk; "lunch, eleven to three; tea, three to six; dinner, six to eight; and supper, eight to twelve."

"What!" shouted the astonished visitor. "When am I going to get time to see the town?"—*Congregationalist.*

To the Lot Holders and others interested in Fairhill Burial Ground:

GREEN STREET Monthly Meeting has funds available for the encouragement of the practice of cremating the dead to be interred in Fairhill Burial Ground. We wish to bring this fact as prominently as possible to those who may be interested. We are prepared to undertake the expense of cremation in case any lot holder desires us to do so.

Those interested should communicate with William H. Gaskill, Treasurer of the Committee of Interments, Green Street Monthly Meeting, or any of the following members of the Committee.

William H. Gaskill, 3201 Arch St.
Samuel N. Longstreth, 1218 Chestnut St.
Charles F. Jenkins, 232 South Seventh St.
Stuart S. Graves, 3033 Germantown Ave.

Please help us by patronizing our advertisers. Mention the "Friends' Intelligencer."

The Friends' Intelligencer

ESTABLISHED 1844 | EIGHTH MONTH 12, 1922 | VOLUME 79 NUMBER 32

Contents

THE FRIENDS' INTELLIGENCER

Published weekly, 140 N. 15th Street. Philadelphia, Pa., by Friends' Intelligencer Association, Ltd.

PAUL W. WAGER, *Editor.*
SUE C. YERKES, *Business Manager*

Editorial Board: Elizabeth Powell Bond, Thomas A. Jenkins, J. Russell Smith, George A. Walton.

Board of Managers: Edward Cornell, Alice Hall Paxson, Paul M. Pearson, Annie Hillborn, Elwood Hollingshead, William C. Biddle, Charles F. Jenkins, Edith M. Winder, Frances M. White.

Officers of Intelligencer Associates: Ellwood Burdsall, Chairman; Bertha L. Broomell, Secretary; Herbert P. Worth, Treasurer.

Subscription rates: United States, Mexico, Cuba and Panama, $2.50 per year. Canada and other foreign countries, $3.00 per year. Checks should be made payable to Friends' Intelligencer Association, Ltd.

Entered as Second Class Matter at Philadelphia Post Office

REGULAR MEETINGS

OAKLAND, CALIF. — A FRIENDS' Meeting is held every First-day at 11 A. M., in the Extension Room, Y. W. C. A. Building, Webster Street, above 14th. Visiting Friends always welcome.

PASADENA, CALIFORNIA — Orange Grove Monthly Meeting of Friends, 520 East Orange Grove Avenue. Meeting for worship, First-day, 11 A. M. Monthly Meeting, the second First-day of each month, at 1.45 P. M. First-day School (except Monthly Meeting days) 9.45 A. M.

FUN

Our idea of dangerous occupations is the attempt of some newspapers to select the twelve greatest women in America.—*Asheville Times.*

Life will never be comfortable for the pedestrian until he invents some kind of disguise that will make him resemble a tack.—*St. Joseph News-Press.*

Professor's wife.—"I suppose you have forgotten that this is the anniversary of your wedding day?"

Absent-minded husband (abstracting himself from conic sections)—"Eh, what? Dear me! Is it really? And when is yours, my dear?"—*Boston Transcript.*

The Friends' Intelligencer

The religion of Friends is based on faith in the "INWARD LIGHT," or direct revelation of God's spirit and will in every seeking soul.

The INTELLIGENCER is interested in all who bear the name of Friends in every part of the world, and aims to promote love, unity and intercourse among all branches and with all religious societies.

ESTABLISHED 1844 — PHILADELPHIA, EIGHTH MONTH 12, 1922 — VOLUME 79 NUMBER 32

Those who learn to love their enemies soon discover that they have no enemies.

⌘

A very good index to a man's character is the way he spends his leisure time.

⌘

Do you ever find yourself secretly exulting in another's misfortune? If so, it would be well to pray to God for a sweeter spirit.

⌘

It is poor policy to join more societies or movements than one can actively support. It is better to be a live member of one organization than dead wood in several.

⌘

Many of our exchanges are very much alarmed as a result of the students' movement against Christianity in China. They see in it a revolt against God and the restraints of religion. They foresee the work of the missionaries brought to naught, the Christian church overthrown and the salvation of China indefinitely delayed or perhaps rendered impossible.

Various explanations for this reaction against Christianity are offered. Some attribute it to the teaching of agnostic and atheistic professors in the Chinese schools. Others think they see in it the hand of Bolshevism.

While the situation is undoubtedly grave and to be regretted, we cannot agree with these others as to the causes of the movement, nor share their apprehension as to its dire results. We do not believe that it is the principles of Christianity that the Chinese are rejecting but the practices of Christianity. They see the Christian Church powerless to prevent the great war, and only feebly remonstrating against it. They see the inequalities, the exploitation, the class conflicts within the membership of the church. They see the many evils of our western civilization and they decide that if they are the products of Christianity, they don't want that religion.

Fred B. Smith, a well-known Y. M. C. A. leader, who has just spent eight months in the Far East says, "The organized 'Non-Christian Society' of China is only a symptom of what is found in varied forms in Japan, India and Egypt. Their leaders are saying Christianity is a western religion and ought to stay in the Occident. It does not fit the Orient or the Oriental.

"I venture to say," he continues, "that Christianity never will be a universal religion if its leaders persist in trying to persuade the Far East to adopt the western mannerisms of ecclesiastical nomenclature, dress, hymns, prayers and sermons.

"I venture to say that Christianity will never be universal so long as the attempt is continued to make denominationalism a part of the Foreign Missionary plan.

"I venture to say that universality will not be realized till western Christianity has rid itself of its war traditions and its historical war theology.

"I venture to say that the world-extended dream of Christian hope will never come till western Christianity accepts a better definition of Christ than the one most commonly held now. Nations called Christian whose people are rampant with desire for material greed and sensual display are poor advertisements for the religion the missionaries are asking the Orientals to adopt. If the Sermon on the Mount were a real thing to the western church members the question of this faith eventually becoming world-wide would not be mooted."

To the Chinese Christianity has ceased to signify righteousness and purity. It has become rather a symbol for greed and strife and hypocrisy. In our opinion the Non-Christian Movement is really nothing immoral or irreligious but a new Protestantism. It is not directed at Christianity in its pristine purity but at Christianity in its corrupted form. It is not directed at the Christian church but at the iniquities of the Christian church. It may result not only in saving China for Christ but the western world also.

First and Third Beatitudes

Amidst the clash and clamor of the world as it is today, where "the man who fights is the man who wins" let us settle down to think for a few moments of the first and third beatitudes; Blessed, or I will put it *happy,* are the poor in spirit, and *happy* are the meek.

We find these the opening sentences to the most powerful sermon ever preached, "The Sermon on the Mount." The whole discourse translated into human activities would destroy all war, feed all hungry children, clothe all people, settle all disputes, and "the crooked would be made straight and the rough ways smooth." This sermon lived out in our lives, would usher in the Kingdom of God, which Jesus established, and which people have been so slow to recognize or to develop.

You know the time and place—Jesus sitting on the mountain side, His followers eagerly waiting for His words of help, and cheer, and wisdom, and by the largeness of His discourse, we know how responsive was His heart to their need.

He opened His mouth and taught them, First by telling them who were the blest or the happy people.

Happiness is what they were seeking; it is what we are all seeking. From his discourse they learned that happiness is an attitude of mind. It is not what we possess outside ourselves, nor what we hope to have in the future, nor the state of mind we will attain in the future that makes us happy, but our present attitude here and now. Jesus had been living the ordinary life of a village carpenter, but that did not prevent Him from learning from all the varied experiences that came to Him, the inner-hidden truths of things. So, he says, are the poor in spirit.

The whole statement is negative. The word *poor* signifies a lack. Commonly speaking the poor man lacks money. A poor workman lacks ability. Here it is a spiritual quality that is lacking. Obviously it is one of the lower qualities Jesus meant and I am going to name it "the aggressive spirit." The dictionary tells us an aggressive person is one who leads an attack, begins a quarrel, oppresses, or gives pain. Jesus says if you lack this aggressive spirit you are happy. His words on this occasion were of comfort and cheer rather than admonition. You, who are poor in spirit, are happy if you only knew it. You have no high worldly ambitions to overcome. You have no haughty spirit to subdue. You have no unjust gains on your hands to worry you. You are not troubled by feelings of envy, jealousy, or self-vanity, but you are peaceable, gentle, easy to be entreated, and, under my guidance, you may become full of mercy and good works, without hypocrisy and without partiality.

James says "hath not God chosen the poor of this world rich in faith." The aggressive man heaps to himself this world's goods and has no faith in anything except himself. The things that God would give him are foolishness to him.

The quiet, receptive mind has all the qualities to develop the Kingdom of God here and now and hence Jesus says: Happy are the poor in spirit for theirs is the Kingdom of heaven." Why are we so slow to learn the true value of things? Worldly fame, riches,—these are not the things that will teach us to be meek and lowly in heart. The best things follow love out of a pure heart.

Let us hear what the prophet says: "Thus saith the Lord your God, Remove the diadem, take off the crown, this shall not be the same, exalt him that is low and abase him that is high; I will overturn, overturn, overturn it and it shall be no more." Is not that what is being done all down through the ages down to these present times? Are not worldly human affairs being overturned and overturned, till at last the people will of necessity learn the truth, that the life is more than meat, and the body more than raiment? The first thing to seek is the Kingdom of God and his righteousness, which means right living, and it is only by right living that we can learn the truth, that blessed are the meek and lowly in heart. When we have learned this, then will the fruits of the spirit be enjoyed by all, namely, love, joy, peace, long suffering, gentleness, goodness, faith, meekness, temperance. It is then we will perhaps begin to realize something of what Jesus meant, when he spoke of the greater things that we should do.

These greater things can only be appreciated and worked out by those who are meek and lowly of heart, and for such there is great need today. Some of these greater things are the establishment of peace on the earth, the recognition of the qualities of a man's mind rather than the fatness of his pocketbook, the ready, outward expression of that heart of sympathy that all true followers of Jesus must have, and the giving of ourselves to a life of service. For Jesus came not to be ministered unto but to minister to others. NANIE WEBSTER.

Read at Pelham Half-Yearly Meeting.

He that loveth God keepeth His commandments, but still the love of God is something more than keeping the commandments.—*Paley.*

To All Young Friends Everywhere

The Thirteenth Annual Conference of the American Young Friends brought together over two hundred delegates. Differing consciously in traditions and customs, we yet found that here our separate lives united in the life of God. It is our earnest desire to express to you who could not share with us this rich experience, the purpose with which we came and—the harder thing—to express the result of this fellowship together.

Our conditions had in them elements of difference according to our several past experiences, but a vision of a united purpose seems to us to have been no less evident. In so far as we can interpret it, this vision was of reaching a spiritual plane a little higher than the one on which we stood before the conference met. We had in us what we called "The Amateur Spirit," that sincere constructive effort to seek the spirit through actual experience.

To you who are also of this spirit we look for sympathetic understanding. You will know what earnestness of purpose and fullness of love this spirit creates and calls forth. You will realize how we could dare to search for fundamental truths and how in this search we could be bravely frank together. It was with this spirit of consecrated purpose and loving reverence for the feelings and opinions of each other that we entered into the adventure of a wider spiritual life. Unknown sea-paths of knowledge and experience lay before us and we gave ourselves to their discovery with Columbus courage.

A letter from Rufus Jones to the Conference called us to this task: "If there is to be any great Quakerism in the future it will be because these who are now at the Conference learn to go down into the deeps of life with Christ and because they rise with kindled personalities to tackle the practical tasks of the world."

A sense of individual responsibility was felt by every one of us who made the high resolve to accomplish this thing. We earnestly believed that each one of us must find God for himself and feel the unity of his life with the life of God. Therefore it seemed necessary to us that we have a fresh experience here of the presence and character of Christ. Our work and play and particularly the meeting for worship at eventide gave to us unlimited opportunity for this experience. We strove for clear-sighted truth along the way and believed that God would guide us.

The practical contact between young Friends of East and West made such a quest possible. As we grew to know each other by sharing simply and generously the life of the spirit we found that our problems were met and were at least partially solved. This is, we feel, the true test of fellowship. We dared go forward in sincere comradeship with God and with each other toward the goal we were so earnestly seeking.

In Paul's own words, we count not ourselves to have apprehended. But this one thing we did—forgetting the things which were past, and pressing forward to that which lay before us with our eyes fixed on Him who is eternal love and truth, we pushed on to secure the prize of God's heavenward call in Christ Jesus.

To seek Him is to know Him and to love Him, and through service as an integral and normal part of our lives we hope to apprehend further. This conference has called us to two aims: One is to deepen our spiritual experience and the other is to serve. Thus we know we shall find Him.

In the quiet adventure of this search, let us continue together. Let us break down the barriers that separate man's God from man. And may the part of this work that falls to each one of us be laid hold of with joy and earnestness. Great opportunities await us at home and abroad, challenging Christians who do things for love of God and not for love of self. We shall find neither happiness nor God by any easier way than this. And so with humility of mind and bravery of heart we shall press on and on, searching the mist for lands still unknown, but which hold for us the joy of discovery. May God keep us close together in this search.

Freedom

I covet not the sordid power of gold.
The city's grinding roar holds ne'er a charm,
For hov'ring o'er the cursing, seething mob
I see the god of Greed, whose grasping arm

Above the whirring wheels of countless mills,
Half hidden mid its tangled web of guile,
With selfish, ruthless spirit rules men's hearts
And turns their souls from God, and things worth while.

I long to flee to peaks whose heav'n borne slopes
Pierce through the drifting fleece that hides their crests;
Where clear, cool streams glide idly past green vales,
And shelt'ring oaks bid song birds build their nests.

I'd wander mid wild blossoms where they bloom
Unhindered, and I'd view the sunsets rare
From lonely crags. Oh, there I'd happy be
To feel God's love about me ev'rywhere.

P. M. F.

The Cantonese and the Political Mix-up In China

By Wm. W. Cadbury

A British Admiral declared before the Washington Conference met that "there is only one problem and it is the problem of the coming conflict between the two halves of the human race, the white and the colored; it will be in the Pacific. In this conflict Asia could draw upon 1000 millions of the colored races as against some 500 millions of the white people."

"Undoubtedly, the scene has shifted from Europe to the far east and the Pacific. The problems of the Pacific are, to my mind, the world problems for the next fifty years or more" are the words of General Smutz, and John Hay declared years ago that: "China is the key to the future of the world."

The truth of these statements is evident to all who have followed the proceedings of the recent conference in Washington.

If, then, the Chinese, numbering one-fourth of the population of the globe are to be such an important factor in the history of the world, it behooves us to consider for a moment the forces at work in this great nation.

The Empire itself covers an area one-sixth larger than that of the Continental possessions of the United States and the population is more than three times that of our own country.

The history of China begins in the third millenium before Christ, but with the reign of the Emperor Yu in the Ha dynasty in 2205, there is a transition from the legendary to the historical period.

But to Europe China was almost unknown until Marco Polo made his remarkable journeys to the Court of Kublai Khan in the 13th Century and from that time on China became of ever greater importance in the eyes of the West. It should be recalled that Columbus was endeavoring to find his way to China when he accidentally hit on the shores of America.

The history of the nation is full of romance,—one great dynasty follows another until in 1911 the Emperor abdicated and the Republic was declared. Sun Yat Sen, the first President, and the leaders in this revolution were Cantonese and from this time on the influence of Canton has been of growing importance in the counsels of the nation.

Who are these Cantonese? They are the inhabitants of the Province of Kwangtung, in the Southeastern corner of the Empire. This province is the richest in China. It is watered by three large rivers, the East, the West and the North, converging at the capital city of Canton and forming there a great delta with its fertile plains.

The population of this province is estimated at 32,000,000 or about 320 persons to the square mile.

These people are shorter of stature than their brothers north of the Yangtze. In a recent study I found that the people of Kwangtung province average only 5 feet 4 inches in height, while the Chinese north of the Yangtze average 5 feet 6 inches, or more.

Ages ago the ancestors of the Cantonese came as conquerors to South China. They drove the Aborigines before them and became the dominant race. These Aborigines, known as the Miaotze, are still to be found in the mountains where they lead a more or less independent existence.

Later, another people came from the North, chiefly from Fukien Province, and these were known as the Hakkas. They also were an inferior race, and were allowed to remain, but as subjects to the dominant Cantonese people.

The superiority over these two tribes may have much to do with the fact that the Cantonese are such a proud and progressive people.

Before the 10th Century there were settlements of these Chinese on the Coast of Africa and from the two districts, San Ning and San Wui of this province come 90 per cent. of all the Chinese who have emigrated to Canada, the United States, Mexico, the West Indies and South America.

It is chiefly the Cantonese who constitute the important Chinese element in the population of Australia, New Zealand, the East Indies and the Malay Peninsula. They are to be found in Africa and Honolulu.

It is estimated that more than 9,000,000 Chinese live outside the limits of the Empire and almost all of them are Cantonese from Kwangtung.

Wherever they have gone they have proved themselves an industrious, peaceable folk, attending to their own business.

Shanghai, which is rapidly becoming the greatest foreign settlement in China, owes its present commercial importance to the Cantonese merchants there, and its trade is but an expansion of that which started in Canton.

In the Philippine Islands there are some 70 or 80 thousand Chinese, all from South China—Canton and Amoy. According to Walter Robb, in "Asia," among the 10,000,000 Filipinos this handful of Chinese carry on 80 per cent. of the commerce and industry of the Islands. There are 3000 Chinese firms in Manila and 7000 in the provinces.

In Malaysia it is said that 90 per cent. of the mines and estates are in the hands of Chinese from the south of China.

Canton was the first city of China opened to trade with the West. The modern department stores which have grown up in the last two decades, in Hongkong, Shanghai and Canton, are entirely financed and managed by Cantonese merchants. These are known as The Taai San, Chan Kwong and Wing On, Companies.

Canton was the first city of China to tear down her ancient walls and build in their places broad thoroughfares through which automobiles now travel.

It was here that the first hospital was established by Peter Parker in 1835 and the first Protestant Christian was baptized.

One of the remarkable features associated with the initiative and progressiveness of the Cantonese, lies in the fact of their living in a sub-tropical country. No evidence exists of that languor which so often appears among tropical peoples. The Cantonese dialect itself attests to this fact, for final consonants are clearly pronounced and not dropped from the speech, as is the case in Shanghai and generally in tropical countries.

In the South Sea Isles where the white man grows indolent and sickly under the effects of the tropical sun, and the natives live a hand-to-mouth existence, the thrifty and hardy Cantonese settles down, raises a family and carries on the banking and business of the community.

It is needless to recount the long struggle that has been going forward since that day. When one considers the forces at work there is no wonder that a settlement has not yet been attained. As Alfred Sze, Chinese Minister at Washington, recently declared: "China is making the change from a social democracy, which has existed for ages, to a political democracy." It signifies the merging of the ideas of the west with those of old China.

Patriotism in China is not jingoism but a love of one's own people, without hatred of others, declared Admiral Tsai, so the present conflict is not inspired by an intense hatred between leaders of the north and south, but, unlike the American war of the Rebellion, we have in China now a truly "civil" war going on.

It is of interest to note that of 95 delegates to the Washington Conference who came over with Admiral Tsai, 74 were from the Southern Provinces, although appointed by the Peking Government.

Let us not forget that it required six years to prepare the American Constitution, when the population of the United States was but 2½ millions. Sixty years later the question of state rights was still unsettled. China is dealing with a country of 400,000,000 people, 95 per cent. of whom are uneducated.

(To be concluded next week)

A Day in Sussex

One approaches writing of William Penn with a little of the feeling you have when walking across lots with signs "Keep Off the Grass" staring you in the face. Everyone knows that Albert Cook Myers has all of Penn in his keeping and it seems unfair to trespass. However, Albert may tell, when he will, why Penn settled in Sussex, what he did there and why he gave it up, here will be told the simple record of one never-to-be-forgotten day in the Weald of Sussex in the midst of which is Worminghurst.

Wherever you travel through rural England you say "well here is the best." So it was in Derbyshire, in Shakespeare land, in the Lakes, along the Roman wall, through Devonshire and Cornwall and now Sussex claims its own. It is a region of hills and trees, of broad views, quaint towns, hidden villages and nowhere more of interest to the antiquarian and historian. Lying between London and the Channel, across from France, it has witnessed the inroads of Saxons, Danes and Normans and many important chapters in England's history were enacted here.

Roughly it consists of the South downs, mainly treeless, chalk hills along and back from the shore, the rolling hilly land back of these South downs extending to the North downs called the Weald, and the low marsh lands along the channel. Kipling has described the feeling you have about it exactly:

"I'm just in love with all these three;
The Weald and the Marsh and the Down countrie:
And I don't know which I love the most;
The Weald, the Marsh or the White Chalk Coast."

We had slept at a clean, little inn at Battle, the hill where Harold and his Saxons gave way before the trick of William the Conqueror. Battle Abbey, which William built over the exact spot of his victory, in fulfillment of a vow, was closed to visitors, but we walked the two miles around the park and stood on the hill where the Normans stood. Perhaps no spot in England has more significance than this so-called battlefield of Hastings which is eight miles from the town of that name. It was one of the turning points in the history of our race.

Returning from our walk we found a flat, characteristic stone for the historic walk in Germantown picked up within two hundred yards of where Harold fell.

Eight miles from Battle, through back roads with many turns and lanes lined with hawthorn bloom brought us to Hurstmonceaux, the land of Augustus Hare, the author of "The Gurneys of Earlham" and his "Memorials of a Quiet Life," its pages filled with the rural beauty of Sussex.

Then down to the coast three or four miles to Pevensey, now by the silting of the sands way back from the sea, where William landed. It has a great Roman wall and a well where the salt water used to rise and fall with the tide. Readers of Kipling will remember how Sir Richard Dalyngirdge hid his gold in the bottom of this well and how the Jew found it and rowing out into the Channel buried it beneath the waves. Inside the deserted castle walls, seated on the grass in the sunlight, an old man was playing his violin to himself, a typical picture of age and contentment.

From Pevensey we journeyed on to Lewes, through Wilmington (Dover was not far away), names which show from whence came some of the early settlers of little Delaware. At Lewes we break through the South Downs. A few miles beyond at Plumpton a giant "V" of fir trees was planted in a fold of the steep north slope of the down to commemorate Victoria's jubilee. Soon another great landmark came in view—the Chanctonbury Ring. It was a prehistoric circular fortification in the stone age and later used by the Romans and Saxons. The circle is now filled with fir and other trees, making it look like some vernal castle while everywhere else on the down there is nothing but grass. The Ring is visible from almost every part of Sussex.

It was probably eighteen miles from Lewes as an English crow would fly, through back country roads with many turns and constant exclamations of pleasure that we came to the little church at Worminghurst. It contains a remarkable brass to Edward Shelley, his wife and nine children with the date 1554. And this reminds me that the poet Shelley was born in Sussex at Warnham two miles north of Horsham, and his admirers are planning this summer to commemorate the one hundredth anniversary of his death.

Almost facing the Worminghurst church is the lane which leads into William Penn's Sussex home. It was here he lived from 1672 to 1702, dates which covered both his visits to Pennsylvania. The farm of some two hundred acres belongs to the Duke of Norfolk, England's great Catholic nobleman, but it is now leased to a Friend named Robinson who lives down Lewes way.

But little if anything remains of the house in which Penn lived. Mrs. Lillywhite, the shepherd's wife, said the tradition was that the present kitchen with its two-foot thick walls was part of the old house. A part of the barn is thought to have been there in Penn's time and we climbed through the chaff bin to see the rooms where the grooms had their sleeping quarters with great open fire places. The old garden wall is also thought to be contemporaneous with Penn. Across the Weald Chanctonbury Ring stood out a conspicuous landmark. A few miles away to the south is Steyning with a meeting-house said to have been built from the timbers of the Welcome, and five miles to the northwest is the Blue Idle meeting-house, surely one of the quaintest as well as the oldest in England.

We imagined we were following the road and making the turns that Penn on horseback and his family in the lumbering carriage, took on First-day morning, through Thakeham and Coolham to the old Blue Idle meeting-house. Why this should be so called there seems no very good explanation except that it was originally painted blue and was idle for many years. The larks were singing as we passed along. Surely rural England should be blessed with this canopy of song which covers her.

Two miles beyond the Blue Idle is the little town of Billinghurst the ancestral parish of the Buckmans who came to Pennsylvania with their friend and neighbor Penn in the Welcome and who are the ancestors or connections of nearly every Friend in Bucks County. There are still some of the name remaining in the neighborhood. About one-third of all the passengers in the Welcome came from Sussex.

The climb over the South down by Arundel Castle, placed there to guard the pass through the hills, the coming down into Chichester with its interesting cathedral and market cross and the ride along the channel toward Southampton soon carried us out of Sussex over into Hampshire, which next day we were again ready to vote was "the best yet," but our day in Sussex will be a never forgotten one.

Lyndhurst, May 30, 1922. C. F. J.

Parenthood and Child Nurture

Edna Dean Baker. Macmillan Co., $1.50.

It is always a comfort to find the completed product to conform to the prospectus. This book is a good example for I find the Editor's introduction a really excellent review of the book. It says:

"It's scope includes the physical, mental, social and spiritual life of the child from birth to twelve years of age. It contains unusually helpful suggestions regarding songs, games, stories and other material suitable for the child. The collateral reading recommended would enable any parent or parent training class to build up a library on the training of children."

It had not occurred to me before how suitable such studies and discussion would be for adult First-day School work, but since reading this, I want to recommend it as a suggestive basis for study. The whole attitude of the author is sane and wholesome. The bibliography seems complete and would be very helpful. LUCY G. MORGAN.

The Withdrawal of the Friends from Serbia

It is with regret that we report the withdrawal of the Friends from Serbia after three years of service. In April, 1922, Dr. Charles L. Outland turned the picturesque hospital at Petch over to the Serbian authorities. It was felt that the need for emergency relief was over and that the responsibility for future work should be carried by the Serbian government. The service rendered has tended to bring Montenegrins, Serbians, Albanians and Turks closer together; and though we have not done much towards solving the Balkan problem we have been able in one city to bring all factions together in a bit of humanitarian work. The following paragraphs are extracts from Dr. Outland's report:

"In looking back over our years' work and the eighteen months Dr. Russell spent in Serbia, we can not fail to see the amount of real good accomplished. The poor and unfortunate were never turned away and our aim was to try to stimulate in the people a wholesome regard for medical services. So many of them had never known what it was. We often had patients sixty and seventy years old, and several at the age of eighty and ninety, who had never seen a doctor in their lives.

"Diseases consisted of the usual kind seen in America, with some typhus and other Eastern diseases. A lot of malaria was noted which responded very readily to treatment.

"The nurses (all English) gave us their co-operation and seemed to throw themselves wholeheartedly into the work. The Serbian help was as a rule very good.

"It might be interesting to know that we also had a fair number of Turkish women in the hospital most of the time. Their custom of remaining veiled in a man's presence was respected; some of them, however, did not adhere strictly to this custom.

"No history of the hospital would be complete without mention of the clinics, five of which were held each week. Here we got all kinds, from those who thought themselves sick to those who were really quite ill. Cases which could have been treated at home were often taken into the hospital for the reason that they could be taught the value of cleanliness, preparation of food, etc., in order that they might be better prepared to care for ill members of their family, and others.

"We sincerely hope that the work will be carried on. Ample supplies for several years were left in the hospital.

"We mention with pleasure the land settlers and how appreciative most of them are of their little cottages. This is evidenced by the improvements being made on them, the planning of yards and gardens. Many of the owners have added several rooms to the cottage and built large barns. Each settler has goats, pigs, chickens, ducks, cows and oxen. A school has been opened in the village nearest Petch (Vitomerica) renamed "Amerikanovac" by the settlers, while in the other village a very large, roomy school building is under construction.

"The settlers have been given employment on the roads through the villages as well as on the road being built across the mountains which will connect Montenegro with Serbia. This has been of immense help to them as it has given them the ready cash with which to improve their homes and lands and buy stock. Their advancement and progress is most encouraging.

"Serbia being an agricultural country must progress and advance steadily to the front. The money is down but at the present better than it was in November of last year when it reached the low level of one hundred dinars to the dollar; in normal times we reckon five dinars to the dollar.

"Serbia is a most interesting country, with many excellent laws which only need carrying out. To watch the future development of Jugoslavia will be indeed interesting. One wonders whether the union will exist. Though of the same race in most instances they are quite different in many respects, and one can appreciate how the progressive parts of Jugoslavia may resent being ruled by a less progressive country, such as Serbia has been in the past. Their King, however, is respected by all and we can only hope that by the aid of Parliament he may be able to bring peace and prosperity out of war and chaos. Given ten years *without war* we would see a much different country from the present."

Under-nourished Children in Mining Regions

The work of feeding the under-nourished and under-developed children in mining regions in West Virginia and Pennsylvania is progressing slowly but satisfactorily. About $6,000 has been received, especially earmarked for this purpose, and the units have been authorized to feed up to a total of 500 children a month for three months if the strike lasts that long. There are four workers in West Virginia and five in Pennsylvania. At the present time they are feeding in each section about 150 children and are opening up new stations as rapidly as possible.

No statistics are yet available which indicate the real condition among these children. The medical examinations show that over one-third of the children are in a condition that calls for supplementary food and a good proportion of this number are in very bad physical condition.

Before the work was undertaken a letter was sent to all the mine owners and operators explaining that our object was to feed the neediest of the children and to do what we could to bring a message of good will to both sides. Responses from the mine operators have been very friendly. In fact, considerable sums of money have already been received from such sources. A few of the operators have protested but all the opposition has been in a kindly spirit. It is encouraging that the work is being so well received.

Friendly News Notes

W. Greenwood Brown, who for some time has been living at Calgary, Alberta, has returned to his former home, 83 Silver Birch Avenue, Toronto, Canada.

The following Eastern Friends expect to attend the sessions of Illinois Yearly Meeting: Isaac Wilson, of Biglerville, Pa.; Charles H. Harrison, of Ardmore, Pa.; Grace Clevenger, of Stephenson, Va., and Arabella Carter, of Philadelphia, Pa.

On the 16th of last month, friends and relations to the number of 70 called on Elizabeth H. Coale to congratulate her on having reached the 96th anniversary of her birth. They found her in good health and spirits.

William Wistar Comfort, President of Haverford College and head of the Department of Romance Languages, is traveling in Spain and France and expects to return to the college on September 15th.

The wedding of A. Jeannette Flitcraft, Executive Secretary of Chicago Monthly Meeting, and Sherman H. Stetson, formerly of Brooklyn, N. Y., will take place at "Greenlawn Farm," Clear Creek, Illinois, the Wilson homestead, on Eighth month 19th. The bride and groom expect to attend the Conference at Richmond.

According to a special dispatch to the *Public Ledger*, Philadelphia, Oxford debaters are coming to the United States to contest with several Eastern College teams, among them our own Swarthmore. In the list are Harvard, Yale, Princeton, Cornell, Columbia, New York University and Bates.

The two subjects chosen for debate are America's abstention from the League of Nations, and the effect of trade unionism on the industrial development of the two countries. The Americans have agreed to adopt the English system of debate, in which extemporaneous speeches are substituted for set addresses.

CONFERENCE NOTES

One of the distinctive young Friends' features at the General Conference, which will be held in Richmond, Ind., August 26th to September 2nd, will be a Forum each morning lead by William J. Reagan. At this Forum there will be opportunity to consider together the different questions that arise during the week.

A large group of young Friends will be in attendance, representing most of the meetings in the east as well as the west, and some of the meetings of the Five Years Meeting.

George A. Walton will lead three Round Tables on John William Graham's book, "The Faith of a Quaker." It is suggested that Friends who will be interested to attend this Round Table prepare by reading as much as possible of the book in advance.

FRIENDS' GENERAL CONFERENCE, RICHMOND, IND.

August 26th to September 2nd.

Special transportation arrangements have been made for Friends going to the Conference, at Richmond, Ind., via Pennsylvania Railroad.

Special Pullman sleeping cars will be attached to train No. 21 leaving Pennsylvania Station, New York City, Sixth-day, August 25th, at 1.05 p. m.; Trenton, 2.21 p. m.; Broad Street Station, Philadelphia, 3.28 p. m.; Harrisburg, 6.10 p. m.; Tyrone, 8.40 p. m.; Altoona, 9.17 p. m.; Pittsburgh, 12.40 a. m., Standard time.

The fare from New York City one way is $26.74; from Philadelphia, $23.50; Harrisburg, $19.75; Chicago, $8.12.

A reduction of one and one-half fare on the certificate plan will apply for the round trip, providing there are 250 traveling with certificates by the various railroads. Please note: *"Certificates are obtained from the agent when ticket is purchased."*

It is very important for all Friends going to the Conference and wishing Pullman accommodations on the special cars to write to Robert Seaman, Transportation Chairman, Jericho, N. Y., at once, stating whether lower or upper berth is wanted so that reservations may be made in the special Pullman cars for Friends attached to train No. 21. Those going on other trains and by other routes make their own reservations and all secure Conference Certificates when tickets are purchased.

WOODSTOWN FRIENDS ENTERTAIN PITMAN AUTOMOBILE CLUB

The annual visit of the Pitman Automobile Club to Friends' Meeting at Woodstown is looked forward to from time to time with ever-increasing interest and real joy by all who enter into the spirit of friendliness and Christian fellowship which the occasion richly affords. On First-day morning last, Seventh month 30th, the Club arrived promptly at the hour of service and all were comfortably seated by 11 o'clock. The visitors came in larger numbers than upon any previous visit, filling the two central sections of the big, roomy house, and overflowing into the side and rear seats, and they are always cordially welcomed.

To George H. Tyler, former president of the club, may be given the credit of having established this annual pilgrimage to Woodstown Meeting. As a small boy, George was a member of Friends' Meeting and First-day School here.

After the opening period of silence, living silence, so dear to the heart of the Society of Friends, Friend Joel Borton spoke at length on "A New Note in Christianity," and welcomed these friends who had come in among us from Pitman and other places where members of the club have scattered since their initial visit to the Meeting here a number of years ago, representing as they do various denominations, but all aiming to some day reach the "Home of Many Mansions."

Walter Harris, "dear to the hearts of the friends of his childhood," was the second speaker and showed without a doubt the beautiful spirit of friendliness and true Christian spirit that makes the living of life worth while, a help and strength to all who are privileged to come in contact with such a life.

A peace resolution to be sent by the Meeting to President

Harding was read, prayer was offered, Meeting closed under the divine canopy of love, and a love-feast of "good will to men" followed. May the visit by the Pitman Automobile Club be repeated *ad infinitum* to Friends' Meeting at Woodstown. E. R. KIRBY.

PEACE MEETING AT BYBERRY, PA.

Our Community Peace Meeting, at Byberry, on the 30th, was an unqualified success. Nearly two hundred persons attended. The Methodist and Presbyterian congregations nearby were represented, while Friends from adjoining neighborhoods took the opportunity to visit also.

The meeting endorsed the sending of a communication to President Harding in support of his efforts to bring about the reduction of armament, and to urge further action in the future to advance the cause of peace. The vigor with which this was voted upon, and the interest with which the speaker was heard, told in no uncertain way the drift of opinion in this locality.

Dr. O. Edward Janney's lecture on "The Educational Approach to a Warless World," which was a counterpart of that given before summer schools at Normal Schools this season, was a practical exposition of how the teacher may teach peace in various departments of geography, history, literature and art, as well as through personal influence in this line. He urged a higher patriotism than that now obtaining.

Franklin Packer and Arthur C. Jackson added brief remarks of a practical character also.

Through special invitation to members, the meeting for worship in the morning and the Monthly Meeting following were much more largely attended than usual, members from Morrisville, West Philadelphia, Haverford and other nearby points swelling the numbers. The majority stayed to picnic lunch, fully fifty gathering under the big oak tree which has sheltered generations gone. A. C.

AMONG THE SUMMER SCHOOLS

There are sixteen Normal Schools in Pennsylvania. Thirteen of them conduct summer schools for the training of teachers, who attend to the number of about 8,000.

It seemed to the members of the General Conference Section of Friends' Disarmament Council that no better work could be undertaken this summer than to give Friends' message on the abolition of war to these teachers, whose influence among their pupils will extend far and wide.

Therefore, application was made to those in charge of these Summer Schools, in the name of the Society of Friends, for the opportunity of addressing their students. Favorable replies were received from eleven of them, no reply having been received from California, in Washington County, and the Principal of Lock Haven declining.

The Executive Secretary, O. Edward Janney, employed the month of July in visiting these schools in Pennsylvania, and addressing the students on the topic, "The Educational Approach to a Warless World." In this service he has visited the Normal School Summer Schools in the following order: Millersville, 600 students; Indiana, 1,146; Slippery Rock, 900; Clarion, 574; Edinboro, 670; Mansfield, 597; Kutztown, 397; Bloomsburg, 855; Shippensburg, 592; West Chester, 360; East Stroudsburg, 460. In all, 6,761 teachers received the message.

To reach these eleven schools it was necessary to travel 1,875 miles by rail, trolley and auto, occupying twenty-four days.

At all points the message was well received, and the courtesy shown by those in charge was delightful. It is felt that this sowing of seed has been well worth while.

In the course of this service the Meeting at Buck Hill Falls was attended, with 400 present; also the Monthly Meeting at Byberry, with a conference on the abolition of war in the afternoon, and on Eighth month 1st, the Quarterly Meeting at Concordville, with goodly numbers present in each instance.

The Executive Secretary has also addressed one Normal School Summer School in Maryland and one in Virginia. He will visit the University of Virginia on Eighth month 13th, and is arranging for visits to other schools.

WESTBURY QUARTERLY MEETING

The address at the afternoon session was made by Robert Bruere, on "Personality and Coal." Mr. Bruere has been working with the Service Committee in the Friends' relief work in West Virginia and Pennsylvania.

In his introductory remarks to Robert Bruere's talk, E. Carleton McDowell spoke of that period in Quakerism when the Society was at a very low ebb, spiritually. But the feeling for the slaves, and of devoted struggle against slavery, revived the Society again, bringing it to deeper spiritual experiences. Our present-day Service Committee was organized a few years ago, simply as an incident; now it is an integral part of our Society. "The problem of the Service Committee, as it should be of all Friends, is to make contacts for the way of Love. If we stand off from making contacts, we cut ourselves off from the way of Love."

In his address Mr. Bruere said, in part: "If I understand your message, it rests fundamentally on the great teachings of Jesus, 'Love the Lord thy God,' and 'thy neighbor as thyself.' This is the supreme doctrine, the clue for us to follow, in our troubled modern life. If this is your message, then it has a definite significance in coal.

"What is coal? It is the result of world upheavals, or tremendous cosmic processes. When coal was first raised in England for use by man, our race, for the first time, directly linked itself with cosmic processes. With the finding of this cosmic force, came the dawn of world civilization. With the coming of coal, came the opportunity for men to be one community.

"Before the coming of coal, we had no control-margin of food, or the forces of the world. Coal, through the release of its energy, gives us the possibility of mastery of the physical forces of life. All through the task of building a society runs coal. No one physical fact in America has had so much to do with our development as the widespread distribution of coal.

Coal should be a service. The coal operators hold the coal in trust; it is God's gift to all of us; and its production should be organized as a service. And so the Friends are trying to go in with both groups, the operators and the miners, trying to 'maintain the spirit of the family, the spirit of love.' Unless we see coal as a means of human development, we miss part of the message of Jesus."

THE YOUNG FRIENDS' EARLHAM CONFERENCE

It is the message that the Earlham Conference wants remembered above everything else, for the things we did there were not so important as the spirit we had there. Yet for those who are interested in the mechanics of an experience like that this brief survey of the conference might well be added.

Alexander Purdy opened the conference with his stimulating lecture on "The Amateur Spirit" as exemplified supremely in Amos, Jesus, George Fox and William Penn, and showed how that spirit throughout all ages had been one of the great moving forces in the history of civilization. With this challenge ringing in our ears we determined to apply the true "Amateur Spirit" to the conference.

Fred Libby's Training Class for The World Peace Movement enrolled a hundred delegates who found in it one way to serve God and humanity in this day. Clarence Pickett's History of the Society of Friends followed Agnes Tierney's Outline and was open to interesting discussions on such subjects as the Quaker testimony of The Inner Light, the circumstances and results of the two separations and the future path of Quakerism. Ward Applegate's class, Young People in the Church, had a large and enthusiastic attendance. Study Groups and other organizations for young people were discussed, as well as the practical problem of how the meetings for business and the meetings for worship could be made interesting and valuable to the younger members of our Society. William Reagan and Edith Wildman held classes for the "teen-age" boys and girls respectively. Combined with the evening meetings for these two groups these classes were no doubt extremely valuable for the High School boy or girl attending such a conference for the first time. Dr. Edward Nourse conducted a Bible Study Class for several enthusiastic adherents who claim they got a new conception of The New Testament in the light of the scholarly study made by the class. The Mission Class led by Amelia Lindley was also highly interesting. Conditions in supposedly Christianized America were taken up along with the too-little known conditions in countries further from our own door-step. Isadore Wilson helped many who were studying the problem of teaching. E. T. Albertson, General Secretary of the Indiana State Sunday School Association, gave a very enlightening course on The Modern Sunday School.

These classes were held in the morning, each delegate selecting two consecutive ones. An open lecture by Miles Krumbine, pastor of the First Lutheran Church, Dayton, Ohio, was given after a restful half-hour recess. His discussion of "Leadership" in this series of seven lectures was acutely stimulating, dwelling on the requirements for true Christian leadership, and the need in this day for such leadership.

The Open Forums which came directly after the lectures were conducted by and for the conference under the skillful leadership of Paul Furnas. It was at this time that we talked about music in meetings for worship and discovered how different our forms of worship were and yet how alike in spirit. Useful magazines and books and other topics of general interest were taken up in other Forums.

The afternoons, devoted to committee meetings and community games, were a welcome feature of the conference. William Reagan's absence for the latter five days made us realize how much his dynamic enthusiasm added to our games.

The evening Vespers, perhaps the most precious part of the whole day, were live meetings for worship, filled as they were with the reality of God's presence. When the darkness had fallen we gathered for the last lecture. Fred Libby, Kirby Page and Murray Kenworthy completed our day for us and sent us home with a deep yearning to attack the problems of this hour with the same spirit and faith that have made each of them such useful servants of God.

E. A. W.

Illinois Yearly Meeting of Friends

Eighth month 19th to 24th, 1922

PROGRAM

SEVENTH-DAY, THE 19TH

10.00 a. m.—Meeting for Oversight and Counsel.
3.00 p. m.—Sunday School Session. Topic: Talks and General Discussion on Beginners' and Primary Divisions of the Sunday School.
Talk by Grace Clevenger: Activities of the Sunday School at Stephenson, Va.
8.00 p. m.—Social Evening. Everybody invited.

FIRST-DAY, THE 20TH

10.00 a. m.—Meeting for Worship.
2.00 p. m.—"Why I Joined the Friends," by Charles H. Harrison.
8.00 p. m.—Young People's Meeting. Talk by Arabella Carter.

SECOND-DAY, THE 21ST

8.00 a. m.—Executive Committee Meeting.
10.00 a. m.—Opening of Business Session, beginning with 15 minute Devotional Period. Reading of Letters from other Yearly Meetings.
1.00 p. m.—Philanthropic Committee Meeting.
2.00 p. m.—Business Session resumed. Committee appointments and reports.
7.30 p. m.—Advancement Committee Meeting.

THIRD-DAY, THE 22ND

10.00 a. m.—Business Session, preceded by 15 minute Devotional Period. Report from Central Committee of General Conference.
11.40 a. m.—Memorial Period.
2.00 p. m.—Business resumed. Report of Committee of Advancement of Friends' Principles.
8.00 p. m.—Program in charge of First-day School Committee.

FOURTH-DAY, THE 23RD

9.00 a. m.—Executive Committee Meeting.
10.00 a. m.—Meeting for Worship.
1.00 p. m.—Women's Meeting.
2.00 p. m.—Philanthropic Committee Report on Peace, Child Welfare, Indian Affairs, Industrial Conditions, Proper Publications, Equal Rights, Purity, Temperance, Anti-Narcotics, Colored People, and Prison Reform.
4.30 p. m.—Auto Trip and Picnic Supper.

FIFTH-DAY, THE 24TH

9.00 a. m.—Meeting for Oversight and Counsel.
10.00 a. m.—Business Session, beginning with 15 minute Devotional Period. Reports of Committees.
2.00 p. m.—Closing Business Session. Final Committee Reports.

Dinners and suppers will be served at the dining hall on the grounds.

Children's Story Periods, with competent persons in charge, at 11.30 a. m. and 3.30 p. m. daily, beginning with Monday, unless otherwise announced.

Local Committee of Arrangements

Mildred S. Whitney, Magnolia, Ill.
Edna Wilson Wolf, Magnolia, Ill.
Arthur Wilson, McNabb, Ill.
Howard Mills, McNabb, Ill.

Items From Everywhere

The King of Belgium, the Queen of Holland and the President of France are to be invited to come to the United States next year to participate in the Huguenot-Walloon Tercentenary which will be celebrated at New York and other points where these people settled.

According to statistics gathered by the Federal Council of Churches, of every 106 persons in the United States, 10 have no religious affiliation and 96 are affiliated through membership, financial support, attendance or other ties with various religious bodies, as follows: Protestant 75, Roman Catholic 18, other faiths 3.

To further international goodwill and understanding and world-wide co-operation among the churches, friendly visitors are being sent this summer to the churches of Europe and the Near East by the Federal Council of Churches. The list of visitors includes some of the most prominent ministers and laymen of the country.

Water companies, owners of mining properties, and clubs of sportsmen in Pennsylvania planted more than 1,200,000 young forest trees on their holdings during the spring of 1922, according to an announcement made by Major R. Y. Stuart, the state's chief forester. During the last eight years the same groups have set out about 5,217,000 seedlings.

The General Assembly of the Presbyterian Church of the United States has gone on record in favor of the proposed celebration to mark the fiftieth anniversary of the first formal meeting of those eminent American scholars who constituted the American Bible Revision Committee, and whose persistent labors during the ensuing thirty years resulted in the publication of the American Standard Bible.

One of the most unequivocal militant calls to action ever issued by a large and diverse group of labor organizations and leaders has just been launched in behalf of Nicalo Sacco and Bartolomeo Vanzetti, the Italian workers awaiting death in Massachusetts on what is believed to be "framed" evidence. The call is in the form of a letter to American Labor and is signed by fifteen central labor bodies and many prominent labor leaders.

THE OPEN FORUM

This column is intended to afford free expression of opinion by readers on questions of interest. The* INTELLIGENCER *is not responsible for any such opinions. Letters must be brief, and the editor reserves the right to omit parts if necessary to save space.

To the Editor:

There will be an informal conference of persons interested in the teaching of History, at the Friends' General Conference, Sixth-day evening, September 1, 7.00 to 8.00 p. m.

I am not running this conference, but I should like to hear persons who are teaching history discuss some such things as "Why Teach History?" Second, "What classes of things in the field of History are really worth teaching?" Third, "What results from the history class should the secondary school teacher expect to find in the pupils' minds twenty years after school has adjourned?"

As a matter of fact, the class in History offers the greatest opportunity in all education for teaching international relations, which have their two great manifestations in trade and war, especially war.

J. RUSSELL SMITH.

To the Editor:

I presume that those Friends who have been maintaining in the Open Forum that capital employed in industry produces nothing, would, to be consistent, also claim that labor can be very productive without employing capital. But the progress of our race in civilization would not have been possible without the use of implements; and all implements are capital. A savage might raise a crop of corn with his bare hands, but if he should take the time and trouble to fasten a clam shell or a sharp stone firmly and durably to a stick he would have a hoe that would enable him to increase his agricultural yield several hundred per cent. The question raised by our Friends, whether the hoe produces the crop or the man behind it is of no consequence whatever.

S. S. GREEN.

To the Editor:

I am surprised and disappointed that THE FRIENDS' INTELLIGENCER should print such a socialistic article as that which appeared in a recent issue, entitled "What is Meant by Wage Slavery?"

It is a sad state of affairs when people who think along the same lines as our friend, J. Paul J. Williams, do not seem willing to think practically and clearly. The whole trend of the times among a certain group of people (of which, I am sorry to say, Friends form no small proportion) seems to be toward building up between employer and employee a spirit of distrust and hatred, instead of the confidence and co-operation upon which the principles of our faith are founded.

There is nothing new in the ideas advocated by friend Williams, and many of them have been in practice in Russia for a few years, with the disastrous results that we are all familiar with.

There is no excuse for either the coal strike or the railroad strike, and both were inflicted upon us by a selfish group of labor leaders who care not for the welfare of the workers, but only for their own ends. Friends should always uphold the principle that, while no one should be forced to work, everyone who wants to work has a perfect right to do so, without any interference whatsoever.

Let Friends support the fair play principle to all—employers, union workers and a great mass of American workers who do not belong to any labor unions.

WALTER CLOTHIER.

To the Editor:

The writer was particularly interested in the letter by S. S. Green printed in "The Open Forum," Seventh month 29th. His statement that the fundamental principles of the present industrial and economic system, as he has well formulated them in his letter, are "inalienable rights," is a little amusing. In the article in the same issue of the INTELLIGENCER entitled "What Is Meant by 'Wage Slavery'?" this writer tried to show the new "master and servant" relation which has developed in our present system as a result of his first principle, "the right of every one to sell his services and to hire the services of others." If this is really a God-given and inalienable right, why are millions of workers in this country who sincerely desire to sell their services unable to do so? And why is it an inalienable right for the owner of capital to receive usurious interest in the form of exorbitant profits?

If those Friends who think that there is no better system than the present one which is admittedly based on fundamental principles that are a direct incentive and temptation to greed and self-interest, would read more widely and seek more sincerely they could never make such statements as the following, taken from your correspondent's letter, "The only alternative to the one (system) we are suffering under is in operation today in Russia." This is followed by a heart-rending picture of "pestilence and starvation." These Friends never seem to have realized that the rulers of capitalistic nations who decreed war and an inhuman blockade against the Russian people are largely responsible for these conditions. Those who support a system which puts property and profits first, and abundant life for the many second, have yet to prove that their Golden Rule panacea is at all compatible with the principles of the system they uphold. In fact, the rarity of its application in a few isolated instances is proof to the contrary.

The writer hopes that reason and prayer will be enlisted in this crisis. Chaos and war lie at the end of our present pathway; order and peace lie on a different road, a path of good will and mutual service instead of greed and the mad contest for success. May we each one take our places in the critical days to come, and stand for the right and Christian way in industrial and economic relations as well as in home and school and state. J. PAUL J. WILLIAMS.

Scranton, Pa.

BIRTHS

CLOUD—On Sixth month 7th, near Doe Run, Pa., to J. Blaine and Dora Edna Webster Cloud, a son, named Townsend W. Cloud, a birthright member of Center Monthly Meeting, Hockessin.

HILTON—On Seventh month 2nd, to Armydis and Rebecca Taylor Hilton, a daughter, named Alice Rebecca Hilton, a member of Camden Meeting. Great-granddaughter of Rebecca Nicholson.

WALTON—On Seventh month 30th, to Joel M. and Frances Baker Walton, of Kennett Square, Pa., a daughter, named Lois Catherine Walton.

MARRIAGES

HOOD-HUGHES—At the home of the bride's mother, at West Chester, Pa., on Seventh month 31st, Harold Dutton Hood and Elsie M. Hughes.

SUPLEE-BROWN—At Malvern, Pa., on Sixth month 24th, Clarence E. Suplee and Margaret Whitaker Brown.

DEATHS

CARVER—At Friends' Home, Germantown, Pa., on Eighth month 7th, Sarah M. Carver, in her 89th year. A member of Philadelphia Monthly Meeting of Friends.

ECK—At Berwick, Pa., on Sixth month 22nd, Anna E. Eck, in the 69th year of her age. A daughter of the late Reece M. and Phœbe Hicks Eck.

ELLIOTT—At Wrightstown, Pa., on Sixth month 22nd, Annie T. Elliott.

COMING EVENTS

EIGHTH MONTH

12th—Blue River Quarterly Meeting, at Benjaminville, Ill.

12th—Picnic on the Palisades, given by New York Friends to Quaker students at Columbia University Summer School. All Friends are invited.

13th—Certain members of Philadelphia Quarterly Meeting's Visiting Committee will visit Germantown Friends' Home, at 7.30 p. m.

13th—Annual Meeting at Peach Lake, N. Y., 3 p. m. (Daylight Saving time). J. Augustus Cadwallader and other young Friends are expected to be present.

14th—Indiana Yearly Meeting, at Waynesville, Ohio.

14th—New York Monthly Meeting, at 7.30 p. m., at 110 Schermerhorn street, Brooklyn. Supper will be served at 6 o'clock.

16th—Monthly Meeting of Friends of Philadelphia, 15th and Race Streets, 7.30 p. m.

17th—Green Street Monthly Meeting of Friends of Philadelphia, School House Lane, Germantown, 7.30 p. m.

19th—Short Creek Quarterly Meeting, at Emerson, Ohio.

19th—Pelham Half-Yearly Meeting, at Sparta, Ontario.

19th-21st—Fairfax Quarterly Meeting, at Lincoln, Va. O. Edward and Anne W. Janney and La Verne H. Forbush expect to attend.

20th—Duanesburg Half-Yearly Meeting, at Quaker street, N. Y.

20th—Certain members of Philadelphia Quarterly Meeting's Visiting Committee expect to attend meeting at Schuylkill, at 10.30 a. m. Others expect to attend Valley Meeting, the visit appointed for Seventh month 9th having been postponed to this date.

American Friends' Service Committee

WILBUR K. THOMAS, EX. SEC.
20 S. 12th St. Philadelphia.

CASH CONTRIBUTIONS
WEEK ENDING JULY 31ST.

Five Years Meeting	$530.00
Other Meetings:	
Frankford Friends	103.00
Burlington Monthly Meeting	5.00
Little Britain	6.00
Ram Allah	50.00
Swarthmore (group)	10.00
Birmingham, First-day School	18.00
	$192.00
Contributions for Germany	18.25
For Austria	25.75
For Poland	686.50
For Russia	1,405.15
For West Virginia	591.25
For Central Pennsylvania	434.25
For General	152.50
For Syria	9.00
For Refunds and payments	5.20
Clothing Department	8.00
	$4,057.85

Shipments received during week ending July 29th: 32 boxes and packages received; 3 anonymous.

WANTED

RIVER CROFT, CLAYMONT, DEL. Special home care for invalids, or rest and physical upbuilding. Booklet on application. E. H. Speakman.

WANTED — A FRIEND TO TEACH Buckingham Friends' School at Lahaska, Pa. 15 pupils—grades 1-8. Apply to Mary A. Watson, 277 Maple Ave., Doylestown, Pa.

POSITION WANTED—BY WORKING housekeeper; married woman, thirty, with small child. Country or suburbs. Refined, experienced, capable. Address B. 310, Friends' Intelligencer.

WANTED — A GRADUATE NURSE to have charge of the Infirmary in a Friends' School. An assistant nurse is employed. Address G. 311, Friends' Intelligencer.

WANTED—COMPANION OR PRACTICAL nurse for elderly lady. Address L. 304, Friends' Intelligencer.

FOR RENT

FOR RENT—THIRD STORY HOUSEKEEPING apartment in central location, Philadelphia. Four rooms and bath, two open fireplaces. Furnished or unfurnished. Electricity. Apply W. P. S., Friends' Intelligencer.

FOR RENT—AT OCEAN CITY, N. J.—Attractive furnished rooms; ocean view; fine location near Boardwalk. Address Laura H. Brosius, 820 Sixth St.

TO RENT — FURNISHED, AT Swarthmore near College, comfortable 13-room house; all conveniences. Porch, shaded lawn, large and small fruits and vegetables. No garage. References exchanged. For terms, write M. S. B., 503 N. Chester Road, or phone, Swarthmore 572.

NOTICE—Concise statements of the principles of the Religious Society of Friends and their application to the problems of every day living, including "The Spirit of Quakerism," by Elbert Russell; "Preparation for Life's Greatest Business," by Rufus M. Jones; and other articles by Henry W. Wilbur, Howard M. Jenkins, Elizabeth Lloyd, Jesse H. Holmes, O. Edward Janney, Edward B. Rawson, etc., to be had free on application to Friends' General Conference Advancement Committee, 140 North Fifteenth Street, Philadelphia, Pa.

FUN

Grad—"This university certainly takes an interest in a fellow, doesn't it?" Tad—"How's that?" Grad—"Well, I read in the graduate magazine that they will be very glad to hear of the death of any of their alumni."—*Siren.*

To the Lot Holders and others interested in Fairhill Burial Ground:

GREEN STREET Monthly Meeting has funds available for the encouragement of the practice of cremating the dead to be interred in Fairhill Burial Ground. We wish to bring this fact as prominently as possible to those who may be interested. We are prepared to undertake the expense of cremation in case any lot holder desires us to do so.

Those interested should communicate with William H. Gaskill, Treasurer of the Committee of Interments, Green Street Monthly Meeting, or any of the following members of the Committee.

William H. Gaskill, 3301 Arch St.
Samuel N. Longstreth, 1218 Chestnut St.
Charles F. Jenkins, 232 South Seventh St.
Stuart S. Graves, 3033 Germantown Ave.

ADVERTISING RATE in the FRIENDS' INTELLIGENCER, for Help Wanted, Positions Wanted, Rooms for Rent, Notices, and other classified advertisements without display, for each insertion, 2 cents per word, including name, initials and address. Answers may be sent to a box at the INTELLIGENCER office, if so directed.

For display advertising the rate is 10 cents per agate line, or $1.40 per column inch, each insertion. On ten or more insertions in a year from date of order, ten per cent. discount. Thus a four-inch single-column or two-inch double-column advertisement costs $5.60 each insertion, less ten per cent., or 5.04 net each time for ten or more insertions. Matter may be changed whenever desired, without extra charge.

Experience has proved the INTELLIGENCER to be a remarkably good advertising medium. All advertisements must "pass the censor!"

Address 140 N. 15th St., Philadelphia

Please help us by patronizing our advertisers. Mention the "Friends' Intelligencer."

The Friends' Intelligencer

ESTABLISHED 1844 | EIGHTH MONTH 19, 1922 | VOLUME 79 · NUMBER 33

Contents

THE FRIENDS' INTELLIGENCER

Published weekly, 140 N. 15th Street, Philadelphia, Pa., by Friends' Intelligencer Association, Ltd.

PAUL W. WAGER, *Editor.*
SUE C. YERKES, *Business Manager*

Subscription rates: United States, Mexico, Cuba and Panama, $2.50 per year. Canada and other foreign countries, $3.00 per year. Checks should be made payable to Friends' Intelligencer Association, Ltd.

Entered as Second Class Matter at Philadelphia Post Office.

FUN

Melville—What is economy, father?

Father—Economy, my son, is a way of spending money without getting any fun out of it.—*Answers.*

Father (from upstairs)—"Helen, isn't it time for the young man to go home?"

Young Man—"Your father is a crank."

Father (overhearing)—"Well, when you don't have a self-starter a crank comes in mighty handy."—*Boston Transcript.*

New Thought—Do you believe in mental suggestion?

Old Thought—Yes. Last week I told my husband that I was going to start my house cleaning, and the next day he left town on business.—*Judge.*

It is in the cemetery at South Bethlehem, Pennsylvania, by the way, that the sign appears: "Persons are prohibited from picking flowers from any but their own graves."—*American Lumberman (Chicago).*

Granny (who doesn't like modern manners)—"You girls are so useless nowadays. Why, I believe you don't know what needles are for!"

The Youngest—"What a dear old granny you are! Why, they are to make the gramophone play, of course." —*London Mail.*

A shopkeeper had in his employ a man so lazy as to be utterly worthless. One day, his patience exhausted, he discharged him. "Will you give me a character?" asked the lazy one. The employer sat down to write a noncommittal letter. His efforts resulted as follows: "The bearer of this letter has worked for me one week and I am satisfied."—*London Telegraph.*

The Irish lad and the Yiddish boy were engaged in verbal combat. First one would insist that his father or mother was better than the other's. Then it was their pet bulldogs and their teachers. Finally the subject came down to respective churches.

"I guess I know that Father Harriety knows more than your Rabbi," the little Irish boy insisted.

"Sure, he does; vy not?" replied the Jew boy. "You tell him everything." —*Treat 'Em Square.*

The Friends' Intelligencer

The religion of Friends is based on faith in the "INWARD LIGHT," or direct revelation of God's spirit and will in every seeking soul.

The INTELLIGENCER is interested in all who bear the name of Friends in every part of the world, and aims to promote love, unity and intercourse among all branches and with all religious societies.

ESTABLISHED 1844 — PHILADELPHIA, EIGHTH MONTH 19, 1922 — VOLUME 79 NUMBER 33

A smile is the same in all languages.

⌘

Alcohol has engraved many a tombstone with the words "it might have been."

⌘

The only way that Friends can convince the world that "pacifism" is not "passivism" is to demonstrate.

⌘

Ninety-five per cent. of the population get no summer vacation and the five per cent. who do are the ones who need it least.

⌘

Those who claim that the masses could not appreciate culture are careful to see that they don't have a chance to develop a taste.

⌘

What a fine feeling it is to be able to say at the close of the day, "Something accomplished, something done, I have earned a night's repose."

⌘

A group of Young Friends possessed with the spirit exemplified in their Epistle, which we published last week, is a credit to the Society. They have the vision, the courage and the energy to undertake large tasks. They have, moreover, a true sense of humility and they appeal to older Friends for counsel and guidance.

The successful movements of history have been those which were supported by the vigor and enthusiasm of youth tempered and directed by the experience of the elders. It has been characteristic of the Society of Friends that, though often pioneers, they have seldom, if ever, had to backwater. It may be that the secret of their success has been due to the close co-operation between the older and younger elements of the Society.

The present body of Young Friends is ambitious, courageous, spiritually-minded, straining at the leash and eager for action. It is the duty of the Society to give them something to do, something hard, something that will challenge their resourcefulness; then, having done so, it must not fail to "back" them. They have addressed their Epistle to "To All Young Friends Everywhere" but it is as truly directed to all Friends who have optimism and vision. It is a challenge to the whole Society to harness and use the latent energy among its younger members.

⌘

Beginning with this issue the INTELLIGENCER is publishing a series of twelve or more articles dealing with the Book of Discipline. These articles are prepared under the direction of the Committee on Revision of Discipline and are for the purpose of giving information about and creating interest in the Book of Discipline.

There are some Friends who believe that there are features of the Discipline which need to be clarified and brought up-to-date. There are others who believe that the present instrument is clear and flexible enough to meet present needs and that revision is unnecessary and unwise. There are a great many others who are not familiar enough with the Discipline to have an intelligent opinion in the matter or even to be interested in the question of revision at all.

It is primarily to educate this third and largest group that the present work is undertaken. When the Society as a whole is better informed about the Discipline as it is, the subject of revision can be more intelligently discussed.

⌘

One of the most unwholesome conditions in America today is the spirit of class consciousness and class rivalry which prevails. It is partly due to corporate industry with its trade unionism and collective bargaining, partly due to the growth of cities and the increasing disparities of wealth, and partly due to the numerous and diverse peoples which make up our population. Whatever the causes it is a situation that is to be deplored. Now that the goal of political equality is almost achieved we must not permit society to be divided along new lines.

We don't want classes in this country but a true

democracy. There must be social and industrial democracy as well as political democracy. This means that the bulwarks of privilege must be torn down and the channels of opportunity kept open. It means that honest toil, however menial, shall always be a badge of honor. It means that no man must be denied the right to work nor deprived of the product of his labor. It means that opportunity must be given for men to assume a proprietary interest in their occupation, become the owners of their own homes and responsible members of society. It means that wherever possible capital and labor should be supplied by the same persons and thus Capital and Labor as separate classes disappear. It means that there be less of servitude of every form, for a master and servant relationship does not make for self-respecting manhood either way. It means that the alarming increase in farm tenantry must be checked if we would avoid an American peasantry. In short, it means that we must preserve and strengthen that middle class which is the bone and sinew of our nation. Indeed, we must so foster its growth that it will eventually absorb both extremities and America become a genuine democracy.

Concerning the Origin of the Book of Discipline

Prepared at the request of the Committee on Revision of Discipline of Philadelphia Yearly Meeting by Anna J. F. Hallowell.

Only by taking a brief survey of the political conditions in England over a considerable period, can the rapid rise of the Society of Friends be comprehended. While for more than two centuries there had been individuals, and here and there small groups of men, to whom the Bible was a living book, yet practically England was a Catholic country until Henry VIII declared it free of the jurisdiction of Rome (in 1532); but that did not separate church and state, and the people were taught to look to the king for religious authority. The changing angles of Henry's mind at different periods were reflected in the education given his children, and hence upon their attitudes to their subjects. Upon the young Edward's accession to the throne the real power passed into the hands of the Protestant leaders, Cranmer and Ridley. Though this reign lasted but six years the effect was indelible. With the succession of Mary, daughter of Catherine of Aragon, the extreme Roman Catholic party was again in the ascendency; and with Mary's marriage to Philip of Spain, came the introduction of the methods of the Inquisition. Her early death, however, in 1658, brought Elizabeth, daughter of Anne Boleyn, to the throne and she turned sharply from the policies of her sister and brought so long a period of comparative religious peace that two generations had the opportunity to develop a sense of steadiness and rightful possession of their own souls. Into this security came the Stuarts (in 1603), with their more or less open Roman leanings, and with their political untrustworthiness; so, when, at last, the Commonwealth took over the civil government, the church revolt was completed. The people had been led by these see-saws of more than a century to think for themselves, yet not quite far enough for an insistence upon a complete separation of church and state.

When George Fox began to preach in 1647, he had no idea of adding a new denomination to the already long list of England's nonconformists, but desired only to help his struggling brothers to the peace which he had found, and "to promote charity and piety."

To quote from the Introduction of London Discipline: "It cannot be said that any system of discipline formed a part of the original compact of the Society. It was an association of persons who were earnestly seeking after the saving knowledge of Divine truth (p. xi., P. III.). The members who lived near to each other, and who met together for religious worship, immediately formed, from the very law of their union, a Christian family or Church. Each member was at liberty to exercise the gift bestowed upon him in that beautiful harmony and subjection which belong to the several parts of a living body. Of this right exercise of spiritual gifts, and thereby of an efficient discipline, many examples are afforded in the history of the Society (p. xiii., P. III.). As the number of members increased those mutual helps and guards which had been, in a great measure, spontaneously afforded, were found to require some regular arrangements for the preservation of order in the Church" (p. xiv., P. III.).

The first meetings for other than religious matters were concerned with the sufferings of such Friends, and of their families, as were persecuted in various ways and on various pretexts, and their goods taken from them illegally. A frequent cause for persecution was the holding of meetings for worship, either in public or private. These meetings seem to have

Attitudes in Worship

II

Fourth article on Worship by Elbert Russell

In addition to the *waiting* and *seeking* attitudes in worship there should be the *outgiving* attitude. We worship not for ourselves alone. We should not seek merely to get truth and strength for ourselves. We should seek to give to others according to the measure of our ability. We should think of them, and pray for them, and bear them on our hearts. The consciousness of our neighbors' needs should be with us, and in our hearts should be a desire that God would help them to find the supply of their needs and the offering of ourselves as His instrument in so far as He can use us. In meeting as well as out of it, we should "bear one another's burdens and so fulfil the law of Christ."

The Protestant doctrine of the universal "priesthood of believers" means not only the privilege of each to come to God directly without priestly mediation; it also includes the privilege and responsibility each of us has to help others to come to God, to seek and find Him; to use all our powers to clarify the vision, quicken the conscience, and strengthen the will of our fellows who are a little more weak or sinful, a little more blind or indifferent to the Ever-present Father than we have been favored to be. We have only what has been given us. And it has been given that it may be shared. If we have in some respects higher attainments, they give us the privilege of reaching helping hands to those below or pointing the way to those whose feet have not yet grown familiar with the paths that lead to God.

All sorts and conditions of people come to meeting, in all moods and with widely different needs. Men and women come with a vague unrest: they need our help to focus it unto a definite aspiration; our words may help them to phrase it in a prayer. They come burdened by sorrow that seems too grievous to be longer borne: we may show them how to cast their burden upon the Lord and let Him sustain them. They come with a sense of defeat in the struggle to keep clean in the contacts of life: we can help them to examine their motives in the light of God's countenance and find with Him both diagnosis and healing. Youths come with pulsing life which they have not yet learned to translate into songs of praise. They come with their loves, their ambitions, their happy secrets, their successes, which we dare not tell to men and have not yet learned joyously to confide to God. "The heart knoweth its own bitterness, and a stranger doth not meddle with its joy." But it is our privilege to be priests unto these, not to stand between them and God, but to offer the sacrifices of sympathy, care, love, and spiritual travail through which they may come into His fellowship. We may not share the solitude of their supreme hours of love and grief and decision, but we may watch and pray with them just inside the gate of their Gethsemanes.

There are no rules to determine when or what we should speak in meeting. Each must follow his leading. But there are certain principles which are helpful in times of uncertainty as to what our duty is. Both Paul and John remind us of our responsibility for determining which of many impressions, thoughts, and impulses is of God. "Beloved, believe not every spirit, but prove the spirits whether they are of God." (I Jno. 4: 1.) "Prove all things; hold fast that which is good." (Thess. 5: 21.) We are also to judge of the fitness of time and place for the giving of a definite message or doing other service. We may do this with assurance, because as Paul reminds us, "the spirits of the prophets are subject to the prophets." (1 Cor. 14: 32.)

Two principles I have found particularly useful. One is Paul's "Let all things be done unto edifying." (Cor. 14: 26. Compare verses 1-5.) One may not take the time and distract the attention of the meeting for purely private ends, or merely to "relieve his own mind." One can attend to purely private worship in silence or at home. (I Cor. 14: 28.) The vocal exercises should have reference to the common welfare. Their purpose should be "edification and exhortation, and consolation." They should "build up" the faith, fellowship, and effective service of the church.

In attempting this we Friends are liable to one great handicap. We are likely to be ignorant of our neighbors' needs. One great advantage of the combination of preacher and pastor in other denominations is that the minister who prays for the congregation and preaches to them is the one who has the most intimate knowledge of their spiritual state. According to his ability and faithfulness, he knows their state, voices their half-felt needs, and speaks to their condition "edification, exhortation, and consolation." The danger of our more democratic system is that "what is everybody's business" may become "nobody's business." Unless we take time to come sympathetically unto fellowship with our neighbors and care truly for their state, how shall we be able to minister to their needs in the service of worship?

The second principle is one which I learned of one of my college teachers whose ministry was among the most helpful influences of my youth. The principle which, by his own confession, guided him most in his public utterances was that when anything had been especially helpful to him, he must share it with others. Sometimes we cherish the belief, in fear or pride, that we are essentially different from others; that no one else ever doubted, or questioned, or was tempted, or beset by such passions as ourselves; or that we have visions and ideals no one else can comprehend, or ecstacies that none may share. We *do* have the peculiarities both inward and outward that mark off our individuality. But at bottom our needs are alike. Our neighbors are of like passions with ourselves, and no temptation befalls us but such as is common to man. We are fed by the same food, hurt with the same cold. In general, other men love and hate and fear; they sin and repent; they aspire and fall short; they feel after God, and cry out to Him in the hours of their pain and extremity, even as we.

Whatever light or consolation, or strength we have found may be expected likewise to minister to other's needs. We may, therefore, give to the meeting confidently all that to our best leading seems then and there suited to the needs of the meeting and of a kind likely to prove edifying.

The Cantonese and the Political Mix-up In China

By Wm. W. Cadbury

(Concluded from last week)

In 1912 after the Republic had been established, a most enlightened and progressive government was formed in the Province of Canton.

General Chen, who at the present writing is in control at Canton, was the military governor and the most capable and well fitted men were placed at the heads of the Departments of Justice, Education, Public Health, etc.

In 1913 it became evident that President Yuan Shi Kai was not in sympathy with this progressive movement in the South. There was a revolt and the leaders in the South were driven out and a servant of the Peking Government was placed in power.

All preparations were worked out for Yuan Shi Kai to assume the throne of the Empire. The Cantonese discovered that they had been deceived and so definitely separated themselves from the Peking authorities. This separation only became complete in 1920 when Sun Yat Sen and General Chen returned to Canton, having driven out General Mok, who represented the military leaders of the North.

At the opening of the present year there were three dominant factions seeking for first place in the affairs of China.

In the North was the bandit governor of Manchuria, Chang Tso Lin. It is well known that he was firmly allied with the Japanese militarists and in view of his controlling influence over President Hsu Shi Chang at Peking, the situation appeared the more ominous.

In Central China, as governor of the Provinces of Hupeh and Hunan, was Wu Pei Fu. He is unique among the military leaders of China, in that he is educated, a keen student of foreign affairs, and honest.

Finally there was the Southern Government, or Canton faction. The leading spirit and most capable administrator here was General Chen Chiung Ming, a native of the Province. With him was Sun Yat Sen, the recently elected President of the Southern Government and the first provisional President of the Republic, until he resigned in favor of Yuan Shi Hai.

While Sun Yat Sen was aspiring to a national consolidation, Chen's ambition was more modest. As Nathaniel Peffer said of him in "Asia": He is determined to let the national government take care of itself. He desires to make of Kwangtung one province that would be administered decently and with some regard for the people's interest—a model province. Already a municipal government has been set up in Canton, the first of its kind in China, and free rein is given to the American-trained young men who are administering it.

There is the Municipal-Executive composed of the Mayor and the Commissioners of Finance, Public Safety, Education, Public Health, Public Works and Public Utilities, all appointed by the Governor.

Then there is an Advisory Council composed of 30 members, 10 appointed by the Governor, 10 chosen by general election and of the other 10, 3 are selected by the Chamber of Commerce, 3 by the labor organizations and one each by the medical profession, the engineering profession, the educational association and the lawyers' association.

Finally there is an Audit Bureau with a chief auditor appointed by the Governor, empowered to audit all municipal accounts.

When the new Governor entered Canton, he found the city depleted of money by the former Governor Mok, and yet one of his first acts was to abolish the gambling monopoly, one of the chief sources of revenue to the Government.

As further evidence of the liberal policy of Governor Chen, he has promised to give to the Agricultural Department of the Canton Christian College the sum of $100,000 silver currency, annually for 10 years, with the object of thereby helping to promote progress in the Agricultural development of the Province.

The adjoining province of Kwangsi was added to the Southern Government, and four other provinces have indicated their sympathy with the Southern leaders. Thus more than half the population of the Empire may be said to be on the side of the Southerners.

The other dominant personality of China is Sun Yat Sen. While his ambitions are more outreaching than those of General Chen, they worked together without open breach up until a few weeks ago.

It is President Sun's ambition that each of the provinces shall be organized along the lines that Kwangtung is now following; and when this is accomplished there shall be a federation of these commonwealths under a common head, along lines similar to those which led to the formation of the United States.

No more impressive scene could be imagined than that which occurred at the inauguration of Dr. Sun in Canton, on May 4, 1921. For many hours students, labor organizations and the representatives of the various guilds, filed past the President and his wife expressing their admiration of the man of their own choice.

Such was the situation in the early part of the present year, but during the past few months marked changes have occurred. Wu Pei Fu has moved from his position in Central China against his chief rival Chang Tso Lin. The latter was completely routed and with his defeat President Hsu was compelled to resign and Li Yuan Hung, who succeeded Yuan Shu Kai as President, has been reinstated.

Genuine efforts have been made to win over Sun Yat Sen, but although he offered his aid to Chang Tso Lin he has held out against Wu Pei Fu. In spite of this, his chief supporter, General Chen, has shown a strong inclination to yield to the Peking forces under certain conditions and so bring about a reunification of the country. On this question Sun and Chen have broken with one another, so that President Sun was forced to flee from Canton. He is now seeking to return and there are rumors of a reconciliation between these two southern leaders.

Much criticism has been made of Sun Yat Sen in this country and by foreigners in China because of his obstructionist tactics in the present crisis. It has been said that he has outgrown his usefulness and is actuated solely by selfish ambition for personal advancement. One must recall, however, that on a previous occasion when he yielded the Presidency to Yuan Shi Kai, he was completely deceived, and it was a mere chance which saved the Republic from losing every vestige of the democracy which Sun had devoted his life to achieve. The educated men of Canton and the Cantonese in this country still believe in Sun Yat Sen.

It is to be hoped that through compromise north and south may be once more united, for it appears that Wu Pei Fu is at one with the Southern leaders in desiring to mould the government along liberal constitutional and democratic lines.

Such are the forces working within China, but there are always the more sinister influences from without.

Japan in the north and Great Britain in the south, have seemed only too ready to continue the internal strife for their own political ends.

The United States, on the other hand, is generally considered a true friend by the Chinese. While there are many incidents in our relations with China, of which we have no reason to be proud, yet the return of the Boxer Indemnity and the generally sympathetic attitude of Americans toward China have given us a place in the confidence and affection of the Chinese people unequalled by any other nation.

The situation has been to a large extent clarified by the Washington Conference, and China is left to work out her own internal salvation. If the other nations do not interfere, we look with hope at the experiment so successfully inaugurated by the Cantonese. In their government and their initiative lie the real hope for the future of China.

Many of the young leaders of modern China have received their education and their ideals from America. It would appear then to be peculiarly the work of America to foster a closer friendship and sympathy with the people of this young sister Republic.

As Wm. H. Seward declared as far back as 1852: The discovery of America and its development were but preliminary to "the more sublime result now in the act of consummation,—the reunion of the two civilizations which, parting on the plains of Asia 4,000 years ago and traveling ever after in opposite directions around the world, now meet again on the coasts and islands of the Pacific Ocean." . . . "Who does not see that this movement must effect our own complete emancipation from what remains of European influence and prejudice, and in turn develop the American opinion and influence which shall remould constitutional laws and customs in the land that is first greeted by the rising sun!"

You

By Frederick J. Libby

Who are you? You are in your own eyes an insignificant member of God's great family, and lost in the crowd. What you do does not seem to matter much in regard to the welfare of any considerable portion of the vast host of your brothers and sisters. When you were young, you expected to make some impression at least upon your day and generation—to leave "Footprints on the sands of time." Perhaps you still cherish this ambition. Perhaps you gave it up long ago.

Yet who are you? You are a child of God, sharing the eternal life with Him, busy with Him in the creation of the heaven of good will and peace promised in Jesus Christ. You are creating heaven in your own community by little deeds and words of kindness which give outward form to the blessed spirit that fills your being.

You are not confined in range to your little circle, because the spirit of man, like the spirit of God, roams more widely than his body does. In the fullness of your love of God and man, you have cast bread upon the great waters. You have made a contribution from time to time, according to your means, to the relief of the suffering in Europe. Like the blessed in Christ's parable, you have forgotten your good deed. God received it, however, and blessed it. He broke the little loaf into fragments for the feeding of a multitude. The multitudes have been fed, and will be fed with bread given by you and others in the same spirit. Little children will rise up on the Last Day to call you blessed. They will relate what great things God has done for them through you.

They will speak, those children, languages which you do not understand—Polish and Russian and German—but they will point to you, and all will look at you and smile. You will blush and stammer and deny having served them. Then the gentle face of the great Saviour will break into a smile, too, and He will say: "Come, ye blessed of my father, inherit the kingdom prepared for you from the foundation of the world; I was a hungered, and ye gave me meat; naked, and ye clothed me. Inasmuch as ye have done it unto one of the least of these my brethren, ye have done it unto me."

The Never-Old

They who can smile when others hate,
Nor bind the heart with frosts of fate,
Their feet will go with laughter bold
The green roads of the Never-Old.

They who can let the spirit shine
And keep the heart a lighted shrine,
Their feet will glide with fire-of-gold
The green roads of the Never-Old.

They who can put the self aside
And in Love's saddle leap and ride,
Their eyes will see the gates unfold
The green roads of the Never-Old.

—*Edwin Markham.*

Those who bring sunshine to the lives of others, cannot keep it from themselves.—*Barrie.*

Friends' General Conference, Richmond, Ind.

August 26th to September 2nd.

Special transportation arrangements via Pa. R. R.

Special Pullman sleeping cars will be attached to train No. 21 leaving Pa. Sta., N. Y. City, August 25th, at 1.05 p. m.; Trenton, 2.21 p. m.; Broad St. Sta., Philadelphia, 3.28 p. m.; Harrisburg, 6.10 p. m.; Tyrone, 8.40 p. m.; Pittsburgh, 12.40 a. m., arriving at Richmond, Ind., 8.40 a. m., Standard time.

All Friends taking train No. 21 at Broad St. Sta., Philadelphia, apply at once to James H. Atkinson, 421 Chestnut St., Philadelphia, Pa., for Pullman reservation; state whether lower or upper berth is wanted.

Special Pullman sleeping cars will be attached to train No. 53-31 leaving Washington, August 25th, 4.50 p. m.; Baltimore, 5.53 p. m., arriving at Richmond, Ind., 9.39 a. m., Standard time. All Friends taking this train, apply at once to Dr. O. Edward Janney, 825 Newington Ave., Baltimore, Md., for Pullman reservation; state whether lower or upper berth is wanted.

All Friends taking the train at other points than Philadelphia, Washington and Baltimore, apply at once to Robert Seaman, Jericho, N. Y., for Pullman reservation; state whether lower or upper berth is wanted.

It is most important that all Friends from both east and west get a Certificate when they purchase their ticket, as a reduced rate on basis of one and one-half fare for the round trip on the Certificate plan will be granted on condition of an attendance of 250 or more presenting Certificates showing the purchase of one-way ticket over the different railroads from which the one-way fare to Richmond, Ind., is 67 cents or more. Ask the agent for a ticket to Richmond, Ind., on the Certificate Plan.

Certificates must show the purchase of tickets on August 23 to 29, inclusive.

Present the Certificate to Robert Seaman on your arrival at Richmond, and if there are 250 or over he will have them endorsed and returned to you; then they will be honored for tickets returning at one-half of the one-way fare.

The only way to secure reservation in the special cars is to apply to one of the three persons mentioned above, then on the 25th inst. purchase your ticket and berth (not forgetting the Conference Certificate) at your nearest large depot at least one hour before train time so there will be no delay.

Conference Notes

George H. Nutt will lead a series of three Round Tables on Friends' Principles at Friends' Conference at Richmond, Ind. Those who knew Mr. Nutt at George School, or remember his Round Tables at Cape May Conference, will appreciate this opportunity to take part in a good discussion, and to get at the kernel of some of our vexing problems.

Over 200 names have been received at Headquarters of the Conference in Philadelphia of people going to Friends' General Conference at Richmond, Ind., Eighth month 26th to Ninth month 2nd. Since these names are mostly from the east, and there will be a large attendance from the middle west, the prospect is for a full crowd at Richmond.

A cordial invitation is extended to all Friends, and also to people from other churches, and those who are not members anywhere.

Among the plans being made for Recreation and Social Activities at the Conference at Richmond is an occasion when a "stunt" will be presented by each Yearly Meeting delegation.

There will be tennis courts available both at Earlham College and the public playgrounds, and tournaments are to be arranged. Golf at the Country Club will be open to all who care to take advantage of it. There will be motor trips over the beautiful country around.

The Conference comes at the season when Hoosiers just naturally have watermelon parties. The Music Committee has the offer of the services of a Young Friends' Orchestra from one of the meetings of the other branch. They are to play the first evening at the reception. The Richmond High School Orchestra, which became famous when they appeared at the Music Teachers' Convention of the United States at Nashville, Tenn., last year, will be one of the attractions. Other activities will be arranged spontaneously on the spot.

Purchase Meeting-House

Beautiful the journey thither—
Beautiful the way-side hedges—
Rocky, green and rose-grown hedges—
Beautiful the rambler roses—
Climbing, blooming o'er the hedges,
Making pink and green the roadside,
And to automobile passing,
Seeming mound of living beauty
Clear from Larchwood on to Purchase.

There, in all its simple grandeur,
Purchase Meeting-house is standing—
Standing in its peace and quiet:
Few the years since flame and fire
Marred and ruined wall and casement—
Marred its ancient roof and casement—
But full-soon, with strength unbounding,
Was restored its old-time grandeur—
'Most exact, its old-time grandeur.
And that summer day we met there—
E'en the singing birds, too, met there—
Other Friends, from other Meetings,
Also sought its peace and quiet—
Beautiful and perfect quiet.

Glad the words that broke the silence
Glad the hand-clasp at the closing,
And the gladsome cordial greetings.
Much we prize the kindly feelings
Of the Friends, with automobiles,
Great the joy that they are giving
To the lovers of "Old Meetings"—
Well beloved and distant Meetings.

ELIZABETH BIDDLE CONROW.

Friendly News Notes

An effort is being made to gather into a group all Friends who expect to attend the University of Chicago. Any Friends, or friends of Friends, who are interested in this movement should communicate with Garfield V. Cox, 1347 E. 62nd street, Chicago, Ill., who will be glad to assist with finding housing accommodations, etc., among Friends.

David H. Wright, of Philadelphia, who is spending the summer at Newport, R. I., has launched a movement to hold a peace convention in the Friends' Meeting-house in Farewell street, Newport, in August of each year. Since the cessation of the peace conventions that were held in the Peace Temple at Mystic, Conn., for some years, it is the desire of many Friends that they be continued yearly at Newport, R. I.

Owing to continued ill-health, Charles S. Zavitz, former Clerk of Genesee Yearly Meeting, was unable to preside at the sessions this year. He is at present at Buck Hill Falls. His place at Yearly Meeting was filled this year by C. Harold Zavitz.

Bliss Forbush reports that at the date of his writing, which was about two weeks ago, fifty-five people have stayed at Camp Keewadin in the "family parties, their visits ranging from four days to two weeks in length. The Camp is engaged until the 21st of August.

Every summer for a period of eight weeks, the New York Monthly Meeting conducts vacation schools in Manhattan and Brooklyn on their school properties. These schools come in contact with over two hundred boys and girls. A very excellent work is done. The financial support for this work comes almost wholly from voluntary subscriptions. Sufficient money has not yet been raised to carry this summer's work to a conclusion. Any Friends desiring to aid this work may send their subscriptions to Samuel B. Williams, Jr., Treasurer, Friends' Summer School, 332 Schermerhorn street, Brooklyn, New York.

As was hoped would be the case, the New Part I of the Book of Discipline, "Christian Life, Faith and Thought," is evoking a good deal of interest in circles other than Quaker ones. The Rev. V. D. Davis, speaking as Visitor at Manchester College, Oxford, on "The Open Way of the Spirit," emphasized the importance of its appearance in "confirmation of the truth of the view of religion without a formulated creed."

He described the book's contents and quoted passages, remarking that "it is a confession of faith in freedom and in the demonstration of the Spirit and of power."

At Abington Quarterly Meeting held at Gwynedd, on Eighth month 10th, messages were given by Alfred W. Wright, Isaac Michener, Elizabeth Walter, J. Barnard Walton, William Eves, Eleanor Scott Sharples and Marion DeVictor.

It was decided to change the time of the Meeting of Ministry and Counsel permanently to meet on Fifth-day morning of Quarterly Meeting, at 9 a. m., Standard time.

Elizabeth Walter gave an account of the Conference at Earlham, and J. Barnard Walton told of the plans for the General Conference at Richmond. Isaac Michener, on behalf of the representatives to the Yearly Meeting, gave a most interesting report of the work of the Yearly Meeting, calling attention to the message there of William Littleboy, of England. (The message is printed in the Extracts.)

PURCHASE QUARTERLY MEETING

About the usual summer number of from 350 to 400 were present at Purchase Quarterly Meeting on Eighth month 6th, to enjoy the sessions and the social mingling. At the meeting for worship, Anna T. Speakman gave a beautiful message, enlarging on the text, "The things of the spirit quickeneth, and the things of the flesh profiteth nothing." Arthur James urged for more thought on spiritual things and closer communion with God, quoting that poem about two ships sailing in opposite directions under the same wind, showing that it is not the "gale but the set of the sail" that determines the paths they go. William W. Cocks gave a strong plea for greater tolerance and good will among men.

In the business session an interesting written report of the New York Yearly Meeting was submitted by our delegates who attended. Friends were urged to attend the Richmond Conference, if possible.

The afternoon meeting was addressed by Arthur James, Professor of Chemistry at Lincoln University, on the question of Negro education. He made the following points:

1. There is nearly as much difference between light and dark negroes as between whites and negroes, and also some hard feeling.

2. The Garvey movement, "Back to Africa," does not come from the best element of the Negro race in this country, and does not have their support.

3. The best way to educate the colored people is to teach them to teach themselves. E. M. B.

LOBO

The Genesee Yearly Meeting of the Society of Friends was held at Coldstream from Eighth month 5th to 10th, inclusive. Delegates from various points in Ontario and western New York State, and also from Baltimore and Philadelphia were present.

A description of this little gathering here in its rural surroundings might be of interest. Sports, picnic, convention,—what is it, thinks the casual passerby. It is all. To the children it is one whole week of picnic. To the young men and maidens, it is an opportunity for sports, hikes and the forming of new friendships. To the older Friends, it is a convention planning for the improvement of human conditions in the world. For all, it is a Pentecostal outpouring of the Holy Ghost, and renewal of consecration and zeal for Christ.

The most vital concern of our Society in this period of reconstruction after the great war is that the new Christianity may be permeated and dominated by the love that was in Jesus Christ. We have little groups of Friends in all the so-called enemy nations spreading this love as they administer food and clothing to the starving, half-clad children and women of these countries. O, that men and nations might forget past hatreds and practice the command of Christ to "Love your Enemies." He knew that only by love can the human race be saved. Let us believe in Him. EDGAR M. ZAVITZ.

(A fuller account of Genesee Yearly Meeting will appear later.)

CONFERENCE AT WRIGHTSTOWN, PA.

Large was the gathering of Friends who came from all the nearby meetings as well as from West Chester, Wilmington and Philadelphia to hold a very interesting conference on the historic old meeting-house grounds at Wrightstown, Pa., on First-day, Eighth month 6th.

The subject presented by Samuel Bunting, chairman of the Yearly Meeting's Committee on First-day Schools, was "The Closer Co-operation of the First-day School and the Meeting." Julius Hund, of Wrightstown, gave a short outline of the start of First-day schools.

Thomas Foulke, of Gwynedd, said the First-day School should serve three purposes: First, it should teach expression; second, it should teach the child to understand worship; and, third, it should teach Biblical history and the basis of all religions.

Marguerite Hallowell told how the meeting should aid the First-day School. It can give financial aid, plan the work and keep in touch with its problems.

Herbert Way, of Wilmington, continued with the obligation of the meeting to the school.

Herbert Worth gave a very helpful talk containing, from his store of ripened experience, much that the younger workers could enjoy and profit by.

The discussion which followed showed the widespread interest in the subject, and not until late afternoon did the assemblage break up and go to their homes.

ELLA M. TOMLINSON.

HAVERFORD SCHOLARSHIPS

Haverford College announces sixteen Corporation scholarships, at an annual value of three hundred dollars each, awarded to the four men in each class receiving the highest scholastic averages. The recipients of the awards are as follows:

1923

Edward K. Haviland—Port Deposit, Md.

Norman E. Rutt—914 Old Lancaster Rd., Bryn Mawr, Pa.

Dudley M. Pruitt—Hwanghsien, China.

G. Randle Grimes—333 Vassar Ave., Swarthmore, Pa.

1924

George W. Howgate—414 Cartaret St., Camden, N. J.

John F. Blair—Winston-Salem, N. C.

Howard Comfort—Haverford, Pa.

Philip G. Rhoads—Moorestown, N. J.

1925

Frederic R. Prokosch—Bryn Mawr, Pa.

Edward L. Gordy—Chambersburg, Pa.

Leigh E. Chadwick—16th and R Sts., N. W., Washington, D. C.

Edwin P. Laug—701 Beechwood Ave., Collingdale, Pa.

1926

Dalzell F. Hartman—Lancaster, Pa.

Francis H. Ale—1162 Murray Hill Ave., Pittsburgh, Pa.

Frederick Roedelheim—Elkins Park, Pa.

Daniel C. Lewis, Jr.—Millville, N. J.

WESTBURY QUARTERLY MEETING

Elizabeth Powell Bond, Isaac Wilson, Anna Travilla Speakman and a number of Friends from Purchase Meeting were visitors at Westbury Quarterly Meeting held on Seventh month 29th.

Isaac Wilson's message was that Christianity is the practical application of Jesus' teaching, and the very essential of Quakerism is faith in God. Have we the courage to invite the world to "come and see" this faith?

Anna Travilla Speakman dwelt on the impressiveness of the silence in meetings, a living silence in which all participate. As Friends, now is the opportunity to live before the world and share with others the peace that comes "away from noise and voices."

William W. Cocks spoke of spiritual currents surrounding us, and it is only our lack of knowledge of the code which keeps us from the true understanding.

"Personality and Coal" was the fourth subject in the series on Problems of Human Relations discussed at the afternoon sessions of Westbury Quarterly Meeting the past year. The address was given by Robert Bruere, head of the Bureau of Industrial Research, who is co-operating with the Friends' Service Committee in the Pennsylvania coal field with which he has been familiar for several years. The discussion that followed his talk, on why miners remain in the industry, the waste in mining, and the question of union interference in non-union districts, was on an unusually objective level, and consequently of more than usual interest and value.

Among the significant statements made were the following: "For every ton of coal mined a ton is wasted; and of every ton burned only 25 per cent. is used. Our lack of thrift as a nation means less education for all the children of America and therefore less wise use on their part of all the resources of the country.

"We use between five and six million tons of coal, but keep up equipment for eight or nine millions on the theory that he who has may use and destroy. The results in terms of human relations are suggested by Mr. Bruere's outline of conditions in the coal industry: an average work year of 215 days instead of the possible production year of 308 days; work full tilt while the order is on, but the working force held all the time, though in some districts they work less than 150 days a year. Perhaps 500,000 of the 700,000 miners are married; if we allow four to a family, this means two million people dependent on the coal industry, one-third of whom never know when work is to be had. Out of work in this case does not mean mere idleness and the consequent demoralization of uncertainty; it means also a muscular stiffening up after a few days in the outside atmosphere, and the miner's work and the effect of periods of unemployment ages men very prematurely. Last year the average year's wage of the coal miner was between $700 and $800, and a 30 per cent. cut was proposed. Yet we demand decent living conditions for our children.

"A great basic industry like coal could and should be organized effectively for *service* by reducing the number of miners by one hundred and fifty to two hundred thousand, regularizing the industry, and utilizing the product fully."

Coming to the present crisis, Mr. Bruere said he had been asked to come and help the hungry children because he knew the miners. In one town where the mine war was on, the co-operation of operators and miners was won in two days, so that the miners' hall is used for relief work and a mine superintendent's wife prepares the food. Other towns will prove more difficult, but if we follow the Friendly way of going in with both groups and maintaining, "in the midst of the controversy, the arithmetic of love," we cannot tell what we may reap.

Items from Everywhere

Capital punishment is to be abolished in Queensland, Australia. By a vote of 33 to 30 the legislature there has passed a bill to deprive the hangmen of their jobs. Holland and Portugal also have abolished the death penalty; Roumania has never employed it; and it is rarely inflicted in Belgium, Denmark, Sweden and Switzerland.

Nearly all of the wheat in the great belt stretching from Oklahoma to the Canadian border is harvested by migratory labor, the bulk of which is concentrated in the membership of the Industrial Workers of the World. Thousands of migrants who work at construction jobs during the winter stream into Southern Oklahoma when the crops begin to ripen and push northward, cutting, binding and threshing the grain in 500-mile swathes.

Christian workers all over the country will be glad to learn that the Bible at least is getting back to pre-war prices. For the first time in almost five years the American Bible Society is able to offer Gospels with heavy paper cover for one cent. An edition of the Gospel of St. John is already off the press and the other Gospels will be prepared in the same style and in various languages. One is amazed that a book of 64 pages, so attractively covered, is issued for the price of one cent.

The American Bible Society distributed 4,855,464 Bibles and parts of Bibles last year, at a cost of $1,172,756. From the sale of books there came in $462,832. It cost 24 cents a copy to produce the volumes and place them in the hands of the ultimate consumer, who paid on the average 9 cents a copy—of course many were given away. The 15 cents difference is paid by churches and individuals who wish to help the society.

A campaign has been successfully carried out in Kansas City, Mo., for the erection of an "Interdenominational Home for Girls." The fund amounts to $225,000 or $25,000 more than was anticipated. At present 28 girls are being cared for in an eight-room house sustained by Protestant churches in which neglected girls from 12 to 18 years of age are given motherly care and Christian training. In the home, the girls are taught to be domestic. They learn housework, cooking and laundering. In the last few months 78 have been turned away because of inadequate accommodations.

THE OPEN FORUM

This column is intended to afford free expression of opinion by readers on questions of interest. The INTELLIGENCER is not responsible for any such opinions. Letters must be brief, and the editor reserves the right to omit parts if necessary to save space.

To the Editor:

I am a Friend by birthright and by conviction. Therefore, I believe in the idea that it is the right of every person to worship God in the manner that to him seems best.

Being a Friend, I am strongly opposed to all wars and fightings, individual, national and international. Also, being a Friend, I am in favor of free speech and free press, when the liberty which these give is not used as a license for treasonable speech or action against the Government that throws its protections over its citizens irrespective of color, political creed, religious belief or nationality.

And, therefore, as a Friend, I could not sign a petition asking President Harding to pardon and liberate political prisoners who are affiliated with organizations whose purpose it is to destroy the Government which protects them, endeavoring to substitute in its place one of Bolshevistic tendency, and does not hesitate to inflict murder on those who differ in opinion, as witnessed in the terrible affair enacted in one of our large western cities some time ago when peaceable men were shot down from roof and upper chamber windows because of their disagreement in politics.

It were better for our country that such persons were kept secluded from the outward world with no opportunity, either by tongue or pen, to spread their infamous propaganda to the detriment of the Government and the safety of its people. ELIZABETH H. COALE.

Holder, Ill.

To the Editor:

When it comes to a question about "lions and lambs," that is something about which I do not have to speculate, I know. I know because I live in the country, and while I have no descendant of a lion, as they are not fashionable in this particular section, I do have one descendant of a wolf and two of tiger ancestry, and they all eat out of one dish, and at night the tiger kitten sleeps curled up close to the wolf puppy! And that is not all; while I do not have lambs, I do have beautiful kids, and one mother tiger had her kittens in the stall with a mother of kids, and all laid safely side by side. They were as happy together as everyone who has *seen nature changed by love knows they would be.*

And someone calls farmers "dupes," and he makes the claim on the ground that they do not get all the money they *might*. Money—money—what is money? Why, farmers *already have* all the things that money can buy, and more, yes, infinitely more. They have power, too. They could starve all the city people to death, *if* they wanted to. But such people,—real humans—do not do all the mischief they *can*. Yes, farmers have all that money might buy, and infinitely more. I am a farmer myself and I know. I do not need an oil painting of a sunset, though I do admire them, for I have the sunset itself! And not merely one sunset, no, many, many, many. I am a real millionaire when it comes to sunsets, the ones God paints, and sunrises, too. I have all those that my eyes see and all that are stored up inside of me to look at on cloudy days. No, it is not the farmers, the real farmers, who are dupes.

Could we not get those "surplus workers," about whom we moan so frequently, and on whom we claim so many evil powers prey, into the country? Could we not transplant *at least some* of that surplus, who keep down the price of "labor," out on to the soil? There is a great deal of *it* that *needs* working. Friends are proud of their ability as educators. Suppose *we taught* these people *how* to feed themselves and their children, instead of merely giving them our money, and berating the "class" that oppresses them. No one ever changed a "class" *to which he did not belong*, by standing and shouting names at it. *Human nature* and *every kind of nature changes by another method than that.* It is the *method*, not the aim, that is giving us trouble.

Suppose some of *us Quakers* were to provide the land, there are many ways of securing land in this country, and suppose some of us gave seed, and some gave a cow, and some of us a plow or a chicken. Could we not get them started, and change, at least, that tendency to *huddle too close* and tramp and starve each other, like chickens in an overcrowded brooder? That is very different from the instinct that prompts *intelligent working together*. If *we* would come out of our studies and try, I think we Friends, we farmer Friends, could help, *could really do it.* ELEANOR SCOTT SHARPLES.

To the Editor:

A unit of value of a day's work would appear to be what one man can earn a day at farm work, after deducting other expenses, counting the days in a year when he can do work on the crops and also when weather conditions permit; then add to that for skill, for risk in work, and the value of the labor contributed by the rest of the family and it will show the unjust demands of union labor. H. P. HUSBAND.

BIRTHS

THOMPSON—On Eighth month 3rd, to Theodore and Marion Pyle Thompson, of Kennett Square, Pa., a son, named Theodore Richards Thompson, Jr.

TOMLINSON—On Seventh month 22nd, at Jenkintown, to C. Ernest and Frances Sharpless Tomlinson, a son, named Robert Lloyd Tomlinson.

MARRIAGES

HENDERSON-BROOKE—On Eighth month 12th, at Sandy Spring, Md., Dorothy Brooke, daughter of Mr. and Mrs. Charles F. Brooke, and Robert Neel Henderson, of Germantown, Pa. The certificate was read by Stanley Yarnall, principal of Friends' School, Germantown, Pa.

DEATHS

CARVER—At Friends' Home, Germantown, Pa., on Eighth month 7th, Sarah M. Carver, daughter of Sarah and Jacob Richards, in her 89th year. Her long chain of years was spent in no small way in endeavors to make the large class of those "whom ye have always with you" a little brighter and happier. She served on the Board of Managers of the Temporary Home for Women and Children for over fifty years, and was also a member of the Board of Managers of "The Home for Aged and Infirm Colored Persons" and "The Home for Destitute Colored Children."

EVES—At Millville, Pa., on Seventh month 19th, Morris E. Eves, aged 61 years.

COMING EVENTS

EIGHTH MONTH

19th—Short Creek Quarterly Meeting, at Emerson, Ohio.

19th—Pelham Half-Yearly Meeting, at Sparta, Ontario.

19th-21st—Fairfax Quarterly Meeting, at Lincoln, Va. O. Edward and Anne W. Janney and La Verne H. and Bliss Forbush expect to attend.

20th—Duanesburg Half-Yearly Meeting, at Quaker street, N. Y.

20th—Certain members of Philadelphia Quarterly Meeting's Visiting Committee expect to attend meeting at Schuylkill, at 10.30 a. m. Others expect to attend Valley Meeting, the visit appointed for Seventh month 9th having been postponed to this date.

21st—Illinois Yearly Meeting, at McNabb, Ill.

22nd—Burlington Quarterly Meeting, at Mt. Holly, N. J.

26th—Quaker pageant will be given at Willistown Meeting-house, at 3 p. m. All invited. Bring box supper. See notice.

26th-28th—Warrington Quarterly Meeting, at Menallen, Pa. Thomas B., Helen L. and Anna W. Hull expect to attend.

27th—Members of Philadelphia Quarterly Meeting's Visiting Committee will attend Merion Meeting at 11 a. m.

31st—Bucks Quarterly Meeting, at Falls, Pa.

NINTH MONTH

2nd—Nottingham Quarterly Meeting, at East Nottingham, Md.

2nd-4th—Center Quarterly Meeting, at Half Moon, Pa. O. Edward Janney expects to attend.

3rd—First-day at 2.30 p. m., Eastern Standard time, a meeting for divine worship will be held at the Wayside Chapel, Cheyney, Delaware County, Pa. A community meeting for all interested persons. Thornbury Young Friends' Association will co-operate. A pleasant pilgrimage from West Chester trolley or by train from Broad Street Station.

5th—Whitewater Quarterly Meeting, at Lincolnville, Ind.

7th—Salem Quarterly Meeting, at Woodstown, N. J.

11th—Baltimore Quarterly Meeting, at Gunpowder, Md.

14th—Haddonfield Quarterly Meeting, at Haddonfield, N. J.

NOTICE—The Representative Committee of Ohio Yearly Meeting will meet at the home of Lindley and Miriam B. Tomlinson, 111 McKinley avenue, Salem, Ohio, on Ninth month 9th, 1922, at 10 a. m., instead of on Eighth month 26th, on account of the Conference at Richmond, Indiana.

NOTICE—A Committee of Salem Quarterly Meeting have arranged to hold the annual Meeting for Worship at the old Cape May Meeting-house at Seaville, Cape May County, New Jersey, on First-day, Eighth month 27th, at 11 o'clock a. m., Standard time.

NOTICE—"Children of Light," a pageant of Quaker History, will be given by the children and grown-ups of Newtown Square, Birmingham, Malvern, Concordville, and Willistown First-day Schools, at Willistown Meeting-house on Seventh-day, Eighth month 26th, at 3 p. m., Standard time. All are cordially invited to attend and bring a box supper. Games will be played after supper. Willistown Meeting-house is one mile from the William Penn Hotel on the Philadelphia and West Chester trolley line from 69th street.

American Friends' Service Committee

WILBUR K. THOMAS, EX. SEC.

20 S. 12th St. Philadelphia.

CASH CONTRIBUTIONS

WEEK ENDING AUGUST 5TH

Five Years Meeting	$31.61
Other Meetings:	
Philadelphia Yearly Meeting (4th and Arch Sts.)	3,986.51
Providence, Pa., Children's Sunday-school	10.00
Gunpowder Monthly Meeting	40.00
Frankford Friends	24.00
Rahway and Plainfield	8.68
Winona, Ohio	13.00
	$4,082.19
Chalons—France	5.00
Austria	380.75
Germany	292.75
Poland	511.81
Russia	2,013.50
West Virginia	347.50
Central Pennsylvania	207.50
General Fund	142.51
Clothing	25.00
Refunds and payments	103.09
	$8,143.21

Shipments received during week ending August 5th: 44 boxes and packages; 2 anonymous.

Auditors' Report

OF THE AMERICAN FRIENDS' SERVICE COMMITTEE FOR THE YEAR ENDING MAY 31ST, 1922.

The books of the American Friends' Service Committee have been audited by Certified Public Accountants, Moyer & Schectman, of Philadelphia, and the following extracts will be of interest to American Friends:

Receipts

Balance June 1, 1921:

Cash	$243,304.06	
Securities	29,585.02	
Cash securities on hand June 1, 1920		$272,889.08

Contributions Received During Year:

Philadelphia Yearly Meetings (Arch Street)	$38,051.62	
Five Years Meetings	11,042.23	
Race Street Meetings	18,519.26	
Other Meetings of Friends	3,460.89	
Individual contributions	72,283.75	
Interest on securities and bank deposits	8,446.76	

Earmarked Contributions:

Austrian relief	82,431.91	
Armenian relief	903.96	
China relief	340.13	
Clothing department	6,363.29	
German relief	177,646.26	
German overhead	5,084.65	
Home service	638.14	
Polish relief	46,230.97	
Russian relief	1,012,058.20	
Russian overhead	53,645.07	
Religious work in Europe	3,100.00	
Serbian relief	3,065.90	
Syrian relief	6,246.11	
James E. Speyer, Treasurer American Relief Administration, European Children's Fund	45,000.00	
Total contributions		1,591,559.10

Disbursements

Administration expense	$101,307.97	
Food drafts	13,306.45	
Reconstruction unit	1,518.44	
Clothing department	9,712.57	
Relief work in Russia	636,718.31	
Relief work in Armenia	487.80	
Relief work in Germany	434,405.20	
Relief work in Serbia	4,070.39	
Relief work in Austria	123,265.32	
Relief work in Poland	80,903.06	
Relief work in Syria	9,694.40	
Home service	632.90	
Friends' European Commission	220.19	
Allowances to workers	3,192.31	
Total disbursements		1,419,435.31
Balance cash and securities May 31, 1922		$445,012.87

Additional Contributions

	Gift Value
Donations of food by the American Relief Administration for work in Austria	$35,408.00
Donations of cotton-seed meal by the American Relief Administration for increasing fresh milk supply in Poland	50,000.00
Food draft profits delivered by the American Relief Administration in Germany	192,000.00
Food delivered in Germany by the American Relief Administration on account of the European Children's Fund Drive in order to bring the total average feeding to 700,000	354,875.00
Corn rations donated by the American Relief Administration in Russia for adult feeding in Friends' area (approximate)	25,200.00
Food credit contributed by the Joint Distribution Committee for work in Minsk	115,000.00
Gifts in kind for relief work in Russia contributed by the American public—Food	261,104.59
Flour donated by American public for work in Germany	510.00
Clothing contributed by the American Red Cross and the American public for relief work in Austria, Poland, Germany and Russia (approximate)	253,046.27
Supplies for delivery in France	250.00
Supplies for delivery in Syria	829.00
Food purchased with money contributed by the $3,000,000 German Child Feeding Campaign Committee for child feeding work in Germany—Food	858,298.13
Purchase of new clothing	100,000.00
Purchasing food in Europe for child feeding work	110,000.00
	$1,068,298.13

The German Government delivered flour and sugar for the child feeding work to an approximate value of	$800,000.00
Grand total in gifts in cash and kind for all fields of work	$4,748,080.09

It is also interesting to note in connection with this that contributions for the month of July were $34,340.32 as against collections for the same month last year of $25,072.51. Contributions for the last three months total more than for the corresponding months of 1921—$252,594.48 as against $107,322.62. Readers should give special attention to the contributions of the various groups of Friends. Some of the money in "Individual Contributions" represents money contributed by Friends who are not definitely affiliated with any particular Yearly Meeting, but most of the sum was contributed by people who are not Friends.

To the Lot Holders and others interested in Fairhill Burial Ground:

GREEN STREET Monthly Meeting has funds available for the encouragement of the practice of cremating the dead to be interred in Fairhill Burial Ground. We wish to bring this fact as prominently as possible to those who may be interested. We are prepared to undertake the expense of cremation in case any lot holder desires us to do so.

Those interested should communicate with William H. Gaskill, Treasurer of the Committee of Interments, Green Street Monthly Meeting, or any of the following members of the Committee.

William H. Gaskill, 3801 Arch St.
Samuel N. Longstreth, 1218 Chestnut St.
Charles F. Jenkins, 232 South Seventh St.
Stuart S. Graves, 3023 Germantown Ave.

HOTELS.

Please help us by patronizing our advertisers. Mention the "Friends' Intelligencer."

The Friends' Intelligencer

Established 1844 | EIGHTH MONTH 26, 1922 | Volume 79 Number 34

Contents

REGULAR MEETINGS

OAKLAND, CALIF. — A FRIENDS' Meeting is held every First-day at 11 A. M., in the Extension Room, Y. W. C. A. Building, Webster Street, above 14th. Visiting Friends always welcome.

PASADENA, CALIFORNIA — Orange Grove Monthly Meeting of Friends, 520 East Orange Grove Avenue. Meeting for worship, First-day, 11 A. M. Monthly Meeting, the second First-day of each month, at 1.45 P. M. First-day School (except Monthly Meeting days) 9.45 A. M.

THE FRIENDS' INTELLIGENCER

Published weekly, 140 N. 15th Street, Philadelphia, Pa., by Friends' Intelligencer Association, Ltd.

PAUL W. WAGER, *Editor.*
SUE C. YERKES, *Business Manager*

Editorial Board: Elizabeth Powell Bond, Thomas A. Jenkins, J. Russell Smith, George A. Walton.

Board of Managers: Edward Cornell, Alice Hall Paxson, Paul M. Pearson, Annie Hillborn, Elwood Hollingshead, William C. Biddle, Charles F. Jenkins, Edith M. Winder, Frances M. White.

Officers of Intelligencer Associates: Ellwood Burdsall, Chairman; Bertha L. Broomell, Secretary; Herbert P. Worth, Treasurer.

Subscription rates: United States, Mexico, Cuba and Panama, $2.50 per year. Canada and other foreign countries, $3.00 per year. Checks should be made payable to Friends' Intelligencer Association, Ltd.

Entered as Second Class Matter at Philadelphia Post Office

SCHOOLS.

NOTICE—Concise statements of the principles of the Religious Society of Friends and their application to the problems of every day living, including "The Spirit of Quakerism," by Elbert Russell; "Preparation for Life's Greatest Business," by Rufus M. Jones; and other articles by Henry W. Wilbur, Howard M. Jenkins, Elizabeth Lloyd, Jesse H. Holmes, O. Edward Janney, Edward B. Rawson, etc., to be had free on application to Friends' General Conference Advancement Committee, 140 North Fifteenth Street, Philadelphia, Pa.

The Friends' Intelligencer

The religion of Friends is based on faith in the "INWARD LIGHT," or direct revelation of God's spirit and will in every seeking soul.

The INTELLIGENCER is interested in all who bear the name of Friends in every part of the world, and aims to promote love, unity and intercourse among all branches and with all religious societies.

ESTABLISHED 1844 | PHILADELPHIA, EIGHTH MONTH 26, 1922 | VOLUME 79 NUMBER 34

Much of the world's unhappiness is due to covetousness.

✖

Freedom, and not oppression, is the right way to meet anarchy. At least, this was the conviction of Edmund Burke.

✖

Does the business meeting fail to appeal to the membership? First, ask them why: it may be a very small matter that tips the balance on the side of staying away. Second, is the business *real* business? If not, an "inspirational" session would do more good.

✖

One sentence in Maxim Gorky's letter of thanks to Herbert Hoover is worth remembering: "The charity of the American people kindles the dream of brotherhood among mankind just at the time when brotherly love and sympathy are very much needed." Such words should be passed on to the contributors, great and small, to the funds of the American Friends' Service Committee. Gorky has also written to Jane Addams, to the same effect.

✖

A few months ago the Motion-picture Producers and Distributors of America called a religious man, a Presbyterian elder, from his seat in the President's Cabinet to become president of their association and to help them produce and put before the people cleaner and better pictures.

The motion-picture business had a phenomenal growth. Within a few years from its birth it had grown into one of the most gigantic industries in the country. It is not surprising that, with its rapid development, the spiritual aspects of the institution (for it is now recognized as an institution as well as an industry) were neglected. The result was that the type of picture was not always clean and wholesome; indeed, it was sometimes degrading. State Boards of Censorship were created to "weed out" the objectionable films but pictures that have been made will be shown. Furthermore, it was not enough to make the films negatively good; they ought to be positively good. Therefore the only sensible policy was to see that only good pictures were produced. When public opinion was sufficiently aroused it was not difficult to secure the audience of the producers. They were soon convinced that the future of the "movies" would be secured by elevating them to this higher educational and moral plane. In this mood they called Will H. Hays to be the Judge Landis of the film world.

He brought to his new task his usual enthusiasm, idealism and integrity, and he has already made splendid progress. The producers are backing him loyally and have stated their new policy in these words: "We wish to establish and maintain the highest possible moral and artistic standards in motion-picture production, and to develop the educational as well as the entertainment value and the general usefulness of the motion-picture."

Mr. Hays recognizes the tremendous influence exerted on youthful minds by the screen and he says, "We estimate that within every twenty-four hours 20,000,000 men, women, and children look for an hour or two on the motion picture screen. They come, not actuated by duty, but with mind relaxed, as a master psychologist would have them come if he desired to make the most lasting impression on them. The influence of the screen on our national life is absolutely limitless—its influence on our taste, conduct, aspirations, and on our youth and consequently its immeasurable influence on our future. Its integrity must and shall be protected. In the name of the producers and distributors of America let me say that we accept the demand of the American youth and mother, the challenge of educator and preacher. We accept it as service—service which is the 'supreme commitment of life.' "

We have reason to believe that the producers under Mr. Hays' direction are sincerely trying to raise the "movies" to a new level and to make them a real force for good in the life of the nation. They should be guided and stimulated in this worthy ambition by the opinion and encouragement of all good citizens.

Lives That Live: Some Thoughts on Recent Quaker Biographies

By Hubert W. Peet

An ingenious German writer has recently written a treatise on the theme that Richardson and the other early English novelists really based the plan and form of their stories on the Journals of early Friends. The theory, right or wrong, at least shows an appreciation of the manner in which the true artist's aim, the revelation of character, is displayed in these writings.

My recent reading, though not actually in early Journals, has brought me up against the value of our Quaker biographies, for the germ of the Journals, not of the pillar Friends of the first era but such as Samuel Bownas, Thomas Shillitoe, Daniel Wheeler, Levi Coffin, and a host of others, are one of the outstanding features of Rufus Jones's latest contribution to our literary store, his two volumes on "The Later Periods of Quakerism" (Macmillan 30/-). But even more immediately helpful are the two latest life-stories of modern Friends. Agnes Fry's "Memoir" of her father, Sir Edward Fry, Lord Justice of Appeal (Oxford Univ. Press, 12/6), and "George Lloyd Hodgkin" by his sister, Violet Hodgkin (Friends' Bookshop, 10/6), form a study in contrasts—the lawyer who died at 90, and the young Friend absolutist C. O., who died at Bagdad, aged 38. Yet each was the seeker after truth and each followed the gleam to the end.

One of the finest tributes to Sir Edward Fry was the saying by a fellow-member of the Bar, that he never overstated a case. The remark sums up his precisian's attitude to life which made him so valuable a jurist.

With our present revolt against much that is termed "law and order" we want reminding that to Edward Fry the members of the Bar and the Bench were "engaged opon one of the noblest of human callings—the promotion of justice and honesty among mankind." While many of us to-day feel that there is a difference between the merciful justice of God and the legal justice of man, we can be thankful to the high place men like Edward Fry have raised the latter, because they sought, though perhaps not always successfully, to attain the higher through it.

Law and formalism whether of the courts or of a rigid Quakerism did not crush out of Edward Fry the mystic or the man. Speaking of his earlier life he wrote, "My religion was then, if you will, rather pagan than Christian; but as time went on, I found more and more in the New Testament which nourished my inward nature. I applied to myself sometimes the words of Christ—'Ye believe in God, believe also in Me.' The basis of my religious belief was the inner conscience of men—nay my own individual inner conscience." And later Agnes Fry records—"My father was wont to dwell on what he called 'the smallness of religion'—the fewness of the essentials to a true life. . . He felt no one could go far wrong who held to the spiritual meaning of the Universe."

No one can think of Sir Edward Fry without thinking of his international work. "Before his seventieth year he had duly played four out of the five of the 'many parts' allotted to man: the infant, the schoolboy, the lover (the soldier omitted) and the justice, but when the sixth age should have shifted him into the 'lean and slippered stage' a wider and unsought scene of activity opened before him, that of international arbitration." This culminated in his mission as "a Minister Extraordinary and First British Plenipotentiary" of the second Hague Conference. As he himself wrote to one of his daughters while the Conference dragged on its weary course, "Many of the deputies are clever men and a chaos of clever men is not likely to get on fast." We all know how the hopes of the Conference have been dissipated then and in subsequent similar gatherings.

The human side is brought out in many a delightful touch. The story for instance of the Highgate neighbor who knowing his children only by sight from her window, as she was an invalid, sent one a birthday present addressed to "Sir Edward's little playfellow." Also a saying of his concerning babies which will appeal to some bachelor and maiden young Friends called upon to admire the new arrivals of their married comrades, that he "expected they would improve with keeping."

"It is the type of life which arrests the Friend of today." It is a vision, an ideal, a spirit which possesses his soul. It is the inalienable impression of Christ's venture which holds him. He may be wrong in his interpretation of life, of this ideal, of this Divine Person, but whether right or wrong, he sees what he sees and he cannot do otherwise than follow his vision."

These words of Rufus Jones' appear at the beginning of the Life of George Lloyd Hodgkin. They might equally be applied to Sir Edward Fry. I would have Friends young and old read both.

This is not the place to tell again the story of the "unfolding of the Quaker self" of the youngest son

felt that for them the call had yet come. Had he and she been able to make a decision now, they might have crossed the seas, or like the majority of those who today have to give an answer, they might have believed that for them at any rate the corner of "the field of the world" in which they must labor, is to "build Jerusalem in England's green and pleasant land." But whatever the decision might have been for them, may we make our own his desire in his last letter to his wife "to pray for a greater spirit of hopefulness. I think a bigger ideal of what our country stands for is the thing to ask for. And then the element of hope and usefulness and eagerness to work will follow."

Reprinted from *Friends' Fellowship Papers*, obtainable from the Friends' Bookshop, 140 Bishopsgate, London, E. C. 2, price 20 cents, postage extra.

Thoughts

These gems of thought were written by Nathan T. Brown, of Lincoln, Va. They were written on the back of a calendar a short time before his death, which occurred on April 5th.

The foundation of virtue and religion is in no book, but in God, in the nature of things, in the soul of man.

If you would serve God, cultivate that seed of Divine Grace within you. It is your birthright. According to its growth will you be able to discern right from wrong.

As your thoughts are, so are you. Help your spiritual being to overcome the many evil fascinations or temptations that beset you in the pathway of life, that you may win the battle in the end and be glorified by the Father, as was Jesus.

"Prayer is the soul's sincere desire," and it is only by prayer and watching that the goal may be attained.

Others may declare things as truth, but take them to the judgment seat within you before you accept them.

Christ in you will guide you if you will let him. "No man can save his brother or give a ransom for his soul." Your salvation comes from within you.

"Accursed is the man who trusteth in man and leaneth on the arm of flesh, and departeth from the Lord."

"Faith without works profiteth nothing. Within the Spiritual man is the true Mount of God where the Eternal One comes down to reveal himself." Revelation is Light.

Concerning the Origin of the Book of Discipline

By ANNA J. F. HALLOWELL

(Concluded from last issue)

The establishment of the various meetings was irregular, the need for their functions leading to their development "as way opened." The first mentioned were the "morning meetings," which seem to have been for the strengthening and encouragement of each other by the ministering Friends. With the persecutions, which so promptly followed the gathering of the meetings, came the need to care for the victims and their families, and all these cases seem to have been referred (when Friends in the immediate neighborhood could not meet the need) to the Morning Meeting. It was gradually felt that these meetings should be relieved of these duties, so at last, in 1675, the Meeting for Sufferings was created. Its sessions were held weekly for many years, then less frequently until in 1794, when, its original functions almost obsolete, it had given to it the duties which have made it what we now call it, Representative Committee.

Under date of 1666, George Fox says in his Journal, "Then was I moved of the Lord to recommend the setting up of five Monthly Meetings of men and women Friends in the city (London) besides the women's meetings and the Quarterly Meetings, to take care of God's glory, and to admonish and exhort such as walked . . . not according to truth." These meetings so answered to the need that had been felt, that others were at once "set up throughout the nation," answerable to the Quarterly Meetings, already established.

There was one "General Meeting" held in London in 1668, attended by ministers only, which requested the Quarterly Meetings "to make a collection for the service of Truth beyond the seas, and for the distribution of books." Again in 1672 a General Meeting of ministers, representing the various Quarters, made this minute: "It is concluded, agreed, and assented unto, by Friends then present, that for the better ordering, managing, and regulating of the public affairs of Friends relating to the truth and the service thereof, that there be a General Meeting of Friends held at London once a year, in the week called Whitsun-week, to consist of six Friends for the city of London, three for the city of Bristol, two for the town of Colchester, and one or two from each of the counties of England and Wales respectively"; nevertheless, the Yearly Meeting, as such, was not settled till 1678, since which date there has been no break.

America had a Yearly Meeting of all members—not exclusively ministers, earlier than the mother-

The Bluffton Conference

The National Conference of Religious Bodies which hold that Peace between Nations can be maintained by following the teachings of Jesus, held at Bluffton, Ohio, August 4-7, was an inspiring gathering. We Quaker pacifists are now assured for all time that we have in the field true co-laborers for Peace. Never again can we speak of our peace testimony as tho' we as Friends had exclusive right thereto when we know of the long-time devotion of our Mennonite and Dunkard brethren who have suffered untold hardships for this testimony as precious to them as to us! From the opening session in the First Mennonite Church to the closing in the chapel of Bluffton College (Mennonite) the way was marked by such devotion, earnestness, consecration and sincerity as to elicit our deepest thanks. The cordial welcome accorded us on our arrival at Bluffton, the homes freely offered and the courtesies extended left an impression of whole-hearted hospitality not soon forgotten.

Now as to the Conference itself. There were one hundred members registered from a distance, not including the large numbers attending from nearby. Of those registered 57 were Mennonites, 31 Friends, 5 Brethren, 2 Schwenkfelders, 2 Congregationalists, 1 Christian, 1 Reformed Church in United States and 1 Methodist. The poll of states revealed seventeen states and two provinces in Canada.

Of the Friends twelve were members of the two Philadelphia Yearly Meetings, each meeting sending five regularly accredited delegates. Others were from New York, New England, Baltimore, California and Indiana Meetings.

As the call carefully set forth, the object of the Conference was twofold: To come together for a season of conference and prayer, and to discuss ways and means of furthering the cause of peace. It was not expected that any permanent organization would be effected. In fact, we were admonished over and over not to think of accomplishing great things here, but rather out of the inspiration gained to go back home to work with renewed vigor—to be touched "as with a live coal from this holy altar" and be purified and consecrated anew. How inadequate are words to convey the spirit of this assembly! Truly it was a holy place, where there were heart revealings and soul searchings, where the oil of consecration made easier the way of the future.

At the opening session the evening of Sixth-day, Eighth month 4th, Elmer E. S. Johnson, of Hereford, Pa., a Schwenkfelder, declared: "If there ever was a time when the Christian people were faced with a challenge to make impossible a repetition of the late war, it is now." This was the key-note of the conference. President S. K. Mosiman, of Bluffton College, in his address of welcome, likewise declared "if Christian people had held as diligently to their real purpose as in building up church organizations, we would now have the Age of Peace." Wilbur K. Thomas in stating the object of the conference told of the greater knowledge and closer relationships growing out of the war, which made desirable a gathering of the denominations believing war to be inconsistent with the teachings of Jesus. Bishop S. E. Allgyer, of West Liberty, Ohio, who will be remembered as serving with his son in the Friends' Reconstruction Unit in France, told of "The Basis of the Christian Testimony against War."

In discussing the subject for Seventh-day morning, "Christian Service—Its Obligations and Opportunities," the speakers were respectively Mennonite, Brethren and Friend, one of each also being heard in the afternoon, when "Methods of developing Peace Sentiment" was the theme. In this way, as perhaps in no other, was shown the real unity of purpose. Sub-divisions of the subject were discussed by each speaker. H. P. Krehbiel, of Newton, Kansas, dealt with "Obligations of the Christian in Times of National Danger"; J. H. Henry of Washington, D. C., discussed "Christianity and Patriotism"; and Alexander C. Purdy of Earlham College, Indiana, chose as his subject "The Heroic Appeal of Christian Service."

The general subject of the afternoon session was education for peace and how the Sunday-school, the churches, the schools and colleges, the press and the "movies" may all be avenues for the dissemination of peace sentiment.

Elijah E. Kresge of Allentown, Pa., in his address on Seventh-day evening on "The Key to a Warless World," declared "Jesus Christ holds the key to this as to every other problem, and he took the first step when he said "Our" Father. The spirit of love between brothers precludes war.

On First-day morning members of the Conference divided attendance among the various Mennonite Churches in and near Bluffton. The afternoon was devoted to the discussion of "How Young People can further the Peace Testimony." Six young men whose experiences in camp as C. O.'s and as Reconstruction Workers abroad had more strongly grounded them in the peace faith, took part.

The evening session was filled by Frederick J. Libby on "The Outlook for Permanent Peace" after the Joint Peace Letter of Philadelphia Friends was read by William B. Harvey. The declaration of General O'Ryan that "the American people can end war in our generation if they get on the job" was emphasized, as was the great activity of women in this line. The Anti-Saloon League was cited as succeeding in its campaign, by driving nail after nail into the saloon's coffin, and three nails were mentioned as effective for the war coffin: World organization, world-wide reduction of armaments and education for peace. Quoting the last of the Peace Letter the speaker closed with the query: "Do you want to leave the next war as your legacy to the church? America must lead the way to abolish war and Christians must lead America."

As we came to the closing session on Second-day morning, surely all felt with the leader that we had been on the mountain top, and the need was to carry the vision home, and make it visible to others. As a means to this end it was desired that the addresses given at the conference should be assembled and distributed.

Encouragement was given to the efforts to secure Peace Lessons in the International Sunday-school Lessons, and as other definite means of service the following resolutions were adopted.

Resolved: That this conference encourages Peace Oratorical contests in the Colleges of the United States and that the following committee be directly responsible for the promotion of such contests: Stephen R. Weston, Antioch College, Yellow Springs, Ohio; Alexander C. Purdy, Earlham College, Richmond, Indiana; Payson Miller, Bluffton College, Bluffton, Ohio.

As a group of members of various denominations meeting in a conference at Bluffton, Ohio, we wish to record our approval of the efforts of the Canadian Mennonites to bring Mennonites from Russia for settlement in Canada. We believe the plan is sound and therefore, recommend that Mennonites, Friends, Dunkards and other related bodies do what they can to provide the necessary funds.

While there had been a strong feeling against a possible tendency to pass resolutions and to feel in so doing that something definite had been accomplished, yet there was an expressed desire that what had been gained in knowledge and fellowship should serve as a nucleus for the future. Accordingly the following resolution was adopted:

Resolved: That this conference approve of the continuation of the efforts to unite in Christian fellowship all denominations and individuals who by faith or practice hold that peace between nations can be maintained by following the teachings of Jesus. We believe that the concern now resting upon us should be given further consideration and we look forward to a meeting to be held a year from now or some convenient time when we can meet for further consideration of this great theme. The Committee responsible for calling this conference is authorized to invite other denominations or individuals to become associated with us in the work.

The Committee—Wilbur K. Thomas, Elmer E. S. Johnson, Samuel K. Mosiman.

Under covering of the Spirit manifested so wonderfully throughout, this unique Conference came to an end. ARABELLA CARTER.

Bluffton, Ohio.

Age

If Age could retain the fair dreams of gay Youth,
The vision of things that should be,
And courage to laugh at grim fate, as of yore,
With spirit that dares to be free;
If Age might cast off the restraint of its years,
And march with the Youth of today,
What strides would be made by a heart-gladdened world,
Where strife and vain fears now hold sway!

P. M. F.

A Wayside Garden

The automobile traveler in Massachusetts may have the unexpected pleasure of coming suddenly upon a well-kept garden-plot beside the stone-wall separating the flower-garden proper from the highway. It was a very happy afterthought of the gardener who doubtless had many times been disappointed when the farmer's stone-wall quite hid the gay garden's treasures. This gardener, now released from the exacting claims of earlier years, is presenting unconsciously to the public, an object-lesson in sharing with the passer-by the delights of the flower-garden.

A rather rough stone-wall—not a thing of beauty in itself, is easily made a minister of beauty. If it had eyes to see, it would certainly be glad that it is made the highway of the graceful ampelopsis creeping here and there over the irregular surface; and that it is the support of the slender hollyhocks with their cheerful blossoms of gayest color. While these dear blossoms, cherished for themselves and for their associations are garnishing the stout stone-wall, at its foot our eyes are gladdened with phloxes and larkspurs and marigolds. For the later season, asters and gladioli and chrysanthemums are making ready.

The protection of the gray wall will doubtless extend somewhat the period of bloom of these flowers of combined delicacy and hardihood; and it must be that the passers-by will give silent thanks for the prolonged feast of pure delight. And some passer-by will recall the poet's lines:

"Were I, O God! in churchless land remaining,
Far from all voice of teacher and divine,
My soul would find in flowers of thy ordaining,
Priests, sermons, shrines."

ELIZABETH POWELL BOND.

A Peace Message by Radio

The following are extracts from a message from the Women's Peace Society which was broadcasted on "No More War" Sunday from the Newark Westinghouse Radio Station.

Today is No More War Sunday. Yesterday, July 29th, the eighth anniversary of the declaration of war by Germany, men and women in eight countries came together to declare as Abraham Lincoln did at Gettysburg, "that our dead shall not have died in vain." Yesterday they held public meetings everywhere and today they have come together in the churches believing that the best way to honor the dead who died for their countries is to see to it that the war to end war shall be followed by none other. With every year it is expected that this day with its greater and greater observance of those ceremonies will send in increasing measure thrills of hope for permanent world peace to the hearts of all those who believe that war is inexcusable in modern times, that it is a sin against the Saviour Himself, and that the great masses of each country must speak out louder and louder to obtain freedom from armies and navies and to put an end to the dreadful waste of money and national resources which armies and navies carry with them.

The world longs for peace. Peace will come when some great nation dares to abandon the outworn traditions of international dealing and to stake all upon persistent good-will.

We are the nation and now is the time. This is America's supreme opportunity.

War to end war has failed. War has not been abolished by war. And yet it is essential that we shall end war before war ends the human race.

The causes for which men fight—liberty, justice and peace—are noble and holy causes. But the method of war is not only unholy, it is ineffective for these ends. Civilization will advance only by good-will and by recognizing the sacredness of human life.

Unpractical though such ideals may seem, experience has taught that ideals can be realized if we have faith to practice now what all men hope for in the future. As a more perfect union of states, as a melting pot of races, as a repeated victor through peace, the American nation has proved practical the methods of generosity and patience. In the face of war's colossal failure in Europe nothing could seem more unpractical than war. Unflinching good-will, no less than war, demands courage, patriotism and self-sacrifice. To such a victory over itself, to such a leadership of the nations along a better way, to such an embodiment of the matchless and invincible power of good-will, this otherwise tragic hour challenges our country.

Jesus Christ and the World Today

By Grace Hutchins and Anna Rochester. New York: George H. Doran Company.

What can we learn from the decisions and experiences of Jesus in relation to the social and economic problems of His day to guide us in the solution of the social and economic problems of our day? This is the question that the authors of this little volume have attempted to answer.

Without making the common error of reading into Jesus' words a support for their own pet panacea, they have given us the data and permitted us to draw our own conclusions. Of course, to a great extent, there can be only one conclusion if we approach the subject with Christian humility and open-mindedness. We must recognize as they do that 'in Jesus Christ we have still the hope of the world, but that Christians have not followed the way of Jesus. One insistent question faces us when we read the gospels, pursues us as we see the contrasts in our cities, haunts us when we remember the millions killed and maimed and starved by the war: What visible witness are Christians bearing today to the way of Christ in the apparently impersonal but actually powerful relationships that make the web of our industrial and national fabric? Are we really following where Jesus leads?"

One is surprised to discover how many of our modern evils had their counterpart in Jesus' time. There were the disparities of wealth, there was domination by one group over another. There was rare prejudice, there was caste within the church, there was religious intolerance and repression of free speech, there was corruption in politics and subversion of the courts, there were radicals and there were reactionaries. There was, in miniature, a society much like our own. Indeed, we marvel at the short distance we have traveled in nineteen hundred years.

"Jesus came that people might have life and have it abundantly. He meant life in its fullest sense—health, mental development, spiritual understanding—the harmony of the whole nature of a person. Every single human life was to Him of equal value, because He was sure that His Father had no favorites. No prosperity was worth so much as the life of a man. Judged then by the principle of Jesus that the life and personality of every individual is of supreme value, any mechanical system that means the subordination of human beings to provide more property for other human beings is unchristian. Any conditions of work that leave the body abnormally tired, the mind dulled and stupified, or the spirit broken are contrary to the will of God as Jesus understood that will. Any organization that gives a few men the right to dominate over the many does not provide for every one the abundant life that Jesus came to bring.

"We are children of God, a great human family. That is good which unites us with God and with each other and that is evil which makes us forget God and draw apart from one another. The desire to possess is in direct conflict with the desire to share. Keeping possession of that which another needs is a direct contradiction of love. Can the Christian acquiesce in the exaltation of self-interest as the necessary basis of society without denying the fundamental truths of the life and teachings of Jesus? Can we enthrone covetousness and think we are serving Christ? Do we trust God enough to believe that the race can be fed and clothed and housed by mutual service without conflict and greed? Do we share the faith Jesus lived and taught that goodness—imaginative, constructive, actively loving, unyielding goodness—embodied in the individual lives of His disciples will rouse the goodness in others who seem to us evil and will spread the contagion of belief that righteousness is fundamental in the universe? Do we expect Christ to accomplish without the active co-operation of every one of His disciples the transformation of our relationships from the self-interest on which the world depends to the desire to serve on which the Kingdom of God depends?"

These are heart-searching questions and whether or not we would unqualifiedly reject the motive of self-interest, we must agree that we have fallen far short of the ideals of Jesus. His life is the best pattern which we have to follow. What would He do if He were here now? Would we be with Him or with the Pharisees and Herodians? His risen life is with us still. Through prayer and through careful study of the gospels we may know his position on many of the great issues of today.

We are much indebted to these two women who, through this book, have helped us "to more clearly understand His dominating purpose, His method of approach to injustice, His conflict with the established order, and His personal decision at various crises in His life." P. W. WAGER.

Friendly News Notes

J. Rowntree Gillett, of England, one of the fraternal delegates to the Five Years Meeting, contemplates extensive service here, covering six or more months.

Margaret S. James, who has for two or more years been principal of a school at Lansdowne, Pa., goes this month to help in the school in Friends' Mission, Japan. She expects to stay two years.

Radnor Monthly Meeting receives $500 under the will of Anna P. Walker, to keep in repair the burying grounds of the Valley Friends' Meeting.

The annual meeting of Danish Friends was held at Copenhagen on July 16th, and was attended by Alfred Kemp Brown, Fred J. Tritton and Winifred Cramp from England, and Jane Bell and Ernst Lorenz from Berlin. An account by Peter Guldbrandsen will be published later.

Frederick J. Libby is preparing in booklet form for the use of Bible Classes and study groups the course of lectures on preparation for peace work presented by him at the Earlham Conference.

The Friendly group at Dewey, Oklahoma, is about to build a meeting-house. The site has been donated and $10,000 in cash. There are about one hundred who will worship in the new building, and it is hoped that Friends who are within reach of Dewey will get in touch with this group. Inquiries in regard to this meeting should be directed to R. C. Slayton, Dewey, Okla.

Plans for Friends' General Conference, to be held in Richmond, Ind., Eighth month 26th to Ninth month 2nd, are practically completed. About 200 Friends are expected from the east, and a large group from the region around Richmond. The sessions will be held in the Grace Methodist Church through the courtesy of that congregation. The social life of the group will be centered about the Meeting-house on North A street, on the ample lawn of which will be living a tent colony of 100 young Friends.

Three hundred and eighteen persons, representing nearly every section of the country, and every trend of thought among Friends, attended the Young Friends' General Conference at Earlham. Foreign points of view were represented by two Chinese students—one from the United States and the other from England—while returned missionaries and American Friends' Service workers brought messages from the fields where they had been working.

The birthday list of political prisoners for September is as follows:

5th, Harry Lloyd; 7th, Sam Searlett; 10th, Francis Miller; 12th, Siegfried Stanberg; 12th, H. Streenick; 13th, Roy Conner; 13th, Peter Di Bernardi; 16th, Ricardo Flores Magon; 27th, Clyde Hough. The address for all these men is P. O. Box 7, Leavenworth, Kansas.

The following resolution was recently circulated among the members of the Orchard Street Meeting, Dayton, Ohio. It was drafted by Fred C. Sawin, who says that he believes that after one signs a resolution embodying such a sentiment he is filled with a stronger sense of being closer united to the Universal Brotherhood movement:

Whereas, There is required consciousness of unity of all people of all the world who believe in Universal Brotherhood, to the end that all peoples may live *for* one another instead of being obliged to live *on* one another; and

Whereas, Such unity is necessary to bring about conditions such that there cannot be war any more; therefore

Be it Resolved, That we, the undersigned, "With malice toward none and charity for all," are believers in the *Universal Brotherhood of Man*, and hereby announce that we are world citizens here and now.

From July 14th to 21st Woodbrooke became a home to past, present and future students of many different terms and many different countries. About 100 took part at one time or another, 40 being there for the whole week. There were 12 Dutch, 4 German, 4 Chinese, 3 Norwegian, 3 American, 2 Danish, 1 Swedish, 1 Indian; and it did not take long to become one family where everyone seemed to know what to do, and did it. The first International Reunion took place in Holland at Barchem, the centre of the Dutch Woodbrooke movement which has 670 members—90 of them Old Woodbrookers. The second was in Norway where there are 50 Old Woodbrookers—next year the fourth is to be at the International People's High School in Denmark. At this, the third meeting in England, the German group of Old Woodbrookers was founded "with deep joy and thankfulness."—*The Friend (London)*.

At Friends' General Conference at Richmond, Ind., there is being planned an interesting series of discussions on Educational Problems. The first will be an Educational Round Table, Second-day morning, with the following subjects:

Are Friends Going to College?—George A. Walton.

Are Friends Becoming Teachers?—William Eves, 3rd.

The Training for Citizenship in Friends' Schools—Edwin C. Zavitz.

The Training for Leadership in Friends' Schools—Elbert Russell.

The next morning there will be an address by Frank Aydelotte, President of Swarthmore College, on Quakerism and Democracy.

On Sixth-day comes the discussion of the next step toward peace in the teaching of history and kindred subjects.

Those who follow this discussion will realize that going to school is not a matter of getting a superficial polish, but has a vital connection with the conduct of individuals and nations.

We are informed from Copenhagen through the World Alliance for International Friendship Through the Churches that "one of the most noteworthy addresses" before the International Conference of Churches in session this month at the Danish capital was made by our friend and well known Friend, Prof. William I. Hull, of Swarthmore College, on the subject, "The Reduction and Limitation of Armaments." The report states: "Prof. Hull, who is a Quaker, acted as official observer for the World Alliance at the Washington Conference on Limitation of Armaments, and his report was authorized and endorsed by the American Branch of this organization, which is represented here (at Copenhagen) by nearly a score of prominent American clergymen and laymen." In emphasizing the present deplorable world situation our friend cited the careful estimate that there are one million *more* men under arms in Europe today than just previous to the beginning of the war in 1914, and this in spite of the fact that the armies of Germany, Austria and Hungary have been greatly reduced. The two baneful elements in the situation he pointed out to be those of fear and imperialism. "It is time for some one to break through the vicious circle," he declared, and pressed the urgent necessity of organized and immediate action by the churches of the world to guard the world's peace. The World Alliance has widely distributed Prof. Hull's address through the press of the country.—*American Friend*.

A BREEZE FROM GENESEE YEARLY MEETING

Beside our own members we had with us from Baltimore, Isaac Wilson and Grace C. Clevenger; from Philadelphia, Charles H. Harrison; from Canada Yearly Meeting, the other branch, Phebe J. Wright, Editor of the *Canadian Friend*, Toronto; Prof. Arthur C. Dorland, of Western University, London; Fred J. Ryan, from Pelham; Josephine Ridley, from New Market, and Charles Walker and wife, from Norwich. All these Friends added greatly to the interest of our Yearly Meeting.

One of these visitors sends her thought thus: "We are having a lovely time here, but nothing can dim the pleasant memories of Coldstream. The mingling of different branches augurs well for the future. One in aim, spirit and fellowship seemed to characterize all the activities of the occasion, in the meeting-house, in the dining-shed and in the grove of sports." Edgar M. Zavitz.

Items from Everywhere

No less than 12,850,000 barrels of oil were destroyed by fire in the United States, within the ten-year period of 1908 to 1917, according to careful estimates of the Bureau of Mines.

Two or three hundred farms containing 20 acres each are to be laid out in eastern North Carolina as Farm City. These farms are to be sold to men and women of means, who are weary of schoolroom and office and eager for an independent farm home.

Permanent peace in South America was brought one step nearer when on the twenty-first of Seventh month, in the Pan-American Building in Washington, delegates from Chile and Peru signed an agreement whereby the President of the United States is to arbitrate the claims of the two countries to the province of Tacna, on the Pacific Coast between Chile and Peru.

Canada has settled 27,000 Canadian ex-soldiers on farm land and has lent $85,000,000 to these men. The full purchase price of the land and up to $3,000 for buildings, equipment and stock has been advanced to each. Only seven per cent. of the men thus aided have abandoned their property and last year's crops from soldier lands were valued at $15,000,000.

James H. Maurer, President of the Pennsylvania Federation of Labor, finds few signs of progress in the American labor movement. He referred, however, to the increased interest in co-operation, the labor banks of the railroad brotherhoods and the Amalgamated Clothing Workers, the co-operative mines of the United Mine Workers, workers' education, and the new interest in political action. The "intellectual," he says, is only now beginning to function effectively in the labor movement, serving it as statistician, accountant, economist, engineer or teacher.

A number of the far-seeing public citizens of the United States have been thinking seriously of how to promote active interest in better homes, better public buildings, better structures for all purposes. It seems to have been left for Mr. Hoover's fertile and practical mind to "think up something." And he has done so. At his suggestion an "American Construction Council" was recently formed in Washington, D. C. Franklin D. Roosevelt, well and favorably known as an able public spirited citizen, is president of this new organization.

THE OPEN FORUM

This column is intended to afford free expression of opinion by readers on questions of interest. The INTELLIGENCER is not responsible for any such opinions. Letters must be brief, and the editor reserves the right to omit parts if necessary to save space.

To the Editor:

I feel that the best reply to the letter by Walter Clothier printed in the INTELLIGENCER of Eighth month 12th, which is typical of the viewpoint of those who uphold the present capitalistic profits system, is a series of questions. First, however, let me express the hope that the editor will not be disturbed by the first sentence of the letter in its characteristic implication that such a "socialistic article" (which it was not) as my "What Is Meant by 'Wage Slavery'?" should never have been printed. Censorship and coercion are a habit of mind with those in pleasant places under the present system.

The first point in the letter is that the writer and those like him do not think "practically and clearly," and are building up distrust and hatred between employer and employee. On this point I ask:

Did Jesus think practically? or did George Fox? or John Woolman? Just what is "practical thinking"?

How can distrust and hatred between employer and employee be built up by those who have almost no contact with either, and are listened to by neither? What part do present living conditions, profiteering, and the effort of owners of the tools of industry to reduce wages to a level below the "saving wage" for standard American family life have in this distrust and hatred? How can confidence and co-operation exist when the employer keeps for himself and his associates all that he can and gives the working producers who make possible his big profits as little as he can?

The second point (I pass over the reference to Russia which is as pointless as the similar reference by S. S. Green, the answer to which I have already suggested in a letter printed in "The Open Forum" immediately following Walter Clothier's letter) is that there is no excuse for the coal strike or the railroad strike, that both are due to a selfish group of labor leaders and that everyone who wants to work should have the right to do so. On this point I ask:

Are the owners of capital setting a good example of unselfishness and renunciation to the workers and labor leaders? Is it a stimulus to unselfishness when the workers find that something like 20,000 new millionaires were created in this country during the World War? What kind of men are taking the jobs of workers on strike? Are the ethics of strike-breakers, ambitious company tools, and the company unions superior to the ethics of the labor unions whose members are suffering privation (really living the "simple life" that we preach about) in a brotherly effort to improve their standard of living? Is Walter Clothier aware of the fact that the great employing corporations after the war started a deliberate drive to crush union labor and to deny to the man with a union card the right to work so feelingly urged by him as a "fair play" principle? Just what is "fair play" and who shall decide what is "fair"?

J. PAUL J. WILLIAMS.

To the Editor:

I am pleased to learn from the Open Forum that our friend J. Paul J. Williams has found a recent communication of mine both interesting and "a little amusing." I take great pleasure in answering the two questions he asks:—

Question:—If the right of every one to sell his services and to hire the services of others is really an inalienable one, why are millions of workers in this country who sincerely desire to sell their services unable to do so? *Answer*:—The question is quite irrelevant; the fact that a man cannot find employment does not prove that he has not a moral right to seek for it, and to accept wages for it when he finds it.

Question:—Why is it an inalienable right for the owner of capital to receive usurious interest in the form of exorbitant profits? *Answer*:—It is not, and I believe I have never heard anyone even intimate that it is.

I do not believe our friend would have asked either of the above questions had he not failed to notice my statement that human rights must be modified by law. Human society would not otherwise be possible. This statement applies to the three rights enumerated in the American Declaration of Independence as inalienable, with the exception of the right to life, which should be regarded as inviolable. Is our friend prepared to deny that my statement of rights is correct? Would he contend that no one has a moral right either to pay wages or to accept compensation for services rendered? Has he conscientious scruples against accepting interest from money loaned or from money invested in the stocks of industrial establishments?

When our friend, alluding to what he sneeringly calls "the Golden Rule panacea," speaks of "the rarity of its application in a few isolated instances," I imagine he is not aware how large a number (estimated at 17 per cent.)

of our large establishments have ended industrial unrest by giving those who work a voice in the management and a satisfactory share in the annual dividends. Can he name one among the great number of very successful co-operative establishments that is not managed upon a plan essentially similar? S. S. GREEN.

Bartow, Fla.

Friends' General Conference

PROGRAM

EIGHTH MONTH 26TH

11.00 a. m.—Advancement Committee.
2.00 p. m.—Sub-Committees.—Philanthropic.
First-day School.
Educational.
3.30 p. m.—Central Committee—in the Meeting-house.
7.00 p. m.—Reception.
8.00 p. m.—Opening address by the Chairman, Arthur C. Jackson.
"Fundamentals"—Wilson S. Doan.

EIGHTH MONTH 27TH

10.30 a. m.—Meeting for worship.
3.00 p. m.—Young Friends' session—"The High Road."
William J. Reagan.
Alan C. Valentine.
Grace T. Warren.
Bliss Forbush.
8.00 p. m.—Meeting for worship.

EIGHTH MONTH 28TH

8.30 a. m.—Devotional meetings.
9.00 a. m.—Round Table on John William Graham's book, "The Faith of a Quaker," George A. Walton.
Round Table—Social Morality, Dr. Emma G. Holloway.
Young Friends' Forum, led by William J. Reagan.
10.00 a. m.—Educational session:
Are Friends Going to College?—George A. Walton.
Are Friends Becoming Teachers?—William Eves, 3rd.
The Training for Citizenship in Friends' Schools—Edwin C. Zavitz.
The Training for Leadership in Friends' Schools—Elbert Russell.
Discussion.
2.30 p. m.—"Christian Ideals for Industry"—Alva W. Taylor.
8.00 p. m.—"Enforcement"—Commissioner Roy A. Haynes.

EIGHTH MONTH 29TH

8.30 a. m.—Devotional meetings.
9.00 a. m.—Round Table on John William Graham's book, "The Faith of a Quaker," George A. Walton.
Round Table—Enforcement of the Prohibition Amendment.
Young Friends' Forum, led by William J. Reagan.
10.00 a. m.—"Quakerism and Democracy"—Frank Aydelotte.
11.00 a. m.—Round Table on President Aydelotte's address.
2.30 p. m.—Sub-Committees.
8.00 p. m.—"The Quaker Faith"—George A. Walton.

EIGHTH MONTH 30TH

8.30 a. m.—Devotional meetings.
9.00 a. m.—Round Table on John William Graham's book, "The Faith of a Quaker," George A. Walton.
Round Table—Anti-Narcotics, Pauline W. Holme.
Young Friends' Forum, led by William J. Reagan.
10.00 a. m.—"Future Peace Work of the Society of Friends"—Jesse H. Holmes.
11.00 a. m.—Round Table on Future Peace Work of the Society of Friends.
2.30 p. m.—Central Committee.
8.00 p. m.—"How Can We Abolish War in Our Time?"—Frederick J. Libby.

EIGHTH MONTH 31ST

8.30 a. m.—Devotional meetings.
9.00 a. m.—Round Table—Friends' Principles, George H. Nutt.
Young Friends' Forum, led by William J. Reagan.
10.00 a. m.—"Future Service of the Society of Friends"—Speaker to be announced.
11.00 a. m.—Round Table on Future Service of the Society of Friends.
2.30 p. m.—General session on "Conference Activities."
8.00 p. m.—"The Basis of Christian Unity"—Charles Foster Kent.

NINTH MONTH 1ST

8.30 a. m.—Devotional meetings.
9.00 a. m.—Round Table—Friends' Principles, George H. Nutt.
Round Table—Methods of First-day School Teaching.
Young Friends' Forum, led by William J. Reagan.
10.00 a. m.—"The Solution of Industry's Problems"—Charles Foster Kent.
11.00 a. m.—Round Table on Prof. Kent's addresses.
2.30 p. m.—"The Causes of War and the Next Steps Toward Peace"—J. Russell Smith.
"A Next Step—The Teaching of History"—Harlow Lindley.
7.00 p. m.—Conference of those interested in the teaching of history.
8.00 p. m.—"Recreation and Religion"—Charles Foster Kent.

NINTH MONTH 2ND

8.30 a. m.—Devotional meeting.
9.00 a. m.—Round Table—Friends' Principles, George H. Nutt.
Young Friends' Forum, led by William J. Reagan.
10.00 a. m.—"The Way to Find Happiness"—Charles Foster Kent.

BIRTHS

AMBLER—On Eighth month 10th, to Chester W. and Eva J. H. Ambler, a son, whose name is Chester William Ambler, Junior.

HARNED—At Agricultural College, Mississippi, on Seventh month 1st, to Horace H. and Harriet Harned, a daughter, named Helen Robey Harned.

LONGSHORE—On Seventh month 30th, to Russell E. and Anna Knight Longshore, of Elkins Park, Pa., a daughter, named Lydia Knight Longshore.

WATSON—On Eighth month 5th, at Neponset, Long Island, to Dr. Rudolph B. and Rachel Hicks Watson, a son who is named Benjamin Hicks Watson.

DEATHS

DeCou—At Modesto, California, Seventh month 30th, Franklin DeCou, youngest brother of the late Samuel C. DeCou, of Moorestown, N. J. He was born near Trenton, in the year 1845. He attended school at Westfield and later Haverford College, but was obliged to leave shortly before the completion of his Senior year because of hemorrhages of the lungs. Most of his life was spent in the West, but he passed on to the Great Beyond longing for the old associations and the peaceful quiet of a Friends' Meeting. He is survived by a widow and six children.

Elliott—At Wrightstown, Pa., on Eighth month 6th, Anna T. Elliott, aged 60 years. A member of Wrightstown Monthly Meeting of Friends.

Heacock—At Wyncote, Pa., on Eighth month 20th, Jane, daughter of the late Joseph and Esther Heacock, aged 82 years.

Moore—At Avondale, Pa., on Eighth month 14th, Shirley Merrill Moore, daughter of Dr. Lawrence C. and Helen Paschall Moore, aged two years and five months.

Norcross—At Mt. Holly, N. J., on Eighth month 14th, 1922, Anna M., widow of Joseph Norcross. Funeral and int. private.

COMING EVENTS

EIGHTH MONTH

26th—Quaker pageant will be given at Willistown Meeting-house, at 3 p. m. All invited. Bring box supper.

26th-28th—Warrington Quarterly Meeting, at Menallen, Pa. Thomas B., Helen L. and Anna W. Hull expect to attend.

27th—Members of Philadelphia Quarterly Meeting's Visiting Committee will attend Merion Meeting at 11 a. m.

31st—Bucks Quarterly Meeting, at Falls, Pa.

NINTH MONTH

2nd—Nottingham Quarterly Meeting, at East Nottingham, Md.

2nd-4th—Center Quarterly Meeting, at Half Moon, Pa. O. Edward Janney expects to attend.

3rd—Meeting at Swarthmore, Pa., to be addressed by Dr. Henry E. Jackson. See Notice.

3rd—First-day at 2.30 p. m., Eastern Standard time, a meeting for divine worship will be held at the Wayside Chapel, Cheyney, Delaware County, Pa. A community meeting for all interested persons. Thornbury Young Friends' Association will co-operate. A pleasant pilgrimage from West Chester trolley or by train from Broad Street Station.

3rd—Certain members of Philadelphia Quarterly Meeting's Visiting Committee expect to attend Race Street Meeting at 10.30 a. m.

3rd—At 2.30 p. m.—Friends' Meeting in the old Meeting-house at Adams, Mass., under care of the Advancement Committee of New York Yearly Meeting co-operating with the Adams Society of Friends' Descendants. Reuben P. Kester and other Friends will attend.

On the following day, Labor Day, there will be a picnic lunch under care of the Society of Friends' Descendants at the old Browne Homestead, at which historical subjects of Friendly interest, including a short pageant, will be presented.

All Friends and others interested are invited to attend.

9th—The Burlington First-day School Union will be held at Mansfield, near Columbus, N. J. Sessions at 10.30 and 1.30. An interesting program is being arranged. Friends from other localities are always welcome.

NOTICE—The Representative Committee of Ohio Yearly Meeting will meet at the home of Lindley and Miriam B. Tomlinson, 111 McKinley avenue, Salem, Ohio, on Ninth month 9th, 1922, at 10 a. m., instead of on Eighth month 26th, on account of the Conference at Richmond, Indiana.

NOTICE—A Committee of Salem Quarterly Meeting have arranged to hold the annual Meeting for Worship at the old Cape May Meeting-house at Seaville, Cape May County, New Jersey, on First-day, Eighth month 27th, at 11 o'clock a. m., Standard time.

NOTICE—For the convenience of those desiring to attend Bucks Quarterly Meeting at the Falls on Eighth month 31st, automobiles will meet the train leaving Broad Street Station at 7.03, at Morrisville station, and the trolley leaving Newtown at 8.45 at Stockham's Corner, Morrisville. For meeting of Ministry of Counsel, the day preceding, take 9.45 trolley at Newtown. All standard time.

NOTICE—On Ninth month 3rd, a meeting under the care of Concord Quarterly Meeting's Philanthropic Committee will be held immediately following the morning religious meeting which is held at 10.30. The meeting will be addressed by Dr. Henry E. Jackson, of Washington, D. C. His subject will be "One Way to Industrial Peace." Dr. Jackson has a special message for the Society of Friends and it is hoped that all those that can attend will do so.

American Friends' Service Committee

Wilbur K. Thomas, Ex. Sec.

20 S. 12th St. Philadelphia.

CASH CONTRIBUTIONS

Week Ending August 13th.

Five Years Meeting	$22.97
Philadelphia Yearly Meeting, 15th and Race Sts.	967.00
15th and Race Sts., Monthly Meeting	1,000.00
Providence Meeting	2.00
	$1,971.00
Contributions for:	
Austria	15.00
Germany	422.58
Poland	658.93
Russia	1,851.52
West Virginia	241.50
Central Pennsylvania	226.50
General	127.00
Syria	20.00
Clothing	158.07
Refunds	548.27
Total	$6,263.34

Shipments received during week ending August 12th: 15 boxes and packages received.

WANTED

RIVER CROFT, CLAYMONT, DEL. Special home care for invalids, or rest and physical upbuilding. Booklet on application. E. H. Speakman.

COUPLE WANT TO LEASE OR BUY small country home with enough land for vegetable and fruit garden. Delaware County preferred. First-class credentials furnished. Please give description, and lowest cash prices. Address P. O. Box 4047, Philadelphia.

WANTED — A COMPANIONable house worker for family of three adults and one child. No laundry. country home with conveniences, no farm work done in the house. Home privileges to the right person, moderate salary. Residence near Ercildoun and Coatesville, within walking distance to R. R. Station and bus line. Address Minnie Bush Brinton, Glen Rose, Chester Co., Penna.

EXPERIENCED PRACTICAL NURSE wishes care of semi-invalid or feeble person. Willing to assist in the home. Address, Mary Alice Brown, Route No. 3, Nottingham, Pa.

WANTED—PAYING GUESTS IN Friends' private home at seashore. Terms reasonable; no objection to children. Address E. Mabel Trafford, Manasquan, N. J.

WANTED — POSITION — HOUSEmother or Matron in Institution or School. Gentle woman, age 45, widow, unincumbered, Quaker (English Rowntree family); thorough business experience; finest reference as to character and ability. Address Mrs. Olive P. Hawley, Room 305, Chamber of Commerce, Brooklyn, N. Y.

WANTED—OCTOBER 1ST UNTIL July 1st, a middle-aged woman who doesn't object to a quiet life in the country, to live with another. Much time to read or sew; easy position; small salary. Address M. 330, Friends' Intelligencer.

WANTED—A HOUSEKEEPER FOR the Friends' Boarding Home, West Chester, Pa. Address Matron.

WANTED—BY SMALL FAMILY with school-going children, board, small furnished house, or housekeeping apartment until January or February, in Swarthmore or neighborhood. Address B. 331, Friends' Intelligencer.

EXPERIENCED TEACHER WOULD like position as governess, or companion to an elderly lady. Good reader. Address P. O. Box 4, Middletown, Maryland.

FOR RENT

FOR RENT—THIRD STORY HOUSEkeeping apartment in central location, Philadelphia. Four rooms and bath, two open fireplaces. Furnished or unfurnished. Electricity. Apply W. P. S., Friends' Intelligencer.

FUN

Pat was helping the gardener and observing a shallow stone basin containing water, he inquired what it was for.

"That," said the gardener, "is a bird bath."

"Don't ye be foolin' me," grinned Pat. "What is it?"

"A bird bath, I tell you. Why do you doubt it?"

"Because I don't belave there's a burrd alive that can tell Saturday night from any other."—*Our Dumb Animals.*

To the Lot Holders and others interested in Fairhill Burial Ground:

GREEN STREET Monthly Meeting has funds available for the encouragement of the practice of cremating the dead to be interred in Fairhill Burial Ground. We wish to bring this fact as prominently as possible to those who may be interested. We are prepared to undertake the expense of cremation in case any lot holder desires us to do so.

Those interested should communicate with William H. Gaskill, Treasurer of the Committee of Interments, Green Street Monthly Meeting, or any of the following members of the Committee.

William H. Gaskill, 3201 Arch St.
Samuel N. Longstreth, 1218 Chestnut St.
Charles F. Jenkins, 232 South Seventh St.
Stuart S. Graves, 3033 Germantown Ave.

ADVERTISING RATE in the FRIENDS' INTELLIGENCER, for Help Wanted, Positions Wanted, Rooms for Rent, Notices, and other classified advertisements without display, for each insertion, 2 cents per word, including name, initials and address. Answers may be sent to a box at the INTELLIGENCER office, if so directed.

For display advertising the rate is 10 cents per agate line, or $1.40 per column inch, each insertion. On ten or more insertions in a year from date of order, ten per cent. discount. Thus a four-inch single-column or two-inch double-column advertisement costs $5.60 each insertion, less ten per cent., or 5.04 net each time for ten or more insertions. Matter may be changed whenever desired, without extra charge.

Experience has proved the INTELLIGENCER to be a remarkably good advertising medium. All advertisements must "pass the censor!"

Address 140 N. 15th St., Philadelphia

The Friends' Intelligencer

ESTABLISHED 1844 | NINTH MONTH 2, 1922 | VOLUME 79 NUMBER 35

Contents

REGULAR MEETINGS

OAKLAND, CALIF. — A FRIENDS' Meeting is held every First-day at 11 A. M., in the Extension Room, Y. W. C. A. Building, Webster Street, above 14th. Visiting Friends always welcome.

PASADENA, CALIFORNIA — Orange Grove Monthly Meeting of Friends, 520 East Orange Grove Avenue. Meeting for worship, First-day, 11 A. M. Monthly Meeting, the second First-day of each month, at 1.45 P. M. First-day School (except Monthly Meeting days) 9.45 A. M.

THE FRIENDS' INTELLIGENCER

Published weekly, 140 N. 15th Street, Philadelphia, Pa., by Friends' Intelligencer Association, Ltd.

PAUL W. WAGER, *Editor.*
SUE C. YERKES, *Business Manager*

Editorial Board: Elizabeth Powell Bond, Thomas A. Jenkins, J. Russell Smith, George A. Walton.

Board of Managers: Edward Cornell, Alice Hall Paxson, Paul M. Pearson, Annie Hillborn, Elwood Hollingshead, William C. Biddle, Charles F. Jenkins, Edith M. Winder, Frances M. White.

Officers of Intelligencer Associates: Ellwood Burdsall, Chairman; Bertha L. Broomell, Secretary; Herbert P. Worth, Treasurer.

Subscription rates: United States, Mexico, Cuba and Panama, $2.50 per year. Canada and other foreign countries, $3.00 per year. Checks should be made payable to Friends' Intelligencer Association, Ltd.

Entered as Second Class Matter at Philadelphia Post Office.

SCHOOLS.

NOTICE—Concise statements of the principles of the Religious Society of Friends and their application to the problems of every day living, including "The Spirit of Quakerism," by Elbert Russell; "Preparation for Life's Greatest Business," by Rufus M. Jones; and other articles by Henry W. Wilbur, Howard M. Jenkins, Elizabeth Lloyd, Jesse H. Holmes, O. Edward Janney, Edward B. Rawson, etc., to be had free on application to Friends' General Conference Advancement Committee, 140 North Fifteenth Street, Philadelphia, Pa.

FUN

No one in Ireland is running for the presidency on the slogan "he kept us out of war."—*Financial American.*

"Pop," inquired little Clarence Lilywhite, "what am a millennium?"

"Sho," said the parent. "Doan' you know what a millennium am, chile? It's jes about de same as a centennial, on'y it's got mo' legs."—*Reformed Church Messenger.*

The Friends' Intelligencer

The religion of Friends is based on faith in the "INWARD LIGHT," or direct revelation of God's spirit and will in every seeking soul.
The INTELLIGENCER is interested in all who bear the name of Friends in every part of the world, and aims to promote love, unity and intercourse among all branches and with all religious societies.

ESTABLISHED 1844 PHILADELPHIA, NINTH MONTH 2, 1922 VOLUME 79 NUMBER 35

Love is patient and kind.

⌘

Religion is a partner that will always carry half the load.

⌘

Only once in the life of Jesus was His pathway strewn with flowers.

⌘

Peace is not an end in itself, but a means to international co-operation.

⌘

Real honesty consists in doing the square thing when no one but yourself will ever know.

⌘

We want to remind our readers that the book "Christianity and Economic Problems" on which we based the series of articles running from Fourth month 1st to Seventh month 8th is published by the *Association Press,* New York. Price 50 cents. It would be well to read this excellent treatise in its unabridged form.

⌘

We are indebted to the *Boston Transcript* for an account of the Congress on Social Christianity held recently at Strasburg. "The place of meeting, itself," states this paper, "was enough to make the meeting impressive in its international aspect, being virtually the dividing line between the belligerent nations of the Great War. The international problem naturally excited the greatest attention and it is a hopeful sign of the future that there was an encouraging spirit of rapprochement between the erstwhile enemies."

One prominent French speaker reminded his hearers, "Thou shalt love thy Prussian neighbor as thyself, and that in the kingdom of God there cannot be Frenchman, German, English or American, but one man in Christ Jesus."

Such an event and such a spirit casts a gleam of light amid the darkness of European discord and bitterness. Its momentary illumination reveals the one path of escape from chaos and despair. If the diplomatic conferences could be pervaded with this spirit of Christian unity there is little doubt but that a satisfactory basis of settlement could be reached.

⌘

The Conference is on. At its sessions are gathered representative men and women from all quarters of Quakerdom. Whatever its visible achievements such an assemblage can not fail to bring great social and spiritual benefits. The mingling of the scattered elements of the Society must give a fuller sense of unity and of a common purpose. The corporate worship of several hundred devout souls must create an atmosphere charged with spiritual power. Its reflected influence will be felt in all the meetings to which the delegates return. The Conference would be well worth while if only its inspirational value were considered, but there will no doubt be other gains.

In this disordered world there is need for constructive statesmanship along all lines. Friends can at least state their position clearly and unequivocally. In the field of international affairs they can draft a platform that breathes the spirit of justice and brotherhood. In the interest of peace they can work for the establishment of arbitration tribunals and the outlawing of war in our generation. And finally of great importance is the position taken in the field of industrial relations. Are there practices in modern industry which are inconsistent with the teachings of Christ and, if so, what is to be the attitude of the Society of Friends toward them? Isaac Sharpless characterized Friends as a "God-fearing and money-making people." We trust that the first quality will always dominate the second rather than the reverse.

There is perhaps more danger of division on this industrial issue than any other that has ever faced the Society. May it be faced soberly, prayerfully, heroically, without fanaticism, yet without compromise. There will be extreme divergence of opinion but if the spirit of Christian humility and brotherly love prevails a Divine Guidance will continue to lead the Society into paths of usefulness and honor.

Labor Sunday Message for 1922

Prepared by the Commission on the Church and Social Service of the Federal Council of Churches.

The Church has a message applicable to human conduct in all its phases and to every variety of human relationships. Industrial relations are but one form of human relations and industrial problems are very largely human problems. A gospel that does not embrace life in its entirety, is not sufficient to save men or to express the full meaning of religion.

Not only so, but the industrial and economic factors in the life of our people condition, to a very great extent, their religious interests and activities. Health and happiness are, generally speaking, necessary to the attainment of the higher life. The Church cannot be indifferent to the physical well-being of its people which depends so largely on their economic status, nor to those relationships within industry which constitute for vast numbers of people the chief sphere of moral activity.

Christian teachings as applied to industry include three cardinal principles: the worth of personality, brotherhood as between all those engaged in industry, and the motive of service. The first principle requires that every person shall be treated as a spiritual end in himself. Christianity aims at the progressive liberation of human life so that every individual may have a share in the life abundant.

Brotherhood in industry expresses itself in co-operation between workers and employers as between human beings who possess immeasurable spiritual worth. It is the spiritual content of democracy. The supremacy of the service motive relegates competition for gain to an inferior place in human endeavor. From the Christian point of view industrial power and privilege are justified only on the basis of the service that they render to those who participate in the industry and to the entire community.

We are still in the period where the dominant note in the industrial world is one of strife and controversy. There probably never was a time when there was more bitterness and conflict, some of it due to misunderstanding between employers and workers, and some of it, unfortunately, due to a very clear understanding of hostile aims and purposes. Employers and workers have too commonly arrayed themselves in hostile camps, and have been inclined to fight out their differences by sheer economic force. This has been manifest especially during the last twelve months.

The Church has a very patent opportunity to study and interpret the moral issues of industrial controversy, to interpret each group to the other and to the public at large, and to teach the principles of sound human relationships in industry. It is probably safe to say that the majority of our people have an ill-informed attitude of hostility to one or the other, or to both of the parties in any industrial conflict which interferes with the public's convenience. Much is made of the practices of labor organizations, some of them reprehensible, which seem to be dictated by class interest and by a disregard of the welfare of the entire community. The labor movement itself is but little understood. Likewise there is a tendency on the part of many people to attribute, sometimes with reason and justice, predatory self-interest to the employing class. Not only is public opinion, which should be the most potent factor in the settlement of industrial disputes, often ignorant of the major facts, but the judgment of the public is too commonly dictated by considerations of self-interest rather than of justice and right. An increasing recognition of these difficulties is leading to a new appraisal on the part of the public generally of the possibilities of the Church and of the ministry in furthering the aims of justice in the industrial world.

The two outstanding industrial crises of the year —the coal strike and the railroad strike—have grown in the main out of inadequacy of earnings. The plight of the coal miners, due to scant employment, is at last receiving public recognition. The reductions in the earnings of railway workers have placed many of them in almost a desperate situation. This is especially true of the maintenance of way workers. That the finances of certain of the roads may have made such reductions appear desirable only adds to the seriousness of the problem. One of the most significant developments of the year has been the publication of statistics by eminently competent and impartial authority which show that our industries as at present managed are not producing enough wealth to raise the income of the working people to the level of health and comfort. This is a challenge to our entire industrial regime.

It is most unfortunate that no more general effort has been made to approach a settlement of disputes in a co-operative spirit and to appeal to justice and to fair play rather than to trial by economic combat. In a moral world, force can settle nothing permanently. The conferences by which most disputes end, would contribute much more to the stability of industrial relations if they were held at the begin-

promise. The press, sharply criticised and often justly so, for partisanship in labor disputes, shows signs of greater fairness and discrimination and in some instances, of moral leadership. The new role that is being played by the religious press in this connection is especially gratifying. And withal, the voice of the Church is being heard with unquestionably greater respect and influence.

Looking back on the year and into a future which is uncertain and turbulent, is it not clear that the Church is called upon to exert itself to the utmost to bring the Christian spirit of fairness and good-will into the economic order, to teach Christian principles and to insist upon their application to industry? Above all, the churches are privileged to give Christian leaders to the forces of capital and labor and to the public, which is exerting a growing influence in industrial affairs.

The Refiners Fire

He sat by the furnace of seven-fold heat,
As He watched by the precious ore,
And closer He bent with a searching gaze,
As He heated it more and more.
He knew He had ore that could stand the test,
And He wanted the finest gold
To mold a crown for the King to wear,
Set with gems of a price untold.
So He laid our gold in the burning fire,
Though we fain would have said Him "Nay,"
And He watched the dross that we had not seen,
As it melted and passed away.
And the gold grew brighter and yet more bright,
But our eyes were so dim with tears,
We saw but the fire—not the Master's hand,
And questioned with anxious fears.
Yet our gold shone out with a richer glow,
And it mirrored a Form above
That bent o'er the fire, though unseen by us,
With looks of ineffable love.
Can we think that it pleases His loving heart
To cause us a moment's pain?
Ah, no! but He saw through the present cross
The bliss of eternal gain.
So He waited there with a watchful eye
With a love that is strong and sure,
And His gold did not suffer a whit more heat
Than was needed to make it pure.

From "The Methodist Protestant."

"Character training means the gradual substitution of intelligent self-guidance for rule of thumb; not a sudden pitchforking into chaos at the beginning of adolescence."—*Arthur Rowntree.*

The Usefulness of Our Queries

Prepared at the request of the Committee on Revision of Discipline of Philadelphia Yearly Meeting by Elbert Russell.

In the present Book of Discipline the Queries are of two kinds: those that care for specific information and those that call for self-examination. The latter are to be answered to oneself and to God: they require for their answering a spiritual inventory on the part of the membership. The former are the more modern development of the Queries. They contemplate the keeping of records on the part of the subordinate meetings and ask for statistics. These Queries might be replaced by a simple direction of the Yearly Meeting to the Quarterly Meetings to keep records, gather statistics and report the desired information annually.

But there is no substitute for the other class of Queries. They are an original and unique feature of our Society. Their character and use are responsible in a large degree for the well-rounded ideals, sanity of outlook, and sobriety of character, which have characterized Friends as a whole. Their chief usefulness seems to consist in three things.

First, they continually remind us of the practical phases of our interpretation of Christianity. We live in a world that puts the emphasis elsewhere or else ignores phases of Christianity altogether. Other denominations make much of creed, ritual, and sacrament. We hear them discuss apostolic succession, episcopal ordination, modes of baptism, the rights of clergy and laity, orthodoxy and fundamentalism. Then our Queries recall us to the fruits by which true followers of Jesus are to be known and ask us whether we are bringing forth fruits suited to our profession. There is much in our environment which tends to draw us away from Christian practice or to make us forget the "weightier matters of the law, justice, mercy, and faith." A people trying to live "in the midst of the world but not of it" need the constant reminders which the Queries give of the essential things the world does not stress.

In the second place, among ourselves we need constant reminders of the whole circle of Christian truth and life. Our preaching is apt to dwell on theoretic phases of the faith. Religious discussions are usually about new applications of the Gospel or disputed phases of truth, which are often of secondary importance. Duties that are generally acknowledged are rarely mentioned just because they are not disputed; but may easily be overlooked by the younger generation. Some truths may be overlooked because no one has a concern for them; and others may not be mentioned because some influential member is sensitive about them.

The Queries thus serve for us the purpose of a periodical review of the range of the practical expression of religion, somewhat as the Episcopal "Christian Year" or the succession of special Sundays (such as Easter, Mother's and Peace Day) in other Protestant denominations.

In the third place, the Queries provide for a spiritual inventory for the members and the meeting as a whole. If it is important frequently to inspect our outward affairs, it is more valuable to take account of our inward state, note our tendencies, progress, and failures, and draw upon the Divine strength and wisdom for the better ordering of our ways. This is the result, when we gather together in worship, solemnly and sincerely listen to the Queries, and answer to ourselves and God whether we are fulfilling our duties and deporting ourselves properly as members of the household of God.

An Opportunity to Help China

The following letter speaks for itself. The INTELLIGENCER *feels that Dr. Hodgkin's appeal deserves the earnest attention of Friends, for every seed planted in China promises to yield a hundred-fold. If anyone cares to contribute to this cause, contributions may be sent to Charles J. Rhoads in care of Brown Brothers & Co., 328 Chestnut Street, Philadelphia.*

On Board S.S. "Majestic"
July 9, 1922.

Charles J. Rhoads,
J. Henry Scattergood.
DEAR FRIENDS:—

I am writing to you in order to follow up the suggestion that arose as we came away from the meeting in Twelfth Street last Fourth-day.

I then mentioned the problems being faced by the new National Christian Council for China of which I have been asked to become secretary. Its hope is to unite in a far more intimate fellowship, if not in organic union, the various Christian bodies in China. This is to be done under Chinese leadership in the main and if I go it will be as a colleague to two or more Chinese Christians. Thus a step towards the development of a truly indigenous Church is being taken at the same time as one towards closer union. Both are very significant and hopeful.

It is strange to me that a Quaker should be chosen as an officer of such an organization, but I put this down to the fact that already it is seen that the Spirit is more important than the forms under which unity can be achieved and also to an openness of mind towards the position we take on war and other questions greater than we usually find in ecclesiastical bodies in the West.

but also in the fundamental question of the status of the worker in industry. Thus it came about that there were many of the future Conscientious Objectors who had come to feel that "it is chiefly by the expression of religious impulses through political effort that we may hope to change men's hearts and practice."

And so it happened that when the war broke out there were a number of men who were questioning whether an economic society organized for profit could possibly be administered in the interests of the many. The society which they envisaged could do no violence to personality. Then came the war and later, conscription. Conscription seemed to be the crowning attack of a vicious system upon personality. To yield to it, to make any compromise with it, was to recognize the right of the State to force the individual to render certain service against his will. This the absolutist would not do. The military seemed dimly to realize that here were a group whose ideas struck at the very foundations of military power and the established order of society, and they pursued them with relentless cruelty. The story of this conflict between the government and the 16,000 Conscientious Objectors of different convictions and types is the theme of John W. Graham's book. The author by careful selection of material not only lets the men tell the story of their sufferings, but he also lets them explain the ideal for which they struggled, that we also may see something of the vision they caught in many an English prison cell.

J. HOWARD BRANSON.

"Conscription and Conscience," by John William Graham (Allen and Unwin, 12/6d), may be secured through the office of Walter H. Jenkins, 140 N. Fifteenth St., Philadelphia, Pa.

The Work in the Coal Fields

The child feeding is progressing satisfactorily in both Pennsylvania and West Virginia. Four feeding centers are now open in Bedford County, Pa., where 195 children were being fed the week ending August 12th. It is expected that feeding in Somerset County will begin this week. Francis Walton and Esther Dunham of Philadelphia and Dr. Emily Seaman of New York are taking the places of workers who must leave shortly.

In West Virginia 182 children are being fed at 5 centers and 115 mothers and babies are receiving fresh milk. Richard Cadbury, who recently returned from Poland, will succeed Philip Furnas, who leaves September 1st.

There appears to be much greater need in West Virginia than in Pennsylvania. The conclusions arrived at by Walter Abell and Drew Pearson in their investigations in April of this year, are borne out by the reports from the workers. They write:

"In trying to find where there is need for relief work, one should guard against judging by appearance. Here in West Virginia there appeared to be poverty and need; but whether that was a mere appearance and not a fact was at first a question. The question seemed to be answered in a decisive fashion by the first medical examinations which were made here. The children were weighed and their height taken, and the results were compared with the norms given by Dr. L. Emmet Holt and the Child Welfare Station of the State of Iowa. The children examined were divided into four classes: I, Normal; II, Undernourished; III, Seriously undernourished; IV, Diseased and seriously undernourished. Less than 50 per cent. of the children were in Class I. A child was not put in Class II or III unless he was more than 8 points below normal, a number that would indicate that he was from six months to a year below the average development or was from ten to fifteen pounds underweight. Of the 211 children in three different camps examined at the time of this writing, 108 or over 50 per cent. were in Class II, 47 or 22 per cent. were in Class III and two were in Class IV.

The work seems to be just in time to do the most good. Help must come when undernourishment begins if it is to be effective. The conditions here are especially hard on little babies, many of whom examination shows belong in Class II or Class III. We are providing them or their mothers with pure fresh milk. We feel that this is one of the most helpful services we can perform. In addition to this, our workers give the mothers advice as to feeding and taking care of their babies, matters with regard to which there is great ignorance.

For the other children who show conditions of undernourishment we have organized, through the co-operation of women and men in the local camps, feeding centers to which the children come for one good supplementary meal each day. Any one who cared to examine the clothes of the children and see how they eat the food provided for them would be assured of the need which the stations are attempting to meet.

It is certainly true that ignorance as well as the present industrial situation has contributed to the condition in which the children now find themselves. The schools in most of the camps are not well equipped; and we are told that they are not well administered. In one of the camps we were told that there were no trustees now. Many of the men and women as well as the children cannot read. I began reading a few lines from a paper to a man in a small store yesterday; and in a moment there were a dozen or more standing around anxious to hear what the news was, but in many instances quite incapable of finding out for themselves what it was. The people naturally, as the result of their ignorance, are easily made to believe foolish and bizarre matters. They can only with difficulty read even a recipe for cooking, and consequently the women have no means for improving their standards. Ignorance is one of the great handicaps of the communities.

The need for some kind of help is universally admitted. Appreciation of our work is expressed as soon as it is understood. Any one who cares to try relief work in these communities will be astounded at times by the remarkable response which supposedly unimpressionable people make. As one of our workers expressed it: "It is wonderful how easy it is to do things when you are trying to help people instead of trying to get something away from them."

The Heart of Virginia

From Washington the C. and O. Railroad stretches away to the southwest, passing through the center of the state. Located on this line, 107 miles from Washington, is the interesting little town of Charlottesville, the seat of the University of Virginia, which may be said to be, in an educational sense, the heart of Virginia.

As one travels along this railroad and notes the character of the country, it easily falls into three sections. The first forty miles consists of forest lands, with small pines and maples, with neglected fields, and is rather hilly. Here the road passes across the field of the Battle of Bull Run, disastrous to the Union forces. It looks quite peaceful now.

The next section of thirty-five miles is quite flat, almost prairie land, with large fields, not well cultivated, some few cattle and horses grazing in them.

In all this extent of territory very few good dwellings are to be seen from the car window. One looks in vain for "the big house" of plantation days, although these may be located at a distance.

As we approach Charlottesville, the country is seen to be more hilly and better cultivated, and beyond that point the Blue Ridge Mountains are approached and finally climbed by the train, until, passing through four tunnels amid the clouds, the beautiful and fertile Shenandoah Valley spreads wide before the eye.

The hills at this point bear large apple orchards, now in bearing. Here a girl entered our train, carrying a basket full of wonderful summer Rambo apples, rich in color and as large as two fists.

The University of Virginia is unique in its plan and a thing of beauty. Founded by Thomas Jefferson, the general plan is his. The original buildings are placed on the sides of an oblong "lawn" and extend a distance of some 300 yards. The buildings are one-story high, except where the professors' houses run up one more floor. These are marked by high white columns. Smaller columns form a corridor, which extends the whole length, forming a covered walk upon which the students' bedrooms open.

Closing the "lawn" at one end is an imposing building of rotunda form with approaches of high and wide flights of steps. This is the library. At the other end is Cabell Hall, a circular auditorium, designed by Stanford White. Further away there is an out-of-door auditorium, capable of seating 2,000 persons and usually filled at "Vespers" and First-day evenings. On the occasion of my visit, being rainy, Vesper service was held in Cabell Hall, where 300 gathered.

All but one of the buildings are of the Georgian style of architecture—red brick, with high columned porticos. The feature that strikes one especially is the enormous number of white columns seen everywhere. Being so old an institution the trees have grown to enormous size, making the campus most attractive, added to by the wide spaces of green grass and the vine-covered walls. In one courtyard are some fine magnolia trees. Several groups of statuary are to be seen: one of Jefferson, standing on what seems to be a replica of the Liberty Bell, and one of Clark, the explorer.

One leaves this historic spot with a feeling of increased respect and admiration for its founder, charmed by the University, itself and what it stands for, and grateful for the many noble lives which have here gained their inspiration. O. EDWARD JANNEY.

The Evolution of Long Island

By Ralph Henry Gabriel. New Haven, Yale University Press, 1921. 194 pages.

Lovers of Long Island will appreciate this book. And who, having any knowledge of its civil and religious history, its marvelously level plains, its rolling northland, its winding lanes and hospitable old houses, does not love this bit of terminal moraine?

The most noticeable feature of this volume appears to be, as our Hibernian friends might say, something which was left out. The author in his survey of the Island and its inhabitants through the centuries, says little about politics, and no word regarding religion. Politics, in the larger sense, has evolved, as elsewhere in America, into what appears to be a settled faith and form. Religion, again in the larger sense, has seemingly evolved, there and in the "hinterland," into a greater tolerance, and possibly into a more intelligent faith in personal and civic righteousness. Why does he disregard them? In other matters he has made excellent use of material from original sources and based thereon reasonable conclusions. He shows how the development of the agricultural and industrial revolution, which brought to an end the age of homespun and changed the motive power on the farm from the slow-moving ox to the quicker, more specialized horse, which produced highways, canals, and later railways, thereby took from the Island that supremacy which contiguity to the large city had theretofore maintained.

Well does he entitle the chapter on the railroad as "Wars and rumors of wars," for the ninety-six-mile line built in 1844 to Greenport, to carry passengers on their way to Boston, and the other little railroads of the Island, suffered all the vicissitudes common to the early history of our railroad systems.

The influence of the high-wheel bicycle on the development of good roads, now remembered only by L. A. W. survivors, here finds a worthy pen. He must have been one of us. The earlier phases of turnpikes and plank roads, with their frequent tollgates, and the social effects of these improvements, is ably shown. This may recall that our cemetery, now hidden in the midst of Prospect Park, was, in 1847, established on the "Coney Island Plank Road."

The "game" in which the sea and the land have tossed back and forth that sand which is Long Island, is not ended. The sea still adds to or takes from the southern beaches; the ice may again advance with relentless creep from the polar cap, and it doth not yet appear what changes this pleasant moraine may undergo in the coming ages. He does not even try to guess. A useful map shows the Island of today. The citations of authorities are numerous and useful, but one source is, surprising, "Gazateers."

The book fails in so little and succeeds in so much, that no Long Islander, no lover of its past or present, can well afford to neglect the pleasant task of reading it.

JOHN COX, JR.

Friends in Madagascar

Wilfrid Allott, a Dublin Friend, now home on furlough, writes in the Friends' Fellowship Papers of the work of the Friends' mission in Madagascar:

The Friends' Church in Madagascar is the most striking achievement of our Society under the guidance of God in this last fifty years. Twenty thousand people meet week by week in our two hundred and seven meetings. It takes time to realize that; but any map of this vast tract of country with our meetings marked is a stimulating sight in these depressing days. Neither meeting-houses nor schools are provided by foreign money. But all these communities are still ultimately dependent on our faithfulness for their intellectual and spiritual life. But the present trend of policy made at home—not only in our mission of course but generally—is to condemn past help as injudicious and preach independence to the native Church. As long as any considerable portion of that church knows little and can know little of the historic Christ, all this theorizing seems cruel neglect of the child by the parent. Or does anyone claim that the Inward Light will invent the Christ of the Gospels for a Church that cannot find Him in the printed page?

Life in Madagascar is very drab. We at home are so used to beauty of all kinds that it is difficult for us to imagine a life deprived of these commonplace blessings. There are no singing birds in Madagascar; no buttercups and daisies. For three months now at home there has been no rain to speak of, yet still Ireland is green and England covered with splendor. But the first three months of the dry season in Madagascar reduce all vegetation to a sorry condition, parched and brown and lifeless. Year in and year out there is no escape from heat and light. Both limit human life narrowly. Sitting on the shore here at home, as the sea breaks lazily on the stones and the children bathe and splash together, one can't but think God has been very partial to most of us. Of course the Malagasy have no idea of the fuller life we live; they are used to a very drab existence. For most of us, that settles it. We are content with the station in life to which it has pleased God to call us. But once we actually *see* the Malagasy this attitude develops and most of us thank God thoughtlessly that we were not called to be Malagasy—and then realize something unacceptable in such a prayer. We are thankful for what the Christian Church has been able to do to break the monotony of life in that island.

The hymns of the Christian Church mean more to the Malagasy than to us. They are a first revelation of the feeling of oneness and fellowship to those whose lives from various reasons are very lonely. Capacity for self-expression and interchange of thought, is not much developed in the Malagasy people. Their letters witness to that, being regularly formal and meagre, quite bare of news, quite without the warm personal touch a good letter always has. The letters are characterless and so often are the people. Music of any kind brings new vibrations into these still lives.

Usually in the evening our boys that live with us, about twenty as a rule, gradually gravitate to the kitchen door and sit round inside, and before long the chorus begins. They have learned part singing and do it pretty well. When these boys scatter down country, among other things they will, in the old phrase, take with them words, but in song form. They have wonderful memories for recitation as have most peoples unused to paper, and this fact helps our hymns as a means of grace. Light has come in this way to many a soul too late reached for light to find any other way home; and in death our hymns have been a comfort to many of those who in the prophet's words hardly knew right hand from left. We are thankful for the wide appeal and reach of hymns. I shall never forget the first time I heard five hundred Malagasy boys sing together: "What a friend we have in Jesus"—nor shall I forget in a lost villege in the west a meeting-house full of children and adults sitting in a stolid silence not knowing how to sing at all, and yet coming together vaguely seeking light. That village was one where they used to sing, but the tide of darkness rose again when the Friends' schools over a large area were closed. Little by little things were forgotten. We had lifted the pall a little and held it a few years only to let it drop again. Heathen customs that had been driven out come back again. "My people perish for lack of knowledge."

A Tribute

In Maurice Hewlett's little book, "Wiltshire Essays," recently published, there occurs the following beautiful tribute to the Society of Friends:

"I have said that Christ's teaching has never been followed, His way of life never attempted. That is true of nations, with which so far I have been dealing. Obviously, it is not true of individuals, nor altogether of groups of individuals. Groups have attempted it: Cathart, Patterini, Franciscans, Hussites, Wycliffites, Albigenses, Friends of God, Port-Royalists, Doukhobors, and such-like. Most of them have failed owing to internal weakness, and the nature of men; some, like the Albigenses, have been crushed out or worn down by the hostility of governments. One only, English in origin, has endured for three hundred years. That is a group large enough to be called something else. It does not claim to be a Church, and calls itself the Society of Friends. By a term of mockery, now become one of affection, men outside it call it the Quakers.

"Founded by George Fox, an uninstructed man illuminated by close and literal reading of the Gospels, outliving both a time of persecution and one of moral collapse, that Society has presented to the world for three hundred and more years the nearest approach to the Christ-like way of life which has ever been known. It is based upon neighborly love, it is strictly pacifist; in the face of government it is quietist. So far the likeness is exact. It does not, however, observe the counsel of Poverty, and is in no sense Communistic. In those two points, and in the fact that it has not been zealous to proselytize, it falls short of the teaching of Jesus Christ. But essentially it resembles that teaching in being an enthusiasm, an illumination and a Way of Life. . . . . . Its doctrine is idealistic and undogmatic.

"What is now extremely noteworthy is that since the late war began the Society of Friends has broken down the defenses which screened it from the world, and definitely ranged itself in Europe as a Christian body with work to do correspendent with the faith which it holds. With no bridge-making to be done, with no gulf between Belief and Conduct, the Quakers of America and Britain, ever since the Armistice, have been steadily at work throughout Europe, and particularly in Germany and Austria, mending the fortunes of broken people, feeding the hungry, clothing the naked, showing forth Goodwill among men who of late years have shown forth none of their own."

Mr. Hewlett then quotes some figures of the money spent in European relief by Friends in the year 1919-20, and continues:

"These figures tell their own story; and if we call the work which they represent 'loving our enemies,' as we well may, it is not what they would call it; for they say that it takes two to make a quarrel, and that Quakers quarrel with no sons of men. The matter for the concern of Christendom is that it is a work which I believe I am right in saying no other Church, no other society of Christian people, as such, is doing."

The above appeared in the *New York Evening Post* for Fifth month 6th, 1922. ANNA L. CURTIS.

An Interesting Report for Workers

I wonder how many Friends can tell, without specially searching, to what organization this motto belongs: "The well-being of mankind throughout the world"? It is the key-word of an organization whose reports should be familiar reading to all who are also engaged in work with that purpose, for this organization has "blazed a trail" where many were unable ever to make a track. It includes in its report for 1921 the following items:

1. Continuing a quarter million annual appropriation to the School of Hygiene and Public Health of Johns Hopkins University.
2. Pledged two million to Harvard for a School of Health.
3. Contributed to Public Health Training in Czecho-slovakia, Brazil and the United States.
4. Aided the Pasteur Institute of Paris to recruit and train personnel.
5. Promoted the cause of nurse training in America and Europe.
6. Underwrote an experimental pay clinic in the Cornell Medical School.
7. Formally opened a complete Medical School and Hospital in Peking.
8. Assisted 25 other medical centres in China.
9. Promised a million dollars for the Medical School of Columbia University.
10. Contracted to appropriate three and one-half millions for the rebuilding and reorganization of the Medical Schools and Hospital of the Free University of Brussels.
11. Made surveys of Medical Schools in Japan, China, the Philippines, Indo-China, Straits Settlements, Siam, India, Syria and Turkey.
12. Supplied American and British Medical Journals to 112 Medical Libraries on the Continent.
13. Supplemented the Laboratory equipment and supplies of five Medical Schools in Central Europe.
14. Defrayed the expenses of Commissions from Great Britain, Belgium, Serbia and Brazil.
15. Provided 157 fellowships in hygiene, medicine, physics and chemistry, to representatives of 18 countries.
16. Continued a campaign against yellow fever in Mexico, Central and South America.

17. Prosecuted demonstrations in the control of malaria in ten states.
18. Co-operated in hookworm work in 19 governmental areas.
19. Participated in rural health demonstrations in 77 American countries and in Brazil.
20. Neared the goal of transferring to French agencies an anti-tuberculosis organization in France.
21. Provided experts in medical education and public health for counsel and surveys in many parts of the world, and rendered many minor services to governments and voluntary societies.

The detailed reports, of which the above are but headings, read like a fairy tale, with their bits of human interest among people all over the world. And they do not tell merely of dreams and hopes—they are accomplished facts, work done, *done* during 1921. These reports can be had by libraries and interested individuals merely for the asking, by addressing the Rockefeller Foundation, New York.

ELEANOR S. SHARPLES.

Friendly News Notes

The "OCL Book," which gives a full account of the 250th Anniversary of Baltimore Yearly Meetings, is ready for distribution. Orders for these books should be sent to O. Edward Janney, 825 Newington Ave., Baltimore, Md. As the price is only $1.00 a copy, every Friend should have one, and as they are beautiful books they will make welcome gifts.

The engagement of Blanche Elizabeth Smith, of Denver, Colorado, and Dr. Edwin W. Perrott, Jr., also of Denver, is announced. Dr. Perrott is a son of Edwin W. and Hannah F. Perrott, of Germantown, Pa., and has been a practicing physician in Denver for several years.

Prairie Grove Quarterly Meeting, held on Eighth month 17th, near Winfield, Iowa, was small and very little apparently could be accomplished. The spirit, however, which draws together these Friends in an effort to keep alive the meeting is very worth while.

Mary N. Chase, Secretary for the Promotion of International Amity, Proctor Academy, Andover, New Hampshire, writes us that she is seeking a place for a Mexican correspondent who desires to come to this country to perfect herself in English. Miss Chase writes that her client is a bright, attractive young lady who has been working for the Bureau of Education in Merida. She would be willing to sew, care for children or do typewriting. If possible she would like to go to school part of the time. Miss Chase prefers to get her into a Friends' home or a Friends' school.

The new conference Committee selected by the Young Friends at their recent conference at Earlham consists of the following: Helen Hawkins, New Vienna, Ohio (chairman); Sumner Mills, West Newton, Ind. (business manager); Arthur O. Rinden, Oskaloosa, Iowa; Clarence E. Pickett, Richmond, Ind.; and Ruth Hoskins, Indianapolis, Ind. Heretofore the officers have been the same as those of the Young Friends' Executive Committee of the Five Years Meeting.

CONCORD QUARTER PICNIC

A representative group of Concord Quarter Young Friends met at Westtown, Pa., on Eighth month 19th, to enjoy the Concord Quarter Picnic of the Young Friends' Movement. After a refreshing dip in the lake, games, and a box supper eaten on the green sweep of the Westtown Friends' School campus, the gathering settled down to a discussion of the purpose and ideals of the Young Friends' Movement.

Lindsley Noble began this discussion with the following points: I. That the Young Friends' Movement designs to arouse active interest in the First-day meetings for worship. II. That it aims to promote fellowship among the younger Friends, so that each individual may realize that the ideals of love and service are dear to others beside himself.

Elizabeth Walter, carrying out the preceding trend of thought, spoke of the ideal "service." Two kinds of service are open to young Friends, she said: service for the world at large and service within the Society of Friends.

One of the great opportunities for young Friends to help strengthen the Society is in the uniting of the Orthodox and Hicksite branches, not in form at first, but in spirit. That such a reunion is possible and practical was shown by the Earlham Conference, when both eastern and western Friends studied the same questions, each inspiring the other.

RICHARD ABELL.

TO ENCOURAGE FRIENDS EVERYWHERE

At the close of an annual meeting held in the old Quaker Springs Meeting-house near Saratoga, New York, *eight* concerned Friends in the neighborhood requested that the building, which has been closed for years, be opened again on First-day the 27th for regular meetings for worship, and promised to attend. The faithfulness of two Friends in the locality is thus rewarded in seeing their devotion bear fruit; one of them has cared for the grounds and opened the doors many times when no one came, and the other has planned and kept alive the annual meetings.

A similar experiment will be tried in Amawalk, Westchester county, on Ninth month 17th, when three devoted families will again open their meeting-house to the community, even though it is small, for regular meetings for worship, through the pleasant weather at least. Albert R. Lawton will attend this first meeting.

" 'Courage!' he said, and pointed toward the land,
'This mounting wave will roll us shoreward soon.' "

FRIENDS' OPPORTUNITY IN THE ORIENT.

In order that permanency may be assured, and a wider circle of interest and financial support established for the work of Friends in the Orient, Alfred W. Wright, chairman of the committee that has had this work in charge, has appealed to the General Conference now in session at Richmond, Indiana, to take over this work officially. It is not intended that the General Conference shall undertake financial responsibility, but rather that voluntary contributions may be solicited under the authority of the General Conference.

As a result of two appeals made during the years 1921 and 1922, this committee has paid to Canton Christian College $3,000 for the full support of Margaret H. Riggs as teacher for two years, and also $800 through John R. Mott, Secretary, as partial support for Joseph and Edith S. Platt. These young people having allied themselves with effective interdenominational agencies, it seems to be more practical to support them in this way than to undertake a sectarian mission of our own. In acknowledging the receipt of the $800, John R. Mott, who is General Secretary of the International Committee of Young Men's Christian Associations, wrote to Alfred W. Wright: "I believe that investments in personality, made in China in these days, will have perhaps more far-reaching value than that of any other part of the world with which I am familiar."

THE PEACH LAKE MEETING.

The annual meeting at Peach Lake, this year, held on the afternoon of First-day the 13th, was an experiment of faith on the part of Mary Emma Hunt, of Goldens Bridge, who always plans it; because she offered to an audience of nearly six hundred people, a representative group of almost all Young Friends' Movement speakers.

Following last year's precedent, the seats were again arranged out-of-doors under the trees, that all might enjoy the beautiful afternoon in the open. A wall of autos, enclosing the benches and camp-chairs, supplemented the seating capacity; while Albert Lawton and Mary Travilla gave inspiration by their company to the line of young Friends on the facing seats.

Albert Lawton opened the meeting by referring to a question some one in attendance had put to him: "If the old meeting-house could only speak, what would it say?" Augustus Cadwallader, of Yardley, Pa., then spoke on "Seek ye the truth." He referred to the work of Friends abroad and how our message carries freedom from the bondage of fear and prejudice and by the fruit of its sowing is carrying the spirit of Truth into political and social problems as the new solution. Grace Warren followed his inspiring talk with Keats' line:

"Beauty is truth; truth, beauty,"

in a plea that we allow the power of beauty, such as one sees in the effect of beautiful music on a crowd, have more sway in our lives,—substituting it for some of our cheap sensations,—so that our individual influence on the unrest about us may be harmony-infecting and calming. Howard Carey, of Brooklyn, president of the Young Friends' Movement of New York Yearly Meetings, was reminded, he said, by the neighboring reservoirs, of the source of power and supply in the all-pervading Spirit of God upon whom, if we will, we can draw unceasingly as in the city we open the faucet and find no limit to the flow of water. Arthur James then added a helpful thought, and Anna Curtis dwelt on the perfect laws of God, physical and spiritual, to which this universe gives constant witness, adding some very apt, true, Quaker stories of the present day to illustrate the infallibility of the law of love and friendless. Then in a beautiful closing address, in which she emphasized the omnipresence of God and the necessity of carrying to our homes and our daily lives the inspiration of the uplifting thoughts we had just heard, Mary Travilla placed a seal to the experiment of faith and brought to a fitting close one more treasured Peach Lake Meeting.

G. T. W.

BALTIMORE NOTES

We are very glad to receive again the News Letter of Baltimore Meeting of Friends sent out by Bliss Forbush. About one-half of it is taken up with a description of the work at the Asquit Street Playground during the last four months. Owing to a shorter season due to the CCL Celebration at the beginning and the General Conference at the end of the summer, the total number in attendance is not quite as large as in 1921, but the work went on enthusiastically and the financial needs were well taken care of this year. This year there were 3,383 children who enjoyed the playground, while last year the total number was 4,844. During July and parts of June and August the playground was directed by Jessie Hill, and much of the success was due to her efficient work.

The new entrance to the School and Meeting is rapidly nearing completion. The new addition provides an open-air study room 70 feet by 25 feet, four new offices, a greatly improved entrance and hall, a large locker room, a larger kitchen, pantry and cold storage room. The excavating in the cellar under the meeting-house has also nearly doubled the size of that space. The new office of the Monthly Meeting Secretary is being made in the northwest corner of the building in the so-called Buffington Room, and will be very convenient. Edward Wilson has offered us the use of the new offices on First-day for our Primary Classes.

On looking over the Honor Roll of Friends' School for 1921-1922, we are very glad to see how well our Friends' children are represented. Here is the list: Williamson Scholarship to Swarthmore College, Elizabeth F. Sharples; Leading Scholars—Senior Class, Edith D. Hull, first place. Class enrollment, 30.

First Year High—Bertha Hull, third place; Thomas Sharples, fourth place; George Carter, fifth place. Class enrollment, 53.

Intermediate, Third Year—Omar Pancoast, Jr., third place. Class enrollment, 41.

Second Year—Charles Whitby (our FDS.), first place; Allan J. Harper, fourth place. Class enrollment, 49.

Primary, Third Year—Arthur E. Taylor, Jr., among first five.

We might also call attention to the fact that Eugenia Merryman and Elizabeth Sharples have not been late for eight years at school; that Thomas Sharples has not been late for seven years, Barton Skeen for six years, or Omar Pancoast and Dorothy Luebbers for five years.

FAIRFAX QUARTERLY MEETING

Fairfax Quarterly Meeting of Friends was held at Lincoln, Eighth month 19th to 21st, the sessions starting on Saturday afternoon with the meeting of Ministry and Counsel. On Sunday a large crowd gathered for the morning session. The meeting was opened by a Bible reading, after which Dr. Janney gave an impressive sermon. Anne W. Janney, William Eves, Thomas B. Hull, Obed J. Pierpont and George Hoge developed further the thought of love and neighborliness with short talks and quoted selections. The meeting closed with prayer.

A bountiful lunch was served on the lawn. The bright sunshine and delightful breeze aided in the enjoyment of the repast and the social intercourse with both old and new friends.

The First-day School Union meeting in the afternoon called forth the usual responses from delegates and representatives of the various schools in the quarter. The primary class of the home school furnished enjoyable exercises.

The topic for the afternoon, "Religious Training in the Home," was ably handled by Bliss Forbush. He described the training which the young Jewish and Catholic child received and asked what the Friend's child had to take the place of the rich store provided for these other children. He then went on to tell some of the things which he thought could be given: the home background of daily Bible reading, of vocal thanks for meals, of bedtime and morning prayers. Short discussions followed in which several joined.

Monday morning a devotional meeting preceded the business session. The theme of self-sacrifice even unto the giving of life itself with the added thought of the living sacrifice as furnished by lives of service was developed by O. Edward and Anne W. Janney and Rev. Branch, a visiting minister.

The business session, which took up answers to all the queries, was a long, but interesting, one. The query on temperance called forth discussion from several in regard to law enforcement, and while it was felt that much had been gained in obtaining our present laws, there is urgent need for assistance in having these laws enforced.

The Peace Committee reported active work accomplished. A series of lectures arranged by them had been given at Normal Schools and various public functions throughout the state this summer. Besides this, posters and peace literature had been distributed.

Memorials were read to the memory of Cornelia Janney and Phineas Nichols, valued members of Goose Creek Monthly Meeting. These, with a message from one of our dear absent members, seemed to bring all present together in a closer bond of unity.

MARY E. NICHOLS, *Assistant Clerk.*

Items from Everywhere

The Canton Christian College of South China is importing American domestic animals and numerous plants and fruit and nut trees in an effort to improve the agricultural situation in that section.

Among the significant happenings of the last few months is the formation of the Progressive Party in Idaho, which had its origin in the conference held in Boise last December at the instance of the Committee of 48. Since then the Progressive Party has been legalized, and now has a place on the ballot.

After printing a weekly serial from the Bible for three months, Arthur J. Carruth, managing editor of the Topeka *State Journal*, declares that the publication of the Bible has proved to be the greatest success of any "feature" ever printed by the *State Journal*. Each installment includes about 3,000 words. The Weymouth text of the New Testament, a translation in every day English, is used. Already publication of the book of Mark has been completed and the book of Luke is well under way.

A treaty was made with the Navajo Indians in 1868 wherein was promised a school-house and teacher for every thirty children of school age. Notwithstanding that promise, today there are over 6,000 such children without school facilities!

There is now an opportunity for meeting that need, in part at least, at slight expense, if the conscience of the people demand it. Hon. Charles H. Burke, Commissioner of Indian Affairs, has requested the Secretary of War to transfer to the Interior Department the virtually abandoned military post at Fort Wingate (near Gallup), New Mexico, for school purposes. This military post is in the heart of the Navajo country, and it can be equipped, at comparatively slight expense, to accommodate fully 500 Indian pupils. Moreover, the climate is well suited to the health of the children of these Navajos.

A more fitting and practical use of Government property can scarcely be conceived. The merging of the implements of war into the arts of peace and education will be a veritable fulfilment of the prophecy that "they shall beat their swords into ploughshares." The War Department has thus far declined the request.

THE OPEN FORUM

This column is intended to afford free expression of opinion by readers on questions of interest. The INTELLIGENCER is not responsible for any such opinions. Letters must be brief, and the editor reserves the right to omit parts if necessary to save space.

To the Editor:

One can only marvel that some calling themselves "Friends" sanction the imprisonment of those who have made the same protests against war and denial of liberty to criticize the Government that sent the founders of our Society to jails and dungeons.

I hope the letter of Elizabeth H. Coale in the INTELLIGENCER of Eighth month 19th will not confirm any in their reactionary and un-Friendly beliefs. Such often do much harm. LOUISA T. PRICE.

Wellfleet, Mass.

To the Editor:

Why need our friend Walter Clothier be surprised and disappointed by a logical explanation of society as it is and a higher ideal of it as it should be contributed to the INTELLIGENCER under the title of "Wage Slavery"? Calling things socialistic certainly cannot be accepted as indisputable argument by clear-thinking Friends who want to know the truth. Why does he not point out wherein the error lies? Most Friends still believe in the old anti-slavery motto, "Let truth and error grapple." I challenge our friend to prove his assertion that these socialistic articles that have appeared encourage a spirit of distrust and hatred. As I understand them, they have, on the contrary, been full of the Christian spirit of co-operation and a higher, more unselfish view of life for all men.

It certainly is not thinking clearly and practically to intimate that constructive justice and peace-promoting socialism has had a fair trial in Russia. The whole capitalist world has done everything it dared do to prevent the success of the revolutionary soviet government in Russia, from furnishing millions of dollars' worth of arms and ammunition to its enemies to establishing starvation blockades. By an appeal to the nobler sentiments and principles of humanity in our own country, true education in real democracy and peaceable nationalization of all great natural resources and basic public utilities, etc., we aim to prevent in the future just such a monstrous debacle of corrupt capitalism and its bloody fruit of revolution. We see in the present outgrown profits system endless hatred and war engendered by its international and class struggles. We believe in an industrial system in which most productive capital is collectively owned and under the direct democratic control of those who by their brain and hand produce it. We believe that the whole people have a fundamental undivided interest in all the great natural resources of the earth. The only way for all to benefit to the fullest is through public or collective ownership and operation at the actual cost of production, with humane working conditions and ample reward for labor. No stock gambling, stock watering profiteers to draw billions of wealth unearned from the necessities of the producers. Under the co-operative commonwealth the Brotherhood of Man conception of the Master would cease to be a far-off ideal and become an accomplished condition.

Right here some readers will wag their heads and say, "impractical idealism." Yes! Just as impractical as applying Christianity in big business. Are war and the class struggle which amounts to civil war practical? Most friends profess to believe in peace. What most of them do not comprehend is the fact that outgrown capitalism cannot continue without increasing injustice, repression and war. A deeper study of economic laws and conditions will certainly bring them to the parting of the way from old political organizations that are under the control of capitalism and militarism. I. K. W.

Oxford, Pa.

BIRTHS

ATKINSON—At Wrightstown, Pa., on Eighth month 16th, to Robert E. and Beulah Elliott Atkinson, a son, named Edward Krusen Atkinson.

DEATHS

ALBERTSON—On Eighth month 22d, Martha H. Albertson, daughter of the late Chalkley and Annie Stokes Albertson, of Magnolia, N. J.

ALLEN—In Philadelphia, Pa., on Eighth month 24th, William E., husband of the late Mary Lane Allen, and son of Samuel and the late Sarah D. Allen, aged 70 years.

GREEN—On Eighth month 17th, at Chappaqua, N. Y., Phebe C., wife of Harvey Green. She was a real mother in Israel, and the five daughters and two sons whom she bore and reared, though they live long, yet their most beautiful memory will ever be that of her love and service.

JOHN COX, JR.

RAMSEY—At Bellefonte, Pa., on Eighth month 27th, Miriam, wife of Dr. William G. Ramsey and daughter of the late Edward D. and Mary E. Eyre.

SHELDRAKE—On Eighth month 24th, C. Anna Sheldrake, daughter of the late Charles and Phoebe Sleeper. Interment in Darby Friends' Burial Ground.

COMING EVENTS

NINTH MONTH

2nd—Nottingham Quarterly Meeting, at East Nottingham, Md. James W. Harry will attend and address the Conference on "The Christian in Public Life."

2nd-4th—Center Quarterly Meeting, at Half Moon, Pa. O. Edward Janney expects to attend.

3rd—Meeting at Swarthmore, Pa., to be addressed by Dr. Henry E. Jackson. See Notice.

3rd—First-day at 2.30 p. m., Eastern Standard time, a meeting for divine worship will be held at the Wayside Chapel, Cheyney, Delaware County, Pa. A community meeting for all interested persons. Thornbury Young Friends' Association will co-operate. A pleasant pilgrimage from West Chester trolley or by train from Broad Street Station.

3rd—Certain members of Philadelphia Quarterly Meeting's Visiting Committee expect to attend Race Street Meeting at 10.30 a. m.

3rd—At 2.30 p. m., Eastern Standard time—Friends' Meeting in the old Meeting-house at Adams, Mass., under care of the Advancement Committee of New York Yearly Meeting co-operating with the Adams Society of Friends' Descendants. Reuben P. Kester and other Friends will attend.

On the following day, Labor Day, there will be a picnic lunch under care of the Society of Friends' Descendants at the old Browne Homestead, at which historical subjects of Friendly interest, including a short pageant, will be presented.

All Friends and others interested are invited to attend.

5th—Whitewater Quarterly Meeting, at Lincolnville, Ind.

7th—Salem Quarterly Meeting, at Woodstown, N. J.

9th—The Representative Committee of Ohio Yearly Meeting will meet at the home of Lindley and Miriam B. Tomlinson, 111 McKinley avenue, Salem, Ohio, at 10 a. m.

9th—The Burlington First-day School Union will be held at Mansfield, near Columbus, N. J. Sessions at 10.30 and 1.30. An interesting program is being arranged. Friends from other localities are always welcome.

10th—Certain members of Philadelphia Quarterly Meeting's Visiting Committee expect to attend Reading Meeting, at 11 a. m.

11th—Baltimore Quarterly Meeting, at Gunpowder, Md.

14th—Haddonfield Quarterly Meeting, at Haddonfield, N. J.

NOTICE—On Ninth month 3rd, a meeting under the care of Concord Quarterly Meeting's Philanthropic Committee will be held immediately following the morning religious meeting which is held at 10.30. The meeting will be addressed by Dr. Henry E. Jackson, of Washington, D. C. His subject will be "One Way to Industrial Peace." Dr. Jackson has a special message for the Society of Friends and it is hoped that all those that can attend will do so.

American Friends' Service Committee

WILBUR K. THOMAS, EX. SEC.

20 S. 12th St. Philadelphia.

CASH CONTRIBUTIONS

WEEK ENDING EIGHTH MONTH 21ST.

Five Years Meeting	$65.00
Other Meetings:	
Orange Grove Meeting, Pasadena, California	20.00
First Friends' Church, Cleveland, Ohio	10.00
Alexandria Monthly Meeting	20.00
College Park Association of Friends, San Jose. Cal.	112.43
	$162.43
Contributions for—	
Chalons	10.00
Austria	25.00
Germany	282.43
Poland	322.00
Russia	1,508.28
Home Service Overhead	10.00
West Virginia	518.25
Central Pennsylvania	518.25
General Fund	559.00
Syria	5.00
Clothing	4.04
Money in Transit	24.90
Refunds and Payments	1,776.57
Total Contributions	$5,791.15

Shipments received during week ending August 19th; Packages, 14; anonymous, 2.

FUN

A New Kind of Amusement.—A Chicago editor once received some verses with the following note of explanation:

"These lines were written sixty years ago by one who has for a long time slept in his grave merely for a pastime."—*Exchange.*

A man who was wanted by the police had been photographed in six different positions, and the pictures were circulated among the police. The chief in a small town wrote headquarters a few days later, saying, "I duly received the pictures of the six miscreants whose capture is desired. I have arrested five of them; the sixth is under observation and will be taken soon."

To the Lot Holders and others interested in Fairhill Burial Ground:

GREEN STREET Monthly Meeting has funds available for the encouragement of the practice of cremating the dead to be interred in Fairhill Burial Ground. We wish to bring this fact as prominently as possible to those who may be interested. We are prepared to undertake the expense of cremation in case any lot holder desires us to do so.

Those interested should communicate with William H. Gaskill, Treasurer of the Committee of Interments, Green Street Monthly Meeting, or any of the following members of the Committee.

William H. Gaskill, 3201 Arch St.
Samuel N. Longstreth, 1218 Chestnut St.
Charles F. Jenkins, 232 South Seventh St.
Stuart S. Graves, 3033 Germantown Ave.

ADVERTISING RATE in the FRIENDS' INTELLIGENCER, for Help Wanted, Positions Wanted, Rooms for Rent, Notices, and other classified advertisements without display, for each insertion, 2 cents per word, including name, initials and address. Answers may be sent to a box at the INTELLIGENCER office, if so directed.

For display advertising the rate is 10 cents per agate line, or $1.40 per column inch, each insertion. On ten or more insertions in a year from date of order, ten per cent. discount. Thus a four-inch single-column or two-inch double-column advertisement costs $5.60 each insertion, less ten per cent., or 5.04 net each time for ten or more insertions. Matter may be changed whenever desired, without extra charge.

Experience has proved the INTELLIGENCER to be a remarkably good advertising medium. All advertisements must "pass the censor!"

Address 140 N. 15th St., Philadelphia

HOTELS.

Buck Hill Falls

For fifteen years or more Friends and Guests of Pocono Manor and Buck Hill Falls have met in strenuous contests on Labor Day on the golf field, in the tennis courts and bowling alleys. Their visits have alternated and this year all Buck Hill will journey over to the Manor to try if possible to bring home the silver cups for the various events.

The first cup played for was a tin cup with three handles, which, old and battered, was permanently won by the Manor young folks. It reposes, or did for many years, on their mantel as a cherished relic. The spirit of friendship and hospitality that has always prevailed on these occasions is grateful and comforting.

The Friends' Intelligencer

ESTABLISHED 1844 | NINTH MONTH 9, 1922 | VOLUME 79 NUMBER 36

Contents

REGULAR MEETINGS

OAKLAND, CALIF. — A FRIENDS' Meeting is held every First-day at 11 A. M., in the Extension Room, Y. W. C. A. Building, Webster Street, above 14th. Visiting Friends always welcome.

PASADENA, CALIFORNIA — Orange Grove Monthly Meeting of Friends, 520 East Orange Grove Avenue. Meeting for worship, First-day, 11 A. M. Monthly Meeting, the second First-day of each month, at 1.45 P. M. First-day School (except Monthly Meeting days) 9.45 A. M.

THE FRIENDS' INTELLIGENCER

Published weekly, 140 N. 15th Street, Philadelphia, Pa., by Friends' Intelligencer Association, Ltd.

SUE C. YERKES, *Managing Editor*.

Editorial Board: Elizabeth Powell Bond, Thomas A. Jenkins, J. Russell Smith, George A. Walton.

Board of Managers: Edward Cornell, Alice Hall Paxson, Paul M. Pearson, Annie Hillborn, Elwood Hollingshead, William C. Biddle, Charles F. Jenkins, Edith M. Winder, Frances M. White.

Officers of Intelligencer Associates: Ellwood Burdsall, Chairman; Bertha L. Broomell, Secretary; Herbert P. Worth, Treasurer.

Subscription rates: United States, Mexico, Cuba and Panama, $2.50 per year. Canada and other foreign countries, $3.00 per year. Checks should be made payable to Friends' Intelligencer Association, Ltd.

Entered as Second Class Matter at Philadelphia Post Office.

SCHOOLS.

NOTICE—Concise statements of the principles of the Religious Society of Friends and their application to the problems of every day living, including "The Spirit of Quakerism," by Elbert Russell; "Preparation for Life's Greatest Business," by Rufus M. Jones; and other articles by Henry W. Wilbur, Howard M. Jenkins, Elizabeth Lloyd, Jesse H. Holmes, O. Edward Janney, Edward B. Rawson, etc., to be had free on application to Friends' General Conference Advancement Committee, 140 North Fifteenth Street, Philadelphia, Pa.

HOTELS.

FUN

Six-year-old Dora returned unusually early from school the other day. She rang the door-bell. There was no answer. She rang again, a little longer. Still there was no response. A third time she pressed the button, long and hard. Nobody came to the door, and she pressed her nose against the window-pane and in a shrill voice, which caught the ears of every neighbor, called: "It's all right, mother; I'm not the installment man."—*London Telegraph.*

The Friends' Intelligencer

The religion of Friends is based on faith in the "INWARD LIGHT," or direct revelation of God's spirit and will in every seeking soul.

The INTELLIGENCER is interested in all who bear the name of Friends in every part of the world, and aims to promote love, unity and intercourse among all branches and with all religious societies.

ESTABLISHED 1844 | PHILADELPHIA, NINTH MONTH 9, 1922 | VOLUME 79 NUMBER 36

Why War? At Last An Answer

Before 1914 it was not difficult to believe the world was getting better and war a vanishing shadow. Then came the terrible explosion. But many of us, perhaps most of us, were foolish enough to believe that an effective League of Peace or League of Nations would arise at the end of it, and so we hoped.

For the last two years the material for pessimism has been abundant. Future wars aplenty point their deadly fingers at us, and where is the basis of hope?

At last I see a ray—the only really optimistic big thing for humanity that I have seen for months. It is an idea. This idea is presented by James Harvey Robinson, a historian of much note, in a book called "The Mind in the Making!" That book is an intellectual event, the greatest that has happened to me for many moons, not to say many years. It shows a contrast and the possibility of revolution (by evolutionary process which is the only effective process of real rather than nominal revolution).

Dr. Robinson explains his point thus:

"When the intellectual history of this time comes to be written, nothing, I think, will stand out more strikingly than the empty gulf in quality between the superb and richly fruitful scientific investigations that are going on, and the general thought of other educated sections of the community. I do not mean that scientific men are, as a whole, a class of supermen, dealing with and thinking about everything in a way altogether better than the common run of humanity, but in their field they think and work with an intensity, an integrity, a breadth, boldness, patience, thoroughness, and faithfulness—excepting only a few artists—which puts their work out of all comparison with any other human activity. In these particular directions the human mind has achieved a new and higher quality of attitude and gesture, a veracity, a self-detachment, and self-abnegating vigor of criticism that tend to spread out *and must ultimately spread out to every other human affair*. (The italics are mine.)

"No one who is even most superficially acquainted with the achievements of students of nature during the past few centuries can fail to see that their thought has been astoundingly effective in constantly adding to our knowledge of the universe, from the hugest nebula to the tiniest atom; moreover, this knowledge has been so applied as to well-nigh revolutionize human affairs, and both the knowledge and its applications appear to be no more than hopeful beginnings, with indefinite revelations ahead, if only the same kind of thought be continued in the same patient and scrupulous manner.

"But the knowledge of *man, of the springs of his conduct, of his relation to his fellow-men singly or in groups*, and the felicitous regulation of human intercourse in the interest of harmony and fairness, *have made no such advance*. (Italics are mine.)

* * * *

"When we compare the discussions in the United States Senate in regard to the League of Nations with the consideration of a broken-down car in a roadside garage the contrast is shocking. The rural mechanic thinks scientifically; his only aim is to avail himself of his knowledge of the nature and workings of the car, with a view to making it run once more. The Senator, on the other hand appears too often to have little idea of the nature and workings of nations, and he relies on rhetoric and appeals to vague fears and hopes or mere partisan animosity. The scientists have been busy for a century in revolutionizing the *practical* relation of nations. The ocean is no longer a barrier, as it was in Washington's day, but to all intents and purposes a smooth avenue closely connecting, rather than safely separating, the eastern and western continents. The Senator will nevertheless unblushingly appeal to policies of a century back, suitable, mayhap, in their day, but now become a warning rather than a guide. The garage man, on the contrary, takes his mechanism as he finds it, and does not allow any mystic respect for the earlier forms of the gas engine to interfere with the needed adjustments."

* * * *

"A savage can give all sorts of reasons for his belief that it is dangerous to step on a man's shadow, and a newspaper editor can advance plenty of arguments against the Bolsheviki. But neither of them may realize why he happens to be defending his particular opinion."

Why do we believe as we do about human relationship?

In brief, Robinson's great point is this. In 300 years time man has come to act in the light of the *facts* in material things. Prejudices and inherited notions go down before the facts in *material* things *but they still dominate human relationships.*

We are now ready to begin the same revolutionary process to the other half—to human relations. But go read the book. Optimists should read it for delight. Pessimists from a sense of duty.

J. R. S.

*(Since receiving this editorial, a review of the book, "The Mind in the Making," has been received and appears on another page in this issue.—*Ed.*)*

The article "Adventurous Quakerism in New York" which appears in part in this issue deals mainly with the work of the Friends of Twentieth Street Meeting, although Fifteenth Street Friends no doubt were included in the "adventures" undertaken before the separation, and we are happy in the knowledge that they have joined in some of the recent "adventures" such as the Town Hall and the Carnegie Hall meetings. They have also worked unitedly in the American Friends' Service Committee relief work and in their Young Friends' groups. We should be very glad to have some member of Fifteenth Street fill the gap between 1827 and the present joint undertakings, by writing up the history of what that group of New York Friends has "adventured."

Friend O' Mine

By Albert D. Belden

Of all ideas concerning God there is none so remarkable as that in which the teaching of the New Testament culminates, the idea of God as Friend. What in the Old Testament is the sublime privilege of one man—"Abraham was called the friend of God"—becomes in the New Testament a privilege offered to all. If we did not know how comprehensive in the mind of Jesus was His favourite term "Father" we might be tempted to think this word "Friend" the richer description of the two. For many, however, seeing that the value of words is dependent largely on our personal experience, this word carries greater weight than any term drawn from the domestic circle. It is a sad reflection that many a home-life is so impoverished that a friend from without may mean more to a soul than a brother or a parent from within. So often "friend" stands for one who both loves and understands as distinct from a home-circle that may certainly love but does not understand. Appreciation is a matter of perspective and one's relatives are often too near to be rightly measured. "Is not this the son of the carpenter?" was doubtless a thought in the mind of *His* brothers before it was the utterance of His fellow-townsmen.

But dare we use this word? Think of its inevitable suggestion of equality! Even between the greatest unequals the word "friend," when used with serious meaning, always carries that value. It dispenses essentially with rank and formality. Unless it means that one is sought for one's own sake it loses all its virtue. The least trace of patronage is blight upon its bloom. Reverence, profound, sincere, there is, there must be, in real friendship, but for that very reason it must be *mutual.* Could there then be any more daring thought of God than that man, any man, may be His friend!

It is here that the full measure of the Divine grace manifests itself in God's relation to man. For this astounding fact is as true of God's Fatherhood as it is of His Friendship, God is so perfect a Father that His parenthood ripens into friendship. When He desired to show us His Fatherhood how did He do it? Did He play that heavy-father part which some parents play—asserting authority bombastically, and widening the gulf between child and parent? Not He! *He came to us as a Brother!* In One utterly like unto ourselves, except for our sin, He came saying "He that hath seen Me hath seen the father." "I and the Father are One." This is no new or strange method of revealing fatherhood, at least, not to fathers who know their business. Woe to the father who does not become a friend to his children. He will lose even his fatherhood.

This is a warning that humanity may well heed in regard to all relationships. It is said of Charles Silvester Horne that he had seven children and "the youngest of them was ever himself." That is true fatherhood. But that is true motherhood, true wifehood, true husbandhood also. Every human relationship must discover a heart of friendship to mature and to endure. Brothers who are content only with their physical relationship and seek no relation of soul will find themselves brotherless at last. Think how true this is of marriage. The husband and wife who do not become, if possible from the beginning but certainly soon, true chums, will find their relationship barren and their home but an empty shell at last. In the Province of God we are called during life into special relationship with other personalities. That relationship, either Divinely fashioned through circumstances over which we have no control, or else created by our own solemn vows, is not meant to displace the need for friendship with those particular souls but rather to give us unique opportunity for making perfect friendship with some at least of our fellow-children of God.

So far indeed from this "friendship" being remote from the family it is actually the reason of its being. Man is ever seeking his other—the one who shall mirror his own features in a perfect sympathy. Every man, says Emerson, passes his life in the search after friendship. Marriage in its ideal meaning is the quest by the soul of its perfect companion. Moreover, our seeking of each other is due to vital spiritual needs. Every soul seeks a spiritual shelter, a spiritual rest and a spiritual renewal. We must interpenetrate and be interpenetrated by some other spirit before we ourselves can fructify and be our best. And He who made us for Himself as well as for each other is the Perfect Home, the Ultimate Rest of us all. "The Eternal God is thy dwelling-place." How lacking then the revelation of God would have been if the great idea of Fatherhood had not been rounded off by the conception of Friend. "Henceforth I call you not servants, for the servant knoweth not what his lord doeth, but I have called you friends."

No worthier resolution could any soul form than to take some part of every day to meditate upon this sublime truth—to call God friend! "Friend o' mine!" and *feel* what it means till its glory lights the mind and fires the heart. It is a truth to intoxicate the soul. Well might Browning burst out, as he thought of it:

"The very God! think Abib! dost thou think?
So, the All-Great were the All-Loving too,
So, through the thunder comes a human voice
Saying, O heart I made, a heart beats here,
Face my hands fashioned, see it in Myself!"

"Our chief want in life," says Emerson, "is somebody who shall make us do what we can. This is the service of a friend." That is the gospel of friendship. To possess a companion who calls to all the good in you—who is ever constraining you to realize your better nature—this is to be in very process of salvation. Happy is the man whose friends believe in him, especially when he loses faith in himself. All this Jesus makes Himself to the least worthy soul, if that soul will have Him for a friend. His aim is to save by friendship. No words have ever described His method better than those of the popular song "Friend o' mine."

"When you are sad and heart a' cold,
And all your skies are dark,
Tell me the dreams that mocked your hold,
The shafts that missed the mark.

Am I not yours for weal or woe?
How else can friends prove true?
Tell me what breaks and brings you low
And let me stand with you."

To "stand with us," that is just God's way of saving us. He our Father is just the Big Brother, our Eternal Chum, the most "understanding" Friend of all. And so far from injuring our reverence for Him it is this exquisite grace of condescension, this magnanimity, lifting us to His side, which stirs within us the final deep of devotion and commands at last all our heart.

Can God then be so really a friend as to see in us a value that can command His reverence? Yes. His valuation of the vilest human soul is simply astounding. "He gave His only begotten Son." Moreover His heart is set on realizing that value. If He is the "Friend of sinners" it is because of His faith that you, the sinner, can yet be His friend. Damon did not believe more implicitly in Pythias, nor Jonathan in David, than does God in you. This faith of God in human nature has made it possible for tens of thousands to recover confidence in themselves. What Emerson wrote of his friend many souls can say of God:

"Me too thy nobleness has taught
To master my despair,
The fountains of my hidden life
Are through thy friendship fair."

The last and worst enemy of friendship is not death but sin. No hour is so bitter in human experience as when friendship is betrayed and nothing shuts out a friend like an alien spirit. Yet it is to just this worst enemy Christ peculiarly addresses Himself. He refuses to surrender His friends to the foe. Nothing will make Him believe in our final apostasy. "The bruised reed He will not break, the smoking flax He will not quench." There is that in us, He insists on believing, which can yet be retrieved for God. This is one of the great meanings of the death of Jesus. It asserts more eloquently than any words could do His absolute belief in the salvability of every soul, yours and mine included. At the point where most human friendships break down—the friendship of God in Christ holds fast.

"What does it mean, this wood
So stained with blood,
This tree without a root
That bears such fruit,
This tree without a leaf,
So leaved with grief?

"Tho' fool, I cannot miss
The meaning this,
My sins' stupendous price,
His sacrifice.
Where closest friendships end,
One friend! My friend!"

Reprinted from "The Friend" (London)

The Sum of Living

If you have a friend worth loving,
Love him. Yes, and let him know
That you love him, ere life's evening
Tinge his brow with sunset glow.
Why should good words ne'er be said
Of a friend 'till he is dead?

If you hear a song that thrills you,
Sung by any child of song,
Praise it. Do not let the singer
Wait deserved praises long.
Why should one who thrills your heart
Lack the joy you may impart?

If you hear a prayer that moves you
By its humble pleading tone,
Join it. Do not let the seeker
Bow before his God alone.
Why should not your brother share
The strength of "two or three in prayer?"

* * * *

If your work is made more easy
By a friendly helping hand,
Say so. Speak out brave and truly
Ere the darkness veil the land.
Should a brother workman dear
Falter for a word of cheer?

Scatter thus the seeds of kindness,
All enriching as you go—
Leave them. Trust the Harvest Giver,
He will make each seed to grow.
So, until its happy end—
Your life shall never lack a friend.

Anon.

"Particular Advices"

(Prepared at the Request of the Committee on Revision of Discipline of Philadelphia Yearly Meeting by Elizabeth Powell Bond.)

It is characteristic of the Society of Friends, that in the conduct of life, emphasis is placed, not so much upon theological beliefs as upon the ruling requirements of daily living. When a man or woman not born to membership in the Society, wishes a place in this fold, it is hardly likely that the first inquiry concerning interest in the Society would be "What *believest* thou concerning the Unity or the Trinity of the God-head?" It is far more probable that the question would be 'What ***thinkest*** thou of the *teachings* of Christ?" This inquiry would probe far more deeply into the depths of his soul, and reveal the controlling law of his daily life. For further knowledge of his inmost interest, perhaps there would be placed before him the testing questions that are presented at stated times to the entire membership of the Society. He might find very illuminating and testing, the questions: "Do you hold your meetings in a reverent spirit?" "Are love and unity maintained among you?" "Do you encourage the frequent reverent reading of the Bible?" "Do you bring up those under your care in sincerity of speech and conduct?" "Do you fulfill the obligations of citizenship?" "Are you clear of the manufacture, sale and use of intoxicating liquors as a drink?" "Do you maintain a faithful testimony in favor of the peaceful settlement of differences, and against war?" "The Society of Friends have ever regarded the marriage contract as one of a religious nature, needing the approval of parents, and of the Divine Counselor." "And Time—'rich gift of God,' is it so used as to renew our strength for the things that endure?" "Friends are earnestly advised to inspect the state of their outward affairs at least once in the year."

From the founding of the Society of Friends, their controlling principle of life has been a dedication to such activities as insure an unfailing harvest of peace and joy and strength. Thus it comes to pass that the emphasis of daily life is not so much upon what we say, as upon what we do. Thus it comes to pass that in the Book of Discipline there are "Particular Advices" preceding the inquiries into the vital matters of conduct in daily life. The convcition is strongly brought home to us, that if all the world were to be held to individual responsibility for its work and its play, there might be realized the peace and joy that belong to God's gift of Life.

If your center of ideals is all right, then the circumference of service is bound to come right.—*Selected.*

The League of Nations and Opium

It is worth while for Friends to note what has been the decision of the League of Nations Council regarding the recommendations put before it by the recent Opium Commission in Geneva. Briefly their resolutions have been as follows:

(1) To urge on all states which have not yet done so and in particular on Switzerland, Persia and Turkey, the desirability of bringing into force in its entirety without delay the Opium Convention of 1912 (described in *The Times* on May 16th in a valuable letter from Sir William Collins).

(2) To press upon the governments the importance of universally adopting the system of Importation certificates in Europe, America, Africa, and Australia not later than September 1, 1922, and by other countries not later than January 1, 1923. That system makes it impossible, legally, to import into any given country dangerous drugs except by the express certificate of the Government of that country for every business order sent.

(3) To ask all governments signatory to the 1912 Convention and all members of the League to furnish the League with a statement of their total requirements per annum of opium and its derivatives, and to empower the League to notify states which are parties to the Convention to facilitate joint investigations by commissions appointed partly by the League into any questions arising under the Opium Convention.

(4) To recommend co-operation between Japan and the Chinese Maritime Customs to trace the source of contraband morphine. The Japanese Government promised during the sittings of the Commission in April to make the strictest possible investigations into the illicit traffic in morphine in the Far East.

(5) That a scheme for tracking the manufacture of cocaine be adopted, together with a series of further administrative and police recommendations.

An important step forward was taken by the acceptance of offers of help in educational work by the Red Cross Societies and of both information and educational work by the missionary societies of the world.

M. Hymans in his speech in presenting this report emphasized strongly the need of co-operation of countries not yet in the League, and especially of the United States of America, which he described as one of the largest morphine manufacturing and exporting countries in the world, and the necessity that as the ratification of the Opium Convention of 1912 was one of the terms of the Treaty of Sevres, the League asks that in any fresh treaty with Turkey similar provisions will be made.

It will be clear from these recommendations but more especially from the absence so far of steps really to check production that a strong insistence by the public opinion of the world will be required to put these comprehensive international plans through to a successful issue.

H. W. PEET.

Prohibition Leaflets

The Women's National Christian Temperance Union has recently published some literature that ought to be widely circulated. These leaflets, of which there are seven in the series, are called "Facts" with the following captions: Manufacturers Favor Prohibition; Family Life Benefitted by Prohibition; Bankers Believe in Prohibition; Health Experts Favor Prohibition; Educators Commend Prohibition; Labor Leaders Outspoken for Prohibition; and Women Want Prohibition. The leaflets give statistics collected from authorities, and the opinions of leading men as to the value of Prohibition.

The following quotation from a recent editorial in the Louisville (Ky.) *Herald* shows that if we are to effectively oppose the forces that are so actively organized in conducting a campaign to modify the Volstead Act and repeal the Eighteenth Amendment, we must arouse to a sense of the danger, those citizens who seem to think that everything has been attended to and nothing further is needed.

> "*The Christian Monitor* is concerned to arouse right-thinking citizens from a false sense of security in regard to prohibition. . . . It is printing a series of articles which reveal that the liquor interests have organized and are conducting a well-planned campaign to modify the Volstead Act and repeal the Eighteenth Amendment. The procedure to be followed: 1. Maintenance of a force of lobbyists. 2. Steady propaganda through the press to the effect that the Volstead law is breaking down and that prohibition is a failure. 3. Careful selection of candidates for public office with the intent of obtaining a working force made up from all parties and hostile to prohibition control of the next House of Representatives in Washington. 4. An effort to bring political pressure to bear on amenable officeholders of whatever rank to the end that the interests of liquor may be served."

The leaflets mentioned may be obtained from the National W. C. T. U. Publishing House, Evanston, Ill. Special price, 30 cents per 100; $2.50 per 1000.

However, leaflets will not do all the work. Let us take a lesson from the organization of the opposition and note how they are carrying on their campaign through the press and through political pressure, both state and national.

"PROSPERITY seems to be hardly safe unless it is mixed with a little adversity."

A Word About Slates and Slate-Pencils

About the time you are reading this article your own children or your neighbor's children will be thinking about school and talking about books, paper, pencils and slates. Away over in Russia where the Friends are trying so hard to feed the starving people, are thousands of little boys and girls who need to start to school this fall but cannot, because of the lack of proper equipment. The Soviet Government has made splendid plans and arrangements for a public school system; but on account of the depletion of all supplies by the great war and the inability of that government to get the co-operation of other countries so that they could buy things that they needed, they have not been able to supply their public schools with the needed physical equipment. Robert W. Dunn, one of the members of the American Friends' Service Committee unit in Russia, in writing to the children of America says that in one school he found only "a stub of a pencil cut in four pieces to be used by sixty children (this was an extraordinarily lucky school—there was a pencil)." He further says that practically all the children have to do sums and write compositions" on the margins of used newspapers and old record books, on the backs of labels from American condensed milk cans," and that little children learn "to spell with one set of paper letters passed on from one to the other."

"I have seen little girls crying because they had nothing to write with, nothing to write on. More strange still I have seen old men cry because they could find no school supplies for the malcheeks and devouchkas in their town whom they wanted to learn to read and write. For these old men had caught a glimpse of what a more interesting life it could be to one who could read and write. They wanted the children to have what they of course had missed, brought up under the serfdom and darkness of Tsarist days.

"Perhaps you will ask me: 'Why doesn't the Soviet Government do something about it?' I answer you, 'It is.' This impoverished country has done much already for the children; it is planning to do much more. For instance in the village in which I happen to be writing the local government is giving wood and repair materials and window-glass and fuel and other things to make the school-houses habitable next winter. But it has no money with which to buy slates and pencils. The schools here will be opened in September; the really devoted and competent teachers will be ready; the building will be all stuffed up in every crack ready for the coldest weather; the children will be more eager than you could ever conceive of being about anything connected with a school—but all the necessary little things that make a school will be missing. It is to help some of these children to enjoy just one of these little things—a slate—that I suggest that you save your pennies for a week and then send them to the Quakers who will either set people to making slates in Russia or if they cannot be made here they will be bought in Germany or some nearby country and hurried in.

"As a matter of fact the Friends' Mission is already doing something for the children in the schools. In some of the villages we are giving little felt boots, the warmest things you can wear in winter. Without them no child can think of going to school. We are giving them some other clothes. We are going to keep giving the actually starving some food from the kitchens throughout the coming winter. We are feeding a good many of the school-teachers. We are paying some of the workers who repair the school buildings. All this we are doing at the request and with the finest co-operation from the people and their government representatives. But we shall not feel that we are doing much until we have those little things in the hands of the scholars—until we have those slates.

The greatest need is for food. Next and almost parallel with it is clothes. The supplying of these schools with paper and pencils is one of the great things which should be done next. Any money contributed for this particular purpose will be gladly spent in purchasing school supplies for these Russian children.

Adventurous Quakerism in New York

A paper read before the Business Meeting of the Twentieth Street Congregation.

By Edward Thomas.

When asked to speak on what would be a suitable adventure for a Christian Church, I felt it was an opportunity to remind Friends that adventurous belief in the brotherhood of man is a foundation stone of Christianity and that Quakerism stands out as the great adventurous belief in modern times. To understand what are to be called adventures we must recall the past, so I will begin by reviewing some of the adventurous episodes of New York Quaker history.

Quakerism in New York began with an adventure when of the five Friends who first came to New York, two women, Mary Wetherhead and Dorothy Waugh preached in the streets, were arrested, kept in a noisome, filthy dungeon, and after eight days sent with their hands tied behind their backs to that "sewer of heretics, Rhode Island." Later one of the two men arrested at the same time was chained to a wheel-barrow with a negro and severely maltreated, left in the hot sun all day, and, still unrepentant, tied up by his hands and whipped.

Time will not allow us to dwell on the exciting experiences of John Bowne and other Long Island Friends. We must confine ourselves to this meeting and its predecessors in New York County and even omit much of its Quaker history for though Friends held few public offices they have had a profound effect on the city life. In 1672, earlier than any record of a regular meeting in New York County,

Friends refused to contribute to the building of a fort in New York harbor on the ground that it was preparation for war. There is little record of the next hundred years on which we can draw, though we know there was a Meeting here.

There was a Society for the Manumission of the Slaves organized in 1775. I have seen no record of the struggles of Friends here with slavery among their own members, but doubtless the idealists had many struggles with the property committee,—at least we know they had such struggles in other places. By 1776 all the Monthly Meetings were investigating the individual members who held slaves, and the Yearly Meeting directed that no contributions be received from any slave-holder. Already the war cloud of the Revolution was on the horizon and Friends had declined to furnish a list of members of military age.

Out of Revolution grew many problems of which we have no record, perhaps because it was unwise to make official records of them. Friends declined to raise a fund for supplying troops with stockings and other necessities in lieu of going as soldiers themselves.

In 1781 was established a school, apparently for the children of Friends. It is recorded that the teacher had every Seventh-day, or Saturday, off. This school was followed by others, for Friends' children, but it also appears to have been the beginning of a great adventure in a different line. In March, 1798, a few women organized an Association for the Relief of the Sick Poor, based on the rules that all members must be Friends and that no relief be afforded to any of the people called Quakers. In June, 1801, a free public school was opened by this Association as the result of a suggestion made earlier that year. A room was rented for £16 a year and a "widow woman of good education and morals" hired as instructor at £30 a year, subject to advance. It is said that Friends opened school after school continuing this for many years. This is the beginning of free education in America. Previously there had been good schools open to the public in various places, but none were free. In the course of time this adventure had other vicissitudes to which I may be able to refer. Apparently the schools depended a good deal for support on the Public School Association which was organized within four years, largely by Friends.

A meeting had been started perhaps many years earlier at Manhattanville, probably not far from where the 129th Street Subway station or the Fort Lee ferry is now. I only know of this because Thomas Shillitoe speaks of visiting it. It may have been the "indulged" Meeting which W. H. S. Wood says was laid down in 1828, made a hopeless adventure by the Separation.

Perhaps stirred by unrecorded Quaker adventures during the war of 1812 an unpopular move was made in 1815 by a group, mostly women Friends, in opening the first school for colored persons in the city. The group was called the Clarkson Association and maintained a mission school for colored women.

This was the first of an active four years among Friends; for the following year the Society for the Prevention of Pauperism was started by Friends and others. Out of this eventually grew the House of Refuge. The same year saw the organization of the American Bible Society, in which Friends played a prominent part, as they have done to this day. Perhaps the war of 1812 had roused them from their apparent lethargy when the New York Bible Society was started seven years earlier. This year of 1816 also saw the organization of the first savings bank, the Bank for Savings, of which the President and five out of twenty-four directors were Friends.

In 1817 two Friends established the first regular packet ship service to Liverpool, the famous Black Ball line. Then in 1818 young men Friends established a school for negroes in Flatbush, meeting every Sunday. In those days there were no subways or even steam ferry-boats. The teachers crossed the river in row-boats and walked four-and-a-half miles to the school. No wonder their courage gave out after about two-and-a-half years.

For a few years after 1820 the spirit of adventure seems to have found no outlet in constructive Christian work, so the adventurous minds turned to controversy, with the resulting disastrous Separation in 1828. Friends had always been quick to find fault in others,—the record books are full of disownments for various causes, trivial and grave alike. They disowned James Lancaster, now regarded as a great Quaker, who persuaded the world that free public education was financially possible. They disowned the man who really carried to fulfillment the work of the Public School Society, and whose name is writ large in every history of education as the great and successful adventurer in universal education. Let us beware lest we regard the saints of our times as heretics. In 1828 Friends lost much of the outlet for their energy because the State refused further financial aid to their public schools, and the city took over the work of education.

New York Friends are said to have been the back-bone of the New York Prison Association which may have been part of the Society for the Relief of Distressed Prisoners, a Friends' Organization. The latter was founded by Thomas Eddy of this meeting before the Separation. Fifteenth Street Friends were the active workers, at least in the later days of the Prison Association, but were strongly supported by members of this Meeting. It was this Association which was led by Abbie Hopper Gibbons who felt that a farm was needed for prisoners. Her father was the only Friend who ever became Mayor of the city. He, too, was deeply interested in prison work. When over eighty years old she finally secured through Choate a hearing before the legislative committee. The committee seemed cold. She finally said: "I must defer to your judgment. I have given my life to the unhappy women of New York City. The Quakers have done all that they can. You must care for them now." She left, but a favorable report started the Bedford Reformatory.

With the Separation of 1828 finally accomplished, the spirit of adventure broke out again. In the Henry Street Meeting-house May 5, 1830, men Friends met to urge the starting of a school for advanced education. This grew out of articles appearing in the *Friend* (called the *Square Friend*) and led to a similar meeting in Philadelphia. Out of this grew a joint committee which founded Haverford at a cost of $42,500.00. The history of this, from the Philadelphia point of view, is set forth in the history of Haverford College,—those interested found their course by no means all plain sailing.

The older women Friends in 1831 started a Sewing Society, meeting at the homes of the members, which flourished for about twenty years, doing much good for charity. The younger women also had a similar Society at the same time. After these died out a Friends' Lyceum sprang up about 1860, with fortnightly debates, part of the time maintaining a club room where was the book-case now in the Meeting-house dining room.

A Sabbath School, which lived for about ten years, was started in 1833. Another started in 1852, continued as long as children lived near enough to attend.

(To be concluded next week)

Our Political Prisoners

By Richard W. Hogue.

During my recent stay in England, I was repeatedly asked whether statements in the English press to the effect that political prisoners—war-time prisoners—are still confined in the United States, could be true. It seemed almost incredible to English people that these men could still be in prison for *expression of opinion only*, and under war-time legislation now no longer in force.

Again and again I was humiliated to be obliged to admit that my own country is indeed the only one of all that were engaged in the World War that is now in this indefensible position. I use the word "indefensible" advisedly. The government has given no valid or defensible reasons whatever for its action. In writing these words I have in mind the letters sent by Attorney General Daugherty not many months ago in reply to inquiries made on this subject by the Federal Council of Churches. The Council published Mr. Daugherty's letter together with its own findings of *fact* regarding the various statements the letter made (March 11, 1922, Issue Information Service, Federal Council of Churches, 105 East 22nd Street, New York).

I have in mind also the practically invariable remark made by all government officials when writing or speaking of the release of these men—that "No one advocating the overthrow of the government by violence will be pardoned." It seems to me about as relevant to continue to repeat this ancient formula in connection with these particular men as it would be to reiterate that "No one addicted to walking on his head will be allowed at large." Many of these men I knew personally. I know also that the industrial organization to which practically all of them belong is concerned exclusively with industry and is not even interested in the overthrow of any government whatsoever.

It would be amusing, were it not for the tragedy that it connotes, to hear men who hold positions of high responsibility talk in this way, as if they were entirely ignorant of the fact, well known to people at large (apparently well known to thinking, intelligent people even on the other side of the world) that every one of these political prisoners has been legally and completely cleared of *all* the preposterous charges made against them during war-time hysteria, that they are now in prison solely for *opinions* and that none of these opinions have anything to do with violence in any degree or direction, or with the overthrow of any government.

Some one should inform all government officials of these facts so that they will not continue to make so serious a blunder in public any longer. I would not, of course, like to believe that they already know the facts and yet continue to harp on this ludicrous formula disingenuously. I would much rather give them all the benefit of the doubt. No honest government has any need to be intolerant. There is no "agitator" like injustice.

Has not the time come for all of us, regardless of church or political affiliations, regardless of the demands of our own personal affairs, regardless of every consideration except that of the plain justice of this matter,—the inalienable human rights involved, the sheer humanity at stake—to take our stand definitely, emphatically, unequivocally, in behalf of these men in Leavenworth who are standing so courageously by their principles and their consciences, in the face of such odds? These men are bearing the brunt of the impetus toward intolerance and repression begotten by the war and are upholding the best traditions of American manhood, laying the foundation for a more truly American conception of freedom, a freedom that is worthy the name.

Surely too few of us in the churches especially are bearing our share of this burden, this work of foundation-building. These men are living true to their ideals at the cost, literally, of their lives. How many of us are doing anything like this for the ideals we profess to hold supreme? How many of us can measure up in courage, in sheer honesty of purpose, in *faith*, with these men who are giving their lives in the full knowledge that for them individually there is everything to lose and nothing to gain, that no advantage can possibly accrue to them, personally? They are true to their ideals in the hope that "the children of the future" may find a better world to live in.

If any one who reads this does not yet know all the facts—the whole truth—about these man, I shall be glad to send the information I have, if letters are addressed to me in care of this paper.

I feel indeed that the political prisoner situation as a whole is one of the very gravest issues that confront us today, and that we should all, especially we in the churches, make it our definite and serious concern to inform ourselves fully regarding it in all its bearings.

Friends Urged to Resist Gambling

Newtown Preparative Meeting of Friends recently received a communication from the Yearly Meeting's Committee on the subject of gambling, asking that more attention be directed against this form of evil. The Preparative Meeting therefore hereby calls upon its members earnestly to search their own lives to see if they are entirely free of all forms of lotteries and gambling as queried in the Book of Discipline.

A court decision declares: "It is gambling when it is determined by chance how much one shall receive for one's money." In spite of this decision, however, the chance-taking habit continues to lay hold on society. The small boy plays marbles for keeps. The woman plays cards for a prize which her money helped to buy. The man takes a chance on an automobile and hopes that his quarter invested may make him the owner of a motor vehicle. A doll, an umbrella, a cake, a Victrola are chanced off for a worthy purpose,—the sellers of the chances seemingly blind to the fact that they are engaged in a business akin to that raided by police in dead of night,—the buyers seemingly unmindful that they, under the law, must be classed as gamblers.

No consistent Friend can take part in any such practice whether it be at a social gathering, at a Country Club Bazaar, or along the Boardwalk at Atlantic City. Even if public sentiment has become so careless as to see nothing wrong in buying or selling chances, fortunate be it if a remnant still remains who, like Joshua of old, will declare as for me and my house we shall be free of all forms of lotteries.

Attention must be called to a further need. It is not sufficient to keep one's self unspotted, but one has a responsibility toward the community. Every state outlaws gambling and good legal authorities declare that all citizens who have knowledge of the violation of such laws and yet make no effort to have such violations stopped are themselves accessory to the act.

Senator Depew once stated that ninety per cent. of the defalcations recorded in the daily press are directly due to gambling. An evil that has resulted in so much crime and sorrow must not be passed by and left to flourish unhindered. Let Friends at least attempt to meet their responsibility in causing an arrest of thought against the growing prevalence of all gambling methods.

The Mind in the Making

James Harvey Robinson. Harper & Bros., 1921.

Though the author of this book is a scholar of the first rank, his genial personality has enabled him to make this apparently abstruse subject as readable and interesting as a novel. In considering the modern world he finds that Intelligence "employed in regard to stars, rocks, plants and animals and in the investigation of mechanical and chemical processes has completely revolutionized men's notions of the world in which they live, and of its inhabitants, with the notable exception of himself." In its application to the regulation of human relations Intelligence is largely "as yet an untried hope." The natural conservation of mankind, which leads even men of outstanding ability to "rationalize" things as they are, has prevented the open-minded application of Intelligence to social relations.

After describing the various kinds of thinking and their prevalence, Professor Robinson illustrates "the process by which we gain our convictions" by giving an interesting historical sketch of the development of the mind of man and his dominant ideas, describing an animal inheritance, the savage mind and mode of life, the tremendous awakening of critical thinking among the Greeks, with the later domination of the ideas of Plato and Aristotle, the religious, mystical influence of mediæval times, and the opening of the scientific period with Bacon, Galileo and Descartes. Again and again it is shown that progress involved discarding some "consecrated notion" held by the wisest and the purest. And the crying need of our day is an open-minded unprejudiced application of Intelligence to the various standards and customs that have come down to us, in order to discover how to cure the sickness of our modern society. The "sacred notions" are particularly in need of examination because the awe in which they have been held has prevented their being an object of thought; the heretics are usually the real benefactors of mankind.

For this reason, the book should be of particular interest to Friends, because we have always been heretics, an insignificant number standing out against the opinions of the world at large for the sake of democracy, or religious liberty, against war or slavery, or feeding the children of the enemy. While most religions look for authority to the past, and so tend to hinder rather than help progress, we are taught to "take truth for authority, not authority for truth," to be ever seeking new light. Consequently, if we live up to our faith we will always be examining old standards and customs and "consecrated notions," and standing with a small minority for that which is newer and better. Professor Robinson's book will strengthen our faith in the value of our mission to the world.

MARY S. McDOWELL.

Friendly News Notes

The many friends of Dr. Charles Foster Kent will be glad to know that he arrived safely in New York and was taken to the Post Graduate Hospital. A severe case of malaria is well in hand the doctors report.

Dr. Kent and his wife wish to express their sincere gratitude for the kindness of Conference Friends.

President Frank Aydelotte, of Swarthmore College, has cabled Ralph M. Carson, President of the Oxford Union, the debating society at Oxford University, accepting the date of October 2nd for a debate between the Oxford team and Swarthmore representatives. This is the first time representatives of the union have crossed the Atlantic, and they will tour the eastern states this fall. Swarthmore College is the only Pennsylvania institution on their list.

An editorial in the New York *Times* of August 27th, commenting on the work of the International Conference of Churches recently held in Copenhagen, quotes Dr. William I. Hull, spokesman for the American group, as saying: "The present peace has been noteworthy for pestilence, famine, disorders, political, industrial and financial, and a litter of little wars."

There has just been published a new and revised edition of "The Parables of Jesus" by Elbert Russell. This booklet lifts the study of the parables above guesswork and explains the correct method of interpretation. The parables are of the greatest importance in the gospels for they contain the gist of Jesus' message in a language of his own creation.

The recent No More War demonstrations and other attempts made by Friends in England to carry on open-air work have shown the imperative need of "give away" leaflets giving very briefly some aspects of our message. The Home Mission and Extension Committee (15, Devonshire Street, Bishopsgate, London, E. C. 2.) is to be congratulated, therefore, in the issue of three "Wayfarer" leaflets (1/— a hundred) which will be excellent for this purpose, especially if the address of the local meeting is stamped or printed on them before distribution.

SERVICE NOTES

Cornell Hewson, who, with his wife, has been in charge of the Relief Work of the American Friends in Minsk, Russia, expects to land in New York on September 1st.

William Albright has left England for Moscow, where he will spend three months helping in the reorganization of the Moscow office.

Harrison Barrow has joined the English Unit at Buzuluk for an extended period of service in the famine area.

Douglass L. Parker and wife are moving to Mexico City, where they will take charge of the Embassy Work for the American Friends' Service Committee. It is hoped that they will be able to do something toward cultivating better feeling between the peoples of the United States and Mexico.

Reports from Moscow indicate that Arthur Watts, who has rendered such splendid service in Russia, and who has been sick with typhus for some time, is in a very serious condition. The latest reports are that he was in Petrograd. He has a recurrent fever and his lungs are affected. Dr. Mackenzie has been attending him; and his mother and nurse are now with him. Arthur Watts has been giving his life for others. It is not our custom to build monuments to those who serve, but friends everywhere can engage in prayer for him.

Since June 1, 1922, $11,167 has been sent to Poland for use of the Friends' unit. The Field Committee asked the

American Friends' Service Committee to find $45,000 in order to complete the work undertaken by November 1, 1922. English Friends, who number 20,000 men, women and children, have been able to find their share. The American Friends, numbering 100,000, have much to learn from the English Friends.

THE CONFERENCE

My impression of the General Conference here in Richmond?

Well, it seems to be a decided success. Richmond is a clean city, having a good business centre, and well laid out streets, with pretty homes. But what is more striking is the polite and kindly manner of the people in their business and other relations. It is significant that in this comparatively small city there are five Friends' Churches, besides our own meeting-house. This may be a matter of cause and effect.

With regard to the Conference itself, although it is not as large as those held at the seashore, there is a goodly gathering here. There are almost 500 names registered and it is estimated that about 500 persons are present.

One marked feature of the Conference is the prevalent youthfulness of spirit everywhere apparent. It is not merely that there is a larger proportion of young people present than on former occasions; they are here, not as onlookers, but to take hold of things. They are a dynamic force which promises much for the future life of our Society.

An account of the proceedings will be published in due form in the INTELLIGENCER. It is enough here to say that the addresses so far delivered have been of a high order, while the Round Tables have been well attended and full of interest. This is particularly true of the Young People's Forum, ably led by William J. Reagan.

Among the high lights may be mentioned Wilson S. Doan's eloquent statement of "Fundamentals" and George A. Walton's presentation of "The Quaker Faith." Commissioner Roy A. Haynes gave an optimistic and convincing account of "Prohibition Enforcement," while Dr. Jesse H. Holmes gave an enlightening world view in pointing out the "Future Work of the Society of Friends." Frederick J. Libby treated "How Can We Abolish War in Our Time" in his usual trenchant style.

By good fortune, the English Friends, Dr. Henry T. Gillett, J. Rowntree Gillett and M. Catharine Albright, who are here to attend the Five Years Meeting, are present at the Conference. T. Edmund Harvey also brought a message of greeting from the London Meeting.

As a matter of course, the young people are having all sorts of "stunts," sometimes in rival groups and at other times collectively. Last evening the young Friends of Richmond gave a watermelon party, and it was astonishing to see how quickly a wagon-load of melons vanished!

The weather has been perfect, and so far "All's well."

DANIEL BATCHELLOR.

Items from Everywhere

Wisconsin has passed a law which grants women equal rights with men in every respect.

The Australian Peace Alliance has sent a circular letter to all parts of the world urging that a world-wide referendum on disarmament be held. Their suggestion is that the votes be taken simultaneously and that the identical question be asked in each case. The question to be put before the men and women of each country would be in substance: "Are you willing that your country should disarm completely, on condition that all the other states specified below do the same?" In the event of a universal reply in the affirmative, governments could at once abolish all preparations for war.

Under the United States Government Savings System, recently adopted, approximately $58,000,000 has been saved and invested in the Treasury Savings Certificates during the first six months of this year by the people of this country. The underlying idea of this plan is to increase thrift and savings, and to provide safe and profitable means for safeguarding the people's money, particularly of those who have not yet formed the habit of dealing with financial institutions. The securities available are Postal Savings and the new issue of Treasury Saving Certificates; the first offered for deposit, the second for investment.

The issue of June 30, 1922, of *The Reform Bulletin*, published by the New York Civic League at Albany, N. Y., is a League anniversary number, reviewing briefly the great moral battles fought in New York State in the last twelve years in which that League has had a leading part. Several pages are also devoted to describing some of the exciting law enforcement battles which the League has fought.

It is a long and creditable record of success and many of the good moral measures passed by the New York Legislature are such as are needed in every state in the Union, and it would be well for people interested in such matters living in other states to look over the long list of good bills passed by the Legislature of New York, as well as the many bad bills defeated, and help secure the passage of many of these same good bills in their own states and be on the watch for the appearance of bad bills in their Legislatures such as they have had to meet year after year in New York. Send five cents in stamps to New York Civic League, 452 Broadway, Albany, N. Y., and get a copy of *The Reform Bulletin* for June 30, 1922. It contains much valuable information.

THE OPEN FORUM

This column is intended to afford free expression of opinion by readers on questions of interest. The INTELLIGENCER *is not responsible for any such opinions. Letters must be brief, and the editor reserves the right to omit parts if necessary to save space.*

To the Editor:

Those Friends who advocate industrial communism as the only cure for the many abuses that have been permitted to grow up in our economic and social life appear to resent bitterly any allusion to the disastrous failure of the gigantic Russian experiment in a similar direction. But have not conditions in Russia been more favorable to the success of the experiment than they could ever become in this country? Has there not been, for one thing, a complete elimination of both domestic and foreign competition with the more efficient capitalist system, as they call it; which competition in this country, they profess to regard as a great obstacle to the successful operation of their scheme even on a small and experimental scale? Are they justified in claiming that the tyrannical methods employed to accomplish this elimination invalidates the Russian experiment, when methods equally drastic and arbitrary employed to overturn the industrial system of our Southern States were followed by immediate and enduring prosperity? If the result in our Southern States has proved even to the satisfaction of its former supporters that the displaced system was unsound economically, what is proved by the fact that the only gleams of prosperity in Russia are due to the return in sporadic cases of certain industries to the discarded capitalist system? How can our Friends claim that the failure of the Russian experiment is largely due to the disastrous effects of the World War when nations like Belgium, France and Italy that suffered more relatively than Russia did, are slowly recovering under the capitalist system, just as our Southern States did after disasters greater than any experienced by these European nations, while Russia, which was a food exporting country under a sound economic system, is now with all her boundless resources at the point of actual starvation, after having consumed the accumulated capital of centuries.

S. S. Green.

To the Editor:

It appears from some articles in the Intelligencer and from some addresses in our meetings, that a number of Friends are interested, not only in Social Reform, but in one aspect of it, the aspect that they believe to be pro-labor, so much so that they may even express themselves as being "amused" at the remarks of those who differ from them.

Now it seems to me that words like "wage slavery," "capitalism," "capitalist," "Socialist," should not be used as epithets, barring the functioning of our minds and hearts, but should stand for definite ideas to which our minds are not closed; we can be slaves to words as well as to wages, and we should keep our minds free to weigh, consider and determine. It need not be assumed to be wrong to be either a capitalist or a socialist,—perhaps it is perfectly ethical to have capital, it may be the just reward of thrifty labor; perhaps it is perfectly ethical to be a Socialist, he may hold to theories of just reward to labor, thrifty or unthrifty. I presume that a brief, but correct, definition of capitalist is a person having capital, and a similar definition of capitalism would be such a social order as permits a person to have capital; under such definitions there can be no question that we live under a capitalistic social order, for it permits persons to have capital and use it. It seems to me that we need not assume that such an order is unethical; but when one uses terms such as capitalistic and capitalism as epithets, indicating that he considers the having and using of capital to be unethical, we must assume that he is opposed to permitting persons to have or use capital. The question may remain whether we must go with him when he says that the church must accept his view. It may be that we think the church has other functions.

The promotion of justice among men is unquestionably one of the functions of the church, but perhaps it is an inner thing, to so stir the minds of men that they will passionately desire justice, desire to do justice to all men they meet, in all exigencies, not to steal, not even to covet, not to misrepresent, not to misunderstand, not to be one-sided, but to keep the mind free; instilling in men's minds the idea that, no matter what the social order, men should be just and fair and give every man his due, may be as far as the church can go in that direction, but when one urges the church to adopt and promote a particular political course, such as single tax, government ownership of railroads, mines, factories, and even of small production units (by which is probably meant small businesses), as being more just to the laborer by giving him a better return for his labor, several questions may arise.

One might be: How do we know that it will? Has such course been found to give prosperity wherever tried? Has it been found to clothe the naked and feed the hungry?

But I think there is a deeper question before we decide questions between capital and labor:

Who made us judges among men?

I understand that one of the reasons that Friends were able to do good work abroad among warring or war-worn nations was that the Society was known not to judge or take sides between the peoples filled with animosity toward one another, but was known to stand for peace and good-will among all men. It seems to me that that is or should be the true function of the church as an organization, and that it should be broad enough to include among its members those who take diverse and opposite views on social questions, and however diverse may be their several callings to work in social matters outside the church, yet inside they meet as friends, democratically, seeking those eternal things that apply to the hearts and consciences of all men, so that there may be one place at least where all men, employer and employe, capitalist and laborer, Republican, Democrat and Socialist may sit down in peace, with their differences left outside, and in common worship the Father of all.

Jesus, once upon a time, was approached by a man who asked Him to make his brother, who possibly accompanied him, divide the inheritance with him. Jesus declined, saying: "Who made me a judge and divider over you?" And he said to them: "Beware of covetousness, for a man's life consisteth not in the abundance of things which he possesseth." It seems to me that that saying is typical of Jesus' attitude, reminding that it is the spiritual things that count most.

It may be that capitalists are covetous and grasping; it may be that those not rich may covet the richer man's goods; it may be the function of the church not to determine how the division shall be, but to warn both of covetousness, which would prevent a fair division.

I know that there are many earnest young Friends full of enthusiasm for social reform who would lose heart in the Society if they felt there was no sympathy for them in it. I think they should have sympathy and God speed, but I think they and all Friends should consider whether the function of the church is to be, not a divider of the things which man possesses, but a reminder that a man's life consists of other things, and that its function is not to better what a man has, but what he is.

H. M. H.

BIRTHS

Clark—On Eighth month 19th, at Street, Somerset, England, to Roger and Sarah Bancroft Clark, a daughter, who was named Mary Priestman.

Wilson—At Sunnyside Farm, Richboro, Bucks Co., Pa., on Seventh month 12th, to Lloyd R. and Mary Smith Wilson, a daughter, named Jane Twining Wilson.

DEATHS

Bunting—In Philadelphia, Pa., on Ninth month 2d, Elizabeth M., daughter of the late Josiah and Anna G. Bunting.

Cloud—At Oxford, Pa., on Eighth month 26th, Edward P. Cloud, husband of Roselda Kester Cloud, in his 63rd year.

Cornell—At the residence of his son, Randall, Langhorne, Pa., Absalom Cornell, aged 83.

Longstreth—At Glenside, Pa., on Ninth month 4th, Morris Longstreth.

Wood—In Germantown, Pa., on Eighth month 30th, Mary

Caroline, daughter of late Joel and Elizabeth C. Wood, aged 78.

ANNA T. ELLIOTT

Anna Thomas Elliott, daughter of the late Thomas R. and Ellen H. Smith, was born near Lincoln, Virginia, Sixth month 4th, 1862, and here in Goose Creek neighborhood was her home until she was married to Eli Elliott, Third month 14th, 1889, when she went to West Liberty, Iowa, helping to build up the Meeting there and becoming an interested member of Illinois Yearly meeting, serving as chairman of their Philanthropic Committee at the time she moved to Wrightstown in 1916, where she actively affiliated with that Meeting.

Though a member of the Advancement Committee, vitally interested in the INTELLIGENCER and untiring in her work for the Friends' Service Committee as long as her strength permitted, it is through the sunshine radiated through her daily life and the little deeds of kindness scattered all along her path, that Anna Elliott will be most tenderly remembered by her host of friends where ever her lot has been cast.

A friend has contributed the following in an article to the Newtown *Enterprise*: "A woman of vigorous mentality and refinement, devoted in her home relationships and untiring in her efforts for others, she speedily made a place for herself in each new environment and leaves a large circle of friends. From her earliest years her joyous and loving spirit awakened the admiration and love of all with whom she came in contact, and in spite of years of ill health and almost constant suffering her fortitude was unvariable, and she was an inspiration to those about her. Keenly interested in all the activities of the meeting she was a leader in the reconstruction work as long as her failing strength permitted. And this example of zeal in her Master's service was but one of many similar instances. A number of friends spoke at her funeral, paying tribute to her high Christian ideals, her charity, serene faith and unselfishness, her wisdom and courage, and prayers were offered asking for comfort and the strength to carry on the work she had so cheerfully done and so uncomplainingly laid down.

So passed from our midst one who being dead yet lives."

L. S. H.

COMING EVENTS

NINTH MONTH

9th—Salem First-day School Union. See Notice.

9th—The Representative Committee of Ohio Yearly Meeting will meet at the home of Lindley and Miriam B. Tomlinson, 111 McKinley avenue, Salem, Ohio, at 10 a. m.

9th—The Burlington First-day School Union will be held at Mansfield, near Columbus, N. J. Sessions at 10.30 and 1.30. An interesting program is being arranged. Friends from other localities are always welcome.

10th—Certain members of Philadelphia Quarterly Meeting's Visiting Committee expect to attend Reading Meeting, at 11 a. m.

10th—W. J. and H. L. MacWatters expect to attend meeting at Solebury, Pa.

11th—Baltimore Quarterly Meeting, at Gunpowder, Md.

14th—Haddonfield Quarterly Meeting, at Haddonfield, N. J.

17th—Special meeting at Gwynedd, Pa., at 10.15 a. m., Daylight saving. See Notice.

17th—W. J. and H. L. MacWatters expect to attend meeting at Mickleton, N. J.

NOTICE—In recognition of a religious concern to observe a "Gwynedd Day" in a spirit of veneration for Gwynedd's historic meeting and its revered honor roll, and with a view to spiritual strength and uplift, it is hoped that all interested Friends within reach of Gwynedd Meeting will attend the meeting for divine worship at Gwynedd, on Ninth month 17th, at 10.15 a. m., Daylight Saving time.

NOTICE—Salem First-day School Union meets at Mullica Hill, N. J., on Ninth month 9th, at 10.30 a. m. and 2 p. m., Standard time. After the business of the meeting, the members will separate into three groups, Primary, Intermediate and Adult, each with a prepared leader to discuss the work suitable for each. The afternoon session will be addressed by E. Vesta Haines. Subject, "Dramatization of Bible Stories for Primary, Junior and Intermediate Classes." Any interested person will be very welcome at these meetings. Bus service is available, or the Reading Railroad.

American Friends' Service Committee

WILBUR K. THOMAS, EX. SEC.

20 S. 12th St. Philadelphia.

CASH CONTRIBUTIONS

WEEK ENDING AUGUST 28TH.

Five Years Meeting	$63.00
Other Meetings:	
Baltimore Yearly Meeting	149.50
Solebury Monthly Meeting, New Hope, Pa.	25.00
Contributions for Germany	6.75
For Austria	131.35
For Poland	145.23
For Russia	821.50
For West Virginia	54.75
For Central Pennsylvania	54.75
For Syria	100.00
For General	124.75
For Home Service Overhead	200.00
For German Overhead	204.44
Refunds	423.50
	$2,544.92

Shipments received during week ending August 26th. 30 boxes and packages received; 2 anonymous.

FUN

MAYBE AN OSTRICH

An Englishman was once persuaded to see a game of baseball, and during the play, when he happened to look away for a moment a foul tip caught him on the ear and knocked him senseless. On coming to himself, he asked faintly, "What was it?"

"A foul—only a foul!"

"A fowl!" he exclaimed. "A fowl? I thought it was a mule."

WANTED

RIVER CROFT, CLAYMONT, DEL. Special home care for invalids, or rest and physical upbuilding. Booklet on application. E. H. Speakman.

COUPLE WANT TO LEASE OR BUY small country home with enough land for vegetable and fruit garden. Delaware County preferred. First-class credentials furnished. Please give description, and lowest cash prices. Address P. O. Box 4047, Philadelphia.

WANTED—PAYING GUESTS IN Friends' private home at seashore. Terms reasonable; no objection to children. Address E. Mabel Trafford, Manasquan, N. J.

POSITION WANTED—AS ATTENDant, companion for elderly woman, semi-invalid. Light duties; plain sewer. Suburbs. References. Address B. 340, Friends' Intelligencer.

WOMAN OF HOTEL EXPERIENCE and ability is available for engagement. Southern hotel preferred. Lydia Van Voorhees, 1725 Oxford St., Philadelphia.

POSITION WANTED—BY WOMAN OF refinement, as companion to elderly lady, or one with impaired vision. Good reader, experienced. Congenial home rather than large salary. References. K. B., 744 Carlton Ave., Plainfield, N. J.

WANTED—IN SWARTHMORE, PA., competent assistant to mother of four children, ages 4 to 12, in home where cook is employed. Address J. 350, Friends' Intelligencer.

LADY WITH BOY, 6, WANTS POSItion as housekeeper for adult family or gentlemen, suburbs preferred. References exchanged. Mrs. J. R. Manning, 2100 West Chestnut Avenue, Altoona, Penna.

WANTED—ASSISTANT MATRON Friends' Home for Children, 4011 Aspen Street, for charge of the girls and Superintending Childrens' Study Room, salary $45.00. Apply Mrs. J. Lee Hall, 5301 Woodbine Avenue. Phone, Overbrook 0411.

WANTED—MOTHER'S HELPER willing to assist with light upstairs work. Home in Germantown, Philadelphia. Address E. 351, Friends' Intelligencer.

WANTED—COMPANION (FRIEND preferred) for elderly blind woman. Reading aloud, assist with housekeeping, family of two. State salary. Address Box 24, Wrightstown, Pa.

PRACTICAL NURSE, EXPERIENCED, wishes care of semi-invalid or elderly person. Assist in home if case permits. Address B. 352, Friends' Intelligencer.

YOUNG MAN, colored, desires position evenings; or will accept steady daily position if lucrative. References. 911 S. 15th Street, Philadelphia.

FOR RENT

FOR RENT—THIRD STORY HOUSEkeeping apartment in central location, Philadelphia. Four rooms and bath, two open fireplaces. Furnished or unfurnished. Electricity. Apply W. P. S., Friends' Intelligencer.

NEW YORK—ROOM TO RENT NEAR Columbia University. E. W. Taber, 44 Morningside Drive has a large double room to rent to two girls. Homelike surroundings. Six minutes' walk from Teachers' College. Meals if desired.

INGHAMDALE, ON THE OLD YORK road, has pleasant rooms, for guests in need of rest and quiet. A week or longer, a week-end, or for a Sunday dinner. Mrs. Howard Knight, New Hope, Bucks Co., Pa.

FOR RENT—FURNISHED TEN-ROOM house, two bath rooms, modern conveniences. Can rent entire or as two apartments. Call or phone from one to five P. M. until Ninth month 12th. 759 Corinthian Avenue. Phone, Poplar 6251J.

FOR RENT—Sunny furnished room in Friend's family, near business section, Philadelphia. Electric lights. communicating bath. Young men preferred. Address M. 353, Friends' Intelligencer.

To the Lot Holders and others interested in Fairhill Burial Ground:

GREEN STREET Monthly Meeting has funds available for the encouragement of the practice of cremating the dead to be interred in Fairhill Burial Ground. We wish to bring this fact as prominently as possible to those who may be interested. We are prepared to undertake the expense of cremation in case any lot holder desires us to do so.

Those interested should communicate with William H. Gaskill, Treasurer of the Committee of Interments, Green Street Monthly Meeting, or any of the following members of the Committee.

William H. Gaskill, 3201 Arch St.
Samuel N. Longstreth, 1218 Chestnut St.
Charles F. Jenkins, 232 South Seventh St.
Stuart S. Graves, 3033 Germantown Ave.

ADVERTISING RATE in the FRIENDS' INTELLIGENCER, for Help Wanted, Positions Wanted, Rooms for Rent, Notices, and other classified advertisements without display, for each insertion, 2 cents per word, including name, initials and address. Answers may be sent to a box at the INTELLIGENCER office, if so directed.

For display advertising the rate is 10 cents per agate line, or $1.40 per column inch, each insertion. On ten or more insertions in a year from date of order, ten per cent. discount. Thus a four-inch single-column or two-inch double-column advertisement costs $5.60 each insertion, less ten per cent., or 5.04 net each time for ten or more insertions. Matter may be changed whenever desired, without extra charge.

Experience has proved the INTELLIGENCER to be a remarkably good advertising medium. All advertisements must "pass the censor!"

Address 140 N. 15th St., Philadelphia

The Friends' Intelligencer

ESTABLISHED 1844 | NINTH MONTH 23, 1922 | VOLUME 79 NUMBER 38

Contents

REGULAR MEETINGS

OAKLAND, CALIF. — A FRIENDS' Meeting is held every First-day at 11 A. M., in the Extension Room, Y. W. C. A. Building, Webster Street, above 14th. Visiting Friends always welcome.

PASADENA, CALIFORNIA — Orange Grove Monthly Meeting of Friends, 520 East Orange Grove Avenue. Meeting for worship, First-day, 11 A. M. Monthly Meeting, the second First-day of each month, at 1.45 P. M. First-day School (except Monthly Meeting days) 9.45 A. M.

NOTICE—Concise statements of the principles of the Religious Society of Friends and their application to the problems of every day living, including "The Spirit of Quakerism," by Elbert Russell; "Preparation for Life's Greatest Business," by Rufus M. Jones; and other articles by Henry W. Wilbur, Howard M. Jenkins, Elizabeth Lloyd, Jesse H. Holmes, O. Edward Janney, Edward B. Rawson, etc., to be had free on application to Friends' General Conference Advancement Committee, 140 North Fifteenth Street, Philadelphia, Pa.

THE FRIENDS' INTELLIGENCER

Published weekly, 140 N. 15th Street, Philadelphia, Pa., by Friends' Intelligencer Association, Ltd.

Subscription rates: United States, Mexico, Cuba and Panama, $2.50 per year. Canada and other foreign countries, $3.00 per year. Checks should be made payable to Friends' Intelligencer Association, Ltd.
Entered as Second Class Matter at Philadelphia Post Office

SCHOOLS.

FUN

An American politician, who at one time served his country in a very high legislative place, passed away, and a number of newspaper men were collaborating on an obituary notice. "What shall we say of him?" asked one of the men. "Oh, just put down that he was always faithful to his trust." "Yes," answered another of the group, "that's all right, but are you going to give the name of the trust?"—*The Argonaut.*

FUN

Architect: "Have you any suggestions for the study, Mr. Newrich?" Newrich: "Well, I'd like to have it brown. Great thinkers, I understand, are generally found in a brown study." —*Boston Transcript.*

Small Boy—Lions have big appetites, haven't they, daddy?

Father—Yes, sonny.

Small Boy—They'd be sure to go for the biggest piece of meat, wouldn't they?

Father—Certainly.

Small Boy—I'm not a bit afraid of lions while you're with me, daddy.—*Selected.*

A babu, or native clerk in India, who prided himself on his mastery of the English tongue and skill in its idioms, sent the following announcement of his mother's death:

"Regret to announce that the hand which rocked the cradle has kicked the bucket."

Newsboy (on railroad car, to gentleman occupant): "Buy Edgar Guest's latest work, sir?" Gentleman: "No! I am Edgar Guest himself." Newsboy: "Well, buy 'Man in Lower Ten.' You ain't Mary Roberts Rinehart, are you?"—*Writer's Monthly.*

The telephone in a well-known surgeon's office rang and the doctor answered it. A voice inquired, "Who is this?"

The doctor readily recognized the voice of his seven-year-old son. Although an exceedingly busy man, he was always ready for a bit of fun, so he replied:

"The smartest man in the city."

"I beg your pardon, sir," answered the child, "but they have given me the wrong number."—*The Methodist Protestant.*

A regular reader sends this one, the origin unknown: The prosecuting attorney had encountered a somewhat difficult witness. Finally he asked the man if he was acquainted with any of the men on the jury. "Yes, sir," announced the witness, "more than half of them." "Are you willing to swear that you know more than half of them?" demanded the lawyer. "Why, if it comes to that, I'm willing to swear that I know more than all of them put together," came the emphatic reply.—*The Christian Register.*

The Friends' Intelligencer

The religion of Friends is based on faith in the "INWARD LIGHT," or direct revelation of God's spirit and will in every seeking soul.

The INTELLIGENCER is interested in all who bear the name of Friends in every part of the world, and aims to promote love, unity and intercourse among all branches and with all religious societies.

ESTABLISHED 1844 | PHILADELPHIA, NINTH MONTH 23, 1922 | VOLUME 79 NUMBER 38

If it were possible to punish the man who sells the liquor for the crime committed by the man who drinks it, there would be less trouble about enforcing the Eighteenth Amendment.

⌘

Many church conventions are passing official resolutions showing their concern in regard to conditions in the Near East. Not only the Armenians but apparently all the Christian minorities in the Near East are in danger of extermination. To stand calmly by and see them massacred after giving fifty millions to save them from starvation is hard. Is there no way of prevention to be found?

⌘

The report of Centre Quarterly Meeting in this issue mentions a story related by E. Howard Blackburn in regard to the death of a neighbor boy in the late war which showed that hate between individuals was not the moving factor. A note in an exchange which states that "the will of a veteran of the Union Army of the Civil War provides for a monument to be erected in Washington, D. C., in memory of General Robert E. Lee" seems to us to make the same point.

⌘

An event of historic significance for the Protestant churches was the gathering in Copenhagen, Denmark, August 10th and 12th, of official representatives of the churches of Europe. It marks the beginning of a co-operative movement within European Protestantism, and owes its origin to the work of the Federal Council of Churches of Christ in America. That the Conference was regarded in Europe as one of the most significant gatherings in the history of the modern church is illustrated by the extensive comment in the European press. Provision was made for continuing co-operative relationship in the matter of relief work.

⌘

Those of us who have felt discouraged about the results of the Washington Conference may find encouragement in the following extract from a letter from Isamu Kawakami, General Secretary of the International Service Bureau in Japan and representative in Japan of the World Alliance for International Friendship through the Churches. Since his return from the Conference, Mr. Kawakami has noticed a change and heard clearly the voice of a new Japan.

"But certainly the national sentiment in Japan has changed, and this change has crystallized in the proposal in the Japanese Parliament for the reduction of the army.

When the large army goes, with it go the chief reason for hatred of Japan, the unrest of the country, and the hindrances to national economic development. Japan's best internal development demands a change in her external policy. Her real needs are industrial and educational progress, social reform and the development of social service, all of which can be much aided by saving of money now expended for armaments. And especially Japan needs the reconstruction of her government so that militarism will not be favored by putting the ministers of the army and navy on a different basis from the other ministers."

Our legislators would do well to note that Japan has learned that *real* needs like "industrial and educational progress, social reform, and the development of social service" are not promoted by militaristic governments, with their emphasis on large armies and navies.

⌘

The report of the proceedings of the Friends' General Conference held recently at Richmond, Indiana, is begun in this issue. We are using as our leading article the opening address of the Chairman as it is a concise setting forth of the work of the Society for the last two years. The material which will appear on extra pages in several issues of the INTELLIGENCER will be assembled after the report is complete, and this address will be included in its proper place. Paper bound copies of the complete report will be available by application to the Advancement Committee headquarters, 140 N. 15th Street, Philadelphia, at a cost of fifty cents.

Friends' General Conference

Richmond, Indiana, 1922

Opening Address

By Arthur C. Jackson, *Chairman*

Friends' General Conference met at Richmond, Indiana, in 1898 and at Winona Lake, Indiana, ten years later. Now, after a period of twenty-four years, it comes back to Richmond again to hold its various sessions. Although the great majority of our members reside in the East, it has been thought wise this year to bring the Conference into closer proximity to our Western members, even though the attendance will naturally be lessened considerably. We see many new faces this year and anticipate a Conference of social enjoyment; of positive, constructive and progressive effort and of deep searching for spiritual truth. It is my desire to outline some of the important activities in which all Friends have been working together and then to mention lines of work undertaken by our conference committees and last to venture a few suggestions for future work.

Since we last met at our biennial Conference at Cape May, New Jersey, in Seventh month 1920, the "All Friends' Conference" has been held in London, England. That great Conference consisted of about one thousand delegates representing nearly twenty countries of the world and including the various sections of the Society of Friends in the United States and Canada. The "Official Report" of that Conference consisting of a volume of slightly over two hundred pages, should be read by Friends everywhere. From it I quote the following: "Looking back at the Conference as a whole, it is impossible to be too thankful for the spirit of love and unity that prevailed, for the stimulus given to the Society of Friends, the world over, in its work for healing and reconciliation among men, and for the drawing together, in the sense of a common task for humanity, under the control and direction of the living Spirit of Christ, of the various branches of the Friends. It is not too much to hope that the Conference will mark a new departure for the Society in learning and delivering to the world the message which has been given it for bringing nearer the coming of the Kingdom of God."

The "All Friends' Conference" held in London appointed a "Continuation Committee" of twenty-two members with provision for four additional members to be appointed at the Conference of Young Friends from all over the world to be held at Jordans the week following. The complete committee consisted of ten members from England, twelve from the United States, two from Ireland and two from Canada. Corresponding members have since been appointed in Australia, Japan and other countries. One of the several duties of this committee was to make provision for another All Friends' Conference at some future time if thought advisable.

The members of the Continuation Committee include Thomas A. Jenkins, Vice-Chairman of this Conference; Lucy Biddle Lewis, who is on our programme, but unfortunately prevented from attending as the result of an accident early in the summer; Walter C. Woodward, Editor of the "American Friend," and Sylvester Jones of the Five Years' Meeting, who is the present Chairman of the Committee.

The American Friends' Service Committee has formed an important avenue through which all Friends in the United States and Canada worked unitedly, both during and since the War. The work of Friends in Europe during the past eight years in assisting to save life and relieve suffering along the front lines, to rebuild devastated homes and in feeding starving children, instead of going to war, is Christian Service as Friends see it. These activities have been guided by the broad Christian leadership of Rufus M. Jones and Wilbur K. Thomas. On the first of Sixth month, 1922, the Service Committee adopted the following minute:

"The members of the Committee are all united in believing that the American Friends' Service Committee should seek to maintain the interest in improving international relationships so greatly enlarged by recent joint work of Friends, and either under its present name or another, continue the organization as a channel for the expression, at home and abroad, of the Christian ideal of service. While it is not expected that such great emergencies as have existed in the past few years will confront us in the next few years, it is felt that there will be many calls for united action on the part of the Society of Friends, outside of any of the existing organizations. No matter how large or small the organization may be at any time, it would then constitute a nucleus which could be expanded as occasion demanded and thus enable the whole group of Friends to give united service on any particular occasion."

May we all continue our deep interest in this work and watch for opportunities for enlarging its usefulness.

Friends participated actively in the work of the National Council for the Reduction of Armaments through the Friends' Disarmament Council. This "National Council in co-operation with similar groups in other countries is working for some form of world organization as a mode of settling international disputes, for the reduction of armaments to a police status, and for permanent peace securely grounded in an educated public opinion." The headquarters of the National Council are located at 532 Seventeenth Street, N. W., Washington, D. C., and Frederick J. Libby, a convinced Friend, is the Executive Secretary. Let us support nobly this important work.

Friends' General Conference Section of Friends' Disarmament Council solicited the co-operation of and appointed a representative in every Monthly Meeting of the Seven Yearly Meetings here represented and received support in both effort and money, so that we have paid more than our required share of the Twenty-five Thousand Dollar budget set up for the first year. We have had the advantage of the services of Dr. O. Edward Janney as our executive Secretary. He has kept every Monthly Meeting advised of the possibilities as they occurred and has himself visited many of our meetings and inspired us to greater activity. During the summer he has rendered a most valuable service by addressing more than eight thousand teachers in sixteen State Normal Schools in the Eastern States.

According to the present organization, our Friends' General Conference has Committees on the Advancement of Friends' Principles, Philanthropic work, First-day Schools and Education. In these departments there are sub-committees to meet the various needs of the work, as for instance there are in all, no less than ten sub-committees in the Philanthropic Committee alone.

Since the last biennial meeting of the Conference, work has been going on along the lines of our organization. Brief references are here made to two or three special lines of work which have been accomplished.

The Advancement Committee arranged for a Summer School in 1921. This was held at George School, Pa., and was successful almost beyond our highest expectations. To the success of this gathering, Dr. Charles Foster Kent contributed in generous measure. His spiritual interpretation of the teachings of Jesus, in combination with the practical experiences in the industrial world as given by Whiting Williams, left a deep impression upon the minds of those in attendance that will not soon be forgotten.

Woolman School is the result of Henry Wilbur's conception of the need for Religious Education. It was originally under the care of a Committee appointed by the Advancement Committee, but has been incorporated under the laws of Pennsylvania and is now managed by a Board of Directors, consisting of members of various branches of Friends. It depends upon individual contributions to make up approximately ten thousand dollars annually—the difference between tuition receipts and cost of operation. During the past school year there have been fifty-two students in residence at the School. Thru nine extension courses, over eight hundred persons have been benefitted by Elbert Russell's inspiring lectures. At the week-end conferences, a special feature of the Summer term, about three hundred different people have been in attendance. I heartily commend Woolman School to anyone feeling a concern for deeper Religious Education.

A sub-committee of the First-day school Committee of the General Conference published two volumes of selected hymns which are now available for those wishing to secure them. These are especially desirable for First-day School exercises. Under the jurisdiction of the First-day School Committee, the publication of the First-day School graded lesson leaves has been continued, with, I believe, great helpfulness to all our schools.

It seems to me that this Conference might give special attention to a few features of its work which have been with me for sometime and which I take the liberty of here stating briefly as follows:

1. The preparation by some committee representing all of our Yearly Meetings of one Book of Discipline, which might in time take the place of the seven books of Discipline which we have at present.

2. The encouragement of all our young members, both in the United States and Canada to devote at least one year each in special service in connection with the work of the Society of Friends. The Home Service Committee of the American Friends' Service Committee will be found to be of great assistance to every Friend convinced of a desire to render a year of Christian service for the benefit of others. This section is under the able care of Clarence Pickett.

3. The appointment of a Committee representing the Young Friends' Movements to co-operate with the Central Committee of the General Conference and to co-ordinate the young Friends' activities of the different Yearly Meetings.

4. The careful consideration by this Conference of any changes in our methods or organization which might make our work more effective.

Quakerism stands for a way of life. It is Christ's way of life for each individual. It surely has a great message for the troubled world of today. Are we one and all willing to be true Spiritual Messengers? If we are, the influences of this Conference will assuredly be far reaching in its results.

Duty

'Tis true the human soul doth need such seasons, when
It communes alone with God, as did our Elder Brother;
But like Him, too, our duties lie amid the haunts of men,
For our love of God, it must be shown by love to one another.

So we must then go down among the weary throng
And help the heavy laden bear his burden through the day;
Bind the wounds of him, who has been torn by selfish wrong,
Then we will know, He is our Light and Way.

Where war and death spread wide their awful pall,
And foul disease and famine swept millions to their end;
Where strike and bitter hatred hover over one and all,
It is our duty, a message of relief and love to send.

When we have done our duty to all our fellow-men,
O, friends, we need not fear the sordid power of gold.
We will have felt a heaven-born freedom then.
Following the footsteps of the Christ will make us bold.

W. W. C.

The Meeting for Ministry and Counsel

Prepared at the request of The Committee on Revision of Discipline of Philadelphia Yearly Meeting by WILSON M. TYLOR.

The very name of our meeting for Ministry and Counsel carries with it all the latency of the gospel of Jesus. It is the potency of this gospel about which Friends should feel concerned; that it be made more effective in the Society at large.

To this end the Discipline of the Philadelphia Yearly Meeting, 1918, pp. 18-23, sets forth a beautiful and harmonious procedure in the conduct of this essential meeting.

The meetings for Ministry and Counsel are in no manner a substitute for other religious meetings, but are designed to perform a distinctive service for spiritual reinforcement to the body corporate, as other religious meetings should reinforce the individual worshiper.

The effective procedure is first to make a survey of the field through proper interrogations, the Queries, to gather in the sheaves of grain bound up in the spiritual exposition and outward conduct of those who register their impress upon the Society and upon the world as "ministers"; and second, with the result obtained, prayerfully consider the perfectness of the harvest, not in the spirit of intellectual judgment alone, but with heart-searching favor of Divine Wisdom to counsel by way of encouragement or admonition to the effect that the Society might grow in the knowledge and power of God.

It were better to confine the membership of these meetings to those whose qualifications enable them to enter into the deeper spiritual concerns, so that the waters of Truth may not only be kept continuously bubbling up, but be kept pure and free from non-spiritualized obstruction.

The development of these qualifications gives value to the process by which they are developed. If the Society of Friends has a process, unique or otherwise, by which men may be led to Divine Truth, its perpetuation must rest entirely upon the fruits brought forth. The failure of the crop reflects upon the process of cultivation. God's laws are immutable. He gives the increase where the planting and watering has been properly attended to.

It is the proper cultivation of the Spirit in meetings and in groups of meetings that concerns the Meeting for Ministry and Counsel. The church cannot save, but it makes a good vessel in which to carry passengers fit for the Port of Entry. To perfect this vessel, with all the powers capable of development under Divine guidance, should be the conscientious concern of all true Friends.

If that were the case there would be fewer empty benches in our meetings; there would be more than simply "conforming to the discipline" so far as our interest in the Meeting for Ministry and Counsel was concerned; there would be more spiritual vitality throughout the membership; more recognition in the world at large that Friends were not mistaken in their dependence upon and their guidance by the Indwelling Spirit as manifested in Jesus. It would be a wonderful boon to the Society as a whole could the smaller meetings, and smaller groups of meetings, be made to consciously feel, through the Meeting for Ministry and Counsel, the responsibility of revitalizing the corporate body.

Hate has no place in any life that is perfectly well and normal. It is gross ignorance to harbor it for if, like God, we could understand all that leads up to it on both sides and all that will grow out of it, we would not waste good brain tissue on it. There is such a pile of loving and other good things for each of us to do every day. Let us get busy on the little things. Some day, if not now, we will thank God for all he has led us into of great blessings.

E. H. S.

The Modern Missionary

n address given at one of the Week-end Conferences at Woolman School

By WM. W. CADBURY

(Concluded from last issue)

The Life of a Missionary

The daily life is not unlike that of men and women in the home lands. There are daily tasks to perform.

As a teacher he has the routine of the school room.

As a physician he has the daily clinic and the rounds in the hospital, only the need is greater. As a sample of what may befall the doctor in his daily rounds, we quote the following from a medical missionary:

"A boy of eleven who fell over a cliff and broke his arm eleven months ago asks to make the bones grow together again. There was no treatment given at the time of the accident. They bound some vile smelling concoction to the arm with bamboo splints and put another plaster of the same mixture on the back to "draw the bone up." The arm is of course useless. An amputation was suggested but was refused. The boy tried to prove that the arm was not dead by opening and shutting the hand.

An old woman, bedridden for many years, lies in the rain on a stretcher made of sackcloth and bamboo poles, with her half blind husband, who almost fell into the water when he tried to walk up the plank. He pleads to give his wife some medicine to make her feet walk, her tongue talk and her fingers able to hold her chop sticks.

A leper, blind, footless and without hands, is sitting on the bank begging for relief from the terrible disease that is slowly killing him. He promises to spend the rest of his life in making prostrations before me if I will condescend to heal him.

A girl with tubercular sinuses in her bound foot tells me that she is to be married soon and that her future husband says he will beat her if she comes to him in poor health.

A poor woman held out her emaciated baby on the bank and asked me to make it see. Some native medical practitioner had run needles into its eye to drive a demon out of its stomach. The mother offered to bow before every shrine within a radius of three miles if I would only give the baby power to look into her face."

In the missionary hospital the medical man gives hope and healing to many of these otherwise incurable patients.

In social intercourse, in the home life, in the daily routine of every day, the missionary endeavors to exemplify the Christian life. As Rauschenbusch declares: "Whoever uncouples the Social and the Religious life has not understood Jesus."

Thus an Embassy of the Kingdom of God is built up and it is the life of the Missionary which is best qualified to show forth the nature of that Kingdom. In contrast with a diplomatic embassy, the object is to promote the material and spiritual welfare of those in whose midst it exists.

Students have often told me that the lives of the foreigners as they see them day by day give the final stamp on the true significance of the Christian religion.

This life is by no means all sacrifice, for having once set his heart upon this task, the missionary finds much to encourage and enthuse.

Mission Stations are arranged on a community basis. Each missionary is paid according to his need. All extra earnings go into the common fund. Thus one may never look forward to increased wealth and perhaps here is a sacrifice according to the world's view of life. But the desire for monetary gain is more than satisfied by the absorbtion of the task.

Beside the daily routine there are great opportunities for study and research. Many of the great explorers of the world have been Missionaries. In medicine and the other sciences, valuable investigations may be carried on. For the economist and sociologist there are countless problems awaiting to be solved, and so the Missionary may add his contribution to the world's stock of knowledge.

In the field of education, a broad and liberal program must be followed. The wide-reaching scope of such work in a missionary college is shown by Prof. John Dewey, after spending two years in China. He says: "Build up a China of men and women of trained independent thought and character and there will be no far Eastern problems—no need of conferences to discuss and disguise the problems of the Pacific."

A Missionary is no extraordinary man, whether he be evangelist, teacher, doctor, nurse or social worker. All have their counterpart in the home land. The work is one whether it be at home or abroad.

Whatever be the task, let it be done well for only the BEST is worthy of the Christian and a man's religion is judged by his daily life and the way he performs his job.

The Missionary's Influence

With methods and ideals such as these, the missionary does more to bring about world peace than any other single agency. Can we make an impress on the East? Has the Christian faith a dynamic which marching armies and commerce have found impossible? These latter have only changed the outward form. It remains for Christianity to mould the heart.

Christianity has a force which is fully appreciated by the leaders of the Orient. Sun Yat Sen declared:

"The Republic of China cannot endure unless that righteousness for which the Christian religion stands is at the centre of the national life."

There must be a true foundation laid in these lands which are so rapidly opening to the institutions of the West, or chaos will surely come.

Sectarianism, nationalism and a narrow dogmatism concerning the teachings of Christ will cause failure. The Church of Christ for China, for Japan, for India is what we must strive for. The Oriental must be trusted to lead his people in the interpretation and practice of the Christian message. As Christ gave to his disciples all authority and power so must we do to our Christian converts.

The following quotations will indicate the profound influence which Christianity is having in the minds of the youth of China:

A sick boy writes from his home: "Surely I am glad to learn that thirty of the boys have come to the right side and took the stand for Christ's sake. This recalls my decision of 1919. Since that time I came to know Christ more truly and to appreciate the very Christian life, and I realize it myself that I have built my foundation of religion upon my Will, Feeling, Belief and Intuition, exclusive of superstition and blindly following; as Tagore has once said that he knows God as one who knows light.

And another boy writes of his idea of Christianity as follows: "Some religions teach men to care for nobody except themselves, and the others treat men unequally, but the religion of Jesus is the only religion which teaches men to love every one even enemies, just as a father loves every one of his sons, even bad ones."

It is the social gospel that appeals to the young men of China, and they are turning the searchlight of criticism upon the Christian faith. Is it worth while? Has it accomplished aught in the West? Can it do for the people of China what Buddhism and Confucianism have not done? Can Christianity transform lives, uplift the down-trodden, improve the economic systems—in short, add a newer and fuller life to the Nation? These are the questions the modern missionary must try to answer in the affirmative.

With this point of view the missionary, as he assumes his tasks in a strange land, may be looked upon as the "pioneer" of the present day. There may be no new lands to be discovered, but the problems of an awakened civilization, new friendships and bonds are awaiting him among peoples of many colors and tribes.

Moreover, he will no longer be looked upon as a different sort of being, but rather as one of the world's workers. On the other hand the element of sacrifice and the unique nature of his work will have its reflex influence on himself and on the Church at home. As Elihu Grant recently said: "Mission work touches lightly those for whom it is done, but is the salvation of those who do it."

By service for others we can best appreciate God. The people of the Orient need the Christian message, but the Church at home needs the inspiration that comes from service, and this comes to the supporter at home as well as to the missionary on the field.

Not alone in the Orient, but also in Europe, in our own land and throughout the world men are seeking for more light, for fuller knowledge. Christ's message is the one sure hope to the world. We need not fear searching inquiry into the "deep things of God," only let us be ready to heed the challenge to prove by our lives as well as by our teaching that at the heart of Christianity will be found the remedy for all the world's ills.

John Oxenham has beautifully voiced the call in his poem "Bring us the Light":

"I hear a clear voice calling, calling,
Calling out of the night;
O, you who live in the Light of Life,
Bring us the Light!

We are bound in the chains of darkness,
Our eyes received no sight;
O, you who have never been bond or blind,
Bring us the Light!

We live amid turmoil and horror,
Where might is the only right;
O, you to whom life is liberty,
Bring us the Light!

We stand in the ashes of ruins,
We are ready to fight the fight;
O, you whose feet are firm on the Rock,
Bring us the Light!

You cannot—you shall not forget us;
Out here in the darkest night.
We are drowning men—we are dying men,
Bring, oh, bring us the Light!"

In Vienna Now

Kronen at 66,000 to the dollar have caused among the Viennese an amount of suffering difficult to exaggerate. What Chancellor Seipel said at Geneva —"I am knocking from door to door for bread"— is true not alone of the government, but of the people.

This summer did not bring the customary relief from acute misery. The rapid depreciation of the krone produced an unprecedented rise in prices, a

Supplement to "Friends' Intelligencer"

Proceedings of

Friends' General Conference

Held at

Richmond, Ind., Eighth Month 26th to Ninth Month 2d

1922

Program of the Conference

EIGHTH MONTH 26TH.

11.00 a.m.—Advancement Committee.
2.00 p.m.—Sub-Committees—Philanthropic.
First-day School.
Educational.
3.30 p.m.—Central Committee—in the Meeting-house.
7.00 p.m.—Reception.
8.00 p.m.—Opening address by the Chairman, Arthur C. Jackson.
"Fundamentals"—Wilson S. Doan.

EIGHTH MONTH 27TH.

10.30 a.m.—Meeting for worship.
3.00 p.m.—Young Friends' session—'The High Road."
William J. Reagan.
Alan C. Valentine.
Grace T. Warren.
Bliss Forbush.
8.00 p.m.—Meeting for worship.

EIGHTH MONTH 28TH.

8.30 a.m.—Devotional meetings.
9.00 a.m.—Round Table on John William Graham's book, "The Faith of a Quaker," George A. Walton.
Round Table—Social Morality, Dr. Emma G. Holloway.
Young Friends' Forum, led by William J. Reagan.
10.00 a.m.—Educational session:
Are Friends Going to College? George A. Walton.
Are Friends Becoming Teachers? William Eves, 3d.
The Training for Citizenship in Friends' Schools, Edwin C. Zavitz.
The Training for Leadership in Friends' Schools, Elbert Russell.
Discussion.
2.30 p.m.—"Christian Ideals for Industry"—Alva W. Taylor.
8.00 p.m.—"Enforcement"—Commissioner Roy A. Haynes.

EIGHTH MONTH 29TH.

8.30 a.m.—Devotional meetings.
9.00 a.m.—Round Table on John William Graham's book, "The Faith of a Quaker," George A. Walton.
Round Table—Enforcement of the Prohibition Amendment.
Young Friends' Forum, led by William J. Reagan.
10.00 a.m.—"Quakerism and Democracy"—Frank Aydelotte.
11.00 a.m.—Round Table on President Aydelotte's address.
2.30 p.m.—Sub-Committees.
8.00 p.m.—"The Quaker Faith"—George A. Walton.

EIGHTH MONTH 30TH

8.30 a.m.—Devotional meetings.
9.00 a.m.—Round Table on John William Graham's book, "The Faith of a Quaker," George A. Walton.
Round Table—Anti-Narcotics, Pauline W. Holme.
Young Friends' Forum, led by William J. Reagan.
10.00 a.m.—"Future Peace Work of the Society of Friends" —Jesse H. Holmes.
11.00 a.m.—Round Table on Future Peace Work of the Society of Friends.
2.30 p.m.—Central Committee.
8.00 p.m.—"How Can We Abolsh War in Our Time?"—Frederick J. Libby.

EIGHTH MONTH 31ST.

8.30 a.m.—Devotional meetings.
9.00 a.m.—Round Table—Friends' Principles, George H. Nutt.
Young Friends' Forum, led by William J. Reagan.
10.00 a.m.—"Future Service of the Society of Friends"—Speaker to be announced.
11.00 a.m.—Round Table on Future Service of the Society of Friends.
2.30 p.m.—General session on "Conference Activities."
8.00 p.m.—"The Basis of Christian Unity"—Charles Foster Kent.

NINTH MONTH 1ST.

8.30 a.m.—Devotional meetings.
9.00 a.m.—Round Table—Friends' Principles, George H. Nutt.
Round Table, Methods of First-day School Teaching.
Young Friends' Forum, led by William J. Reagan.
10.00 a.m.—"The Solution of Industry's Problems"—Charles Foster Kent.
11.00 a.m.—Round Table on Prof. Kent's addresses.
2.30 p.m.—"The Causes of War and the Next Steps Toward Peace"—J. Russell Smith.
"A Next Step—The Teaching of History"—Harlow Lindley.
7.00 p.m.—Conference of those interested in the teaching of history.
8.00 p.m.—"Recreation and Religion"—Charles Foster Kent.

NINTH MONTH 2ND.

8.30 a.m.—Devotional meeting.
9.00 a.m.—Round Table—Friends' Principles, George H. Nutt.
Young Friends' Forum, led by William J. Reagan.
10.00 a.m.—"The Way to Find Happiness"—Charles Foster Kent.

The Story of the Conference

"On to Richmond"

In Richmond, Indiana, where stand five Quaker meeting-houses—no, four of them are Quaker *Churches*—and many churches of other denominations; where an auto seems to go with every home; where while there are some large factories there are no slums; where every house has its own plot of ground, and a chief "outdoor sport" is watering the lawns; where a tempting waste-basket is fastened to every third tree in the trim and beautiful park—well, in Richmond, Indiana, the Friends' General Conference of 1922 was held, Eighth month 26th to Ninth month 2nd.

This Story of the Conference is written frankly and entirely from the viewpoint of an Easterner and a visitor. It would be well worth while to have some word from the plucky Indiana group that took upon itself the burden of supplying the material needs of several hundred visitors; who arranged for the housing of all, with a tent colony on the meeting-house grounds; who established a cafeteria in the meeting-house which served breakfast, dinner and supper to all comers, set up a temporary telephone, arranged for a song-leader, and for watermelon *ad libitum;* who were always on hand, always busy, but never admitting weariness—after all, Indiana has already spoken, and very fully, in her deeds.

The Tent Colony

To some of us it gave a proud and thrilling sensation to travel in a special train. To be sure, we had a special train of day-coaches from Philadelphia to Cape May a couple of years ago. But this was different. From Philadelphia to Richmond a special Section of Quaker sleeping-cars, with our own engine and diner. To see the dining-car filled with your own party; to go from engine to rear platform, seeing only Friends—all that gives a very delightful sense of importance. Coming back, we had all these joys, and, in addition, our own time, for the whole *train* was a special! And still another joy with which the railroad had nothing to do. The Baltimore car left the special at 8.45 A. M. Several hours later, as the morning grew hot and people thirsty, the word was passed along—"Watermelon!" Robert Seaman and William C. Biddle had smuggled several of the luscious "berries" aboard, and were cutting them in a smoking-room, first covering the floor with paper. "We had no other use for the smoking-room, so we thought we'd eat watermelons in it," said Robert Seaman.

On the 26th of Eighth month it was an emphatic fact that all roads led to Richmond. The local trains, the New York-Philadelphia contingent, the Baltimore-Washington carload, and automobiles from every direction and every distance! Autos came from Wilmington, Del., from Easton and Purchase, New York, from Canada, Virginia, Illinois and from all over Indiana. The native automobile population was increased by scores, but they were utterly lost in the crowd. Richmond is an automobile city, and a few hundred, more or less, make no impression.

Arrival

It was in the middle of the morning—what with Eastern Time, Daylight Saving Time, and Central Time, most of us hardly knew what time to call it—when we arrived in Richmond, to be met by an enthusiastic group composed partly of Easterners who had been "doing" the Yearly Meetings. There were some Indianaians among them, but few from Richmond. The Richmond people were at their posts in the meeting-house and elsewhere, struggling with the stern facts of lodging—made all the sterner, because only a quarter of the bedding promised for the tent colony had arrived, and a delegation was forced to go out into the town that afternoon and borrow enough for seventy-five people.

"To the meeting-house first" was the marching order, and the procession of Conferees, loaded with bags, suit-cases, umbrellas, tennis-rackets, and coats, obediently followed its guides by autos and on foot to the pleasant, wide-spreading, tree-shaded meeting-house, where on porch and in lobby, cards, files, and cash-boxes bore witness that this was the place to register and be directed to rooms. It was a surging, though peaceful, mob for a time, but everybody was cared for at last. The hundred who slept in the tent colony were fortunate. Once assigned, all they had to do was to step down from the porch, and their encampment was before them. The Westcott, the hotel in which a large number were accommodated, was only two blocks away, and a stream of Conferees moved steadily in its direction. All over the town the others were scattered, housed in ones and twos and half-dozens, in private houses. Several autos worked overtime in conveying Friends and their baggage to their destinations.

Officially the Conference did not open until evening, although five large committees held meetings that afternoon, when all were washed, brushed, unpacked, and some were already well acquainted with the town. After supper, there was for an hour a pleasant gathering and social at the meeting-house, while one busy group attached name-tags to everybody, and another sold Conference badges to all who had not already secured them.

Opening of Conference

At ten minutes of eight, the gathering became a procession again. These processions were of tri-daily occurrence between the Meeting-house and Grace Methodist Church, one block away, where the sessions were held. As the crowd seated itself, and quieted to silence, Arthur C. Jackson, Chairman of the Central Committee, came forward, and delivered the opening address printed as leading article in this issue.

The Conference of 1922 had begun!

Grace Methodist Church

Striking the Keynote

Wilson S. Doan followed with his address on "Fundamentals." This address, frequently referred to throughout the week, struck the keynote of the Conference in this sentence, "Let us bury our surface differences, and recognize that the great fundamental of beauty, truth and righteousness is Love. Make this a realized fact, a controlling force of life."

Again and again during the week this thought was emphasized. Said Murray Kenworthy, fresh from Russia, "Within our two organizations, we need to learn the art of living together. If we can not live in peace, we can not say to Poland and Russia, 'You must live together.' "

The English Friends brought the same message of unity. Others spoke it; the Five Years Meeting Friends who joined in our sessions, lived it. But of all the messages brought none was more forceful than that of 94-year-old Timothy Nicholson, "the grand old man of Quakerism."

This aged Friend who sat upon the platform at several sessions, deserves a special paragraph. Born in the year of the separation, he told the Conference one day, that the differences of that sad period did not descend to him. Throughout his long life, he has been a leader among Friends, and an influence for unity, and among the foremost in all upward movements in the State. Yet, in spite of these long years of service, he is young in spirit and in body. It is said that this summer, two middle-aged Friends saw him running wildly to catch a street-car. "Will thee do that when thee is his age?" asked one. "I don't do it now," replied the other, sadly. Timothy Nicholson gave to the members of the Conference a most cordial invitation to attend the Five Years Meeting, which would convene in Richmond on the Third-day after the Conference closed.

Over a dozen Eastern Friends, old and young, responded to this invitation, remaining to attend nearby Meetings on First-day, and then a part or all of the Five Years Meeting. Of their membership William J. Reagan, Elbert Russell, Murray S. Kenworthy, Clarence Pickett, and Harlow Lindley, all held prominent places on our Conference program. We were pleased to see many other Five Years Meeting Friends present at the sessions.

The day after the opening was First-day, which meant two Meetings for Worship, at 10.30 and at 8, and a session at 3, addressed by four young Friends, on "The High Road." William J. Reagan, principal of Oakwood Seminary, Poughkeepsie, N. Y.; Alan C. Valentine, of Glen Cove, N. Y.; Grace T. Warren, Secretary of New York Yearly Meeting; and Bliss Forbush, Secretary of Baltimore Monthly Meeting, each stressed a particular fact to consider in following "The High Road" of life.

That night, after the evening meeting for worship, everybody rushed to his abiding-place, and made up sleep. Nobody would have missed on any account, the additional social hour which followed the opening session on Seventh-day night, or the lemonade and wafers which accompanied it. But

First-day night, for many people, Morpheus had sued positive orders to "collect all arrears" of eep.

Laziness Not Encouraged

It was necessary, for with Second-day morning, ıe serious work of the week began. As George Valton said, in beginning his series of Round ables on John William Graham's "The Faith f a Quaker":—"This is no book for a lazy mind." here was little balm for a lazy mind at any time uring the Conference, and, judging by the steady ttendance, and the wide-spread use of note-books, o lazy minds were present. Is it not likely that he fact that so many of the younger generation vere assisted to come, made them feel much more "responsible" to those at home? Nearly everybody, it seemed, was expecting to report the Conference, at Monthly or Quarterly Meeting, to First-day School, Study Group, or Young Friends' Movement. By the time this story appears, scores, perhaps hundreds, of such reports will have been made, bearing the message and the inspiration of the Conference into the farthest corners of our Conference territory.

What the Register Showed

By the way, sixteen States, Canada and England and the District of Columbia appeared on the registration list. India should have been represented, but our eloquent friend, Haridas Mazumdar, preferred to register as from New York. California, Delaware, Florida, Illinois, Indiana, Iowa, Kentucky, Maryland, Missouri, New Jersey, New York, Ohio, Pennsylvania, Virginia, Washington and Wisconsin, were the States represented, ranging in number of members, from 97 from Pennsylvania to 1 each from Kentucky, Missouri and Washington. According to the register, which showed about 400 names, only 50 Indiana Friends were present. But there is more than circumstantial evidence to show that many, perhaps nearly all who returned to their own homes at night, omitted this little formality.

Haridas Mazumdar,—the name looks comparatively easy, but has a certain inflection that nobody but Dr. Janney attained—is a young native of Bombay, India, and a firm adherent of Mahatma Gandhi. He started out to walk to the Conference from New York via Philadelphia and Baltimore. The tale goes that he carried a placard on his shoulders, "New York to Richmond. Please help me along," —and walked only 25 miles of the entire distance. Mazumdar, who speaks English fluently and accurately, conducted a Round Table one day upon the non-violent Revolution in India led by Gandhi.

Education

The Educational session of the Conference was fittingly placed early on the program,—"The purpose of Education," said the presiding officer, Thomas A. Jenkins, "is to make our minds give better service in the purposes for which we intend them." Four different angles of the question were discussed,—the getting of higher education by Friends, the imparting education, and the training for citizenship and leadership in Friends' Schools. These were presented by George A. Walton, William Eves, 3rd, Edwin C. Zavitz, and Elbert Russell. President Frank Aydelotte, of Swarthmore College, presented still another viewpoint in his address on "Quakerism and Democracy." Declaring that the key to the full realization of the ideals of both lies in education, he said that "neither group has provided enough educational facilities."

The gist of these addresses, and of all the others, will be given in later Supplements. Service and Preparation for Service,—that was one thread that ran throughout the Conference. Service, Unity, Faith, were the three words which might best sum up the inspirational thought of the week.

Peace

Peace work was well represented on the program by Jesse H. Holmes' address on "Future Peace Work of the Society of Friends," a work which he said should begin with study of the world problems for which no inertia can remove our responsibility; by Frederick J. Libby's set address on "How can We Abolish War in our Time?", and his Round Table on "What Shall We Do at Home?"; by J. Russell Smith's talk on "The Causes of War and the Next Steps Toward Peace," by Harlow Lindley's paper, "A Next Step—The Teaching of History," and the Round Table on the teaching of history.

Perhaps the talks by Murray S. Kenworthy and Clarence Pickett on the "Future Service of the Society of Friends" should be included with the preceding. What better Peace work can we be doing than carrying clothes and food to Russia, learning factory-life from the inside, teaching in schools for colored children, working in prisons, or serving as United States Consuls.

Industrial Relations

Industrial Relations appeared three times on the program:—in the address by Alva W. Taylor, of Cincinnati, on "Christian Ideals for Industry"; in the Round Table on "Industrial Relations," and in the address on "The Solution of Industry's Problems," which should have been given by Charles Foster Kent, but was delivered by Elbert Russell, on account of the illness of the former.

Professor Charles Foster Kent, of Yale University, set an example of faithful devotion to his word which should be an inspiration to all. He was scheduled to give four addresses on the last three days of the Conference. He arrived in New

York from Palestine the day before the Conference began, with a son sick with the fever of Palestine, and, as it proved, with the seeds of malarial fever in his own system. He reached Richmond, however, and against all medical advice, insisted on giving his first lecture, although obliged to sit while he did so. Suffering though he must have been, he yet smiled at the close of his address, and said, "This has been one of the pleasantest hours of my life."

The next morning he had a very high fever, and was obliged, sorely against his will, to give up all hope of continuing his addresses. Seventh-day evening, however, his temperature was nearly normal, and, as he was most anxious to return home, it was decided to take him on the special train, under the care of Dr. Nathan Thorne, of Moorestown, N. J. At one session when he was to have spoken, the Conference sat in silence, prayerfully remembering him.

The three empty places on the program were filled by Elbert Russell and William J. Reagan, Elbert Russell giving, in addition to the one already named, the closing address of the Conference. William J. Reagan gave a talk on Professor Kent's announced topic, "Recreation and Religion."

Enforcement

National Commissioner Roy A. Haines gave a stirring address on the Enforcement of the Eighteenth Amendment. While in no way discounting the opposing element, he declared himself fully convinced that "they that be with us are more than they that be with them." This address will probably be printed as a leaflet.

Forums and Round Tables

William J. Reagan was really a rather overworked man during this Conference. He not only filled in for Professor Kent, but he was one of the four speakers on First-day afternoon, and every day throughout the Conference, he led the Young Friends' Forum in the mornings, and had charge of games in the afternoons. The Young Friends' Forum attracted young Friends from fourteen years of age to seventy-four. It discussed a number of vital topics, with great freedom. In fact, the number who took part in the discussions was one of the striking features of the Forum, another being the number and variety of the leader's illustrative stories.

George H. Nutt led three Round Tables on Friends' Principles, his topic of two years ago. Round Tables on "Social Morality" and "Anti-Narcotics" were led by Dr. Emma G. Holloway and Pauline W. Holme respectively, the latter having given to hers an added attraction in the presence of John Huddleston and Chas. M. Fillmore.

These two gentlemen, the night before, made several good Friends hastily gulp down their last mouthfuls of watermelon, as William C. Biddle's stentorian voice called everybody back from the side-lawn to the Meeting-house steps,—"Hurry up! We've a treat for you." It was. Mr. Huddleston, who cheerfully proclaimed himself as weighing 325 pounds, and being six feet, four inches tall,—we expected him to give his circumference, but he didn't,—in addition to his fine singing, and generosity with encores, interspersed jokes and quips among the songs.

After the Evening Lectures

Watermelon was perhaps mentioned a little prematurely. But now it must be said that on one unforgotten night, the 29th, the Conference enjoyed a watermelon party. How many melons were cut, nobody knows, but everybody had a chance, at least, at one large pink crescent, and some who kept closest to the carvers, had more. One English Friend, Catharine Albright, counted herself fortunate at being here for watermelon,—almost an unknown delicacy in England, except in small cubes in the "smart" shops. Her only grief was that she could not take a picture of the scene.

This watermelon party was only one of the evening after-lecture festivities. On three nights, there was group-singing, as many as possible of the crowd packed on the steps, the remainder seated at the sides. Mr. Barton, whom we judge to have been a very active, and successful cheer-leader in his college days, led the singing on two nights. On one night, Betty Walters and James Bogardus cast themselves into the breach, succeeding in beating time almost unanimously. On another evening, Daniel Batchellor arranged a musical program, of flute, violin, piano and voice. He himself recited "Herve Riel." The whole performance was most delightful. Still another night, games such as "Three Deep" appeared, and various "stunts" engineered by William Reagan.

Yearly Meeting Stunts

But after all, the climax of the Conference sportiveness was reached on Fourth-day afternoon when each Yearly Meeting was invited to give a "stunt" for the edification of the others. Indiana, leading off, gave one act of a play written for the purpose of raising money for Laing School, S. C., and showed a session of a business meeting at which was considered the establishment of such a school. The Quaker costumes were complete and delightful, whether worn by snowy-haired Martha Warner or by 16-year-old Gladys Lawall, the two men coming from the Men's Meeting being equally complete.

Illinois presented its entire delegation in a "deestrick" school, whose scholars were quite as stupid as could have been desired. A chief feature was the lining up of eight of the group, each wearing a large letter forming the word "Illinois," each scholar then telling what he stood for, in terms of the Conference. A bit of verse, one of several, thrown off by this group, was

There is a Doctor named Janney,
Whose head is busy and planny.
He lets no one shirk,
Finds each one some work,
With an insight that's almost uncanny.

Philadelphia, thanks to its large delegation, was able to aid its chosen actors, by a large and energetic chorus, under the leadership of William Eves, 3rd. To the tune of "Where, oh where are the Verdant Freshmen," the chorus inquired, successively for the Quaker babies, the Quaker children, the smart young Quakers, and the Overseers, responding joyously to themselves that they were "Safe now in the First-day School," "the Y. F. M.," "among the Overseers," and "on the facing bench." For each verse an appropriate bit of drama was enacted, the most taking, perhaps, being the Monthly Meeting scene.

A Group of New Yorkers

New York gave a few pantomimes of events in the history of its Young Friends' Movement in the last year. Each pantomime was prefaced by a descriptive verse, of which this is a sample:

AT GLEN COVE.

Water, water everywhere,
Sky and ground and sea,
All the elements conspired
To see how wet they'd be.
We waded to our seaside tent,
We danced o'er pools of rain,
But pancakes served for breakfast brought
The smiling sun again.
We sailed until the sail gave out,
Then rowed with our best licks,
And for a climax visited
The grave of Elias Hicks.

Baltimore, not to be outdone in poetic fervor, sang a song concerning their 250th anniversary. And then,—in came the birthday cake, a wonderful cake covered with white frosting, and dotted so thickly with tiny candles that the cake could hardly be seen. Isaac Wilson, O. Edward Janney, and Daniel Batchellor lighted the candles. Then, with a puff from all the party, the flames went out, and the cake was cut, and handed about, with a candle in each tiny piece,—tiny, but Oh, how good!

Richmond Courtesy

Individual hospitality to the Conference gave us two organ recitals, one by Mary Carman, Organist of the Grace Methodist Church, in which the sessions were held, and the other at the South Eighth St. Friends' Church, by Halcy J. Harold. Here, too, Letha Peckham, of Idaho, sang a sacred solo, which added much to the program. Both recitals were well attended by members of the Conference, and were much appreciated. The Public Art Gallery in one of the high schools, which is a very remarkable collection for a city the size of Richmond, was also opened for the Conference one day.

Group Meetings

As always at a Conference, there were various group-meetings called at in-between times, after lunch, or supper, or the afternoon sessions, in addition to the regular Committees, which met at all hours and long hours. The George School contingent came together one day, sixty strong. The call for a Swarthmore gathering brought out thirty-eight Swarthmoreans, ranging from Faculty, Board of Managers, and the class of 1873, with three representatives, down to the future classes of 1928 and 1831. In all, twenty-eight classes were represented. A Woolman School gathering on the lawn brought together a large number of past and prospective students, some terms having four members present to sing its praises. The future hostess, the Director, and others interested spoke, the meeting only closing for a regular Conference session. The London Conference Delegates ate supper together one night in the Meeting-house cafeteria, and enjoyed a delightful reunion,—all but one, who visited the new Richmond swimming-pool that afternoon, and found it so delightful that she missed the reunion. There were twenty or more present, many choice reminiscences being retold. The sound of hearty laughter heard outside testified to the fun. Dr. Janney achieved the desire of his heart one evening, when a group of Secretaries came together to discuss the problems of Monthly and Yearly Meetings!

Another "in-between" occasion was the taking of the Conference picture. The picture of the Conference of 1898 had been posted for all to admire. Isaac Wilson happened to sit very near the center front of this earlier group. "And," said George Walton, in announcing the sitting, "We want to have him right in the same place. The rest of you can gather around, and be a halo for him." Those who see the Conference picture will observe how well this plan was carried out. The halo is worthy of its center.

Response to Appeal

The two high-water marks of the Conference were: the period when the English Friends presented their letters and their "concerns"; and the night when the Conference members vied with each other in giving over $4,000 for the National Disarmament Council.

This sum was raised after Frederick Libby's address on "How Can We Abolish War in our Time?" which was followed by an earnest appeal for funds for the work of the Council. The Conference responded to the appeal, slowly at first, and then with a rush. Individuals pledged what they could give. Little groups representing various Meetings, First-day Schools, and Young Friends' Movements, laid their heads together, and then announced what they would pledge. Cards were passed around, giving those who were too modest to "speak in meeting" a chance to give, nevertheless. "For the first time in my life," said Herbert Corder, "I have seen a legitimate appeal to the gambling instincts of us all."

Our English Friends

Our love-feast with the English Friends was held on Fourth-day morning. There were five present, —Catherine Albright, Herbert Corder, Henry and Rountree Gillett, and T. Edmund Harvey. The first four of these presented their Minutes addressed to the Five Years' Meeting, while T. Edmund Harvey, the leading worker on the Friends' War Victims' Relief Committee, brought a Minute addressed directly to the General Conference, the first Minute to that body ever brought by an English Friend. All five of these Friends spoke briefly, bearing testimony to the need of a deeper Christian fellowship among Friends, and the desirability of a closer union. "No truth need be sacrificed, but new gained, in the pooling of all."

Special Concerns

A letter from the "Committee on Friends' Opportunity in the Orient" was read by Elbert Russell at the business session, accompanied by a personal appeal for the work being done by Margaret Riggs, and Joseph and Edith Stratton Platt.

At the same session Edgar Zavitz read to the Conference his special concern for constructive peace work.

"One of my chief concerns in coming to this Conference, being a Canadian in the United States, was that I might plead with you to carry out one especially practical phase of our work towards world peace. We boast of no armaments for a century between Canada and the United States, but we have high and still rising tariff walls. Tariff walls are built on greed, and tend toward international irritation and war. Let us on both sides of this barrier pledge ourselves to do all we can to tear it down, and establish trade relations that tend towards peace. Also, I appeal to you to help your nation to resume, with heart and soul, its place within the League of Nations."

Nearing the Close

The Conference drew finally toward its close. People began to look overfed with wisdom and good advice. Note-books were written full. The Conferees were asking each other, "Is thee staying over?" Easterners, in their haste to do all that they wanted to, "cut the corners" more than ever, thus shamelessly betraying their Eastern origin to the square-stepping Westerners.

There was, too, a deepening sense of union, of having been near to spiritual realities, a sense which remained with us on our homeward way. In each of the four cars on the speeding train at 10.30 on First-day morning, Friends gathered into a silence no less real because of the noise and clatter about. To very many, this was as truly a part of the Conference, and as vital, as anything else that had taken place in the course of the week.

Closing

"We have the opportunity to carry into our social and religious world the process of civilization." With these words, Elbert Russell concluded the last address of the Conference. The next hour was filled to overflowing with expressions of good-will and of farewell, and of deep gratitude for the spiritual uplift of the week. There was a rising vote of thanks to the Richmond Friends for their hospitality and their efforts on behalf of the Conference. Last of all spoke T. Edmund Harvey, calling us to the dedication of heart in which we may feel the Divine presence, and may again hear the words of the Master, "My grace is sufficient for thee."

The gathering sat in reverent silence for a few moments. Then came the Closing Minute, and the ending of the Conference.

scarcity of food and an appalling amount of unemployment. Mothers found it impossible to purchase milk for their babies and proper food for their children. Everywhere the financial collapse brought hardship. There were empty beds in the children's hospitals because parents could not meet the cost of hospital care. Holiday homes in the country for sickly children, and welfare centers, could not pay their staffs. The government had to discontinue its help to the land settlements.

The Mission was overwhelmed with calls for help. With only 12 members it did its best to meet the situation. It cabled for additional personnel and funds, and large consignments of clothing. It promptly subsidized the milk supply; it issued numbers of kitchen dinner tickets; it stretched its resources to the utmost to meet the emergency that has become almost a fixed condition. The hope that it would not be necessary to appeal for further relief vanished. There is nothing to indicate that Vienna does not face a winter of perhaps as severe suffering as Russia. All the departments of the Mission will need to be continued on the largest possible scale; and every effort will go toward building up the constructive side of the work.

The Agricultural Department will endeavor as its first object to increase the milk supply. Most of the cows previously placed with the farmers have been paid for, so that there is not a sufficient quantity of milk coming to the Mission to provide a daily allowance of a pint of milk for the 10,000 children who have been receiving it. It is estimated that it will be necessary to purchase 350 cows and 50 tons of oil-cake to insure an adequate supply during the winter. Unfortunately, the hay crop was poor because of drouth; and its consequent high price made another problem for the farmers and the Mission.

The most promising means of giving permanent help is through the land settlement movement. Two hundred and sixty houses have been built by the settlers; and it is expected to bring the number to 500 by the end of October. All is not hopeless when children are active and healthy and gardens are yielding remarkably well. But this fortunate condition applies only to a few hundred people; and there are literally tens of thousands of people in Vienna who again face a winter without fuel, or clothing or adequate food.

The Mission is appealing for funds for the fresh milk scheme, children's institutions, anti-tuberculosis work, clothing and the land settlements. If the depreciation of the krone continues, starvation must result; and the government has no resources with which to avert it. It is to be hoped that such fears will not be realized. It cannot be that Vienna will knock in vain at our door for bread.

The Mothers' Meeting at Crown Hill

The social life in a mining-camp in West Virginia is well pictured by Anna Owers, a member of the Friends' Unit. The camps may lack material things; but they do not lack a spirit of neighborliness.

"The Crown Hill Mothers' Club Meeting had no beginning nor ending. Mrs. Clements' home was a natural place to meet for her big hospitable heart made every one welcome. The children in the camp needed undergarments for the approaching school-days; therefore, the regular club program was put aside and the mothers sewed. Two women were kept busy cutting, five kept the machines humming, a dozen made buttonholes. Girls and boys of ten or twelve years held the babies; and a few mothers with small babies, who claimed all their attention, were there that they might not miss the friendly neighborly conversation.

"The conversation of the women ranged among those ever fruitful topics, of religion, home and work. The religious discussion was heated but good-spirited. In a community where all the men were idle, what amusements were legitimate? Was card-playing an invention of satan; or, was that "all right, so long as he worked and was a good provider and kind to his family." Or, was his soul endangered, as some most stoutly contended? Here one member burst forth with a strain of a song learned in meeting—"Jesus saves my soul." And the checker-boards? No one could complain of checkers but were they "fair" when up in the rough places in the hills grew thousands of blackberries—spread like the manna of old, one said—that could be put up for the winter. What is goodness, anyway?

"One young mother of nineteen years told me she had lost her parents when she was two and had lived "here and yonder" with relatives until she could "work around." At sixteen she had married because "it was better to have your own home"—didn't I think so?

"No one spoke of work save from the point of view of the community. No one spoke of her husband's work but rather of the work of our men. Individual comfort apart from the comfort of all the workers was counted the gravest of sins; and every hope expressed was "for us," the community.

The sewing continued as the conversation ranged back and forth; and at the close of the evening there were twenty finished garments, and a score of garments ready for the hand sewers."

Give a man power over my subsistence and you give him power over the whole of my moral being.

—*Alexander Hamilton.*

Shall We Prevent War?

Sentiment will not end war. Organization, and Education will, and without "changing human nature." In '49 Californians "toted guns." In '59 they had stopped. Why? Had human nature changed? No, they had set up courts which commanded confidence and gun-toting had become intolerable.

How We Can End War Now

We can end war permanently when we have set up a better way of settling international disputes. "What else could we do?" will continue to be the pretext for wars until the present unbridled international anarchy with its fierce nationalism has given place to sufficient world organization to assure to all nations justice with security.

The Way to Peace

1. *World organization under any name*—League of Nations or Association of Nations—both political parties are committed to the principle.

2. *World wide reduction of armaments to police status,* an inseparable accompaniment of world organization and an economy demanded by world needs.

3. *Education for peace and better international understanding* through every known channel used in educating for war.

America's Next Steps Politically

1. Recognition by the American government of the Permanent Court of International Justice at The Hague, commonly known as the "World Court at The Hague." Its decisions will determine the development of international law. The old Hague Tribunal has established no body of law.

2. A Conference on the Reconstruction of Europe to meet in Washington before Christmas with *Reduction of the Inter-Allied Debts* to *practicable* figures *on condition* that European countries join with us in accepting Hoover's five points:

(1) Reduction of *German reparations* and *all* intergovernmental debts to practicable figures.

(2) Drastic reduction of armaments.

(3) Balancing of budgets by reduction of expenditures and increased taxation.

(4) Lowering of trade barriers.

(5) Cessation of the printing of paper money and stabilization of currencies at a gold value.

What You Can Do

Secretary Hughes says that America is "ill prepared" for its present commanding position. This means *you* and *your community.*

1. Educate yourself and your club on world problems.

2. Ask your local editor to print more world news.

3. Offer prizes of $10 and $5 in your schools for the best essays on "The Prevention of War" or "The Reconstruction of Europe" or a similar topic.

4. Provide your library with a shelf of books such as Will Irwin's "The Next War," Philip Gibbs' "Now It Can Be Told" and "More That Can Be Told," Frederick Palmer's "The Folly of Nations," Bass and Moulton's "America and the Balance Sheet of Europe," George Gleason's "What Shall I Think of Japan?" J. M. Keynes' "A Revision of the Treaty," and his earlier book, "The Economic Consequences of the Peace," Norman Angell's "The Great Illusion" and "The Fruits of Victory," Samuel Guy Inman's "Problems in Pan Americanism," G. Lowes Dickinson's "Causes of International War," Prince Kropotkin's "Mutual Aid," Hendrick Van Loon's "Story of Mankind," Kirby Page's "The Sword or the Cross," and other books on Europe and Asia and the philosophy of peace as they appear.

5. Get up book clubs for the purchase and exchange of books like these.

6. Form study groups to inform themselves on the problems that must be solved to insure peace.

7. Elect to Congress men and women who are intelligently waging peace. Every candidate will claim to *want* it but some have never thought on the problem of *getting* it and are blindly advocating again the discredited way of universal "armed preparedness" which got Europe into *war.*

8. Prevent duplication of effort locally by organizing a local Council representing all groups that agree on this issue. An Executive Board composed of representative "live wires" will complete the organization. This body can arrange community mass meetings, pageants and other big affairs and see that the other points of the program are fully covered.

9. Armistice week, November 5-12, will be the next rallying point. Send us some good ideas for its adequate observance. Send us a good constructive *slogan.*

10. We want the best possible *Pageant,* simple enough for use in schools, yet artistic and valuable enough to be wanted everywhere. It should be designed either to promote better international understanding or to picture the War on War that is now being waged.

11. Good speakers should be listed and their names sent to us until your State Council is formed. Then we should prefer working through your State Council.

12. Stick together! If the foes of the movement succeed in dividing us, the cause will suffer. Differences in detail must not prevent our firm co-operation on the main practical lines. Keep the issue above partisan politics. We cannot go so fast as some groups wish nor can we be so cautious as some feel.

With a little tolerance, however, we can stick together and if we do, America will lead the world in our generation into permanent peace.

(Copies of this article in leaflet form for distribution can be obtained from The National Council for Reduction of Armaments, 532 Seventeenth Street, Northwest, Washington, D. C.)

Proposed Child Labor Amendment

Senator Medill McCormick, of Illinois, introduced in the United States Senate on July 26 a resolution which proposes an amendment to the Federal Constitution providing that:

"The Congress shall have power to limit or prohibit the labor of persons under eighteen years of age, and power is also reserved to the several states to limit or prohibit such labor in any way which does not lessen any limitation of such labor or the extent of any prohibition thereof by Congress. The power vested in the Congress by this article shall be additional to and not a limitation on the powers elsewhere vested in the Congress by the Constitution with respect to such labor."

This is Senate Joint Resolution No. 232. It has been referred to the Committee on the Judiciary, the membership of which is as follows: Senator Knute Nelson, of Minnesota, Chairman; Senators William P. Dillingham, of Vermont; Frank B. Brandegee, of Connecticut; William E. Borah, of Idaho; Albert B. Cummins, of Iowa; LeBaron B. Colt, of Rhode Island; Thomas Sterling, of South Dakota; George W. Norris, of Nebraska; Richard P. Ernst, of Kentucky; Samuel M. Shortridge, of California; Charles A. Culberson, of Texas; Lee S. Overman, of North Carolina; James A. Reed, of Missouri; Henry F. Ashurst, of Arizona; John K. Shields, of Tennessee; Thomas J. Walsh, of Montana.

The National Child Labor Committee is urging that communications be sent to Senator McCormick, to the Chairman of the Judiciary Committee, and to other Senators, in support of this resolution. Messages to Senators coming from their own constituents are especially effective.

The McCormick resolution follows the wording of the draft amendment agreed upon after several successive meetings of the Permanent Conference for the Abolition of Child Labor, which was formed in Washington in May, by representatives of numerous civic, religious and labor organizations interested in child welfare, following the decision of the Supreme Court declaring unconstitutional the federal child labor tax law.—*Federal Council Bulletin.*

Fellowship of Reconciliation Conference

This is the season abounding in conferences. Richmond, Indiana, has been host to three Friendly gatherings, the inspiration of which the INTELLIGENCER is passing on to those of us who could only go west in spirit. George School has just had its turn in entertaining the general conference of the Fellowship of Reconciliation September 7th to 11th. The occasion was for those present an experience difficult to describe, because, quite above and apart from the topics appearing upon the program under the general subject of "Creating the Co-operative Life," breathed that elusive Fellowship spirit that can be felt, but not analysed. The purpose of the Fellowship, uniting a remarkably diverse group of people, is the application of the spirit of Jesus to the social problems of today. With this basis of agreement the discussions, even when most spirited, were entirely free from intolerance of opposite opinion.

The main subject of the conference was education in the largest sense. An evening, led by Jerome Davis, of the Department of Sociology, Dartmouth, was spent on an analysis of those factors in the present social order which determine the moulding of personal character. Ideals of modern education, with emphasis on the child's right to self-development and expression, and experiments in co-operative communities, such as Brookwood, Arden and Shelton, were discussed at other sessions. Carrying co-operation to the widest margins, J. Nevin Sayre, editor of the *World Tomorrow*, spoke on "Building the International Mind." He came to the conference directly from Europe where for several months he has been furthering the establishment of branches of the Fellowship, known collectively as the Movement Towards a Christian International. He found throughout the Old World a depth of despair and bitterness which he thinks will lead inevitably to greater disaster unless some such spirit of brotherhood can be widely diffused within the next few years.

At a business session new wording of the paragraph on war in the statement of principles was adopted; ten new members of the Board elected; and activities outlined for the coming year. But more important than the routine was the human, friendly feel of the Conference which will stick in our memory, when between sessions we jostled elbows on our way to the kitchen in a practical demonstration of co-operation in table-clearing, or encouraged each other to new and daring feats down slippery slides in the swimming-pool. During both the absorbing discussions and the playful interludes this heterogeneous group was dominated by a common deep yearning for a finer and fairer social order.

Among the many men and women present who are widely known for their lives of applied fellowship were:— Gilbert Beaver, Chairman F. O. R.; Bishop Paul Jones, Secretary F. O. R.; A. J. Muste, Roger Baldwin, Director Civil Liberties Bureau; Mary McDowell, Office Secretary F. O. R.; Scott and Nellie Nearing, of the Rand School for Social Work; Stanley R. Yarnall, Principal Germantown Friends' School; O. Edward Janney, Abby Mary Hall Roberts, Martha P. Falconer, former head of Sleighton Farms and now prominent in social hygienie work; Norman Thomas, Assistant Editor of the *World Tomorrow;* Lucy Biddle Lewis, Florence L. Sanville, of the Women's Trades Union League, and James Maurer, President Pennsylvania State Federation of Labor.

Friendly News Notes

A letter from Mrs. Charles Foster Kent states that Professor Kent is recuperating rapidly from his attack of malaria. He was able to leave the hospital and is at his home in Mt. Carmel, Ct.

Walter H. Abell, formerly editor of the FRIENDS' INTELLIGENCER, has spent several months travelling in Europe visiting the various fields of Friends' work. On his return to Philadelphia, about Ninth month 26th, he will be in charge of the publicity work of the American Friends' Service Committee, having been appointed Publicity Secretary.

Murray S. Kenworthy, formerly chief of the Friends' Mission in Russia, is now connected with the work of the Service Committee at headquarters in Philadelphia. Anna B. Griscom, of Moorestown, N. J., is another addition to the Service Committee staff this fall.

Clarence E. Pickett has resigned from his position as Secretary of the Young Frineds' Movement of Five Years Meeting. He has been appointed as teacher of the Bible at Earlham, succeeding Alexander Purdy, who goes to Hartford Theological Seminary.

Friends of Montclair E. Hoffman, of Happy Grove School, Jamaica, will be interested to know that one of his pupils, Osmond Pitter, whom he has prepared for college, has been invited to enter Haverford College this fall.

William E. and Caroline S. Walter, of Swarthmore, Pa., have announced the engagement of their daughter Elizabeth Ann Walter, to Paul J. Furnas, of New York, son of Mr. and Mrs. William Furnas, of Indianapolis. "Betty" Walter is at present Secretary of the Young Friends' Movement of Philadelphia Yearly Meeting.

We are also informed that Edmund S. and Mary F. Holmes, of Riverton, N. J., have announced the engagement of their daughter, Esther Fisher Holmes, to Edward Morris Jones, of Germantown.

At Haddonfield Quarterly Meeting held recently at Haddonfield, N. J., Ruth Conrow and Elizabeth Walter gave interesting accounts of the Richmond Conference, the Young Friends' Conference at Earlham and the Five Years Meeting.

Under the direction of Concord Quarterly Meeting's Philanthropic Committee, Henry E. Jackson spoke after the morning meeting at Swarthmore on First-day, the third, on "A Way to International Peace." The key-note of his plea was for the education of children in national ethics by courses on the subject in the schools. The first need is for a text-book and his concern is for Friends to help in the compilation of one as there must be those among us especially fitted for this work.

According to "Gathered Gossip," the Flitcraft publication of Oak Park, Ill., Wilmer A. Jenkins, son of Thomas A. Jenkins, graduated from the University of Chicago at the Convocation of September 1st, having majored in chemistry and mathematics. He is contemplating a post-graduate year at the University of Michigan. Francis Jenkins, another son, appeared on July 15th, last, in the public amphitheatre of the University of Toulouse, France, to defend his thesis in Chemistry. He spoke for about 25 minutes in French and was awarded the diploma with "very honorable" mention. He will complete his chemical studies at the University of Chicago. His engagement to Miss Henrietta Smith, of Seattle, Washington, has beeen announced.

A letter from Effie Danforth McAfee from West Pawlett, in the green hills of Vermont, where she and her husband James R. McAfee have been summering, tells of the pleasant times they have been having "neighboring" with the Friends of Granville. James R. McAfee has given two talks on his recent experiences in Austria and Poland in the Granville Meeting-house.

Effie D. McAfee writes, "In speaking before the D. A. R. of Granville recently (and this is all historic ground) the speaker recalled how a local family was massacred by the Indians. When called upon I felt it incumbent upon me to give a Quaker viewpoint, so I related two stories of Easton told me in London by Violet Hodgkin, during Friends' Conference. One when the Indian Chief and followers visited a meeting at Easton and surprised to find us unarmed, the Indians sat down themselves to worship the Great Spirit and went home with the Friends. The other story, how Indians surprised a company of Friends and forming a war circle, handed around a Quaker baby. But finding all peaceful and unarmed, returned the baby safely to the arms of its mother.

I asked if anyone present could substantiate these stories. Lemoyne D. Allen arose and said 'The baby handed around was my direct ancestor.' Hannah R. Thorne-Warren, Lemoyne D. Allen and Elizabeth Hoag's sister each arose and testified to the truth of each story."

AN OPPORTUNITY FOR FIRST-DAY SCHOOL TEACHERS

Woolman School is offering a special week-end course of lectures on The Teaching of Jesus extending over six week-ends beginning Seventh-day, Ninth month 30th. The lectures will be given by Dr. Russell at 7.30 Seventh-day evening and at 9 o'clock First-day morning. This will enable young Friends who are not free to attend the regular course to get some instruction at Woolman School, and the course closes in time for those who take it to organize and conduct classes in the same subject in their First-day Schools the remainder of the year.

This course on The Teaching of Jesus follows naturally after the special course on The Life of Christ given in the early fall last year, and which was so well patronized.

The special fee for this course is $20 including tuition, board and lodging from Seventh-day afternoon to First-day afternoon for each of the six week-ends.

CENTRE QUARTERLY MEETING

Centre Quarterly Meeting of Friends was held Ninth month 2nd to 4th, inclusive, at Centre, Pa. Because of the Richmond Conference and our Quarterly Meeting dates overlapping, the number of representatives was smaller than usual. However, Dr. Janney and our Friend, Elisha M. Davis, of West Branch, omitted one or two closing sessions of the Conference and arrived here on Seventh-day morning in good time for Quarterly Meeting.

The First-day School Conference met at 2 p. m., and consisted of the usual reports from the different schools. Following the routine business the primary class of the home school rendered an interesting exercise supplemented by volunteer service by representatives from other schools. The meeting of Ministry and Counsel followed.

At First-day morning meeting, Dr. Janney delivered an impressive sermon upon "Christian Ideals," using the text, "This is Life Eternal to know thee the only true God and Jesus Christ whom thou hast sent."

At the afternoon conference, Dr. Janney gave an address on "The Hope for a Warless World." Opportunity was then given for discussion or questions.

E. Howard Blackburn related a very touching story with which he was familiar, relating to the death of a neighbor boy in the late war, illustrating that there was no hate or animosity between individuals of the contending armies.

This very full First-day was rounded out by a Parlor meeting or "Round Table" at the home of Darlington and

Nina Way, where the question was considered, "Is there any use or service for the Society of Friends in the world today?" It was very positively answered in the affirmative. This being true, what are the best methods to pursue to enable the Society to perform this service? This was not so easily answered, but absolutely necessary to be considered.

The Second-day morning meeting consisted of routine Quarterly Meeting business. ISAAC UNDERWOOD.

Items from Everywhere

During the year since the passage of the Wisconsin Equal Rights bill no litigation has arisen because of its effect on welfare laws, and Wisconsin legislators and judges and women all over the state have united in endorsing the measure.

There were 140,197 accidents reported in the state of Pennsylvania during 1921. 62 out of every 100 were due to carelessness. 82 out of every 100 were preventable. The amount of wages lost in this state in 1921 because of accidents was nine million nine hundred thousand dollars.

The National Board of Fire Underwriters, 76 William St., New York, has issued a leaflet on "The Dangers of Anthracite Substitutes." Recognizing that the shortage of anthracite coal will force people to use bituminous coal, oil, gas and electricity in its place, they have issued this warning in order that proper precautions may be taken to prevent loss of life and property by fire.

Alice Paul, vice president of the National Woman's Party, will report to a conference of National Party leaders November 11 that the organization's "Equal Rights" program has brought legislative victories in nine states, removing discriminations affecting more than 4,000,000 women. The victories in these states concerned the right of women to serve on juries, to hold public offices, control of property, guardianship of children, choice of voting residences, and equal rights with the father to inherit from a deceased child.

In regard to the benefits of Prohibition, Dr. John Dill Robertson, Health Commissioner at Chicago, gives these statistics:

Alcoholic cases in House of Correction (Bridewell):

1918 (last license year) 1,772
1921 151

Total alcoholic cases reported:

1918 1,921
1921 1,040

Miss Edna Foley, superintendent of the Visiting Nurses' Association, said:

"We have never seen so many families to whom we minister so well dressed, and so many children with shoes and stockings.

"Statistics from records of the 'United Charities of Chicago' show a drop from 499 intemperance cases in 1918 to 61 in 1921."

John J. Abbott, vice-president of the Continental and Commercial Trust and Savings Bank of Chicago, said:

"Since the date on which National Prohibition went into effect the savings deposits of this bank have increased approximately $10,000,000 or 30 per cent."

What has happened to all the breweries of the country is a question often asked by visitors to America. From a recent survey it was found that 667 former breweries are now making non-intoxicating near beer; 431 are making other drinks; 118 plants are making soft drinks; 63 are making malt syrups; 145 are manufacturing ice; 50 are cold storage warehouses, and 152 are idle.

THE OPEN FORUM

This column is intended to afford free expression of opinion by readers on questions of interest. The INTELLIGENCER *is not responsible for any such opinions. Letters must be brief, and the editor reserves the right to omit parts if necessary to save space.*

To the Editor:

I am one of the group of political prisoners—war-time prisoners—confined in Leavenworth for the past five years for the expression of opinion—opinion against war. During war-time hysteria, we were charged with many wild, incredible things, of all of which we have since been legally and completely cleared. It has been legally and indisputably proven that there was no basis in fact for the charges that were made. I was released last month on the expiration of my five-year sentence, and I am now giving all my time and strength in the interest of those I have left in prison; for though we were all sentenced under the same indictment, the sentences (for no reason apparent on the court records) varied from five to twenty years.

From time to time I have seen issues of the INTELLIGENCER. It goes regularly to Leavenworth prison. There is a life of George Fox in circulation there, and several little pamphlets—"The Spirit of Quakerism," "Friendly Fundamentals," etc. I know a few Quakers personally, and I had come to feel that the Society of Friends stands as a whole not only as opposed to war, but equally opposed to hasty, unjust condemnation and prejudice. For this reason I was surprised and very sincerely grieved to read the Forum letter from Holder, Ill., in the issue for August 19. I know these men in prison, especially the group of fifty-two who have refused all offers of release requiring compromise of principle. I know their unselfishness, their strength of character, their splendid loyalty to their ideals even at the cost of their lives. And I know that they are wholeheartedly opposed to violence of any sort, for any purpose. It is for this reason that we refused to take part in the organized violence that the government calls war.

It is true that Government officials and newspapers have continually coupled with mention of these men, such words as "violent overthrow of the government," "bolshiviki," etc., but this only shows that those who do this have not taken the trouble to inform themselves accurately regarding the facts as shown in the legal records of the case. The Federal Council of Churches found it necessary to investigate some of these many misstatements, and in the March 11 (1922) issue of the Council's Information Service, gave a most illuminating statement of *facts*. I will be glad to send this statement to anyone who will take the trouble to read it—anyone fairminded enough to want to learn the facts on both sides, and to be just.

It is not true that these political prisoners ever used violence or desired violently to overthrow anything. They —we—are interested in work, industry, economics, not in politics. We are interested in trying to have every overworked mother, every hungry, pitiful baby, decently and humanely cared for. We wish that the ninety per cent. of this country's taxes that now go toward war (under what ever name) were used for health and education instead. I turn the pages of that same issue of the INTELLIGENCER, and I see that Quakers are learning (p. 523) that miners average only some two hundred days of work in the year instead of the full number that they *want* to work, and that this means under-nourished, hungry mothers and children. Does the writer of this letter from Holder know that more than seven million little children all over this country go hungry to bed every night, *now?* That more than two million ill-nourished children are now, today, as I write, as you read, toiling long hours in factories, for a pittance?

We all know now that the World War did not "end war," nor make the world "safe" for anything at all. It was because I was convinced that no war could do this, or any good thing, that I was opposed to that war and was imprisoned in consequence. I believe that in my opposition to war I was true to the spirit of the best traditions of America. My people were with Washington in our own Revolution, and have been identified with our Government in various offices in succeeding generations. And I feel that as one of this group of men in Leavenworth I was upholding the traditions and the principles of my family and my country. Does the writer of this letter before me think it just to associate without discrimination, those she calls "political prisoners" with those who "seek to destroy government—and shoot peaceable men from roofs," without even ascertaining whether there is the slightest connection in facts between these two groups? There is no such connection. I speak with authority, because I know the facts. It is a deep disappointment to me to know that a Quaker could judge so hastily and could be willing to speak without due consideration and full knowledge of all the facts.

May I add this one more word regarding many letters that have appeared in this paper, on different angles of this whole vital question. In talking with at least the few Quakers whom I now know, I find them practically agreed on these simple, basic principles—that the earth is, in the beginning, God-given to all humanity; that there is nothing in all the world that has not, at some time, been derived from the earth by means of human labor; and that the goal of all life and work should be the development of character, of personality. This is what I, too, believe, and this is why I spent five years in prison. Is there not some common ground on which all who so believe, may meet, without misunderstanding. PIERCE C. WETTER.

DEATHS

BARTRAM—At Media, Pa., on Ninth month 13th, Susanna P., widow of Thomas P. Bartram, aged 86.

COMING EVENTS

NINTH MONTH

23rd—The 25th Anniversary of the Friends' Home, 6300 Greene Street. Germantown. See Notice.

23rd—Bucks First-day School Union at Wrightstown Meeting-house, at 10.30, Standard time.

24th—An appointed meeting under care of Gwynedd Monthly Meeting will be held in the Providence Friends' Meeting-house, at 3 p. m.

24th—A meeting under the care of both branches of Friends will be held at Centre Meeting-house, near Centreville, Del., at 2.30 p. m., Standard time. All interested are invited to attend.

24th—Certain members of Philadelphia Quarterly Meeting's Visiting Committee will attend meeting for worship at Fairhill, at 3.30 p. m. In the evening at 7.30, they will attend a meeting at Germantown Friends' Home.

25th—Canada Half-Yearly Meeting at Newmarket, Ontario.

TENTH MONTH

1st—First-day, at 3 p. m., a meeting for divine worship at Birmingham Meeting-house, Chester County, Pa., under care of a Committee of Concord Quarterly Meeting. Young Friends generally are asked to co-operate, and all interested persons are invited to attend.

1st—A special meeting, under the care of a Committee of Burlington Quarterly Meeting, will be held at Mansfield, at 3 p. m. Elbert Russell expects to be in attendance. It is hoped that all Friends within a reasonable distance will attend and help to make this meeting a success.

1st—Annual Meeting at the old Randolph Meeting-house near Dover, Morris Co., N. J., on D. L. & W. R. R. Basket lunch and social hour at 12.30; meeting for worship at 2 p. m. J. Bernard Walton and Grace T. Warren will be present.

NOTICE—The Committee having care of Philadelphia Quarterly Meeting's Boarding Home invite the members of that meeting to attend the 25th anniversary of the Home (6300 Greene Street, Germantown), on the afternoon of Ninth month 23rd, from 3 to 6 o'clock. Caroline S. Jackson, Clerk.

American Friends' Service Committee

WILBUR K. THOMAS, EX. SEC.
20 S. 12th St. Philadelphia.

CASH CONTRIBUTIONS

WEEK ENDING SEPTEMBER 11.

Five Years Meetings	$260.00
Philadelphia Yearly Meeting (Orthodox)	2,188.90
Other Meetings:	
Oakland Monthly Meeting of College Park Ass'n.	26.30
Skaneateles Meeting	10.00
Cambridge Group of Friends	725.00
Easton Monthly Meeting	21.00
Contributions for Germany	19.25
For Austria	337.91
For Poland	17.81
For Russia	1,611.48
For Russian Overhead	32.50
For Central Pennsylvania	58.00
For West Virginia	116.00
Home Service Overhead	3.15
For General	236.75
Clothing	376.46
Refunds	203.73
	$6,244.24

Shipments received during week ending September 9th, 49 boxes and packages.

WANTED

WANTED—MOTHER'S HELPER FOR child two years old. Give references and state terms. Mrs. J. M. Griscom, Moorestown, N. J.

WANTED—A POSITION AS COMPANION, care of invalid or housekeeper. Address Y. 360, Friends' Intelligencer.

MOTHER'S HELPER OR CHILD'S nurse, Protestant; companion for three small children. Assistant nurse kept. Good salary, good home. Address Mrs. Frederick V. Geier, 2319 Grandview Avenue, Cincinnati, Ohio.

WANTED—BY ELDERLY WOMAN (Friend) a capable, companionable woman to share my convenient home and do my housekeeping. Moderate salary. Mrs. Mary F. Browning, 15 Sunnyside Avenue, Pleasantville, New York.

WANTED—IN HOUSEHOLD WHERE additional service is desired, woman of excellent character to help with different kinds of work including either washing and ironing or mending. Good home in suburbs. Two lines of trolleys. Address Miss M. L. Wharton, N. W. Cor. York Road and Chelten Ave., Philadelphia. Telephone, Oak Lane 3578.

WANTED—ELDERLY OR MIDDLE aged woman to assist with care of five-year-old child and light household duties. Moderate salary and pleasant home. State age. Address B. 362, Friends' Intelligencer.

WANTED—YOUNG WOMAN AS COMPANION and helper in care of elderly gentleman, semi-invalid in Swarthmore, duties light, $10.00 week. Address J. 361, Friends' Intelligencer.

FOR RENT

FOR RENT—THIRD STORY HOUSEKEEPING apartment in central location, Philadelphia. Four rooms and bath, two open fireplaces. Furnished or unfurnished. Electricity. Apply W. P. S., Friends' Intelligencer.

INGHAMDALE, ON THE OLD YORK road, has pleasant rooms, for guests in need of rest and quiet. A week or longer, a week-end, or for a Sunday dinner. Mrs. Howard Knight, New Hope, Bucks Co., Pa.

FOR RENT—FURNISHED TEN-ROOM house, two bath rooms, modern conveniences. Can rent entire or as two apartments; 759 Corinthian Avenue, Philadelphia. Address B. 354, Friends' Intelligencer.

FUN

Ex-President Taft told at a literary dinner the story about a colored man. "A colored man," he said, "knocked at Mrs. Brown's back door and asked for work. 'What's your name?' Mrs. Brown asked, for she liked the man's looks. 'Mah name's Poe, Ma'am,' he answered. 'Poe, eh?' said Mrs. Brown. 'I suppose some of your family once worked for Edgar Allan Poe—did they?' The colored man's eyes bulged, and he struck himself a resounding whack on the chest. 'Why, Ma'am,' he said, 'Ah is Edgar Allan Poe.'"—*St. Thomas Times Journal.*

To the Lot Holders and others interested in Fairhill Burial Ground:

GREEN STREET Monthly Meeting has funds available for the encouragement of the practice of cremating the dead to be interred in Fairhill Burial Ground. We wish to bring this fact as prominently as possible to those who may be interested. We are prepared to undertake the expense of cremation in case any lot holder desires us to do so.

Those interested should communicate with William H. Gaskill, Treasurer of the Committee of Interments, Green Street Monthly Meeting, or any of the following members of the Committee.

William H. Gaskill, 3801 Arch St.
Samuel N. Longstreth, 1218 Chestnut St.
Charles F. Jenkins, 232 South Seventh St.
Stuart S. Graves, 3033 Germantown Ave.

ADVERTISING RATE in the FRIENDS' INTELLIGENCER, for Help Wanted, Positions Wanted, Rooms for Rent, Notices, and other classified advertisements without display, for each insertion, 2 cents per word, including name, initials and address. Answers may be sent to a box at the INTELLIGENCER office, if so directed.

For display advertising the rate is 10 cents per agate line, or $1.40 per column inch, each insertion. On ten or more insertions in a year from date of order, ten per cent. discount. Thus a four-inch single-column or two-inch double-column advertisement costs $5.60 each insertion, less ten per cent., or 5.04 net each time for ten or more insertions. Matter may be changed whenever desired, without extra charge.

Experience has proved the INTELLIGENCER to be a remarkably good advertising medium. All advertisements must "pass the censor!"

Address 140 N. 15th St., Philadelphia

The Friends'
Intelligencer

ESTABLISHED 1844 — TENTH MONTH 7, 1922 — VOLUME 79 NUMBER 40

Contents

REGULAR MEETINGS

OAKLAND, CALIF. — A FRIENDS' Meeting is held every First-day at 11 A. M., in the Extension Room, Y. W. C. A. Building, Webster Street, above 14th. Visiting Friends always welcome.

PASADENA, CALIFORNIA — Orange Grove Monthly Meeting of Friends, 520 East Orange Grove Avenue. Meeting for worship, First-day, 11 A. M. Monthly Meeting, the second First-day of each month, at 1.45 P. M. First-day School (except Monthly Meeting days) 9.45 A. M.

BELL, PRESTON 23-74
KEYSTONE, WEST 2661

S. D. HALL

39th and Parrish Streets

Place your order for COAL at once and get in line for delivery.

H. F. BRUNER & CO.

16 North 21st Street

Bell, Locust 0243 *Keystone, Race 5661*

FUN

"Sambo, what's a university?" "A university am a place where they teaches yuh how to stawve to death in a gentlemunly an' cultured mannah."—*Life.*

THE FRIENDS' INTELLIGENCER

Published weekly, 140 N. 15th Street, Philadelphia, Pa., by Friends' Intelligencer Association, Ltd.

SUE C. YERKES, *Managing Editor.*

Editorial Board: Elizabeth Powell Bond, Thomas A. Jenkins, J. Russell Smith, George A. Walton.

Board of Managers: Edward Cornell, Alice Hall Paxson, Paul M. Pearson, Annie Hillborn, Elwood Hollingshead, William C. Biddle, Charles F. Jenkins, Edith M. Winder, Frances M. White.

Officers of Intelligencer Associates: Ellwood Burdsall, Chairman; Bertha L. Broomell, Secretary; Herbert P. Worth, Treasurer.

Subscription rates: United States, Mexico, Cuba and Panama, $2.50 per year. Canada and other foreign countries, $3.00 per year. Checks should be made payable to Friends' Intelligencer Association, Ltd.

Entered as Second Class Matter at Philadelphia Post Office.

SCHOOLS.

Woolman School

Special Week-end Course on "The Teaching of Jesus"

Six Weeks—Twelve Lessons

Begins Ninth Month 30

ELBERT RUSSELL, DIRECTOR,
Swarthmore, Pa.

GEORGE SCHOOL
Near Newtown, Bucks County, Pa.

Under the care of Philadelphia Yearly Meeting of Friends.

Course of study extended and thorough, preparing students either for business or for college. For catalogue apply to

GEORGE A. WALTON, A. M., Principal
George School, Penna.

FRIENDS' CENTRAL SCHOOL SYSTEM

Write for Year Book and Rates.

L. RALSTON THOMAS
Principal.
15th and Race Sts., Philadelphia.

FRIENDS' ACADEMY
LONG ISLAND, N. Y.

A Boarding and Day School for Boys and Girls, conducted in accordance with the principles of the Society of Friends. For further particulars address

S. ARCHIBALD SMITH, Principal,
Locust Valley, N. Y.

WALTER RHOADS WHITE,
Attorney and Counsellor-at-Law
Lansdowne Trust Co., Lansdowne, Pa.
Also Member of the Delaware County Bar

GENEALOGIST

ELIZABETH B. SATTERTHWAITE,
52 N. Stockton St., Trenton, N. J.

ELLWOOD HEACOCK
FUNERAL DIRECTOR
2027 NORTH COLLEGE AVENUE
PHILADELPHIA
CALLS OUT OF CITY ANSWERED PROMPTLY

WE BUY ANTIQUE FURNITURE and antiques of all kinds; old gold, silver, platinum, diamonds and old false teeth. Phila. Antique Co., 633 Chestnut, cor. 7th. Phone Lombard 6398. Est. 1866.

HOTELS.

Buck Hill Falls

There is now an opportunity to enjoy the Pocono mountains during the delightful Fall season. After the middle of October we will have accommodations available you would desire and would be happy to have you visit us at that time.

You will find the country more beautiful than at any other time with the foliage changing from day to day, which makes motoring thru these mountains a real pleasure. The Golf Links and tennis courts will not be so crowded. Riding horses will be available and by walking one can appreciate more fully the beauties which are missed by those who pass thru the region more rapidly.

THE INN
"Wealth in Health"
BUCK HILL FALLS, PA.

HOTEL WARWICK
SOUTH CAROLINA AVENUE
ATLANTIC CITY, N. J.
OPEN ALL THE YEAR

First house from beach and boardwalk. Steam heat, electric lights, elevator. Excellent cuisine, quiet, dignified surroundings and attentive service.

Reasonable rates. Write
SARAH H. FULLOM, Prop.

THE WHEELER
Boardwalk at Massachusetts
ATLANTIC CITY, N. J.
Ocean Rooms—Table Guests
MRS. A. W. WHEELER

STRATH HAVEN INN
SWARTHMORE, PA.

Attractive Suburban Hotel. 20 minutes from Broad St. Station. Free auto to morning and evening trains. Garage. Spacious grounds. Special Winter rates. Entertaining features for guests and their friends.

Telephone—Swarthmore 680. F. M. Scheibley.

SOUTH CAROLINA

PINE RIDGE CAMP, Actually Mid the Pines. Ideal place for outdoor life in winter. Main house and cabins with sleeping porches. Modern improvements. Pure water. Excellent table. Rates moderate. Open all the year. Write Miss SANBORN or Miss CROCKER, Aiken, South Carolina.

FRANK PETTIT
ORNAMENTAL IRON WORKS
Iron Fencing, Fire Escapes, Stairs and Ornamental Iron Work.
1505-15 N. Mascher Street Philadelphia, Pa.

Please help us by patronizing our advertisers. Mention the "Friends' Intelligencer."

The Friends' Intelligencer

The religion of Friends is based on faith in the "INWARD LIGHT," or direct revelation of God's spirit and will in every [s]eeking soul.

The INTELLIGENCER is interested in all who bear the name of Friends in every part of the world, and aims to promote love, [u]nity and intercourse among all branches and with all religious societies.

[E]STABLISHED 1844

PHILADELPHIA, TENTH MONTH 7, 1922

Conference Echoes

"Why do we hold so many Conferences?" said [o]ne Friend to another. "All the time conferring, [t]alking, discussing, and debating; nothing but prob[l]ems and questions, addresses, talks and round-[t]ables: what does it all amount to?"

"Hard to say," answered the other Friend. "I [g]o to get ideas; and then it is so pleasant to meet old [f]riends and to make new ones."

"Ideas? what ideas," persisted the Doubter; "it [a]ll seems to me talk—talk, and words—words."

"Some of it does seem heated atmosphere, as the [b]oys say, but once in a while a thought, an idea is [e]xpressed which changes a person's life—changes it [f]or the better. At Richmond, I witnessed one such [c]ase. Dr. A. W. Taylor said: (I don't remember [t]he exact words): 'Marxian socialism and capital[is]m are much nearer to each other than either is to [a]pplied Christianity, for both are absolutely ma[t]erialistic, while Christianity is not.' I saw that [i]dea hit a young man Friend as plainly as if it had [b]een a bullet; he had been bothering his home Meet[i]ng a good deal with what *he* thought were whole[s]ome economic truths but which *they* thought were [n]either true nor wholesome, and here, from the plat[f]orm, he heard a veteran speaker and writer, an [u]ndoubted authority, calmly putting the Marx phil[o]sophy in its right place. Wasn't that worth while?"

⌘

Friends are reluctant—too reluctant—to praise [e]ach other for good works done, for fitting words [s]poken at fitting times, for timely aid extended to [d]eserving persons or causes. It was told about at [R]ichmond that a concerned Friend had said to [y]ounger Friends living in the East, "If you will go [t]o Richmond, I will see to it that it costs you no more [t]han if the Conference were held at Cape May or [a]t Saratoga Springs." Many, evidently, took ad[v]antage of this generous offer; the young people [w]ere furnishing at least one-half of the numbers [a]nd at least three-fourths of the energy at Rich[m]ond, and who would venture to estimate the results to them and to the Society? Will the anonymous Friend accept these thanks? Or, are such expressions of sincere appreciation not quite Friendly good form?

And then, how we shrink from naming persons! (except on committees). We rightly hesitate to dismiss long and faithful services with what we fear may seem a few complimentary phrases, painfully inadequate to the willing work done, often for a life-time, in the Lord's vineyard. Yet, before these valued Friends help in their last Conference, before the younger persons (whom they have trained) assume the old, familiar duties whose performance has brought no material rewards, is it not permissible to say publicly how much the Conference owed (once more) to the veterans, the wheel-horses, the stand-bys? Old, familiar faces at Richmond were numerous—and welcome: James H. Atkinson, Harry Hawkins, Dr. Janney, Herbert P. Worth, Josephine H. Tilton were all present, on duty, to the benefit of all concerned. (Does that compliment exceed the decorous bounds permitted to Friends?) In the ministry, Samuel Zavitz and Isaac Wilson were most helpful.

⌘

Richmond, the headquarters of official Quakerism, the seat of the somewhat dreaded and mysterious Five Years' Meeting, the center of American Friendly population—Richmond could hardly fail to revive thoughts, questions, and reminiscences of the great Separation, now nearly a full century old. Why was it? What caused it? Whose fault was it? How could Friends professing forbearance and loving peace quarrel so openly and so outrageously? These questions were often asked and answered with more or less accuracy—oftener perhaps with less than more—but always with curiosity rather than heat, with mild astonishment rather than regret. One Friend said: With me, and with my father before me, the Separation is an Inheritance; it was none of my doings, it was "wished upon me" by my ancestors. I do not feel bound to accept such an inheritance. I am like a group of young people

I heard of who want to join the Root and not a Branch of the Society of Friends. It makes me impatient that any interest of organization should in any way divide me from the Quakerism of people like William J. Reagan and Frederick J. Libby. In what I do and say, I propose to ignore the Separation.

We doubt if ignoring facts is just the right way of dealing with them; we are sure that nothing but good can come from acting upon one's personal convictions of what is right, and we have a good deal of sympathy with those who are protesting against an unwelcome inheritance, against a condition not of their own making. It would seem that these are called to create a new set of conditions.

T. A. J.

⌘

"The world knows more of the Quaker faith today than it ever did before." This expression by Wilson S. Doan at the beginning of the "Conference" strengthened my courage and raised my hope to a fresh roseate hue. Then the query, what has transformed our small, insignificant, atrophied Society so suddenly into full life and world-wide fame? Of course it was its stand of non-violence during the great war; and the work of groups of faithful young Friends who took their lives in their hands, and went, in the spirit of love, and clothed the naked and fed the starving in allied and enemy lands alike. They proved to a doubting world, what Jesus plainly taught, the invincible power of love to overcome hate and make our enemy our friend.

From every branch of Friends there blossomed forth the love that has made the name of Quaker a household word beloved throughout all Europe and the world.

But our work has just begun. What Friends have done in Europe reveals still greater work for us to do. The millions whose bodies have been nurtured back to life are asking and craving for a spiritual home where they can know more of this saving love of Jesus so exemplified in the lives of these His followers. Shall we let their souls starve whose bodies we have saved? This further and greater lack we dare not evade. Love is today re-making the world more to her liking. But she must have men and women, *our* young men and young women. Yes, she is calling for you. Will you go?

EDGAR M. ZAVITZ.

Coldstream, Ont., Canada.

⌘

We are beginning this week the publication of a page of "First-day School Methods," edited by Bliss Forbush. Many Friends are already acquainted with the ability of Bliss Forbush in getting things going, and just now when so many of our schools are open-

Religion and Public Life

By Carl Heath

"Ecclesiastical paddocks and spiritual preserves for the righteous, belong to an age which is past. A new conception belongs to the men of our day, a conception of no New Atlantis, a Utopia, or City of the Sun, but of an international Society with its common will bent towards the socially righteous, the politically free; and with its union rooted in the fellowship of a common religious bond."

In these words Carl Heath, secretary of the Friends' Council for International Service described the ideal of Humanity today, speaking on "Religion and Public Life"* at the annual Swarthmore Lecture, with which the Yearly Meeting of the Society of Friends opened at Devonshire House.

The lecturer pointed out the intimate connection between religion and public life from the dawn of history onward, and in particular their close association in the story of Israel; the place in national life of priest and prophet; the mission of the old prophets in combating public wrong and appealing for the ideal of a purified community. He noted the contrast between the free and unorganized primitive Christian fellowship, dominated by the ideal of the Kingdom of God, and the institutional church which soon took its place. Facing "The tragedy the Church has made of heathen Europe and the tragedy heathen Europe has made of the Church," he found reassurance in Amiel's saying: "When Christianity dies, the religion of Jesus will still live."

The Church Must Speak, or Die

"The European War of 1914-1918 found both the Church and the World unexpectant, and the new City of Humanity must be planted on a firmer foundation than that which satisfied the last generation. The failure of the Church is felt by her own members as well as those outside. Her appeal has been too exclusively to the side of life which is personal. Yet the teaching of Christ laid equal emphasis on the social side. The Christian Church must speak overtly to the public life as well as to the private, *or die.*"

Some would prefer the Church to die. But the Church in Carl Heath's view, is not an outward institution, but "primarily an inward and spiritual fellowship of the souls of men, whose life should run in and through the inner fibres of the whole fabric of society."

The gospel of Jesus is one of new relationships. "He has seen and revealed to men the very nature of God. This nature of God, seen and embodied in the life of the Son of God, is the power station for all Christian activism." All social relations must be tested by Christ's conception of the Fatherhood of God, and all that it implies. The substitution of the Greek idea of Salvation for the Hebrew idea of the Kingdom of God involved the loss of "a corporate and social conception essential to the Gospel."

In the true conception of Christianity there is no antagonism between spirit and matter, as in its monastic perversion. Jesus "is Himself the synthesis of the Spirit and of Matter . . With Christ all material things take on another aspect. In His Human life He expresses in the simplest way a relationship to material things, human in its enjoyment, divine in its sympathy and mastery." He does not, like other teachers, seek to free mankind by getting outside life, by separating spiritual and material. "The purpose of the Spirit to penetrate and transfuse the phenomenal and material does indeed lie at the very heart of the great doctrine of the Incarnation." Similarly "the spiritual community is not to be thought of as something antagonistic to the material one."

With the materialistic ideas of the Reformation, the Church has taken up a separatist attitude towards the material world. The Catholic ideal is right in emphasizing the sense of community and the importance of social order, and the equality of Christians in the presence of that order; wrong in its claim for ecclesiastical authority, in its denial of freedom, above all in the pagan worship of power, inherited from ancient Rome. The Protestant ideal is right in its assertion of personal freedom as a spiritual and political mainspring, but wrong in its neglect of the corporate life.

Carl Heath went on to discuss the place of the Reformation, the liberating work of Luther and its limitations, the tragedy of the ineffective struggle of the proletarian reformers of the early Anabaptist movement to achieve both the corporate and individual ideal of Christianity, the consequent narrowing of the greater Protestant communions into nationalism and individualism, resulting in that divorce between corporate religious ethics and social and political practice, against which "the European proletarian is in a world-wide revolt."

Compromise

Penn's "Holy Experiment" in Pennsylvania of a colony, based not upon mere toleration but religious freedom was next dealt with, and the subsequent withdrawal of the Quaker Community from political life through their desire to avoid compromise.

"What is the content of this word Compromise that gives it an ill sound in religious or in moral conduct?" the lecturer asked. "The streams of life produce an endless series of complicated knots in conduct in which at most we see truth relative to mixed conditions. It is not political compromise that is the enemy of religion but the method by which such compromise is reached; the method that is falsely called democratic, of reaching an agreed end by immoral surrender of principle, and by voting down and coercing one another. A nobler way of transcending differences has been achieved in the Quaker method of reaching a decision, without vote or counting of heads, by a spirit of co-operative search for the best. This Christian method needs to be applied to all the problems of corporate life."

The range of religion is far wider than politics. But "the Gospel must be social. Religion holds a message which is both inward and outward. It binds in a perfect unity a body of ideas which go to make a way of faith, and a body of actions which constitute a way of life. No merely outward reconstruction of the social order will bring us peace. The true functional society is a kingdom of right living, mutual freedom. Parliaments, Councils, Commissions of experts may plan with most effective wisdom. But efficiency is not righteousness."

Modern paganism is built on a *Machtidee*—a theory of the joy of outward power. The Church of Laodicea, though it does not bless this, stands by and has no great affirmation of right to make. The Church must have a *Realpolitik* of its own to face the drink curse, the sex evil, the war trade, industrial domination, the opium traffic and the other problems of the modern world. Everywhere men have a new vision of a better social order. Mankind is incurably religious. The Church must not think of God "as the patron of a Church apart." All men are citizens of Christ's Kingdom, though they do not realize the implications of citizenship. We pray, "Thy kingdom come." Why not now?

"The fellowship of believers is not a credal group, but a society of doers of the word. A prophetic Church is above all human needs the greatest."

"What is to be the future of the Society of Friends?" said Carl Heath in conclusion. In its essence, as the lecturer saw it, the Society of Friends was neither a sect nor an institutional Church, but a free and catholic fellowship, which must translate its vision of the eternal order into the activities of the material world. "Such a community must see Christ as no exclusive possession of an ecclesiasticism, nor even of the grouping known as Christendom;" it must look upon the functions of social human life, not under the narrowing classification of sacred and secular, but as parts of a life which is expressing God's life.

* The lecture is published in book form by the Friends' Bookshop, 140, Bishopsgate, E.C.2. Price 1/6 in paper and 2/6 in cloth.

Life

"Life is a gift to be used every day,
Not to be smothered and hidden away,
It isn't a thing to be stored in the chest
Where you gather your keepsakes and treasure your best;
It isn't a joy to be sipped now and then
And promptly put back in a dark place again."

"Life is a gift that the humblest may boast of
And one that the humblest may well make the most of.
Get out and live it each hour of the day,
Wear it and use it as much as you may;
Don't keep it in niches and corners and grooves,
You'll find that in service its beauty improves."

—Edgar A. Guest.

An International Economic Conference

(The following information was taken from the National Council for Reduction of Armaments Bulletin, Frederick J. Libby, Executive Secretary.)

The press on September 1st carried the news that the *French Premier* is seeking a conference "of all nations interested" in the reduction of intergovernmental obligations, at which *"reciprocal sacrifices"* shall be made "in the interest of *humanity."* The same day *President Harding* told the Washington correspondents that the Administration will co-operate in such a conference "at the proper time." Well-informed papers have since then reported the growing sentiment in favor of holding this conference *in Washington after election.*

The European Deadlock

The policy of France towards Germany has brought things to the place where she can collect no more from Germany and can only wreak vengeance upon her. This would mean permanent war in Europe. It would mean bankruptcy for France herself, and disruption everywhere. It would justly isolate the offending nation and no conceivable defense could prevent the blame for the world-wide disaster from falling where it would mainly—not exclusively—belong.

Moreover, the antagonistic interests of Great Britain and France have created a dangerous breach which grows wider daily. Most recently, France has helped the Turks against the Greeks until today their success threatens again to embroil Europe. England encouraged in Greece a mad ambition. Germany and Russia have been driven into each other's arms. Russia is an ally of Turkey. The Balkan States are stirred with alarm at the menace of Turkey revived. Militarism is rampant. Famine threatens countries besides Russia.

Europe seems to contain no savior. Neither Poin

care nor Lloyd George can break the deadlock. Both see the imminent danger and national considerations make both powerless to avert it. Both look to America and both *seem ready now to co-operate with America* in the "reciprocal sacrifices" that will be required.

America Must be Prepared

Let us look now at America's position at this conference. The sacrifices will have to be genuinely "reciprocal." *Press* and *people* must prepare to *do our part* and yet *not in a gush sentiment*, but with full knowledge of the facts. Our share in the conference is bound up with the Interallied Debts.

THE INTERALLIED DEBTS

1. Purpose of the Loans Must be Considered

Bernard M. Baruch, in a letter to Senator Borah dated September 12th, called attention to differences in *the purposes* for which America lent money to her allies which are bound to be considered in the final settlement. Oscar T. Crosby, former Assistant Secretary of the Treasury, discussed these differences at the recent Institute of Politics in Williamstown, dividing the loans from this standpoint into three classes: A. Loans for the purchase in this country of *munitions* used by our allies *because our soldiers were not yet ready* to use them. B. Loans for the purchase in this country of raw materials and other supplies which were *resold* in Europe *and the money kept*, or else became a *permanent* part of the *commercial* equipment of the purchasing Government. C. Loans for the purchase of supplies in Argentina and other countries, our loan being made because of our superior credit, to prevent the demoralization of the exchange.

2. Differences in Ability to Pay Must be Considered

Just as Class B above would be deemed by every fairminded person a different kind of obligation from Class A, while Class C would require expert study and treatment in detail, so an examination of the debts of the different countries reveals great differences as to their *respective worth on a business basis*. Nearly every country in Europe owes us, but the largest debts are these (in millions of dollars):

Country	*Principal*	*Interest*	*Total*
Belgium	377	51	428
France	3341	430	3771
Great Britain	4136	611	4747
Italy	1648	243	1891
Poland	136	23	159
Russia	193	35	228
Czecho-Slovakia	92	12	104
Serbia	51	7	58
Roumania	36	5	41

Great Britain despite great unemployment and economic depression is balancing her budget. France, suffering less from these causes, has been borrowing money to pay both for the restoration of the devastated area and for the pensions of her soldiers and widows, both being charged under the Versailles Treaty to the German account. Her debt has *doubled* since the war and her *taxes* cover, according to David F. Houston, less than 45 per cent. of her present expenditures. Italy is paying 60 per cent. of her expenses by taxation but her exchange rate is much lower than that of France. Poland's finances are only nominally better than those of Austria and Russia. Without going into further detail, it is clear that the *relative solvency* of our debtors is decidedly pertinent to the discussion.

(Concluded in next issue)

Obstacles to World Union

"The first obstacle which we meet is the enormous difference in race, language and culture among civilized nations. The second obstacle is no less formidable and that is the different levels of civilization. The great majority of humanity is still not yet not self-governing in any real sense of the word.

"Then there is a third obstacle, that is the sheer problem of numbers. The present machinery of democracy does not seem to be very appropriate for dealing with the world problem. Then there is a fourth obstacle. If ever the world is to have unity and liberty and peace, it must be on the basis of the self-government of all its parts.

"The sovereignity of the world should be constitutionally vested in the whole people of the world. That statement, at first sight, may appear somewhat meaningless. But constitutional lawyers will see that if it is made effective, it will end war and make the reign of law universal over every aspect of human affairs, city, state, national and international.

"We are faced with two alternatives and two only —steady progress in the direction of world unity, or another world war. We can have which we choose. But the choice itself is, in my judgment, inexorable. If we sit still and murmur, 'Well, it's a beautiful dream, but we cannot do anything about it now,' then we are in fact casting a vote for another world war.

"It is really a great adventure which lies before us, if we have eyes to see it. It is an adventure far greater and calling for far more moral courage than the physical courage needed for fighting a war. There is no risk of our becoming effete if we really attempt it. It is for the civilized peoples to take the lead. Without them nothing can be done."

Philip Kerr, at the Williamstown, Mass., School of Politics.

Milk for West Virginia Babies

Milk-fed babies will no longer be a novelty in the mining regions of West Virginia where the American Friends' Service Committee has been working. After the feeding centers for the older children were established it was decided that the best way of overcoming malnutrition among the babies was by furnishing fresh milk to them and their mothers. Luella Jones' account of the fresh milk program shows how valuable it has been, both in improving the condition of the babies and in educating their parents.

"The people of these districts have not been educated to the value of fresh milk. During good times most families have their own cow which roams up and down the roadside of the narrow valley. But since the strike few of them have been able to keep a cow. The milk at best is tainted from the bitter weeds upon which the cows feed; it is further contaminated by poor facilities for keeping it fresh, since very few families have basements or can afford ice. For this reason it is little wonder that, as we are told, "the children don't like milk."

"Our Committee supplied good milk from a Charleston dairy. The mothers were urged to use this early in the morning while it was still in good condition. Simultaneously with the milk feeding was begun a plan of house to house visiting to weigh the babies. From listless indifference or friendly tolerance the mothers soon stirred to lively rivalry to see whose baby gained most. Too often there was a pitiful failure to gain, and the mother had to be urged to increased care. Sometimes she would say: "I never did like milk, but I think of my baby and take it down like medicine. Now I like it, and I know it helps me and baby both." With the third week of weighing came gratifying results. The whole family and often neighbors watched for our coming and gathered around to see if baby had gained.

"One of our families owns a pair of emaciated twins of five months old. They weighed only eight pounds, were too young and too delicate to be weaned. The mother had only coarse unsuitable food to eat. Steadily the register fell from week to week and it looked as if the twins would not be able to get through the hot weather. We induced the mother to drink the milk. This she did reluctantly at first. Then there was a happy day when it was discovered that Pauline, the littlest twin had gained two ounces! Mother and grandmother beamed at us happily, garrulously congratulating themselves and thanking us. Brothers and sisters fawned over the babies arguing over the health of each. Then the father appeared, a big burly miner, claiming his share of the infant's attention. He reminded one of a big bear playing with a kitten, and one might have concluded that poor little scrawny Pauline was the most precious bit of humanity on Cabin Creek.

"We were much gratified when a local doctor and nurse told us that our plan of weighing the babies and of distributing milk had taught the mothers more about child care than years of practice had accomplished. Some of the mothers say they will not again try to do without milk for their children if there is any possible way to get it. The doctor tells us there have been fewer deaths and less sickness than usual among the babies of our district."

Even though the feeding centers closed when school began, the fresh milk distribution was continued. Now that the families see the good results from the use of milk it is hoped that it will continue to be the staple article of diet for babies in this region.

Friends' Agricultural Show in Poland

On Tuesday, August 15th, an Agricultural Show was organized says W. Carleton Palmer, one of the Friends' workers at Holoby, Poland. The place chosen was an old platform and buildings formerly used as a rail-head by the German Army during the war. A report from the field reads:

"Part of the proceedings consisted of a long procession of villagers from the different villages in which Friends Mission help had been given and of the horses in the ploughing columns. These horses were ridden by the peasants who were being helped and for one village several women were riding. The whole scene was very attractive and reminiscent of the wild west, very stimulating when one knew of the work lying behind it all,—the special help which was given to returning refugees. There were special exhibits of vegetables, grain and flax, much of it grown entirely from Mission seed. A Government official was present and warmly thanked the Mission for the work which has been done. It is said to be the first agricultural show which had ever been attempted in the agricultural districts of Poland. We think it very probable it will not by any means be the last. . . .

Florence Barrow reports that there may be no seed rye for the fall planting. The fall of the Polish mark and the decrease in contributions from the United States have both played a part in bringing about this catastrophe. Unless additional relief is guaranteed, 7,000 families including many children will remain destitute and without bread to eat for another two winters. If we send help in this crisis, they may hope to again become self-supporting, self-respecting citizens.

The Quaker Faith

The Faith of a Quaker

Three Round Tables, conducted by George A. Walton, on the book of that name, by John W. Graham, published in 1920.

(Concluded from last issue.)

Most of us have intimate friends with whom we may say and do things which neither would stand from anybody else. To appreciate a book like this, it is worth while to appreciate the spirit in which it was written. Let us not expect the same system that we get in scientific books. The book is like a fine house, full of the richest treasures. But you go from one floor to the next by a secret staircase. In thus judging it, we must remember that the central thought of Friends is too great for any one person to express.

The attitude of the author is that of a poet rather than of a prose writer. He was brought up on Browning, Tennyson and Wordsworth, and we can see their influence throughout. We may well take the book something from the point of view of a good stiff poem of Browning.

The book is divided into four parts. The first part is J. W. G.'s philosophy. It is all solid, so solid that we cannot read much of it at once. It is not a book for a sedentary mind, not because it is so complicated, but because it is so solid and concentrated. Book I is on "The Foundations" of the Quaker Faith. Book II treats of "The Founders," its chapters being George Fox, Isaac Penington, Some Writings of William Penn, and Barclay's Apology. Book III on "The Superstructure," sets forth the secondary phases of the Quaker Faith. This tells of the testimonies and ministry of the early church, while Book I tells of God, Christ, and human personality. The Chapters in Book III are entitled, Separate from the World, Art and Education, The Reward of the Ascetic, Ministry in the Early Church, The Decay of Prophecy, Ministry as a Profession, Silence in Worship and the Workshop of Ministry, The Lord's Supper, Baptism, Organization and Discipline. Book IV, "The Outlook Upon the World" treats of Social Service, War, Religion and the State and Evangelicalism.

Book I, in Graham's own words, is a "high essay to tell in part what can never be told in full; to hold out what little light from the eternal radiance has come my way." If we want to describe Quakerism, we must make up our minds that it is something different. It has been said that there are three types of religion today, Catholic, Protestant and Quaker. Historically, Quakerism is the last extreme offshoot of Protestantism. It was a split-off from Puritanism, which was a split-off from Catholicism. "Our religion bases whatever it builds on the sure foundation of experience." We can not give inquirers an idea of our religion in the ordinary theological framework. In Graham's first chapter, "The Father," he gives three religious experiences which he thinks common enough to use as a basis. These are Consecration, Love, and Prayer, the result of the revelation of God in the human soul. Some may say that Prayer is but the development of fear in the lower animals, and that Love is the development of the sex instinct; "what" says Graham, made simple lowly instincts turn into such glorious gifts?"

The spirit of consecration leads up to the purer thought of God. "Religion is the accumulated spirit of our fathers and mothers." Consecration is constantly submerging self. We are called to spend and be spent in the service of the home, the family, the church, the nation, the larger whole. So we find ourselves consecrated to the interests of a larger whole, and thus led to consecration to the whole, in a sense of completeness with God, the cause of all. The same process by which we consecrate ourselves to anything, brings us to realize that we stand in the presence of God, who is larger than family, church, nation, or race. The way to meet God is not through theological books or ideas, but through Consecration, Love, Prayer. When two people love, the usual barriers of personality are taken down, and the two personalities mix. A person who loves his fellow-men finds himself led into the personality of God. Of course, that is mysticism,—Quaker mysticism.

One can see the naturalness of prayer manifested in real children. Prayer is not a messenger sent to the store to get a desired article; it is a sense of the power of God, and our weakness. In this first chapter he shows how irresistibly each phase of our nature points on to God. We are conscious of the future, but do not know it; and so we turn to God, who is conscious of the future, and knows it. The very handicap suggests God. This experience points in the direction of thinking of God as an infinite personality of which we are a part, as a leaf is part of a book. John W. Graham insists on the oneness of man and God, but carries it farther than the old idea of man's being as a hand to God. The hand is but a part of the body, but the body is made up of countless cells. "May it be that we are like cells forming a greater Whole, entering somehow into the total personality of God?"

II.

Where does Christ come in, in J. W. G.'s scheme? He quotes the 1st chapter of John, "The Word was made flesh, and dwelt among us." The mind of Christ is one that man is unable to distinguish from the mind of God. This point of view leaves no room for a system which lays down the boundaries between man and God.

Book III deals with the superstructure which the founders built on the basis of our connection with God. The first chapter, "Separate from the World," tells of that period of being "a peculiar people." When did that period stop? How recently were we wearing the plain garb? [Not within the memory of the oldest person in the group. About 1850 was decided upon, after discussion, as the end of this general period.] From 1725 until 1850 or thereabouts, the Society of Friends, then, was consciously a "peculiar people," set apart by its dress, language, etc., from the rest of the world. J. W. G. thinks this was unavoidable but did much harm. Rufus Jones has pointed out that this aloofness, together with lack of education, brought about a littleness of mind that allowed the Separation. J. W. G. even says that "thee" and "thou" were a heavy baggage to carry.

The second chapter in this Book III deals with "Art and Education." We know that the Friends were opposed to many forms of Art. We did not originate this; it was an inheritance from the Puritans. J. W. G. thinks that knowledge of art, music, etc., develops a person, and makes him more qualified to live a human life. Yet, after criticising Friends for suppressing art, J. W. G. writes on "The Reward of the Ascetic." "Doubtless," he says, "the absence of music from our meetings has kept many away from our fellowship. But I claim this ascetic habit as a sign of reality and a source of spiritual strength." "For better or worse, Silence, as a means of expression, has made us what we are." And again, "Esthetic sensibility lies nearer the surface of our nature than religious perception." There is danger in using music and art to stimulate religion; they may only excite the outer layers, and not touch the deeper nature at all. The Church which is most full of ritual and beautiful music is the most degraded. The most stupid man alive can see more of God in his own nature than in any ritual, no matter how beautiful. Our sensitive-mindedness is destroyed by constant attacks upon it, by books, papers, pictures, etc.

Now there may be two different effects from our asceticism. One may become narrow, or saintly. "I believe in the case of the man whom asceticism narrows and sours, pride is mixed in with his habit of mind." But the world of music, drama, art, is ours. Our religion is within ourselves, independent of music or priest. "The mistake of the churches has been to confuse the quests for Love and Truth with that for Beauty." "Beauty is not put into the Quaker service; it comes out of it." A Friends' meeting is to an arranged service as a hand-made article is to a machine-made one. The hand-made articles may not be as uniform, but they have their distinctive charm, and bear the marks of loving care. "It is much cheaper to join in the elaborate ecclesiastical machinery . . . but the meeting has for us a charm . . . in comparison with which the ordinary worship of the churches is as moonlight unto sunlight."

J. W. G. turns next to the ministry. One chapter is a long historical digression, showing how the ministry in the Christian church of the first century was like that of the Quakers. Then came three centuries in which it was like that of the Protestant churches. Then it became Catholic. First, Quaker; then, Nonconformist; then Catholic.

Chapter VI: "Ministry as a Profession." Friends say that they have no clergy. That is a false idea; we have no laity. We all belong to the clergy. We are all set aside as definitely for religious service as the clergy in the Roman Catholic Church. We did have a clergy as long as we recorded ministers, indicating these as people with a special gift. "Ministry, as understood by Friends . . . comes from a deeper stratum of our being . . . than the streams of current consciousness." "Our meetings are much more than a convenient plan by which the ministry of several may be substituted for the ministry of one; they are a well-considered provision for the silence of the outward, inasmuch as that is a condition for the inward to find a voice."

"Ministry comes to me by waiting. . . . As I sit down in meeting, I think of what has struck me during the week,—a text, a book, an incident. If nothing flames, silence is my portion, and I turn from ideas of ministry to my own private needs."

III.

[This session occupied much time with discussion of some of the points previously brought out. A summary of this discussion is given first, names of speakers not being mentioned.]

At the Richmond Conference of 1898, it was said that when the plain language disappears, the end of the Society of Friends will be at hand. Yet J. W. G. says this has been a heavy burden. If we lose the intimate words that we use in prayer, we lose much of the tenderness of it. If we do not use these words in our homes, they become unreal in prayer. If we use the plain language on all occasions, we have opportunities of attracting to Quaker principles the attention of those who notice our words. Are we not brothers; should we not use the same words to all? 'You' was a word of superiority. It was a great step in democracy to use 'thee' to all. Now, there is no real religious thought in it; there is fraternity, a peculiar tenderness.

Is the prophetic ministry dying out among us? It is among the older members, but we have a new group coming on. The first prophetic ministry of Christendom was in the first century, and only lasted about a century. There has never been a time when there was no prophetic ministry whatever. Each new outburst of religion has brought a fresh access of prophetic fervor. How long did the prophetic zeal of Friends last? It began to fade about 1750. Most of the sermons of the Friends of that time would be unreadable, now, except those of John Fothergill and Job Scott. A perfect ministry is one which meets the immediate, conscious need of any group of persons. This is prophetic ministry.

The fourth book of the volume, "The Outlook Upon the World" is the least original, and probably the least vital of all. The chapter on War is very long, full of thought, and bears marks of having been written, re-written, and worked over. The interest of the chapter on Religion and the State is to us Americans rather academic. The chapter on Evangelicalism is most pertinent, because it deals with theological ideas that have been so vital to religious history. In the chapter on Social Service, he points out that the philosophy of kindness to one's neighbor has been from the beginning a characteristic of the Qukaer faith, and a protest against social abuses. He refers to John Bright, Joseph Sturge, William Allen, and to other social-minded Friends who blossomed in England before the Great War.

In the War chapter, J. W. G. says: "We must distinguish between war and force. Force is a poor expedient. . . But we use it with horses and dogs, criminals and lunatics, and in the last resort, with children." But war is absolutely wrong. "Christ would win men, not conquer them. . . He would not try to turn enemies into corpses, but into friends." The Christian scheme is not to overthrow evil, but to undermine its' foundations, to turn it into good.

Round Tables on Friends' Principles

GEORGE H. NUTT, *Leader*

These three round tables perhaps did not give out anything definitely new, but served to clarify thought among those attending as was voiced by some.

The first session dealt with the Quaker idea of God. In introducing this, George H. Nutt desired there should be recognized the distinction between principle and practice—the latter often being but a temporary expression of age-old principles. "Most of the trouble," he said "in the religious world is caused by inability to distinguish between the two." "We pump children full ofttimes of things we want them to know and they must spend a long time getting rid of them." "But," another said, "we get our bearings from the past—today depends on the day that is gone, and the child of yesterday is the father of tomorrow." Wilson Tylor said, "If God is all truth then there is no truth outside him. We partake of truth according to our ability—the truth is unchanged." Chauncey Shortlidge spoke of Friends as steering clear of creed; Samuel Zavitz felt too much emphasis was laid on the past and future—too much glorifying of our sect rather than on service to our fellow men. Barclay Spicer referred to theology as "canned goods," which are not "bad because they're canned but because poor goods have been put in. We repeat creeds rather than our own experience. The trouble is not that we deal with formalities but there should be experience also."

The second of the course dealt with the "Inner Light" which it was declared was the foundation stone of Quakerism. This, however, was objected to by some who felt this to be not the exclusive possession of Friends. If God is the source and center of all strength and light, it is only our interpretation—the peculiar way Friends have of expression that is wholly ours—not the thing itself. The feeling was expressed that the young people do not want the former loose-jointed method of expression but want that which can readily be understood. "It is difficult," said Daniel Batchelor, "to get away from the Man idea of God, and the troubles arise from trying to limit him." Wilson Tylor felt we were lost in a search for terminology, but it takes positive and negative to make light—so the differing views tend to bring light to our vision. Isaac Wilson from years of experience of leaning on the Voice queried that there should be a question of what and where God is! Elizabeth Chandler put it clearly by declaring the same toys do for new children—the thing itself is unchanged but new minds and aspirations need re-statements for themselves. It was largely a matter of language which is not capable of expressing just what is desired.

"Ministry and Counsel" was the topic for the last of this series, in which it was felt complaints need not be laid to the lack of ministry. "I've never tried a real silent meeting," said one "for there's always something being said to me if I go in the right spirit whether there's a word said outwardly or not." Edith Winder felt the rapid modern life was in itself responsible for lack of ministry. The auto is a blessing yet the fast going prevents impressions from forming, so it is with modern life. "We'll never get powerful ministry until we have time to concentrate." The only need for preaching is to bring people to the true Teacher, and as the people best acquainted do not have to talk to convey their feelings, so in meeting. Pastoral visiting was felt to be fully as much a necessity as vocal ministry. Mary Whitson declared her belief that young Friends today are not waiting for someone to speak but are experiencing a deeper feeling than mere speech.

Attention was called to the need of the silent ministry which precedes the vocal, and the opportunities offered in farm life for meditation. The inspiration received while pruning fruit trees or walking between plough handles is as surely inspiration however far it may be from the meeting-house. Accepting personal responsibility and the making of kitchen, shop or farm preparatory schools for service in the meeting was the main thing. It was felt there would be no lack of vocal ministry if this were done.

Education

Educational Session

Opening remarks by Thomas A. Jenkins, who presided:— One of the fundamentals spoken of in our first session was Truth. There is inward Truth and outward Truth. The discernment of Truth is not easy, our minds are fallible and liable to error. They need direction, that is to say, Education—construction.

Lawyers know how vaguely and inaccurately we observe. Almost any lawyer could give stories out of his own experience as surprising as this of a group of twenty school-girls. They had heard a lecturer the day before. "What color was his beard?" they were suddenly asked. Fourteen of them said it was black, four that it was brown; two could give no answer. As a matter of fact, the speaker had no beard whatever.

The purpose of education is to make our minds give better service in the purposes for which we intend them. We want to be well-equipped in the great war on disease, error and ignorance. If I am to "speak to the conditions" of men, I must have knowledge of those conditions. Does the Society of Friends know just where it is going in educational matters? We have arranged for four short addresses to answer some of the possibilities.

Are Friends Going to College?

George A. Walton

When I was asked to undertake this talk, I thought I would stick to statistics on Friends going to College. But it is evidently intended that I shall not trouble you with statistics, for when I got out here, I found that I did not have any of the figures I had collected. I have only one statistic that is reliable, and that I secured out here.

The Chairman said that the Society of Friends has never been opposed to education. That may be true, so far as elementary education is concerned. But I feel that we have been, and are still, indifferent to liberal education. There is a difference between education for business, and the education which brings out the humaneness and divineness of the Spirit for whatever service may come to us. I think we have been even opposed to such education as this, from a misunderstanding of George Fox's saying that "neither Oxford nor Cambridge will help us to serve God."

In a certain Yearly Meeting Discipline, one of the queries once read, "Do Friends partake freely of learning to fit them for business?" I am glad to know that this now reads, "Do Friends partake freely of learning to fit them for a life of service?"

Because a genius like George Fox needed not such help, shall we assume that we can all go without it? It is interesting to see that when he reached out to people beyond his own personal touch, he took the educated men,—Penn, Penington, Barclay,—among the very best-educated of their time. Penington, by the way, had difficulty in finding himself at home among Friends, because of the intellectual poverty of the group, in general. An ignorant and unspiritual body thus sprang up, so that the Society of Friends became, in time, a Society of Enemies. They then woke up, and became better fitted for service. The first Friends' Schools, as Ackworth and Moses Brown, were mainly to keep their children apart from the world. Beacon lights today are Earlham, Haverford and Swarthmore, and others which are endeavoring to undo the mistakes of the former time.

About 300 of the young people of our group went to college last year, or 1 and ½ per cent. of our entire number. At a rough guess, we have about 750 young people of college age. Therefore, about 40 per cent. of our eligible group are attending college. Of course, this is far greater than the average of the country. From 5 to 6 per cent. only, of those of appropriate age in the country at large, go to college. About 42 per cent. of the students in private college preparatory schools go to college. I think, that we are increasing the percentage of our members who attend.

Of the 750 of eligible age, there will be some who have not the right kind of intellectual ability for college, and there are some who are needed at home for the support of their families.

The thing I wish is that our attitude might be so changed toward education that our boys and girls might go to college for more than the learning of a gainful profession. Many of our boys and girls do not realize that their home meetings might be enriched by their college courses.

If a boy or girl goes to normal school, or a school for nursing, etc., I do not consider it a college; there is not time in professional courses for a truly liberal education in service to others. Some are sent to college to make good connections for society or business. I have heard parents say "Yes, I want her to go to college. She will have a good time, and make better friends than elsewhere." Going to college for such a motive does not pay for the money which has been put into the college. Everybody who goes to college should be expected to bring something back to his community or meeting. If this were definitely expected of all who go, it would stop off the triflers, and by easing the pressure, would be a help to college presidents.

Are Friends Becoming Teachers?

William Eves, 3rd

All college graduates do not become teachers,—not all are fitted to be. Nor is it true that one may not be a good teacher without being a college graduate. The answer to the query, "Are Friends becoming teachers now, in as great porportion as in the past?" is partly to be found in Philadelphia Yearly Meeting, and the Friends who are teaching in the Friends' Schools therein. Twenty years ago, there were thirty-one schools in Philadelphia Yearly Meeting; ten years ago there were twenty-four; one year ago, eighteen. Twenty years ago there were in these 167 teachers; ten years ago, 149; one year ago, 133. Twenty years ago, 61 per cent. of these teachers were Friends; last year 33 per cent. In George School, however, the proportion of Friends who are teachers has remained about the same during this period.

These figures are significant. They show that Friends are teaching in smaller numbers in Friends' schools. Many, of course, are in other schools, but I feel, though I have nothing to show it, that there has been a decrease in the number of Friends who are teaching.

In the Five Years' Meeting, there are 1100 people registered as teachers. All teachers are not registered, so there are, perhaps 1500, in all, or one person in each 68 of their membership is a teacher. To meet the needs of our schools in Philadelphia Yearly Meeting, we should have one teacher to each sixty members. I am not trying to give the impression that *all* the teachers in our Friends' Schools should be Friends.

Here are some of the reasons why heads of Friends' Schools do not have more Friends as teachers, as given by the "heads" themselves in their answers to the questionnaire sent out by Elbert Russell a couple of years ago. In only three Schools out of the thirty included in the questionnaire were 100 per cent. of the teachers, Friends. In very many, the number was less than 50 per cent. "Other positions more lucrative"; "Not qualified"; "Few men qualified to teach special subjects"; "Not enough in existence"; "Low salary and lack of concern"; "Scarce at salaries offered."

These answers show: first, that there are not enough qualified Friends to fill the jobs; and second, that the salaries offered are lower than in other schools (non-Friends) for the same qualifications. We need more concerned Friends to teach in Friends' schools.

Recently I looked over the list of graduates of George School (up to 1917, because graduates since that time are mostly continuing their education), and picked out those who are now teaching. Fifteen per cent. of the Alumni are now teaching and 20 per cent. of the first graduates are now teaching. Of course, many more have taught, and there is good reason for many women giving it up, and good reason for some men giving it up. I wish I could find evidence that more of our young Friends are becoming teachers now than in the past. But I did not find any such evidence at George School.

I found, on examination, that nearly 50 per cent. of the Earlham College graduates taught for a time after graduating. Of course, it is not fair to compare a college with a preparatory school. But just now there is a concern that more young men and women take up teaching as a service.

I believe we Friends should turn out better trained teachers than some other groups. This puts on us an even greater responsibility. At the present time, during the summer, thousands of teachers have been training themselves further, in the Summer Schools. They have begun to realize that ability alone does not make teachers. It is capacity *and* training that are needed. I would urge all young Friends here to decide upon their life work, not as the one which will bring in most money, but as the one which will give most service. Let them consider if they are capable of carrying out the concern that Friends have for education. For the past few years Friends have had a chance to be of service abroad, and this especial home field should not be overlooked.

Thirteen out of twenty-six Friends' Schools gave the answer "No" to the question, "Is there religious instruction given in the schools?" We need more religious instruction in our Schools, in addition to the reading of the Bible. And if we believe Friends' schools are needed, we must man them with the best teachers available. Friends must be teachers if we are to carry out our concern for education.

The Training for Citizenship in Friends' Schools

EDWIN C. ZAVITZ

Training for citizenship should be in every school. Our training for citizenship should be to prepare people for the most valuable service they can render to those among whom they live. The best way to prepare for life is to participate in it. Schools should be lifelike, should be natural, afford natural reactions between children and teachers. In the past we have thought of schools as places where information was handed out largely pre-digested.

Handicapped because schools have been considered as information factories, we must turn our best attention to the conscious effort of developing the qualities of citizenship. What do we mean by citizenship? What qualities do we want to develop among our students? We must join them in co-operation for this work.

Let us teach the boys and girls to co-operate. There are three things innate in every child. He loves to do things, he loves to do things that he has thought up himself, and he loves to do things in co-operation with others. We must train boys and girls to take part in government, and we can not do that by preaching, or by books. Let them have a share in the government that concerns them. We should give them the power to choose their leaders. If we can give them some chance to try out government in school, they will develop judgment which will help later. They soon learn to follow their peers, and to lead their peers. We can train them to sidetrack personal interests for the interests of the group.

The type of citizenship that is developed under compulsion will not stand. The children must work on their own initiative. A very important thing to teach is to do the last 2 per cent. of a job as well as the first 2 per cent. Teach them not only to see through things but to see things through.

A good citizen will always have a good sense of humor. He will see a joke even when it is on himself, as well as when on another. We teachers have frequent opportunity to develop this sense. We can also develop in our future citizens the ability to get on with people. We do not want to make everybody alike. We must give equal opportunity for the boy and girl to develop into the extraordinary man or woman.

I think we need to consciously prepare our boys and girls for business ideals which will make business what it ought to be—ideals for service in business, with the monetary goal omitted.

We must make our boys and girls realize that it is necessary to keep pace in spiritual development with material and scientific realities. The real citizen of the future must make spiritual discoveries.

This is the new ideal for scholarship. Let us teach our boys and girls to be scholars in co-operation, in initiative, in personality, in humor, and in spiritual affairs. Such a scholarship will create a new type of citizenship.

Training for Leadership in Friends' Schools

ELBERT RUSSELL

A few days ago I walked through a certain street in Chicago, which was lined with employment agencies. The windows of these were filled with papers telling of jobs, and the street was filled with men wanting jobs. I wondered why this should be, and then I noticed that most of the jobs required some degree of technical training, and I decided that most of this group on the street were without jobs because they had not the training.

The world needs the kind of things that is our spiritual heritage, and I wonder if we have the training, the leadership that is needed in the Society of Friends today. The world needs today, not so much a George Fox as a modest leadership—not brilliant but such as will usher in the new order. What the world will be fifty years from now depends on what people are doing in their own communities today. This leadership the Society of Friends can supply if we know how. It will be a tragedy if we stand on the sidewalk while the world advertises for publishers of truth, healers of wounds, because we do not know how.

Leadership in a democracy like our own depends on these things:

Force of character
Intelligence
Initiative
Knowing how to do.

The Friends' schools can do something in training toward such leadership. It is a matter partly of heredity and partly of environment. I think the Friends' schools can give the general training of which we have heard this morning, so that when the great opportunity comes, we will not have to stand at the open door, and say, "I'd like to go in, but don't know enough." If they have the character and initiative and spiritual force needed, the schools should give the training.

I think we serve the world best through an organization. The best chance that Friends have to do their work in the world is through the Society of Friends, and so it seems to me that all our young people should find in our schools, training in loyalty to the best in our Society. The Y. M. C. A. is growing in many colleges, and is attracting loyalty. Our own Society should attract just such loyalty.

We should be trained for whatever we do. We can not have the training that George Fox had. He had a religious education the equal of which Woolman School can never give. For twenty years he heard long lectures weekly on theology. He was saturated with the Bible, and according to his friends, if it were destroyed, he could have reproduced it from beginning to end. He knew the religious history of the sects of the day. Whenever he heard of any sect, he went and found out about it. He knew the language of religions, their history and ideals. The young folks of today can not have such a training.

I want to urge the young people of the Society today to take time to study and training for leadership. Of course, we have to make a living, but one hundred years from now, it will mean nothing if you left an estate of $10,000 or $100.000, but it will mean much to civilization if you were able to interpret the message of Christianity! Think of the group of young people that Fox gathered and trained. Within ten years after Fox's vision on Pendle Hill, his followers had reached America, Austria and the Sultan of Turkey. That is the important thing that is before us—training for leadership in the Society of Friends.

You can not do more for yourselves and humanity than to take the three months of the kind of training we try to give at Woolman School. Business is important, living is important, but not as important as this. We must not rest on what has been accomplished. If God calls for us to preach we must be able to do it and not stand dumb.

In the discussion which followed, a number of Friends were heard briefly, regarding:—the necessity of maintaining Friends' Schools; teaching in the home; one pleaded for loyalty to Friends' Schools, and another for the public schools, that they should mean more to the community generally, and that they be made more Friendly. It was felt that to put education within the easy reach of all is the highest duty of the community.

The question was asked, "How many here have been or still are teachers?" A large number rose in response. The reply was equally gratifying when those who are expecting to take up that profession and are now preparing for it, were asked to rise.

Quakerism and Democracy

Frank Aydelotte, *President of Swarthmore College*

George Walton, presiding, said:— A Quaker college established one hundred years ago would have embodied the spirit of the eighteenth century. It would have had no music, art or science. Twentieth century Quakerism is showing a new and broader spirit,—a sense of obligation to human needs. It has broadened so that it transcends the narrow limits of sectarianism. It tries to translate the spirit of present-day Quakerism into actual fact. Twentieth Century Quakerism must have suitable leaders.

Before I went to Swarthmore I had thought much of a college which might embody the spirit of modern democracy. When we plan an educational system, we allow for growth; we do not want to embody only the moment. In planning for education for democracy, we want to consider what kind of education will minister best to the highest principle of democracy. If a college education is confined too narrowly to the idea of a single sect, it is narrowing.

My idea of a college education for democracy is one that keeps up communication for the future. Oxford kept up such communication because it dared to have dreamers—so may a Quaker college hold with the future. When I came to Swarthmore last year, I thought it part of my duty to study education in Quakerism. I find that there is a fundamental similarity between Quakerism in the religious sphere, and Democracy in the political sphere. In both there is a revolt against the setting apart of one man to lead.

The members of the Society of Friends chose as a religious ideal the ministry of all believers as opposed to the ministry of a small group especially trained for the priestly office. The Quaker ideal implies a whole group sharing with one another religious insight and inspiration in a manner that implies the highest degree of individual independence and responsibility.

The ideal of Democracy, in the political sphere, is somewhat similar,—the ideal of the rule of the whole people as opposed to government by a small, specially trained ruling class. It implies far more widespread responsibility and independence than is required in other forms of government.

Both Quakerism and Democracy have set for themselves high ideals, the key to the full realization of which lies in education. Both depend upon a very high level of character, ability, and training.

George Fox criticised education only as an insufficient means of leading the people to Christ. He advised Friends to set up schools, and they did so. Last year I visited the first meeting-house in Pennsylvania, at Merion, built about 1690. Part of the upper floor was set aside for a school. I am told that this was built like the meeting-houses in England of that time. The meeting-house and the school stood together in their estimate. Probably no single group has done more, or so much, for education as the members of this religious body. In the same way, democratic education has come to mean education for all.

In no other country is there so much given for education, in no other country are colleges so endowed, in no other country is there such a belief in education as in this new democracy, and that belief comes direct from the belief *in* democracy. There was not much difficulty in starting a system of elementary schools here. But there was a great struggle here in Indiana, at least, when it came to establishing high schools; that was different.

Both groups have laid special stress on elementary education, as was necessary, since both advocated the extension of educational privileges to people who had had them before. Both laid great stress on practical education, as was inevitable, for practical needs are first felt and must first be met; and both have laid much stress on making education universal, since only thus could their spiritual and political ideals be realized.

Education must be universal. That is the common ground of Friends and of democracies. Friends first established schools for themselves; then schools for poor children in the towns where they lived. Before the Civil War they were not content with helping negroes at the South, but started schools for them in the North. In New York, for instance, the schools were open to all races and colors, and when taken over by the city, were carried on in the same way.

Nevertheless, both groups have under-estimated the difficulty of the problem. Neither group has carried its educational training far enough, or made it fine enough.

De Tocqueville, a learned Frenchman who visited here once, and admired our institutions, said that we could not have the highest education for all, but it is better to sacrifice the few highest, and give all something.

I know there are countries in Europe that bring a few people up to a higher level than we bring any. Democracy must get to this level for the capable few without sacrificing the education of the many. I think that the first thing to do is not to improve the education of the masses, but to improve the chances of the few who have ability. I would educate all as far as they can go, and have ambition to go. Perhaps that is the next step in our democracy.

It is a common idea that universal education is incompatible with the highest educational standards; that nations and religious bodies must choose whether they will have education for all of a low quality, or a high quality of education for the few. The fact is that they must have both. The success of such religious ideals as those of the Quakers, or such political ideals as those of democracies, demands the education of all, each individual being carried to the highest point to which he can profitably go. These points will not all be equal. But there is no less necessity for the highest training of the best than there is for the adequate training of the masses.

The defect of universal education is this:— Our intellectual standards are set by the average. The pace is such as the average can attain. The very stimuli provided for persons of average intelligence and ability are a hindrance to those who have the will and the power to go further and faster. In our colleges we are sacrificing the best training of the best to the adequate training of the majority. We are giving valuable college training to as many men and women today as received high school training half a century ago. But, because we put all our students through the same regime, we are, in my opinion, sacrificing the best.

We take our college race-horses and work them at the plough with the others, and slow them down, and bring them to the level of the great majority. We have a plan for separating the race-horses from those who are average.

At Swarthmore College, as in a number of other colleges and universities, we are planning to remedy this situation by allowing students who wish and are able to do more work than the average to do it. We are not proposing to coddle a few at the expense of the many. As it is, we coddle the many. We propose to let these few take up the harder tasks, and if they succeed, we propose to give them degrees with suitable honors to mark their success. To these students we shall not apply the ordinary elaborate machinery of regulations, tests, etc., designed to curb the wayward and stir the laggard student; rather, we shall refuse to admit to this more difficult work any students except those who have the ability and the moral stamina and the ambition to do it for themselves. But having admitted them to read for honors, we shall leave them a far greater measure of freedom than is at present enjoyed by any of our undergraduates.

In making this provision for better training for our best minds, we shall, of course, not slacken any of our efforts with students of more modest ability. But in supplementing the work that we are doing with the average by this more intensive training for those who have the ability and ambition to undergo it, we are, I hope, doing something to meet one of the gravest educational problems alike of the Society of Friends and of our American Democracy.

(Round Table on this subject will be found in next issue.)

The Literary Digest's Postcard Vote

The *Literary Digest* claims to have sent ballots for a Prohibition poll to 38.7 per cent. of the electorate in New York State, including all telephone subscribers. But, according to William H. Anderson, State Superintendent of the Anti-Saloon League of New York, of the adults of voting age in the church congregations, only 6.7 per cent. received ballots, and of those having telephones only 18.6 per cent. received them.

Waiting until the *Digest's* announcement that the returns were all in, on September 13th the Anti-Saloon League of New York mailed to the 3,647 State pastors on its "working lists" (of denominations committed to prohibition and enforcement) a request that on Sunday, September 17th, each pastor at his most representative service count the adults of voting age present, the number of those having telephones, and of those who received the *Literary Digest* ballots.

Responses have come from 377 churches. In 63 no ballots were received. In 90 more only one or two were received. A very few have responded for more than one church. About the same number could not be counted because they gave merely a percentage without figures or reported "no ballots received" without reporting the voters present. This is as large a percentage of returns from pastors the first week as the *Digest* received on its ballots in about ten weeks after unparalleled advertising both paid and free. And as the *Digest* says on September 9th, "A careful balancing of the whole poll * * * justifies the * * * observation that 'variations and divergences have a way of neutralizing each other, and experts recognize that in the general average there is an indication of almost uncanny accuracy'."

These letters, the originals of which are on file in the New York office of the Anti-Saloon League and subject to inspection by any person having a legitimate interest, show that of 29,364 voters counted and reported as present by these hundreds of pastors, only 1,980 received *Literary Digest* ballots, as reported by the voters themselves, counted and transmitted by the pastors when the 38.7% claimed by the *Digest* would have reached 11,363 out of this number of church voters. There were 9,692 telephones reported, with 33 churches omitting this item. Using the average for those omitted, the total number of telephones from the churches reporting would be 10,622. That is, 17.4% (seventeen and four-tenths percent.) of THE CHURCH PART of the claimed 38.7% of New York State voters received ballots, and 18.6% (eighteen and six-tenths percent.) of the claimed total of telephone subscribers received them.

The Superintendent of the New York State Anti-Saloon League received no ballot, although there are both residence and office telephones in his own name and he is a subscriber to the *Literary Digest* and a book customer of the publishing house that issues it.

This statement ignores all discussion of the vagueness of the first question and the impropriety of the second one or the reasons why the drys might ignore what they believe to be an improper and at best an inconclusive poll whereas the wets have every incentive to make a showing, and is confined to the fundamental proposition that ballots utterly failed to reach dry and enforcement voters so they even had a chance to vote in anything like the claimed and advertised proportions.

Having proved by the laws of averages enthroned by the *Digest* itself that less than a fifth of the dry telephone subscribers of the State (the *Digest* claimed that the telephone lists gave the drys the better of it and diluted the vote with wet factory workers of foreign birth or extraction) actually received ballots, it is in order to call attention to an illuminating fact. Out of approximately a million ballots sent into New York State with the known outstanding drys of the several communities receiving only a small fraction of their proper proportion, with all the efforts of the wets, the combined wet votes show only 75,866 persons who took the trouble to get finally recorded in favor of either repeal or a nullification brand of modification, whereas with less than a fifth of those constituting the real dry strength receiving their quota of ballots, the vote was 30,204 against any change even in this so-called wet state.

Free the Seventy-six

(The following article, an editorial appearing in the New York *Evening Post*, Ninth 1st, 1922, is reprinted at the request of F. Ernest Johnson, Secretary of the Research Department of the Federal Council of the Churches of Christ in America.)

Was the United States ever in as dire danger from the enemy as Italy, France, England, or Belgium? Is there any reason why American political offenders should stay in jail longer than British, Belgian, Italian, or French political offenders? To state these questions is to answer them. We were never in as much danger as our allies. Our Government is safer now than are their Governments. Yet the United States continues to hold seventy-six political prisoners long after the jails of Western Europe have been cleared of such offenders.

Our allies issued general amnesty proclamations on the following dates: Italy, November 19, 1918; France, October 24, 1919; Belgium, October 31, 1919; Canada, December 30, 1919. British sentences were short and terminated soon after the armistice. "For nearly three years," to quote the Joint Amnesty Committee, "the United States has had the unenviable distinction of being the only country to keep prisoners of this [political] character in jail."

This is shame enough and argument enough; the case might be rested here. But the American people should know that all the German spies and agents imprisoned by our Government during the fevered days of the war have long since been released, and that the seventy-six remaining prisoners stand convicted not of deeds dangerous to life and property, but merely of expressions of opinion against the Government's course in the war. Their offences were not crimes *per se*, but actions not criminal in peace which became criminal by definition during an emergency long since passed. Common sense has struck the espionage act from the book of laws, but these men convicted under it get no relief thereby. Better for the seventy-six if they had actually run amuck, dynamiting and burning, instead of confining themselves to talk. The wreckers go free; the conversationalists remain in Leavenworth.

The fact that fifty-two of the seventy-six are I. W. W. members who refuse to sue for pardon individually ought not to weigh in the scales for or against release. Their refusal to plead is so much propaganda, but only the Government's harshness furnishes opportunity for that propaganda to win a sympathetic hearing. Whatever the attitude of the imprisoned individuals, all who are held simply on the ground of words uttered, written, or circulated four or five years ago, in the extraordinary circumstances of those distraught days, should be released forthwith. Keeping them in prison this long has been a mixture of cruelty and folly unparalleled in American history.

First-day School Methods

By Bliss Forbush

How To Reach New Scholars

It is useless, of course, to ask people to join our First-day School if we have not provided for their needs before hand. But taking for granted that the First-day School is fairly well graded, the lessons good, and the teachers regular in attendance and in the preparation of the day's work, how can we reach new people who have shown no desire to attend our School in the past? Every locality will have its different problems along this line, and its different answers, yet there are several methods that all our Schools might try with success.

New members must come either from the Meeting membership or from people outside its present range of influence. At first it is best to work for those within the influence of the Meeting itself and to branch out into wider fields later. It is better to provide first for the needs of our own people than to look after the needs of others.

The Superintendent of the School, and one or two others, ought to come together with a directory of the Meeting membership at hand, and go carefully over it, listing every one not already in a class, under the name of the class to which they would logically belong. Those who could not possibly attend because of age, or other similar reasons, need not be added, but all who might have the faintest chance of being interested should be included. Next, the Superintendent should write each member on this list a personal letter telling of the work of the class which he has in mind, what its teacher is trying to do, what special problems they have to work over, and invite the prospect to join the class and help with the work. The list should then be given to each teacher and they in their turn should write a brief invitation to the person and follow it up when ever possible with a personal call. This call should be made in a tactful manner, basing the proposition rather on the class's need of the new person, rather than his need of the class. The teacher must be the salesman, selling the course to the prospective member.

If the work of the Superintendent and Teacher do not bring results—and nothing must be forced—a class member may call and repeat the invitation, and perhaps offer to call the next First-day and go with the interested person to the School. This latter person should be responsible for the prospect assigned to them; he or she should call, and repeat the call; and if he is successful in having the new member go with him the older member must see that the latest arrival is introduced to the class individually, is made at home, and this especial welcome repeated for several weeks until the new member is fully conscious of how glad the class is to welcome him.

This method has been followed the past two years in our School with remarkably good results. Last year a number of new members joined because of these letters and personal visits; and this year another group whom we failed to get last year have responded and are joining enthusiastically in with our older members.

With the younger children of the Kindergarten and Primary grades it is best to have the work done by the Teacher, that is, all but the first letter which the Superintendent writes. She should visit the home of the child and explain to the mother what the class work consists of, who is in the class, and assure her that her little one will be made to feel perfectly at home. The argument most used by the parent of the stay-at-home child will be that it is impossible for her to take her child to and from the First-day School because of home cares or younger children. The teacher can meet this objection by volunteering to call and return the child herself, or to have someone else do so in whom the mother will have perfect confidence. Often some of the children in the older classes will undertake to call for one or two children each First-day, or the teacher may have one or two assistants who will help with this work. Each First-day a teacher of the Primary grades passes my home with four little children from different homes in tow, and below our house she adds two more, and goes around the corner to pick up I don't know how many more little tots. Surely we can follow her example.

In the Intermediate, Junior, and Senior Grades the personal work, after the letter of invitation and a visit of the teacher to the parents has taken place, can well be done by the scholars themselves. Boys and girls of these ages are often enthused about having their class grow in numbers, especially if a score, or competition is held. They will be perfectly willing to ask other children of their own age to join with them, and will stop by on their way to pick someone up. In two cases with which I have come in contact, the teacher of boys' classes of grammar and high school age, have gone to the home of every member of their classes before hand to see that the boys were up in time to eat their breakfast and be off to the First-day School; and one young friend, who taught a group of high school girls, made a practice of calling every one of them up on the phone in the morning to see that they were prepared to be present on time. True, many teachers will say that they are too busy for this kind of close personal work. But are they? If they take a class at all, with all the work it means in the preparation of lessons and being on hand, why not do a little more and make a tremendous success of it. How would you like to double or triple the size of your class? Many classes have done so, and you can do likewise.

The question of reaching people outside our own membership is more difficult because it is harder to find a method of approach. After this has been found, the treatment may be the same. For instance, if a new family has moved into your neighborhood, call on them and in a friendly way see if the parents would care to send their children to your First-day School, and come with them to an older class. Do not be afraid that they will think it proselyting on your part. You do not know whether they have any church connection or not. If they do have, they will tell you so and thank you for your friendly interest; if not, they may indeed be glad of the opportunity of having their children placed under your care, and to come and meet some pleasant people of their own age.

Where the entire family cannot be reached the children may be reached individually, and possibly the parents interested later. Ask your boys and girls to look about and see if there are not other children of their age who do not go to other churches whom they might interest. They will do this and often bring a companion to the class themselves. If they do, welcome this new member in a frank way and as soon as convenient call at the home and tell the parents that you are very glad to have their child become a member of your class and that you will look after him and report to them of his interest and progress. Do not make any effort at this time to interest others in the home, but quietly find out what other children are in the home and whether they go elsewhere to Sunday School or not. Treat each case separately and in time the matter of asking the parents to join an adult class may be taken up. If the child has enthused over the work of his class, the chances are that the parents may be glad to come, sometimes simply out of curiosity, and if they come it is up to you to make it so pleasant and worth while for them that they will be glad to return again.

Friendly News Notes

Letters from Dr. Joseph Swain received by his friends in the faculty tell that he and Mrs. Swain have been having a most enjoyable and interesting time in Japan. He is gradually returning to perfect health.

Eugene M. and Sarah R. Chambers, of Media, Penna., have announced the engagement of their daughter Edith Hazel to Charles Henry Craig, son of Mr. and Mrs. Ira N. Craig, of Dixmont, Maine.

Invitations are out for the wedding of Dorothy Ellinor Dilks, of Richmond, Indiana, and Dr. Elisha Roberts Richie, of Brewster, N. Y. The marriage will take place on Tenth month 14th, at the North A Street Meeting-house, Richmond, Indiana.

Friends will be glad to hear that Arthur Watts, who has been so long and dangerously ill with typhus, is now on the way to recovery and is at the Convalescent Home near Helsingfors, Finland. His mother and Rebecca Thompson, who has nursed him through this long and trying illness, are with him.

The last issue of *Friends' Fellowship Papers* gives a more optimistic view of the possibility of making "fresh effort to give *Friends' Fellowship Papers* a new lease of life." There were so many letters of regret, some of them containing definite promises of financial help, that a new start is to be made to put the publication on a stronger footing. Those interested in this work are trying to get 700 subscribers, who will pay promptly, and also to get donations of even small amounts to help wipe off their debt. For the information of those Friends who have not been in touch with *Friends' Fellowship Papers*, they are issued bi-monthly, at a cost to American subscribers of $1 per annum, post free. The American agent is Grace W. Blair, Media, Pa.

According to the London *Friend*, William Littleboy, at the meeting of the Young Friends' Central Committee, held at Birmingham recently, expressed the hope that a visitation of English Young Friends to America would take place next summer. We shall certainly be glad to have them come and if the visitors who have come from the older group are a criterion, we have a treat in store for us.

Did the pioneer Friends believe that there was anything sacred in high places, or was it an outcropping of the suppressed instinct for beauty that led them to locate their meeting-houses in such scenic places? The pilgrims who climbed the hill to the old Randolph Meeting-house outside of Dover, N. J., on First-day, Tenth month 1st, felt the impression of the spirit that guided their ancestors to this location.

The house is maintained by an Historical Association. Two of the members, both of whom are descendants of Friends, Eugene Carroll and Charles Brotherton, welcomed the visitors. Among others who contributed to the meeting were Grace T. Warren, J. Barnard Walton, Margaret Vail, Jane Washburn, Edith Palmer, and Edward D. Hutchinson.

The spirit of the pioneer Friends certainly has a message which is timely today.

BALTIMORE NEWS

Our First-day School opened in a most enthusiastic manner, one hundred and ten teachers and scholars being on hand. Tho some of our classes lost members to distant schools and colleges, the loss was more than made up by other people who enrolled for the first time. We started our competitive contest which this year is to be in the form of a transcontinental auto race and all seem very much interested in it.

The work of the Home Department begins this week and will be a study of the Old Testament as taken up in the Bible Class of the regular school. A mimeographed lesson sheet will be sent to the Home Department members each week covering the work for that time.

Last Fifth-day the Queens of Avalon held a reunion at the home of one of the girls. Many were the tales told of summer camps and travels. The boys' clubs are also getting under way, the younger ones going down to Camp Keewadin over Sixth-day night.

Tho the News Letter put out by the Monthly Meeting's Advisory Committee is a local affair, we have had a number of people outside our Meeting express a desire to receive it regularly. To meet these requests, the Committee has decided to send the News Letter to anyone interested in the same on payment of the cost of publishing, which is one dollar a year. Send names and checks to Bliss Forbush, Park Avenue and Laurens Street.

YOUNG FRIENDS AT RICHMOND

Many of the accounts of Richmond mention the contribution which the young Friends made to the conference this year. There were young Friends there in larger numbers than there have been at previous conferences and the meetings no doubt gained in interest and vitality because of this fact. However the young Friends at Richmond not only gave but received. It would be hard to state what had been the individual benefit derived from such an experience. But the young Friends as a whole profited in certain definite ways, and they ought to know what happened there.

For some time there has been felt a need for a closer amalgamation of young Friends in all our Yearly Meetings, and for a better co-operation between this group and the Central Committee. In order to discuss these two needs a mass meeting of all young Friends was called early in the conference. A definite proposition, made by the Chairman in his opening address, was brought to this meeting. In brief his plan was: to have a committee of representative young Friends incorporated in the Central Committee. The young Friends approved this plan in general and left it to a smaller committee to work out the details with the Chairman of the Central Committee. The following plan was adopted: to increase the number of the Central Committee from 100 to 125, the extra 25 to be elected proportionately by the Young Friends' Movements in six of our Yearly Meetings; these 25 to be elected at the Yearly Meeting nearest to the holding of the Biennial Conference, and to serve for two years. Twenty-five young Friends selected at the conference were made members of the Central Committee at that time.

Also it should be known that three young Friends are members of the Executive Committee of the Central Committee. It is hoped that in this way the young Friends will feel that they have an active and integral part to play in the business of the Society.

A large part of the benefit received by the young people at the conference was the inspiration and encouragement they were given to enter a practically new field of service. The problem of uniting all branches of Friends in America was directly and bravely faced by the Conference. It was felt that this task falls peculiarly to the young Friends who are learning the lessons of tolerance and love, the two most-stressed principles of Christianity at this time. The necessity for the strength that is in unity is felt most strongly by those on whom the world problems weigh so heavily just now. This problem in our own Society summons all the spiritual strength that is in us. That is why young Friends are particularly grateful for all that the Richmond Conference has done for them. E. A. W.

CHILD WELFARE WORK

The Child Welfare Committee of Philadelphia Yearly Meeting now has on file in the Central Bureau, 154 N. 15th Street, Philadelphia, literature on subjects relating to Child Welfare work. This literature will be forwarded to Friends if they will write to the Bureau expressing their needs and desires.

This Committee has also arranged with various organizations to provide speakers for communities desiring to hold public meetings to consider phases of Child Welfare work. Such meetings are essential to make people realize the need of organized effort to make the coming generation stronger physically, mentally and morally. Through the Home Economics Department of State College, Pennsylvania, through the National Committee on Visiting Teachers and through the Public Education and Child Labor Association of Pennsylvania, speakers can be obtained for this work. Hannah F. Perrott, Executive Secretary of the Child Welfare Committee, 459 Winona Avenue, Germantown, will take pleasure in arranging for speakers. Friends must remember, however, that these speakers are in demand and as much time as possible should be given in which to make the arrangement.

The material which is on file at the Central Bureau has been procured from the Public Education and Child Labor Association of Pennsylvania, the Pennsylvania State College Extension Department, the Child Health Organization of America and the National Committee on Visiting Teachers.

GEORGE SCHOOL NOTES

George School opened for the 30th/year on the 12th and 13th of this month, with 128 boys and 123 girls as boarding students. There were also 30 day students from the neighborhood. About 55 per cent. of these are children of Friends, an increase of 10 per cent. over the previous year.

The number of students has been somewhat increased the last two years. The financial conditions of 1920 and 1921 prevented the completion of the campaign for the additional endowment of $500,000.00 and the number of students had to be increased to avert financial disaster. The buildings are crowded but the freshly painted walls and new floors in dormitory rooms give great satisfaction.

In order to make it easier for the students to keep their rooms in order hardwood floors were laid last summer on the second floor of Drayton Hall and the Main Building. The upper floors will be completed as finances permit.

In addition to the regular college preparatory curriculum a short curriculum is now offered. In quantity it requires 25 per cent. less work, but in quality, the same. It conforms to the minimum requirement of the State of Pennsylvania for a first class High School diploma, but does not entitle one to a recommendation to college. It is not open to all students, but only to those who, in the Principal's judgment, should not undertake the long curriculum.

A large class is studying Quakerism with George A. Walton as teacher.

Ethel Brinton Phillips, Pomeroy, Pennsylvania, a member of Caln Quarterly Meeting and a graduate of Smith College, is now teaching Bible and English in the place of Edith M. Winder, who has gone to Woolman School as hostess. Alfred J. Wright, a graduate of George School, and the University of Michigan and a member of Indiana Yearly Meeting, is teacher of English and Civics. Other additions to the faculty are Marion Vincent, of Barnard College, French and Spanish, and Rebecca Townsend, Yale School, Youngstown, Ohio, teacher of fundamental processes. Students of ability who have not mastered the fundamental processes of spelling, reading, writing, figuring and grammatical analysis will receive special instruction instead of their regular class work.

The new Director of Athletics is Stanley B. Sutton, formerly of Virginia Polytechnic Institute and Germantown Academy. He is organizing the boys so that all will receive the discipline of athletic exercise.

Under direction of S. Wynne Keever, a class in newspaper work has been formed, which will publish a weekly newspaper of George School life.

Student participation in government has been extended by the election of a student council of five girls and five boys. They are to co-ordinate and support the dormitory government associations, authorize other student activities, and labor for the best development of individual students. The chairman is Garrett Kirk. Other members are Thomas G. Best, Edith Branson, Gardiner DeCou, Barbara Jenkins, Sarah E. Percy, J. Roland Pennock, Earl T. Potts, Barbara B. Sayen and Edna M. Shoemaker.

Eleanor M. Peters, of the class of 1921, won the State competitive scholarship to college from Adams County, Pennsylvania, and is now at Gettysburg College. She took competitive examinations with over a thousand applicants from all counties of the State. Her marks ranked fourth in this State-wide competition.

GEORGE A. WALTON.

Items from Everywhere

According to the *Dearborn Independent*, only 16 out of 142 institutions in the United States formerly known as "drink cures" are now conducting a business similar to that which they pursued before the advent of national prohibition of the liquor traffic.

Fire Prevention Week which is being celebrated October 2-9, has been endorsed by the President of the United States and the governors of virtually every State in the Union. Fires in the United States average one a minute. Last year the burning rate rose to a staggering total of $485,000,000. More than 15,000 lives are lost each year by fire, most of the victims being women and little children. A large percentage of this loss of life and property is due to ignorance and carelessness.

The *Press Bulletin* of the Philippine Commission of Independence reports Edwin Denby, Secretary of the Navy, as saying in his parting statement before sailing for home, "To me, judging from what I have seen here, Manila, and the surrounding country, appears to be keeping well up with the best of our cities in the United States. The schools are excellent and so are the roads and other developments upon which all good cities pride themselves. I shall never forget my welcome at the University of Philippines and the quick intelligence of the students. They will have a far-reaching influence over the future of their own country and of all the Orient."

In view of this statement, does it not seem as if it were time for America to fulfill its pledge of self-government when the people showed they were ready for it?

THE OPEN FORUM

This column is intended to afford free expression of opinion by readers on questions of interest. The INTELLIGENCER is not responsible for any such opinions. Letters must be brief, and the editor reserves the right to omit parts if necessary to save space.

FRIENDS' SCHOOLS

To the Editor:

R. P. K in THE INTELLIGENCER of Ninth month 16th, calls attention to the desirability of extending the influence of the publications and of the schools and colleges of our Society. I agree with all that R. P. K. has said, and would emphasize one phase of Friends' Schools; viz., the teaching of respect for women.

Friends were pioneers in considering women to be the equals of men. Meeting business was effected only when approved by the women. In religious meetings, women had the same rights and the same considerations as men.

It was quite natural, therefore, that Friends' schools and that Swarthmore and Earlham Colleges should be co-educational, and that Friendly boards of trustees should be composed of both women and men.

All of which results in an educational system that considers the boy and the girl of equal value and of equal ability. The boy who goes to such a school and college has a respect for girls that is not easily gotten in any other way.

There comes a natural friendship, as in a family where there are boys and girls. There is better understanding between the two sexes, and I believe the men from Friends' Colleges have the greatest respect for women.

Among Friends generally there is less romancing and more real love. Marriages are almost without exception happy—due, I believe, to the fact that the husband considers his wife as his equal. Even in this year of political freedom, the men of the world need to be taught respect for women.

Therefore, for the good of a Nation, as well as the strength of our Society, I urge we help extend the number and the size of Friends' Schools and Colleges.

New York, N. Y. W. W. J.

REGARDING THE VOLSTEAD ACT

To the Editor:

Your note, which is first on the page of your issue of Ninth month 23d, suggests a query.

When and how was it made a crime to sell liquor?

Was the writer ignorant of the lawful right to sell liquor under definite regulations as permitted by the law?

The apparent desire to punish the man who sells liquor may be inspired by a sincere opinion that all liquor is unfit for consumption as food or stimulant.

May a man who has used liquor of all kinds as a tonic, prescribed by his physician, venture to assert that it was always beneficial to him, and in his opinion to a large majority of persons who used it.

Persons who commit crimes while under the influence of the intemperate use of liquor should not be regarded as any less guilty. Temperance in all meats and drinks is a virtue, and intoxication is a crime.

Total abstinence from any food or drink which is known to be injurious to any person should be practiced by the individual, and an amendment to the Constitution may be thought justifiable to restrain individuals in the dangerous exercise of their freedom, but there are still honest objections to what are known as sumptuary laws.

Selling liquor to any intoxicated person is a crime, and was so defined many years before the *crime-provoking* statute known as the Volstead Law was enacted, but public opinion prevents complaints being made in legal form.

Honest liquor dealers were driven out of their legitimate business by a law which has resulted in stimulating persons to supply the wants of hypocrites and cowards, who want liquor, and do not care who breaks the law.

If intoxication was punished as a serious crime, and no consideration or sympathy was shown to the intemperate, some crimes might be prevented.

It has been my good fortune to have friends who sold liquor to those who had a right to buy it, until the Eighteenth Amendment interfered with the proper right of every person to eat and drink without injuring himself or his neighbor.

Much more might be said, and you need not fear that I am ignorant of the danger which must be avoided by the temperate use of all food and drink containing stimulants.

Total abstinence is the safe remedy for the tendency to excessive indulgence, but legal restraint has been clearly shown to be ineffective, and *crime-provoking* to a dangerous extent. FRED P. GORDON.

Pleasantville, N. Y.

BIRTHS

BROSIUS—On Ninth month 22nd, to Malcolm Acker and May Whittaker Brosius, a daughter, named Ruth Elizabeth.

HOOD—Near West Grove, Pa., on Seventh month 20th, to Brinton L. and Anna Pusey Hood, a son, named Robert Chambers Hood.

MARRIAGES

MAMMEL—KESTER—In Newtown Friends' Meeting-house, on Ninth month 23rd, under care of Makefield Monthly Meeting, Albert Conard Mammel, of North Wales, Pa., and Lucretia Mott Kester, daughter of Reuben P. and Myrtle Kester, of Newtown.

DEATHS

BARTON—At Haddonfield, N. J., on Ninth month 24th, Sarah Barton, aged 78 years.

LAWRENCE—At Rancocas, on Ninth month 4th, Rebecca Evans, widow of Thomas Lawrence, in her 84th year. A birthright member of Haddonfield Monthly Meeting and an elder for several years.

PRICE—At his home in Punta Gorda, Florida, on Ninth month 19th, Benjamin D. Price, formerly of Philadelphia, aged 77. Interment in the local cemetery.

WALTER—At Swarthmore, Pa., on Ninth month 25th, Emeline S., widow of William H. Walter.

COMING EVENTS

TENTH MONTH

6th—An unusual opportunity to hear the Rt. Hon. Sir Gilbert Parker, Bart., is offered under the auspices of the Somerville Forum. The lecture on "The World—Whither Now?" will be given at Swarthmore College, at 8 p. m. Cards, $1. Sir Gilbert Parker was for eighteen years a leading Member of Parliament and was head of American Publicity for England during the war. He is a distinguished British novelist and publicist.

7th—Farmington Half-Yearly Meeting, at Farmington, N. Y.

8th—Scipio Half-Yearly Meeting, at Scipio, N. Y.

8th—Philadelphia Quarterly Meeting's Visiting Committee will visit Radnor Meeting at 3 p. m.

8th—Conference Class at 15th and Race Streets, Philadelphia, at 11.40 a. m., at the close of the meeting for worship. Subject—Prophets of Pagan Religion. Leader—Charles H. Harrison.

9th—Opening meeting of the P. Y. F. A., 15th and Cherry Streets, at 8 p. m. Selections from Plays, Songs and Folk Dances.

11th—Annual Meeting of the Young Friends' Aid Association, at Friends' Seminary, 226 East 16th Street, New York, at 8 p. m.

15th—Brooklyn First-day School will re-open.

16th—Easton and Granville Half-Yearly Meeting, at Easton, N. Y., at 11 a. m. Meeting of Ministry and Counsel at 10 a. m.

21st—Concord First-day School Union will be held at Concord Meeting-house. See Notice.

21st—Pelham Half-Yearly Meeting, at Sparta, Ont. See Notice.

21st—Trip to Germantown for benefit of Building Fund of Neighborhood Guild. See advertisement.

NOTICE—Concord First-day School Union will be held on Tenth 21st, at 10 a. m. and 1.30 p. m. The morning session will be occupied with reports from the summer schools, the report of the Committee on Field Secretary and a report of Vesta Haines' summer work, followed by discussion. Lunch at 12.

At 1.30 there will be an opening song by Concord First-day School, followed by reports of Delegates and various committees. Concord First-day School will give a dramatization of a Bible story, which will be followed by a talk by Vesta Haines.

A cordial invitation is extended to delegates from the other Unions. Concord Friends will meet busses on the Wilmington and West Chester line before 10 a. m. and 1.30 p. m., if so requested. Please drop a card to Bertha L. C. Darlington, Darling, Pa.

NOTICE—Pelham Half-Yearly Meeting was changed from Eighth month 19th to Tenth month 21st, at Sparta, Ontario, due to the holding of Yearly Meeting in Eighth month.

American Friends' Service Committee

WILBUR K. THOMAS, EX. SEC.

20 S. 12th St. Philadelphia.

CASH CONTRIBUTIONS

WEEK ENDING SEPTEMBER 25TH.

Five Years Meetings	$175.40
Other Meetings:	
Ladies' Aid of Dayton Friends' Church	7.00
Friends at Coldstream, Canada	10.00
Salem Monthly Meeting	50.00
Green Street Monthly Meeting	10.00
Cornwall Monthly Meeting	10.75
New Garden Preparative Meeting	36.00
Minneapolis Monthly Meeting	11.25
Contributions for Germany	22.25
For Austria	1,009.75
For Poland ($4,000.00 of this to go to Jewish Organization. Money in transit)	4,165.25
For Russia	953.90
Russian Overhead	17.00
For General	119.60
For Clothing	35.00
German Overhead	8.02
For Armenia	.25
Refunds	61.14
	$6,702.56

Shipments received during week ending September 23rd: 75 boxes and packages; 1 from Mennonites.

WANTED

WANTED—A POSITION AS COMPANION, care of invalid or housekeeper. Address Y. 360, Friends' Intelligencer.

REFINED MIDDLE-AGED MAN AND wife desire position as caretakers of home or position of trust. Best references given. Address C. 380, Friends' Intelligencer.

HOUSEKEEPER WANTED—FAMILY of two. A good home in a country town. Reference desired. Chas. S. Pyle, Rising Sun, Md.

WANTED—MIDDLE-AGED WOMAN to help care for invalid; also assist with light housekeeping. Three adults. Address Louisa T. Wright, Newtown, Pa.

BOY 15 WANTS PLACE ON FARM AS general chore boy, good bed and board and one dollar a week. Answer C. 381, Friends' Intelligencer.

WANTED—BY AN ELDERLY WOMAN, experienced, a position with light household duties or care of invalid. Apply 910 Clinton Street, Philadelphia.

WANTED—TWO EXPERIENCED girls, one for child's nurse or mother's helper, other for housework. Good wages. G. L. Cowan, Edgewater Park, New Jersey.

WOMAN OF REFINEMENT SEEKS position as companion to lady living alone, or managing housekeeper in widower's home where kindness and interest would be appreciated. Reference. Address D. 382, Friends' Intelligencer.

MAN AND WIFE DESIRE POSITION in a home of elderly couple; capable of taking full charge. Experienced in care of invalid. Address S. 383, Friends' Intelligencer.

WOMAN OF MIDDLE AGE, NURSE, wants care of invalid. Address P. 374, Friends' Intelligencer.

WANTED—MIDDLE-AGED WOMAN for general housework in country. Three in family. Address Friends' Intelligencer, M. 384.

GRADE TEACHER (FRIEND) DEsires position. Address Friends' Intelligencer, H. 385.

FOR RENT

FOR RENT—SEVERAL PLEASANT rooms. Willing to serve breakfast. Business men preferred. Mrs. Elizabeth B. Champion, 4911 Royal Street, Germantown. Telephone, Wyoming 4426-M.

FOR RENT—PRIVATE ADULT family have two pleasant furnished rooms near train and trolley. 6336 Jefferson Street, Germantown.

Apartment Without Cost!

Ivy Lodge, 29 East Penn Street, Germantown.

Attractive unfurnished apartment, 2 rooms, sleeping porch and bath, with light and heat included, to be let, preferably to a man and wife in return for partial service.

Man to care for furnace and hot water heater, woman to prepare simple breakfast at cost for 12 teachers, and to perform a few other simple housekeeping duties.

Apply to Emma Thorp, Germantown Friends' School. Phone Germantown 4020.

To the Lot Holders and others interested in Fairhill Burial Ground:

GREEN STREET Monthly Meeting has funds available for the encouragement of the practice of cremating the dead to be interred in Fairhill Burial Ground. We wish to bring this fact as prominently as possible to those who may be interested. We are prepared to undertake the expense of cremation in case any lot holder desires us to do so.

Those interested should communicate with William H. Gaskill, Treasurer of the Committee of Interments, Green Street Monthly Meeting, or any of the following members of the Committee.

William H. Gaskill, 3201 Arch St.
Samuel N. Longstreth, 1218 Chestnut St.
Charles F. Jenkins, 232 South Seventh St.
Stuart S. Graves, 3833 Germantown Ave.

ADVERTISING RATE in the FRIENDS' INTELLIGENCER, for Help Wanted, Positions Wanted, Rooms for Rent, Notices, and other classified advertisements without display, for each insertion, 2 cents per word, including name, initials and address. Answers may be sent to a box at the INTELLIGENCER office, if so directed.

For display advertising the rate is 10 cents per agate line, or $1.40 per column inch, each insertion. On ten or more insertions in a year from date of order, ten per cent. discount. Thus a four-inch single-column or two-inch double-column advertisement costs $5.60 each insertion, less ten per cent., or 5.04 net each time for ten or more insertions. Matter may be changed whenever desired, without extra charge.

Experience has proved the INTELLIGENCER to be a remarkably good advertising medium. All advertisements must "pass the censor!"

Address 140 N. 15th St., Philadelphia

The Friends'
Intelligencer

ESTABLISHED 1844 | TENTH MONTH 14, 1922 | VOLUME 79 NUMBER 41

Contents

THE FRIENDS' INTELLIGENCER

Published weekly, 140 N. 15th Street, Philadelphia, Pa., by Friends' Intelligencer Association, Ltd.

SUE C. YERKES, *Managing Editor.*

Editorial Board: Elizabeth Powell Bond, Thomas A. Jenkins, J. Russell Smith, George A. Walton.

Board of Managers: Edward Cornell, Alice Hall Paxson, Paul M. Pearson, Annie Hillborn, Elwood Hollingshead, William C. Biddle, Charles F. Jenkins, Edith M. Winder, Frances M. White.

Officers of Intelligencer Associates: Ellwood Burdsall, Chairman; Bertha L. Broomell, Secretary; Herbert P. Worth, Treasurer.

Subscription rates: United States, Mexico, Cuba and Panama, $2.50 per year. Canada and other foreign countries, $3.00 per year. Checks should be made payable to Friends' Intelligencer Association, Ltd.

Entered as Second Class Matter at Philadelphia Post Office.

FUN

One of the advantages of living on Long Island is that on one side of the island you SEE the SOUND and on the other HEAR the SEA.—*New York World.*

The Friends' Intelligencer

The religion of Friends is based on faith in the "INWARD LIGHT," or direct revelation of God's spirit and will in every seeking soul.
The INTELLIGENCER is interested in all who bear the name of Friends in every part of the world, and aims to promote love, unity and intercourse among all branches and with all religious societies.

ESTABLISHED 1844 | PHILADELPHIA, TENTH MONTH 14, 1922 | VOLUME 79 NUMBER 41

The Need for Quakerism

(The following editorial was published in the Friends' Intelligencer and Journal, of Fourth month 20th, 1895. Though written more than twenty years ago, we feel its message is quite as timely now as when it was written.)

"There never was greater need for Quakerism than there is today," was the energetic exclamation of a young woman whose earnest spirit had been stirred by a revelation of some of the weaknesses and corruptions of modern society. Quakerism, in her estimation, stood for what is right; not what is expedient. For courage of conviction; not a weak submission to incipient evil. For love and forbearance, not hatred and strife. For cheerful obedience to those in authority; not rebellion against wholesome rule. For good taste and simplicity; not dead conformity or display. For neat, tasteful homes; not ostentatious mansions. For wholesome recreations; not corrupting diversions. For cordial hospitality; not elaborate entertainments. For honesty and fair dealing; not injustice and avarice. For moderation in all things; not extravagance in many things. For pure every-day living; not spasmodic goodness. For broad, cultured minds and warm hearts; not selfish intellectualism and coldness. For self-respecting aid to the needy; not demoralizing charity. For simplicity in worship; not formality and grandeur. For sincerity and freedom in belief; not cant and narrowness. For toleration; not assuming judgment. For the inward revelation of truth; not dependence upon dogmatic theology. For faith in God and the divine Christ in men; not faith alone, or works alone, but both combined.

Do these things represent true Quakerism? Then is there need for it. And however we who profess it may fall short of this ideal, we believe it to be the true standard towards which we all should aim. And countless are the Friends of the past—many of them obscure, self-denying heroes—against whose characters, judged by this formula, could be placed the record, "well done." And shall there not be a succession in the line of these Christ-like lives? If the world needs us, what right have we to falter and to think others can do our work? Let us renew our strength and welcome the young, whose fresh inspiration and zeal—though these may need the directing hand of the experienced in many ways—will infuse new life. A little band, compared to the vast numbers of many of the religious bodies, yet if "the neighborhood was once shaken for miles around" by its influence, it may be again. Let us have faith and courage, remembering it is the Lord that "strengthened the weak hands," that "confirmed the feeble knees," and his promise is over us all now as in the olden time.

LYDIA H. HALL.

⌘

Everywhere as we go about through the country at this season of the year, we see the dark purple clusters of the Concord grapes hanging from the green-leaved arbors in beautiful profusion, but as we enjoy at our tables their delicious flavor, we seldom stop to think of the patient work which developed this luscious grape from its wild ancestor. The man who painstakingly chose the earliest and best of the wild fruit, planted the seed, and again waited and took the best, gave to the country a material contribution of great value and along with it an ethical thought which in the hurry and flurry of this work-a-day world, it is all too easy to overlook. He watched for the best and took that to perpetuate. Do we watch for the best in our fellow human beings and strive to develop that, passing by the things which we do not like. Would not this method, practiced with love and patience, bring a new era to humanity?

A. H. P.

⌘

Are we as much in earnest about getting ourselves in shape to co-operate with others as we are about demanding that they be ready to co-operate with us?

⌘

It may not be a sin to be pious, but we verily believe it is a sin to be merely pious. We dare not be ignorant of the great Christian movements of the world.—*Edgar L. Killam.*

Jesus in the Temple

By O. Edw. Janney

It was early morning in Nazareth. For weeks the family of Jesus, with their relatives and friends, had been looking forward to going up to Jerusalem to the great annual feast and holiday, the Passover, and now they were ready to start on their journey.

In accordance with the custom of the Hebrews the boy, now twelve years of age, had been taught the main points of Jewish history. He was familiar with the stories of Abraham, Isaac and Jacob and had been given a good knowledge of the Hebrew Scriptures.

He knew that Moses had led his people out of Egyptian slavery and through the Arabian deserts to the Promised Land. From the hills above Nazareth he had seen the great plain of Sharon sweeping westward to the sea. To the north the mountains rose in terraces until crowned by the cedars of Lebanon. To the south two paths led to the wonderful City of Jerusalem. One of these followed the valley through which flowed the River Jordan, and then at Jericho turned steeply to the west to the city. The other, more direct, followed its rough course over the hills and vales to its destination.

It was along one of these roads that the company with which Jesus traveled wended their slow and tedious way. There can be no doubt that he, who had never before been many miles from home, viewed everything with keen interest.

As they drew near to the great city other companies joined theirs, many of them having come from a great distance, with strange garb and language.

Much had been told Jesus of the City of Jerusalem towards which they were journeying. He knew its history, its many thousands of population, its palaces and public buildings and its central mount crowned by the beautiful Temple.

It was not long after arrival in the city that Jesus, not attracted, as other boys would have been, by the strange sights of the town, found his way to the precincts of the Temple. While wandering about among its many courts and buildings he heard the murmur of voices and, drawing nearer to this sound, he saw before him a room, open to the sky and furnished with rugs on which a group of some twenty men were sitting or reclining.

They were men gathered together from many widely separated parts of the country, who took advantage of the Passover to hold a conference on subjects of religious significance. There were some among them of middle age, but for the most part they were old and reverend in appearance.

As the boy Jesus looked through the archway that led into the court where these men were holding converse, he could not help hearing some of their words and these at once caught his attention, for they were talking about holy things, which, from very early years had had a deep attraction for him. So he at once realized that from these men he might get the knowledge which he was seeking. For already, altho only twelve years old, he had begun to have visions of the work that lay before him and for which he was beginning to prepare himself.

It is a beautiful picture that we have of him as he stands in the sunlight of the archway, hesitating whether to draw near to the wise men in the court. Tall for his age and dressed in the simple garb of a Jewish boy of the time, his beautiful face glowing with eagerness, his large dark eyes beaming with intelligence and his rich auburn hair thrown back in wavy masses from his broad white brow.

Attracted by the voices and the interest that he felt in the subjects that were being discussed, the boy drew nearer and nearer to the group. The men noticed him but made no objection to his approach. At length he found himself sitting close to one of the younger men whose appearance attracted him, and for awhile he listened quietly to the conversation of the men. At a pause in the discussion Jesus gently touched the arm of the man who was near him and said:

"I heard you talking about God. Can you tell me where He lives?"

"Oh, yes," was the reply, "We can tell where he lives." The others had heard the question and the reply and listened in silence while the speaker continued, meanwhile looking with interest at the boy who had asked the question.

"Dost thou see that blue sky overhead? Well, that we call the firmament, and above that is heaven where God dwells in the midst of glory and surrounded by companies of bright angels who minister to Him. We know how wonderful and glorious it is because at night there are spots where the light shines through and we call these places stars. Up there is where God lives."

The boy looked very thoughtful for a moment and then said:

"My fathers, may I say how it seems to me?" The men looked a little startled at this, for they were altogether unused to having boys at their council, but his face was so eager and his manner so respectful that the oldest man in the group said, "Speak on, my son," and Jesus then spoke as follows:

"Sometimes, when I have been out on the hills

"Oh, he will come in great clouds of glory, with multitudes of angels all about him. There will be a loud sound of trumpets and the souls of all men will quake with fear at his majesty and power. And the good he will gather together, but the wicked he will utterly destroy and cast into destruction. He will sweep away the Roman power and reign over all the kingdoms of the earth, and the hearts of all his enemies will melt with fear of the ruthless destruction that will await them."

Hearing a sob, the men looked at the boy, and to their surprise they saw tears rolling down his face, which was full of sorrow. One of them called the boy to him and asked what was the trouble. Then he said, "Oh, I had thought of the Messiah coming in such a different way from that which you have described. I thought of him coming as a little child and growing up among his people, finally to become their leader. I thought of him as one who would be kind to all, even his enemies, if he should have any, and gain his kingdom by winning the hearts of all and not as you describe."

"If he should come that way," said the man who had last spoken, "that would be a terrible disappointment to everyone, for all look for him to come as a powerful ruler. Boy, should he come as thou sayest, how would we know him to be the Messiah?"

"I am only a child," said Jesus, "and do not know much, whilst you are good and wise, but may it not be that when he comes and moves about among the people, he will be so filled with goodness and wisdom, and his talks to the people will show a wisdom that is higher than that of other men, that they will recognize him as the Messiah? And if, perhaps, he would have power given him to heal the sick and lame, would not this show who he was? And now I remember that once in our home in Nazareth, my father read to us children these words from our Scriptures: 'The spirit of the Lord is upon me, because He anointed me to preach good tidings to the poor; He hath sent me to proclaim release to the captives, and recovering of sight to the blind, to set at liberty them that are bruised.' And he would talk of love and show the people how to live together in peace and with good-will to all, and not wish to destroy the wicked but to save them. Oh, I think all would know that this is the Messiah."

In such discourse the time passed rapidly, and when the eventide had come, one of the men took the boy to his home and took care of him. And so a day or two passed and one morning Jesus saw his parents standing in the archway and beckoning to him.

He went to them at once and his mother said, "We have been looking for thee everywhere. Thy father and I have sought thee, sorrowing."

"Why did you not come to the Temple at once? Wist ye not that I would be in my Father's house and about my Father's business?"

And soon they took up their journey along the road to Nazareth, and though their feet grew weary their souls were aglow with the consciousness of the immediate presence of God.

Poems of War-time

Book Review

By Henry Ferris

One of the interesting memorials of the Great War is a dainty little volume of poems and reminiscences of travel by Margaret Cope, a Friend of Germantown, just published by the John C. Winston Company, Philadelphia, (75 cents). The poems include "Pictures from the Pyrenees," and "Cathedral Reveries," written while the author was traveling in France and Italy in 1914, just before the outbreak of the war. They are followed by an interesting prose account of her terrible journey from Italy to England after war was declared. Then comes another collection of poems, "Seven Years After," largely descriptive of English life and scenery, written after a second journey to Europe in 1921.

The poems are pervaded throughout by deep religious feeling, as shown by one of the "Pictures from the Pyrenees," entitled

Light and Shade

The western light is flooding all the vale
While round me shadows deepen,
And the cliffs on either side
A frame-work make to scenes beyond.

So may we, when God His picture paints,
Of light and shade, be patient in the shadow
And content to be a frame-work to our brother's joy,
Knowing His Sun will shine upon us in the morn.

The religious feeling is beautifully expressed also in another of the "Pictures from the Pyrenees," entitled

On the Mountain

The blooming chestnuts cast their shadows o'er me,
The mountain air is blowing in my face;
Father, I thank Thee that the way before me
Is lighted by Thy love in every place.

In light and shade Thou paintest well Thy picture
With skilful hand, nor makest a mistake;
Can we not trust that Master hand, whose nature
Knows well from first to last what tints to make?

The flowers bright are blooming mid the grasses,
The grasses tall are blowing in the wind,
The light falls softly down the mountain passes
Casting blue shade from trees: Ah! who so blind
That cannot see God's hand in all the picture
The Master stroke that gives the touch divine
Painting it well, that every human creature
May look and love—and worship at His shrine.

Another poem, entitled, "The Quiet Hour," written on "Sunday morning, July 5th, 1914," seems to convey in a peculiar degree the Quaker spirit of worship:

The Quiet Hour

Father, I thank Thee that the morning light
Is soft with shadows blue,
I thank Thee for the snowy mountain height,
And valleys drenched in dew.

The blooming chestnuts on my wayside path,
The bracken and the grass,
The little clouds that fleck the morning sky
And let the shadows pass.

The rivulet pouring from its mountain spring
Still babbling o'er its stones,
The birds above, that still Thy praises sing
Who all creation owns.

Thine is the kingdom, and the power is Thine
And Glory over all!
And we whose hearts are tuned to thoughts divine
Listen—to hear Thy call.

The almost incredible difficulties and terrors of the author's journey from Italy to England are lightened by occasional touches of humor. On arriving at Aosta she found a friend awaiting her. "Finding that a private car was quite beyond my means," she writes, the bank refusing to honor my "letter of credit," I engaged the last seat on, I think, the last trip of the public motor to the old Hospice of the Grand St. Bernard.

The "diligence" there had ceased running, all men having been mobilized, but I found two English ladies—one New Zealander—who with me procured a conveyance, down as we hoped, into the little village of Orsieres, by misty moonlight. Half way down we were turned out in perfect darkness; but I bethought me of my luggage in a separate van, and with some trouble regained it—my hot-water-bag being an object of suspicion to the Custom House officials who held it up, exclaiming gruffly, "Was ist das?" On the way down a burly Swiss who had boarded the front seat of our carriage, fell off half-drunk—I hope at his home—and from there on, everywhere from their chalets, the men, young and old, were turning out with such equipment as they could muster. On arriving late at night in the little village of Orsieres, the "Place" was soon crowded with men and horses equipped for the frontier; and as I watched from my window of the little hotel looking down into the square, the names of all were called out and responded to as they filed out, one man leading two laden horses or riding in the middle —the farm horses that were to have reaped the grain of Switzerland; while the women, standing on seats and benches crowded against the walls, wept and wrung their hands, exclaiming, "Jamais! jamais! jamais!" and the horses, as if prescient of the horrors of war, sent forth unearthly screams.

Arriving at Paris at last, she writes, "The next morning I left my hotel about 4 a. m. in order to obtain a seat in the train for Boulogne. The streets of Paris were being washed as usual, and had I had any breakfast I could have taken it off any of them. I was put on the wrong train by a porter, but through kind Providence I found my mistake before it was too late and was allowed a seat "not reserved," on the right one. This was shortly before the great battle of the Marne, and on our way, near Amiens, we saw many Red Cross tents and the first poor bleeding soldiers, while train after train rushed by with the English Tommies waving. At Boulogne all was confusion—people crowding each other out of place in efforts to obtain passage, and I shall never forget the behaviour of some young men, and their language when appealed to, who tried to break the line—the little babies having to be passed back for safety, and many women almost having their arms broken carrying their dress-suit cases in the crush.

On board, a pretty young French-Irish girl asked me for my protection to escape the rudeness with which she had been treated. It is times like these that show the character of those "tried in the fire."

The author's vein of humor is perhaps best shown by verses in "Seven Years After," entitled "Immigration in 1492," which will be appreciated by readers who have wrestled with passports and other troubles of travel since the war:

Immigration in 1492

Columbus went out on a little sea trip—
Do you hear?
He thought he would go on the "Saxonia"—
Never fear!
She's as steady a boat as any afloat,
And when near
To the Quarantine Station the doctor is sure
To appear.

Said the doctor to him, "You can't land here this Spring,
Do you hear?
You've a hole in your stocking, it simply
Is shocking!
Go back cross the water,
Me dear."

"Besides this, perhaps you're aware
That who lands here will have to declare
What he's eaten this year,
For it all must appear
On his card in the Custom House here."

Said Columbus to him, "By your life and your limb,
I *must* land here this Spring.
Is that clear?
For I'm 'booked' ninety-two,
So you must let me through,
Or the histories will think it is queer;

"And the time's nearly up—
For the water was rough,
And the 'Saxonia'—it is so slow!"
Said the doctor to him,
"I will let you pass then—
The 'Saxonia' never could go!"

Here is one of the descriptive poems which will be appreciated by those who have heard the overwhelming clash of church bells in London on a Sabbath morning:

"Ears Have They but They Hear Not, Neither do They Understand"

Hear the ringing, ringing, ringing
Of the bells of old St. Paul's
Clashing down upon the pavement,
Ringing, swinging, swinging, ringing—
As the music downward falls
On the pavement near the portals;
And the sound our heart enthralls
Where the children feed the pigeons
'Neath the steps below the walls.

Hark! the bells have ceased their calling,
And the great clock booms the hour—
While the choristers are trooping
Up the steps below the towers—
And the children feed the pigeons—
And the city's traffic roars.

Hark! the solemn organ pealing,
Jewelled light is downward stealing,
In the choir the boys are kneeling,
Enter in and pray—
While the city, like the ocean,
Roars outside in swift commotion,
Leave the din, and with devotion
Enter in and pray.

Hushed is all the din and roaring,
As the music upward soaring
Falls again:—with hearts adoring
Bow your heads—and pray.

(The book is just published, and will be on sale by Walter H. Jenkins, Friends' Bookstore, Wanamaker's, and other stores.)

The Representative Committee

(*Prepared at the request of the Committee on Revision of the Discipline of Philadelphia Yearly Meeting and approved by* HORACE ROBERTS, *Clerk of Representative Committee.*)

The year which elapses between the closing session of one Yearly Meeting and the gathering of the membership again the next year, is too long an interval to be without a body with ability and power to transact business for the Meeting. A group of 44 persons (as our Representative Committee is now composed) hesitates somewhat to act for the body, except in matters which would suffer by waiting for the entire Meeting to consider them. When the number of pressing matters is small, a tendency toward passivity on the part of the Committee is natural.

Do we not need to revise our ideas somewhat as to what a Representative Committee should do? Our Yearly Meeting sessions are crowded with business. There is little time for the introduction of new concerns. In recent years, the consideration of the state of society has received scant attention. To meet these conditions, would it not be wiser for the Representative Committee to expect to act on just as many matters as possible instead of the few that are necessary? This Committee might very fitly consider all phases of the society's present and possible work, receive the reports of Committees appointed by the Yearly Meeting, help subordinate meetings plan for increased efficiency, and in general keep in close and sympathetic contact with every phase of the Yearly Meeting's work and of the field which it covers. It might also be depended on to make recommendations to the Yearly Meeting, so that this body would have the benefit of suggestions based upon the mature deliberations of its representative body. A Representative Committee, to meet these demands, must meet frequently and should include the responsible workers in the meeting. In order to secure major attendance at frequent meetings, it is probable that a new basis of appointment should be considered by the Committee on Revision of Discipline. It is also doubtful whether appointments for a single year are calculated to develop far-reaching plans. In our other Committees, we have found it best to make the Committees continuous by appointing for a term of years and so arranging that only one-fourth of the members' terms expire each year. London Yearly Meeting appoints for that portion of life during which members are able to meet the obligation. Absence from a series of meetings without adequate excuse automatically releases members from appointment and leaves vacancies to be filled.

An International Economic Conference

(The following information was taken from the National Council for Reduction of Armaments Bulletin, Frederick J. Libby, Executive Secretary.)

(Concluded from last issue)

3. Our Ability to Receive Must be Considered

The little book by Bass and Moulton, two Chicago professors, "America and the Balance Sheet of Europe," discusses in a manner intelligible to laymen another problem which is equally important to us: How much of this debt *can we receive* without closing our factories and producing greater unemployment than we have been having? *Debts between countries*, as is coming to be known generally, have to be paid ultimately either *in gold* or *in goods*. Paper is only a temporary expedient. Our debtors have no gold to speak of. We have most of it now. So they would have to pay us in goods and it seems to be with the purpose of keeping out these very goods that our new Tariff Bill is drawn.

The total annual interest alone on our debt would be approximately $500,000,000. Since practically all nations owe us money, we should have to *cut our exports* till they were surpassed by our imports by practically this amount, in order to receive *even the interest*. How much we can absorb in goods without excessive injury to ourselves and how the tariff should be adjusted to meet this situation would be a third consideration for us if from the standpoint of enlightened selfishness alone.

4. The Terms of Peace in Europe

Every observer agrees substantially with Secretary Hoover on the terms of *real* peace in Europe. These terms concretely put and brought down to date are as follows:

1. *Reduction of German Reparations* to a sum which Europe's leading economists now estimate between four billions and ten billions. It now stands at thirty-three. *Pensions for Allied soldiers* must, in other words be *stricken from the bill* against Germany. She must be held to the full restoration of the devastation of Belgium and France. She will probably provide for this willingly. Force will become unnecessary. A sullen debtor will become a willing debtor. We shall be returning here to the terms of the Fourteen Points.

2. *All intergovernmental debts* must be dealt with like our own in the light of *all* the facts.

3. *Armaments* must be cut. This means that *Russia's* presence at the conference is *badly needed*, though it may be deemed impracticable till other questions between Russia and ourselves are settled. A 50 per cent. reduction of *battleships* and the extension of the naval terms to include *all nations;* limitation of *air* forces—our government is now looking forward to an air force of 42,000; abolition of *sub-*

Quakerism and Democracy

Round Table

In the discussion which followed, a question brought out detailed information concerning the Historical Library at Swarthmore College, with its six or seven thousand volumes. "We are trying to build up this collection," said President Aydelotte, "and get as many books as possible, concerning other sects as well as the Society of Friends, in order to get religious backgrounds. Also we need material about the history of Pennsylvania, as this is so connected with the Friends and the various movements in which they have been active. We are trying to get as many early letters and objects of historical interest as possible. If this Historical Library develops as we hope, it should become a place of great interest to students of religious history, philosophy, prison reform, etc."

The query was voiced as to whether Swarthmore was sufficiently sectarian,—whether enough opportunity is given the students to learn about the Society of Friends, its principles and its work, and the opinion was prevalent that there should be more accomplished along this line. A Chair of Quakerism was suggested. While it was felt that sectarian education was not in good taste in a college such as Swarthmore, yet it was felt that something more might be done.

Mention was made, however, of the unobtrusive action taken by the residents of Swarthmore to make students who are Friends feel they are still in a Quaker atmosphere, and at home with Friends. It was stated by a member of the Faculty that the principles for which Friends stand are far from being theirs exclusively.

Arthur Morgan, President of Antioch College, said: "Recently, I visited several Friends' meetings. In all, the average age of the members was about fifty years. I have heard of a universal solvent, remaining itself unchanged. What kind of a vessel, then, can hold the chemical? We can not keep the spirit of Truth in a sectarian vessel. Whenever an earnest search for Truth is made, it dissolves the vessel. There cannot be a Baptist or Presbyterian or Quaker truth. That is the beautiful reason why Friends tend to disappear,—because they are dominated by the earnest critical search for Truth. It is not a catastrophe if this spirit which works in Friends has tended to disintegrate the group. This same spirit wants to be carried over into democracy.

It is part of our theory that everybody should have some chance. We may have to revise that by saying we will give each of our young people a chance according to how greatly they can profit by it. Increase the amount now paid for education as we may, we cannot get enough to give *all* the same education. But some cannot profit as much as others. Many people have the idea that education consists in handing down the inheritance of the past. The new idea is that minds are organisms which it it our duty to develop. The aim of life is not discipline. It will not be possible for us to have a philosophy of education in this country unless we have a philosophy of life that will be valid for this modern life. It is in Swarthmore and similar institutions, with inspirational ideals behind them, that we hope to find this for our future education.

Peace

Future Peace Work of the Society of Friends

Jesse H. Holmes

We all appreciate the urgency of the call that has come to the Society of Friends to study. Yet there is a danger in study. We may study so much that we do nothing. We avoid doing it by means of appointing committees to investigate. I have seen one committee after another appointed to investigate matters, and have seen their enthusiasm and life fade away. I want to ask you to study the world situation, but not to stop there. This world is something of a looking-glass country. We have to look backward, instead of going forward. Yet I can conceive of nothing more inefficient than a Society of Friends which knows all about our past, and nothing of our work. We study history to understand the world, not to know history itself. The Society of Friends is not an end but merely a bit of machinery. If we are trying to make the Society strong for the sake of the Society, it is futile. Life is the supreme value. The only valuable thing is ourselves—this is not modest but it's true! But if we begin to think of our own lives as of great value, they become valueless. The value of life is in its contacts, its activities.

Our opposition to war should not be based on killing. Everybody dies. We should consider death as a great experience given to all. Death is a part of life. To keep alive is not the object.

I urge the Society of Friends to have a larger knowledge of its work, and that we take the peace problem beyond the sentimental stage; it is not because people get killed that we want war stopped, but because it engenders hatred, malice—meanness inexpressible. It makes a whole people hate even the innocent. It puts a bitterness in the cup of life which nothing else can. Unless people are in some way lovable, Christianity is a mistake. The very basis of Christianity is a loving society.

We owe loyalty to our government as long as it stands for the things that we believe, so far as it does the things that build up the best in the nation. We do not owe loyalty to government which assumes a personality, as "Columbia the Gem of the Ocean." The government is the people, and should be supported as long as it does what the people desire. When it does not uphold the best, we owe it to ourselves and to the country to oppose it, even if this means standing against the crowd. That capacity for standing against the crowd is what I covet for my people; that they can see what is needed, and stand like a rock for it. The time has come today for the Society of Friends to stand, for I think we have had a great slump lately in the free rule of the people. Everything tends toward centralization of authority; our citizens are saying, 'Let the President settle the difficulty,' or 'Let Congress handle it.' This is laziness. It is time for us to study world conditions, and know individually what should be done with the world problems.

In America we are not experiencing the horrors that Europe and Asia are, yet we are no better than they.

There are about a billion and a half people in the world. Right here in the United States we could give two acres of land to every family in the world. Now why are we crowded, if the United States alone could thus hold the entire world population, with less crowding than there is in Japan? We are not really crowded; something is wrong with the adjustment. So a part of the work for peace is to recognize that there is plenty of room, plenty of work for all; we need a readjustment. It is our job not to sentimentalize over the horrors of war, but to look for the causes, and help to straighten them out.

Japan is a yellow people, but has caught the white man's disease of imperialism. How impertinent that is! She has not enough land to feed her people. So, like England a few years ago, she reached out for trade. But Japan had no coal and iron, so seized Formoso, Manchuria, and other land. Her armies have been centers of disorder wherever they have been. They have tried to keep hold of any wealth they could buy in China. And China was in such a condition for years, remember, that many people were glad to sell.

China has a very interesting people. Most of its nationalities are not native to the country. It has been conquered again and again, but in the course of centuries, the conquerors have always disappeared; they have been absorbed by China. In 1912, China suddenly became a republic. We have some responsibility for this. After the Boxer Rebellion, when the United States returned thirteen millions of indemnity to China, that country was so astonished that any white nation should return money which it once had its hands upon that she never got over it, and they still think America their friend.

What is our policy in regard to China and Japan? If we have a republic, we have also a responsibility. I want us in this group to feel a duty in knowing, and in helping to govern. If you only have one year of life left to live, make it interesting. Know what you are doing. Let's go about this business of living, and not sit in a rocking chair and read papers.

An imperialistic nation does not like to see how good its claims are; only how strong its armies are. We do the same as Japan. Our claims to Mexican property are no better than theirs in Manchuria. We bought property in Mexico when the President was driven out. If the Mexican Government were strong, we would not find our titles good. Nations have no honor when their "interests" are in question. They say that they are trying to civilize the inferior peoples. But no nation is a good judge of what makes an inferior people. We have no right to govern any country against its will. An imperialistic nation will do anything to carry out its will. Sherman's march to the sea is a classic example. Virtues have no place in war.

Today in Asia Minor there is a petty little war between Mohammedans and alleged Christians. This may become a very dangerous little war, because the Mohammedans are anxious for a Christian War. There is no Mohammedan nation which has not been exploited by Christian nations,—as Morocco, Algeria, Arabia, Egypt. The Turks have not accepted the Treaty of Versailles. Practically all that is left of Turkey is under the mandates of other nations. The Turks, therefore, have been fighting the Greeks ever since the Treaty. Every promise made by France and England to keep their subject nations in the war has been violated, and apparently there was no intention of carrying them out. Every Mohammedan country in the world has been oppressed by Christian nations. A few missionaries go to them to preach Christ, and the nations meanwhile steal their wealth, and fight about it. What do they think about Christianity? It is a matter of history that the Christian nations are the fighting nations. The Mohammedans think we are robbers and thieves, and that Christianity is a low-grade religion.

Try to be real citizens. Don't just accumulate. Give up getting rich, there is no fun in that. The fun is in living. One thing that Friends ought to do right away is to get away from partisanship. Nothing is more dangerous. If you find one scrap of partisanship about you, get rid of it. Treat a party as you do an auto, get in it when its going where you want to go!

Now here is the League of Nations. There are fifty-one nations in it. It is rather effective, but weakened by the absence of the United States. It has established an international court with fifteen judges, which the majority of the nations have accepted. It has presented a general scheme for disarmament, and has done many other things. Partisanship keeps our country out of it.

We in the Society of Friends should be students for the sake of being active citizens. We have no right to sit in the reserved seats, and watch the tragedy of the world. There is danger in being active in matters that we don't understand. World policies are intricate in detail, but not in general. They are Christian and honorable, or they are not. We can tell about if we know what is going on. What stands in the way of our knowing? It is ignorance, cowardice. A good many of you after you leave College, let yourselves deteriorate until you read only easy things. It is inertia and conservatism that stand in the way of reaching the land of heart's desire. We have kept some old leaders that have led us to the brink of the abyss. We want new leaders, who will try new plans. In science, when a thing doesn't work one way, we try another. Let us try that in politics and life. Discard that which is bad. A system that depends on the welfare of property is bad. We need a system that depends on the welfare of people—that centers round the principle of love.

How Can We Abolish War in Our Time?

Frederick J. Libby

Dr. O. Edward Janney, who presided, said:—"Whatever subject is on my mind at the time is the most important in the world. This subject is tremendously important for us. All the world is thinking about the happy time when war shall be no more. Some of our live men think that we can do away with war in this generation. When we began this work we found Frederick Libby ready to take part in it. Then he went into the Council for Limitation of Armaments, and has been in it ever since."

I received a letter the other day which gives point to our meeting. It was from a "gold-star mother," who said she would be glad to help make war forever again impossible. "I am hoping that the mothers of America will never more have to suffer as I have suffered," she said:

Edison was asked if the city of London could be destroyed by gas in twelve hours. He said, "No, it could be done in three hours." No way has been found to keep gas waves from destroying great cities in incredibly short spaces of time. It must not be forgotten that when General Bliss spoke in Philadelphia last year, he said that a perfectly possible quantity of a certain new gas in a certain area would have wiped out the entire American army of one and a quarter million men. Now, if there should be a war, each country would try to end it on the first day.

Do you remember the words of Lloyd George:

"If the churches of Christ in Europe and America allow such ideas to fructify, they should close their doors." "War has become so destructive," says Lord Bryce, "that we must abolish war, or war will abolish us."

General O'Ryan has said that he was made a soldier by a picture of General Sheridan on his black steed,—"Turn, boys, turn, we're going back." He thought of war as a glorious thing, but real war made him know better, and he said in New York City, "The American people can end war in our time if they get on the job." Why "the American people?" Because of our possibilities of leadership. As America goes in the next twenty years, we may almost say "so goes the world." Nothing is impossible when it is right. We can end war in our time if we get on the job.

Make war unnecessary and it will become impossible. In California in 1849, everybody carried pistols. In 1859, nobody carried pistols. Just one thing made the difference:—they had established courts in which they had confidence, and which proved the better way for establishing justice.

The history of America's relations with Canada is an instance in point. There have been causes of war; there have been disputes; but our joint history shows that disputes can be settled in other ways than by war. We had "causes of war," but settled them without war because we established courts of arbitration, and all disputes were settled in orderly fashion. We do not have to change human nature to end disputes. We shall stop war when we have established confidence in the better way.

The W. C. T. U. created a tremendous sentiment against the saloon. Without its untiring work of years the saloon would not have been abolished. But sentiment alone was not enough for the abolishing of the saloon. When the Anti-Saloon League also entered the field, and worked step by step toward this end, the battle was won. Has human nature changed? No. They tried to do one thing, and one thing only, abolish the saloon as an institution. When your fathers tried to abolish slavery they did not try to raise the negro until his chains were off. They abolished slavery as an institution in the national life. Some say that the Civil War ended slavery. After the Civil War two Amendments were added to the Constitution:—one of these abolished slavery; the other gave suffrage to the negro. Public opinion accepted one of these; the other is hardly even yet accepted. The War did nothing even for the abolition of slavery. Public opinion decided it.

Therefore, as we conceive our task, it is not entirely to bring peace into the hearts of all men. We and our children's children will be working at this. But we can abolish war as a means of settling international disputes, if we wish. World organization, world courts, world education, are the three ingredients for the most permanent peace.

There are elements in the League of Nations that will remain in the ultimate world organization. It is the boldest expression yet made of this organization, it is a great step forward, and yet it is not final. World organization is essential for the abolition of war. Disputes will continue. Courts of arbitration are only a makeshift; there must be a court which will build up a body of international law, which will settle disputes in the future.

There must be a world-wide reduction of armies to a police status. How much that will be, we cannot tell. This means all the nations, including our own. Last winter, there was a plan in military and navy circles to increase enormously our expense for navy and aeroplanes; and this immediately after the Washington Conference. Our Council waged a vigorous campaign against this, and brought down the navy personnel to 86,000 instead of 100,000. It was a step.

The naval limitations established at the Conference were epoch-making. They have made war between Japan and the United States impossible as long as they are kept in force. We were fortifying Guam. but have given up the work. We were fortifying the Philippines, but have stopped. All possibility of war between the two nations has thus passed away, for the United States has and will not have, any naval base within two thousand miles of Japan, while Japan has none within 5,000 miles of this country. Our naval "experts" tell us that Japan could come down on the Philippines, and we could not prevent her. True, but all the white races would be upon her within a year, if she did this unlikely thing. There is no likelihood of war for the United States for ten years, unless she is drawn into war in Europe. And even in Europe, it will be twenty years before the country is built up enough for war. We have twenty years in which to build for peace.

We must educate our people. The slogan "No More War" appeared in thousands of cities and towns of the country on "No More War" day. The press, almost without exception, carried editorials and articles about it. Ministers and speakers told of the movement. The "No More War" movement was bitterly attacked, called "Bolshevistic," etc., by the National Security League, and several prominent papers, as the *Philadelphia Record* and *North American*, and the *Boston Transcript*, carried the League's letter. But a most encouraging feature of the day was that most of the papers threw the Security League's letter into the waste-basket, and carried our material. They are with the campaign to end war.

We must use schools, churches, mass-meetings, bill-boards,—every instrumentality that can be used for carrying propaganda must be used now. We must begin with the children, who are growing up in the midst of hostility and bitterness. They must be brought up free to love, as God tells us we must love, our fellow men. Narrow nationalists in your communities will try to frighten you as to the way schools should be carried on. It is time for these people to fail. It is time for us to organize for peace. We are at the parting of the ways. The day has gone for narrow nationalism. The day has dawned when the flag of America should stand for service. Standing side by side, we should go forward for service in all countries.

Some in this audience may be alarmed for fear we may go too fast in relation to other nations. Fear not. In England there were demonstrations on "No-More-War" day in one hundred cities which put the biggest of ours in the shade. In London, 15,000 people came together in Hyde Park, with 55 speakers at different platforms. In Germany three hundred cities and towns held these demonstrations, and practically the whole population of these places took part. In Berlin between two and three hundred thousand people cried "War, Never Again," while the speakers on every platform declared that working-men must never be drawn into war, and warned all against the militarists.

The schools in Germany once taught boys to be militarists first, then men; they are beginning to be different now. The same is true of Japan. Next June the World Congress of Educators will be held in this country. Why? In order that they may plan for world-wide education against war. We must have peace. We must end war. We owe it to our children to make that "next war" impossible. We can stop it. Politicians know how we forget, how we let things drift, and they think we can be influenced to prepare for war again.

What are we going to do? Are we going to put an end to war? From whom should we expect leadership in this struggle more than from the Society of Friends? And why? Because we have the history, because we have the traditions against war. Is there the spiritual power, is there the capacity for sacrifice among us that our ancestors had? Have we still the vision that was theirs? The next ten years will show whether the Friends will get behind this thing, and bring the movement forward to a successful conclusion. If you don't do it, who will? Think, is there anybody who will be more concerned for the prevention of future war than you? I want you to feel that for the next ten years, there is little else that matters for you. If you are privileged to give your life to this cause for the next ten years, it will not have been spent in vain.

General Smuts said recently, "Doubt it not, we are at the beginning of a new century. The old world is dying around us. Let it die in us." Friends, we are called to give ourselves in devotion. How much will you give to leave a warless world? No one can answer that for you. You must answer it for yourselves, as though the responsibility for "the next war" rested entirely on you. It all rests on you.

Dr. O. Edward Janney, said:—I am sure this thrilling appeal has reached our hearts. I wonder if it would not reach a little deeper. I wonder if Frederick Libby would not tell what he would like.

Frederick Libby:—We want to organize and to educate: we want you enlisted in this cause until you die.

We want money? We want a budget of $250,000 for the coming year. On how much smaller scale can a nation like this be covered? We have the fight of our life before us this winter. It is not a little thing we are doing. We spent $30,000 last winter, and we need $250,000 this year, and as much more next year. In England one man has given $250,000 for the work. They are getting alive to the greatness of the problem.

"To start a conflagration, begin with the dry stick," is an old saying. We shall start our "warless world" campaign with the Society of Friends. We do not minimize the thirty other organizations in the Council for Limitation of Armaments. But if we Friends are not yet absolutely in the movement, we cannot expect that bodies which supported the war will go farther than we.

The bills of the Council are paid up to September. Now in answer to your question,—I wish a contribution could be taken up right here and now.

(It was at this point the $4,000 was raised for the Council, in the manner portrayed in the Story of the Conference.)

A Next Step—The Teaching of History in the Light of National Consciousness

Harlow Lindley

Dr. O. Edward Janney, in his introduction, said appropriately, "greatness consists in constructive service to humanity."

At this time, just after the terrible World War, the public mind is possibly considering the problem of permanent international peace more than any other question. International conciliation is not today a subject for pacifist pens alone; it is the burning issue of the day. Our greatest minds see that an end of war is imperative if we are to preserve our civilization.

There is probably no one way to attain universal peace. No doubt, a multitude of ways must be employed to realize the ideal of amicable international understandings. Not many years ago, many statesmen believed that the way to *prevent* war was to *prepare* for war, and that the most heavily armed nation was the safest. Today we have learned at a terrible cost that this system has failed. Now the nations are trying arbitration, a League of Nations, and armament reduction. Another avenue of approach toward this goal of universal peace has thus far been little traveled,—through the teaching of history in the nations of the world.

History is one of the most universally studied subjects in the curriculum. It has great possibilities for influencing the thinking of future generations in regard to peace and international relations. As it *is* taught and *has been* taught, our minds are filled with distrust and hatred for the citizens of foreign nations. The placing of emphasis, the insertion and omission of material, and the manner of its write-up, have been tools in the hands of the authors of histories, and the governments of nations, for instilling into children suspicions which make good foundations for the reception of war propaganda.

There are many ways in which the histories of the past and present engender a love of war. Wars and the glory of battle have been given too prominent a place, while generals are held up as the highest type of hero. If we can cut down the space that is given to wars, give economic and social history more fully, and paint the glories of peaceful pursuits in more attractive colors, the youth of today will have less of the militaristic spirit. The fact should be emphasized that, even after the disrupting of homes, the killing and maiming of the best men, and the bankruptcy of the warring nations, the question in dispute must, finally, be settled in the only way disputes are ever *settled*,—by the meeting of minds in discussion.

American children have been taught that England oppressed the colonies, and was altogether in the wrong. They have been taught to despise the yellow race. Similar historical teachings appear in every country. The race and national prejudices thus engendered bear fruits of war and international animosities. H. G. Wells says that history is the great humanizer. "We have taught history too much as English history, or German history, the history of this nation or that, cut and dried flowers indigenous to this country or another, with no roots or meaning. Hardly ever have we taught human history. The result of this kind of teaching has been a separation, hostility, hate.

We have been apt to accept one man's opinion as sufficient authority in our teaching of history. But no matter how honest, that opinion may be mistaken. Teachers should have the historical attitude of mind, showing that in nearly all international disputes, there are two sides to the question, and no nation need think itself the only people on the earth.

History is not only a record of the past; it is living and dynamic. Current events should be taught, so as to relate the past to the present. No longer can we afford to teach history as a record of the past, with no intimate relation to our social existence of today. History can be taught so that nations see that they have a common history and a common destiny. Mr. Wells says, "History is—should be—the most powerful influence in unifying the world."

Ignorance is the soil in which prejudice grows, and so is the greatest hindrance to international good-will. Society is more ready to abolish war today than ever before, so it remains largely with teachers to foster the spirit of antagonism to war, and a broader understanding of the peoples of other countries.

Nationality must flow beyond frontiers, and must extend so that *citizenship,* as well as trade and industry and commerce, goes beyond the outer boundaries of one's own country, and becomes continental and inter-continental. We have considered nations as rival units, but have in this, ignored a great economic law, which is that, the politics of a nation being closely interwoven with economics, the economics of nations are closely interdependent.

During the war we put in common our men, our goods, our food, and our means of transportation. After the Armistice, instead of pooling what was left, we returned to the old traditions of an obsolute nationalism. As students, we have seen the results, and are learning the lesson that we must give up our tradition of nationalism in the old acceptance of the term, that we shall not get out of this tangle unless we adopt a policy of good-will and co-operation based on sound economic sense and understanding.

Land, race, language, religion are the great factors usually mentioned as promoting nationalism. Lacking any one or all of these, a people may still have a strong spirit of nationalism. The Poles have lived for a century and a half with no land they could call their own. In America we have fully forty nationalities represented in our population. Yet the spirit of nationality in America during the late war was tremendous. In Switzerland, three languages are spoken, but nobody doubts the unity of the Swiss national spirit. The one indispensable factor for the spirit of nationality is the possession of a common history, the memory of great personalities, of sufferings, victories, and of sacred places wherein the national memory is enshrined. Every people worthy of a life of its own, and a place in history will nourish this priceless heritage, this indestructible quality of nationhood.

America has only a brief history, but that history has been marked with enough notable achievement to give us the spiritual power of a national life. This came to America by a slow growth, through trial and tribulation, from heroic names and great endeavors. Seventy years of union had passed before we could be sure if we were a nation or mere federated states.

The love of country is a spiritual conception that is unconquerable and indestructible. The heroes who in all ages have been willing to give to their country the last full measure of devotion are worthy of the praises of men and the emulation of the ages.

But true national patriotism is not inconsistent with a higher loyalty to mankind. Mazzini, the outstanding patriot of the 19th century, inculcated love of country, but was moved by a larger faith in the unity of the human race. He held that fatherland and humanity are inseparable terms with every people striving to become a nation.

Extreme nationalism may lead a people to a career of conquest under the conviction that they have a superior life which they should impose upon the world. Nationalism should eschew the spirit of dominance. The life of small nationalities is as precious as that of large ones. To boast of one's country is not patriotic. Modesty is still a human virtue, whether among individuals or among nations. A man is not a patriot because he wishes the community to which he belongs to be aggrandized at the expense of a community to which he does not belong. "My country right or wrong" is no more patriotic than "myself right or wrong" is unselfish.

National selfishness and national self-will and national injustice are no better than are these qualities when manifested in an individual. The patriot is one who will sacrifice himself for the good of his country; who will take pains to find out the right and wrong course. If convinced that the rulers of his country are wrong or unwise, the patriot will have the courage to say so, and, if need be, to undergo pains and penalties, legal or social—that man is the patriot!

Man was first loyal to his family, then to his village, then to his clan, his tribe, his city, his commonwealth, his nation. May he not now rise to a higher loyalty? The nations of the world are now confronting the question whether they can rise above their national egoism for the service of humanity. This nation, along with others, has an opportunity. Can we overcome sordid selfishness and materialism, the deadening reaction and partisanship that followed the war, and demand that our national powers shall be used so as to make our nation an instrument to promote the welfare of mankind?

There are two ways of settling disputes among men:—by force and by law. Courts have long been established for the hearing of disputes within the domestic life of every civilized nation. In a breach between nations, a dispute can only be settled by force of arms. War is still lawful among nations. Has the time not come to make it an outlaw? If the statesmen can not do it, the people must demand it. Here is the next step in the long progress of man from savagery to civilization. History shows one certain mark by which evidence of human progress may be known,—the degree by which law and courts have supplanted the methods of force and violence.

What the world needs now is not more "laws of war," but *laws against war*. War should be declared abolished as a means of settling disputes among nations, as duels have been abolished among individuals. Reduced to simple terms, this is a proposal to substitute reason for brute force in the settlement of international disputes. Individuals have united in community and state to preserve good order and the peace of society. Why should not nations unite and submit their differences to an international court of reason and equity?

Every great adventure carries with it uncertainty and danger. Should America tremble at a new adventure? A century ago our pioneer ancestors faced the dangers of the wilderness. In 1789 our fathers launched their Ship of State for a trial trip. It was not a battleship; it was statesmanship. When the gospel of doubt and fear was preached to Washington, he answered that he would erect a standard to which the wise and prudent could repair, and would leave the result in the hand of God. We need more of the spirit of Washington. We should take counsel of our faith, not of our fears.

At such a time as this, the teachers and students of our colleges and universities should feel it their duty to impress on themselves and others a positive and active sense of personal responsibility for our international policies.

What part is the study of history to play in developing this international mind? Its influence will have to begin at the top of society and work downward, for the average man knows little and cares less about history. But if we eliminate the old type of Fourth-of-July history, and if we can substitute a fair history of people throughout the world's lifetime, we can expect succeeding generations to be more and more broadminded in international affairs. History will show the fallacies of jingoism, while proving that human nature does change along lines of progress, and that war can be suppressed, now that it has outlived its usefulness. History, after percolating through all society, can help to bring the common man to the point where he will no longer be swayed by some demagogue shouting "My country, right or wrong!" When that point is reached, citizens of the world will look back in astonishment at the days when men set out at more or less regular intervals to destroy each other in wholesale fashion.

Future Service of the Society of Friends

MURRAY S. KENWORTHY

William C. Biddle, in his introduction said, "The subject we have today interests us all. But more than merely interesting us, we have an active part in it, I sometimes think this word 'service' has been terribly overworkd, but used in the right way, it is a wonderful word. Jesus almost exalted the servant above the master. We have with us today one who has served, who has spent about nine months in the country which has suffered most in the world."

I have a difficult task before me to say all that I want to in the time given me, so I think I will give the latter part of my message first, so as to be sure to give it.

A woman in Poland asked some time ago, "Why are the Quakers in Poland?" The interpreter answered, "To relieve suffering." "But why?" she insisted. He turned to the Friends and explained the question. They answered, "To help restore comfort and prosperity, because they are sorry for the people." "But why?" she still insisted. "Because we want to show our good-will," answered the Friend. "We have worked in France, Germany, and Russia, helping the people who need help." The woman was satisfied at last. "Well, I always thought there ought to be people like that, but I did not know there were any."

I cannot help but feel that we have one of the most difficult problems to solve yet before us, that we have had in a long time, if we stand as people who with practical ideals, demonstrate the kind of life that

Jesus wanted his followers to live. We must first learn to live, and live together. There were some who thought that American and English Friends could not work together, but they did, and with either an American or English Friend as chief, and the others as subordinates.

One of the greatest tasks is before us here in America. Within our own organizations we need to learn the art of living together, and that is one of the greatest contributions we can give to the world. Then, as separate groups, we want to give this demonstration. If we cannot live in peace, we cannot go to a foreign field, and say to Poland and Russia, "you must live together."

It was embarrassing in Russia because the people believed in us so. One of the most embarrassing situations there was brought upon us when some supplies intended for another relief organization were delivered to us. The provisions had been already distributed when the mistake was found out, and we had to try to prove to the other organization that we did not steal the provisions intentionally!

We have practically left France, Poland, and Serbia. We have practically completed the work for which we went. Our workers have left a reputation behind them. Now, dare we go back, and carry a religious message? I know of one great religious organization that went into Poland to do relief work, on purpose, by their own confession, to get a foothold for religious propaganda. I am not content to leave these countries without doing something like this, but how can we do it consistently. We are embarrassed by the feeling that such work may carry the idea that we are hoping to profit in membership by our war service. An editor asked me the other day, "Why don't you Friends start a great membership campaign in the United States and Europe." It was explained to him that it would look as though we had been using the relief work as a stepping-stone. How can we carry our message, and yet not seem to have meant to? These peoples look to us for a demonstration.

In Russia today, the Greek Church is the largest. Many other sects are represented, however,—Mennonites, German Lutherans, Baptists, Molykani, Doukhobors, Friends or Druses, and two groups of Tolstoyans, one organized, the other quite unorganized.

The Molykani, or "milk-people" take their name from their searchings after "the milk of the word." These people are mostly interested in the same way of life as ourselves. They are pacifists, and, moreover, vegetarians, some of whom would be willing to starve to death rather than to eat meat. They will not kill anything, not even a mouse; some of them would not even kill body-lice or bedbugs. Life is life, and, therefore, sacred!

Not only do the people have confidence in us, but the Government of Russia has confidence in us. Again and again the question has come up of Friends taking over large tracts of land, and setting up model farms for the teaching of the Russians. They would have given us unlimited opportunities, unhampered by taxes or regulations. They would have placed many orphans under our care on these farms, giving us a free hand in instructing them. I said to one of the men who pressed the thing, "What if we taught more than agriculture or domestic science; what if we taught religion?" "That is all right; we know you Quakers. Teach them what you want." There is a call, and it is a pressing one.

At Termel, the buildings for an agricultural school are already there, waiting for us, if we want them. A certain man was appointed by the government to take charge. "I would gladly turn the work over to you if you would take it," he said to me.

The Russian type of mind is peculiarly fitted to our message. Millions of Russians are not satisfied with formal religion, they are not satisfied with the Greek church. Friends have already made an impression, and the people are ready for more.

I want to say of the work we did in Russia, that no account of the need has been exaggerated. I have seen a pile of dead in a cemetery, as long as this platform, and as tall as I, all the bodies stripped of clothing, and incredibly emaciated. Everywhere we went, it was like that. I left Samara on the 2nd of June, and dead bodies, stripped and decaying, were lying on heaps of refuse, because the living were still too weak to bury them. In our area it is estimated that 23 people in every 100 died of famine; in another, 25. In still another volost, 49 per cent. of the children and 47 per cent. of the adults perished. Out of 4,000 horses in one volost, only 500 are left, and the same proportion of cows and camels have died.

People have died, and they are still dying. I want to emphasize that the Russian government did not take relief food for the Red Army. The Russian Government has showed us exceeding courtesy. They have given free transportation for ourselves, our Russian workers and our food. They have given us free gasoline, and in many other ways have shown their good-will. Even the bandits have been courteous. In the south of Russia, a group of bandits came to one of our store-rooms, and demanded that it be opened. In fact, they enforced the command with a pistol. They looked at the food. "Sent by the Americans, to feed the hungry. Close the doors." And the doors were closed, with nothing taken out.

Now, with all the opportunities that are before us, it remains to be seen if we are sufficiently devoted, sufficiently free, to carry to this people what they still ask of us,—the message of good-will!

marines; limitation of *cruisers*—these are steps for which the people are ready; and with this such immediate limitation of *armies* as European conditions permit with the prospect of further steps later.

4. Reduction of expenses and increase of taxes all around *till budgets balance.* Our own deficit next year will be $500,000,000. This cannot be saved out of the pitifully meager expenditures for peace. It can largely be saved out of the preparations for further wars. *The printing of paper money* can stop in Europe only when budgets balance.

5. Some kind of a *gold basis* must be agreed upon for every European currency. Some of them are now dropping in the bottomless pit.

6. *Impassable trade barriers* in Europe need to be lowered for any body to do business there. We shall soon be embarassed about bringing this subject up by *our own tariff bill,* which is not calculated to encourage trade.

Preparation by Experts Necessary

It should be clear to those who have considered carefully the complexity of the situation as sketched above that *neither Balfour nor Clemenceau* can settle the European tangle by appeals to our generous idealism. We are idealists but our idealism has a thoroughly practical tinge. We, as a nation like to get our money's worth *in one coin or another.* Senator Borah spoke for the man on the street when he assured Europe that we shall reduce its obligations to us only if the money goes *towards the purchase of permanent peace.*

The Conference on Limitation of Armaments was a success because our naval board, acting under the direction of Secretary Hughes, prepared in detail a *concrete proposal,* as a basis for discussion whose *reasonableness* won it instant support from the peoples of the world. The second great Washington Conference will be a success *only if similarly prepared for.*

Bold Leadership Imperative

The initial proposal will need to be bolder even than that which on November 21, 1921, electrified the world. Europe is very sick. She needs heroic treatment to save her. Secretary Hughes has never lacked courage. We believe that the peoples of the world are ready to support a proposal that, conceived in even-handed justice and in the interest of all humanity, will lift Europe's problems at one stroke out of the mire of national selfishness into which they have fallen and put them where they must be discussed in the light of the permanent needs of the world.

LET PRESIDENT HARDING KNOW THAT AMERICA WILL SUPPORT HIM IN MAKING THIS CONFERENCE A SUCCESS. OUR CIVILIZATION WILL BE AT STAKE.

Austrian Land Settlements

During the two years since its inception, the Austrian land settlement movement has attracted worldwide attention as one of the most constructive programs now being carried out toward European reconstruction. The rapidly increasing distress in Austria, due to the catastrophic depreciation of the krone, renders these settlements at present both more hard-pressed for support than they have ever been, and at the same time more vitally necessary to suffering Austria. The Friends' Austrian Mission is accordingly asking for an appropriation of about $44,000 for the support of the land settlements during this critical period, and it is important that Friends be in touch with the latest developments of the movement.

How the Movement Began

The land settlement movement grew out of the garden allotment plan by means of which supplementary food was produced in war-gardens surrounding Vienna. A group of war invalids who had worked some of these gardens, formed a co-operative society, took possession—after having informed the Government of their intentions so to do—of a corner of the former royal hunting grounds, and set to work building homes for themselves and so reconstructing their lives. Following their leadership, other similar groups were begun until there are now forty settlement societies which are either actually building or planning to build land settlements in the vicinity of Vienna. All these groups are joined in a central settlement league. The greater number of the settlers are workmen who previously lived in Viennese tenement houses.

The land for the settlements is loaned by the Government. Each group of settlers, organized in the form of a co-operative society, pledges its own members to perform a large amount of the unskilled labor of construction. Skilled labor is hired, where necessary, from funds which the settlers themselves contribute to the extent of their ability, and which have been largely increased by government loans and by loans and gifts from the Friends' Mission in Vienna. Co-operative carpenter and blacksmith shops have been established on many of the settlements, while the settlers themselves in many cases manufacture the hollow concrete bricks of which the houses are built. An interesting glimpse of both the methods and the spirit of the land settlement movement is afforded to visitors by the chains of women settlers who pass these bricks from the sheds in which they are molded to the surrounding fields to dry. All the buildings constructed belong to the settlement co-operative society and are simply leased to the individual settlers.

Nature of the Settlements

In most cases the houses are built in closely joined rows for the sake of economy. They are two stories high, with a garret above; trim in external appearance and tastefully decorated within. Ample gardens surround them; and they are provided with sheds in which poultry, goats and pigs may be kept. Visiting teachers go from one settlement to another, instructing the settlers in the care of their gardens and livestock.

By the end of October it is expected that the number of houses ready for occupancy in the 16 land settlements assisted by the Friends' Mission, will total 500, sheltering approximately 3,000 settlers. This number, owing to the shortage of funds, is only about 50 per cent. of the building program arranged in January for the year 1922. The spirit in which the settlements have been conceived and carried out, is in itself one of the greatest promises for Europe's future. Self-help, production and co-operation are its key-notes and these must be the key-notes of all permanent European reconstruction.

Present Needs

Owing to the acute shortage of state and municipal funds, further government loans to the land settlements are at present impossible: Building operations have consequently had to be cut in spite of the willingness of the settlers to do all the unskilled manual labor. With a comparatively small number of families yet housed, while many hundreds of men have already contributed their unpaid labor in the hope of getting their homes before winter, this limitation is a serious setback to the settlement movement. Unless Friends and others interested can provide sufficient funds to carry the movement through the coming winter, many of the settlements will be forced to dismiss their paid workmen and some will entirely break up. It is now proposed to build small wooden or brick huts which could later be enlarged, and the hut plans formerly used by the French Mission are being sent to Vienna for possible use in this connection.

Funds are thus first of all urgently needed for the maintenance of the actual building program. A second need is for the establishment of non-alcoholic canteens for the workmen of the settlements; canteens which can later be converted into co-operative stores for the settlers. Six such canteens have already been established. Gifts of food from the Friends' Mission have made possible the establishment of these canteens. Five of them are provided with soda water fountains—through the generosity of a visiting American Friend. The soft drinks sold are discouraging alcoholism, and at the same time they form a source of profit for the community. A co-operative clothing union will be formed this winter for the purchase of sewing-machines and the cheap production of clothes for the settlers.

Funds for the aid of the settlement movement should be so marked and sent to the American Friends' Service Committee.

First-day School Methods

By Bliss Forbush

Use of Competitions

To children competition is the spice of life. They compete with their fellows in studies, in athletics, and in any line of interest two or more of them take up. This trait of children and young people might well be taken advantage of in the First-day School and used to stimulate their regular attendance and to encourage them to bring new scholars to the school.

The most common form of competition is a race for better attendance and new members. Most schools extend such a plan over a term of six months with a weekly report as to the standing of each class. The individual teacher enthuses her scholars to hold the attendance of their class to a hundred per cent. standard, and to hunt for new members. It is customary for a new scholar to count for the class that introduces him into the school tho he may join another group. The class scoring the highest average attendance and bringing in the greatest number of new members of course wins the contest.

Another interesting form is to have an older class challenge the school to see which class can have the highest average attendance of its members at the morning meeting over a period of three weeks or six months. It is surprising to see that a class of thirteen-year-old boys often come out ahead in this race.

The best form of competition I have yet seen is known as the Lincoln Highway Sunday School Auto Race. This is a standard Sunday School supply and the material can be obtained from any store carrying religious educational material, or from the *Pilgrim Press*, 14 Beacon Street, Boston, Mass. The cost is $5.00, including all supplies. However a small school that does not have sufficient funds to spend this amount on a novelty can make the material to serve their purpose nearly as well.

The plan is as follows: A map of the Lincoln Highway, three feet wide and twenty feet long, is the basis for this contest. The road is divided into miles by short marks, and has cities such as San Francisco, Salt Lake City, Denver, Chicago and New York located along the way. Each class then chooses the auto in which it wishes to make the trip, and elects a chauffeur. This person, who the previous year has been regular in attendance, will act as recorder for the class, marking their points each week on a slip provided for the purpose by the secretary in charge of the contest.

The Lincoln Highway can be expanded or contracted according to the length of time the contest is to last. If the race is to run a school year about six hundred miles will be needed. If it is to run only six months double the mileage given or reduce the number of miles marked on the map. At the beginning of the contest the cardboard autos will be pinned on the map at the starting point, either San Francisco or New York.

The rules for the race must be carefully arranged so as to make it as fair for the class of boys or girls who come every week as it is for the conference class which, having many housekeepers and other busy people, can seldom have a perfect attendance. Points for a six hundred mile contest should be given as follows: for a new member 15 miles, for a perfect class attendance 10 miles, for punctuality at the opening exercises 5 miles, for each member of a class present at the morning meeting 1 mile. Thus a class of ten members having a perfect attendance, all on hand at the opening exercises, one new scholar, and eight at the morning meeting, gains 38 miles on a single First-day. Another class with a membership of thirty, having twenty present, one new scholar, someone late to opening exercise, and sixteen at the morning meeting, gains 31 miles on a single First-day.

Each week the autos will be arranged on the map by the secretary in charge, showing the total mileage of each class. The report will necessarily be one week late. The secretary will also announce each week any especially good records, and give encouragement to all.

It should be clearly understood at the outset what constitutes a new scholar, and how irregular people are to be counted. A class does not receive credit for a new member until he has attended the school three times. If a member is absent more than three consecutive times his name is placed on a separate list and his continued absence does not count against his class. For instance, if someone is absent for five weeks for any reason, he keeps his class from a perfect attendance mark for three weeks, the fourth and fifth weeks, however, his absence does not count against his class. On his return he is marked as any other scholar.

Things to Be Avoided

There are several dangers in connection with the use of contests which should be guarded against. Competitions should not involve financial matters as they do not encourage right ideals, nor are they fair. This method does not stimulate generosity, it simply fosters a desire to win regardless of the purpose for which the money is to be used. Some young people have larger allowances than others, while others have a greater opportunity to earn money, thus such competition is not on a fair basis.

Competitions in which class room work is judged, or preparation of lessons, are not satisfactory in First-day Schools. A common basis to judge different ages and conditions has not been found.

Competitions will lag and interest will be lost unless they are referred to each week by the secretary in charge, the results named, and the goal pointed out anew.

A Quarterly Meeting Contest

An interesting contest can be arranged between First-day Schools in a Quarter having similar conditions. If there are seven schools in a Quarter four of which have a membership of fifty to one hundred, and three with a membership of twenty to fifty, there should be two divisions each having the same rules. A banner should be given to the school scoring the highest number of points for the month. Each superintendent should report the number of points scored by his school to the secretary of the Quarter, or some one appointed by the First-day School Union, at the close of each month. The points might be scored per week as follows, tho any Quarter could vary them to fit its conditions: perfect class attendance five points, each new scholar ten points, school with the highest average attendance 20 points. Thus if a school in either division has on a given week two classes with a perfect attendance, three new members, and the highest average attendance of any school that week, it scores sixty points.

These contests will arouse the interest of the different schools in one another, and cause backward schools to take a new lease on life.

Friendly News Notes

Helen Hawkins has been appointed to succeed Clarence E. Pickett as Secretary of the Young Friends' Movement of the Five Years Meeting.

Dr. John A. Miller, vice president of Swarthmore College, has been elected a fellow of the Royal Astronomical Society of England. Dr. Miller's election came in recognition of his work at the Sproul Observatory at Swarthmore.

The department of astronomy at Swarthmore College also has been honored this year by the assignment to it of the Isaac Newton studentship of the University of Cambridge, England, for research in astronomy. The holder of the studentship, who is designated as research assistant, is L. J. Comrie, F. R. A. A., of New England, and St. John's College, Cambridge.

Another Swarthmorean to be honored recently is Edward B. Temple, '91, who has just been appointed to be chief engineer of the Sesqui-Centennial.

Chicago Monthly Meeting is growing. At the last meeting there were nineteen present. The date for holding the Monthly Meeting has been changed to the second Second-day on each month. As it is planned to have supper before the meeting, those who expect to attend are requested to notify Jeannette F. Stetson, 225 North Pine Ave., Chicago, three days before the time of the meeting.

An after-meeting discussion class has been formed, and all Chicago Friends and their friends are urged to attend and help make it a success.

On Tenth month 2nd a company of about twenty gathered at the home of Hannah Clothier Hull, Swarthmore, Pa., and observed the 85th birthday of Rachael W. Hillborn. This dear Friend was for more than 34 years one of the active editors and managers of the INTELLIGENCER and she still retains a deep interest in its affairs. Her wise judgment and good common sense have been valued factors in the conduct of the above since her active retirement some years ago.

The team of English debaters from the University of Oxford visited Swarthmore on the evening of October 2nd. The question for debate was "Resolved, that the United States should enter the League of Nations immediately." In order that the debate should not assume an international character, one of the Oxford men debated on the negative side and a Swarthmore woman took the affirmative. An interesting feature was the difference in manner of presentation of facts and of the speakers themselves. The Swarthmore team was earnest, stuck closely to facts and arguments, taking a serious view of this important question. The Englishmen indulged in humor and persiflage and had a lightness of touch that kept the audience in smiles a good part of the time. They were accustomed to public speaking, having, we understand, all been president at different times of the Oxford Union, a miniature debating Parliament of the University.

The question was decided not on the merits of the debate, but on the opinions of the audience. After the debate, tellers were stationed at the doors which were marked "affirmative" and "negative" and the audience passed out through the door of their choice. Four hundred and fourteen voted in the "affirmative" and three hundred and seventy-four in the "negative." The occasion was a thoroughly enjoyable one.

MEETING IN SARATOGA MEETING-HOUSE

First-day, Tenth month 1st, the old Saratoga Meeting-house, near Quaker Springs, was again the scene of activity, when about seventy-five people gathered in Friendly fashion. Isaac Wilson was in attendance and presented clearly the lessons to be drawn from the incident of Jesus meeting the women at the well. Among other things he said that while religion may have failed in its purpose, Christianity has never been fully applied, and His kingdom has not been established on earth.

Edgar Brown called attention to the necessity of overcoming evil with good.

In the afternoon a union service was held in the Methodist Church at Quaker Springs, where Isaac Wilson again spoke with wonderful strength and clearness from the parable of the prodigal son. He said that personal examination was a good way to open a religious service, and proceeded to apply personally the lessons to be drawn from the text.

There seems to be a little Quaker leaven working in the Saratoga neighborhood, the Meeting-house, closed for many years, has been opened each week since the Annual Meeting held Eighth month 20th, which was attended by Grace Warren and Effie McAfee. While the attendance has been small it indicates an awakening of interest.

PHEBE A. HOAG.

BALTIMORE NEWS

On First-day we were fortunate in having Dr. Joseph Spencer, President of Morgan College, and O. Edward Janney with us. Both gave very inspiring addresses.

In the closing exercises of the First-day School the different play activities of the School were summed up by having slides thrown on the screen. These included slides taken of the camp, playground and different members of the School on their vacations.

Several classes have taken up various activities outside the School work, the Conference Class appointed a committee to look into the political situation, the Senior Class appointed a social committee and a basket-ball manager, and the Bible Class is planning to help with the work of the Home Department, which now has twenty members, both resident and non-resident.

Last week Thomas Hull and Charles Whitby, Sr., took the boys down to Camp Keewadin to stay over Sixth-day night. Meals were cooked out of doors, and everyone had a fine time.

WOOLMAN SCHOOL

The first two week-ends of the special course at Woolman School have made a delightful beginning. Those in attendance who expect to be present for the six week-ends are: Florence Ely of Solebury, Dorothy Michener of Unionville, Mary Walker of Kennett Square, Anna Smedley and Sarah Pratt of West Chester, Mary Magruder of Sandy Spring, Elizabeth Jamison and Byron Conrad of Philadelphia, Floyd Warrington and Raymond Thompson of Mickleton, Ernest Votaw of Lansdowne, J. Macklin Beattie of the Wilmington Y. W. C. A., and Anna Owers of Philadelphia, also of the Y. W. C. A.

The first week-end group was greatly increased by the members of the Young Friends' Committee, meeting in Swarthmore, most of whom attended the lectures. During the second week-end, we have had some of the students for the fall term, who are just arriving. These regular students are Sarah and Margaret Pennock, Emma Lippincott Higgins, Martha Jamison, Letitia Webster, Caroline Smith and Alice Allen. Henrietta Bulla, an Irish delegate to the Five Years Meeting, is also a guest at the school, and we are making good use of the opportunity to compare notes with her on Friendly affairs.

Since the first lectures of the week-end course are more or less introductory, we hope others may be encouraged to share the opportunity from now on.

THE OPEN FORUM

This column is intended to afford free expression of opinion by readers on questions of interest. The INTELLIGENCER *is not responsible for any such opinions. Letters must be brief, and the editor reserves the right to omit parts if necessary to save space.*

WHAT IS "CAPITALISM"?

To the Editor:

The letter of H. M. H. in the Open Forum of Ninth month 9th is an excellent presentation of the point of view held by many Friends on a subject of vital importance, and as such it deserves an adequate answer; but it is impossible to do this in the brief space of an Open Forum letter. Therefore, I would urge the editor to ask some competent person, such as Lewis Abbott, who has been a student along the lines of economics and sociology, to write an article on what "capitalism" is and its influence on personal character. For that is the crux of the matter. Capitalism as defined by H. M. H., "such a social order as permits persons to have capital and use it," is not "capitalism" as the term is usually employed today, and gives no clue to what is criticized in it. It is one of the rather unsatisfactory terms used to designate our complicated modern industrial and financial system, which has developed so naturally in the course of years and we are so familiar with it that we are apt to take it for granted as something necessary and right. If, as some of us believe, an examination of this "capitalist" system shows that it tends to develop in men a character at complete variance with the way of life taught by Jesus, and if it tends to produce situations that easily lead to violence in industrial conflict and to war, then those who are deeply imbued with the Christian spirit will naturally try to study out some better system; just as in the early days when Friends came to realize the evil of slavery, they first freed their own slaves, and then agitated to abolish the whole slave system.

Changes in our social system are bound to come, sooner or later. But it is not inevitable that the changes will usher in a more Christian and happy society. In fact, how can we expect a Christian society, or the "Kingdom of God," to come on earth unless the people who believe in Christian principles study about it, plan for it, and try to carry it out by Christian methods, without bloodshed or dictatorship?

M. S. M.

Brooklyn, N. Y.

BIRTHS

BRINTON—At Richmond, Indiana, September 6, to Howard H. and Anna Cox Brinton, a daughter, Lydia Shipley.

DISNEY—On Ninth month 30th, to James L. and Maude Disney, of Germantown, Pa., a son, who is named Robert Gordon Disney.

MILLER—At Fishertown, Pa., on Eighth month 14th, to E. Blair and Mary J. Miller, a son, who is named John Robert Miller.

MARRIAGES

BARNEY-CORSE—At Baltimore, Md., in the Park Avenue

Meeting-house, under the care of the Society of Friends, on Tenth month 7th, Maynard V. Barney, of Enfield, Thompsonville, Conn., and Helen Frances Corse, daughter of Frank E. and Sarah M. Corse, of Baltimore, Md.

DEATHS

LOVETT—At Bristol, Pa., on Tenth month 4th, Benjamin T., husband of Abbie F. Lovett, in his 77th year.

WOOD—At Greensboro, Indiana, on Ninth month 30th, Margaret K. Wood, aged 97 years. She was a birthright member of the Society of Friends and for many years has been a devoted member of Fall Creek Monthly Meeting.

COMING EVENTS

TENTH MONTH

15th—Brooklyn First-day School will re-open.

15th—Elbert Russell will address a special afternoon meeting to be held at the Haverford Meeting, at 3 p. m. Thee and thy friends are cordially welcome.

16th—Easton and Granville Half-Yearly Meeting, at Easton, N. Y., at 11 a. m. Meeting of Ministry and Counsel at 10 a. m.

17th—At 7.30 p. m., in P. Y. F. A. Building, meeting of all interested in forming Study Groups.

18th—Monthly Meeting of Friends of Philadelphia, 15th and Race Streets, 7.30 p. m.

19th—Green Street Monthly Meeting of Friends of Philadelphia, School House Lane, Germantown, 7.30 p. m.

21st—Abington First-day School Union. See Notice.

21st—Concord First-day School Union will be held at Concord Meeting-house. See Notice.

21st and 22nd—Pelham Half-Yearly Meeting, at Sparta, Ont.

21st—Trip to Germantown for benefit of Building Fund of Neighborhood Guild.

22nd—Southern Half-Yearly Meeting, at Camden, Del.

24th—Western Quarterly Meeting at London Grove, Pa., at 10 a. m. In the afternoon, Western First-day School Union will be held at the same place.

25th—Address by Frederick J. Libby at the Meeting-house, Lafayette and Washington Avenues, Brooklyn, at 5.15 p. m., on "How We Can Abolish War in Our Time." All interested are cordially invited.

26th—Caln Quarterly Meeting, at Christiana, Pa.

26th—Donation Day at Chapin Memorial Home for Aged Blind. See Notice.

27th—All-Day Educational Conference on Proper Inter-Racial Contacts in Our Schools to be held at 15th and Race Streets, Philadelphia. Full notice next week.

28th—Westbury Quarterly Meeting, at Flushing, N. Y. Meeting for worship and business meeting at 10.30; lunch at noon; afternoon session at 2.30.

29th—New York First-day School will re-open.

30th—Baltimore Yearly Meeting, at Baltimore, Md.

31st—Concord Quarterly Meeting, at Darby, Pa.

NOTICE—The Representative Committee of Philadelphia Yearly Meeting will hold a conference to consider our meetings for worship, on Sixth-day, Tenth month 27th, at 10 o'clock, in Room No. 4, 15th and Race Streets, Philadelphia, Pa.

All members of the Meeting for Ministry and Counsel and others especially interested in the subject are invited to attend.

NOTICE—The Abington Young Friends' Fair has been postponed from October 28th to November 18th. The proceeds of this Fair are to be divided between the Norristown Friends' Home and the Service Committee. Other details will be published later.

NOTICE—Abington First-day School Union will be held Tenth month 21st, at Quakertown, Pa. Morning session at 10.30. "First-day School Materials" will be presented by Marguerite Hallowell, followed by general discussion of the subject. Current Events will be given by William Eves, 3rd, of George School. Lunch at 12. Afternoon session at 1.45 will be addressed by Wilbur K. Thomas, on "The Problem of Religious Education."

NOTICE—On Tenth month 16th, Easton and Granville Half-Yearly Meeting will be held at North Easton Meeting-house at 11 a. m. Meeting for Ministry and Counsel same day and place at 10 a. m.

First-day, the 15th, a meeting for worship will be held in the old South Meeting-house at Easton, at 11 a. m. A pilgrimage from New York and vicinity will attend this meeting; there will be a box lunch at 12.30, a meeting of the Social Reconstruction Committee at 1.30; and an afternoon meeting of interest especially to young people and the community at large at 3 o'clock. This will be addressed by a speaker from the American Friends' Service Committee.

NOTICE—Concord First-day School Union will be held on Tenth 21st, at 10 a. m. and 1.30 p. m. The morning session will be occupied with reports from the summer schools, the report of the Committee on Field Secretary and a report of Vesta Haines' summer work, followed by discussion. Lunch at 12.

At 1.30 there will be an opening song by Concord First-day School, followed by reports of Delegates and various committees. Concord First-day School will give a dramatization of a Bible story, which will be followed by a talk by Vesta Haines.

A cordial invitation is extended to delegates from the other Unions. Concord Friends will meet busses on the Wilmington and West Chester line before 10 a. m. and 1.30 p. m., if so requested. Please drop a card to Bertha L. C. Darlington, Darling, Pa.

NOTICE—Donation Day—Chapin Memorial Home for Aged Blind, 6713 Woodland Avenue, Philadelphia, Thursday, October 26, from 11 a. m. to 10 p. m. Luncheon 12 to 2, supper 5 to 7 o'clock (75 cents). Music, entertainment, sales of candies, cakes, flowers, fancy and useful articles. Donations of cash, provisions and anything for use or sale will be thankfully received.

A long list of waiting applicants emphasizes the need for increased accommodations but this requires larger resources. The personal, self-sacrificing efforts of Managers and Committees have, so far, provided the shortage of fixed income, but this appealing work needs to be enlarged, at least doubled, to take care of pressing, urgent cases of needy blind men and women of the highest respectability, who should not be left without suitable provision. Church and Beneficial Homes fear to assume the care of the blind and do not take them.

Donations may be sent to the Treasurer, the Home, or the following Committee members: Miss Ella Headman, *Chairman*, 6420 Overbrook Ave.; Mrs. William H. Woodward, *Chairman of Auxiliary*, Stoneleigh Court.

Baltimore Yearly Meeting, 1922

The Yearly Meeting will be held this year as usual, commencing on Seventh-day, Tenth month 28th.

Lodgings will be provided for Friends at Park Avenue Meeting-house as usual. Applications for this accommodation are to be made through the Friend who may be appointed in each Monthly Meeting, and should be forwarded by him as promptly as possible to the Chairman or Secretary of the Committee in Baltimore.

Accommodations at moderate cost may be provided elsewhere, for those who desire such, when specific applications are made.

The dormitories will be ready for occupancy on Sixth-day, Tenth month 27th for those who may have early meeting engagements. Meeting for Worship convenes at 10 o'clock on First-day.

Annie L. Lewis, Chairman, 731 Linwood Avenue, Tuxedo Park, Baltimore.

Bertha Janney, Secretary, The Plaza, Baltimore, Maryland.

FRIENDS' NEIGHBORHOOD GUILD needs an additional building. To raise necessary funds,

BUY A TICKET
for the
TRIP AROUND THE WORLD

starting from School Lane Meeting-house, Germantown, between 5 and 7 P. M., Seventh-day, Tenth Month 21st, 1922. Supper, transportation, entertainment, dancing—Price $1.50

Tourists will touch at Holland, China, Egypt, United States, Dance Land.

Tickets for sale at Friendly Centres or Guild Committee.

American Friends' Service Committee

WILBUR K. THOMAS, EX. SEC.
20 S. 12th St. Philadelphia.

CASH CONTRIBUTIONS

WEEK ENDING OCTOBER 2ND.

Five Years Meeting	$102.67
Other Meetings:	
Middletown Meeting	15.00
Oakland Branch of the College Park Association	9.50
Purchase Meeting	100.00
Newtown Service Committee	20.00
Contributions for Germany	20.00
For Austria	35.47
For Poland	860.48
For Russia	748.00
For Russian Overhead	254.25
For Central Pennsylvania	20.00
For West Virginia	7.50
For Message Committee	10.00
For General	217.50
Refunds	88.50
	$2,508.87

Shipments received during week ending September 30th: 79 boxes and packages received, 1 anonymous.

LUKE 2. 14—AMERICA'S ANGELUS

"Glory to God in the highest, and on earth peace, good will toward men."

Stand back of President Harding in Prayer for Universal Peace by meditating daily, at noon, on the fourteenth verse of the second chapter of Luke.

Ask your friends to help make this a Universal Meditation for Universal Peace

Pass it on *Friends in Christ*

WANTED

WANTED—A POSITION AS COMpanion, care of invalid or housekeeper. Address Y. 360, Friends' Intelligencer.

WANTED—TWO EXPERIENCED girls, one for child's nurse or mother's helper, other for housework. Good wages. G. L. Cowan, Edgewater Park, New Jersey.

WOMAN OF REFINEMENT SEEKS position as companion to lady living alone, or managing housekeeper in widower's home where kindness and interest would be appreciated. Reference. Address D. 382, Friends' Intelligencer.

HOUSEKEEPER WANTED—FAMILY of two. A good home in a country town. Reference desired. Chas. S. Pyle, Rising Sun, Md.

WANTED—MIDDLE-AGED WOMAN to help care for invalid; also assist with light housekeeping. Three adults. Address Louisa T. Wright, Newtown, Pa.

BOY 15 WANTS PLACE ON FARM AS general chore boy, good bed and board and one dollar a week. Answer C. 381, Friends' Intelligencer.

WOMAN OF MIDDLE AGE, NURSE, wants care of invalid. Address P. 374, Friends' Intelligencer.

WANTED — MIDDLE-AGED WOMAN for general housework in country. Three in family. Address Friends' Intelligencer, M. 384.

GRADE TEACHER (FRIEND) DEsires position. Address Friends' Intelligencer, H. 385.

WANTED—RELIABLE WOMAN FOR general housework. Family of two, all conveniences. No washing. No objection to woman with small daughter. Mrs. Penrose Robinson, Hatboro, Pa.

WANTED—GOOD HOME OR BOARDing place with cheerful surroundings for middle-aged lady, mentally somewhat deficient. State probable terms. Address P. 390, Friends' Intelligencer.

$2250 WANTED ON FIRST MORTgage for five years at 6% interest. Property is a new frame bungalow with two acres of land in Bethel Township, Delaware County, Pa. Loan desired is about one-half the value of the property and the owner is a young man of excellent reputation. Apply to Charles Palmer, 12 East Fifth Street, Chester, Pa.

ELDERLY WOMAN DESIRES POSItion assisting Mother with children, plain sewing and light duties. Miss Hannah G. Garwood, 1630 North 17th Street, Philadelphia.

WANTED—BY YOUNG WOMAN WHO has lived in a Friends' Home fifteen years, position as a Mother's helper in city home, or as caretaker of linen room or the like in a school or institution. Miss Carrie Scrimger, 3017 Cambridge Place, Washington, D. C.

WANTED—WHITE WOMAN OF REfinement for maid in apartment in Atlantic City, to care for apartment and clothes. Very little cooking. Write Mrs. J. W. Mott, Traymore, Atlantic City.

WANTED—WORK AT HOME, ADdressing and general circularizing or keeping books for Dentist, Doctor or private concerns by young lady. Twenty-five years with last employer. Address L. 392, Friends' Intelligencer.

EXPERIENCED NURSE WANTS care of elderly lady. Best references. Address G. 393, Friends' Intelligencer.

WANTED — PRACTICAL NURSE under forty. Good reference. Phone Lansdowne 200.

WANTED

WANTED—MOTHER'S HELPER FOR child two years old. State experience and salary desired. References requested. Mrs. J. M. Griscom, Moorestown, New Jersey.

POSITION WANTED—AS COMpanion-nurse to invalid, or elderly woman; management of home, help kept. Capable; references. Address B. 394, Friends' Intelligencer.

WANTED—IN HOUSEHOLD WHERE additional service is desired, woman of excellent character to help with different kinds of work including either washing and ironing or mending. Good home in suburbs. Two lines of trolleys. Address Miss M. L. Wharton, N. W. Cor. York Road and Chelten Ave., Philadelphia. Telephone, Oak Lane 3578.

To the Lot Holders and others interested in Fairhill Burial Ground:

GREEN STREET Monthly Meeting has funds available for the encouragement of the practice of cremating the dead to be interred in Fairhill Burial Ground. We wish to bring this fact as prominently as possible to those who may be interested. We are prepared to undertake the expense of cremation in case any lot holder desires us to do so.

Those interested should communicate with William H. Gaskill, Treasurer of the Committee of Interments, Green Street Monthly Meeting, or any of the following members of the Committee.

William H. Gaskill, 3201 Arch St.
Samuel N. Longstreth, 1218 Chestnut St.
Charles F. Jenkins, 232 South Seventh St.
Stuart S. Graves, 3033 Germantown Ave.

The Friends' Intelligencer

Established 1844 — TENTH MONTH 21, 1922 — Volume 79, Number 42

Contents

EDITORIAL

REGULAR MEETINGS

OAKLAND, CALIF. — A FRIENDS' Meeting is held every First-day at 11 A. M., in the Extension Room, Y. W. C. A. Building, Webster Street, above 14th. Visiting Friends always welcome.

PASADENA, CALIFORNIA — Orange Grove Monthly Meeting of Friends, 520 East Orange Grove Avenue. Meeting for worship, First-day, 11 A. M. Monthly Meeting, the second First-day of each month, at 1.45 P. M. First-day School (except Monthly Meeting days) 9.45 A. M.

FUN

The front door-bell was out of repair. Mother instructed John to put up some sort of notice to that effect. John is better at athletic games than punctuation. He finally evolved this sign, which a startled neighbor neighbor presently brought in to the mother:

"Please Knock the Door Bell Out of Order."—*Bombay Examiner.*

Once a friend of Mark Twain's was conversing with him regarding a terrible affliction of a person known to them both. The friend said:

"Can you imagine anything worse than having diphtheria and scarlet fever at the same time?"

"Yes," replied Mark; "I can easily imagine some things worse than that —for instance, rheumatism and St. Vitus's dance."—*Everybody's Magazine.*

THE FRIENDS' INTELLIGENCER

Published weekly, 140 N. 15th Street, Philadelphia, Pa., by Friends' Intelligencer Association, Ltd.

SUE C. YERKES, *Managing Editor.*

Subscription rates: United States, Mexico, Cuba and Panama, $2.50 per year. Canada and other foreign countries, $3.00 per year. Checks should be made payable to Friends' Intelligencer Association, Ltd.

Entered as Second Class Matter at Philadelphia Post Office.

The Friends' Intelligencer

The religion of Friends is based on faith in the "INWARD LIGHT," or direct revelation of God's spirit and will in every seeking soul.

The INTELLIGENCER is interested in all who bear the name of Friends in every part of the world, and aims to promote love, unity and intercourse among all branches and with all religious societies.

ESTABLISHED 1844 | PHILADELPHIA, TENTH MONTH 21, 1922 | VOLUME 79 NUMBER 42

Luxuries—Who Shall Have Them?

Many times during the war when the working man was getting a salary far beyond any he had ever received before, we heard much criticism of the way in which he spent his money. People who had always ridden in vehicles, either horse drawn or motor driven, were appalled at the recklessness of the working men who, as soon as he had a little nest egg, coupled it with a comparatively large mortgage and bought a car. And his wife and children demanded player-pianos and fur coats. People who had been accustomed to fur coats and player-pianos were further horrified at this additional evidence of the improvidence of the working class.

In reading the following extract from an editorial in the Christian Register, we ask our readers to substitute the word "Friends" for Unitarians; or better still, read it first with the word Unitarian and then re-read it with the word "Friends" inserted. The editorial is headed "Workers' Silk Shirts."

> "A man writes a letter to a New York newspaper complaining bitterly of an editorial which says it is "the crowning iniquity of 'labor' that the workers during the war received wages that 'blossomed and flourished in silk shirts, furs, and automobiles.'" He says, "Let us grant the abuses and tyrannous exactions of labor at a time when the only question seemed to be whether the worker should get it first or the profiteer." Then this question, "What of your inference that the worker should never be allowed to enjoy the finer things which he produces? Shall we assume that only men who do their work in offices and on revolving chairs have a right to silk shirts?" This attitude of "mingled cynicism and contempt" for the "worker's" desire for some of "earth's finer and more beautiful things is almost tragic in the face of our need today for a social understanding and sympathy."
>
> We submit this as our own true but not overworked gospel. If we Unitarians do not get more of it in actual force in our organizations, we shall fail of saving civilization from the greatest of all wars. Mark that. How many of us realize that the country at this moment is two armed camps, on one side capital, on the other side labor? How many realize that we are, and for a decade have been, in an actual state of war? How many Unitarians are there, apart from the ministers, who feel with the writer of the letter given above? How many have been taught to believe that labor is a monster, and that all the sins and ills are on one side?

In connection with this we quote from a report on social and economic life given at an Episcopalian convention held recently in Chicago:

> "A fundamental change in the spirit and working of our social and industrial life is necessary to restore the world to peace and order. The fundamental change can be effected only by accepting on the basis of all our relations the principle of co-operation in service for the common good, in place of unrestricted competition for private or sectional good."

Even those who sympathized with the workingman in his desire, when he had the chance, to share in the finer things of life, felt that he did not use good judgment. But with his education and background, would we have done any better? Is not the responsibility really ours to see that he gets a fair share of the profits of his labor all the time so that he will be better balanced in times of crisis?

⌘

A recent issue of the Christian Register contains an article by E. Stanton Hodgin on "The Quaker: Radical and Pacifist" with a sub-title of History and Influence of Disciples of "Inner Light." The article is very interestingly written by one who sees our weaknesses as well as our strength, as illustrated in the following quotation:

"The Quakers thought to safeguard themselves against any possibility of idolatry by abolishing every vestige of external form or expression of worship, and now we see some of them complacently reverencing the vacuum or absence of form with all the zeal of devotees. Here we have driven home to us the essential truth that it is neither the external form nor the lack of form that is the essential thing, but the constant renewal of the inner life, either through the one or the other."

The Religious Ter

By Rufus

It would take a real prophet to deal adequately with the above subject. There are many tendencies at the present time, and not a single well-defined *one*, and these tendencies are complicated and interlocked rather than direct and simple. In any case the old alignments are a thing of the past and the old rubrics and spellwords are strangely out of date.

There is at the present moment an appalling number of persons, both young and old, who show no interest in religion at all. It is apparently to them no longer a *live hypothesis*. The world is accepted for what it is at its face value—a material world where men can get food and clothes, houses and lands, stocks and bank accounts, certain items of pleasure and finally a grave. They propose to make the most of this kind of a world and let all fine hopes and fancies die. They say with Omar,

"Myself when young did eagerly frequent
Doctor and Saint, and heard great argument
About it and about: but evermore
Came out by the same door as in I went.
* * * *
"Into this universe, and *Why* not knowing,
Nor *Whence*, like Water willy-nilly flowing;
And out of it, as Wind along the Waste,
I know not Whither, willy-nilly blowing."

It is a pathetic and ominous tendency, because there is no hope of maintaining lofty morality, high standards, sound ideals, fine manners, pure hearts and clean lives in a world where faith in God and reverence for His will have died out and vanished. The nobler traits of character and conduct last on for a little while by the momentum of the past. We still have a good stock of inherited virtue which was transmitted to our generation from the spiritual heroes and saints of the past, but how pitiable would be a world which had no spiritual saints and heroes still radiating their lives! When there is no longer a fresh stream of transmission the deluge may as well come!

One of the most vigorous tendencies at the present moment is undoubtedly that which has been called by its leaders and advocates "the fundamentalist movement." It corresponds very definitely to the apocalyptic movement which was a strong feature in the first century of this era. Its leaders, like those ancient writers of apocalypses, have lost all hope of a better world, or of a Kingdom of God, coming by slow moral and spiritual processes. They do not consider this world to be God's world, they do not believe in evolution, they are hostile to the idea of

is we produce fruit—the fruit of His spirit. He revealed His will in a Book. It *is* there in that Book, but God's revelation is unending and continuous. Not once in a single startling day of Judgment has His righteousness flamed out like lightning for all men across the world to see. Human history is always revealing days of Judgment. The decisive drama of the historical movement, with its stern siftings and its selection of those who line up on the side of righteousness and truth is one of the most impressive words the universe has yet spoken, though some seem to miss it or misinterpret it.

The most complete expression of divine beauty and forgiving love and compelling goodness that has yet touched the race came in the life of Jesus Christ. It has settled forever for our minds and hearts the question: What is the character of God? We rise up and say with glowing conviction: He must be like *that.* Through Him we have found God as One who loves and understands and forgives and vitalizes us. But the revelation which He has brought us in the light and glory and power of His life has made us suddenly see that God can be truly revealed only through life and in terms of character. And we see, then, that these lesser lives of ours—like the bruised reed which He would not break or the smoking flax which He would not snuff out—may also reveal Him and be organs of His Life and Spirit, and so we hold up our little cup to be filled or our tiny torch to be kindled.

According to this way of thinking religion is as natural as breathing, as much a necessary part of life as love is. Not to find God and not to be an organ of His revealing and creative purpose is to miss the main thing that makes life life—it is to be in the backwash and not in the forward-moving current. The real heresy that matters is to have dull eyes when the divine light is shining, unkindled hearts when God's fire is burning—"the unlit lamp and the ungirt loin.

A Garden Is a Little Child

A garden is a little child
That must be tended;
Befriended;
Mended.
Befriended from sly weeds;
Tended with more seeds;
Mended. Oh, near and far
They are the same! Not worth it, to your view?
But think of what a comfort gardens are
When they're grown up, and *they* take care of *you!*

—*Youth's Companion.*

The Worth of Art

(An address given by Professor Alfred Mansfield Brooks, at Collection. Professor Brooks is head of the revived Department of Art at Swarthmore College.)

I have been asked to Swarthmore to teach art. To do this thing with any degree of success, here, and the country over, must mean, first of all, making art respected. At present it is not respected either in fact, or as a subject for serious study. By this I mean that, with rare exceptions, the mere mention of art to undergraduates, faculties, society in general is to speak of what is unimportant, or of that kind of importance which can always be put off to a more convenient time.

To the great majority of our people art signifies things of unnecessary beauty. In a word, luxuries which can be foregone until wealth and leisure warrant them. And the widely held opinion is that art is effeminate. This I suspect is because many more women than men have had the fineness of perception to sense its worth to mankind.

Those who think of art in any of these, or other similar ways, are quite right in not respecting it. The point is that such thinking is all wrong. It is wrong with the wrongness of ignorance.

As best I can, I shall now tell you what art is, calling to my help one or two from the company of those who have held a different view, and are known by their works; the sort of men Browning meant when he wrote:

> "God uses us to help each other so,
> Lending out our minds";

men who, by common consent, are acknowledged to be chief among the lasting benefactors of civilization. It is the company that numbers such as the author of the Iliad, builder of St. Peter's dome, painter of the Sistene, creator of Hamlet, composer of the Pastoral Symphony, and many more.

Art is wholly a matter of accurate description; of truth telling;—about the world, and all that in it is, as it appears to our senses and as it appeals to our sympathies. The worth of art is in proportion to the keenness of our senses and the depth of our feeling. As I use worth I mean whatever is identical with beauty. In this sense is the Iliad a matter of description; a most wonderful piece of truth-telling. The same of the dome of St. Peter's, of the Sistene; of Hamlet, the Pastoral Symphony and many more.

Listen now to what I have been saying laboriously, said perfectly;—itself a work of art because a completely truthful description of what he knew, and what he felt about what he knew.

The great French sculptor but recently dead, Rodin, says:

"Art is the expression of thought seeking to understand the world, and to make it understood."

John Galsworthy says: "Art is the one form of human energy in the whole world which really works for union and destroys the barriers between man and man. It is the continual replacement of oneself by another; the real cement of human life; the everlasting refreshment and renewal."

And what it is to be without art, or to have an aversion to it, was never more powerfully put than when Thackeray compares Warrington and Paley in the thirtieth chapter of Pendennis.

"The one could afford time to think, and the other (Paley) never could. The one could have sympathies and do kindnesses, and the other must needs be always selfish. He could not cultivate a friendship, or do a charity, or admire a work of genius, or kindle at the sight of beauty or the sound of a sweet song—he had no time and no eyes for anything but his law-books. All was dark outside his reading-lamp. Love, and nature, and art (which is the expression of our praise and sense of the beautiful world of God), were shut out from him."

Few are those who understand art in this way who would deny its importance, but the fact remains that the great majority do deny its importance. The end of any teaching worthy the name must add to the smaller number and take away from the greater.

A Newspaper Clipping

Just before I started for Matveevskaya Volost this morning I read another of those clippings from an American paper. It told of a Russian harvest of a billion and a half bushels. It spoke of a grain tax worth several hundred million gold rubles. It painted the rosiest picture of Russia I have seen since the Soviets began to command the respect and the business dealings of the Western capitalist governments.

I felt quite proud of Russia as the motor-cycle hammered along over the hard black road running south toward the Cossack lands. The fields were green from the late—the too late—rains, the sun was performing miracles with the hillsides, and the clouds over them. August morning without a black crow on the horizon—I felt peaceful, self-satisfied, official, prosperous. I felt so because, for the moment, I was being tricked into the illusion that Russia was rich and affluent and flowing with milk and honey.

Then I rode into Matveevska and engaged the Volost Mutual Aid Committee in conversation. And I learned from these serious, honest peasant committee men certain facts. I learned:

That dozens of families are preparing to leave the volost—bound for Tashkent or any place where there is the least rumor of a harvest—because they know they have not a fraction of the bread they need to feed themselves over the winter.

That the people who survived last winter were able to do so because they had household goods and so forth to sell, but this winter they have nothing that could be called a reserve.

That dozens of families in Matveevska Village, as well as in the poorer village, Medvedka, where the horse statistics read "1921—120; 1922—0," possess altogether but a few pounds of grain with which to live eleven months! These few pounds were acquired by painfully gleaning kernels from the fields of the peasants in other and slightly more fruitful volosts.

That the recent rains have not only delayed the threshing of the grain, thus preventing the peasant who had any from realizing his riches earlier, but they have caused much of the grain to mould in the field and in the stack. . . (It will be remembered that the big sheds—*rigas*—where the unthreshed grain is ordinarily stacked—were unroofed and unthatched by the hungry stock and people last winter.)

That the few people who had any grain for seeding were reluctant to plow for it because they are not sure that they will receive pyoks from the Quakers. If they sow their rye they will need Quaker flour for their bread pots next month or the next. If they save their rye to eat they might be able to get along until Christmas.

Having learned these facts I told the committee to advise the peasants to sow all for which they could prepare the soil, to sow for the harvest of 1923 when the Quakers may have gone, to sow for the time when they can rely on self-help and not on charity. Having given this advice, which in a sense amounted to a promise involving life and death and thousands of bushels of flour, I rode out of Matveevska leaving behind me for a few yards a trail of bits of newspaper clipping.

ROBERT W. DUNN.

Help In a Chinese Emergency

Those who sent contributions to the American Friends' Service Committee to be used for famine relief in China, provided a means of serving in an unexpected emergency. During the spring and early summer, seventy-six dollars and sixty-five cents were sent to the Service Committee office for this purpose. As there was no American organization then engaged in famine relief in China, a check for this amount was forwarded to Margaret Hallowell Riggs a member of the Fifteenth and Race Streets Philadelphia Yearly Meeting of Friends, who, in response to a missionary call, is serving on the staff of Canton Christian College, Canton, China. She was requested to see that it reached the proper Chinese relief agency.

A letter from Margaret Hallowell Riggs, dated Kuliang, Foochow, China, August 20, 1922, contains the following account of the way in which these funds were employed:

"The generous check of $76.65 from the Service Committee for famine relief in China reached me August 16th, having been forwarded from Canton. It gave me the greatest satisfaction and joy, for it came most opportunely at a time of great need.

"On the night of August 2nd, a terrific typhoon, the worst in the history of this coast, struck Swatow, a town half way between Foochow and Hongkong. The typhoon raged all night and by morning all was desolation and destruction. About 50,000 Chinese lost their lives either by being washed out to sea by the tidal wave or by being crushed under their falling houses. . . .

"The first steamer that could get into the harbor after the storm came four days after and I happened to be on it on my way here for two weeks. All around us bodies were floating of people and cattle and on shore the people were working feverishly burying the dead by thousands. The heat was extreme and all feared cholera. Plague has broken out since.

"Upon my arrival here at Kuliang Mountain, the Red Cross Chapter of the American Association immediately took action and we were able to raise about $2900. The very day after the meeting came your check for $76.65 and you can imagine how glad I was to turn it over to the Committee for you. It brought the total from this one place to over $3000. This amount was immediately cabled for relief. . . . Your gifts, therefore, are now feeding the hungry of those desolate villages and giving a little hope to the broken-hearted who have lost all.

"The Chinese have shown remarkable courage and efficiency all through these terrible days since the catastrophe and are worthy indeed of our help."

Women as Law Makers

At the very first meetings of the League of Nations, efforts were made to reach agreements so that traffic in women would be suppressed.

At the meeting of the League at Geneva, September 23, a report on white slavery was presented. Mrs. Coombe Tennant, a representative of the British Government, again pressed the need of international agreements on this subject, and urged that every nation send women with their delegations to arouse more interest in the work of the association. The strength of the League, she declared, is based on public opinion, in which women, especially mothers, take a considerable part.

She said: "The League of Nations must become in some real sense a league of mothers. This is necessary if the League is to accomplish the task of bringing about an enduring peace."

Mrs. Margaret Dale, of Australia, also supported the white slave report, which asks the advisory committee to consider whether, pending the abolition of state regulation, it cannot agree that no foreign women shall be admitted to licensed places.

It is gratifying that women are being admitted to these Councils. In our own country, women have the right to vote, but as yet have small representation in the making of laws, or in formulating international treaties.

W. W. J.

First-day School Methods

By Bliss Forbush.

The Opening Session

The opening session of a First-day School can often be taken as an indication of the spirit of the entire school. If our opening exercises begin in a haphazard fashion and lead to no definite end, the lessons to follow, and the closing period later, are apt to be disconnected and meaningless. If they are conducted in a business-like manner, with a well thought out aim, the entire school hour will be well worth while.

One great difficulty with many opening exercises is that very often they are made a time filler, a period of waiting until every one is present before going to classes. Our opening exercises should be religious services, conducted in a way acceptable to children and young people. Unnecessary tardiness disturbs these services of the school, whatever form they may be taking. The Superintendent should check this tardiness by giving short talks stressing the need of promptness, and on the value of punctuality.

Opening exercises should be brief. They should be an introduction to the class work to follow if possible, and should send the scholars to their classes in the best possible frame of mind to take up their individual work. If, as is often the case, many of the younger members have been present for ten minutes, discussing questions of interest and engaging in lively arguments, it is well to make the opening exercises of a quiet nature. The hymns should be worshipful, such as "God Is In His Holy Temple," "Mysterious Presence, Source of All," or "Unto the Calmly Gathered Thought." But if the school is lifeless or lacks enthusiasm, the exercises should be sprightly and full of life. The Scripture reading might be chosen from the heroic passage telling of the high spots in Hebrew history, or inspiring passages from the words of Jesus. The hymns should be of a stirring nature, as "Come Thou Almighty King," "On Our Way Rejoicing" or "We Plough the Fields and Scatter."

If the school possesses a piano or an organ, as most of our schools do, it is a pleasant plan to have a march played while the classes are going to their separate rooms. This helps the pupils to go more quickly and quietly.

Two hymns, one at the opening and one at the close of the exercise, is sufficient and all that time will allow. When the closing exercise is the general assembly period and the time set aside for speakers or special purposes, the opening exercises should not take over ten minutes.

We have come to recognize that music in the First-day School is a thoughtful instrument for religious feeling. All children have a desire for music, even when they are three or four years of age. It is ridiculous to presume that we will let our children sing popular music on the streets and in our home, and not allow them to sing of God in the place where they are to learn about Him. There is nothing magical, however, about music and there is no danger that it will crowd out the idea of silent worship in our Meeting.

Our hymns should not be chosen hit or miss. Not only should we consider the feeling we wish to cultivate in our work for the day, but we should be careful not to pick out hymns which are unsuitable for the occasion. "Abide With Me" and "Softly Now the Light of Day" were written as vesper or evening hymns and should not be used in a morning exercise. "Lo, the Earth is Risen Again" and "Spring is Come" are spring songs. When there comes a time sacred with personal or general association children should follow the example, as someone has said, "of the Master, who closed his Gethsemane with the pascal song on his lips, flung forth in the face of death."

Our General Conference First-day School Committee has published two volumes of hymns. These are suitable for most occasions and should meet our needs. It is better to use these exclusively than to use a variety of hymn books. If we could sing twelve of these hymns correctly from beginning to end it would be far better than if we sang forty of them indifferently. We were quite dismayed to find at the Richmond Conference that without hymn books very few of us could sing more than one verse of half a dozen hymns. The members of most denominations, having had a longer musical history than we, can in their assemblies sing thirty or forty hymns without any books at hand. Indeed, many Sunday Schools require each grade of the school to memorize a number of hymns, beginning with two a year in the Primary Classes to six a year in the Intermediate and Junior Grades. Something of this nature might well be emulated by us and made a part of our curriculum. If we sing, let us sing well.

Many of our schools have added to the attractiveness of the exercises by gathering a small orchestra together to lead the singing or to play instrumental selections. It is surprising to find what a variety of instruments can be introduced into such an orchestra. Often there is a piano, violin, a guitar or mandolin, and a saxophone. A cornet or other wind instrument may seem rather loud for First-day School, but if the room is fairly large, and the windows open, even they are acceptable! These orchestras have often proven an excellent way of interesting young people in the school, and their rehearsals are usually made very pleasant social occasions.

The lack of audible prayer is to be deplored in First-day School exercises. While we must leave space for silent prayer, especially at the close of the school, there ought to be more vocal prayer than is customary. A part of the First-day School work is to train the child to commune with his Heavenly Father. With our silent graces at home, with silent prayer in Meeting, our children cannot grow up to be praying adults unless the First-day School shows them the way. Prepared prayers, with the one exception of the Lord's Prayer, do not fit the needs of the children, nor do they accomplish that which we desire; but spontaneous prayers by the Superintendent, by the teachers, or even the crude expressions of the children themselves, can be very helpful and are very necessary to the religious life of the children.

Friendly News Notes

Dr. and Mrs. Henry Erdmann Radasch, of Hedgewood Farm, Malvern, announce the engagement of their daughter, Marie Turner, to F. Lawrence Pyle, son of Mr. and Mrs. T. Norman Pyle, of Malvern.

According to the *Bethlehem Globe*, Raymond Walters, dean of Swarthmore College, former registrar of Lehigh University, is writing a book on "Bethlehem Long Ago and Today," which is scheduled to be published about December 1st. This is a short history of the city in all its phases.

A letter from Joan Mary Fry, an English Friend who is with the "Quaker Embassy" in Berlin, tells of the truly international nature of the work being carried on there. There English, Irish and American Friends are working side by side with German Quakers. In one afternoon the visitors included two parties of English people, a well-known Oxford don, an American, a Rumanian, a Korean, an Indian, a Polish lady and a Chinese student.

Alfred C. Garrett and wife have been given a Minute of their Meeting (Germantown, Philadelphia) for service in Germany and Austria under the auspices of the American Friends' Service Committee. It is understood that Alfred Garrett's service will be in the line of a teaching ministry, and in the distribution of Quaker literature.

Flushing Friends will continue their support of the relief work carried on through the Service Committee, by working in their Sewing Club, which will meet every other week.

Earlham College is to have a brand new Indoor Athletic Field, one hundred by two hundred feet, and walls 24 feet high. It will have a seating capacity at games of 3,000. This splendid indoor athletic field will supplement the two outdoor fields already in use, one for men and one for women. The building is in process of erection and will, when completed, afford a room large enough to accommodate any audience that may come to the campus. It is situated a little to the south and east of Earlham Hall.—*The Canadian Friend.*

A letter from Alfred W. Nicholson, President of Bettis Academy, Trenton, S. C., tells of the trouble schools for colored people in that section of the south are having on account of the continued ravages of the boll weevil.

This school depends largely for its support upon the colored people of the district. They have not yet learned to substitute other crops for cotton, and the cotton crop this year has been almost destroyed.

Alfred Nicholson was a friend of Henry W. Wilbur, and will appreciate greatly the support of any Friends who wish to continue this interest.

Margaret McIntosh Linton, 6417 Harper Avenue, Chicago, Ill., has a deep concern about bringing the ten- and eleven-year-olds of different countries to know more about each other so that they will be well armed against the years of prejudice that may be ahead, and as all children of that age are ripe for collecting, and many take to collecting stamps, she has established an International Stamp Collectors' Club. The membership now includes children in Canada, Egypt, Scotland, Austria, France, England, China, Germany, Holland and the United States.

This is really a very important work, and has grown to such proportions that Margaret Linton would be glad to enlist the interest and help of Friends who desire to promote better international understanding and who recognize that it is on the children that the hope for the future rests.

Peace

Future Service at Home

Clarence Pickett

William C. Biddle in introducing the speaker said: "Some of us have been so favored as to work abroad. I say 'favored' because abroad we could work at it body and soul and were not distracted as at home. But there is work at home, too, which is worth doing."

I have never yet heard of anyone who has done our work in France or another country speak of it as anything but a privilege. To the great body of our young people this privilege has been denied. Yet there is the same interest today as yesterday in the Society of Friends and in the building of a new world order in the shell of the old. Among those in college classes, I think the interest is just as great. The American Friends' Service Committee has felt this, and believed the opportunity should be given for service at home. Within the last year, opportunities have begun to offer, which will give young men and women:

1. Opportunity to serve without remuneration, or with little pay.

2. Opportunity to make contact with spots of social irritation.

Moreover, this home service will tend to restore to the whole body of Friends, the great interest in the social order which the first friends had. It is suggestd that people ought to give more than a year to such work as this. But those who did the work in France and elsewhere, do not show any tendency to let their service stop there, to settle down and do nothing. They have a keener interest in life, in all its phases.

Work in Social Service is offered us. We have now two persons in such work, a boy at Ellis Island, working under the direction of the Home Missionary Society, and one girl in the Friends' Neighborhood Guild of Philadelphia. Three are in work with negroes, one at Hampton Institute, and two at Southland Institute. Also there will be at Friendsville Academy in Tennessee this year, a young woman helping where she has opportunity. These people will not take the places of the regular staff, but will be added to the staff. They will do social service work.

Two young women are going to Porto Rico as teachers. They will receive a small salary,—more than mere living expenses—nevertheless, they are going with the true Home Service spirit. One young woman is doing missionary health work, visiting the scattered Indians in North Dakota, riding her pony here and there over about fifty miles of country.

Two young women of Penn College spent six weeks this summer in industry in Cleveland. One was taken sick before the time was up, but even this was worth while,—it was part of the experience.

The Service Committee has felt that there were opportunities in the consular service of the United States Government, for persons who desired to truly serve both the Government and many individuals. Many of the usual applicants for such positions are quite undesirable. When spoken to about this matter, officials in Washington were quite insistent that if young Friends could pass the consular examinations, they should be urged to do so. About fifteen or sixteen young men have entered for the examinations. Of course, there are temptations in such work, but I feel that we can have a dozen or more worthily representing the Society of Friends.

This service has cost the Service Committee about $500. It is not expensive, you see, and this is only the beginning. You older Friends have a great responsibility in keeping the ideal of service before the young people.

I would like to speak just a word about the feeding of the miners' children. We have been feeding about 150 children near Altoona. This has been done by two young men. In West Virginia, two young women have been caring for more. The operators have been consulted, and practically every one gave cordial approval, and even help. In fact, the work brought about a better feeling between the operators and the miners. The work is diminishing now, as the miners go back to their work. What is still done in West Virginia will be carried on in the homes now instead of at centers. It has been worth while; it has been setting an example of good-will in the midst of warring groups.

In the discussion, William Eves said: I realize now, as I did not when I left College, that it is not very important to set right about earning. I feel that if I had spent a year at that time in some such Service work, my future life would have been greatly affected. My year's work in Germany recently has deepened my life, and yet my material prosperity is not affected.

We can not leave those countries. We have made contacts which must not be broken. In these countries where we have done relief work, people have had their souls stirred as never before. They do not know what the future holds for them; they look to the Quakers for balm for their disturbed souls.

They feel that there must be something back of the food, which will restore their souls. They come to us, they gather about us, they ask so many questions, that we in Germany were forced to organize a special group to address meetings, to distribute literature, etc. From June 3rd to July 12th there were 684 pieces sent in response to such requests. This work is not done to seek members, but to answer those who are seeking. In many countries, seekers are seeking, and we dare not break this contact.

During the past year, the Service Committee has organized a sub-committee—the Message Committee. This is also connected with London and Dublin Friends. We have Quaker centers or embassies at Berlin, Frankfort-on-Rhine, Geneva, and other places. This Message Committee is seeking people who are concerned to carry this Message. A broad knowledge of the language is not necessary, though helpful. There are many lines in which we feel there are openings for persons to do this work.

I often feel ashamed when I receive reports of the literature distributed as the result of direct requests from seekers after knowledge of Friends. "Quakers and War," "The Belief of Quakers," "Relief Work of Quakers" have been put into German. Children's stories are being translated, and many other Quaker leaflets, articles and stories. Our English Friends have taken this matter to heart more than have we. They are trying to spread Truth, and we want to help spread Truth, also.

Joseph Stubbs, saying that most of us only scratch the surface of our lives, urged that we plow deep enough to raise the best things.

Frederick Libby said: We get perspective when we come into a group like this. Seventy Quakers changed the spirit of Vienna. Yet in Philadelphia, the large numbers of Friends there do not make a dent. They live like machines, and are satisfied to work in the city, live outside of it, go home at night, and let Philadelphia go to the devil. There is a far-sighted need, for which we have only near-sighted vision. International strife, industrial strife, racial strife, are the three great questions in our world. And fraternally, inter-racially, industrially, we have only begun to make a dent. If we really begin our work in the world, we shall work at our tasks at home and everywhere, carrying the same spirit of service.

E. Edmund Harvey said: We have been profoundly stirred by the messages of this morning, and by this appeal. I am glad we have been able to link up in the new service your Committee and the Yearly Meetings of London and Dublin. I hope we will be more helpful in the future, sharing our knowledge and experience. It is not our work, but the work that we are to do for God that is the need and the purpose of all our lives.

Causes of War and the Next Steps Toward Peace

J. Russell Smith

So far as war was concerned, I grew up in a Fool's Paradise of platitudes, believing that the combined forces of trade, industry, finance, decency and education had placed nations under restraints too strong to break. The war proved our delusion. The way it swept nation after nation before it can only be likened to the way a sweeping fire engulfs the forest or the tall dry grass of the prairie.

War is the result of two classes of causes, one psychological, the other economic. Among the psychological, are revenge, lust of power and empire. The second class of causes, the economic, all sift down to one base: land hunger, which arises when a people does not have as much land as it likes, and becomes a dangerous factor when they know of other peoples who have relatively more, and whose conquest would therefore enrich the conquerors. The point, then, is density of population in relation to resources. Not sheer, absolute density of population, because a rich country with 100 people to the square mile may be under-populated, and a poor country, with two people to the square mile may be over-populated. Hunger does not breed good morals. The removal of the war temptation, therefore, requires some balance among the peoples of the world with regard to their degree of pressure of man upon resources.

Human numbers tend to increase geometrically. If unchecked, this produces astonishing results. In India, for instance, where it is the custom for people to marry young, a couple marrying at eighteen, may double their numbers by the time they are twenty-five. The United States had 3.9 millions of people at the first census, in 1790. One hundred and thirty years later, we were 105 millions. If that rate of increase should be maintained for a second period of 130 years, our population would be 2,800,000,000, nearly double the present population of the world.

Human numbers have been kept from such increase by five factors, chiefly the first four: famine, pestilence, unsanitary conditions, war, and voluntary control.

1. *Famine.* The story of Joseph's brethren is only one of many references to sheer starvation in the Old Testament. In 1891, the Russian Government spent seventy million dollars carrying food to the people of the lower Volga basin. In 1922, the whole world contributed to repeat this aid, but many persons perished. Last year also millions perished in two provinces of China because of crop failure. Not long ago there was such a famine in India, that

people died by hundreds of thousands. There are many examples of famines that have wiped out single blocks of people as great in number as the entire population of the United States at the time of the establishment of the Republic.

2. *Pestilence* follows famine; it also stalks by itself. The chronicles of Europe and Asia bristle with stories of scourges of the past:—the black death, smallpox, typhus, typhoid, bubonic plague, yellow fever and the flu which we have seen in our country take a greater toll of American life than the World War did. Then there are the diseases like tuberculosis, venereal diseases, and malaria, which last alone has done much to keep large sections of the world empty of people.

3. *Unsanitary conditions,* whether produced by ignorance, laziness, or malnutrition, have steadily reduced human numbers. Among the Indians in the north woods of Canada, it is common for a woman to have had ten or fifteen children, but uncommon for her to have more than one or two living.

4. *War.* As though these other three were not enough to keep us down, war has ravaged mankind for an unknown time. We are inclined to think that the World War was unique. It was uncommon in size only. It was tame and gentle in its proportion of destruction. Look at one of the recent more primitive wars. Between 1885 and 1898 a native ruler called the "Mahdi" had possession of a part of Africa called the Anglo-Egyptian Sudan. During these fifteen years, war and its attendant famines, pestilences, and slave trade, reduced the population from eight millions to two. Since then, under the peace created by the British Government, their numbers almost doubled.

The nineteenth century has abolished in great extent the checks on population. Famine has been checked by the organization of transportation and world trade. Pestilence and unsanitary conditions are being conquered by medical and sanitary science, and a good food supply. The results of these three great improvements are: A twenty-seven fold increase in the population of the United States since 1790; the approximate doubling of the world's population in the last hundred years; and the World War.

Man is still an organism, and in the struggle for survival, food, and space he fights to the death every other organism, whether visible plant or animal, invisible bacteria, or his own kind. Rapidly expanding population means, if the people are unorganized, famine and pestilence. If it is organized into effective groups, it goes and gets lands and wealth of the weaker groups. Witness the expansion in the nineteenth and twentieth centuries of England, Russia, Germany and Japan. The Japanese produce, at the expense of almost unbelievable labor, five bushels of grain per capita per year, whereas we produce fifty bushels, and do it with less labor. A nation with such a dense population, driven to the limits of toil and poverty, often hungry, was ripe for famine and pestilence at any time of crop failure. These conditions are the background, the dynamic forces that caused Japan to rise as a disturbing factor in world peace, because she has seized upon western machines, science and mechanism. The people of the United States can throw no stones at any other nation, for during the twenty years before 1919 we took more land than any other empire in the world. We control the Philippines, Porto Rico, Cuba, Haiti, Santo Domingo, Nicaragua and Panama. At an earlier time we brushed the Indian relentlessly aside, and took his land.

When expanding peoples come in sight of undeveloped resources, there lurks the seed of war. I have joined with others in pointing with pride to our American-Canadian boundary, 3000 miles long, unfortified, and with no rumor of war along it in a hundred years. But I now realize its real significance. The temptation to war does not exist across this boundary because similar population ratios on both sides of it remove the temptation to war.

It is a sad fact that while it may take two to make a quarrel, it takes but one to make a war. When human numbers increase beyond easy support by the land in which they live, relatively empty land nearby becomes a continuing temptation to war. Witness the Indians and the Mexicans in our own history. The real basis of the European chaos at the present moment is the deadly fear that France, with 40,000,000 people and a static population, has of Germany, with nearly 60,000,000 people, still rapidly increasing.

If one takes a long view, perhaps the greatest peril in all the world today is China, actuated by the Chinese religion,—ancestral worship. Where this religion prevails, the state of heaven is attained by those who have children to revere them; therefore, the institution of early marriages and children promptly, and enough of them to guarantee the parents against childlessness, even if some of the children should not grow up. Contemplate the future of China, with 300,000,000 people, healthy, vigorous, increasing by natural tendencies, plus a religious impulse. Note that Western science, philanthropy, education, and finance are combining to remove from this people the ancient checks of famine and pestilence and bad sanitation which in the past have held down their numbers. We are further preparing our own undoing by teaching them the arts of war.

The Next Steps Toward Peace

a. *Voluntary control of human numbers.* Since the involuntary controls of famine, pestilence and bad sanitation are being removed, the checks must be furnished by war or by human volition. I salute Mrs. Sanger as the prophet of the anti-militarist campaign of this century. Since we have achieved death control, we must also achieve birth control. The year 1921 has two great events leading toward eventual peace. One was the conference in Washington upon limitation of armaments. The other was a commission of representatives of various bureaus of the Japanese Government to America and Europe to study the birth control movement.

At the Washington Conference, the Japanese delegation insisted upon this assumption: Japan, having a population increasing by several hundred thousand per year cannot feed them on her own resources. We cannot, therefore, discuss anything that prohibits us from having access to the natural resources of Asia. If population continues to increase, Asia will not be large enough to hold them. Then what? The answer to that question is not pleasant, but if the Japanese government should deliberately persuade its people to check their numbers, the thing would take care of itself. Birth control is not a mystery. Witness the long static population of Iceland, the static population of France, the declining numbers of the Friends, whose birth rate in Philadelphia Yearly Meeting is seven per thousand, and whose death rate is twenty-two.

The whole background of any discussion of ultimate peace must have as its background the concept of a society of nations and peoples. One of the best clauses in the constitution of the League of Nations provided that if any nation showed signs of breaking the world's peace at a future time, the matter should be the subject of discussion. Under this, if Japan or Germany should say, 'Here, we have an increasing population; therefore, we must have the earth,' the answer might be, 'start an educational campaign to check increase of your population.'

b. *Improve the human quality.* Any society of nations that can be organized on a basis to control war will need a large number of persons of high intellectual and moral caliber. There is surprising evidence in America of the proportional decline of the best and most competent elements among our people. Intelligence tests applied to the draft army showed 24.9 per cent. illiterates. There were only 4.5 per cent. of the so-called A grade intellect, capable of doing very well in college. Group B, 9 per cent., capable of average record in college; C+, 16.5 per cent., inferior college material. Then came group C, comprising 25 per cent., rarely capable of finishing a high school course. Most astonishing of all was that 47 per cent. had a mental age of twelve years or less. We have a rapidly increasing population. But family records of the graduates of Harvard, Vassar, Yale, Smith, and Barnard Colleges show that the college graduates are having such small families that "if the Harvard of the future were limited to sons of Harvard men, it would shrink in half a dozen generations from 5000 to 250." The two great things, therefore, to be achieved if we abolish war are:—

1. Voluntary control of human numbers.

2. Along with this control, the increase of the best rather than the worst of us.

c. *War symptoms.* Limitation of armaments, the League of Nations, arbitration treaties, poison gas, military training in colleges, conscription, and other things which speak directly of war and preparation for war are only symptoms. The important thing is to remove the causes which produce the war fever with its many symptoms.

d. *Education.* There was a time when I thought that the increase of education among the nations would remove the tendency to war. I know now that this is one of the best preparations for extensive war. Witness highly educated Germany, and highly educated Japan. It takes an educated nation to make war, and the war arises from the peoples' necessities, or their concepts of their necessities, and their ideals.

e. *Scientific point of view.* This is praised as an age of Science. What is this science? It is finding out the facts, and then acting in the light of the facts, rather than in the light of notions that came, we know not how, and have no rational defence, however sweet they may be to us. We have all heard the sad story of Galileo, who was made to forswear his scientific discoveries about the universe, so shocking was his idea to the prejudices of the people of his age. In the course of three hundred years, we have come in material things to act very largely in the light of the facts, but in human relationships, we still act very largely in the light of our prejudices, and in none of these, perhaps, more than in matters pertaining to war.

f. *The conference habit.* One of the surest rays of light in the dark world of the present is the international conference habit. If we can increase our tendency to act in the light of the facts, and increase our international conference habit, the world may yet be saved. Take France and Germany today. They are embroiling the world in commercial hardship because France is afraid the more potentially powerful Germany will soon turn around and annihilate her. Germany's population was deliberately fomented by the militarists, the picturesque Kaiser preaching that women's place was covered by three words, *Kinder, Kucken, Kirche* (children, kitchen, church), which in being interpreted, meant infantry, food supply, obedience. A conference of nations needs to tell the Germans they need a campaign to reduce their birth rate to the point where the country can support her people without the deliberate expectation of conquering half the world to make room for them.

g. *The habit of international action.* Since the ultimate end of international peace seems only possible through some kind of international government, I commend to all persons interested in opposing war the serious study of international activity. Before the World War, I understand that there were about 250 of such lines of activity. The cause of peace is promoted by every international organization, or any other thing whereby people of different nations can come together to talk over things or to do things. Knowledge of what the nations are doing together is most effective propaganda for peace.

h. *"No More War" agitation.* Thus far I have mentioned specific things that need to be done. But people are not going to do things until they believe they need to be done, and the person who devotes his time to creating a dread of war as an unendurable thing is creating the background from which action may finally spring. Getting children to grow up with such a slogan as "No More War" gets them in the position where finally in a crisis they will really stand for things that mean no more war.

In conclusion; let the good work go on in any and all ways, for what we want, down back of it all, is a public opinion against war, which will finally forge the necessary intellectual implements, and stop the creation of the physical implements of war.

Round Table on Teaching of History

Led by J. Russell Smith

This Round Table opened with some discussion of population pressure. In England even during the war, there were 100 births to every 97 deaths. In France there were 157 deaths to every 100 births. In such countries as England, the strain of population is tremendous.

Does the surplus population of other countries affect us? it was queried. We are building a navy, and paying taxes because of Japan's surplus population.

There is hardly anything that offers greater variety in choice than the teaching of history. What should we emphasize and what not? Most of our United States histories are practically lists of wars. Quaker teachers have a great opportunity in choosing material. It is a good idea to teach history and geography together.

Our histories have stressed political events to the exclusion of other things. A child's interest is not in the records of the past, he is interested in the present and future.

The social side is stressed much more than it used to be, but that is only a part of history. There is social, political and religious history. We want to show children that history is dynamic and alive.

What should a teacher emphasize? Whatever he emphasizes is propaganda. But what he believes in he will put across, he can't help it. Of all the means of social education, history stands first with geography not far behind. We need more industrial history. Good teachers do not try to teach wars, as wars. They try to teach bigger things. They are getting their material from near, far and everywhere. Unfortunately, it was feared, there are not many teachers of real efficiency in their field. The majority of school teachers are just students of books. These should use the newspapers and magazines that are the aristocracy of education, and thus make the best of the text-books that we have.

Round Table on Work Against War

[This period, regularly belonging to the Young People's Forum, led by William J. Reagan, was given over by him to Frederick Libby.]

If we can take this spirit of fellowship with us, we shall not be working alone, but in the great strength that makes all tasks easy. God is all-powerful but He has limited himself to working through his children. Our standard of right must rise to the point where we believe that war must cease.

I want to tell you some of the things that have been done, and to remind you that some of the suggestions in the last *Bulletin* of the *Council for Limitation of Armaments* are practical for us all.

The two great days to celebrate in the war against war are: the anniversary of the beginning of this war, July 29th, when we swear "No More War," and second, Armistice Day, November 11th. "No More War" day was celebrated in various ways. In St. Louis there was a big mass meeting. In some places they had peace pageants, using the children playing in the parks. There were parades in various places, New York's being one of the smallest in the country, only from 600 to 1000.

Enlist the press.

If you see misleading statements in the papers, write to the editor yourself, and ask your friends to write, explaining the facts. You may change his mind by your letter. The National Security League will try to discredit us this winter. We depend on you to protect us. We must expect opposition of this kind. A newspaper will always publish an answer to an attack if it comes promptly, while the matter is still news. We will be on the spot. The Council is in Washington, and we will provide you with all the statements in regard to it that you need.

Our *Bulletin* comes out every two weeks. It gives material which can be put into letters which the papers would take because it would be newsy. The editors will publish letters when they will not publish the *Bulletin*. We stand behind the facts in the *Bulle-*

Industrial

Christian Ideals for Industry

ALVA W. TAYLOR

"Dr. Alva W. Taylor," Dr. Janney announced, "has been for twelve years Professor of Sociology at the University of Missouri, and is now Secretary of Social Welfare of the Disciples of Christ. He was a member of the Federation of Churches' committee which investigated the Steel Trust, and is a frequent contributor to the *Christian Century*."

I make no pretense of being an industrial expert, but for thirty years I have qualified as something of a specialist in Christian ethics. I have had manufacturers say, "What do you know about managing men?" I answer, "What do you know about the relations of Jesus Christ to the management of men?" I am doing my best, with many others, to find what relation the Saviour of the world has to all human relations.

We shall never have the kingdom of God here, as Jesus taught it, until we have it in factory and mine. We shall never have brotherhood until we are brotherly in the common relations of the Almighty Dollar. The mission of the church should be to transform the atomic mass. We are to become working units in a church whose duty is to bring in the kingdom of God.

There are three or four fundamental principles of Christianity. First, the sacredness of life. Every human being's life is sacred. We have the spirit of God in us, and our spirits, our lives, are sacred. Jesus said that the final test at the Great Assize would be how we had ministered, not only to our own race, or family, but "unto the least of these," the outcast, the humblest—the Lazarus at the gate, though he may be there because of his own vices. There is no sacredness attached to *property*, but to the beggar at the gates.

makers. Many men get by their consciences by saying, "Everybody does it." Sam Jones once said: "You've got to live, and you've got to lie to live? Well, you haven't got to live, and you'd better die than live by lying."

Human life is sacred. Is our modern industrial system giving every man an equal chance? Would you think that every child born in the drab, dreary houses of a mining-town has an equal chance with your child or mine? What kind of inheritance has the tenement-house child as against the farm-house child? Seventy to 80 per cent. of the leaders in our life come from farm homes, 90 per cent. of the ministers, and 95 per cent. of the missionaries. If you can't give the children a Christian environment, what hope is there for them? Take a man whose wage is that of the textile worker, or the packing-house worker—$18.00 a week, and even at that, the man knows that he cannot work every week. He earns $900 a year. Say he lives in the City of Chicago. I pay $900 a year for five rooms in a middle-class district in Indianapolis. Where is this man who earns $900 a year going to live, and bring up his children? What do you think of an award that gives to thousands of railway workers an average wage of two and a half dollars a day? What chance are they going to have to bring up their children in the culture of good American citizens?

We hear sometimes of skilled workers who get $36.00 or more a day. But they didn't strike! No $7.00-a-day men struck! It was the men who were getting $2.50 a day who struck. Where is the margin of opportunity for a man to bring up children on that? We shall never have a Christian foundation for industry until the men who have the greatest need have opportunity to give their children the schooling that they must have, the cultural opportunities that ours have. It is a man in a million, like Andrew Carnegie, who says it is an advantage to be born poor. There are thousands of others who are borne down by circumstances. Give everybody a chance!

If every non-productive person in our modern society would cut out the non-essentials, and set free the men at the machines producing these goods, they could make enough essentials to give to all, the comforts that the middle class now enjoys. Twelve years ago in the Pittsburgh steel mills, when a man was killed, $300.00 was the average sum paid to his family, while $50 was the usual compensation for a hand or foot. There has been a great change in that respect even in the steel mills. But they can still get rich by the 12-hour day, when they choose. Ours are the only steel mills in the world that work twelve hours a day. American enterprise vies with Chinese industry.

When our American genius really gets to work, we shall make as great results on the human side as we have on the material side. We need some prophets today to show forth the social meaning of our gospel, until the men who work little children, and who work men twelve hours a day feel as Jonathan Edwards used to make sinners feel—as though flames were leaping about them! And we must come out for experimentation. Happily there are many experiments being made. It does not matter so much about the kind of machinery that we use; it is the spirit with which we work.

The second fundamental of Christianity is Service. Service, not Profit, should be the dominating motive of business. It is too often thought that self-interest must be the controlling interest of modern life. "Economics has no more to do with ethics than geology has to do with ethics." "God in His divine wisdom has so planned that if a man does his best for himself, he is doing his best for the race." It would be a nice world, indeed, if this motive moved it! What did Jesus say? "He is greatest who ministers most." The terms of service are self-sacrifice. The whole fabric must be permeated through and through with the life-blood of the Christ spirit. Our feeling must be that we are giving or contributing something to the common weal. There is something in the spirit of emulation that may drive us to the highest degree of service. We can make service of the highest meaning, and self-interest only secondary to it.

Socialism and Capitalism are more alike than either is like Christianity. Both are materialistic, but different in their concepts. If we go on as we are, we shall end in anarchy. One in every nine marriages in America is broken by divorce. In Ireland, the number is one in 3,000. In Canada it is one in 1,200. There is no nation to compare with us in this respect except Japan. There one in six is broken, but they are improving, while we are getting worse. Why? Our crass individualism that results in divorces, and in an autocratic business system that fights the right of millions of men to organize. I am ready to fight for the right of both laborers and owners to unite and work together. The man who puts either brawn or brain into a factory has some claim on that factory.

I do not know what the solution will be, but I am sure that we will find one. The inventive genius that invented the air-plane, the enterprise that organized the steel mills and all their workings, can also organize the human factory. We will slay our state if we do not change.

In the discussion, Arthur Jackson told of a joint committee in Philadelphia, which has for several years been making a study of industrial conditions.

"I would advise any Friends in industrial centers to make a similar study," he said.

In response to a query concerning the matter a number of firms and organizations were named that were applying successfully the principles advocated by the speaker.

The Christian Solution of Industry's Problems

ELBERT RUSSELL

(Dr. William Swain, of Indiana University, presided at this session.)

These problems are not new; they existed in the time of Jesus. The thing that is new is the extension of power that our modern industry has given, and the new instruments with the resulting complexity of life. But the fundamentals are the same. Our power for good or evil has outrun our imagination. That is what makes it so hard for us to understand how to apply the Golden Rule. When men understand the results of their acts, they will do right. There are people who would not steal a penny, but would not hesitate to steal a railroad. There are men who would not think of inoculating a man with deadly disease, yet would let tenants go into an infected house, and get the germs of deadly disease.

Modern machinery has so greatly extended our power that most of the victims of our sins lie beyond our knowledge. I know a young fellow who was trained in a military college for the artillery. It was all mathematics for him until finally he went into action, and, to his horror, saw for the first time what it meant. Aeroplanes dropping bombs over cities recorded the hits, but they did not know what those hits meant in terms of humanity. If a Russian baby lay on our doorstep, we would see that it did not die for lack of food. But thousands of miles away, we do not see the effects of the famine, or hear the wails of the victims. We are so linked with people everywhere that we heal, or kill, or help, without knowing it. The mine-operators in the struggle do not see the babies starving. To them, hunger is only a part of the game. They do not mean to kill.

Measles does not kill babies in rich families. But 10 per cent. of the babies of the poor who have it die. Ninety thousand babies die each year in the United States because of low incomes. Would you take 7 per cent. instead of 8 per cent. dividends, to save these babies? We are all involved in a social system that is beyond our knowledge, and we may well wonder what lies ahead. We need to make our imaginations active, and realize our responsibilities. There is room for differences of opinion among us as to the effect of our acts. We must learn to discuss fairly what is the effect of the twelve-hour day, autocratic system of industry? We must be ready to follow the teachings of Jesus.

As Jesus sums up these teachings, there is one chief goal of life—free, self-determined spiritual personalities. "What doth it profit a man if he gain the whole world and lose his own soul?" Jesus never attached any value to compulsory goodness. Personality must be self-determined. We must become spiritual personalities. These should be our great goals. Our activities and our industrial processes can be tested by this: If they tend to make men spiritual personalities, and self-determined personalities, they stand approved; if not, they are condemned. Take the matter of the working-day; shall it be twelve hours, or eight hours? A man cannot be a good citizen and work twelve hours a day; nor a good father. He can develop neither mind nor spirit if he has to give his full life to making a living. Education means a margin from the demands of the body in which to build up the mind and soul. The eight-hour day means to men the opportunity to become human beings. What do they do with the extra four hours? Many will answer, "Squander it." Do we take away the money of the rich because some of them only waste it? The way to develop character is to give a chance for choice; not to take away the opportunity, but teach them how to use it.

Thrift is an excellent quality. But have you ever thought how much it may mean to the United States to have men saving money? If a man is earning eight or nine hundred dollars a year, and laying by fifty dollars,—what may it mean? A child may be sick, but because the father needs to save a dollar a week the doctor is not called, and the child may die or be disabled.

A certain young lady was to be married; her father found it necessary to raise $20,000 for the wedding expenses. He made the money by cutting the wages of the girls who worked in his factory fifty cents a week each. That meant cutting off the recreation in those girls' lives, and it led directly to the prostitution of five of those girls.

Then in addition to the needs of the body, we have to pay our tobacco bill. We are taking that out of our souls. We have children on half-time in the schools, because our cities cannot get money enough to pay the teachers proper salaries, or to build enough school-houses. Yet we pay two billion dollars for tobacco. I do not say that it is wrong or harmful to use tobacco. I do say that it is a mistake to take this out of our children. What does it profit a nation to gain money, and starve the souls and minds of its children?

(To be concluded in next issue)

The following paragraph appeared in a Richmond paper:

The advent of a number of our British cousins this week, during the Five Years Meeting, has helped to impress on many of us the wonderful unity and sincerity which has characterized this unusual gathering of people from so many lands. It has, too, brought to some of our people strange and unfamiliar phrases. One waitress welcomed a couple of distinguished looking visitors and the husband gave the order for "two dishes of ice." The waitress stunned by the unfamiliar request finally made out that they really wanted vanilla ice cream, when the husband, reconsidering, asked his wife: "Or would you rather, dear, have yours in a biscuit?"—And what d'ye s'pose he wanted—"in a biscuit, mind you!—you'd never guess in all the world. Why, he meant an ice-cream cone!—*The American Friend.*

On Tenth month 12th the Numismatic and Antiquarian Society of Philadelphia, under the leadership of J. Henry Scattergood, made an historical pilgrimage to Montgomery, Delaware and Chester Counties. Their first stopping place was at Merion Meeting-house built in 1695, and the oldest house of worship in Pennsylvania. It is also unique as being the only meeting-house in all the Society built in the form of a Tau Cross or Cross of St. Anthony. The peg which succeeds the peg on which William Penn once hung his hat, the old horse block, the date stone and other features of the house were pointed out to the visiting Antiquarians by Charles E. Hires, who also distributed a handsome booklet, which he had prepared, with views of the meeting-house and grounds, as a souvenir of the visit. Charles F. Jenkins made a short historical address covering the founding of the meeting and the Welsh Friends who settled in Merion and adjoining townships. After an interesting visit the Antiquarians proceeded to old St. David's Church, General Anthony Wayne's home and the scene of the Paoli Massacre, completing the excursion with lunch at the home of J. Henry Scattergood.

The meeting that was held at Haverford Meeting-house on Tenth month 15th, was one of those occasions which are so spiritually beneficial to all that we sadly realize that they come all too seldom in our lives. Not simply was Elbert Russell's address an inspiration, but the well-filled house added much. Friends from three branches were present as well as neighbors from the community, among them being the Catholic priest from the church across the way.

In his address, Elbert Russell showed us that there was something better than justice. Decisions rendered according to the laws of justice as we have generally interpreted it have resulted, in many cases, in adding needless suffering for innocent relatives and Friends. Not by such decisions has the world been made better, but by those loyal persons who have worked and not required a just wage, by those who have labored on and sacrificed themselves unstintingly, out of love for humanity. We have all received, to a much greater extent than we deserved, the benefits of such love. Having received bountifully, so should we give.

Charles Harrison added a few words, pointing out that only as we give do we receive; if we are not receiving, it is a sign that we are not giving.

On September 23, 1867, at Lincoln, Va., in the Old Friends' Meeting-house, according to the custom of Friends, a double wedding took place. The couples were Barclay Eyre, of Bucks County, Pa., and Emma D. Taylor, of Lincoln, Va.; Thomas E. Taylor, of Lincoln, Va., and Mary J. Taylor, of Silcott's Springs, Va. More than one hundred persons signed the wedding certificates as witnesses. Of that number only fifteen are still living.

On September 23, 1922, at the hospitable home of Henry J. and Laura S. Hoge, Barclay Eyre and wife celebrated the fifty-fifth anniversary of their marriage. Barclay and Emma Eyre, who for many years lived near Dolington, Pa., on the farm bearing the name of Mont Eyre, but now of Washington, D. C., went to Virginia that they might be with their relatives on the occasion.

Sara E. Hoge, of Virginia; Furman and Edith Mulford, of Washington, D. C.; Charles and Martha Platt, of Pennsylvania; Howard and Sara Hoge and Mary J. Taylor, of Virginia, and H. B. Taylor and family attended this anniversary and all present enjoyed the feast of good things and the stories and reminiscences of by-gone days. The bride and groom of the occasion received a number of cards and telegrams bearing congratulations and good wishes.

"Bright is the glow of the evening sky
When clouds are entangled by sunbeams golden;
Sweet are the thoughts of well spent lives
Woven with threads of memories olden.

Calm be the days passing swiftly bye,
Whether glad or gay, or serene and sober;
Restful the years that before you lie,
Filled with the peace of life's October."

BALTIMORE NEWS

This week the Young Friends meet for the first time this fall. A Firelight Supper is planned, with a discussion following of the plans for the year. The older boys' club also gets under way this week, the younger group already having had three meetings.

Sixty-four people attended our Monthly Meeting supper last week.

Next week, autos are to call at the homes of our families and collect all manner of garments for the Reconstruction Group, and those interested in the colored schools in the south.

Our Community Service Department is asking the Federation of Churches to send a delegation to the Commissioner of Police and encourage him to enforce the laws to the utmost.

The Recreation Department recently reported that our summer camp cleared all expenses and paid ninety dollars toward the equipment it purchased.

FRIENDS' LIBRARY NOTES

At the meeting of the Committee of Management of the Library Association of Friends, 15th and Cherry Streets, Philadelphia, the report of the previous month showed such an increase in the use of the Library and its opportunities that plans for further work were discussed.

In September, 1921, the number of books circulated was 109; the borrowers classified as follows: Friends, 45; non-Friends, 16; pupils, 17; school teachers, 5.

September, 1922, the number of books circulated was 226; the borrowers: Friends, 58; non-Friends, 26; pupils, 117; school teachers, 7.

The marked increase in the juvenile circulation shows the opportunity for its greatest development. It would cover reference for the Friends' Elementary School,

Friends' Central School and the Public Schools of the neighborhood, and supply books for supplementary and recreational reading.

A rearrangement of the shelves will make the books of especial interest and value more accessible. The Friends' Works will be replaced and kept up to date and thereby give the Library its place among the historic as well as the modern libraries of the city.

At present, it is possible for any Friend to use the Library for reference and study. The books may be borrowed and kept for use as long as there is no other demand for them. The Library is free to the public and open for use on week-days from 1 to 4.30, Seventh-day 1 to 4. MAUDE A. LAWS, *Librarian.*

NOTES FROM THE "SWARTHMORE PHOENIX"

During the summer there appeared in the Sunday *Public Ledger* a tribute to the genius of Professor J. Russell Hayes. It was written by Lee Weiss, '21, who was at that time on the staff of the *Ledger.*

The special article showed a fine sense of appreciation of the man and his works. One quotation of special interest follows:

"Many volumes of J. Russell Hayes' poems are dear to the hearts of all lovers of nature as well as to those of the people of Chester County; particularly, "The Brandywine." "Brandywine Days," "Old Fashioned Garden." "Swarthmore Idylls."

"Mark Sullivan recently told a Swarthmore friend that Hayes' volume, "Old Quaker Meeting Houses," is a favorite book of himself and Herbert Hoover in their quieter hours.

"That volume," says Prof. Hayes, "was written with deep affection for Quaker shrines which I inherit from my ancestors on both sides."

"He wanders across the campus, a solitary figure with Van Dyke beard, a cap, and a greeting for all the signs of life about him.

"All his poems speak the spirit of Prof. Hayes' life, which is: "We live by admiration, hope and love." He believes that the nature of the out of doors and of human beings—particularly of girls—is all of the same harmony of life."

The *Phoenix* reports the following marriages of former Swarthmoreans:

Mary Truman and Bernard Welsh, on June 3rd, at Collingdale, Pa. Their home is at Ridgeway, Pa.

Oswald Wallwyn Darch, of England, and Margaret Barber Marr, in Hongkong, China, on June 28th. They will be located temporarily in Manila.

Raymond Taylor Bye and Virginia Lippincott Higgins, at West Chester, Pa., on Ninth month 7th.

Roger Bacon Owings and Lucy Marie Penrose, at Ocean City, N. J., on June 16th. They are at home in Parsons, Kansas.

Ruth Agnes Lacey and Cyrus Spicer Tandy, Jr., on July 9th, at Pen Argyl, Pa.

Josephine Murray Griffiths and Harrison Weber, on June 10th, near Norristown, Pa. They are living at Port Indian, Pa.

Helen Elizabeth Sigler and George Chester Carpenter, Jr., on June 17th, at Indianalo, Iowa. They are at home at Des Moines.

Doris Maria Hays and Frederick Craig Fenton, on June 8th, at Ames, Iowa, where they are now living.

George Earnshaw and Grace Stockton, on June 26th, in Philadelphia.

Ruth Elizabeth Pownall and Charles R. Russell, on September 4th, at Swarthmore, Pa., where they are now living.

Joseph Powell and Ida Dutton, at Media, Pa. Joseph will complete his course at Bucknell and they will live at Lewisburg.

Kathryn Elizabeth Madden and Charles L. Hammell, of Collingswood, N. J., on July 12th, at Baltimore, Md.

AMERICAN QUAKER ACTS AS PEACE AMBASSADOR IN CHINA'S CIVIL WAR

The story of how an American Quaker, Mr. J. E. Platt, of the Y. M. C. A., Mukden, and a Scottish Medical Missionary, Dr. W. A. Young, senior doctor of the Mukden Medical College, were instrumental in arranging an armistice which led to peace in the Civil War in North China has just reached London by the China mail.

Some three months ago the armies of Wu-Pei-Fu and Chang-Tso-Lin were facing one another with every prospect of the long continuance of the strife. General Chang's son when on a visit to Mukden, keenly feeling how injurious for the best interests for China was a further continuance of the Civil War, brought his troubles to his old friend, Mr. Platt.

"Will you help us to put an end to useless slaughter?" he begged. "There is nothing to be gained by fighting. My father is distracted. Not knowing which way to turn. Will you come to try to open negotiations at the front?"

Dr. Young was brought into consultation, and the American and the Britisher finally acceded to Chang-Han-Ching's urgent request.

They had no light task in front of them. No Chinese would accept the risks. Foreign ministers had forbidden their Consuls to intervene, and foreign business men felt they must hold aloof.

On the understanding that their task was that of bringing the peace delegates together, Mr. Platt and Dr. Young unprotected and without any documents, made three strenuous journeys from Mukden to the front. Chang-Han-Ching was not allowed to accompany them for the parley, and twice General Wu, entrenched as he was in a favorable position, refused all suggestions of peace. On the second visit the trip from Shinhaihuan to Chinwangtao and back had to be made in a Chinese junk over a stormy sea in the dead of night, amid all the risks incident upon the resumption of fighting which had taken place.

At last their importunity was rewarded, and a parley was arranged which took place at 2.30 a. m. on a Sunday morning on board the British cruiser Curlew. Here the final negotiations were carried through, while the bluff British captain harangued the bargainers of the Chihli and Fengtien armies on his quarter deck.

"Peace was declared. North China breathed freely. Manchuria was spared the letting loose of hell," commented the *North China Herald.* The courage, perseverance and wisdom of our two Mukden comrades, the humanity of their cause, their intrepid bearing and entire detachment from political and personal matters carried their point."

"I can quite imagine the way in which Platt would carry out work like this," commented his friend, Mr. Harry T. Silcock, Secretary of the English Friends' Foreign Mission Association in London, who has himself had long experience in China. "He is an extremely fine chap and is a regular 'Chinahand' and can speak the language to some purpose. Last time I saw him was in Philadelphia last summer just before his marriage to Edith Stratton, of the well-known Quaker family there."

HUBERT W. PEET.

Recent Publications

"THE WAYFARER," by J. E. Ward. MacMillan Co. of Canada, Toronto. A beautiful little volume of prose poetry from the pen of a gifted Canadian writer. In these days of materialistic tendencies such a book as this dealing largely with things spiritual, the building up of character, and the sanctifying of the commonplace happenings of everyday life, should make a great appeal to the thoughtful reader.

PICTURES FROM THE PYRENEES, CATHEDRAL REVERIES, AN ACCOUNT OF JOURNEY FROM ITALY TO ENGLAND, AUGUST, 1914, AND SEVEN YEARS AFTER, by MARGARET COPE. Winston Company, Publishers, Philadelphia, .75. This book was reviewed under the heading "Poems of War-time."

The title of Margaret Cope's second book is "AMERICAN DESCRIPTIVE AND THOUGHTFUL VERSE.". It deals with nature in its picturesque and emblematic phases in many parts of Eastern America, beginning with bird and flower songs. The thoughtful verse is written in this period, fruitful of thought along many lines induced by the war and contrasts in social life, beside much of a more varied character.

Both of these books can be procured through Walter H. Jenkins, 140 N. 15th Street, Philadelphia.

"THE MEANING OF THE CROSS," by Edward Grubb, M. A. George H. Doran Company, Publishers, New York. $1.50.

Edward Grubb is one of our leading English Friends and the author of "The Bible: Its Nature and Inspiration." In this book, "The Meaning of the Cross," he points out some of the difficulties of the Substitutionary doctrine of the Atonement; sketches the different strains of teaching in regard to Atonement in the Old and New Testaments, and the main theories developed by Christian thinkers at different times; and concludes with an attempt to indicate the lines along which thought is moving toward a more satisfying solution of the problem of the relation of Christ's death to human salvation. The book will be serviceable to those who are seeking for light on the subject, and should prove specially useful as a brief text-book for study groups.

"THE CHILDREN'S BIBLE." Selections from the Old and New Testaments, translated and arranged by Henry A. Sherman, head of the Department of Religious Literature of Charles Scribner's Sons, and Charles Foster Kent, Woolsey Professor of Biblical Literature in Yale University. Charles Scribner's Sons, Publishers, New York. $3.50.

Those Friends who have read Professor Kent's Shorter Bible will know what to expect in this book which is arranged especially for children. The illustrations are well selected and beautifully printed. The whole make-up of the book is such as to make it attractive to children.

"CHRISTIANITY AND PROBLEMS OF TODAY." Charles Scribner's Sons, New York. $1.25.

"Christianity and Problems of Today" is a collection of addresses delivered at Lake Forest College on the occasion of the inauguration of Herbert McComb Moore as President of Lake Forest University.

The contents include the following: From Generation to Generation, by John Huston Finley, LL.D., L.H.D.; Jesus' Social Plan, by Charles Foster Kent, Ph.D., Litt.D.; Personal Religion and Public Morals, by Robert Bruce Taylor, D.D., LL.D.; Religions and Social Discontent, by Paul Elmer More, Litt.D., LL.D.; and The Teachings of Jesus as Factors in International Politics, with especial reference to Far-Eastern Problems, by Jeremiah W. Kenks, Ph.D., LL.D.

Items from Everywhere

The Near East Relief is making a special appeal for funds to aid the 500,000 or more refugees made homeless by the advance of the Turks and the burning of the Christian sections of Smyrna. The condition of the innocent women and children is most pathetic. Contributors to this emergency fund are asked to mark their checks "Smyrna." Checks may be mailed to Near East Relief, Cleveland H. Dodge, Treasurer, 151 Fifth Avenue, New York.

According to the *World League Clip Sheet*, the movement to discredit the eighteenth amendment and the Volstead act was hard hit when President Albee of the Keith theaters circuit issued the following order: To the managers of all Keith theatres; also houses booked through the Keith Vaudeville Exchange: There have been many complaints from patrons in reference to jokes about the Volstead act. I feel that the humor in this has been overdone and to continue is irritating to those who favor prohibition. Inasmuch as theatres should not be used for political propaganda, would like to have you notify the artists that any reference to prohibition should be eliminated from their acts. (Signed) E. F. ALBEE.

The passage by the Senate of the Cable Equal Citizenship Bill may be hailed as a great victory for women.

The wording of the bill is "that the right of any woman to become a naturalized citizen of the United States shall not be denied or abridged because of her sex or because she is a married woman." The bill also provides that a foreign woman who marries a citizen does not, as heretofore, become a citizen merely by such marriage, but must comply with the naturalization laws, except that she need not file a declaration of intention, and that the five-year residence required of foreign men is reduced to one year in the case of foreign women married to citizens. Finally women shall not cease to be citizens because of marriage.

Dr. Robert R. Moton, principal of Tuskeegee Institute, was recently re-elected, by unanimous vote, president of the National Negro Business League, at its 23rd annual business meeting. Nearly 5,000 white and colored citizens of Norfolk and the adjacent territory crowded into the Norfolk Armory to hear Doctor Moton deliver his annual address.

Within the Norfolk district there are, according to Doctor Moton, about 150,000 Negroes who spend annually $15,000,000 for food and clothing, and $1,000,000 for shoes.

The average Negro, it has been discovered, spends his dollar for the following items: clothing, 36 cents; food, 32 cents; shelter and insurance, 12 cents; luxuries, amusements, education, and benevolences, 17; savings, 1 cent.

Dr. Moton outlined clearly his program: the effective organization of a bureau of business promotion, a bureau of public education and co-operation, and a bureau of health. He recommended the revival of "trade-boosting campaigns," through the assistance of the National Negro Business League as a clearing-house of information and a source of inspiration.

THE OPEN FORUM

This column is intended to afford free expression of opinion by readers on questions of interest. The INTELLIGENCER *is not responsible for any such opinions. Letters must be brief, and the editor reserves the right to omit parts if necessary to save space.*

To the Editor:

In Elizabeth H. Coale's hypothetical question on Free Speech in a recent INTELLIGENCER, she is evidently referring to Pierce Wetter's superb letter in an earlier issue; but she makes a serious mistake in not stating that she is opposing a person who has been imprisoned five years for opinion's sake.

To use the epithet "Incendiary" is an ancient and convenient substitute for reason. Hers is the mental attitude which at the time of the crucifixion of Jesus held both thumbs down; or at the time of George Fox, upheld the magistrates in their course of imprisonment and persecution of the Quakers for their opinion's sake. And all the way down that has been the attitude of things-as-they-are toward progress, to call ideas a false name (Incendiarism) and then *without discussion, and unable to refute it*, to thrust its disciples into prison.

For here is the point: Elizabeth H. Coale *did not discuss the ideas she called incendiary.* It is her duty to take the *real ideas these men teach* (not the falsehoods attributed to them), *and show that they are evil.*

Opposition to free speech is, as it always has been, the acme of privilege, and tyranny, and cowardice. How can so many otherwise intelligent people persistently ignore what is so obvious and self-evident? Because of the universal propaganda of plutocracy, in the popular press and pulpit and platform.

So refute "Incendiarism" if you can. If you can't, you are probably wrong and your antagonist right. At any rate, you can't imprison an idea; although of course you can make a reputation for yourself by imprisoning and crucifying the prophets. JONATHAN C. PIERCE.

Brooklyn, N. Y.

To the Editor:

May I suggest to Elizabeth H. Coale that she is hardly correct in paralleling the man with a torch and even the agitator whose words are an offense to reason and decency, much less to the man who protests against an existing order as unjust to himself or others? Incitation to lawlessness is an offence against the law, and punishment is provided for without reference to the commission of the crime itself. The constitutional guaranty of freedom of opinion, of speech and of the press is fundamental in a free government and cannot be too sacredly guarded. That it has been violated in all times when public opinion has been excited beyond reason is a fact, and the innocent have often suffered. Martyrdom for conscience's sake has been the fate of the good since time began. It was the spirit, to which your correspondent has lent unconscious aid in her comparison, that erected the Cross, that caused the intolerance against the Christian religion until this day, and under which the Friends have suffered and are suffering. You do not believe in war, nor do I. The law defends your pacificism in specific terms, but as I cannot claim the benefit of that law, I have been compelled to "do my bit." Yet there are those who consider both of us guilty of treason when we preach against war, although armed conflict is rarely justified and never save in defense of home and country.

Comparisons should never be made between actual crime, which calls for resistance, and presumptive crime, participation in the actual suggestion is not compulsory. Abraham Lincoln, indignant at the reception his appeal for funds to pay the soldiers met in New York, said of the eastern bankers, "They ought to be shot." He committed no crime; but if someone had heard him and had committed the crime, would your correspondent have considered the President guilty?

Who is to say what is criminal speech? The Constitution says treason may not be protected, and this little loophole in the protection of free speech has permitted Congress to enact laws by which many a crime against liberty has been made possible and has been supported in the highest court in the land. Do you realize that even such language as I am using now might, during the Civil War, have caused Secretary Stanton to press his office bell and commit the writer to prison without a hearing? The writ of habeas corpus was suspended. The same power was exercised in the recent World War, in addition to the meanest espionage ever conceived.

Pardon my plainness. I do not imagine you would wittingly justify such tyranny, but—one must think to what end an expressed opinion may lead.

Dearborn, Mich. MARCUS T. WOODRUFF.

HERE AND HEREAFTER

To the Editor:

It seems to me that there are men who do not understand the fundamental principles of Christianity. It is unquestionable that hereafter only those willing to treat their fellowmen equally as well as themselves in the matter of meat, drink, clothing, shelter, etc., can exist where Jesus Christ is. God is our father, Jesus our elder brother, and *then* we shall live as we are willing now in this time to live. The fact of the matter is that if we want to live as brothers, children of one father hereafter, we must be willing to do so here. There is no other way to gain the life that persists through death into that future life with Jesus Christ.

All the law and the prophets are summed up in a statement of the unalterable fact. All the teachings of the New Testament reiterate the same unalterable fact that those willing now to live that way can be enabled to do so.

The good news or gospel of the New Testament is the fact that the risen, living Spirit of Jesus Christ will enable whosoever is willing to do it, and only they live with him hereafter.

It seems strange to me that men will call themselves Christians and utterly refuse to act Christlike towards their brothers; utterly refuse, unwilling, to see that their fellowman has as good meat, drink, clothing, shelter, fellowship, etc., as they have.

The coal and railroad strikes were caused by the moneyed classes as Henry Ford has proved beyond the shadow of a doubt. All the misery in the world is caused by the refusal of man to act Christlike, and the wonder is that the refusers think they will live with Christ hereafter.

God from creation has urged man to act brotherly because this universe is so constituted that the law of brotherly fellowship is as binding upon man as the law of gravity or electricity. All laws work, when obeyed, for man's good, and, when disobeyed, for his harm.

Under the new dispensation the present living Spirit of Jesus Christ enables whosoever will. The projection into life of the family relationship as exemplified by the fatherhood of God and the brotherhood of man with Jesus Christ as elder brother is accomplished by Jesus' help now and hereafter. J. A. WEBSTER.

Highland Park, Mich.

COMING EVENTS

TENTH MONTH

21st—Abington First-day School Union. See Notice.

21st—Concord First-day School Union will be held at Concord Meeting-house.

21st and 22nd—Pelham Half-Yearly Meeting, at Sparta, Ont.

21st—Trip to Germantown for benefit of Building Fund of Neighborhood Guild.

22nd—Southern Half-Yearly Meeting, at Camden, Del.

22nd—Philadelphia Quarterly Meeting's Visiting Committee expects to attend meeting for worship at Merion, at 11 a. m., First-day School at 10 a. m.

22nd—Conference Class at 15th and Race Sts., Philadelphia, at close of meeting for worship, 11.40 a. m. Murray S. Kenworthy will address the class telling of his experiences in Russia. He is expected to attend meeting for worship at 10.30.

24th—Western Quarterly Meeting at London Grove, Pa., at 10 a. m. In the afternoon, Western First-day School Union will be held at the same place.

25th—Address by Frederick J. Libby at the Meeting-house, Lafayette and Washington Avenues, Brooklyn, at 5.15 p. m., on "How We Can Abolish War in Our Time." All interested are cordially invited.

26th—Murray S. Kenworthy will address a Community Meeting at West Grove, Pa., on Russia.

26th—Caln Quarterly Meeting, at Christiana, Pa.

26th—Donation Day at Chapin Memorial Home for Aged Blind.

27th—All-Day Educational Conference on Proper Inter-Racial Contacts in Our Schools to be held at 15th and Race Streets, Philadelphia.

28th—Westbury Quarterly Meeting, at Flushing, N. Y. Meeting for worship and business meeting at 10.30; lunch at noon; afternoon session at 2.30.

At the afternoon session, John Nevin Sayre, editor of The Fellowship of Reconciliation paper, "The World To-Morrow," will speak on "Conditions in Europe Today, and The Christian International." Mr. Sayre was in Europe during the past summer, attending this gathering, and should give a most interesting address. All are cordially invited. Isaac Wilson, of Biglerville, Pa., will attend. Mary Travilla also expects to attend the Quarterly Meeting, and will remain over night and attend the meeting for worship on First-day.

29th—New York First-day School will re-open.

30th—Baltimore Yearly Meeting, at Baltimore, Md.

31st—Concord Quarterly Meeting, at Darby, Pa.

NOTICE—The Spiritual Way of Peace for This Generation, is the topic of six lectures by Miss Bertha Conde, to be given in Philadelphia under the auspices of the Y. W. C. A.

These talks are held Second-day afternoons at 2.45, at the League Branch, 1222 Locust Street. The dates are as follows:

October 23rd—The Social Hunger."
October 30th—"The Social Centre."
November 20th—"The Social Fabric."
November 27th—"The Social Principle."
December 4th—"The Social Service."
December 11th—"The Social Life."

Tickets $5.00, admitting Ticket Holder and Guest.

Friends might not be able to bring Miss Conde to Philadelphia for our group alone, but are invited to share in this opportunity.

NOTICE—John Cox, Jr., 507 Fifth Avenue, New York, has a copy of the first volume of FRIENDS' INTELLIGENCER. Anyone who knows of a library where the file is incomplete, or that would be interested in having this volume, is requested to communicate with him.

NOTICE—The Representative Committee of Philadelphia Yearly Meeting will hold a conference to consider our meetings for worship, on Sixth-day, Tenth month 27th, at 10 o'clock, in Room No. 4, 15th and Race Streets, Philadelphia, Pa.

All members of the Meeting for Ministry and Counsel and others especially interested in the subject are invited to attend.

NOTICE—Abington First-day School Union will be held Tenth month 21st, at Quakertown, Pa. Morning session at 10.30. "First-day School Materials" will be presented by Marguerite Hallowell, followed by general discussion of the subject. Current Events will be given by William Eves, 3rd, of George School. Lunch at 12. Afternoon session at 1.45 will be addressed by Wilbur K. Thomas, on "The Problem of Religious Education."

On account of the Bethlehem pike being closed to automobiles, the Quakertown Friends would like to inform those wishing to come to the Union by autos that it is quite possible to make the detour by way of Doylestown. Another way is to take the Sumneytown pike to Spinnerstown and from there over to Quakertown.

NOTICE—All-Day Educational Conference on Proper Inter-Racial Contacts in Our Schools to consider: The Importance of Teaching Modern Sociology Squarely; The Preparation of Up-to-date Texts for Civic Classes; How to Teach Inter-racial Understanding and Co-operation; Qualities Needed in Civic Teachers; Problem of Segregation, and Other Kindred Topics.

Friday, October 27, 1922, in Friends' Meeting-house, 15th and Race Streets, Philadelphia, Pa. Morning session, 10 a. m. to 12.30 p. m. White educators of Southeastern Pennsylvania, New Jersey and Delaware, by invitation.

Afternoon session, 2 to 4 p. m. Speakers: Dr. Thomas E. Finegan, State Superintendent of Public Instruction, Pennsylvania; Dr. Edwin C. Broome, Superintendent of Public Schools, Philadelphia; Dr. Joseph H. Odell, Director of the Service Citizens of Delaware; Dr. James Hardy Dillard, of Virginia, President of Jeanes and Slater Funds, Rector of William and Mary College. Discussion from the floor.

Evening session, 8 p. m. Open public meeting.

Speakers: Professor Leslie Pinckney Hill, Principal Cheyney, State Normal School; Mrs. Alice Dunbar-Nelson Associate Editor of *Philadelphia-Wilmington Advocate.* Spirituals by Cheyney Octette.

You are cordially invited to attend or to send a delegate, and to extend this invitation to others interested.

It is especially important that you plan to stay for the evening session.

Lunch and dinner will be provided at very moderate cost in an adjacent building. R. S. V. P.

By order of the Philadelphia Yearly Meeting Committee on the Interests of the Colored Race, Raymond T. Bye, Chairman, and of the Philadelphia Inter-Racial Committee, Anne Biddle Stirling, Chairman, 4517 Kingsessing Avenue, Philadelphia.

Baltimore Yearly Meeting, 1922

The Yearly Meeting will be held this year as usual, commencing on Seventh-day, Tenth month 28th.

Lodgings will be provided for Friends at Park Avenue Meeting-house as usual. Applications for this accommodation are to be made through the Friend who may be appointed in each Monthly Meeting, and should be forwarded by him as promptly as possible to the Chairman or Secretary of the Committee in Baltimore.

Accommodations at moderate cost may be provided elsewhere, for those who desire such, when specific applications are made.

The dormitories will be ready for occupancy on Sixth-day, Tenth month 27th for those who may have early meeting engagements. Meeting for Worship convenes at 10 o'clock on First-day.

Annie L. Lewis, Chairman, 731 Linwood Avenue, Tuxedo Park, Baltimore.

Bertha Janney, Secretary, The Plaza, Baltimore, Maryland.

FRIENDS' NEIGHBORHOOD GUILD needs an additional building. To raise necessary funds,

BUY A TICKET
for the
TRIP AROUND THE WORLD

starting from School Lane Meeting-house, Germantown, between 5 and 7 P. M., Seventh-day, Tenth Month 21st, 1922. Supper, transportation, entertainment, dancing—Price $1.50

Tourists will touch at Holland, China, Egypt, United States, Dance Land.

Tickets for sale at Friendly Centres or Guild Committee.

Be Loyal

to the concerns that advertise in our paper. It is of vital importance to its success and we can't urge too strongly. Read the ads when you read the paper. They often contain valuable suggestions that will help you in your shopping. They frequently point to a possible saving. There is always something there that might interest you.

PATRONIZE OUR ADVERTISERS—IT WILL PAY YOU.

American Friends' Service Committee

WILBUR K. THOMAS, EX. SEC.
20 S. 12th St. Philadelphia.

CASH CONTRIBUTIONS
WEEK ENDING OCTOBER 9TH.

Five Years Meeting	$399.74
Philadelphia Yearly Mtg. (Orthodox)	1,621.50
Philadelphia Yearly Mtg. (Hicksite)	2,418.50
Other Meetings—	
Orange Grove Friends, First-day School	5.00
Gunpowder Monthly Meeting	51.00
Chester Monthly Meeting, Moorestown, N. J.	10.00
Oxford Monthly Meeting, Baltimore	100.00
Little Britain Monthly Meeting	4.00
Eastland First-day School	1.50
Contributions for Germany	32.00
For Austria	2,161.61
For Poland	1,517.80
For Russia	1,200.46
Russian Overhead	2.00
For Armenia	35.00
For West Virginia	27.50
For Central Pennsylvania	27.50
For German Overhead	74.00
Message Committee	111.00
For General	840.75
For Clothing	92.82
Refunds and Payments	20.50
	$10,754.18

Shipments received during week ending October 7, 1922: 129 boxes and packages received; 13 anonymous.

STATEMENT OF CASH CONTRIBUTIONS FROM MEMBERS OF THE PHILADELPHIA YEARLY MEETING OF FRIENDS HELD AT FIFTEENTH AND RACE STREETS, PHILADELPHIA, DURING AUGUST AND SEPTEMBER.

Penna. Peace Society by Arabella Carter (Russian Rel.)	$32.00
Lansdowne Mo. by C. C. Lippincott	30.00
A. G. Thatcher	100.00
Mary H. Thatcher	100.00
Wilmington Mo. by S. H. Stradley	1,022.00
Abington Mo. by D. L. Lewis	100.00
"A Friend"	39.50
Middletown Prep. by Frances W. Broomall	40.00
Swarthmore Mo. by E. J. Durnall	5.00
Wilmington Mo. by S. H. Stradley	952.00
	$2,420.50

WANTED

REFINED MIDDLE-AGED MAN AND wife desire position as caretakers of home or position of trust. Best references given. Address C. 380, Friends' Intelligencer.

HADDONFIELD, NEW JERSEY—Room and Board. Second floor, bath, electric light, good cooking, refined environment. Reference required. Bell phone 69-J. 15 Grove Street, Haddonfield, N. J.

REFINED SURROUNDINGS AND Mother's care may be had for infant, small child or small family. No other children. References exchanged. Address L. 400, Friends' Intelligencer.

WANTED—Single room in central part of city by a young Friend in social work. Address C. 403, Friends' Intelligencer.

WANTED—BY AN ELDERLY WOman, experienced, a position with light household duties or care of invalid. Apply 910 Clinton Street, Philadelphia.

WANTED—WORKING HOUSEKEEPer. Family of two. No washing. Country, right on trolley line. City conveniences. Address J. 401, Friends' Intelligencer.

WANTED—MOTHER'S HELPER, VILlage near Wilmington. To be member of family. Address S. 402, Friends' Intelligencer.

WANTED—RELIABLE WOMAN FOR general housework. Family of two, all conveniences. No washing. No objection to woman with small daughter. Mrs. Penrose Robinson, Hatboro, Pa.

WANTED—GOOD HOME OR BOARDing place with cheerful surroundings for middle-aged lady, mentally somewhat deficient. State probable terms. Address P. 390, Friends' Intelligencer.

$2250 WANTED ON FIRST MORTgage for five years at 6% interest. Property is a new frame bungalow with two acres of land in Bethel Township, Delaware County, Pa. Loan desired is about one-half the value of the property and the owner is a young man of excellent reputation. Apply to Charles Palmer, 12 East Fifth Street, Chester, Pa.

WANTED—WHITE WOMAN OF REfinement for maid in apartment in Atlantic City, to care for apartment and clothes. Very little cooking. Write Mrs. J. W. Mott, Traymore, Atlantic City.

NURSE, PRACTICAL, WISHES PERmanent care of lady or gentleman; 5921 N. Broad St. Wyoming 4518-W.

WANTED—MOTHER'S HELPER FOR upstairs work and care of three children. Phone, Moorestown 66. Lester Collins, Moorestown, New Jersey.

WANTED—MOTHER'S HELPER FOR child two years old. State experience and salary desired. References requested. Mrs. J. M. Griscom, Moorestown, New Jersey.

POSITION WANTED—AS COMpanion-nurse to invalid, or elderly woman; management of home, help kept. Capable; references. Address B. 394, Friends' Intelligencer.

WOMAN OF MIDDLE AGE, NURSE, wants care of invalid. Address P. 374, Friends' Intelligencer.

WANTED—MIDDLE-AGED WOMAN for general housework in country. Three in family. Address Friends' Intelligencer. M. 384.

WOMAN OF REFINEMENT SEEKS position as companion to lady living alone, or managing housekeeper in widower's home where kindness and interest would be appreciated. Reference. Address D. 382, Friends' Intelligencer.

FOR RENT

FOR RENT—A WELL FURNISHED second story room in private family of Friends, at 2727 North 11th Street, Philadelphia. Convenient to Trolleys and Restaurants.

FUN

A bellboy passed through the hall of the hotel, whistling loudly.

"Young man," said the manager, sternly, "you know it's against the rules to whistle while on duty."

"I am not whistling, sir," replied the boy; "I'm paging Mrs. Jones' dog." —*Epworth Herald.*

To the Lot Holders and others interested in Fairhill Burial Ground:

GREEN STREET Monthly Meeting has funds available for the encouragement of the practice of cremating the dead to be interred in Fairhill Burial Ground. We wish to bring this fact as prominently as possible to those who may be interested. We are prepared to undertake the expense of cremation in case any lot holder desires us to do so.

Those interested should communicate with William H. Gaskill, Treasurer of the Committee of Interments, Green Street Monthly Meeting, or any of the following members of the Committee.

William H. Gaskill, 3201 Arch St.
Samuel N. Longstreth, 1218 Chestnut St.
Charles F. Jenkins, 232 South Seventh St.
Stuart S. Graves, 3033 Germantown Ave.

Please help us by patronizing our advertisers. Mention the "Friends' Intelligencer."

The Friends' Intelligencer

ESTABLISHED 1844 — TENTH MONTH 28, 1922 — VOLUME 79, NUMBER 43

Contents

EDITORIAL

THE FRIENDS' INTELLIGENCER

Published weekly, 140 N. 15th Street, Philadelphia, Pa., by Friends' Intelligencer Association, Ltd.

SUE C. YERKES, *Managing Editor*.

Editorial Board: Elizabeth Powell Bond, Thomas A. Jenkins, J. Russell Smith, George A. Walton.

Board of Managers: Edward Cornell, Alice Hall Paxson, Paul M. Pearson, Annie Hillborn, Elwood Hollingshead, William C. Biddle, Charles F. Jenkins, Edith M. Winder, Frances M. White.

Officers of Intelligencer Associates: Ellwood Burdsall, Chairman; Bertha L. Broomell, Secretary; Herbert P. Worth, Treasurer.

Subscription rates: United States, Mexico, Cuba and Panama, $2.50 per year. Canada and other foreign countries, $3.00 per year. Checks should be made payable to Friends' Intelligencer Association, Ltd.

Entered as Second Class Matter at Philadelphia Post Office

The Friends' Intelligencer

The religion of Friends is based on faith in the "INWARD LIGHT," or direct revelation of God's spirit and will in every king soul.
The INTELLIGENCER is interested in all who bear the name of Friends in every part of the world, and aims to promote love, ty and intercourse among all branches and with all religious societies.

TABLISHED 1844 | PHILADELPHIA, TENTH MONTH 28, 1922 | VOLUME 79 NUMBER 43

Pastoral Work in Our Meetings

We Friends need more pastoral work, in order to ld together our Religious Society. When we com- e our present condition with the past, we see that too many cases our meeting-houses, which in mer days were filled with worshippers, now have a small and gradually decreasing attendance at First-day meetings.

It is not that we have outgrown the old faith, nor t our members have, to any great extent, left us join other churches. Their names still stand on r roll of membership; but many of them have got t of the habit of attending our meetings, and so ve at best but a languid interest in meeting affairs. All will admit that our fundamental principles ve lost none of their fitness to human needs. In- d, there never was a more urgent call for the ap- cation of Friendly ideals to the problems of life ich confront us. The weakness is not in the prin- les which we profess, but in ourselves. We have t something of the moral earnestness of the old iends, with whom duty was such an impelling tive.

The meeting was to them the centre of interest, which all other affairs had to be adjusted. It was one thing which held them together in close fel- ship. Is it not true that with many of us, going meeting is largely a matter of convenience? We willing to go, and rather enjoy going, when it s not interfere with other arrangements! In the en time, going to meeting meant more than that.

Another thing which served to bind the Friends ether was the visiting among their homes, es- ially at the times of the various meetings. The rit of hospitality is still alive among us, but it s not find such free expression now as it did ong the early Friends. In the multiplicity of our agements we do not seem to have time for the et family visitings, and so we lose a great co- ive influence.

The difficulty of holding together the members churches is everywhere felt, and to meet this most of them have some pastoral system of ministers, deaconesses, nurses, etc. In our Society, such a course is not possible, nor, as most of us think, would it be desirable. A few of our meetings are able to have a trained leader to co-ordinate the different branches of service, and to keep in touch with the whole membership; but with most of the meetings this pastoral work must be done voluntarily by the members themselves.

One important line of service is the periodic visitation of those who are sick, or enfeebled by age. It is hard for us who are well and actively engaged to realize what these visits mean to those who are shut in all the time, often with pain and weariness. Hear the call—"I was sick, and ye visited me: I was in prison, and ye came unto me." Those who have automobiles can render Christian service in this way.

Another good service to which automobiles may be put is to call around for those who otherwise would not be able to attend meeting. This is being done in many cases; but it might be made more general.

The Young Friends' Movement may prove a valuable aid in pastoral work. Their pilgrimages to the country meetings have done much to arouse interest, and to bring out some of the habitual absentees, and this work should be systematically followed up. Can they not also, in small groups, visit those who are confined to their homes and there hold meetings for worship? By doing this, they would not only carry blessing to others but they would also be developing in themselves a spirit of consecrated service.

The pastoral work is a matter in which every member of the meeting should feel an individual responsibility. There are many kinds of service, which require different talents, and there is always something for each of us to do. Given the *will* to do something, a way will be found. It is only when every one is engaged in the service that we can have "a free gospel ministry." When we get that our meetings will wake up and again become sources of spiritual power.

D. B.

Some Reasons for Attending Meetings for Worship and Business

Example

To a greater extent than we realize our conduct is watched by the people about us, and regular attendance of Meeting on our part will encourage others to do the same. The reverse is also true.

To Increase Our Faith

In this life, with all of its dangers, temptations and doubts, we need to avail ourselves of every source of strength. Social religious worship is one of these sources. There is engendered in the Meeting a spirit of worship which passes from one to another in an uplifting way that is not often felt when one is alone. While there are inspiring moments when alone, it is not often true that one can worship as well at home as in Meeting, when that Meeting is performing its high function.

When a thought is expressed by someone present in the Meeting, this may start a train of thought in the minds of others, the expression of which may e inspiring and helpful to all.

To Add to the Life of the Meeting

The sight of many empty seats is deadening, vhile, on the other hand, a full Meeting is pretty ure to be a good Meeting. Under the latter condition religious feeling will the more easily develop and this will be felt by all thoughtful attenders. In this way the real value and helpfulness of a Friends' Meeting will be made evident.

To Manifest the Presence of God

God is present everywhere, yet there are times when He seems nearer to us than at others. A full Meeting is often such an occasion; and to such we would be more willing to invite the attendance of our visitors and neighbors. Then, even if no sermon is preached, the presence of the Spirit of the Lord will be impressively felt.

To go to Meeting in a spirit of prayer will insure a helpful gathering. Then the thoughts of business and the cares of the day drop away and the channel is opened whereby we may feel the impress of God's Spirit.

To Encourage a Ministry

In such a meeting as this, with many thoughtful souls present, each seeking to communicate with the Father, there will surely arise a vocal ministry by some whose lips have been touched by a live coal from God's radiant altar. Then, in addition to the value of the silent waiting together upon God, there will come to the Meeting a message that has passed through the crucible of some inspired soul thrille with the thought of being God's messenger to men

Nothing, perhaps, is so needed just now as me and women vibrant with such a vital message to th world; and full attendance at Meeting is one way t encourage the coming forth of these Publishers o Truth, these Torch-bearers of Progress within ou ranks.

To Preserve the Society of Friends

Does it seem to thee that Quakerism is a goo thing? Has it a prospect of usefulness? If so, the do thy part in insuring its future by regular attend ance at Meeting.

How long can any organization exist if its mem bers remain away from its meetings? If the Societ of Friends is to continue to live and to perform it service, each member must do his part, not only b attendance at all its meetings, but also by enterin into its service with a whole heart and untirin energy, undeterred by unpromising conditions.

To Encourage the First-Day School

When parents and children attend the First-da School and not the Meeting, there is a vital loss t the Meeting. Herein lies a source of weakness.

Parents and children should attend Meeting an thus the habit of attendance will be formed, an gradually the children and young people will come t take their part in the work of the Meeting.

The experience, so common, of seeing childre attend First-day School and desert the Meeting i most discouraging. This is usually the fault of t parents, who should attend Meeting accompanied t their children.

Incidentally, it may be remarked, that those wh wish to enter into Christian work, need not depa to foreign lands for the purpose, for they may fir a fertile field in First-day School teaching, right home.

To Encourage the Attendance of Non-Membe

In many communities there are persons who wou be interested to attend Meeting and, who, later o may become members.

With the prospect of small attendance there often a hesitancy to invite such to come to Meetin Here is another reason why our members shou secure a full attendance. Naturally, we wish tl Society to grow in numbers and in influence, for v believe, many of us, that it has a great service to pe form. Not from births among us can it grow, b only by attracting those not in membership.

They had recently founded a new school (Weston or Westtown), built a great new Meeting House (Fourth and Arch Sts.), launched a Tract Association, and had undertaken work for the Seneca Indians (Tunesassa), and for the Negroes and other poor people of their home city. Bonds of Christian love and understanding linked Philadelphia with London. There was an open door; the opportunity for a people to go forward.

Beneath a sky so fair and with such auspicious beginnings, it is sad that the current of Quakerism in Philadelphia should so soon plunge into the backwater of a whirlpool of separations. Perhaps the trouble was not primarily due to the preaching of rationalistic philosophy, nor to tactless repression. It is doubtful whether the wreckage was caused either by a too narrow conservatism in mere forms, or by ultra-evangelical enthusiasms. These appear symptoms, rather than procuring causes. The real malady, we must confess, to have been a partial *deadness* in the body itself, a coldness in too many hearts towards God.

* * * *

A century has passed. Observers at home can tell whether in 1922 the situation of Philadelphia Friends and of American Quakerism, largely viewed, has (or has not) some of the same strengths and weaknesses. None of us may read the future, but we can face it confidently if our trust (and hope too) is set in the revelation of God to the soul. Against this foundation nothing can prevail. My desire then follows the concern of our friend M. I. Reich, that in extending, we may also be deepened; that as the cords are lengthened, the stakes may be strengthened; that with works we may also have faith; that in busy lives, we may not neglect the Life that is life indeed. Christ says, Seek The Kingdom.

Beyrouth, Syria.

Love

Oh, love is not a mild desire
 That wishes a general good,
Love is a personal, passionate thing
 That will not be withstood.

The heart of Man, when it learns to love,
 Is the Bride of God, the King,
And out of that love will the New World grow,
 As flowers out of the Spring.

Love gives its all, its very self,
 Love gives, it cannot withhold,
And out of that love will the New Birth come,
 A new Man for the old.

ELEANOR SCOTT SHARPLES.

Help Uphold the Standard!

Few religious organizations have been afforded such an opportunity for the effective expression and advancement of their ideals as lies open to the Society of Friends today through the work of the American Friends' Service Committee.

The article by Robert W. Dunn, published below, gives a graphic instance of the kind of results which the work is producing: "Mile after mile of flat river-bottom land—*plowed.*" When one realizes that this land lies in the famine zone of Russia, that it means not only emergency famine relief, but permanent agricultural reconstruction, and that it was plowed by Friends' workers, one is thrilled with a vision of the possibilities which lie in Friends' service work.

By serving as a "good Samaritan" to thousands upon thousands who are stricken in body and soul, it is not only administering relief, but is demonstrating that there are those for whom service and love are realities, and so is stimulating new faith in the ideals which the present international situation so often tends to crush out.

But the Service Committee can realize these great opportunities only in proportion as the Society of Friends realizes *its* opportunity by continuing to render wholehearted support to the service work. That work was begun in response to a great emergency. Great emergencies still call for its help. But so far as concerns the Society of Friends itself, the work can no longer be regarded as of simply an emergency character. It has become one of the Society's permanent concerns.

Every Friends' Meeting should have its local service committee, and should be working in the cause as a part of its regular religious activities. The many communities which have served so splendidly in the past, are urged to continue their support this winter with renewed zeal. Many other communities have taken comparatively little share in the work thus far, and it is hoped that they will now realize the opportunity which it opens to them, and will enter wholeheartedly into it.

Last year the Society of Friends in America contributed approximately $250,000 to the work. This served as a base upon which the Service Committee was able to raise total contributions valuing more than $4,700,000. This year, with Russia facing a new famine crisis, the committee hopes to obtain and distribute relief having an even greater total value, and it depends upon Friends to continue their support upon as large a scale as heretofore. Will not every Friend give, and every Friends' community raise, at least as much for the service work this year as last?

If Jesus were among us today, and were seekin means to carry healing and cheer to the destitute an the suffering, what Friends' Meeting would not mak every effort and sacrifice in order that His missio might be fulfilled? Every Friends' Meeting ca help to carry on that mission by supporting its shai of this work which was inspired by His ideals, an which it is attempted to carry on in His spirit.

From a Car Window

If you happen to be a passenger on a Moscov Tashkent express and if you happen to be awal when your train is clicking off the distance betwee Totskoye and Sorochinskoye on the single-track lir between Samara and Orenberg, you will see som thing that will make you certain that you are not the famine area. You will simply not understand i especially if you have heard of the appalling casua ties among horses this last year in Buzuluk Count

This is what you will see. Mile after mile of fl river bottom-land—*plowed.* A broad black str along the railroad. It begins just beyond the 25 acre millet field where they are now cutting ar threshing the clean native millet—millet for whic land was turned by Quaker tractors last May ar June—and it stretches up the gentle slope towa the horizon and farther than the eye can follow. B you will be able to get the sweep of it from the wi dow of your wagon for it runs parallel with the tra for a distance of two or three miles.

This black *plowed* land is neither the work of G nor of thrifty peasants. Neither must it be tak as an index of the amount of land plowed in th parts. It is entirely abnormal. It is not a mirac but it would not be there but for one fact—the pr ence of the Quaker tractors. It is their work. It the land they have plowed for the fall seeding. is the biggest single accomplishment and certai the most visible evidence of the presence of Friends' Mission in Sorochinskoye.

Two carloads of seed rye have arrived from Gubernia Agricultural Department in Samara. harrows and seeders, also pulled by the four Fc sons are already at work. The process of plow and seeding farther and farther west along the will continue as long as the fall sowing season l till the end of September. With the 1750 poods rye available for the sowing it will be possible, a poods to the small dessiatine to sow 350 dessiati or some 560 acres this fall. Then there will be s eral hundred acres left over for the spring sow of wheat.

And the products from these long furroughs, grains from this vast stretch of black, where they go? By agreement with the Soviet Governn

He said a friend of his who smoked cigars probably spent just about twice as much, and even this is below the amount spent by others, I am told.

While he knew it might seem like a little thing yet he realized that if anyone said, "Well, if it is such a little thing, why don't you give it up?" that he would find then it was a very big thing.

It would be ridiculous to write a long article for *The Friend* on the harmful effects of smoking, but are there any smokers who would be willing to give it up when they realize it is keeping others from joining? It seems like a challenge to the smokers.

In Kent's "Shorter Bible" he translates Paul's advice to the Corinthians as, "Therefore if what I eat proves a hindrance to my brother, sooner than injure him I will never eat meat again as long as I live. In all things I can do as I like, but they are not all good for me. In all things I can do as I like, but they do not all build up character. Each of us must seek not merely his own good, but that of his neighbor."

I heard a university professor telling his class of students that Friends had the highest ideals and more nearly lived up to them than any other set of people he knew.

I wonder if people haven't an idea we are better than we really are?

I realize that it is a delicate subject to touch because some of our wealthiest members smoke, and some of those in our "best families," but shall we follow the ministers who dare not preach as they might because of the wealthy pew holders? If anyone objects to this article let him read John xv:18: "If the world hate you, ye know that it hated me before it hated you." SARAH B. LEEDS.

Reprinted from *The Friend.*

The Shame of the Near East

By JOHN HAYNES HOLMES

Now that the ashes of Smyrna are cooled and its dead buried, and the menace of another world war for the moment apparently removed, it may be well to set down, in as concise form as possible, some facts about the Near East horror which have been pretty successfully obscured by the daily press. The New York *World* and a few other intelligent and fearless newspapers, as well as the radical journals generally, have published the truth, but this is still largely hidden in the chaos and confusion of a vast upheaval of disaster.

The facts are these—

(1) The war between Greece and Turkey is in reality a war between England and France.

(2) Greece went to war at the suggestion and with the support of the English government; the Turks, under the triumphant Mustapha Kemal, went to war with the support, the ammunition and the guns of France.

(3) England rushed troops and warships, to defend Constantinople and the Dardanelles, because her arms—i. e., the Greeks—were beaten; France remained inactive and unexcited, not because she was more wise and less militaristic than England, but because her arms—i. e., the Turks—were victorious, and she could therefore afford to stand pat.

(4) England and France are now rivals after the Great War, just as England and Germany were rivals before the Great War. These two nations will plunge Europe into another "world war" whenever, to either side, the hour seems to be propitious.

(5) Asia Minor is the center of disturbance because of the gross injustice done to Turkey, in the Treaty of Sevres, by the victorious Allies.

(6) The talk of Greece about "a holy war" to save the Christian world from the Moslem, the appeal of the English cabinet to the dominions across the seas to join hands in protecting civilization again from the barbarians, is the same kind of "bunk" that was foisted upon mankind at the oubtreak of the war against Germany; this crisis, like the crisis of 1914, is purely imperialistic, and has no remotest connection with Christianity, civilization, democracy, or any other genuine humanitarian interest.

(7) The dreadful Turkish atrocities, reported from Asia Minor, are just like the dreadful German atrocities reported from Belgium and France in 1914 and 1915. Some of them undoubtedly took place, for atrocities invariably accompany war. Of these, we may be sure that the Greek Christians committed quite as many as the Turkish Moslems; says Mark O. Prentiss, special representative of the Near East Relief in Smyrna,

"I hear and firmly believe many stories of Greek atrocities, and I have abundant evidence that the Greek army distributed enormous quantities of ammunition among the civilians in Smyrna, and encouraged and organized sniping and bombing."

Of all these tales, however, the majority are sheer imagination or deliberate invention. Thus, in the sack and burning of Smyrna, a city of about 375,000 population, it was reported on the first day that 120,000 were killed. That this number was later reduced to 2,000, and later still to 1,000, only proves the truth of our assertion.

(8) The dead in Asia Minor, like the dead in Flanders, are the innocent victims of an ignorant and cruel imperialism. They died to serve the interests of gold and steel and oil, and therefore "died in vain."

(9) Europe today is governed by the same men, controlled by the same forces, as those which were dominant in 1914. The "next war" is definitely and swiftly on the way.

When, or if, this "next war" comes, will the people be duped again as they were duped before? Will they again take up arms, and again fight and kill and die, for no purpose of imaginable good? Or will they revolt and say—and mean what they say!—"Never again"? There were at first encouraging signs in England that the people, especially labor, would refuse to follow the Coalition Cabinet in its mad career. But how long did these signs last? Within three days, a New York *World* signed despatch gave the cheerful news, that there was a complete change of front.

"Nothing more is heard from labor," wrote the correspondent, "of 'not a gun, not a man, not a ship,' the stubborn slogan so popular three days ago. Instead is published a series of statements by labor leaders placing the necessity of maintaining the freedom of the Dardanelles as the main plank in labor's platform. . . . It is also noted that the elaborate preparations for a great nation-wide protest of labor against war have been quietly halted. . . In fact, war feeling is growing."

The same old story! The Great War not four years gone, and the world all ready for another fight! "How long, O Lord, how long?"

Reprinted from *Unity*.

The master forces are the need for bread and the need for God.—*W. E. Orchard.*

Industrial Problems

The Christian Solution of Industry's Problems

ELBERT RUSSELL

(Concluded from last week)

There is this advantage about democracy; we can- get any higher than the rank and file. In an au- racy, the only need is a good ruler. In a democ- y, to raise the standard of efficiency, we must se the level of education. This is true of industry, well. There are some who think that the ability manage is limited to certain privileged classes. t the reason the masses do not show this ability that they rarely have a chance. Many men can nothing but obey the boss; they should be given a ince to develop their managing ability. I think re is much ability of this kind in the ranks, be- ise many of the managing men have come up from bottom. Make it easier for them to come up. It uld make us more efficient, and more Christian, l would develop character.

Race prejudice comes in here. Take the negro race. ey have very little chance to show if they have nagerial ability. But the darky mammy in the plantation kitchen showed that ability. The d waiter in some of our big hotels, who has, three ies a day, to seat, feed, and keep in good humor ee or four hundred people surely has it for it takes nagerial ability to do this. But our industrial sys- i tends to prevent the development of ability of kind, or of the individual.

The creative impulse delights in making things utiful. There are some things necessary to our lization which we can turn out by machine, all e, but this standardization of production has ely destroyed the artistic impulse, and the delight vork. One of our problems is how we shall give a chance to express their souls. The creative im- se is largely latent in those who tend machines, it may be possible for us to change our civiliza- so that each worker will know the finished prod- and take pride in it. Perhaps each person will a turn at each machine, giving all a chance to elop the creative impulse.

The American people as a whole have little sense he proper proportion of things. We talk about American standard of living, which we fear will verthrown by the incoming races. By the Amer- standard, *we* mean silk shirts and piano players, meat every day. We don't want our children to go to church unless they are dressed up. It is material comfort and luxury that the American standard of living looks for. Southern Europeans live on much less. They are often willing to give up outward comfort for the other thing. In art-galleries, I have often been interested to see the large proportion of this group. *We* sacrifice the cultural things to the material. Fine houses often mean a sacrifice of art, books, music. Our accumulated wealth is often a scaffold on which the soul is hung.

I think that Jesus laid the emphasis on brotherhood for the help of each. No person can be complete alone; social feelings follow social actions. Justice should be a principle of action. Do justice to people whom you do not know; treat people in a brotherly fashion whether you feel it or not. Jesus calls on us to treat each other as though God were our father, and we recognized each as our brother. We know that the division of food and comforts in the family is never on the competitive system. Grandfather and grandmother, who earn nothing, are not set off with a piece of bread, while the husky young son takes it all.

Booker Washington has said, "The worst thing any man can do to me is to make me hate him." John Woolman would not stoop to any means of contention. He went to the Quaker slave-owners in all love and friendliness, and asked them if it was right for them to live by unpaid labor? This was the beginning of the work of emancipation among Friends; they got rid of their slaves without war.

Experience shows that it is very difficult to manitain brotherhood across great differences in life. You remember the rich young ruler. I think the simplest explanation of Jesus' demand that he give away all his goods is this:—The other disciples had given up everything to follow Jesus. If this young man had come in, with all his wealth, there would have been difficulty. Where a few people in a Meeting have money, I know how hard it is to keep brotherhood. I remember a Meeting where one family was very rich. They were pathetically eager to get into brotherhood with the others; they might forget their wealth, but the others could not.

The first tendency of the brotherly life is to create a sort of communism—a spiritual fraternity. This is the sort of thing we see in a college dormitory. I was worried about it at one time, but as one boy said, "If he wants what I have, why shouldn't he have it?" The spirit of fraternity was there. The spirit of sharing goes with love.

Our American democracy is nearing a new and

dangerous stage. The rich men of the first generation had come up from the ranks. They could eat with a working-man and feel at ease. Their children cannot; they do not know how.

The principle of brotherhood will carry us far. Let me speak of some of the ways in which the Christian spirit is obliterating differences, leavening the lump. We are rather determined that all our children shall have some education, rich or poor. We have found that mothers in cities often have to go to work, leaving their children,—so we give them their breakfast. This is Christian charity, trying to wipe out the differences. Christian charity is wiping out pew-rents. Books, parks, etc., have been the prerogative of the rich. Very well, we will make public parks for all, and build great art-galleries open to all. Christian philanthropy establishes great libraries all over the land, where all may read. Christian charity is trying to equalize inequalities.

But it is our industrial system that makes these inequalities, and all these efforts are as though we left a faucet running, and tried to prevent a flood by dipping up the water with a cup. I wonder if some day we will not turn to the other end of the industrial organization, and give all the children of God a chance to share in the heritage which He has given us. I believe in giving every human being the fullest possible chance to develop the qualities which God has given him.

In the discussion it was said that when Seebohm Rowntree visited this country, he was impressed by our managerial ability, our efficiency in making things, but also by our lack of interest in individuals. He suggested that the captains of industry divide their profits as follows:—first, set aside a sum for capital; next, a sum for labor's security, in the form of insurance against unemployment; then a share for social insurance; after that a lower cost of the product to the consumer; and finally a profit-sharing plan for the workers.

There is a great group of banks, which controls much of the present industrial situation, for if businesses do not play into their hands, the banks can refuse to give them credit. The problem is thus tremendously involved.

Seebohm Rowntree puts into practice what he preaches. It would be a good thing for American employers to study his works. The papers give little space to the idea which he represents.

Round Table on Industrial Relations

Led by E. Morris Burdsall

The slogan of America has been material prosperity. The luxuries of one hundred years ago are considered necessities today. The mere fact that this is so, shows that we are giving more and more thought to material things.

Constant production increases the wealth of the community, but it increases it disproportionately. It all comes down to what our ideals are. Should not the mass of the people have a right to what a few have? Why the unequal distribution? Ford has the ideal of supplying the needs of the many instead clothes, etc., at a reasonable price? Because so many of the wants of a few. Why can't we get food, are making things that are wanted by a few.

Is there any difficulty in the production of the necessities of life? Is it not more a problem of distribution? When apples are rotting on the ground because it costs more to get them to the city than the farmer would be paid for them, yet are ten cents a pound in the city market, it seems that there is something wrong with distribution. One part of the responsibility of the producer is the proper distribution. The farmer does not understand distribution, as he should, and there are many things which it now costs more to distribute than to produce. So far as distribution is concerned, we may well be compared to Russia.

Production has exceeded demand in this country so that we have to export, said one, while another queried whether we should not rather say that production has exceeded the monetary demand? It may fall far below the real need. A family cannot buy more than the wages allow, no matter how great it need.

Industry should be for both profit and service it was declared. Self-interest is the main thing tha keeps business going and we must try to change ou attitude so that the motive will be different, sai another.

It was recently stated at a meeting of the Amer ican Federation of Labor that the leaders of or ganized labor realize the problem of carrying me who are not up to the standard and do not feel th should be forced upon the employers.

The church plays no part in labor which is goi through a great change. Shall Christianity not ha a part in it? This is one of the great problems the day, and the church has here fallen dow Church people must stand on the same level wi the working men, not let them feel that they thi themselves superior. We Friends have had lit contact with working men. The only church th touches them to any purpose is the Catholic. W must make contacts.

The human being in industry is more import than the industry itself. We want to look towa the betterment of all engaged in industry.

Philanthropic Interests

Enforcement—The Signs of the Times

Commissioner Roy A. Haynes

As an appropriate introduction to the address by mmissioner Haynes, Dr. O. Edward Janney read 6th chapter of 2nd Kings, laying emphasis es- ially on the passage "Fear not, for they that be h us are more than they that be with them."

Wilson S. Doan, making the introduction, said:— 'e are glad to have a 'captain of the base' here to- ht."

Many long centuries have passed since the young n saw the Armies of Syria, but failed to see the rioteers of fire; that partial vision of the young n seems to be an inherent trait of ours. Most n fail to see the splendid background that com- tes the vision, and deeper still the triumphant pur- e or cause that remains unveiled. The Golden e is either in the past or in the future; the sent is accepted as commonplace. In other words, the young man, our attention is directed towards charioteers of iron and steel to the exclusion of charioteers of fire that form a part of our age. rhaps it is difficult to interpret the times in which live because of the fact that we are so close to own age and proximity has a tendency to dim lustre of things or at least to obscure part of their ndeur. The traveler can scarcely catch a vision Mt. Shasta that does not challenge his attention the abstraction of all else, but it is not at the foot this mountain that you catch the glimpse that quers your memory. As the train winds north- rd and the shadows lengthen eastward, the moun- seems to rise in grandeur as it recedes; the foot s seem to sink downward toward the horizon line the mountains to climb up to solitary splendor. So in every age great men, great events, great vements come and go and those who touch them sely scarcely sense their greatness.

Many of us crossed the threshold of the new cen- y; but how few of us really sensed the greatness that century.

We look back upon a wonderful century. Lord red Russell tells us that there were thirteen great coveries during the Nineteenth Century, and only en great discoveries during all the centuries be- e that, but it scarcely seemed marvelous while the s were lengthening into years. What is true of past is true of today. We are living in a great . The hour is tremulous with the shock of con- . To some it seems as if the destiny of our ntry hangs upon the outcome of the conflict that being waged in this land today. Yet there are e who do not sense the importance of this ggle, and who dwell upon the past.

Let us, my friends, not overlook the importance of the struggle now going on to make the 18th Amendment effective. As a great American recently said: "In view of the attempts, sometimes success- ful, to misinterpret the Constitution, the efforts to change it and the danger involved in disregarding its provisions, the time has arrived for us to put on the armor of patriotism as our forefathers knew and applied it."

It is only the man who knows the far-reaching moral influence of the former liquor traffic, legalized and protected, who knows something of the debauch- ing and prostituting effects of the former brewery and distilling interests in politics, who knows the foreign un-American element that champions the liquor business, who can today interpret the signifi- cance of the struggle that wages about the Volstead Act.

The man who understands the temperance reform, who visualizes its far-reaching influences upon the life of our nation, who contemplates the benefits it must confer upon the rising and unborn generations, must be thrilled with the events that are daily staged. If he is not blind to the determined opposition that this reform daily meets, the importance of this hour must give him pause. With this insight into the contest he must surely be led to feel with Kathleen Norris, who recently said: "The Eighteenth Amendment has given us one of the greatest oppor- tunities of our lives. Wars will come and wars will go, administrations will rise and fall, but the work we may do now to build up this cleansing and strengthening and constructive law into our life will never be undone."

There are those who see only one side of this con- flict. Like the young man in his morning vision, they see only the forces that are arrayed against them, and, seeing but this side, they become pessi- mists, saying that the law can't be enforced or there is no use in trying to make the Eighteenth Amend- ment effective; prohibition is a faliure. Then there is another class, who, like the young man, sees the charioteers of fire. To them the fight is won. They cry out "They that are for us are more than they that are against us," and this class of optimists does nothing because their optimism destroys the neces- sary effort and pauses the nerve of action.

What we need to do is to see not only the hosts of Syria that are against us but also the charioteers of fire who are for us,—to get a vision of the struggle as it is and to find that there is an urgent need for our effort. Let us for a moment first see some of the forces that are against us in our effort to make America safe and sober—law-abiding and loyal to our Constitution.

Some of the militant forces against us include—

1. A highly developed propaganda.

2. An unfavorable attitude on the part of a small minority of public officials.

3. Apathy on the part of a good many Christian citizens, but this element, I am glad to report, is rapidly decreasing.

4. An organized attack upon the efforts of enforcement and an effort to discredit the service.

But, my friends, do not fail to look also for a brief moment at the chariots of fire—those elements that are for us;—

1. Great organizations, church and secular, great leaders of thought.

2. Those not originally prohibitionists but who are staunch supporters of the law.

3. The population of the great rural sections, particularly of the West, Central West, and South.

4. The fathers and mothers of the citizens of to-morrow.

5. The women of the Union, now a part of our political parties, and their tremendous force for every righteous cause.

So, in interpreting this hour, we must see clearly the forces that are for, as well as the forces that are against us. While imbued with faith and hope and confidence, we should remember that the failure on the part of our best patriotic citizenship to function and co-operate in enforcement may bring dire results. Many good citizens seem to regard the Republican form of Government as imperishable, and yet our own America is less than 150 years old. Venice had a Republican form of Government for 1100 years; Carthage for 700 years; Athens for 900 years, with varying intermissions; Florence for 1300 years; and Rome 500 years. What caused the downfall of these ancient Republics?—The people began to disregard their own laws. When law ceased to reign, the Governments crumbled and fell.

There is no question as to where the leaders of this administration stand on law-enforcement. Attorney-General Daugherty recently said: "The Government will endure on the rock of law-enforcement or it will perish in the quicksands of lawlessness."

No less drastic is the conviction of Assistant Attorney-General Goff: "The law must and shall be enforced as it is conceived and written, and always without fear or favor. So far as it lies within the power of the Department of Justice to execute and enforce the law of the land, there will be no backward step, no retreat, in preserving the Constitution and carrying out the mandate of the people."

Our great Secretary of State, who has rendered service to the whole world in his recent leadership at the Conference for the Limitation of Armaments, has also voiced with characteristic clearness and patriotism this thought when he said: "Everybody is ready to sustain the law he likes. That is not in the proper sense respect for law and order. The test of respect for law is where the law is upheld even though it hurts."

And there is no question as to where we will locate the President of the United States on this great issue, for with the same constructive statesmanship with which he has viewed the distracted conditions of Europe, he has keenly penetrated to the very heart of the great problems at home and has spoken the word that leaves no doubt as to the large place which he has given law-enforcement. He recently said: "Whatever breeds disrespect for the law of the land, in any particular department of our community relations, is a force tending to the general breakdown of the social organization. If the people who are known leaders, as directing influences, as thoroughly respected and respectable members of society, shall in their respective communities become known for their defiance of some part of the code of law, then they need not be astonished if presently they find that their example is followed by others, with the result that presently the law in general comes to be looked upon as a set of irksome and unreasonable restraints upon the liberty of the individual. Every law involves more or less of this element of restraint. Nearly every individual will find some part of the code that to him seems an unreasonable inhibition upon his personal freedom of action. Our only safety will be in inculcating an attitude of respect for the law, as on the whole, the best expression that has been given to the social aspiration and moral purpose of the community."

These words are eloquent; they are pregnant of thought; they have couched in them great and far-reaching truths, but to me, entrusted, as I am, with the enforcement of this law, the attitude of this great President toward my problems has been eloquent beyond even these most brilliant periods. In the very hours when he has been carrying a burden perhaps larger than that of any other man in the world, he has found time to encourage me in the task that lay before me. While he was wrestling with questions of world-wide importance, he has at no time been too busy to interest himself or to render every possible assistance within his power.

I say there is no question as to where these great men stand, or where the great forces of our national life are to be found. The question is where *you*, as an individual citizen, shall be located and what is *your* attitude toward the law?

I think little is to be feared from those who are positively hostile to law-enforcement. I think there *is* danger in those who are negative or fail to express themselves. If the question of law-enforcement is as these good men see it to be—fundamental to the life of the nation—then the individual citizen imme diately is placed in a position where *he must become militant in its defense.* To assist in the enforcement of the law must become his duty toward his country.

The average American is a law-abiding citizen. The idealism which actuated the fathers in the establishment of this Republic recognized the need for a high regard for law and order and constituted authority.

Every good American citizen, whether he be native-born or adopted, recognizes that he has entered into a contract with the Government of which he is a part, to observe the law of the land and to contribute to the best of his ability to the support of the fundamentals of the Government. Only so may the objects of the founders, the hope of the world and the general good of the people obtain. In the final analysis, regard for the sacredness of contract is the basis of all stability in all relationships. If the sacredness of contract is not observed in business, commerce and industry becomes chaotic. If the sacredness of contract of capital with labor or labor with capital is not observed with sincerity, at once there is chaos. If the sacredness of contract is not observed in the family, at once domestic tranquillity disappears. If there should be a general disregard for the sacredness of contract by our citizenship with the Government, nothing but anarchy could result. *In other words, stable civilization is built upon the foundation of covenants and the keeping of them.*

The prohibition law is the product of evolution and education covering almost a century and marks one of the greatest strides ever taken by any country in a great moral reform in all the history of the world. This law, a part of our Constitution and made operative by legislative enactment, by an overwhelming majority, mechanically becomes a part of the contract entered into by every citizen of the republic and a part of the contract, the whole of which, every good citizen is bound to observe.

I admit that it is very difficult for the alien to understand this law because of the fact that he has been reared under institutions hoary with years; he has been surrounded with customs that are ancient; he has lived in a country where the population is homogeneous, and so a law that touches one's personal habits as closely as the Prohibition Law, is quite foreign to his thought. On the other hand, we are a very heterogeneous population; our institutions are new and our customs are largely in the making, and we must of necessity have laws that are character-forming and directing, as to conduct, in order that we may develop the American type of character, which alone insures our perpetuity as a free people.

Some of our citizens protest that the Eighteenth Amendment infringes upon their personal liberty by restricting one's personal habits. Every law does that to a larger or smaller degree. The Narcotic law interferes with the personal habits of the drug addict; the traffic law seriously restricts the speed-fiend; but these restrictions do not seriously limit the man who places the community good above self indulgence nor do they greatly embarrass the man who places the public welfare above his personal convenience. Liberty is after all personal habits restricted by law for public good, and license the same impulses unrestricted. Our laws in this great Republic are more than line fences marking the boundaries of liberty and license. They must be because of the many elements entering into our national life—forces, to form the American character and type. The obvious task of our country is to take the same forces, impulses, and characteristics of all those races that come to our shores and shape them into the American type and form the American character. Our laws are restricting, directing, and character-forming, and in them lies the secret of America's future.

Tennyson says that the dragon fly began its career in the bottom of a well in a cocoon that is juglike in shape. Soon the impulses of life awakened in it and the law of growth forced it on, outward, and upward, but the aperture of the juglike cocoon is so small that it restricts and restrains the struggling creature, but in the very struggle the little creature sends the color to the tips of its wings, discovers its latent power, develops its type and evolves into a creature of higher sphere. So the foreign standards of life, types of citizenship, ideals, and customs are not sufficient for us. America must inspire with its ideals, direct and restrict by her laws until she has remodeled and remade the foreigner into the American type with the American character. If any of the pampered sons of American wealth, or un-American sons of Europe, revolt against the very forces from which has sprung our greatness, let them leave our shores, but let them leave to us those institutions and laws which have conspired to make America in its ideals and in moral grandeur, unique among the peoples of the earth.

But, my friends, the difficulty is not altogether with that group of our population which may have sprung from foreign shores. There is also some difficulty with a group of our population—a certain group, if you please, of our citizenry made up of respected business and professional men, who have been slow to realize that there is just one question involved in prohibition law-enforcement, and that question is whether or not the individual citizen is *for* or *against* the Constitution of the United States.

There are proper methods whereby laws may be modified, *but there is no proper method by which our laws,* so long as they are laws, may be nullified.

Almost every election held in this country emphasizes the fact that the American people were thoroughly conversant with what they were doing, when by direct vote or through their representatives, this great law was made a part of the organic law of the United States and made operative through subsequent legislation. In my judgment, there is little, if any, cause for belief that there will be a recession from the advanced position already taken, for with the passage of the Nineteenth Amendment the women of the country came into their long-delayed rights of citizenship, and at that moment there entered into the realm of our political life a force that can always be relied upon to exert itself on the right side of every moral or social question. Beyond the peradventure of a doubt the women of this country can be depended upon either at the polls, or in the jury box, to cast their vote for law and rigid law-enforcement.

There is another predominant trait in the American character and that is the trait of impatience. Many have suggested that this law has been tried and found wanting. My friends, this statement is most frequently made by *those who desire to find the law a failure,* and yet some of those considered friends of this law have been led into error by just such adverse criticisms. This law has been operative for comparatively a short time, and yet there are those who desire to judge it a complete success or a complete failure at this early hour.

One of the greatest difficulties, especially facing us in the east today, is the type of propaganda met. Nothing is being left undone to impress upon the public the idea that this law is not operative. Surely there is grave danger to the Republic in the attitude that the *minority* need not submit to the *will of the majority,* and the question arises at once as to the security of our free institutions. I am frank to admit that I am inclined to believe that the source of this propaganda is not to be found in the unwillingness of the minority to submit to the dictates of the law, but that this propaganda has its origin in a well-defined purpose to nullify the law in the interest of large personal gains on the part of a comparative few, who have felt most forcefully the effect of the law, and it is significant that at such a time when liquor is the most difficult to obtain in all our history, when drunkenness has been decreased to a very appreciable degree, when convictions of violators are becoming most numerous,—that at such a time the largest amount of space is given in some of the unfriendly newspapers to articles most flimsy of fact which set forth the idea that prohibition is a failure.

Over 12,000 convictions for the violation of this law have been obtained in the Federal Courts during the past year. It would not be strange if some of the hue and cry "Prohibition is a failure" might have arisen from some of the very ones who have felt the force of the law either in the temporary loss of their property or their liberty, or in the loss of their social standing.

My friends, it is not to be expected that certain citizens of this country will submit to the will of the majority without making a determined effort to regain some of the sources of revenue of which they have been deprived.

The chief cry of the anti-prohibition law propagandist is that prohibition is a failure and the question arises in the mind—"Wherein has it failed?" No one expected 100 per cent. enforcement. What law can you suggest that is enforced 100 per cent.? But again, wherein has it failed? The drunkard has almost disappeared from the streets of our great cities; arrests for drunkenness have decreased 60 per cent. under prohibition; legal consumption of red liquor has been reduced in America from about 130,000,000 gallons before prohibition to *twelve and one-half million gallons* in 1920, *three and one-half million gallons in 1921,* and perhaps about *two million gallons* this calendar year; scores of institutions for the treatment of inebriates have closed their doors; the open saloon has disappeared, and the influence of sober workmen is evident everywhere in the industries of our country; and it is safe to say that for every job lost by prohibition two others have been created. Economically, the biggest thing the prohibition law has done was to destroy a parasitic business. This in itself has been one of our greatest sources of strength during a period fraught with financial peril. And yet the cry is that "Prohibition has failed."

Foreign observers visiting America recently have expressed astonishment at the evidence of improved conditions. They point to the extent of drunkenness in their home lands, not only men but women, and see almost no evidences of it on the streets of our great cities. The fad of home-brewing is rapidly disappearing as was expected and illegal distillation is rapidly becoming an unpopular and dangerous pastime, and yet this is no hour to determine whether or not the law is a failure. Every law requires the test of time and, as Chief Justice Taft is reported to have said, "not until after we have tried this law for at least ten years, may we with propriety discuss whether or not the law is a failure. At least the law should be given a fair chance and the enforcement of it should be entrusted to the friends of the law and then its value determined by its good or bad results."

Among the most subtle and deceptive of all the propaganda directed against the enforcement of the Eighteenth amendment is the persistent cry that the

one of the greatest essentials of the American people —that the law is but an expression of the nation's will, and the will power of America has ever met apparently insuperable difficulties and changed them into world-amazing achievements. It is no mere expression of pride to say that when *America wills to do that which other nations have not done, she will not fail of that achievement.*

Before the American will, every obstacle to law shall disappear, every doubt of authority take flight, and America become a nation without a slave or saloon, sober and safe for all generations to come.

Let us confess that the Eighteenth Amendment leads the way for all the nations of the earth in moral achievement; that America is the pathfinder for the race in this legislation; but let us also remember that the majority has spoken and that American backbone is as strong today as it was when the world laughed at the experiment of independence, or scorned the prophecy of Lincoln, or doubted the dream of Roosevelt of the Panama Canal.

Never was there greater necessity for the great law-abiding forces of America to be a unit than at the approaching elections in their support of those candidates who have come out wholly and patriotically on the side of law and order. The day has come for all good citizens to make plainly apparent just where they stand on the great fundamentals which are essential to the perpetuity of the American form of Government. There is no magic wand by the waving of which lawlessness and crime will disappear, but it is only through the co-operation of good citizens and the processes of evolution and the course of time that conditions will more nearly approach the high standard which has been set for all American community life.

Particularly do I desire to call the attention of this great audience tonight to the fact that one of the most insidious weapons being used today by the opposition is the effort to discredit the prohibition service. In my judgment, taking it as a whole, the force of about three thousand people engaged in the prohibition work in all parts of the United States is as high type a force as is found in governmental service. You may be pretty well assured that when an official engaged in this work is doing his duty, he is hurting somebody and that he is making some enemies. The law violator will go to any extremity to "get" that official. That official will be lied about, that official will be misrepresented in the hostile press. In other words, every effort will be made to make that official so discouraged, so tired out and so weary in the task of trying to do his duty, with carping criticisms hounding him on every side, that he will give up in despair, unless he is made of that material of which most of the prohibition forces of the United States are made, namely, of grit, perseverance, and red-blooded American patriotism. All honor to those officials who are going through this experience to the end that final victory may come as the majority on this question will be increased and as the minority shall diminish. Then will this law, come to be looked upon in much the same regard as all other laws and will be as successfully enforced.

You may ask, "What can I do to express my patriotism and place myself positively upon the side of law-enforcement?" As citizens you can give your co-operation and assistance to all enforcement agencies. You can help in the enforcement of this law by publicly and privately registering your sentiment in favor of vigorous enforcement of the law; you can greatly assist by serving upon juries, as every good American citizen should do. You can render assistance by expressing your opinion to the editor of your paper and by encouraging the faithful public servant who is doing his best to help enforce the law; you can register yourself in favor of law-enforcement by affiliating yourself with those societies and organizations that have for their purpose the inculcating of the spirit of reverence for law in both young and old. You can support at the polls those candidates whose records are sound on the law-enforcement program. And not the least among all the things to be observed that will place you on record is your daily conduct where, in strict obedience to the law, you will create an example that will point to a proper attitude toward the law.

Let us, then, my countrymen, enroll ourselves in the cause of our country's safety and the securing of our Constitution. Let us renew our courage and strengthen our hope that our country shall endure. Let us listen to the heroic voices of the past and dedicate ourselves anew to their unaccomplished task. Before the altar of our nation, let us consecrate our lives and our love in the service of one God, one Country and one Flag. Let us be militant, but full of faith, remembering always that "They that are for us are more than they that are against us."

At the close of the address, the chairman, Wilson S. Doan, pledged the message should be carried to the neighborhoods whence the people came; and he stated his belief the Conference would stand as one man, pledged to hold up the hands of Commissioner Haynes in Law Enforcement.

Round Table on Enforcement

Led by WILSON S. DOAN

In introducing the subject, the leader referred to the fact that many do not believe in the Volstead Act; some of these are against all law, others are sincerely in earnest in not wanting *liberty* interfered with,—who honestly cannot discriminate between license and liberty. "We have relied on the school as a melting-pot, while the home and the church have responsibilities, as well. Lawlessness is not all to be attributed to the foreigners, however."

Lack of uniformity of law works against law enforcement, it was said, and the divorce law was held up as an example of the sanctity of the law not being observed. "What can we do as Friends?" was asked, and it was felt that every Meeting should be a factor and Friends should never rest until courts are free from politics, and a statute placed eliminating politics from the judiciary.

Justice, instead of being sure and speedy, is usually tempered with politics, and made slow. This is often the secret of lack of respect for law. Loyalty to the Constitution was emphasized, and various evidences of good produced by prohibition were mentioned by Ida W. Keever, Oren Wilbur, Dr. Nathan Thorne, Chauncey Shortlidge, Pauline W. Holme, Caroline S. Engle, William Griest, and Miss Stradling.

Round Table on Anti-Narcotics

Led by PAULINE W. HOLME

This was principally in the hands of Charles M. Filmore, National Superintendent of the No-Tobacco League, who, with John Huddleston, whose splendid voice won him friends, had been secured to bring a vision of the work to Friends. Mr. Fillmore declared man could not attain the best against the hindering influence of tobacco. There is a need of example to be set to both men and legislature, but education of the young is most necessary.

Speaking of the tobacco business, which the speaker considered a scheme of Satan, he spoke of the great increase in smoking among minors. He declared 75 per cent. of high school boys are now smoking, and more than half of the fourth grade, and even third grade boys, and cited a second grade boy whose father taught him, at three years of age, to smoke. "Boys too young to start school pick up stubs men have thrown away," he said. Quoting Government statistics of the increased manufacture of cigarettes, he gave the following table:

1900	2 billions
1910	8 "
1918	39 "
1919	47
1920	53
1921	63 "

which last means that more than five billion cigarettes are used in this country each month.

Thirty-five per cent. of High School girls now smoke, he declared, and many American women smoke in public. Of the eight States now organized to fight the cigarette, Illinois was the last.

(Round Table on Social Morality in next issue.)

der of such a group would have on the lives of the young ›ple would be of lasting value.

BOOKS

Will you send me a list of books that girls and boys in early high school years would enjoy, and that would be ›d literature and perfectly safe."

Edward Everett Hale once said, "All girls like boys' ›ks. Almost no boys like girls' books." The following contains many more boys' books, the only distinctly ls' book being "Little Women," which many a boy has en a great deal of pleasure in reading! These are all sidered good literature, and are perfectly safe for boys l girls to read.

Captains Courageous," by Rudyard Kipling.
Little Women," by Louisa Alcott.
The Widow O'Callaghan's Boys," by Gulielma Zollinger.
The Deerslayer" and "The Last of the Mohicans," by nes F. Cooper.
Masterman Ready," by Frederick Marryat.
The Half-Miler," by A. T. Dudley.
Kidnapped" and "Treasure Island," by Robert Louis venson.
The Lance of Kanana," by Harry W. French.
Men of Iron," by Howard Pyle.
Rob Roy," by Sir Walter Scott.
Richard Carvel," by Winston Churchill.
A Tale of Two Cities," by Charles Dickens.
Stover at Yale," by Owen Johnson.
Westward Ho," by Charles Kingsley.
Green Mansions," by W. H. Hudson.
Seventeen," by Booth Tarkington.
The Lost World," by Conan Doyle.
The Efficient Life," by S. L. Gulick.
The Home Book of Verse," by Burton E. Stevenson, ted.
The Making of an American," by Jacob A. Riss.
The Call of the Twentieth Century," by D. S. Jordan.
Life of Jesus for Young People," by W. B. Forbush.
The Monster Hunters," by Francis Holt-Wheeler.
Boys' Book of Exploration," by Tudor Jenks.
Boy Mineral Collector," by J. G. Kelley.

Friendly News Notes

t a meeting held on Tenth month 15th, at the Eastland ting-house, J. Chauncey Shortlidge, Principal of the ›lewood School for Boys, at Chester Heights, Pa., gave illustrated lecture on the Friends' General Conference at Richmond. After the lecture there was general ussion of the subjects considered at the Conference.

omen Friends who have always been granted equal :age with men in their meeting affairs must be watch- :hat not only they, but their women friends and neigh- as well, take advantage of their right of suffrage in fall elections. If we do not measure up to our respon- ities in going to the polls, we are sanctioning and ting the political corruption, wastefulness and misuse ıblic funds, fraud and graft for which we have hitherto the men responsible.

ıymond Walters, Dean of Swarthmore College, in an :le on "The Scope of Collegiate Registration Statistics" ished in "School and Society," makes the statement "as large a percentage of our population obtain a college education today as obtained a high school education 50 years ago. The increase in college attendance in the last quarter century has been several hundred per cent." Dean Walters is an authority on this subject, due to his long experience as Registrar of Lehigh University. He and Professor W. Carson Ryan, Jr., head of the Education courses at Swarthmore College, are co-editors in the publication of "School and Society."

There are probably many of the readers of the INTELLIGENCER who are either permanently associated with Buck Hill Falls or who have been transient guests of that attractive mountain resort; among these there may be some who have not already known of the illness of our beloved and revered cottager, Dr. Gannett.

The latest information received is that he is making progress toward convalescence, though very slowly. He is still imbued with his love for Buck Hill and all its charms, but on account of the cold weather, is happy in the prospect of leaving in a few days.

We trust that the long journey to his Rochester home may not prove irksome to this dear friend, whose bright cheery face, unbounded faith, and helpful spiritual messages have proved an inspiration to all who know him.

The Pittsburgh Quaker Round Table met on the evening of October 21st, at the home of Mr. and Mrs. Carl Vandervoort, in Allegheny, with a good attendance. The meeting was begun with the usual brief period of silence, and, after transaction of regular business and the annual election of officers, Henry Moore gave an interesting account of the contrasting conditions and "atmosphere" in two large manufacturing plants which he had recently inspected. He then read reports of relief work and present economic conditions in Russia. During the lengthy discussion of this latter subject which followed, the members and friends present were favored with informal and highly interesting accounts by Mr. Demetri Verogradoff.

The Friends' Historical Society was entertained by Swarthmore College on Seventh-day, Tenth month 21st. There was an exhibition of Quaker bibliography and relics in the library, the various exhibits being made most interesting through the information given in a talk by Albert Cook Myers. The guests then visited the Benjamin West house, going on to the College, where an exhibition of Benjamin West's paintings were exhibited and explained by Professor Alfred Mansfield Brooks. After a visit to the Sproul Observatory, where Professor Miller showed the guests how the telescope worked, all were entertained at tea by President and Mrs. Aydelotte. The whole affair was delightful and the members who were fortunate enough to be present greatly appreciated the courtesy extended and the opportunity of visiting the College in this way.

A private letter from Nora Wain, who is in Shanghai, China, contains two items of interest to a large circle of Friends. She writes:

"Who does thee think I have just been seeing off on a boat to Hongkong? Dr. and Mrs. Swain. It has been so nice to see them and to have them seeing the China that I like so much even though I am not at all satisfied with their visit. It has been far too brief, but they have promised to return and spend several months later and let me be the conductor. I should like that and I feel sure I can make China more real to them because the language barrier and the old formal courtesies of the life of a Chinese family are impassable walls to the tourist. It was really as good as a trip home to talk with President and Mrs. Swain. They are having such a happy time and both look ten years younger than when I saw them before. Mrs. Swain is in perfect health now and they say that they have enjoyed every minute of the time—they are as enthusiastic as a young bridal couple and as eager to do all the things they have planned since the days of their youth, that I felt as I left them today that they had in reality discovered and recaptured youth.

Aileen Goddard, an English girl who is my best friend out here, and I had lunch with them on the President Wilson just before the ship sailed, so I have just within the hour waved them southward. They plan to go to Hongkong, then to Singapore, then on to Java, India with Spain as an objective in the spring and possibly Scotland for the summer."

The second item is that Nora Wain has become engaged to an Englishman, G. E. Osland-Hill and expects to be married in Shanghai the first week in December. Mr. Osland-Hill is the Chinese Postal Commissioner stationed at Nanking, which presumably will be their home. Nora expects to be able to continue her literary work and at the present time she has seven stories which are presently to appear in various magazines.

Samuel T. Tyson, of Los Angeles, California, has written and printed privately a "Contribution to the history and genealogy of the Tyson and Fitzwater families." The Tysons are descendants from Reynier Tyson, one of the thirteen heads of families, who, following Pastorius, settled Germantown in 1683. There were thirty-three souls in the little party of Germans who came from Crefeld in the lower valley of the Rhine not very far from the border of Holland. At the time of his arrival, Reynier Tyson was unmarried. His sister was the wife of Jan Streypers, one of the six original purchasers.

About 1708 Reynier Tyson removed to Abington township, Montgomery County, purchasing a large tract of land, part of which is now covered by the village of Glenside. He became an active and important member of Abington Meeting. His children intermarried with the Potts, Jenkins, Lukens, Naylors, Lewis, Hallowel, Thomas, Kirk, Roberts and Harker families, so that today thousands of descendants, particularly in Montgomery and Philadelphia Counties, trace their ancestry to this sturdy pioneer. The writer has gathered together more information relating to the Tysons than has heretofore been found in any one place and he has traced down his own line of descent in full.

Thomas Fitzwater, who gave his name to Fitzwatertown, and his son Thomas were fellow passengers with Penn on the "Welcome." The son married Mary Tyson, the widow of Matthias Tyson, the oldest son of Reynier Tyson mentioned above.

We have no information as to whether Samuel T. Tyson has copies of his book for sale, but anyone interested in these two families will certainly desire to obtain a copy.

C. F. J.

BALTIMORE NEWS

The Conference Class recently had a round table on the Daily Newspaper, with different members of the class discussing assigned parts, such as General News, Editorials, Treatment of Crime, the Funny Page, Advertisements.

In our closing exercises of the First-day School we are having once a month a talk, illustrated with slides and maps, on Biblical Geography.

The Young Friends' Movement has adopted a program for the Study Group which is divided into Religious Discussions, Home Service, Foreign Service, and Carol Singing. This Seventh-day they are all going on a straw ride to Fallston.

The Calling Committee of the Advisory Committee is going to all our members in the near future with another set of canvas questions. This time it is to secure the names of people who might be interested in our activities. Only 45 per cent. of the American people are church members. There must be, therefore, many people living near our friends who are not church goers. We want to have a chance to interest them.

NOTES FROM THE ADVANCEMENT COMMITTEE

The Advancement Committee will bring out as a pamphlet for distribution Wilson S. Doan's address, "Fundamentals," at the Conference at Richmond. The Committee also looks forward to printing "The Quaker Faith," by George A. Walton.

It was reported that the students living in the house at Pennsylvania State College have decided to retain the name "Friends' Union." There are 31 young men living in the house, filling it practically to capacity. Dr. Henry T. and J. Rowntree Gillett visited the Friends' meeting there on October 22nd.

The Committee considered ways of securing new members in the Society of Friends. Evidence was given that in some meetings where there had been a distinct growth this was attributed most of all to the cordial welcome given every stranger who attended. The Committee desired to call to the attention of Advancement workers and Friends everywhere the importance of the personal contact both in welcoming those who come to our meetings, and in taking the initiative to invite those of our acquaintance who may be in the attitude of a seeker, but may not have broken the barrier of our artificial life to speak about it.

FRIENDS' GROUP AT PENN STATE COLLEGE

The third year of existence of what is believed to be unique among college organizations was begun when the Quaker students of the Pennsylvania State College reopened their club house for the new college year which began September 13th. About thirty boys, over half of whom belong to the Society of Friends, are living at the Friends' Union. Their teams meet the fraternities of the College in athletic competition, although the Union is not a Greek letter fraternity.

The Friends' Union was organized by a group of interested members of the Society of Friends, in 1920, in order that there might be a recognized home for the sons of Friends and for others who desire to join with them. William C. Biddle and Dr. O. Edward Janney were largely responsible for the organization of the Union. At present there are eleven men on the active roll who were in attendance together at George School, one of the institutions at which the group first met.

The house is owned by the Friends' Student Hostel, a corporation composed of Friends and graduates of the Pennsylvania State College. Members of the Union upon their graduation may become members of the corporation and eventually it is planned that the club will belong t

it was frantically semaphoring. The yells were about as intelligible to me as the sis-boom-bah we hear at home. I suppose they were telling each side they were swinging like a rusty beer sign or something equally complimentary.

"—It was as close a game as I have seen. Both teams fielded and threw the ball in a way that would have done credit to a big league bunch. But neither side could hit. Although the umpires made two or three close decisions, there was not a kick from any player nor the sign of a protest from the crowd.

"—Tokyo won in the seventh and eighth innings—final score two to nothing. After the game the losing team sat in silence around their dressing room, some of them crying. The winning team will now give a tea to the losing team, and will serve tea cakes with the crest of the school embroidered upon them."—*The Swarthmore Phoenix.*

Baltimore Yearly Meeting
1672—1922

Program

OCTOBER 28TH TO NOVEMBER 2ND, INCLUSIVE.

SATURDAY, OCTOBER 28th.

2.00 p. m.—Meeting of Ministry and Counsel.
All who may be interested are invited. Main Room.

4.00 p. m.—Annual meeting of the Committee on Social Service. All invited. Main Room.

5.00 p. m.—Executive and Nominating Committee of Young Friends. Room 3.

7.00 p. m.—Business meeting of Young Friends. Room 3.

7.00 p. m.—Executive Committee of Philanthropic Section of Friends' General Conference. Principal's Office.

7.15 p. m.—Executive Committee of the Yearly Meeting. High-school Room.

8.15 p. m.—Addresses by Dr. Henry F. Gillett and J. Rowntree Gillett, of England. Lecture Room.
Reception.

SUNDAY, OCTOBER 29th.

10.00 a. m.—Meeting for Worship. Main Room.

10.00 a. m.—Story Hour for children under ten years. In charge of Ada E. Tucker. Girls' Gymnasium.

2.00 p. m.—General Nominating Committee. High-school Room.

3.00 p. m.—Young People's Meeting. Address by Dr. Samuel C. Schmucker, of West Chester, Pa. Topic, "The Interrupted Feast." All invited. Main Room.

4.00 p. m.—Executive Committee of Friends' General Conference. Room 3.

8.00 p. m.—Meeting for Worship.

MONDAY, OCTOBER 30th.

9.00 a. m.—Committee on Education and the Fair-Hill Fund. Room 3.

9.30 a. m.—Devotional Meeting. Main Room.

10.00 a. m.—Business Session.
Opening Minute.
Minutes of Visiting Friends.
Reports from Quarterly Meetings.
Report of the Committee on Program.
Reading of Epistles from other Yearly Meetings.
Report of the General Nominating Committee.
New Business.

1.15 p. m.—Advancement Committee. Members of Monthly Meeting Advancement Committees invited. High-school Room.

3.00 p. m.—Business Session.
Minutes.

Report of Representatives on Clerks, etc.
Reading of Epistles continued.
Report of the Committee on the 250th Anniversary.
Reading and Answering of the Queries.
7.00 p. m.—Committee on Friends' Home. Room 5.
7.00 p. m.—Committee on the Indians. Principal's Office.
7.00 p. m.—Committee on First-day Schools. High-school Room.
8.00 p. m.—Address on "How Can America Help Europe?" By Dr. Wm. I. Hull, of Swarthmore College.
Address on "America at Work for the Abolition of War." By S. Edgar Nicholson, of the National Council for the Reduction of Armaments.
Discussion.

TUESDAY, OCTOBER 31st.

9.30 a. m.—Devotional Meeting.
10.00 a. m.—Business Session.
Minutes.
Report of the General Nominating Committee.
Statement of the General Secretary of the Advancement Committee of the General Conference, J. Barnard Walton.
Statement of the Chairman of the Advancement Committee of the Yearly Meeting, Thomas B. Hull.
Statements of Monthly Meeting Representatives.
Discussion.
Statement of Young Friends' Movement.
1.15 p. m.—Round Table on Narcotics. Pauline W. Holme, Superintendent, Leader. Main Room.
3.00 p. m.—Business Session.
Minutes.
Statement of Chairman of Committee on Social Service, Anne W. Janney.
Consideration of the Work of the Committee.
4.00 p. m.—Address on "Inter-racial Problems," by Peter Ainslie, Minister of the Christian Temple.
4.30 p. m.—Address on "Conditions in Leavenworth Prison observed during a recent visit," by J. Rowntree Gillett, of England.
8.00 p. m.—Conference.
Topic: "True Citizenship: Its Imperative Present Need."
Address: Lavinia Engle, Director of the Maryland League of Women Voters.
Address:
Discussion.

WEDNESDAY, NOVEMBER 1st.

9.30 a. m.—Devotional Meeting.
10.00 a. m.—Business Session.
Minutes.
Minutes of the Executive Committee of the Yearly Meeting.
Report of the Committee on Friends' Home.
American Friends' Service Abroad.
Statements by John K. Harper on work in the Yearly Meeting. Thos. B. Hull, The American Friends' Service Committee. Murray S. Kenworthy, Chief of the work in Russia.
Report of the Indian Committee.
The Richmond Conference—Account of.
Co-operation with the Anti-saloon League. Benj. H. Miller, Representative.
Emergency Committee on Peace and the Limitation of Armaments. Arthur K. Taylor, Chairman.
1.15 p. m.—Advancement Committee. High-school Room.
2.00 p. m.—Conference on First-day Schools. All invited. Main Room.
4.00 p. m.—Conference on Social Service. All welcome. Main Room.
7.00 p. m.—Executive Committee. High-school Room.
8.00 p. m.—Meeting for Worship.
8.30 p. m.—Address on "The Christian Foundation of the Social Order," by J. Rowntree Gillett, Dr. Henry F. Gillett.

THURSDAY, NOVEMBER 2nd.

9.30 a. m.—Devotional Meeting.
10.00 a. m.—Business Session.
Minutes.
Education and the Fair-Hill Fund.
First-day School Committee. Statement by Henry R. Sharpless, Chairman.
New Business:
Action of the General Conference on a uniform Discipline.
Petitions or resolutions.
3.00 p. m.—Business Session.
Minutes.
Auditing Committee Report.
Report of the Treasurer.
Proposed Epistles to other Yearly Meetings.
The Minute of Exercises.
Unfinished Business.
Adjournment.

THE OPEN FORUM

This column is intended to afford free expression of opinion by readers on questions of interest. The INTELLIGENCER *is not responsible for any such opinions. Letters must be brief, and the editor reserves the right to omit parts if necessary to save space.*

PROHIBITION DEFENDED

To the Editor:

In the issue of the 7th inst. there appeared an article in the form of a letter, entitled "As to the Volstead Law," which was so unusual an article for the pages of the INTELLIGENCER as to call for a reply.

The writer begins by asking: "When did it become a crime to sell intoxicating liquor?" and then proceeds at some length to offer excuses for the licensed liquor traffic. One can not help wondering where the writer can have been during the past 30 or 40 years to ask such a naive question. It has certainly been that long and even longer in some States that the infamous liquor traffic has been outlawed, first by Statute Laws and then by Constitutional Amendments, thus placing the ban against it in the fundamental law. The Amendment to our National Constitution, the greatest forward step that humanity has ever taken, is so recent that it seems scarcely worth while to look up the exact date.

But no doubt the question which the writer wished to ask was this: "*Why* was the liquor traffic, so dear to many thirsty souls, prohibited by the underlying law of the Nation?" The best answer to this question that I have recently seen has recently been published, and is the work of one of the most active Y. M. C. A. Secretaries in the City of New York. Men engaged in his line of work among young men have a right to answer this question for they know whereof they speak. As it seems to fully answer all that there was to answer in the communication published in the INTELLIGENCER I append it to this letter, hoping it may meet the requirements of the writer who asked the former question:

"Now why did the people arise in their might and land a knockout blow on this mighty dragon, that was supposed

Instance the case of Sacco and Vanzetti and others. If our government as constituted guaranteed protection to all loyal citizens it would long ago have freed these noble idealists who have suffered a vicarious atonement for peace-professing Friends and others.

Is not this spirit of suppression of honest, conscientious conviction advocated by Elizabeth H. Coale the same spirit that jailed, tortured and burned millions of the noblest men and women for opinion's sake all through the ages past, among them many early Friends? That same spirit of intolerance crucified Jesus of Nazareth for "stirring up the people" for teaching them the true democratic religion of the "divinity of man," of brotherhood and self respect.

Was Mary, the Mother of Jesus, as interpreted by Luke, "using the priceless gift of Freedom of Speech" as a license or a cloak to cover up a treasonable plot" in aiming to put down the mighty from their seats of ruling and exalting those of low degree? Read these declarations in the light of today.

"He hath shown strength with his arm. He hath scattered the proud with the imagination of their hearts."

"He hath put down the mighty from their seats and exalted them of low degree."

"He hath filled the hungry with good things and the *rich* he hath sent empty away."

Not one of our prisoners for opinion's sake was guilty of expressing more revolutionary ideals than these. Our rich criminals who constitute the invisible government back of the apparent one, with their corrupted courts, who have trampled under foot the people's guarantee of rights in our Constitution and our Declaration of Independence, would have given Mary, the Mother of Jesus, a twenty-five years' sentence in jail. I. H. W.

Oxford, Pa.

BIRTHS

BROWN—On Ninth month 22nd, at Coldstream, Ontario, to Pearson C. and Emily MacKellar Brown, a son who is named Mervin James.

MARRIAGES

HOUGH-HOLLINGSWORTH—On Tenth month 14th, at Gwynedd Meeting-house, under the care of Gwynedd Monthly Meeting, Phoebe Atkinson Hollingsworth, daughter of Robert A. and Elizabeth Atkinson Hollingsworth, and Israel Ely Hough, son of Mary P. H. and the late Charles Hough, all of Ambler, Pa.

STANTON-SHOTWELL—At the home of the bride's parents, near Coldstream, Ontario, on Tenth month 14th, James Stanton and Mary Shotwell, daughter of Thomas and Phebe Shotwell.

VAIL-BARRETT—At the home of the bride's parents, at New Market, N. J., on Tenth month 14th, Harvey Adelbert Vail, of Plainfield, and Mildred Barrett.

DEATHS

EVANS—In Pasadena, California, on Tenth month 11th, Elizabeth Passmore Evans, daughter of the late Thomas Passmore and Phebe Smedley Evans.

HOOD—In the Delaware Hospital, on Tenth month 22nd, Robert Chambers, son of Brinton L. and Anna Pusey Hood, age 3 months and 2 days.

PEARSALL—At "The Pennington," New York, on Tenth month 13th, Antoinette G. Pearsall.

COMING EVENTS

TENTH MONTH

29th—Members of Philadelphia Quarterly Meeting's Visiting Committee expect to attend meeting for worship at Germantown Friends' Home, at 7.30 p. m.

29th—Conference Class at 15th and Race Sts., Philadelphia, at close of meeting for worship, 11.40 a. m. The subject for discussion will be "The Prophetic Mission of Jesus."

29th—New York First-day School will re-open.

30th—Baltimore Yearly Meeting, at Baltimore, Md.

31st—Concord Quarterly Meeting, at Darby, Pa. The Meeting of Ministry and Counsel will be held at Darby on the 29th at 2 p. m.

ELEVENTH MONTH

4th—Philadelphia Quarterly Meeting, at Reading, Pa. See Notice.

4th—Prairie Grove Quarterly Meeting, at Marietta, Iowa.

4th—Stillwater Half-Yearly Meeting, at Richland, Ohio.

5th—Purchase Quarterly Meeting, at Chappaqua, N. Y. Meeting for worship at 10.30 a. m. Afternoon session at 2. William J. Reagan, Principal of Oakwood School, expects to attend both meetings, giving an address at the afternoon session on "Religion and Recreation." Conveyances will meet at Chappaqua the 10.18 northbound train, and 8.54 southbound.

5th—First-day at 3 p. m. The usual semi-annual Community meeting for worship will be held at Chichester Friends' Meeting-house under care of a Committee of Concord Quarterly Meeting. All persons welcome and young people particularly invited. Train leaves 24th and Chestnut Streets, Philadelphia, for Boothwyn at 1.30 p. m.; Darby, 1.43; Chester, 2.00, returning about 4.29 p. m. Trains will stop at cross-road near Meeting-house.

6th—Nine Partners Half-Yearly Meeting, at Oswego, N. Y.

9th—Abington Quarterly Meeting, at Byberry, Pa., at 10.30 a. m. See Notice.

11th—Salem Quarterly Meeting, at West, near Alliance, Ohio.

11th—Fall Conference of Friends' Associations, Makefield, Pa.—afternoon and evening.

12th—Theatre Meeting, South Broad Street Theatre, Philadelphia, Pa., under auspices of Sectional Committee, Y. F. A., 3 p. m. Subject, "Quaker Ideals." Speakers: Dr. Henry T. Gillett, Oxford, England; Jos. Rowntree Gillett, London, England; Jesse H. Holmes, Swarthmore, Pa.

NOTICE—Abington Quarterly Meeting at Byberry, on Fifth-day, Eleventh month 9th, at 10.30 a. m. The 9.17 train from Reading Terminal will be met at Somerton Station. The Quarterly Meeting of Ministry and Counsel will be held the same day at 9 a. m. As there is no available train for the earlier meeting, persons wishing to attend will be obliged to go by private conveyance.

NOTICE—Reading Friends hope there will be a large attendance at the Philadelphia Quarterly Meeting to be held for the first time in Reading, Penna., on Eleventh month 4th, at 2 p. m. Those having automobiles are requested to come with no empty seats. There is a train leaving Broad Street Station, Philadelphia, at 11.40, arriving at Franklin Street Station, Reading, at 1.20. Other trains are as follows:

A special train leaves the Reading Terminal at 1.00 p. m., reaching Reading at 2.32; a short walk from the Franklin

To the Lot Holders and others interested in Fairhill Burial Ground:

GREEN STREET Monthly Meeting has funds available for the encouragement of the practice of cremating the dead to be interred in Fairhill Burial Ground. We wish to bring this fact as prominently as possible to those who may be interested. We are prepared to undertake the expense of cremation in case any lot holder desires us to do so.

Those interested should communicate with William H. Gaskill, Treasurer of the Committee of Interments, Green Street Monthly Meeting, or any of the following members of the Committee.

William H. Gaskill, 3201 Arch St.
Samuel N. Longstreth, 1218 Chestnut St.
Charles F. Jenkins, 232 South Seventh St.
Stuart S. Graves, 3033 Germantown Ave.

ADVERTISING RATE in the FRIENDS' INTELLIGENCER, for Help Wanted, Positions Wanted, Rooms for Rent, Notices, and other classified advertisements without display, for each insertion, 2 cents per word, including name, initials and address. Answers may be sent to a box at the INTELLIGENCER office, if so directed.

For display advertising the rate is 10 cents per agate line, or $1.40 per column inch, each insertion. On ten or more insertions in a year from date of order, ten per cent. discount. Thus a four-inch single-column or two-inch double-column advertisement costs $5.60 each insertion, less ten per cent., or 5.04 net each time for ten or more insertions. Matter may be changed whenever desired, without extra charge.

Experience has proved the INTELLIGENCER to be a remarkably good advertising medium. All advertisements must "pass the censor!"

Address 140 N. 15th St., Philadelphia

The Friends' Intelligencer

ESTABLISHED 1844 | ELEVENTH MONTH 4, 1922 | VOLUME 79 NUMBER 44

Contents

EDITORIAL

GENERAL ARTICLES

THE FRIENDS' INTELLIGENCER

Published weekly, 140 N. 15th Street, Philadelphia, Pa., by Friends' Intelligencer Association, Ltd.

SUE C. YERKES, *Managing Editor.*

Editorial Board: Elizabeth Powell Bond, Thomas A. Jenkins, J. Russell Smith, George A. Walton.

Board of Managers: Edward Cornell, Alice Hall Paxson, Paul M. Pearson, Annie Hillborn, Elwood Hollingshead, William C. Biddle, Charles F. Jenkins, Edith M. Winder, Frances M. White.

Officers of Intelligencer Associates: Ellwood Burdsall, Chairman; Bertha L. Broomell, Secretary; Herbert P. Worth, Treasurer.

Subscription rates: United States, Mexico, Cuba and Panama, $2.50 per year. Canada and other foreign countries, $3.00 per year. Checks should be made payable to Friends' Intelligencer Association, Ltd.

Entered as Second Class Matter at Philadelphia Post Office

The Friends' Intelligencer

The religion of Friends is based on faith in the "INWARD LIGHT," or direct revelation of God's spirit and will in every seeking soul.

The INTELLIGENCER is interested in all who bear the name of Friends in every part of the world, and aims to promote love, unity and intercourse among all branches and with all religious societies.

ESTABLISHED 1844 | PHILADELPHIA, ELEVENTH MONTH 4, 1922 | VOLUME 79 NUMBER 44

Prohibition in Danger!

One of the greatest needs of the present time is for people who believe in the Eighteenth Amendment and the Volstead Act to arouse themselves to a realization of the powerful movement on foot to repeal them. There is no question in our minds that Friends are apathetic, when a letter to the Open Forum such as appeared in the issue of Tenth month 7th, after a period of several weeks, has been answered by only one Friend. We had expected to be deluged with indignant protests. Does this mean that Friends agree with the sentiments there expressed?

Will Irwin, one of a group of eminent California authors whose influence was said to be adverse to prohibition in the Golden State, said recently in an article in the *Saturday Evening Post:*

"Lately I have talked over the general situation with several social-settlement workers of New York. They all report their people doing well under prohibition. In general, they find less desertion, less thriftlessness, fewer crimes against women and children. One or two lament a recent increase of home-brewing which affects the sobriety of the women, but they seem to regard this, at its present extent, as a minor evil. Of late the traffic in women and commercialized vice in general have dwindled almost to the vanishing point."

The following expression is only one of many as to the good which has resulted to the working man and his family:

"While I am not a believer in prohibition, particularly in the way the law has been carried out in the past two years," says D. C. Blakewell, President Duquesne Steel Foundry Company of Pittsburgh, Pa., "nevertheless, there is no question in my mind that it has been a great help to industry as a whole. Very few men are now absent after pay-day, whereas, in the old days, we used to count on a fairly large percentage of absentees. This money is undoubtedly being spent in a wiser manner than it was in the past, and I believe it will be for the ultimate benefit of the country to have some sort of prohibition in effect."

William Bennett, city street sweeper of Los Angeles, is reported in the Los Angeles *Record* of September 8, 1922, to have said: "I want things just as they are. I don't want any more of the saloon business. I know about it. I used to run one. We can get along without light wines and beer. It's all right just as it is."

The return of beer and wine means inevitably the return of the old-time saloon, or the licensing of certain places for the sale of alcoholic beverages. The alternative is the distribution of these liquors by means of groceries, soft drink establishments or coffee shops—a method that would stamp them as "respectable" and make them even more accessible to the youth of the nation than they were before. The experience of years has proved that the beer drinking habit is certain in most cases to create an appetitie for the strongest distilled liquors.

The return of the traffic in beer and wines would make the enforcement of the prohibition law immeasurably more difficult, if not impossible, and would eventually mean the return of the control of politics, in city and state, by the brewers. Chief Justice Taft has said: "Any such loophole as light wine and beer would make the Eighteenth Amendment a laughing stock."

Inadequately as the national prohibition law has been enforced in some sections of the country, there is abundant evidence of the most reliable kind to show that it has lessened the consumption of liquor, improved home life and social conditions, and by branding the drink traffic as an outlaw, reduced tremendously the temptation to the young people to acquire the drink habit.

Shall we Friends not make every effort to vote for men at the coming election who as candidates have expressed themselves as opposed to the modification of the Volstead Act? Right now is a critical time and all our influence should be brought into play *at once.*

Our Peace-Work : What Next ?

By William I. Hull

The peace work familiar to members of our Society has been pursued mainly along three lines. The first of these has led our efforts direct to Washington where we have endeavored to influence the executive branch of the government to enter into what seemed to us just and righteous international relations, and have striven to prevent the Congress from indulging in a variety of militaristic experiments. This line of endeavor is perhaps the least fruitful of any, since the government pays not nearly so much heed to what is told it in Washington as it does to what is thought and said by "the folks back home." It is a work which must be done, however, and, to be effective at all it must be done by those in as largely a representative capacity as possible.

The second line of endeavor has led us into a campaign of education within the schools, the press, the moving picture exhibitions and from the public platform. This campaign of education is slow but fundamental, and like temperance instruction a generation ago will yield in time rich harvests. Those engaged in it may well recall Whittier's words:

Knowing this, that never yet
Share of Truth was vainly set
    In the world's wide fallow;
After hands shall sow the seed,
After hands from hill and mead
    Reap the harvests yellow.

It is, however, the third line of endeavor which peculiarly belongs to the Society of Friends. This is the placing of the Peace Movement upon the religious basis, and in particular the interpretation and the application to it of the peace message of Christianity. This message we conceive to be, first, a negative one, and second, a positive and constructive one. The negative part of the message, "Thou shalt not kill," "Thou shalt not resist evil with evil," may not be so attractive to ardent minds; but it is nevertheless of fundamental importance and in fact a prerequisite to the successful accomplishment of the positive and constructive part of our program. Through war and peace, through good fortune and ill fortune, it has been the historic task of our Society, performed by unnumbered and unknown men and women through the generations, to proclaim to a warring world that war is wrong and that preparations for war are also wrong in themselves and inevitably lead to war. When Christendom is thoroughly convinced of the unchristian character of war and preparations for war, and turns its back definitely and finally upon war as a method or an agency in the conduct of human affairs, then and then only can we hope to accomplish thoroughly successful and permanent peace work of a constructive kind.

It was not until the Christian consciences of our fellow-countrymen were thoroughly aroused to the iniquity of human slavery, and not until slavery was abolished that the colored people of the South could be led successfully along the pathway of progress. Ceasing to do evil must ever come before learning to do well.

Do we desire the substitution of judicial settlement for the arbitrament of the sword? If so, we must definitely discard the sword, or judicial settlement cannot be given a fair chance to succeed. Both reason and experience convince us of this truth, just as they did Isaiah and Micah who proclaimed to an unwilling generation that swords must be beaten into plowshares and spears into pruning-hooks before the nations can learn war no more.

Are we eager for our country to join hands with all others and participate in the co-operative performance of the world's international tasks of sanitation and hygiene, industry, transportation, communications, morality and charity? If so, we must turn our backs definitely upon the use or threat of military force in *any* phase of international life. Otherwise the co-operative effort for which we are eager will be stifled in its spirit, robbed of its incentive, and deprived of its resources.

Whether then we are intent on the prevention of war by the adoption of peaceful means of settling international disputes, or whether we are keen upon the international accomplishment of the world's great tasks; we must pave the way for this constructive program, and indeed make it possible, by persuading the world to discard the entire system of war.

Of him to whom much is given, much is expected. Is it not Christendom then upon whom rests the duty of preaching the doctrine and setting the example of eliminating war? Is it not the duty of the Christian church to convict, convince, and persuade the mind and conscience of Christendom to accept this leadership? And what more heavenly mission can the Society of Friends endeavor to perform upon earth than that of inducing our sister Christian churches throughout the world to sieze the present opportunity, the most critical perhaps and the most hopeful in the world's history to undertake this great task?

Christ at the Bar

Christ stands at the bar of the world today,
As He stood in the days of old.
And still, as then, we do betray
Our Lord for greed of gold.

Not alone did Judas his Master sell,
Nor Peter his Lord deny,
Each one who doth His love repel,
Or at His guidance doth rebel,
Doth the Lord Christ crucify.

Like the men of old, we vote His death,
Lest His life should interfere
With the things we have, or the things we crave,
Or the things we hold more dear.

Christ stands at the bar of the world today,
As He stood in the days of old.
Let each man tax his soul and say,—
"Shall I again my Lord betray
For my greed, or my goods, or my gold?"

—*John Oxenham, in "All's Well."*

War!

By James Logan Mosby.

(The following is the prize essay, which appeared in the October 2, 1918, issue of *Life*, which was a War Number. It was sent to us by Charles S. Gerrish, who adds that the main picture in the issue shows a little girl looking into her father's face, with her arms around his neck, while a military figure stands in the roadway holding a horse by the bridle, and the young wife holds an army hat in her hand as she leans pensively against the high back of a chair. Under the picture it reads, "Daddy, are you going to kill some other little girl's father?")

I was conceived in passion, hatred, envy and greed, born in the morning of antiquity, and have a genealogy whose every page drips with the red blood of murdered innocence. I respect neither the feebleness of gray hairs, the helplessness of infancy nor the sacredness of virtue, and walk, iron-shod, ruthlessly and impartially over the form of the weakling or the form of the giant.

I paint the midnight skies a lurid glow from the burning homes I have ravaged, and I turn peaceful scenes of rural beauty, where God's own creatures dwell together in amity, into a raging hell. I set neighbor against neighbor in deadly combat, and I incite the brother to slay his brother.

I make puppets of kings, princes of paupers, courtiers of courtesans and thieves of respected subjects, and empires melt before my breath as does mist before the morning sunlight.

I make of religion fanaticism; the heathen I make a fiend incarnate; and of all men I make playthings devoid of reason and justice. Through intrigue I make the intelligent powerful, the unscrupulous wax fat on the spoils of blood-won victories gained by others, and the less learned suffer for their own ignorance.

Famine, want and misery follow in my path; I lay waste green fields and still the hand of industry. I pillage the land of its resources but contribute nothing of benefit to mankind, leaving pestilence to stalk ghost-like in my wake and complete the work of destruction.

I lay a heavy tribute upon my most loyal subjects for the maintenance of my establishment; I squander the vitality and lives of those who serve me faithfully, yet return to the world nothing but ruin and ashes. The baubles of fame I confer on some are the empty shells of false standards wherein the license to commit murder and rapine is held to be the insignia of glory by a mistaken civilization.

I can offer no excuse for my having come into existence, nor can I give one plausible reason why I should not cease to be, other than that so long as men who weild influence are permitted to gratify their selfish desires and ambitions at the expense of the many who must carry the burdens and endure the suffering, that long will I continue to exact my toll of sorrow, devastation and death. For I am pitiless—devoid of all feeling; I fear neither man nor God; I am amenable to no law, and I am in myself the Law and the Last Resort.

I AM WAR!

Baltimore Yearly Meeting

Under especially favorable conditions of wind and weather Baltimore Yearly Meeting opened its Ministry and Counsel session on Seventh-day with good attendance of its own membership with a number of visiting Friends from other Yearly Meetings present as well. Dr. Henry T. Gillett and James Rowntree Gillett, from London Yearly Meeting, were present with minutes from their respective Meetings, which were read, and a cordial welcome extended. William W. Cocks, of New York Yearly Meeting, also presented a minute. Anna Braithwaite Thomas, a member of the "other branch" in Baltimore, was also given cordial greeting. Reference was made in the early part of the meeting to Martha Townsend, 95 years of age, who, from her sick bed, sent a message by Dr. Janney: "Give them my love and ask for their prayers." Her exemplary life was dwelt upon lovingly; other absentees also were kindly referred to. Later in the meeting a message of loving remembrance was sent from this meeting to Martha Townsend. The welcome extended to the English Friends by Daniel Batchellor, who 45 years ago came to this country from England, contained a peculiar quality of fellowship. The ideal of a closer union among Friends permeated the session to a very great extent, especially was this dwelt upon by J. Rowntree Gillett, who spoke of the work abroad during the war when no one asked to what "branch" you belonged, but only "can you do the work?" "A great fellowship was built up during the war," he said, and he felt Friends have a big cause before them in spreading the Gospel of Peace." "In England so widely is our testimony against war known that a Quaker who fights is considered as not playing the game." Henry T. Gillett followed the same line in urging the openness to all truth and common work which brings unity of spirit.

Concern was manifested by many Friends that participation in the vocal ministry was necessary to the growth and strength of the meeting, and the feeling was expressed that the duty of sharing in spiritual matters was as great as sharing the products of the farm, which is done so willingly. The providing of proper soil for the germination of seed was emphasized as a clear duty also. The withholding from others of a message found helpful to the recipient was deplored. Not so much prepared sermons as prepared men was the need of the hour and the warning that in addition to training for service the constraining spirit be added. In this busy life Friends were urged to "take time to be holy," and not devote too much time to material things. Obedience to the Golden Rule was emphasized by Elizabeth Passmore, who despite her 84 years, is more active and earnest in the service of her Society than many whose years number a score less, and without her richer experience. War would have been impossible, to her mind, had this Rule been obeyed. The giving of approbation to those young in the ministry and the withholding of destructive criticism of their messages was emphasized.

In answer to the query concerning evidences of religious life, these were not wanting in any Quarter. Increased membership, increased attendance, increased interest in and work for the First-day School were among these evidences noted, an added responsibility being shown among the young people. And in these, as Rowntree Gillett expressed it, lies the hope of the future of the Society.

The evening was devoted to addresses by Dr. Henry T. and Joseph Rowntree Gillett. In introducing them Dr. O. Edward Janney spoke of earlier English visitors to this country: John William Graham in 1896, Edward Grubb later, E. Maria Bishop and others, and "now two more messengers of God have come to us." Dr. Henry T. Gillett dwelt briefly on what the Society of Friends stands for, although a small part of the world at large. The world he felt was turning from a religion of authority to a religion of experience, as exemplified by Friends. He spoke of the scientific butchery of a few years back and the unscientific expenditure of today. "The state of things today," he said, "is not due to the war, but to the lack of Christian teaching before the war." All countries were responsible for the war, not Germany alone. Force is no remedy,—love is. Indemnities are the boomerangs that fly back and hit us. If the forgiveness advised by Jesus Christ obtained there would be no indemnity. "The world needs capital today, but needs spiritual capital more," said the speaker. "If a thing is wrong it cannot turn out right."

"The Outlook of our Society Here and Abroad" was discussed by J. Rowntree Gillett, who declared the immanence of God is the greatest doctrine of early Friends. "Our best men," he said, "are going into making money today—thus becoming the greatest slaves of money instead of developing themselves intellectually and spiritually. Character of men is greatest value in life. They are judged by character, not by dollars. Quakerism is a faith," he said, "not a church," and emphasized three main points in this faith: 1—A lay ministry; 2—Equality of men and women in the church; 3—Peace testimony.

The meeting for worship on First-day morning was an especially large and satisfying one, judging by the earnest comments of those attending, many of whom were non-Friends.

The impressive opening silence was broken by Dr. Henry Gillett, whose message was centered around the thought, "I give Thee back the life I owe," following which J. Barnard Walton appeared in supplication.

Isaac Wilson drew from the story of the Woman of Samaria the lesson of finding the Christ spirit in common humanity today. From the text, "All things are possible to those who know God," Anna Jackson Branson, of Germantown, drew a practical lesson, likening life to a race for which we need careful training, and emphasizing the necessity of keeping the goal in sight. The world needs a religion applicable to the practical things of life. Asking our Heavenly Father to help us with our plans is a very different matter from placing our lives under His direction. The impossible things of today may be the inevitable things of a future day.

J. Rowntree Gillett, from the text "I am the Good Shepherd. I lay down my life for my sheep," emphasized the shepherd instinct in our lives. He dwelt upon the sacredness of family life. The care of the young life entrusted to the father should act as an invisible spur to urge him to develop the best of which he is capable, since failure in this would react upon the life of the child as well as upon himself.

William W. Cocks, of New York, said: "The spiritual life is not an abnormal or unusual thing. We are growing tired of bickerings in the church—it matters not by what name we call it so long as we possess the spark of Divine Life within us.

Reuben Kester and others added to the life of the Meeting by brief messages.

The Young People's Meeting at 3.00 p. m. was addressed by Dr. Samuel Schmucker, of West Chester. His topic was "The Interrupted Feast." From that portion of the story of the "handwriting on the wall" he drew a lesson applicable to present-day conditions and needs.

ARABELLA CARTER.

Thanks for a Shawl

"For American Friends' Service Committee. A bit of comfort, I trust, to Russian refugees or others—A shawl brought by my parents from Scotland."

We find this note pinned to a warm grey shawl that comes out of one of the bales from Philadelphia. The Quaker worker in the Gamaleyevka warehouse along the Tashkent railroad, holds up the shawl and remarks: "What a serviceable, lasting thing this will be. What a big all-enveloping piece of cloth."

Just then the Director of the new Children's Patronat No. 91 at Novo Sergeefka steps up and hands us a carefully-drawn list of the clothing needs of his 115 orphaned famine children, for the coming winter. They expect to have beds, real beds, at least one for every two children. That makes 57 plus bed-covers needed. "Do you have any covers suitable for the winter?" the Quaker worker inquires. "Not a thing," answers the Director apologetically.

A few moments later the Director and his assistant are loading on to three deep-bottomed *telegas* piles of clothes. I suppose there must be at least two full bales in the lot. Among the other things they pile on are some bed-covers. The warm, grey Scottish shawl is one of them.

Tomorrow night it will be covering the bed of Ivan Petrovitch, an "all-around orphan" and a member of the Children's soviet at the new Patronat in Novo Sergeevka.

These early days of September are cool and rainy and the nights are cold. You need bed-covers in Novo Sergeevka these nights. Ivan Petrovitch thanks the American lady who sent him his.

Other little Russian orphans are still waiting for theirs. Has thee a shawl or a warm coat to send them? If so, send it to American Friends' Service Committee—Store Room, 15th and Cherry Streets, Philadelphia, Pa.

R. W. D.

A Human Document

The following letter appeared recently in one of the daily papers of New York City. It is a most appealing and convincing human document. It presents the *moral side* of the Prohibition issue concisely and strongly, and coming as it does from a woman who has suffered, should appeal to all men and women who can sympathize with those who suffer; and should influence them to vote aright:

To the Editor of the Evening Journal:

I read that the Democratic platform declares for beer and wine, and that the *Evening Journal* will support the Democratic party.

I have read the *Evening Journal* for more than twenty years. I kept many of the editorials that you published about whisky and the saloon, because I found in them hope and comfort. I have four boys, and I have known the sorrow and shame of drunkenness in my house.

Since whisky and the saloon were outlawed, my boys have been sober. Money that was spent in saloons late at night is now brought home early. Not one of my boys drink, in spite of all the talk I hear about bootlegging. They save their money, they have bank accounts, and they are better paid than they were in the old days.

I for one will never vote for any party or any candidate that tries to bring back the days of the saloon, no matter how the plan may be disguised by fair words and promises.

The bootlegger is bad for those that hunt him out; he is poisonous and criminal. The government should take care of him.

But the bootlegger is not a saloon, OPEN ON EVERY CORNER, with its bright lights, its music, its vicious, poisonous "hospitality," inviting young men and old in to spend their hours and their wages on whisky and on each other.

After all the good work that the *Evening Journal* did for so many years against whisky and against the saloon, I hope it will not now advocate any policy that would bring back the old days, when so many mothers' hearts were broken, so many fathers left at the corner saloon the money that should have bought clothes, shoes and food for their children. I ask you to reprint as a warning to mothers one of your old editorials that I enclose. It is an editorial that I have kept all these years, and I value it. Please return it to me whether you print it or not.

There are tens of thousands of mothers, wives, sisters and daughters that will join with me in my determination to work against any effort to bring back the saloon, no matter how disguised, and I for one shall vote against any party that proves itself to be the party of the corner saloon by trying to bring that saloon back under false pretenses.

As an old reader I have a right to ask that you print this letter. And I ask you to publish again the editorial that I send with it.

It is an editorial that you may well be proud of; it is one of many that did good to the hearts of many poor women like myself. Now that the victory is won and the saloon is gone, it is your duty to fight against its coming back, as you fought for so many years and successfully against the evil that it did.

Thank God I have a vote, so have other women. Any man is mistaken who thinks that women's votes will be cast for any friend of the saloon, however smoothly he talk or disguise himself.

Yours sincerely,

Mrs. E. D.

P. S.—I am 65 years old, with four sons and three daughters. This means that from my family there will be eight votes cast against the effort to bring the saloon back, whether that effort comes disguised as "light wines and beer" or as "whisky and damnation."

Another letter which should help to a right decision at this time is the following, which appeared also in a New York paper:

* * * The sanity of the majority in passing and maintaining the dry law is already demonstrated by the vital statistics of the State of New York for 1921, which prove that it has done just what it was expected to do. As compared with the averages of the five wet years 1913-17, inclusive, with an increase of population of 8 per cent., the total death rate decreased 19.7 per cent. and that of children under 5 years of age decreased 31 per cent. In the City of New York alone, with an increase in population of 10.1 per cent., the decrease in the total death rate was 23.3 per cent., and that of children under 5 years decreased 37.1 per cent. What might have been the record had every one united to keep and enforce the law!

As further evidence of the sanity of the majority, Dr. Alexander Lambert, discussing pneumonia, says: "There has been a great change in pneumonia in New York City. When we had all the alcohol that was desired in life, in Bellevue Hospital one-third of the 10,000 patients were in the alcoholic wards, with or without delirium tremens. That made a strong alcoholic group among pneumonia patients, and the death rate was 63 per cent. for the alcoholic group and 23 per cent. for the non-alcoholic group. The type has changed. One does not see the thoroughly poisoned, chronically soaked alcoholic person in the hospital. The change in pneumonia has also been distinct. We had two groups of fifty patients each; in one group alcohol was given, and the death rate was 40 per cent.; in the other group alcohol was not given, and the death rate was 14 per cent." * * *

MARY BREESE SHARPE.

Brooklyn, N. Y., Sept. 15, 1922.

The following figures have been gathered by the Committee on Philanthropic Labor of Philadelphia Yearly Meeting of Friends, and are convincing evidence that Prohibition *is effective:*

Arrests for Drunkenness

Boston	
Average 1912-1918	59,308
Average 1920-1921	26,293
Massachusetts	
Average 1912-1918	108,123
Average 1920-1921	48,372
New York City	
1907	95,529
1921	11,472
Jersey City	
In 58 cities, including most of the large ones	
1917	316,842
1918	260,169
1919	172,659
1920	109,768

Deaths from Alcoholism

Massachusetts	
Average 1913-1918	225
Average 1920-1921	78
New York City	
1918	252
1920	98

California Jails

1918	3,601 inmates
1921	2,898 inmates

Juvenile Court in Chicago

1918	3,036 boy and girl delinquents
1921	2,415 boy and girl delinquents

Spreading the Message

Who is there among us who is not proud of his Quaker heritage? How many of us are really concerned to deliver the Friendly message to a soul-hungry world, bowed down in dejection, yet groping for light,—for religious light, for social light, for industrial light, for international light?

Is there not a danger that we indulge ourselves in pride, when we can consider that today Quakers are international figures; yesterday practically unknown in Europe, while today they are loved and revered throughout the continent. Something in the Quaker spirit at home, something in the souls of the little groups, who went abroad, to feed and shelter the stricken, carried the healing message of love and reconciliation. Yesterday a great section of the world was mostly concerned with its empty stomach and naked body; today all the world is realizing the pangs of a starving soul and is casting about for new spiritual shelters.

Europe is looking to the Quakers as it would to a prophet. We can hardly take up any of the better class magazines without reference in some article to the wonderful work of alleviation which Friends have accomplished or are now pursuing. The time has come when we should be concentrating more and more on preventive work, rather than upon remedial. Industrial clashes, international and inter-racial wars, poverty and immorality, none of these are causes, they are results. A hateless world, a warless world, a forebearing and forgiving world, a comfortable world, a Christian world, or, in other words, a sane world, is the ideal toward which we must strain our energies. "Real political economy is that which teaches nations to desire and labor for the things which lead to life; which teaches them to scorn and destroy the things that lead to destruction," said John Ruskin. The political economy of the Sermon on the Mount, believed honestly

Philanthropic Interests

Round Table on Social Morality

Led by EMMA G. HOLLAWAY

In this Round Table, much that was pertinent and helpful was discussed. Dr. Holloway felt there were too many Topsies in the world who were let "grow" without proper oversight. "People are prepared for everything save parenthood, the most vital business of all" she said. There is a laxness of morals sad to behold, and she urged that a falsehood should never be told a child when it asks questions. "If it is old enough to ask questions, it is old enough to be told *a part of* the truth at least."

It was felt that all were doubtless convinced of the right thing to do, and each, as parent or teacher should serve as an apostle. Dr. Janney felt the United States was getting no better, and outside, other peoples were getting worse. This was questioned, and statistics were quoted to show that young men from Oregon were the best from the social morality standpoint of any in the army, showing the result of teaching along this line. Many entered into live discussion concerning actual experiences, mostly regarding girls. The question as to whether ridicule might not aid in the cure of an over-dressed young girl brought out the use of love as a winning factor, though it was felt good-natured "chaffing" was also expedient.

Miss Stradling, of Indianapolis, a teacher, felt that the teacher had to cope with this question today, as never before, in place of the parent. She emphasized the dress of the teacher as a factor not to be despised, that she not be deemed an "old fogy" when dealing with up-to-date questions. Dr. Brown spoke of the primal instinct which we must not refuse to face, and urged better teachers be secured to set the pace both in dress and dances. The teachers, he declared, were not trained to give necessary teaching any more than were children fitted to receive it, and he advocated the right foundation be laid.

While it might seem much of the discussion was of a pessimistic tone, yet the standpoint of a young girl present gave another side, when she declared the young today were asking questions, and getting knowledge, so the future generation would not have to flounder as this has done, because the parents did not have the information to pass on.

At a session of the Conference, Dr. Holloway urged that the moral education of a child begin at home, "for by homes and mothers are men made. On our personal relations with God himself depend our hopes of social morality. If a home starts out in the right way, with the joining of two consecrated minds and ideals, its children will be well-born. A race is built through the individual, and every child has the right to be well-born, and the character and disposition of a child depend on the home from which it comes. The children say, 'You can make us what you will: save us from ignorance and wrong-doing, and we may become the mightiest creatures in the world.' Do we realize that the young folks of today are but following out their natural instincts? They need to be guided and guarded with love, charity, and sympathy.

So dress and carry yourself, that your personal appearance will not detract from your personality. Some little thing may turn the whole scale in the work with children. We should not only know our own children, but their associates. The young do not want to be bad, but just to have a good time. Let us help them to have the right kind of a good time. Work with children should be a great part of the future work of the Society of Friends."

She closed with the appropriate selection, "The Gospel According to You."

Young Friends' Sessions

The High Road

This session was in care of the younger Friends attending the Conference. Waldo Hayes, the presiding officer, reminded the Conference, in his opening remarks, that "It is the young Friends who must in the future carry on the work which the older Friends are doing today. The Conference, therefore, would not be complete without a word from the younger Friends."

The four speakers, William J. Reagan, Alan C. Valentine, Grace T. Warren and Bliss Forbush, each stressed a different point on the journey along "The High Road."

William J. Reagan said: "In the days of the Puritan in New England, children were forced to go to Meeting, and listen to sermons two hours' long, with prayers lasting half an hour; and this twice a day. The school during the week was conducted on the same Spartan basis. 'Those who survived became great.' We admire the Puritans, but we do not envy them. I myself remember going to Quarterly Meeting from 10 to 4 o'clock, and no lunch in between. We do not do that any more. Puritanism has passed for ever, I suppose.

On the contrary, we have today perhaps an exaggerated idea of freedom. We now believe that the child's life should be made more smooth. At the gang-period of a boy's life, we must not try to get him away from the gang; we must win the gang, or lose the boy.

There are three big things on the new 'High Road of Life.' The determination to worship will be the most significant fact that life has to offer us. The crying need of the hour is the need for worship in every phase of our active lives. Every sensible teacher begins the class in an attitude like that of prayer. We Friends have not practiced the psychology of worship; we have gone so far in our informality—we have become so formal in our informality—that it may be asked if we have not defeated our own ends.

We must have a new doctrine of personal righteousness. I can not tell you exactly what you ought to do. But no one can be happy unless his religion costs him something. We must have a code of personal righteousness. I know a man who thought it right to feed the German children, but not the children of the miners. Yet both are children of the common Father.

The new 'High Road' will give no substitute for duty. We will talk less about our rights, and more about right and duty. Some people talk about a new social order who have no conception of righteousness. Personal righteousness and the new social order depend on our each becoming attuned to hear God's voice whenever it calls. The 'High Road' must be the road to God's righteousness. Take your places on the Road."

Alan C. Valentine said: "What will Friends stand for fifty years hence? This question is of very definite importance to the younger Friends. Where are we trying to go and how will we get there? Can we find any sign posts along the 'High Road' of Quakerism? But before we speculate upon where we are going, let us ask ourselves who we are. Every Friend has a dual relation to society in general; his obligations as an individual member of society, and his obligations as a Friend. What should we stand for as Friends, apart from our obligations as individual human beings? What is the essence of Quakerism?

One thing seems certain. We must lay more emphasis on the essential things of our religion. There is danger of letting some of the flowers of our religion conceal its main stalk from whence comes our strength. People often think of Quakerism as the sum total of a number of its external evidences and fail to see the fundamental religious conception that lies back of these externalities.

For example, the whole spirit of Quakerism is not embodied in silent worship. Silent worship is not the distinct religious contribution of Quakerism; it existed before the Society of Friends, and still exists elsewhere. Neither is Quakerism embodied in simplicity of dress, style of Meeting-houses, or antagonism to war or drink; these things are all external evidences of the individual Quaker's interpretation of the dictates of his Inner Light.

The essence of Quakerism is the fundamental religious ideal which the Quakers contributed to the world,—the idea of the individual being guided in his convictions, and hence in his actions, by an Inner Light which is the spirit of God. Quakerism is based first of all on the sovereignty of the individual, and may vary with the individual in proportion to his closeness with the Inner Light, or the accuracy with which he interprets his guidance. Let us not feel, therefore, that our meeting is at fault when its members cannot agree; let us rejoice that they are thinking for themselves. The Society can present certain views as its representative religious convictions, but cannot present a unanimous front upon all questions. Let us recognize this as an element of strength, growing directly from our adherence to an Inner Light.

This right to an individuality of religious conception is the great contribution of Quakerism, with its corollary, toleration of the beliefs of others. If there is any message needed in the world today it is this,—firmness of religious conviction in oneself, and tolerance of the efforts of others. The spreading of this message seems to me the chief duty of every young Friend on the 'High Road.'

Perhaps conduct along the 'High Road' comes under three heads; my attitude toward the Society of Friends, toward society in general, and in securing my individual aims. Some suggest that we assure the future life of the Society of Friends by more attention to its organization. But too much attention to organization and too little to spirit will make any organization die of its own weight. Jesus did not organize his followers; he knew there were other things more important. Let us perpetuate the spirit of Quakerism, and the organization will care for itself. Let us foster the spirit, remembering three things:—that we must make a conscious effort to get away from material things; that no religion can live unless it have a definite meaning in daily life; that Quakerism must be based on a fundamental religious unity rather than on a social unity. Here is a concrete danger for Quakerism. We tend to discourage the entrance into our body of one of another stratum, who makes us uncomfortable because he breaks up our social unity. We must not throw up social barriers against the spread of religious truth.

Let us be more tolerant to society in general. We are not set apart; perhaps we do not even know all the truth. We are Quakers, but we have no obligation to Quakerism that can conflict with our primary obligation as citizens of a world made by God who created all human beings equal in His eyes.

In the realizing of our individual aims, perhaps Quakerism may be applied most effectively. Let each young Friend here review his choice of a career from the point of view of Friends. Does his choice help not only his material wants, but also his aims as a Friend? If not, let him think again. How many of us carry our Quaker ideals into business, family and political life? This job of being a good Quaker requires real moral bravery,—the power to say what ought to be said, and do what ought to be done. Each young Friend on the 'High Road' of Quakerism must ask himself these questions:—Are we as Friends going forward? Where are we headed? If we know our own aims, and they are good, do we know how to reach them? We are proud of the ideals of Quakerism our fathers handed down to us. Shall we discard their trust, or shall we stand up and play the game?"

Grace Warren said: "The 'High Road' for Friends to take today is the road of a fixed purpose. George Fox, with his eyes fixed on the 'ocean of light and love' which flowed over the 'ocean of darkness,' had 'great openings' as he traveled.

The 'High Road' is one of purpose and determination, for which great equipment is not necessary. We do not need material things. We need not travel by the auto of wealth to join the caravans there; nor do we need a great baggage-train of intellectual attainments. Education is an advantage, but truth is its basis. The true equipment is in ourselves; it is just what God has given us, if we will use it. It consists in the powers of loyalty and endurance which added together spell the word 'devotion.'

Our endurance must show in our ability to use well and persistently whatever poor tools we have with which to work. It is our determination that counts. And our loyalty must meet the challenge of adverse conditions in our little fields of service at home, bickerings and prejudices and criticisms. It is a journey which calls one spiritually to such a campaign as Garibaldi promised when he said to his little band of patriots: 'I promise you forced marches, short rations, bloody battles, wounds, imprisonments and death,—let him who loves home and fatherland follow me.' In our meetings, we may say, 'I promise you insufficient ministry, and a lack of leadership, discouragement, and lack of vision.' Let him who loves Christianity after the manner of Friends learn devotion.'

We look back and draw inspiration from the devotion of the old-time Friends. Our hope is that we may catch the gleam of light from their highway. Let us start after our fiery pillar on the High Road of Purpose, determined that 'ere it vanish over the margin we will

'After it, follow it, follow the Gleam!'"

Bliss Forbush said: "If we are to live by the 'High Road of Life,' we must open our eyes to all the wonders that are about us. We must live our lives to the uttermost. We must interest ourselves in things about us, and not narrow our lives to a single business and a single hobby. We should know, wherever we live, of the great movements that are going on in the world today, we must know what each new prophet of reform is teaching his followers, we must be interested in all that tends to make the human family better and nobler.

We live by the side of the 'High Road of Life,' yet its greatest wonders escape our attention. We who live in great cities often have never visited their historic spots; we who live among God's great nature pictures often find them only mirrors reflecting nothing but our own faces. And we often close our ears to the beauties of music because we have not a musical ear. But worse than lacking the beauties of eye and ear, we often lack the beauty of the heart because we have not developed the spiritual side of our being. We have seen the great efforts of little men, and have not been thrilled by them; we have seen brave ones make the supreme sacrifice, and not wished to emulate them; we have seen glorious ones turn from the gain of material things to the path of hardship, for the good of humanity, and we have not followed them; and we have had moments of great exultation when we felt we discerned a little of God's great plan for us, yet we turn our backs to it all because the road seems long and the way long. We remain blind because we do not wish to see.

When Jesus was asked, 'Where dwellest thou?' he said, 'Come and see.' And they followed and saw him heal the sick and comfort the poor in heart, and give the guide of life in the Beatitudes. But the story does not say where they decided He dwelt. Where do you think was His home? And where along the 'High Road' dwellest thou?"

Young Friends' Forums

Led by William J. Reagan.

(These Forums were held each morning at the time of the other Round Tables, and were confined to no set topics. The trend of discussion, however, covered such topics as the relationship between play and work, our preparation for the meeting for worship, our business meetings, our friendships, and the maintenance of our personal ideals. The notes given below are consecutive, without dividing line between the different sessions. Practically all the material given is quoted from the leader. There was much discussion, free and frank and general, but as a general thing, the leader's summing-up of the general idea covered the ground as clearly and much more briefly than if the entire discussion were given; and is, therefore, used here.)

The Forum opened by a discussion of three questions: 1. Is it legitimate to use play as a bait to get young people to attend Quarterly Meeting? 2. Should we *not* use play as a bait?. 3. Should we play at Quarterly Meeting at all?. A discussion taken part in by many resulted in answering the questions as follows: 1. No. 2. Yes. 3. Yes.

The discussion brought up the question of the distinction between work and play. Work and play are distinguished by the mental attitude; if a thing is regarded as necessary, or is unpleasant, or if one thinks it *must* be done, such a thing is usually thought of as Work; but if the thing to be done is pleasant, or if one really wants to do it, it is regarded as Play. Play, moreover, is for its own sake, while work is for something else.

To really know a person well, one must both work and play with him, as both bring out certain characteristics which would otherwise remain unknown. Many homes have been broken up simply because their occupants did not both work and play together, and so missed the comradeship and co-operation which go with both. Then, too, we often forget all those little formalities which make life away from home so pleasant. At home, it is easy to forget to say "Good morning" when we see the rest of our family for the first time.

Work makes play, and play makes work.

Hard work and play are necessary.

Never use play as a means to an end.

Play is a bad bait.

Always play when it is possible.

Old and young need to play together.

Never make work of play.

The younger person is always controlled by others. They copy, even if pretending to be independent. Young men whose lives have been wrecked have followed in the steps of older ones. One of the lovely things about this Conference is that the older people and the younger are playing together. How many of us know an older person "who makes a difference to me"? I wish every young person here would put down in his note-book "When I get home, I will go to an older person, and tell him all about the Conference." That will help make a friend, and will make the Conference more vivid.

A whole host of people think that they have to "fix their faces" to pray, or to talk about worth while things.

Most of the trouble in the world comes because we do not get together in the right way. A young minister played basket-ball with a group of boys, but did not win them. But he got them to keep an old woman in wood for a winter, and won them entirely. We need to get together right. How can we live our own lives, and yet take the help our

Speak to the small boy. Any adequate talk about the Message will be built on a fundamental basis of real love for all mankind. When the other impressions of the Conference have gone from me, I shall remember the black porter in my Pullman car; he will continue to speak to me.

We have been talking this week about some very costly ventures of life. I think that if we are in earnest, our technical blunders will be more seeming than real. We have enjoyed this Conference, but we can not say yet that it is a success. Very often the Conference makes more difference to people who never say anything about it. We shall be tired when we get home. But the first task ahead of us will be to tell about the Conference when we want to sleep. The real test of anything is the reaction that it carries closest home. Wouldn't it be fine if a lot of these young people would go home, and seek out others, and fill them with the radiance of these days?

I heard once of an architect who scrimped a house he was building. Then he married the daughter of its owner, and was given the house as a wedding present. Each of us is building all the time the house we have to live in, for thirty, forty, fifty years, or more.

There are certain books which will be very helpful in building our houses.

"The Manhood of the Master," Fosdick.

"The Meaning of Prayer," and other books by Fosdick.

"Prayers of the Social Awakening," Rauschenbusch.

"What and Where is God?" Swain.

"Elizabeth Fry," Richards; which is accepted by the Board of Regents for English work.

"George Fox," by Rufus M. Jones, which is required at Oakwood for the work in English.

Woolman's Journal.

"What is Quakerism?" Edward Grubb.

One very valuable thing we can do is to use literature of this kind:—read it ourselves, and put it where it can be read.

In telling of the Conference we ought to show that we have had a good time, and that we have had serious thoughts. We can do harm by giving only one side of the thing. Many of you who have never taken part in the morning Meetings will have to after these days, or else reject the urge within; when the time comes, I hope you will be brave.

There are many Monthly Meetings where there seems nothing real to take part in. Our difficulty is the difficulty of getting together and doing what we can. As young Friends, we must be willing sometimes to be bored a little, and we must all, old and young, try to make the meetings more real than ever before.

(Here came a discussion of how voting should be carried on in the meetings, the majority preferring the present system.)

In voting by "Aye" and "No," there is great danger of being ruled by majorities. At the Lake Mohonk Conference, in which the participants were of very different opinions, they used the Friendly method of writing and re-writing statements until all could agree upon them.

In every community there are boys and girls who are unhappy because they have not friendship. I wonder if there are not some in this group who would help someone like this in real friendship, not in superiority. Nobody gets from anybody anything worth while, unless we share those worth while things.

At the close of the Conference, various young Friends were privately asked to tell what impression was uppermost in their minds when they thought of the Young Friends' Forums. Here are the replies:

1. The tremendous earnestness of the young people.

2. The large number of young people who have a definite concern to take part in the vocal ministry of their home Meeting, but who hesitate to do so.

3. The contagious enthusiasm and concern of William Reagan.

4. The fact that the present generation will witness a great re-birth of Quakerism.

5. The enthusiasm and loyalty of convinced Friends.

6. The essential relationship between work and play.

7. The unity of purpose of both younger and older Friends.

8. The renewed encouragement to continue work in the smaller and more isolated meetings.

9. The practical value of the topic discussed.

10. The ability of the leader to draw out general discussion.

11. William Reagan talked WITH us rather than AT us.

Recreation and Religion

William J. Reagan.

Bliss Forbush, Executive Secretary of Baltimore Monthly Meeting, who presided, hinted at insincerity on the part of those who condemn Sunday base-ball and golf, yet take out their high-powered machines for a trip to the country. "Is it fair to stop the Sunday movies when we go autoing?" he said.

People complain today of lack of time for what they wish to accomplish, yet when was there ever so much pastime as today—giving vitality to some, and nervous prostration to others, in the glare and rush of life. There is an old tale of a traveler in a desert who was pursued by a wild beast. In fleeing, he tried to climb down into a well, but saw at the bottom a horrible dragon, and clinging to a bush, dangled just out of reach of the beast above, but in danger of dropping into the dragon's jaws. And as he hung there, two mice came, and nibbled away the earth around the roots of the bush. But in this deadly danger, he saw some honey on the leaves of the plant, and eagerly devoured it. This is a parable of Life, and the honey is the pleasure that men snatch as they pass along.

We shall not be merely negative in our attitude toward religion. We can not live long just by not doing things that hurt us. The church has too long said: "No, No, No." People are still interested in religion, and organized religion has a vital part to play; but we want a new outlook. We cannot longer refuse to realize play as re-creation. The thing we think about is the thing we finally do. To cut off the outward expression of a thing drives one to it.

At Oakwood we have decided not to let the boys and girls dance. It is not wrong, perhaps, but it seems to us inexpedient. Now, our danger is that they will think, think, think dance, and that may be worse for them than to dance and forget about it. I think the best way to keep a boy from smoking cigarettes is not to tell the evils of cigarettes, but to tell of the beautiful body that would result from not using them. We must do something more than that. We must teach them to eat and live properly, and to have respect for their bodies,—and that is where the churches have the field. They are different to-day from the time of Jesus and Paul.

There are many boys and girls, who want a good time, but have no money.

Three such boys were brought to Judge Lindsey's court. "What are you here for, boys?" asked the Judge. "Judge, did you ever steal a watermelon?" asked one of the boys. "I'm asking the question," answered Lindsey, and they both laughed. Then Judge Lindsey took the boy out for a walk. The youngster showed a cherished possession. "Perhaps sometime somebody will steal that," said Lindsey. "No, the law won't let him," said Micky. "Micky, if boys steal anything at all, there won't be any law when you grow up." Micky saw the point, and became one of the Judge's good friends, and an upholder of law.

Another boy found recreation in turning the frog on a car-track so that cars turned a corner unexpectedly. "Why did you do that?" he was asked, in court. "I learned a new cuss-word every time," he answered.

We dare not be merely negative in our pleasures; we must make recreation profitable if we can, but we must make play-life possible for boys and girls. And we misunderstand and misjudge our young when we attempt to substitute play for legitimate work. I think I am opposed to the kindergarten system. You can't make a backbone grow on the outside of a boy; it must grow on the inside. It is fair to a boy to make him realize the responsibilities of the future. One of the crimes of the hour is that people feel they must constantly entertain their children. A man said recently, "It paid me to lose my income, because I found my family." Every boy and girl needs parents much more than things.

There should be a positive program of recreation. Play should be thrilling. The difference between play and work is not the difficulty of the thing. The foot-ball men work at it, and get hurt, too. It is the spirit which tells.

The great rowing-coach, Courtney, had very high standards. No member of his crews could dissipate. One man, on the very day before a race, went out, and drank, thinking he could not be left out. But Courtney said, "Boy, you can not go in this race." Then to the others, "Sorry, boys, but we can do nothing else." And the other oarsmen said, "We'll win for you, anyhow."

Boys and girls, don't demand easy things. One of the reasons that homes are sometimes unhappy is that we forget the little things. I pity the woman who stays at home day after day with the children, whose husband comes in at night, and forgets common courtesy, and the tokens of love.

Learn to do the ordinary things of life playfully, and not be sour or grouchy. Why should we be so somber? The spirit of prayer should hallow all our lives.

For a year, I went to the movies twice a month. I only found a few that did not do one of the other of these things:

Make fun of home and family.
Make fun of church and the minister.
Get rich without working.

Think what would happen if the only things we think about were what we see in the movies. It is up to us to make the movies good. Our recreations should be harmless, and it is up to all of us to go into our amusements and make them good.

Hosts of people are in despair tonight because men and women have been careless about their relations with each other, because they have not chosen their recreations wisely.

We can make over the aspects of recreation that are bad. There are certain dances that have to be barred. They are positively bad, and the people who dance should be brave enough to put them down. We must help solve that problem. If people who do not dance have no social life, Christian people should be strong enough to get along without dancing. Our amusements should be simple, we ought to dress more simply,—the more a dress costs, the fewer times it can be worn. The chair that costs ten dollars is good to sit in, but one that costs fifty is no use in particular.

One of the crimes of the church is that it has used socials to pay its bills. If a person pays money for a social, he thinks he has a right to say what he shall get. He doesn't need the blessing of realization.

If I were an old man, I would want to be as young as the old man with whom I once worked in the field day by day. "Does thee like poetry?" he said to me. I began to recite "The Waterfowl" and he joined in. The beautiful years behind him joined in with the poem, and when we had finished, we were sworn friends. Two or three years later, when I last saw my old friend, he said, "Boy, I don't know what thy life will be, but I tell thee to be true, faithful, and hopeful."

This was a man who bought books and music that his children might find happiness at home, and who radiated love and pure happiness. Side by side with the task of the church of Christ in serious problems is their task of shedding joy and happiness in true re-creation.

First-day School Methods

Round Table led by William Eves, 3rd.

The principles underlying First-day School methods are important and yet too often neglected. The methods used in our day-schools should be applied. We should get the co-operation of parents. We must find incentives that rouse more interest than day-schools, because we lack the incentives and habits that exist there. Consultation with parents may reveal better ways of reaching and understanding pupils.

In some grades the coming lesson should be opened up the week before, leaving unfinished work to be done or thought over during the week. Not a lecture from the teacher, but the combined thought of all should constitute the lesson, with illustrations and applications to every-day life by the teacher. If hand-work is done, it should not be entirely done in class, but some during the week.

First-day School Unions may find more value in discussing problems than in having a stated address.

The record-book provided by the Central Committee should be used by all schools. Contests of various kinds between classes should be used wisely after advantages and disadvantages have been considered. Several schools are trying to show the pupils the meaning of the Meeting for Worship, and considerable progress is being made. This, and the Young Friends' Movement, may remove the old-time "vanishing point" which generally came in the late 'teens of the pupils.

Mahatma Ghandi

A Round Table, conducted by Haridas Mazumdar.

This Round Table was almost entirely an address by the leader upon the character and life-work of Ghandi, the new social and religious leader of the people of India. Many incidents were told of his early life to show his strength and force of character in a new path to gain freedom from oppression, not by the old way of brutal war, but by non-violent and peaceful methods.

The boy Ghandi had an inquiring spirit, and was baffled in his search after truth by the superstition of the Indian people and the binding influences of the Caste system. Nevertheless, he early began to think things out for himself, and when convinced that a thing was right, had the courage to try it even in the face of great opposition. As an example of this: it was considered by his people a sin to eat meat; it was, therefore, sinful to cross the waters in a boat, as the sailors ate meat. He came in contact with Christian missionaries, but so strong was the opposition of his people to the missionaries, who ate meat and drank wine, that Christianity did not make a favorable impression upon the boy.

Nevertheless, to his imagination, meat-eating made the English strong, and he had the courage to try it for himself. Later, the religious ceremonies of his people did not satisfy him, and he ceased to be a believer in God. He determined to study law, although this was against the wishes of his mother. To satisfy her, on another point, however, he made a vow to abstain from eating meat, or indulging in any intemperate practices.

His father was a well-known statesman of India, who belonged to the better class of the social Caste system, and the boy had prospects of leading at least a comfortable life, perhaps one of approved leadership. But he chose the stony path, and resolved to give his life for the uplifting of the social and spiritual condition of his people. With other Indians, he observed the revolution in Russia which began in 1917, but soon began to despair of it, and saw the great failure that it was. This to him vindicated his stand for the great moral principle that violence and blood-shed do not lead to righteousness.

Three years he spent in England, in the successful study of law. Here he came in contact with the Ethical Culture Society, and others of like nature. He studied the principles upon which all the religions are based, and, discovering the Sermon on the

Mount, became converted to a belief in God as the Creator of Society. This was the great turning-point in his life, and he became convinced that wars are the worst of barbaric institutions, and that the only way to achieve righteousness is by means of love and non-violence. This belief he determined to put into practice, as a believer in the power of suffering.

He returned to India, became a Barrister, and, at the age of twenty-four, had bright prospects for a prosperous career. But he chose to share the sufferings of the oppressed, and was requested to go to South Africa to conduct a law-suit, in 1889. While on this business, he was insulted many times, and personally abused. However, he demonstrated his belief that true beauty consists in doing good for evil, and remained in South Africa for twenty years, endeavoring in every way to mitigate the race prejudice there. During his stay he was imprisoned four times, and attacked and wounded twice. Once he was knocked down and left bleeding on the street. Never did he show unforgiveness, however.

He negotiated with General Smuts to do away with an unjust law which reflected upon the honor of his countrymen. He arranged the settlement, and saw to it that his people kept their side of the agreement. The African Government, however, at first, did not keep faith. Imprisonments were made by the Government, and other violent measures taken, but the Hindoos kept up their non-violent attitude, and the law was taken from the statute-books. At another time, a judge refused to recognize Hindoo marriages, by demanding a certificate which the Hindoos could not give. This greatly enraged the Hindoo women, a number of whom organized themselves into a peaceful army to travel from place to place afoot, and make known the cause for which they stood.

These happenings were of great value to the people of India, and Ghandi became convinced that his people could rise to the level of divinity. The absence of hatred among those whom he led was his greatest achievement in those twenty years. Returning to India, in 1916 he established schools for truth-seeking children, where they might be trained to become fit citizens, learn home-industries, and, above all, learn the principles of non-violence.

In 1919, all of South India had come to have the spiritual heritage of non-violence, but the forces of dissatisfaction became still greater, and the people became very bitter over the imperialism that was held over them. About this time the crops were below one-fourth of the normal yield, and the law required a confiscation of a great part of the crops to pay the taxes. The people revolted against this crushing burden, and some violence occurred in the province of Bombay. It was apparent that a revolution was under way, but Gandhi insisted that there must be no fighting, and restricted his activities to this province, in order to restrain the people. He agreed with them that they should be free, but they must take a vow to do no violence, even though the law was broken. As additional means of winning the non-violent revolution, the people were instructed to give up all titles, to keep their children from undergoing military training, to boycott all British-made goods, to provide for their own necessities, and to abandon the use of liquor and opium, which last is a vast source of revenue to the English Government.

In this way, they were to get freedom, not by the bayonet, but by a peaceful program of non-co-operation with the ruling power. Former demonstrations had shown what great things could be achieved by appealing to the soul-force instead of to the brute-force. This non-co-operative program began in 1920. Many arrests were made, and the people were insulted by the police, but Ghandi gave instructions that these hardships must be endured, and that most important of all, was to demonstrate the principle of non-violence. Though this leader of India does not call himself a Christian, on account of the attitude of the so-called Christian nations, he quotes accurately from the Bible, is essentially a Christian, and agrees with Friends in his great idea of carrying out the testimony against war, and in achieving a solution of the great problems of today by means of love and non-violence.

Conference Activities

At the General Session on Conference Activities, the report of the Central Committee spoke of the English Friends who were in fellowship with us. There was an outpouring of welcome and friendship for them, with the entire Conference standing in token of greeting.

To this, T. Edmund Harvey replied, saying: The spirit of friendship is wrapped about us. We are here only as representatives of many others who send messages to you,—living links binding Friends together. American Friends have meant so much to us in the past that we rejoice to become better acquainted with them now.

William C. Biddle, of Advancement Committee, called attention to the fact that Woolman School, whose original idea comes from Woodbrooke in England, is now under a Board of Directors representing all branches of Friends.

(Concluded in next issue)

and lived conscientiously, is not the political economy taught very generally either in our colleges or in our churches. Our ministers, or scholars, our diplomats, our captains of industry, our labor leaders are endeavoring to evolve some method of human relationships which at the same time will keep peace and still yield the lion's share to each contestant.

Our little Quaker experiments in practicing the "Sermon on the Mount," in Germany, Poland, Russia, Serbia and France and in the coal fields of West Virginia during the past strike, have been successful. We need to educate the world in the efficiency of such experiments. We need to encourage a sense of spiritual daring. Manhood and womanhood have proven their physical bravery, their willingness to sacrifice their lives if need be; now let them take a grand step in faith. If they die, they will die, like Jesus, conquerors.

In our quiet retiring way, Friends have been waiting for God to speak within our being. The world calls and the Word comes; we must be about our Father's business.

For the fourth time we are going to carry our message to the general public. On First-day afternoon, Eleventh month 12th, at 3 o'clock, in the South Broad Street Theatre, we will present a series of talks, "Quaker Ideals." There will be three speakers and subjects: Dr. Henry T. Gillett, of England, on "Family Life"; J. Rowntree Gillett, of England, on "Industrial Life"; and Dr. Jesse H. Holmes, on "International Life."

It is our reverend hope that there may be a great outpouring of the Word. The Sectional Committee of the Philadelphia Young Friends' Association, under whose care these meetings are held, urge that all Friends make this occasion their personal concern, particularly the spiritual side. However, as the cost of the theatre and advertising is very considerable, the committee will appreciate financial aid. Checks should be mailed to Arabella Carter, 140 N. Fifteenth Street.

For the Committee,

JOSEPH HAROLD WATSON,
Chairman.

Notes from the Service Field

Impartial American investigators have confirmed the reports on the Russian famine situation which the American Friends' Service Committee has been circulating since July. The Philadelphia *Public Ledger* of October 18th, in a special cable dispatch from Moscow, summarizes the findings of Graham Taylor and Allen Wardwell, of the Commission on Russian Relief of the National Information Bureau. These men went to Russia to conduct an investigation of the Russian famine situation for the benefit of the contributing public in the United States. They now report that the famine during the coming winter will be as bad in some districts as it was last year.

They agree with the Friends' workers that relief must be continued through the coming winter and that animals to cultivate the ground must be imported to terminate the vicious circle of famine years.

A survey being carried on under the supervision of the Friends' Mission likewise points to the need for continued relief in Russia. This survey aims to make a complete analysis of the food resources of each family in the Friends' district. The results from three of the volosts (townships) are now completed. In the best of these volosts, 84% of the population will need to be fed by the end of the year; while in the worst, practically 100% will depend for their existence upon relief administered by the Friends.

After two joint meetings of the Executive Board and the Finance Committee of the American Friends' Service Committee, the budget for the coming year's work has been decided upon. This budget totals $4,350,000 in cash and kind, to be used for relief and reconstruction in Russia, Austria and Poland. The enthusiastic support of every Friend is needed to carry forward the program as planned. In no way can the Society of Friends more effectively express its ideals than in helping to carry on the service of love which this program embodies.

All kinds of letters come to the Service Committee office. Here is one just received:—

"Gentlemen: Yours of September 6th just at hand and in reply will say we have come to the conclusion that helping the Russians only adds to their misery. If they cannot get down to peaceful living when being helped, it may be better to discontinue helping them until they do so. We want to better the needy, but do not favor kindling a fire."

This letter indicates just two things: first, how much more responsibility for loving service of relief lies upon those whose eyes are not blinded by prejudice; and secondly, what a great service Friends can render by counteracting such misunderstandings with their larger knowledge of the field and vision of its needs.

Solomon E. Yoder was one of the members of the French Mission who was charged with aiding the families of the German prisoners who were associated with the work in France. During the past summer he has received many letters, calling for relief, from the families of former prisoners. The Service Committee will be glad to forward to such families any donations made for the purpose.

A recent letter from Edith M. Pye (London) gives most encouraging news of the Maternity Hospital at Chalons, France, which was built by the Friends as a permanent memorial of the work of the French Mission. This letter is based upon a report given by Lily Mason, who has just visited the hospital. She reports that the wards are all full; that the patients are so satisfied that many of them make voluntary donations for the upkeep of the hospital; and that the money received from the Prefeture and the patients has, so far, practically covered running expenses. The weekly baby consultations are increasing in number; and home visiting will soon be undertaken in connection with them. The staff includes French, English, American, Peruvian and Alsatian girls. Edith M. Pye concludes: "I believe that great developments for the welfare of infants and children in that part of France will take place as a direct result of the Friends' gift."

The American Friends' Service Committee has sustained a great loss in the death of Cecil Cloud, a former member of the Unit in Serbia. He went to Serbia with the first group of workers. His loyalty, ability to work harmoniously with government and local officials, and his keen insight into relief and reconstruction problems, made him of great value to the Unit. Mission members who knew him will miss his boyish face and his man's presence. It is good, however, to think of him still

"..........faring on, as dear
In the love of there as the love of here.

First-day School Methods

By Bliss Forbush.

A Thanksgiving Play

The use of dramatics is now an accepted fact in many of our First-day Schools, some using them frequently for closing exercises and others producing longer plays for special occasions. Thanksgiving time is a very favorable time to produce a short dramatic performance that will take the place of the closing exercises and recall to the children's minds the fact that in the fall, the time of harvest, we can all be especially thankful to our Heavenly Father for his good gifts.

The following little play can be produced after one or two rehearsals, should not take more than ten minutes to give, and the costumes should present no difficulties. It is to be given either on the raised platform so often found in our Meeting-houses, or in a corner of the First-day School room set off by screens for the purpose. Home-made costumes, patterned after pictures in our history books of the Puritans, may be effective. The collars and cuffs of the Governor, Elder, and Father are made of heavy white drawing paper. Miles Standish is dressed in a hunting costume, and the Indians wear feathered head dresses and Indian blankets. The Mother and Ruth should wear plain work dresses with kerchief and caps.

The First Thanksgiving

Time—The Thursday before the first Thanksgiving. Place—A Puritan Home.

Mother: Stir up the fire, Ruth, the air grows sharp. We must have a bright fire for Father when he returns from town meeting.

(Ruth stirs up the fire. Looks out the door.)

Ruth: Here comes Father. Governor Bradford and Elder Brewster are with him.

Mother: Run quickly, child, and open the door.

(Enter Governor Bradford, Elder Brewster, and Father Endicott.)

Governor: Good day, Mistress Endicott; good day, Ruth.

(Ruth curtsies.)

Mother: Good day. Come sit by our fire a little while.

Elder: How warm and comfortable you are.

Mother: Yes, things are much better with Plymouth Colony than a year ago.

Ruth: Oh, what a terrible winter! I shall never forget it!

Mother: It is better to think of the good we have than to grieve over what we cannot change.

Father: We have much to be thankful for. Less than a year ago we were doling out our rations of five kernels of corn each, and fearing that soon even that would be gone.

Mother: How thankful we should be that our lives were spared in that dreadful time, and that our harvest has been abundant.

Elder: That is what Governor Bradford said today in town meeting, and so he has set a day for public thanksgiving. We are to gather at the Meeting House for prayer and praise. Afterward there is to be a great feast. For three days we are to make merry.

Governor: Every one is to take part in the thanksgiving. Even the Indians are to be invited. That thus they

Friendly News Notes

According to *The Friend* (London), Dr. Henry T. Hodgkin has decided to accept the invitation of the National Christian Council of China to act as one of its five Secretaries, the others being Bishop Roots, of America, and three Chinese Christian leaders (one of them a woman). It is understood that he contemplates sailing again for the East in January.

We are glad to hear of the greatly improved condition of Dr. Gannett's health.

The long journey from Buck Hill Falls to Rochester, N. Y., was not so fatiguing as might have been expected, although the last forty miles was by ambulance. Our regard and affection are extended to Dr. Gannett and his family. May his physical condition soon be restored to the extent of keeping pace with his mental activity.

According to the *Public Ledger* (Philadelphia), "Twelve Quakers are listed among the hundreds who are seeking seats in the next Parliament. Members of the faith are found in only two parties, the Labor and Liberal, seven of them running on the former ticket and five on the latter.

The Quaker women candidates, two in number, are Lady Barlow, who is contesting as a Liberal the High Peak Derbyshire constituency, and Dr. Ethel Bentham, who is out for one of the London seats as a Laborite."

Lansdowne Monthly Meeting has sent a letter to the editors of the leading Philadelphia daily papers protesting against the undue prominence given to unsavory news matter in the reporting of social misdemeanors of persons of this and other states. Such news is not demanded nor desired by the self-respecting and law-abiding readers and is considered by them as undesirable reading for the young and inexperienced members of their families. They urged these editors to use their influence to have their respective papers emphasize not the evil, but the things of good report.

This is an important move in the right direction and other groups of Friends would do well to make protests of a similar nature in their home communities.

STRAW RIDE AT BALTIMORE

Last week the Young Friends went on a straw ride to Fallston, twenty miles north of the city. There they were met by the Fallston people, had a pleasant social time, ate a picnic supper, and came back after dark.

The competitive plan in the First-day School has worked very nicely so far this fall. Our average attendance has been one hundred and seven. Last week the highest number were present, one hundred and fifteen. Three classes have had a perfect attendance for four weeks, and at least four classes have had a perfect attendance on every First-day. There are thirty-five new scholars on the rolls this year with additions every week. The teachers are very enthusiastic about their work, are using much outside material, and are spending a good deal of time each week on preparing their lesson.

The McKim Free Kindergarten, which the Meeting maintains in the foreign section of the city, has an enrollment this year of fifty-two.

A card was sent out a few days ago to all our members asking them to gather together any garments they might have for the Russian Relief Work, or for the Southern Schools. On a given day autos went to the homes and collected all the material. Three large boxes of things were secured.

SOUTHERN HALF-YEARLY MEETING

Southern Half-Yearly Meeting convened at Camden, Del., on First-day, Tenth month 22nd, with a larger representation from the smaller meetings than usual. Among visiting friends was Joel Borton, of Woodstown, N. J., whose message of good will to men reached the hearts of all present. He was followed by Wilson M. Tylor upon the general theme of charity for well-directed efforts even though the theological viewpoint differed.

The room was filled to capacity and the day was ideal. In the business meeting which followed the religious hour a plea was made by Mary Ida Winder, associated with Frederick Libby in the anti-war crusade, for greater support. At the close of the session all present were invited to partake of lunch, bountifully provided by the members of Camden Monthly Meeting. This was in the Woman's Club building at Wyoming, three-quarters of a mile distant. About 4 o'clock the one hundred and more Friends began to disperse, many driving to their homes 45 to 60 miles distant. Enthusiasm and life is not abating, but on the contrary increasing, as one is permitted to scan the receding decades of Southern Half-Yearly Meeting.

WILSON M. TYLOR.

CONCORD FIRST-DAY SCHOOL UNION

Concord First-day School Union opened its Fall Meeting at Concordville on Tenth month 21st, with a very good attendance.

The Thirteenth Chapter of First Corinthians reminded us that we might have any amount of Faith or Hope, but, without Love, life is not worth living.

The annual reports of Birmingham, Newtown Square, Willistown and Concord First-day Schools were read, while that of Malvern was deferred until after lunch. Concord and Newtown Square were blessed by a very greatly increased attendance and the latter so encouraged that it is considering remaining in session on into the winter. Birmingham was very grateful for the aid and enthusiasm brought them by the summer Field Secretary. Willistown felt the Pageant "Children of the Light," a story of Quaker History from George Fox through the present Reconstruction period, had created for their school a great amount of enthusiasm. This pageant was participated in by all five summer schools. Malvern has few in attendance, but all are enthusiastic.

A very interesting discussion followed in which many points brought out in the reports were discussed. Singing has found a place in nearly all schools with much benefit derived therefrom.

The report of the summer's Field Work as prepared by E. Vesta Haines was read by Ethel Gates Coates, Chairman of the Field Secretary Committee. The report itself will be available a little later. Many expressions of the encouragement, instruction and the general helpfulness of this experiment were heard. One First-day School teacher said, "I am extremely grateful for the visits of the Field Secretary, for it was not any strikingly new thoughts she brought, but old ones in new garments which return to my mind as the weeks go by, bringing me not only increased vision for the instruction of my First-day School children, but for my week-day school ones as well." The only objection heard was one of finances, and it seemed overshadowed when we were reminded that Friends get their *religion* for a mere pittance. We were asked if it seemed fair or wise to be miserly in our expenditure for the religious training of our children when not one of us would withhold any legitimate amount for secular training.

Upon convening after a very appetizing lunch prepared and served by Concord Friends, the delegates reported that we were invited to hold our next session at Providence Meeting, Media, Pa., in Fourth month, 1923.

The Summer Visiting Committee's report was rather disappointing in that delegates from only two schools visited and one school only was visited.

E. Vesta Haines, a member of the Germantown Friends' School Faculty, and our Summer Field Secretary, gave us a very interesting talk on "The Need of Working in the First-day School." (We hope to publish this paper in an early issue.)

A full discussion followed this excellent paper.

Owing to the newness of the experiment and the fact that circumstances made it impossible to secure the same Field Worker or any other sufficiently trained one to carry on the work in the winter schools this winter the Union directed that the subject of Field Work be handed over to the Yearly Meeting's First-day School Committee for further action.

The expense of the summer's work amounted to $284. This amount was raised pro rata amongst the entire Union.

The sessions of the Union concluded by the reading of the Minutes of the Union held at Swarthmore in Fourth month last.

WILLIAM T. COPE,
ETHEL GATES COATES, *Clerks.*

THE OPEN FORUM

This column is intended to afford free expression of opinion by readers on questions of interest. The INTELLIGENCER *is not responsible for any such opinions. Letters must be brief, and the editor reserves the right to omit parts if necessary to save space.*

AS TO THE VOLSTEAD ACT

To the Editor:

The name of the author of the ten reasons why the liquor traffic was outlawed by the 18th Amendment was omitted through oversight, in my letter of the 17th inst. His name is Charles W. Dietrich, Secretary of Central Y. M. C. A. of Brooklyn, N. Y., which has the distinction of being the largest in the world, having a membership of nearly 10,000.

Immediately after giving the ten reasons, their author continued by making the following strong statement, which has universal application and will find a ready response and approval in every mind and heart that can feel sympathy with suffering and a desire to oppose the evil that causes it:

"In the light of these facts, which cannot be disproved, every man with the least spark of human sympathy and interest would surely be willing to forego the pleasure of occasional indulgence in alcoholic liquors in order that the sorrow and suffering and inestimable loss following in the train of this vile traffic might be permanently eliminated, or at least reduced to a minimum."

ISAAC ROBERTS.

BIRTHS

CONROW—On Tenth month 11th, to A. Engle and Ann Zebley Conrow, of Rancocas, N. J., a son, who is named William R. L. Conrow.

JAMISON—On Tenth month 18th, to Alfred Roberts and Athalia Crawford Jamison, of Lower Merion, Pa., a son, who is named Alfred Roberts Jamison, Jr.

ROGERS—On Sixth month 29th, to Howard M. and Inez Vance Rogers, of Crosswicks, N. J., a daughter, who is named Hannah.

SPACKMAN—On October 14th, to George Donald and Elizabeth Worth Spackman, of Coatesville, Pa., a son, who is named John Worth Spackman.

DEATHS

DUTTON—On Tenth month 26th, John F., husband of Lauretta Smedley Dutton, in the 50th year of his age, a son-in-law of Lewis V. Smedley. Interment at Willistown Friends' Burying Ground.

EELLS—In Philadelphia, on Tenth month 22d, R. Frances, wife of the late Herbert Eells, aged 74.

STILES—Near Bordentown, N. J., on Tenth month 11th, Benjamin Stiles, in his 55th year, a member of Chesterfield Monthly Meeting.

COMING EVENTS

ELEVENTH MONTH

4th—Philadelphia Quarterly Meeting, at Reading, Pa. See Notice.

5th—Purchase Quarterly Meeting, at Chappaqua, N. Y. Meeting for worship at 10.30 a. m. Afternoon session at 2. William J. Reagan, Principal of Oakwood School, expects to attend both meetings, giving an address at the afternoon session on "Religion and Recreation." Conveyances will meet at Chappaqua the 10.18 northbound train, and 8.54 southbound.

5th—First-day at 3 p. m. The usual semi-annual Community meeting for worship will be held at Chichester Friends' Meeting-house under care of a Committee of Concord Quarterly Meeting. All persons welcome and young people particularly invited. Train leaves 24th and Chestnut Streets, Philadelphia, for Boothwyn at 1.30 p. m.; Darby, 1.43; Chester, 2.00, returning about 4.29 p. m. Trains will stop at cross-road near Meeting-house.

5th—West Philadelphia Bible Class at 10 a. m. Subject—"Is Religion a Democracy or an Autocracy?" The phase under consideration is Ritualistic Protestantism.

5th—Conference Class at 15th and Race Sts., Philadelphia, at close of meeting for worship, 11.40 a. m. Subject—The Prophetic Contribution of Paul. Leader—Henry Ferris.

5th—Nine Partners Half-Yearly Meeting, at Oswego, N. Y. (Moore's Mills). Social hour and lunch. Public meeting at 2 o'clock.

9th—Abington Quarterly Meeting, at Byberry, Pa., at 10.30 a. m. See Notice published last week.

11th—Salem Quarterly Meeting, at West, near Alliance, Ohio.

11th—Fall Conference of Friends' Associations, Makefield, Pa.—afternoon and evening.

11th—Miami Quarterly Meeting, at Waynesville, Ohio.

11th—Shrewsbury and Plainfield Half-Yearly Meeting, at Plainfield, N. J.

11th—Blue River Quarterly Meeting, at Clear Creek, Ill. It is hoped that Friends will not fail to attend the business meeting as well as the meeting for worship.

11th and 12th—Conference of New York Young Friends' Movement, at Fifteenth and Twentieth St. Meeting-houses.

11th to 13th—Baltimore Quarterly Meeting at Little Falls, Md. Isaac Wilson expects to attend.

12th—Theatre Meeting, South Broad Street Theatre, Philadelphia, Pa., under auspices of Sectional Committee, Y. F. A., 3 p. m. Subject, "Quaker Ideals." Speakers: Dr. Henry T. Gillett, Oxford, England; Jos. Rowntree Gillett, London, England; Jesse H. Holmes, Swarthmore, Pa.

12th—Preparative Meeting in New York and Brooklyn, after the Meeting for Worship.

13th—Chicago Monthly Meeting at the Y. M. C. A., 19 S. La Salle St., Chicago, Ill. Dinner will be served at 6.30 p. m. This meeting has been changed from the first to the second Second-day of each month. A cordial invitation to all.

13th—New York Monthly Meeting at 221 East 15th St., New York, at 7.30. Supper will be served at 6 o'clock. The exhibition of articles made by children in the Vacation Schools will be held in the Seminary Gymnasium, at 5 o'clock and after.

17th and 18th—Thirty-fourth Annual Fair of the Young Friends' Aid Association and the Friendly Hand, from 3 to 10 p. m., in the Gymnasium of Friends' Seminary. There will be the usual articles for sale, a Russian Tea-room, and a "straight dinner" served. Entertainments will give variety, and an unusual number of side-shows. One of these will be Professor Morse's first working model of the telegraph.

NOTICE—Anyone knowing Friends living in Detroit, Michigan, is requested to send names and addresses to L. Oscar Moon, 2574 2nd Blvd., so that an effort may be made to connect them with our Meeting.

NOTICE—Bishop McConnell (Francis J. McConnell, Methodist Bishop) will address a meeting under the auspices of the Social Order Extension Committee at 8 o'clock on the evening of Sixth-day, Eleventh month 24th, at Friends' Select School, 17th and Parkway, on the subject of "Christianity and Industry."

NOTICE.—Friends' Monthly Meetings of Salem, New Jersey, will celebrate the one hundredth and fiftieth anniversary of the East Broadway Meeting-house, Eleventh month 11th, 1922. Morning session, 10 a. m. "Local History of Early Friends" and other exercises. Lunch served at noon.

Afternoon session, 2 p. m., at which Rufus M. Jones will speak on "The Need of the Hour." Interested Friends are invited to attend.

NOTICE—Reading Friends hope there will be a large attendance at the Philadelphia Quarterly Meeting to be held for the first time in Reading, Penna., on Eleventh month 4th, at 2 p. m. Those having automobiles are requested to come with no empty seats. There is a train leaving Broad Street Station, Philadelphia, at 11.40, arriving at Penn Street Station, Reading, at 1.20. Other trains are as follows:

A special train leaves the Reading Terminal at 1.00 p. m., reaching Reading at 2.32; a short walk from the Franklin Street Station to the Meeting-house. A special train leaves Broad Street Station at 12.48 p. m., arriving at Reading at 2.40. Exeter Meeting will serve refreshments to the visiting Friends. Friends desiring to remain over night are requested to notify John B. Bowers, 205 Windsor Street, Reading, Pa., by Eleventh month 3rd.

Return trains leave at 6.00 and 7.30 p. m. The Meeting-house is located at Sixth Street above Washington Avenue. The Touring Bureau advises that the road through Norristown, Collegeville and Pottstown is fair.

NOTICE—The Best Interests Committee of Philadelphia Monthly Meeting will give a supper preceding Monthly Meeting on November 15th, in the lunch room of Friends' Central School. Tickets 65 cents, can be secured from Almira P. Harlan, 154 N. 15th Street, or the following: Race Street, Clara H. Barnard; West Philadelphia, Myra H. Blackburn and Mary L. Griscom; Girard Avenue, Sarah J. Wolfe and Elizabeth H. Jamison, Jr. All reservations must be in by the morning of Eleventh month 13th.

Co-operation

It is hard to realize the wonderful possibilities of this word "co-operation," but there is just one little phase of it we want to call to the attention of our readers. Our advertisers place before you the advantages of dealing with them in the purchase of certain commodities. They are helping you by giving you this information, they are helping us by placing their advertisements in the INTELLIGENCER. And right here is where the CO-OPERATION comes in! Will you not help us both, the advertiser and the INTELLIGENCER, by dealing with them to as large an extent as possible? The firms here represented are all first class, and if you will make it known when you deal with them that you are doing so because you saw their advertisement in the INTELLIGENCER it will be an additional evidence of your desire to help us both.

American Friends' Service Committee

WILBUR K. THOMAS, EX. SEC.
20 S. 12th St. Philadelphia.

CASH CONTRIBUTIONS

WEEK ENDING OCTOBER 23RD.

Five Years Meetings	$131.25
Fifteenth and Race Streets Meeting	10.00
Other Meetings:	
Alexandria Monthly Meeting	150.00
Moorestown Junior Mission Board	30.00
First Friends' Church, Cleveland	5.00
Norristown Preparative Meeting	50.00
Wrightstown Monthly Meeting	185.21
Contributions for Austria	310.36
For Poland	2,125.85
For Russia	4,271.63
Russian Overhead	57.00
For Armenia	25.00
For Syria	28.00
West Virginia	5.00
For General	364.00
For Message Committee	273.00
Clothing	3.32
Refunds	121.98
	$8,146.60

Shipments received during week ending October 21st: 116 boxes and packages, 10 anonymous.

REGULAR MEETINGS

OAKLAND, CALIF. — A FRIENDS' Meeting is held every First-day at 11 A. M., in the Extension Room, Y. W. C. A. Building, Webster Street, above 14th. Visiting Friends always welcome.

PASADENA, CALIFORNIA — Orange Grove Monthly Meeting of Friends, 520 East Orange Grove Avenue. Meeting for worship, First-day, 11 A. M. Monthly Meeting, the second First-day of each month, at 1.45 P. M. First-day School (except Monthly Meeting days) 9.45 A. M.

SCHOOLS.

HOTELS.

Buck Hill Falls Company

FIRST MORTGAGE 6% GOLD BONDS

Notice is hereby given that pursuant to the Sinking Fund provisions of the Mortgage dated June 5th, 1913, five of the above bonds, each for $500.00, have been drawn for redemption on December 1st, 1922, at 102½% and accrued interest to that date.

The Bonds drawn and numbered as below, with all unmatured coupons attached, should be presented for payment at the office of the Treasurer on or after December 1st, 1922, when all interest thereon will cease.

The Bonds so drawn are numbered 37, 113, 132, 136, 180.

MORGAN BUNTING, Treasurer,
603 Chestnut St., Phila. Pa.

Apples By Parcels Post

For One Dollar Money Order I will deliver at your door One Half Bushel of the finest hand-picked Smokehouse, Golden Delicious, or Gano Apples.

WILLIAM CANBY FERRIS
Wilmington Delaware
R. F. D. No. 2

WE BUY ANTIQUE FURNITURE and antiques of all kinds; old gold, silver, platinum, diamonds and old false teeth. Phila. Antique Co., 633 Chestnut, cor. 7th. Phone Lombard 6398. Est. 1866.

WANTED

WANTED—BY AN ELDERLY WOMAN, experienced, a position with light household duties or care of invalid. Apply 910 Clinton Street, Philadelphia.

WANTED—RELIABLE WOMAN FOR general housework. Family of two, all conveniences. No washing. No objection to woman with small daughter. Mrs. Penrose Robinson, Hatboro, Pa.

WANTED—GOOD HOME OR BOARDING place with cheerful surroundings for middle-aged lady, mentally somewhat deficient. State probable terms. Address P. 390, Friends' Intelligencer.

GOOD HOUSEKEEPER WANTED—Small home, all conveniences; two in family. Good home for the right party, if reasonable. Call or address, M. Marple, Hatboro, Pa.

WANTED—SINGLE ROOM IN CENTRAL part of city by a young Friend in social work. Address C. 420, Friends' Intelligencer.

WANTED—A POSITION AS COMPANION, care of invalid, or housekeeper. Address L. 421, Friends' Intelligencer.

WANTED—POSITION BY YOUNG woman, Friend; as mother's helper, light house duties or companion, in congenial home. Answer in full. E. R., 331 East Chestnut Street, Coatesville, Pa.

WANTED—PERMANENT POSITION, middle-aged woman experienced with lady, or children, or invalid. Reference. Address T. 422, Friends' Intelligencer.

"RIVERCROFT," CLAYMONT, DEL. Special home care for invalids, or rest and physical upbuilding. Reference on application. E. H. Speakman, R. N.

Strawbridge & Clothier

Men's and Young Men's Suits, $23.50, $29.50, $32.50

—And Two Pairs of Trousers to Every Suit

Yes, this Store does by far the greatest Men's Clothing business in Philadelphia. And the Clothing sold is **all** good Clothing, which is one of the main reasons for the large business!

For instance, the Suits in these three groups, $23.50, $29.50 and $32.50, are all with two pairs of trousers, and excellently tailored of fine serge, worsted and cassimere in a remarkable variety of patterns and styles.

Every man can be properly fitted, be he short, thin, stout, tall or of the average figure. Come in and pick your Clothes from a stock numbering thousands of the handsomest Suits and Overcoats you men ever want to see.

We are exclusive Philadelphia distributors of the nationally famous Hart, Schaffner & Marx and Stein-Bloch Clothing, and have in stock at all times a representative collection of garments from these manufacturers.

Strawbridge & Clothier—Second Floor, East

STRAWBRIDGE & CLOTHIER
MARKET STREET EIGHTH STREET FILBERT STREET
PHILADELPHIA, PA.

FOR SALE

FOR SALE, OR LEASE—TWO BEAUTIFUL seashore properties in Maine, situated in well known health resort, Kittery Point. Each has splendid waterfront on Portsmouth harbor. One vacant location adjoins home residence of famous American family. The other includes a building of nearly 30 rooms, suitable for dwelling or for summer boarding rooms. Address Charles S. Gerrish, 8 Hoffman Ave., Oil City, Pa.

FOR SALE—MODERN SUBSTANTIAL frame dwelling. Good location, lot 80x180. Large living room with fireplace, dining room, pantry, kitchen, 6 bedrooms, sleeping porch, bath, steam heat. Price $13,000. E. C. Walton, Swarthmore, Pa.

FOR RENT

FOR RENT—A WELL FURNISHED second story room in private family of Friends at 2727 North 11th Street, Philadelphia. Convenient to trolleys and restaurants.

To the Lot Holders and others interested in Fairhill Burial Ground:

GREEN STREET Monthly Meeting has funds available for the encouragement of the practice of cremating the dead to be interred in Fairhill Burial Ground. We wish to bring this fact as prominently as possible to those who may be interested. We are prepared to undertake the expense of cremation in case any lot holder desires us to do so.

Those interested should communicate with William H. Gaskill, Treasurer of the Committee of Interments, Green Street Monthly Meeting, or any of the following members of the Committee.

William H. Gaskill, 3201 Arch St.
Samuel N. Longstreth, 1218 Chestnut St.
Charles F. Jenkins, 232 South Seventh St
Stuart S. Graves, 3833 Germantown Ave.

The Friends' Intelligencer

ESTABLISHED 1844 | ELEVENTH MONTH 11, 1922 | VOLUME 79 NUMBER 45

Contents

THE FRIENDS' INTELLIGENCER

Published weekly, 140 N. 15th Street, Philadelphia, Pa., by Friends' Intelligencer Association, Ltd.

SUE C. YERKES, *Managing Editor.*

Subscription rates: United States, Mexico, Cuba and Panama, $2.50 per year. Canada and other foreign countries, $3.00 per year. Checks should be made payable to Friends' Intelligencer Association, Ltd.

Entered as Second Class Matter at Philadelphia Post Office

The Friends' Intelligencer

The religion of Friends is based on faith in the "INWARD LIGHT," or direct revelation of God's spirit and will in every ding soul.
The INTELLIGENCER is interested in all who bear the name of Friends in every part of the world, and aims to promote love, ty and intercourse among all branches and with all religious societies.

ſABLISHED 1844 | PHILADELPHIA, ELEVENTH MONTH 11, 1922 | VOLUME 79 NUMBER 45

Increasing Quaker Efficiency

Recently a Philadelphia lady of much philan-opic activity, and a member of one of the evan-ical churches, was utterly astonished to find out w few Friends there were in the so-called Quaker y. "Why," said she, "I thought there must be least 300,000 of you, because I never was on a nmittee in my life on which there were not some iends present." This is typical of our excellent ord in work for social welfare of the communi-; in which we live.

Society is now in a period of rapid change and requirements for effective social service have inged, too. To be successful in the practice of therly love, and to be an efficient worker in the rch-helpful has become a more difficult service the individual member.

o be kind hearted, well meaning, and generous indispensible attributes, but now even more is ɪired. This was well shown by a recent episode New York, in which a lawsuit brought out the : that a certain legless beggar had been securing 5 a day in alms on one of the New York streets. the close of his day's lucrative business he put his artificial limbs, called his chauffeur and re-shed himself with automobiling before going to suite of rooms in one of New York's palatial els. Think what it would have meant if the ostor's $125 a day could have gone to your pet anthropy!

he new charity, the new philanthropy, the new ʒion, acts not from impulse alone, but is guided he light of the facts. In business, men are ceas-to act on what they call "hunches," taking instead findings of a research department as their guide. s is necessary because of increasing complexity ocial structure, and widening fields of knowledge. efficient society (or industry) is the result of rts who, by investigating, get the knowledge that back of efficiency.

Vhat does this mean for the Society of Friends? any one who has spent many hours on Friends' Committees review the proceedings and he will see that he has spent a good deal of time listening to and helping other good people as they discussed subjects about which many had not thought much.

It is very inefficient to serve for a few meetings on this committee and a few meetings on that committee and a few meetings on the other committee, to none of which we can, because of the scattering of attention, bring good intent backed up with *good knowledge*. Surprising things, in many cases, great things, are in progress in almost every field of our Society's activity, whether it be First-day School, secular education, prison reform, or any of the many philanthropic activities in which we have earned so enviable a reputation. Furthermore, these new and suggestive things are constantly being described in print, and are available, so that a Friend who may select one of them as his real avocation can in a few months or a few years become highly informed, if the time that goes to a scattered philanthropic effort and to scattered readings could be devoted to this one subject.

The efficient Friend should become expert on one subject or a few related subjects, because expert knowledge on many subjects is impossible. But people should not therefore, become "single tracked" or narrow. They should be broadly informed, particularly in practical principles that underly society, so that the meeting can intelligently consider the advice of its specialists.

Think what it would mean to a meeting to have one person who really knew to the very bottom the situation with regard to prisons and the treatment of those for whom prisons are built. The Monthly Meeting, the Quarterly Meeting, or Yearly Meeting committees on prisons could then act in the light of the facts. With its work thus guided month by month and year by year, the "weight of the meeting" in society would be most effectively felt.

It takes time to produce social results. A committee is not going to do much in the course of a winter or spring on a big thing like prison reform but if it has one member who really knows and if it keeps on year after year, most astonishing results may come, not only to a county jail, but to a state or even to the national penitentiaries.

The Friends who have made the Society famous by their philanthropic achievements have been persons who stuck to their lasts.

This editorial is an appeal, therefore, to Friends to pick their topic, stick to it, inform themselves gradually but thoroughly—in short, to become authorities. Naturally, a Friend would work mainly on one thing only, thus making his or her effort much more effective than if it were divided among three or four fields. Such a Friend would doubtless give *money* to many good causes—it is safe to scatter money. But to scatter one's self is neither safe nor effective. If the motto, "Choose thy topic and stick to it," were

Wayside

By WALTER

They also serve, who only

Like many other legends on the "miracles of Our Lady," the story has come down to us in the form of an old-French metrical romance. In Bartsch's rhymed translation, from which are taken the lines quoted below, we may enjoy at least a suggestion of the simplicity, the earnestness, the charming *naivete,* of the mediaeval original.

A knight both courteous and wise,
And brave and bold in enterprise,

was journeying toward the lists on the day set for a tournament, when the bells announced that mass was to be said in a wayside chapel. Although he had been hurrying to reach the field before his rivals, the knight immediately

drew rein and entered there
To seek the aid of God in prayer.

High and clear they chanted then
A solemn mass to Mary Queen.

No sooner was the first mass concluded than a second was begun; and following immediately upon the second, a third.

Lost in his prayers, the good knight stayed,

but his squire, who realized that the hour for the tournament was drawing near, could no longer hide his impatience at the delay. Accordingly, he made bold to whisper in his master's ear:

"The hour of tournament is near;
Why do you want to linger here?
Come on at once! Dispatch your prayer!
Let us be off to our affair!"

Lines more beautiful than those in which the knight replied have never been written.

meet these in a spirit of sincere love as for those affected by them to gather in daily communion with the ideal, and to make their first concern the application of the ideal to their own lives. Where one is separated from any group with which he might meet, however, he may still derive great benefit from a devotional period. In this case, he may find it helpful to devote a portion of the time to communion in spirit with those who are absent. Sometimes when our own group has been separated, we have found it helpful to agree upon the same daily readings, and then to share with each other, through correspondence, the thoughts to which the latter give rise.

We have found that in general the period was most helpful when divided between three forms of activity: reading, discussion and prayer; though special circumstances should always be allowed to alter any fixed program. A reading is helpful to begin with because it brings the stimulus of contact with another strong personality that has known the meaning of the ideal; and because it affords the mind, at the outset, definite material upon which to base its spiritual exercise. *What* one reads is not important, provided it carries real spiritual stimulus; but few works compress so much that is spiritually stimulating into so small a space as does that epic of idealism which we call the Bible.

New translations of the latter are especially stimulating because they bring the message home to us in the simple tongue of our own day, and make the speakers seem more our fellow-seekers and less the mystic heroes in some drama of the dim past.

The *object* of the reading is inspiration, *illumination*. We should begin by fixing in our minds the main facts of the passage read, but the retention of facts is the least important part of the exercise. What we want is help in meeting the problems that confront us today; real incentive to live highly and buoyantly. Often, if we read from the Bible, the particular matters discussed will be dead letters—problems of a different age, conceptions which have long since passed away. But the laws of the spirit which they almost invariably involve are universal and unchanging. It is these laws of the spirit which we should seek to discover and retain. And we should not be content unless we find them; unless we see and *feel* their vital bearing upon our own lives. To each chapter, each story, each statement and doctrine, we should put the unceasing question: "What is the reality behind these words, and what is its bearing on the problems of present-day individual and social life?"

We have found it a most successful practice in conjunction with our devotional reading to select each day one thought from the passage read—a thought which brings us definite inspiration—and to adopt that thought as a kind of motto to hold with us during the day which follows. Such a thought helps to keep our souls growing all through the day, and if we keep it before our minds when we are beset with difficulties, often has magical powers in tempering our spiritual fibre and strengthening us to meet the situation in the light of our highest ideals. It is helpful to read from an edition which we can mark for future reference, and to underline the thoughts which strike us in each passage, adding marginal notes of interpretation or application whenever these suggest themselves.

Following the reading should come a period of thoughtful discussion of the passage read. Each one present should give his impression or interpretation of it, and whatever present-day applications he may perceive of the laws which it involves. This is really a part of the reading itself; an assimilation of the thoughts which the latter has brought forward.

It will then frequently be helpful to discuss, in the same spirit of impersonal truth-seeking, any problems which may present themselves in our individual, family or group lives. There is no difficulty which cannot be happily overcome, if we will seek earnestly and unselfishly for the light to overcome it. It is a good rule never to leave the devotional period as long as there is any imperfect adjustment in spirit between any members of the group present; or between any one of us and the brotherhood of men which makes up the world. ". . . first be reconciled to thy brother, and then come and offer thy gift."

Finally, we may conclude our devotions with a period of prayer—an effort to transmute all that we have gained into spiritual power that is focused on the path before us, and that will carry us forth joyously and confidently into the day's tournament.

The entire exercise, as outlined, does not require nearly as much time as one might suppose from reading this somewhat detailed discussion of it. From twenty minutes to half an hour should suffice to render it entirely satisfying. And we may be assured that when we emerge from the chapel of some such spiritual exercise as this, we shall have gained infinitely more in power than we gave in time. Define "God" as you prefer, or as you are able, the fact still remains that His—or its?—strength is ready to tourney for us today as was the case for our knight of the middle ages. If we more often followed the knight's example by entering the chapel and remaining until the end of the last service—until we had forged real spiritual force and vision for ourselves—we should marvel at the miracles that would often follow.

The world today is beset with problems and diffi culties. Men are attempting nearly every metho of overcoming them; every method, at least, fro commissions of experts to poison gas. But th method of dismounting at the wayside chapel r mains almost untried. Who knows but that humanity would try it today as earnestly as th knight in our legend, tomorrow we might not fin that an irresistible ideal had battled for us while w prayed, and had won for us the victory of real pea and an abundant world life?

Baltimore Yearly Meeting

A Summary of the Proceedings

(Continued from last issue.)

With not the slightest abatement of the life of th previous days Baltimore Yearly Meeting assembl in business session on Second-day morning: Isa Wilson said, "We have met as we promised one ye ago, the engagement then made to meet our Heaven Father here." Responding to welcome extende the English Friends spoke of the change in Lond Yearly Meeting during the last few years. N longer is there a warning against this branch Friends, but a real love expressed for them. Th had been brought about by the working togeth overseas; the lack of knowledge had caused th aloofness. More visitation would, it was felt, st further enlighten. William W. Cocks spoke of b ing a Quaker free-lance, untrammeled, as only Friend could be, by the need of pleasing either co gregation or vestry.

Much time naturally was consumed with the usu detailed work incident to the occasion:—calling representatives and presentation of Minutes visiting Friends. The epistle from London Year Meeting gave rise to grateful comment; its origi ality and absence of platitudes was remarked as w its general helpfulness. Following the New Yo Epistle, Wm. W. Cocks queried as to what w really being done by Friends in various localiti to fill empty meeting houses,—to regain the inter of now indifferent members. He confessed he h no panacea himself but desired one. As one Frie expressed it, "There's surely something for us Qua ers to do," and a number of suggestions were c fered, among them being one by Walker Bond as fewer committees with a working membership th the present larger number of committees.

The need of new life was emphasized, and it w felt an exchange of living delegates between Yea Meetings would be beneficial. At a later session t took concrete form in the appointment of six de gates as follows:—To attend Genessee Yea Meeting, Walker and Grace Bond; New York, Verne Forbush and Mary Blackburn; Philadelph

when the military cry peace and missionaries cry war? It is important that America's policy be right, for she can lead the world." He made a plea for world education and organization and understanding.

Education in its various ramifications claimed the larger part of one session, being introduced by the consideration of the query regarding the interest of Friends in their own schools and those of the community as well, which was shown to be well maintained. The age-old question of securing Friends as principals and teachers, and of having Friends' children placed in Friends' schools instead of public or other institutions here claimed attention —although the discussion dealt largely with New York rather than the Baltimore situation, a larger number of teachers who are members being now on the staff of Park Avenue School than heretofore. The appreciation shown non-members who sent their children to Friends' schools was evidenced in ever-increasing numbers. Many teachers, it was said, could not afford to teach in Friends' schools, however much they might so desire, because the low salaries paid by Friends in comparison with other schools prevented. President Aydelotte's enthusiasm concerning Friends' contribution along educational lines to real Democracy was mentioned.

Woolman School was brought to the attention of the meeting, a former pupil, Mary Magruder, feeling no member should miss a term there, and urged the matter be given serious attention.

The First-day school as an aid to the meeting was dwelt upon, being considered the largest work done. One of the local schools, Hopewell, Va., was mentioned as a real community school, being composed of both branches of Friends, Baptists and Presbyterians, the latter congregation deeming it unnecessary to start a Sunday School of their own, since "the Quakers had such a good one."

J. Rowntree Gillett told of the Adult School Movement in England which had accomplished so much in the way of fellowship. Two thirds of the new members recently received in their meeting were traceable to the Adult Schools. The thought was emphasized that too many Friends' Meetings here in America formed an aristrocracy, never having acquaintance with democracy.

Doctor Gillett spoke of the advance made by the labor movement in England, and felt it was well to get in touch with labor and see if the church has not a contribution to make. The Adult School formed a fine point of contact. Doctor Janney touched briefly on the different situation in this country with its many nationalities, incapable of the closer mingling as in England.

The statistical table of membership this year showed a small net loss instead of the gain shown in recent years, there having been a gain of 100 in five years. But this deficit was explained by the fact that in two Quarterly Meetings there had been dropped from membership quite a number who apparently had no interest in the Society, since repeated communications, remained unanswered. So it was felt that while numerically smaller, the meeting was really stronger.

The report of Yearly Meeting's Advancement Committee dwelt on the work for disarmament done by its Secretary within and without its borders, the work in Summer Schools of Pennsylvania, Virginia and Maryland to the number of sixteen which had reached 10,000 teachers with the gospel of peace. Ninety-two visits to the sick and a reception to thirteen new members in one meeting had been given. Pastoral, publicity religious and educational work had characterized the year's report.

The aim for the next year is to add 100 new members, give increased attention to Meeting and First-day School; form study groups; interest non-Friends and increase the feeling of fellowship. Bliss Forbush spoke of the steadily rising attendance at Baltimore Meeting, the average rising from 80 to 125 in three years. He believed the taking of a census was a good thing, and that work, inspiration and enthusiasm—with more work than talk—were needed to secure results.

A Round Table on Anti-Narcotics with Pauline W. Holme, leader, brought out a tribute to women's activity by Chauncey Shortlidge, and a plea by another Friend to women to use their newly acquired ballot for the forwarding of reforms in which they are interested. She declared against a woman's party, believing there was too much party politics now. "We cannot hope to convert men," she said, "but we can educate the children."

A number of addresses completed the activities of Third-day. Peter Ainslie, Minister of the Christian Temple of Baltimore, spoke on "Inter-racial Problems." He felt this was the greatest problem of the day, and queried whether by evolution or revolution would come the answer. He declared it the greatest misfortune that slaves were freed by war, saying in his opinion in ten years more all slaves would have been freed without war. His lost confidence in the white man must be restored, for the two races are further apart to-day than ever. "Will the church deal with this," he asked, "for it never faced a bigger task. Only by becoming more moral itself can the white race help its darker brother to a higher level. We must meet the question where we are and judge the race by its best, not its worst."

J. Rowntree Gillett spoke on "Conditions in Leavenworth Prison" as he saw them in a recent visit when he talked at length with some 72 political prisoners still there, and gave it as his opinion that lib-

Edith Cavell

(At the request of a number of Friends, this poem is published in full. It was read by the author at a meeting for worship on Eighth month 27th.)

There once was a nurse
In a small English town,
Who won by her graces
Much fame and renown.

Her classmates adored her;
Her teachers had praise
For the love in her heart
And the calm in her ways.

And she grew up in favor
Of angels and men
Till her cup of contentment
Seemed brim full; and then

There came the great war—
O, the crime and the curse,—
And she went to the front
Did this brave English nurse.

There she bound up the wounds
And she spoke words of joy
To many a homesick,
Death-stricken boy.

Till one day she was captured,
And held as a spy,
Court-martialled, condemned,
And sentenced, "to die."

The name of this maiden,
You know it full well;
Enshrined in all hearts
Is Saint Edith Cavell.

And this is the message
She leaves with her friends,
As she waits at the gate
Where earth's pilgrimage ends.

"To limit our love
By the bounds of our land,
Falls wofully short
Of the Master's command,

Who said, 'Love your foes';
Let your love be unfurled
Till it spans and encircles
The whole human world.

Wreak, my foes, what you can,
It's beyond your control

To put hate in my heart
  Or embitter my soul."

"O, Father, forgive them,"
  Thus Jesus once prayed,
And breathing that love
  The great sacrifice made.

Shall we, too, learn the lesson
  Supremely to dwell
In the love lived by Jesus
  And Edith Cavell?

EDGAR ZAVITZ.

Applied Christianity

The Basis of Christian Unity

CHARLES FOSTER KENT

One of the most basic things now before the world is: Is there a basic unity in the teachings of Jesus? I have gone back in my study with most profound misgivings, for the people are not yet awake to the necessity of unity. I need not discuss the spiritual question of unity. As we study the situation we can see its fruits, in the unquestioned fact that the situation now is very different from that of a year ago, and perhaps worse, rather than better. There seems little Christian unity, for there are sad divisions even in Protestantism, and against the pressure of our most tremendous problems, the modern church has failed. As regards the undernourished children, peace, labor problems, the great war, the church has failed. It has no message, because it is not united. If it were united, it would be irresistible; but it has failed, and has been the undoing of many communities. In one place, several different denominations are sending ministers each to its own little group of worshippers, for eight or ten Sundays a year. And the like is true of very many other places.

In some places, a united church furnishes the recreative life, as well as the spiritual life for the community. How has the movement for community churches spread? There are two or three hundred community churches in America to-day, and they are growing apace. The relationship of church with church is not the only unity required. Unity must be a development. There can be no undermining influences to stay the progress of Christian unity. Every Protestant Church should be a united Protestant church.

Christian unity does not depend on the similarity of forms of worship. Paul got different kinds of Christians to worship together. During the war, Jewish rabbis gave the last sacrament to Roman Catholic soldiers, and vice versa. Strip away the conventions that bind us, and feel the great reality. Church unity is no more impossible than was prohibition or other things that have come to pass. Church unity will be a fact if you take off your coats and work for it. I hear some talk of junking the old machinery, and building a new brotherhood. That is not necessary. The three things that are necessary are:

1. A common working faith.
2. Unity of aim.
3. Working together.

What about the working faith? What is the real foundation of the differences in faith? The chief form of difference is in creed. And creeds grew up largely in the third, fourth and fifth centuries, when Greek thought and mysticism came sweeping into the young church. Calvin put more yokes on the shoulders of men than has any other man. Almost without exception, the differences that lie at the bottom of our churches are the individual differences of men.

What sort of a working faith do we need for to-day, for this modern scientific age in which youth must live? Our philosophy of life is not that of the early church teachers, with their Greek and Roman training. The whole gospel of Jesus is that we shall be perfect "even as our Heavenly Father is perfect." We have gone far in living instead of preaching, yet there are certain aspects in the gospel of Jesus which even you good Friends have not fully applied. It is what each church admires in the gospel of Jesus that it builds upon—as for instance, the Baptist Church has taken for its own the symbol of baptism. Is the contribution of our Unitarian friends to religious thought entirely negative?—They call attention to the wonderful charm of character of Jesus.

Unity is not a question of any church giving up its faith; it is a matter of making clear the value of that upon which it builds, and of all others having joy in this vital contribution to unity. We would do well to ask each church what its secret is. Our Methodist brothers—how much we need their outstretched hands, and their missionary zeal! Our Christian Science friends—Science can do nothing but reveal the power of God in the life of man! We and our children need the faith of the Roman Catholic church, its ministry to the needy and suffering.

The teaching regarding the future life is the step where the uncertain light has made many churches lose members. There should be a call for a new orthodoxy, an orthodoxy that depends not upon Luther, but on the great Founder of his faith. I had a class last year, in which I asked each boy to bring in his idea of what the different churches had done for the life of mankind. The result was most interesting. They went back to a common basis and a common working faith.

As far as aims are concerned, take those of the Master himself—"That you may know the Truth and the Truth may make you free." "I come that you might have life, and have it more abundantly." Yet there is cause for depression to-day, in that so few seem to be finding life "and that more abundantly." The Church is gathering wealth, but, giving no life to the people, is sad and dreary. Jesus went and sought the people on the mountain-side. We have forgotten that part of his life—"to seek and to save." Did Jesus have other aims? Yes, one which includes the others—to found one great family at Capernaum, which would give everybody an opportunity for self-expression and development of life. The common aim and common movement of getting together is part of the work of the Master. He found no need of founding a church.

The Germans in talking about the work of the Quakers in that country, said, "They have come with no bluster. They have fed our children. They bound up our wounds. They have done these things, expecting no recognition, and asking no remuneration. Is it possible that Christ is again on earth?" There can be no higher praise than this paid your representatives.

Bankrupt Europe is calling on America. Yet most of the churches pass by. If all the churches could only be a part of this work. The laboring classes need your help. We must take up the spirit of Mastery. Give the other races justice. The question has been asked why Jews are better off in England than in America. We have not treated them as men, but as members of a despised race. They are probably the most susceptible of all races, and have been made what they are by the treatment of others. It is many long centuries of unchristian treatment that have made them a people apart.

The Spiritual Adventure

Elbert Russell

Quakerism was a spiritual adventure from the beginning, and especially in America. In the settlement of America there was a twofold aspect. There were among its settlers those, who, like John Smith, came in the love of adventure or of gain; and there were those who came like Penn, because they believed that in the New World was a place for spiritual adventure. For about one hundred years, the American people gave themselves to clearing the continent. For years after 1787, the movement of the people was westward, and about 1850, the last phase of this movement was entered upon. Now the task and turmoil of moving people and homes bodily is over, and the American people are face to face again with social problems. The frontier is behind us, but we are faced with a new frontier. I do not think the American peple, as a whole, have begun to realize the influence of the frontier on our life. We are a frontier people, for the men and women, in past years, who lacked the spirit of adventure, stayed in Europe. Those who believed that a new world could be carved out of the forests came here. This frontier life developed what Dickens called "the hideous versatility" of the American life, and it is this that lies behind our "spoils system," our distrust of the "expert," and the idea that one man can do a thing as well as another.

These characteristics have been bred into us. We are the children and grand-children of pioneers. In the West, it is only fifty or a hundred years back to the beginning. In the East, it is not more than three hundred years. So we have some of the initial spirit of courage of the pioneer. What will we do with it? Shall we use it in any way?. Shall we take it out at the "movies," or dare we follow its impulse to break away from the conventions? This blood of the pioneers that is in us demands the thrill of adventure. We might easily break up our civilization just by sinning for the sake of sinning. But there are plenty of other opportunities for us to satisfy this call of the blood. The very desert brings us a challenge to make it blossom as the rose. There are plenty of other places in the world that offer opportunities for spiritual adventure. I wish you might feel the call. There is the international call of desolate Europe and the East. There are whole tracts in Europe where civilization, as we know it, has disappeared. Money has ceased to function, transportation has broken down, each family is toiling for itself. There is need of America to help rebuild the life of civilization. And unless America responds to the call of Europe to preach the gospel of love, and exorcise the demands of hate, our duty is not done. Get the spirit of men right, and the rest will come.

The men and women that came to America two hundred years ago, or a hundred years ago, did not bring much with them except the creative spirit, and they made everything from that. If we of to-day want thrills, if we want to get out of the rut, there is a challenge to us. We may not need to bring furniture over the mountains, but we need to bring courage, and build civilization, and start a new growth, in place of the stumps that confront us. I pity anybody who is willing to settle down for a humdrum life, content, not willing to risk anything in the great experiment for freedom, when there are such opportunities ahead.

The wild beasts have gone, but to-day we have ignorance and superstition to fight against. There was almost a mass movement toward Christianity in Korea a few years ago, simply because the Korean found that there were no devils in Christianity, and they wished to be freed from the terrible fear of devils. There is terrible pain and suffering in the non-Christian world. We never see running sores here; in heathendom, they are everywhere. Toothache rarely lasts more than twenty-four hours here; it may last for months there. Daniel Oliver with his rusty forceps, cures the toothache and allays fear. Everywhere, European doctors are thronged by the sick, in long, hopeful lines. I think the story of the man who, hour by hour, fights back disease in a population of a million souls, is much more thrilling than that of the man with a machine-gun.

There is a hospital in Tokio waiting for Friends. There comes a call from Mexico. The Mexicans do not hate us yet, but they fear us. Powerful interests are working for "intervention" there, and if they get it, thousands of American boys will be called to the colors, and will go, for the love of adventure. Yet under the banner of God, this may be prevented. Cannot we get there first? There are schools there needing Christian teachers; our opportunity is open for us.

You have heard of the beginning of industrialism in China and Japan. I told you the other day of the struggle to protect workers in this country against the greed of the machine. The process is beginning in China and Japan. Children are being worked many hours a day, and this sacrifice of humanity must be stopped. Capitalists are not all alike, but some of them are looking for a place where they can get unlimited labor at ten to thirty cents a day. And there is a great attraction in China for manufacturers of cotton goods. If her population of 450 millions only bought a yard a year apiece it would strain the looms of this country to supply that demand. The chance to get in there, to stop the slaughter which is already beginning, to Christianize them, and lay the foundations of a human social order, is before us.

I read the other day, "The Rising Tide of Color," a book whose utterly hateful and un-Christian assumption is that the white race must be dominant. The assumption is un-Christian, but full of interest. The Pan-African Union is only one evidence of the growing consciousness of race forced on other races by our attitude toward them. There is a feeling in the world that the Japanese and negroes are both suffering from our prejudice. In the Soudan, there are forty millions of the finest physical specimens of humanity. If the negroes of the Soudan, the Japanese, and the Hindoos should make common cause, and learn to hate us, there would be a great danger to peace.

Make an adventure in Philadelphia. Try treating the colored people there just as you would whites

things, we must seize hold on the powers that God offers us. Let us be worthy of our parentage, good children of Abraham. Ordinary people have done great tasks unafraid and undaunted. We set out, not knowing where, but trusting, and taking Jesus' teachings as guide—faith, consecration, and love, and remembering Jonathan's speech to his armor-bearer: "It may be that the Lord will work for us; for there is no restraint to the Lord to save by many or few."

I said that in a hundred years the American people have done a thing unparalleled in history: they have taken a virgin wilderness and reduced it to civilization. Each man took the quarter-section nearest him, and cleared it, each man doing what came next, each doing his part—a great people with a common purpose and fidelity. We need the same common purpose and fidelity for the redemption of mankind. We need a group of people who will share the Gleam, and share what they see, each one faithful in his own place ,and at his own task.

A commission recently studied the best way to avert floods in a section of the Mississippi River valley. It had been thought that great dams might have to be built, to feed the water down gradually. But the Commission reported that if the people living in the water-shed would be careful not to denude the mountains of vegetation, and if the farmers would plow on the mountainsides, back and forth, instead of up and down, the floods could be stopped. It is very simple. We must cultivate the good in our own souls, and dam the hate and sin that cut furrows in our own souls which endanger humanity. In the wide fields of our own souls and our own country there is a great opportunity for spiritual teachings.

Now that the work of pioneering is done in America, and we have laid the material foundations of our civilization, we may adventure again into the jungles of inhumanity and heathenism which confront the world. All these spiritual frontiers offer us opportunity to give expression to the love of adventure we inherit from the pioneers, and to carry into our social and religious world the process of civilization. When we recall what George Fox and his companions did in ten short years, it is a call to us of this generation to dedicate ourselves, in their faith and their energy and their power, to the great spiritual adventure of the day, as knights-errant of the Kingdom of God.

The Unity Session

The Conference session on Fourth-day, the 30th, which had been originally intended for a general discussion of the problems suggested by Jesse H. Holmes' address, was used instead as a time for welcoming the English Friends, and for listening to the messages of unity with which they came freighted. The Minutes of four of them, addressed to the Five Years' Meeting, were read, T. Edmund Harvey presenting in addition a Minute addressed directly to the Conference, being the first of its kind, and much appreciated.

T. Edmund Harvey was the first speaker of the hour, after the reading of the Minutes. He said, "It is a great responsibility to-day to be a Friend. It is a great privilege, as well as a responsibility, to be here, to see you face to face, and give you this message of Christian fellowship. I feel this the more because this is my first visit here, and I have longed to come to America. I have longed for the time when there shall be no separation among Friends.

"And I am especially anxious for a union of Friends, because my great-grandfather, Thomas Shillitoe, was here at the time when the Separation took place. I remember reading in his journal how he sat with Elias Hicks in 1827, and again I remember that when matters reached a crisis, he was in Jericho, and passing by the home of Elias Hicks, he saw the door open, and Elias Hicks beckoning him to come in. But he felt that his place was not there. I have often wondered what would have happened if that invitation of love had been accepted. But, as my great-grandfather was invited by Elias Hicks to partake of his hospitality, so have you given me a cordial invitation. The door is open, and I come in with joy which approaches sorrow.

"Our message, which seemed so big, shrinks into insignificance beside the wonderful response of the wide world. It was a joy in the devotional exercises to hear the prayer of one Friend for unity. Let us take a further step for unity—break down all barriers, and tread the path of common worship, and love, and loyalty to all our fellow men. We have seen the unifying effect already of our first steps on this path. The common struggle for peace ideals is giving a new vision of life. After all, this is only part of the world service that needs to be done. A great world may be ours, for the world has need of the Quaker vision of love.

"How shall we worship together? The path to unity is shown by that wonderful meeting in France, where Friends from all parts of the world came together as members of the society of Friends, sharing the deliberative life of our Meeting, just as we had shared the work. And then, deepest of all, and without which all must fail, they expressed their common love and loyalty to the one Master, Christ, who has broken down all walls and barriers."

Herbert Corder said: "There is in our minds the thought of that common basis of unity which should unite the Society of Friends. Being an insurance broker and accustomed to cover other people's risks, I could not help but think when Jesse Holmes spoke to us that what lies behind it all is the taking of risks—the taking of other people's risks! The greater the hazard the greater the joy! In the colleges of America, there is no student who does not choose games with the element of risk in them. The Christian church has been enervated because it has thought too much of security in this world and the next.

"'I have thought of the Society of Friends as a God-fearing, money-making people,' says somebody, and surely the organization does pay attention to external affairs. All of us are apt to pay excessive homage to the property side of life. But money is like manure—it is no use in heaps, and is only useful when spread over the land.

"The whole question of what God wants us to do is a question of taking risks. I think the Society of Friends has been led in a most wonderful way. We have followed our leader into the stricken countries of Europe. It is not the clothes, or money, or food that we have taken there that count; it is the love that went with every tin of milk. That was the human touch, and it is in that ministry that we must be united.

"Young men and young women, the future is yours, and the present. Remember what Paracelsus said: 'I am young. I can devote myself. I have a life to give.'"

Dr. Janney offered a prayer for the dedication of the hearts and lives of all present to the service of God and the spreading abroad of His truth.

Elizabeth Walter told of the message of the Earlham Conference, at which 318 young people came together. One representative from each delegation met each day of the Conference to consider the future of the organization. "We met in prayer, and in prayer found a common life together. Emptied of selfishness, a spiritual unity seemed born among us. As we left the Conference, Frederick Libby said, 'Don't give up the vision of the united Society of Friends.' We do not hope that organic unity can be achieved at once, but the spiritual unity has already been begun."

Catherine Albright said: "The question of unity has been much with me since I first came to this country. To talk about unity does not mean dropping the things that are real and vital to either; we need not sacrifice truth, but find a new aspect of it. We are apt to over-emphasize the value of a particular truth. But Truth is bigger than any of us know, for the part of it that each holds is only a small part of it, no matter how vital it may be to us. If we pool Truth, not a whit will be dropped. It is mainly a matter of language; we must ask not what people say, but what they are trying to say. The truth that lies behind is the important thing."

J. Barnard Walton said: "The thing that binds us together more than truth is love. Can we not take from this thought the feeling of the love that will hold us together, no matter how different our ideas of the truth. It is not the understanding of Truth, but the understanding of Love, and each other's understanding of the Truth that counts."

Henry T. Gillett said: "There is only one thing more important than your opinion, and that is your fellowship. 'The truth shall make you free.' True, and yet, instead of keeping truth in front of us, let us remember that fellowship is more important. We have just lost one of our great writers, William Charles Braithwaite, who, with Rufus M. Jones, has given us much of our history. There are still tasks confronting us, calling for all the ability and love that our small community can give. Anyone who has traveled in Germany knows how the word 'Quaker' opens the doors anywhere. But the feeling we have is of profound inadequacy in talent, in spirit, in faithfulness. Let us use what we have as God gives it to us."

Frederick J. Libby said: "I did not join Friends at first, because I did not want to joint a *branch*. Now I see how much the branches need each other. The greatest desire for service can not come until all are united in spirit; external unity is not essential. The spirit is all in all. I have just been in Ohio Yearly Meeting, which is perhaps the most Orthodox of all. They are interpreting their Christian experience in the language of fifty years ago. Christian experience is the same in all times, but it should be interpreted in the present-day vocabulary. The essential unity is to be at one in heart, not to be tied up by any misunderstanding or grudge, and in that way we shall conquer. Let us be above differences in our own hearts. I told Nebraska Yearly Meeting that I cannot urge the French to love the Germans, if the Friends do not love each other. There are Germans who want to come and see us here. Let them wait until we are ready for inspection. We do not love each other as they think we do. If we have unity, we shall bceome an instrument of service for God, to be used in His name. Let us be ready when He comes to us."

Isaac Wilson spoke of Whittier and his desire for unity among Friends, which he expressed shortly before his death.

George Wood told how he had carried religious enmity through school and college, and had later found out his mistake. At the Meeting in Buffalo an old Friend of 83 said one day, 'I think we ought to get more of the Hicksites in with us; they are just as Orthodox as we are.' You see we Orthodox Friends do not know what you are; we do not know the spirit of love among you. We are all working for Truth, and it is a great privilege to attend the Meeting at Pelham, where you can not tell one kind of Quaker from another. Let us get together and have that unity of spirit which we can not have

ing, my brother?" said, "If it is, its light must fall on the way that we and others tread. We who are older must feel that there is still something for us to do. God's light is shining for us, and if we look to Him, He will light us into the Kingdom."

A prayer, earnest and sincere, was offered by Henry T. Gillett.

Caroline Worth said: "'Build thee more stately mansions, O, my soul.' These words are an expression of life. As we leave our outworn past, we come into a realization of God's greatness and lovingness of spirit, giving each one of us a sense of the meaning of life."

Herbert Corder reminded Friends that, as children of men, we must all be born again, as children of God.

Charles Harrison said: "There are three kinds of surfaces. One kind absorbs light, one reflects, and one catches fire. The occasional surface may serve to absorb, or to reflect light, but if Quakerism is really the pearl of great price to us, we shall be ready to catch fire and give light. We must both receive and give light. We must not be afraid to throw away the things that hinder the work of light in our own souls. Make it possible for all to live with us peaceably, the spirit of Christ being a part of our own lives."

It was said by a Friend: "The missionary spirit is a call to go out to serve, but few go. Each one should start the missionary spirit in his own soul and in the community. Let us clear out the selfishness that bars the light of Christ."

Chauncey Shortlidge said: "I have felt that this Conference is sowing seed that will bear fruit. 'Plant love, and love will spring up. Plant hate, and hate will grow.'"

Frances Robinson said: "We have built a Tabernacle in which to assert our own spirituality. What would Jesus do in our day and generation? He would do those things that need to be done. That then is our task; let us promise to do them."

Edgar Zavitz said: "Learn the law of retribution. We shall sow what we reap."

Darlington Hoopes said: "We must go home and show what the Conference has done for us. Many of us young Friends must express in this way our appreciation and thanks to those who made it possible for us to be here. It is not what we receive or what we give that counts so much as what we share. In the community life, we can not rise high above our surroundings. We must all rise together."

Rowntree Gillett said: "'To whom then wilt thou liken God?' In Jesus we have seen God. 'He that hath seen Him hath seen God.' Every man and woman among us may see God. Each must decide for himself the high service that he will do. The world is full of problems; Christ calls to us on every side, but our eyes are blinded. It is the way we act and the things we do that testify to our belief. There is a great hunger in the hearts of men everywhere. Can we as a people testify to the life and truth of Jesus Christ?"

Wilson M. Tylor said: "Our hearts are filled, yet there is more food left than when we began. But we need to focalize on one objective point. Let us have faith. There is a beautiful spirit who can not be with us this morning. Let us think for a few moments of him, and earnestly desire the speedy restoration to health of our friend, Charles Foster Kent."

In response to this loving thought, the entire Conference sat for a few moments in prayerful remembrance of Dr. Kent.

T. Edmund Harvey said: "There come sometimes to us moments of vision when we get glimpses of the divine glow, and realize the possibilities that are in us through the goodness and love of God. In some such moment we can make a tremendous affirmation that we would not otherwise dare to make. The love of God stretches out an all sides; it takes up all that is good in our lives, our love for our friends or our families. We have to think for God, for our Meetings, for the problems of the world, and not be afraid of thinking. We must have dedication. It is part of God's plan that we shall think, that we shall use the faculties He has given us; the faculties of prayer and faith and thought. There have been prophets in the past: are there to be none for the problems of today,—prophets who will send us from Meetings with our hearts aglow as never before? It can be if we will but dedicate ourselves to His service, and listen to the Divine appeal.

This little branch of the Kingdom of God that we call Friends demands in a unique degree this dedication to the service of God and man. It may be that in this group there are some to whom the greater dedication for deeper work in the name of the Master may come. We may feel how helpless we are, how unworthy messengers for the word of God. Centuries ago, from one praying that his weakness might become strength, we hear, 'My strength is made perfect in weakness.' We feel the weakness and poverty in our Meetings, and in our own hearts. but through these we know the dedication of the heart, feeling the Divine Presence about us. And we may receive again the benediction of the pierced hands, and hear again the words of the Master, 'My grace is sufficient for thee.' "

Closing Minute

The Friends' General Conference in session in Richmond, 8-26 to 9-2 in 1922, might well be called an epoch-making Conference, the theme of which developed into spiritual unity through fellowship. It opened with a clear setting forth of what various stages of society have called fundamentals and has been characterized throughout by a sincere search for those cornerstones upon which we can build today:—truth, righteousness and love.

The practical application of these principles was considered in the fields of education, industry and international, inter-racial and social relations. We are deeply concerned as we behold the strife and bitterness between races, nations and classes all over the world. Yet we have faith to believe that amid the universal turmoil, the seeds of enduring peace have been sown and are growing wherever individuals and peoples are seeking better mutual understanding and a spirit of Christian co-operation.

Feeling, as Friends, our urgent need to express our ideals in the life of our times, we are in sympathy with and endorse the Friends' Disarmament Council, the National Council for the Reduction of Armament, the Eighteenth Amendment and the enforcement of law.

The keynote of spiritual unity has found furthe expression in some measure of achievement in th tasks definitely set before us at the beginning of th Conference. We have taken preliminary steps toward the preparation of a uniform discipline an the reorganization of the Conference for greate effectiveness. The Young Friends' Movement ha been recognized and incorporated as a part of th Central Committee by increasing the membershi of this committee from one hundred to one hundre and twenty-five, the additional members being ap pointed by the Young Friends of the various Yearl Meetings.

The attendance of an unusually large number o young Friends, made possible by the generosity o an interested friend and their active interest in se sions of the Conference, have helped to create a re fellowship, not only among our number but with a Friends and, in fact, with all seekers of Truth. W acknowledge, with profound gratitude, the livin message of love and the spirit of good will and fe lowship brought to us by our very dear Englis Friends, T. Edmund Harvey, Catherine T. A bright, Herbert Corder, Joseph Rowntree Gille and Henry Tregelles Gillett. We have been bless by their consecrated spirit.

This Conference has awakened a deep sense spiritual unity through fellowship. In closing v pray that we may be granted strength to carry hon the inspirations received, that we may brighten o homes, strengthen our meetings and cheer all wi whom we come in contact by reflecting in our liv the presence of God.

"Grafskaya Volost is one of the better ones. Here is a population of 7,632. Our survey shows 3,085 should be fed at once, and that by the end of the year we should be feeding 6,422, or 84%."

The second confirmation of the famine emergency was made by trained American investigators entirely independent of Friends. It is outlined in the following despatch which was cabled from Moscow, and which was published in the Philadelphia *Public Ledger*:

Special Cable Despatch
Copyright 1922, by Public Ledger Company.

Moscow, Oct. 17.—Graham Taylor and Allen Wardwell, of the Commission on Russian Relief of the National Information Bureau, who came to Russia to conduct an investigation of the Russian-famine situation for the benefit of the contributing public, are returning to the United States with the report that the famine during the coming winter will be as bad in some districts as it was last year.

Mr. Wardwell, in an interview with your correspondent, said the splendid work of the American relief organizations will have been in vain unless relief work is continued. The famine area is more limited than last year. It covers the Tartar, Bashkir and Kirghiz republics and other districts east of the Volga with millions of peasant inhabitants. The famine in those regions, he said, would be more severe than in the winter of 1921-1922 because the population has already eaten all the livestock, dogs and cats.

The commission traveled miles without seeing plowed or planted fields. Men and women were seen here and there pulling plows themselves or wielding hoes and spades.

The members of the commission, who visited Samara, Kazan and Orenburg in the Urals, said that though the optimistic crop reports of the Soviet authorities and various relief organizations might have been justified when the crops first began to appear above ground, there was no question now that the harvest was insufficient for the needs of the population.

There will be no surplus and no grain for export purposes.

The population above all, Mr. Wardwell said, needs animals to cultivate the ground and thus terminate the vicious circle of famine years.

(The Friends' Mission, as one phase of its work, has already begun importing horses for the above purpose.)

Shipping Here and There

Last winter the American papers harped on the demoralization of Russion shipping and the interference with relief work arising therefrom. There was at times delay in the expedition of goods in Russia; but that this was only to be expected, is indicated by the fact that there was, and still is, similar delay in America. Almost two months have been lost as a result of lack of cars due to the railway shop strike; while a considerable amount of flour has been damaged by being shipped in cars that were out of condition. Now a dockmen's strike may still further delay shipments which the Service Committee is trying to get off to Russia for the winter. Word from the field says that there is now no congestion on the Russian railroads and urges that relief shipments be made at once, before the winter snows make transportation more difficult.

For Christmas Gifts:
Polish Folk-Embroidery

Here is a chance to relieve suffering in Poland by means of your Christmas shopping! The Service Committee has just received a fresh consignment of embroideries made by Polish refugees. These goods, which consist mainly of runners, pillow-covers, and square table-covers, possess the simple beauty of folk-embroidery. They make Christmas gifts or personal possessions of high value, while the funds received from their sale will be used to aid the Polish refugee women during the hard winter which is before them.

These embroideries are on exhibition at 20 South 12th Street, Philadelphia, Pa. Interested persons who are unable to come to Philadelphia will be sent samples for selection upon request to the Secretary of Women's Work, c/o American Friends' Service Committee, at the above address.

The Service Committee also has for sale copies of two Christmas post-cards containing reproductions of drawings by Viennese children.

Speak Out!

I do not think that all is good and wise,
I cannot watch the world with tranquil eyes
And say "thy will be done" to all I see;
To foolish pride, to greed and cruelty.
It was not meant that men should thus submit,
Should see deep wrongs, yet still in silence sit.
Speak out! Speak out! Though nations curse thy word,
Better a crown of thorns than truth unheard;
Better the rack, the cell, the martyr's stake
Than speech suppressed for black oppression's sake.
Who knows but what in thy lone heart shall break,
A light to guide men further on that way
That leads far onward toward the glowing day?
And who can say but what thy feet shall tread
A surer path than time's immortal dead?

—PAUL ARCHER CHADWICK

First-Day School Methods

By Bliss Forbush

The Closing Exercises

The closing period of the School can be made the most attractive feature of the day. It is here that the reports of the School come in, where visitors speak to the boys and girls, and where special features are mentioned.

The School should assemble rapidly and quietly from their class rooms. Especially should the older classes, that are so fond of dallying on the way, be prompt in taking their places. The Secretary should make the report of the collection and attendance, emphasizing an unusually good record; and if any contests are going on they should be enthusiastically summed up by the Director. A stirring hymn should be sung and then the special feature of the day be presented.

Sometimes the Superintendent will give a talk on some topic the news of the day or the season of the year brings to mind. For instance, the recent registration day in Baltimore gave our Superintendent an opportunity to speak on how Friends can affirm instead of swear when they go to the polls; and why therefor we should all be careful to tell the truth, as the word of a Friend must never be doubted. The coming of winter, and later the approach of spring, give the Superintendent an opportunity to speak on nature, thankfulness, and other kindred subjects.

Those Schools that are fortunate enough to own lanterns can make frequent use of them in the closing exercises. Any photographer will make slides for you from films of the school taken on special occasions. One of our Assistant Superintendents has charge of the slides one First-day a month when he shows slides of his own making, or that he has secured from outside, together with a talk appropriate to their use. One interesting thing he does is to have a slide with the names of all the scholars on it who have not missed attending the School during the month, together with the names of those in the banner class for the same period. This always creates interest.

Such companies as the Keystone View Company, 91 Seventh Avenue, New York City, and Beseler Lantern Slide Company, 131 East 23rd Street, New York City, have many slides, which they rent for a moderate figure, that are suitable for First-day School work. Among these would be slides for different seasons, such as Christmas, Thanksgiving, etc.; slides of famous paintings of religious subjects, such as those of Holman Hunt, the Old Masters, and the Tissot series; or slides of Palestine and the surrounding country.

BIBLICAL DRAMATICS

Once a month, or at longer intervals, Biblical dramatics would make very attractive and worth while closing services. These should be very simple, the wording taken intact from the Bible, and with costumes that can easily be made at home. Some of the more familiar stories that might be given are, the Infant Moses, Naomi and Ruth, the Good Samaritan, the Wise and Foolish Virgins, Samuel, King David, and many more that can be selected.

SPEAKERS

The School often likes to have new people address it. These can be chosen from the men and women in the Meetings who are interesting speakers to children and young people, and from outside men and women who come

vited will be held at the Twentieth Street Meeting House at 3 P. M., and will be addressed by a well-known speaker.

STUDY GROUP PROGRAM

The following program is prepared by the Young Friends' Movement of Philadelphia Yearly Meeting. While the groups are especially designed for young people, we hope that anyone who is interested in the subjects will feel free to attend the meetings. The group organized to study the discipline is the only one in Philadelphia Quarter so far, and we hope many Friends who are concerned about this matter will attend. Different members of the Revision Committee will be present each meeting and will be ready with suggestions for discussion.

The class studying the Quaker separations in the Nineteenth Century will use original sources as far as possible and will strive to get at the truth of the matter through personal study, and the able leadership of Elbert Russell.

The groups start this week. It is hoped that there will be considerable interest in them and that the attendance will not only be large but regular.

STUDY GROUP PROGRAM
1922-1923

I. An Unpartisan Study of the Separations in the Nineteenth Century.
Meets with Elbert Russell once a month.
Begins November 7th, at 7.15 P. M.
Meets every Tuesday in Room No. 4, Race Street Meeting House.

II. A Training Class for the World Peace Movement.
Follows the outline prepared by Frederick J. Libby, Executive Secretary of the National Council for the Reduction of Armaments.
Begins November 9th, at 7.15 P. M.
Meets every Thursday in Room No. 1, Race Street Meeting House.

III. Study Class for the Revision of the Discipline.
Using London Discipline and others for comparison. Following outline prepared by the Discipline Committee of Philadelphia Yearly Meeting.
Begins November 8th, at 7.15 P. M.
Meets every Wednesday in the Association Room, P. Y. F. A., 140 North 15th Street.

IV. The Christian Solution of Industrial Problems.
Using 'Christianity and Economic Problems," Kirby Page.
Begins November 9th, at 7.15 P. M.
Meets every Thursday in Room No. 4, Race Street Meeting House.

These Study Groups are under the auspices of the Young Friends' Movement of Philadelphia Yearly Meeting, headquarters at 154 North Fifteenth Street.

All persons interested are cordially invited to take part. Meetings begin promptly.

The hour and place of these meetings are subject to change.

ELIZABETH ANN WALTER, *Secretary.*

WESTBURY QUARTERLY MEETING

Those who attended Quarterly Meeting at Flushing, on Tenth month 28th, were privileged to hear inspiring messages from Isaac Wilson and Mary Travilla.

Isaac Wilson said we should consider ourselves co-laborers with God to bring the Kingdom of Heaven on Earth, and just as the Disciples were prepared to hear Jesus on the mountain because the "spiritual eye had been rightly annointed," so we should listen to the real word of God as spoken to the inner ear. "Ye believe in God, believe also in me," is the exhortation of Jesus urging people to have faith in human strength of which He was the exponent. We should realize that omission of right doing is as bad as commission of wrong. Are we ready to serve the world? Are we willing to adjust our ears better to hear God's voice so that the inward light may shine more brightly, and not for ourselves alone, but with an out-going of spirit?

Mary Travilla, linking her message with the Sermon on the Mount, said that Christ was sent to encourage humanity. Not sorrow but kindness comes from God and forces of righteousness must prevail in the end. Let God's love flood our souls and sickness of spirit and body will be healed. E. A. P.

CONFERENCE ON INTER-RACIAL RELATIONS

"Proper Inter-racial Contacts in Schools," was the subject of an all-day conference in the Friends' Meeting-house at Fifteenth and Race Streets. The morning session was conducted by J. Henry Scattergood, who said that the inter-racial problem was no longer confined to the Southern States, but was one that vitally concerned the whole nation.

The subject was introduced by Anne Biddle Stirling, chairman of the Philadelphia Inter-racial Committee. She said that the root of the difficulty between the white and colored races was a sense of suspicion and fear. This was not a natural condition, for the little children played together on terms of equality and goodwill. They wanted an education which would preserve this mutual understanding and sympathy.

The Rev. Dr. Joseph H. Odell, director of Citizens' Service Association of Delaware, gave an address on "Equal Opportunities for the Colored Race in Delaware." He said that up to 1919 the colored schools of that State were in a deplorable condition, but great advances had been made, until now the colored people there had equal educational opportunities, and by means of better schools and surroundings the colored people remained in the country instead of herding into the neighboring town.

Dr. Gregg, of Hampton Institute, said in the South they were watching the work of Negro education in Delaware. He spoke also of the great educational advance being made in North Carolina and other places. There was a growing feeling that Negroes should be given a square deal.

Mr. William Anthony Aery said in the South they were developing an intelligent public opinion. There were now 800 inter-racial committees working together for a better understanding between the races.

In the afternoon session Dr. Thomas E. Finegan, State Superintendent of Public Instruction, spoke on "The Responsibility of the State for the Education of the Colored Race." He showed the advance that has been made from slavery and said that during the last fifty years it was wonderful what the race had accomplished. The educating of the future generation was a great public duty, Dr. Finegan said, and he believed the public schools should be free for all races and conditions. The colored people must be afforded the means to raise themselves to the status of citizenship. With good education they were a splendid asset, but without education they were a menace. He wished that one of their outstanding men should be on his staff at Harrisburg.

Dr. James H. Dillard, rector of William and Mary College, Va., and president of the Jeanes and Slater funds, spoke on "How to Promote Inter-racial Understanding and Co-operation." Like Dr. Finegan, he thought that the whole country should share the responsibility of universal education. He showed how year by year there had been a forward educational movement in the South, and great improvement in the number and status of colored teachers. Racial conditions were getting better in the South and he believed that they would also get better in the North.

A lively discussion followed, in which George A. Walton, Anna B. Pratt and Robert T. Kerlin took part.

the Norristown Friends' Home, and the American Friends' Service Committee. Any donations will be appreciated, and the support of all Friends interested in these causes is solicited.

NOTICE—The Best Interests Committee of Philadelphia Monthly Meeting will give a supper preceding Monthly Meeting on November 15th, in the lunch room of Friends' Central School. Tickets 65 cents, can be secured from Almira P. Harlan, 154 N. 15th Street, or at Race Street, West Philadelphia and Girard Avenue Meetings. All reservations must be in by the morning of Eleventh month 13th.

Walt Whitman has been dead thirty years. Is his popularity as a poet increasing or decreasing?

I am asking this question of all Friends who are interested in Whitman's life and work. If you, dear reader, are one of these, will you kindly send me your opinion in care of "Unity," 700 Oakwood Blvd., Chicago, Ill.?

It is possible that a book may be made of the replies received in this symposium.

JAMES WALDO FAWCETT.

CORRECTION

During the session of the Meeting of Ministry and Counsel of Baltimore Yearly Meeting last week the age of Martha Townsend was mentioned as 95 years and was so reported. Later information proved this to be an error. She is 85 years old.

American Friends' Service Committee

WILBUR K. THOMAS, Ex. SEC.
20 S. 12th St. Philadelphia.

CASH CONTRIBUTIONS

WEEK ENDING OCTOBER 30TH.

Five Years Meeting	$72.00
Other Meetings:	
West Grove First-day School	3.00
Green Street Monthly Meeting	10.00
Cambridge Group of Friends	588.50
Easton Monthly Meeting	22.75
Contributions for Germany	19.00
For Austria	59.00
For Poland	81.59
For Russia	1,424.40
For Russian Overhead	75.60
Central Pennsylvania	200.00
For Syria	214.00
For General	93.10
For Clothing	15.54
Refunds	28.31
	$2,906.79

Shipments received during week ending October 28, 1922: 76 boxes and packages, 3 anonymous.

Strawbridge & Clothier

Wonderful New Purchase of

Heavy All-Silk Crepe de Chine $3.00

Thousands of yards of this highly fashionable Silk, of a quality that only through an extraordinary trade circumstance, could possibly be sold at this remarkably low price.

All-silk, heavy, beautiful finish, 40 inches wide, and in black and every desirable shade of the season.

Get here early—a similar great lot, not quite equal to this in value, was bought up in a surprisingly short time, not long ago.

Strawbridge & Clothier—Aisle 6, Centre

$75,000 WORTH OF DECORATIVE LINENS AT ATTRACTIVE PRICES

Think of choosing Decorative Linens for your home and for gifts from such a wonderful assortment as this, gathered from the Linen centres of the world, just for you.

Choice, new and original designs in Doilies, Centrepieces, Lunch Cloths and Sets, Napkins, Scarfs and other pieces. Finished in various styles, plain hemstitched, scalloped and hemstitched, embroidered, lace-trimmed and in combinations of lace and embroidery. These outstanding values illustrate the scope of savings in the entire collection:

Doilies—18c to $1.10
Centrepieces—75c to $1.35
Lunch Cloths—$3.00 to $4.00
Pillow Shams—$2.50
Scarfs—$1.75 to $2.25
13-Piece Lunch Sets—$4.50

All of these of plain round-thread linen, with spoke-stitched inserts and scalloped hems.

Doylies—20c to $1.00
Centrepieces—85c to $2.00
Lunch Cloths—$5 to $11.50
Pillow Shams—$3.75
Scarfs—$2.50 to $3.50
13-Piece Lunch Sets—$6.00

All of round-thread linen with spoke-stitched inserts, combination solid and eyelet work, embroidery-finished and with linen cluny lace trimming.

Madeira rose-scalloped Linens: Doilies—50c to $2.00; Centrepieces—$1.15 to $2.50; Scarfs—$3.00 to $5.25.

Madeira hand-embroidered and hand-scalloped 13-piece Lunch Sets, in choice designs and dainty effects—$5.00, $6.50, $8.00, $12.00, $13.50 a set.

Strawbridge & Clothier—Aisle 11, Centre

STRAWBRIDGE & CLOTHIER

MARKET STREET EIGHTH STREET FILBERT STREET

PHILADELPHIA, PA.

To the Lot Holders and others interested in Fairhill Burial Ground:

GREEN STREET Monthly Meeting has funds available for the encouragement of the practice of cremating the dead to be interred in Fairhill Burial Ground. We wish to bring this fact as prominently as possible to those who may be interested. We are prepared to undertake the expense of cremation in case any lot holder desires us to do so.

Those interested should communicate with William H. Gaskill, Treasurer of the Committee of Interments, Green Street Monthly Meeting, or any of the following members of the Committee.

William H. Gaskill, 3201 Arch St.
Samuel N. Longstreth, 1218 Chestnut St.
Charles F. Jenkins, 232 South Seventh St.
Stuart S. Graves, 3033 Germantown Ave.

FOR SALE

$12,000 CASH WILL PURCHASE acre and half of ground (250 feet frontage, paved, curbed and macadamized) in desirable suburb 13 miles (half-hour) from City Hall. $500 will fully redecorate house. $5,000 will redecorate and change into five apartments with total of 28 rooms. House alone, with 15-inch walls, and splendid steam-heater in high semi-basement (in which there is room for apartment for janitor) could not be duplicated for less than $20,000. Near good public school, one of the best Friends' Select Schools in the country and half-mile from Meeting-house. Enough frontage can be sold to more than reimburse for changing to apartments. ONLY CASH WILL BUY AT ABOVE FIGURES. Please do not reply unless fully in earnest. X. Y. Z., Friends' Intelligencer.

The Friends' Intelligencer

ESTABLISHED 1844 | ELEVENTH MONTH 18, 1922 | VOLUME 79 NUMBER 46

Contents

EDITORIAL

GENERAL ARTICLES

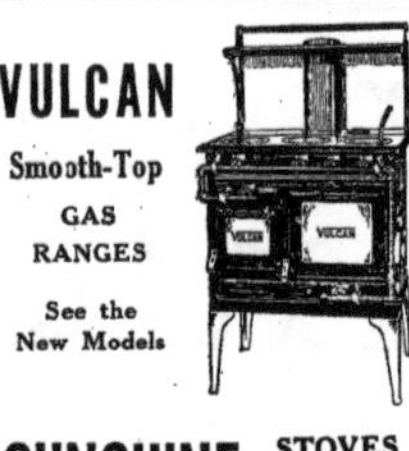

THE FRIENDS' INTELLIGENCER

Published weekly, 140 N. 15th Street, Philadelphia, Pa., by Friends' Intelligencer Association, Ltd.

Subscription rates: United States, Mexico, Cuba and Panama, $2.50 per year. Canada and other foreign countries, $3.00 per year. Checks should be made payable to Friends' Intelligencer Association, Ltd.

Entered as Second Class Matter at Philadelphia Post Office.

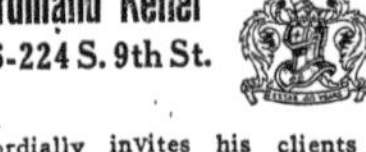

The Friends' Intelligencer

The religion of Friends is based on faith in the "INWARD LIGHT," or direct revelation of God's spirit and will in every ...king soul.
The INTELLIGENCER is interested in all who bear the name of Friends in every part of the world, and aims to promote love, ...ity and intercourse among all branches and with all religious societies.

...TABLISHED 1844 PHILADELPHIA, ELEVENTH MONTH 18, 1922 VOLUME 79 NUMBER 46

The Inter-racial Committee

In our last issue, the editorial by J. Russell Smith ... "Increasing Quaker Efficiency" pointed to the ...ed for specializing along a certain line rather than ...reading our energies over a number of subjects. ...e conference on "Inter-racial Contacts in Our ...hools," held at Fifteenth and Race Streets, Phila...lphia, recently, a report of which appeared in our ...st issue, is the result of just such concentration on ...e part of the members of one of our Yearly Meet...g Committees. The Inter-racial Committee of ...iladelphia Yearly Meeting, Anne Biddle Stirling, ...airman, called together educators from New York, ...ew Jersey, Delaware, Virginia, Maryland and the ...istrict of Columbia, as well as leading teachers and ...perintendents from nearby schools and colleges, to ...nsider the immensely important question of proper ...ter-racial contacts between the white and colored ...ces.

This small gathering should be the nucleus around ...ich a great movement shall develop to create a ...tter understanding and a broader toleration of the ...egro race. A future conference was recommended ... this meeting, to be held in Philadelphia in the ...urse of a few months to discuss the means of im...oving inter-racial relations. It is recognized in ...is effort, as in many others, that it is a matter of ...ucation, and the place to begin is with the children ... the schools. We find them mingling freely and ...thout thought of color in the lower grades. This ...ndition should continue as they grow older, but ...r instruction is one-sided, in many cases bringing ...t the inferior or lower qualities of the Negro race, ...ile enlarging upon the achievements of the white ...ce. It would be well for us to stop and consider ...metimes such incidents as the following:

Mrs. Mary Church Terrell was the first colored woman ... serve on a Board of Education in this country, and ...rved for eleven years, a longer service than that of any ...er person, white or black, on the Board of Education ... our National Capital. Mrs. Terrell was the only one ... the American delegates to the International Congress ... Women in Berlin some years ago who addressed the convention in German. She followed it by an address in French. It carried the audience literally by storm, and she was recalled three times.

As Dr. Finegan, State Superintendent of Public Instruction of Pennsylvania, said at the conference: "Now men and women must face the Negro problem as a national problem, which must be solved according to the principles of right and justice."

If it were possible to put into this editorial the achievements of the Negro race during the last fifty years, we would stand back in amazement and awe at the progress they have made. To quote from the remarks of Leslie Pinckney Hill, Principal of the Cheyney State Normal School, "The most wonderful feat of Negroes has been their securing of vast amounts of land. Negroes have bought and paid for over 32,000 square miles of land. In Georgia, for example, Negroes own 1,500,000 square acres, which are worth $16,000,000. . . . Negroes have also shown a deep interest in education. In 1866, the Negro illiteracy was almost 100%. In 1920, there was less than 28% of illiteracy among Negroes. In 1866, there were about 15 schools for the higher training of Negroes. These schools cost less than $500,000. In 1920, there were 500 schools of this type, which cost more than $18,000,000. This amount included $1,800,000 given by the Negroes themselves."

In closing his address he said, "Among the modern Negro leaders there are few hot-headed Negro radicals. The Negro leaders to-day study the facts of life. They are saying: 'We shall take the middle course. We shall do what we can here and now. We shall not lose faith or patience. We shall win our way forward. We shall be sure to put ourselves on the side of the right.'

"If Negroes can think *over* difficulties that loom so large and can continue to believe that there is good in others, they will surely rise. Intelligent Negroes are everywhere saying, 'God forgive them for they know not what they do.'

"We must have two planks in our platform, namely, 'We will believe in ourselves,' and 'We must unite with all seekers after truth.' Negroes everywhere are anxious to ally themselves with those who seek to help them. Hate has no end. Love is stronger than hate. God is God. All men are brothers. Christianity will possess the earth."

If we will but join our Negro brothers in an effort to put into practice the rules that they have made for themselves there is little doubt but that the question of inter-racial contacts can be settled to their mutual advantage in such a way that the white and colored races may live side by side in peace and harmony.

The Chicago Commis

(The Chicago Commission on Race Relations was appointed by Frank O. Lowden, then Governor of Illinois, following the most destructive riot, in both lives and property, that has taken place since freedom came to the Negroes of America. The following extracts are from an article which appeared in the Literary Digest of October 28, under the heading "The Light Turned on a Race Riot." —Editor.)

On a Sunday afternoon in July, 1919, there were fights between the white and colored bathers over the crossing of an imaginary line in the water that divided their recreation privileges. A negro boy, riding on a piece of timber, floated over this line. He was stoned and drowned. In the excitement that followed, the police made arrests only among the negroes. The officers refused, the negroes claimed, to arrest the white men pointed out as those who stoned the negro victim. Then the riot broke. It lasted with varying intensity for seven days, and extended down to "the loop"—Chicago's business district—for even there negroes were attacked by pursuing whites. The 38 deaths brought nine indictments and four convictions—and these mild prison sentences.

Governor Lowden, "appalled by the rioting and murders," appointed the Race Relations Commission—a "mixed committee composed of prominent men of both races." Among its members were Victor F. Lawson, owner of the Chicago *Daily News*, and Julius Rosenwald, head of the Sears-Roebuck Company. The negro members were selected from the ablest of the colored population in the city. The Commission studied its problem for three years before its report was complete. The "gist of the opinion of the Commission" is thus given by the New York *Tribune:*

"There is no reason inherent in the mental, moral or physical make-up of the negro race which would prevent its attaining its full stature as a component part of the American commonwealth if certain environmental conditions that handicap it at present were to be removed. At the same time, there are no short-cuts to the solution of the problem of fitting Caucasian and Ethiopian into their

vailing misconceptions as: that negroes have inferior mentality; that negroes have an inferior morality; that negroes are given to emotionalisms; that negroes have an innate tendency to commit crimes, especially sex crimes.

"We believe that such deviations from recognized standards as have been apparent among negroes are due to circumstances of position rather than to distinct racial traits. We urge especially upon white persons to exert their efforts toward discrediting stories and standing beliefs concerning negroes which have no basis in fact but which constantly serve to keep alive a spirit of mutual fear, distrust, and opposition."

The *Chciago Defender,* the negro daily of that city, says that "this body, composed of trained, public-spirited men of both races, finds at the end of its task that there is no panacea or quick overnight remedy to a solution of all the various questions that go to make up what we call a race problem," and proceeds:

"But its members are convinced that if thinking men and women will study the facts and abandon the slavery to prejudices built up on myths and ignorance, a long step will be taken toward mutual confidence and understanding. It ought to be a matter of encouragement to members of the race to find that when white men of high character and ability are compelled by circumstances to sit down with colored men of equal character and ability to study this question they come out of the baptism of fire as converts to our cause and point of view."

To N. H.

Beyond the Wall—where all are one—
Is she who tried to tear it down,
Beyond the Wall, where all is love
And one is neither white nor brown.

Her face so fair to look upon,
The soft, rich tints of Autumn's tone.
But in those dark, dark depths of eyes
There always, always sadness shone.

The Wall is high and dark and cruel;
She tried to span it, and she found
'Tis ignorance—fear—that keeps it there,
And only love can tear it down.

Was the task too great, the hands too few?
And love withheld this side the Wall?
Is that the why her Youth was spent?
Then we must answer to her call!

The Wall is high and dark and cruel;
Arise! O ye of little love!
Tear down the Wall with that great Force
That only comes from God above.

RACHEL DAVIS-DUBOIS.

Baltimore Yearly Meeting

A Summary of the Proceedings

(Concluded from last week)

Samuel Brosius, agent of Indian Rights Association, gave a most interesting talk early in the session on Fourth-day morning, concerning the 340,000 Indians, most of whom he felt were unable to take care of themselves, though 101,000 belong to what is known as the civilized class. The speaker advised citizenship for Indians, though he felt the Government should keep the property until Indians were able to assume charge. He told of work done in Arizona in building of dams for irrigation, but declared the Government had been too stingy in this. The matter of peyote, the drug which is enslaving so many Indians, was discussed, the Indian Committee being given power to enter protest or to otherwise act in the interests of the Indian.

Benjamin F. Miller gave report of work of the Anti-Saloon League, on which he is Friends' representative, and gave it as his opinion that the enemy is neither dead or sleeping, and declared officials cannot do all the work. Individuals must feel the responsibility.

Anne W. Janney reported the work of the Social Service Committee, which she felt to be much more important than many think. Twelve Monthly Meetings have committees, three have no committees, but report work done; only one Monthly Meeting sending no report. There are nine departments, viz.: Temperance, Anti-Narcotics, Child Welfare, Peace, Purity, Prison Reform, Anti-Gambling, Colored People and Social Hygiene. While work has been done in all, only a few of these departments were touched upon. Very practical work on the line of Prison Reform was reported. Eight essay contests, with 300 contestants, was an item mentioned in the department of Anti-Narcotics; 5,000 leaflets having been distributed in public schools. Thomas B. Hull, in reporting work done for American Friends' Service Committee, spoke of it as "Our Society in Action." He touched lightly on the various fields of labor abroad and spoke of the nine meetings now being held in France, Switzerland, Germany, Austria and Poland. He read a letter from Caroline Norment, a member of this meeting, now on the Russian field, which told of the harrowing situation there. A further report from John K. Harper told of sewing, knitting, collection of partly worn clothing, etc.

Murray S. Kenworthy was to have continued the subject further at this session, but so little time remaining he was given opportunity at the opening of next day's session, when for a brief half hour he graphically portrayed conditions in Russia as he saw them. The statement that only 1% of the food sent

ness were taken up and woven into a completed web. Announcement was made that the Young Friends' Movement of the Yearly Meeting would see to the collections of American Friends' Service work for the next year, and Mary F. Blackburn was named to represent with Thomas B. Hull, this Yearly Meeting on the Service Committee.

At the instance of Pauline W. Holme, a letter was adopted, asking Senators in the districts represented in the Yearly Meeting to vote for the Dyer Anti-Lynching Bill to the end that the wide-spread evil of lynching be checked.

The Peace Section of Social Order Committee offered a resolution, which was adopted, endorsing the action of the National Educational Association in asking that text-books hereafter give as much consideration to the heroes of peace as to heroes of war.

The "Letter to Christian Churches," prepared by the two Philadelphia Yearly Meetings, was given the endorsement of Baltimore, thus completing the endorsement of our branch of Friends.

Elizabeth H. Bartlett reported the work of the First-day Schools, with a field secretary in every Quarter. A Teachers' Training Class at Hopewell, Va., where a Community School is held, with members of both branches of Friends, Baptists and Presbyterians, the pastor of the latter denomination refusing to have a school started at his church because "the Friends had such a good one, theirs was unnecessary." Oxford had installed a lantern, the first school to be so equipped.

The remaining Epistles from Dublin, Genesee, Indiana and Illinois were read, as was the report of the Committee on Education and the Disposition of the Fair Hill Fund. The playgrounds at Winchester, Va., with an enrollment of 140 children had been a great boon to the community. The Park Avenue Friends' School had graduated a class of 30, 21 of whom are continuing study elsewhere now. There are 543 students now enrolled, only 45 of whom are members of the Society. The addition to the building, though not large of itself, seems to give a roominess to the entrance hall very delightful, as are the new offices and out-door study room. Tributes were paid to Jonathan K. Taylor and Eli M. Lamb for their long and untiring labor in the cause of education—"In the uplifting of lives as well as instructing the mind."

The reports of the Treasurer and Auditors were received, and after some discussion, it was agreed to have a budget committee for the future and for this next year the quotas were raised 5 per cent. over the present tax. One could not help but notice the readiness with which the members took on the increased assessment, although they are paying 50 per cent more per capita for Yearly Meeting expenses than are we of Philadelphia Yearly Meeting!

Memorials for Uriah Blackburn, Phineas Nichols and Cornelia Janney were read. The matter of Uniform Discipline was approved, as was the proposition to celebrate the Tercentenary of the birth of George Fox, with the hope that such procedure might have a cementing influence throughout the Society. There was a warning extended, however, that there not be too great tendency to celebrate, especially since George Fox was himself opposed to "celebration of days and times." Edward C. Wilson suggested a program be gotten out suitable for small meetings, which was approved.

The report of the "Hallowell" (Friends' Home) was most satisfactory, and the Matron, Mary E. Griest, commended. It was said her method of managing was asked for by the Baptists.

Martha Farquahar and Pauline W. Holme were named as Fraternal delegates to the Worlds' and National W. C. T. U. Convention to convene in Philadelphia.

Under a new regime the officers for next year were named at the last session and Wm. S. Pike, Presiding Clerk; Laura S. Hoge, Recording Clerk, and Isabel C. Roberts, Reading Clerk, were presented, appreciation being voiced of the seven years of service given by Edward C. Wilson, who retires now.

As the Epistle was read to other meetings, one phrase seemed to stand as keynote of the Yearly Meeting: "It is not enough to keep unspotted from the world, but we must keep the world unspotted,

---

After the first installment of the Proceedings had been mailed on First-day night, Tenth month 29th, a great treat was given in the Lecture Room. Chauncey Shortlidge took us to Richmond Conference again! Pictures taken by the way recalled the beautiful scenery; the views at Richmond made us live again the happy days, while his brief comments on the address gave the heart of the messages. With Roy A. Haynes' picture on the screen, he gave a summary of his splendid "Enforcement" address—gave it in a way to impress people with a sense of duty they must not evade. Looking at Dr. Holmes, Arthur C. Jackson, Dr. Janney, Dr. Aydelotte and the rest as they gazed down characteristically, we were filled anew with a realization of what the Conference contained, and what this hour's portrayal might mean to people unable to be there. ARABELLA CARTER.

"Because George Fox lived two and a half centuries ago, we think of him as an old man, while in reality he, and his fellow workers were in their twenties when all England was shaken by their 'Forward Movement.' "—*Canadian Friend.*

The New Message Work: a Spiritual Service

"The withdrawal of the Friends from Germany is a source of deep regret to me. We need them. The state churches are as empty as our hearts, and the longing for a new and intensive contact with the World-Father is, in my opinion, universal.

"We cannot do it alone. We lack the traditions which you have, and which we cannot make up in a moment."

Such words as the above—in this case written from Darmstadt, Germany, when Friends were closing their child-feeding there—express the call which has given rise to the Message Work of the American Friends' Service Committee. In several countries where Friends' service has been carried on, groups of seekers, who had previously found no satisfying religious associations, have turned to Friends for new hope and inspiration.

Such groups need the service of the Society of Friends just as much as famine sufferers, and a concern has arisen that they should not appeal in vain. English Friends began work through the Friends' Council for International Service in pre-war days, and now have centers in many parts of Europe. To further the American concern, the Service Committee last year appointed a sub-committee which is known as "Message Committee"—its interest being the spiritual message resultant from Friends' service.

The work of the Message Committee can in no sense be regarded as sectarian propaganda. It is an attempt, not to proselyte, but to serve; and divides itself into two main phases.

The first consists in visiting those who are interested in the Friends' message, translating and publishing literature explaining Friends' ideals, and co-operating with English Friends in the work of Friends' centers in Europe. Under a concern for such types of service, Agnes L. Tierney, and Alfred and Eleanor Garrett—all of whom are members of the Fourth and Arch Streets, Philadelphia, Yearly Meeting—have just sailed to spend the winter in Europe. They will make their headquarters in Germany, but will also visit a number of other countries. Other Friends will probably follow them at a later date.

The second division of the work is that of building upon the foundations of international good will laid by Friends' service abroad. The Message Committee's activities in this respect include encouraging American teachers who are in sympathy with Friends' ideals to accept positions in Europe; and suggesting that professors who spend their sabbatical year abroad, and also American Friends who are students in foreign universities, locate where they can keep in touch with one of the Friends' centers. Furthering international visits is another aim. Under the latter heading the committee is now making itself responsible for a visit to the United States of Pani (Mrs.) Maria Rachel Jagmin, a Polish lady who has been active among the "Friends of Friends" in her country.

In order to carry on its work, the Message Committee is appealing for contributions to the extent of $5,000, and also for a special fund with which to finance Pani Jagmin's visit.

A Bulletin (No. 53), dealing with the aims of the work, will be sent upon request. The committee would appreciate it if all Friends going abroad would concern themselves to make as many contacts as possible with this work; while those interested in any of the opportunities for service suggested above are requested to correspond with the committee through the office of the American Friends' Service Committee, 20 S. 12th Street, Philadelphia, Pa.

A Chance to Serve

A national campaign is just getting under way to raise funds for the Service Committee's annual budget for European relief work, which has this year been set at a total of $4,350,000. Murray S. Kenworthy, former chief of the unit in Russia, has been speaking almost daily for the last month and will be doing so for two months to come. His engagements stretch all the way from Boston to Chicago; and in each community, committees are being organized to follow up his work with a definite local campaign. Beulah Hurley and Miriam West, who have also just returned from Russia, will likewise undertake speaking tours.

Committees have been organized in several sections in the East and the Middle West. A Boston Committee consists of more than fifty prominent residents under the chairmanship of Dr. Charles W. Eliot, ex-president of Harvard University. The committee in Baltimore includes the Governor of the state, the Mayor of the city, the Archbishop of the Catholic Church, several prominent representatives of other denominations, the presidents of Johns Hopkins University and Goucher College and three prominent physicians. In Chicago, Jane Addams is a moving spirit of the work. A nucleus of Friends in Indiana is just preparing to organize that state for campaign purposes, and has set out to raise $100,000 for the service work. In North and South Dakota, the Governors of the states are appointing committees to collect funds that will be distributed through the Service Committee.

The committee has faith that every Friends' group will do its part in helping to carry out the year's program; for without the active support of Friends

Summary of Minutes

Central Committee

Friends' General Conference

Richmond, Indiana, 8-26 to 9-2, 1922.

At the first meeting of the Central Committee held at Richmond, Indiana, on Eighth month 26, 1922, the membership and proxies of those present were:—

Philadelphia	23
New York	7
Baltimore	8
Genesee	1
Illinois	2
Indiana	6
Ohio	1
Making a total of	48

Eleven had sent excuses.

The business of this meeting was mainly one of routine, reading the reports from the sub-committees (which reports are printed following this) and also from those who had the Conference in charge.

A letter from Ellwood Burdsall, Clerk of New York Yearly Meeting, was read, containing a proposition from the Joint Committee on Affiliated Service of the two New York Yearly Meetings, that in some suitable way the Tercentennial of the birth of George Fox be celebrated by Friends of all branches, and that the Conference be requested to take up the matter.

The subject was referred to a small committee appointed for the service, which, at later sessions of the Central Committee and the Conference, reported that hearty response to the idea had been received and that in the near future a letter, signed by the Chairmen of the Special and the Central Committees would be sent to Friends' Meetings of all branches requesting their co-operation in the celebration. At the suggestion of one of the English Friends, the Meetings of New Zealand, Australia and South Africa will be included.

The Executive Committee presented the following report from the Treasurer:

Balance Sixth month 22, 1921	$2,576.61
Total receipts since last report	12,289.21
	$14,865.82
Total disbursements during the year	13,009.82
	$1,856.00
Reserved for Richmond Conference expense	1,250.00
Balance Eighth month 22, 1922	$606.00

(Signed) HARRY A. HAWKINS,
Treasurer.

After the death of Henry W. Wilbur, at the Saratoga Conference in 1914, some interested friends subscribed to a fund for the benefit of his widow, to be known as the Henry W. Wilbur fund, and this was invested in the name of the Friends' General Conference; the income from said fund was to be paid to Eliza M. Wilbur during her lifetime by the Treasurer of the Friends' General Conference, and after her death the fund, which amounts to $2,700, was to be at the disposal of the Friends' General Conference.

As Eliza M. Wilbur has recently died, the Central Committee now directs its Treasurer to pay to the Treasurer of the Advancement Committee the income of that fund.

At the second meeting of Central Committee, held Eighth month 29th, the report of the Nominating Committee was received in regard to the organization and sub-committees.

The pleasure of the meeting on Eighth month 30th was increased by the presence of T. Edmund Harvey, whose minute to Friends' General Conference was read, after which he gave to us a message of love and good will from the parent Meeting, expressing, too, the conviction that differences between us were disappearing, that fellowship and unity were increasing between the countries, a fellowship that will ultimately break down the barriers which have existed during the past years. His words carried conviction to his hearers, and, also, the blessed hope of a greater unity among Friends here and in the parent country. He was warmly welcomed by the Chairman and other members of the Committee.

The question having arisen as to better and greater possibilities for the work of the Conference, the Executive Committee was requested to appoint a Commission who would study possible methods for the reorganization of the Conference and report at the next meeting of the Central Committee in 1923.

The following is a letter received from the Young Friends' Movement:—

8-30-1922.

"To Central Committee of Friends' General Conference:

Dear Friends:—Our young Friends have long desired a closer co-operation with the older Friends in the business affairs of our Society. At the last two Conferences, particularly, a greater number of young people have shown their willingness and eagerness to participate fully in the work of the various committees. So, in response to the suggestion given by the Chairman in his opening address, the young Friends of this Conference called a meeting on Eighth month 26, 1922, to discuss what means of co-operation they could adopt. This meeting expressed the desire to ask the Central Committee of Friends' General Conference to consider the following plan:—To increase the number of Central Committee to 125, the additional 25 members to be young Friends elected proportionately by the Young Friends' Movement in each of the active Yearly Meetings, and those members to serve for two years. Believing that such a step would be a valuable means of bringing the young Friends into a more active co-operation with the older Friends, we ask, on behalf of the young people of our Meetings that such a step should be taken by the Central Committee of the Friends' General Conference."

(Signed) LINDSLEY H. NOBLE,
E. MORRIS BURDSALL,
ELIZABETH ANN WALTER.

The proposition was unanimously endorsed by this Committee, so the membership of the Central Committee will now number 125, and the Executive Committee will add three of the Young Friends to its number, thus making its members at large six instead of three.

Another concern presented to the Committee was that a more uniform book of Discipline for all the Yearly Meetings might be prepared. Consideration of this important subject is to be referred to a special Committee to be appointed by the Executive Committee.

The following letter was read:

8 mo. 22, 1922.

Friends' Opportunity in the Orient.

To Friends' General Conference:

Dear Friends:—We have found among Friends a growing concern to carry the Friendly message to the people of the Orient, particularly to the people of China and Japan. This interest has been developed greatly by Margaret Hallowell Riggs, a member of Phila. Monthly Meeting, teaching in Canton Christian College, Canton, China, and by Joseph E. Platt, a member of Gwynedd Monthly Meeting, serving as Secretary of the Y. M. C. A. in Moukden, China.

Joseph E. Platt's wife, Edith Stratton Platt, also in the same work, is well known through her connection with the Young Friends' Movement.

The Committee on whose behalf this letter is written, as a result of two appeals made during the years 1921 and 1922, has paid to Canton Christian College $3,000, for the full support of Margaret H. Riggs as teacher for two years, and $800 through John R. Mott, Secretary, as partial support for Joseph and Edith Platt. These young people, having allied themselves with effective interdenominational agencies, it appears to us more practical to support them in this way rather than to undertake a sectarian mission of our own.

As time goes on others among us may feel inclined to enter this field of service. We believe a self-appointed committee should not delegate to itself so great a responsibility; so now we ask the General Conference to take this matter in charge, and thereby afford opportunity of support to Friends who are called to Christian service in foreign lands. We do not propose that the Conference undertake financial responsibility but rather that voluntary contributions may be solicited under the authority of the General Conference, and that permanency may be assured, a wider circle of interest and financial support established.

(Signed) ALFRED W. WRIGHT,
Chairman.

This letter and subject were later brought before a Conference session, and after discussion it was proposed that it be referred to the Committee to be appointed on "Friends' Opportunity in the Orient" to express to religious movements in the Orient, as way may open, the fellowship of our religious body —which was approved.

JOSEPHINE H. TILTON,
Secretary pro tem.

Report of the Committee on Philanthropic Labor—1922

In presenting this report of work accomplished during the past two years the chairman wishes to acknowledge the faithful work of the superintendents of the various departments. The plan adopted four years ago of laying out a suggestive program of work and encouraging the subordinate meetings to make use of as many of the suggestions as fitted their needs has been generally followed. Lists and samples of suitable literature have been distributed by the superintendents from time to time and they have always been ready with encouragement and help when called upon.

After a brief summary of the work of each department a few observations will be presented which grow out of the past years' experience. It is hoped that the Conference will take time to consider them in the light of future activities.

Child Welfare

It is a satisfaction to report the final passage by congress of the Sheppard-Towner Bill and this department has been active in enlisting the support of all meetings for the measure. Some meetings have also worked in their states for the passage of enabling acts to make the national law effective.

While some meetings support their own schools and recreation centres, most meetings find that they can work most effectively by co-operating with local committees of schools, parent-teacher associations, mothers' clubs, day nurseries, etc. One of the notes of particular interest in connection with the maintenance of play grounds in some of our meeting-house yards is the arrangement whereby colored children are given an opportunity to use the facilities provided. Another interesting item reported in connection with school lunches which are encouraged by this department is that in one month when the lunches were discontinued the children lost on an average of a half pound each.

The sewing for relief of distress both at home and abroad has been continued and coal has been given and sold at half price to widows with children. Some Friends are serving as probation officers in an effort to reduce juvenile crime and guide offenders of tender age in better paths. In these hurried days thought for the child is of utmost importance, and no meeting can give too much attention to its welfare.

Equal Rights

The vote having been secured by women, the need of this department has ceased as pointed out two years ago. The chairman was continued for the purpose of representing Friends in the dissolution of the National Women's Suffrage Association. The department will not again report to this conference.

Indian Affairs

At the last session of the Central Committee Philanthropic Section a deep concern was expressed that an investigation of the real condition of the American Indian might be made. Plans were considered whereby Dr. Janney might visit some of the reservations and a special committee was appointed. The work in connection with the Disarmament Conference made this service on Dr. Janney's part impossible, and there has been very little done to report.

Marianna Burgess has been active in working for the abolition of the Bureau system which she feels destroys the Indian's initiative and prevents him from becoming a self-reliant and self-respecting citizen. The use of the drug peyote is also proving very injurious, but no effort is made to stop the sale, which is a profitable trade for a few people. The Society of Friends with their record of former interest in the fair treatment of this ward of the nation should give greater evidence of a desire for information on this subject and endeavor to arouse public sentiment in behalf of our red brother.

Industrial Conditions

The work of this department is still so new to many Friends that the chief effort is in the direction of education. An effort has been made to hold discussions in various meetings calling attention to the fundamental basis of industry and the mal-adjustment which has grown out of a disregard for the fundamental principles. It is the desire of this department to encourage Friends to examine their position and beliefs from a Christian standpoint and develop a leadership in these matters just as our forefathers did in respect to war and slavery. This department has no solution to offer for the unrest and bitterness which seems to be developing in the industrial world. None of the isms of which much has been heard will cure the condition which maintains today. A slow evolution, however, as a result of enlightened leadership may save the world much suffering and chaos.

Peace

The reaction against war which had been expected set in during the past two years, and for the first time since 1916 the militarists were brought to book. The part played by Friends in this movement has been very important. The Friends' Disarmament Council, representing all Friends, carried out an active program of education throughout the country. But more important than the work done as Friends was the work made possible by loaning Frederic J. Libby and making funds available to launch the campaign of the National Council for Limitation of Armament. This movement focused the sentiment of the country on the Washington Conference, and made articulate the voice of many and various organizations which otherwise would never have been heard.

For three months Dr. Janney devoted all of his efforts to the arranging of meetings in the communities represented by this conference and in collecting funds to make possible the work nationally. Some eight thousand dollars was contributed by members of the seven yearly meetings.

A serious effort was made to put the Message of the Society of Friends adopted at the London Conference in every household in all of the Yearly meetings. In this all but one Yearly meeting co-operated, and the work was successfully accomplished. An inter-collegiate peace essay contest with prizes amounting to one hundred and twenty-five dollars was held by Illinois Yearly Meeting. Special attention was paid to the opportunity presented at state and county fairs to interest people in the disarmament movement by Philadelphia Yearly Meeting, and much literature was prepared and distributed on these occasions. Baltimore and New York report the arranging of large mass meetings addressed by prominent speakers and generally much useful work has been accomplished.

William I. Hull reported and interpreted the Washington Conference for Friends and also for the Church Peace Union. His letters were sent to 100,000 pastors in the United States and widely published in newspapers and magazines. Another notable service was rendered by Paul M. Pearson, who as chairman of the National Association of Chautauqua and Lyceum Lecturers and president of the National Association of Lecturers, was able to arrange that every lecturer on whatever subject he was speaking should make a place for a brief statement for the disarmament plans. He also made extended use of the chautauqua and lyceum platform for a more adequate presentation of the case. Millions of people were reached in this fashion.

The work for peace has aroused the Society of Friends to new life and activities, and there is open to us a service of great usefulness in the future if we will listen to the call.

Prison Reform

For many years Friends have been leaders in the movement for prison reform. It is to be hoped that they will continue this leadership. There is a pressing need for intelligent and enlightened leaders in every community who can bring the situation of local penal institutions to the attention of the thinking people. Often our jails are schools of crime, rather than corrective institutions. Where the county prison has been replaced by the state farm marked improvement has been noted in the results secured. The abolition of the county jail, except as a place of temporary confinement, is a reform in which Friends might profitably interest themselves.

Two services which offer opportunity in nearly every community are visiting the prisons with the purpose of improving conditions and attempting to find work for discharged prisoners to prevent them from again falling into the ways of crime due to social ostracism.

Social Morality

A suggestive program for this department has been sent to all meetings, together with a questionnaire to stimulate interest in the problem of social morality and possible avenues of service which are open to meetings. Some communities are interesting themselves in good motion pictures, some in having lectures on sex hygiene given to the boys and girls of the schools, others are working through mothers' clubs, etc. Where possible co-operation has been given the public health departments of the states and much literature has been distributed. It is hoped that with a concrete program before them that the meetings will next year give more serious attention to this important field.

It is with deep regret that we mention the death of the former head of this department, Rachal Knight. We have lost an interested and able worker whose usefulness to the Society, because of her training, was unlimited.

Twenty-two dollars are reported as being used for literature, etc. The Public Health Film, "End of the Road," was shown in two localities, brought through a member, though not especially under the auspices of the Meeting. Two Yearly Meetings are working toward better movies, and one against gambling at fairs, etc. At least one state has laws requiring reports of venereal diseases. One meeting reports policewomen, and that some women usually attend trials of women. One locality has been very active in the past, and obtained much in Juvenile Court work. One boys' First-day School class formed a study class, using "Human Conduct," by Peters. Two Yearly Meetings report members giving lectures, one giving, among others, a course to boys at George School, and the other one engaged by her State W. C. T. U. principally. Lectures reported by these are: 27 to about 900 parents or mothers, 61 to 4,361 girls, 30 to 1,847 boys, beside the George School Course, 15 to 1,245 of general public; 10 others have not specified the approximate audiences, making a total of 148 lectures to over 8,300 people. Over 7,000 pages of literature have been given out, and one Yearly Meeting reports posters and books for loan, and publish "Social Progress," a compilation of valuable information on literature, etc., and carry subscriptions for all the Committee of "Social Hygiene." Approximately 500 pages of public health literature distributed, and several public health venereal clinics in one state. Three community playgrounds reported, and another tells of interest in increasing the number of them. Eleven parent-teacher associations reported. Among especial features reported are good team work for the community, and a Community Chest, which includes service for white and colored. Leaflets and books most used are: "The Making of a Man," "God's Nobleman," "The Nurse and the Knight," "The Angel's Gift," "The Heart of the Rose."

Proper Publications and Amusements

Since the death of Stella Allen there has been no superintendent for this department. With the moving pictures today taking the place, to a large extent, of books in the lives of many children this department is more important that ever. We see today children in their teens putting into practice the moral laxness which they see portrayed on the screen. It is a question whether the suggestions of frivolity which are so largely presented in the desire for sensational pictures have not also had a serious effect in removing moral restraints among adults as well.

Temperance and Anti-Narcotics

When the Eighteenth Amendment and the Volstead Law became effective, it seemed that soon the work of the temperance department would be becoming less urgent. This has not been the case. The attention formerly given to education must now be directed toward law enforcement. The powerful financial interests behind the whiskey and beer business are doing everything in their power to discredit the prohibition act. This and the extensive bootlegging traffic which has developed in defiance of law make the work for temperance as important and arduous as before. Pauline W. Holme, who has long and faithfully served in this work, recommends that the two departments again be separated.

Not only does the law enforcement work present a pressing need, but the onsweep of the tobacco habit calls for the wisest and broadest educational program. The war contact of American and European women and the moving pictures have introduced this destructive habit among the girls and women of our country. The importance of sound education as to the injurious effect of tobacco make it wise to have an interested and able leader for this work alone.

We congratulate the Friends of Genesee on the successful vote in the province of Ontario for prohibition. This adds another large territory to the dry area and will aid in the enforcement of our law.

Much literature has been distributed, some essay contests have been held, and members have co-operated with the W. C. T. U. and other local groups working for enforcement and education.

Work Among Colored People

A letter asking for contributions to the work of Laing and Schofield Schools was sent out. It met with a generous response upon the part of some meetings. The importance of the work of these schools continues to grow and more funds are needed to take advantage of the opportunities which are ours. The Schofield School suffered a serious loss in the destruction by fire of the Wharton Hall dormitory for boys.

Some work in the interest of the colored race is being done in most of our meetings, and many have given their support to the Dier Anti-Lynching Bill now before the Senate. It has already been passed by the House.

Future Activities

The object of a Conference Philanthropic Committee is to serve as a clearing house for ideas developed in the various meetings. It is not right or proper that it should be expected to carry on the work which Yearly and Monthly Meetings should do for themselves. If meetings appoint persons who are not interested or who for any cause do not co-operate with the Conference Committee then the purpose of this committee must fail.

There seems to be less interest in the philanthropic work in many meetings each year. Members will not make the sacrifice necessary to do this type of work. Either the concerns and principles of the past rest more lightly upon our members or there is a refusal to give that free service which has marked the leadership of the Society.

Respectfully submitted,
J. AUGUSTUS CADWALLADER.

Report of Educational Committee

Between the time of the Conference of 1920 and that of this Conference, this committee has been able to hold only one meeting, a state of things which has led some to raise the question whether the committee should not be discharged at this time. At the same time, much has happened of importance and interest in the educational field; a survey of these events may prove the best background against which to discuss the usefulness of an Educational Committee.

A useful survey of all the Friends' Secondary Schools of the Society of Friends (both branches) was compiled, late in 1920, by Elbert Russell, of Woolman School, and published in *The Quaker*. This survey revealed the facts that Friends were unexpectedly weak in numbers upon the teaching forces of our Secondary Schools, and that there was a very general lack of religious instruction of any sort provided for. Those in charge of schools reported that suitably-prepared Friends were nearly impossible to find. While there may have been some improvement in the latter respect in the last two years, it probably remains true that if more young Friends prepared themselves for teaching, places would be found for them. One thing imperatively needed is a directory of Friends now engaged in teaching, both in colleges, secondary and primary schools. If such a directory were kept up to date and issued annually, school boards and principals would know where to look when vacancies occur in their staffs.

The campaign for additional endowment conducted by George School resulted in the subscription of some $165,000. The income from this added endowment is being applied in the form of scholarships to enable the children of Friends to attend the School. This leads to the remark, in passing, that a complete and accurate list of funds now held by Friends' Meetings for educational purposes would be very helpful both to schools and to parents.

Joseph Swain, for nineteen years President of Swarthmore College, laid down the duties of that arduous office in 1921, and was succeeded by Frank Aydelotte, of the Massachusetts Institute of Technology. President Aydelotte already gives evidence of a warm interest in Friends, and of a sincere desire to promote the welfare of the Society through his important office. Two of the Swarthmore faculty, Messrs. Ryan and Walter, are Editors of the important weekly periodical, "School and Society," which has a national circulation and wields a great professional influence. Much might be done to bring the problems of Friends' Schools to the attention of the editors of this journal, and to promote support of the journal among Friends' Schools and teachers.

Ida P. Stabler, for the Educational Committee of Philadelphia Yearly Meeting, reports that she has had good success in aiding and encouraging Friends' teachers to continue their professional training at summer schools and otherwise, bringing to their attention the well-tried principle of Herbert, "Thou that teachest others, teachest thou not thyself?"

The success of the Students' Hostel at State College, Pennsylvania, suggests the idea that similar centers might be opened at other places; their existence would act to encourage young Friends to attend college, although it is true that the activities of these college Friendly centers is a matter which belongs rather to the Advancement Committee.

It is evident that "a good, rousing Educational Committee" could find plenty of useful—nay, vital—work to do: but it is likely that little could be accomplished without some funds. Continuity of effort is what has been lacking. If the Secretary of the Committee were paid so that he or she could stay with the work several days of every week, preparing material for the meetings of the Committee, making surveys, and gathering facts and figures, we should not be so slow in seeing results.

It was the opinion of the committee at its last session, that, in view of the Educational work being done by other agencies throughout the Yearly Meetings represented in this Conference, there is little which could be done profitably by this committee except what might be accomplished by an expert and well-paid Secretary, for whom there is, at present, no fund.

The committee feels, therefore, that it might be laid down.

In order, however, to be ready to continue, should the Central Committee so desire, the committee reorganized by appointing Geo. H. Nutt, Chairman, and Edith Wilson Jackson, Secretary.

GEO. H. NUTT, *Chairman.*

Report of Committee on First-day Schools to Friends' Central Conference—1922

During the past year the Committee on First-day Schools has transacted more than the usual amount of the usual kind of business. The responsibility for issuing a second collection of Hymns, entrusted to us, has been met and a collection of forty-two hymns was made available about December 1st. We have distributed thus far 1,882 copies to 49 First-day Schools and other Friendly organizations.

At the request of the Young Friends' Movement we printed a Study Outline on "The Life and Teachings of Jesus," covering the Woolman School weekend course given by Elbert Russell. It has been quite extensively used. After the close of our fiscal year our first work was the printing of the third Adult Quarterly on "The Idea of God."

Our Executive Committee took up the matter of new material and decided upon two new courses, viz.: first, an adult series on "Christianity and World Democracy," all three quarterlies of which have been prepared and printed; and second, a series for Primary classes on New Testament Stories. This series provides a notebook for each pupil and pictures where they are indicated for use. Two of these quarterlies have been issued, and schools have begun to use them with apparent satisfaction.

We found it necessary to reprint "Life of Jesus No. 1," "New Testament History, series No. 2," and the "Beginners Stories," separate leaflets Nos. 1-20. The total number of separate quarterlies and leaflets issued by our committee during the year was 38,200. We have also continued the publication of the *First-day School Bulletin*, which we believe is increasingly used by First-day School workers.

While we always have some schools which do not find our publications quite what they want, the evidence of our large correspondence is that they are increasingly satisfactory. The steady demand of schools for the material is, of course, the best evidence of its usefulness. We have filled, over a twelve months' period, 590 orders to 100 First-day Schools. These orders run from about 6 to 100 copies.

From letters received, we cite the following comments:

"The Christmas number of the *First-day School Bulletin* has greatly appealed to me as something we might use to advantage."

A request to have a name put on the mailing list for the *First-day School Bulletin* says:

"I am eager to have her receive a copy of the *Bulletin* each time it is published for I find them most helpful and inspiring. I use the suggestions given and the lesson material we use almost entirely. I look forward to its coming and read and study it with great interest."

Another says:

"I wish to express my appreciation of the *First-day School Bulletin*. It always contains something worth while. 'Christianity and World Democracy' we consider one of the biggest set of lessons we have undertaken."

Another says of the new Primary series:

"The class seems interested in the work; and we want more copies of note-books. I believe the lessons will be both interesting and profitable."

During the year we have supplied a large number of sample copies to our own Friends, a few to members of the other branch of Friends, and made up complete files for the Hartford School of Religious Education, and the Department of Religious Education of Teachers' College, New York.

While we do not do this work on account of receiving credit or recognition for it, we believe Friends generally ought to have a better understanding of the amount of labor and planning that it requires to prepare, print and distribute so large a volume of varied materials.

We endeavor to obtain complete reports from the First-day Schools within our Yearly Meetings. We regret that in some localities those in charge do not seem to feel that it is important to make detailed up-to-date reports. For this reason our information concerning certain sections is not as recent as we wish that it was, though full reports have been received from a larger number of schools than usual. All schools have had one or more requests to fill blanks this summer and 7 have still failed to respond. We apparently have 100 organized First-day Schools and, in addition, classes, either for children or adults, which operate some part of the year at Byberry, Camden, Doylestown, Stroudsburg and Woodbury in Philadelphia Yearly Meeting; Purchase and Westbury in New York Yearly Meeting; Lancaster within the limits of Baltimore Yearly Meeting; Pennville and Lincolnville in Indiana Yearly Meeting; Chicago in Illinois Yearly Meeting. Indications are that First-day School interest has been revived in some localities where such work had been suspended. This is true of Byberry, Doe Run, Doylestown, Woodbury, Jericho and Purchase.

The young Friends' study groups are also undertaking work which it is a concern of First-day Schools to promote. While none of them are officially under our care we endeavor to keep in sympathic contact with them and supply material needed as far as we are able.

Interest in the New York Yearly Meeting field has been shown by increased activity during the year. Baltimore has felt the enthusiasm developed by Bliss Forbush and his wife in the city of Baltimore and radiated to some extent into other parts of the Yearly Meeting. Philadelphia Yearly Meeting's Committee has undergone thorough reorganization and appears to be ready for effective work. We note two compilations of Questions prepared by this committee, endorsed by the Conference Committee on First-day Schools. We believe these will be helpful in setting definite standards towards which First-day Schools may aim.

Several First-day School unions have tried the experiment for a portion of the year, of placing regular secretaries in the field, including all the Quarterly Meetings within the limits of Baltimore and Concord, the largest Philadelphia Union. The latter has employed a field secretary for three months' full time. It is too early yet to estimate justly the value of this method of work. It indicates an earnest desire to improve our First-day Schools. We are sometimes very much dissatisfied with our schools as they are. This is wholesome whenever the discontent takes the form of earnestly seeking to improve them. They are better as schools than they used to be, more of our teachers are equipped for their work, regularity of attendance has improved, we are working in more definite way to secure the results of instruction, more money is locally spent to provide materials and equipment, and we are much more critical of the way our schools are conducted and of the partial successes which crown our best endeavors. We need the enthusiastic support of all our members. It is increasingly apparent that leadership and effective followers, under our democratic form of organization, must be supplied through more earnestness in pursuing Religious Education. Woolman School is doing its best, Summer Schools are helping on the cause, week-end conferences contribute their share, but it still remains true that not only our children, but the greater part of the adult membership of the Society of Friends must depend upon our First-day Schools for advancement in Religious Education.

The feeling of our committee is not that we have done our work particularly well, but that we have a realizing sense of this opportunity and this responsibility, and we have tried to put more into it than simply to print and mail Lesson Leaves. Our headquarters at the Central Bureau gives constant and prompt attention to the needs of this committee's work. In accordance with the direction given us by the Conference we have provided for the publication and distribution of "Scattered Seeds," a separate report of which will be presented.

We have striven to administer our appropriation of $2,500 with care and have kept our expenditures within its limits, partly by the advantageous buying of paper, and in very considerable measure through failure to keep pace with the necessary increase of expenses at the Central Bureau upon which we depend for efficiency in our work. We have also been obliged to defer the printing of the last quarterly of one series of lessons until the next fiscal year. In order to make progress, including the development of some needed field work, we estimate that we will need $3,000 for next year, while $2,800 would probably enable us to continue comfortably on the present basis.

On behalf of the committee.

HERBERT P. WORTH,
Chairman.
EDITH M. WINDER,
Secretary, pro tem.

Report of Scattered Seeds for Year 1921 to Friends' General Conference, Held 8-26-'22

The publication of the *Scattered Seeds* has been continued under the direction of the same editors and with the same business management. The financial report for the fiscal year ending Twelfth month 31st, 1921, shows a slightly larger balance than reported a year ago, due to a large reduction in the cost of paper. The other expenses have remained the same. The cost of labor, either in the editorial department or that of business management, does not enter to any extent into the expense of issuing the *Scattered Seeds*. Both ends of the work are done at a nominal rate which bears little relation to the actual market value of the service rendered.

We have advertised the *Scattered Seeds* in *The World Tomorrow*, the *Swarthmore Phoenix*, the *Quaker*, and the *American Friend*, but have had very little tangible result. The number of subscriptions discontinued are, as always, a little greater than the number of new names placed and the management up to this time has found no way of changing this trend. The older generation of Friends were attached to the *Scattered Seeds* and very loyal in its support. The young people who live in a world better supplied with Children's literature are, as a whole, quite indifferent as to whether we have such a paper or not. The editors do their best and the business management has made the kind of effort which it knows how to make without brightening the prospects for the future of the paper. As usual the Committee on Education of Philadelphia Yearly Meeting of Friends donated $500 from the Jeanes Fund toward the support of the paper. We received from the Conference $200 to replace the money from the Jane Johnson Trust Fund carried in the current expense account and have placed the same in a Savings Fund for the protection of the paper in the future. First-day Schools have generally well maintained their subscription lists. The paper needs a wider field of individual subscribers, but we feel we are fortunate in living for the time being, at least, without the financial embarrassment which handicapped the paper for the first fifty years of its existence.

J. B. Hilliard, *Chairman.*

Scattered Seeds Statement
12-31-1920 to 12-31-1921

Balance, 12-31-1920		$963.44
Receipts:		
From Subscriptions	$1,398.83	
Donations—F. D. S. Unions, etc.	122.25	
Committee on Education	500.00	
Advertising	100.00	
		$2,121.08
Interest on deposits		17.76
Total receipts		$3,102.28

Expenditures:		
Business Management*	$229.16	
Printing and mailing	1,252.32	
Paper supply	191.84	
Editorial services	233.39	
Office expenses — postage, etc.	16.90	
Addressograph plates	13.76	
Advertising	4.00	
Total expenses		$1,941.37
Balance, 12-31-1921		$1,160.91

Additional $200 received from Friends' General Conference and deposited in Savings Fund.

I have audited the foregoing account and find it correct.

Dated Second month 8th, 1922.

J. B. Hilliard.

7-15-1922.

J. Bernard Hilliard, Chairman of Scattered Seeds Committee.

Dear Friend:

On account of largely increased expense for housing and clerical service, the Central Bureau Committee feels it necessary to request the *Scattered Seeds* to increase its annual payment for business management from $250 to $300, beginning Eleventh month 1st.

Very truly,
Herbert P. Worth,
Chairman of Central Bureau Committee.

In view of the accompanying letter, and on account of the wisdom of depositing each year a small sum in a sinking fund for *Scattered Seeds*, we feel justified in asking the Conference to make an annual appropriation of $100 to the *Scattered Seeds.* We believe this amount will enable us to meet our expenses and to add a few dollars—fifty, we hope—to a sinking fund already established. This course will be a protection to the Conference against possible bills for deficits which may occur in the future.

*January work paid for in 1920.

none of the work can go forward. Upon request to 20 South 12th Street, Philadelphia, Pa., suggestions will be sent to any community as to definite ways of co-operating in the service. The program outlined for the year is a big one, but the needs in Europe are bigger yet. Biggest of all is the opportunity for service open to the Society of Friends.

First-day School Methods

By Bliss Forbush

Teaching Biblical Geography in the Closing Exercises

If the Superintendent of the School, or some one appointed in his place, would take one First-day of each month to teach Biblical Geography in the closing service it would prove of great interest to the scholars and well worth while.

The teacher must first read such books as "Historical Geography of Bible Lands," by John B. Calkin; "Students' Historical Geography of the Holy Land," by William W. Smith, or the standard work by George Adam Smith, "The Historical Geography of the Holy Land." Then he must divide his subject into lessons to fit the number of periods he is to have. In most schools, if the subject were taken once a month, it would be eight and he might divide the work as follows: 1. Form of the Land, Fertility, Climate. 2. The Coast. 3. Maritime Plain. 4. Judea. 5. Samaria. 6. Galilee. 7. Jordan Valley and Dead Sea. 8. Eastern and Northern Syria.

If the School has a lantern the work can be well illustrated by slides rented for the occasion. But if not, an excellent way to impress the subject on the minds of the scholars is to make a large outline map, six feet by four feet, on heavy brown paper, using ordinary crayons to make the outline. The teacher will pin this map to the wall, drawing upon it only those things to be taken up on a given day.

For instance, the map need show for the first day the outline, the Dead Sea, Jordan Valley, Sea of Galilee, Mt. Taurus, Gaza and Damascus. As the children learn in the day school to first bound a country the teacher does likewise with this subject and shows them the boundaries of Palestine, desert on the south and east, the Great Sea on the west, and Mt. Taurus on the north. The teacher makes the size of Palestine real to all, 400 miles by 70 to 100 miles, by comparing it with the State the school is in or by a neighboring one, such as Maryland or Massachusetts, which are about the same size as the Holy Land. The general lay of the land, plains, mountains, seas, should then be referred to, and next the great variety of climate which enables the Bible to speak of lions getting caught in snow storms, and of prophets standing on cold mountains gazing down into valley towns which are corrupt largely because of their enervating climate.

Two other interesting points to bring out in the first lesson would be the barrenness of the land from March to October due to lack of rain, and the fertility of the land during the rainy spell from October to February. The other is the fact that the oldest road in the world runs through the country from Gaza to Damascus. The teacher, by reference to old trails and roads near their home, and by describing the people upon them, makes much more real the ancient road and those who traveled upon it.

The second lesson on the Coast, of course, explains why the Hebrews were not sailors. It tells of the famous cities of Tyre and Sidon and their part in history. It also tells of how the coastland served as a bridge between Asia and Africa for marching armies through many centuries.

The Maritime Plain contains the richest land of all Palestine and the history of the Israelites long centered there when they were warring with the Philistines for possession of the land. Judea, with its Holy City and its many stirring scenes, would crowd an hour, to say nothing of a fifteen-minute period: Samaria, so familiar to Jesus, and Galilee have interesting stories. The Jordan Valley with John the Baptist, the hermits who lived along its bank, and the marvelous Dead Sea, contains much of rich interest. Eastern Palestine takes the land first won and first lost by the twelve tribes, Damascus; and further north the majestic Lebanons which gave up their treasures for King Solomon's temple.

Each of these lessons would see some new places marked on the map, new stories of interest told, and brief reviews of what had gone before.

If the School has a large set of maps, such as the Kent and Marsden Maps, Charles Scribner's Sons, they could be used in the last lesson or two to tie the locations together better, but the home-made map with its weekly additions would keep the places more clearly in the minds of the students than to use a printed map from the beginning.

JERUSALEM AND ITS ENVIRONMENT

This same method of teaching could be used with the city of Jerusalem itself. A map might be made on the plan of our ordinary city maps, and large enough to be seen from the platform. As with the other, the lessons could be divided among the places of interest, and the teacher locate each place on the map as he tells about it. Eight divisions might be: 1. Mt. Zion, the old city which contained Herod's and Agrippa's palaces, and is now the Armenian Quarter. 2. Acra, the lower, or Christian city, containing the Church of the Holy Sepulchre, and the Pool of Hezekiah. 3. Northeast, the Moslem Quarter, containing the Pool of Bethesda, Via Dolorosa, and St. Stephen's Gate. 4. Mt. Moriah, containing the Temple site and Hill of Orphel. 5. Mt. of Olives with the garden of Gethsemane. 6. Calvary. 7. Pool of Siloam. 8. The Six Roads leading out of Jerusalem.

As different locations are mentioned it would be wise to illustrate them with pictures if possible. Many famous paintings of the life and times of Jesus contain as backgrounds these places, and there are modern photographs of the city as it is today that can be secured. These illustrations, after the talk, might be pinned to the wall beside the map, numbered with a corresponding number on the map, and so bring out clearly the location. The following companies could supply pictures for this course: Perry Picture Co., Malden, Mass.; W. A. Wilde Co., Boston, Mass.; American Tissot Society, 27 East Twenty-second St., New York City, and George P. Brown Co., Beverly, Mass.

QUESTION AND ANSWER BOX

If Teachers and Officers of our First-day School will submit their problems to the Intelligencer we will have them taken up through our column on FIRST-DAY SCHOOL METHODS.—*Editor.*

Friendly News Notes

Robert L. Simkin, missionary to West China, now on furlough, is taking a half-year of post-graduate study at Union Theological Seminary, and would be glad to visit meetings within easy distance of New York as far as he is able. His address until January 20th will be 600 West 122nd Street, New York.

At Abington Quarterly Meeting held at Byberry on Eleventh month 9th, the meeting for worship preceding the business session was full of life. There were a number of speakers, among them being Annie M. Jarrett, Eliza Ambler, Elizabeth Walter, Esther M. Jenkins, Isaac Michener, J. Barnard Walton and Elizabeth H. Ely. Dr. Henry T. Gillett, who presented a minute from his home meeting in England, was warmly welcomed and spoke with force and feeling on our duty to become "fishers of men." He pointed out that we were still largely going on in the light of the God of the Old Testament, a God of force, rather than following the leadings of the God of the New Testament, a God of love and suffering.

The business session was occupied largely with the consideration of some of the Queries, the summary answer of the sixth bringing out some discussion of the question of Prohibition. Friends were urged to be more active in its support, as the enemies of the Volstead Act and the 18th Amendment are working hard to undermine them.

The fourth of the Theatre Meetings held under the auspices of the Philadelphia Young Friends' Association was held Eleventh month 12th in the Broad Street Theatre, Philadelphia. The attendance was larger than at any of the previous meetings, and while the meeting was nearly two hours in length, the speakers held the close attention of their hearers throughout. The meeting was in charge of J. Harold Watson, chairman of the Sectional Committee, and presided over by J. Eugene Baker.

The discussion centered about "Quaker Ideals," Dr. Henry T. Gillett, of England, discussing "Quaker Ideals in Family Life," J. Rowntree Gillett, also of England, "Quaker Ideals in Industrial Life," and Jesse H. Holmes, of Swarthmore, "Quaker Ideals in International Life." As we hope to publish these addresses in full, we will not attempt to summarize them here.

BALTIMORE NEWS

Now that Yearly Meeting is passed all our organizations are beginning their winter's work. The women of the Meeting are gathering each week for the Russian relief sewing, the Women's Gymnasium Class begins its course this week, the boys' clubs are active again, and the Young Friends' program is well under way.

During October, 62 members of First-day School did not miss a day, nor were any teachers absent. The average attendance for the month was 106. A set of Kent and Madsen maps have recently been purchased. Each scholar is planning to bring next week two pencils and a note book to send to the Russian orphans.

Last First-day evening Anna Griscom of the Home Department of the Service Committee gave us a talk on the "Home Work of the A. F. S. C." under the auspices of the Young Friends. Next week Louis Moon, Executive Secretary of Baltimore Yearly Meeting (Orthodox), will address us on "Foreign Mission."

THE NEW YORK FRIENDS' SCHOOLS

Three or four years ago, the reports of the Trustees of the Schools carried on by the New York Monthly Meeting in New York and Brooklyn were rather gloomy. Expenses were mounting, and the deficit was much larger than any members of the Meeting liked to look in the face. Matters have changed, "since the Armistice." The report made at the Monthly Meeting of Tenth month showed both schools crowded to their capacity of nearly six hundred children, and more applicants for admission than can be accepted, with a financial balance of nearly $19,000. Moreover, an addition to the New York school buildings is planned, to be completed for the next school year, which will greatly increase the capacity of the school.

WESTERN QUARTERLY MEETING

"Life and religion are one or neither is anything," was the dominant thought at Western Quarterly Meeting held recently at London Grove Meeting-house. With all the representatives appointed by the seven constituent meetings present except one, absent because of sickness, the meeting was live and interesting from first to last, a number of vital questions claiming attention.

Two English Friends, Dr. Henry Gillett and J. Rowntree Gillett, were present with minutes from their respective meetings of London and Oxford, both of whom were heard in the Meeting for Worship which preceded the business meeting.

Daniel Bachellor, of Washington, was also a visitor, being the first speaker. His text being "Be not conformed to this world, but be ye transformed," he took a pebble and an acorn as samples of elements acted upon by outward influences and the other transformed by power from within. "Noble lives," he said, "do not come in a day nor does the acorn become an oak over night."

J. Rowntree Gillett, following the same thought, declared the transformed condition is evidenced by service. "Prohibition," he said, "seemed an impossible thing, but victory has come because reformers have caught the vision. The triumph of woman-cause is another evidence from which we may now reap advantage, for the call is now to woman to come out not only to enjoy political freedom, but to take her legitimate place in democracy."

Alice P. Sellers urged against allowing fear as a barrier in the way of service. Henry T. Gillett declared the Society of Friends does not need history or the expression of truth so much as the devotion of the spirit. Edith M. Winder, of Swarthmore, felt prohibition did not seem so much a miracle to the teacher in the district school who had taught the children the evils of liquor and prepared their minds for its coming.

Frank M. Bartram, of Kennett, and Elizabeth Mitchell, of Hockessin, Del., served as clerks in the business meeting. Robert Pyle emphasized the need of an international Quaker movement, for on both sides of the Atlantic there is a common vision.

During the consideration of the "queries," Jane P. Rushmore urged that Friends gather promptly at meeting hour, in reverent spirit, setting aside worldly affairs. The efficacy of prayer was dwelt upon by Emma C. Bancroft and Elizabeth F. Newlin, both of Wilmington.

The special question under consideration was "How the Meeting and First-day School can come into closer touch." Edith M. Winder was the first speaker, declaring both had common interests, and instead of the First-day School being a feeder for the Meeting, both were feeders for the world.

J. Rowntree Gillett gave some account of adult school movement in England. ARABELLA CARTER.

OUR MEETINGS FOR WORSHIP

The following is an abstract of the proceedings of a meeting of the Representative Committee of Philadelphia Yearly Meeting, with members of the Meeting for Ministry and Counsel and others, held at Race Street on Tenth month 27th:

The concern before the meeting was presented by Hannah Clothier Hull. She outlined the conditions of indifference toward our Meetings for Worship and other service in the Society, which often prevails, and restated the basic needs of our Meetings and their relation to social service. She also reviewed the considerations of the Special Committee appointed to devise means of arousing our membership to greater activity and efficiency.

Attention was called to making external arrangements connected with Meetings for Worship as favorable as possible—e.g.—Facing seats may be dispensed with in order to bring about a closer feeling of unity, or they may be filled with people of all ages and occupied in rotation by different groups. The length of the Meeting should be determined by its apparent profit to those assembled.

A portion of the work of the members of Ministry and Counsel is to help make a right spirit felt in the Meeting. The cultivation of a spirit of fellowship among the members either through personal visits or letters, may be important service for this group.

Ministry was defined as a simple giving of self or sharing with others. Those who come to Meeting with a real desire to help and with the spirit of earnestness and prayer upon them, will both help and be helped by the Meeting.

The silence of our Meetings should be active, not passive, occupied with earnest search for a better understanding of God's relation to us.

Expression was given to the fact that many young Friends are apparently not interested to attend Meeting. A young Friend thought young people felt a subtle barrier between themselves and the older people when gathered for worship and mentioned the distaste which youth has for being allied with discouraging or unsuccessful organizations. She believed separate Meetings for Worship for the young might help. This thought was not generally concurred in by the Meetings, though sympathy was expressed with the difficulty of making a religious Meeting thoroughly homogeneous and democratic.

Our attention was called to the primal aim of all Church organization, viz., to establish the kingdom of God on Earth. Service to man is the practical outcome of becoming filled with God's spirit. The Meeting is a place of vision and a means of gaining power. Our work among men makes us feel the need of God, and our communion with God makes us better able to do our work among men.

A plea was made for care in having children share in our Meetings for Worship. An English experiment was noted of having the children remain half an hour and then quietly withdraw, while the adults settled into a longer period of devotional search.

Especial emphasis was placed on the desirability of breaking down the formality and hardness of our Meetings which often interferes with the feeling of unity, warmth, and fellowship which should characterize our religious groups.

We were enjoined to each assume fully our responsibilities, and with determined purpose, try to make our Meetings personally and socially helpful.

Recent Publications

"A SHORT HISTORY OF QUAKERISM," by Elizabeth B. Emmott, with introduction by Rufus M. Jones. Illustrated. George Allen and Unwin Ltd., London.

This book is based upon the Rowntree Series of Quaker History by Rufus M. Jones and William C. Braithwaite, and is an attempt to bring within smaller compass, for the use of busy people, the store of interesting material and the spiritual message of those wonderful volumes.

"PATHWAYS TO GOD," by Alexander C. Purdy. The Woman's Press, New York.

The book is written simply, so simply a child may understand it, and makes a direct appeal to the young student who vexes himself and his elders with doubts they cannot dispel and questions they cannot answer to his satisfaction. Alexander Purdy has practically been all his life in close contact with student life and knows the student's problems and longings as they are known by few. He would take this eager, restless and somewhat skeptical youth of today by the hand and lead him back to the Bible. In no simpler or surer way will he find an answer to his questions; in no other way will he find God.

"THE BOY JESUS AND HIS COMPANIONS," by Rufus M. Jones. MacMillan Company, New York. $1.25.

These stories will be read with interest by children and parents alike. They will be especially useful for parents and teachers to read aloud. The book pictures the childhood and early life of the great figures of the Gospel narratives. The birth and early life of the central character awaken our interest at the very start, and that interest keeps on growing to the last great scene on the shore of Gennesaret. The book is illustrated; and Rufus Jones uses the scenery and circumstances of actual history and geography, and makes us feel these people, around whom the mists of tradition have gathered, more vividly than ever. It would be a suitable gift for either boys or girls of from 8 to 10 years, or can be read to children of from 6 to 8.

"SPIRITUAL ENERGIES IN DAILY LIFE," by Rufus M. Jones. MacMillan Company, New York. $1.50.

This is a companion volume to "The Inner Life" and "The World Within" with both of which many of our readers are familiar. In his introduction, Rufus Jones says, "In saying that religion is energy I am only seizing one aspect of this great experience of the human heart. It is, however, I believe, an essential aspect. A religion that makes no difference to a person's life, a religion that *does* nothing, a religion that is utterly devoid of power, may for all practical purposes be treated as though it did not exist. . . . . Faith has come to be recognized as an energy in many spheres of life. We know what a stabilizer it is in the sphere of finance. Stocks and bonds and banks shift their values as faith in them rises or falls. *Morale* is only another name for faith. Our human relationships, our social structures, our enjoyment of one another, our satisfaction in books and in lectures rest upon faith and when that energy fails, collapses of the most serious sort follow. We might as well try to build a world without cohesion as to maintain society without the energy of faith."

Items from Everywhere

Churches throughout the country will observe the last Sunday in November as Bible Sunday.

A statement sent out by the Pennsylvania Anti-Saloon League immediately after the recent elections stated that "Wayne B. Wheeler reports that the next Senate will be the driest in the history of the country and the House of Representatives at Washington will be practically the same as it is at present."

A campaign text-book entitled "War on War," prepared by Frederick J. Libby, is now ready for use by study groups, peace committees, First-day School classes, and all workers for peace. It consists of four chapters: I. We Must End War or Perish. II. We Can End War Now If We Will. III. How Can We End War? IV. Answers to Skeptics Sixty-four pages, 10 cents a copy. Twelve copies for one dollar. Order through the National Council for Reduction of Armaments, 532 Seventeenth St., N. W., Washington, D. C.

The New York State Council of Churches became a reality on September 21, 1922, at Utica, N. Y., and will become a working reality by June, 1923, if the hopes of the Utica Meeting of delegates are realized. Forty representatives of eight denominations spent the forenoon reporting on the attitude of their respective constituencies and hearing what the Ohio Federation and the Massachusetts Federation were doing, from their respective Secretaries. There was no opposition to the organization of the Council, the necessity for such a work being scarcely a debatable question in the minds of those present. The action called for the raising of a budget of $10,000 per year, which will be only 1¼c per member of the interested constituencies.

The total membership of the twelve leading denominations of New York State in 1916 was 1,317,154.

The Philippine Independence Mission, which recently left for Manila, issued a statement through Mr. de Veyra, the Philippine Commissioner, reiterating the desire of the people for self-rule, which declares that:

"All the expenses of the Philippine Government are borne by the Filipino people. . . . With the exception of the offices of Governor-General, Vice-Governor, and insular Auditor, all of the important executive and administrative offices in the islands are in the hands of native Filipinos. All members of both branches of the legislature are Filipinos, as well as all provincial and municipal officials. There has been established in the Philippines a stable government of, by, and for the Filipinos, the condition precedent to the granting of their independence. The time for America to fulfill its pledge has already come. . . ."

THE OPEN FORUM

This column is intended to afford free expression of opinion by readers on questions of interest. The INTELLIGENCER *is not responsible for any such opinions. Letters must be brief, and the editor reserves the right to omit parts if necessary to save space.*

FACING THE FACTS

To the Editor:

It is a well-known fact that we can get figures to prove nearly any proposition, so it is perhaps not surprising two of our conference speakers hold such different views on possible over-population. Dr. Holmes' address was so splendidly stimulating that I have wished ever since that he had not partly spoiled it for me by his statement, "Right here in the United States we could give two acres of land to every family in the world." That sounds fine and liberal, perhaps, to anyone who has not had first-hand knowledge of the sad struggles of the "dry farmers" of North Dakota and Colorado. This land is classed as arable, but to expect any family to exist on two acres of it is surely offering a stone instead of bread, and the same is probably true of much of the western farm land. There are very impressive statistics to prove that population depends finally not so much on soil as on water supply, and in the west this seems self-evident.

With this viewpoint, I welcome Russell Smith's address, printed in the INTELLIGENCER of Tenth month 21st, as a distinctly worth-while contribution to our thought. All his suggestions are good, but it seems to me that it is especially important that we read the facts and face the issue squarely and that we advocate a benevolent segregation and isolation of the feeble-minded that their race may die out; that we try to increase the birth-rate in the A, B and C groups and that we use our influence against the unjust laws under which Margaret Sanger has been persecuted. In this connection, I want to add a thought from an article in the *Century* last year on "The Decalogue of Science." To follow the Golden Rule as we should, we must include as our neighbors all the unborn generations of children and so order the world that their biological inheritance may qualify them for abundant life.

Yellow Springs, Ohio. LUCY G. MORGAN.

FREE SPEECH.

To the Editor:

I have been an interested reader of the "Open Forum" in your paper, and without wishing to write on the real merits of the case would suggest that people who hold such extreme views on freedom of speech as have been expressed by certain writers to the Open Forum should migrate to some ocean island a thousand miles from any other human being, and then they can talk, act and write as they please.

It is an indisputable fact that as population becomes dense each individual's freedom to do as he pleases is limited somewhat, and the denser the population the less individual liberty one enjoys. This principle obtains in regard to the right of so-called freedom of speech as to any other right. It, freedom of speech, is, if used on any and all occasions, indiscriminately, as likely to cause trouble as other violations of law and if we expect to preserve our traditions and principles, we must protect ourselves against lawlessness of speech as well as any other thing.

Bloomington, Ill. G. E. COALE.

BIRTHS

HAINES—On Tenth month 29th, at Chester, Ohio, to Corwin and Jane Eva Underwood Haines, a daughter, who is named Marcia Jane.

MARRIAGES

DURNALL-FEW—At West Chester, Pa., by Friends' ceremony, Anna L., daughter of Mrs. Benjamin Few, of West Chester, Pa., and J. Dilwyn Durnall, of Swarthmore, Pa.

DEATHS

DUTTON—On Tenth month 26th, John F., husband of Lauretta Smedley Dutton, in the 50th year of his age, son-in-law of Lewis V. Smedley, and son of James B. Dutton, formerly of Waterford, Va. Interment at Willistown Friends' Burying Ground.

HARVEY—At the home of her sister, Lavinia C. Hoopes, at West Chester, Pa., on Eleventh month 2nd, Ada B., widow of Charles T. Harvey, of Philadelphia. Daughter of George D. and Susan W. Cock, she spent a happy girlhood in Baltimore and in Yardley, Pa. Of a retiring nature, her character was marked by honesty, sincerity and an exceptional devotion to her own family. Keen in her sympathies, little children were to her an especial delight. A son, Herman Harvey, survives her, in addition to two sisters and a brother.

TOWNSEND—On Eleventh month 6th, at her residence in Baltimore, Md., Martha S., in the 85th year of her age, for many years a beloved minister in the Society of Friends.

VERLENDEN—At Darby, Pa., on Tenth month 22nd, Jean Parker, wife of Jacob Serrill Verlenden.

WYNNE—In Philadelphia, Pa., on Eleventh month 11th, Thomas Wynne, aged 73 years.

COMING EVENTS

ELEVENTH MONTH

17th and 18th—Thirty-fourth Annual Fair of the Young Friends' Aid Association and the Friendly Hand, from 3 to 10 p. m., in the Gymnasium of Friends' Seminary. There will be the usual articles for sale, a Russian Tea-room, and a "straight dinner" served. Entertainments will give variety, and an unusual number of side-shows. One of these will be Professor Morse's first working model of the telegraph.

18th to 20th—Fairfax Quarterly Meeting, at Waterford, Va. Isaac Wilson expects to attend.

18th to 20th—Centre Quarterly Meeting, at Grampian, Pa. O. Edward Janney expects to attend.

19th—Conference Class at Fifteenth and Race Streets, Philadelphia, at close of meeting for worship, 11.40 a. m. Subject—The Prophets of the Social Order. Leader—Charles Paxson, of Swarthmore, Pa.

19th—A meeting for worship at Greenwich, N. J., to be held at 2.30 p. m., has been arranged by the Committee of Salem Quarterly Meeting.

19th—Philadelphia Quarterly Meeting's Visiting Committee expects to attend meeting for worship at Valley, at 10.30 a. m.

19th—Chester (Pa.) Monthly Meeting at Providence, at 2.30 p. m.

21st—Burlington Quarterly Meeting, at Trenton, N. J. Meeting-house, corner of Montgomery and Hanover Streets. General invitation to all to attend. Dinner served at Meeting-house.

21st—Germantown Friends' Association, 8 p. m. An illustrated talk on the Passion Play by Rev. William B. Lower.

25th to 27th—Warrington Quarterly Meeting, at Menallen, Pa. O. Edward Janney expects to attend.

26th—Certain members of Philadelphia Quarterly Meeting's Visiting Committee expect to attend meeting for worship at Schuylkill, at 10.30 a. m.

NOTICE—An illustrated talk on The Passion Play, by Rev. William B. Lower, will be given under the auspices of the Germantown Friends' Association, School House Lane, Germantown, on Thursday evening, November 21st, at 8 o'clock. A cordial welcome to all.

NOTICE—J. Chauncey Shortlidge, principal of Maplewood School for Boys, will give his illustrated address on the Richmond Conference at the Birmingham Meeting-house on First-day afternoon Tenth month 26th.

NOTICE—Anyone knowing Friends living in Detroit, Michigan, is requested to send names and addresses to L. Oscar Moon, 2574 2nd Blvd., so that an effort may be made to connect them with our Meeting.

NOTICE—A Fair, Supper and Entertainment will be given by the Young Friends' Movement of Abington Quarterly Meeting, at the Abington Friends' School, Jenkintown, Pa., on Saturday, November 18th. Supper at 5.30. Tickets, 75 cents. Proceeds for the Neighborhood Guild, the Norristown Friends' Home, and the American Friends' Service Committee. Any donations will be appreciated, and the support of all Friends interested in these causes is solicited.

American Friends' Service Committee

WILBUR K. THOMAS, EX. SEC.
20 S. 12th St. Philadelphia.

CASH CONTRIBUTIONS

WEEK ENDING NOVEMBER 6TH.

Five Years Meetings	$115.20
Philadelphia Yearly Meeting (Orthodox)	3,867.00
Other Meetings:	
Ladies' League of First Friends' Church, Cleveland	10.00
Westtown Monthly Meeting	5.00
Chester Monthly Meeting	150.00
Friends of Lincoln, Virginia	75.00
High Street Friends' Meeting, West Chester, Pa.	15.00
Orange Grove Friends' Sewing Society	5.00
Westerly Meeting	30.00
Concord Friends	25.00
Mansfield Meeting and Columbus Community	112.25
Baltimore Yearly Meeting	507.50
Menallen Meeting	10.00
Fairfax Meeting	10.00
Centre Meeting	13.00
Little Britain	95.00
New York Meeting	185.00
Cambridge Group of Friends	50.00
Contributions for Germany	13.00
For Austria	442.50
For Poland	35.40
For Russia	3,371.04
Russian Overhead	727.00
German Overhead	71.27
For General	60.00
For Clothing	229.95
Refunds	143.25
	$10,373.36

Shipments received during week ending November 4th: 90 boxes and packages received; 1 from Mennonites, 2 for German relief, 6 anonymous.

Buck Hill Falls Company

The annual meeting of the stockholders of the Buck Hill Falls Company will be held in the auditorium of the Philadelphia Young Friends' Association, 140 N. 15th Street, on Fourth-day afternoon, Twelfth month 6th, 1922, at 2 o'clock.

MORGAN BUNTING, *Clerk.*

FUN

A man, all out of breath, recently rushed into a general store and said to the clerk: "A nickel mouse-trap, please, and let me have it quickly. I want to catch a train."—*Continent.*

"I asked you to send me young lettuce." "Yes, ma'am. Wasn't it young you got?" "Young? It's almost old enough to wash and dress itself."—*Boston Transcript.*

"Shall I go over the top?" asked the talkative barber, poising his shears.

"Yes, as soon as your gas-attack is over," answered the weary customer. —*The Traveler's Beacon.*

WANTED

WANTED—GOOD HOME OR BOARDING place with cheerful surroundings for middle-aged lady, mentally somewhat deficient. State probable terms. Address P. 390, Friends' Intelligencer.

"RIVERCROFT," CLAYMONT, DEL. Special home care for invalids, or rest and physical upbuilding. Reference on application. E. H. Speakman, R. N.

WANTED—POSITION, MIDDLE-AGED practical nurse, experienced housekeeper and companion. Willing to go South. Reference. Address T. 431, Friends' Intelligencer.

POSITION WANTED—BY REFINED middle-aged woman as companion and nurse to semi-invalid or elderly woman. Address W. 430, Friends' Intelligencer.

REFINED PRACTICAL NURSE would like position as companion. Address M. 440, Friends' Intelligencer.

NURSE GOING TO CALIFORNIA would accompany children or an invalid for fare one way. Phone Wyoming 8646-W.

SALARIED STENOGRAPHER, NIGHTS free, can report occasional daylight meetings. George B. Cock, Bell (Philadelphia) phone directory.

WANTED—FOR A FEW WEEKS OR longer, a settled woman for chamberwork and waiting, in a suburb of Philadelphia. Small family, no washing, good wages. Address P. O. Box 1632, Philadelphia, Pa.

Fine Newtown Property

at Private Sale

The residence of the late Thaddeus S. Kenderdine, corner State and Sterling Streets, near George School.

Large brick house, with all conveniences; frame barn; surrounded by large shade trees. One of the best properties in town. Sold to settle the Estate.

Robert Kenderdine, Louis R. Kenderdine } Executors

Christmas Cards—Hand Colored

Three for 25 cents

Bertha Sellers, Y. F. A., Phila., Pa.

REGULAR MEETINGS

OAKLAND, CALIF. — A FRIENDS' Meeting is held every First-day at 11 A. M., in the Extension Room, Y. W. C. A. Building, Webster Street, above 14th. Visiting Friends always welcome.

PASADENA, CALIFORNIA — Orange Grove Monthly Meeting of Friends, 520 East Orange Grove Avenue. Meeting for worship, First-day, 11 A. M. Monthly Meeting, the second First-day of each month, at 1.45 P. M. First-day School (except Monthly Meeting days) 9.45 A. M.

FUN

Henry Ford is still talking about his currency scheme. What we want, Mr. Ford, is a dollar which resembles your well-known flivver in that it will go a long way, but won't go very fast.—*Charleston News and Courier.*

Strawbridge & Clothier

Overcoats That Appeal to Lively, Manly Boys

Such Overcoats as these please the youngsters because of the mannish tailoring, sensible colorings and smart styles and please parents because of the economical prices.

Little Boys' Overcoats

—Attractive little models, of warm chinchilla cloth and mixed cheviots. Sizes 3 to 10 years—$10.75.

—All-wool-lined Overcoats of chinchilla cloth, mixed tweeds and herringbones. Sizes 3 to 10 years—$13.75.

—Exceptionally fine Overcoats, handsomely tailored, of thick, all-wool chinchilla cloth in all wanted shades. Sizes 3 to 10 years—$15.

Overcoats for Older Boys

—Full-lined all-wool Overcoats, in sizes 9 to 18 years—$15.00.

—Excellent assortment of sturdy, all-wool Overcoats in a wide range of colors and styles. Sizes 9 to 18 years—20.00.

—Fine plaid-back Ovrecoats in the choicest colorings and fabrics. Sizes 9 to 18 years—$25.00.

Strawbridge & Clothier—Second Floor, Filbert Street, East

FINE HEMSTITCHED LINEN DAMASK DINNER CLOTHS, $5.00

Unusual value indeed are these beautiful Cloths in sizes for 48-inch or 54-inch round or square tables. Designs are handsome and each Cloth is finished with a two-inch spokestitched hem. Women who know Linens will be eager to secure these at such a price advantage—$5.00.

Sets of Cloth and Six 20-inch Napkins to Match, Boxed—$10.00

Strawbridge & Clothier—Aisle 11, Centre

STRAWBRIDGE & CLOTHIER

MARKET STREET EIGHTH STREET FILBERT STREET

PHILADELPHIA, PA.

To the Lot Holders and others interested in Fairhill Burial Ground:

GREEN STREET Monthly Meeting has funds available for the encouragement of the practice of cremating the dead to be interred in Fairhill Burial Ground. We wish to bring this fact as prominently as possible to those who may be interested. We are prepared to undertake the expense of cremation in case any lot holder desires us to do so.

Those interested should communicate with William H. Gaskill, Treasurer of the Committee of Interments, Green Street Monthly Meeting, or any of the following members of the Committee.

William H. Gaskill, 3201 Arch St.
Samuel N. Longstreth, 1218 Chestnut St.
Charles F. Jenkins, 232 South Seventh St.
Stuart S. Graves, 3035 Germantown Ave.

FOR SALE

$12,000 CASH WILL PURCHASE acre and half of ground (250 feet frontage, paved, curbed and macadamized) in desirable suburb 13 miles (half-hour) from City Hall. $500 will fully redecorate house. $5,000 will re-decorate and change into five apartments with total of 28 rooms. House alone, with 15-inch walls, and splendid steam-heater in high semi-basement (in which there is room for apartment for janitor) could not be duplicated for less than $20,000. Near good public school, one of the best Friends' Select Schools in the country and half-mile from Meeting-house. Enough frontage can be sold to more than reimburse for changing to apartments. ONLY CASH WILL BUY AT ABOVE FIGURES. Please do not reply unless fully in earnest. X. Y. Z., Friends' Intelligencer.

The Friends' Intelligencer

ESTABLISHED 1844 | ELEVENTH MONTH 25, 1922 | VOLUME 79 NUMBER 47

Contents

EDITORIALS

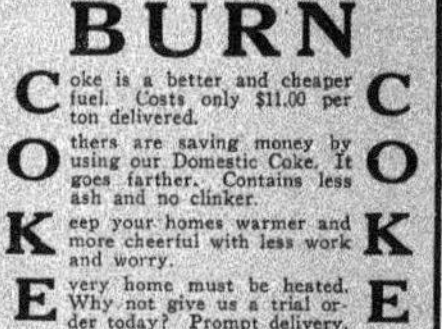

THE FRIENDS' INTELLIGENCER

Published weekly, 140 N. 15th Street, Philadelphia, Pa., by Friends' Intelligencer Association, Ltd.

SUE C. YERKES, *Managing Editor.*

Subscription rates: United States, Mexico, Cuba and Panama, $2.50 per year. Canada and other foreign countries, $3.00 per year. Checks should be made payable to Friends' Intelligencer Association, Ltd.

Entered as Second Class Matter at Philadelphia Post Office

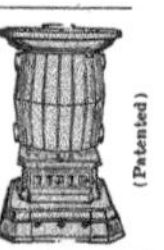

The Friends' Intelligencer

The religion of Friends is based on faith in the "INWARD LIGHT," or direct revelation of God's spirit and will in every eking soul.
The INTELLIGENCER is interested in all who bear the name of Friends in every part of the world, and aims to promote love, ity and intercourse among all branches and with all religious societies.

STABLISHED 1844 | PHILADELPHIA, ELEVENTH MONTH 25, 1922 | VOLUME 79 NUMBER 47

Thanksgiving Day

It is quite necessary, if we are true to the principles e profess, for us to consider very soberly our :lebrations of these "days set apart." The early uakers cried out against special times feeling that ıch day should be "lived unto the Lord." We have ıme, however, to observe more or less actively, the ırious holidays which come. Are we in danger of sing our sense of a really vital point in the matter? his is not an argument that we should pass by ınoticed all appointed seasons but it is an appeal ıat we should on these days take an account of ock, as it were, earnestly and individually and try ı make sure that our observances are of the right ırt.

I am reminded just here of the old Scotch woman ho, lame with rheumatism, was no longer able to ork and saw ahead of her the poor-house and the ss of her loved little thatched cottage-house with ; dooryard and flowers. However, through the :neficence of a kindly gentleman, a small stipend as given to her each month and she was enabled to ıntinue living in her home. But to express her ankfulness she would every now and then put on :r best and, taking her cane, go to walk up and ıwn in front of the Poor House and show the mates that she was not like them—exclaiming as e hobbled back and forth, "An awfu' thankfu' art, an awfu' thankfu' heart!"

What was it Jesus said about the man who gave anks that he was not as other men were?

Rather let us pray with George Herbert:

Thou that hast given so much to me,
Give one thing more, a grateful heart.

* * * *

Not thankful, when it pleaseth me;
As if thy blessings had spare days,
But such a heart, whose pulse may be
Thy praise.

A. H. P.

Thanksgiving—1922

As Thanksgiving comes again, America has infinitely much to be thankful for—and much likewise for which thanks cannot be rendered.

We should be thankful that our country today is not facing a famine such as confronts millions of Russian peasants this winter, or the combined devastation and destitution against which hundreds of thousands of Polish refugees are struggling, or the national poverty which is bringing suffering to all classes in Germany and Austria. But we should not be thankful that in our country in the State of Pennsylvania industrial feuds have led to the eviction of countless families of miners from the only homes that are available to them, and that they are being forced to face the approaching winter in tents and rough board barracks. We should not be thankful that of the 550 little American citizens, between the ages of 8 and 14 years, who were recently examined by a Friends' worker in five of these camps, 86% were found to be undernourished.

We should be thankful that our country is not at present plunged into the fiery furnace of destructive and self-destructive war. But we should not be thankful that our government is spending $630,000,000 this year on its military and navy appropriations—$630,000,000 which will help stimulate militarism abroad and make other nations our potential enemies rather than our friends. We should not be thankful that America has thus far denied official recognition to the Permanent Court of International Justice at the Hague, an institution in keeping with the highest American ideals, and one which stands as a step toward the settlement of international disputes by justice rather than by force.

We should be thankful for the million dollars worth of relief which generous hearted individuals in our country, often at a sacrifice to themselves, have sent to help their less fortunate brothers in stricken Europe. But we should not be thankful, that, as a nation, we have followed the policy of "splendid isolation," instead of offering wholeheartedly to give Europe the help by means of which she can alone recover; and which, given in a spirit of true good-will, might do more than anything else to heal her hatred as well as to reconstruct her material life.

We should be thankful that freedom of speech and press is one of America's traditions. But we should not be thankful that there are still in Leavenworth prison today, 64 men whose only offense was an expression of opinion against the course which our government took in entering and carrying on the war. We should not be thankful for the ordeal of confinement which these men are undergoing without just cause, nor for the sufferings which many of their families are experiencing during their imprisonment.

But among the things for which we should, or should not, be thankful this Thanksgiving Day, there is one which rises above all others, and which swings the balance emphatically on the side of thankfulness. It is the fact that, above the strains and stresses of our individual and social lives, there is a spirit which can give us "life more abundantly"—a spirit which will lead us to disband armies and which in return will give us real peace, a spirit which can find food and clothing for the miners' children of Pennsylvania and for all other hungry and destitute human souls, a spirit which will free the prisoners from Leavenworth and make prisons themselves unnecessary.

May Thanksgiving Day this year be a day of consecration on which we lay aside the little interests of self, and dedicate ourselves to this spirit of hope and faith and love. Under its guidance, we can so recreate the life of humanity's great family that at some future Thanksgiving we shall have only thanks to give.

W. H. A.

Thanksgiving

By Frances B. Damon

A woman came down from her chamber and stood with her hand on the hall door. "It is hard to be thankful," she thought, "for thanksgiving days that were good and have gone." She flung the door open to the sweet November morning. The village in the valley was softly wrapt in mist, over which stretched a high, glowing sky flecked with purple and rose. She smiled, thinking that here at least was something to be thankful for—that she had eyes to see and a heart of love for what she saw. But before the words were formed in her mind she recalled dear, dim eyes that grew unable to see the beauty of life. The woman felt the iron in her soul, and she turned quickly away and plunged into the work of the day. She knew that to give thanks because one escapes for a brief season the losses and mishaps that have overwhelmed and are still overwhelming others is but an act of ungrateful selfishness or gross heedlessness. "O my Father," she murmured, "I can thank thee today only for this—that some day we shall all thank thee together."

* * * *

Before night the glory had vanished from the sky and a wild, dark storm had broken loose. The woman sat alone and thought——

Gross and vain
Soundeth all song if thou hast heard the rain.

Oh, might there be
My own tonight under this roof with me,
Under this rain-wet roof with me!
(His keeping grace
Is sure but I would see my loved ones face to face.)

All are at home:
Some by the ingle-side,
Some on the stormy tide,
Some in the mad, hot races,
Some in the heavenly places,
But all, all at home;
All in the Father's hand
Who knoweth each by name,
Mindeth the poor and lame,
Letteth nor great nor small
Out of his hand-grasp fall,
With his own mantle covereth all:—

Forgiveth, so I trust,
The cry (knowing our frame, remembering we are dust),
"Oh, might there be
My own tonight under this roof with me,
Under this rain-wet roof with me!"

* * * *

Later, she lay in the darkness and reasoned with herself: You know thanksgiving is after all only "sharing the joy of the Creator" over what has been brought up out of chaos and disorder. It's only being glad of what is good, along with him, and so inevitably, one would think, increasing the amount of satisfaction and well-being in you—in the whole world! How can loveliness of spirit and health of body, and prosperity, and harmony on earth b brought about—be increased—if we do not recogniz and heartily rejoice in what has already been attained? How else shall we build on it and make i grow? Why not share the joy of the Giver of ever good and every perfect gift? Why not be full o thanksgiving?

Simplicity and Moderation

One reason for favoring simplicity is that simple things are usually more beautiful. Artists and people who have seriously studied beauty say that where there are ostentation and display there is no beauty. To that extent there is a moral relation in esthetics. But a Friend whose "simplicity" is merely an expression of good taste misses the real meaning in the query.

A simple life is one that has a main central purpose. Such a purpose with a Friend is supposed to be the following of God's will as revealed in the heart, and trying to bring the Kingdom of God on earth. With such a dominant purpose, one has not time or money for a multiplicity of things. One with such a purpose will arrange his life so as to have time to think, time for devotion, time to study conditions on this earth and find out how the Father's Kingdom may be brought here. John Woolman, for instance, did not choose the occupation that would bring him most money, but one that would leave him time to devote to the ministry and God's work. A person with such a dominant purpose will not have many or expensive clothes, for he will save all he can to send to those who are suffering for lack of clothes, in the Near East, Austria, and even in our own country. It will be the same with food and furnishings, amusements and luxuries generally; we cannot be lavish or careless in spending money while others are in dire need of it.

It seems to be impossible to set a definite standard for simplicity. We cannot say that so many things and no more are required by the simple life. But there is a theoretical standard which is worth considering, though it is one that cannot be computed. All the people in the world need food, clothing, shelter, etc.; some of these people are not able to work because they are infants, or are ill, or feeble with age. Therefore, on the average, each able-bodied adult should work enough to supply his own needs and more, for he must help support the dependents. In modern times, of course, people all over the world are working to supply our needs; the average person should try to see to it that the sum of the hours and minutes these scattered workers work for him in a year is less than the time he spends in productive work for society. You may say that time spent is not a good unit of comparison, because some kinds of work are more valuable than others. But it is hard to measure values; and it is a question whether a man deserves to be paid more for unusual native ability, which is God-given. Moreover, the statement referred to average people. If a man considers his own work of unusual value, let him consider how much more valuable it is than supplying his own physical and intellectual needs and desires; if he concludes the work done for him is not very important, then he probably will be content with only the average amount of things to consume, and will rejoice that he is a benefactor to mankind, one who gives more than he receives. A person who performs service of ordinary value to society, but has, for instance, two servants at his personal disposal is certainly taking from society more than he gives; in fact, that would be the case if he had one servant for himself, because there are besides hosts of people in factories, stores, mines, freight cars, in orchards and dairies, lumber camps, etc., who devote some minutes to his needs, to say nothing of the painters, sculptors, authors, singers, actors, lecturers who minister to his enjoyment.

As has been said, the standard here indicated cannot be measured with any accuracy in these days of complicated industry. But to consider it may help us to realize our proper position in the society of the world. A person with a real concern for simplicity would naturally consume for his personal use less than such an average consumption.

MARY McDOWELL.

The Call from Poland

The following quotation from a recent report of one of the Friends' workers in Holoby, Poland, shows why those who know the extent of the needs in that country are concerned to have the Mission continue work there during the coming winter. The worker writes:

"The industries have shown decidedly during the last two weeks that, after a short time of rather better conditions during the harvesting, the people are beginning to dread the winter.

"One widow in Zajaczowska asked me to 'Please write this week and thank the people who send the money to keep the industries going.' Another tried very hard to persuade me to keep her money towards a horse. I explained that this was impossible, as I could not in any way promise any horses, and suggested that she should put the money on one side herself. 'But,' she said, 'When one is hungry, one just has to buy food for the children if the money is in the house.'

"This woman's final sentence is indicative of the conditions of thousands of Polish peasants. They need food, they need implements for clearing their devastated land, they need horses with which to plow, many of them need even homes to shelter them. The slender means at their command are insufficient to provide for more than a fraction of all these needs. Only as they are aided by their more fortunate brothers in other countries can they survive the hardships which they are now enduring.

In the Vilna district which the Friends' Mission is entering this winter, there are 40,000 people living in dugouts, trenches and branch shelters. In many of the villages whole families were wiped out last winter by starvation. Into this stricken district, the Friends' Mission plans to bring food for those who are in dire need of it, home industry work by which the women refugees can help to support themselves, horses for the plowing, and for hauling timber that will be used in housing re-construction.

The American Friends' Service Committee has had special difficulty in raising funds for the work in Poland, because of the fact that most of those of Polish descent in America are affiliated with the Roman Catholic Church and are not in sympathy with the inhabitants of Eastern Poland, which was formerly a part of Russia, and which comes under the Greek Catholic Church. Others have declined to support the work because of certain policies of the Polish government.

But the peasant sufferers are not responsible for any of these conditions, and they deserve every bit of help which can be sent to them. The very fact that we may disagree with some of the policies of their government is all the more reason why we should endeavor to demonstrate the ideals of service and good will among them. "Not they that are whole need a physician, but they that are sick." Funds for the work in Poland, contributed now, can render unlimited service in relieving distress and saving life this winter.

Pennies That Helped Save Lives

Some months ago a little American girl, having heard that Russian children were starving, took her pennies from her bank and gave a dollar to a Quaker relief worker who was just leaving for Russia. She wished it to be used in helping some little Russian girl. The American girl has just received a letter from the Quaker worker, in which he tells how the dollar was used. His letter, in somewhat abridged form, is as follows:

"Dear Hester:

The dollar which you gave I put some time ago into the hands of a poor little fatherless Russian girl. At the rate of exchange then current, your dollar brought 4,000,000 rubles, and I can assure you that it did a wonderful lot of good for the little girl and her mother. It was enough to buy 50 lbs. of rye flour to make delicious Russian rye bread, or to go a long way in buying warm woolen clothes for the winter. The Russian winters are terribly severe.

"The little girl has given me a note of thanks to you. It was written by her mother; for the girl, although 8 years old, cannot read nor write. There

less Evil." In the meantime we must give the nation and people our sympathy and help, and look forward to the not distant future when the country will again be free from the ravages of opium and its accompanying evils.

The magnitude of the present recrudescence is not the chief cause of alarm for at worst it is not more than one-tenth of that of the old unrestricted days, but the practically universal reversion to its use in all provinces. Some parts of the country have always been worse than others and they are so now, but that opium should have returned to the homes of rich and poor in town and village throughout the whole land calls indeed for serious reflection, and the encouragement of all forces working for the elimination of this evil should be given without reserve.

Typical of the conditions in the country is the statement from Yunnan:

"Opium is a cheap and popular stuff here. Except women about sixty per cent. of the people have the habit of smoking it. You will find the opium plant everywhere in the province. I hear that the local Government, instead of trying to prevent the people planting poppy, always reckons the opium tax as a big income."

A more detailed picture is supplied from Kansu, of which a recent visitor says:—

"Never have I seen opium exhibited with such nonchalance and complete absence of fear as on this trip. Opium was produced in railway trains and native inns, and its quality and price openly discussed before a foreigner without the least reticence. The new Tutung at Suiyan found one-third to one-fifth of the best land in the rich Paotow valley planted with poppy and guarded jealously by the Chihli soldiers of the late Tutung. Even the privates of the Paotow garrison are said to be rich. They have gone out through the villages and appropriated each man several acres of land, upon which they have forced the peasants to plant poppy. Each soldier "protects" his "own" poppy field, in return for which protection he collects two-thirds of the yield from the farmer. If the yield is very poor he takes all, and instances have occurred in which he has forced the peasant to sell his personal goods to make good the disappointment of a bad crop."

In one case at least famine relief has had to be refused by the International Famine Relief Committee, whose funds are restricted to relief of famine caused "by Act of God," for the appeal came from an area in which food shortage has been caused solely through compulsory cultivation of poppy instead of grain.

The Government is honestly trying to do what it can to cope with the situation as the record of the destruction at Shanghai of 130,000 dollars worth in one-quarter of contraband drugs from Japan (incidentally the product of British, American, German and Swiss factories) testifies.

In Fukien cultivation has been eradicated, but smuggling and secret manufacture at Amoy are hard to cope with. At Peking last January 8,932 ounces of drugs were burnt, while seizures in one month at Tientsin included 300 lbs. of morphia, two years totals of seizures amounting to 113,000 ounces—estimated at about 10 per cent. of the undetected mass. Tons of opium were burnt in Hunan and Hupeh.

Great trouble is caused by smuggling from Siberia, but it appears that generally, partly because of its cheapness, opium is more used than morphia, and in most cases the Japanese authorities really seem to be trying to grapple with the smugglers from their country.

Dr. Aspland concludes:— "We would be without hope, were we not absolutely convinced that this is but a passing phase in the life of this nation and one for which every national, social and religious force must be urgently and sympathetically used to deliver the people. We foreigners can assist by rousing the conscience standard of our own countries. There is no room for stone throwing. The subject is international and as such producers and consumers, the debauching and the debauched must take equal responsibility."

H. W. Peet.

Street Speaking for Peace

Are we going back—or going forward—to the days of George Fox and William Penn? That we are beginning to follow their methods of advancing our ideals is indicated by the fact that on Armistice Day, in Philadelphia, Friends spoke on the streets in behalf of abolishment of war and about steps that would bring world peace.

The Society of Friends cannot claim the honor of having organized this movement. It was planned and carried out by the Women's International League for Peace and Freedom, but a majority of the speakers were members of our Society. Those Friends who spoke were Frederick Libby, Jannet Payne Whitney, William I. Hull, Jesse H. Holmes, Rowntree Gillett, J. Augustus Cadwalader, Walter H. Abell, Walter C. Longstreth, J. Harold Watson, Ernest Votaw, Henry Ferris, Samuel J. Bunting, Ruth Conrow, Leslie Frazier and Edward Evans. The other speakers were Dr. Frederick Griffin, Rev. Edward Shelton, Rev. Jos. Morris, Henry Close, and Allen S. Olmsted, 2nd. A "chairman" was stationed at each speaking point to supervise arrangements, to briefly introduce speakers when this seemed desirable, and to hold the crowd between speakers if any delays should render this necessary. Of these chairmen, four were Friends: Ruth Verlenden, Grace Watson, Mary Hannum, and Mrs. Jonathan Steere. The remaining two chairmen were Miss Sophie Dulles and Mrs. Liverwright.

The speaking points were as follows: City Hall Courtyard; the Bandstand on the City Hall Plaza; 9th and Chestnut Sts., in front of the Central City Post Office; Broad St. and Columbia Ave.; Broad and South Sts., in the Negro section; and 5th and Bainbridge Sts., in the Jewish section.

The affair had been so arranged that each speaker spoke successively in at least three of these places, and by this process of rotation, the twenty speakers kept all six meetings going from approximately noon to 3 o'clock.

The reaction on the part of the public was surprisingly favorable. Crowds gathered at practically all of the speaking points, that in the City Hall Courtyard averaging 200 persons at a time, newcomers constantly taking the places of those who left. One of the aides at one point heard a remark made by a man who was just leaving to one who had just arrived. The former exclaimed in regard to the message which a Friend had just finished giving: "You ought to have been here to hear him! That was *real* stuff he gave!" At one of the other points, one man said as he left, *apropros* of a speech which involved the Friends' attitude toward war, "That's right about war. I know what it is. I have been in three of them myself."

On the whole, the experience indicated how ripe the fields are for harvest, and how great is the need for workers. It is not to be doubted that as a result of these street talks on Armistice Day new thoughts about war and peace entered thousands of Philadelphia homes that night. One visitor from Pittsburgh, who happened to be present, declared that he was going to do the same thing in his city in the near future. Most of those who were connected with the undertaking are asking themselves the same question as the result of it: "Why limit this work for peace to special days a few times a year, when there is such a great need for it all the time? Why should we not be doing this sort of thing continually?"

WALTER H. ABELL.

The Later Periods of Quakerism

A year ago the HIBBERT JOURNAL devoted an important review to W. C. Braithwaite's "Second Period of Quakerism." The October issue this year deals at length with the concluding volumes of the series: "The Later Periods of Quakerism," by Rufus Jones. The writer praises the work, but there is an interesting note of enquiry and criticism at the end which in these days of commendation should not be ignored.

The reviewer says:

"There are two questions we have had constantly in mind as we have followed the course of this history. One is with regard to the practice of corporate silence as the basis of worship among Friends, and their 'fundamental faith in Spirit-guided ministry.' Dr. Jones has a warning note against the danger of supposing 'that inspiration and illumination must come, if at all, during the meeting-hour,' and he points to the growing recognition among Friends of the fact that education is required, and there must be a serious preparation, if the standard of effective ministry is to be maintained. Must we not therefore conclude that inspiration has wider aspects and other channels beyond those maintained with such devoted consistency by Friends, and that the witness and guidance of the Spirit may be as real and unmistakable under other methods of administration in the Churches?

"Then as to the Spirit that guides, that is present as the Light of all our seeing, what are we to say? What actually is that 'Christ revelation' of which the concluding word of the history speaks? The mission of Friends, we are told, is to bear personal testimony to the real presence of God. There must be 'first-hand experience of direct relation with the present inward revealing God.' Evidence of God 'comes in quiet ways to the soul through the moral and spiritual tasks of a life-time,' and while the testimonies of prophets confirm our own discovery 'one historical Figure stands out in solitary splendour. In Jesus Christ we have the supreme confirmation of our most significant inner intimations and discoveries. The conviction of connection with God reached in Him its highest certainty. He felt himself to be the instrument and organ of Divine manifestation in unparalleled degree.'

"His was 'a representative life and death.' 'He is thus the head of a new race, the first of a new series, the founder of a new kingdom, the revealer of a new way of living.' What a man needs is 'spiritual illumination and moral reinforcement. Christ is the source of both these. He is the Light of Life. He reveals and exhibits life in its full and complete measure.' Salvation is 're-living the life of Christ in His power and in His Spirit.' All this we can understand as falling rightly into the order of a world of progressive spiritual illumination; but when we are told at the same time that 'Christ is God eternally revealing Himself—God in immediate relationship with men,' and that Friends both of the earliest and of the latter time have regarded 'the living Christ as the ground of their faith, the source of their power, and the central fact of their message,' we ask whether the spiritual fact is rightly discerned, and whether there is no distinction of being between this living Christ and the Father in whom Jesus trusted and taught his followers to trust, to whom he prayed and taught them to pray."

Central Literature Council of the Society of Friends.

Concerning the Collections

(The following article appeared in a recent issue of The Friend (London) and is here reprinted with the thought that it may be helpful in solving the problem with which some of our Yearly Meetings are struggling.)

Year after year most of our meetings have had to consider the raising of sufficient money to pay their own way, and send contributions to the Yearly Meeting Fund, and the various organizations connected with the Society.

Appeals have been sent out, but the result has been disappointing. Minutes have been passed suggesting that means might be considered of raising funds other than once a year. But we are still inclined to consider ourselves as a cheque book Society and to think that it is inappropriate to take steps when we meet for worship to make it easy to contribute towards the support of the activities of Friends. It seems strange that when so many Friends pay the train or tram fare *on Sunday* which enables them to get to the meeting-house, they should object to give voluntarily a contribution to enable the various bills to be paid by the treasurer. However, the collections taken for the War Victims' Relief Committee have proved that we can give after meeting without losing either our spiritual power or our self-respect!

Many meetings are now adopting improved means for raising funds; and I venture to suggest one which has been adopted by one meeting by means of which most of the bodies connected with the Society will benefit. It has been decided to have weekly collections, and the year has been divided to enable contributions to be made to the following purposes.

Local expenses (12 times) 1st Sunday in each month.

Home Mission* (12 times) 2nd Sunday in each month.

War Victims † (8 times) 3rd Sunday—1st, 2nd, 4th, 5th, 7th, 8th, 10th, 11th months.

Yearly Meeting Fund (6 times) 4th Sunday—1st, 3rd, 5th, 7th, 9th, 11th months.

Friends' Boarding Schools (5 times) 4th Sunday—2nd, 4th, 6th, 8th, 12th months.

F. F. M. A. 5th Sunday when it occurs.

Local Hospital 4th Sunday in 10th month.

R. H. SMITH.

*Monthly contributions on account of help rendered by the Committee.

†So long as need lasts.

"If you cannot at the Meeting
Speak with grace to move the heart
You can come with cheer and greeting
Helping on the social part.
Though you're timid in the forum,
Or command no powers rare,
You can help to make a quorum,
You can occupy a chair."

BLISS FORBUSH.

Statistical Report

COMMITTEE ON FIRST-DAY SCHOOLS TO FRIENDS' GENERAL CONFERENCE HELD AT RICHMOND, IND., EIGHTH MONTH 26 TO NINTH MONTH 2, 1922

hool Superintendent Address	Term	Enroll-ment	Adult	Minor	Friend	Are Friends' Lesson Leaves used?
gton—Wm. A. Longshore—Elkins Park, Pa.	10—6	90	40	50	60	Yes, some classes
ingham—Marian P. Cope—West Chester, Pa.	5/29—9/11	34	15	19	20	Yes
ingham—Joseph C. Watson—Lahaska, Pa.	5/1—10/1	33	14	19	24	Some are used
rry—Elizabeth H. Bonner—Torresdale, Pa.		Children's Class				
len		Young People's Conference Class				
ter—Charles Palmer—Chester, Pa.	10—5	52	7	45	10	Yes
ord—Pennock E. Sharpless—Ward, Pa.	4—12	70	30	40		Yes
swicks—Laura N. Rogers—Crosswicks, N. J.	9—7	42	11	31	13	With one exception
y—Mary A. Yarnall—735 Church L., Yeadon, Pa.	10—6	36	9	27	8	To some extent
Run		Reorganizing				
estown—Elizabeth Watson—277 Maple Ave., Doylestown		Children's Class				
doun—Elizabeth W. Moore—Coatesville, Pa., R. D. No. 5	Entire year	35	17	18	22	Yes
Hill—Stuart S. Graves—3033 Gtn. Ave., Philadelphia, Pa.	10—5	105	20	85	18	Yes
kford—Leslie Griscom—1522 Overing, Frankford	10—6	29				Yes
antown—Emily H. Taylor—239 Gowen Ave., Mt. Airy, Pa.	10—5	101	33	68	63	Yes
'd Avenue—Albert E. Conrad—2134 N. Uber, Philadelphia, Pa.	10—5	69	39	30	37	Yes
awich—Grace B. Ewing—Greenwich, N. J.	All year	6	6			Yes
nedd—Wm. Hibbs Tomlinson—Hatfield, Pa.	9/15—6/15	45	31	14	39	Yes
rford—Garrett Kirk—30 Tenby Rd., Llanerch, Pa.	All year	12	11	1	12	Yes
essin—Elizabeth T. Mitchell—Hockessin, Del.	4—2	42	26	16	28	Yes
ham—John P. Williams—Willow Grove, Pa.	9—7	40	15	25	30	Yes
ett Square—Florence N. Cleaver—220 S. Broad, Kennett Sq.	9—6	162	46	116	95	Yes
horne—George R. Ambler—Langhorne, Pa.	9—6	45	23	22	43	In two classes
sdowne—Frederick P. Suplee—Lansdowne, Pa.	10—6	79	21	58	60	In some classes
on Grove—Thos. L. Passmore—Chatham, Pa.	4—1	142	71	71	118	Yes
field—Edith T. Ely—Washington Crossing, Pa.	All year	79	39	40	47	Yes
ern—Helen A. Passmore—Malvern, Pa.	9—7	33	21	12	26	Yes
field—Eugenia N. Harvey—Columbus, N. J.	Spring and Summer	27	17	10	26	Yes
ord						
n—W. Russell Green—225 Iona Ave., Narberth, Pa.	9—7	15	7	8	10	Yes
leton—Rebecca A. John—Mickleton, N. J.	9—7	136	61	75	93	In 8 classes out of 11
ille—Ellen R. Eves—Millville, Pa.	Entire year	67	46	21	44	Yes
estown—William C. Coles—400 Chester Ave., Moorestown, N. J.	10—6	231	124	107	220	Yes
Iolly—Franklin S. Zelley—Mt. Holly, N. J.	9—6	25	15	10		Yes
ca Hill—J. Omar Heritage—Mullica Hill, N. J.	9—7	89	45	44	70	Yes
Garden—J. Norman Pusey—Avondale, Pa.	4—12	134	78	56	69	In four classes
own—William T. Wright—Newtown, Pa.	All year	97	42	55	72	
town Square—Ella B. Elliott—Newtown Square, Pa.	5/22—10/30	24	20	4	22	Yes
stown—Anna G. Wood—232 Jacoby St., Norristown, Pa.	9—7	88	40	27	39	Yes
Kennett—Elwood Nichols—Kennett Sq., Pa., R. D. No. 3	5—12	26	14	12	18	Yes
ge Grove—F. T. Hartley—1817 Monte Vista, Pasadena, Calif.	All year					None at present
outh Meeting—N. Esther Shoemaker—W. Conshohocken, Pa.	9—6	40	17	23		No
dence—Laura A. Reynolds—234 E. 3rd, Media, Pa.	10—7	29	10	19	20	Yes
Street—Charles H. Harrison—The Gables, Ardmore, Pa.	10—5	80	75	5	72	In one class
and—Annie B. Roberts—409 E. Broad St., Quakertown, Pa.	9—7	30	20	8	20	Yes
ury—George W. Jackson—Christiana, Pa., R. D. No. 1	5—10	45	25	20	45	Yes
—Elizabeth T. Smith—Salem, N. J.	9/15—6/30	107	47	60	71	Yes
ary—Marion R. Ely—New Hope, Pa.	Entire year	40	16	24	36	Yes
lsburg—Anna W. Palmer—517 Thomas St., Stroudsburg, Pa.	Entire year	Conference Class				
hmore—Ethel G. Coates—223 Vassar Ave., Swarthmore, Pa.	10—6	137	54	83	77	Yes, espec'y in prim'y
Haven—Wilson M. Tylor—Easton, Md.	Entire year	46	35	11	44	Not this year
on—John R. Satterthwaite—Trenton, N. J.	9—6	130	35	90	100	In some classes
—Winfield W. Conard—829 Swede St., Norristown, Pa.	4—1	49	37	12	46	Yes
ville						
Chester—Herbert P. Worth—West Chester, Pa.	9/15—6/15	136	74	62	88	Yes
eld—Bertha L. Parrish—Riverton, N. J.	10—6	90	53	37	73	Yes

—

:e report was submitted Charles J. Suplee, 146 Hilldale Rd., Lansdowne, Pa., has been made Superintendent.

e report was submitted Hanna M. B. Hipple, Broomall, Pa., has been made Superintendent.

School Superintendent Address	Term	Enroll-ment	Adult	Minor	Friend	Are Friends' Lesson Leaves used?
West Grove—Anna R. Beitler—West Grove, Pa....................	Entire year	70	25	45	30	Yes
West Philadelphia—Joseph J. Baily—1122 N. 63rd St., Phila., Pa...	10—5	108	44	64	62	Yes
Willistown—William W. Evans—Edgemont, Pa..................	5—11	65	24	41	35	In Adult Class
Wilmington—D. Herbert Way—305½ W. 19th St., Wilmington, Del..	9—6	125	64	61	90	Partially
Woodstown—H. Milton Flitcraft—Woodstown, N. J...............	9—6	158	75	83	110	In several classes
Wrightstown—Joseph S. Parry—Rushland, Pa....................	4—10	95	41	54	46	Yes

NEW YORK

School Superintendent Address	Term	Enroll-ment	Adult	Minor	Friend	Are Friends' Lesson Leaves used?
Brooklyn—Will Walter Jackson—50 Beekman St., New York City............		56	14	42	52	In 3 out of 5 classes
Cornwall—Gilbert T. Cocks—Cornwall, N. Y......................	Entire year	27	14	13	24	Yes
Flushing—Grace K. Hubbard—109 N. 14th St., Flushing, N. Y.....	10—6	28	12	16	23	Yes
Jericho—Helen W. Underhill—Jericho, L. I......................	Entire year		4	40	6	No
Manasquan—George F. LaFetra—Manasquan, N. J..................	Entire year	54	18	25	11	Yes
Matinecock—Florence J. Willits—Glen Cove, N. Y................	Entire year	15	5	10	9	Occasionally
Newark—Henry M. Woolman—54 13th Ave., Newark, N. J....................		20	20		20	Yes
New York—J. Hibberd Taylor—Larchmont, N. Y..................	10/30—5/14	45	1	34	15	Yes
North Easton—Phebe A. Hoag—Greenwich, N. Y., R. D., No. 1....	5—12	25	6	19	7	In Adult Class
Plainfield—Ruth S. Vail—721 W. 4th St., Plainfield, N. J..........	10—7	36	19	17	21	Yes
Purchase		Conference Class				
Westbury		Children's Class				

BALTIMORE

School Superintendent Address	Term	Enroll-ment	Adult	Minor	Friend	Are Friends' Lesson Leaves used?
Park Avenue—Thomas B. Hull—3510 Duvall Ave, Baltimore, Md..	9/25—6/4	172	78	94	142	Yes
Eastern District—Thomas O. Matthews.....................................		Thinking of discontinuing				
Broad Creek—James W. Harry—Juvenile Ct., Baltimore, Md................		58	33	22	29	Yes
Centre						
Deer Creek		Adult Class				
Drumore—Ann Amanda Lamborn—Holtwood, Pa., R. D. No. 1....	5—10	14	10	4	10	Yes
Dunning's Creek—E. Howard Blackburn—Bedford, Pa............	Entire year	54	36	18	48	Yes
Eastland—Robert K. Wood—Nottingham, Pa......................	1/15—12/31	87	28	59	25	Yes
East Nottingham—Charles R. Brown—North East, Md., R. D.................		40	15	25	14	Yes
Goose Creek—Henry B. Taylor—Lincoln, Va	5—11	123	61	62	94	Yes
Gunpowder—Ella Scott Bosley—Sparks, Md....................................		54	20	34	20	No
Hopewell—Lewis Pidgeon—Wadesville, Va........................	Entire year	82	59	23	53	In 3 classes
Little Falls—Dora Curtiss—Bagley, Md.........................	Entire year	23	15	8	16	In Children's Class
Menallen—E. Belle Weidner—Arendtsville, Pa..................	Entire year	55	25	30	44	Yes
Oxford—Harold B. Earnhart—155 Pine St., Oxford, Pa.......................		70	34	36	70	Yes
Penn Hill—Wm. P. King—Peach Bottom, Pa......................	4/16—10/1	92	48	44	65	Yes
Sandy Spring—Mariana S. Miller—Spencerville, Md...............	10—6	50	30	20	46	Yes
Unionville						
Washington—Furman L. Mullford—2552 Tunlaw Rd., Wash., D. C..	9/25—6/18	92	37	55	63	Yes
West Branch—Edwin A. Spencer—Grampian, Pa..............................		62	27	35	40	In 3 out of 5 classes
Winchester—D. S. Mattison—Winchester, Va.....................	Entire year	51	30	21	43	In one class
Woodlawn—George C. Gillingham—Accotink, Va............................		40	15	25		No

INDIANA

School Superintendent Address	Term	Enroll-ment	Adult	Minor	Friend	Are Friends' Lesson Leaves used?
Camden						
Fall Creek—Ollie Haines—Pendleton, Ind..................................		72	37	35		Yes
Green Plain—Leland S. Calvert—Selma, Ohio..............................		18	11	7	15	Yes
Lincolnville—Margaret K. Shoemaker—Wabash, Ind.........................		Adult Class				
North A Street...						
Waynesville—Seth E. Furnas—Waynesville, Ohio.................	Entire year	55	25	30	35	In four classes
Westfield—Levi T. Shoemaker—Camden, Ohio, R. D. No. 2........	4—12	41	7	34	14	No

ILLINOIS

School Superintendent Address	Term	Enroll-ment	Adult	Minor	Friend	Are Friends' Lesson Leaves used?
Clear Creek—Laura W. Smith—McNabb, Ill.		78	35	43	28	Yes
Chicago—Jeannette Flitcraft		Discussion Class				
Highland Friends—Elwood Brooks—Salem, Ind..................	Entire year	135	74	61	58	Mostly

GENESEE

School Superintendent Address	Term	Enroll-ment	Adult	Minor	Friend	Are Friends' Lesson Leaves used?
Coldstream—Edgar M. Zavitz—Ilderton, Ont.	Entire year	70	20	50	65	Yes
Sparta—Isaac A. Willson—Union P. O., Ont., Canada.........................		25	20	5	20	

Report of the Advancement Committee

For several years the Advancement Committee has been feeling its way. The cause for which it was appointed, and the reason for its existence is to spread the Quaker message beyond our borders. From the first the Committee felt the need for strengthening our own meetings to which we wish to invite people to come. With this object, week-end conferences, pilgrimages, and interchange of visits have been arranged. More and more this work is being cared for by local agencies, Meetings for Ministry and Counsel, Young Friends' Movement, Monthly Meetings' Advancement or Best Interest Committees, with which groups we are convinced this responsibility rests. This leaves the Advancement Committee free to devote itself to the outside work which is its own task.

Need has also been felt for more training for those who are to express the message. The Summer Schools, Woolman School, and some beginnings of a program of religious education is the result.

The Advancement Committee still carries many of the details of these activities, including the management of the bi-ennial Summer School.

We are deeply interested in the progress of Woolman School, which is now managed by a Board representative of all Friends, and are doing all we can to increase its attendance. The young Friends who have attended are among our best assets for Advancement work. They should not be looked upon as Meeting leaders from the mere fact of their having been to Woolman School, but they are all serving in their fields, and have expressed most emphatically how much Woolman School has meant to them. The past year has seen three very successful terms, and also three distinctly progressive steps: (1) the inauguration of the special week-end course, which was adapted to meet a need felt by young Friends, and was carried through enthusiastically with the co-operation of the Young Friends' Movement; (2) the series of special week-end conferences during this summer term, with especially valuable programs, and (3) the carrying of the Extension Lectures to a greater distance from Swarthmore by giving a program of several lectures over a week-end. Further development of Extension Work with a wider variety of subjects is announced for the coming year. Edith M. Winder has been appointed Hostess and begins her work immediately following the Conference.

Part of our program of education is the printing and distribution of clear-cut and modern statements of the Friendly faith. There is an increasing call for this material. During the year we have issued "Preparation for Life's Greatest Business," by Rufus M. Jones; "Quaker Worship—an Invitation," and reprinted "Friendly Fundamentals," by Henry W. Wilbur; "Our Faith and the Causes of War," by J. Russell Smith; and shared in the publication of two editions of "The Quaker Challenge to a World of Force," by Elbert Russell, through the Friends' Literature Council.

The Committee's routine work includes the maintenance of an office in the Philadelphia Young Friends' Association Building, and the meeting of calls for information about the Society of Friends and its activities. Through this office a link is formed to keep our Society in touch with the National Federation of Religious Liberals, the Federation of Churches, and other national movements.

At the office is kept a list of speakers, and help is frequently given in connecting a meeting with the person they wish to invite. We appreciated very much the visits of William Littleboy, Elizabeth B. Emmott, and E. Maria Bishop to several of our meetings this past year, and were glad to help them in arranging for their travels. We are grateful also for the delegation that responded to the call to go to Genesee, Indiana and Illinois Yearly Meetings this summer: Isaac Wilson, Grace E. Clevenger, and Charles H. Harrison for all three, and Arabella Carter for two and George H. Nutt for one of them.

There is also kept at headquarters the list of non-resident members of the different Meetings, and by correspondence, Friends are put in touch with other Friends in the place to which they have moved. The office keeps in touch with the meetings that have been started informally in new places, and helps as there is opportunity. The Committee has been interested especially in the efforts of the groups at Buffalo, N. Y., and Oakland, Cal. We have sent names and recommended visitors for the groups at Lancaster, Harrisburg, and Pittsburg, Pa. A new group is proposed at Toledo, Ohio, to include Friends of all branches. The meetings at Cambridge, Mass., San Jose, Cal., and the winter meeting at St. Petersburg, Fla., are well established. The one at Des Moines, Iowa, has held some meetings.

There are very strong Friends' groups now in some of the colleges. The fact that a house was provided at Pennsylvania State College through the interest of Friends, has given a meeting-place and solidarity of spirit to the group there which is a real contribution to our cause and to the college life, as well. The other colleges where Friends are getting together in a more or less formal way, in addition, of course, to the Quaker Colleges, are: Cornell, Vassar, Smith, Holyoke, Wellesley, Columbia University, University of Pennsylvania, Oberlin, University of Michigan, University of Iowa, Ontario Agricultural College, Summer School.

The office has cared for much of the work in preparation for the General Conference. The Committee is deeply grateful for the generous fund placed in its treasury for helping to have as good a representation of Young Friends at Richmond as if distance were no factor. The Conference will, we have no doubt, show the result.

Through all this routine work we have tried to keep clear our purpose to advance Friends' principles into new territory. For the past few years, the Committee has been experimenting with different methods. We concentrated in one place for a time—Buffalo—with the idea of developing the possibilities of a strategic center. More recently we have been interested in Advancement Work in Chicago with the same idea. We selected an industrial community—Newark, N. J.—where we might try to present our message in a series of meetings to the non-church-going factory workers. Our efforts in that field did not meet with success, due to the lack of natural contacts. We have been interested in the theatre and town hall meetings held in Philadelphia and New York, with the idea of reaching a different audience than that which will come to a church building. This past year we have been carrying a little advertising offering "A Quaker Challenge to a World of Force" by Elbert Russell, to be sent on request. In response 428 requests have been received. Over half of these have led to further correspondence, and many to very interesting points of contact. One of the results is the starting of a reading-circle in St. Thomas, the Virgin Islands of the United States. The office is following up this correspondence, and making individual points of contact with Friends, or meetings wherever it is possible.

As a result of this experimenting we are convinced that now is the time to go forward vigorously. The call for our Quaker message is imperative. The opportunity is particularly open just now because of the reaction from the war, and the wide search for a true and fundamental basis for peace, because, also, of the interest aroused by Friends' relief work in Europe, because of the cry of the world for a religion that will meet its needs. It is not a new denomination the world is calling for. It has too many church organizations already. It is not doctrine it wants, although it needs the truth. It is the spirit of Christ, the spirit of love and good-will in the hearts of men. The spirit of good-will the world has come to associate with the name "Quaker."

The opportunity is therefore open to Friends, as to no other body, to spread a message which is not ecclesiastical nor dogmatic, but full of brotherhood and the love of God; to spread by example and precept a way of life that will mean peace and inspire definite constructive progress toward better relationship between races, industrial and social groups, and all of the warring factions in our social life.

Does this seem too great a task? It is too great for one Committee. It is too great for the Society of Friends, except by the divine enabling. Our recommendation to the Conference is that we face the task, and attempt it. We recommend that all our Meetings and all our members undertake a part. By combined effort we can go forward all along the line at once.

Such a program would involve the following:

For the General Conference Advancement Committee.

1. Advertising in national periodicals.
2. Following up by correspondence.
3. Concentration on student communities.
4. Find natural points of contact with industrial groups, and use them.
5. Serve as a clearing-house for methods and materials between the different Yearly Meetings.
6. Co-operate with the Message Committee of the American Friends' Service Committee by working through them in extending the Quaker message in other countries.

For Each Yearly Meeting Through its Appropriate Committee.

1. Strengthen its weak meetings.
2. Raise the tide of life in the stronger meetings to zeal for service beyond their borders. (Detailed programs are being worked out in some Yearly Meetings, and will not be repeated here.)

For Each Local Meeting.

1. Make the most of the possibilities of every member, and deepen the unity of spirit in the Society of Friends.
2. Use the First-day School, Young Friends' Association, and meeting for worship, and special lectures for inviting others from the community.
3. New types of meetings like that in the Broad Street Theatre, Philadelphia.
4. Public meetings of this type in smaller cities.

For Each Member.

1. Develop the individual points of contact that come to every one. The Friend of whom a question is asked has a better opportunity to answer than will ever come to another.
2. Co-operate with the work of the meeting and the Advancement Committees.

On behalf of the Advancement Committee:

WILLIAM C. BIDDLE, *Chairman.*
J. BARNARD WALTON, *Secretary.*

Appendix

Members of Central Committee, 1922—1924

PHILADELPHIA YEARLY MEETING

James H. Atkinson
Mary C. Atkinson
Joseph J. Bailey
Frank M. Bartram
William C. Biddle
Joel Borton
Ruth Smedley Bowers
Samuel J. Bunting, Jr.
T. Augustus Cadwallader
Arabella Carter
William C. Coles
Rebecca W. Conrow
Myra M. Eves
William Eves, 3rd
Henry Ferris
Martha E. Gibbs
Anna B. Griscom
Ellen Pyle Groff
Annie Hillborn
J. Bernard Hilliard
Elwood Hollingshead
Jesse H. Holmes
Hannah Clothier Hull
William I. Hull
Arthur C. Jackson
Edith W. Jackson
Sarah W. Knight
Lucy Biddle Lewis
William A. Longshore
Rebecca B. Nicholson
George H. Nutt
Sara J. Packer
Charles Palmer
Hannah F. Perrott
Florence Hall Philips
Robert Pyle
Chester Roberts
Emmor Roberts
J. Russell Smith
Elizabeth A. Walter
George A. Walton
J. Barnard Walton
Mary H. Whitson
Herbert P. Worth

NEW YORK YEARLY MEETING

E. Morris Burdsall
Mary R. Burdsall
Isaac M. Cocks
Jessie Wright Cocks
Edward Cornell
Harry A. Hawkins
Tacy Clark Jackson
Charles McDowell
Elizabeth S. Percy
Ethel A. Post
Mary Hutchinson Savage
Robert Seaman
J. Hibberd Taylor
Josephine H. Tilton
Florence J. Willits
Frederick E. Willits
Ella H. Williams

BALTIMORE YEARLY MEETING

Gladys Brooke
T. Janney Brown
Margaretta B. Heacock
George Hoge
Mary B. Hull
Anne W. Janney
O. Edward Janney
William P. King
Rebecca T. Miller
Caleb J. Moore
Furman L. Mulford
Susan T. Pidgeon
Rachel T. Thom
Alban G. Thomas
Ella W. Thomas
E. Belle Weidner
Edward C. Wilson

GENESEE YEARLY MEETING

Wm. Greenwood Brown
Emma H. Landon
M. Camilla Zavitz
Samuel P. Zavitz

OHIO YEARLY MEETING

Charles F. Branson
Mabel A. Clark
Marietta Hartley
J. Franklin Lamborn

ILLINOIS YEARLY MEETING

Elwood Brooks
Ruth Bumgarner
Harold W. Flitcraft
Thomas A. Jenkins
Clarence C. Mills
Clara Pyle
Theodore Russell

INDIANA YEARLY MEETING

Wilson S. Doan
Thomas M. Hardy
Emma G. Halloway
Ida W. Keever
Susan M. Roberts
Benjamin Rogers
E. Annie Wilson
Edith M. Winder

ORGANIZATION OF THE CENTRAL COMMITTEE

Chairman, Arthur C. Jackson, 4530 Tacony St., Frankford, Pa.

Vice-Chairman, Elwood Brooks, Salem, Indiana.

Secretary, pro tem., Josephine H. Tilton, 120 South Second Ave., Mount Vernon, New York.

Treasurer, Harry A. Hawkins, 57 Pierrepont Ave. West, Rutherford, New Jersey.

EXECUTIVE COMMITTEE

James H. Atkinson (Chairman), 421 Chestnut St., Philadelphia, Pa.
Dr. O. Edward Janney, 825 Newington Ave., Baltimore, Md.
Dr. Charles McDowell, 310 Kenmore Place, Brooklyn, N. Y.
Elizabeth Ann Walter, 154 N. 15th St., Philadelphia, Pa.
Eleanore Miller, Sandy Spring, Md.
E. Morris Burdsall, Port Chester, N. Y.
With Officers of the Conference and Chairmen of Standing Committees.

TRANSPORTATION COMMITTEE

Robert Seaman (Chairman), Jericho, Nassau Co., N. Y.
James H. Atkinson, 421 Chestnut St., Philadelphia, Pa.
Wilson S. Doan, 1106, I. O. O. F. Building, Indianapolis, Ind.
Thomas B. Hull, 614 Equitable Building, Baltimore, Md.
Clarence C. Mills, McNabb, Ill.
Howard V. Zavitz, R. D. No. 2, Ilderton, Ontario, Canada.

EDUCATION COMMITTEE

Chairman, George H. Nutt, George School, Pa.

Secretary, Edith W. Jackson, 6445 Greene St., Germantown, Pa.

William C. Biddle, 107 Chambers St., New York City.
Mary R. Burdsall, 381 Irving Ave., Port Chester, N. Y.
Charles F. Branson, 6013 Greene St., Germantown, Pa.
Rebecca W. Conrow, Riverton, N. J.
Edward Cornell, 43 Willow St., Brooklyn, N. Y.
Elwood Hollingshead, Moorestown, N. J.
Thomas A. Jenkins, 5411 Greenwood Ave., Chicago, Ill.
Ida W. Keever, Centreville, Ohio.
Lucy Biddle Lewis, Lansdowne, Pa.
Rebecca T. Miller, Ashton, Md.
Florence Hall Philips, 910 Van Buren St., Wilmington, Del.
Susan T. Pidgeon, Wadesville, Va.
Ethel A. Post, Westbury, Nassau Co., N. Y.
Robert Pyle, West Grove, Pa.
Chester Roberts, Swarthmore, Pa.
J. Russell Smith, Swarthmore, Pa.
George A. Walton, George School, Pa.
Frederick E. Willits, Glen Cove, Nassau Co., N. Y.
Edward C. Wilson, 1925 Park Ave., Baltimore, Md.
E. Annie Wilson, N. W. 5th St., Richmond, Ind.
M. Camilla Zavitz, R. D. 2, Ilderton, Ontario, Canada.

COMMITTEE ON FIRST-DAY SCHOOLS

Chairman, Herbert P. Worth, West Chester, Pa.

Secretary, Elizabeth A. Walter, 154 N. 15th St., Philadelphia, Pa.

Joseph J. Bailey, 1122 N. 63rd St., Philadelphia, Pa.
Frank M. Bartram, Kennett Square, Pa.
Ruth Smedley Bowers, 205 Windsor St., Reading, Pa.
Elwood Brooks, Salem, Ind.
Ruth Bumgarner, McNabb, Ill.
Samuel J. Bunting, Jr., 6386 Overbrook Ave., Philadelphia
Mabel A. Clark, Bridgeport, Ohio.
Jessie Wright Cocks, Old Westbury, Nassau Co., N. Y.
Myra M. Eves, Millville, Pa.
William Eves, 3rd, George School, Pa.
Henry Ferris, 151 W. Hortter St., Germantown, Pa.

Harold W. Flitcraft, 633 Maple Ave., Oak Park, Ill.
Ellen Pyle Groff, London Grove, Pa.
Thomas M. Hardy, Pendleton, Ind.
Margaretta B. Heacock, Bedford, Pa.
J. Bernard Hilliard, Salem, N. J.
Annie Hillborn, Swarthmore, Pa.
Mary B. Hull, 3600 Duvall Ave., Baltimore, Md.
Tacy Clark Jackson, East Williston, Long Island, N. Y.
William P. King, Peach Bottom, Pa.
Emma H. Landon, Angola, N. Y.
William A. Longshore, Elkins Park, Pa.
Furman L. Mulford, 2552 Tunlaw Rd., Washington, D. C.
Elizabeth S. Percy, 1014 Park Place, Brooklyn, N. Y.
Susan M. Roberts, South Charleston, Ohio.
Theodore Russell, Winfield, Iowa.
J. Hibberd Taylor, 17 Summit Ave., Larchmont, N. Y.
J. Barnard Walton, 140 N. 15th St., Philadelphia, Pa.
Mary H. Whitson, 1005 N. Main St., Kokomo, Ind.
E. Belle Weidner, Arendtsville, Pa.
Edith M. Winder, Woolman School, Swarthmore, Pa.
Florence J. Willits, Glen Cove, Nassau Co., N. Y.

COMMITTEE ON PHILANTHROPIC LABOR

Chairman, Anna W. Janney, 825 Newington Ave., Baltimore, Md.

Secretary, Mary Hutchinson Savage, 215 East 15th St., New York City.

James H. Atkinson, 421 Chestnut St., Philadelphia, Pa.
Mary C. Atkinson, 423 E. State St., Trenton, N. J.
Joel Borton, Woodstown, N. J.
Gladys Brooke, Sandy Spring, Md.
T. Janney Brown, Woodward Building, Washington, D. C.
W. Greenwood Brown, 83 Silver Birch Ave., Toronto, Ontario, Canada.
E. Morris Burdsall, Port Chester, N. Y.
J. Augustus Cadwallader, Yardley, Pa.
Arabella Carter, 1305 Arch St., Philadelphia, Pa.
Isaac M. Cocks, Cornwall-on-Hudson, N. Y.
William C. Coles, Moorestown, N. J.
Wilson S. Doan, 1106, I. O. O. F. Building, Indianapolis, Ind.
Martha E. Gibbs, Columbus, N. J.
Anna B. Griscom, 331 Chester Ave., Moorestown, N. J.
Marietta Hartley, 250 Rice St., Alliance, Ohio.
Harry A. Hawkins, 57 Pierrepont Ave. West, Rutherford, N. J.
George Hoge, Lincoln, Va.
Jesse H. Holmes, Swarthmore, Pa.
Emma G. Holloway, 206 S. Sycamore St., North Manchester, Ind.
Hannah Clothier Hull, Swarthmore, Pa.
William I. Hull, Swarthmore, Pa.
Arthur C. Jackson, 4530 Tacony St., Frankford, Pa.
O. Edward Janney, 825 Newington Ave., Baltimore, Md.
Sarah W. Knight, Somerton, Pa.
J. Franklin Lamborn, Sebring, Ohio.
Charles McDowell, 310 Kenmore Place, Brooklyn, N. Y.
Clarence C. Mills, McNabb, Ill.
Caleb J. Moore, Fallston, Md.
Rebecca B. Nicholson, 217 Washington Ave., Haddonfield, N. J.
Sara J. Packer, Newtown, Pa.
Charles Palmer, Box 218, Chester, Pa.
Hannah F. Perrott, 459 Winona Ave., Germantown, Pa.
Clara Pyle, Rt. 3, Marshalltown, Iowa.
Benjamin Rogers, Pendleton, Ind.
Emmor Roberts, Moorestown, N. J.
Robert Seaman, Jericho, Nassau Co., N. Y.
Ella W. Thomas, Oxford, Pa.
Rachel T. Thom, 6315 Connecticut Ave., Chevy Chase, Md.
Alban G. Thomas, Ashton, Md.
Josephine H. Tilton, 120 S. Second Ave., Mount Vernon, N. Y.
Ella H. Williams, 340 West 86th St., New York City.
Samuel P. Zavitz, R. R. 2, Ilderton, Ontario, Canada.

ADVANCEMENT COMMITTEE

Chairman, William C. Biddle, 107 Chambers St., New York City.

Secretary, J. Barnard Walton, 140 N. 15th St., Philadelphia, Pa.

Frank M. Bartram	Emma G. Holloway
Joel Borton	Jesse H. Holmes
Charles F. Branson	Hannah Clothier Hull
T. Janney Brown	Arthur C. Jackson
Samuel J. Bunting, Jr.	Edith W. Jackson
E. Morris Burdsall	O. Edward Janney
William C. Coles	Thomas A. Jenkins
Isaac M. Cocks	Sarah W. Knight
Rebecca W. Conrow	Clarence C. Mills
Wilson S. Doan	Emmor Roberts
Myra M. Eves	Elizabeth A. Walter
William Eves, 3rd	George A. Walton
Henry Ferris	Mary H. Whitson
Anna B. Griscom	Edith M. Winder
Harry A. Hawkins	Herbert P. Worth
Margaretta B. Heacock	Samuel P. Zavitz

Also the following not members of Central Committee:

Elwood D. Allen	Marian H. Longshore
Eliza M. Ambler	Sara T. Marshall
Ortis Baynes	Harriett Cox McDowell
Abigail Blackburn	Hadassah J. Moore
Bertha L. Broomell	Jane P. Rushmore
Marianna Burgess	Henrietta S. Smith
Grace E. Clevenger	Ida P. Stabler
Anna L. Curtis	Jeannette F. Stetson
Dora Curtiss	Lydia F. Taylor
Julia D. Eves	R. Bentley Thomas
Bliss Forbush	Charles H. Trafford
Warren C. Gregg	W. Russell Tylor
Carolyn H. Greist	Grace Tower Warren
Edgar Haight	D. Herbert Way
Charles H. Harrison	Oren B. Wilbur
W. Waldo Hayes	Cordelia Wilson
Dorothy Brooke Henderson	Amy Willets
Thomas B. Hull	Martha Cocks Willets
Susan W. Janney	Richard D. Williams
Reuben P. Kester	Edna Wilson Wolf

C. Harold Zavitz

Pursuant to the action of the Central Committee th following members of the Young Friends' Movement hav been added:

Philadelphia—
Mary Atkinson, 423 E. State St., Trenton, N. J.
Thomas A. Foulke, Ambler, Pa.
Frances Griscom, Salem, N. J.
Edith M. Hayes, Moorestown, N. J.
Waldo Hayes, Moorestown, N. J.
Ethel W. Martin, Kennett Square, Pa.
Lindsley H. Noble, 201A Penn St., Camden, N. J.
Joseph S. Parry, Rushland, Pa.
D. Herbert Way, 305½ W. 19th St., Wilmington, Del.

Baltimore—
Alice Allen, Darlington, Md.
Edith Blackburn, Melrose Ave., Govans, Md.
Eleanor Blackburn, Bedford, Pa.
Bliss Forbush, Park Ave. and Laurens St., Baltimor Md.

Eleanor Miller, Spencersville, Md.
Evan Stubbs, 39th and Woodland Ave., Phila., Pa.

New York—
Richard Burdsall, Port Chester, N. Y.
Marion Cocks, Cornwall, N. Y.
Phoebe N. Seaman, Jericho, N. Y.
Victor Wilson, 1030 East 7th St., Brooklyn, N. Y.

Illinois—
Jeanette F. Stetson, 225 N. Pine Ave., Chicago, Ill.
Sherman Stetson, 225 N. Pine Ave., Chicago, Ill.

Indiana—
Esther Allen, Pendleton, Indiana.
Russell Lewall, 244 S. 4th St., Richmond, Ind.

Genesee—
Edwin Landon, Angola, N. Y.
Lorena Zavitz, Ilderton, R. D. No. 2, Ontario, Can.

[The young people of the Central Committee, including the twenty-five listed above, have organized into a Young Friends' Committee of Friends' General Conference, with the following officers:
Chairman, Elizabeth A. Walter;
Vice Chairman, E. Morris Burdsall.
Secretary, Lindsley H. Noble.

This Committee is for the purpose of binding more closely together the Young Friends' Movement of the various Yearly Meetings and to help plan young peoples' activities at future Conferences.]

Our Conference Picture Gallery

Commissioner ROY A. HAYNES

GEORGE A. WALTON

CHARLES FOSTER KENT

J. RUSSELL SMITH

ELBERT RUSSELL

FRANK AYDELOTTE

J. ROWNTREE GILLETT
HENRY T. GILLETT

ARTHUR C. JACKSON
Chairman

PAULINE W. HOLME

JAMES H. ATKINSON

DR. O. EDWARD JANNEY

ROBERT SEAMAN

First-day School Methods

By Bliss Forbush

Question and Answer Box

"Will thee send me a list of prayers suitable for little children?"

1.

"Father, we thank thee for the night,
And for the pleasant morning light,
For rest and food and loving care,
And all that makes the world go fair."

—*From "Songs and Games for Little Ones," Walker and Jenks.*

2.

"Help us to do the things we should,
To be to others kind and good,
In all we do in work or play
To grow more loving every day."

—*Walker and Jenks.*

3.

"Father of all in heaven above,
We thank thee for thy love.
Our food, our homes, and all we wear
Tell of Thy loving care."

—*Hill, Song Stories for the Kindergarten.*

4.

"O Father, help thy children,
Do thou our footsteps guide,
We walk in peace and safety,
While keeping at Thy side."

—*Mrs. Edwards.*

5.

"Guide up, protect us, Show us the way.
Help us, dear Father, just for today."

6.

Now I lay me down to sleep,
I pray thee, Lord, my soul to keep.
When in the morning light I wake,
Help me the path of love to take,
And keep the same for Thy dear sake.

7.

"Now I lay me down to sleep,
I pray thee, Lord, my soul to keep;
Thy love be with me thru the night,
And bless me with the morning light."

A Grace at Table.

"We thank thee for this bread and meat
And all the good things which we eat;
Lord, may we strong and happy be,
And always good and true like Thee."

—*James M. Yard.*

Pendleton, Indiana, writes for suggestions concerning hymns to be used in the First-day School. They state their problem as follows:

1. They have the two pamphlets the General Conference First-day School Committee puts out and consider them excellent, but not to compare with the hymns used by other denominations in the interest of young people.

2. They object to so many catchy tunes which the public like to hum and are of the Methodist militant type.

3. They do not want a Unitarian Hymnal.

4. They want a song book fitted to the needs of the young people, one that shall contain tunes with words that have more action than are now found in tunes in books that appeal to Friends.

5. They are asking the department of music of the National Federation of Woman's Clubs for advice.

We wish that some of those Friends who have made a study of music and have any suggestions along this line would write them to Elwood D. Allen, Pendleton, Ind.,—the writer is out of his depths.

Would it not be a good idea to appeal to the Community Service, 1 Madison Ave., New York City. They publish several song books for community singing and are authorities on this subject. It was one of their song books that we used at the Richmond Conference. Another source of information would be the Russell Sage Foundation, 130 East 22nd St., New York City.

It might also be wise for the Pendleton people to secure the hymnals of the liberal churches, such as the Congregationalist, and see if they can find what they need among them.

Friendly News Notes

"The Chocolate Uncle" with which the November Number of *The Wayfarer* (the little Quaker Monthly, 15 Devonshire Street, E. C. 2., 1d) opens is a delightful appreciation of the late George Cadbury from the pen of the talented Austrian Poetess and Educationist, Frau Scheu Riesz. This tribute from an "ex-enemy" is a fitting one and shows one of the many little (but not by others unremembered) acts of kindness which filled so large a part of George Cadbury's life.

West Philadelphia First-day School has arranged for an "Automobile race" from Thirty-fifth and Lancaster to Orange Grove, California, and the first to arrive is to wigwag the news to Margaret Riggs in China. Lewis Kirk, Superintendent, has already assigned the "Autos" to each class. The course or journey is laid out and charts each mile. 10 miles for perfect attendance, 5 miles for a new pupil, 2 miles for a visitor and a percentage attendance at meeting is credited as mileage. Lewis H. Kirk, Jos. J. Bailey and W. J. MacWatters were chosen as a highway committee to settle all disputes and act as a repair gang. The Christmas celebration is to be on Second-day, Twelfth month 18, for which preparations have begun.

The sub-committee on Prison Reform of the Philanthropic Committee of Philadelphia Quarterly Meeting has joined, with representation on the Council, the Penal Reform Society of Pennsylvania. Dr. Kirchway, who succeeded Thomas Mott Osborne at Sing Sing, is Director of the Penal Reform Society of Pennsylvania. He is now traveling over the state starting local organizations.

Don't miss the chance to hear him when he comes to Philadelphia!

The Young Friends' Movement of Philadelphia Yearly Meeting is having its annual Membership Campaign at this time. The need for funds is only one reason back of this campaign. The bigger reason is the desire to increase the active membership by bringing into a fuller co-operation a large group of young Friends who are now only nominal members. The Movement feels that it has a work to do that is bounded only by the number of people old and young who believe that the Society of

Friends depends upon its younger members for its future strength and influence. To keep the young Friends interested in the Society, united in Quaker fellowship and engaged in Christian service is the three-fold aim of the Movement. To do this requires a certain amount of money for printing outlines to be used in Study Groups, for sending delegates to Conferences and Yearly Meetings, and for postage and other materials used in keeping young Friends in touch with each other and with Quaker activities of today.

We gladly receive and deeply appreciate contributions from older Friends who believe in this work and who have faith in the young Friends. Anyone interested in sending subscriptions to the Movement may do so by visiting, or communicating with, Elizabeth Ann Walter, Executive Secretary, 154 N. 15th Street, Philadelphia, Pa.

Women's organizations all over the world are being asked to send delegates to the Women's International Conference, convened by the Women's International League for Peace and Freedom at the Hague, December 7-9, 1922.

The following names of those who are going as Friends' delegates have been sent in: Lucy Biddle Lewis, Lansdowne, Pa.; Hannah Clothier Hull, Swarthmore, Pa.; Frances M. White, Cardington, Pa.; Caroline Roberts, Baltimore, Md.; Agnes Tierney, Philadelphia, Pa. (now in Europe); Effie D. McAfee, New York, N. Y.; Caroline Norment, Baltimore, Md. (on way home from Russia); Rachel Davis DuBois, Pitman, N. J.

The Peace Treaties have failed because they were based on greed and revenge. It is this basis that must be changed. In this conference the political, military, economic and psychological aspects will be considered. The appeal is made to every one who is in sympathy with the objects of the Conference to attend the Conference as a delegate, or if this is not possible, to send a subscription for the Conference to the U. S., Section of the W. I. L. P. F., 1403 H. Street, Washington, D. C., where you can also apply for further information. Also, help these women who are helping the world by discussing the object of the Conference with your friends and through the press.

William C. Rowland, of Germantown, member of Green Street Monthly Meeting, has been elected a Manager of the Grandom Institution in place of Thomas P. Bacon, who has resigned on account of ill health.

The Institution is an unique organization, having been established in the will of Hart Grandom about 1840. It possesses two funds of considerable amount, one of them for the purpose of loaning money to "Young men who arrive at manhood and want assistance to commence the various vocations they have learned and whose parents are unable or unwilling to aid them." The other portion of the fund is to be devoted to "Alleviate the most prudent of poor, not intemperate, in procuring fuel, clothing and other necessities, which such persons want in winter." The administration of the latter fund consists in supplying coal at greatly reduced prices to widows throughout the city.

The managers are of almost equal numbers of Friends of 15th and Race Streets and 4th and Arch Streets Yearly Meetings. They are as follows: William H. Haines, T. Morris Perot, Jr., George M. Wainer, Edward M. Wistar, John Story Jenks, J. Henry Scattergood, George Vaux, Jr., William S. Ingram, Charles F. Jenkins, James A. Bunting, Hugh McIlvain, Isaac H. Clothier, Jr., James Buckman, William C. Rowland.

feature was the planting of a young oak tree in the Meeting-house yard, with appropriate exercises by a group of children. J. Bernard Hilliard said that the young tree might be considered a birthright member, since it was a scion of the famous tree, believed to be 400 years of age, which still flourished in the Friends' burial ground.

After this, a bountiful lunch was provided, including a huge birthday cake, on which there were one hundred and fifty candles.

At the afternoon session, eight ministers from the various churches of Salem were seated side by side in the speakers' gallery. The kindly greetings from all of these, including two young colored ministers, were delivered with excellent taste, laying emphasis on their points of agreement with Friends' principles.

Dr. Rufus M. Jones then gave one of his inspirational talks, the subject being "The Need of the Hour." Only one or two points can be touched upon in this limited space. He said that the first of the world's needs was the *vision of a better social order.* Four years had elapsed since the signing of the armistice, which was to usher in an era of peace,—and international relations were now in a worse condition than before. Our statesmen lack vision, and "where there is no vision the people perish."

Every great advance was due to some one who had vision—who had *faith in the invisible.* As instances in the realm of science, he cited Sir Isaac Newton with the law of gravitation; Edison with electricity, and Marconi with wireless transmission.

The next need was *a dynamic faith.* As a Society of Friends, they must not be content with a passive belief that things would be better at some future time; but an energetic faith that would strive against all odds—and overcome them. They must attempt the impossible. In this connection, he quoted an epitaph from an old tombstone which read, "*She hath done what she couldn't.*"

The celebration was well planned and carried through without a hitch, thanks to the able management of J. Bernard and Sarah A. Hilliard, backed up with the hearty co-operation of the Salem Friends." D. B.

WOOLMAN SCHOOL NOTES

The Week-end Course at Woolman School closed on the 4th and 5th. Dr. Henry T. and Rowntree Gillett were there and lead a discussion preceding the Seventh-day evening lecture in which the "thrashing meetings" of early Quakerism were seen to be an effective way of sharing our message with seekers outside our membership.

The following expressions of appreciation show how the opportunity has appealed to the week-enders who have become a vital part of this term's family life.

"Six week-ends is an excellent length of time for the growth of social spirit among a group of twenty or thirty people of varying ages from different towns. The Woolman School Week-end students discovered this to be true. The first two week-ends one became acquainted with one's table neighbors and room-mate; the general conversation of the table being extended on short strolls in the woods or after Meeting. By the third week-end the students were ready to be welded into a real party if the right event occurred and the Camp Fire supper on Alligator Rock proved the right event. No people are strangers who have eaten food and sung old songs around a log fire among great trees as the night comes on.

The Hallowe'en Celebration and the closing Party with charades and one sketch from "The Book of Quaker Saints" were real family parties with the spirit of a family that enjoys making merry together."

ANNA OWERS.

"We feel that our course at Woolman School was very successful. It has given us a better understanding of Jesus' teachings, combined with a better knowledge of the Bible. We will not soon forget, also, the kind hospitality our hostess gave us. Then here's to our term at Woolman!"

MARY WALKER,
DOROTHY MICHENER.

"Hello! Hello! Jim there?—

Hello, Jim! How's thee?—

I say, Jim, I see there's to be another week-end course out at Woolman School this year, starting next Seventh-day. Doesn't thee want to take it with me? I was there in 1922 and it certainly was great. Nice crowd. Very lively bunch of girls. And it sure is a fine place to be that time of year. Wonderful scenery up and down the Crum. If you want to, you can take in the games at the College and perhaps angle a bid to a College soiree after the Saturday evening lecture.—

You bet I did! Only there turned out to be none that night, worse luck.—

No, you don't have to go to Alligator Rock. There're lots of places just as pretty, if not prettier, and not so thickly populated.—

Yes, we all eat together and have jolly good times, too.— Yes, and plenty of it.—

No. I haven't an idea who's going this year, but it's worth taking a chance.—

Oh, yes. A lecture Seventh-day evening and another First-day morning. Mighty fine, too. Elbert Russell leads them. Might be more discussion, but that's the fault of the class and not his.—

That's fine, Jim. Then I'll meet thee next Seventh-day, on the one o'clock train.—So long."

ERNEST N. VOTAW.

"I have just finished the six-week Week-end Bible study course at Woolman School, Swarthmore, under Dr. Elbert Russell—and I wish I had it to do over again! I consider it one of the most worthwhile courses, for so short a period that I have ever attended; unique in its comprehensiveness and completeness. Teaching the meanings of the Parables as contained in the Gospels. Dr. Russell took for the basis of the study, eight chapters of Charles Foster Kent's book, "The Life and Teachings of Jesus," adding, however, much not to be found in text books as he drew treasures of his rich experiences of the Christian life.

As a course for teachers, for Sunday School workers, social workers and others whose tastes and professions make them leaders of young people, I do not know where anything similar so satisfactory could be found. Certainly, the pleasant week-end spent in the school is an inspiration itself. In this way the group touches the life of the school and absorbs its quiet temper and before the actual evening lecture begins, is imbued with its "atmosphere." I would that all who have to do with teaching or leading the young might have advantage of such a school. It is like a refreshing spring in a thirsty land out of which one may drink to his soul's comfort.

In the varied group in the quiet study, were men and women of vastly different ages, interests and experiences, and yet, in the absorbing work a sense of unity, of common thinking, was produced under the skillful leadership of Dr. Russell. Not a small part of the plan is the discussion which occurs, sometimes during the lecture itself or at other intervals following the more formal instruction. No point is too trivial for consideration of the class; no intricate question too difficult to be discussed. Nothing is ever passed over until the questioner is satisfied. Enough ground is covered in twelve lectures to form the basis of a winter's study with a class. I consider it a great privilege to have been one of the week-end students this fall and shall endeavor to take advantage of such a course whenever it may be offered at Woolman again."

J. MACKLIN BEATTIE,
General Secretary,
Wilmington Young Women's Christian Association.

Items from Everywhere

The American Red Cross during the year ending June 30, 1922, expended more than $1,441,000 in responding to seventy-two disasters, in which 674 persons were reported killed and 521 injured.

A monumental English dictionary, on which Oxford lexicographers have been at work for thirty years, will be issued sometime during next year.

The Rockefeller Foundation spent $8,666,813 during 1921 in the promotion of public health and medical education throughout the world.

Of the 530 men and one woman who are at present members of the House of Representatives and the Senate, more than 300 are lawyers.

American Education week is to be observed December 3rd to 9th. In order that the campaign might be concentrated upon phases of education, which are of outstanding significance, the following topics have been arranged for certain days: Sunday, December 3, God and Country; Monday, December 4, American Citizenship; Tuesday, December 5, Patriotism; Wednesday, December 6, School and Teacher; Thursday, December 7, Illiteracy; Friday, December 8, Equality of Opportunity; and Saturday, December 9, Physical Education and Hygiene.

THE OPEN FORUM

This column is intended to afford free expression of opinion by readers on questions of interest. The INTELLIGENCER is not responsible for any such opinions. Letters must be brief, and the editor reserves the right to omit parts if necessary to save space.

BROTHERHOOD

To the Editor:

Will the following thoughts mean anything to some of the recent writers in the Forum? They mean much to me.

I think we are all aiming at Brotherhood, whatever our name, or the limit of our human vision, whatever our fears, or our suffering.

But one says: Brotherhood cannot come until the I. W. W. is controlled or annihilated. And one says: Brotherhood cannot come until Capitalism is controlled or annihilated.

And our Father, He who loves us *all*, in spite of our sins and our imperfect vision, what does He say? I think He says: Ye *are* brothers *now*, love each other. Not I. W. W. only brothers to those who agree with them; not Capitalists only brothers to those who agree with them; but now brothers to each other, and each therefore bound not merely to love those who love them. Who was it said that, about loving only those who love us? And what else did He say, He, our elder brother, what did He say about loving enemies? He did not say merely loving our own set, but enemies. Who are enemies? He did not say if we annihilated our enemies, imprisoned them, blew them up with bombs, that then, when they were gone, all gone, it would be easy for those who were left to be brothers. No, He did not say that; what did He say? Did He not mean we *are* brothers *now*, good or bad, wise or foolish, *poor* or *rich*, and that we *must act* to each other *like brothers*, both sets of us, neither one hating the other? And if we do that, all of us, how will things be then? Just think of it!

ELEANOR SCOTT SHARPLES.

To the Editor:

So splendid is the poem "Speak Out" in this week's INTELLIGENCER that I feel moved to congratulate you on being able to offer your readers such a message. It thrills like a trumpet blast that summons all those who would be of God's army to clothe themselves in the whole armor of Christ, and advance valiantly against the hosts of evil.

West Chester, Pa. ROBERT T. KERLIN.

AMERICA ON THE DEFENSIVE OR OFFENSIVE

To the Editor:

Elizabeth H. Coale, in her letter to the Open Forum, compares the propagandism of radical theories in the United States with criminal barn burning. I believe I can show her that she has lost faith in her own country, lost faith in the principles of liberty and justice for which the Republic advances, lost faith in the Constitution, even tho she calls it "the best the world has ever witnessed."

I say she has lost faith in the United States because she thinks such a principle as political liberty is endangered by what she believes to be false doctrines. The false cannot supplant the true. America is not on the defensive! America must not try to be on the defensive. America must have enough faith in her own ideals, to continue on the offensive.

The founders of the Republic were on the offensive. They promoted an idea of democracy which ever since has been winning the acceptance of increasing numbers of mankind. Let us continue to advance our own liberties, and no false propaganda can hurt us.

America is not a below-sea-level country needing dykes to keep out a flood of Bolshevism. Rather, let Bolshevism look to its dykes before the flood of American principles! Will not Elizabeth Coale agree with me as to which has more reason to fear the other, Americanism or Bolshevism?

If, in our Courts, we "deny justice to millions" as Elihu Root says we are doing, if we deny freedom of speech and of press, we give radicals a just basis for their arguments against us.

Without the first ten amendments, which guarantee freedom of speech and assembly, etc., the Constitution would not have endured thus long. As for its being "the best the world has ever witnessed," modify the statement to " the best the eighteenth century produced." Several twentieth century Constitutions, notably Mexico's, have had the advantage of time and have improved upon ours. Before long, we will improve upon ours by constitutional amendment, if we keep our faith alive.

FREDERICK J. POHL.
Brooklyn, N. Y.

BIRTHS

JENKS—On Eleventh month 9th, to Barton Loag and Elizabeth Andrews Jenks, of Rutherford, N. J., a son, who is named Barton Loag Jenks, Jr.

PARRY—On Eleventh month 7th, to Henry Crawford and Mary Knight Parry, of Langhorne, Pa., a son, who is named William B. K. Parry.

PEASLEE—To Amos Jenkins and Dorothy Quinby Peaslee, of 1169 Park Avenue, a daughter, who is named Dorothy Waddington Peaslee.

DEATHS

HOLLINGSWORTH—Near Wilna, Harford County, Md., on Tenth month 29th, Rebecca G. Hollingsworth, in her 82nd year. A life-long and deeply interested member of Little Falls Monthly Meeting.

MAGILL—At New Hope, Pa., on Eleventh month 5th, Caroline L. Magill, wife of Ezra C. Magill, aged 78 years.

RICHARDSON—On Ninth month 16th, at Friends' Boarding Home, West Chester, Pa., Alice A. Richardson, in her 88th year.

STACKHOUSE—Near Oxford Valley, Pa., suddenly, on Eleventh month 13th, Henry Stackhouse, aged 61.

COMING EVENTS

25th to 27th—Warrington Quarterly Meeting, at Menallen, Pa. O. Edward Janney expects to attend.

26th—Certain members of Philadelphia Quarterly Meeting's Visiting Committee expect to attend meeting for worship at Schuylkill, at 10.30 a. m.

26th—Conference Class at Fifteenth and Race Streets, Philadelphia, at close of meeting for worship, 11.40 a. m. Subject—Prophets of Education. Leader—Jane P. Rushmore.

26th—West Philadelphia Bible Class, 35th and Lancaster Avenue, 10 a. m. Subject—Liberalism.

26th—Thanksgiving will be celebrated in advance by the Brooklyn First-day School, on First-day the 26th. Several of the children, of different classes, will give, as a part of the First-day School exercises, the little Thanksgiving play which appeared in the INTELLIGENCER for Eleventh month 4th.

28th—The Brooklyn Fellowship group will meet, as usual, at the meeting-house. Supper will be at 6.30. All who wish to attend the supper will please notify Caroline Underhill. At 8 o'clock Charles McDowell will give a talk on "Europe After the War," to which all are cordially invited.

30th—It is planned to have a meeting of all Friends at the meeting-house, 144 East Twentieth Street, New York, on Thanksgiving Day morning, at 11 o'clock. The presence of a large number from the meetings in Greater New York and vicinity is hoped for.

30th—Bucks Quarterly Meeting at Langhorne, Pa.

TWELFTH MONTH

1st—West Philadelphia First-day School Fall Social, 7.30 p. m. An evening of fun and pleasure. Everybody invited. Refreshments.

2nd—Nottingham Quarterly Meeting, at Little Britain, Pa.

2nd—Whitewater Quarterly Meeting, at Fall Creek, Indiana.

4th—Millville Half-yearly Meeting, at Millville, Pa.

7th—Salem Quarterly Meeting, at Woodbury, N. J.

14th—Haddonfield Quarterly Meeting, at Moorestown, N. J.

18th—Christmas Entertainment and exercises at West Philadelphia First-day School, 35th and Lancaster Avenue. Bring your gifts for the poor and hear the children sing. 7.30 p. m.

NOTICE—Anyone knowing Friends living in Detroit, Michigan, is requested to send names and addresses to L. Oscar Moon, 2574 2nd Blvd., so that an effort may be made to connect them with our Meeting.

American Friends' Service Committee

WILBUR K. THOMAS, EX. SEC.
20 S. 12th St. Philadelphia.

CASH CONTRIBUTIONS

WEEK ENDING NOVEMBER 13TH.

Five Years Meetings	$162.00
Other Meetings:	
New Garden Prep. Meeting	50.00
Baltimore Yearly Meeting	220.00
Westerly Meeting	100.00
Dayton Monthly Meeting	12.70
Chester Monthly Meeting	100.00
Minneapolis, Monthly Meeting	12.40
Contributions for Germany	1,406.39
For Austria	4,121.56
For Poland	3,353.05
For Russia	8,040.55
Russian Overhead	130.00
For Syria	190.15
Message Committee	5.00
For General	203.50
Miscellaneous Sources for General	645.00
Refunds	235.75
	$18,988.05

Shipments received during week ending November 11th: 41 boxes and packages; 1 from Mennonites.

CASH CONTRIBUTIONS RECEIVED FROM MEMBERS OF THE PHILADELPHIA YEARLY MEETING OF FRIENDS, 15TH AND RACE STS., OCTOBER.

Swarthmore Mo. by Jesse H. Holmes	$50.00
Lansdowne Mo. by C. C. Lippincott, general	60.00
Wilmington Mo. by S. H. Stradley	1,022.00
Abington Mo. by W. L. Lewis	50.00
Millville by Bernice Eves	13.00
Individual Friends	50.00
	$1,245.00

Buck Hill Falls Company

The annual meeting of the stockholders of the Buck Hill Falls Company will be held in the auditorium of the Philadelphia Young Friends' Association, 140 N. 15th Street, on Fourth-day afternoon, Twelfth month 6th, 1922, at 2 o'clock.

MORGAN BUNTING, *Clerk.*

REGULAR MEETINGS

OAKLAND, CALIF. — A FRIENDS' Meeting is held every First-day at 11 A. M., in the Extension Room, Y. W. C. A. Building, Webster Street, above 14th. Visiting Friends always welcome.

PASADENA, CALIFORNIA — Orange Grove Monthly Meeting of Friends, 520 East Orange Grove Avenue. Meeting for worship, First-day, 11 A. M. Monthly Meeting, the second First-day of each month, at 1.45 P. M. First-day School (except Monthly Meeting days) 9.45 A. M.

FUN

"Are you sure you have shown me all the principal parts of this car?" asked the fair prospective purchaser.

"Yes, madam, all the main ones," replied the dealer.

"Well, then, where is the depreciation? Tom told me that was one of the biggest things about a car."—*Exchange.*

A writer of popular stories was one day being shown through a book-shop in New York. A small table was devoted to the new books, and all the rest of the space was taken up with gorgeous editions of Stevenson, Dickens, Scott, Thackeray, Fielding, etc.—fine leather-bound volumes at very modest prices.' The writer indicated with a sweep of his arm this collection of books and observed, "Literature would pay better if there were not so many dead men in the business."—*Harper's Magazine.*

A lady who had just received an interesting bit of news said to her little daughter: "Marjorie, dear, auntie has a new baby, and now mamma is the baby's aunt, papa is the baby's uncle, and you are her little cousin." "Well," said Marjorie, wonderingly, "wasn't that arranged quick!"—*Boston Transcript.*

Three little boys began to brag about the ability of their respective fathers. One boy said, "Well, my father can write a song, take it down street, and sell it for $10 any time, and he does it, too." The second boy earnestly insisted that *his* father could, and did, write an article for the daily paper, which brought him $25 for each article. The third boy, a minister's son, calmly announced, "Ho. *My* father can go to the attic on Saturday afternoon, get an ole sermon out of his box, and the next morning after he has preached it, it takes four men to carry the money up to him."

WANTED

.NTED—GOOD HOME OR BOARDng place with cheerful surroundings iiddle-aged lady, mentally somewhat ent. State probable terms. Address 0, Friends' Intelligencer.

.VERCROFT," CLAYMONT, DEL. Special home care for invalids, or and physical upbuilding. Reference iplication. E. H. Speakman, R. N.

NTED—FOR A FEW WEEKS OR longer, a settled woman for chamork and waiting, in a suburb of delphia. Small family, no washing. wages. Address P. O. Box 1682, delphia, Pa.

S. GOVERNMENT UNDERWEAR— 2,500,000 pc. New Government Wool rwear purchased by us to sell to the direct at 75c EACH. Actual retail $2.50 each. All sizes, Shirts 34 to)rawers 30 to 44. Send correct sizes. Postman on delivery or send us y order. If underwear is not satis-y, we will refund money promptly request. Dept. 24, Pilgrim Woolen 476 Broadway, New York, N. Y.

.ARIED STENOGRAPHER, NIGHTS se, can report occasional daylight ngs. Geo. B. Cock, (Phila.) phone ory.

ITION WANTED—BY REFINED iddle-aged woman, experienced keeper and companion to one or lderly people. Reference. Address M., Moorestown, New Jersey.

ISTMAS CARDS — HAND COLed. Twelve sent on approval. One if retained (or ten cents each). a Sellers, Young Friends' Associa-Philadelphia.

NTED—SUMS OF $900 AND $400 in first mortgages in the City of er. Security ample. Charles Palmer, st Fifth Street, Chester, Pa.

'ine Newtown Property

at Private Sale

'esidence of the late Thaddeus S. erdine, corner State and Sterling ts, near George School.

brick house, with all conveniences; barn; surrounded by large shade trees. the best properties in town. Sold to the Estate.

Robert Kenderdine
Louis R. Kenderdine } Executors

FUN

, easy it is to mistranslate an ard remark. Said Mrs. A, "They have been to the zoo, because I her mention 'a trained deer.'" Mrs. B: "No, no. They were g about going away, and she said n, 'Find out about the train, ' Said Mrs. C: "I think you th wrong. It seemed to me they discussing music, for she said, ned ear' very distinctly." A few s later the lady herself ap-, and they told her of their dis-ient. "Well," she laughed, certainly funny. You are poor rs, all of you. The fact is, I'd at to the country overnight, and sking my husband if it rained last evening."—*Boston Tran-*

To the Lot Holders and others interested in Fairhill Burial Ground:

GREEN STREET Monthly Meeting has funds available for the encouragement of the practice of cremating the dead to be interred in Fairhill Burial Ground. We wish to bring this fact as prominently as possible to those who may be interested. We are prepared to undertake the expense of cremation in case any lot holder desires us to do so.

Those interested should communicate with William H. Gaskill, Treasurer of the Committee of Interments, Green Street Monthly Meeting, or any of the following members of the Committee.

William H. Gaskill, 3201 Arch St.
Samuel N. Longstreth, 1218 Chestnut St.
Charles F. Jenkins, 232 South Seventh St.
Stuart S. Graves, 3033 Germantown Ave.

ADVERTISING RATE in the FRIENDS' INTELLIGENCER, for Help Wanted, Positions Wanted, Rooms for Rent, and other classified advertisements without display, for each insertion, 2 cents per word, including name, initials and address. Answers may be sent to a box at the INTELLIGENCER office, if so directed.

For display advertising the rate is 10 cents per agate line, or $1.40 per column inch, each insertion. On ten or more insertions in a year from date of order, ten per cent. discount. Thus a four-inch single-column or two-inch double-column advertisement costs $5.60 each insertion, less ten per cent., or $5.04 net each time for ten or more insertions. Matter may be changed whenever desired, without extra charge.

Experience has proved the INTELLIGENCER to be a remarkably good advertising medium. All advertisements must "pass the censor!"

Address 140 N. 15th St., Philadelphia.

The Friends' Intelligencer

Established 1844 | TWELFTH MONTH 2, 1922 | Volume 79 Number 48

Contents

EDITORIALS

GENERAL ARTICLES

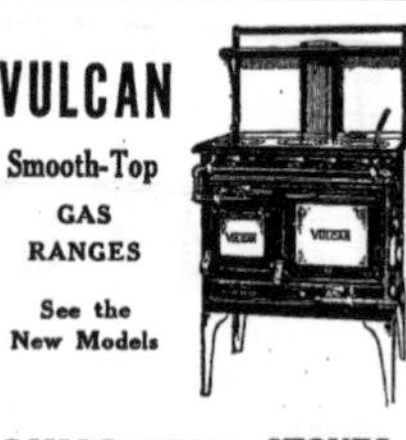

THE FRIENDS' INTELLIGENCER

Published weekly, 140 N. 15th Street, Philadelphia, Pa., by Friends' Intelligencer Association, Ltd.

SUE C. YERKES, *Managing Editor.*

Editorial Board: Elizabeth Powell Bond, Thomas A. Jenkins, J. Russell Smith, George A. Walton.

Board of Managers: Edward Cornell, Alice Hall Paxson, Paul M. Pearson, Annie Hillborn, Elwood Hollingshead, William C. Biddle, Charles F. Jenkins, Edith M. Winder, Frances M. White.

Officers of Intelligencer Associates: Ellwood Burdsall, Chairman; Bertha L. Broomell, Secretary; Herbert P. Worth, Treasurer.

Subscription rates: United States, Mexico, Cuba and Panama, $2.50 per year. Canada and other foreign countries, $3.00 per year. Checks should be made payable to Friends' Intelligencer Association, Ltd.

Entered as Second Class Matter at Philadelphia Post Office

The Friends' Intelligencer

The religion of Friends is based on faith in the "INWARD LIGHT," or direct revelation of God's spirit and will in every seeking soul.

The INTELLIGENCER is interested in all who bear the name of Friends in every part of the world, and aims to promote love, unity and intercourse among all branches and with all religious societies.

ESTABLISHED 1844 — PHILADELPHIA, TWELFTH MONTH 2, 1922 — VOLUME 79 NUMBER 48

"Modern Hunters for the Truth"

Under this title there appears in the *Literary Digest* of November 18th an article setting forth the tentative program of the Modern Churchmen's Union of America, recently formed in New York by a small body of Episcopal clergymen who claim the right to put their own spiritual interpretation on the creeds, in accordance with the results of modern science and of Biblical scholarship.

The tentative program of the Union includes the following purposes:

"To maintain the right to interpret the historic expressions of our faith in accordance with the results of modern science and Biblical scholarship.

"To advance, as an aid to the ultimate reunion of Christendom, co-operation and fellowship between the Protestant Episcopal Church and other Protestant churches.

"To promote a new evangelism among the unchurched classes of our population, which shall win their allegiance to the religious and moral demands of the Kingdom of God.

"To further the application of Christian principles in all industrial, social and international relations.

"To promote the adaptation of the church services to the needs of the time.

"To emphasize afresh the nature of the Christian life as personal fellowship with God and to study with sympathy those movements and tendencies of thought which are mystical in character."

"Sincere and deep religious conviction, a spirit of honest and unhampered search after the truth, practical interest in the problems of social life and a purpose as churchmen to enlarge and inspire the company of believers," comments the Springfield *Republican*, "are connoted by the program in its entirety. Whether it is entirely 'orthodox' depends, perhaps, upon its application."

This action on the part of a group of Episcopal clergymen is merely an indication of the trend of thought in all religious denominations. The attack by certain Presbyterians on Dr. Harry Emerson Fosdick, a Baptist minister preaching in a Presbyterian pulpit, is paralleled by the dismissal of the Rev. J. D. M. Buckner, of Aurora, Nebraska, an honored clergyman who has served in the ministry of the Methodist Episcopal Church for nearly forty years, by the Nebraska Conference last September because they objected to his opinions with regard to the "verbal inspiration of the Bible."

All denominations are recognizing that within their ranks are the two groups, the Progressives and the Fundamentalists. Is the church, as at present organized, big enough to hold them both? The last session of the Five Years Meeting of Friends passed through this ordeal in a way to give all Friends satisfaction and cause for rejoicing. We are, perhaps, better equipped to meet this test than other religious denominations for we are not hampered by any set creed, thus each member may have consideration for and tolerance of the other's point of view.

As Dr. Fosdick says, "Intolerance solves no problems," and it is only as we give freedom for expression of opinion on these as well as all other matters, that we may hope to reach a right conclusion. The steam boiler which has no safety-valve explodes, and the Church which tolerates no differences of belief and no freedom of expression defeats its own purpose.

The Indian Needs Our Help

In the Nation (London), issue of August 12th, 1922, appeared the following, in a letter from C. E. Maurice:

"If I thought that M. Poincare and Mr. Lloyd George had Europe at their mercy, I should indeed despair. But since the war, I have been more and more impressed with the powers of small and comparatively obscure bodies to affect both public opinion and the course of events. Bodies like the Friends' Relief Committees, the Save the Children Committee, and the League of Nations (which is still scorned by so many for its smallness and incompleteness), have done more to influence the minds of men, and therefore, to guide events, than any Prime Ministers, or Field Marshals, or millionaires, and I think it is most dangerous for private citizens to underestimate their own importance."

This extract was sent us by Edward Thomas, of New York, who wrote, "I think the extract is too flattering to be published without comment." It is, indeed, most encouraging to feel that we have had a part not only in caring for the material relief of the suffering world, but that we also have been of assistance in "influencing the minds of men."

While the tribute is flattering, there is nothing but the truth in the statement that "it is most dangerous for private citizens to underestimate their own importance" in the matter of helping in the shaping of the policies of their respective countries. In view of this fact, we wish to urge all Friends to read carefully the article in this issue "Arise Quickly and Help," and then follow the suggestions there outlined to help the Indian in this his fight for life. We must remember that, *with millions in prospect, no effort will be spared to get possession of the Indian's land, and it is a duty we should not dare neglect, to at least record our protest.*

Arise Quickly and Help

Recently an Indian was haled before a court in New Mexico by a white man. The Indian was about seventy years of age, with snow-white hair and the finely chiseled, sensitive, self-respecting face which naturally commands the respect of persons of fine feeling. The interpretor, after much questioning, got this story.

"All my life," said the Indian, "I have been going ten miles from my home at the pueblo to work in my corn patch, where the big gully runs into the canyon. My father and my grandfather tilled that corn patch, and no one has ever disturbed us. One day, as I went with my baskets to bring home on my back a load of corn and beans and pumpkins, I saw this white man driving stakes in my garden. 'What are you doing?' I asked. 'You get out of here, you Indian, or I will fill you full of buckshot. That's what I am doing!' "

"Did you strike the white man?"

"No."

"Did he strike you?"

"No."

But the white man had haled the Indian into court for assault. This is but one of the many cases that now keep some of the courts of New Mexico busy in the attempt to prove the bad character of the Indian. *The Indian has land.*

For 5000 years, perhaps 10,000 years, the Pueblo Indians have lived in their stone houses on the mesas of the southwestern plateaus, laboriously winning a living from a dry and desolate country. Sometimes the Indian travels ten, twenty, or even thirty miles to a place where a little trickle or seepage of water enables him, with the most arduous toil, to produce the few bushels of grain that feed his family until the next harvest.

In one of those many treaties which we have so often made, and much too often broken, we set apart as the permanent home of these Indians a reservation in the dry (and generally considered worthless) lands of New Mexico and Arizona. But now these reservations are fairly swarming with white men, squatters, who have moved in and are driving stakes for the boundaries of pieces of land. *There are rumors of oil!*

Behold! Suddenly a law has passed the U. S. Senate. It is called the Bursum Indian Land Law, and if it becomes a law it will "stultify the government and add another failure to its record in dealing with dependent people." This Bursum law proposes to remove the Indians from under the care of the National government, which as guardian has done some helpful things for these dependent people, and t place them under the jurisdiction of the state of New Mexico. In New Mexico, the Indian is regarded and treated very much as is the negro in some of the southern states. Yet more! This Bursum law gives the squatters who have claimed land in this territory such land as they have claimed. This drives out the Pueblos, as paupers, into the desert. This is unspeakable.

Fortunately, this bill is not yet a law. First, it must pass the House of Representatives, then it must be signed by the President. What can the readers of the FRIENDS' INTELLIGENCER do to stop this wholesale robbery and eviction, this driving out into the desert to perish a people who have occupied their homesites for a time longer than history and have developed an admirable and unique culture? *We can do the following things and we must do them quickly.*

1. Every Monthly Meeting in the Society can within the next thirty days send protests to H. P. Snyder and Clyde M. Kelly, House of Representatives, Washington, D. C., telling them of our opposition to the Bursum Indian Land Bill (Senate Bill No. 3855) which is now before the House Committee and should be killed in committee by an avalanche of protest.

2. Every man and woman voter who reads this

can send a personal letter to Hon. Clyde M. Kelly and Hon. H. P. Snyder and can spend an afternoon or evening asking their friends to send protests. Every copy of this issue of the INTELLIGENCER should be good for at least five letters of emphatic protest. This is one of the most effective ways of voting, the only way by which we can speak our minds and ask our government not to commit an act which parallels the driving out of Christians for which the Turk is blamed.

This Indian situation should serve as a convincing statement of the necessity of more Quaker memberships in the Indian Rights Association, an organization with a secretary whose task it is to let the rest of us know when we can help to do some thing to prevent the annihilation of a harmless and innocent people who have already fared badly enough at the hands of our race.

This fight at best is one between the poorly equipped and the well equipped. The forces of exploitation, with prospective millions that the Indian's land may give, can well afford to hire expert attorneys and skillful lobbyists to get bills through legislatures, and, furthermore, spend money to poison the public mind by false propaganda. Our answer to this is to fight this bill at once and to support the Indian Rights Association, at least with cash and memberships and here and there, with the more precious aid of personal service, which selects this as the cause for that *active opposition to evil* which John Morley points out as the factor that differentiates good people from others.

Persons desiring to become members of the Indian Rights Association should present their names and addresses to the President, who will submit them to the Board of Directors for election. An annual fee of two dollars is required of members, in return for which they are entitled to all publications of the society. Herbert Welsh, President I. R. A., 995 Drexel Building, Philadelphia.

J. RUSSELL SMITH
JESSE H. HOLMES
WM. I. HULL

Copy of letter of protest sent by Swarthmore Monthly Meeting.

November 23, 1922.

HON. H. P. SNYDER,
House of Representatives.
Washington, D. C.
ESTEEMED FRIEND:

At the regular business session of Swarthmore Monthly Meeting of Friends, held Eleventh month twenty-first, 1922, the status of the Pueblo Indians as affected by the Bursum Indian Land Bill (Senate Bill No. 3855) was gravely and earnestly discussed.

It appears that there are conflicting interests between the Indians and outsiders who have settled on much of the best land to which the Indians have title. If the bill becomes a law these trespassers will be given title to the land upon which they now reside. Furthermore, this bill, if passed, will subject the Pueblo Indians to the partial and antagonistic jurisdiction of the courts of the State of New Mexico, instead of the Federal courts.

We want to see this bill utterly and wholly defeated We regard it not only as grossly unjust, but also as fatal to the physical welfare and cultural development of a race whose fate lies in our hands. Swarthmore Monthly Meeting will use every means within its power to extend a knowledge of the facts concerning Senate Bill No. 3855 and will co-operate with others who are working to that end.

We pray that our government may not add another failure to its record in dealing with dependent peoples, but that justice may prevail.

Very truly thy friends,
SWARTHMORE MONTHLY MEETING OF FRIENDS.
HENRIETTA STEWART SMITH, *Clerk.*

If I Were a Spirit

If I were a Spirit, and gifted with might
To lift up the fallen, or carry the Light
To those heavy-laden, or blinded by sin;—
Think you I would falter, or fail to begin?

If I were a Spirit, and gifted with love
To comfort the sorrowing, to point them above
To the Source of all comfort, the strength of whose grace
Would cheer and uplift them;—would I fail in disgrace?

If I were a Spirit, and gifted with power
To open the eyes of the blind, or to shower,
Through the blessing of God, His gifts on His poor;
Would I hesitate, think you, my own joy to ensure?

Behold; I *am* Spirit! and gifted with Light,
And with love, and a share of His glorious might.
His work lies before me;—how then shall I dare
Be idle, or faithless, or sink in despair.

By the word of His grace, and the strength of His might;
By the power of His love, and His inshining Light,
The work that He shows me, that work will I do,
And praise Him forever that I can be true.

R—.

Cowardice asks, Is it safe? Expediency asks, Is it polite? Vanity asks, Is it popular? But the conscience asks, Is it right?—*Selected.*

"Meeting for Sufferings"

By Anna J. F. Hallowell

A number of study classes having asked for the meaning of "Meeting for Sufferings," and the functions of the original meeting, the following article has been prepared for use.

In a wonderful old volume there is a very long and full account of the "Institution of the Discipline," and so beautifully worded a description of the meeting for sufferings that it ought to be copied in full, but time is lacking. Briefly, the early followers of George Fox soon found the need for mutual brotherly care, and "Disciplinary" meetings were the ultimate result. Most of the early members were people of small means, but the definite form of their testimonies were not very acceptable to their neighbors, many of whom refused to trade with them, thus cutting off their means of livelihood. In many places the priests (of the English Church) forbade their congregations to have any dealings with the Quakers, who were constantly in trouble because of their refusal to take the oaths of Allegiance (to the Crown) and of Conformity (to the English Church).

"It seldom happened that the storm fell with equal violence on all parts at once. Sometimes it was severe in one county, while others adjoining it would be comparatively exempt, so that some were mostly in a condition to extend help to the sufferers. The occasions for the exercise of brotherly kindness were numerous and pressing, and they were met in a spirit of noble liberality, which has seldom been surpassed. None appeared to regard what they had as their own exclusively, but as a trust for the general benefit of all, to be freely applied in relieving the wants of their more destitute brethern." "The exercise of the spirit of kindness and accommodation toward each other, established a habit of benevolence, which showed itself in their conduct toward others, and became proverbial."

The number of imprisonments became so great that Friends could not keep up with personal knowledge of them, so a "meeting" (we would call it a Committee now-a-days) was appointed in 1675, to which all "sufferings" by Friends were to be reported.

"They (the meetings) were for the purpose of inquiring what Friends were prisoners, or from other causes needed relief—what wives had been made widows, and what children orphans, by the death of their husbands and parents in prison, and to take care that suitable provision was made for such. Another object was, to collect accounts of the sufferings of Friends by imprisonment, distraints, and other penalties for their religious principles, and prepare them for laying before those in authority. This gave opportunity for examining who were illegally imprisoned, and adopting such measures for their liberation, as the circumstances rendered proper."

The original minute reads as follows:—"Agreed, that certain Friends of this city "(London)" be nominated to keep a constant meeting about sufferings four times a year, with the day and time of each meeting here fixed and settled. That at least one Friend of each county be appointed by the Quarterly Meeting thereof, to be in readiness to repair to any of the said meetings at this city, at such times as their urgent occasions of sufferings shall require."

Nevertheless, within the next year the "urgent occasions" grew so numerous that from 1676 to 1794 the meetings took place *weekly*. Could any name be more truly descriptive than Meeting for Sufferings?

The minute of 1794 reads:—It is agreed to be sufficient, that the meeting for sufferings be held in course on the first Sixth day in each month; subject nevertheless, on any emergency, to the call of any five members thereof."

Very slowly other duties were assigned to the Meeting for Sufferings; the very first being the "inspecting, ordering, regulating the press, and printing of books; and that no books be reprinted, without the said meeting's direction"—1679.

Then the correspondence with "foreign countries" during the intervals between the Yearly Meetings to "be signed by the Meeting for Suffering on behalf of the Meeting" was added in 1730. In 1800 a minute was adopted directing the *annual* collection and printing of "a correct list of meetings for worships and discipline, and the times and places of holding them, the meetings of ministers and elders," etc.

Austria, 1922-23: Poverty-Stricken

Professions

The plight of Austria to-day illustrates the fact that war devastation is not limited to the destruction of walls and bridges. Austrian buildings were not shattered by cannon fire; but the nation's economic fabric has been disrupted by the conditions imposed by the treaty of "peace."

How real is the resultant social devastation may be judged from an incident reported by a Friend who visited Vienna last summer. She was out walking with one of her Austrian acquaintances, the wife of a well-known Viennese lawyer. They passed a spot on the sidewalk over which coal had been shot into a cellar window. A few grains of coal-dust remained on the sidewalk; and a woman of the laboring-classes was scraping it up with her hands. On seeing her, the lawyer's wife exclaimed:

"I wish *I* could do that! We need coal just as much as she does; but we cannot get it in that way. We are forced to suffer in silence."

Due to the depreciation of the krone, which is now quoted at 75,018.75 kronen to the dollar, and to the consequent rise in the cost of living, adequate salaries are practically unknown in Austria, and the salaried classes are for the most part suffering acutely. Doctors, lawyers, professors, lack the means to provide themselves and their families with the common necessities of life. Visitors to Vienna are brought down to reality with a shock when they are shown a "professor-feeding." When university professors are in need of relief feeding, one realizes that the nation is suffering in a way unheard-of in the past.

The permanent reconstruction of Austria, and of Europe, depends upon precisely these trained and thinking classes which are now caught in the grip of national poverty.. Unless they can be kept in efficient condition during this trying period, permanent reconstruction will be set back a generation. For this reason it is planned to enlarge the middle-class relief work of the American Friends' Service Committee in Austria. Most of the professions in that country are organized in the form of brotherhoods; and help to those families most in need can be tactfully rendered through such organizations. Funds for this work are urgently needed by the Service Committee, and should be sent to its treasurer, Charles F. Jenkins, at 20 South 12th street, Philadelphia, Pa.

The New Vilna District in Poland

Members of the Friends' Relief and Reconstruction Mission in Poland have just completed their third visit of investigation to the new district of Vilna, where work is being undertaken this fall and will be continued through the winter.

This district is located about 350 kilometers northeast of Warsaw, along a battle-front more completely devastated, and more difficult to repair, than any met with in France or Belgium. Its remoteness from industrial centers makes the reconstruction slow, while the Polish peasants have not been aided by the rest of the world to nearly the same extent as were the refugees on the western front. Most of the land in the Vilna district, which has not been cultivated for years, is overgrown by young birch forests.

Housing needs are terrible in the extreme. There are 40,000 people in the district without houses, living in dugouts, trenches and branch shelters. One of the investigators writes:

"I have measured dugouts in different places, but they seldom vary in size: three by four yards, and a tall man cannot stand upright without striking his head on the beams. The stove occupies most of the floor space, the heat and constant damp create an atmosphere fetid enough to strangle most people, without the addition of the 11 to 15 human beings who herd into it with all their possessions, the family cat, a chicken or two and sometimes a pig."

In one township eighty families were entirely without shelter, and this number did not include families living in dugouts or crowded into houses with other families. Lack of food is acute. In many villages, large numbers died last winter from starvation. Skerele, for example, possessed 34 families, of which four were completely wiped out. In another village 25 people died of starvation. In the village of Viszniczo, the priest said that 20 adults in his church died of starvation last winter, while children's deaths were not counted.

The investigators concluded that the northern part of the Vilna district is a genuine famine area; and that it will be necessary, if life is to be saved, to have some sort of feeding scheme this winter. The workers state that even the richest of the peasants with whom they talked were so poor that they would be fed if they were in the Russian famine zone.

Conditions such as these breed epidemic diseases Typhus has not yet appeared in epidemic form; but isolated cases are beginning; for instance, 10 teachers out of 350 have it.

It is in such a district, then, that the Friends' Mission is opening the new portion of its work for the winter. Its program will consist in providing food rations to those who would otherwise starve, establishing home industry work by which the women can help to support themselves, giving medical relief, and lending horses to the peasants for plowing and for hauling timber that will be used to reconstruct their homes. The difficulties which beset the population of the Vilna district are probably as severe as any which must be encountered in Europe this winter—for in addition to famine, they must face the devastation of the battle-front.

The American Friends' Service Committee will be glad to receive contributions, allocated especially for use in Poland, to help these innocent victims of war and European post-war conditions.

Light or Shadow?

"I'm a Quaker," I said.

"*Yes*, you are," he replied, smiling.

Such insinuating scepticism has often met my declaration of membership in the Society of Friends. However, I insisted

"Sure, I'm a Quaker."

"Well you're a fine Quaker! You dance, you play cards, you don't say "thee" and "thou." You're no more a Quaker than I am."

"I'll admit," I answered "that I may be a black sheep as regards some of the time honored customs of Quakerdom, but I believe in the fundamental principle on which the Society is founded."

"And what is that?"

I explained to him the Friends' conception of divinity and the inner light.

"Why," he said, greatly surprised, "that's exactly what I believe, but I never knew there was a religious society based on it."

The fellow to whom I was talking was a student at Yale. He was typical of thousands of young men and women of college education.

It has been my experience that the majority of those college men and women who are not atheists believe essentially what the Quakers believe. This is because the Friends' belief is perfectly compatible with the scientific theories nowadays generally accepted, and requires no exceptions, evasions, or ingenious interpretations to reconcile it with these theories; and because at the same time it completely fills the spiritual needs. George Fox was two hundred years ahead of his time. Popular religious thought has now caught up to his conceptions, and people everywhere are coming to believe what he believed. Why then is the society which is based on these ideas becoming yearly weaker when it should be experiencing the most phenominal growth of any modern Christian sect?

I believe the reasons are four:

First, many people to-day feel that declaration of faith is a matter of form, to be recited with fingers crossed, and thus continue their connections, formed thru family, with churches whose doctrines they certainly do not accept literally.

Second, many others believe that they can live their religious life fully and righteously without identifying themselves with any religious organization.

Third, many of those who believe as the Friends do, and would gladly associate themselves with some body of their own belief, do not know of the Quakers; or, having heard of them, know them only by their peculiarities and not by their principles.

Fourth, those who do believe as the Friends, who wish to associate themselves with a religious body, and who know that the Friends and they have common principles, are held off by the clannishness and age-old customs and traditions of a large number of our society.

When George Fox was alive the use of "thee" was the heroic expression of one of the logical correlaries of his basic axiom. To-day it is neither heroic nor logical, but merely sentimental. And it is one of the customs which cause outsiders visiting our society to feel like strangers in a foreign land.

Furthermore, such rather quaint customs catch the public eye to the exclusion of more important characteristics, so that, as illustrated in the conversation with which I began, Quakers are known to the world more by their peculiarities than by their beliefs. Of course they are not alone in suffering from misunderstanding in Public Opinion. Most people associate Christian Science with miraculous cures, Mohammedanism with polygamy, and Buddhism with fat squatting idols, but few know of the fine fundamental principles of these religions.

Why are religions generally known more by some non-essential characteristics than by their principles? Is it because the succeeding generations take more pride in their society's individualities than in its fundamentals? Are we ourselves thus maintaining customs which obscure from the world our real message, and at the same time keep outsiders away?

GEORGE BEMENT JACKSON

First-day School Methods

By BLISS FORBUSH.

A Christmas Service

This service is arranged for the average small school which has no platform other than that on which the benches for the ministers and overseers sit, or perhaps only a cleared space in the front of the room. No curtains are required, although they would make the scenes more effective.

Costumes

Shepherds: Either grey or brown blankets pinned around the arms and covering the body, or burlap sacks, cut kimona style, with a hole to slip over the head, to be worn over the boy's clothes. The head dress should be a shawl or strip of dark cloth wound around the head and falling down over the shoulders. Legs and arms are bare with cardboard sandals for the feet. Each shepherd has a long staff.

Wise Men: Oriental garments made of couch covers, or rich colored shawls. Turbans of purple, green, and blue. One carries a bag of money, one a treasure box, and one a box of ointment.

Arrangement

It is very pleasant to turn the entire First-day School period over to the Christmas service. The service as given would take about a half hour; the rest of the time may be used in the telling or reading of a Christmas story, or by individual or class activities. Some of these stories and activities will be mentioned in a later issue.

The only properties needed are several screens which can be borrowed from the homes of members, and material to make a fire. The fire is made by covering an electric light bulb, or a flash light, with red paper on which small sticks of wood are piled tent-like.

The Carols

"O Little Town of Bethlehem," and "It Came Upon the Midnight Clear" are in the first volume of the General Conference Hymns and Songs; "Calm on the Listening Ear of Night" is in the second volume. Music for the others can be found in other hymn books.

The opening and closing carols are to be sung by the whole school. The second and fourth are sung by a special group placed at one side of the room, in a connecting room, or behind screens. When possible, the third carol is sung by the three wise men themselves; if this is not possible, then by a male chorus. The small group which sings most of the carols should practice singing the carols together several times.

Prelude

All present sing the first three verses of "Calm on the Listening Ear of Night."

Superintendent reads (standing at one side), Luke 2:8, 9.

SCENE I.

Screens are drawn aside, showing four shepherds asleep about the fire, their heads resting on their arms, with their staves at their sides.

Chorus sings, "The First Nowell."

"The First Nowell the angel did say
Was to certain poor shephreds in fields as they lay;
In fields where they lay keeping their sheep
On a cold winter's night that was so deep.
Nowell, Nowell, Nowell, Nowell,
Born is the King of Israel."

SCENE II

Superintendent reads Luke 2: Verses 10, 11, 12, 13, 14.

Shepherds wake in consternation, gaze upward, rise, and bow in reverent prayer over their staves, while the

Chorus sings "Silent Night."

"Silent night, holy night,
All is calm, all is bright;
Round Thy children, Father on high,
Beams the light of Thy starry sky,
Sleep in heavenly peace.
Sleep in heavenly peace.

Silent night, Holy night,
Shepherds pray at the sight,
Glories stream from heaven afar,
Golden beams from the eastern star;
Comes the glorious morn,
Comes the glorious morn."

Superintendent reads Luke 2:15, 16, as shepherds walk away, gazing upward expectantly.

SCENE III

Superintendent reads Matthew 2:1, 2, 3; Matthew 2:8, 9, 10, 11, 12.

Enter three Wise Men, singing "We Three Kings of Orient Are."

Three Wise Men:

"We three kings of Orient are;
Bearing gifts we traverse afar
Field and fountain, moor and mountain,
Following yonder star.

CHORUS

O Star of wonder, Star of night,
Star with royal beauty bright,
Westward leading, still proceeding,
Guide us to Thy perfect light.

First Wise Man:

"Born a King on Bethlehem's plain,
Gold I bring, to crown him again,
King forever, ceasing never,
Over us all to reign.

CHORUS: All three.

Second Wise Man:

"Frankincense to offer have I,
Incense owns a Deity nigh.
Prayer and praising, all men raising,
Worship him, God most High.

CHORUS: All three.

Third Wise Man:

"Myrrh is mine, its bitter perfume
Breathes a life of gathering gloom;
Sorrowing, sighing, bleeding, dying,
Sealed in the stone-cold tomb.

CHORUS: All three.

Go off as they sing the last chorus.

SCENE IV

Superintendent reads Luke 2:15th through 20th verse.

Shepherds and Wise Men return, slowly cross the stage with arms outstretched, as chorus sings "O Little Town of Bethlehem." Chorus sings first two verses.

POSTLUDE

All present sing first three verses of "It Came Upon a Midnight Clear."

Christianity and Industry

"Jesus' denunciation of the Pharisees could have been edited by a committee of ministers so as to have been made entirely unoffensive," said Bishop Francis J. McConnell in his address at Friends' Select School on Eleventh month 24th.

The church is sometimes urged to stick to general principles. When we do this nobody makes the application. It is the concrete application which drives the subject home and which hurts.

Bishop McConnell told of visiting a silk mill in Shanghai on his recent trip to China. There he saw an eight-year-old girl moistening cocoons with her hands in water that would scald one of us. She worked thirteen hours a day with no time off at noon, but could eat her lunch as she stood at her work. Her wages were seven to ten cents per day, and the mill paid 100 per cent. profit on the English and American capital invested.

This story was told to illustrate Bishop McConnell's meaning when he said that the missionary today is blocked by the glaring contrast between the teaching and life of the missionary and the aggressiveness of western capitalism.

The church is told not to criticise industrial or political conditions, unless it can propose a solution. "That is the business of the technical engineers," said Bishop McConnell. The church can see the social results of a given condition and has a duty to call attention to it.

It is admitted that the twelve-hour day still exists in the steel industry. It is admitted that the spy system exists. The engineers of industry will find the way to remove these evils as they did the dangerous stove in the railway cars when our enlightened conscience demands it.

We cannot get rid of war and leave out the economic causes of war. No young men in the United States would volunteer for war in Mexico for oil; but the treasures in oil are the economic cause that puts us in constant danger of a war with Mexico. American missionaries can do nothing in Mexico because of the standing contradiction to their teaching in the fact that the United States army may at any time swoop down across the border.

Bishop McConnell said that the personal and social gospel must go along together. He recognized that the "radical" groups are ahead of the church at many points, and pleaded for a recognition of the light which they see.

J. BARNARD WALTON.

Friendly News Notes

Edward Thomas, of New York City, formerly of Haverford College, has written an article recently on "Compulsory Publication of Labor Turnovers." It appeared in an engineering magazine and has been printed in tract form for distribution.

A beautiful little folder has come to our office containing an account of the memorial service to Robert W. Maxwell, including a poem by J. Russell Hayes, and an address delivered by Cullen Cain on "Bob" Maxwell, of Swarthmore. An effort is being made to raise a Maxwell Memorial Fund under the auspices of *The Phoenix*, students and alumni of Swarthmore College. Contributions ranging from five cents to five dollars are being sought, and may be mailed to *The Phoenix*, Swarthmore, Pa.

A reprint of the account of the second Conference of the International Federation of University Women written by Isabelle Bronk, of Swarthmore College, is at hand. This report appeared in the September 16th issue of *School and Society*, and is full of interest not only to college women, but others as well.

Isaac Roberts, a New York Friend, is connected with the Municipal Credit Union, of the City of New York, which is really a Co-operative Bank. It is a co-operative association incorporated under the banking laws of the State of New York, and its purposes are to promote thrift among its members by encouraging the investment of their savings in its shares, and to make loans to its members for productive purposes or to relieve cases of need.

In 1916 there were 19 members, while there are at the present time 5,800 members. In 1917, new loans made during the year amounted to $40,251.00, and in 1921 they reached the sum of $607,460. Anyone interested in further information in regard to this sort of co-operative work can get it by writing to Isaac Roberts, Room 1730, Municipal Building, Manhattan.

A meeting was held recently, in Oxford, Pa., under the care of a committee appointed to get better co-operation for religious training for the children, by the parents and teachers of the First-day school.

Ethel Reynolds opened the meeting by Scripture reading. Bliss Forbush and wife, of Baltimore, were present. In his address was shown the result of the care and environment thrown around the Jewish and Roman Catholic child, from infancy on and he wondered whether we should not be more filled with the Christ spirit, through prayer, and start with the child just as early in life.

The question was asked—Are Friends so afraid of "vain repetition," in audible prayers, that we fail to teach the child the value of prayer? It was thought we need to teach the child to pray in words he can understand and in the same way to show a thankful heart by repeating a few lines before a meal and for blessings in life. The meeting was very helpful to all present.

E. G. WRIGHT

The "Open Letter to President Harding" which was sent by the 52 members of the I. W. W. in Leavenworth Penitentiary who refused to apply for individual clemency is a splendid exposition of the ideas and beliefs held by these men, the severity of the punishment meted out to them for remaining true to their ideals in opposing war, the great difficulty of getting a fair hearing and finally the injustice of keeping them in custody when all other war-time prisoners have been pardoned. Every Friend should get a copy of this Open Letter and read and consider it carefully. They can be obtained by application to "The General Defense Committee," 1001 West Madison Street, Chicago, Ill.

SINGING CAROLS IN BALTIMORE

This First-day evening the Young Friends begin a series of five delightful evenings together. They have arranged to spend an hour each First-day evening singing carols under the direction of a paid leader who has had much training in group singing. All those in the Meeting interested in this program will be invited to attend. The series will probably culminate on the evening of December 24th when we plan to hold an outdoor community sing, and on the evening of the 25th when a smaller group will go through the neighborhood singing before the homes of Friends.

The Morgan College Quartette will give a concert in the Meeting-house one evening this week for the benefit of the Young Friends.

BLUE RIVER QUARTERLY MEETING

Blue River Quarterly Meeting was held at Clear Creek on Eleventh month 11th, with the following delegates present: Thomas A. Jenkins, Miriam Jenkins, Albert Miller, Alice Miller, Clement B. Flitcraft, Luella W. Flitcraft, and Paul Douglas from Chicago, Nellie Baynes and Helen May Brooks from Salem, Indiana.

Paul Douglas gave a very inspiring talk on "Faith." Thomas A. Jenkins compared the story of the good Samaritan with the work of the American Friends' Service Committee. The First-day School gave an interesting program.

Chicago Monthly Meeting, which is now held on the second Second-day of each month, is growing in attendance and interest. At the last meeting, after the regular business had been transacted, Dr. Thomas J. Allen led an informal discussion on reforming the newspapers.

The Monthly Meeting dinners are proving very successful and a cordial invitation is extended to all, but reservations must be made to the Executive Secretary three days in advance of the meeting.

JEANNETTE F. STETSON

"A WORLD WITHOUT WAR"

"In America they are considering sixty different kinds of gasses for destruction, any one of which would wipe out Bewdley in a few minutes. Is this a practical way of conducting the life of the world, quite apart from morals and religion? Does it not seem to make true someone's description of the earth as 'the lunatic asylum of the Universe'? asked Carl Heath, Secretary of the Friends' Council for International Service, at a public meeting on 'A World Without War' at the Friends' Meeting-house, Bewdley, recently. The meeting was arranged by the Friends' Home Mission and Extension Committee, which had been holding a week-end conference at Bewdley, Worcestershire.

"The League of Nations needs many improvements, and every nation should be in it by right; but it marks the parting of the ways. It can do many things if it is sure of an instructed public opinion behind it. When the League at Geneva the other day was deciding to put Austria on its feet, one big country was making difficulties. After Lord Balfour had stated that if an agreement were reached all the documents and discussions should be made public, Lord Robert Cecil asked whether they would also be published if no agreement were come to. After a moment's hesitation Lord Balfour said they would, and this certainty that the world would know which country had obstructed a settlement, led the representatives concerned to come into line and help save Austria. The obstructors felt that they could not stand the inevitable criticism which would follow disagreement.

But deeper than the political, international and social roots of war and safeguards against it, were religious and moral ones.

"The Gospel—the good news—is having the courage to try trust, and to appeal to that of God in every man. Is it dangerous? Yes, but is it dangerous compared with the war method? Whether French, German, Russian, Dutch or English you will find men everywhere very much alike, just struggling human beings with something of the life of God within them."

Mrs. Janet Braithwaite, wife of the late William Charles Braithwaite, the well-known Quaker historian and Adult School leader, appealed strongly to "everyday people like herself" to help to create public opinion against war by joining the League of Nations' Union.

Recent Publications

"WHAT IS THERE IN RELIGION?" by Henry Sloane Coffin. MacMillan Co., New York, $1.25. A series of lectures on experimental religion, which are also practical. "Dr. Coffin has instanced the experience of sane, strong and well-poised leaders in all departments of human endeavor, and his book might be called "What the ordinary, normal man may expect in the way of a religious experience."

"THE COUNTRY FAITH", by Frederick F. Shannon. MacMillan Co., New York. $1. A Series of addresses by Dr. Shannon, pastor of "Old Central" Church in Chicago. According to The Biblical World, University of Chicago, "His addresses cannot be measured by the ordinary yardstick; they can hardly be criticised; it is better to enjoy them. They are in a class by themselves and the product of a unique mind."

"THE CHRISTIAN CRUSADE FOR A WARLESS WORLD," by Sidney L. Gulick. MacMillan Co., New York. $1. Dr. Sidney L. Gulick is Secretary of the Commission on International Justice and Goodwill, of the Federal Council of the Churches of Christ in America. This book has been prepared in order to put into the hands of pastors and Christian leaders the material which the churches must have if they are to deal effectively with the great task of establishing permanent peace.

"PUBLIC RELIEF OF SICKNESS," by Gerald Morgan. MacMillan Co., New York. While this book deals largely with legislative proposals and investigations originating in the states of New York and Illinois, the importance of the subject of public relief of sickness is fully recognized throughout the greater part of the United States.

"ON THE TRAIL OF THE PEACEMAKERS," by Fred B. Smith. The MacMillan Company, New York. $1.75.

Fred B. Smith, well known as international Y. M. C. A. secretary, traveled to the Far East as the representative of the Federal Council of Churches and the World Alliance of Churches for International Friendship. He met and talked with men and women in every walk of life in many countries of Europe and the Orient, and "On the Trail of the Peacemakers" is his record of conditions as he found them, and his view of future possibilities of international good will. After having thrown himself ardently, with so many of his fellows, into the World War, led on by the ideal of the better world that was to emerge from the chaos, he now says, "Never again under any circumstances can I say the things about war which were expressed many times during the years of 1916 to 1918." He now says, "1. War is an enemy of all human progress. 2. War is an enemy of sound economics and prosperity. 3. War is an enemy of the Kingdom of God." Towering above all other issues now confronting the Church, without a single exception, he sees this: Will it outlaw war by educating the world to build up other means of settling international disputes?

"THE UNSOLVED RIDDLE OF SOCIAL JUSTICE," by Stephen Leacock, B.A., Ph.D., Professor of Political Economy at McGill University, Montreal. Reviewed by John C. Trautwine, Jr.

Our author realizes the defects of our individualistic social and economic system. "Something must be at fault with our social order. It won't work." He realizes also that that system is passing. "The average citizen of three generations ago was probably not aware that he was an extreme individualist. The average citizen of today is not conscious of the fact that he has ceased to be one."

But our author maintains that what is going to replace individualism is not socialism. "The one thing that is wrong with socialism is that it won't work. That is all."

In its beneficence, our modern socialism is like the air we breathe. Its existence is generally ignored. Our life today depends upon the maintenance of our socialistic highways, railways, post offices, water supplies, etc. Yet the average man, like our author, says:—"Socialism won't work."

Under the profit system, which makes individual material gain the one thing needful, the heart of man is *of course* deceitful above all things and desperately wicked; but the world is being rapidly socialized; not by propaganda but by the *selfish* demand of each person for better service than individualism can give him; and this socialization, by eliminating the institution of private property, is removing the inducement to anti-social activities, and is thus sweeping us into a new heaven and a new earth, wherein dwelleth righteousness.

This our author seems not yet to have perceived.

Items from Everywhere

"*Everyland,*" the missionary magazine of World Friendship for girls and boys, has almost completed its first year under the new management. This magazine is gotten out in very attractive form, with interesting stories and pictures of children of this and other lands. The price is only $1.50 a year.

The corner-stone has just been laid for the Center Avenue Branch Building of the Y. M. C. A. in Pittsburgh, Pa., which will be the second largest establishment of its kind in the country for colored men and boys. The new building will represent a total cost of $250,000.

It is interesting to note that of the $600,000 spent by colored Associations in this country last year, $500,000 was given by their own group.

The friendly visitors sent last summer by the Federal Council of Churches to the churches of Europe included clergymen, college presidents, educators, business men and women of prominence. Now most of them have returned and in a joint statement declare "that the moral and political problems of continental Europe are fundamentally economic. They are unanimous in saying that the nations overseas can never meet the situation caused by the war, in which the United States took part, without the sympathetic counsel, advice, and economic help of America."

A vote was recently taken on the wet and dry question among the inmates of the prisons in the United States. More than 133,000 voted dry and only 909 voted wet, which shows that even the lawbreaker is capable of right thinking and dreads the results of drink.—*Dearborn Independent.*

There are at least 30,000 mental defectives or feeble-minded in the community in Pennsylvania with little or no protection. There are institutional accommodations for only about 4,000 of these. Mental defectives are apt to develop bad habits, become dependents, prostitutes or other delinquents or felons, involved in the most serious crimes, such as murder. They are easily led astray and become the tools of designing persons.

The Bureau of Mental Health in Pennsylvania is establishing mental health clinics for early identification, study, advice and supervision of mental defectives. They are co-operating with the Department of Public Instruction in promoting the establishment of special classes in the schools, where mental defectives may receive training in proper habit formation. They are also working along the lines of Community Supervision, the increasing of institutional accommodations, and also in establishing developing institutions especially as Training Schools from which a certain percentage of the mental defectives may from time to time be safely returned to the community to make room for those in urgent need of training or custodial care.

THE OPEN FORUM

This column is intended to afford free expression of opinion by readers on questions of interest. The INTELLIGENCER *is not responsible for any such opinions. Letters must be brief, and the editor reserves the right to omit parts if necessary to save space.*

OUR SOUTHERN SCHOOLS

To the Editor:

Our Friends have been interested ever since the Civil War in two Southern Schools for the Colored race, one called the Lang School and one called the Schofield Normal and Industrial School, Aiken, S. C. The writer has made two visits to this Aiken School during the present year. This school lost by fire in April, the Deborah Fisher Wharton Hall.

This loss amounted to $13,000, of which $8000 was covered by Insurance. This school has been completely rebuilt, and is now better equipped than ever before, the fire risk is much less owing to better construction. The Management has had enough money from insurance, gifts and some other sources to pay for the Construction of the new building. However, they estimate it will take $1500 to furnish 30 rooms for the boys, or $50.00 each. Through the kindness of our friends, we have been able to raise more than one-half of this. We are still short about $750.00. This appeal is to our Friends to raise this amount, and Friends may send checks to Mary A. Jenkins, Gwynned, Pa., or Annie Hillborn, Swarthmore, Pa.

While the former generation of Friends born before the Civil War and readers of "Uncle Tom's Cabin" had more intesest in the education of the colored youth than the present generation, however, it is interesting to know that the local interest in the School has strengthened with the years. We have on the Board residents of Aiken, Mrs. Sheffield Phelps, Rev. Mr. McLean, and Mr. Woolsey, all are very much interested and very helpful. We are very fortunate in having as Superintendent, Miss Georgia Crocker, formerly of Boston, but a resident for sometime past of Aiken, and formerly assistant to Martha Schofield.

ALBERT G. THATCHER.

POPULATION VS. LAND

To the Editor:

One of your correspondents has entirely misunderstood my use of figures as quoted in a recent letter. I do not at all differ from J. Russell Smith as to the dangers of over-population. My statement was nothing more than a calling attention to the fact that the present population of the world is not such as to make wars necessary. The figures are as follows:

Population of the world (about)..........1,500,000,000
Families (5 to a family)..................300,000,000
Total acerage of U. S. 1,903,000,000
Acreage in farms in U. S...................878,000,000

This is about three acres per family, and would seem to indicate that nations need not fight for standing room. It is perhaps unnecessary to add that I am not in favor of having them all come here. It would be possible to give each person in the world over a hundred square yards in Pennsylvania.—but it isn't desirable to have them.

In spite of the great spread of land in the U. S. and our comparatively small population we are afflicted with an artificial land scarcity which is an artificial over-population and is due to our system of land ownership. The gradual settlement of a country hides from its people the essential iniquity of *ownership* of the surface of the earth. By the time it is all owned the system is established and its evils seem inevitable. Those evils are essentially the same whether the ownership is in few hands or many, so it is short of the whole. As all *must* live on the earth why toil in it, those who own *must* control those who do not. Freedom is impossible when all the usable parts of the earth's surface belong to any less group than the whole. So long as there were great unused stretches of available land the labor question could never become a very difficult one. Men will not submit to oppression if a safety valve of free or near-free land relieves the pressure. But this last generation has seen the last of the free land, and as the land is all owned, tho not half used, we may expect to see constantly increasing tensions and frequent explosions.

And we are not intelligent enough or courageous enough to apply the very simple remedy of taxing all land to its full rent value.

JESSE H. HOLMES

To the Editor:

I would like to call the attention of my critics to the definitions of the words "Incendiary" and "Incendiarism," as given in Webster's Unabridged Dictionary, and after giving them careful thought, read from the Associated Press items the alleged confession of a former head of the I. W. W. in his trial in Sacramento, California. Then having given this their thought, read from the same source later, the opinion of U. S. Attorney-General Daugherty, on Liberty of Press and Speech.

Holder, Ill. ELIZABETH H. COALE.

MARRIAGES

THATCHER-WOOD—In Plainfield, N. J., at the Crescent Avenue Presbyterian Church, on Tenth month 21st, William Hibbard Thatcher and Gertrude King Wood.

EVANS—On Tenth month 11th, at Pasadena, California, Elizabeth Passmore Evans, daughter of Thomas Passmore and Phebe Smedley Evans, formerly of West Chester, Pa.

DEATHS

CHALFANT—At Kennett Square, Pa., on Eleventh month 4th, Sarah W. Chalfant, widow of William Chalfant, in her

93rd year. She will be sadly missed by all on account of her kindness and generosity.

ENGLE—On Eleventh month 25th, at the Covington, Philadelphia, Jane Darnell, wife of the late Robert B. Engle, aged 84.

JOHNSON—At the home of Mary Cadwallader, Wycombe, Pa., on Eleventh month 2, 1922, Benjamin E. Johnson, aged 72 years. Interment in Buckingham Friends' ground.

KIRBY—At Philadelphia, on Eleventh month 25th, Sallie A., widow of Robert J. Kirby, aged 81.

ROBERTS—On Eleventh month 21st, at Willow Grove, Pa., Rowland, husband of Sarah Anna Roberts.

UNDERHILL—On Eleventh month 16th, at his residence in Brooklyn, Robert, husband of Grace D. Underhill, in the 70th year of his age. Funeral in Brooklyn Meeting-house on First-day, the 19th of Eleventh month, at the hour of Meeting.

COMING EVENTS

3rd—Conference Class at Fifteenth and Race Streets, Philadelphia, at close of meeting for worship, 11.40 a. m. Subject—The Prophets of Adventure. Leader—David G. Paul.

3rd—West Philadelphia Bible Class, 35th and Lancaster Ave., 10 a. m. Subject—Sin.

3rd—Members of Philadelphia Quarterly Meeting's Visiting Committee will attend Reading meeting for worship, at 11 a. m.

4th—Millville Half-yearly Meeting, at Millville, Pa.

7th—Salem Quarterly Meeting, at Woodbury, N. J.

14th—Haddonfield Quarterly Meeting, at Moorestown, N. J.

17th—Amawalk Friends' Meeting will be held at the home of Louisa Loder, north of Amawalk Meeting-house, at 2.30 p. m.

18th—Christmas Entertainment and exercises at West Philadelphia First-day School, 35th and Lancaster Avenue. Bring your gifts for the poor and hear the children sing 7.30 p. m.

NOTICE—The Children's Aid Society has in their care an unusually intelligent colored boy, ten years old, whom they are anxious to place with a white family. The boy was cruelly treated and it has been difficult for him to adjust in colored homes in which he has been placed. He needs kindly but firm ard intelligent supervision. Board will be paid. If any Friend is interested in giving this boy the benefit of their intelligent effort will they kindly address M. M. Rogers, 1430 Pine Street, Philadelphia, Pa.

NOTICE—On December 3rd there will be a debate on "Resolved, that a measure conferring Equal Rights before the Law upon Women is both just and expedient," in the Broad Street Theatre, Philadelphia, at 3 p. m. Admittance free. Auspices Philadelphia Young Democracy.

American Friends' Service Committee

WILBUR K. THOMAS, EX. SEC.

20 S. 12th St. Philadelphia.

CASH CONTRIBUTIONS

WEEK ENDING NOVEMBER 20TH.

Five Years Meetings:	$110.00
Philadelphia Yearly Meeting (Hicksite)	1,245.00
Philadelphia Yearly Meeting (Orthodox)	50.00
Other Meetings:	
Orange Grove Friends of Pasadena	35.00
Cambridge Group of Friends	190.00
Four Meetings of Friends of New York	103.60
Birmingham Monthly Meeting	10.00
First Friends' Church, Cleveland	5.00
Providence Meeting	6.00
Abington Friends' Meeting	5.00
Fallowfield Monthly Meeting	50.00
Contributions for Germany	39.00
For Austria	1,050.00
For Poland	515.25
For Russia	2,439.52
Russian Overhead	77.50
For Syria	70.00
Central Pennsylvania	50.00
For General	1,570.88
For Clothing	2.00
Refunds	120.55
	$7,744.30

Shipments received during week ending November 18, 1922: 111 boxes and packages received, 1 from Mennonites.

LUKE 2. 14—AMERICA'S ANGELUS

"Glory to God in the highest, and on earth peace, good will toward men."

Stand back of President Harding in Prayer for Universal Peace by meditating daily, at noon, on the fourteenth verse of the second chapter of Luke.

Ask your friends to help make this a Universal Meditation for Universal Peace

Pass it on *Friends in Christ*

REGULAR MEETINGS

OAKLAND, CALIF. — A FRIENDS' Meeting is held every First-day at 11 A. M., in the Extension Room, Y. W. C. A. Building, Webster Street, above 14th. Visiting Friends always welcome.

PASADENA, CALIFORNIA — Orange Grove Monthly Meeting of Friends, 520 East Orange Grove Avenue. Meeting for worship, First-day, 11 A. M. Monthly Meeting, the second First-day of each month, at 1.45 P. M. First-day School (except Monthly Meeting days) 9.45 A. M.

FUN

"Did you have any difficulty with your French in Paris?"

"No—but the French people did."—*Karikaturen (Christiania).*

FUN

The young daughter of the household was celebrating her birthday anniversary when she suddenly turned to the interested old colored mammy and asked: "Hannah, when is your birthday?"

"Law, miss," Hannah replied, "I ain't got no birfday; I was bawned in de night-time."—*The Ladies' Home Journal.*

Buck Hill Falls Company

The annual meeting of the stockholders of the Buck Hill Falls Company will be held in the auditorium of the Philadelphia Young Friends' Association, 140 N. 15th Street, on Fourth-day afternoon, Twelfth month 6th, 1922, at 2 o'clock.

MORGAN BUNTING, *Clerk.*

WANTED

WANTED—GOOD HOME OR BOARDING place with cheerful surroundings for middle-aged lady, mentally somewhat deficient. State probable terms. Address P. 390, Friends' Intelligencer.

U. S. GOVERNMENT UNDERWEAR—2,500,000 pc. New Government Wool Underwear purchased by us to sell to the public direct at 75c EACH. Actual retail value $2.50 each. All sizes, Shirts 34 to 46—Drawers 30 to 44. Send correct sizes. Pay Postman on delivery ,or send us money order. If underwear is not satisfactory, we will refund money promptly upon request. Dept. 24, Pilgrim Woolen Co., 1476 Broadway, New York, N. Y.

CHRISTMAS CARDS — HAND COLored. Twelve sent on approval. One dollar if retained (or ten cents each). Bertha Sellers, Young Friends' Association, Philadelphia.

WANTED—SUMS OF $900 AND $400 on first mortgages in the City of Chester. Security ample. Charles Palmer, 12 East Fifth Street, Chester, Pa.

MIDDLE-AGED LADY, THOROUGHLY experienced, managing housekeeper, matron, hotel or institution. Excellent reference. Mrs. H. B. Cox, 3801 Walnut Street, Philadelphia.

SALARIED STENOGRAPHER, NIGHTS free, can report occasional daylight meetings. George B. Cock, Bell (Phila.) phone directory.

PRACTICAL NURSE WOULD LIKE care of semi-invalid, or feeble person. Willing to be generally useful in home if case permits. Address B. 440, Friends' Intelligencer.

GENTLE WOMAN, EDUCATED, REfined, pleasing personality, unusually capable, would like position as companion or managing housekeeper for one or two. Mrs. M. E. Green, 6410 North 11th Street, Oak Lane.

WOMAN OF MIDDLE AGE, NURSE, wants care of invalid. Address P 441, Friends' Intelligencer.

WANTED—REFINED YOUNG WOman for clerical work. Knowledge of telephone exchange desired. Friend preferred. Address B. 443, Friends' Intelligencer.

POSITION WANTED—BY REFINED middle-aged woman as companion and nurse to semi-invalid or elderly woman. Address W. 442, Friends' Intelligencer.

MAY WE COUNT ON THY HELP IN our advertising campaign? As a friend of the INTELLIGENCER will thee not patronize our advertisers, and mention the FRIENDS' INTELLIGENCER when making inquiries or purchases?

FOR SALE

FOR SALE—NEWTOWN SECTION—Desirable Homes. I have for sale in Newtown a variety of properties from $3,000 up. One within five minutes' walk of George School, a lovely home, all conveniences; garage, poultry house and yard, garden. If interested inquire promptly. Also some of the finest farms in Bucks County. W. T. Wright, Newtown, Pa.

Fine Newtown Property

at Private Sale

The residence of the late Thaddeus S. Kenderdine, corner State and Sterling Streets, near George School.

Large brick house, with all conveniences; frame barn; surrounded by large shade trees. One of the best properties in town. Sold to settle the Estate.

Robert Kenderdine
Louis R. Kenderdine } Executors

Strawbridge & Clothier

Correct Shoes for Children Fitted by Experts

When you bring the children to see Santa Claus, bring them to the Children's Shoe Store—the opportunity to have them properly fitted.

Children's Shoes

Sizes 8½ to 11

Children's tan calf Lace Shoes, sturdy leather soles—$3.75 and $4.50.

Children's tan calf Lace Shoes, fawn buck tops—$6.00.

Patent leather Button or Lace Shoes—$5.00 and $5.50.

Children's patent leather Lace shoes, with gray nubuck tops, flapper cuffs—$5.00.

Sizes 11½ to 2

Misses' tan calf Lace Shoes, some with rubber heels—$4.50, $5.00 and $6.50.

Misses' tan calf Lace Shoes, with fawn buck tops—$7.00.

Misses' patent colt Lace Shoes, kid tops—$6.50.

Misses' patent colt Lace Shoes, gray nubuck tops, flapper cuffs—$6.00.

Misses' tan grain Blucher Scotty Oxfords, wing tips, just the shoe to be worn with woolen stockings—$6.50.

Sizes 2½ to 7

Growing Girls' tan Elko Lace Oxfords, rubber heels, medium or round toe lasts—$5.50.

Growing Girls' gun-metal calf Oxfords, with shield tips, rubber heels—$6.00.

Growing Girls' tan calf Lace Oxfords, with shield tips, rubber heels —$6.50.

Growing Girls' tan grain Lace Oxfords, with shield tips and low flat heels—$7.00.

Growing Girls' tan grain Lace Blucher Scotty Oxfords, wing tips, full round toes—$8.00.

Growing Girls' tan calf one-strap Grecian Pumps, shield tips—$8.00.

Growing Girls' patent colt One-strap Pumps, welted soles—$7.00.

Growing Girls' patent colt One-strap and Buckle Pumps, shield tips—$7.50.

Boys' Shoes

Boys' dark brown Elk Blucher Shoes, full round toes; sizes 11 to 2 and 2½ to 6, $5.50.

Boys' dark tan Brogue Shoes, with rubber-slip soles; sizes 2½ to 6—$6.50.

Boys' tony red calf Shoes, full toes; sizes 2½ to 6—$6.00.

Boys' tan, English and full round-toe Shoes; sizes 2½ to 6, special—$4.45.

Strawbridge & Clothier—Eighth and Filbert Streets.

STRAWBRIDGE & CLOTHIER

MARKET STREET EIGHTH STREET FILBERT STREET
PHILADELPHIA, PA.

To the Lot Holders and others interested in Fairhill Burial Ground:

GREEN STREET Monthly Meeting has funds available for the encouragement of the practice of cremating the dead to be interred in Fairhill Burial Ground. We wish to bring this fact as prominently as possible to those who may be interested. We are prepared to undertake the expense of cremation in case any lot holder desires us to do so.

Those interested should communicate with William H. Gaskill, Treasurer of the Committee of Interments, Green Street Monthly Meeting, or any of the following members of the Committee.

William H. Gaskill, 3201 Arch St.
Samuel N. Longstreth, 1218 Chestnut St.
Charles F. Jenkins, 232 South Seventh St
Stuart S. Graves, 3033 Germantown Ave.

ADVERTISING RATE in the FRIENDS' INTELLIGENCER, for Help Wanted, Positions Wanted, Rooms for Rent, and other classified advertisements without display, for each insertion, 2 cents per word, including name, initials and address. Answers may be sent to a box at the INTELLIGENCER office, if so directed.

For display advertising the rate is 10 cents per agate line, or $1.40 per column inch, each insertion. On ten or more insertions in a year from date of order, ten per cent. discount. Thus a four-inch single-column or two-inch double-column advertisement costs $5.60 each insertion, less ten per cent., or $5.04 net each time for ten or more insertions. Matter may be changed whenever desired, without extra charge.

Experience has proved the INTELLIGENCER to be a remarkably good advertising medium. All advertisements must "pass the censor!"

Address 140 N. 15th St., Philadelphia.

Lansdowne and Darby Saving Fund and Trust Company

LANSDOWNE, PA.
ESTABLISHED 1903

GEORGE FOSTER WHITE, *President and Treasurer*
W. LANE VERLENDEN, *Vice-President*
WALTER RHOADS WHITE, *Trust Officer*
MORGAN BUNTING, *Secretary*
LEWIS LAWRENCE SMITH, *Solicitor and 2nd Vice-President*
M. L. KENNEY, *Assistant Treasurer*
W. RAYMOND EVANS, *Real Estate Officer*

Banking and Trust Service of the Better Class.

Interest Checking Accounts 2% Savings Deposits 3.65%

FRANKLIN NATIONAL BANK

PHILADELPHIA
INCORPORATED 1900

Capital $1,500,000 Surplus and Profits $5,300,000

OFFICERS:

J. R. McALLISTER, President
J. A. HARRIS, Jr., Vice-President
J. WM. HARDT, Vice-Pres. and Cashier
E. E. SHIELDS, Assistant Cashier
W. M. GEHMAN, Jr., Assistant Cashier
M. D. REINHOLD, Assistant Cashier

The Swarthmore National Bank

SWARTHMORE, PA.

Conducts a General Banking Business. Business by mail receives careful and prompt attention. 3 per cent. interest paid in Savings Fund Department.

EDWARD B. TEMPLE, President
J. EVERTON RAMSEY, Vice-President
THOMAS S. SAFFORD, Vice-President
E. S. SPROAT, Cashier
A. M. PASSMORE, Assistant Cashier

DIRECTORS

Edward B. Temple, Thomas S. Safford, Joseph Swain, Charles Paxson, C. Percy Webster, Garrett E. Smedley, John F. Murray, John W. Pittock, J. Everton Ramsey, Joseph E. Haines

SUPPLEE

Cream Buttermilk

HEALTHFUL—REFRESHING

Supplee-Wills-Jones Milk Co.

PHILADELPHIA—ATLANTIC CITY

ABBOTTS CERTIFIED MILK

Produced at Edgewood Dairies, Woodside, Pa.

Approved by Philadelphia Pediatric Society

Contains 4 per cent. Butter Fat

Abbotts Alderney Dairies, Inc.
31st and Chestnut Sts.
Philadelphia, Pa.

WALTER RHOADS WHITE,
Attorney and Counsellor-at-Law
Lansdowne Trust Co., Lansdowne, Pa.
Also Member of the Delaware County Bar

GENEALOGIST

ELIZABETH B. SATTERTHWAITE,
52 N. Stockton St., Trenton, N. J.

SCHOOLS.

Woolman School

Winter Term, First Month 8 to Third Month 23, 1923.

Courses in Bible Study, Church History, Religious Education, Social Problems.

Send for catalog.

ELBERT RUSSELL, Director,
WOOLMAN SCHOOL
Swarthmore, Pa.

GEORGE SCHOOL
Near Newtown, Bucks County, Pa.

Under the care of Philadelphia Yearly Meeting of Friends.

Course of study extended and thorough, preparing students either for business or for college. For catalogue apply to

GEORGE A. WALTON, A. M., Principal
George School, Penna.

FRIENDS' CENTRAL SCHOOL SYSTEM

Write for Year Book and Rates.

L. RALSTON THOMAS, Principal.
15th and Race Sts., Philadelphia.

FRIENDS' ACADEMY
LONG ISLAND, N. Y.

A Boarding and Day School for **Boys and Girls**, conducted in accordance with the principles of the Society of Friends. **For further** particulars address

S. ARCHIBALD SMITH, Principal.
Locust Valley, N. Y.

A new edition of
"The Life and Letters of Elias Hicks"
by Henry Wilbur
just in from the bindery, and selling at the original price $1.50
Everyone should own a copy of this good book.

WALTER H. JENKINS
Successor to Friends' Book Association
140 N. 15th Street, Philadelphia
Bell Telephone—Spruce 2425

CRETH & SULLIVAN

INSURANCE

210 South Fourth Street, Philadelphia.

Estate of Joseph T. Sullivan Marshall P. Sullivan

Please help us by patronizing our advertisers. Mention the "Friends' Intelligencer."

The Friends' Intelligencer

ESTABLISHED 1844 — TWELFTH MONTH 9, 1922 — VOLUME 79 NUMBER 49

Contents

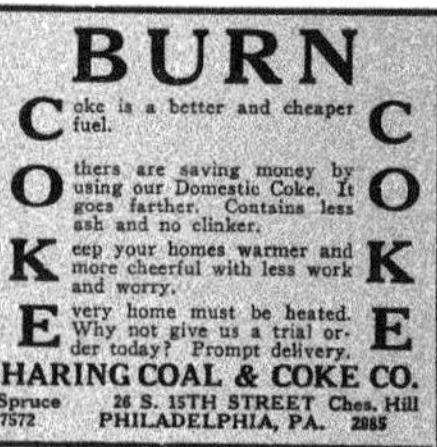

THE FRIENDS' INTELLIGENCER

Published weekly, 140 N. 15th Street, Philadelphia, Pa., by Friends' Intelligencer Association, Ltd.

SUE C. YERKES, *Managing Editor.*

Editorial Board: Elizabeth Powell Bond, Thomas A. Jenkins, J. Russell Smith, George A. Walton.

Board of Managers: Edward Cornell, Alice Hall Paxson, Paul M. Pearson, Annie Hillborn, Elwood Hollingshead, William C. Biddle, Charles F. Jenkins, Edith M. Winder, Frances M. White.

Officers of Intelligencer Associates: Ellwood Burdsall, Chairman; Bertha L. Broomell, Secretary; Herbert P. Worth, Treasurer.

Subscription rates: United States, Mexico, Cuba and Panama, $2.50 per year. Canada and other foreign countries, $3.00 per year. Checks should be made payable to Friends' Intelligencer Association, Ltd.

Entered as Second Class Matter at Philadelphia Post Office.

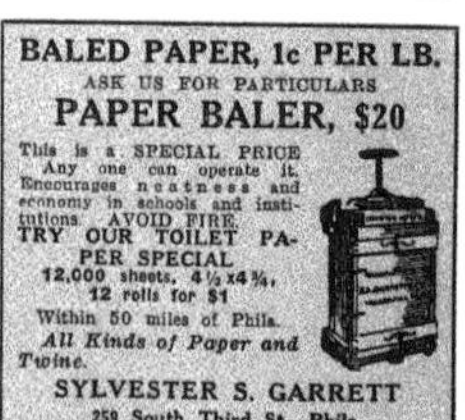

The Friends' Intelligencer

The religion of Friends is based on faith in the "Inward Light," or direct revelation of God's spirit and will in every seeking soul.

The Intelligencer is interested in all who bear the name of Friends in every part of the world, and aims to promote love, unity and intercourse among all branches and with all religious societies.

Established 1844 — PHILADELPHIA, TWELFTH MONTH 9, 1922 — Volume 79, Number 49

Making Our Meetings More Attractive

How to make our meetings for worship more full of life is a problem which many of us would like to see solved. Especially would we like to see them made more attractive to the young, upon whom the future welfare of our Society depends.

We must admit that there is little in the ordinary Friends' meeting to interest the children and young people. The consequence is that they are not drawn to the meeting, altho' they like to attend the First-day School. How can we make them want to come?

Let it be clearly understood that the main purpose of our worship is not entertainment; it is for spiritual uplift. But all do not get this in the same way. Hence the many forms of worship. We cherish the ideal of silent waiting on God: so far as we can attain to that, it is perhaps the purest form of worship, and should have a prominent place in all our assemblies. But the meetings which are habitually silent do not grow. As the aged members die off, there are no new ones to take their places.

A soul-moving silence is pretty sure to find vocal expression. The ideal meeting, as some one has said, is where the spoken messages rise, like beautiful islands, out of a calm deep sea of silence. Such a meeting would have real interest for the worshipers, whether old or young.

We are continually reminded of the need of "a free gospel ministry;" but do we carefully consider all that is involved in this? It is a ministry of the whole group, and one in which each member has an equal share of responsibility. It is only when all present contribute something to the spirit of the meeting that it can be truly called a free gospel ministry. Remember that the spoken word is only one kind of ministry, and even that is largely influenced by the silent devotional spirit which prevades the meeting.

Why is it that our meetings have not more life? Is it not because most of our members came without any preparation for the service? Their mental attitude is passive rather than active. So far as they are concerned, the meeting begins with spiritual lethargy and, unless there be a spirit of life from other sources, it is likely to be a dull meeting. How different it would be if each member came with "an active concern for the advancement of truth."

Probably, in each life during the past week, something had transpired which would be of spiritual interest and help to the meeting. Then, too, how helpful it would be if every one, before setting out for meeting, had spent a brief interval in quiet communion, or still better, had had some simple form of worship at the breakfast table.

But the repressed silence is not all due to apathy; it is sometimes caused by timidity. The delivery of a message is natural enough to one who has been accustomed to it; but to a novice it is an alarming ordeal. Let such remember that there are other ways of contributing to the life of the meeting. It is always appropriate to follow the opening silence of the meeting by reading a carefully selected passage of scripture. Good scripture reading is a rare art, and highly illuminating.

Then there are the beautiful and inspiring words of the poets, prophets and saints of all ages; and these are too seldom heard in our meetings. Probably never a week passes without some one of these great utterances being brought to our attention. Then why should we not bear it in mind and be ready to impart it at a suitable time in the meeting? If each were ready to do this, what a feast of good things we should have! But a word of caution here—*do not let the selections be too long.* In a lengthy passage the interest may be well sustained in silent reading, where it would be tedious to read it aloud. Where the "cutting out" is judiciously done, it is generally more effective to extract the more graphic parts than to read it all through. This holds good also in scripture reading. The mistake is often made of reading the whole chapter, when the lesson to be conveyed is contained in a few verses.

And lastly, let us not be afraid of new methods. Our meetings have gone too much in a rut. We have discarded the old Quaker modes of dress—much as we cherish their associations—but we still cling to old forms of worship which are not suited to the present time. This is not in keeping with the natural course of things. As Tennyson teaches:

"The old order changeth, yielding place to new,
And God fulfils Himself in many ways."

And again:

"Our little systems have their day;
They have their day, and cease to be;
They are but broken lights of Thee,
And Thou, O Lord, art more than they."

We must have full faith in our young people. Their spiritual life is as real as that of the earlier Friends; but it will naturally express itself in other ways. They also are moved by the same living Spirit, for "God is not the God of the dead, but of the living."

In proportion as our meetings answer to the intellectual and spiritual needs of the rising generation of Friends, they will attract them. D. B.

Democracy in Worship

By M. Catharine Albright

"I feel that I am coming home much enriched by all the expériences of Richmond, especially the personal contacts, old friendships renewed and new ones begun, and all the interest of the common causes for which we are all working so keenly." Quoted from a personal letter from M. Catharine Albright, on board the *Olympic*, September 29th.

In the recent conference at Richmond the similarity of principles underlying Quakerism and Democracy was brought out. Both of these movements were shown to be in the nature of revolts against the oppression and limitations imposed by governing officials, whether political or ecclesiastical. Both in the religious sphere and in the political it was shown how men had claimed the right and privilege to self-determination and self-expression.

With regard to Quakerism and Democracy, it was also demonstrated that their needs are the same. If either of them is to function properly, a higher standard of individual intelligence is required. "Everyone must be carried as far as he can go"—(this is the ideal of both the movements under discussion)—and we must have a method of education that will keep this ideal always to the fore.

"Everybody is to be carried as far as he can go," not only for his own satisfaction and for the glory of self-development but because the community of which he is a part needs him and all he can contribute to the common good. Democracy is not the exercise of a vote once in so many years, when certain more or less artificial choices have to be made. It is the daily exercise of the power to judge between the worse and the better course of public action and the daily sharing by the true citizen in the duties and responsibilities of citizenship. The ideal democracy is not one where a vast majority accept a ready-made policy, however wisely thought out, but one in which every member of the democracy has had a share, however humble, in *constructing* that policy and constantly feels his responsibility for the working out of it. It is a perpetual effort and not a periodic excitement.

But it is quite time to ask, "What has all this to do with worship?" for it may well seem that there is something almost crude and irreverent in bringing these thoughts about Democracy alongside any consideration of Worship.

But if Quakerism is a true spiritual Democracy, the principles of that democracy must be operative, not only in our "Church-government," but in the spiritual exercise we call worship. In the same way that democratic government is a co-operative enterprise, everyone taking his share in it according to his capacity, so our Quaker worship should be a co-operative effort, shared in by all who happen to be present.

The mere fact that it is not decided beforehand who is to speak and what is to be said means that the worshippers have to decide it themselves when they come together. Together they have to feel after "that of God" in each other, until the united warmth and the united smouldering fires burst out into a white heat of living silence, or into a flame of burning words. The whole effort of worship is a seeking together, a co-operative reaching out after God. The group, whether small or large, is embarked on a voyage of discovery, there is no one helmsman whose business it is to steer by an authorized chart. Rather everyone must be on the alert for signs of guidance and each contribute what he receives on behalf of the group, however insignificant it may seem. It may be that the most trivial token, only observed by the humblest member of the group, may be used to guide the whole vessel on its rightful course. Each must be receptive, not only of individual guidance, but of the guidance that comes through his fellow-worshippers. He must take account of the revelation that comes to the one that sitteth by. Even if it seems to him to be no true revelation at

Facts About Friends' Service in Russia This Winter

By Wilbur K. Thomas, *Ex. Sec.*

After careful study of the latest information received from the Russian famine field, the American Friends' Service Committee has agreed upon $2,675,000 as the amount of its budget for Russian work during 1922-23. Of this amount, $1,675,000 will be allocated to feeding famine sufferers, and will be in addition to the supplies of food which the Service Committee already has in Russia. The latter are sufficient to feet 75,000 until April 1st, 1923.

Requirements authorize an increase above this number of 25,000 per month beginning December 1st, 1922, and extending until July 1st, 1923. The total number being fed on July 1st will be 250,000. In addition to the feeding of this number in the Friends' area, $75,000 of the appropriation for food will be used to extend relief feeding into adjoining sections which received no help last year.

Medicines and equipment for Children's Homes and hospitals will be sent in to the extent of $500,000, clothing and raw wool and flax for home industries will receive $300,000, while the remaining $200,000 of the budget will be spent upon the agricultural work.

We feel that the budget as thus revised represents our very best judgment of the relief which we ought to provide in our district during the coming year. We, of course, expect to make feeding our first object, and to use funds for reconstruction only after famine relief has been taken care of. It should be realized, however, that our agricultural and other reconstruction work is itself famine relief work in the broadest sense of the term. Until the agriculture of the famine zone is reconstructed, the famine cannot be terminated; and our reconstruction program is just as essential to permanently saving life as is relief feeding.

We have a splendid group of 24 workers in Russia and they are well fitted and prepared to handle a very complete work. We have one doctor, four trained nurses, three agricultural directors, and the rest are social workers supervising the distribution of the food. We feel that we are in position to make the very best use of any and all of the funds that may be contributed for this purpose.

All of our reports indicate that the suffering in the famine area is going to be almost as great this year as last. The great shortage of horses and seeds made it impossible for the peasants to plant enough for their needs, and a very severe drought during the summer of 1922 very seriously affected what little grain was planted. Large numbers survived the famine last year by eating their livestock, but this year little stock remains to be eaten. Last year famine sufferers who had clothing or other valuable possessions sold them for food, but this year they will not have that resource either. They will depend more completely than ever upon outside relief for their lives.

The American Friends' Service Committee has endeavored to get as much food as possible into Russia before the winter sets in. We have, therefore, followed the policy of buying to the limit of our funds and forwarding to Russia for use during the winter. As a consequence, we have thousands of tons of food in storage, guaranteeing a minimum program of feeding for over half of the winter. We are depending on securing other funds for work in the late winter and spring.

The food and medicines which we are sending are not only intended to save life, but to make the individual recipients know that there are people in America who care for them and who desire to give them a message of good will in their time of need. We keep absolutely clear of all political questions involved in the changes in Russia and hold ourselves ready to give relief in the interests of creating a better world in which to live. We want men and women everywhere to feel that they are all children of a common Father and that we ought not to let differences of opinion lead to serious misunderstandings and war. We must do all that we can to get the peoples of the world to have confidence in each other.

We believe that every Friend will feel the importance of this work in serving those who are suffering, in stimulating international good will, and in increasing the usefulness of our own Society by the vision and inspiration which the service brings. We hope that every Friend will take his part in carrying the year's program to a successful conclusion.

Where the Clothing Goes

The following paragraphs are taken from a letter from one of the workers of the American Friends Service Committee in Russia. They indicate how great is the need for clothing, alike for men, women and children, in the famine zone:

"First there are the Children's Homes, where the most pitiful groups of children are to be found, orphans and half-orphans of the terrible famine of last winter. They are in need of everything, and the Homes and the Government are scarcely able to provide them with more than the little frame house they live in and the board beds, where they sleep huddled two and three together for warmth.

"We are trying to give the children in these Homes at least some of the warm clothing that they need for the winter, and then to make a general distribution to children living at home, and to their parents, as far as the clothing holds out. For it is not only the children who lack clothing, but the entire population. If it were not that the need is so terribly great, we should feel almost overwhelmed by the hundreds of bales of strong, warm clothing that keep steadily coming in from home.

"As it is, we look at the lists of the thousands of people whom we must feed this winter or let starve, and wonder how the stocks of clothing will ever be enough for them. It goes without saying that a man who has no crops, no horse, no cow, has long ago sold his clothing and his family's for food. For on the horse and cow the peasant's life depends, and he will part with anything else first. So do not be surprised to know that whole villages are thrown into a turmoil of excitement when the news goes out that the Quakers have American clothing for them."

Bidden to a Feast

Who among us but knows that disinclination to fulfil a dinner engagement, the invitation for which we had accepted gladly? Then the prospect was pleasant. Now, the time has come for action, and 'tis not so easily done as said. We prefer to remain where we are; to be easy in our old clothes; to drift, instead of squarely facing a new situation; to be ourselves, without disturbing constraints. Our own table is in fact very much to our liking. And so, "Better bear the ills we have, than fly to others which we know not of."

Ah! but when one has returned from the dinner, rich in a legacy of kindliness and new experience, how 'worth while' it after all was. Even our very clothes and boots retain a 'post-nuptial' lustre, and we are glad, truly glad, we went.

So simple a parable scarcely needs paraphrasing. Christ's invitation to COME stands. It is likely we have already accepted. God give us grace to take the further step, and help us with the wedding garment.

W. B. EVANS

Address to New York Friends

By T. EDMUND HARVEY

(The following address was given to New York Friends at the Twentieth Street Meeting House.)

We are all linked together by our friendships. When anyone makes a friend, it is for all his friends. I thought I might share with you the impressions of this trip, which is filling up a gap in my education, for I had never been in America before. There is such a beautiful life of hospitality here. When the way seemed to open for me to be here, I thought it would be nice to attend not only the Five Years Meeting, but also to have a liberating Minute to

the General Conference, that I might be a direct messenger of good-will, from the mother Society to both of these great representative assemblies. This was a great joy to me.

At the General Conference, we English Friends were greeted most warmly, and we feel particularly grateful for the discussion of duty that came after we had spoken. A number of members of the Five Years Meeting who were present also took part. Prominent among these was Timothy Nicholson, that lovely old man, who said, "I was born in the year of the Separation, but I have never been able to understand it, and so I invite you all to the Five Years Meeting."

Then came the wonderful sessions of the Five Years Meeting. We had been warned, even in England, that there was bitterness there, and might even be more separation. But from the start there was a sense of opportunity and duty to mankind, before which all else vanished. Then, too, the delegates were nearly all lodged at Earlham, and ate together there, with never the same company at any one table. This meeting together on the human side had much to do with the wonderful result achieved.

A very remarkable session came on the third day of the Conference. There had been a number of resolutions from Western Yearly Meetings, asking for a change in the Richmond Declaration of Faith. When I heard the Minute of the Business Committee read, I felt at first that it was really a step down, but as I heard Rufus Jones explain it, I saw that it was really a step forward. In removing a phrase which had been bitterly opposed, the Five Years Meeting showed that spiritual expression was deeper than intellectual words, and that is what the Minute shows—the spirit of Love, which is over all. It was very touching that in this great meeting no vote was taken. One Western Delegate after another rose to ask that no vote be taken. Is it too much to hope that you may not go back to the old clumsy method of taking votes? A vote so often saves time, and loses everything else. Let us keep our old method, at least for our deepest matters.

The Meeting showed itself full of interest in matters outside the society, Indians, prisons, etc. One touching feature was the appeal made by a member of the Hicksite Friends. It was so beautiful that a Western Friend who is most opposed to any thought of union, went across to her, took her hand and thanked her.

From Richmond I went to the Conservative Meeting in Barnesville, Ohio. It was a long journey back to see a hundred or more real Quaker bonnets, worn, not only by old Friends, but by girls in their teens. On First-day there were nearly a thousand people present, many of them from the neighborhood. So the Spirit still speaks, though somewhat in the language of the early nineteenth century. One was struck with the desire of the older Friends that the younger ones should take part, and with the wonderful simplicity, the beautiful loving home life.

I do not suppose any of us want to do just as the Barnesville Friends do, but underneath is something that we need. In Pittsburgh we met the material. In Barnesville, there is a spiritual life that we need to carry through all our relations. In Europe our civilization is so obviously breaking down that we have this need of the spiritual forced on us all the time. We Friends ought to stand for the other way of living—the spiritual.

In New Jersey I spent a few hours at the birthplace of John Woolman, where I rejoiced to see the same landscape that he saw. Think if we could have a Society of John Woolmans, going out, translating the spirit of Jesus into every-day life! We may differ in theological ideas, but when we think of a life like John Woolman's, we feel the appeal of a life which expressed itself in services to others, always bearing the burden of the world's suffering, though enjoying innocent pleasure keenly.

Friends are to-day called to get into the spirit of John Woolman. We are called to live the simple life, not to get fortunes to serve with. We often try to get money that we may give better service therewith. But the best service is that of self. John Woolman was one of the poorer men of his day, and he made himself poorer, by closing part of his business, so as to have more time for his fellow men. If we are to be real Friends, we must take life in terms of humanity, not of the material. Here in New York, as in any large city, we surely have a message.

Our London Yearly Meeting buildings are like little islands of quiet in the midst of the roar of our civilization. Can we make our lives places from which peace is given out? Over one of the entrances to Devonshire House, there in London, was written a hundred years ago, "Persons carrying burdens are not to use this passage." That sounds rather selfish. We do not want to get peace by separating ourselves. We want to take peace to our brothers and sisters who are in such need. And after all, the peace that is ours, which is the peace that comes from God, is not to be found by shutting out the world. It is found by going deeper into our own lives. We may attain the deeper peace by sharing it with our brothers who mourn.

ANNA L. CURTIS

Disenchantment: A Book Review

By C. E. Montague, Brentano's N. Y., 1922, 280 pages. $2.00

Here is a book, not religious—in any ordinary sense—evidently not intended as a religious book, which none the less must bring profound and searching reflection to the religious mind. It is about the War, its causes (not those mentioned in the Books, White Blue or other color), its course (in human hearts, not in communiques) and its consequences (not to the States of Europe, but to the minds of men).

The theme is the high and holy fervor with which English young men volunteered in the beginning of the conflict, soon to be damped by the follies and excesses of a professional staff; the natural impulse occasionally to joke with the foe or otherwise to show their honest respect for him, this impulse discredited and made ashamed by the non-combatant hater; the Hate which increased directly as the distance from the front trenches and was most virulent in the home newspapers and recruiting centres; and the effect of these causes on the minds which suffered them. It is told in crisp, clear English, with such force and vigor that one no more easily hears the clock strike bedtime than when intriqued in a "best seller" novel.

In the chapter "The Sheep that were not Fed," he scores the average chaplain. The typical working-class man believed, in general, "that whatever Christ said mattered enormously; it built itself into the mind......he felt, all unblunted, the point of what Christ had said about such things as wealth and war and loving one's enemies." "Ever since those disconcerting bombs were originally thrown courageous divines and laymen have been rushing in to pick them up and throw them away......Yet they lie, miraculously permanent and disturbing, as if just thrown. Now and then one will go off, with seismic results, in the mind of some St. Francis or Tolstoy." "But this war had to be won; that was flat......Any religion or anything else that seemed to chill, or deter, or suggest an alternative need not be wholly renounced. But it had to be put away in a drawer. After the war, when that dangerous precept about the left cheek could no longer do serious harm, it might come out again."

In the short and spicy chapter "War Politicians" he satyrizes the old diplomacy and political leadership. "The crust of the political globe seemed to have caked, on the whole, almost as hard and cool as that of the elderly earth. It felt as if it were so firm that we could safely play the fool on it, as boys jump on the ice of a pond and defy it to break under them."

The injury done to the common man's thinking by propaganda of false statements is well shown. "If you cannot hit or kick during a fight, at any rate you can spit. But to be happy in this arm of the service, you have to feel sure that the adversary is signally fit to be spat upon. Hence, on each side in every war, the civilians will-to-believe that the other side are a set of ogres, every man of them." "While their armies saw to the biting, the snarling was done with a will by the press of Berlin and Vienna, Petrograd, Paris and London.* That we were all fighting foul, every man, was the burden of the strain. Phone and anti-phone, the choric hymn of detraction swelled." "The authentic scarecrow, the school of though that ruled the old German State, was not used for half of what it was worth. But the word went forth that any redeeming traits in the individual German conscript were better hushed up...... A war correspondent who mentioned some chivalrous act that a German had done to an Englishman during an action, received a rebuking wire from his employer, 'Don't want to hear about any nice, good Germans'." "So it comes that each of several million ex-soldiers now reads every solemn appeal of a Government, each beautiful speech of a Premier or earnest assurance of a body of employers with that maxim on guard in his mind—'You can't believe a word you read.'"

"The churches, as we have seen, got their chance, made little or nothing of it, and came out of the war quite good secular friends with the men, but almost null and void in their eyes as ghostly counsellors, and stripped of the vague consequence with which many men had hitherto credited them on account of any divine mission they might be found to have upon closer acquaintance. Respect for the truthfulness of the Press was clean gone. The contrast between the daily events that men saw and the daily accounts that were printed was final. What the Press said thenceforth was not evidence...... Neither was anything evidence now that was said by a politician."

"Any weapon you use in a war leaves some bill to be settled in peace, and the propoganda arm has its cost like another. To say so is not to say, without more ado, that it should not be used. Its cost should be duly cast up, like other accounts; that is all. We all agree—with a certain demur from the Quakers—that one morality has to be practised in peace and another in war; that the same bodily act may be wrong in the one and right in the other. So, to be perfect, you need to have two gears to your morals, and drive on the one gear in war and on the other in peace. While you are on the peace gear you must not even shoot a bird sitting. At the last stroke of some August midnight you clap on the war gear and thenceforth you may shoot a man sitting or sleeping or any way you can get him, provided you and he be soldiers on opposite sides."

Under the new dispensation (of the Duty of Lying,) "The most disreputable of successful journalists and 'publicity experts' would naturally man the upper grades of the war staff......the practice of colouring news, of ordering reporters to take care that they see only such facts as tell in one way, would leap forward......when a man feels that his tampering with the truth has saved civilization; why should he deny himself, in his private business, the benefit of such moral reflections as this feeling may suggest?"

As to hatred: at the front "all you want is just to win the war......you are always forgetting to burn with the gem-like flame of pure fury that fires the lion-hearted publicist at home. A soldier might have had the Athanasian ecstasy all right till he reached the firing line. Every individual German had sunk the *Lusitania;* there was none righteous, none...... The relation of actual combatants is a personal one—no doubt a rude primitive one, but still quite advanced as compared with that between a learned man at Berlin who keeps on saying *Delenda est Britannia!* at the top of his voice and a learned man in London who keeps on saying that every German must have a black heart because Cæsar did not conquer Germany as he did Gaul and Britain...... You can never wholly suppress laughter between two crowds of millions of men standing within earshot of each other along a line of hundreds of miles." "Scrofulous minds at home had long been itching, publicly and in print to bomb German women and children from aeroplanes, and to 'take it out of' German prisoners of war."

As to effects of war. "One of the most sweetly flattering hopes that we had in the August of 1914 was that in view of the greatness of the occasion causes were not going to have their effects...... If anyone hints in such days, that causes may still have some control, he is easily seen to have no drop of true blood......they shall see what excellent hothouse grapes will be borne by the fine healthy thistles that we have been planting and watering."

As to a cure for this train of evils. His doctrine is not new to our ears. "Not, I fancy, by any kind of pow-wow or palaver of congress, conference, general committee, subcommittee, or other expedient for talking in company instead of working alone. This is an individual's job, and a somewhat lonely one, though a nation has to be saved by it. To get down to work, whoever else idles; to tell no lies, whoever else may thrive on their uses; to keep fit, and the beast in you down; to help any who need it; to take less from your world than you give it; to go without the old drams to the nerves—the hero stunt, the sob story, all the darling liqueurs of war emotionalism, war vanity, war spite war rant and cant of every kind; and to do it all, not in a sentimental mood of self-pity like some actor mounting in an empty theatre and thinking what treasures the absent audience has lost, but like a man on a sheep farm in the mountains, as much alone and at peace with his work of maintaining the world as God was when he made it."

This is *our* book, written better than we can write it, by one who knew not this fact and who probably knows little of us, except our name, and who undoubtedly would smile at the belief (which some of us appear to entertain) that the principles so vividly enunciated are rather exclusively our own. No one opposed to war, and least of all, no earnest Friend, should be without this truth telling little book.

JOHN COX, JR.

A truck-driver recently stopped to read the message from a certain Wayside Pulpit, which ran as follows: "Religion gave us the Sabbath Day. Will you give one hour of the Sabbath Day to religion?" When he had read it he remarked: "I would if I could. I work seven days a week. Sunday is exactly the same as any other day. Why don't you church people do something about it?" Why don't we?—*The Christian Register.*

*We may add, of New York and Chicago, of Boston and San Francisco, of other provincial towns, little and big, here.

First-day School Methods

By Bliss Forbush.

Question and Answer Box

"Can you give me a list of Christmas stories that would be suitable for use in our First-day School?"

The birth of Jesus—Luke 2:1-7.

Story of the shepherds—Luke 2:8-20.

Story of the Three Wise Men—Matthew 2:1-12.

"The Other Wise Man" and "The Mansion," by Henry Van Dyke.

"Why the Chimes Rang," "Cratchets' Christmas Dinner." and "The Philanthropists' Christmas," from "Children's Book of Christmas Stories," by Ada M. Skinner.

"The Golden Goblet," by Jay T. Stocking has two good Christmas stories in it.

The famous story in Dicken's "Christmas Carols" can be condensed for reading or telling.

There are two excellent stories in the Christmas Number of the *Pilgrim Elementary Teacher*, published by the Pilgrim Press, 14 Beacon Street, Boston, called "A Christmas Story" and "Boniface and Keep-it-all."

There are several suitable stories in the little book, "Child's Christ Tales," by Andrea Hofer.

In Gertrude Lewis' book, "A Designer of Dawns and Other Tales," are a number of stories which breathe the Christmas spirit, though not written especially for that occasion.

Special Christmas Work for the First-day School

Christmas time ought to be the time when the idea of service should be uppermost in the minds of all. To give gifts in the right spirit is splendid, but it is better yet to give one's self. We must not only cultivate a desire among our children to give to others, but we must provide a means for the practical expression of these desires.

Many Sunday Schools apply to the local Federated Charities at this time for families they may help. Why not adopt this plan? The First-day School might apply to a local charity organization for the name of some one in need and then assume the responsibility of taking care of this need.

Would this not be an excellent time for the First-day School to make a drive for assisting the Russian work? It might organize canvassing committees, give entertainments to raise funds, and collect clothing and other things to send to the Russians.

Park Avenue First-day School has an interesting evening when the children gather to pack the bags for the Christmas celebration which is given each year to the McKim children—the fifty little Italian and Jewish children of our downtown kindergarten.

Our children assemble in the main room and at the appointed time march in single file into the library where various tables are set with articles for the bags. At the first table the large paper bags themselves are given out, at the second a stocking of candy, at the third nuts, next apples, then smaller toys, and last a doll for the girls, or a set of reins for the boys. By this time the line has encircled the room, the bags are handed to the Superintendent and his helpers, and by them placed in a large packing box ready for transportation downtown. After this pleasant task has been completed games are played, and refreshments served, thus making a delightful social evening for all—especially as at this time our members absent at schools or colleges are home for their vacations. This celebration takes the place of Christmas gifts to the scholars by the First-day Schools. We feel it is better for the gifts to go to these less fortunate children than to ourselves.

I recently heard of a Sunday School which had the scholars give gifts of service to the Sunday School and Church. This is a novel idea and one we might well adopt. At Christmas time a card is sent to each member on which a "service list" is printed. The member checks those services he will perform and returns the card to the Superintendent. These then form the basis of requests for volunteer workers in different lines where the First-day School or Meeting needs help. Could you not give some of these things as Christmas gifts to your Meeting and First-day School?

Read the Bible more regularly.

Attend Meetings more regularly.

Be a home department visitor.

Act on the Visiting Committee to see the sick and shut-ins.

Be an assistant or substitute teacher in the First-day School.

Help in the closing exercises by telling some suitable stories when called upon.

Being responsible for placing kindergarten chairs and tables, or materials for other classes, where they will be needed on First-day.

Distribute the hymn books, and collect them.

Make a bulletin board.

Furnish, or help furnish, flowers for the Superintendent's desk.

Call on new members of the First-day School or Meeting.

Assist in recreational or social activities of First-day School and Meeting when called upon.

A delightful plan the school might initiate is to go carol singing in the neighborhood Christmas eve. This comes on First-day evening this year which is all the better. Have a group of at least ten people practice the carols such as "O Little Town of Bethlehem," "Silent Night," and "It Came Upon a Midnight Clear," several times. On Christmas eve pick out the homes of those members who would especially be pleased,—such as the more elderly members or the sick and shut-ins, and sing before their homes. You will need some instrument to set the pitch, and a few flashlights will be very handy. Vary the program by having an individual sing the verse, with the others joining in the chorus. Those who hear the carols will be much pleased and you will all have a delightful time.

A Peace Day in Washington

By William I. Hull.

Whenever Friends make expeditions to our Capital City in any representative capacity, it would seem well to make a brief report of such expedition to the Friends whom they represent. We accordingly will present such a report in brief. William B. Harvey and I, representing primarily the Joint Committee of the Philadelphia Yearly Meetings on the Appeal to Churches, spent Eleventh month 17th in Washington with the following results:

We had an interview with Chairman Kelly of the House Committee on Appropriations, who has been holding hearings with naval experts in regard to details of the naval appropriation bill. We had heard that a very vigorous "drive" was on foot for a considerable increase in the naval appropriation for the coming year, and requested the opportunity of presenting both the religious and the American point of view in opposition to such increase. The committee room was filled with officers in their "gold-braid" uniforms and the outlook appeared rather ominous; but our interview with the Chairman of the Committee was quite reassuring and he informed us that the only matters under discussion at present are matters of technical detail, and that there would be no increase in the naval appropriation already agreed upon; that the struggle in Congress last spring and the stand taken by the President and the Director of the Budget had been decisive, and that although the Committee on Appropriations had been at that time unsuccessful in keeping the navy personnel down to 69,000 men and had been obliged to increase the number to 86,000, it was now able to proceed with the policy of standing like a rock against any further increase. Chairman Kelly gave every evidence of being in very great earnest in speaking of his committee's determination to hold the appropriations at their present point. We, of course, assured him to the best of our ability that the Society of Friends would give such a policy their whole-hearted support, and further that we would most gladly welcome and support any further steps such as those taken at the Washington Conference a year ago in the direction of a far more drastic reduction and limitation of armaments on land and sea and in the air.

A second rumor which we had heard led us to the Washington headquarters of the Boy Scouts of America. This rumor was to the effect that the War Department, in the conference which it has been holding this week with representatives of the Boy Scouts, the High Schools, and small colleges, had offered to supply *gratis* tents, guns, and other equipment for summer camps conducted by the Scouts, the schools and the colleges, on condition that military training should be made a feature of them. The Master Scout and his assistant both assured us that such a policy would be impossible of realization for two reasons: That, in the first place, the Boy Scouts' Association at least was irreconciably opposed to military training for boys; and, secondly, because the War Department itself was opposed to such a plan both because of its expense and because of its inefficiency from the point of view of warfare. Both the Scouts and the War Department, we were told, were in favor of an adequate physical and mental training of boys so that the alarming deficiency, both physical and mental, which had been revealed by the draft during the recent war, should be overcome. We, of course, were in full sympathy with the desire for a genuine physical and mental development of our young Americans and expressed our gratification at the information that not only were the Scouts entirely opposed to military training but that their three leading officials were at that moment engaged in drafting a resolution which would preclude any danger of the introduction of military training in their programme. We thought it right, however, to remind them that "eternal vigilance is the price of liberty," and that in their dealings with the War Department it would be simply the part of wisdom to keep in mind the truth embodied in the old Homeric saying: "*Timeo Danaos et donos ferentes*" (I fear the Greeks even though they come bearing gifts).

Our third visit was to Dr. John A. Ryan, Director of the Catholic Welfare Society and a representative of that organization on the Executive Board of the National Council for the Prevention of War. Our interview with him was in regard to the distribution of the Appeal to the Churches which our two Philadelphia Yearly Meetings adopted last spring. It was a prolonged interview, covering various possible methods of procedure and resulted in a promise to write a letter which should bring the concern in a concrete way before the Catholic Welfare Board. Dr. Ryan and Dr. Burke, as well as various other members of this influential Catholic organization, are evidently in very great sympathy with the object of our Appeal, and we received the assurance that most careful consideration would be given to it.

Friendly News Notes

We are glad to be able to report that according to an editorial in the Philadelphia *Public Ledger*, at the instance of Senator Borah, the Bursum Indian Land Law, against which we urged Friends last week to protest, has been recalled from the House.

One Friend, who had sent a protest, received word from both H. P. Snyder and Clyde M. Kelly to the same effect, the latter stating that it was his opinion that this bill is never likely to be enacted into a law.

An editorial in the Harrisburg "Patriot," of December 2nd, pays a high compliment to President Aydelotte, of Swarthmore College, for the conviction and courage shown in his Thanksgiving address, in which they report he said, "that America ought to take a larger share in European affairs, and that it is regrettable that at just the time the world is suffering for lack of leadership, 'a tariff wall which shuts off the importation of a neighbor's goods, the highest ever made by any country, is preventing the economic readjustment of the world.'"

Susanna Gaskill Mahan has presented to Swarthmore College a number of Indian relics belonging to her, in the hope that they may attract other collections to the college. She is also very solicitous that the Dr. Leidy Museum be restored to something like the dignity that he intended. All that had been previously accomplished was destroyed by the fire in 1881.

A number of our Monthly Meetings, among them Centre Monthly Meeting of Western Quarterly Meeting, have entered a protest against the publishing of unsavory news detail by appealing to the editors in their localities to use their influence to "emphasize not the evil, but the things of good report."

In the Book Department of the New York *Evening Post* recently, a correspondent asked for suggestions for literature to read aloud to a child easily "scared." L. G. M., of Yellow Springs, Ohio, responded with a delightful list, including Whittier's "Child Life in Poetry," Kipling's "Jungle Books," Helen Hunt's "Cat Stories," Selma Lagerlof's "Adventures of Nils," and a dozen others, the last named being "The Children's Story Garden," edited by Anna Broomell (Lippincott). L. G. M. makes also this special comment on "The Story Garden": "'The Children's Story Garden' is especially adapted to the needs of such careful people as H. P."

We would add that "The Children's Story Garden" is a book of stories collected by a committee of the Philadelphia Yearly Meeting of Friends, of which Anna Pettit Broomell was chairman. Price $1.50, postage prepaid.

The Pittsburgh Quaker Round Table met at the home of Mr. and Mrs. Henry T. Moore, in Wilkinsburg, on the evening of November 25th. There was a good attendance, and nearly every one participated in the "quiz" and discussion which followed a very interesting informal address on conditions in Russia, by Mr. Demetry I. Vinogradoff. Mr. Vinogradoff, who is an engineer in the employ of the Westinghouse Electric and Manufacturing Company, expressed the hope that some plan may be devised whereby Russian young men will be able to secure the advantages of an American scientific education, as hundreds of them are now receiving technical training in Czeko-Slovakia.

C. E. W.

In the Spring the Friends' Bookshop issued an attractive list of announcements of Quaker and General literature likely to appeal to Friends under the title of "Books You Want." In similar form an autumn list has just been published, which can be obtained free on application to 140 Bishopsgate, London, E. C. 2.

A letter on "Teachers' Independence" which appeared recently in the *New York Evening Post*, contains the following interesting reference to one of our Friends, Mary McDowell, of the Brooklyn Meeting:

Doubtless all your readers who have children of the going-to-school age have been interested in Dr. Patri's articles. But when I read a short time ago of the qualities desirable in a teacher I rubbed my eyes and looked again. "Independence of thought," "fearlessness," "the courage to stand for one's convictions"—desirable qualities to have inculcated in one's children, surely! But to look for these among the teachers of the New York public schools—go to! There's no class of workers in the city that displays greater mental timidity, none in whom mental timidity is so insistently inculcated. . . . . It's not so long ago since an admirable teacher of twenty years' service was dismissed for no other reason than the exercise of her constitutional right of religious liberty. She was a Quaker and declined to change her faith on the ground of expediency. And was there a strike or a protest from fellow teachers at the injustice? Not a peep! When do teachers protest at any civic or national injustice?

ARMENIAN HANDKERCHIEFS FOR CHRISTMAS GIFTS

The American Friends' Service Committee has just received eight dozen handkerchiefs made by Armenian and Syrian refugees under the direction of Mrs. Daniel Oliver at Ras-el-Matn, Syria. The money received from their sale is for the benefit of the Friends' relief work and orphanages at that place. The handkerchiefs are all hand-made, with beautiful lace borders, and will make fine Christmas gifts. They are of two prices: 66c and 72c each, respectively, which prices are considerably below the market value of these handkerchiefs.

FAIRFAX QUARTERLY MEETING

The autumn meeting of Fairfax Quarter was held at Waterford, Loudoun County, Va., the week-end of the 18th to 20th of Eleventh month.

Instead of going to the large Meeting-house for the meeting of ministry and counsel, Friends gathered in a little private school house and the homey atmosphere of this has seemed to have the effect of making it a specially attractive meeting.

The subject of Friends assisting in arrangements whereby the world may be ensured permanent peace drew remarks from several.

Then there was some talk about the proposition to unify our discipline, and several queries were considered relative to their suitability for use in that connection, but no very definite conclusions were reached.

On First-day morning, Daniel Batchellor, Isaac Wilson and Benjamin Miller each presented thoughts along spiritual lines worthy of being carried home for consideration of every one of the large number present.

That evening at a union meeting that crowded the Methodist Church, Isaac Wilson delivered a very touching sermon.

On Second-day the session convened an hour earlier than usual, as many Friends wished to attend, in the afternoon, the burial service of Susanna Davis.

About a half hour was devoted to worship, most of the time occupied with words of counsel from dear ministering Friends. Then followed the business session, and being the first after Yearly Meeting, little was found to claim attention. Permission was given for continuing the annual circular meetings at the four points in Frederick County, and a move made for some further teaching of peace principles. They adjourned to meet next in the Second month, in Washington, D. C.

LEWIS PIDGEON, *Clerk*.

AN EASTERN YOUNG FRIENDS' CONFERENCE

Gerald Littleboy, writing for the English Young Friends' Committee, says, "We are becoming increasingly conscious that The Young Friends' Movement in America and England is one movement. We are one in aim and ideal, and to a larger extent than ever, one in general outlook. And we are one in the realization of the vital importance, both for ourselves and for the world, of a living experience of contact with God.

"And therefore, as we look on the needs of a world that is perishing for lack of knowledge of the power of God's love, we desire to draw closer than ever before with you who are bound on the same quest as ourselves, and who are following it along similar lines."

This appeal for a closer fellowship among young Friends comes at a time when various groups of young Friends in America find themselves appealing to each other for the same thing. For some time now the Earlham Conference in Richmond, Indiana, has been holding together the Western young Friends by bringing them into a ten-day fellowship each summer. Only a few Eastern young Friends have been able to attend because of the expense, but the few who have gone to Earlham Conferences have felt greatly helped and inspired by the experience.

But we feel that the time has come now for Eastern young Friends to hold a conference similar to Earlham—but in the East. The vital importance of Christian leadership and service is apparent in all countries and all classes today. Many and urgent appeals come to us continually to undertake the responsibility that lies upon Christian young people. And we are feeling more and more keenly the need for Christian fellowship and education.

Therefore we are hoping to have a conference next summer which shall give us the training and inspiration that we need so much. A group of young English Friends will probably be with us, also any Westerners who can make the trip. The fellowship made possible by such a conference would give us all a living experience of contact with God and the knowledge of the power of His love.

ELIZABETH ANN WALTER.

THE OPEN FORUM

This column is intended to afford free expression of opinion by readers on questions of interest. The INTELLIGENCER *is not responsible for any such opinions. Letters must be brief, and the editor reserves the right to omit parts if necessary to save space.*

THE WRITINGS OF JACOB BEHMEN

To the Editor:

May one who is not a Friend, but who is deeply indebted to the teaching and practise of Friends, express a "concern" to tell of the little known writings of Jacob Behmen which for 300 years have been the joy of those fortunate enough to know them?

Behmen's books are written in a somewhat, and to us an antiquated, style, but to one familiar with the Friends' spiritual writings of the early times they should not present any insuperable difficulties, and if they should prove hard reading they richly repay study.

Some of the older libraries in the United States have copies of English translations of Behmen made from 1647—1764 or of a London re-print of four of the principal works in 1909—1914, but these are available to very few. After considerable search I have found three publishers of any of Behmen's works in the U. S., G. W. McCalla, N. W. Cor. 18th & Ridge Ave., Phila. issues a vol. of Epistles and three small booklets of selections;—E. P. Dutton, New York, publishes "The Signature of All Things," with which is bound two beautifully plain and simply written treatises;—The Macoy Pub. Co., New York, issues a re-print of F. Hartmann's Life and Doctrines of Jacob Behmen, under the title of "Personal Christianity a Science." The Morris Book-Shop, 24 North Wabash Ave., Chicago, has a few copies of "Six Theosophic Points" newly translated by John R. Earle, a very valuable work.

None of these are expensive, and together they give a good introduction to Behmen, and to those who are ready for him an insight into the profoundest spiritual writings of modern times.

Not all can read him profitably. Those who would try must, he says, have "a totally resigned and yielded will, in which God himself searcheth and worketh, and which continually pierceth into God, in yielding and resigned humility, seeking nothing but his eternal native country, and to do his neighbor service with it; and then it may be attained. And he must begin with effectual repentance and amendment, and with prayer, that his understanding might be opened from within; for then the inward will bring itself into the outward." FLORENCE D. BRATTEN

FREE SPEECH

To the Editor:

In the Open Forum of Eleventh month 18th Mr. G. E. Coale complains of the views of some of your contributors on the subject of Free Speech, and suggests that they should "emigrate to some ocean island a thousand miles from any other human being;" there "to talk, act and write as they please."

We must know what we are talking about before we can discuss the subject. Does Mr. Coale refer to anarchists, who are advocating unlawful measures against government? If so, I freely admit the right of government to defend itself and our institutions by suppressing such speech, although toleration is often a better policy. But I do not believe Mr. Coale refers to this class, because they are not anarchists who have been writing to THE INTELLIGENCER.

The principle of free speech and free press confers the right to think and advocate any change in government whatsoever, so long as the individual is a law-abiding citizen, submits to the will of the majority, and seeks to gain his point by the exercise of his franchise.

The right of free speech is vital and it must not be taken away in the interest of an established order, or we will soon have a static government in a dynamic world.

All political and social evolution depends on the right of free expression else we are wholly ruled by the dead hand of the past.

It is the intolerant who are the proper candidates for ocean islands—the tolerant can live together.

The subject of personal liberty versus personal license which Mr. Coale refers to has no proper place in this discussion. That free speech is a thing to be gradually taken from us because our population grows denser is absurd.

I. D. WEBSTER.

FREEDOM OF SPEECH AND OF ACT

To the Editor:

As the letter of Elizabeth Coale with regard to freedom of speech has recently been severely critized, I feel it a duty to say that it was one of the best utterances on that subject that I have seen. Believing in freedom of speech, as I do, I also believe there are well defined limits for it, laid down by law, and by good morals as well. When freedom of utterance goes so far as to advocate the assassination of public officials, or making overt attacks upon the freest government on earth, then it has gone beyond the limit of tolerance, and should receive the sudden and severe check of organized government.

If seditious utterance, the open and flagrant advocacy of treasonable attacks upon our form of government, are tolerated, then we have no government worthy the name. It is quite time that those who claim such freedom of speech should learn that "thoughts are things," and thoughts expressed in speech leading toward overt acts of violence are, in guilt, but little short of the acts themselves. If I entertained toward the government of my country sentiments that have recently been expressed in letters in the "Open Forum," I would make diligent search for a freer country with a better form of government, and if successful in finding it, would take passage on the earliest steamer possible headed that way. In doing this I would be "leaving my country for my country's good," and so both would be satisfied. ISAAC ROBERTS

BIRTHS

JONES—At Lebanon, Indiana, on Eleventh month 26th, to Professor M. M. and Della Downing Jones, a son, who is named Elbert Downing Jones.

MILLER—At Chicago, Ill., on Eleventh month 6th, to Wyatt A. and Lucile D. Miller, a son named Wyatt Wistar Miller.

ROBERTS—On Eleventh month 15th, at Marlton, N. J., to Byron T. and Lydia L. Roberts, a son, who is named Edwin Kirk Roberts.

DEATHS

BRIGGS—Near Langhorne, Pa., on Eleventh month 29th, 1922, Anna Mary, wife of Edward Briggs, aged 74 years.

HURLEY—On Eleventh month 28th, Wallace P., husband of Elizabeth M. Hurley and son of William W. and Achsah P. Hurley, of Solebury township, aged 39 years.

MOORE—At Elmer, N. J., on Eleventh month 26th, Bertha M., wife of S. Lippincott Moore, aged 47 years. She was a member of Pilesgrove Monthly Meeting.

ANTOINETTE PEARSALL

Antoinette Pearsall has passed on to the Higher Life, and to the reward of a good and faithful servant. Although a great sufferer and physically unable to enter largely into the work of her beloved Society, she was alive to its needs, and interested for its welfare. Being of a deep spiritual nature, she responded to all that was elevating and ennobling, which is indicated in the message she left.

"And this is the Cross of Christ, to bring our wills in reverential subjection to the Life within, which is our God. It was only as Jesus yielded His will unto His Maker, and thus reached the growth when He could say, 'Thy will be done.' Then it was, He took up the Cross.

Again, the deep Living Silence in us is the trysting place with the Divine. It is here we make our vows, it is here we are face to face with our God; and may it be that we can recognize our Creator in and through the life in us."

COMING EVENTS

TWELFTH MONTH

10th—Conference Class at Fifteenth and Race streets, Philadelphia, at close of meeting for worship, 11.40 a. m. Subject—Prophets of Literature. Leader—Dr. Harold C. Goddard, Swarthmore College.

13th—New York Monthly Meeting, at 110 Schermerhorn Street, Brooklyn, at 7.30. Supper at 6 o'clock. Supplementary sale after the Aid Association Fair will be held.

13th—Germantown Friends' Association, 8 P. M. An O. Henry evening given by members of the Emerson Club. A cordial welcome to all.

14th—Haddonfield Quarterly Meeting, at Moorestown, N. J., at 10.30 a. m. Meeting of ministry and counsel at 9.15.

17th—Amawalk Friends Meeting will be held at the home of Louisa Loder, north of Amawalk Meeting-house, at 2.30 p. m.

18th—Christmas Entertainment and exercises at West Philadelphia First-day School, 35th and Lancaster Avenue. Bring your gifts for the poor and hear the children sing. 7.30 p. m.

20th—Monthly Meeting of Friends of Philadelphia, 15th and Race Sts., 7.30 p. m.

21st—Green Street Monthly Meeting of Friends of Philadelphia, School House Lane, Germantown, 7.30 p. m.

22nd—The Brooklyn First-day School will hold its Christmas Festival this evening. There will be supper for all at 6 o'clock, followed by exercises, and the tree and presents.

NOTICE—Friends and Friendly people living in or passing through St. Petersburg are cordially invited to gather on First-day afternoons at three o'clock, at the residence of Sarah E. Gardner-Magill, 850 Sixth St., South, for a Conference and religious meeting.

The first meeting will be held Twelfth month 17th.

As to Subscriptions

Sometimes we wish we had pastors, presiding elders, "'n everything," when we read in the *Christian Advocate*, the official paper of the Methodist Episcopal Church, that Dr. H. A. Butts, presiding elder of the Paris district, Memphis Conference, has secured 385 new subscriptions to that paper.

When we think of what one man has done for that paper, and how badly we want to get the INTELLIGENCER into every Friendly home, we almost jump to the wrong conclusion and think that it is presiding elders that we need. We know that is not so, but we do need more men like Dr. Butts who recognize the value of the official organ to the Church, and are willing to exert themselves to get this idea across to their fellow members. This is the best time of year to get new subscribers, for people are making up their list of magazines for the coming year.

Will thee do 1/385 as much for thy paper as Dr. Butts did for his, and send us one new subscription? All new subscriptions begin at once and continue until First month 1st, 1924.

A Note of Thanks

We want to thank the reader of the INTELLIGENCER who recently patronized one of our advertisers to the extent of several hundred dollars and made the required effort to let the management know that she had seen the advertisement in the INTELLIGENCER. We called on that manager later, and were told that they were "having most remarkable results from that little ad."

This is the sort of co-operation that costs so little and helps so much.

American Friends' Service Committee

WILBUR K. THOMAS, EX. SEC.
20 S. 12th St. Philadelphia.

CASH CONTRIBUTIONS

WEEK ENDING NOVEMBER 27TH.

Five Years Meeting	$113.00
Philadelphia Yearly Meeting (Hicksite)	100.00
Other Meetings:	
Middletown Meeting	25.00
Langhorne First-day School	1.50
Willistown First-day School	25.00
Brooklyn Meeting	20.00
Center Meeting	100.00
Oakland Branch of the College Park Meeting	24.50
Green Street Monthly Meeting	500.00
Contributions for Germany	15.75
For Austria	58.75
For Poland	681.27
For Russia	6,721.59
For Russian Overhead	1,220.40
For Armenia	241.48
For General	200.36
For Syria	220.00
German Overhead	25.00
Clothing Department	322.62
Refunds	89.14
	$10,705.36

Shipments received during week ending November 25, 1922: 104 boxes and packages, 3 anonymous.

FUN

"Mary," said the mistress of the house when she discovered dust on the table, "I can write my name on this table."

"Yes, ma'am," replied Mary, beaming, "I always said there is nothing like education."

When Mr. Spurgeon went to preach for Dr. Clifford, he said in the vestry before the service, "I cannot imagine, Clifford, why you do not come to my way of thinking."

"Well," answered John Clifford, "you see, Mr. Spurgeon, I only see you about once a month, but I read my Bible every day!"—*Methodist Protestant.*

A sturdy backwoodsman returned hearty thanks to a famous bishop for a sermon which had greatly enlightened him. The bishop begged to know what was the subject on which a light had been thrown. "Well bishop," replied the Westerner, "I had always supposed before that Sodom and Gomorrah were two twins."—*Selected.*

Of Sabbath breaking north of the Tweed there are many stories, and an American who has spent a bit of his time there adds one concerning a Scot and his wheelbarrow.

Donald was hammering away at the bottom of his barrow when his wife came to the door.

"Mon," she said, "you're making muckle clatter. What wull the neebours say?"

"Never mind the neebours," replied the busy one. "I maun get ma bara mendit."

"Oh, but, Donald, it's vera wrang to wurk on Sabbath!" expostulated the wife. "Ye ought to use screws."—*Selected.*

WANTED

WANTED—GOOD HOME OR BOARDING place with cheerful surroundings for middle-aged lady, mentally somewhat deficient. State probable terms. Address P. 390, Friends' Intelligencer.

U. S. GOVERNMENT UNDERWEAR—2,500,000 pc. New Government Wool Underwear purchased by us to sell to the public direct at 75c EACH. Actual retail value $2.50 each. All sizes. Shirts 34 to 46—Drawers 30 to 44. Send correct sizes. Pay Postman on delivery or send us money order. If underwear is not satisfactory, we will refund money promptly upon request. Dept. 24, Pilgrim Woolen Co., 1476 Broadway, New York, N. Y.

PRACTICAL NURSE WOULD LIKE care of semi-invalid, or feeble person. Willing to be generally useful in home if case permits. Address B. 440, Friends' Intelligencer.

WANTED—REFINED YOUNG WOMAN for clerical work. Knowledge of telephone exchange desired. Friend preferred. Address B. 443, Friends' Intelligencer.

MAY WE COUNT ON THY HELP IN our advertising campaign? As a friend of the INTELLIGENCER will thee not patronize our advertisers, and mention the FRIENDS' INTELLIGENCER when making inquiries or purchases?

POSITION AS HOUSEKEEPER OR Companion and Nurse to old person. Capable and willing. Address W. 451, Friends' Intelligencer.

SALARIED STENOGRAPHER, NIGHTS free, can report occasional daylight meetings. Geo. B. Cock, Bell (Philadelphia) phone directory.

WANTED—ONE OR TWO PERSONS to occupy a large front room in Friend's family, New York City, modern conveniences. Restricted block. Convenient to bus, trolley and subway. Address F. 450, Friends' Intelligencer.

FOR SALE

FOR SALE—NEWTOWN SECTION—Desirable Homes. I have for sale in Newtown a variety of properties from $3,000 up. One within five minutes' walk of George School, a lovely home, all conveniences; garage, poultry house and yard, garden. If interested inquire promptly. Also some of the finest farms in Bucks County. W. T. Wright, Newtown, Pa.

REGULAR MEETINGS

OAKLAND, CALIF. — A FRIENDS' Meeting is held every First-day at 11 A. M., in the Extension Room, Y. W. C. A. Building, Webster Street, above 14th. Visiting Friends always welcome.

PASADENA, CALIFORNIA — Orange Grove Monthly Meeting of Friends, 520 East Orange Grove Avenue. Meeting for worship, First-day, 11 A. M. Monthly Meeting, the second First-day of each month, at 1.45 P. M. First-day School (except Monthly Meeting days) 9.45 A. M.

FUN

Dr. Grenfell after amputating the limb of a Roman Catholic patient wrote an appeal for a wooden leg to enable the man to move about. This was published in *The Congregationalist* and read by a Baptist woman whose husband, a Methodist, who had worn a wooden leg, had just died. So the Methodist leg given by a Baptist woman in answer to a Congregational appeal is now being used as a perfectly good interdenominational understanding—*Selected.*

To the Lot Holders and others interested in Fairhill Burial Ground:

GREEN STREET Monthly Meeting has funds available for the encouragement of the practice of cremating the dead to be interred in Fairhill Burial Ground. We wish to bring this fact as prominently as possible to those who may be interested. We are prepared to undertake the expense of cremation in case any lot holder desires us to do so.

Those interested should communicate with William H. Gaskill, Treasurer of the Committee of Interments, Green Street Monthly Meeting, or any of the following members of the Committee.

William H. Gaskill, 3201 Arch St.
Samuel N. Longstreth, 1218 Chestnut St.
Charles F. Jenkins, 232 South Seventh St.
Stuart S. Graves, 3858 Germantown Ave.

ADVERTISING RATE in the FRIENDS' INTELLIGENCER, for Help Wanted, Positions Wanted, Rooms for Rent, and other classified advertisements without display, for each insertion, 2 cents per word, including name, initials and address. Answers may be sent to a box at the INTELLIGENCER office, if so directed.

For display advertising the rate is 10 cents per agate line, or $1.40 per column inch, each insertion. On ten or more insertions in a year from date of order, ten per cent. discount. Thus a four-inch single-column or two-inch double-column advertisement costs $5.60 each insertion, less ten per cent., or $5.04 net each time for ten or more insertions. Matter may be changed whenever desired, without extra charge.

Experience has proved the INTELLIGENCER to be a remarkably good advertising medium. All advertisements must "pass the censor!"

Address 140 N. 15th St., Philadelphia.

The Friends' Intelligencer

ESTABLISHED 1844 — TWELFTH MONTH 16, 1922 — VOLUME 79 NUMBER 50

Contents

EDITORIALS

GENERAL ARTICLES

THE FRIENDS' INTELLIGENCER

Published weekly, 140 N. 15th Street. Philadelphia, Pa., by Friends' Intelligencer Association, Ltd.

SUE C. YERKES, *Managing Editor.*

Subscription rates: United States, Mexico, Cuba and Panama, $2.50 per year. Canada and other foreign countries, $3.00 per year. Checks should be made payable to Friends' Intelligencer Association, Ltd.

Entered as Second Class Matter at Philadelphia Post Office.

The Friends' Intelligencer

The religion of Friends is based on faith in the "INWARD LIGHT," or direct revelation of God's spirit and will in every seeking soul.

The INTELLIGENCER is interested in all who bear the name of Friends in every part of the world, and aims to promote love, unity and intercourse among all branches and with all religious societies.

ESTABLISHED 1844 | PHILADELPHIA, TWELFTH MONTH 16, 1922 | VOLUME 79 NUMBER 50

The Near East

One horror succeeds another with such rapidity that our senses become numbed and we seem to forget so quickly the victims of one calamity as we await news of the next. The letter from Daniel Oliver in this issue, brings to us afresh the magnitude of the suffering from the massacres at Smyrna. Here is a man, a Friend, someone we know, living in the midst of these horrors, trying to help relieve this indescribable misery.

He asks, "Over against this flood of destruction and fury, wrong and suffering, what can we do?" Then he answers his own question by saying that we must hold fast to our faith that God reigns, and, in spite of everything, we must believe that love, and only love, can heal the world's wrongs.

"Practical love, sympathy and service are all that we can contribute." In this case, as in many others, the only way in which we can make this contribution is by sending to Daniel Oliver and his co-workers the material supplies by means of which they can pass on to these sufferers evidence of our desire to help them.

We have done much in the way of relief work during the last few years, but how many of us have given "until it hurt?" Have we practiced any real self-denial? Haven't we, every one of us, been comfortably housed, fed and clothed? In fact, we have been so comfortable that we have no experience on which to base any realization of what these people have passed through, what they are now suffering, and how little the future holds for them. Can we, at this time of the year, when we think especially of the Christ spirit, be satisfied to call ourselves "Christians" unless we follow more closely in His footsteps and sacrifice ourselves for the good of others? We have hardly sacrificed our "wants." When we have reached the point where we are sacrificing our "needs," we shall have made real progress in our own development, and the amount thus released for the relief of our suffering brothers will be amazing.

The American Friends' Service Committee will be glad to forward to Daniel Oliver any money or supplies sent to it for that purpose.

The World League Against Alcoholism.

The International Convention against Alcoholism held recently in Toronto, Canada, has placed an immense responsibility on the United States to "make good" in its support of the Eighteenth Amendment. Here were representatives from sixty-five countries gathered to discuss the question of Prohibition, all of them looking to us for inspiration and help in their battle against alcohol.

We cannot begin to comment on the prominent people who are listed as speakers at this convention. With the work of many of them we are familiar, and they all of them are leaders. But of what use are conventions and leaders without followers. That is where those of us who could not attend the convention, but who are heart and soul against the liquor traffic, come in. And we must come in, if the Eighteenth Amendment is to stand. We need to help by seeing that the law is enforced on the rich and poor alike, taking the matter of enforcement out of the hands of politicians.

The following quotation from "The Outlook" appeals to us as being the best possible statement of the situation:

"Stripped of all sophism, the question is simply a problem of social expediency. Is it better for the nation to insist upon the personal liberty of every man to decide for himself about the use of alcoholic beverages or to insist upon the sacrifice of that form of personal liberty in order to abolish the liquor saloon with the alcoholism, the vice, the crime, and the political corruption which it inevitably produces? Prohibition is not a matter of abstract morals; it is a matter of social welfare, like the abolition of the personal liberty of spitting where one chooses or the institution of compulsory vaccination. Viewed in this light, it is the greatest and most interesting experiment that has ever been tried in the history of civilization. It is certainly worth trying fairly and honestly."

The Sense of God's Presence

By ELBERT RUSSELL.

(This article is the fifth in a series of articles on "Worship" which have been appearing at irregular intervals during the year. There will be two more articles in this series which we hope to publish soon.)

The sense of God's presence comes to the few as a rare, overwhelming experience, a turning-point in life, an hour of ineffably sweet fellowship. For such experiences there is no formula. Like the great hours of human fellowship they come without herald or conscious preparation. There is no magic "Open Sesame" that invariably opens the gates of the soul for God; nor can we say: "Lo, here He is," or "Lo, there the beatific visions come." Two of us may grind at the same mill, and one be taken and the other left.

But for the unillumined hours and for those of us uninitiated into the mystic exaltation of such "visions and revelations of the Lord," there is possible a less rapt but more sustaining sense of God's continual presence in His world, and of close fellowship with Him, both in the communion of the hour of worship, and while walking the common paths of duty. This sense of His presence can be "practised," as Brother Lawrence phrased it; it can be cultivated by definite effort and attained by diligent practice. It is to be sought inside the gateways of the soul and found in the paths that thread our normal psychic states. These articles are written not for those who have the abiding consciousness of the Presence, and need no rules for the "Practise" nor directions for the "Way," but for those who are groping after Him in prayer and worship, and still follow afar off.

The sense of God's presence is both more difficult and easier to attain than the sense of present fellowship with our human friends, because of the absence of any bodily symbol of His presence. We associate human personalities with their bodies, which occupy a definite space and can be located with reference to our own bodies. Our sense of their presence is reinforced by the impression of physical nearness, by the sight of them, of their gestures and facial expression, and by the sound of their voices. But God is a spirit; He dwells not in "a house of clay" nor "in temples made by men's hands"; His manifestations are not to our senses. No man hath seen Him at any time, nor does He speak with an audible voice.

On the other hand, the lack of a physical incarnation of the Divine Spirit frees us from any limitations of time or place or physical manifestation in our thought of Him or consciousness of fellowship with Him. We do not have to go to some sacred place to be or feel "near" Him. God is a Spirit. Drawing near in worship is not a matter of pilgrimage to Jerusalem or Gerizin, but of the seeking soul. This indicates how inadequate is the word "presence" to express the reality we are trying to attain. Presence inevitably carries with it a suggestion of physical nearness, of proximity in location. While what we mean by God's presence is a matter of approachability, of possible fellowship, of available help and strength. And these are not wholly nor chiefly even in our human relations matters of physical proximity. "Presence" is, however, the established word. No better one is at hand, and we must keep on using it, doing our best to counteract its continual suggestion of bodily presence and physical location.

The omnipresence of God in religious thought has meant two things: (1) the universality of God's efficient will in the universe; and (2) the possibility of conscious fellowship with God, regardless of our location. The sense of God's "presence" consists chiefly of the latter, but could hardly exist beyond momentary impressions without a conviction of the former, which we may consider first.

As long as we think of God's presence in a physical sense, it is a difficult thing to realize. In thinking of Him, it is hard to escape the tyranny of our senses. Our imagination wishes to give even to God "a local habitation and a name." Few of us, perhaps, attain Whittier's sense of His spirituality:

No picture to my aid, I call;
  I shape no image in my prayers.
I only know in Him is all,
  Of life, light, beauty everywhere,—
  Eternal Goodness here and there!

If God were localized on a throne in heaven or confined to a temple or inhabited a body as our human spirits do, he could no more be everywhere at once than a man can. But if God is a spirit, He can pervade the universe; for a spirit is a self-conscious person who thinks, feels, and wills. The omnipresence of God means that His will is efficient everywhere, manifesting itself in uniform and intelligent law, and in orderly power. This is not easy to imagine; but a consideration of how our own thoughts move and our wills become efficient in wide ranges beyond the limitations of our bodies may help. When we talk of things that are done "in our presence" we mean "within our reach or within range of our sight or hearing." We ourselves are "present" where we can see, hear or do things. Man has continually been extending the sphere of his efficient will by all manner of tools, instruments and machines. A pole or club, an arrow or gun extends a man's reach. The radiophone brings persons within hearing hundreds and even thousands of miles away from us. The telescope enables men to see stars thousands of light-years away. They are in the astronomer's presence. The social and material machinery of modern life extends the range of men's efficient will. We can get things done that we want done all around the globe. Where our agents are at work or our machines are operating, there we are as practically "present" as at the end of our arms. By means of money I can convert my energy into definite activity and have it performed for me in China or Tasmania. As an efficient working will I am present where my money is securing the doing of what I want done. So we think of God's intelligent efficient will as "present" everywhere throughout the universe wherever Force works according to Law and where Order is clothed with Beauty. The very uniformity of Nature is evidence of His universal presence and the universal reign of Law the result of a single all-pervading Control. Worship, prayer, and responsibility are equally possible in all places because His knowledge, control, and power to help are equally efficient in all places. The things that separate us from Him are not matters of time and place, but ignorance, indifference or sin. There is a vast comfort in the thought of His ever-present Fatherly will at work.

"I know not where His islands lift
Their fronded palms in air;
I only know I cannot drift
Beyond His love and care."

The omnipresence of God is also used to express the conscious fellowship and communion which we have or may have with God, regardless of our location. The consciousness of the presence of human personalities is not essentially a matter of physical neighborhood. As a vital influence in our thoughts, and a determining factor in our conduct, a person may be "present" though half a world away.

A friend in Russia may be constantly in our thoughts. We may do or refuse to do dozens of things daily because it would please him, while persons who work beside us in the office or sit beside us on the subway cars are not present to our consciousness at all. One may be lonely in a great crowd, and in solitude feel the vivid comradeship of a far-away loved one.

The sense of God's presence in the universe makes it feel differently. A child comes home from school and finds no one in the house. It feels empty, terrible. She calls, and her mother answers from a distant room. At once the mother's known presence in the house transforms the "feel" of it. The child is no longer lonely or afraid. She goes about her play comforted, though the mother is not visibly present. So the consciousness of God's presence makes the world no longer seem an impersonal mechanism or inexorable "wheel of Nature," but transforms it into the Father's house, a place of co-operation and communion.

The consciousness of God's presence is a source of spiritual power. We can do so many things when someone shares them with us, that we could never do alone. Sympathy gives power to endure pain. It is easier for a child to resist temptation if Mother is along. A man will be a truer gentleman in the presence of a fine, pure woman. Courage comes with comradeship. When I was a little boy, I was mortally afraid of the dark. I could not venture into a dark room alone. But if my little sister would hold my hand and go with me, I could muster courage for the venture. In a similar way the realization of the presence of God brings to each who feels it and lives in it the fullness of spiritual power.

This realization can be developed and strengthened by our own efforts. First, we must harmonize our wills with His. The pure in heart see God. Selfishness, irreverence, vulgarity, and sensuality dim the spiritual vision and cloud the consciousness of God.

We can also cultivate the habit of sensing God's presence in Nature. In an artist's studio or a craftsman's shop, one feels the presence of the worker in his work. It reveals him so intimately—his designs, ideals, skill, character. So through all the varying harmony, beauty, order, and life of Nature we feel God's preesnce, and enjoy the fellowship of "thinking His thoughts after Him, delighting with Him in the beauty of His work, and sharing with Him the creative work of bringing order out of disorder.

More important still is it to cultivate the sense of God's nearness in men and women. I distrust the mysticism which can only work in solitude; which feels farther from God when it comes close to men. We should sense His presence in every act of justice, in all true thinking, in every appreciation of beauty, and in every gleam of self-sacrificing love among His children. Only so can we recognize God in Christ, and feel that we are serving Him in ministering to His brethren.

Then we must form the habit of acting as in His presence. There are persons who vitally influence our conduct, when present. We wish to do and

respect them deeply, we act as if in their presence even when they are absent. We do not wish to do anything that would hurt or displease them, if they should learn of it. So we learn to live, in the presence of God.

> "Holding as in the Master's sight,
> Act and thought to the Inner Light."

We cannot, of course, be thinking constantly of God, but the consciousness of His presence can be carried in the background of our thoughts, dominating all our purposes, even as a range of mountains in the background dominates a landscape. Consciously or subconsciously we learn to live in and for Him, so that we can say with Paul: "For me to live is Christ."

Each In His Own Tongue

A fire mist and a planet—
  A crystal and a cell—
A jellyfish and a saurian,
  And caves where the cavemen dwell;
Then a sense of law and beauty,
  And a face turned from the clod—
Some call it evolution,
  And others call it God.

A haze on the fair horizon,
  The infinite, tender sky,
The ripe, rich tint of the cornfields,
  And the wild geese sailing high—
And all over upland and lowland
  The charm of the golden rod—
Some of us call it autumn,
  And others call it God.

Like tides on a crescent beach
  When the moon is new and thin,
Into our hearts high yearnings
  Come welling and surging in—
Come from the mystic ocean,
  Whose rim no foot has trod—
Some of us call it longing,
  And others call it God.

A picket frozen on duty—
  A mother starved for her brood—
Socrates drinking the hemlock,
  And Jesus on the rood;
And millions who, humble and nameless,
  The straight, hard pathway plod—
Some call it consecration,
  And others call it God.

—*William Herbert Carruth.*

European Relief as a Safeguard to American Health

Dr. Royal S. Copeland, Commissioner of Health of the City of New York, visited Europe last summer on a "health scouting trip." His observations are published in a recent issue of the "Weekly Bulletin of the Department of Health, City of New York." Through his professional eyes Commissioner Copeland sees the present need and suffering in Europe from a new angle—that of its relation to the health of the United States. Commissioner Copeland first visited Austria. He writes of that country:

"The whole population has been so long deprived of food essentials that its powers of resistance are a fraction of that which they should be. All Austria, already suffering dreadfully from disease, is ripe for a great epidemic. Austria is no longer a military threat against her neighbors, but she is a sanitary threat against the world."

Commissioner Copeland then visited Poland and inspected the devastated territory and the points of admission through which the Polish refugees from Russia are returning to their native country. He says:

"Poland especially enchained my interest, for it too easily may become the source of the world's greatest sanitary catastrophe. Hundreds, even thousands, of sufferers from typhus, cholera, relapsing-fever are passed through them (the unequipped admission points) and permitted to mingle freely with the people in the interior of Poland.

"Without the slightest hesitation, I predict that these diseases will sweep through Poland, Germany, Belgium, Holland and France into England. I predict that from every port in the great area whence sail ships, infection will be shipped to the United States unless without delay we take the lead in providing proper measures of precaution there in Poland."

In closing his report, Commissioner Copeland asks what sources of relief from this situation can be found. He says that there is little hope of relief from European governments at present or from the government of the United States.

"Therefore," he concludes, "the only hope I can see is that private funds may be contributed. I can think of nothing more inspiring than giving now, directly for the protection of suffering Poland (and Austria), indirectly for the protection of our own nation, states, cities, homes, wives and children."

Going the "Second Mile"

One of the checks received last week by the American Friends Service Committee for work in Austria was accompanied by the following note:

"I am inclosing my check for $25, which completes the pledge I gave the Committee the first of the year. I promised to send $25 a month from January to December, 1922. I had every intention of stopping after that, as there are so many other things that make demands upon me. However, your report, forwarded the other day, was very appealing! I shall, therefore, keep on with my contribution, $25 a month, up to July, 1923."

This is the spirit which makes possible the continuation of our relief and reconstruction work abroad.

Thanks to the Quakers from a Russian Village

Many of the villages in the Russian famine zone, which have been helped by the relief mission of the American Friends Service Committee have written letters to the Quakers expressing their thanks for the help received. The following paragraphs are taken from such a letter. They illustrate not only how tragic the need is, but also that the Russian peasants appreciate something of the spirit in which the help is given.

After describing the terrible conditions experienced during the famine, the letter continues:

"In the unbearable agony resulting from the fear of immediate death they sought further means of escape from their terrible plight and found none. At last, having lost all their strength in their search for an escape, and having given up all hope of help from any source, they settled back each to await his death. Everything was at a standstill, frozen, quiet as the grave; a deadly silence surrounded all, broken only by the sighs of the dying.

"Then occurred that of which all had ceased to think—a miracle. Help came. Either the ceaseless currents of the air or the stormy waves of the sea had carried to the shores of America the sighs of the perishing. The Humble Saviour died, but his teaching, 'Love thy neighbor,' still lives; with its creative warmth burning in your noble and responsive hearts it brought life to millions of the starving. You, bearing in your hearts the words of the Great Teacher, and with sincere Christian endeavor, fearing not the tempestuous tides of the Atlantic hastened to help your doomed brethren in Russia.

"Your great Christian effort may be compared to the deeds of the noble saints who carried manna to the Children of Israel in the desert. You rescued from death us and our children, those innocent flowers of humanity. Again their young voices rang out, raising to the Eternal their prayers for you, our good Quaker brothers.

"You saved our lives. No human tongue can express the gratitude that we feel toward you. Each of us personally sends to you great Russian thanks."

The Near East

Dear Friends everywhere:

We sent off a cablegram yesterday as follows: "Horrors and massacres at Smyrna, as told by eye-witnesses, are appalling. First steamer, refugees, arrived Beyrout destitute. Large contributions urgently needed if we are to do some part in relieving distress. Olivers and Evans." I hope this cable will have reached your side, as I was able to send it from another country. I must here explain that we are under a very strict censorship, and most items of news in regard to relief work, and especially in regard to Armenians, are suppressed by the censor. I do not know why. In consequence many of my letters have not reached their destination. Will those Friends who have not received answers to their letters, please accept this explanation? The censor will not see this letter for it will go through a channel which he cannot intercept, but if it should ever meet his eye in print, let me assure him that his mind can be perfectly easy, I never write anything about military or political subjects.

The horrors of the massacres at Smyrna were even worse than the reports, I have no words to depict them. We have our information from eye-witnesses, but it is too shocking to go into details. The misery resulting to those still alive is indescribable. This is the fruit of war, of divided counsels, and rivalry among the allied Powers. Hundreds of thousands of women and children, and old men are fleeing in all directions, while the young and able bodied men are taken into the interior, *for what?*

The first steamer load of 1500 refugees has arrived in Beyrout. They are being disinfected at the Quarantine Station and then will be let loose to go where they will. Again, as last year after the flight of refugees from Cilicia, all the caves by the seashore, all spaces under bridges will be occupied by masses of hungry, cold, ragged, homeless individuals. Already there are thousands of Armenians in Beyrout, many of them wandering about the streets looking for work, and a crust of bread. Can Heaven look down today on a sadder sight than the rich fertile lands of Anadolia ruined and devastated, its soil drenched with the blood of its sons, its villages (once full of happy homes, and the children in the streets playing with marbles) now burnt and blackened ruins, and flocks of vultures still hovering over the unburied bones of those who were only so recently living their lives, dreaming their dreams, and looking into the future with hope and faith?

What awful tornado has swept over this beautiful Anadolia? Has hell burst through its boundaries and carried desolation and doom with it everywhere? Have all the traditional devils gathered for a united attack, and to gloat over the agonies of dying and suffering multitudes? My very brain is staggered and reels in front of the facts which I know. The floods of human hate and vindictiveness would seem to have reached a height beyond which they could not rise.

The Greeks in their mad rush from Smyrna, northeast to Eskischehr, their objective being Angora which they were unable to reach, left destruction and ruin in their trail, the Moslem villages being the sufferers. It is futile to hide or deny this. It is a fact. The rising tide of Turkish nationalism, and Mohammedan fanaticism all over the Mohammedan world, made the Turks of Anadolia a new power, and with the force of a cyclone they rushed West and drove the Greek armies into the sea. Then the Moslem wrongs were avenged to an extent that will stagger humanity when it is fully known. But on whom were they avenged? Not on the Greek army, which got mostly away in their fleet. Vengeance fell on the non-combatant population. Between the upper and lower millstones the poor inhabitants of Smyrna, and the villages in the interior, have been crushed, and seen hell in all its awful realities, and suffered agonies worse than death.

Over against this flood of destruction and fury, wrong and suffering, what can we do? What is left to us to do? In the first place, still to hold on to our faith that God reigns. To some even that is no longer possible. Everything has been swept overboard in the storm. And second, in spite of all, to believe that love, and only love, can heal the world's wrongs. Love is the only answer to the wrath of man. Practical love, sympathy, and service are all we can contribute. These will do much to soothe and heal. For many there will be no more sunshine in their lives. Here we are ready to do everything we can to help in measures of relief, and I appeal to all to do what they can to help us to meet one of the greatest emergencies that has yet come to the Near East.

Since the above was written Herbert G. Wood, of Woodbrooke, England, has arrived here, and is sleeping under our roof tonight. He and Dr. Rendel Harris have just arrived from Constantinople and Smyrna. Herbert G. Wood has confirmed all the information we had already, only some things are even worse than we had heard.

The Armenians we brought up here at the beginning of the year have all got settled in the villages around and are in one way and another eking out a living. We propose to repeat the experiment if funds are forthcoming. We could probably find houses for two or three hundred families in the villages around here. It will be something to have people under a roof before the winter storms begin.

Our Syrian orphans are all flourishing, with a few exceptions, who are having attacks of malaria, and these are practically cured. We count on the love, and unity of our friends with us in the work here, and to the many in different parts of the country, and the cities, whose friendship we treasure, we send our love and cordial greetings.

Sincerely thy friend,

DANIEL OLIVER.

The World Against Alcoholism!

How I wish it might be possible to give a bird's-eye view of the great International Convention of the "World's League Against Alcoholism" held at Toronto, Canada, Eleventh month, 24th to 29th.

Attended by over eleven hundred regularly accredited delegates—over four hundred of whom came from the United States—a total of sixty-five countries being represented, one is awed at the immensity, not so much of the convention itself, but of what it portends! The grandeur of the thought that every one of these more than eleven hundred delegates from these sixty-five countries is pledged to wage war against King Alcohol in their respective lands!

As reports came from these delegates telling of success and failure, one could but wonder at their optimistic bravery and energy, for not once had defeat spelled despair, but only victory deferred!

From Australia, Finland, France, India, Ireland, Scotland, Sweden, Newfoundland, countries in South America, and many others, came the same appeal, "stand firm, United States, we are looking to you to make good!"

As we of the United States, listened to this same cry over and over again, all feeling of superiority (because of the 18th Amendment) faded away and we were humbled to the point of realizing our responsibility, not only as citizens of our country but as citizens of the world to make our Prohibition Amendment stand as an ensign to all nations; and we came away pledged to do, as far as in us lay, our part in this tremendous task!

May I speak briefly of one day devoted largely to the problems of the young? At this time students of many colleges and universities, near and far, sat on the large platform, practically filling one side of it, and many of these were called upon to speak briefly. As one after another came out and in good English pledged his life in service to the homeland, whether it be Columbia, Peru, Spain, Japan or India, to the end that prohibition might obtain, one could not but take courage, and feel, indeed, that "they that be with us are more than they that be with them."

At their luncheon conference, where ways and means of enlisting students of colleges and universities in this world movement, were discussed, this same fact was clearly evidenced in the heartiness with which the students responded.

Seated at the same table with me was a young German woman, who had just received her Doctor's degree, and whose thesis when printed will be used as a text book in schools. I was favored to have a number of conversations with her and learned she will remain in this country for sometime, studying prohibition and its beneficent effects, sending her findings to three German newspapers, which have agreed to print the truth as she sends it to them. One day, speaking of the conditions in her homeland she said "We'll never forget the work of Friends there, never."

One,—to me—strikingly strange thing was the apparent universality of the English language, for, of the sixty-five countries represented, only two delegates used their native tongue, one Spanish and the other French, and these not because they did not understand English, but because of the difficulty of speaking it. As evidence of this when the dapper Spanish Dr., was speaking, his aged West Virginia farmer-translator did not always translate to the speaker's entire satisfaction, and he'd shake his head and wait until another word was given which better expressed the thought!

The energetic expression of the French speaker was only matched by his over-time volubility, except at the last session when instead of filling his one-minute period he used the one English phrase he seemed to have mastered, saying "good-bye" as he gracefully bowed himself off, amid applause.

When one heard of two countries, one of which was Bulgaria, where no one is allowed to join church who drinks or uses tobacco, and when another told of the 250,000 members of the Seventh-day Adventist church, which allows neither to its members, I've felt that Quakers must look to their laurels in these regards or we'll be listed away down the line!

In such a brief outline one can say nothing of the addresses separately, save perhaps to mention that of Dr. Saleeby of London, Eng., so masterly as to place it in a class by itself. Not that there were not many exceptionally fine ones for the cream of our speakers from over the world were there! Mrs. "Pussy-foot" Johnson was received with acclaim one afternoon, her eminent husband, being hard at work in Europe at this time. "Ralph Conner," too, was introduced to Convention as "everybody's sky pilot" and spoke briefly but earnestly.

Music, singing, prayer at every session, were all given with devotion that told!

The Banquet, attended by about six hundred; the reception at Willard Hall, W. C. T. U. headquarters; the Royal Winter Fair, to which all delegates were given tickets; the reception by Lieutenant-Governor gave a glimpse of the palatial Governor's House, as well as receiving the hospitality thereof—all these were a part of the mosaic of that closely filled week.

Attendance at Friends' Meeting, First-day morning, where the first sign in the vestibule said "Donations to American Friends' Service Committee," while at the side another less conspicuous notice read "This Meeting is supported wholly by voluntary contributions" made one feel somewhat at home. Even here a Kansan, a Rhode Islander, an Indianian and a member of Dublin Yearly Meeting as speakers gave a cosmopolitan atmosphere.

The Convention as a whole, was too big to describe! It was marked by earnest devotion, humility and steadfastness, yet, withal a spirit of buoyancy and undaunted courage!

ARABELLA CARTER.

I Was In Prison

Christmas again draws near. All hearts beat with quickened pulse at the thought: glowing shop windows, throngs of rushing people, merry greetings on the street, stacks of gifts, Christmas trees, homes decked with holly, visits, parties, games, theatres, high festivals of music and ceremony in the churches: a thousand anticipations of delight.

Again in the churches throughout Christendom will be retold the beautiful story—the most beautiful we mortals possess—of the heavenly splendor on Judean hills, of the angel song to the Judean shepherds, and the marvelous guiding star, and the manger-cradled child. In the light of that child's manhood life, which was the light of men, we shall have that beautiful story interpreted, its meaning unfolded. The words of Isaiah, which the child, grown man, applied to himself, the Gospel passages that bear witness to the fulfillment, will be read. And it will fall like sweet music upon the heart:

The spirit of the Lord God is upon me; because the Lord has anointed me to preach good tidings unto the meek; He hath sent me to bind up the broken-hearted, to proclaim liberty to the captives, and the opening of the prison to them that are bound.

"All hearts," I said. Alas, no! Not all. The heavenly host chanted "On earth peace, good will toward men"; but the earth is filled with strife and distress, the wreckage of war, the bitterness of hate. Millions can think of that song but as Mephistophelian mockery.

But no general picture of the world's distressful state do I wish to suggest here. Quite the contrary. I would draw the curtain upon that. We are wont to escape from the particular, near-at-home call for action by uttering hopeless sighs over frightful situations in far-off lands or the general wreck of civilization.

As Christmas approaches, and the Christmas idea dominates and colors more and more all my thinking, my mind turns more and more insistently towards a certain small number of families in our land who are most unchristianly and unnecessarily denied all participation in the message of Christmas. For these it cannot but be a season of gloom and of distress. I mean the families of our so-called political prisoners—the wives and children, the mothers and fathers, of some sixty men who will soon be spending their sixth Christmas within stone walls and iron bars.

The men themselves are of heroic mould. They have strength within to endure, as they have given proof. They can suffer and not yield. They are witnesses, in times that need nothing so greatly as such witnesses, of the invincible integrity of which humanity is capable. They are unshakably loyal, in times when such loyalty alone can save the world, to their visions and their convictions. He that declared the spirit of the Lord to be upon him "to proclaim liberty to the captives" would exhibit a special sympathy, I doubt not, with these men. He is called the Prince of Peace: they are in prison for opposing war. He was a workingman: such are they. He had strong ideas of justice and honest dealing among men, of a new order of things which He called the Kingdom of God on earth; He denounced the rich despoilers of the toiling poor; He had economic views that would abolish the system of exploitation of class by class. Such ideas and such stories have these men, prompted by similar love for suffering humanity. That is why they are in prison. Exactly for that reason and no other. They are, then, the kind of men Christ required His disciples to be: men who have the vision of a saner order of society and are loyal to that vision even unto death. They are the kind of men history celebrates for independence of spirit, for love of liberty and for heroic resistance to tyranny; the kind that time canonizes and enrolls among the world's prophets and martyrs.

Our duty as a nation, if our country is to be true to its fundamental principles, is clear. But still the Administration at Washington refuses to heed it. Our duty as individual citizens, our patriotic and humane duty, therefore, becomes equally clear. It is to entreat the authorities and petition them without ceasing, to enlist our neighbors in the cause, and to persist as if these were our very brothers in those dungeons of torment, this Christmas time.

That our duty may be rendered convincingly clear, that we may act with the full consent of our consciences and absolute conviction of the rightness of our action, let us reflect upon these facts:—

1. That these men committed no crime, were never accused of overt acts.

2. That some of the most eminent jurists of the country, including two professors of law in Harvard University, and a member of President Taft's Cabinet, assert that these men never should have been convicted and that long since, in any case, they should have been released.

3. That all other countries—Italy, France, England, Belgium, Canada—liberated their politicals within thirteen months after the armistice.

4. That our Government has pardoned out of prison notorious and actual war enemies of the country, who were convicted of plotting harm on a large scale: such desperadoes as Capt. Robert Fay (attempting to blow up ammunition ships); Jacobsen, Freese, Kennedy, and other such conspirators.

5. That the terms of the sixty-two men yet in prison range from five to twenty years.

6. That fifty odd of these prisoners,—namely, the Industrial Workers, who were convicted solely because of their economic theories, refuse to ask for individual pardons, standing upon principle.

7. That the Espionage Act, under which they were convicted—one of the most drastic laws of this character ever enacted—has been repealed for more than a year.

Reflect upon these facts and study what you can do, as you love freedom, as you esteem the good name of your country, and as you value human fortitude and devotion to an ideal. Besides uniting with others in petitioning Attorney General Daugherty and President Harding for the speedy release of these men and their return to their families—this should ever be first with us—study to see if you cannot in the meantime help, by money, gifts, and cheering messages, through the Joint Amnesty Committee, 233 Maryland Building, Washington, D. C., to make the Christmas season a bit less sad for the victims of our war-time hysteria. ROBERT T. KERLIN.

West Chester, Pa.

First-day School Methods

By BLISS FORBUSH

The Use of Questions by Teachers and Superintendents

Sometimes it is hard for a teacher to know just how much the scholars are actually remembering from all she is so patiently teaching them. The best way to find out is for her to write a series of questions covering the work, and have her class take either an oral or a written examination. The answers as given by the students may show that they have not obtained a very clear knowledge of the work. If the latter is true, it is up to the teacher to carefully go over the lessons and see where the fault lies. Taking for granted that the young people give good attention while in the class period the fault must lie deeper. Perhaps the course is not quite fitted to the class; it may be too advanced; or the foundation which should have preceded may not have been carefully laid. Perhaps the presentation is not made in a manner which enables the scholars to pick out valuable points and remember them; the work may be going forward too rapidly; so many things may be introduced at one time that no clear picture is retained in their minds. Whatever the case, the teacher should carefully study the situation and improve on the past effort.

Some Sunday Schools have required written examinations covering the year's work before a class is graduated. Few of our schools have introduced this method as yet, but we are no doubt working toward it. We might introduce the method of written examinations at the close of the year with an announcement of those making especially high marks; but our schools are not large enough to warrant the retention of a scholar in a class for not passing his work, when that class might be composed of boys and girls much younger in age.

There are several interesting ways in which Superintendents may use questions in the closing exercises.

A common way is to have him ask questions of classes in turn. If a member, not counting the teacher, can answer, it counts one for their class; if not, another class has the chance of answering. Perhaps twenty or more questions are asked, depending on the time at the disposal of the Superintendent; then the teachers report how many each class has answered correctly.

Another excellent method is to have two classes of about the same age, or a given number of boys and the same number of girls, see which can answer the most questions. This method would take the form of the old-fashioned spelling bee. The Superintendent has the two sides stand up on opposite sides of the room and addresses questions to first one side, then the other. If a member of one side misses an answer he or she sits down and the same question goes to the opposite side, and so back and forth, until it is answered correctly when a new question is taken. This continues until only one person is left, his side being declared the winner.

Nottingham Quarter of Baltimore Yearly Meeting is to have a Scripture Bee some time this coming spring, at which four or five schools will be represented by their best informed scholars, chosen after long competition. The outcome will be waited for with greatest interest.

In using questions in the closing exercises the Superintendent must take great care that they are all equally fair. He might well begin with a list of commonly known things and gradually go on to harder and harder ones. Catch questions, with obscure meanings, should not be used; nor should questions be asked about things which are not worth remembering.

The following questions are examples of what a Superintendent might fairly ask. These are taken in order from the books of the Old Testament.

Who was Abel's father?
Who gave the animals their names?
Who was commanded to build an ark?
Who was Lot's uncle?
Who was called "Father of the Faithful"?
Who entertained three angels unawares?
Who was the husband of Rebecca?
Who is called the Father of the twelve tribes?
Who was sold by his brothers as a slave?
Who saw a ladder descend from heaven in a dream?
Who led the Hebrews out of Egypt?
What man was buried by God?
Who was the first High Priest of the Israelites?
Who succeeded Moses as leader of the Israelites?
What woman led the Israelites into battle?
What woman became Judge over the Israelites?
Who tested the fitness of his men by the way they drank from the river?
Who was the strongest man mentioned in the Old Testament?
Who was the first of the prophets and last of the Judges?
What prophet annointed the first king of Israel?
What maiden is spoken of as gleaning in the fields?
Who was known as the most patient man in the Old Testament?
Who was the first King of Israel?
Who was the strongest man among the Philistines?
Who slew Goliath?
Who was called the "sweet singer of Israel"?
What shepherd boy was raised to a throne?
Who was David's nearest friend?
Which of David's sons became king after him?
Who was David's best beloved son?
What prophet was fed by ravens in the wilderness?
Who was known as the 'boy king"?
What famous Queen came to Solomon for advice?
Who was the shepherd prophet?
What Bible book is named after a Queen?
What prophet answered the call of God by saying "Here am I, send me"?
What prophet was in Jerusalem when it fell?
Who interpreted King Nebuchadnezzar's dream?
Who was not afraid of lions?
What cup bearer to a king became Governor of Jerusalem?
Name two seas in Palestine.
What is the longest river in Palestine?
What is the outlet of the Dead Sea?
What town did the caravans from Egypt to Palestine first reach?
What was the name of the chief northern sanctuary?

Friendly News Notes

Martha Travilla Speakman, who has participated in Friends' relief work in France and Austria, has been appointed as recreation expert, to the permanent staff of the Children's Bureau of the United States Department of Labor, which has thus inaugurated special service in the field of recreation. She was in charge of the organization of play in the schools of Portò Rico during the "Children's Year" campaign recently concluded by the Children's Bureau.

The Meeting for Sufferings, in its recent sessions in London, submitted a minute cordially liberating A. Neave Brayshaw for religious service among Friends in and near Philadelphia and isolated districts. Ever since his visit to America with J. Wilhelm Rowntree, about twenty-four years ago, he has kept in touch with Friends here and has felt a desire to make a return visit which has now become an urgent call. Many well-known Friends endorsed his concern. He believes his service will be among Friends of a conservative type of mind, not especially among younger Friends, but all sorts. He hopes to visit the schools and colleges and, by interchange of ideas, give and get an understanding of the place of Friends in the world.

We wish to again call to the attention of Friends the fact that Carman Espinosa, a Mexican young woman stenographer, is anxious to come to the United States to work in order to perfect her knowledge of English and so better fit herself to help bring about friendly relations between the two countries. This is a matter in which Friends can help and we trust that anyone who can be of any assistance will get in touch with Mary N. Chase, Secretary for the Promotion of International Amity, Andover, New Hampshire.

Harry T. Silcock and Frederic Rowntree have returned to England after attending the annual meeting of the Board of Governors of the West China Union University, which was held this year at Philadelphia. The building programme of the University, the provision of adequate funds and the admission of women were the three principal matters discussed. Frederic Rowntree is architect of the University and H. T. Silcock was appointed Joint Secretary in place of Henry T. Hodgkin, who has filled this position for some years.

Lewis V. and Selina C. Smedley, of Upper Darby, Pa., celebrated their fiftieth wedding anniversary on Twelfth month 9th. Their marriage took place on Twelfth month 12, 1872. Lewis Smedley is well known to a large circle of Friends through his many years of service as clerk of the Educational Committee of Philadelphia Yearly Meeting.

We note in the News Letter from Pendleton, Indiana, edited by Elwood D. Allen, that they are practicing Christmas songs, led by Louise Swain. Also, that "East Richmond Quakers and West Richmond Quakers joined in with North A. Street Quakers "in collecting large quantities of clothing for the Service Committee, and that they have grown closer together in this common service of love.

A letter from Rebecca B. Nicholson, of Haddonfield, N. J., tells of a very spiritual and delightful visit she had with Frends at Berkeley, California, recently. She was present at their regular Monthly Meeting, and the devotional meeting that preceded it was most helpful. One thought that was brought out was that vocal prayer helped those around you, while the silent prayer helps only ourselves.

These ardent and determined Friends are about to purchase a meeting house, and beside needing all the help that Friends can give them in a financial way for that purpose, they are appealing to First-day Schools that may have books that have outlived their usefulness, to send them to them.

At the request of a member of the First-day School Committee of Philadelphia Yearly Meeting, E. Vesta Haines has sent the following additions to the list of Christmas stories furnished by Bliss Forbush for the use of First-day Schools. All three stories are found in the Children's Story Garden.

An Inventory.
Resourceful Santa Claus.
The Christmas Council of the Winter Folk.

A Thanksgiving service was held in the meeting-house at Penn Hill on Thanksgiving morning and participated in by at least fifty persons. Several vocal expressions, either inspired or read, were given to show gratitude for the blessings of the past and hope for the future. Annie H. Peeples, in well chosen words, painted a picture of the first Thanksgiving and pointed out reasons for our own gratitude. R. J. S. Bullock said the first Thanksgiving service on American soil was that held by Columbus when he landed in 1492. Marguerite Earnhart read a poem by Phebe Cary, "The Woodchopper's Daughter." H. W.

Dr. Alfred Salter, M. P. for West Bermondsey, and C. Roden Buxton, member of Accrington, were the two members of the Society of Friends to be elected to the new Parliament. Another member of the Society, Rt. Hon. John William Wilson, who has represented North Worcestershire for more than a quarter of a century, was defeated. In the late Parliament, he was the only member of the Society of Friends.

In the death of Miss Georgia E. Crocker, Schofield School has suffered another great loss. Her death occurred on November 30th after a short illness of pneumonia. Miss Crocker, who succeeded Louisa Haight as Superintendent, was a woman of fine executive ability, was highly regarded by everyone, and gave great promise of future usefulness.

The school is now under the management of Mary Sanborn, who was secretary to Miss Crocker, and will hold the position until a successor to Miss Crocker is found.

The managers of Schofield School are looking for a successor, and will be glad if Friends having any suggestions will send them to G. Herbert Jenkins, or Albert G. Thatcher.

At the annual meeting of the Board of Managers of Swarthmore College held on December 5th it was announced that the goal of the jubilee anniversary campaign of 1919 had been attained and that the college now has an endowment of three and one-quarter million dollars (3.-250,000). It was stated that practically all of the subsciptions from alumni and friends of the college are now paid in. The General Education Board gave $200,000 and the Carnegie Corporation made a second contribution of $75,000, supplementing its earlier gift of the College Library. Resolutions of warm appreciation of these gifts were passed by the Board and forwarded to the General Education Board and to Mr. John D. Rockefeller personally, and also to the Trustees of the Carnegie Corporation.

The children in Friends' Seminary this year provided Thanksgiving dinners for over forty persons,—not only dinners, but provisions to last the recipient for several days. This is a growing custom in the school. For many years, the kindergarten children have annually brought in gifts of provisions, fruit, etc., which are distributed to families or individuals suggested by the Friends' Employment Society of the Aid Association. Within the last three or four years, several classes,—perhaps remembering the giving of their kindergarten days—have "adopted" families for Thanksgiving or Christmas. This "adopting" means the children bring to the chosen family supplies enough, not only for the one festive dinner, but for days to come, and usually, clothing, toys, games and books. The money for the food is not begged from their parents at the moment. Each class in the school is organized, with a teacher as class adviser, and with small weekly dues. The gifts are made out of the accumulated weekly dues.

This year, three different classes in the Seminary "adopted" families. The First-day School, which is made up entirely of Seminary students, "adopted" three families. And the kindergarten brought in enough supplies to give a dozen old men and women a touch of Thanksgiving cheer. One four-year old girl packed a box with her own hands for "two old ladies," insisting that peppermints be a part of the provision, because "Old ladies like peppermints." Plenty of more substantial food was included, and the two old colored women who received the box had true cause for thankfulness.

A notable occasion in the history of Quakerism in New York was the joint Thanksgiving service held in the Twentieth Street Meeting-house on Thanksgiving morning. The meeting was astonishingly large,—at least, all whom the writer heard speak of its size seemed astonished. Evidently a great number of the New York Friends felt the significance of the occasion, and had come to make it still more significant.

On the facing-seat sat one representative of each of the four Meetings in New York and Brooklyn. Three of them spoke, in terms of love and hope for the present, and encouragement for the future. Elden Mills, of the Lafayette Ave. Brooklyn Meeting, in particular, denounced the lack of love in 1828 which has brought upon Friends a century of disunion and diminution, and called for the Greater Love to-day which shall make itself felt at home and abroad.

Mrs. Donchian, of the Twentieth Street Meeting, sang twice, rising from her place at appropriate times, and singing unaccompanied. It was a touching contribution to what all declared was "a beautiful Meeting."

ANNA L. CURTIS.

NOTTINGHAM QUARTERLY MEETING

Under the favorable circumstances of a beautiful winter day, Friends assembled at Little Britain on Twelfth month 2nd for the annual Nottingham Quarterly Meeting at that place. A large number of persons was present. The speakers in the meeting were R. J. S. Bullock, Dr. O. E. Janney, J. Barnard Walton and Seth L. Kinsey. The unity of thought prevailing in the spoken messages was "What constitutes true greatness." R. J. S. Bullock's text was "And he shall be great in the sight of the Lord." Some people are great in their own sight, but the truly great persons are those who are great in the sight of God. The world will be better to the extent that we have followed the message of Jesus.

Dr. Janney in discussing "Who are the truly great men?" said, "Greatness consists in service to humanity of a permanent character."

Seth L. Kinsey, taking the text, "Know ye not that I must be about my Father's business?" said that our business is to make religion practical and to realize our responsibility to the divine. We are not living for the present but for the future generations. This is one of our great responsibilities.

In his message, Barnard Walton said that as our horizon is broadened by climbing a tree, so it is widened by rising from a lower to a higher plane,—a wider vision is before us. The charm of life is that it is always opening wider visions.

The business session followed in which Woolman School was stressed, and Friends were also urged to live, talk and wage peace. After a bountiful dinner and a social hour, the afternoon session convened to discuss the question of Law Enforcement, or Law Observance." Robert K. Wood presided.

Reports of the World's W. C. T. U. Convention held recently in Philadelphia were given by R. K. Wood, H. Bennett Coates and Helen Wood. The prevailing thought among the foreign delegates was that if the United States can stand firm and make good, the rest of the world will follow.

The discussion brought out the fact that the prohibition law is being enforced better than we think; that the tendency to drink just because it is forbidden is passing away; that we need to go on with the campaign of education to accomplish a peaceful enforcement of the law; and that as a result of the recent elections, the temperance situation in Congress has not been weakened. The Chairman was directed to send to officials in Washington a communication expressing our moral support in their awakening to the realization that more stringent efforts should be made to enforce the law.

HELEN WOOD.

WHITEWATER QUARTERLY MEETING.

Whitewater Quarterly Meeting was held at Fall Creek Meeting House, near Pendleton, Indiana, Twelfth month 2nd. The weather was unusually mild for the time of year which made attendance much more confortable than at some other times. The short devotional period was of that type of silence that is so dear to Friends in which the power of the Spirit operates to the renewing of strength in the individual souls to go forward and manifest to the world the beauties of the Friendly life.

There was but little business outside the regular routine that claimed the attention of the meeting but an interesting and profitable discussion arose in regard to a more strict practice of some of the principles and usages of Friends that are of long standing and have proved to be of importance in the maintainence of the dignity of the meetings for business. A communication was received from Indiana Yearly Meeting requesting that the subordinate meetings engage in a more systematic and thorough effort to strengthen the membership along the lines of permanent peace for which Friends have always stood and for which the world at the present time is in so much need.

A short session of the Quarterly Meeting of Ministers and Elders was held following the regular business session of the Quarterly Meeting.

Fall Creek First-day School is very much alive and the School on the day following Quarterly Meeting is always looked forward to with a great deal of interest by the home people because of the visiting members and others that are always present. Classes were full and very active on this Quarterly Meeting occasion.

Fall Creek Monthly Meeting has been making a special effort the past summer to increase the interest and attendance of meetings for worship by means of a committee appointed for that purpose, as a result of this effort two home members, Chester Anderson and Ray Blakeley contributed exercises to the interest of the First-day meeting, and two visiting Friends, Emma G. Holloway, of North Manchester, Indiana, and Helen Hawkins, of Wilmington, Ohio, Secretary of the Young Friends' Movement of the Five Years' Meeting, took an active part in the services.

The principal discourse of the meeting was given by Wilson S. Doan, in which he portrayed the Christ Spirit operating in the human heart by means of the parable of the Good Samaritan.

The Young Friends' Movement under the leadership of Esther Allen had made arrangements for an afternoon session on First-day. At this meeting Helen Hawkins gave a very instructive talk on the importance of a rigid application of Friends' principles in the every day conduct of life, and William J. Sayres of Muncie, Indiana, gave a very valuable address along the line of the importance of the Young Friends' Movement in giving to the world that advice and assistance for which it is looking in the solution of present day problems. There is the greatest opportunity at the present time there has been since the days of George Fox for Friends to make themselves felt in the world if they will but arise to the occasion and show to the world the way of life as they see it.

FINLEY TOMLINSON, *Clerk.*

THE OPEN FORUM

This column is intended to afford free expression of opinion by readers on questions of interest. The INTELLIGENCER is not responsible for any such opinions. Letters must be brief, and the editor reserves the right to omit parts if necessary to save space.

LIGHT OR SHADOW

To the Editor:

The recent article on this subject makes one pause to consider whether Friends are peacefully sleeping in the shadow of the tree of religious liberty which tree was planted by Fox, or whether we are out in the light, planting and tilling for the benefit of future generations.

It is well to have consideration for custom and for the work of those who are gone; yet Jesus suggested we must not let our minds linger in the past.

It is so difficult for me to decide what *is* right, except I consider what *was* considered right by some one else. I must not do anything to offend my neighbor; yet I cannot be a true Friend if I do not get my own immediate guidance, and mind the Light—and not the Shadow!.

W. W. JACKSON.

COLLECTIVE OWNERSHIP

To the Editor:

I am a little surprised at Jesse H. Holmes' letter of 12 mo. 2nd., wherein he puts the emphasis for our economic troubles entirely on the private ownership and accumulation of *land.* The single tax idea, to prevent the accumulation and holding of large tracts of land by individuals, would have been a great relief, back in the days of hand-tools and small machinery. But now with our big power-machinery, too *expensive* and *too extensive* for the *individual* to *own* and *to use* by *himself*, the *private ownership* of *machinery enslaves* the *average man* more than the private ownership of land ever did.

Of course they are part and parcel of the same problem, and their solution ultimately depends upon the same remedy; but today land counts for little without machinery, and an up-to-date view of life requires railroads to distribute products, great mills to grind the grain, great packing houses to slaughter and prepare food-animals, great mining operations to dig coal, and metal ores, great smelters to convert the ore into metals, etc., etc.

The limitation and cessation of individual or private ownership and goverment of big machinery is much more essential to the solution of the problem, than the doing away with private land-ownership. In fact non-agricultural industry is much farther developed for collective operation, than is agriculture. But Jesse Holmes' idea is right:—*collective ownership* for those big industries and means of making a living, which are *collectively used.*—Prof. Stephen Leacock to the contrary notwithstanding.

Brooklyn, N. Y. JONATHAN C. PIERCE.

A CORRECTION

To the Editor:

Calling me a "New York Friend" seems like "thrusting honors too thickly" upon me, so I wish to correct the statement made in a recent issue of the INTELLIGENCER by saying that I still regard myself as a Pennsylvania Friend, my immediate membership being with Swarthmore Monthly Meeting, Penna. where it has been for nearly 20 years past.

May I also say, with reference to the Municipal Credit Union with which I am connected, that it is not in any way legally identified with this city, as might be implied from the mention made of it,—but is owned entirely by the employees of the city, who alone can be members. It is a private corporation, but under the supervision of the State Banking Department. Every large city in our country should have a Credit Union of this kind.

New York City. ISAAC ROBERTS.

BIRTHS

ABBOTT—On Eleventh month 18th, to Helen Reid and W. Lewis Abbott, of Colorado Springs, Colo., a daughter, who is named Marjory Reid Abbott.

BUNTING—On Eleventh month 27th, to George Miller Bunting, Jr., and Marian Searight Bunting, of Birmingham, Michigan, a daughter, who is named Caroline Keen Bunting.

MARRIAGES

HARVEY-COMLY—On November 21st, at Port Chester, N. Y., Dorothea Birchall Comly, daughter of Walter Seaman and Mary Watson Bosler Comly, and Carroll Sherlock Harvey, of Wellesley Hills, Mass. The bride is a granddaughter of Cynthia G. Bosler, of Ogontz, Pa., and of Samuel and Emma M. Comly, of Port Chester, N. Y

JENKINS-SCRIBA.—At Chicago, Ill., on Twelfth month 8th, 1922, Alice Florence Scriba and Edward Magill Jenkins, eldest son of Thomas A. and Marian M. Jenkins.

DEATHS

ALLEN—Suddenly, on Eleventh month 19th, in Philadelphia, Elizabeth S. Allen.

ALLEN—At Media, Pa., on Twelfth month 3rd, Geo. B. Allen, in his 83d year.

AMBLER—At Langhorne, Pa., Twelfth month 3d, Eliza C., widow of George B. Ambler, aged 86.

CARTER—At his residence in Germantown, Philadelphia, on Twelfth month 1, 1922, John E. Carter, in his 85th year.

HIBBS—In Langhorne, Pa., on December 3, after a long illness, John Aden Hibbs, aged 86 years. Interment in Middletown Friends' Ground.

COMING EVENTS

TWELFTH MONTH

17th—Conference Class at Fifteenth and Race streets, Philadelphia, at close of meeting for worship, 11.40 a. m. Subject—Modern Prophets. Leader—Margaret E. Byrd, Swarthmore, Pa.

17th—Amawalk Friends Meeting will be held at the home of Louisa Loder, north of Amawalk Meeting-house, at 2.30 p. m.

18th—Christmas Entertainment and exercises at West Philadelphia First-day School, 35th and Lancaster avenue. Bring your gifts for the poor and hear the children sing. 7.30 P. M.

20th—Monthly Meeting of Friends of Philadelphia, 15th and Race Sts., 7.30 p. m.

21st—Green Street Monthly Meeting of Friends of Philadelphia, School House Lane, Germantown, 7.30 p. m.

22nd—The Brooklyn First-day School will hold its Christmas Festival this evening. There will be supper for all at 6 o'clock, followed by exercises, and the tree and presents.

22nd—Girard Avenue First-day School, Philadelphia, will hold the First-day School Christmas exercises at the Meeting House, at 7.30 p. m. There will be story-telling by Miss Adair, carol singing by the school, and other musical selections. All invited.

American Friends' Service Committee

WILBUR K. THOMAS, Ex. Sec.
20 S. 12th St. Philadelphia.

CASH CONTRIBUTIONS

WEEK ENDING DECEMBER 4TH.

Five Years Meetings	$1,186.25
Other Meetings:	
Alexandria Monthly Meeting	50.00
Miami Monthly Meeting	30.58
Birmingham Monthly Meeting	25.00
Purchase Meeting, New York	20.00
Chicago Meeting, Bible School	2.88
High Street Friends, West Chester, Penna.	6.00
Flushing First-day School, New York	50.00
Contributions for Germany	21.00
For Austria	413.50
For Poland	87.30
For Russia	3,104.67
Russian Overhead	644.00
For General	300.40
For Syria	13.00
For Chalons	5.00
Refunds	58.20
	$6,017.78

LUKE 2. 14—AMERICA'S ANGELUS

"Glory to God in the highest, and on earth peace, good will toward men."

Stand back of President Harding in Prayer for Universal Peace by meditating daily, at noon, on the fourteenth verse of the second chapter of Luke.

Ask your friends to help make this a Universal Meditation for Universal Peace

Pass it on ***Friends in Christ***

WANTED

MOTHER'S HELPER WANTED in small family located in Germantown (having ample household help) to assist in care of six-year child. Experienced preferred. Address R. 461, Friends' Intelligencer.

WANTED—BY FEBRUARY 1ST, POSITION as Visiting Governess by young Friend with Kindergarten and Primary Training and knowledge of Music and Drawing. Address T. 460, Friends' Intelligencer.

U. S. GOVERNMENT UNDERWEAR—2,500,000 pc. New Government Wool Underwear purchased by us to sell to the public direct at 75c EACH. Actual retail value $2.50 each. All sizes, Shirts 34 to 46—Drawers 30 to 44. Send correct sizes. Pay Postman on delivery or send us money order. If underwear is not satisfactory, we will refund money promptly upon request. Dept. 24, Pilgrim Woolen Co., 1476 Broadway, New York, N. Y.

SALARIED STENOGRAPHER, NIGHTS free, can report occasional daylight meetings. Geo. B. Cock, Bell (Philadelphia) phone directory.

WANTED—ONE OR TWO PERSONS to occupy a large front room in Friend's family, New York City, modern conveniences. Restricted block. Convenient to bus, trolley and subway. Address F. 450, Friends' Intelligencer.

WE BUY ANTIQUE FURNITURE AND antiques of all kinds; old gold, silver, platinum, diamonds and old false teeth Phila. Antique Co., 633 Chestnut, cor. 7th. Phone Lombard 6398. Est. 1866.

WOMAN OF EDUCATION AND ABILITY desires position in refined home as companion to lady or child over 7 years. Music and French, if desired. Highest references. Address G. B., Friends' Intelligencer.

MAY WE COUNT ON THY HELP IN our advertising campaign? As a friend of the INTELLIGENCER will thee not patronize our advertisers, and mention the FRIENDS' INTELLIGENCER when making inquiries or purchases?

TRANSIENT ACCOMMODATIONS

WASHINGTON, D. C.—ROOMS FOR visitors. Near Station, Capitol, Library. Continuous hot water. Electricity. Garage. Mrs. L. L. Kendig, 120 C. Street, Northwest.

Special Meeting

Notice is hereby given that a Special Meeting of the Stockholders of the Buck Hill Falls Company is called to meet at the Philadelphia Young Friends' Association, 15th and Cherry Streets, Philadelphia, Pa., on Third Month, March 7th, 1923, for the purpose of voting for or against a proposed increase to the Capital Stock of the said Company from $200,000 to $400,000.

MORGAN BUNTING, Treasurer.

FUN

One of our country correspondents, telling about a fire in his town, wrote: "The Fire Department was called, but not much damage was done."—*Capper's Weekly.*

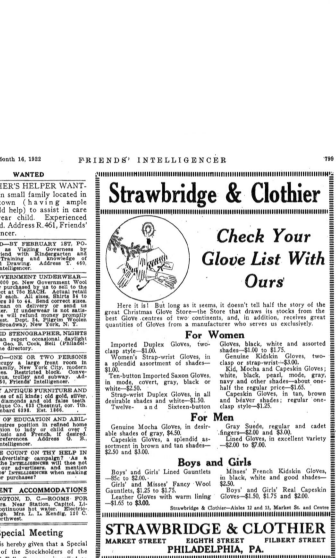

Strawbridge & Clothier

Check Your Glove List With Ours

Here it is! But long as it seems, it doesn't tell half the story of the great Christmas Glove Store—the Store that draws its stocks from the best Glove centres of two continents, and, in addition, receives great quantities of Gloves from a manufacturer who serves us exclusively.

For Women

Imported Duplex Gloves, two-clasp style—$1.00.

Women's Strap-wrist Gloves, in a splendid assortment of shades—$1.00.

Ten-button Imported Saxon Gloves, in mode, covert, gray, black or white—$2.50.

Strap-wrist Duplex Gloves, in all desirable shades and white—$1.50.

Twelve- and Sixteen-button Gloves, black, white and assorted shades—$1.00 to $1.75.

Genuine Kidskin Gloves, two-clasp or strap-wrist—$3.00.

Kid, Mocha and Capeskin Gloves; white, black, pearl, mode, gray, navy and other shades—about one-half the regular price—$1.65.

Capeskin Gloves, in tan, brown and beaver shades; regular one-clasp style—$1.25.

For Men

Genuine Mocha Gloves, in desirable shades of gray, $4.50.

Capeskin Gloves, a splendid assortment in brown and tan shades—$2.50 and $3.00.

Gray Suede, regular and cadet fingers—$2.00 and $3.00.

Lined Gloves, in excellent variety—$2.00 to $7.00.

Boys and Girls

Boys' and Girls' Lined Gauntlets—85c to $2.00.

Girls' and Misses' Fancy Wool Gauntlets, $1.25 to $1.75.

Leather Gloves with warm lining—$1.65 to $3.00.

Misses' French Kidskin Gloves, in black, white and good shades—$2.50.

Boys' and Girls' Real Capeskin Gloves—$1.50, $1.75 and $2.00.

Strawbridge & Clothier—Aisles 12 and 13, Market St. and Centre

STRAWBRIDGE & CLOTHIER

MARKET STREET EIGHTH STREET FILBERT STREET

PHILADELPHIA, PA.

To the Lot Holders and others interested in Fairhill Burial Ground:

GREEN STREET Monthly Meeting has funds available for the encouragement of the practice of cremating the dead to be interred in Fairhill Burial Ground. We wish to bring this fact as prominently as possible to those who may be interested. We are prepared to undertake the expense of cremation in case any lot holder desires us to do so.

Those interested should communicate with William H. Gaskill, Treasurer of the Committee of Interments, Green Street Monthly Meeting, or any of the following members of the Committee.

William H. Gaskill, 3901 Arch St.
Samuel N. Longstreth, 1218 Chestnut St.
Charles F. Jenkins, 232 South Seventh St.
Stuart S. Graves, 3288 Germantown Ave.

ADVERTISING RATE in the FRIENDS' INTELLIGENCER, for Help Wanted, Positions Wanted, Rooms for Rent, and other classified advertisements without display, for each insertion, 2 cents per word, including name, initials and address. Answers may be sent to a box at the INTELLIGENCER office, if so directed.

For display advertising the rate is 10 cents per agate line, or $1.40 per column inch, each insertion. On ten or more insertions in a year from date of order, ten per cent. discount. Thus a four-inch single-column or two-inch double-column advertisement costs $5.60 each insertion, less ten per cent., or $5.04 net each time for ten or more insertions. Matter may be changed whenever desired, without extra charge.

Experience has proved the INTELLIGENCER to be a remarkably good advertising medium. All advertisements must "pass the censor!"

Address 140 N. 15th St., Philadelphia.

HOTELS

Buck Hill Falls

RESOLVED, by the Board of Directors of the Buck Hill Falls Company that a special meeting of the Stockholders of the Company be called to meet at the Philadelphia Young Friends' Association, 15th and Cherry Streets, Philadelphia, on Third Month (March) 7th, 1923, for the purpose of voting for or against a proposed increase of the Capital Stock of the said Company from $200,000 to $400,000, and also for voting for or against proposed amendments to the By-Laws as follows:

Article VII—Section 1. Amended by the insertion of the word "Vice-President" in the first clause, so that it shall read, "The elective officers of this Corporation shall be a President, a Vice-President, a Secretary and a Treasurer."

Article VII—Section 2. Amended to read, "No person shall be elected to any of these offices who is not a Director of this Corporation."

THE WINTER INN

"Wealth in Health"

BUCK HILL FALLS, PA.

HOTEL WARWICK

SOUTH CAROLINA AVENUE

ATLANTIC CITY, N. J.
OPEN ALL THE YEAR

First house from beach and boardwalk. Steam heat, electric lights, elevator. Excellent cuisine, quiet, dignified surroundings and attentive service.

Reasonable rates. Write
SARAH H. FULLOM, Prop.

THE WHEELER

European plan winter months

Boardwalk at Massachusetts Avenue

STRATH HAVEN INN

SWARTHMORE, PA.

Attractive Suburban Hotel. 20 minutes from Broad St. Station. Free auto to morning and evening trains. Garage. Spacious grounds. Special Winter rates. Entertaining features for guests and their friends.

Telephone—Swarthmore 680. F. M. Scheibley.

"New-Idea" Service Table

A sturdy, neat and well finished oak table, unexcelled for general household purposes, carrying entire meal and returning dishes to kitchen. How many steps will this save you?—Shelves 18 x 24 inches covered with cork material, not affected by heat, water, etc. Sent parcel post, with return privilege—not sold in stores. Price $8.50 plus postage or express. Weight 20 pounds. Circular on request.

Rodda Mfg. Co., 10 S. 18th St., Phila., Pa.

Lansdowne and Darby Saving Fund and Trust Company

LANSDOWNE, PA.

ESTABLISHED 1903

GEORGE FOSTER WHITE, *President and Treasurer*
W. LANE VERLENDEN, *Vice-President*
WALTER RHOADS WHITE, *Trust Officer*
MORGAN BUNTING, *Secretary*
LEWIS LAWRENCE SMITH, *Solicitor and 2nd Vice-President*
M. L. KENNEY, *Assistant Treasurer*
W. RAYMOND EVANS, *Real Estate Officer*

Banking and Trust Service of the Better Class.

Interest Checking Accounts 2% Savings Deposits 3.65%

Cream Buttermilk

HEALTHFUL—REFRESHING

Supplee-Wills-Jones Milk Co.

PHILADELPHIA—ATLANTIC CITY

Established 1865

BIOREN & CO.

BANKERS

410 CHESTNUT STREET
PHILADELPHIA

Members of New York and Philadelphia Stock Exchanges

Investment Securities
List on request

JANNEY & CO.

Formerly

MONTGOMERY & CO.

INVESTMENT SECURITIES

133 SOUTH FOURTH STREET
PHILADELPHIA

Joel Berton

SCHOOLS.

Woolman School

Winter Term, First Month 8 to Third Month 23, 1923.

Courses in Bible Study, Church History, Religious Education, Social Problems.

Send for catalog.

ELBERT RUSSELL, Director,
WOOLMAN SCHOOL
Swarthmore, Pa.

GEORGE SCHOOL
Near Newtown, Bucks County, Pa.

Under the care of Philadelphia Yearly Meeting of Friends.

Course of study extended and thorough, preparing students either for business or for college. For catalogue apply to

GEORGE A. WALTON, A. M., Principal
George School, Penna.

FRIENDS' CENTRAL SCHOOL SYSTEM

Write for Year Book and Rates.

L. RALSTON THOMAS
Principal.

15th and Race Sts., Philadelphia.

FRIENDS' ACADEMY
LONG ISLAND, N. Y.

A Boarding and Day School for Boys and Girls, conducted in accordance with the principles of the Society of Friends. For further particulars address

S. ARCHIBALD SMITH, Principal,
Locust Valley, N. Y.

Please help us by patronizing our advertisers. Mention the "Friends' Intelligencer."

The Friends' Intelligencer

ESTABLISHED 1844 — TWELFTH MONTH 23, 1922 — VOLUME 79 NUMBER 51

Contents

EDITORIAL

GENERAL ARTICLES

THE FRIENDS' INTELLIGENCER

Published weekly, 140 N. 15th Street, Philadelphia, Pa., by Friends' Intelligencer Association, Ltd.

SUE C. YERKES, *Managing Editor.*

Subscription rates: United States, Mexico, Cuba and Panama, $2.50 per year. Canada and other foreign countries, $3.00 per year. Checks should be made payable to Friends' Intelligencer Association, Ltd.

Entered as Second Class Matter at Philadelphia Post Office.

Friends' Intelligencer

The religion of Friends is based on faith in the "INWARD LIGHT," or direct revelation of God's spirit and will in every seeking soul.
The INTELLIGENCER is interested in all who bear the name of Friends in every part of the world, and aims to promote love, unity and intercourse among all branches and with all religious societies.

ESTABLISHED 1844 | PHILADELPHIA, TWELFTH MONTH 23, 1922 | VOLUME 79 NUMBER 51

"No offering of my own I have,
Nor works my faith to prove;
I can but give the gifts He gave,
And plead His love for love."

A Real Christian.

We feel that we want to add our tribute of praise to the many which have come from such a variety of sources in regard to the life and work of the late Sir George Cadbury. As we read these tributes our reaction is: "Here was, indeed, a *real* Christian," and, again, "Surely the gates of Heaven opened wide to receive this rich man, even though Jesus said, 'It is easier for a camel to go through the eye of a needle than for a rich man to enter into the kingdom of God.' "

According to *The Friend* (London), George Cadbury was in very truth the father of Woodbrooke. When John Wilhelm Rowntree, twenty years ago, laid before George Cadbury his ideal of an institution which should be devoted to the preparation and equipment of Friends and others who might feel the call to religious or social service, the scheme met an instant and cordial response. Woodbrooke was established and endowed.

At a meeting of the Council held recently, a minute was passed which closed with these words:

"There was a rare simplicity about our friend which restrains any tendency on the part of us, who love him, to indulge in excess of praise. Rather would we join with him in giving glory to God who has given such power unto men. Without George Cadbury, Woodbrooke as we know it could not have been. We can wish for it nothing better than that it may now, and increasingly as the years pass, be penetrated with his spirit of unselfish service and practical devotion."

The Wayfarer, a Record of Quaker Life and Work, recently carried a full account of George Cadbury's interest in the children of Austria, and his sending three tons of chocolate for the reading-rooms in Vienna, which had been started by funds sent by some Swedish friends of Vienna. He later had seventeen of these little Austrians sent to him at Bournville, where he watched them change from pale, sickly bits of humanity to strong happy children, with red cheeks and iron muscles.

One of our exchanges tells of how "the late Sir George Cadbury, Quaker, and cocoa manufacturer, began business with twelve helpers, and left it one of the greatest of British concerns. While teaching Bible classes of his men he became convinced that slum conditions made against a good life. If houses were better, the dwellers were more likely to be righteous. So he built Bournville, a model town for the factory workers. Lady Frances Balfour says of him:

> 'Work he believed in, under circumstances that made it a joy and not a slavery. He loved to tell how hopeless drunkards translated from the slums into Bournville had found in their gardens a resource from the temptation. Bournville had been granted a plebiscite as to whether a public house should be given to its five thousand inhabitants. An overwhelming vote against had disposed of that serpent in their garden of Eden.' "

And then to crown it all, as a fitting tribute to the life and example of such a father, we find comments in many papers on the fact that Mrs. Boeke, daughter of Sir George Cadbury, has transferred her 2800 shares of the stock of her father's chocolate factory to a trust composed of representatives of the employees, the income to be used for their benefit, asking only that the income from the shares be administered for social, international and philanthropic purposes.

Space does not permit our going into further details as to the life and work of this Friend, and anything we can add seems only in the nature of an anti-climax. We can only hope that more of us will so live that when our missionaries sent to convert the "heathen" are met with unbelief, there will be more Christians like George Cadbury to whom they can point as those whose acts square with their professions.

The Face of Jesus Christ

By M. CATHARINE ALBRIGHT.

It has often been discussed whether Paul ever saw Jesus. He does, indeed, speak of having done so, but it is impossible to prove whether when he speaks of His having been "seen of me," he means an outward sight or an inward vision. Anyhow, it is remarkable that he is the only one of the apostles who alludes to "the face of Jesus Christ." To him, whether he had actually seen it or not, his Master's face was the revelation of the glory of God, and the special channel by which God had chosen to make Himself known to men. No doubt we must include in the term "face" the whole personality, but at the same time it must surely have been with Christ as with other men, that the personality was summed up in the face.

The main fact remains the same, that through a personality God has been specially revealed to men. Personality is not the only means He has chosen through the ages, but for us *persons* it is the most important. The Light that lighteth every man is not a vague, abstract thing. It is something that takes shape, and, in fact, can only be known at all in and by personalities. Had it flamed out in unique glory "in the face of Jesus Christ?" It is not, therefore, unseemly to ask what did that face show in the way of deep emotions, such as we know so well in ordinary men and women. We have evidence that it showed pity, grief, anger, love, joy, peace and pain.

It is of the joy and of the pain that, perhaps, we need to take most note at this time.

There is much need that we should bring back into our thought of Jesus the element of joy. Radiance is another good word for that overflowing love and confidence and hope that was His as He compared Himself to a bridegroom going forth to fetch his bride, or to a rejoicing shepherd who brings home his lost sheep from the wilds.

We shall never understand Jesus' power over men till we re-emphasize the joy that must have radiated from Him and made Him such a contrast to the stern prophet of repentance who had preceded Him. What would have been the use of His holding out the promise of joy to others unless they had seen what He meant in His own person? It is, in fact, His own joy, "my joy," which He wants them to have fulfilled in themselves.

But it has been well said that supreme joy is hard to distinguish from supreme pain. The expression "tears of joy" is one we all understand. And we have at least heard and read of the martyr's smile of triumph in the midst of torturing pain.

That joy and pain were deeply united in the experience of Jesus is abundantly clear and is summed up in the words: "Who for the *joy* that was set before him endured the cross and despised the shame." It was an inner impulse of joy that drove him on to choose the cross. He could not turn his back on Love. If He had been willing to *do* less and to *be* less for mankind, He might easily have escaped the drinking of that cup. But He could not turn his back on Himself and deny all that He had been and was yet to be. Therefore, He was called to suffer. The jealousy, prejudice, blindness and hatred of men pursued Him to death.

We cannot get away from the fact that part of the revelation of God to men, "'in the face of Jesus Christ," is the revelation of one whose "visage was marred more than any man," who was actually "bruised" and "pierced" in the cause of Love, and whose being was rent by physical and mental agony. The idea of "'a suffering God" was anathema to the beauty-loving Greek and to the dignified Roman, but no less a stumbling-block to the national pride of the Jew. We in our turn have to ask ourselves what we can make of it. The fact is there, the only question is its interpretation and its meaning, if any, for ourselves. If God could not fully manifest Himself in the personality of Christ without subjecting Himself to suffering and death, was it just an incident, without special significance, a bit of history that might conceivably just as well have not happened, or was it a revelation of some fundamental element in human problems?

In the suffering of the Cross we see the way sinful men deal with supreme Love, and we see the way supreme Love deals with sinful men. We see how sin is met and overcome, but we also see the cost of that overcoming. "He was *wounded* for our transgressions, he was *bruised* for our iniquities;" "He was led as a lamb to the slaughter," and He was Himself "numbered with the transgressors."

It seems that the only way to get rid of sin is to suffer with it and for it, almost to identify oneself with it, so that the casual observer sees the innocent as besmirched with the same mud as the guilty. It seems that the one who would redeem sinners has to be pointed at with scorn as "the friend of sinners." No wonder that Peter, contemplating the mystery of the cross, and feeling the identity of his own sin with that which killed his Lord, breaks out into the words: "He bore *our* sins in his own body on the tree."

We also have to ask ourselves whether we must include ourselves in this word *our,* and whether we need for our redeeming a Love as deep as that which redeemed Peter.

On the face of Jesus Christ there is both joy and pain, but it is the joy that triumphs, for Love is stronger than both Sin and Death.

Peace Through Good Will

Peace on the earth! Our Father, God, inspired
This statement of his will, concise and clear.
Thy will be done. By this we are required
To make God's will our test of conduct here.

Peace is God's will. But war is man's creation.
God gave man vision, power, creative skill.
Man has wrought out each reprobate relation
Which fosters hate, and fans the lust to kill.

Men can achieve relations with each other
Such as exist where love makes sweet the home;
Where brother strives to help and bless his brother.
Then war must cease. Then peace on earth will come.

Fly to your closet. Let God's grace, inherent,
Speak in your heart, and make its mandate clear.
Let heavenly love and heavenly truth, inerrant,
Lead you beyond this hell of lust and fear.

Peace on the earth! For ages men have waited
Hoping that God their dream of peace would fill.
Now, to our task, with powers consecrated,
We must make peace by lives of stark good will.

Rock Creek, Ohio. RAYMAN F. FRITZ.

Discovering God

"God is never sought in vain, even if we do not find him," said St. Bernard. All life leads to God.

"God is a revelation from His side, but from our side He is a discovery." "Blessed are the pure in heart, for they shall see God." No one can make the discovery for us. Sometimes the discovery is no more than the feeling of a great omnipresence which controls life and seems very near, yet not a part of one's self.

Jesus as a teacher endeavored to express God to men as a Father with a loving heart, and that it is possible to commune with that Father. This is an inward relationship.

T. R. Glover explains the relationship by saying, "Jesus has no definition of God, but he assumes God, interprets God; and God is discovered in his acts and relations. He would have us live in God and with God. Whence came his consciousness of God? We do not know. The story of his inward growth is almost unrevealed to us. We are told that 'he learned by the things which he suffered.' He is conscious always of a real nearness to God. Says Jesus, 'God is near and here.' "

Is it too much for us to discover God as near and here? St. Augustine puts it, "Thou hast made us for thyself, and our heart knows no rest until it rests in thee."

Harry Emerson Fosdick, in explaining the meaning of prayer, brings out convincingly that God is seeking each one, and our part is to surrender. He says, "No one is prepared to experience the presence of God until he sees that God is seeking for him. How can man break into an experience of God unless God is seeking to reach down into friendship with man? The deepest necessity of a fruitful life of prayer is the recognition that God's search for men is prior to any man's search for God.

> ' 'Tis rather God who seeks for us
> Than we who seek for Him.' "

"God is forever seeking each man. The promptings of conscience, the lure of fine ideals, the demand of friendship, the suggestion of good books, the calls to service, every noble impulse in hours when

> 'The spirit's true endowments
> Stand out plainly from the false one's'

are all the approach of God to us. Prayer is not groping after Him. Prayer is opening the life up to Him. The prayerless heart is fleeing from God. Finding God is really letting God find us; for our search for Him is simply surrender to His search for us. When the truth of this is really seen prayer becomes real. There is no more talking into empty space, no more fumbling in the dark to lay hold of him. We go into the secret place and there let every fine and ennobling influence which God is sending to us have free play. We let Him speak to us through our best thoughts, our clearest spiritual visions, our finest conscience. We no longer endeavor to escape. We find Him as runaway children, weary of their escapade, find their father. They consent to be found by Him.

The time or times will come, if we earnestly seek through this inward relationship, when an indescribable force holds one bound, it seems, at first, then with liberating power and

> "The beauty, and the wonder, and the power.
> The shapes of things, their colors, lights and shades,
> Changes, surprises—and God."

When this experience comes, all qualifying words for God, as spirit, light, love and life become an illumination of God by which we translate our discovery into every-day living.

"He guides me and the bird
In His good time."

E. R. B.

In the Arts and Crafts Shop At Vienna

There is a long queue standing in the hall of Singer-strasse 16, on Tuesdays and Fridays, and the room in which the Society of Friends receives, judges and distributes the work of this department is crowded to the full.

It is a heterogeneous collection of people waiting there, but the common bond between them is that of a poverty which fights courageously against almost overwhelming difficulties.

A blind orphan girl, Frl. S., is standing at the counter—a thin, anaemic child of about 17. She lives in a home for the blind, paying 20,000 Kr. monthly for her board and lodging and sleeping in a room with 20 other girls. The sitting-room of the home has been unheated until the first of November, and her apology for bringing back her orders so slowly is that her hands are always too stiff and cold to knit quickly. But the woolen jumper and the children's dresses are finished at last, and the money she receives for them will at least assure her board and lodging and a pair of shoes this month.

The wife of General A. stands next, with a bundle of embroidered underwear and ivory carvings; the former her own work; the latter made by her husband, who now works in a factory from 7 in the morning until 6 in the evening, and then adds to the family income by carving hat-pins, umbrella handles, bell-pushes, watch-hangers and belt-buckles.

An old man brings a box of little toys. It is the Baron S., who now devotes his time to carving and painting quaint wooden character figures—they are really delightful both in their humor and delicate workmanship. Poverty has also driven the Baronin B. to turning her artistic talent to batique work, excellent jumpers and very original pyjamas.

Quite at the back of the room, too shy to present herself until the last possible moment, is Fraulein S., very tall, very thin, very nervous, with angular, stooping shoulders and weak ankles, and clad always in a long, narrow, brown ulster. She is utterly dependent on what she can earn by making silk underclothing, but wrapped in her bundle is a small antique, the property of a starving artist friend in Munich, and which she is trying to sell for him.

They work for others, nearly all these people; in their own need they are always willing to try and help others, and any help given to this department of the Society of Friends through buying the work produced there is in no sense charity. It is a practical method of assisting a talented class of people to organize themselves into a self-supporting body, useful both to itself and to other countries who need the result of their labors.

Ethel Cooper.

From Dugout to New Home in Eight Months

It is sometimes said that to contribute to European relief is to "pour money into a sieve." Such is not the case with Friends' work in Poland. The following paragraphs, taken from the report of one of the Quaker workers, show that Friends' Service is not merely relieving the suffering of the refugees, but is enabling them to begin life on a self-supporting basis within a remarkably short time.

"A very poor family returned from Russia in the autumn of 1921. They lived in a dugout, and potatoes were the only food that they had tasted during the winter. I visited the family in April, and decided that the spring crop must reconstruct their lives. The mother came three times to ask for horses to plough the land. When our column reached her village the controller ploughed two morgs of land for her. A week later she received 8 puds of oats to seed the dessiatine.

"The land was of a fine quality and yielded over 100 puds of oats in return. Besides, the family received a number of garden tools from the Mission, and the children worked in the fields for the neighbors, and together earned a substantial sum. Much of the oat crop was sold to buy rye for fall seeding. To seed the fall rye crop the family no longer asked for Mission help in ploughing their field, but were able to pay their neighbour to do the ploughing. Later they were able to buy a sheep and horse from the Mission. Now they are hauling timber to build a new house. It has been a remarkable change in eight months. Not all is the material help received, for they have worked very diligently since the Mission offered to start them, but without this stimulation they might have got no further than during the previous seven months.

"About 100 families have received help from the Mission in this district, and there are a great many who have progressed equally well as the family mentioned above."

"Fly downward to that under world, and on its souls of pain,
Let Love drop smiles like sunshine, and Pity tears like rain!"

What Is Your Program?

The editorial in the FRIENDS' INTELLIGENCER of Eleventh month 11, 1922, urged upon those who wished to better the condition of mankind the necessity of specialization, persistence, and long continued efforts to get results. Two days after the editorial was in print, I came upon an example so apt that I hasten to give it to the readers of this journal.

A dozen years ago Louis N. Robinson was teaching Economics and Sociology in Swarthmore College. His special interest, the subject of his doctor's dissertation, the thing into which he was digging as his specialty, was Penology, the study of the proper treatment of criminals and social offenders.

Some time in the year 1914 we had in the Swarthmore Meeting-house one of those stated public meetings held quarterly by our Quarterly Meeting's Philanthropic Committee. Most persons intimate with the machinery of the Society of Friends know about these meetings and the flitting about here and there which often occurs to find someone who will come and talk. On this particular First-day afternoon we got Dr. Robinson to come and talk about prisons. He convinced us that our system of handling prisoners in Pennsylvania was bad, needlessly bad. He shocked us by showing that prisons were creating criminals rather than curing them. Finally he showed us that the situation, bad as it was, could be remedied if a moderate amount of intelligence and good will were put into it. At that point scores and hundreds of such meetings stop. We get morally convinced and then we go home, but nothing happens. But this meeting was different. Some one with a practical turn of mind asked Dr. Robinson to tell the next step towards reform. He answered that the penal system was wrong and that little could be done until we had a better state law controlling jails, prisons, and the treatment of criminals. Someone then put a motion and the meeting authorized Dr. Robinson to secure information necessary to drafting the right kind of penal statute for the state of Pennsylvania. To this end he was set at liberty to travel in Pennsylvania or even to the distant parts of the United States, and if need be, at the Meeting's expense. It was expected that Dr. Robinson would bring the proposed law back to a future session, when perhaps it might have become a program for united Quaker endeavor and be pushed to success in five years or ten years or twenty-five years. But it went rather faster than we expected.

Within a year one E. M. Abbott, of Philadelphia, a criminal lawyer with long experience in murder trials, was elected to the legislature. He had a feeling that there was something the matter with the conduct of our prisons and the treatment of prisoners, so he got through the 1915 legislature a bill providing for a penal commission of five members. Dr. Robinson seized his opening. He sought membership on the commission, which, however, was impossible because its members were definitely prescribed by professional occupation, but the commission needed a secretary, which position Dr. Robinson, with the assistance of a few of his friends, secured.

Late in the summer, after the legislature adjourned, the commission met for its first business meeting in the country home of one of the members. After a very little talk it was apparent that the members had vague desires but no plans. Then they asked the new secretary what he thought. Now he did not begin to think out loud, committee fashion, and waste a golden opportunity. For months he had been preparing for this moment. He had read everything within reach. He was ready to state the problem. The commissioners were convinced as to what was needed. They gave Dr. Robinson an appropriation, a secretary, and an office. He then set to work to collect facts and to make recommendations. His report was adopted by the penal commission of 1915 as its official report. Embodied in the recommendations were several bills which the commission sought to have passed in the state of Pennsylvania. The bill that was passed, though considerably mangled by amendment, was a distinct step forward.

In his journeys through the state in the preparation of this report, Dr. Robinson visited every state penitentiary, talked with every warden, and found all of them entirely opposed to any improvement. He thought the situation was peculiarly dead and hopeless. It seemed as though the world never would move.

In 1917 another commission was appointed, of which Dr. Robinson was a member. Dr. Kirshway, of New York, prepared the report, which was much like the 1915 report, and no new legislation resulted.

In 1921, the result of Dr. Robinson's fifteen years of study appeared in a volume entitled "American Penology."

I am now old enough to have noticed several times a peculiar fact of social progress. The forces striving for readjustment seem to beat in vain for years against the stony walls of immovable conservatism. Then suddenly the wall gives away. A new idea has won the day. Now this miracle seems to have happened in Pennsylvania. Investigation today shows that most of the wardens of the state penitentiaries are now in favor of the report of 1915. One of them says he has read Robinson's new book twice, and frankly admits that his recommendations for improved methods were taken from that book. Seven years ago there was a State Board of Charities, inactive, uninterested, opposed to any change. Now, through the good work of a few citizens, this board is abolished. In its place is a State Department of Public Welfare which is in favor of the reformation of the prisons of the state. The new governor-elect, Pinchot, says he wishes to reorganize prison finance in the interest of economy and efficiency. In his policy of calling upon experts for advice, he asks Dr. Robinson for recommendations. It is a wonderful opportunity to combine a social reconstruction with a financial reconstruction. It also looks like an example of what democracy ought to be—government by the best. Dr. Robinson is but one of many experts working on plans for the new governor, under expert-adviser-in-chief, Clyde L. King, of the Wharton School, University of Pennsylvania.

The moment looks opportune for real big things. But note the time involved. We are now apparently upon the threshold of results of a plan that started in a Friends' First-day afternoon meeting eight years ago. The world was not made in a day. Humans do not change their minds quickly, but it is surprising how much the group mind can change in a few years.

The particular moral of this interesting experience is this. Reforms or philanthropies are best promoted by definite programs. The making of a program may require some years of time. Its execution may take decades or even generations. To get these things done we need people who stick to work rather than sit in committees and hop about from interest to interest.

J. RUSSELL SMITH.

First-day School Methods

By Bliss Forbush.

Question and Answer Box

Sandy Springs, Md., asks for suggestions as to materials and methods for six and seven year old children.

This is the age when children are strongly individualistic, restless, and impulsive. The body and brain are growing at a very rapid rate and they have not mixed enough yet with other children to readily conform to standards set for the entire group. Their rapid growth and superabundant energy make them very restless, and their lack of mental experience makes them very impulsive.

The fact that children are very credulous at the ages of six and seven places a deep responsibility on the teacher. She must not only be careful that the children understand what she is saying, but she must be very sure that what she is saying is the exact truth. The foundation of ethical and religious ideas begins at this time and if an incorrect idea is learned by the child now it will take years of later teaching to correct it.

It is the time to begin good habit forming. The child imitates the actions of adults around it. If the entire atmosphere of the class is one of kindness, obedience and gentleness it will help the scholars very much to form like habits.

Music

Music should have a large place in the primary classes. At Swarthmore they have worked out the best system I have seen among our First-day Schools. There they have a separate Primary Department which makes it possible to separate these little tots from the older members of the school. Only rarely do they join the rest of the school in opening or closing exercises.

Their method is to have each of the three primary classes meet together for the opening service. A prayer is given by one of the teachers, suitable songs are sung and then each teacher takes her class to its separate room. At the close of the lesson period the three classes unite again for a program of songs, a prayer, and any special exercise that may be scheduled.

If there are two or three primary classes with scholars from four to eight, this is an excellent plan to follow. But even if there is only one primary class it is best to have it meet separately from the rest of the school if possible.

Some of the more familiar songs for the primary classes are "Good Morning to You" and "Weather Song" in "Songs and Stories for Kindergarten," by Mildred and Patty Hill. "Little Lamb so White and Fair," from Song and Games for Little Ones," by Walker and Jenks. "Praise Him, Praise Him," by Hubert P. Main. The following are in our General Conference Hymn Book: "Father, We Thank Thee," "Can a Little Child Like Me?" "God Make my Life a Little Light."

The songs should be few enough for the children to learn, and they should be sung softly. All songs should be pitched high, which will mean that some songs will need to be transposed for them. A good range is between E and F sharp.

Lesson Leaves or Quarterlies

The series published by the General Conference for children four to six is good. This includes "Friendly Helpers," "Our Busy World' and "Beginners' Stories." Each of these provides the teacher with stories and cards or pictures for the children to crayon. With a simple opening and closing exercise, such as they would have if they met with the rest of the school, or by themselves, the stories and the cards to crayon will fill the time.

The Series No. 11 for Primary Classes, age 6 to 9, is fair, but outside material can be brought in to great advantage, and some supplementary material will be needed. Pictures to go with most of the stories in these quarterlies can be picked out from the catalogue of the Perry Picture Co., Malden, Mass., and cheap notebooks bought for the children to paste the pictures into after the teacher has told the story.

As supplementary material or to use in place of No. 11 one of the following would be excellent:

For five year olds: "A Course for Beginners in Religious Education," by Mary E. Rankin. Published by Charles Scribners' Sons, New York City. $1.50. This is a book containing complete instructions for the teacher as to how to handle beginners' classes, suggestions as to hand work, and programs for each Sunday in the year. Each First-day School should have this in its library for reference at least. Pictures of unusual worth may also be purchased to go with the course, and if desired a series of letters which are sent to the parents each week to keep them in close touch with what the children are being taught.

Other proven courses are:

Age 6. "God the Loving Father and His Children." Scribners. Sixty cents for scholars' quarterlies and cards, and eight cents for teacher's material.

"First Book of Religion." The Beacon Press, 25 Beacon St., Boston, Mass., by Mrs. Charles A. Lane, Teacher's material, eighty cents; pupil's, fifty cents. Teacher's book contains explanations and suggestions as well as thirty-six lessons. Pupil's material is crayon work, pasting and directions for handwork, etc.

Age 7. "God's Loyal Children Learning to Live Happily Together." Charles Scribners' Sons. Teacher's manual, eighty cents; scholar's, sixty.

"Living Together," by Frances Dadmun. Beacon Press. Teacher's book contains lessons, stories, memory verses, and suggestions for teaching. The scholar's work is color work, pasting, drawing, and modeling. Teacher's manual, eighty-five cents; scholar's handwork, fifty cents.

Bible Story Books

"Wee Folks' Stories from the Old Testament" and "Wee Folks' Stories from the New Testament." Published by Charles Scribners' Sons, fifty cents each.

"The Children's Bible," by Charles F. Kent and illustrated by Taylor. Scribners, price $3.50.

"Tell Me a True Story," by Mary Stewart.

"Childs' Christ Tales," by Andrea H. Proudfoot.

"Hebrew Heroes," by Rufus M. Jones. $1.50.

Prayer

The primary teacher should place much emphasis on prayer. Her example will give the child a good start on his way toward keeping a free avenue of approach between his Heavenly Father and himself. Have the child learn and repeat in unison such simple prayers as those printed in the "Question and Answer Box" in the Intelligencer of November. It is natural for children to give thanks to God especially if we teach, as Jesus taught His Disciples, that God is our Loving Father.

Equipment

Let the little tots have the sunniest, cleanest spot in the building where there will be no dampness to spread disease and no dim light to strain the eyes while crayoning. Small chairs permitting the children's feet to touch the floor are almost necessary for comfort. A simple kindergarten table may be made for you by a local carpenter. One without folding legs can be made for under six dollars.

Have you problems concerning your First-day School that you would care to receive help with; or are there questions you would like answered? Send them to Bliss Forbush, Park Avenue and Laurens Street, Baltimore, Md. They will be answered through the INTELLIGENCER.—THE EDITOR.

"How We Did It!"

"So that finishes our budget for next year, wife. I think we may congratulate ourselves on fitting things so well. We shan't have much margin, but there's a little."

As my husband spoke he lifted the closely written sheet of paper over which he had been working the whole evening and started to read aloud the items: "House rent, food, clothing, fuel, amusements, books, automobile expenses, Church and charity." Yes, there was that last item. We had set aside for it about as much as we would pay for two automobile tires.

Something in the tone of my husband's voice as he read the last words and laid the paper down made me glance up into his face. A half startled look was there.

"My dear, do you see what we have done? For the amusements and the automobile we have appropriated almost ten times as much as we're planning to give to Church and charities. I never saw the figures that way before."

I glanced over the list. We had made such appropriations, never thinking of the absurd disproportion. For the truth is, we were both interested in our church and in the needs of other people, and we had honestly thought we were giving all we could.

"What are we going to do about it?" he continued. "We've got to fix up that thing right away."

"We can cut out the clothing item," I answered. "You remember it includes a fur coat for me. Cut that out, and we'll give the money to the Church benevolences."

"Really, little woman, can you give up that fur coat?"

I nodded "Um-hm," though I didn't want to. "What sort of Christian do you think I am, to prefer a fur coat for myself to helping other folks when once the thing's been put to me like this?"

He mused a moment. "Well, really, now, I don't need those fancy accessories for the machine. The old car'll go without them. They were chiefly to pamper my pride, anyway. We'll cut those out and transfer the credit to charity."

And so we went through the list, eliminating here and there expensive trifles we had thought we could never do without. After a half hour's work the sum set aside for Church and charity amounted to a little more than one-tenth of our income.

"Now, that's something like it," John murmured. "That'll do for a starter. A tenth is the least we can do. Still it seems kind of a heathenish little bit, but we're learning.

I smiled up into his earnest face. I knew it wasn't going to be an easy thing for us to "carry on" when it came to tithing, but I was as determined as he to see the thing through. And we did it!

Now we have literally "grown up" as supporters of the enterprises of our Church and are no longer mere children giving on impulse. We weigh one claim against another, so as to be sure not to waste our little hoard. Each year we give a definite proportion of our income. A tenth? It was that at first, but now—well, with a tenth we just couldn't do all the things that had to be done. So we've been making it more each year, until now—but there! I shan't tell you all. Try the scheme and find out for yourself how much you'll be giving five years from now.—Reprinted from *The Canadian Friend.*"

Friendly News Notes

Rt. Rev. Paul Jones, formerly Bishop of Utah, who is well known to many Friends through his service as secretary of the Fellowship of Reconciliation, was recently nominated as missionary Bishop of Eastern Oregon. Although he was not elected, his nomination in the House of Bishops caused considerable comment, as he had resigned his jurisdiction of Utah in 1918 because of his views on social questions and on the war. He remains a Bishop without jurisdiction and with a seat and vote in the House of Bishops.

Ralph Howell, an Associate, desires to have articles in the Intelligencer comparing public ownership with private or corporate ownership, as the Municipal owned street car system of Detroit, Michigan. He writes, "The coal and railroad situation as it is in America, paralyzing business all over the nation, is criminal, and shows a lack of statesmanship. If public opinion were strong enough and we had men and women in Congress whose sympathies were with the people's interests, we would soon have a change and a solution."

The Indianapolis News of October 20 reports Vincent Starrett as having said in *The Mentor* magazine that "Black Beauty," the most successful animal classic ever written, was sold by the writer, Anna Sewell, for less than $100, and while in America alone the book has achieved a circulation to date of more than 3,000,000 copies, yet the Quaker author who wrote it on her sick bed, and whose life was one of remarkable bravery and cheerfulness under the most depressing of circumstances, is practically unknown to fame. She was born in Yarmouth, England, March 30, 1820, and died in 1877, one year after the book was published.

Prof. George H. Nutt, of George School, has been the recent guest of Frank C. and Frances Coles Pettit, of Woodstown, N. J., where he addressed a group of about forty Young Friends on Seventh-day evening, 2nd instant. Prof. Nutt attended Woodstown First-day School and Meeting on First-day morning and spoke interestingly at both sessions. He was introduced to the large gathering of First-day school pupils by the young and progressive superintendent of the school, J. Milton Flitcraft, as having been a teacher in George School ever since George School was started. This is Joel Borton's home Meeting and though he and wife have gone to their Philadelphia home for the winter they are very faithful in attendance, having come this snowy First-day morning, 10th instant, to be in their places to serve the Lord with gladness. Surely a fine "example of the believers, in word, in conversation, in charity, in spirit, in faith, in purity." And—let them come! "And let him that heareth say, Come. And let him that is athirst come. And whosoever will, let him COME AND TAKE OF THE WATER OF LIFE FREELY."

E. R. K.

The New York State Commission for the Blind held a sale of articles of every description made by the blind, during the first two weeks of Twelfth Month. The Commission worked in co-operation with the churches of New York City, a denomination supplying saleswomen for each day of the sale, and, of course, advertising the sale among its members. The net profits for the first week were over a thousand dollars, and it is hoped that the second week was as good. "Quaker Day" was Seventh-day, the 9th. A dozen women about equally divided between the two New York Meetings were on duty, and found the day one of pleasure, as well.

Baltimore First-day School has jumped from thirteenth place to second place among the First-day Schools of the General Conference in the last two years. They also claim a very high average attendance. According to the statistical report submitted to the Conference, the ten largest schools are as follows:

Name	Enrollment	Friends
Moorestown, N. J.	231	220
Baltimore, Md.	172	142
Kennett Square, Pa.	162	95
Woodstown, N. J.	158	110
London Grove, Pa.	142	118
Swarthmore, Pa.	137	77
West Chester, Pa.	136	88
Mickleton, N. J.	136	93
Highland Friends, Ind.	133	58
New Garden, Pa.	134	69

One of our readers has sent the following poem, with the suggestion that perhaps others will want to follow his plan this Christmas of sending a copy of this poem to those to whom he usually sends gifts, and then in that person's name he will send two dollars to Russia for feeding orphans. This is a splendid suggestion. We regret that it could not have been made earlier but we can keep the idea in mind for another year.

For Christmas, 1922

Thinking of you in your cozy home,
Sheltered from winter's blasts and sleet.—
With comforts and peace for body and mind,
Good clothing to wear, and abundance to eat,—
My mind veers off to a far-away land,
Where conditions are just the reverse—
To Russia—the country of famine and woe,
Sad victim of war's awful curse.
And instead of bestowing a gift on you,
(Pray don't think me gone quite wild)
In your name I'm sending *its price over sea*
To *help feed a famishing child.*
And tell me, can money better be spent
In honoring our Lord Christ's birth
Than in feeding His hungry little ones
So found on His wonderful Earth?

We cannot resist publishing the following comment. We know that we cannot possibly please everybody with every issue, but we hope that every issue will carry some message of value to some one.

Dear Editor:

I want to thank William I. Hull through your paper for his "Peace Day in Washington." It is so very interesting and proves that *personal interviews are better than "hear-say."* The last number, 12-9-22, has *so much* of good, as "Making Our Meetings More Attractive." "Democracy in Worship" means much to us who have met Catharine Albright, and also the article by T. Edmund Harvey to those who met him at Richmond, with his great concern for our beloved Society. In fact, the paper is "running over."

M. C. W.

The Brotherhood of Mankind

Lewis C. Lawall, of Richmond, Indiana, is circulating cards containing the following thoughts, and we are glad to help him by presenting them to INTELLIGENCER readers.

The BROTHERHOOD OF MANKIND and the FEDERATION OF THE WORLD is fostered by all persons whose loyalty accords with the following:

BASIC PRINCIPLES OF FELLOWSHIP

1. Faith in the power of Truth to supplant error, Good to supplant evil and Love to supplant hate.
2. Conviction that the discernment of and growth in Truth, Goodness and Love are contingent upon cheerful obedience to the Truth already perceived and the exercise of Goodness and Love (God) already experienced.
3. Personal and collective application of these Basic Principles in private, social, business, national and international life at all times and under all circumstances as strength and opportunity afford.

Since the world's great need must be supplied by the foregoing Spirit and Life let us endeavor to daily contribute our part as far as in us lies.

Post this in a conspicuous place to serve as a constant reminder of these duties and privileges. For more copies address Lewis C. Lawall, Richmond, Indiana.

NEAR EAST RUSSIAN RELIEF IN BALTIMORE

On Fifth-day evening a concert is to be given in the Meeting-house for the joint benefit of the Near East and Russian Relief. After the concert Harry G. and Rebecca J. Timbres are to tell of the work in Russia. They returned from the Russian field last week. A number of outside agencies are co-operating.

On the following evening William S. Pike is giving an illustrated lecture on Crater Lake for the benefit of the Advisory Committee.

The group that has been meeting First-day evenings to sing carols together, under the auspices of the Young Friends, has averaged over fifty each time. On the evening of the 24th those of the group in town will go carol singing at the homes of our shut-in and older members.

Last First-day W. Russell Green, of Philadelphia, attended our morning meeting and brought forcefully home to us the necessity of carrying our religion into our daily life.

After this week the clubs and gymnasium classes will suspend operations until after the Christmas holidays.

One hundred and twenty-six pads and notebooks and one hundred and sixty-seven pencils have been sent on for the use of the Russian orphans.

Last month our First-day School had an average attendance of 111, the highest average attendance for a month we have ever had. Sixty-eight scholars did not miss attending during the month; fifty-one have not missed a First-day so far this year.

The New York *World* of November 26th contained an article stating that in the will of Col. Lewis Morris, dated December 7, 1691, an annual legacy of £6 was bequeathed to the Society of Friends in New York. As there was no trace of this legacy having been paid, and as 230 years have elapsed since the will was filed, the article stated the amount due without interest would be $6,468.

As we were interested in following up this matter, we wrote to John Cox, Jr., Chairman of the Joint Committee on Records of the Religious Society of Friends in New York, and received from him the following:

"Colonel Lewis Morris appears to have joined Friends in Barbados, from which place he addressed a letter in 1665 to his friend John Bowne of Flushing stating his determination to remove to Long Island. Another letter to Bowne in 1673 shows him settled at Greenwich, Conn. The earliest meeting records show Lewis and his wife, Mary, signing Quaker documents, as members, in 1680, and in 1865 in a list of contributors to a meeting fund his subscription of five pounds far exceeded that of any of the numerous other signers. He bequeathed an annual fund of six pounds to the meeting. A minute of the 28th of 3rd month (May) 1692, appoints a committee 'to speake with Lewis Moris & Demand ye Legasey given by his uncle unto this meeting an allsoe Receave ye same & give a Lawfull Receipt.' Again, in 1693, a new committee was appointed to desire an account of what he (the nephew) had paid 'of his unckels will.'

The Meeting several times, down to 1700, dealt with the matter. Miles Forster, a member of the first and second committees, received a part of one payment, but refused to pay it over to those of the meeting appointed to receive it. In 1700, when the Yearly Meeting took up the matter, it appears that Miles Forster had also acted as collector of a legacy of Col. West to the poor of Friends in London, and that the meeting advised a suit by Law except Miles submit to a reference. I have no further information at hand on the West legacy, nor anything later on the Morris bequest. The 'answer in writing' of Lewis Morris in 1696 was read, but not accepted. It may have stated that the charge was properly against certain land, and not against him personally, for in 1698 a committee was appointed to speak with James Grayham who lives upon Lewis Morris 'estate 'yt he in Jaged to pay a Legasey of six pounds per an Um Given to ffriends.' The matter is now interesting historically, but not financially.

It will be seen by the above that the account in the New York World-Herald was erroneous in some particulars."

John Cox, *Jr.*

NOTES FROM THE SERVICE FIELD

Reports from the Polish Mission covering September and October, 1922, tell of the successful conclusion of the fall plowing by the Mission plowing columns. Between September 17th and November 4th the columns plowed approximately 2283 acres for 1734 families in 108 different villages.

The Polish Mission is hoping to secure several portable motor-run saws in order to help cut up the lumber that the horses are hauling for housing reconstruction. With mechanical saws under the direction of Mission workers, it will be possible to saw in a day more than a Polish peasant could saw in weeks.

The October reports from Vienna indicate that during September and October 406 cows were imported by the Mission, and sold to various institutions. These institutions are to pay for them in milk, which will in turn be used for relief purposes.

The October report of the Middle-Class Department says: "The outlook for the professional and salaried classes this winter is going to be very difficult. Owing to the reduction of government personnel demanded by the League of Nations, there is sure to be a large number of state officials dismissed and unable to get other work. The first great demand has been for food, and we are giving tickets to the municipal "communal kitchens," where a daily hot meal can be obtained more cheaply than food packets can be made up and cooked."

PILGRIMAGE TO CROSSWICKS

On the afternoon of December ninth the 3.52 train from Camden carried eleven pilgrims to Bordentown, N. J. There we were met by Clara Brick, representative of the Crosswicks Friends, who arranged for our being taken by machines to Crosswicks, where the group was hospitably entertained at various homes for dinner.

Shortly after seven the pilgrims reunited and met with the Friends of Crosswicks in the old historic Meeting House, which was built in 1773. Next year its 150th anniversary will be celebrated. Charles Harrison was to have spoken on "Quakerism Applied to Individual Lives," but, since he was unavoidably prevented from attending, William Kantor read the paper which Charles Harrison had prepared. Betty Walter spoke on "Quakerism Applied to Peace Work," followed by Thomas Philips on "Quakerism Applied to Service Work." After the meeting we all joined in get-together games until after ten o'clock, when we went home with our respective hostesses for the night.

First-day morning meeting convened at 10.30. The half-hour service seemed all too short, for others might have spoken had time permitted. First-day school followed, in which each member of the boys' class gave a recitation of the keenly alive type, appealing to both young and old. Since this was the fiftieth anniversary of the founding of the First-day School, Floyd Platt suitably commemorated the occasion.

After First-day School we were shown over the historic Meeting House, which was used as a British barracks during the Revolution. Evidence of this still remains in the blood stains which can be detected on the floor of the balcony and in the replastered portion of the wall, which was penetrated by a cannon ball during war activities. This seems odd when we consider our adherence to the principle of peace, but the Meeting House was evidently the strongest building for defense in the vicinity. Nowadays only a small portion of the building is used for meetings, but in olden times the entire building was not only used, but filled. This question of the dwindling of Friends' Meetings is a serious one demanding careful study.

After a picnic lunch served in an adjoining building we were escorted over the new fire house and shown the chemical fire engine, both recently donated to the town by the Brick Brothers in memory of their deceased father.

A number of Trenton Friends came down for the afternoon session, which resolved itself into an informal discussion on the subject of "What does it mean to be a Friend in our time?" led by Lindsley Noble. Everybody jonied in making the meeting a success. A short meeting for worship followed, in which the young Friends put into practice suggestions given in the discussion for breaking the quiet of our meetings.

The pilgrims, who included William Kantor, Eunice Roberts, Nancy Shoemaker, Lindsley Noble, Virginia Keeney, Frances Walton, Thomas Philips, Isabelle Bunting, Edith Roberts, Elizabeth Lundy and Charlesanna Coles, express their appreciation for the hospitality so graciously extended them by the Crosswicks Friends, which made the week-end both enjoyable and helpful.

CHARLESANNA B. COLES.

A CHALLENGE TO THE THOUGHTFUL.

In a few more fleeting days the fall term at Woolman School will have become a portion of the past, and its ten weeks will have resolved themselves into a precious memory to those who have constituted the family here.

It has seemed to be an ideal group. Three of the ten are in the middle walks of life, with the experiences which attend those years, and yet with the eagerness of youth for new knowledge; the younger members, all past twenty years of age, with their fresh learning, and earnest, ardent interest, have contributed not only the joyousness of youth, but its vigor and promise.

Our hostess at all times and in all things has been one with us.

It would be very difficult in a brief article to state the advantages of a term at Woolman School. All persons, of whatever age, occupation, or previous educational opportunities—the young man or woman entering upon a life work, the parent, the religious worker, the student and even the scholar may all be benefitted by it.

We find in our instructors, the broadest and most exact scholarship, the deepest spiritual life, a human interest in all phases of life, and a sense of close personal fellowship. From them we have gained new knowledge, and have learned how to restate the old; how better to interpret the Scriptures and to express them in terms of larger truth; we have reveled in the grandeur of Hebrew poetry; we have studied how to tell a story properly; and have delved into social, political and industrial problems. We have visited meetings, institutions and courts. We have had during this term the opportunity of coming into friendly contact with prominent visitors from England, Ireland, India, Russia, and Germany.

Residents of Swarthmore and elsewhere have entertained us in their homes, thus enabling us to establish new friendships.

In short, we all feel that we cannot be too grateful for the privilege which we have had, and we earnestly recommend any one who can possibly do so to make some sacrifice, if necessary, in order to gain a term at Woolman School.

Here is a place to burnish high ideals, to lift the aspirations, to increase knowledge, to rest the body, to strengthen faith and to grow love.

EMMA LIPPINCOTT HIGGINS.

WOOLMAN DEVOTIONAL MEETING.

Judges viii, 4—"And Gideon came to the Jordan and passed over, he and the three hundred men that were with him, faint, yet pursuing."

We have just left the devotional meeting. It is a chilly, dark morning without, but there was an unusual glow of warmth in the meeting. Our director read from the story of Gideon, closing with the verse quoted above: "Faint, yet pursuing," and then he added something like this: There are times in our lives when our purposes seem to run low; there is no special inspiration to make our work easy, but we are enabled to keep on going.

"Tasks in hours of insight willed
May be in hours of gloom fulfilled."

It is sometimes true that a small purpose in life leads us into a life work, which goes clear beyond the original purpose. There was once a boy who loved candy beans. He was poor, and his parents had no money to let him buy such things. So he made up his mind that he would go out and find a job that would bring him enough money so he could have all the candy beans he wanted. He went as a sailor, and, after a while, he became a wealthy planter on the shores of the Caribbean Sea. One day he went back to his little home town, and as he walked along, he saw a jar of candy beans in a confectioner's window. But the desire for candy beans was gone. He cared nothing about them.

There is a story of a man who ran a train through a tunnel. One morning there was water in the tunnel so deep that it put out the fire of the engine. But the steam had previously risen to such a point that the train went through the tunnel in safety.

If our roots go deep into the life of God, we are able to pass through the times of dullness, and are not disturbed. Our kindly interest in people becomes a habit, so that it shows itself even when we do not feel like being kind. We can even be kind to our enemies.

We can not only mount with wings as eagles, in times of inspiration, but in periods of gloom we can run and not be weary; we can even walk and not faint.

The spirit of the two prayers which closed the meeting was as follows:

Our Father, help us to realize that by taking hold of Thy hand we may go through the difficult, dull places with joy, because Thy love and Thy guidance are always with us.

E. W.

Recent Publications

"NIGHTS AND DAYS ON THE GYPSY TRAIL," by Irving Brown. Harper & Brothers, New York. $3. This book by Professor Irving Brown is the work of a man who, like George Borrow of "Romany Rye" fame, has lived like a gypsy, with gypsies, in all parts of the world, who is accepted by them as "Calo"-"black," and who speaks as many dialects of Romanes as perhaps anyone living. The author concentrates upon his most recent adventures with the Gypsies, in Spain, where, he says, they can best be studied and where they play the most important role in the life of the people.

No one but a scholar could have set down these adventures so charmingly, and no one but a young man could have gone out in search of them.

"SOME DISTINGUISHED AMERICANS," by Harvey O'Higgins. Harper & Brothers, New York. $2. Convention prevents the truth from being told about our distinguished Americans in their official biographies. In this book of Imaginary Portraits, the author has escaped the conventional restraints by writing his biographies as fiction so that he might be free to tell the ideal and naked truth about typical Americans and the environments that produced them.

"THE ROAD OF THE STAR," by Walter Russell Bowie, D. D. Fleming H. Revell Co., New York. A book of ad-

safeguarding health and education of their youth, and a new school house equipping the next generation for its presentation of their holy Play.

One of our exchanges quotes from a press report from El Paso, Texas, the following:

"The migration of ten thousand more Mennonites from Canada to Mexico will begin this month, the Mennonite Church having advanced $4,000,000 to families contemplating the trip, J. F. D. Wiebe, their representative, announced here. The sixteen hundred Mennonites who settled in Mexico last year have done well with their crops and have erected adobe barns and granaries and stone houses and are working on churches and schools. Mr. Wiebe said by the time other Mennonites arrive they will have wells dug, roads built, and enough extra houses for temporary shelter. Each new family will bring two to four cows, four to six horses, and some sheep and poultry—all blooded stock."

The reason given for the Mennonites leaving Canada is that the laws of the Dominion do not allow them to be as independent as they want to be.

BIRTHS

MARBLE—On Eleventh month 27th, to Dr. Henry Chase and Alice Ingram Marble, of Boston, Mass., a son, who is named William Ingram Marble.

DEATHS

COMLY—Passed away, on Fifth day, Twelfth month 14th, Anna Comly, daughter of the late Charles and Debby Ann Comly, of Byberry, Phila., in her 78th year.

FELL—At Elkins Park, Pa., on Twelfth month 17th, Robert N. Fell, in his 52d year.

JACOBS—At West Chester, on Twelfth month 15th, Jane B., widow of Francis Jacobs.

MASON—At his home, Lewisville, Pa., Montilion B. Mason passed from this life on Twelfth month 6th, 1922, aged 72 years. He leaves a widow, four married children, seven grandchildren and one sister, the last of the family. A widow of a deceased son survives. Services were held at the house Seventh-day afternoon, the 9th. Interment at Friends' Burial Ground, Brick Meeting House, Calvert, Md.

McCOLLIN—Suddenly, on Twelfth month 12th, at her home, Wallingford, Pa., Lydia Kite, widow of Thomas H. McCollin.

RUDOLPH—At Pasadena, Calif., Twelfth month 10th, Hannah P. Rudolph, formerly of Woodbury, N. J.

NOTICE—The Christmas program at Friends' Neighborhood Guild is as follows: December 18th, at 3.30 p. m., a party of 40 selected needy children; the 20th, 7.30 p. m., a party of Intermediate boys (about 150 boys, aged 12-15); 21st, at 7.30 p. m., party of Junior boys and girls and Kindergarten (about 100 children, aged 3-9); 22d, at 7.30 p. m., exhibition and entertainment of girls' clubs and classes (about 100 girls, 10 to 14 years); 26th, at 2 p. m., party for mothers and babies of clinic. At 8.30 p. m. Christmas dance for Senior boys and girls (about 65).

NOTICE—The First-day School at 15th and Race Sts., Philadelphia, has prepared a special Christmas program for First-day, the 24th, and extends a most cordial invitation to visitors. There will be a tableaux of shepherds and wise men, Christmas carols, violin and piano solos and other music. These exercises will be gvien in the auditorium of the Young Friends' building, at 11.40 a. m.

COMING EVENTS

TWELFTH MONTH

22nd—The Brooklyn First-day School will hold its Christmas Festival this evening. There will be supper for all at 6 o'clock, followed by exercises, and the tree and presents.

22nd—Girard Avenue First-day School, Philadelphia, will hold the First-day School Christmas exercises at the Meeting House, at 7.30 p. m. There will be story-telling by Miss Adair, carol singing by the school, and other musical selections. All invited.

22nd—Annual Christmas Tree Festival of the Brooklyn First-day School, at Schermerhorn St. Meeting House. Supper at 6 o'clock, to be followed immediately by short exercises of the evening, the climax being the arrival of Santa Claus and the distribution of gifts. All Friends are invited.

24th—New York First-day School will hold special Christmas exercises, beginning at 10 A. M. The singing will be led by Edward P. Palmer. Friends are earnestly urged to attend, to join in the singing and encourage pupils and teachers.

American Friends' Service Committee

WILBUR K. THOMAS, Ex. SEC.
20 S. 12th St. Philadelphia.

CASH CONTRIBUTIONS

WEEK ENDING DECEMBER 11TH.

Five Years Meetings		$270.00
Philadelphia Yearly Meeting (Orthodox)		2,633.50
Philadelphia Yearly Meeting (Hicksite)		50.00
Makefield Monthly Meeting	$20.00	
Swarthmore Friends	150.00	
Darby Monthly Meeting	100.00	
Lansdowne Monthly Meeting	30.00	
Social Service Club of Wilmington	25.00	
Wilmington Monthly Meeting	957.00	
Middletown Preparative Meeting	40.00	
Pennsylvania Peace Society	25.00	
		1,347.00
Other Meetings:		
Ram Allah Monthly Meeting, Palestine		50.00
Alexandria Monthly Meeting, Takoma Park, D. C.		90.00
High Street Friends' Meeting, West Chester		5.00
Baltimore Yearly Meeting		74.50
Solebury Monthly Meeting		10.00
London Grove Monthly Meeting		250.00
Cornwall Monthly Meeting		10.00
Contributions for Germany		193.06
For Austria		153.68
For Poland		532.26
For Russia		7,395.68
For Russian Overhead		510.35
For Syria		10.00
For Message Committee		50.00
For General		166.00
German Overhead		2.03
Refunds		117.36
		$13,920.42

Shipments received during week ending December 9th: 84 boxes and packages received, 6 anonymous.

CASH CONTRIBUTIONS RECEIVED FROM MEMBERS OF THE PHILADELPHIA YEARLY MEETING OF FRIENDS HELD AT 15TH & RACE STREETS, PHILADELPHIA DURING THE MONTH OF NOVEMBER.

Makefield Monthly by H. G. Miller	$20.00
Swarthmore Friends by Mary H. Thatcher	100.00
Darby Monthly Mtg. by W. R. White	100.00
Lansdowne Mo. Mtg. by C. C. Lippincott	30.00
Social Service Club of Wilmington by Jesse W. Phillips	25.00
Wilmington Mo. by S. H. Stradley	957.00
Middletown Prep. by F. W. Broomall	40.00
Swarthmore, Mo., by Annie Hillborn (Russian Rel.)	50.00
Penna Peace Society by Arabella Carter "	25.00
	$1347.00

LUKE 2. 14—AMERICA'S ANGELUS

"Glory to God in the highest, and on earth peace, good will toward men."

Stand back of President Harding in Prayer for Universal Peace by meditating daily, at noon, on the fourteenth verse of the second chapter of Luke.

Ask your friends to help make this a Universal Meditation for Universal Peace

Pass it on ***Friends in Christ***

REGULAR MEETINGS

PASADENA, CALIFORNIA — Orange Grove Monthly Meeting of Friends, 520 East Orange Grove Avenue. Meeting for worship, First-day, 11 A. M. Monthly Meeting, the second First-day of each month, at 1.45 P. M. First-day School (except Monthly Meeting days) 9.45 A. M.

FUN

"No, no oysters, lady, only cockles and whelks. We only 'as oysters when there's an R in the month."

"R in the month? An' 'ow do *you* spell Orgust?"—*London Opinion.*

"Edward, you disobeyed your grandmother when she told you just now not to jump down those stairs."

"She didn't tell us not to, daddy. She only came to the door and said, 'I wouldn't jump down those stairs, boys;' and I shouldn't think she would, an old lady like her!"—*The American Boy.*

To the Lot Holders and others interested in Fairhill Burial Ground:

GREEN STREET Monthly Meeting has funds available for the encouragement of the practice of cremating the dead to be interred in Fairhill Burial Ground. We wish to bring this fact as prominently as possible to those who may be interested. We are prepared to undertake the expense of cremation in case any lot holder desires us to do so.

Those interested should communicate with William H. Gaskill, Treasurer of the Committee of Interments, Green Street Monthly Meeting, or any of the following members of the Committee.

William H. Gaskill, 3201 Arch St.
Samuel N. Longstreth, 1218 Chestnut St.
Charles F. Jenkins, 232 South Seventh St.
Stuart S. Graves, 3868 Germantown Ave.

The Friends' Intelligencer

Established 1844 | TWELFTH MONTH 30, 1922 | Volume 79 Number 52

Contents

EDITORIAL

GENERAL ARTICLES

THE FRIENDS' INTELLIGENCER

Published weekly, 140 N. 15th Street, Philadelphia, Pa., by Friends' Intelligencer Association, Ltd.

SUE C. YERKES, *Managing Editor.*

Editorial Board: Elizabeth Powell Bond, Thomas A. Jenkins, J. Russell Smith, George A. Walton.

Board of Managers: Edward Cornell, Alice Hall Paxson, Paul M. Pearson, Annie Hillborn, Elwood Hollingshead, William C. Biddle, Charles F. Jenkins, Edith M. Winder, Frances M. White.

Officers of Intelligencer Associates: Ellwood Burdsall, Chairman; Bertha L. Broomell, Secretary; Herbert P. Worth, Treasurer.

Subscription rates: United States, Mexico, Cuba and Panama, $2.50 per year. Canada and other foreign countries, $3.00 per year. Checks should be made payable to Friends' Intelligencer Association, Ltd.

Entered as Second Class Matter at Philadelphia Post Office.

Friends' Intelligencer

The religion of Friends is based on faith in the "INWARD LIGHT," or direct revelation of God's spirit and will in every seeking soul.

The INTELLIGENCER is interested in all who bear the name of Friends in every part of the world, and aims to promote love, unity and intercourse among all branches and with all religious societies.

ESTABLISHED 1844 | PHILADELPHIA, TWELFTH MONTH 30, 1922 | VOLUME 79 NUMBER 52

We bear the burden of the years
Clean limbed, clear-hearted, open-browed,
Albeit sacramental tears
Have dimmed our eyes, we know the proud
Content of men who sweep unbowed
Before the legionary fears;
In sorrow we have grown to be
The masters of adversity.

* * *

Into one hour we gather all
The years gone down, the years unwrought,
Upon our ears brave measures fall
Across uncharted spaces brought,
Upon our lips the words are caught
Wherewith the dead, the unborn call;
From love to love, from height to height
We press and none may curb our might.

From *"The Fires of God"* by JOHN DRINKWATER.

Life, An Opportunity!

Raining, raining, this is the first impression I receive as I awaken and become conscious of what is going on in the outer world. Gently it patters against my window so that I know the wind is in the West. What is more luxurious and comfortable than to lie in one's warm bed and hear the patter of the gentle rain outside. It brings home to one's consciousness, as nothing else does to mine, the acme of perfect physical bliss—it lulls the senses and soothes the mind until one seems to float in comfort free from all this weary world of hurry and responsibility, of rush and fatigue, of pain and sorrow.

There can be no desperate, despairing pain when one listens to the gentle fall of rain—patter, patter, patter—only a dull ache for all the sorrows of this earth, a sort of vicarious sorrowing such as one gets from reading a sad book.

But oh, this is so different from that real heart sorrow of our own which shakes the body and wrenches the soul and forces us to truly face facts and grasp the fundamentals of life with frankness and despair. Sorrow forces us to do one of two things—to conquer or to shirk—truly faced and bravely met, squarely dealt with, patiently lived, slowly day by day we grow in strength and bearing power. We grasp that Omnipotent Hand and learn in dark and doubt, in tumult and overpowering grief to depend and trust the Everlasting from whom comes strength. Then we know the real meaning of "Our Father."

So as the years pass and I look back on life, I welcome the sorrow and heartaches which I have bravely met, which passing have left me stronger; yet hide my head in shame at those early times which held such promise of discipline and which I slipped through unimproved, unstrengthened and unlearned.

All life is opportunity which broadens as we tread the path for the lessons of today rightly learned prepare us for the lessons of tomorrow. If we study not and read not the Hand of the Maker written large about us when we are young, later life will be to us as to one who seeks to do his college course never having been to high school.

So the hardest way is after all the easiest, for the more difficulties and defeats, sorrows and misfortunes, disappointments and disillusions which come to us and which we meet with the brilliant lamp of an unconquerable spirit brightly shining, help to give us a realizing belief that we are one of the fragments of the Almighty.

Give us that courage which faces danger calmly; when it is in the right, meets opposition with firmness; and which recognizes defeat only to learn a lesson from it. Let the trials and tribulations, frustrated hopes and ambitions, stinging defeat and misfortune, bring us closer to our Heavenly Father, who gives us broader understanding, wider sympathies and strength to press on.

And as the gentle rain falls from Heaven with its soft drip and splash, let gentle calm and quiet fill our souls that we may hear God's voice. He is speaking to us always. His world goes on and on—day after day—year after year—and we with it in harmony or out of harmony. That rests with us, that is for us to decide. He is ready and willing to guide and strengthen, sustain and comfort, refresh and enlighten, if we but do our part and seek his help.

A. J. B.

Resolution

Adopted at the Women's International Conference held at the Hague, December, 1922.

This Conference, composed of 111 International and National Organizations, representing 20,000,000 members, and organized by the Women's International League for Peace and Freedom, declares that the present terrible state of Europe and its reactions on the rest of the world are the result not only of the World War but also in very large measure of the existing Peace Treaties.

These Treaties are contrary to the Armistice Terms (e.g. President Wilson's fourteen points). They are inconsistent with the spirit of the League of Nations as expressed in the Preamble of the Covenant, and do in fact "endanger the peace of the world." (Article 19 of the Covenant). They have proved disastrous alike from the political, economic, military and physical aspects. They have

(a) prevented economic reconstruction on a basis of international co-operation and the satisfaction of international interests by treating this matter as one to be settled by those nations alone which achieved military predominance in the World War,

(b) recognized and created animosities and suspicions which make disarmament by land, sea and air increasingly difficult and the abolition of chemical and bacteriological warfare practically impossible,

(c) retarded the establishment of a League of Nations universal, democratic and fully effective.

THEREFORE

This Conference demands *A NEW PEACE* based on New International Agreements, and its members resolve to work unremittingly by every means in their power to bring about the convening of A WORLD CONGRESS through the instrumentality of The League of Nations, of a single nation, or a group of nations, in order to achieve

A NEW PEACE.

Women's International Conference

Organized by the Women's International League for Peace and Freedom, The Hague, Holland. December 7, 8 and 9, 1922

By Hannah Clothier Hull

The call for a special emergency Conference in December was issued from Freiburg by the Executive Committee of the Women's International League for Peace and Freedom at its meeting in September. The reason for this action was the dire distress of Europe. The women of the twenty-two countries belonging to the League, have felt increasingly burdened by the disastrous consequences of the Peace Treaties, and have helplessly watched the effects upon victor and vanquished nations alike until they were impelled to unite in one strong protest against the world's trying to exist under them any longer.

When the call came to the United States Section of the League, since we as a nation seemed to be so isolated from the conditions which confront Europe and have seemed to the rest of the world so indifferent in trying to discern our duty in the matter, we questioned whether it would be possible for us to help sufficiently in such a conference to make it worth while for us to go. Jane Addams, the InterNational President, had planned to start in January around the world in the other direction, and upon first roll call of our membership scarcely anyone could be found to go to the Hague. The call came so urgently, however, that Jane Addams could not resist it: she changed her plans completely, and upon such an example Lucy Biddle Lewis, National Chairman for the U. S. Section, also decided to go; whereupon others were induced to follow, until a delegation of eleven members was organized and enlarged by those already in Europe, and finally numbered thirty in all. We set sail on November 21st, on S. S. Volendam. The voyage was unusually pleasant in its social opportunities with such congenial company, and after the first few days of adjustment to sea-life, there were daily group meetings for the study and discussion of the objects of the conference.

The Conference was held in Hotel Witteburg on the Grand Canal and opposite a beautiful park adjoining the Hague. It was a disappointment to many not to be able to live at the Hotel which, after arranging to accommodate us, was embarassed by the sudden calling by the League of Nations of a commission of Jurists to meet for some weeks at the

Peace Palace to discuss regulations for making war more humane!

The Conference opened very auspiciously on the morning of December 7th, with 350 delegates present, representing 111 different societies from 22 different countries, and a number of visitors and invited guests, including men as well as women. Among the American organizations represented were the Friends' General Conference, Arch Street branch of Friends, Five Year's Meeting, and the Fellowship of Reconciliation. As is always the case in an international conference, the personnel was one of the most interesting features. It was indeed a study in itself to look around that large room into the faces of the many men and women so varied in type, and yet so united, in the mission which had brought them together, namely, to demand a New Peace for the world. The proceedings were conducted in three languages: English, French and German. When the original address was spoken in any one of the three, it was immediately translated into the other two and so ably and quickly done that it added to the interest rather than detracted from it.

This article will not attempt to quote speeches, but will endeavor to give the gist and spirit of some of the proceedings as the writer interpreted them. Our own Jane Addams presided over all the meetings. In her opening remarks she explained in her direct and simple way the reasons for our coming together. She said that the time has come for some one to speak out. While realizing that nothing is more important in Europe than stability, it is necessary to make a radical change in order to attain it, and to make a fresh start on a new basis before matters will be better. The work of the League of Nations must not be underestimated: it is a child of war-time and has had tied around its neck, things which the Treaties make it very difficult to carry out. One of the five Treaties has already been overthrown by military force and unless the others are willingly revised we shall find that all will sooner or later meet the same fate. In order to have a settlement which is sure to be satisfactory, the victors and vanquished must meet together. Therefore it is our claim that it is in the very interests of stability itself to have a world conference to organize on a broader basis of justice, good will and understanding. We wish to adopt as our slogan a "New Peace" until it echoes and re-echoes around the world.

This conference composed of 111 international and national organizations representing 20,000,000 members and organized by the Women's International League for Peace and Freedom welcomes most warmly the declaration made by the Congress of the International Federation of Trade Unions held in Rome in 1922 that "the Fight against Militarism and War and for World Peace, based upon the fraternization of the peoples, is one of the principal tasks of the Trade Union Movement"; that "it is above all the duty of the International Trade Union Movement to combat the concluding or maintaining of alliances or agreements which might lead to concerted military actions," and to take united and international measures to "counteract all wars which may threaten to break out in the future." The organizations represented at this Conference desire to stand side by side with the workers in this effort, and welcome the initiative taken by the I.F.T.U. in calling an International Congress at the Hague with the object of organizing co-operative international action for the attainment of these ends.

This Conference notes with satisfaction that the I.F.T.U. gives its support to international efforts that are being made to secure control and restriction of the manufacture of munitions and war material of every kind. We, ourselves, go further, standing for total universal disarmament, national and international, and we appeal to the workers of the world to co-operate with us in this demand, and in the campaign we are initiating at this Conference to secure the abolition of the present disastrous Peace Treaties and the calling of a World Congress to achieve A NEW PEACE based on international justice, democracy and goodwill.

PROPOSALS FOR ACTION

1. Great Britain, France, Belgium and Italy propose to take immediate common action in putting pressure upon their respective Governments to bring about a reasonable settlement of the demands made by the Allies upon Germany for reparations. Further to unite in making representations to any International Organization or meeting which has the question of reparations under consideration. Further to appoint for the purpose of joint action a Correspondent in each of these countries for intercommunication.
   Further to prepare and exchange literature and a list of suitable speakers.
   They will invite other members of the Entente countries to co-operate.

2. Great Britain, France, Belgium and the United States propose to take immediate common action in putting pressure upon the respective Governments to withdraw the Armies of Occupation from the Rhineland, and to unite in making representations to an International Organization or meeting which has the question

of the Armies of Occupation under consideration.

3. Resolution for the presentation to the I.F.T.U. Congress at the Hague, December 10th to 15th, 1922.

4. This Conference filled with the greatest apprehension of the military occupation of the Ruhr urges upon the Reparations Conference which is shortly to be held in Brussels that the best way of settling the problem of international indebtedness due to the war would would be to abandon at once both indemnities and inter-Allied war debts and make the restoration of all the devastated areas a matter for international agreement.
It heartily welcomes the suggestion advanced at the Assembly of the League of Nations (1922, Report of the 3rd Commission) that the whole question of reparations should be considered from an international standpoint and urges the Reparations Conference to recommend to the Entente Powers that they should secure the good offices of the League of Nations in bringing together all parties for the settlement of the whole question.

5. (a) that mass demonstrations should be held in co-operation as far as possible with all other friendly organizations and individuals, such as religious bodies, workers by hand and brain, Youth Movements and the International Association of former soldiers;
(b) that this should be accompanied by an intensive press campaign;
(c) that the question of the New Peace should be made a prominent feature of all political and election work;
(d) that deputations should be sent to Members of the Parliament, Governments and Political Parties;
(e) that newspapers might be induced to have a Questionnaire on the question of making completely new international agreements such as was carried out by the French paper *Le Matin*.

6. It is suggested that a Christmas message be issued as from this Conference to all peoples suffering from the results of the Peace Treaties and that Miss Addams be asked to draft it. It would then be distributed to the Press and the National Sections of the Women's International League and Organizations which sent fraternal delegates.

(Report of the Conference will be concluded in next issue.)

Youth

We see him stand with forward face,
Firm limbed and strong,
Ready to start his race,
Full of great courage and adventure fine.
God placed that courage there,
Made him exceeding fair.

But on his path one day,
Grave Wisdom crossed his way,
Sombre and gray,
And, yet, the while,
Showing a faint-traced smile.

Youth looked—then, filled with nameless fears,
Clasped both hands on his ears,
And begged, "Speak not to me,
It chillest all my courage just to see
Thy sober face.
Leave me to run my race,
I cannot bear thee near."
God gave the courage fine—also the fear.

And Wisdom went his way,
Waited another day,
Till, stumbling and forlorn,
Doubting and worn,
The racer groped for light
Out of the lonely night.

Sombre, yet smile the same,
Once more grave Wisdom came,
And hand-in-hand that day
They walked their way.

ELEANOR SCOTT SHARPLES.

Faith With Works

Where there is a will to help relieve the suffering in Europe this winter, there is always a way.

The wife of a well-known biologist and botanist of Harvard University is aiding the Friends' Service work through the sale of "miniature plants." A check for $50 resulting from their sale has already been received.

Another contribution of $50 is accompanied by the following note: "Enclosed is from the Monthly Meeting of Friends in Ram-Allah, Syria, for relief work in Russia. We wish we might pay more. The collections are taken at the morning meeting the first two Sundays in each month." Even the crisis which they are themselves experiencing in the Near East, has not made these Friends forget the great need in Russia.

Many give of their substance at real sacrifice to themselves. One contributor from Ionia, Michigan, who sends $5 from himself and $5 from his wife, writes: "I am a railway worker. I was locked out four months in 1921 and two months in 1922 and have since been out on a strike five months. I have a wife whom we have been raising from the dead almost these last four years. Sounds like a hard luck story—well it is not. When we got your appeal for Russia, we realized how much we have to be thankful for, and we are sending 'our mite' in 'His name.' May the famine sufferers be blessed in receiving as we are in sending."

Agricultural Work in the Famine Zone

Recognizing that the Russian famine was caused by agricultural reverses, and that it can be terminated only by agricultural reconstruction, the American Friends Service Committee is making such reconstruction a part of its work in the famine area.

The original famine of 1921 was caused by crop failures due to drought. The recurrence of famine this year is due to a new drought during the past summer, and also to the lack of livestock in the famine zone. In the area for which the Quakers are responsible, 75% of the horses either starved or were slaughtered to keep alive the famine sufferers last winter. The resulting shortage of draft animals prevented the peasants from plowing sufficiently in the spring, so that the crop would have been inadequate even had there been no drought. Only as they are given means to plow their fields again can the peasants raise normal crops and only then can the famine be completely terminated.

The Friends' Mission, therefore, is importing both horses and tractors into the famine zone. Horses are being bought from the nomads in the Aral Desert and transported to the famine area. They will be sold to individual peasants in return for a portion of the flour which they raise, or its equivalent in some service for the famine community.

Four Fordson tractors have been used by the Mission since last spring. They have plowed some thousand acres which would have otherwise remained fallow, but which will now produce crops next year to help terminate the famine. Twelve additional tractors will be sent at once, while the Quakers are appealing for funds to increase this number to as many as one hundred. The tractors are being shipped to Russia from America.

A plan has been worked out by which the tractors will be sold to agricultural communes and farm schools in return for payments of grain which will be distributed to famine sufferers.

This plan will yield thousands of bushels of grain for distribution among the famine victims, will aid in agricultural reconstruction, and will also encourage the peasants to introduce modern agricultural methods.

Demand for Quaker Literature in Germany

Agnes L. Tierney, who is in Germany in connection with the Message work of the American Friends Service Committee, writes of the demand for Quaker literature in Germany at the present time.

"I must speak of the importance here at this time of having plenty of Quaker literature," she says. "Used as I was to the difficulties of getting any thing serious read at home, I was unprepared for the hunger and thirst here for solid reading. It seems to me that for the spread of Quaker ideals, furnishing literature is really the important work.

"If we could quickly get into all the universities a shelf of our best Quaker literature it would probably be much used. I say "quickly" because of course the interest has been aroused by the feeding, and again because so little new literature comes into Germany now. I pay 350 M each day for my lunch. That is a trifle over four cents. Think how many meals it would cost a German professor to subscribe to the *Atlantic Monthly*. The majority of them can't pay 350 M for a meal—far from it."

In another letter Agnes Tierney throws further light on the great hunger for printed literature of all kinds which is now found in Germany, and on the general conditions being experienced by the middle class. She writes:

"If there is any way in which you could get doctors to send their literature here it would be a wonderful thing. The doctors cannot possibly afford to subscribe to foreign periodicals. Gilbert McMaster tore a leaf out of the *Survey* giving tuberculosis statistics of New York and addressed it to Dr. Rost. He got an affecting letter of thanks from the medical head of all Germany saying how much it meant to them to have a report like that."

You invite people to a meal and find that lack of carfare stands in the way of their accepting. Remember these are educated people used to nice ways of living."

The representatives of the "Message Committee" in Germany are doing all they can to preserve the faith of these hard-pressed people, and to provide them with literature that will satisfy their longing for religious reading along the line of their ideals.

Income Tax Exemptions

All contributions to the American Friends Service Committee are deductible on income tax returns. In case this is questioned, kindly refer to letter from the Treasury Department signed by Mr. Ephraim Lederer under date of 2nd Month 28th, 1921 and confirmed on 12th Month 20th, 1921.

First-day School Methods

By Bliss Forbush.

The Home Department

In every Meeting there are a number of persons who are unable to attend the First-day School sessions, but who would like to do some systematic Bible study. Many of these were once active in the First-day School and Meeting affairs but now, because of age or infirmity, have been forced to relinquish their work and see others step into their places. There are some who because of household duties are unable to attend the First-day School sessions, much as they would like to do so. There are some living on the outskirts of the Meeting district, or in towns and cities at a distance, who would like to be more intimately connected, but cannot because of their place of residence.

To these people the Home Department may come with its organization, and offers a tie that will bind them more closely to the Meeting and will provide for them systematic forms of Bible study.

Organization

The Home Department is organized under the direction of the First-day School Committee, with a Superintendent and such helpers as he or she may need.

The Superintendent keeps a list of those who are enrolled, often going over the membership list to see if others cannot be added; sends out the lesson leaves and reference books; and directs the work of the assistants.

The assistants are known as Home Department Visitors. Their work is to call on such members of the Home Department as are assigned to them once a quarter, if possible, and with them go over the work they are studying. They make recommendations as to reference books and supplementary reading that would be of interest, and they also carry with them general news of the First-day School and Meeting and their recent activities. One assistant, or the Superintendent, looks after all those members of the Department, who live at such a distance that their work must be directed by correspondence.

Members

The Home Department is open to anyone not enrolled in another Sunday School. Sometimes regular members of the school also enroll in the Home Department for Bible study. Their names will therefore appear on two records and must be subtracted from one when the total enrollment of the First-day School is given to the General Conference or the Yearly Meeting First-day School Committee.

The members may be classified as follows:

A. Those members who, because of sickness or infirmity, are unable to attend regular sessions of the school. These should receive the most careful attention. The material should suit their needs and the visitors should call on them as frequently as possible, and besides talking about the Department work should carry to them the remembrance of the Meeting and reports of recent happenings there.

B. Children at a distance whose parents have found the local Sunday Schools inadequate to their needs and so wish to give the children their entire religious training at home. Each child should be supplied with the First-day School Quarterlies which correspond with those the children of their own age have in the regular school, along with any helps they may need. The parents should be supplied with reference books and with other material that will aid them in instructing their children.

C. Those adults who, because of home duties, are unable to come to the regular sessions of the school. These should be supplied with Quarterlies such as classes of their own age are studying. They should be encouraged to attend the school whenever possible, and should be loaned books of interest on the subject they are taking.

D. Those regular members of the school who would like to do systematic Bible reading, or other religious reading, at home under the guidance of the Department.

These may take a Quarterly and study it, or some book recommended to them. Their study should be diligent and good reports given to the visitor.

Materials

For the Superintendent: He should have a book and a card catalogue for the names, addresses, and reports on the Department members. A Department Roll, similar to that used by the Cradle Roll, to be hung in the First-day School assembly room would be attractive, and membership cards for the members if desired. These materials can be secured from *The Pilgrim Press*, 14 Beacon St., Boston, Mass. Either, or both, of these books would be helpful for the Superintendent to own, "The Home Department of Today," by Mrs. Stebbins, 60 cents; and "The Home Division of the Church School," by Agnes N. Wiltberger, 20 cents. These can be purchased from the same house.

For the Members: For the sick and shut-ins—Quarterlies from among those published by the General Conference Committee. "Social Studies in the Teachings of Jesus" and "Social Teachings of the Apostles," by Elbert Russell. "Psalms," by Augustus Murray. "Messages from the Biblical Books." If some of the shut-ins are children they should receive quarterlies and helps suitable to their ages.

For adults who can rarely attend: Same as above.

For those who wish systematic reading on Biblical or other religious lines:

On Biblical Works. Outline Bible Courses, American Institute of Sacred Literature, Hyde Park, Chicago, Ill. "Jesus of Nazareth, How He Thought, Lived, Worked and Achieved," by E. D. Burton. "The Old Testament Books, Their Origin and Religious Values for Today," by G. L. Chamberlain. "The Universal Element in the Psalter," by J. M. P. Smith. These for fifty cents each course.

Charles Foster Kent's two series, "The Historical Bible" and "The Historical Series for Bible Students," the former being better suited to the general student.

The Expositor's Bible—Old Testament Series. 75 cents a volume. Genesis, Samuel, Kings, Isaiah, Psalms, Daniel and the Minor Prophets being especially suitable.

On Quakerism. John W. Graham's "The Faith of a Quaker." Various books by Rufus Jones. "Story of Quakerism," by Elizabeth Emmott.

Devotional: "The Meaning of Prayer" and "Meaning of Faith," Harry E. Fosdick, Association Press.

For Parents: "Religious Education in the Family," Henry F. Cope, University of Chicago Press. "Child Study and Child Training" and "The Boy Problem in the Home," W. B. Forbush, Pilgrim Press.

Disarm the Nursery

Toy pistols, soldiers and guns teach children to tolerate and admire war, and to anticipate killing people in war.

Military clothes for children teach admiration for soldiers' professional clothes. Military uniforms are planned to be decorative so as to impress people. Their miniature imitations impress the young as well as the old. Girls and boys are even taught the stiff, ungraceful gesture of the military salute.

Toy submarines, battleships, airships with bomb-dropping apparatus, and armored automobiles are made and sold.

War is not a pleasant game! War is hideous. There cannot be "civilized warfare." Vast majorities in all countries condemn war. Teaching children that war is a pleasant game is a great mental danger.

The place to begin is in the nursery. Disarm the nursery first. Children's minds are extraordinarily receptive. Impressions are lasting.

Banish all war toys, war clothes, war pictures and war story-books.

No store would put into stock a toy guillotine, or a headsman's ax and block, with puppets to be beheaded. Parents would revolt at the idea of their children playing games with such toys of violence and death. If they would think, they would revolt at the idea of all kinds of war toys and war clothes. Sham battles are both silly and wicked. Uniforms are made to be soaked in gore.

The Woman's International League for Peace and Freedom at its convention in 1921, a congress of mothers from 38 countries, condemned war toys and appealed to all the mothers of all countries to disarm the nursery.

This brief statement is circulated to emphasize the international advice, and to name specifically pistols, guns, soldiers, cannon, submarines, battleships, armored automobiles, armed airships, war pictures and war story-books.
—Palo Alto Branch of Woman's International League for Peace and Freedom, Palo Alto, California.

Friendly News Notes

A teacher in one of the public schools of New York city sends her thanks for the Thanksgiving exercises printed in THE INTELLIGENCER. It was easily presented and was successful in giving pleasure and instruction.

A new edition of Violet Hodgkins' "Quaker Saints" is now available. This is a very interesting book, and those Friends who were disappointed at not being able to get it while it was out of print, can now obtain it.

Friends will regret to learn that on the evening of Thanksgiving Day, while on a visit in Moorestown, N. J., Rufus M. Jones was struck by an automobile and thrown into the street with the result that he has a broken leg and some broken ribs. With characteristic cheerfulness he writes: "I am extremely fortunate to escape without more damage." While recovery will doubtless be slow, there seems to be assurance that eventually all will come back into normal condition.

One of the finest libraries on romance philology in America has been received by Haverford College, a lifetime collection of the late Dr. J. E. Matzke, for many years Professor of Romance Philology at Leland Stanford University. The gift includes 2,000 volumes, which have been presented by Dr. Edith Hedges Matzke, widow of the Professor, and David E. and Robert R. Matzke, recent graduates of Haverford. Professor Matzke was for many years a close friend of Dr. Francis R. Gummere and was greatly interested in the college. Several universities have already made offers to purchase the collection, but it is the present intention to house it in a special compartment in the college library. The majority of the works, both in English and French, deal with the French language, but the literatures of Spain and Italy are also represented. There is a useful collection of dictionaries, unbound fiction and old French theses and treatises on Roman philology. Many volumes are rare or unobtainable. The gift will be known as the "John E. Matzke Memorial Library."

At the recording rooms of the Gennett phonograph building of the Starr Piano Company, Richmond, Timothy Nicholson, on December 7, made two records which will be of interest to all members of the Society of Friends the world over. Both dealt with his own recollections of two great movements with which he had been intimately connected. One was the abolition of corporal punishment in Indiana prisons (a reform which later spread all over the world), and the other had to do with the history of the Richmond Declaration of Faith, and the establishment of the Five Years Meeting. The story of the latter was told very simply and powerfully.

Mr. Adolph Lewisohn, President of the National Committee on Prisons and Prison Labor, writes in a constructive and suggestive way in a letter to the New York *Times* for November 12, concerning the need of concerted action on the problem of employment of prisoners. "It is a hundred years since Elizabeth Fry first set forth the truth that the lot of the prisoner could be made tolerable only by giving him productive work to do, and practically every step of progress in improving the lot of prisoners and lifting the level of prison administration has been brought about by applying Elizabeth Fry's doctrine. . . . The goal at which all efforts for amelioration should aim is that every prison shall be a workshop for restoring prisoners at the end of their terms to civil life in condition to be useful members of the community." Mr. Lewisohn suggests a wider adoption of centralized prison purchases, manufactures and sales within the needs of the State's institutions themselves, in order to free the markets of such goods from political manipulation and to provide adequate wages for the prison workers.

The psychological study of the mysticism of George Fox by the late Dr. Rachel Knight is published this week by the Swarthmore Press under the title, *The Founder of Quakerism*. It was written as a thesis for the degree of Doctor of Philosophy at the University of Iowa, an honour which was conferred on its author in 1919. Dr. Knight had received her previous education in Friends' Schools in Pennsylvania and had taken her M.A. degree at Swarthmore College. She had also studied at Woodbrooke. For five years she taught in private schools and for nine years was Principal of a public school in Philadelphia. In 1917 she held a fellowship at the University of Iowa. At the time of her death in September, 1921, she was Professor of Psychology and Dean of Women at the State College of South Dakota. The work is dedicated to Professor E. D. Starbuck, "my teacher and friend, scientist, philosopher, Quaker, mystic, and master in the art of living." As the author died before she had completed the manuscript for publication, her executors committed to A. Barratt Brown the task of seeing her book through the press, and he contributes a few introductory notes to the volume.

On Sabbath night, November 12th, John Haynes Holmes, pastor of the Community Church, New York City, gave a remarkable address on conditions in Europe at Ford Hall Forum, Boston, Massachusetts.

In a letter to J. Edgar Williams, pastor of Boston Friends Meeting, written after his visit to Boston, Mr. Holmes spoke of the Friends Service work in Europe in the following language:

"I certainly did find evidences in Germany, Austria and Russia of the wonderful work done by your 'American Friends Service Committee.' The Quakers were the one group of people in Europe who held the love of everybody. This work represented the finest vindication of Christianity—pure and undefiled that our age has produced. Indeed it almost seems to me to be about the only living evidence of real Christianity that there is in the world today."

Methuens, the London publishers, announce in their new autumn catalogue of forthcoming books under the heading of "Comfort and Cheer," A DIARY FOR THE THANKFUL HEARTED, edited by our Friend Mary Hodgkin, of Darlington. (6s. net.)

They state that "The central thought in the quotations from writers past and present, which are here collected and presented in an attractive form for each day of the year, is that of thankfulness—a thankfulness unforced and real, and devoid of sham sentimentality or prompted gaiety. The volume is intended to bring refreshment when life seems difficult."

A humorous-minded member of New York Meeting, remarking on the difference between the open and closed backs of the seats in one of the old meeting-houses, remarked that it was probable that the open ones were so made to allow room for the "bustles." Her children told the joke at the Friends' Seminary, and the following is the result:

The New York *Sun* of Tenth month 23rd prints the following item:

"Radical changes in feminine dress inaugurated by the return to long skirts may, some fashion dictators hint, bring the bustle back into vogue. Few of the younger generation remember the days of the bustle, but there will be at least one place where its bulky splendor will not be out of place.

In downtown New York is the city's oldest Quaker meeting-house. Here the benches that held the congregations of the eighties are still in use. The section reserved for men has benches with closed backs. But in the benches in the section reserved for the women there are open backs, built to allow for the bustle."

We would be interested to know what really was the reason for having some open and some closed, since the above explanation was purely in fun and had no foundation in fact so far as the speaker knew.

The following extracts from a letter written by Gudrun Friis Holm, of the Fifteenth Street Meeting, New York, seem of interest as showing one "Friendly outpost." The letter comes from Kandy, Ceylon.

"When I heard about a little settlement of Friends in Makale, only eighteen miles from here, I decided to call on them, and it will interest you to hear about the good work Annie E. Clayton is doing on Mr. Joseph Malcom's estate. The school has forty-two native girls as scholars. All are so happy and attractive. The Friends' Foreign Mission Association supported the school, but on account of the great need in Europe, all contributions stopped, and the school was supposed to be closed.

One of the English teachers left, but the other, Annie E. Clayton, decided to see what she could do. Mr. Malcomson promised her the buildings, and for the little fee the girls pay her she has been able to cover the running expenses. She has four native teachers, young girls educated in the school. Besides these, she is the only educated woman for many miles distance. Mrs. Malcomson died last winter, and as she took active part in many enterprises, she is very much missed.

Mr. Malcomson was called to work in Ceylon when he was young, and was the one to start the Friends' activities here. By native Friends' assistance, there are still three Sinhalese and four Tamil (the principal native tribes) schools that did not close when the English money was withdrawn. Mr. Malcomson and the native Friends support an evangelist, who goes from house to house and keeps open-air meetings."

The Yorkshire 1905 Committee has new editions ready of Edward Grubb's *'Problem of Authority in Religion'* (2d.) and *'Disarmament: The Way to Freedom,'* by Edith J. Watson and F. E. Pollard (2d.), while W. C. Braithwaite's F. Q. E. paper of last year has appeared under the title *'Inspired Leadership,'* upon which subject few were better qualified to speak than he.

One of the great points of value in B. Seebohm Rowntree's essay *'Industrial Unrest: A Way Out'* (Longman's, 1s.) is that he calls it *a* way and not *the* way out. This both shows an absence of dogmatism on his side which makes for sympathetic approach while the course he advocates may be looked upon as possible common ground for peaceful discussion and action for extremists on either side.

Unrest, he says, is as avoidable as medieval plague, and his cures are, sufficient wage for decent comfort (this would mean an increased minimum in most industries); reasonable hours of work; economic security (obtainable by a sum equal to 5 per cent increase on the industry's wages bill to which the State, employer, and worker should contribute); a reasonable share in management; and an interest in prosperity of the industry.

Seebohm Rowntree confesses, with regard to the last time, his conversion to a belief in profit-sharing, but its motive should be not as a spur to industry—a sort of 'donkey's carrot' which should make the worker as much a profit hunter as the owner—but as a mode of creating harmony.

The note which we miss is the call to let all work, whether of owner or worker, be for service. Probably our Friend would take this as implicit, but all readers would not necessarily do so. But I should like to see this essay, the larger book, R. H. Towney's *'Acquisitive Society'* (Bell, 4s. 6d.), and the pamphlet *'Christianity and Trade Unionism,'* by Walter H. Armstrong, with a foreword by Arthur Henderson, M.P. (Epworth Press, 3d.), taken as a basis of common discussion for groups composed of all parties.

HUBERT W. PEET.

In "*The Wayfarer.*"

"CHRISTENDOM FOR A WARLESS WORLD."

A letter from Alfred C. Garrett reports as follows the distribution in England of the "Philadelphia Letter," as they call it there, appealing to Christians for a "Warless World."

"Of the 100,000 printed, 87,000 had been distributed, and they were going so fast that 20,000 more were to be printed. . . . One hundred and twenty-seven preparative meetings are active, and large public meetings are being held. One hundred and twenty-one requests for more came from non-Friends, and 14,000 copies were sent to them. Copies were sent to 189 trade-union and labor papers. All of the 39 English Bishops had been approached, and many other prominent men, and many interesting replies had been received. Only the Roman Catholics repelled the appeal; the Y. M. C. A. also does not co-operate. The other denominations were cordial,—the Wesley Methodists declare they hold that *all* war is wrong. The national body of Sunday Schools promises to distribute the letter to all of their centers."

The Friends' Center in Paris is also taking up the matter although Alfred Garrett says, "there appear to be not over six members of the Society of Friends in France and pacificism is almost an illegal attitude to take. However it was proposed to send the letter to all Protestant pastors and to Protestant religious papers generally, as well as some Roman Catholic papers." Mark Hayler, Secretary of the Quaker center in Paris can use 5,000 copies in France, sending them to Belgium, Switzerland, Poland and some to Constantinople and Syria, as well as distributing them in France as above suggested. Carl Heath wants 6,000 printed that 1,000 may be sent to him for distribution from London.

Alfred Garrett had also heard that the Monthly Meeting in Berlin had taken up the subject and "prepared a shorter letter of their own based on ours, and are preparing to distribute that." We hope to hear more fully from Germany after Alfred Garrett's visit there.

EMMA CADBURY, JR.

CHRISTMAS IN NEW YORK

Pupils of the Brooklyn Friends' School have filled 225 of the large red stockings furnished by Brooklyn associations for children of the poor. Practically every child in the kindergarten and primary departments, and a great many in the grammar and high school divisions have taken the loving trouble to fill these stockings with toys, books, gloves, candy, mufflers, or whatever the fancy of the giver dictates. Each stocking bears the name and age of the recipient, so that it may be appropriately filled, and the Society for Prevention of Cruelty to Children and the Society for Improving the Condition of the Poor gladly see them distributed.

The philanthropy of the New York Seminary is carried on through the Friends' Aid Association, which suggests names of families and children who are in need of help. Three different classes each adopted a family, and gave it provisions, not only for a Christmas dinner, but for several days' living. Another class gave $4.25 to go to a fourth family. And from all over the school came toys, books, dolls, games, clothing, in excellent condition. The classes adopting families usually take those with children of their own age, so that the clothes, etc., brought in by them will go to a definite destination. The classes which did not actually "adopt" children gave their gifts to be distributed at the discretion of the Aid Association.

Over thirty children were thus given Christmas joy by the children of the Seminary. But they had given many more things than could be given to these thirty, even though each received several articles each. The remaining gifts were turned over to the United Girls' Club, the society of working girls which has its headquarters at the Friends' Seminary, and meets there for gymnasium work, or other enjoyment, one evening each week. On the afternoon of the 24th, this Club set up a Christmas tree in the gymnasium, and gave a Christmas party to a hundred children of poverty, a party with ice-cream, candy, and presents. This is becoming an annual event at the Seminary, as it will be the third such Christmas festival held by the Club.

The Brooklyn First-day School held its annual Christmas Tree Festival on the evening of the 22nd. The exercises were simple and short, in order not to keep in suspense too long the small children to whom the coming of Santa Claus was the great event of the year. A few carols were sung, a couple of short Christmas stories told, and a collection was taken up for the Near East Relief, as has been done for several years past. This year the sum taken in amounted to $106. And then Santa Claus arrived, in beard and red and white suit and sleigh-bells all complete, bringing a small gift for each member of the school, and for every child present besides. The most striking part of the program is, always, the presentation of the gifts to the colored superintendent of the building, and his two assistants. All make speeches—good ones, too, and are received with a storm of applause.

OLD STUDENTS AT WOOLMAN SCHOOL

Once more the time has come and gone for all good Woolmanites to gather together to renew old ties of friendship and to form new ones among the newer generations of students at Woolman House. This year the meeting was held on the second of December and all who could be there found many old friends and some new ones among the forty to fifty people who gathered together. We were not all present by four-thirty when the business meeting began but came in by ones and twos as the afternoon wore on. We missed many old faces, but welcome was waiting for us from Dr. Russell, whom we all love, and the new hostess, Edith M. Winder, who performed the functions of her office with all the cordiality of an old hand.

The business meeting was called to order by the President, Edith Winder, and after the very interesting minutes had been read, so vividly carrying the spirit of the last meeting, the election of officers for the next year resulted as follows: President, Isabel Bunting; Vice-president, Richard Taylor; Secretary, Mary Walton; Treasurer, Howard Fussell; Executive Board, William Eves, Louise Hall, Ernest N. Votaw; Scholarship Committee, E. Vesta Haines, Julia D. Eves.

The President read extracts from the letters of a number of our old students who were not able to be present, and we shared their regret that they could not be with us.

The Secretary announced that the correspondents for the last two terms were,—for the class of the winter term, 1922, Mary Magruder, and for the class of the summer term, 1922, Edna Hamacker. Those appointments were approved.

There seemed to be a strong feeling that the old students should be more closely organized to help in the canvass for new students. It did not seem possible to settle the best way to do this in one evening, as so many different circumstances entered in, so it was left with the Chair.

to appoint a committee who should give the matter careful consideration, and see how and what can best be done about it.

After a very good and bountiful supper had been served by the students of the present term, we had a very brief business session to hear the reports of the auditors, and then our President introduced Wilbur K. Thomas to us to speak on the "Place and Need for Woolman School and the Society of Friends in the Future." It would be very difficult to try to put his message on paper. He spoke of the need of a real ministry in our meetings for worship. It is not the intellectual level of the congregation nor the Biblical interpretation of the subject that makes a live ministry, but a real spiritual revival within the heart of each individual. Each one of us is called to some form of public service. A call comes to each of us to serve in the meeting. To this end we must give some definite time to preparation for the ministry, a thing that we are all too apt to neglect. If we store up in our minds lines from fine essays or bits of poetry or phrases that have struck us as fine they will all help in the expression of our thoughts. Only by the cultivation of our hearts and lives can we have more devout spirits.

Following him, Dr. Russell said that only out of the depths of spiritual experience could we benefit the world. The electric current cannot produce lights unless the fixtures are there and properly connected up, for the technical side is also necessary. Woolman School was founded in the hope of meeting that need. The policy of the school has always been to render the next service required which seems to be two things—a certain knowledge of things religious, for the power of the Society of Friends is never higher than the spiritual and intellectual level of the members; and secondly, the training of young people for First-day School, Young Friends' Movement activities in their own communities for social work, and to furnish leadership among non-pastoral Friends.

Now is the time to seize the great opportunity or to make the great refusal. Just now there are two challenges to Woolman School, that of the Home Service Department of the American Friends' Service, and the call for service in the meetings. Of the first, it would seem most advantageous that any one starting out to give the year of service asked for by the Committee should have the background of three months at Woolman School to help them get the proper perspective of the work, and to realize that the fundamental conception of life is from a religious angle. The second of these challenges, the call to service in the meetings, is particularly among the non-pastoral meetings, where the increasing number of meeting secretaries, people who have the leisure to do ministerial work, and the increasing demand for people fitted to do this form of work, give Woolman School an unlimited opportunity. The courses now given at Woolman School are eminently suitable for use in such a position. If to them we can add a course or courses which will give some training along the line of Quaker organization, office technique, publicity, public speaking and the necessary steps in making a community survey, we will be doing much to help the Society of Friends toward a real spiritual efficiency.

Unfortunately, trains, like time and tide, wait for no man, and as a good many of those present were unable to stay over night, we did not have the time we could have wished to discuss these interesting and thought-producing talks. We felt, more than ever sure, that there was a place and a need for Woolman School, and went away rededicated to the task of making our influence count on the side of thorough and prayerful preparation for service in the small world of the meeting as well as in the larger world where there is always need for the loving and understanding heart. J. D. E.

On First-day morning those who had remained over night enjoyed a real treat. Dr. Russell's Bible Class was on the Book of Revelations, this being the only book of the New Testament belonging to the group of books known as the Books of the Apocalypse—which are fictitious writings for a religious purpose. Geo. Adams Smith describes them as "Prophecy that has lost touch with history."

The Book of Revelations is wonderfully mathematical and full of beautiful symbolism. The writer brought a message too subtle to give in words. It is filled with mathematics and music and holds an optimism that appeals to people. It is really a revelation of what Christ means in working for his Kingdom without force and through love. It is the secret of the world's hope and carries much the same message as is found in John, the fourth Apostle, and there is a possibility he may have written it.

The group attended Swarthmore First-day School and meeting and after dinner departed by ones and twos feeling the return visit had been filled with the real Woolman spirit. It is hoped next year a larger group of old students will come for the reunion. S. W. K.

Items From Everywhere

The Vassar Club is the newest Woman's Club in New York. Only those who have graduated from Vassar College are eligible.

Prohibition Commissioner Haynes has estimated that already more than 125 prohibition enforcement agents have been killed by bootleggers and rum-runners since the Volstead Act went into effect.

This is murderous demonstration that the violator of the prohibition laws has no respect for any law—either statutory or moral.

Theodore Bortoli, a former business man of Smyrna, is in Washington to try to arrange with this and other countries for the entrance of refugees who are blood relatives of Armenians and Greeks in this country, and for a mass movement to the Argentine, Brazil, Chile and other South American countries. He has been warned that the interests of those who go to South American countries must be guarded lest they be forced into peonage, but Mr. Bortoli says they would welcome even that to escape their present plight.

Because of the interest in offering a harbor of refuge for the Armenian and Greek refugees of Asia Minor, three bills have been introduced in Congress. They are designed to make some provision for the entry into the United States of Christians seeking to escape the Turks. The first two, one introduced by Senator Walsh (Democrat), of Massachusetts, the other by Congressman Fairchild (Republican), of New York, would relax the operation of the quota law to admit for a limited time all refugees from the Near East.

The third bill, which has considerable support from religious and social organizations, restricts the entrance of refugees to those who are blood relatives of Greeks or

Armenians now in this country, who have become American citizens, or who have declared their intention of becoming American citizens. It was introduced by Senator Keyes (Republican), of New Hampshire. It would allow to come into the United States only the brothers, sisters, fathers and mothers, aunts, uncles, grandparents and grandchildren, but not the cousins, of Armenians and Greeks now in this country who can demonstrate their ability to take care of them, so that they will not become public charges. Most of the support of this bill is due to the belief of many of its advocates that it can be easily passed.

The suggestion has been made to allow a number of orphans now under the care of American relief organizations in the Near East to enter the country under the care of these organizations.

Recent Publications

"THE THOUGHTS OF YOUTH," by Samuel S. Drury. The MacMillan Co., New York. $1.25. This book consists of talks to boys (and their sisters) about how to get the most out of life. The writer, who is rector of St. Paul's School, has had long experience with young people and sympathetically believes in them.

"THE THEORY OF ETHICS," by Arthur K. Rogers. MacMillan Co., New York. $1.50. In this volume, ethics becomes a name for the interest man has in discovering and realizing the ends that make life positively worth living. The later chapters present, from this same point of view, a rather distinctive outlook upon the ethical life in the concrete which is most attractive.

"THE A B C'S OF BUSINESS," by Henry S. McKee. The MacMillan Co., New York. $1. In his discussion of the complex character of our business organization, the misunderstanding of money, wages, and wealth, the elements of banking, the abuse of our railways, and the subject of speculators and markets, the author has picked out the really essential principles, and presented them within the comprehension of the average adult who has had at least a grammar school education.

"HAPPINESS AND GOODWILL," by Rev. Professor J. W. MacMillan, D.D., George H. Doran Company, New York. $1.35. An arresting and original series of essays on human conduct, linked up with the practices and teachings of Jesus. Professor MacMillan is a Canadian, whose ministerial service includes mission work, who is an educator, being now professor of Sociology, Victoria College, Toronto. He is also Chairman of the Minimum Wage Board of Ontario.

THE OPEN FORUM

This column is intended to afford free expression of opinion by readers on questions of interest. The INTELLIGENCER *is not responsible for any such opinions. Letters must be brief, and the editor reserves the right to omit parts if necessary to save space.*

HARRYING THE CLERK OF THE MEETING

To the Editor:

After the business of Monthly Meeting is well under way, there comes a time in the evening when it seems to be considered "open season for clerks" and the gunning is on. She should have said "marriage" instead of "wedding" in such a passage, she had so-and-so's middle initial wrong; and so on. It seems to me questionable taste not to make these corrections to her in private.

But the most unfortunate effect from this portion of the program is upon a certain mis-guided part of the assembly who have come to Monthly Meeting with considerable regrets for work of importance—(so it seems to them)—which they have left behind at home.

While the clerk takes her three minutes of harrying with saint-like patience, these persons are resolving to stay home next month.

CAROLINE H. ROBINSON.

BIRTHS

ZAVITZ—At Coldstream, Ontario, on Eleventh month 11th, 1922, to Helen A. and George M. Zavitz, a daughter, who is named Emily Louise.

MARRIAGES

EDGERTON-MCILVAIN—Mr. and Mrs. Hugh McIlvain announce the marriage of their daughter, Mary Bunting McIlvain, and Charles Willis Edgerton, son of Mr. and Mrs. Charles Edgerton, of Haverford, by Friends' ceremony, at the residence of the bride's parents, Hill Top, Haverford, Third-day, Twelfth month, twelfth, nineteen hundred and twenty-two, at six o'clock.

Miss Edna B. McIlvain, sister of the bride, was maid of honor, Miss Rosabelle Sinclair, of London, England, Miss Isabel A. Swain and Miss Anna M. Reeder, of Philadelphia, bridesmaids; Mr. David R. Edgerton, of Westfield, Mass., brother of the groom, best man, and Mr. Edward L. Webster and Mr. William R. K. Mitchell, of Philadelphia, and Mr. I. Thomas Steere, of Haverford, groomsmen.

WILLSON-BROWN—At Coldstream, Ontario, at the home of the bride's parents, on Eleventh month 4th, 1922, Mabel Phebe, daughter of Samuel P. and Annie L. C. Brown, and W. Raymond Willson, of Welland, Ontario, son of William and Martha Willson.

DEATHS

HARRIS—Suddenly, on Ninth month 22nd, 1922, at her home in Benderville, Pa., Miriam G. Harris, wife of the late Hiram L. Harris, and daughter of Isaac J. and Sarah G. Wright, in her 77th year.

KENT—On Twelfth month 20th, Mary Elizabeth, widow of Major Daniel H. Kent, of Wilmington, Del.

MARSHALL—Suddenly, on Eleventh month 21st, at his residence in Kansas City, Mo., Comly M. Marshall, aged 62 years, eldest son of Dr. Calvin P. and Emily Mather Marshall; and a member of Wilmington, Del., Monthly Meeting.

MOON—At Minneapolis, Minn., on Twelfth month 19th, Everett Moon, in his 62d year, son of James H. Moon. Funeral at Fallsington, Pa.

NUTT—At George School, Pa., on Twelfth month 23rd, Mary L., widow of George H. Nutt, Sr.

ZAVITZ—At Sunnyside Farm, near Coldstream, Ontario, Emily Cornell, wife of Jonah D. Zavitz, on Eleventh month 15th, 1922.

CALEB J. MOORE.

On Third-day, the 14th of Eleventh Month, there passed away at his residence, at Fallston, Maryland, Caleb J. Moore, a life-long member of the Society of Friends. His helpful influence was felt not only in his Monthly Meeting, but throughout his community, and even a far wider circle. He took a deep interest in the affairs of the Society, and it was largely through his interest that the advancement work of Baltimore Yearly Meeting adopted a plan of service which has produced such excellent results.

Our friend had almost reached his 81st year. Remarks and tributes at his funeral, which took place in the Meeting-house at Little Falls, proved the high regard in which he was held by his friends and neighbors. The interment was in the grounds at Easton, Maryland. O. E. J.

COMING EVENTS

TWELFTH MONTH

31st—Conference Class at Fifteenth and Race Streets, Philadelphia, at close of meeting for worship, at 11.40 a. m. Subject—Next Door Prophets. Leader—Anne Biddle Stirling.

FIRST MONTH

6th—At George School, Pa., recital by the Philadelphia Male Quartette.

7th—Philadelphia Quarterly Meeting's Visiting Committee will visit Frankford meeting at 11 a. m. First-day School at 9.30 a. m.

7th—The West Philadelphia Bible Class will take up the study of the Discipline with a view of suggesting changes as requested. All members of Society, whether members of the meeting or class, are invited, that there may be a full expression and report.

7th—At New York Preparative Meeting, after the meeting for worship, a representative of the Anti-Saloon League will speak, telling the latest aspects of the great problem.

8th—New York Monthly Meeting will be held at 7.30, at Fifteenth Street Meeting-house, New York. Supper will be at 6 o'clock, and all are welcome. Meeting for Ministry and Counsel at 5.

14th—Amawalk Friends'. Executive Meeting will be held at the home of Burling Hallock, 1½ miles north of Yorktown Heights, at 2.30 p. m.

NOTICE—The Fortieth Annual Meeting of the Indian Rights Association will be held in the Friends' Meeting-house, Twelfth Street, near Chestnut, Philadelphia, on January 11th (Thursday), at 8.15 p. m. Addresses will be made by Mr. Herbert Welsh, President of the Association, who will also preside, Hon. Clyde Kelly, M. C., from Pennsylvania, and Rev. John W. Chapman, D. D., of Anvik, Alaska.

American Friends' Service Committee

WILBUR K. THOMAS, EX. SEC.

20 S. 12th St. Philadelphia.

CASH CONTRIBUTIONS

WEEK ENDING DECEMBER 18TH.

Five Years Meetings	$350.67
Other Meetings:	
Sadsbury Monthly Meeting	15.00
Muncy Monthly Meeting	5.00
Swarthmore Friends	15.00
Race Street Meeting, Philadelphia	5.00
Camden Friends' School	10.00
New York Meeting	25.00
Cornwall Monthly Meeting	5.00
First Friends' Church, Cleveland, Ohio	5.00
Contributions for Germany	30.75
For Austria	531.36
For Poland	748.55
For Russia	7,192.81
Russian Overhead	205.00
For Armenia	17.00
For General	424.40
Miscellaneous Sources for General	580.00
Central Pennsylvania	801.00
Refunds	13.50
	$10,980.04

Shipments received week ending December 16th: 127 boxes and packages received.

LUKE 2. 14—AMERICA'S ANGELUS

"Glory to God in the highest, and on earth peace, good will toward men."

Stand back of President Harding in Prayer for Universal Peace by meditating daily, at neon, on the fourteenth verse of the second chapter of Luke.

Ask your friends to help make this a Universal Meditation for Universal Peace

Pass it on ***Friends in Christ***

Special Meeting

Notice is hereby given that a Special Meeting of the Stockholders of the Buck Hill Falls Company is called to meet at the Philadelphia Young Friends' Association, 15th and Cherry Streets, Philadelphia, Pa., on Third Month, March 7th, 1923, for the purpose of voting for or against a proposed increase to the Capital Stock of the said Company from $200,000 to $400,000.

MORGAN BUNTING, Treasurer.

Griscom Hall

The regular annual meeting of Stockholders of the Griscom Hall Association will be held at 2.00 p. m., Seventh-day, January 6, 1923, in room No. 4 of the Meeting House, 15th and Race Streets, Philadelphia, Pa.

HARRY S. BONNER, President.

To the Lot Holders and others interested in Fairhill Burial Ground:

GREEN STREET Monthly Meeting has funds available for the encouragement of the practice of cremating the dead to be interred in Fairhill Burial Ground. We wish to bring this fact as prominently as possible to those who may be interested. We are prepared to undertake the expense of cremation in case any lot holder desires us to do so.

Those interested should communicate with William H. Gaskill, Treasurer of the Committee of Interments, Green Street Monthly Meeting, or any of the following members of the Committee.

William H. Gaskill, 3201 Arch St.
Samuel N. Longstreth, 1218 Chestnut St.
Charles F. Jenkins, 232 South Seventh St.
Stuart S. Graves, [illegible] Germantown Ave.

HOTELS

Buck Hill Falls

The Christmas tree in the Exchange, the wreaths and evergreen boughs, the coasting on the hills, the Christmas Carols, the one hundred and fifty "youngsters" gathered around the Christmas turkey—all combined to make the 1922 Christmas the best ever.

We are sorry indeed that we couldn't take all in who wished to be with us. There will be plenty of room over the coming week-ends. Bring your parties then.

THE WINTER INN

"Wealth in Health"

BUCK HILL FALLS, PA.

HOTEL WARWICK

SOUTH CAROLINA AVENUE

ATLANTIC CITY, N. J.
OPEN ALL THE YEAR

First house from beach and boardwalk. Steam heat, electric lights, elevator. Excellent cuisine, quiet, dignified surroundings and attentive service.

Reasonable rates. Write
SARAH H. FULLOM, Prop.

THE WHEELER

European plan winter months
Boardwalk at Massachusetts Avenue

STRATH HAVEN INN

SWARTHMORE, PA.

Attractive Suburban Hotel. 20 minutes from Broad St. Station. Free auto to morning and evening trains. Garage. Spacious grounds. Special Winter rates. Entertaining features for guests and their friends.

Telephone—Swarthmore 680. F. M. Scheibley.

"New-Idea" Service Table

A sturdy, neat and well finished oak table, unexcelled for general household purposes, carrying entire meal and returning dishes to kitchen. How many steps will this save you?—Shelves 18 x 24 inches covered with cork material not affected by heat, water, etc. Sent parcel post, with return privilege—not sold in stores. Price $8.50 plus postage or express. Weight 20 pounds. Circular on request.

Price $8.50
Parcel Post

Rodda Mfg. Co., 10 S. 18th St., Phila., Pa.

Lansdowne and Darby Saving Fund and Trust Company

LANSDOWNE, PA.

ESTABLISHED 1903

GEORGE FOSTER WHITE, *President and Treasurer*
W. LANE VERLENDEN, *Vice-President*
WALTER RHOADS WHITE, *Trust Officer*
MORGAN BUNTING, *Secretary*
LEWIS LAWRENCE SMITH, *Solicitor and 2nd Vice-President*
M. L. KENNEY, *Assistant Treasurer*
W. RAYMOND EVANS, *Real Estate Officer*

Banking and Trust Service of the Better Class.

Interest Checking Accounts 2% Savings Deposits 3.65%

Cream Buttermilk

HEALTHFUL—REFRESHING

Supplee-Wills-Jones Milk Co.

PHILADELPHIA—ATLANTIC CITY

Established 1865

BIOREN & CO.

BANKERS

410 CHESTNUT STREET
PHILADELPHIA

Members of New York and Philadelphia Stock Exchanges

Investment Securities
List on request

JANNEY & CO.

Formerly

MONTGOMERY & CO.

INVESTMENT SECURITIES

133 SOUTH FOURTH STREET
PHILADELPHIA

Joel Borton

SCHOOLS.

Woolman School

Winter Term, First Month 8 to Third Month 23, 1923.

Courses in Bible Study, Church History
Religious Education, Social Problems

Send for catalog.

ELBERT RUSSELL, Director
WOOLMAN SCHOOL
Swarthmore, Pa.

GEORGE SCHOOL
Near Newtown, Bucks County, Pa.

Under the care of Philadelphia Yearly Meeting of Friends.

Course of study extended and thorough, preparing students either for business or for college. For catalogue apply to

GEORGE A. WALTON, A. M., Principal
George School, Penna.

FRIENDS' CENTRAL SCHOOL SYSTEM

Write for Year Book and Rates.

L. RALSTON THOMAS
Principal

15th and Race Sts., Philadelphia.

FRIENDS' ACADEMY
LONG ISLAND, N. Y.

A Boarding and Day School for Boys and Girls, conducted in accordance with the principles of the Society of Friends. For further particulars address

S. ARCHIBALD SMITH, Principal,
Locust Valley, N. Y.

CRETH & SULLIVAN

INSURANCE

210 South Fourth Street, Philadelphia.

Estate of Joseph T. Sullivan   Marshall P. Sullivan

Please help us by patronizing our advertisers. Mention the "Friends' Intelligencer."

Lightning Source UK Ltd.
Milton Keynes UK
UKHW010000220119
335965UK00007B/297/P